RAND McNALLY

TODAY'S WORLD

A NEWLY REVISED

WORLD ATLAS

FROM THE

CARTOGRAPHERS

OF RAND McNALLY

TODAY'S WORLD

A NEWLY REVISED WORLD ATLAS FROM THE CARTOGRAPHERS OF RAND McNALLY

RAND McNALLY

CONTENTS

TODAY'S WORLD

Copyright © 1992 by Rand McNally & Company.

Revised 1996 Edition.

Library of Congress Cataloging-in-Publication Data
Rand McNally and Company.
    Today's world: A new world atlas from the cartographers of
Rand McNally. - 1993 rev. ed.
        p.   cm.
    Shows changes for Europe, Russia, and Eritrea.
    Includes index.
    ISBN 0-528-83778-8
    1. Atlases. I. Title.
G1021.R4867 1993 < G&M : fol. >
912—dc20   93-7143
                                                              CIP
                                                              MAP

Title page photo: Mount Cook, New Zealand, J. Amos/SUPERSTOCK

USING THE ATLAS

MAPS AND ATLASES

Satellite images of the world (figure 1) constantly give us views of the shape and size of the earth. It is hard, therefore, to imagine how difficult it once was to ascertain the look of our planet. Yet from early history we have evidence of humans trying to work out what the world actually looked like.

Twenty-five hundred years ago, on a tiny clay tablet the size of a hand, the Babylonians inscribed the earth as a flat disk (figure 2) with Babylon at the center. The section of the Cantino map of 1502 (figure 3) is an example of a *portolan* chart used by mariners to chart the newly discovered Americas. Handsome and useful maps have been produced by many cultures. The Mexican map drawn in 1583 marks hills with wavy lines and roads with footprints between parallel lines (figure 4). The methods and materials used to create these maps were dependent upon the technology available, and their accuracy suffered considerably. A modern topographic map (figure 5), as well as those in this atlas, shows the detail and accuracy that cartographers are now able to achieve. They benefit from our ever-increasing technology, including satellite imagery and computer assisted cartography.

In 1589 Gerardus Mercator used the word *atlas* to describe a collection of maps. Atlases now bring together not only a variety of maps but an assortment of tables and other reference material as well. They have become a unique and indispensable reference for graphically defining the world and answering the question *where*. Only on a map can the countries, cities, roads, rivers, and lakes covering a vast area be simultaneously viewed in their relative locations. Routes between places can be traced, trips planned, boundaries of neighboring states and countries examined, distances between places measured, the meandering of rivers and streams and the sizes of lakes visualized—and remote places imagined.

FIGURE 1

FIGURE 4

FIGURE 2

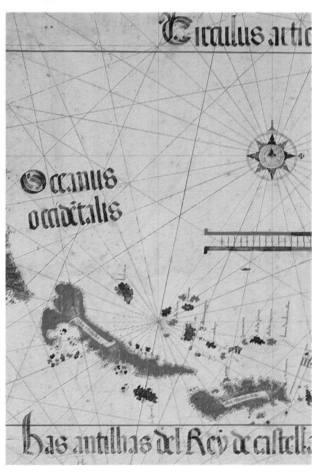

FIGURE 3

FIGURE 5

SEQUENCE OF THE MAPS

The world is made up of seven major landmasses: the continents of Europe, Asia, Africa, Antarctica, Australia, South America, and North America (figure 6). The maps in this atlas follow this continental sequence. To allow for the inclusion of detail, each continent is broken down into a series of maps, and this grouping is arranged so that as consecutive pages are turned, a continuous successive part of the continent is shown. Larger-scale maps are used for regions of greater detail (having many cities, for example) or for areas of global significance.

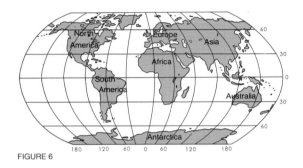

FIGURE 6

GETTING THE INFORMATION

An atlas can be used for many purposes, from planning a trip to finding hot spots in the news and supplementing world knowledge. To realize the potential of an atlas the user must be able to:

1. Find places on the maps
2. Measure distances
3. Determine directions
4. Understand map symbols

FINDING PLACES

One of the most common and important tasks facilitated by an atlas is finding the location of a place in the world. A river's name in a book, a city mentioned in the news, or a vacation spot may prompt your need to know where the place is located. The illustrations and text below explain how to find Yangon (Rangoon), Myanmar.

1. Look up the place-name in the index at the back of the atlas. Yangon, Myanmar can be found on the map on page 38, and it can be located on the map by the letter-number key *B2* (figure 7).

Yangguanpu, China	C4	34
Yangjia, China	I7	32
Yangjiang, China	G9	30
Yangkoushi, China	G7	34
Yangliuqing, China	D5	32
Yanglousi, China	F2	34
Yangon (Rangoon), Mya. ..	B2	38
Yangp'yŏng, S. Kor.	F15	32
Yangquan, China	F1	32
Yangsan, S. Kor.	H17	32
Yangshuling, China	B6	32
Yangtze see Chang, stm., China	E10	30
Yangxiaodian, China	D5	34
Yangyang, S. Kor.	E16	32
Yangzhou, China	C8	34
Yanheying, China	C7	32
Yanji, China	A17	32
Yankdŏk, N. Kor.	D14	32

FIGURE 7

2. Turn to the map of Southeastern Asia found on page 38. Note that the letters *A* through *H* and the numbers *1* through *11* appear in the margins of the map.

3. To find Yangon, on the map, place your left index finger on *B* and your right index finger on *2*. Move your left finger across the map and your right finger down the map. Your fingers will meet in the area in which Yangon is located (figure 8).

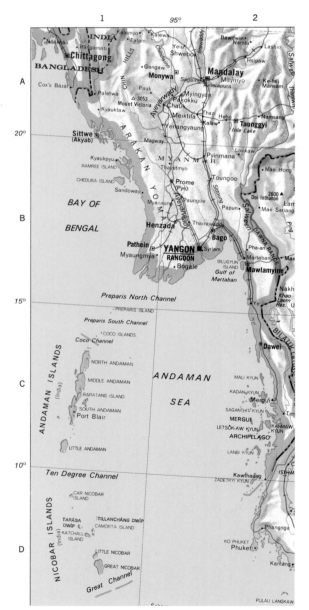

FIGURE 8

MEASURING DISTANCES

In planning trips, determining the distance between two places is essential, and an atlas can help in travel preparation. For instance, to determine the approximate distance between Paris and Rouen, France, follow these three steps:

1. Lay a slip of paper on the map on page 14 so that its edge touches the two cities. Adjust the paper so one corner touches Rouen. Mark the paper directly at the spot where Paris is located (figure 9).

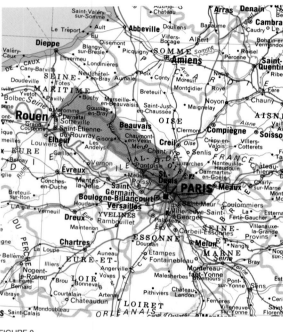

FIGURE 9

2. Place the paper along the scale of miles beneath the map. Position the corner at 0 and line up the edge of the paper along the scale. The pencil mark on the paper indicates Rouen is between 50 and 100 miles from Paris (figure 10).

3. To find the exact distance, move the paper to the left so that the pencil mark is at 100 on the scale. The corner of the paper stands on the fourth 5-mile unit on the scale. This means that the two towns are 50 plus 20, or 70 miles apart (figure 11).

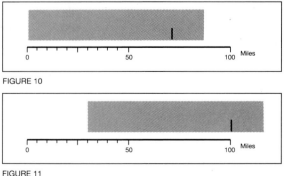

FIGURE 10

FIGURE 11

DETERMINING DIRECTION

Most of the maps in the atlas are drawn so that when oriented for normal reading, north is at the top of the map, south is at the bottom, west is at the left, and east is at the right. Most maps have a series of lines drawn across them—the lines of *latitude* and *longitude*. Lines of latitude, or *parallels* of latitude, are drawn east and west. Lines of longitude, or *meridians* of longitude, are drawn north and south (figure 12).

Parallels and meridians appear as either curved or straight lines. For example, in the section of the map of Europe (figure 13) the parallels of latitude appear as curved lines. The meridians of longitude are straight lines that come together toward the top of the map. Latitude and longitude lines help locate places on maps. Parallels of latitude are numbered in degrees north and south of the *Equator*. Meridians of longitude are numbered in degrees east and west of a line called the *Prime Meridian*, running through Greenwich, England, near London. Any place on earth can be located by the latitude and longitude lines running through it.

To determine directions or locations on the map, you must use the parallels and meridians. For example, suppose you want to know which is farther north, Bergen, Norway, or Stockholm, Sweden. The map in figure 13 shows that Stockholm is south of the 60° parallel of latitude and Bergen is north of it. Bergen is farther north than Stockholm. By looking at the meridians of longitude, you can determine which city is farther east. Bergen is approximately 5° east of the 0° meridian (Prime Meridian), and Stockholm is almost 20° east of it. Stockholm is farther east than Bergen.

UNDERSTANDING MAP SYMBOLS

In a very real sense, the whole map is a symbol, representing the world or a part of it. It is a reduced representation of the earth; each of the world's features—cities, rivers, etc.—is represented on the map by a symbol. Map symbols may take the form of points, such as dots or squares (often used for cities, capital cities, or points of interest), or lines (roads, railroads, rivers). Symbols may also occupy an area, showing extent of coverage (terrain, forests, deserts). They seldom look like the feature they represent and therefore must be identified and interpreted. For instance, the maps in this atlas define political units by a colored line depicting their boundaries. Neither the colors nor the boundary lines are actually found on the surface of the earth, but because countries and states are such important political components of the world, strong symbols are used to represent them. The Map Symbols page in this atlas identifies the symbols used on the maps.

FIGURE 12

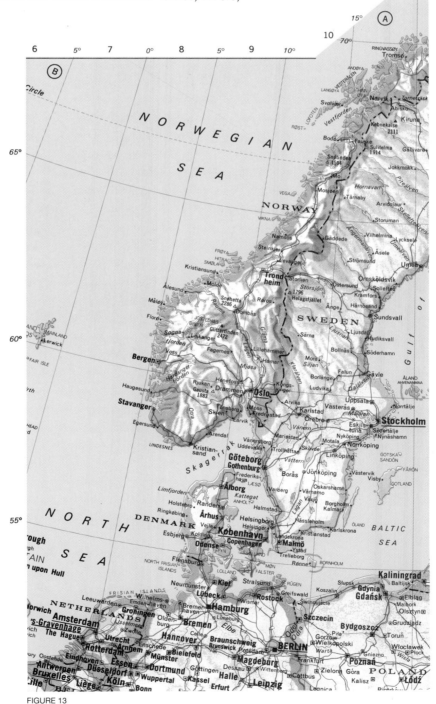

FIGURE 13

World Time Zones

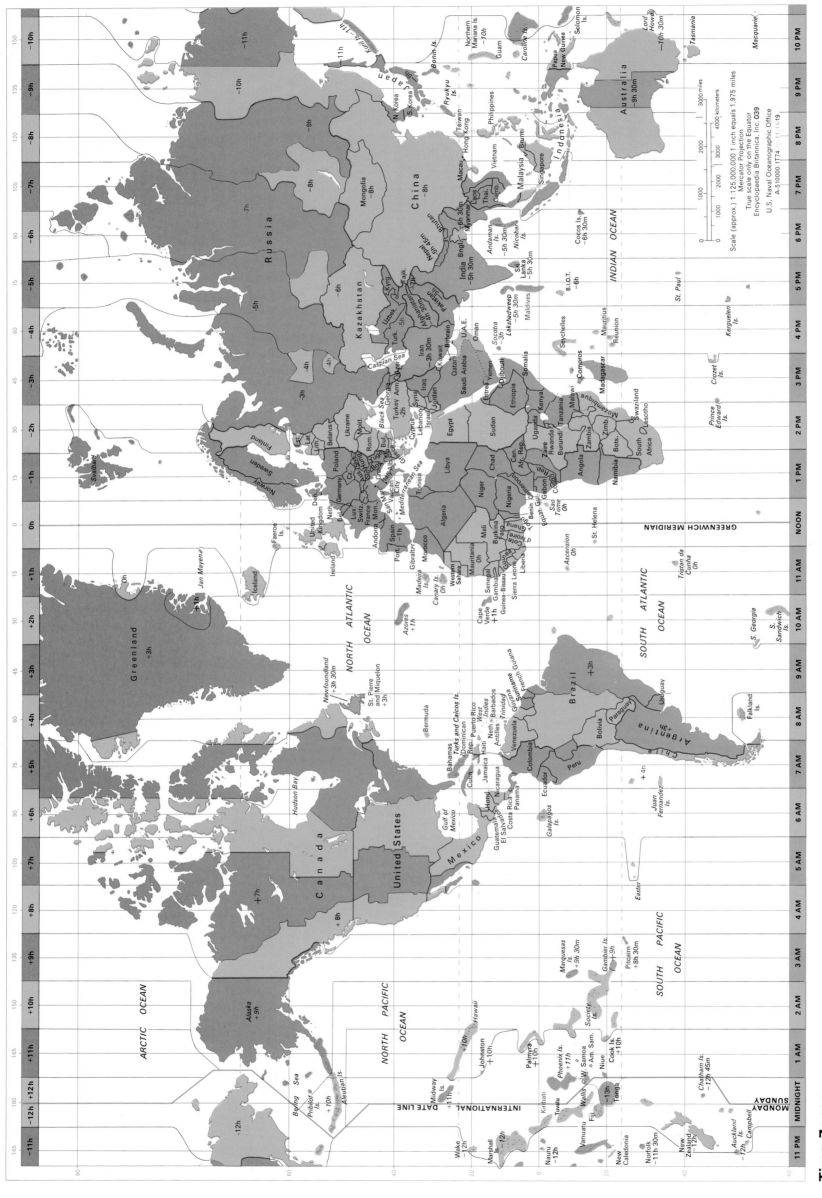

Time Zones

Standard time zone of even-numbered hours from Greenwich time

Standard time zone of odd-numbered hours from Greenwich time

Time varies from the standard time zone by half an hour

Time varies from the standard time zone by other than half an hour

| h | m | hours, minutes

The standard time zone system, fixed by international agreement and by law in each country, is based on a theoretical division of the globe into 24 zones of 15° longitude each. The mid-meridian of each zone fixes the hour for the entire zone. The zero time zone extends 7½° east and 7½° west of the Greenwich meridian, 0° longitude. Since the earth rotates toward the east, time zones to the west of Greenwich are earlier, to the east, later. Plus and minus hours at the top of the map are added to or subtracted from local time to find Greenwich time. Local standard time can be determined for any area in the world by adding one hour for each time zone counted in an easterly direction from

one's own, or by subtracting one hour for each zone counted in a westerly direction. To separate one day from the next, the 180th meridian has been designated as the international date line. On both sides of the line the time of day is the same, but west of the line it is one day later than it is to the east. Countries that adhere to the international zone system adopt the zone applicable to their location. Some countries, however, establish time zones based on political boundaries, or adopt the time zone of a neighboring unit. For all or part of the year some countries also advance their time by one hour, thereby utilizing more daylight hours each day.

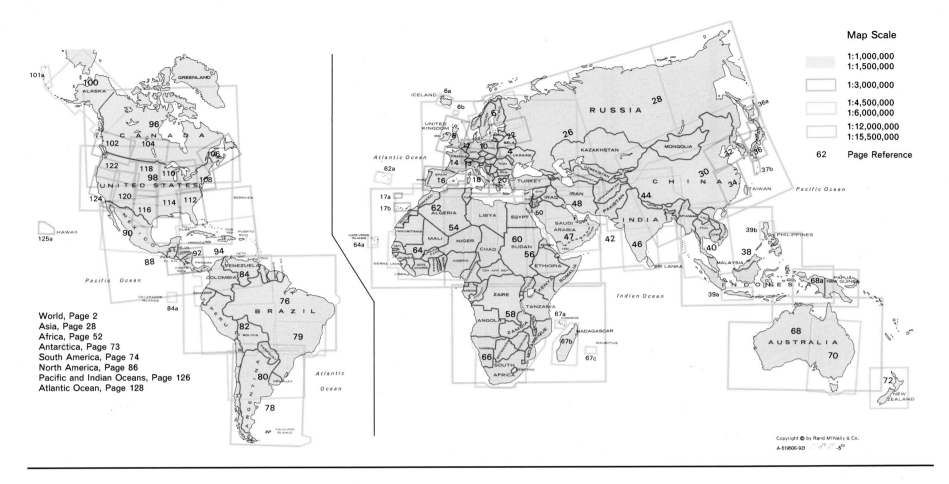

Map Scale

	1:1,000,000
	1:1,500,000
	1:3,000,000
	1:4,500,000
	1:6,000,000
	1:12,000,000
	1:15,500,000
62	Page Reference

World Maps Symbols

Inhabited Localities

The size of type indicates the relative economic and political importance of the locality

Écommoy	Lisieux	**Rouen**
Trouville	**Orléans**	**PARIS**
Bi'r Safâjah °	Oasis	

Alternate Names

MOSKVA
MOSCOW
English or second official language names are shown in reduced size lettering

Basel
Bâle

Volgograd
(Stalingrad)
Historical or other alternates in the local language are shown in parentheses

Urban Area (Area of continuous industrial, commercial, and residential development)

Capitals of Political Units

BUDAPEST   Independent Nation

Cayenne   Dependency (Colony, protectorate, etc.)

Recife   State, Province, County, Oblast, etc.

Political Boundaries

International (First-order political unit)

Demarcated and Undemarcated

Disputed de jure

Indefinite or Undefined

Demarcation Line

Internal

State, Province, etc. (Second-order political unit)

MURCIA   Historical Region (No boundaries indicated)

GALAPAGOS (Ecuador)   Administering Country

Transportation

Primary Road

Secondary Road

Minor Road, Trail

Railway

Canal du Midi   Navigable Canal

Bridge

Tunnel

TO MALMÖ   Ferry

Hydrographic Features

Shoreline

Undefined or Fluctuating Shoreline

Amur   River, Stream

Intermittent Stream

Rapids, Falls

Irrigation or Drainage Canal

Reef

The Everglades   Swamp

RIMO GLACIER   Glacier

L. Victoria   Lake, Reservoir

Tuz Gölü   Salt Lake

Intermittent Lake, Reservoir

Dry Lake Bed

(395)   Lake Surface Elevation

Topographic Features

Matterhorn △
4478   Elevation Above Sea Level

76 ▽   Elevation Below Sea Level

Mount Cook ▲
3764   Highest Elevation in Country

133 ▼   Lowest Elevation in Country

Khyber Pass ⊨
1067   Mountain Pass

Elevations are given in meters.
The highest and lowest elevations in a continent are underlined

Sand Area

Lava

Salt Flat

1

ARCTIC OCEAN

14 30° 15 45° 16 60° 17 75° 18 90° 19 105° 20 120° 21 135° 22 150° 23 165° 24 180° 90°

A

NOVOSIBIRSKIJE
OSTROVA

ZEML'A FRANCA-IOSIFA
Barents
Sea

SVALBARD
(Nor.)

Hammerfest
Narvik
ORWAY
SWEDEN
Murmansk
NOVAJA
ZEML'A
Karskoje
more
Dikson
more Laptevych
75°
Arctic Circle
B
FINLAND
Oslo
Bergen
HELSINKI
STOCKHOLM
Archangel'sk
Salechard
Vorkuta
Noril'sk
Chatanga
Tiksi
Verchojansk
60°
Anadyr'
C
K0BENHAVN
SANKT-PETERBURG
ST. PETERSBURG
Ladozskoje
ozero
Ob'
Jenisej
Igarka
Magadan
Bering Sea
ALEUTIAN IS.
(U.S.)
BERLIN
POLAND
BELARUS
MOSKVA
Nižnij Novgorod
Perm'
Čel'abinsk
Omsk
Novosibirsk
Krasnojarsk
Irkutsk
Lena
Jakutsk
Lensk
Cita
Nikolajevsk
Sea of
Okhotsk
Ochotsk
Petropavlovsk-
Kamcatskij
OSTROV SACHALIN
GERMANY
Bonn
WARSZAWA
UKRAINE
KYYIV
Volgograd
Jekaterinburg
Ural
Samara
KURIL'SKIJE
OSTROVA
45°
D
SWITZ.
ALPS
ITALY
ROMA
Napoli
CZECH
REP.
BUDAPEST
WIEN
HUNG.
SLVK.
ROM.
BEOGRAD
BUL.
SOFIA
Dnepr
Astrachan'
gora El'brus
5642
Caspian Sea
Voiga
Karaganda
KAZAKHSTAN
ozero Balchaš
Ürümqi
ALTAJ
ozero
Bajkal
Ulaanbaatar
MONGOLIA
GOBI
Harbin
Chabarovsk
Vladivostok
Sea of
Japan
Sapporo
JAPAN
Sendai
HOKKAIDO
International Date Line

ALB.
YUGO.
GREECE
ATHÍNAI
Istanbul
ANKARA
TURKEY
GEOR.
ARM. AZER.
BAKU
Aral
Sea
ALMATY
TAŠKENT
TIEN SHAN
KYRG.
UZBEKISTAN
TAJIK.
Shache
CHINA
Hohhot
BEIJING
PEKING
Shenyang
N. KOREA
P'YONGYANG
Tianjin
Dalian
S. KOREA
SOUL
Pusan
Fukuoka
OSAKA
TOKYO
HONSHŪ
Yellow Sea
30°

MALTA
TARĀBULUS
TRIPOLI
Mediterranean Sea
GREECE
CYPRUS
SYRIA
LEB.
ISR.
JORDAN
BAGHDĀD
IRAQ
TEHRĀN
Eşfahān
IRAN
KĀBOL
AFGHANISTAN
Islamabad
Rawalpindi
Lahore
Lanzhou
Xi'an
Chengdu
Chongqing
Lhasa
HIMALAYAS
Mount
Everest
8848
Wuhan
Nanjing
SHANGHAI
Changsha
Fuzhou
NANSEI-
SHOTŌ
OGASAWARA-GUNTO
(Japan)
PACIFIC

LIBYA
EGYPT
Aswān
AR-RIYĀD
QATAR
UNITED
ARAB
EMIRATES
KUWAIT
Abādān
Karāchī
DELHI
New Delhi
Kāthmāndu
NEPAL
BNGL.
Tropic of Cancer
Kunming
Guangzhou
HONG
KONG
(U.K.)
T'AIPEI
TAIWAN
OCEAN
WAKE
ISLAND
(U.S.)
E
HARA
FRICA
NIGER
SUDAN
CHAD
AL-KHARTŪM
SAUDI
ARABIA
OMAN
Masqat
Ahmadābād
BOMBAY
INDIA
Hyderābād
CALCUTTA
DHAKA
MYANMAH
HA'NOI
South
China
Sea
Philippine
Sea
MANILA
NORTHERN
MARIANA
ISLANDS
(U.S.)
MARSHALL
ISLANDS
M
Tamenghest
N'Djamena
ERITREA
Şan'ā'
YEMEN
Adan
Madras
Bay of
Bengal
ANDAMAN
ISLANDS
(India)
YANGON
THAILAND
VIETNAM
KRUNG THEP
BANGKOK
CAMB.
Phnum Penh
GUAM (U.S.)
PHILIPPINES
PALAU
I
Niamey
Kano
Abuja
NIGERIA
DJIBOUTI
ADIS ABEBA
ETHIOPIA
SOMALIA
Bangalore
SRI LANKA
COLOMBO
Cochin
NICOBAR
ISLANDS
(India)
Thanh Pho
Ho Chi Minh
Davao
FEDERATED STATES
OF MICRONESIA
C
R
O
N
E
S
I
A
15°
LAGOS
Porto-Novo
Douala
Yaoundé
CEN.
AFR. REP.
UGANDA
KAMPALA
KENYA
Muqdisho
MALDIVES
MALAYSIA
BRUNEI
KUALA LUMPUR
SINGAPORE
Medan
SEYCHELLES
Equator
F
EQUATORIAL
GUINEA
Libreville
GABON
CONGO
Brazzaville
KINSHASA
ZAIRE
RWANDA
BURUNDI
Bujumbura
NAIROBI
Kilimanjaro 5895
Mombasa
Lake
Victoria
BRITISH
INDIAN OCEAN
TERRITORY
SUMATERA
Palembang
BORNEO
Banjarmasin
SULAWESI
NAURU
KIRIBATI
TUVALU
G
LUANDA
Lobito
ANGOLA
ZAMBIA
Lusaka
Lubumbashi
TANZANIA
DAR ES SALAAM
Dodoma
Zanzibar
Lake
Tanganyika
INDONESIA
JAKARTA
JAWA
Surabaya
Ujungpandang
TIMOR
PAPUA
NEW
GUINEA
Mount Wilhelm
4509
NEW
GUINEA
Port Moresby
SOLOMON
ISLANDS
M
E
L
A
N
E
S
I
A
INDIAN
Windhoek
Walvis Bay
NAMIBIA
Gaborone
BOTSWANA
ZIMBABWE
HARARE
Lilongwe
Lake
Nyasa
Zambezi
MOZAMBIQUE
Mozambique Channel
ANTANANARIVO
MADAGASCAR
MAURITIUS
REUNION
(Fr.)
COCOS
ISLANDS
(Austl.)
CHRISTMAS ISLAND
(Austl.)
Darwin
CAPE YORK
Gulf of
Carpentaria
Cairns
Coral
Sea
VANUATU
NEW
CALEDONIA
(Fr.)
Nouméa
Suva
FIJI
NORFOLK
ISLAND
(Austl.)
15°
H
OCEAN
SOUTH
AFRICA
CAPE TOWN
CAPE AGULHAS
Port Elizabeth
Durban
Johannesburg
PRETORIA
MAPUTO
SWAZILAND
LESOTHO
Tropic of Capricorn
Alice Springs
AUSTRALIA
Rockhampton
Brisbane
30°
BOTSWANA
Perth
Darling
Adelaide
Melbourne
Mount Kosciusko
2228
Canberra
Sydney
Tasman Sea
NORTH ISLAND
NEW
ZEALAND
Auckland
Wellington
I
TASMANIA
Hobart
SOUTH
ISLAND
Christchurch
45°
SOUTHERN
J
ÎLES KERGUÉLEN
(Fr.)
OCEAN
Antarctic Circle
K
ENDERBY LAND
WILKES LAND
75°
Copyright © by Rand McNally & Co.
Map prepared by Rand McNally & Co.
A-510000-264
L
C T I C A
14 30° 15 45° 16 60° 17 75° 18 90° 19 105° 20 120° 21 135° 22 150° 23 165° 24 180° 90°

Kilometers
0 1000 2000 3000 Km.
Statute Miles
0 1000 2000 3000 Mi.

One centimeter represents 750 kilometers.
One inch represents approximately 1200 miles.
Robinson Projection
Scale 1:75,000,000

3

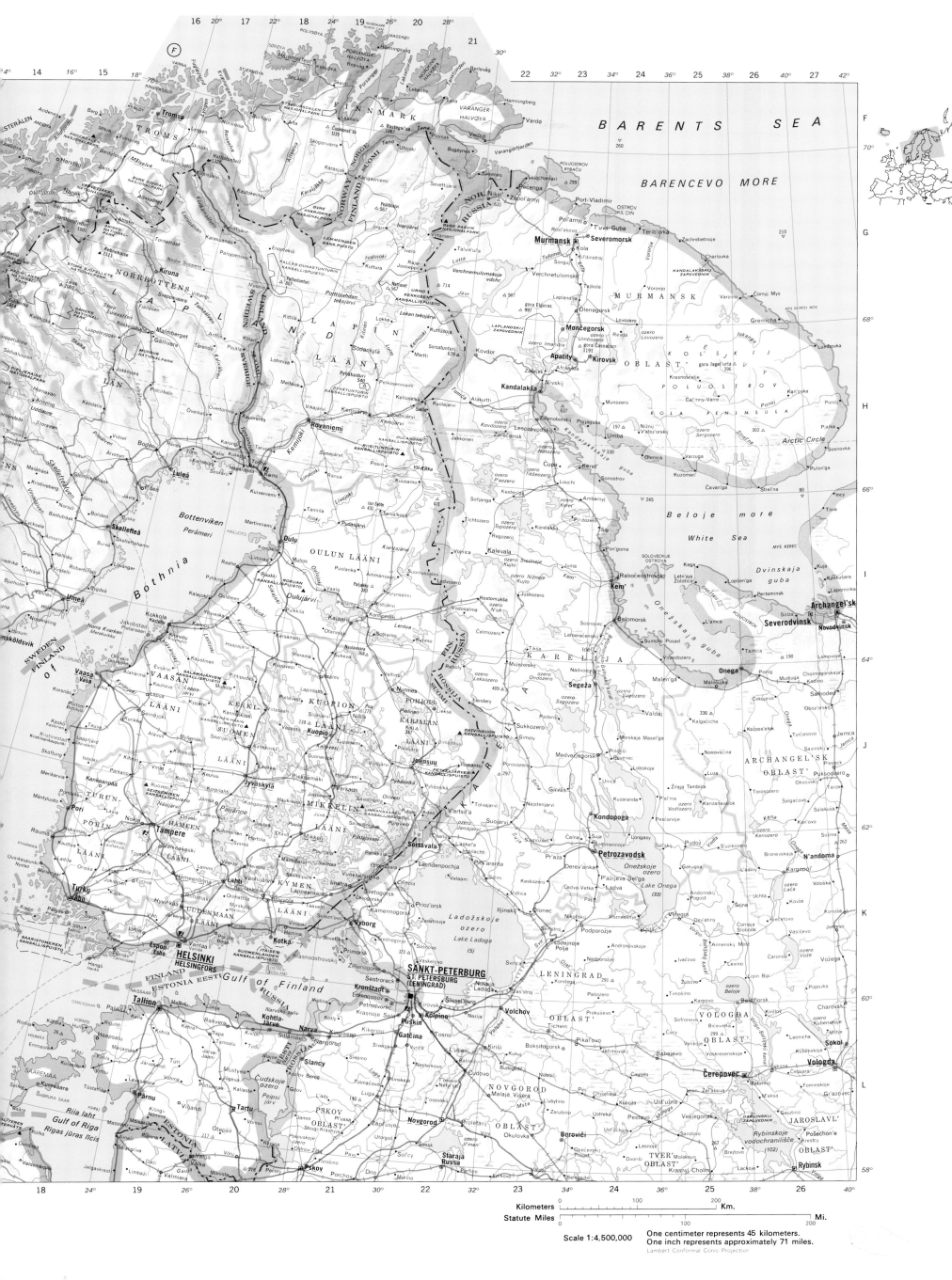

Kilometers
0   100   200   Km.
Statute Miles
0   100   200   Mi.

Scale 1:4,500,000

One centimeter represents 45 kilometers.
One inch represents approximately 71 miles.

Lambert Conformal Conic Projection

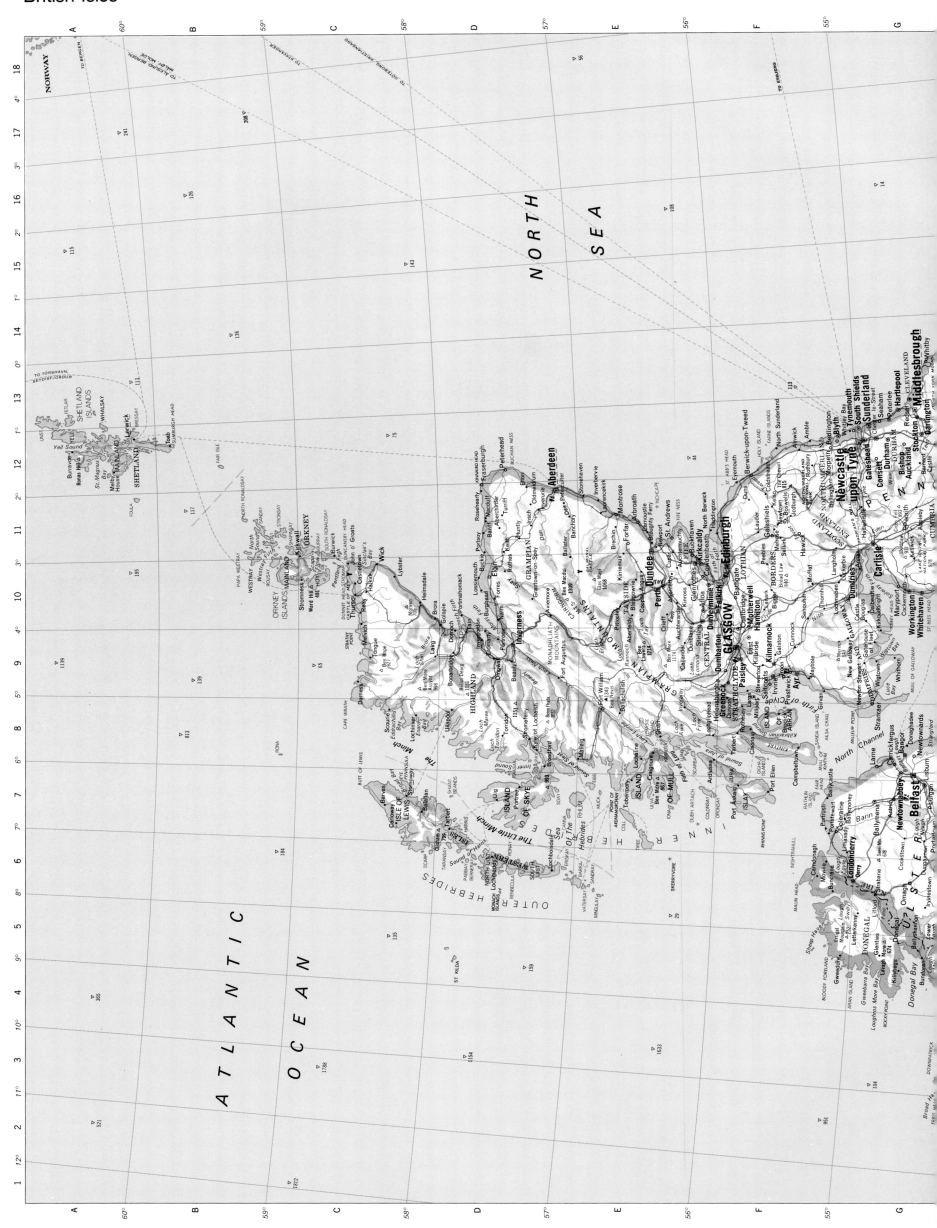

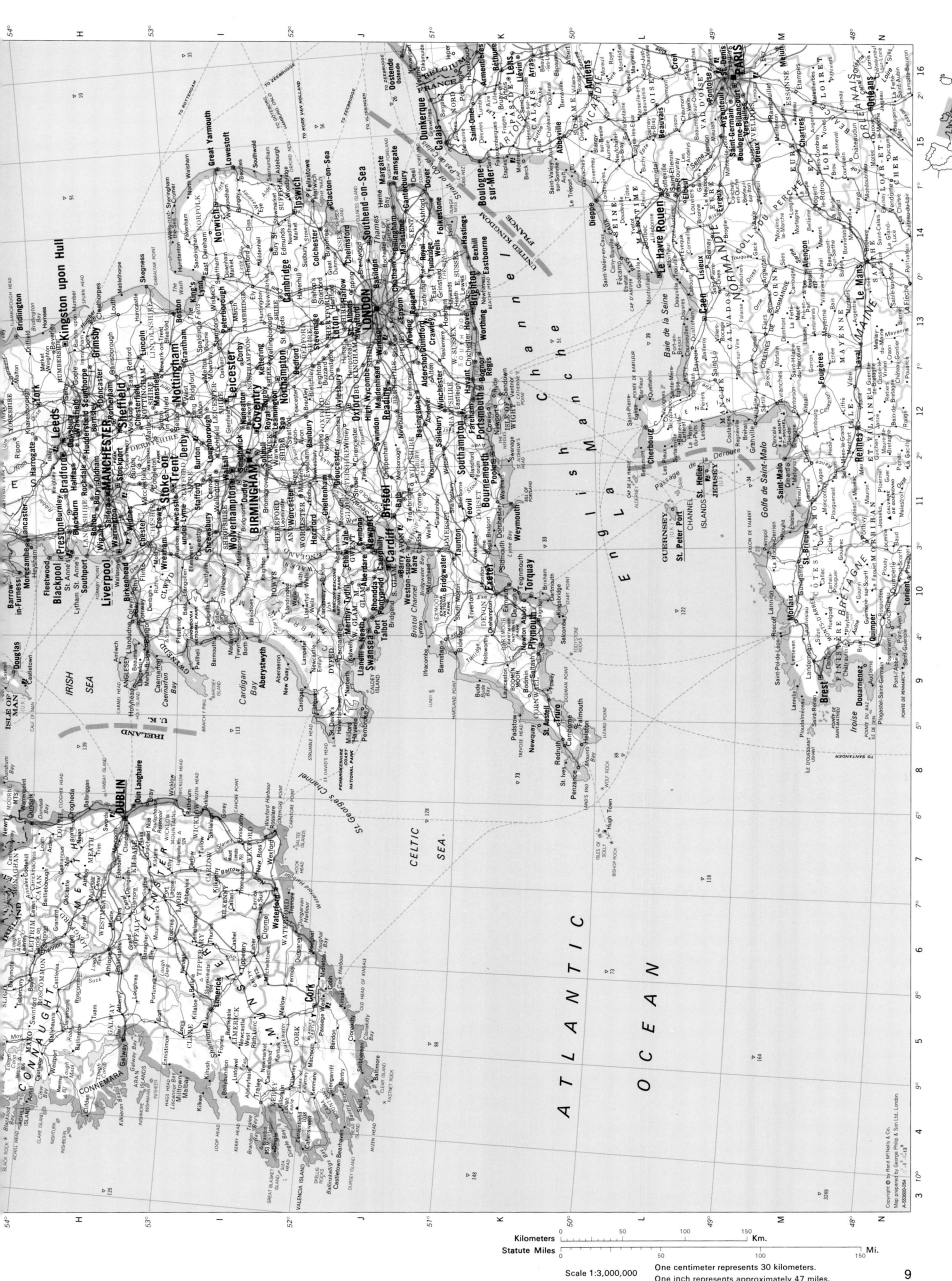

Kilometers
Statute Miles

One centimeter represents 30 kilometers.
One inch represents approximately 47 miles.
Conic Projection, Two Standard Parallels

Scale 1:3,000,000

9

NORTH SEA

FRISIAN ISLANDS

DENMARK

GERMANY

NETHERLANDS

BELGIUM

FRANCE

SCHWEIZ / SUISSE / SVIZZERA

ÖSTERREICH

Flensburg
Kiel
Neumünster
Lübeck
Rostock
Schwerin
HAMBURG
Bremerhaven
Bremen
Hannover
Braunschweig
Magdeburg
Groningen
Leeuwarden
Den Helder
Alkmaar
Haarlem
AMSTERDAM
Utrecht
's-Gravenhage
Rotterdam
Osnabrück
Münster
Bielefeld
Dortmund
Essen
Duisburg
Düsseldorf
Köln
Kassel
Halle
Leipzig
Erfurt
Weimar
Jena
Antwerpen
Gent
BRUXELLES / BRUSSEL
Liège
Aachen
Bonn
Lille
Roubaix
Valenciennes
Charleroi
Namur
Reims
LUXEMBOURG
Trier
Koblenz
Wiesbaden
Frankfurt a. M.
Mainz
Darmstadt
Würzburg
Bamberg
Bayreuth
Metz
Nancy
Saarbrücken
Mannheim
Ludwigshafen
Heidelberg
Karlsruhe
Nürnberg / Nuremberg
Fürth
Regensburg
Strasbourg
Stuttgart
Augsburg
MÜNCHEN
Freiburg
Basel / Bâle
Zürich
Bern / Berne
Lausanne
Genève / Geneva
Innsbruck
Besançon
Dijon
Troyes

Kilometers
Statute Miles

Scale 1:3,000,000
One centimeter represents 30 kilometers.
One inch represents approximately 47 miles.
Conic Projection, Two Standard Parallels.

10

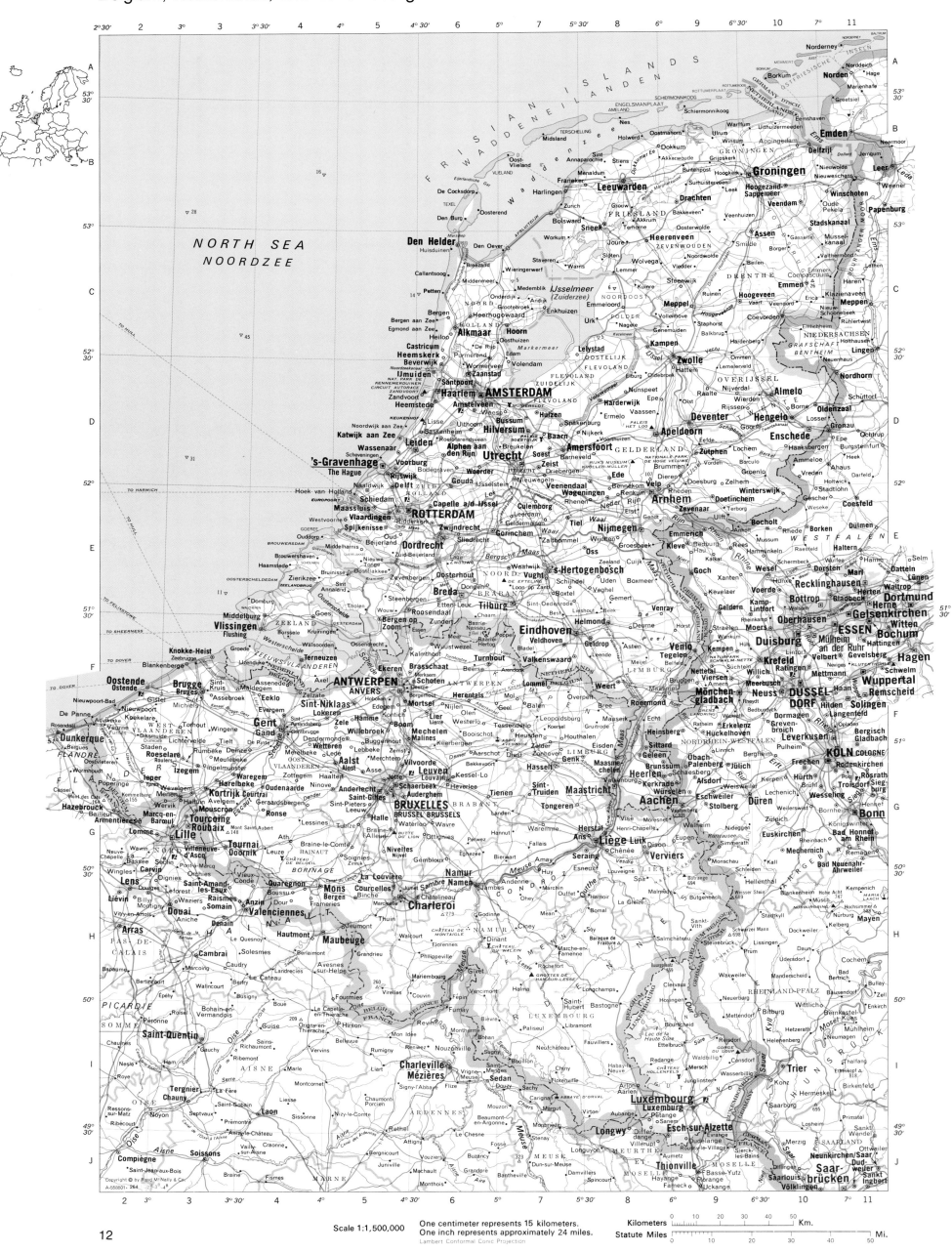

Scale 1:1,500,000
One centimeter represents 15 kilometers.
One inch represents approximately 24 miles.
Lambert Conformal Conic Projection

Kilometers
Statute Miles

Scale 1:1,500,000

One centimeter represents 15 kilometers.
One inch represents approximately 24 miles.

Lambert Conformal Conic Projection

Kilometers |0 10 20 30 40 50| Km.

Statute Miles |0 10 20 30 40 50| Mi.

Kilometers

Statute Miles

Scale 1:3,000,000

One centimeter represents 30 kilometers.
One inch represents approximately 47 miles.
Lambert Conformal Conic Projection

15

MEDITERRANEAN SEA

Golfe du Lion

ILLES BALEARS
BALEARIC ISLANDS

MENORCA MINORCA

MALLORCA MAJORCA

BALEARS

ARQUIPÉLAGO DA MADEIRA
MADEIRA ISLANDS
(Portugal)

MADEIRA

Funchal

ILHAS DESERTAS

ATLANTIC OCEAN

ISLAS CANARIAS
CANARY ISLANDS
(Spain)

LA PALMA

TENERIFE

LA GOMERA

EL HIERRO

GRAN CANARIA

Las Palmas de Gran Canaria

Santa Cruz de Tenerife
La Laguna

LANZAROTE

FUERTEVENTURA

WESTERN SAHARA

ATLANTIC OCEAN

ALGERIA
ALGÉRIE

Wahran
Oran

Sidi bel Abbès

Kilometers
Statute Miles

Scale 1:3,000,000
One centimeter represents 30 kilometers.
One inch represents approximately 47 miles.
Conic Projection, Two Standard Parallels

17

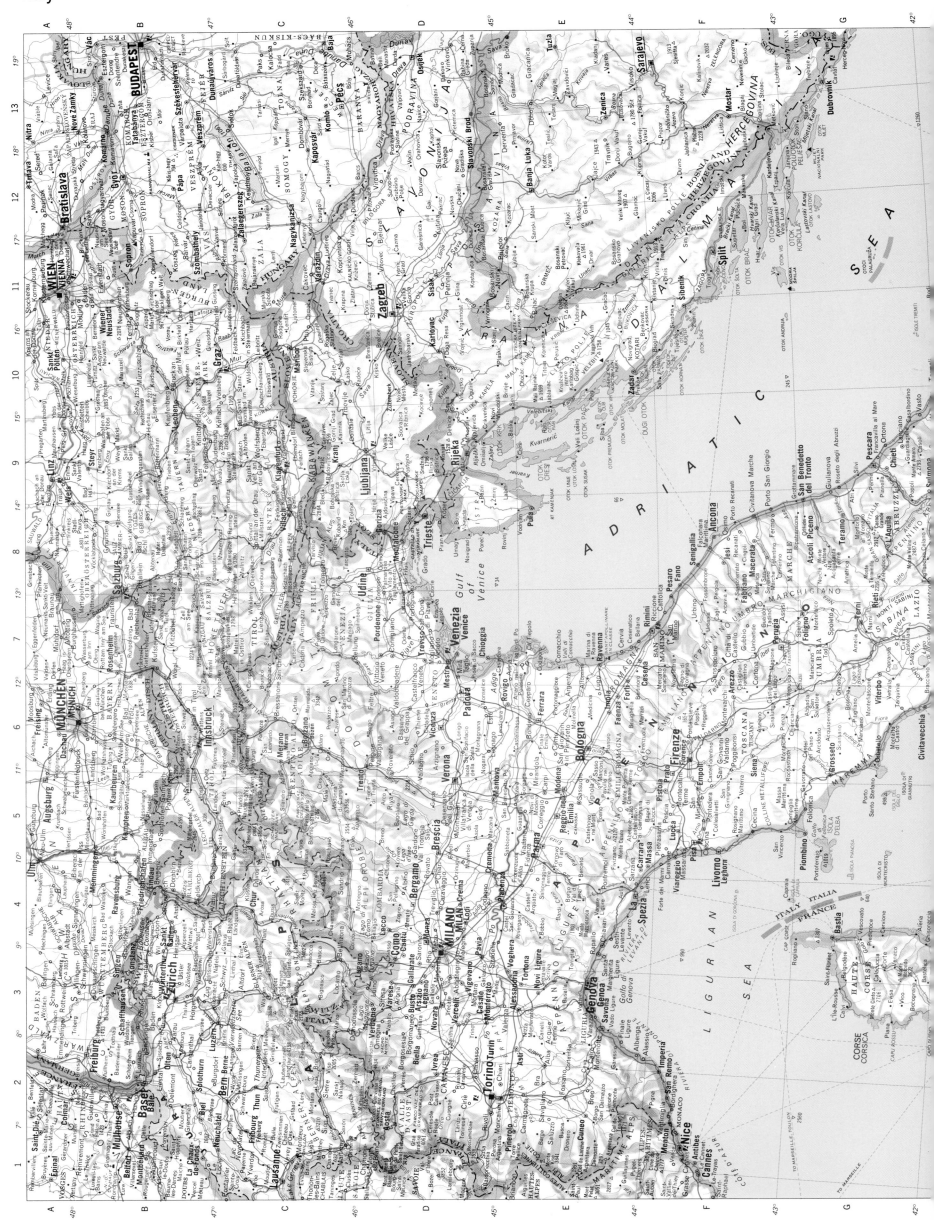

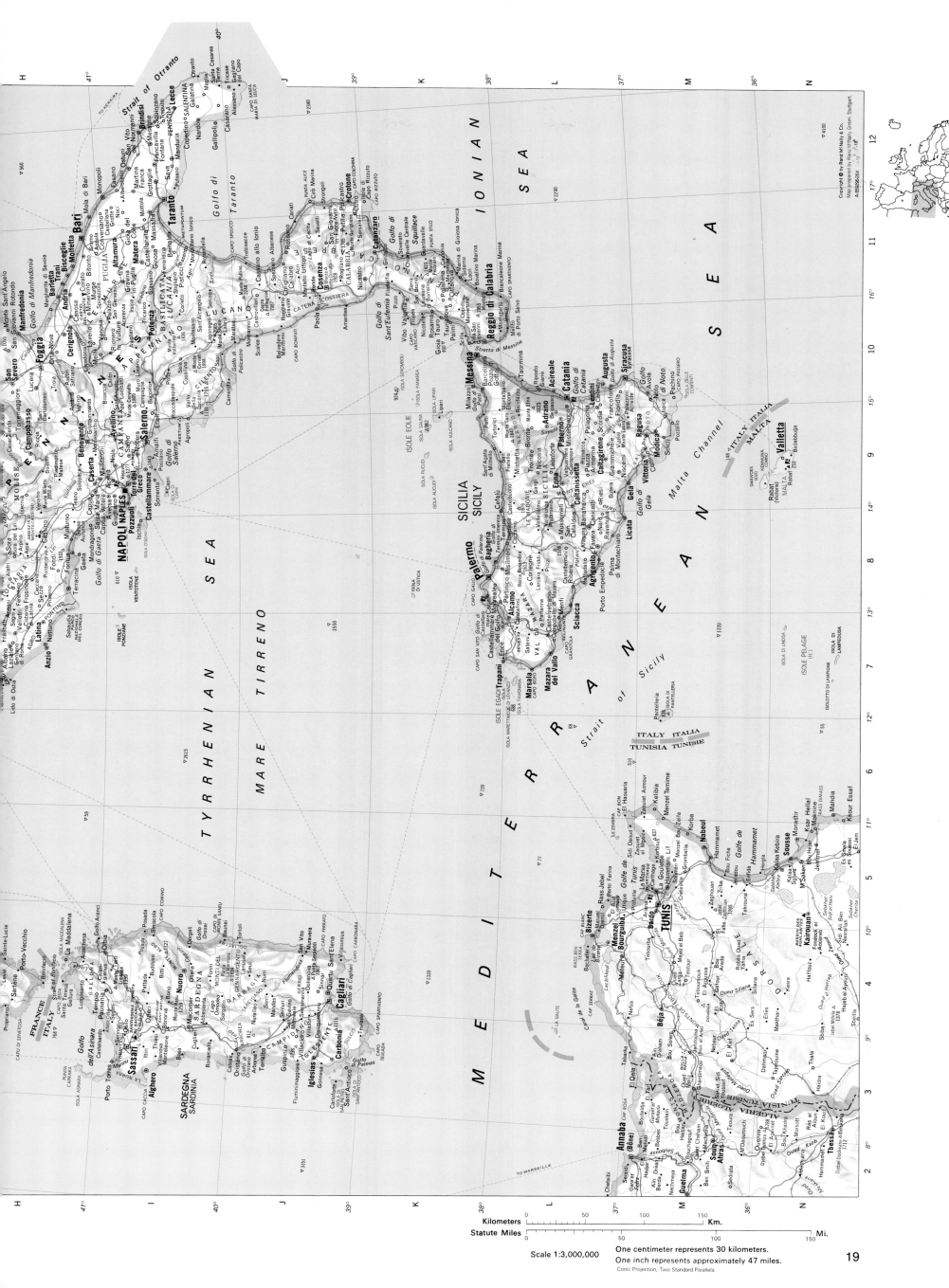

Kilometers
Statute Miles

Scale 1:3,000,000

One centimeter represents 30 kilometers.
One inch represents approximately 47 miles.
Conic Projection, Two Standard Parallels

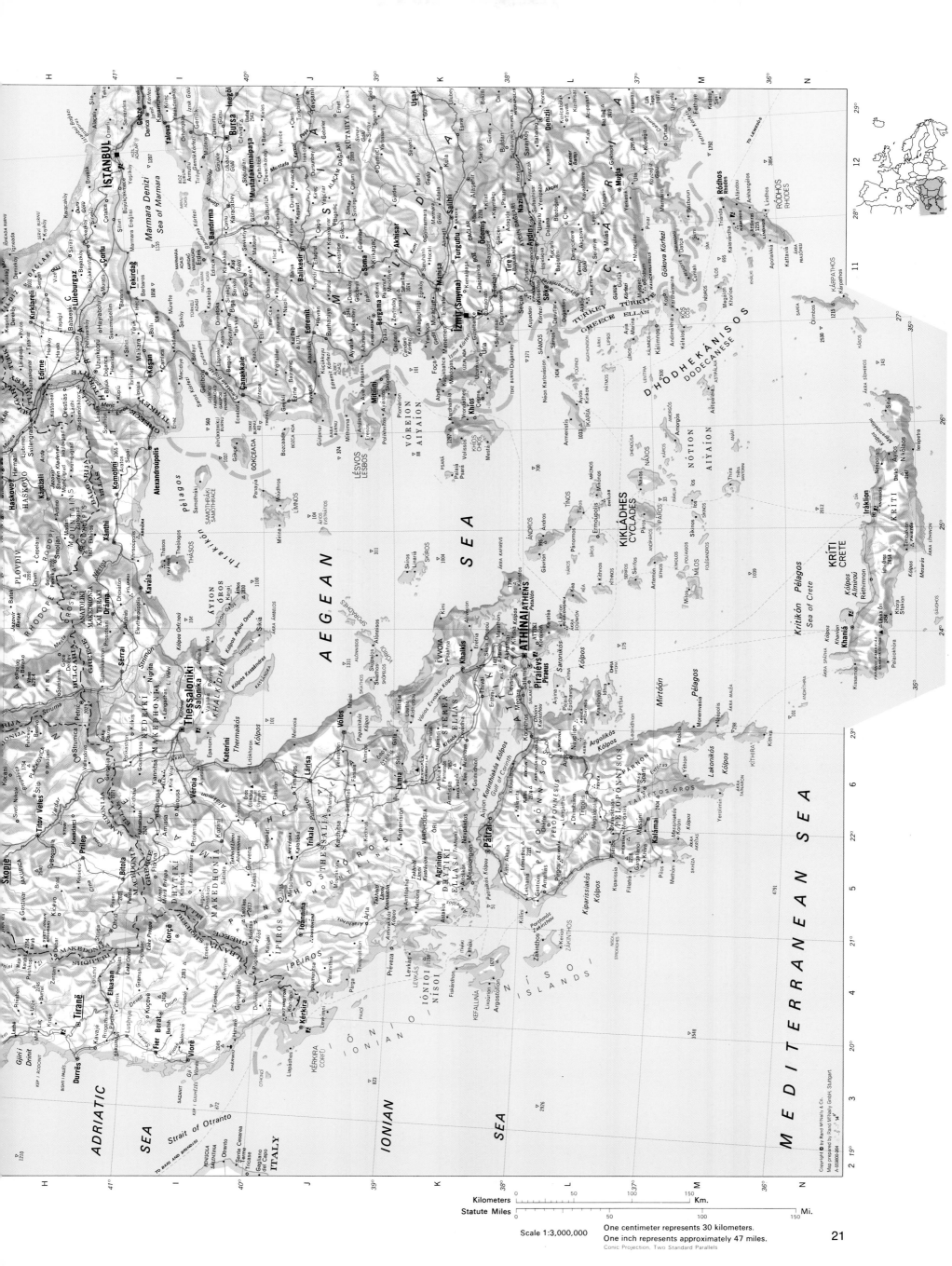

Kilometers
Statute Miles

Scale 1:3,000,000   One centimeter represents 30 kilometers.
One inch represents approximately 47 miles.
Conic Projection, Two Standard Parallels

21

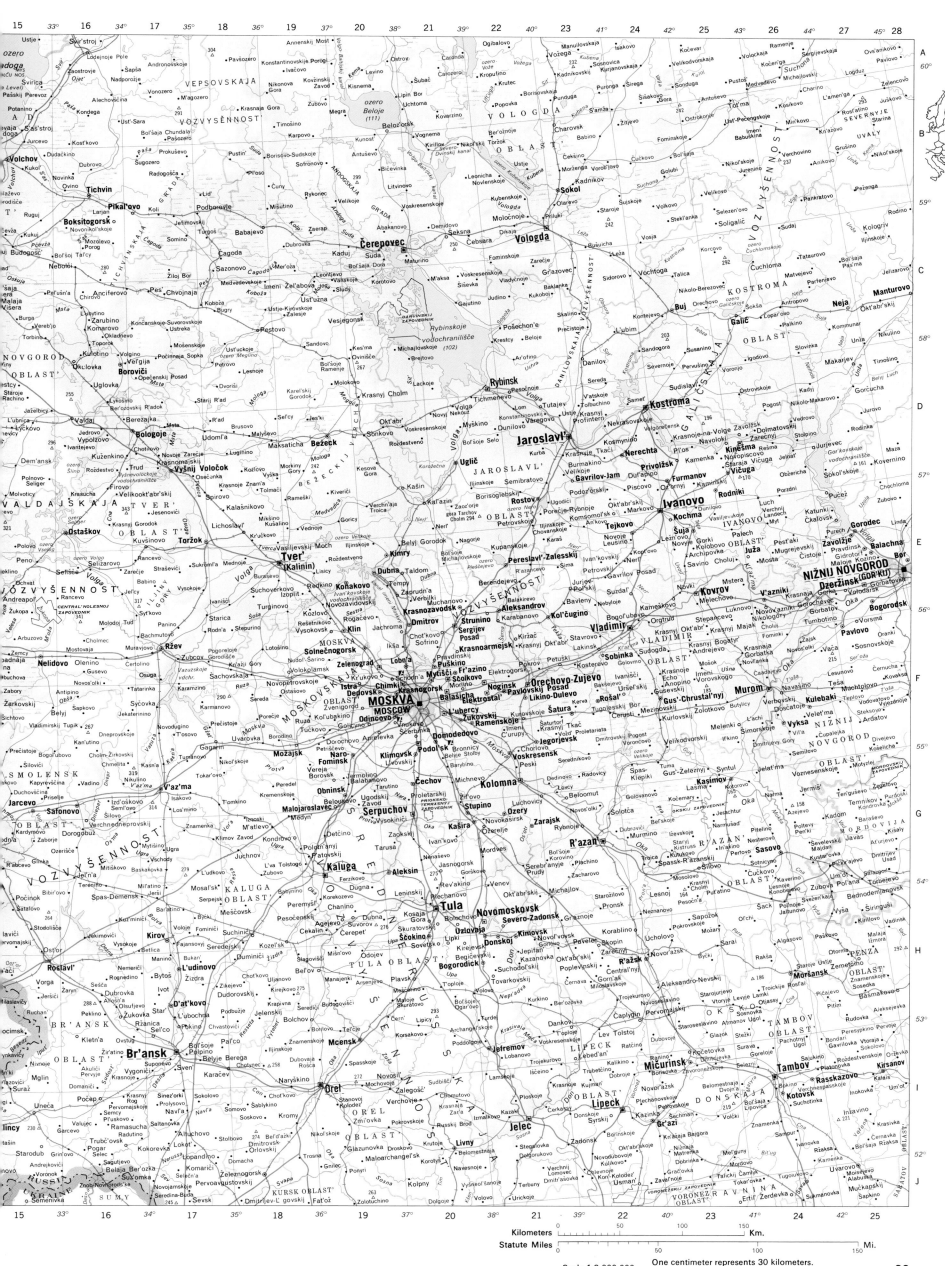

Kilometers
Statute Miles

One centimeter represents 30 kilometers.
One inch represents approximately 47 miles.

Scale 1:3,000,000

Lambert Conformal Conic Projection

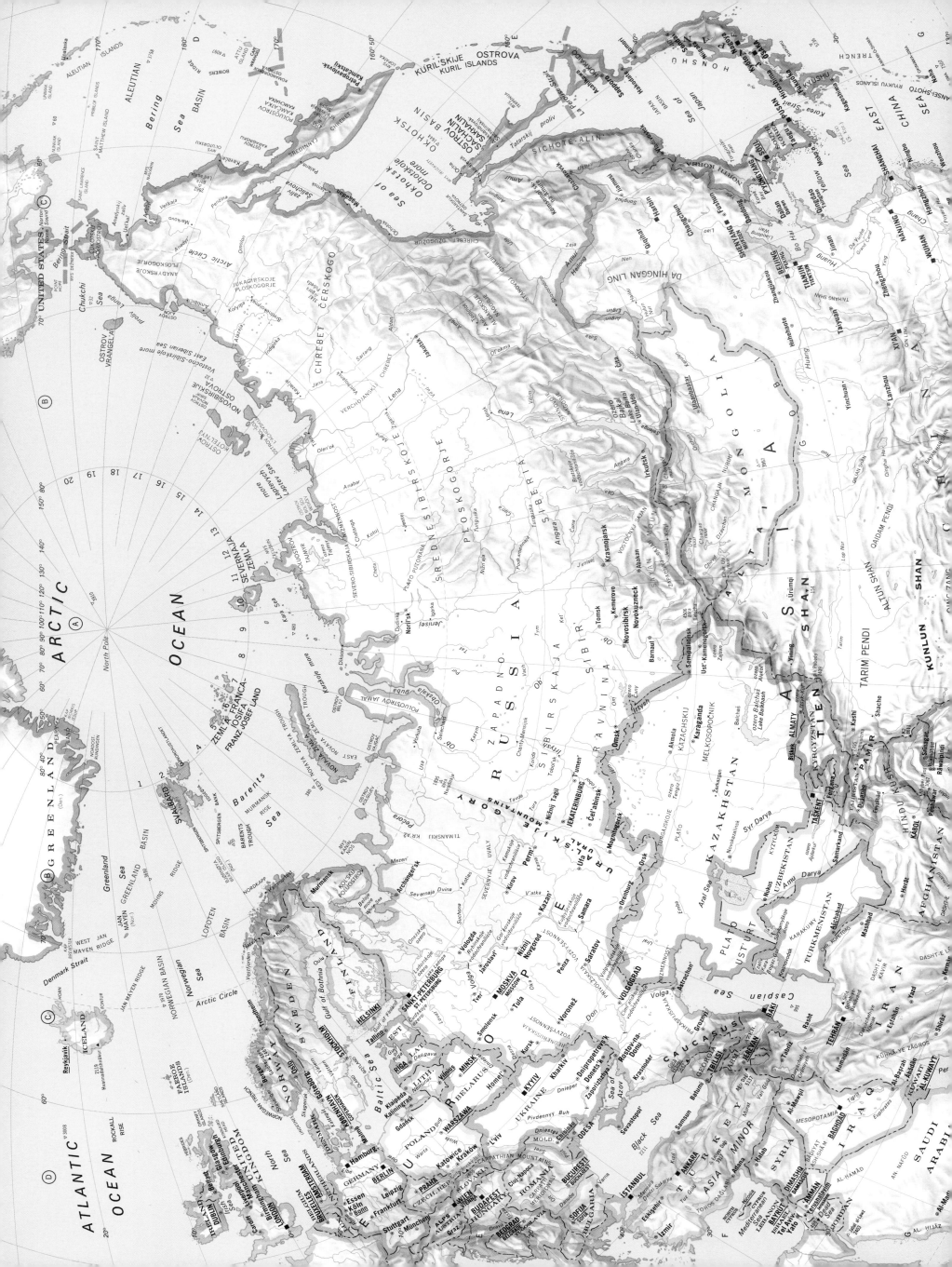

AUSTRALIA

INDIAN OCEAN

ARABIAN SEA

Bay of Bengal

INDIA

PAKISTAN

MYANMAR (BURMA)

THAILAND

VIETNAM

SOUTH CHINA SEA

PHILIPPINES

MALAYSIA

INDONESIA

GREATER SUNDA ISLANDS

BORNEO

SUMATRA

JAVA

SRI LANKA

MALDIVES

MADAGASCAR

SOMALIA

ETHIOPIA

YEMEN

OMAN

ARABIAN PENINSULA

AR-RUB'AL-KHĀLĪ

Kilometers   Km.
0   200   400   600   800
Statute Miles   Mi.
0   200   400   600   800
Scale 1:24,000,000
One centimeter represents 240 kilometers.
One inch represents approximately 380 miles.
Lambert Azimuthal Equal-Area Projection

Copyright © by Rand McNally & Co.
Made in U.S.A.

NEW DELHI
DELHI
BOMBAY
MADRAS
BANGALORE
COLOMBO
CALCUTTA
DHAKA
YANGON (RANGOON)
KRUNG THEP (BANGKOK)
PHNOM PENH
THANH PHO HO CHI MINH (SAIGON)
HA NOI
HONG KONG
GUANGZHOU (CANTON)
MANILA
QUEZON CITY
KUALA LUMPUR
SINGAPORE
JAKARTA
SURABAYA
BANDUNG
KARĀCHI
HYDERĀBĀD
AHMADĀBĀD
PUNE
HYDERĀBĀD
NĀGPUR
KĀNPUR
AMRITSAR
LHASA
MANDALAY
PERTH
ANTANANARIVO
MOGADISHU
ADEN
SAN'Ā'
DJIBOUTI

INDONESIA
CELEBES
SULU SEA
CELEBES SEA
PHILIPPINE SEA
HIMALAYAS

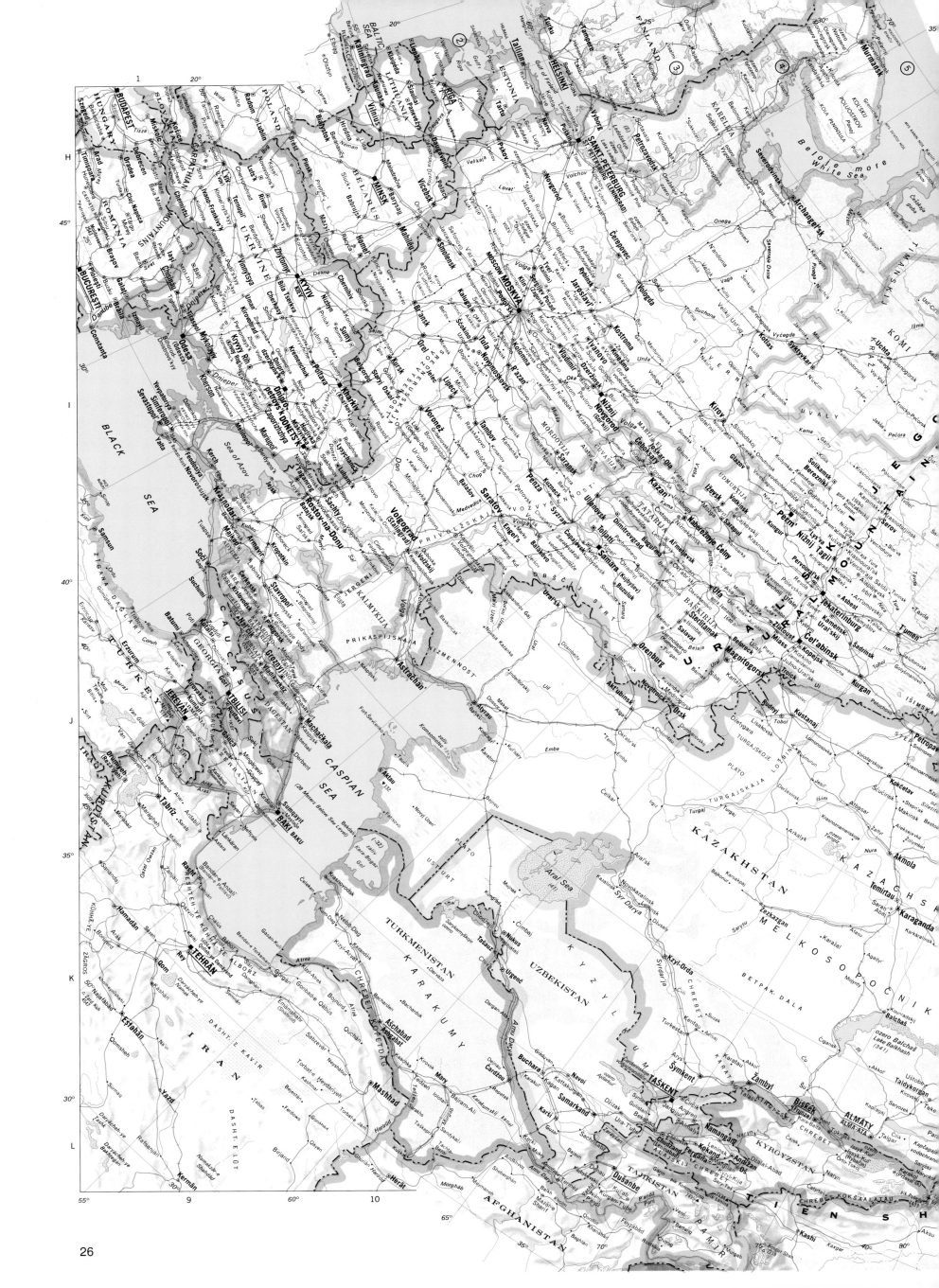

Kilometers

Statute Miles

One centimeter represents 120 kilometers.
One inch represents approximately 190 miles.

Scale 1:12,000,000

Lambert Conformal Conic Projection

Kilometers
Statute Miles

Scale 1:12,000,000

One centimeter represents 120 kilometers.
One inch represents approximately 190 miles.

Lambert Conformal Conic Projection

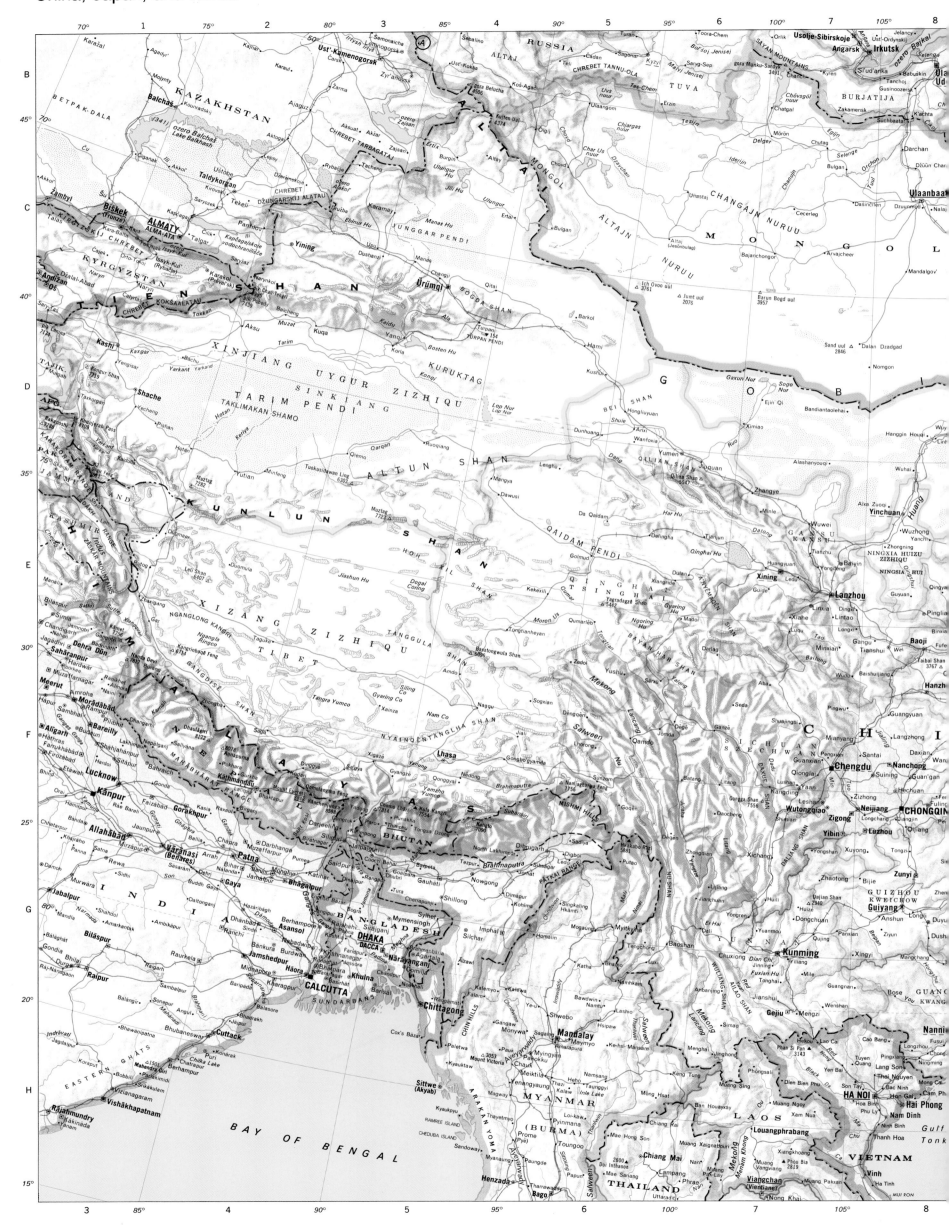

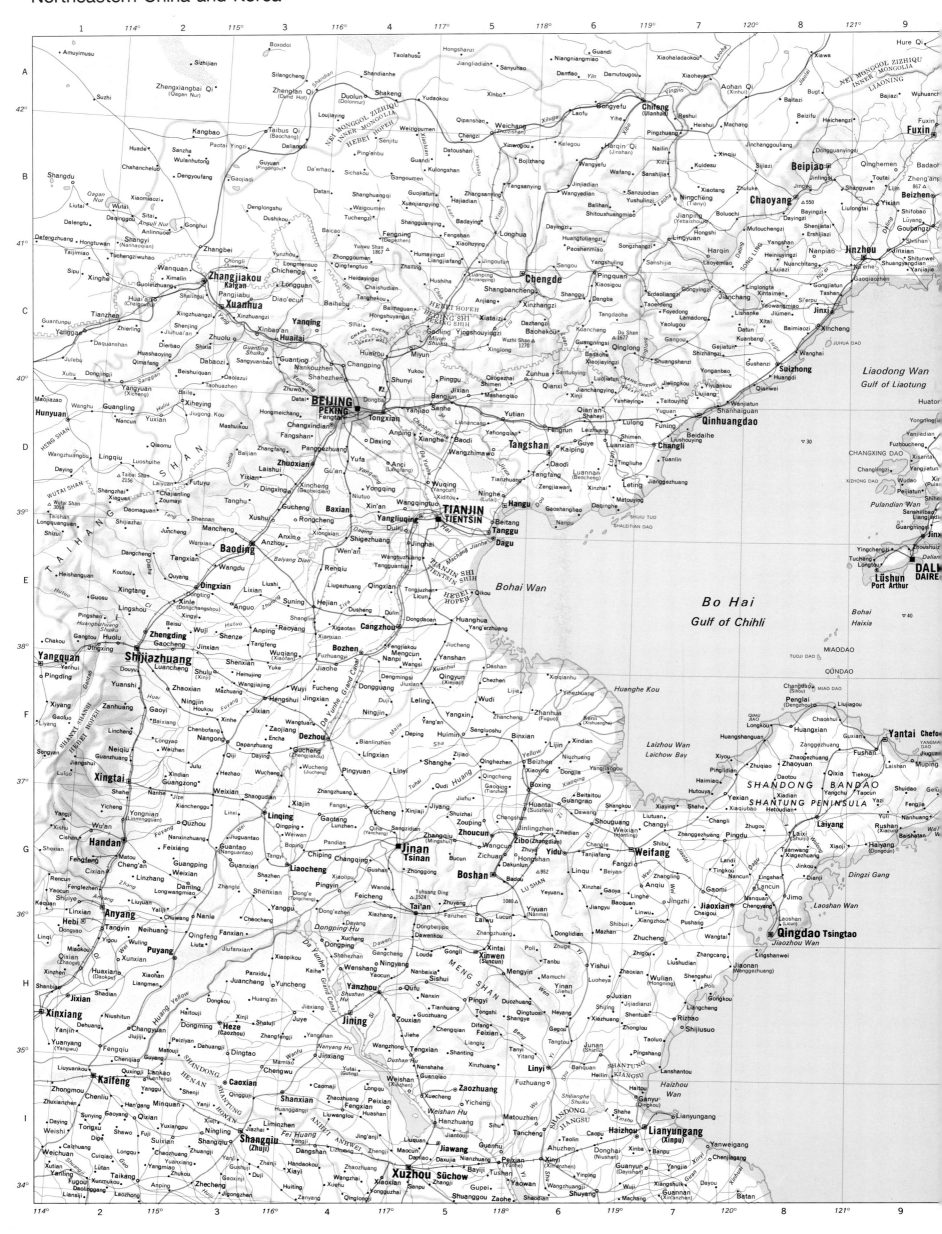

Kilometers
Statute Miles

Scale 1:3,000,000

One centimeter represents 30 kilometers.
One inch represents approximately 47 miles.

Lambert Conformal Conic Projection

Copyright © by Rand McNally & Co.
Map compiled by Cartographia, Budapest.
Map produced by Rand McNally & Co.
A-564400-264

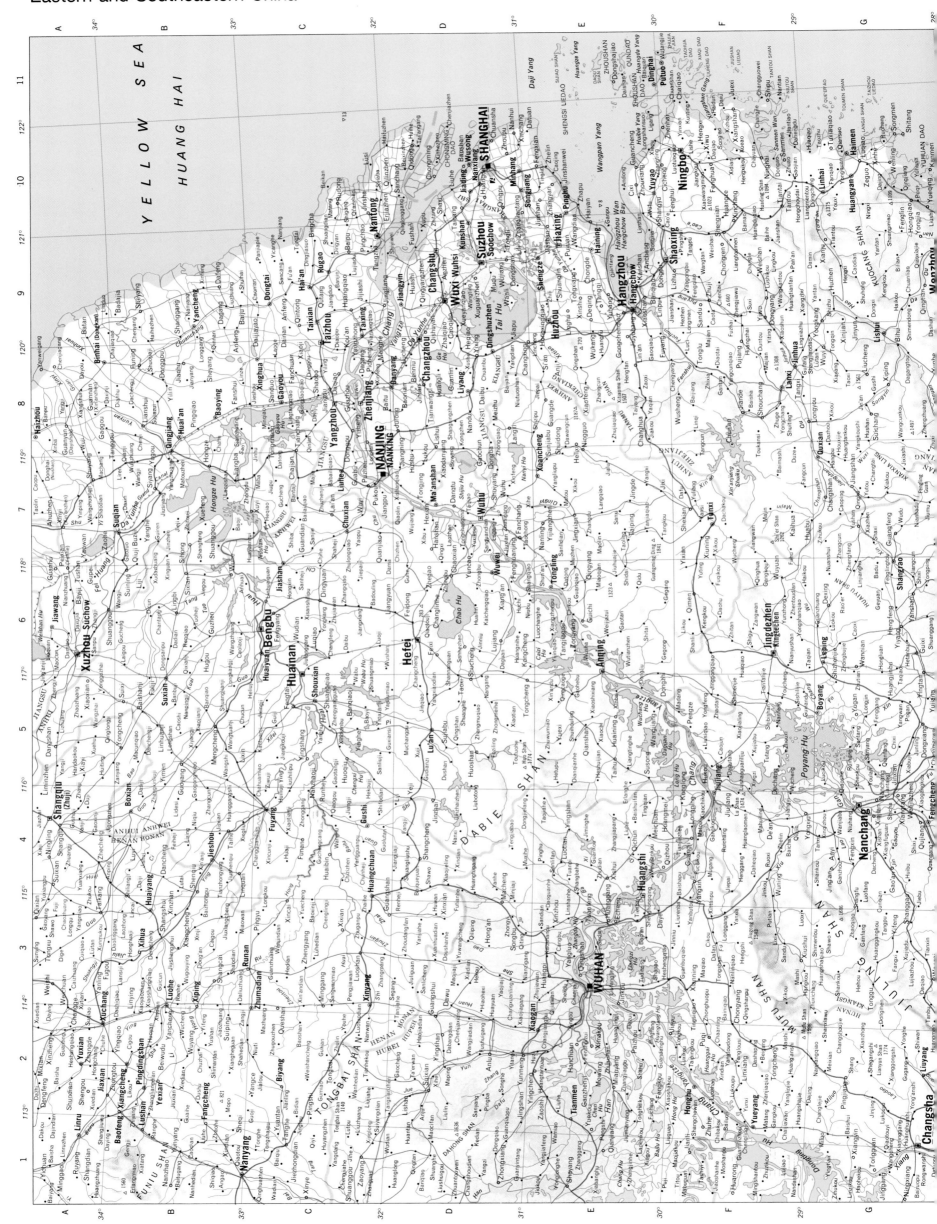

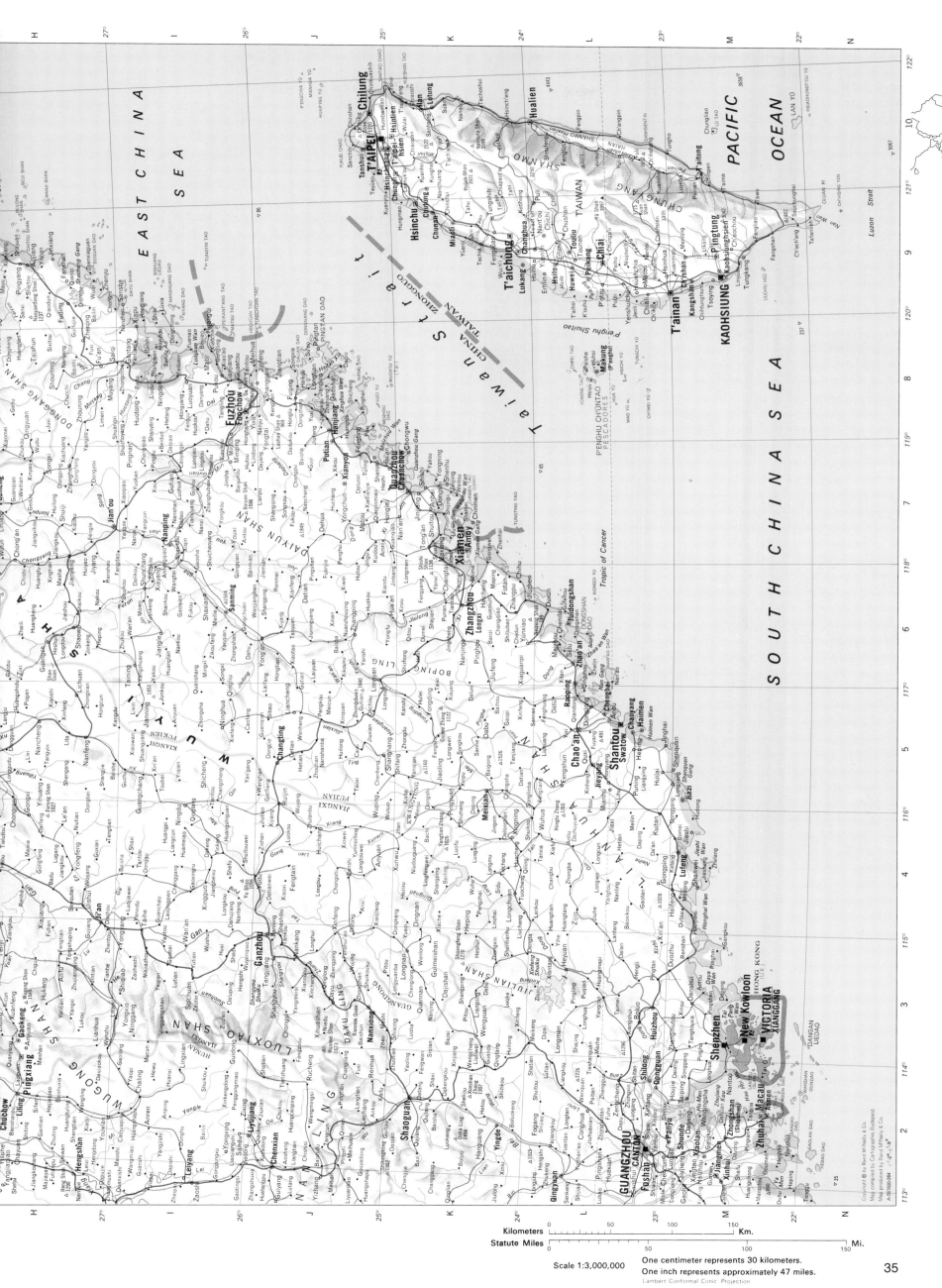

EAST CHINA SEA

PACIFIC OCEAN

SOUTH CHINA SEA

T'aipei

Chilung

Hualien

T'aichung

T'ainan

KAOHSIUNG

P'ingtung

TAIWAN

China Strait / Taiwan Strait / Zhongguo Taiwan

PENGHU CH'ÜNTAO (PESCADORES)

Tropic of Cancer

Luzon Strait

Fuzhou
Foochow

Quanzhou
Chuanchow

Xiamen
Amoy

Zhangzhou

Shantou
Swatow

Chao'an

Nanping

Sanming

Changting

Meixian

Ji'an

Ganzhou

Shaoguan

Nanxiong

Liling
Chuchow

Hengshan

Pingxiang

Lüyiang

Chenxian

GUANGZHOU
CANTON

Foshan

Shunde

Panyu

Zhuhai

Macau

VICTORIA
XIANGGANG

New Kowloon

Shenzhen

HONG KONG

Qingyuan

WUGONG SHAN

NANLING

LUOXIAO SHAN

DAYU LING

JIULIAN SHAN

NAN LING

LIANHUA SHAN

BOPING LING

DAIYUN SHAN

WUYI SHAN

DONGGONG SHAN

GUANGDONG

FUKIEN / FUJIAN

KIANGSI / JIANGXI

KWANGTUNG

Kilometers
0   50   100   150 Km.

Statute Miles
0   50   100   150 Mi.

One centimeter represents 30 kilometers.
One inch represents approximately 47 miles.

Scale 1:3,000,000

Lambert Conformal Conic Projection

35

Copyright © by Rand McNally & Co.
Map compiled by Cartographia, Budapest.
Map produced by Rand McNally & Co.
A-561000-354

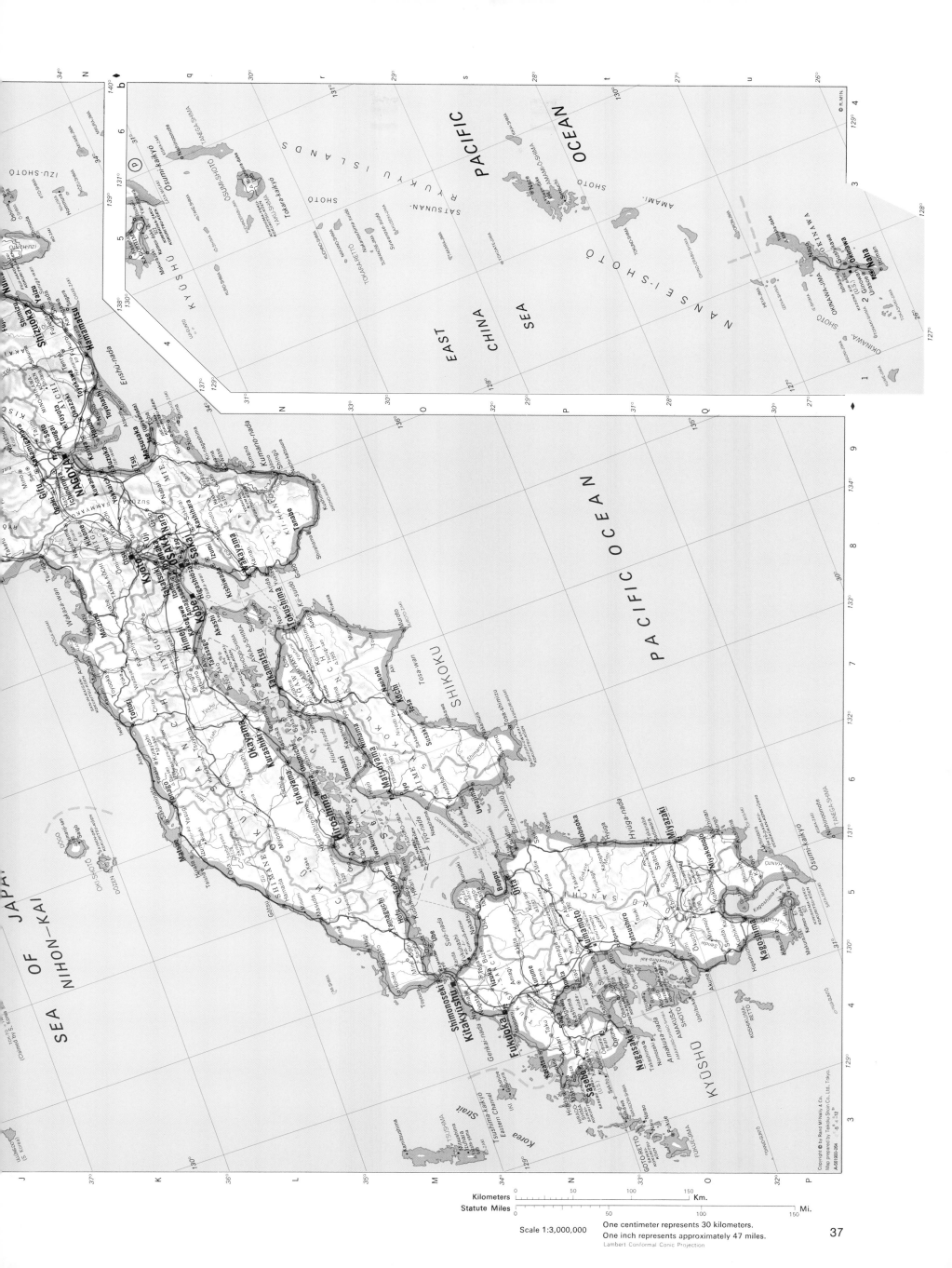

Scale 1:3,000,000

One centimeter represents 30 kilometers.
One inch represents approximately 47 miles.

Lambert Conformal Conic Projection

Kilometers

Statute Miles

37

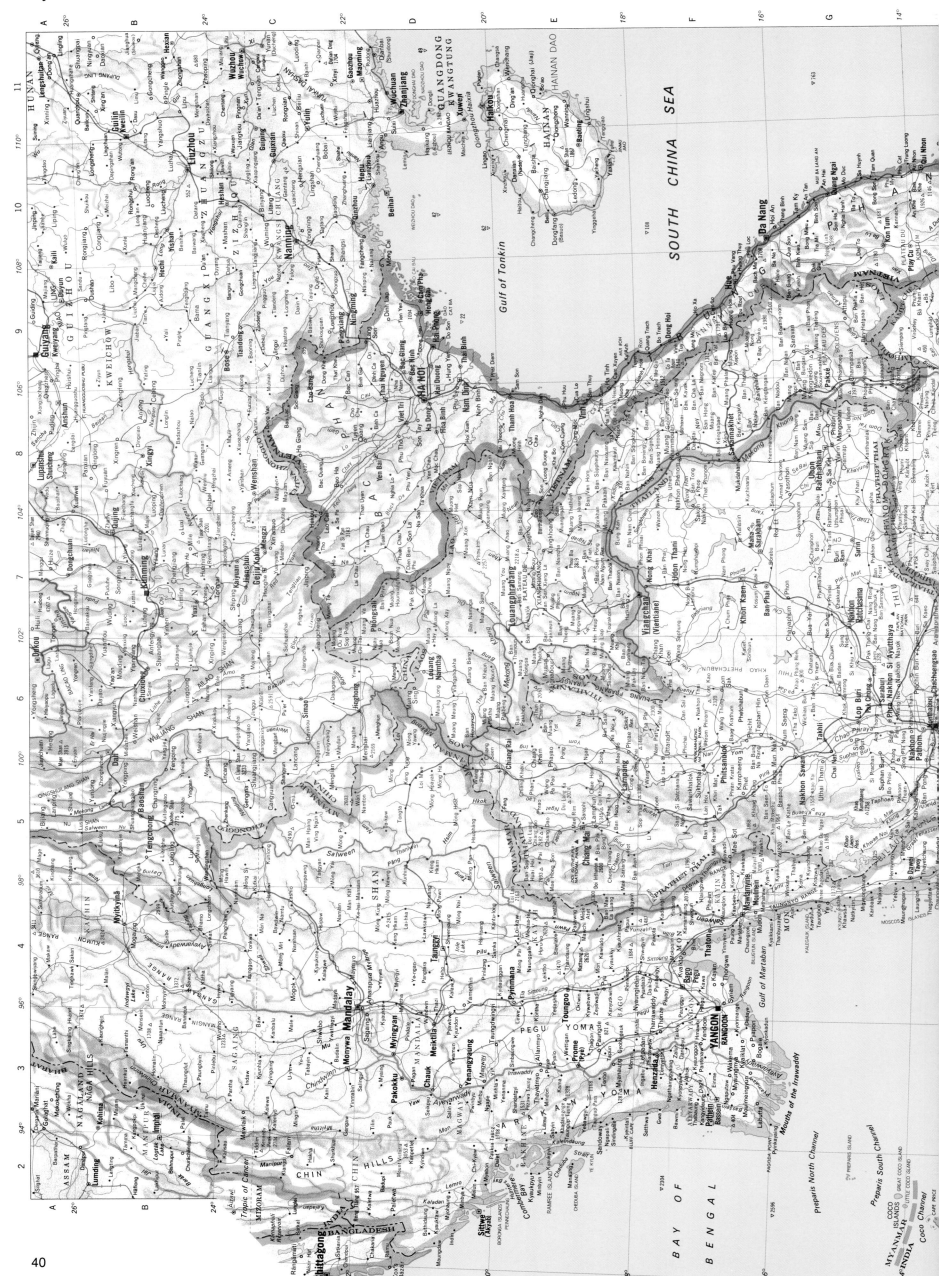

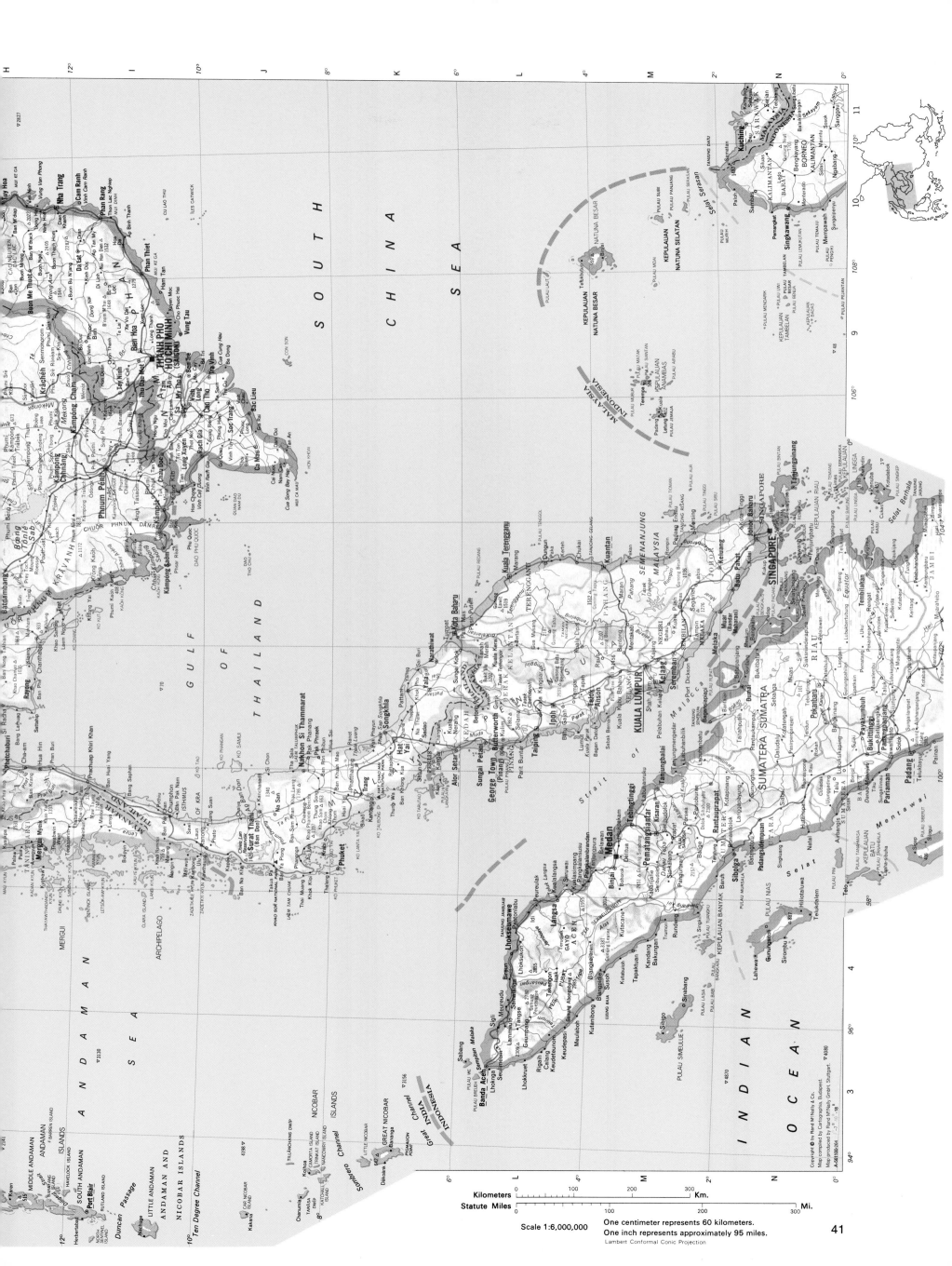

Kilometers

Statute Miles

One centimeter represents 120 kilometers.
One inch represents approximately 190 miles.
Scale 1:12,000,000
Lambert Conformal Conic Projection

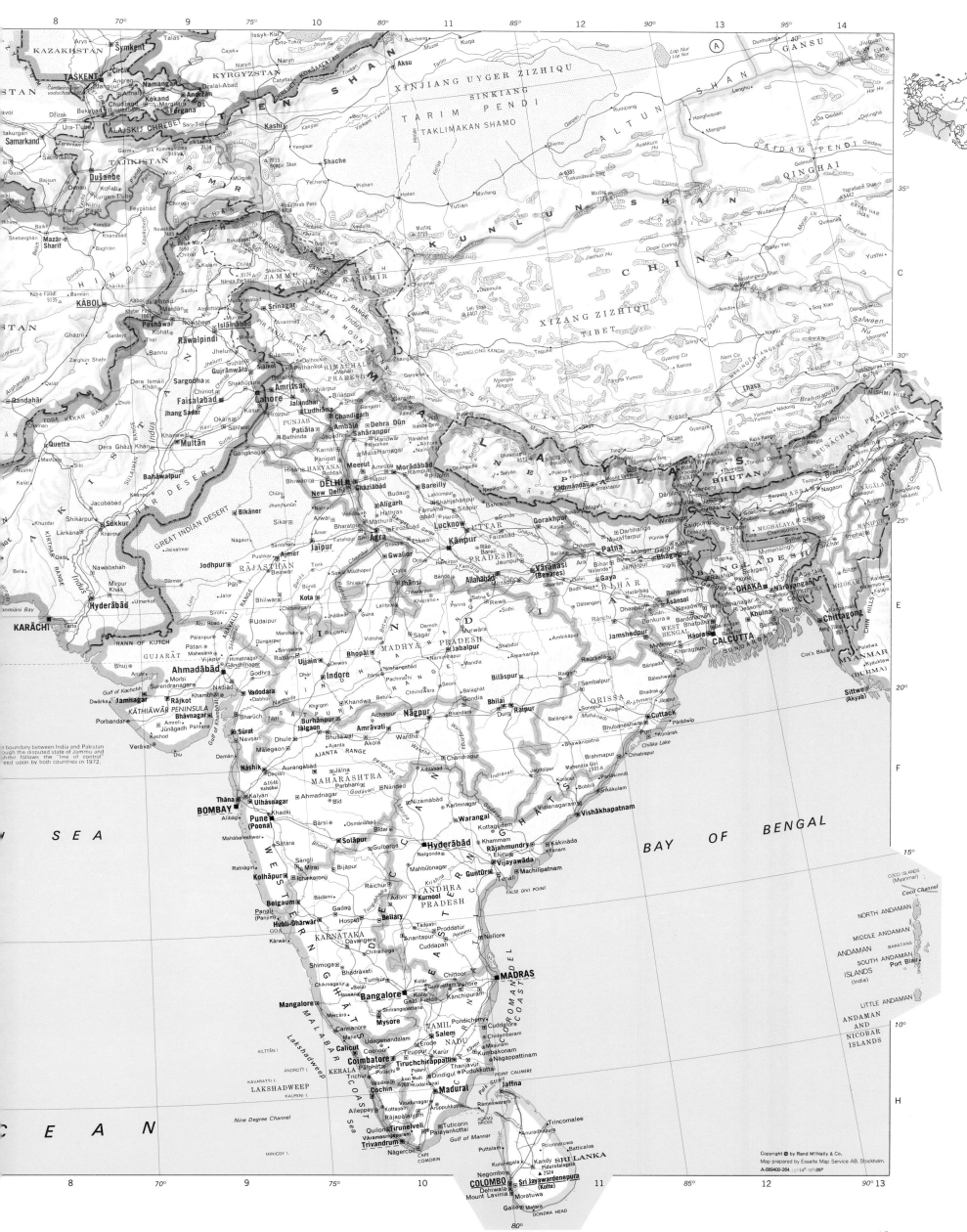

43

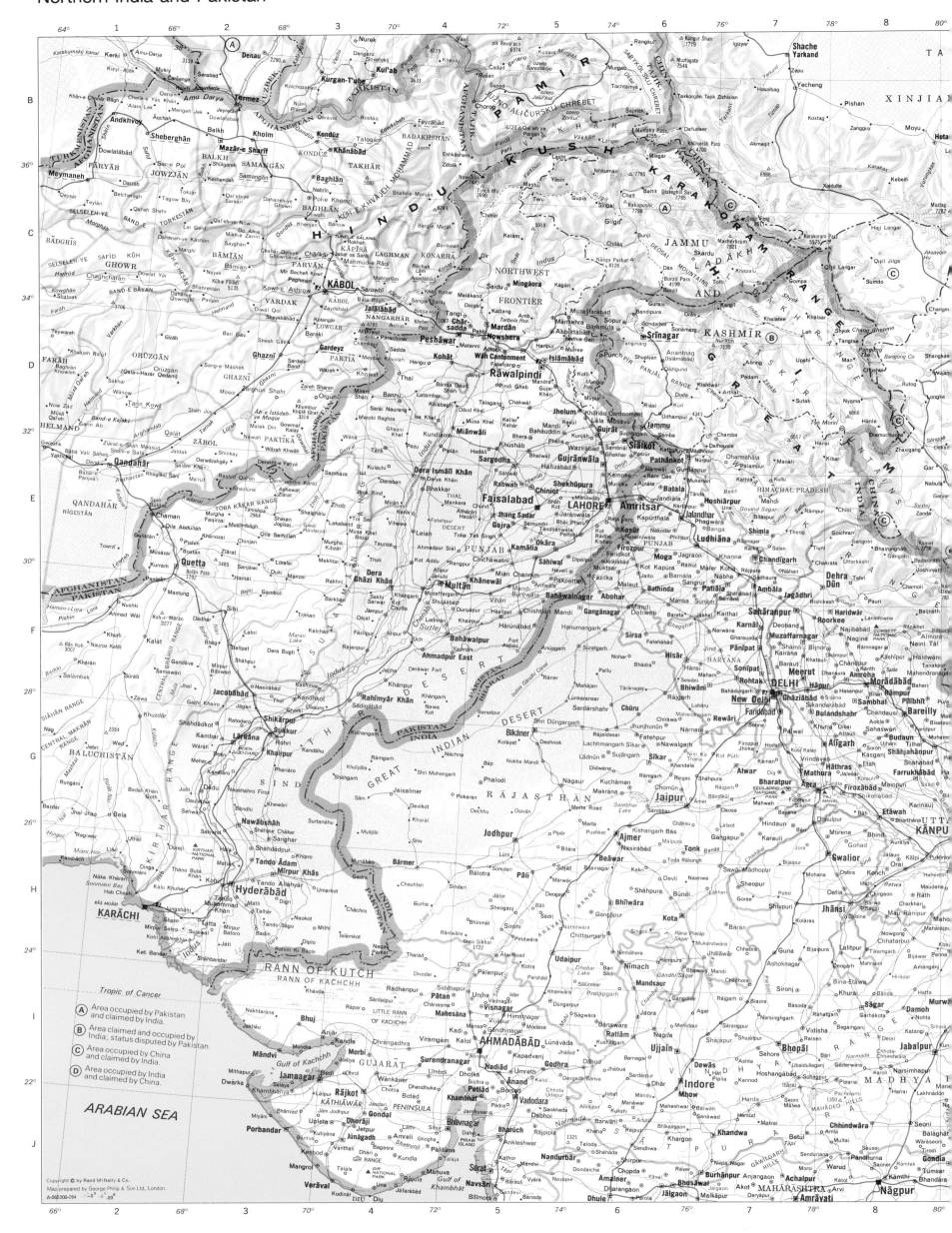

A Area occupied by Pakistan
and claimed by India.

B Area claimed and occupied by
India; status disputed by Pakistan.

C Area occupied by China
and claimed by India.

D Area occupied by India
and claimed by China.

Tropic of Cancer

ARABIAN SEA

Copyright © by Rand M?Nally & Co.
Map prepared by George Philip & Son Ltd., London.
A-566200-264

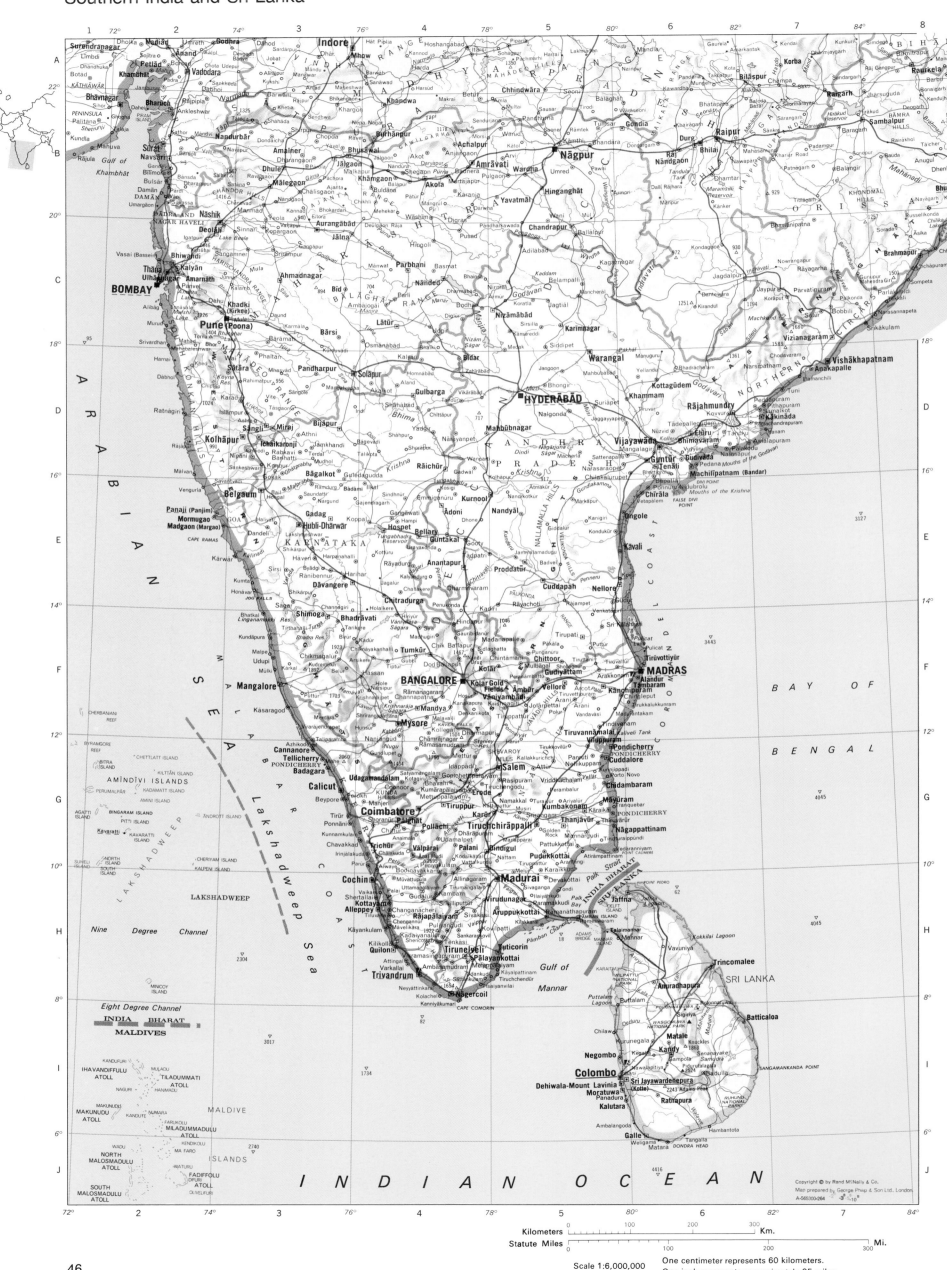

Copyright © by Rand McNally & Co.
Map prepared by George Philip & Son Ltd. London
A-565300-264

Kilometers
Statute Miles

Scale 1:6,000,000

One centimeter represents 60 kilometers.
One inch represents approximately 95 miles.

Lambert Conformal Conic Projection

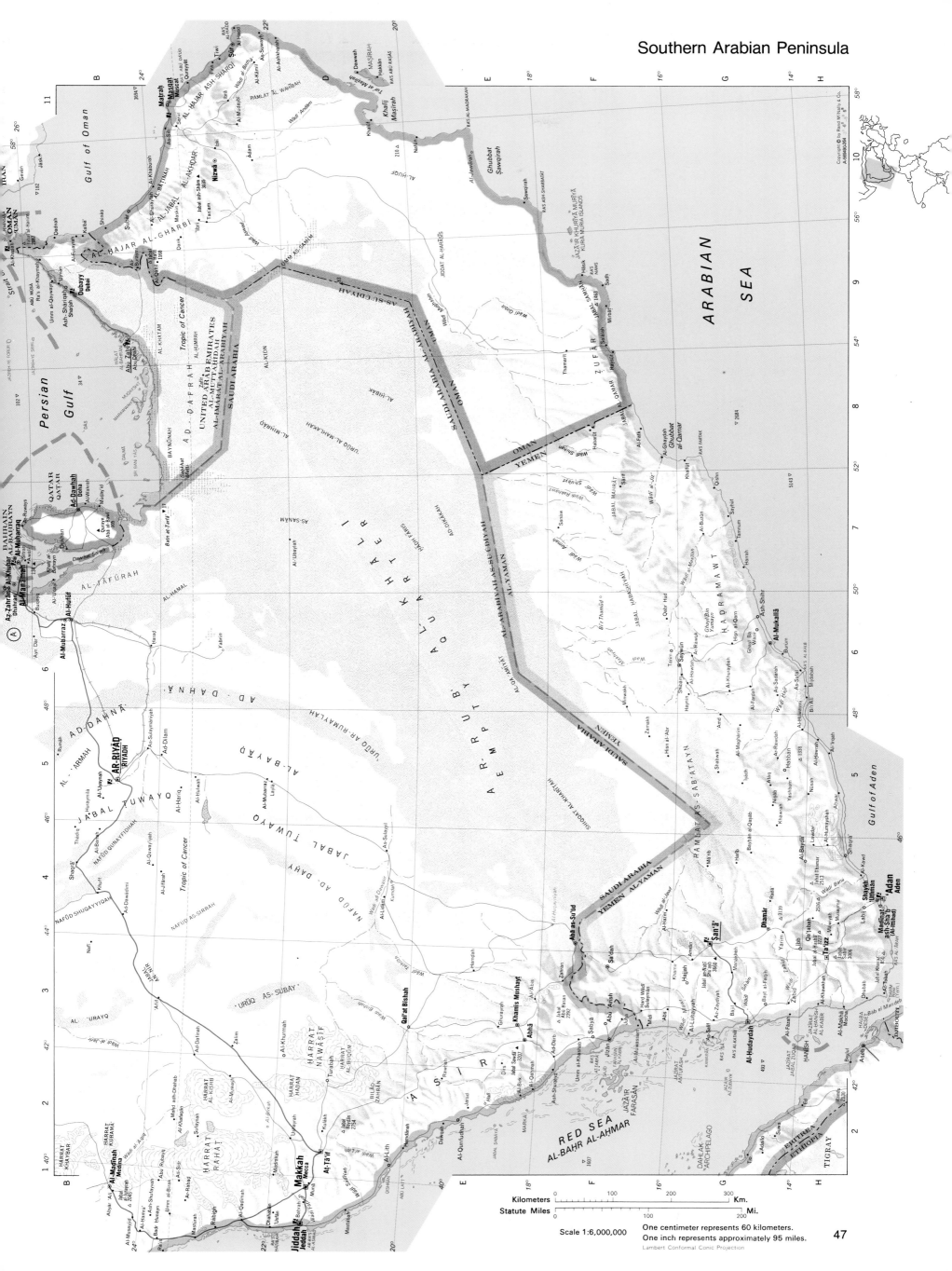

Southern Arabian Peninsula

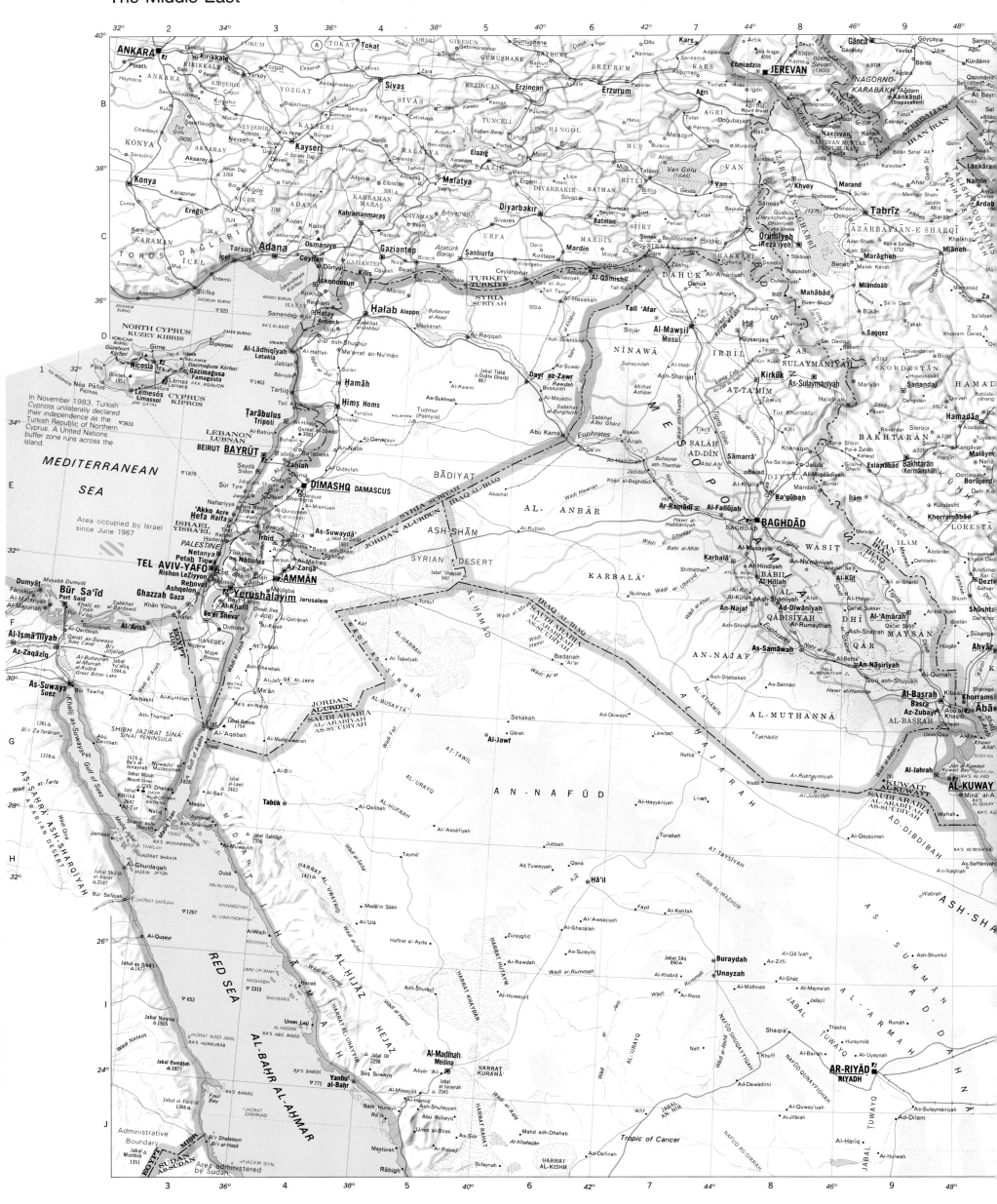

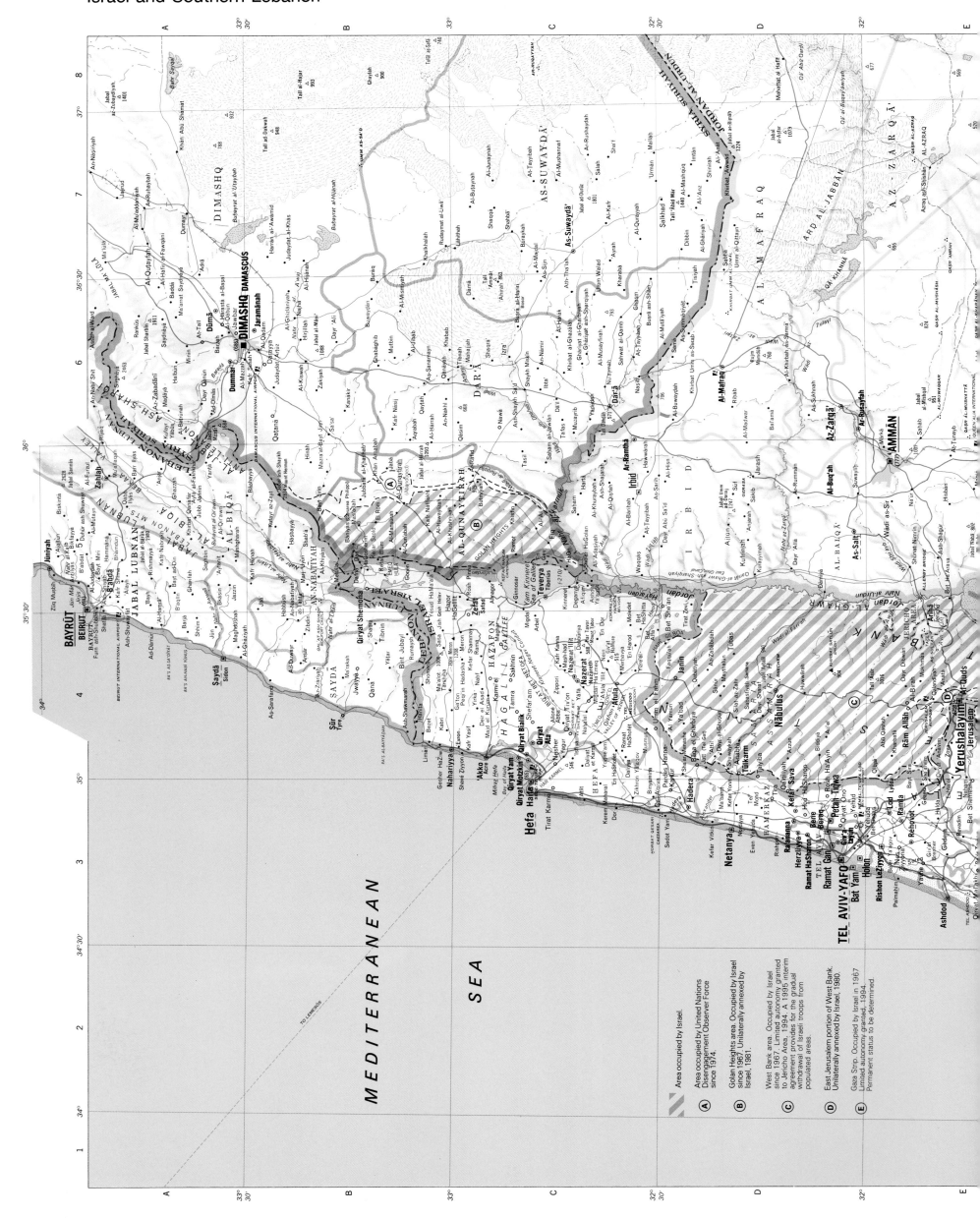

Area occupied by Israel.

Ⓐ Area occupied by United Nations
    Disengagement Observer Force
    since 1974.

Ⓑ Golan Heights area. Occupied by Israel
    since 1967. Unilaterally annexed by
    Israel, 1981.

Ⓒ West Bank area. Occupied by Israel
    since 1967. Limited autonomy granted
    to Jericho Area, 1994. A 1995 interim
    agreement provides for the gradual
    withdrawal of Israeli troops from
    populated areas.

Ⓓ East Jerusalem portion of West Bank.
    Unilaterally annexed by Israel, 1980.

Ⓔ Gaza Strip. Occupied by Israel in 1967.
    Limited autonomy granted, 1994.
    Permanent status to be determined.

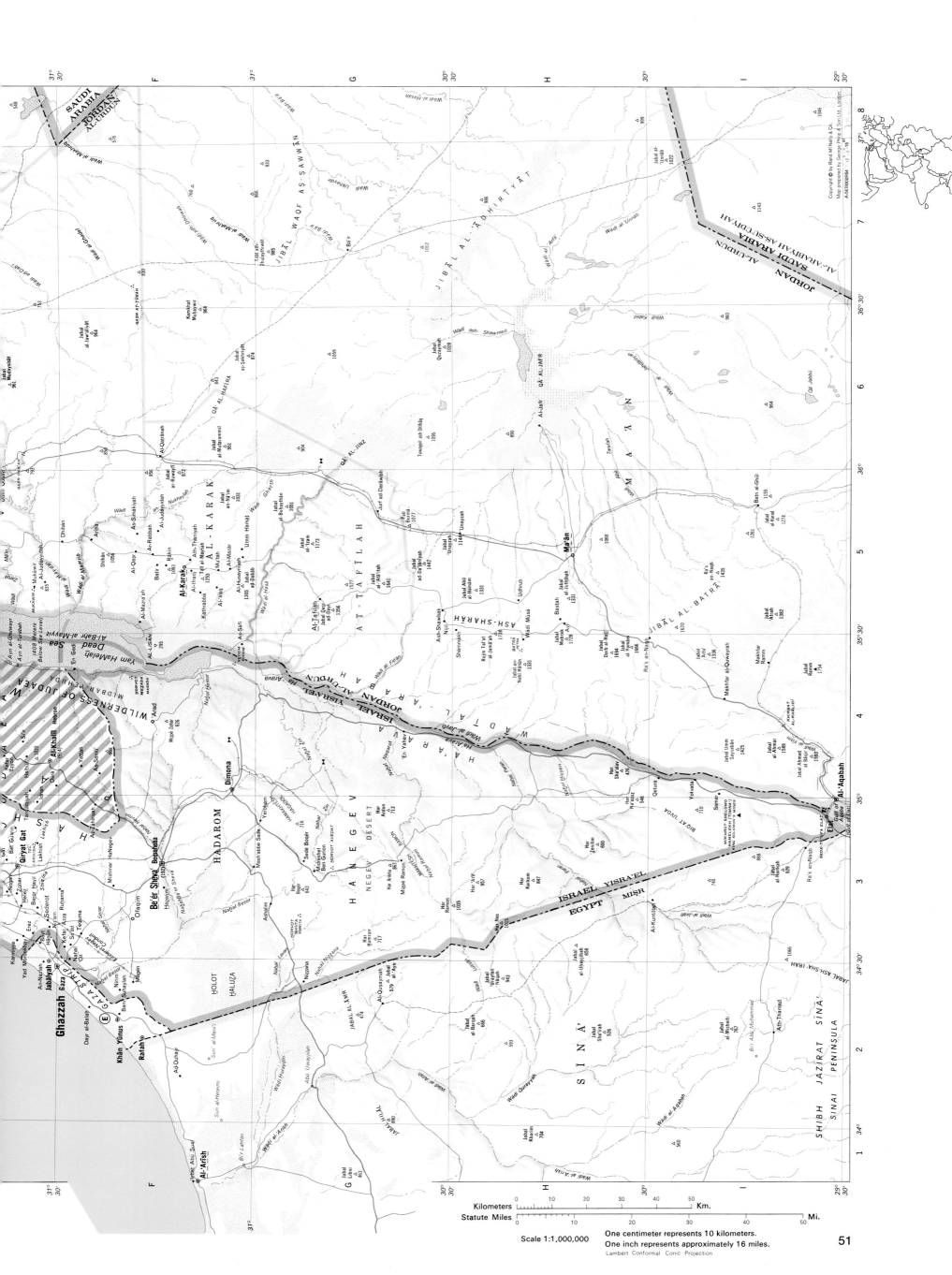

Kilometers
0   10   20   30   40   50   Km.

Statute Miles
0   10   20   30   40   50   Mi.

Scale 1:1,000,000

One centimeter represents 10 kilometers.
One inch represents approximately 16 miles.

Lambert Conformal Conic Projection

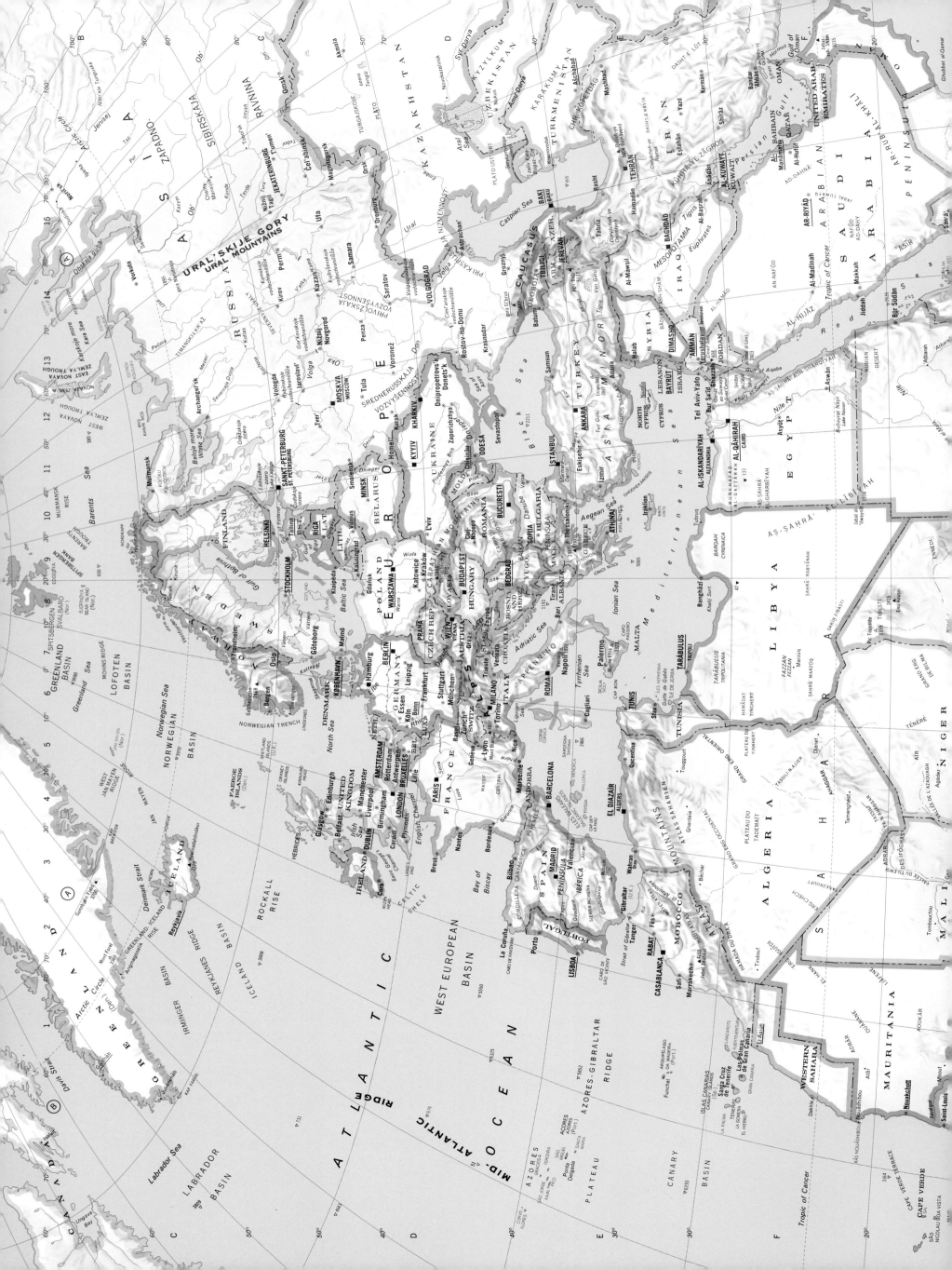

Western Sahara has been occupied by Morocco

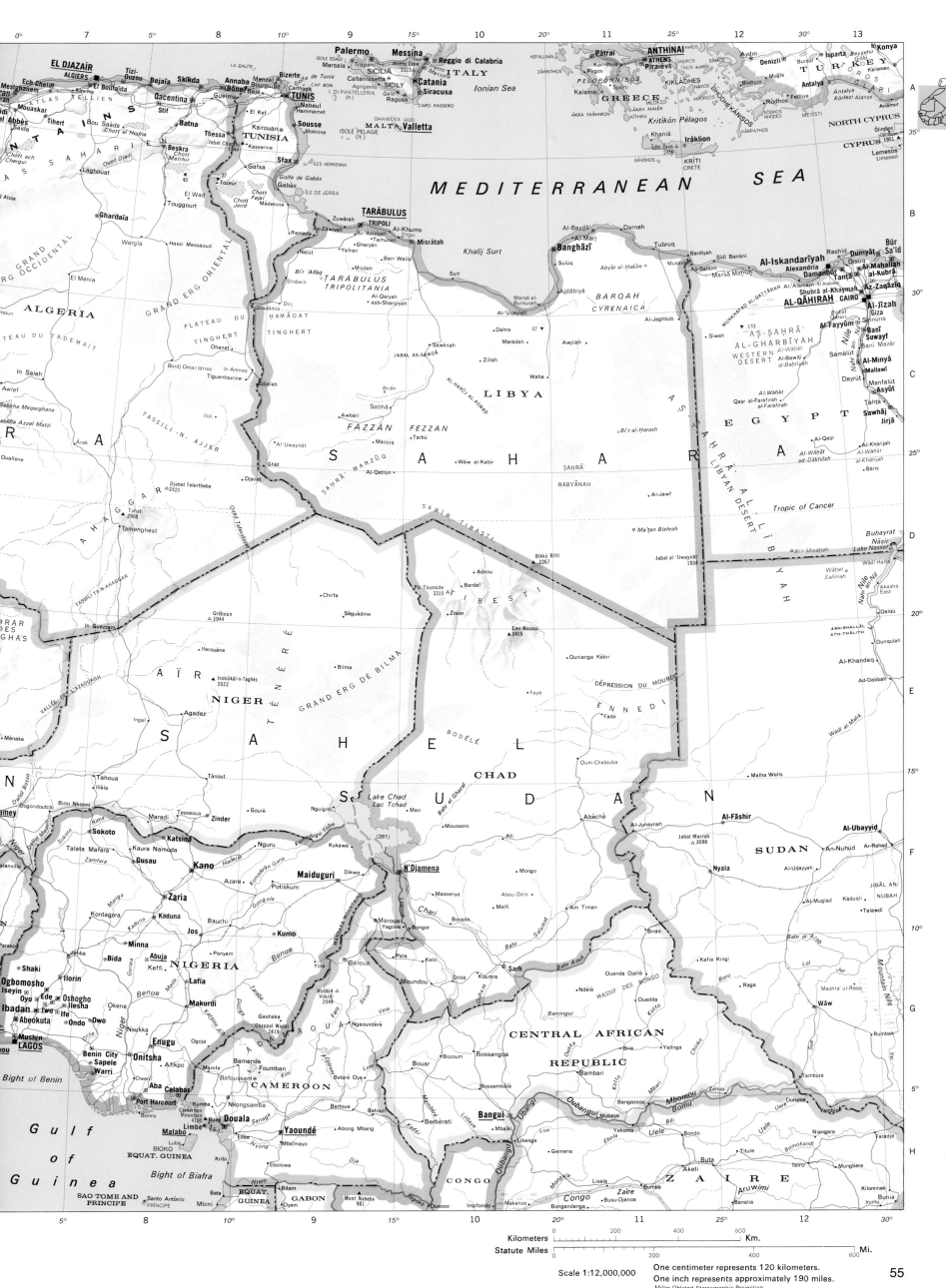

Kilometers 0 ⟶ 200 400 600 Km.

Statute Miles 0 ⟶ 200 400 600 Mi.

Scale 1:12,000,000   One centimeter represents 120 kilometers.
One inch represents approximately 190 miles.
Miller Oblated Stereographic Projection

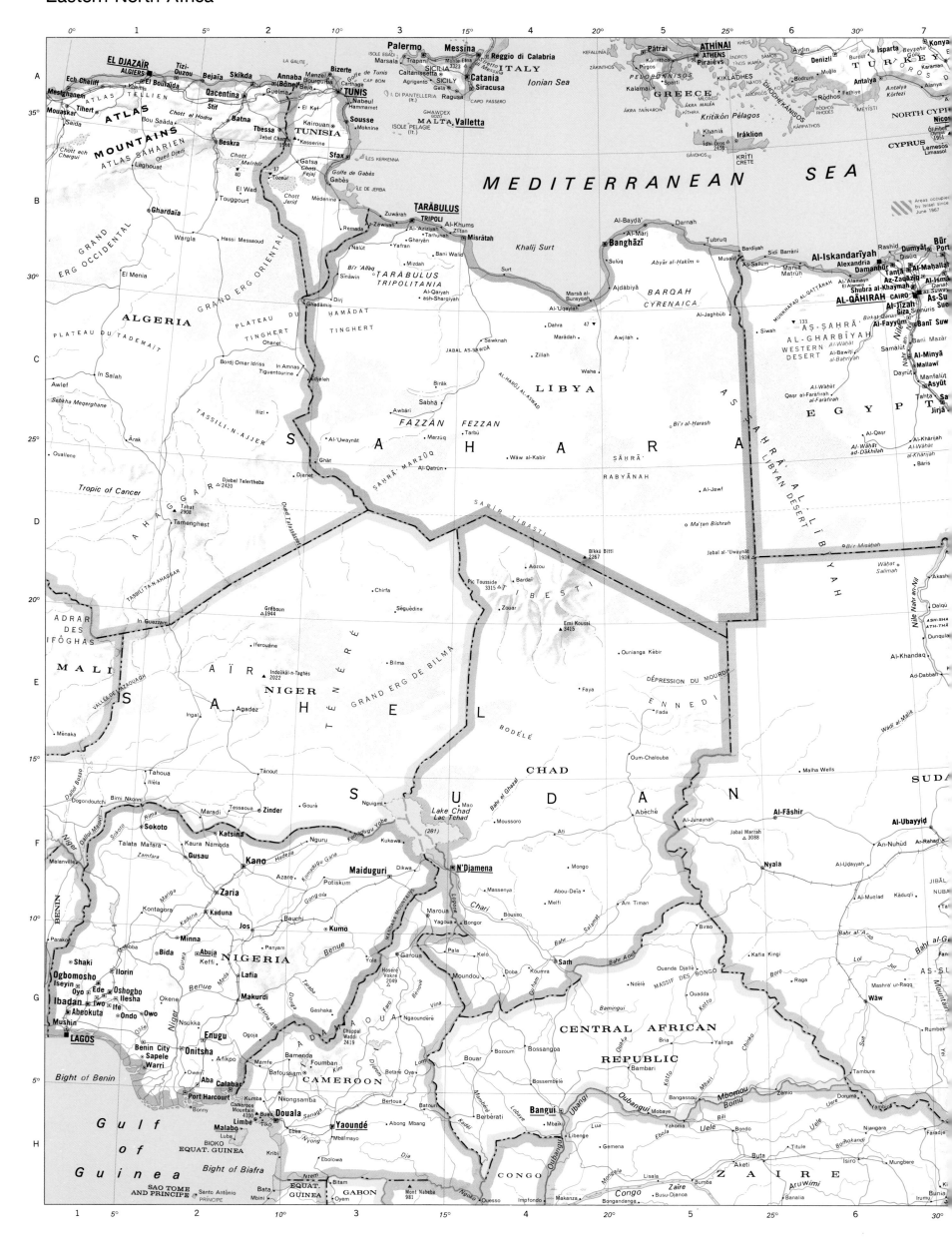

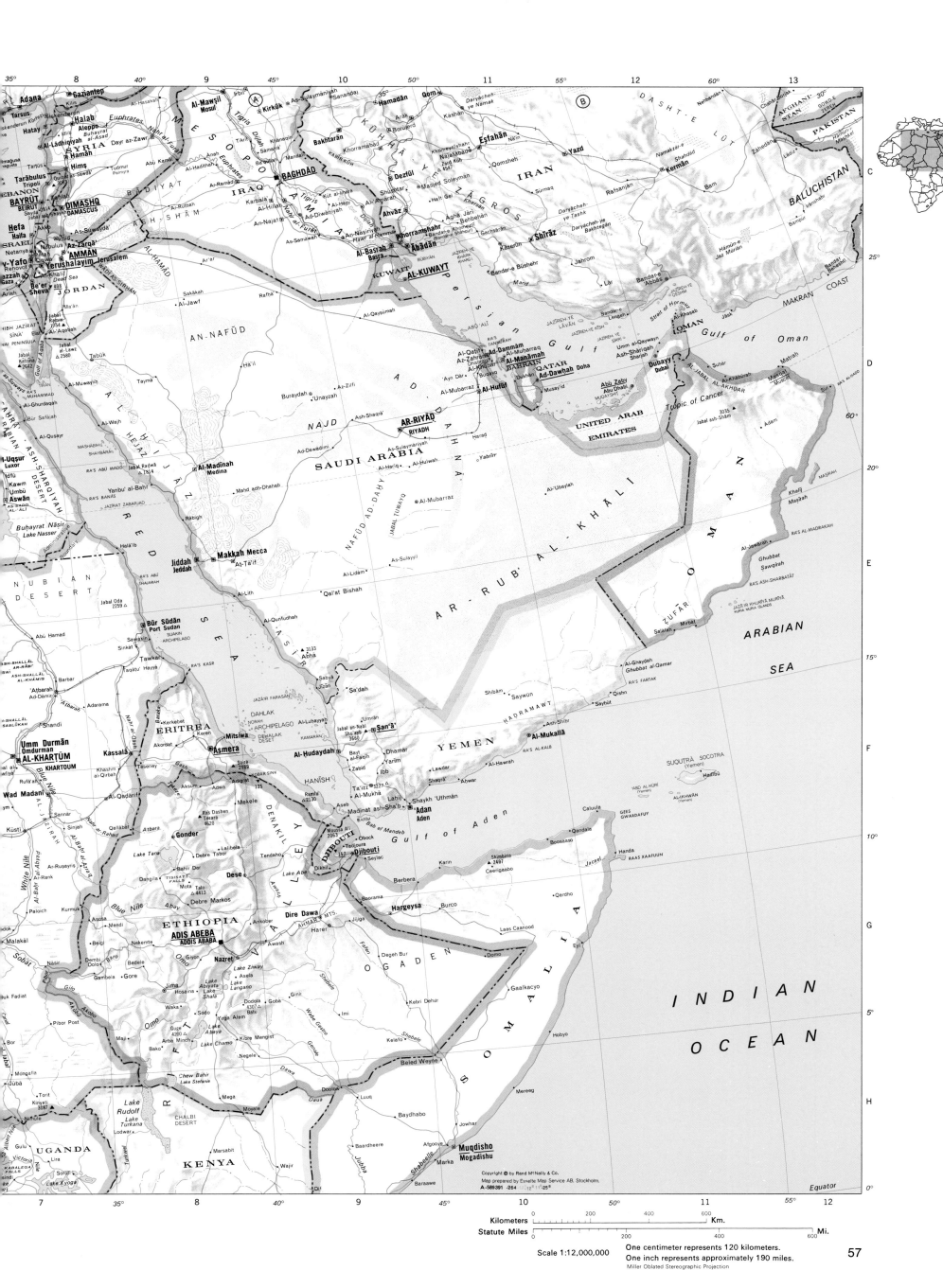

Kilometers 0   200   400   600
                                    Km.
Statute Miles 0   200   400   600
                                       Mi.

Scale 1:12,000,000
One centimeter represents 120 kilometers.
One inch represents approximately 190 miles.
Miller Oblated Stereographic Projection

57

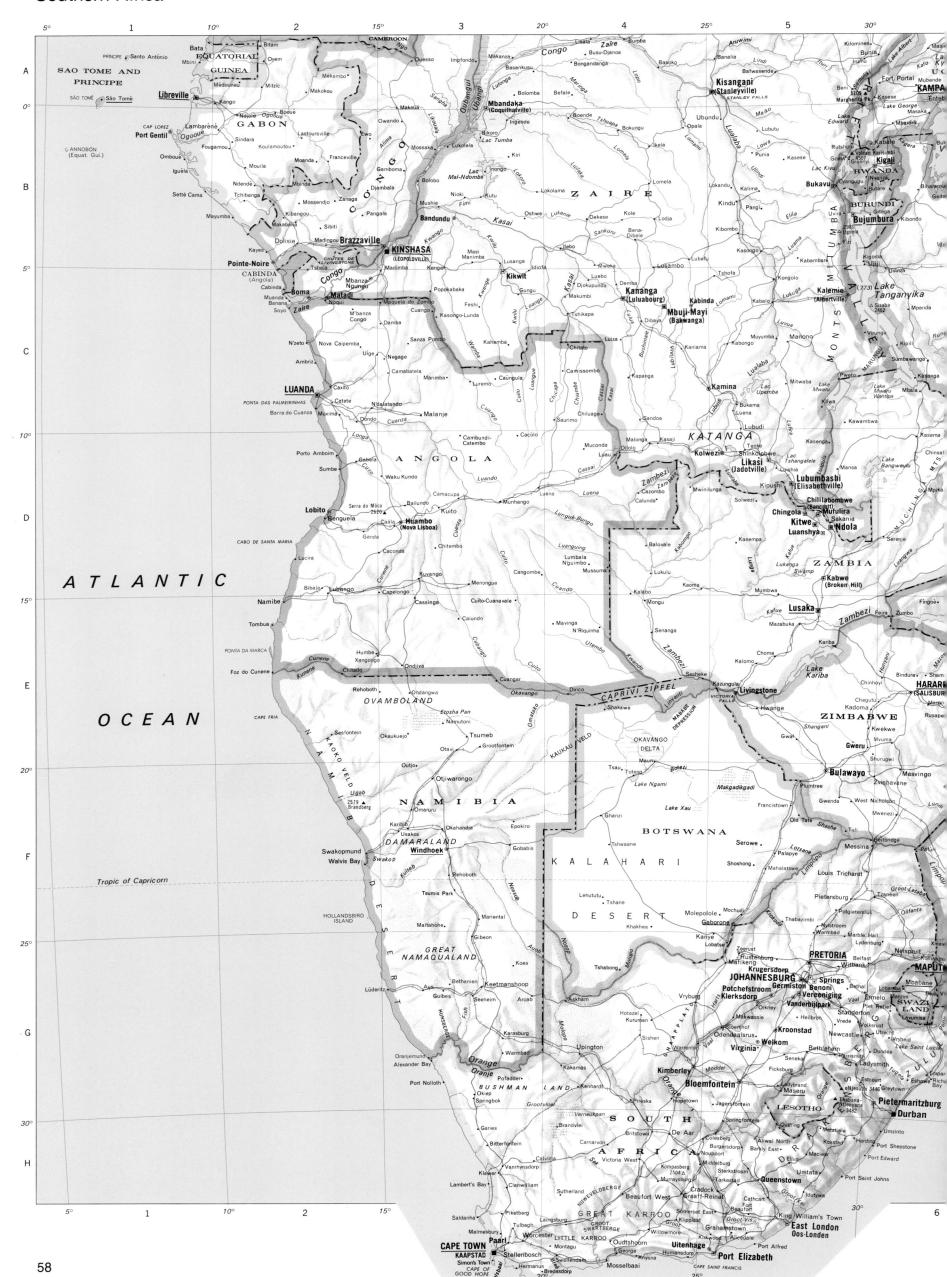

SOMALIA

INDIAN OCEAN

Equator

0°

KENYA

NAIROBI

Mombasa

B

Arusha

Zanzibar

Tanga

5°

SEYCHELLES

Victoria
MAHÉ ISLAND

AMIRANTE ISLANDS
(Sey.)

ÎLE DESROCHES
(Sey.)

PLATTE ISLAND (Sey.)

DAR ES SALAAM

TANZANIA

STEPPE

MASAI

SERENGETI
PLAIN

Dodoma

Morogoro

ALPHONSE ISLAND (Sey.)

COETIVY ISLAND
(Sey.)

C

MAFIA ISLAND

Kilwa Kivinje

ALDABRA ISLAND
(Sey.)

COSMOLEDO I.
(Sey.)

SAINT PIERRE ISLAND
(Sey.)

PROVIDENCE ISLAND
(Sey.)

CERF ISLAND
(Sey.)

Lindi

Mtwara

ASSUMPTION ISLAND
(Sey.)

ASTOVE ISLAND
(Sey.)

FARQUHAR GROUP
(Sey.)

10°

Lake
Nyasa

Lake Malawi

MALAWI

CABO DELGADO

Pemba

AGALEGA ISLANDS
(Mauritius)

ÎLES GLORIEUSES
(Fr.)

CAP D'AMBRE

CAP
SAINT-SÉBASTIEN

Antsiranana

D

COMOROS

Moroni

NJAZIDJA

Mutsamudu

Dzaoudzi

MAYOTTE
(Fr.)

NOSY MITSIO

NOSY BE
Hell-Ville

Ambilobe

Vohimarina

Nacala

Nampula

Zomba

Blantyre

MOZAMBIQUE

Moçambique

MASSIF DU
TSARATANANA

Maromokotro

Sambava

Antalaha

Baie de Narinda

Befandriana

Port-Berge

PRESQU'ÎLE
DE MASOALA

CAP EST

15°

Quelimane

Helodranon' i Mahajamba

Mahajanga

Maevatanana

Marovoay

Mandritsara

Mananara

ÎLE TROMELIN
(Fr.)

MOZAMBIQUE

Zambeze

Beira

Lac Alaotra

Toamasina

E

MADAGASCAR

ANTANANARIVO

Antsirabe

Morondava

Fianarantsoa

Port Louis
Curepipe

Mahébourg

MAURITIUS

20°

Toliara

Le Port
Saint-Paul

Saint-Denis

Saint-Pierre

RÉUNION
(Fr.)

MASCARENE
ISLANDS

BASSAS DA INDIA
(Fr.)

ÎLE EUROPA
(Fr.)

CAP SAINT-VINCENT

Pic Boby
2658

Manakara

Farafangana

Tropic of Capricorn

F

Xai-Xai

CAP SAINTE-MARIE

Faradofay

25°

INDIAN OCEAN

G

Copyright © by Rand McNally & Co.
Map prepared by Esselte Map Service AB, Stockholm.
A-589200-264

30°

Kilometers

Statute Miles

Km.

Mi.

Scale 1:12,000,000
One centimeter represents 120 kilometers.
One inch represents approximately 190 miles.
Miller Oblated Stereographic Projection

59

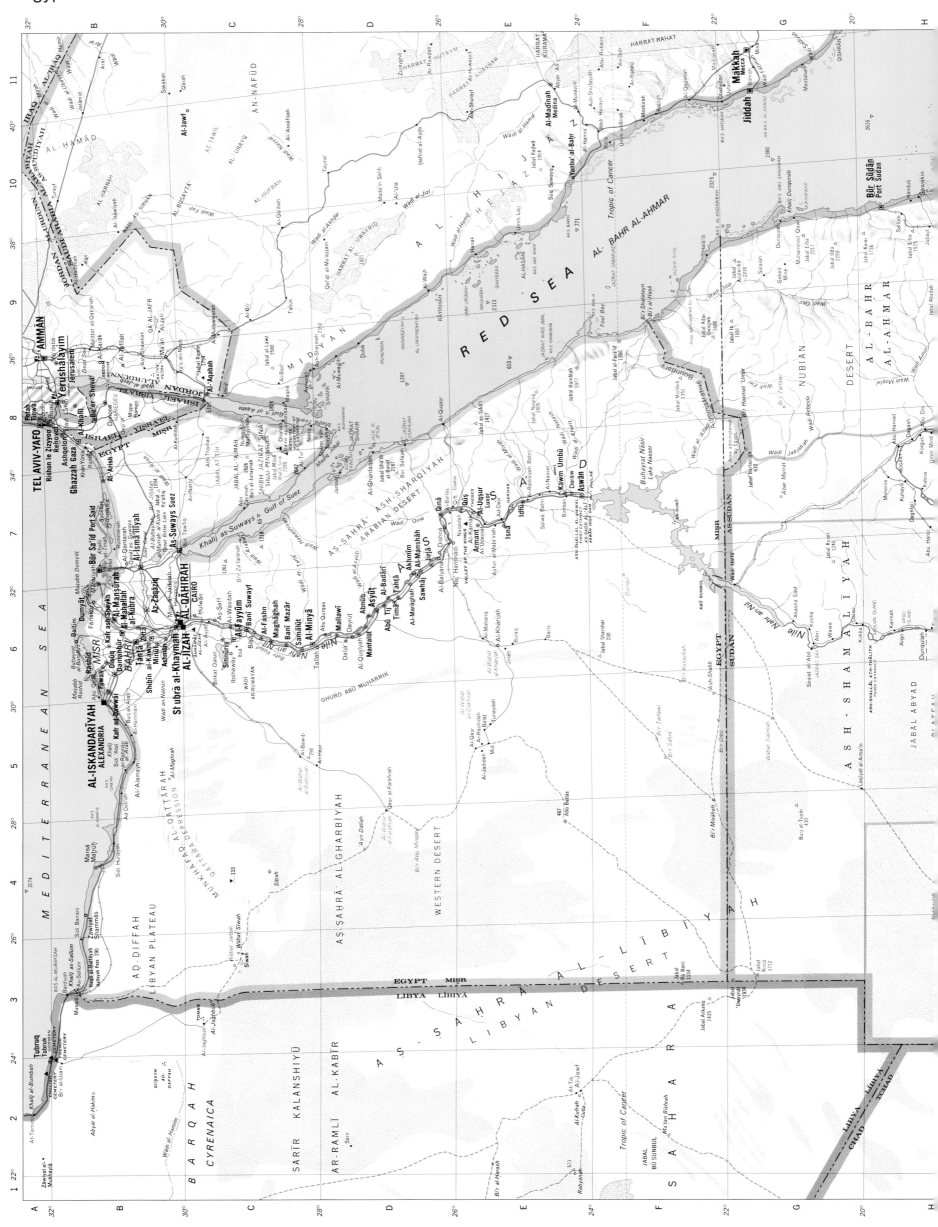

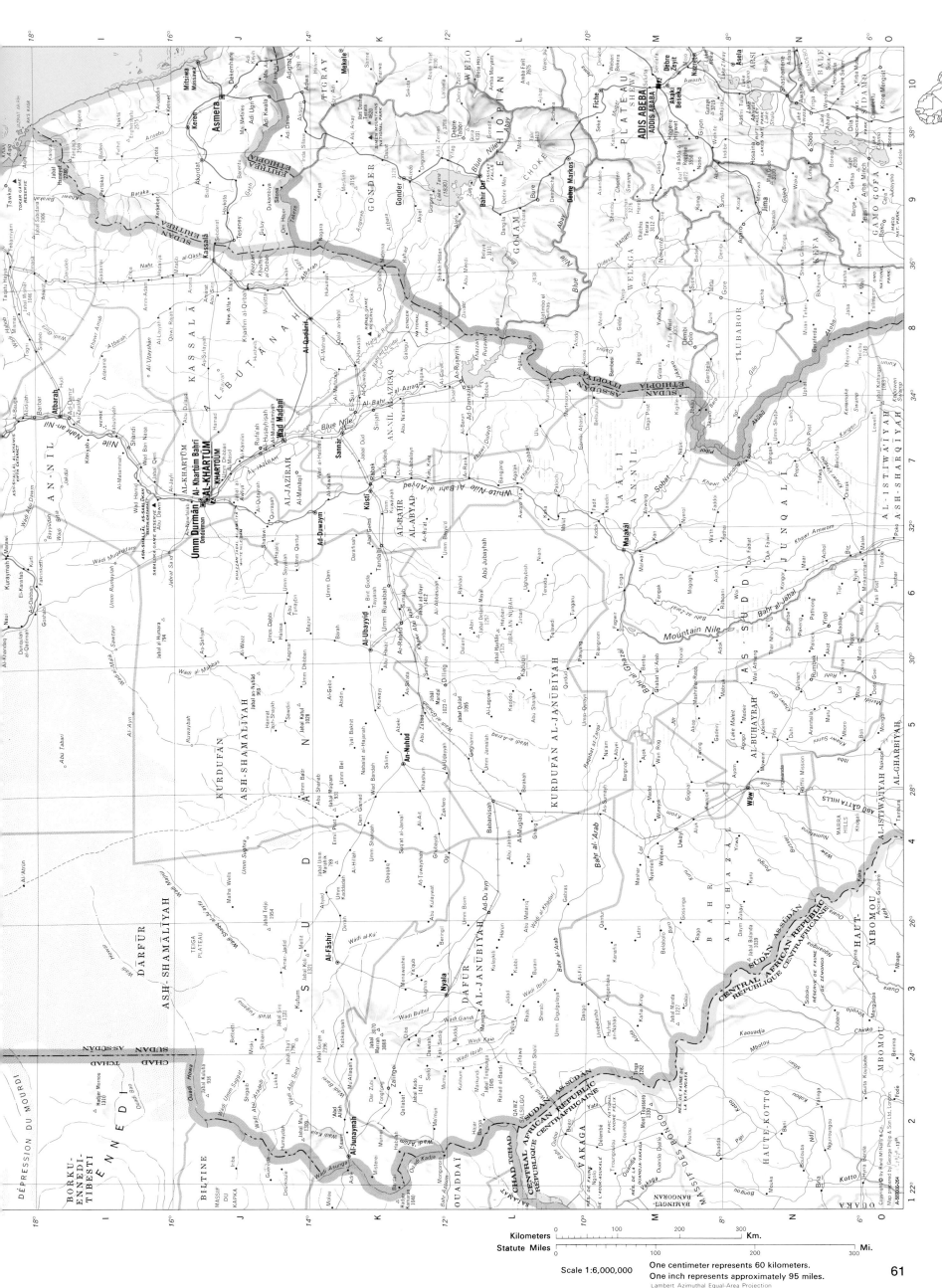

Kilometers

Statute Miles

Scale 1:6,000,000

One centimeter represents 60 kilometers.
One inch represents approximately 95 miles.

Lambert Azimuthal Equal-Area Projection

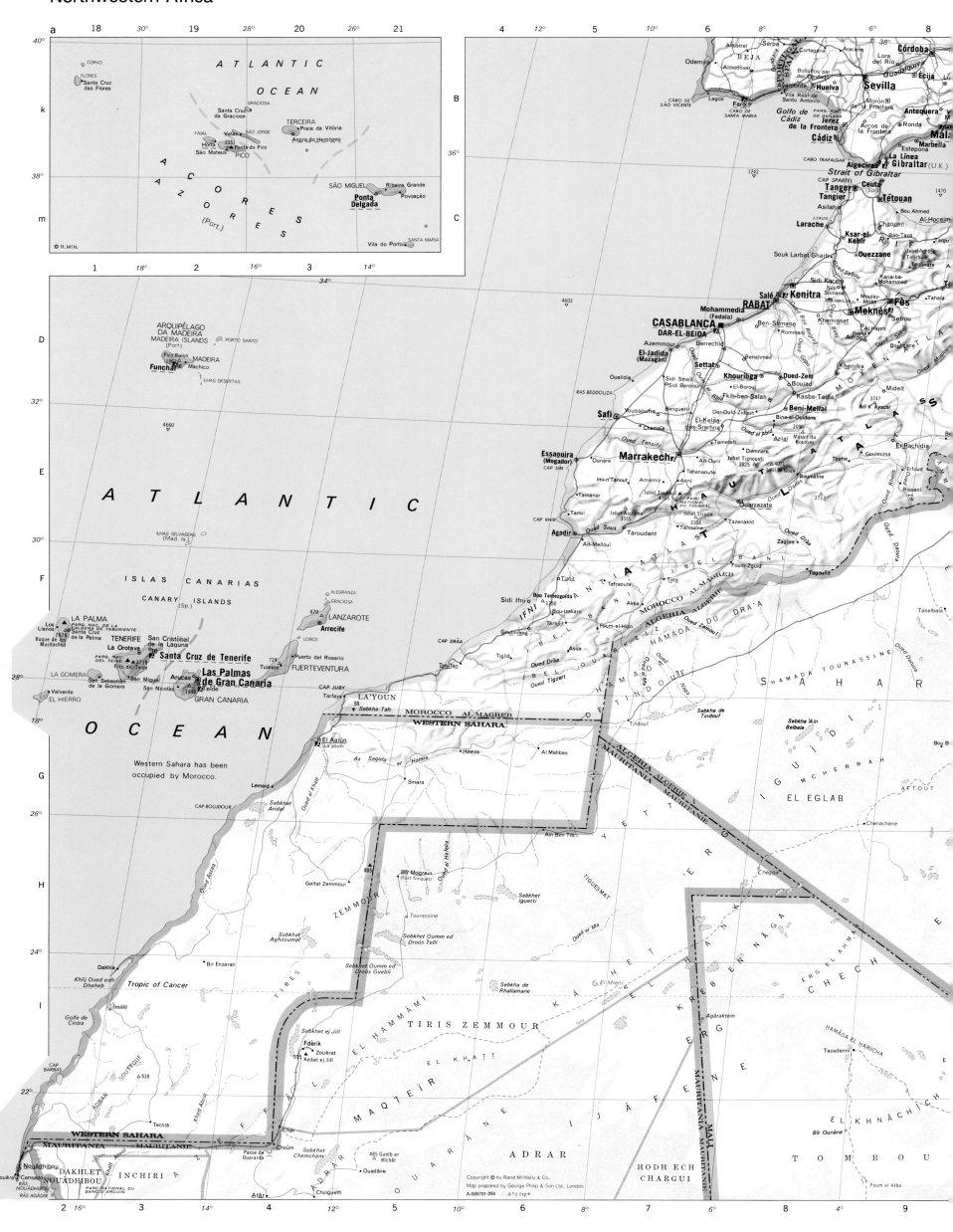

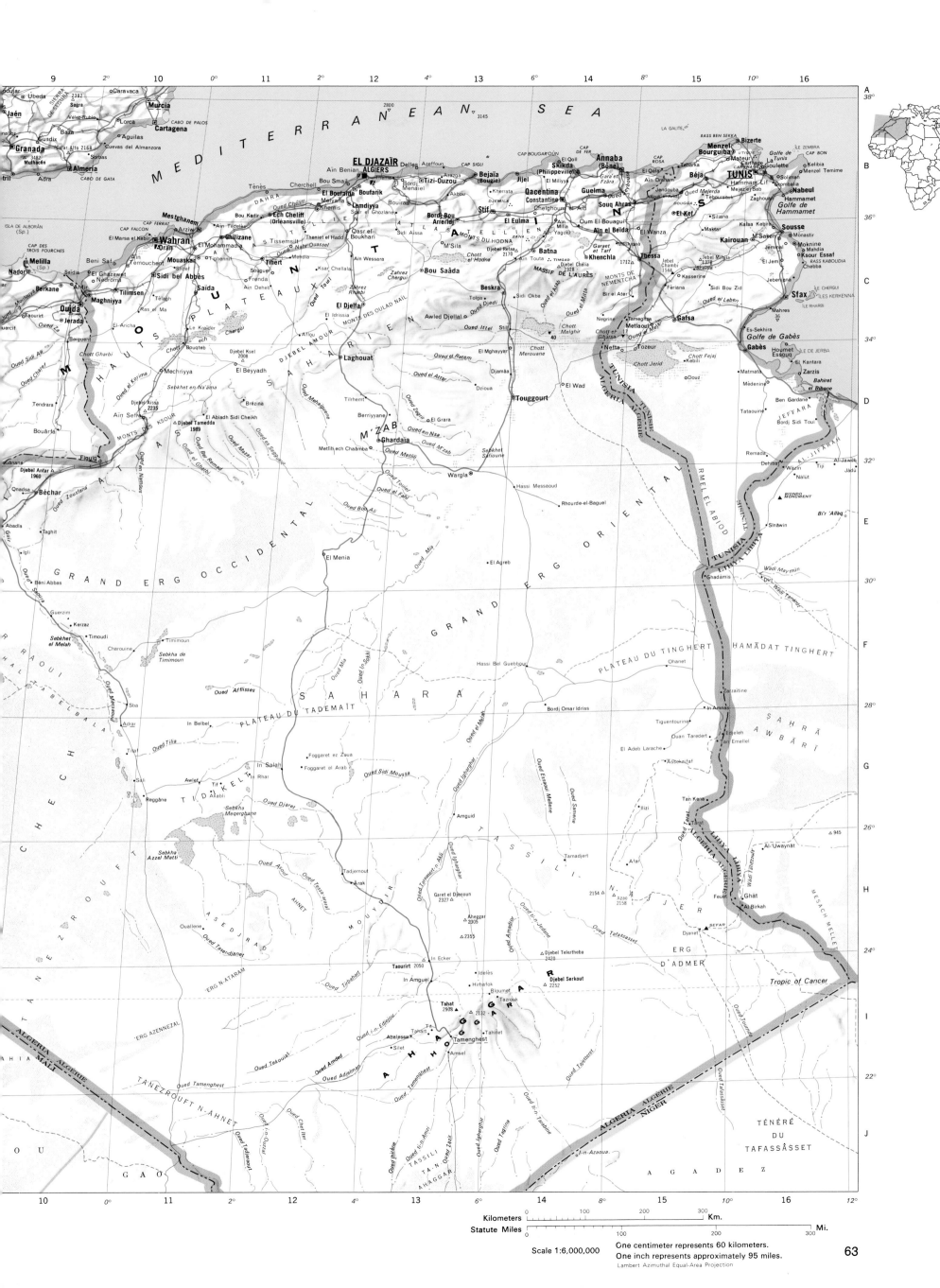

One centimeter represents 60 kilometers.
One inch represents approximately 95 miles.

Scale 1:6,000,000

Lambert Azimuthal Equal-Area Projection

63

Kilometers 0   100   200   300   Km.

Statute Miles 0   100   200   300   Mi.

Scale 1:6,000,000
One centimeter represents 60 kilometers.
One inch represents approximately 95 miles.
Lambert Azimuthal Equal-Area Projection

Copyright © by Rand McNally & Co.
Map prepared by George Philip & Son Ltd., London.
A-589292-264

Kilometers
Statute Miles

Scale 1:6,000,000
One centimeter represents 60 kilometers.
One inch represents approximately 95 miles.
Lambert Azimuthal Equal-Area Projection

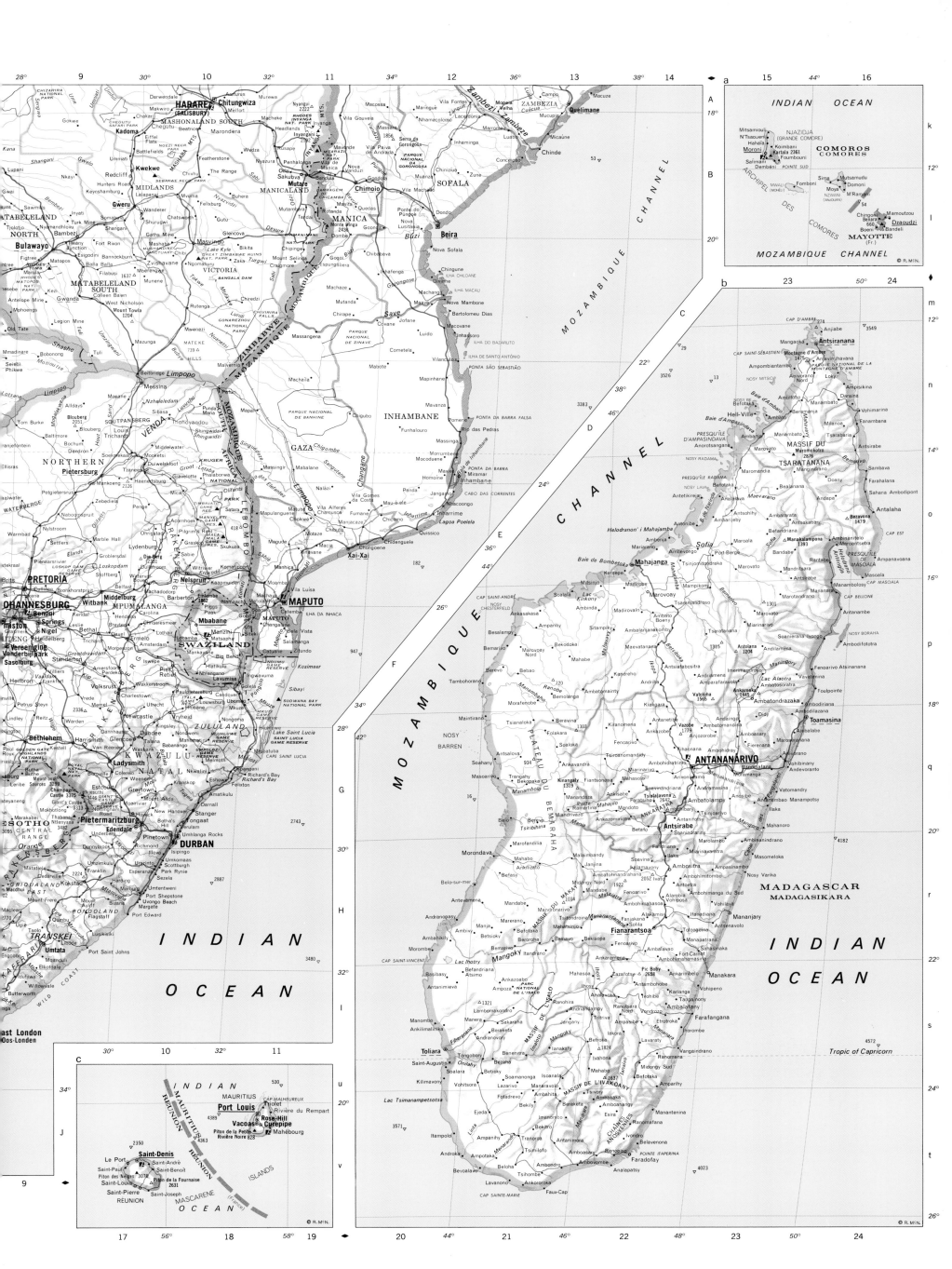

Australia

Inset map (top left)

PACIFIC OCEAN

0 100 200 300 Km.
0 100 200 Mi.

PULAU WAIGEO   Equator
SELAT Dampier
PULAU MISOOL
SALAWATI   Sorong   JAZIRAH   BIAK   KEPULAUAN SCHOUTEN
Manokwari   DOBERAI   PULAU NUMFOOR   PULAU YAPEN
SERAM   Bula   Fakfak   Teluk Berau   Teluk Cenderawasih   Membramo
Kaimana   TANJUNG D'URVILLE   NINIGO GROUP   HERMIT ISLANDS
MUSSAU ISLAND
KEPULAUAN BANDA   KEPULAUAN KAI   PEGUNUNGAN MAOKE   Puncak Jaya 5030m   Puncak Trikora 4750m   Aitape   Wewak   Sepik   ADMIRALTY ISLANDS   MANUS ISLAND   EMIRAU ISLAND   NEW HANOVER   Kavieng   NEW IRELAND   Namatanai
INDONESIA
KAI KECIL   Dobo   PULAU WOKAM   NEW GUINEA   BISMARCK Ramu   Madang   KARKAR ISLAND   WITU ISLANDS   Rabaul   Kokopo
KEPULAUAN ARU   PULAU KOBROOR   PULAU TRANGAN   Mt. Giluwe 4368m   Mt. Wilhelm 4509m   UMBOI ISLAND   Talasea   NEW BRITAIN   Mount Ulawun 2338 m
PULAU YOS SUDARSO   PAPUA NEW GUINEA   Lae   Huon Gulf   Morobe   KIRIWINA ISLANDS
PULAU SELARU   TANJUNG SUARSO   Merauke   Popondetta   MUYUA ISLAND   D'ENTRECASTEAUX ISLANDS
Arafura Sea   Torres Strait   Gulf of Papua   Port Moresby   OWEN STANLEY RANGE   Samarai
MELVILLE ISLAND   COBURG PEN.   CROKER ISLAND   WESSEL ISLANDS   Gulf of Carpentaria   CAPE YORK   GREAT BARRIER REEF   Coral Sea
BATHURST ISLAND   Van Diemen Gulf   Darwin   AUSTRALIA   CAPE YORK PEN.

A-592200-264-1-1-1-2
© 1979 R.MSN

Main map

INDIAN OCEAN

NORTHERN TERRITORY

Timor Sea

Laut Sawu   Savu Sea   TIMOR   Soe
PULAU SEMAU   Kupang
PULAU ROTI
HIBERNIA REEF
ASHMORE ISLANDS   CARTIER ISLANDS (Austl.)   Van Diemen Gulf   MELVILLE ISLAND   CAPE CROKER   CROKER I.   COBURG PENINSULA   GOL
Beagle Gulf   Clarence Strait   Van Diemen Gulf   Darwin   Humpty Doo   Jabiru   ARNHEM LAND
POINT BLAZE   Rum Jungle   Pine Creek   Katherine
BROWSE ISLAND   Joseph Bonaparte Gulf   Wyndham   Ord   Kununurra   Daly Waters
ADÈLE ISLAND   BONAPARTE ARCHIPELAGO   York Sound   Admiralty Gulf   CAPE LONDONDERRY   Victoria   Victoria River Downs
BUCCANEER ARCHIPELAGO   Collier Bay   KING LEOPOLD RANGES   Lake Argyle   Wave Hill   Newcastle Waters
CAPE LEVEQUE   King Sound   Derby   Mount Ord 937   KIMBERLEY PLATEAU   DURACK RANGES   Ord   Lake Woods
ROWLEY SHOALS   Broome   Fitzroy Crossing   Halls Creek   TANAMI DESERT   Barrow
CAPE LATOUCHE TREVILLE   La Grange   EIGHTY MILE BEACH   Fitzroy
DAMPIER ARCHIPELAGO   Port Hedland   Goldsworthy   Shay Gap   GREAT SANDY DESERT   Lake Gregory   Lake White   TERRITORY
MONTE BELLO ISLANDS   Dampier   Karratha   Roebourne   De Grey   Lake Wills   Lake Mackay   Mount Liebig   Mount Zeil
BARROW ISLAND   Marble Bar   Nullagine   Lake Dora   Lake Auld   Mount Leisler 897   1524   1511
MUIRON ISLANDS   Onslow   Pannawonica   Fortescue   Wittenoom   HAMERSLEY RANGE   MACDONNELL RANGES
NORTH WEST CAPE   Exmouth   Exmouth Gulf   Mount Brockman 1132   Mount Bruce 1235   Newman   Lake Disappointment   Lake Macdonald   Lake Neale   Spr
POINT CLOATES   Ashburton   Tom Price   Mount Meharry 1251   Parabardoo   Savory   Lake C?   GIBSON DESERT   Lake Amadeus
Tropic of Capricorn   CAPE CUVIER   Lake Macleod   Lyons   1105   Mount Augustus   906   Mount Essendon   WESTERN   Mount Olga 1069   Ayers Rock 867
Geographe Channel   Carnarvon   Gascoyne   Peak Hill   ROBINSON RANGE   Lake Carnegie   Lake Gillen   AUSTRALIA   Mount Cockburn 1138   Mount Aloysius 1085   Mount Woodroffe 1440
BERNIER ISLAND   DORRE ISLAND   Shark Bay   Wooramel   Murchison   Meekatharra   Wiluna   Lake Wells
Naturaliste Channel   Denham   Nannine   AUSTRALIA   GREAT VICTORIA DESERT
DIRK HARTOG ISLAND   STEEP POINT   Cue   Lake Austin   Agnew   Mount Redcliffe 562   Yeo Lake   Lake Maurice   SOU
Kalbarri   Mount Magnet   Sandstone   Leonora   Laverton   Lake Carey
Northampton   Yalgoo   Lake Ballard   Malcolm   Lake Carey   Maralinga   Ooldea
HOUTMAN ABROLHOS   Mullewa   Pindar   Mongers Lake   Menzies   Lake Raeside   Lake Mingwal   Forrest   Deakin
Geraldton   Lake Barlee   NULLARBOR PLAIN
Dongara   Three Springs   Lake Moore   Kalgoorlie-Boulder   Zanthus   Rawlinna   Haig   Eucla
GREEN HEAD   Moora   Dalwallinu   Bonnie Rock   Coolgardie   Lake Lefroy   CAPE ADIEU   SAINT PETER ISLAND
Wanneroo   DARLING RANGE   Bencubbin   Bullfinch   Southern Cross   Lake Cowan   Eyre   CAPE CULVER
Perth   Northam   Merredin   Kellerberrin   Lake Johnston   Norseman   Lake Dundas   POINT CULVER   INVESTI
Fremantle   York   Beverley   Brookton   Hyden   Newdegate   Esperance   Great Australian Bight
Pinjarra   Narrogin   Wagin   Nyabing   Ravensthorpe   CAPE ARID   ARCHIPELAGO OF THE RECHERCHE
Bunbury   Collie   Katanning   Gnowangerup   Hopetoun   Esperance Bay   HOOD POINT
Geographe Bay   Busselton   Bridgetown   Bluff Knoll 1096   Mount Barker
CAPE NATURALISTE   Augusta   Manjimup   Pemberton   Albany
CAPE LEEUWIN   POINT D'ENTRECASTEAUX   Denmark   CAPE VANCOUVER   King George Sound
WEST CAPE HOWE

SOUTHERN OCEAN

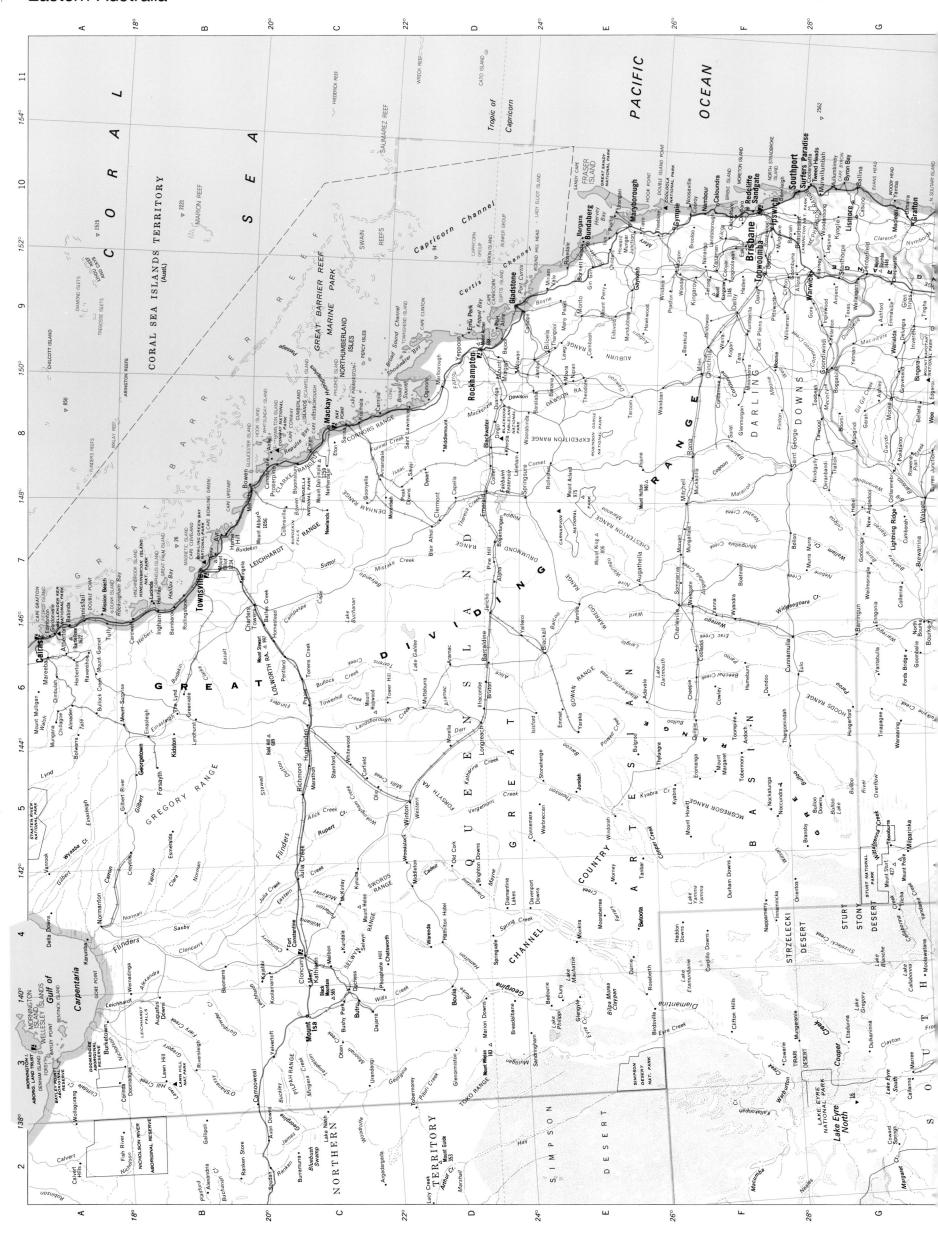

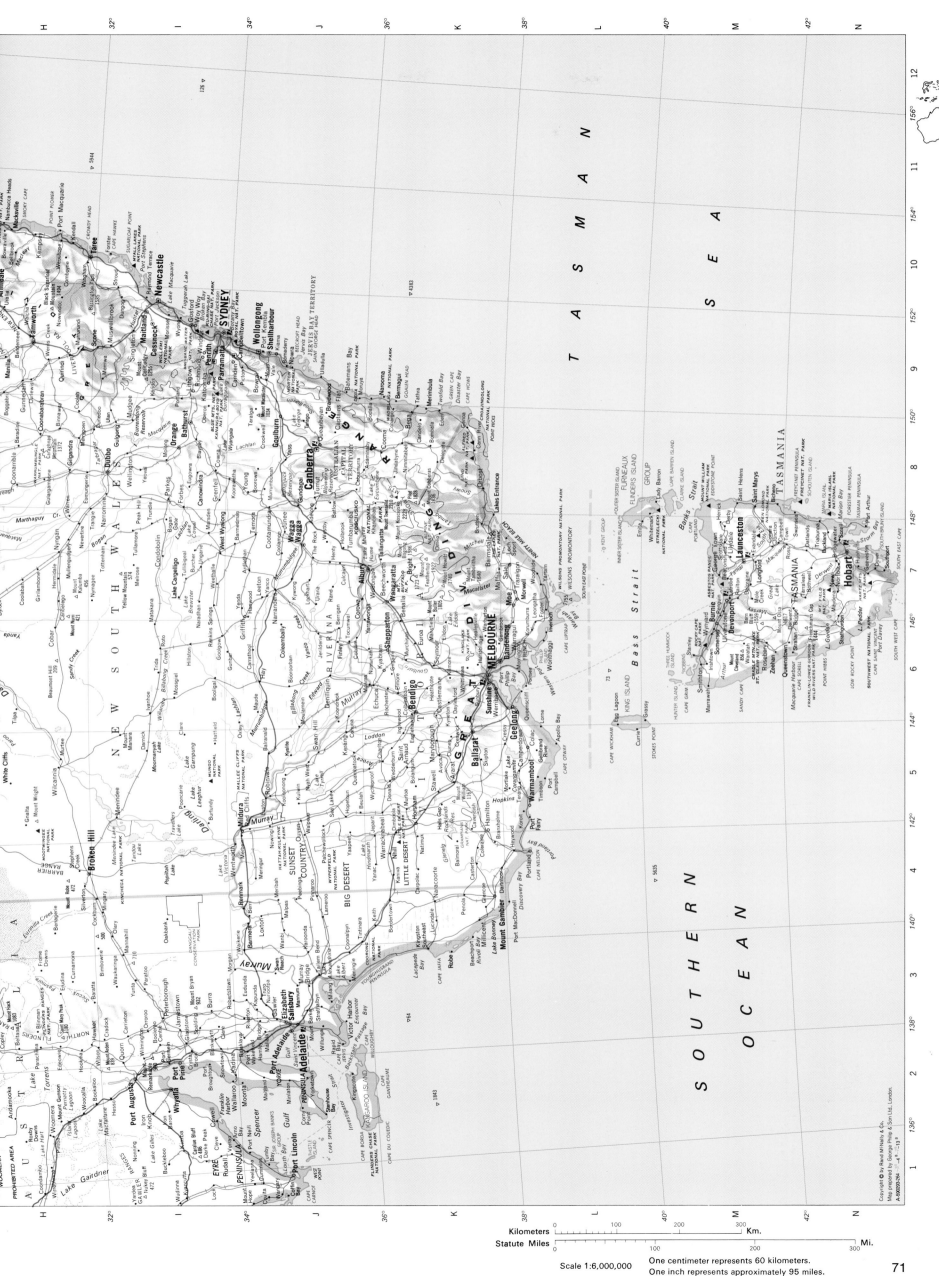

Kilometers 0 100 200 300 Km.

Statute Miles 0 100 200 300 Mi.

Scale 1:6,000,000

One centimeter represents 60 kilometers.
One inch represents approximately 95 miles.

Lambert Conformal Conic Projection

Copyright by Rand McNally & Co.
Map prepared by George Philip & Son Ltd., London.
A-690093264

New Zealand

PACIFIC OCEAN

CAPE REINGA
NORTH CAPE
Raoungu Bay
Ahipara Bay
Doubtless Bay
TAUROA POINT
CAPE BRETT
Okaihau
Opua
Whangarei
Dargaville
Wellsford
Bream Bay
GREAT BARRIER ISLAND
Kaipara Harbour
Hauraki Gulf
COROMANDEL PENINSULA
Takapuna
Devonport
Auckland
Manukau Harbour
Pukekohe
Thames
Waiuku
Waihi

TASMAN SEA

NORTH ISLAND

CAPE RUNAWAY
Huntly
Morrinsville
Bay of Plenty
Hamilton
Cambridge
Tauranga
Whakatane
EAST CAPE
Te Awamutu
Opotiki
Te Kuiti
Toroa
Rotorua
Murupara
RAUKUMARA RANGE
Hikurangi 1754
North Taranaki Bight
Taupo
Lake Taupo
KAIMANAWA MTS
New Plymouth
Waitara
Taumarunui
Tarawera
Wairoa
Gisborne
Mt. Egmont 2518
Stratford
Ruapehu 2797
MAHIA PENINSULA
Opunake
Hawera
Raehi
Hawke Bay
Napier
South Taranaki Bight
Patea
Taihape
CAPE KIDNAPPERS
Hastings
Wanganui
Waipukurau
Palmerston North
Dannevirke
Woodville
CAPE FAREWELL
Golden Bay
D'URVILLE ISLAND
Levin
Otaki
Takaka
Tasman Bay
Cook Strait
Masterton
Motueka
TARARUA MTS
Lower Hutt
Hector 1529
Nelson
Picton
Wellington
Lake Wairarapa
Karamea Bight
Richmond
1875 Mount Owen
Blenheim
CAPE PALLISER
Seddonville
Wairau
Westport
CAPE FOULWIND
Buller
Mt. Uriah 1501
CAPE CAMPBELL
Reefton
SPENSER MTS
Tapuaenuku 2885
Mt. Travers 2337
Runanga
Manakau 2610
Greymouth
Kaikoura
Hokitika
Horaka
Ross
Waiau
SOUTH ISLAND
Mount Murchison 2400
Waipara
Whataroa
Oxford
Pegasus Bay
Sheffield
Kaiapoi
Mount Cook 3754
SOUTHERN ALPS
Lake Tekapo
Mount Somers
Methven
Christchurch
Little River
Haast
Mount Somers
Southbridge
BANKS PENINSULA
Fairlie
CASCADE POINT
Lake Pukaki
Canterbury Bight
Timaru
Mount Aspiring 3035
Lake Wanaka
Omarama
2756 Mount Tutoko
Wanaka
Mount Saint Bathans 2086
Kurow
Waimate
Queenstown
Cromwell
Waitaki
Oamaru
LIVINGSTONE MTS
Lake Wakatipu
Alexandra
Ranfurly
Doubtful Sound
Te Anau
Kingston
Roxburgh
Palmerston
RESOLUTION ISLAND
Lake Te Anau
Mossburn
Beaumont
Port Chalmers
CAPE PROVIDENCE
Nightcaps
Edievale
Clutha
Dunedin
Otautau
Winton
Gore
Milton
Rivarton
Kaitangata
Invercargill
Tokanui
Tahakopa
Foveaux Strait
Bluff
Mt Anglem 978
STEWART ISLAND

PACIFIC OCEAN

Copyright © by Rand McNally & Co.
A-591600-286

Scale 1:6,000,000
One centimeter represents 60 kilometers.
One inch represents approximately 95 miles.
Lambert Conformal Conic Projection

Kilometers
Statute Miles

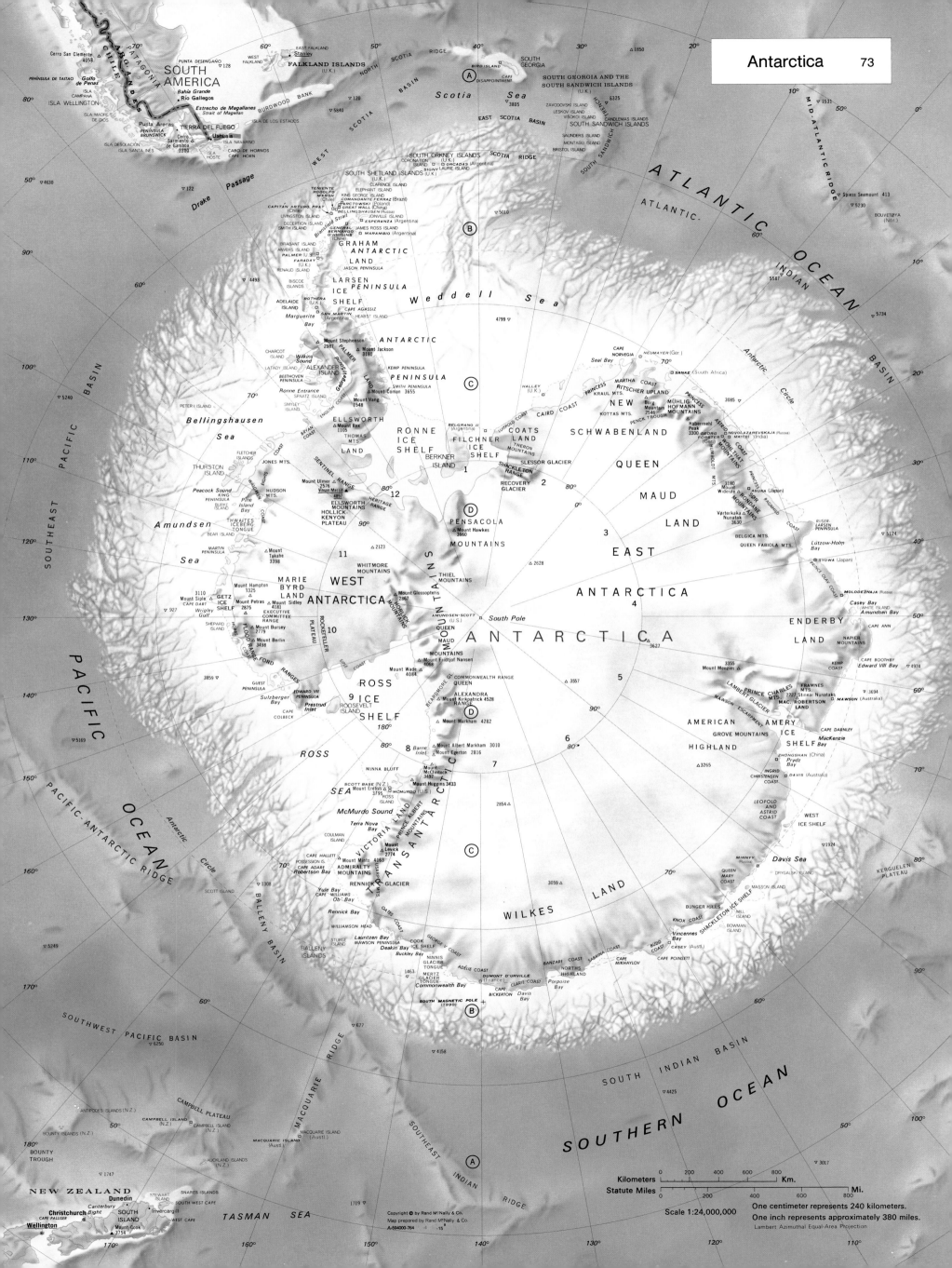

Scale 1:24,000,000

One centimeter represents 240 kilometers.
One inch represents approximately 380 miles.

Lambert Azimuthal Equal-Area Projection

Copyright © by Rand McNally & Co.
Map prepared by Rand McNally & Co.
A-594000-764

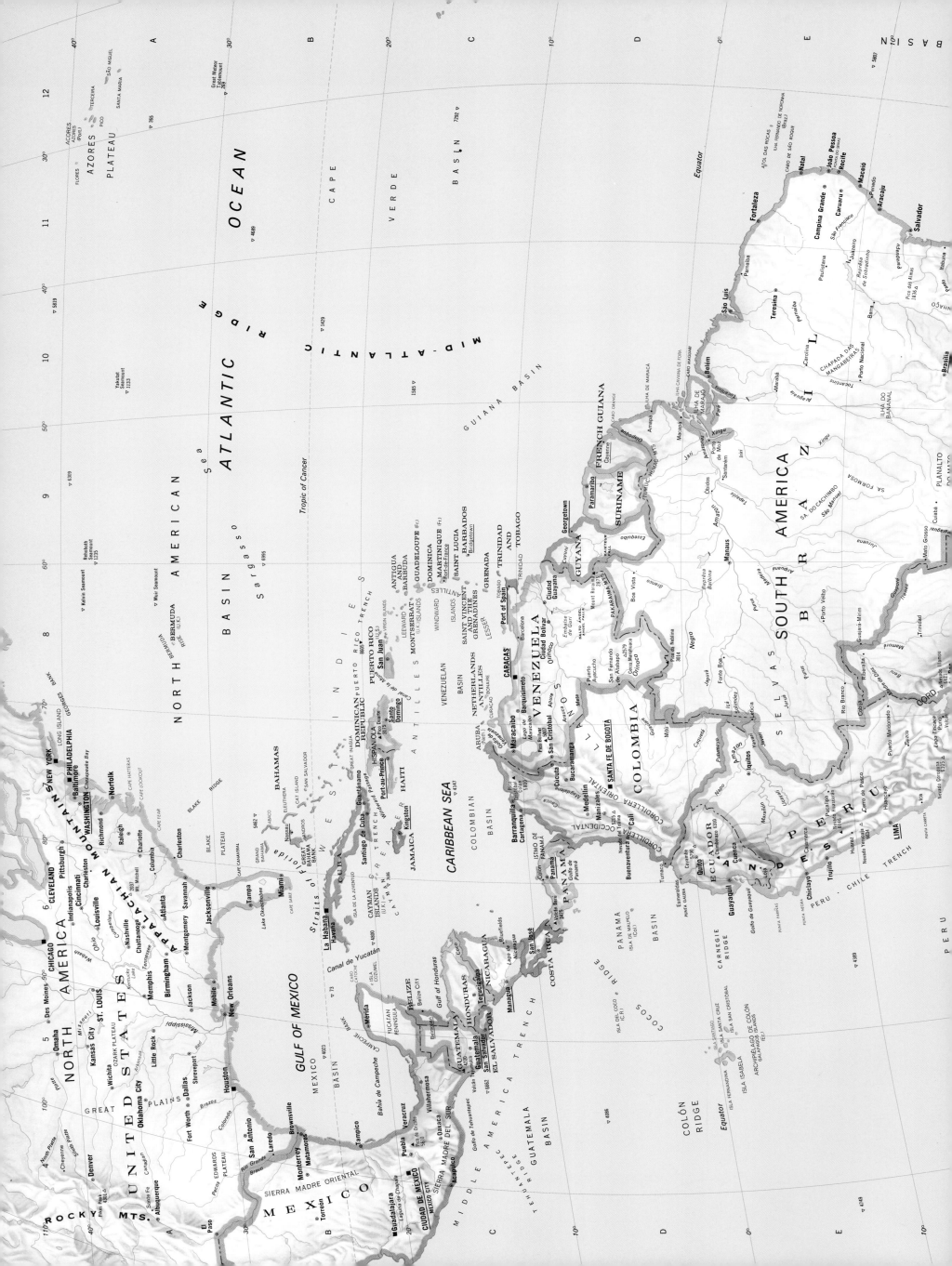

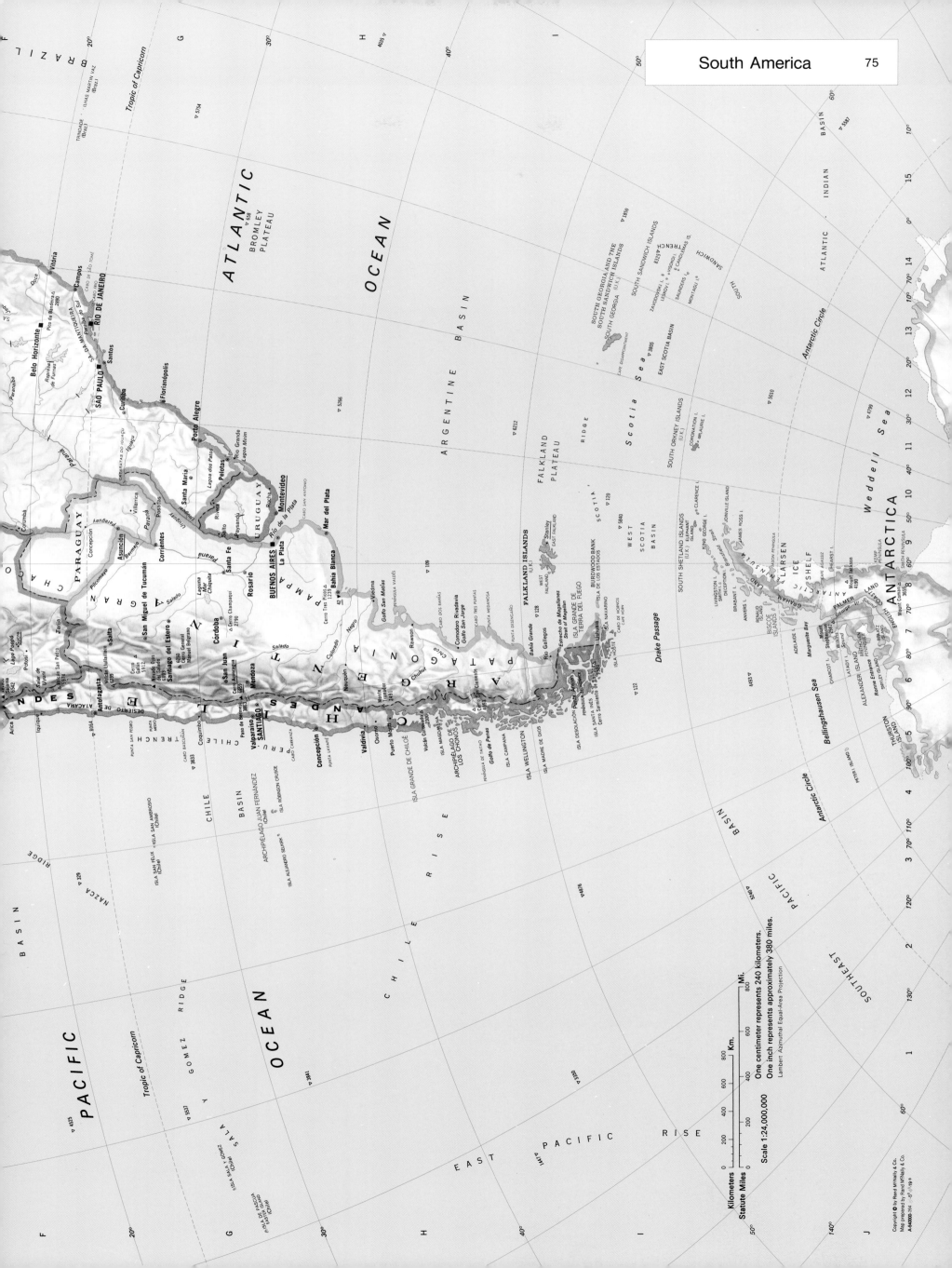

Copyright © by Rand McNally & Co.
Map prepared by Esselte Map Service AB, Stockholm.
A-549100-264
−16°

Kilometers
Statute Miles

Scale 1:12,000,000
One centimeter represents 120 kilometers.
One inch represents approximately 190 miles.
Oblique Conic Conformal Projection

Kilometers
Statute Miles

Scale 1:12,000,000

One centimeter represents 120 kilometers.
One inch represents approximately 190 miles.

Oblique Conic Conformal Projection

Copyright © by Rand McNally & Co.
Map prepared by Esselte Map Service AB, Stockholm.
A-549200-264

ATLANTIC OCEAN

Scale 1:6,000,000

Kilometers

Statute Miles

One centimeter represents 60 kilometers.
One inch represents approximately 95 miles.

79

Oblique Conic Conformal Projection

Kilometers
Statute Miles

One centimeter represents 60 kilometers.
One inch represents approximately 95 miles.

Scale 1:6,000,000
Oblique Conic Conformal Projection

81

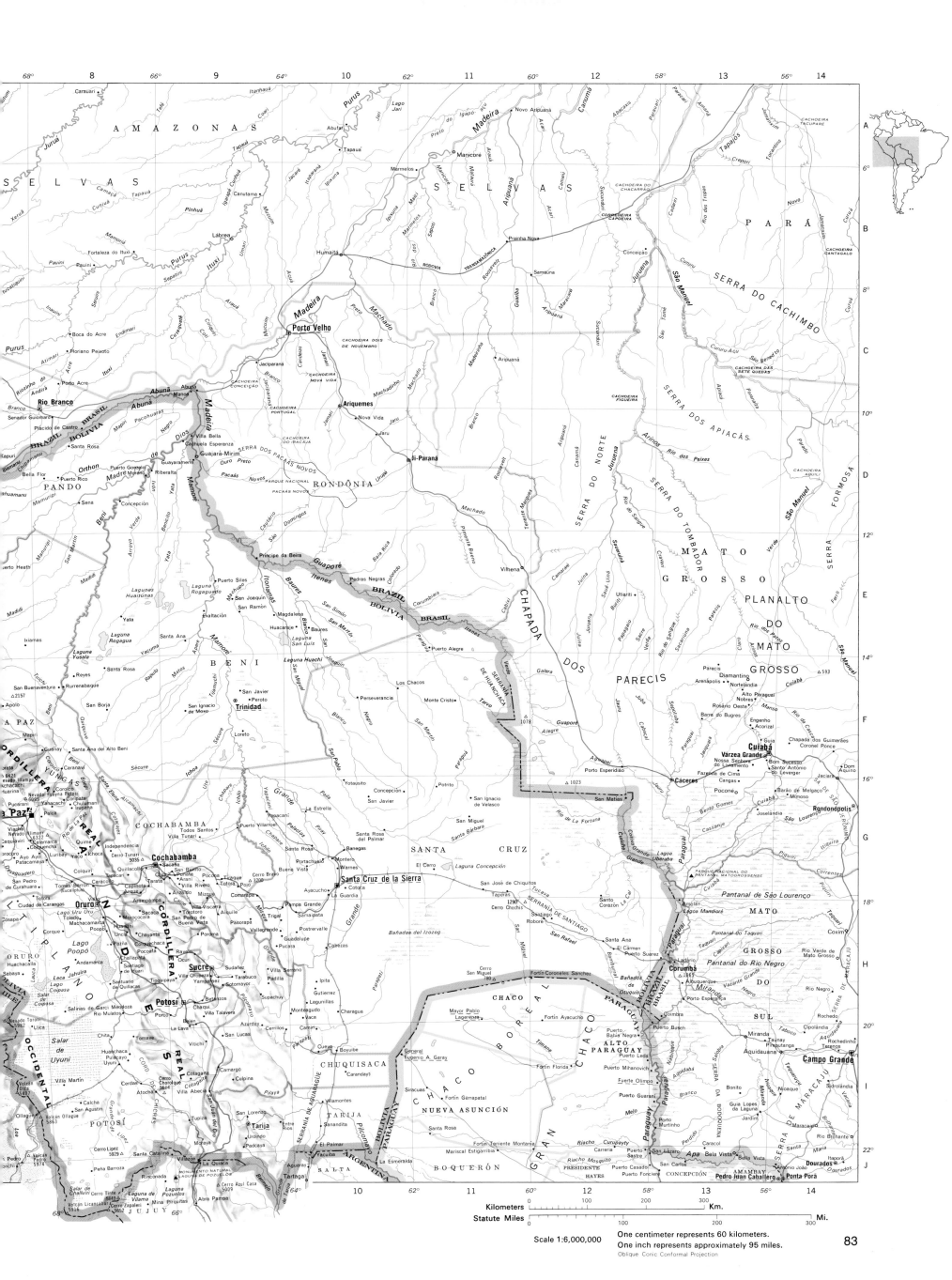

Kilometers | 0 | 100 | 200 | 300 | Km.

Statute Miles | 0 | 100 | 200 | 300 | Mi.

Scale 1:6,000,000

One centimeter represents 60 kilometers.
One inch represents approximately 95 miles.

Oblique Conic Conformal Projection

83

Colombia, Ecuador, Venezuela, and Guyana

Kilometers

Statute Miles

Scale 1:6,000,000

One centimeter represents 60 kilometers.
One inch represents approximately 95 miles.

Oblique Conic Conformal Projection

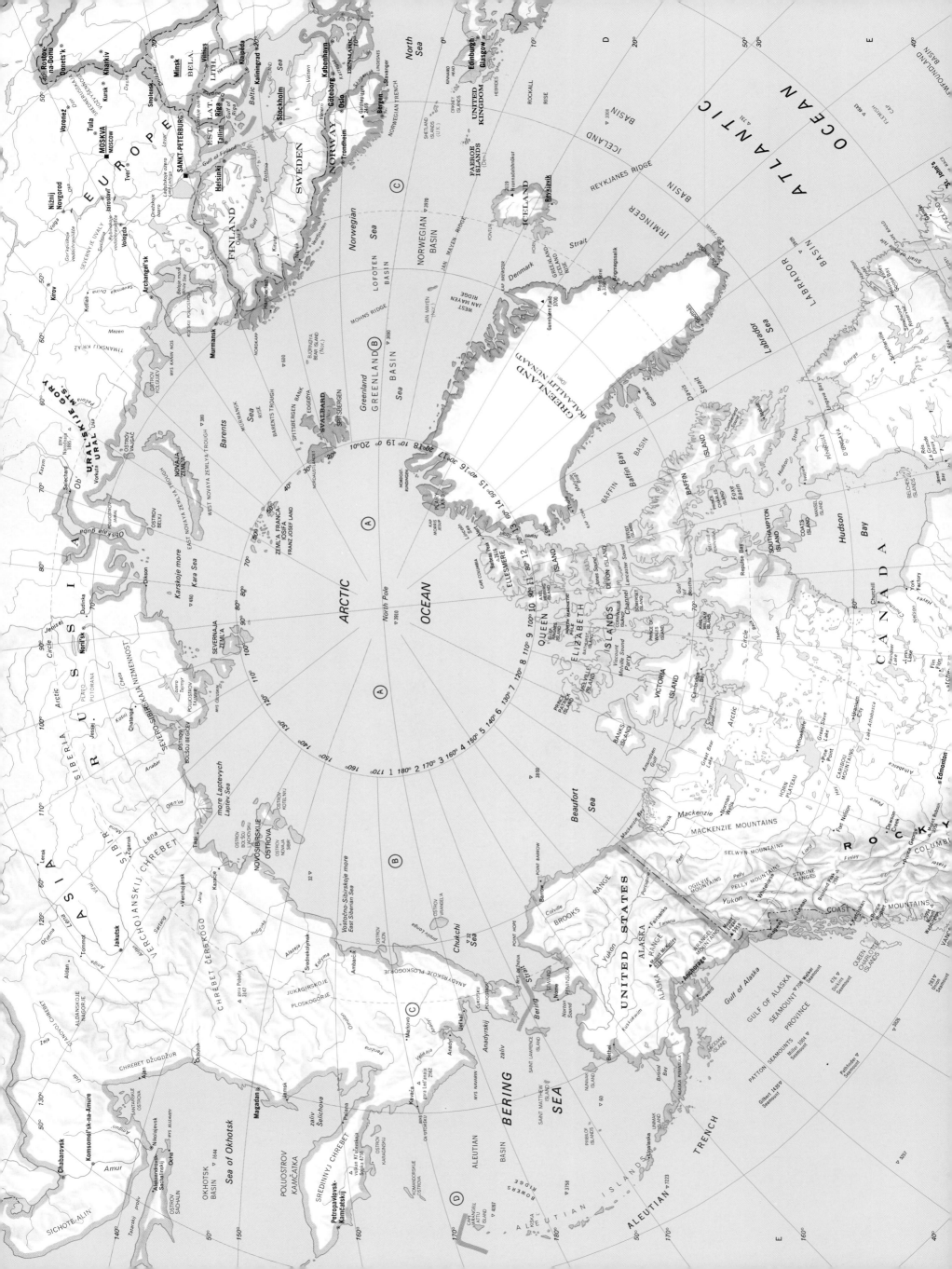

One centimeter represents 240 kilometers.
One inch represents approximately 380 miles.
Lambert Azimuthal Equal-Area Projection

Scale 1:24,000,000

Copyright by Rand McNally & Co.
Map prepared by Rand McNally & Co.
A-520000-264

Scale 1:12,000,000

Kilometers
Statute Miles

One centimeter represents 120 kilometers.
One inch represents approximately 190 miles.

Oblique Conic Conformal Projection

89

Mexico

One centimeter represents 60 kilometers.
One inch represents approximately 95 miles.

Kilometers
Statute Miles

Scale 1:6,000,000
Lambert Conformal Conic Projection

9 85° **10** 84° **11** 83° **12** 82° **13** 81° **14** 80° **15**

A DE GUANAJA
aja

A

∇ 105

CAYOS CAJONES

CAYOS BECERRO

CAYOS VIVORILLO

CAYO DE SERRANILLA
(Colombia)

na de Guaimoreto
Santa Rosa de Aguán
Limón   Iriona   CABO CAMARÓN
Sico   Tinto   Laguna de Brus   PUNTA PATUCA
Cerro Payas   Tinto   Brus   ∇ 22   CAYOS COCOROCUMA
1128   Laguna de Ibans

∇ 40

B

COLÓN   Paya   Patuca   ∇ 145
Cerro Piñas   Sigre   Laguna de Tansin   ARRECIFES DE LA MEDIA LUNA
1035   Dulce Nombre de Culmí   Laguna de Warunta   CABO FALSO   ∇ 356
Esteban   △ 1326   Wampú   Laguna de Tansin
Wampu   Puerto Lempira   Laguna Rohunta

amas

LANCHO   LA MOSQUITIA
GRACIAS A DIOS   CABO GRACIAS A DIOS

15°

MONTAÑAS DE COLÓN   Cabo Gracias a Dios

Patuca   Coco

2590

RÁPIDO PANSIK   Coco   San Ramón   Waspam   Laguna Bismuna   ∇ 87
Valencia   Raiti   Bilwaskarma   Ulang   ARRECIFE EDINBURGH   C
PORTAL DEL INFIERNO   Wiwili   Likus   Misko   Edinburgh Channel   ∇ 5
CORDILLERA   △ 1132   Wawa   QUITASUEÑO
ENTRE RÍOS   Bocay   Waspuk   Wawa   MISKITOS REEF   CAYO DE SERRANA
HONDURAS   Amaka   Bonanza   Yablis   ∇ 105
NICARAGUA   Bocai   CAYOS MISKITOS   14°
JINOTEGA   Cerro Saslaya   La Rosita   Puerto Cabezas
Cerro Kilambé   1650   Siuna   Laguna de Krukira   ∇ 105
1750   La Luz   Kukalaya   ∇ 47   ∇ 1755   CAYOS DE RONCADOR   D
Peñas Blancas   Bambana   Laguna de Wounta
1745   Tuma   Yaoya   Tungla   Wounta   ∇ 534   ∇ 3292

CORDILLERA DARIENSE   13°
atagalpa   Prinzapolka   Prinzapolka
MATAGALPA   ZELAYA   Grande de Matagalpa   San Pedro del Norte
uy Muy   Matiguas   La Cruz de Río Grande   ISLA DE PROVIDENCIA
Dionisio   Kurinwás   La Barra   C A R I B B E A N   E
pulas   ∇ 25
BOACO   Siquia   Laguna de Perlas   SAN ANDRÉS Y PROVIDENCIA (Colombia)
ombacito   1059   Santo Domingo   Mico   ISLA DE SAN ANDRÉS   San Andrés
nzo   Camoapa   La Libertad   Rama   PTA SET NET
Comalapa   Santo Tomás   Muelle de los Bueyes   Escondido   CAYOS DEL ESTE SUDESTE   12°
CHONTALES   Villa Sandino   Rama   PUNTA DE PERLAS   F
Juigalpa   CORDILLERA CHONTALEÑA   ISLAS DEL MAÍZ (Nic.)   CAYOS DE ALBUQUERQUE
anada   PUNTA MAYALES   SERRANÍAS HUAPÍ   El Bluff   3174 ∇   3174 ∇
Mombacho   San Ubaldo   Bluefields   Bahía de Bluefields
Lago de   ISLA ZAPATERA   Morrito   SERRANÍAS DE YOLAINA   ISLA DEL VENADO
Concepción   1616   Punta   Punta Gorda   2633 ∇   S E A
Altagracia   ISLA DE OMETEPE   San Miguelito   Punta Gorda
San Jorge   Volcán Maderas   Tule   Bahía de Punta Gorda
as   1394

(31 Meters Above Sea Level)

RÍO SAN JUAN   ARCHIPIÉLAGO DE SOLENTINAME
n Juan   Cárdenas   San Carlos   El Castillo de La Concepción   11°
Sur   Indio   San Juan del Norte   G
a Cruz   PARQ. NAC. GUANACASTE   Los Chiles   Caño Negro
ena   Volcán Orosí   Upala   Río   Colorado   ∇ 3381   ∇ 2116
ago   1487   PARQ. NAC. RINCÓN DE LA VIEJA   NICARAGUA   Sarapiquí
a de   Santa   Hacienda   Volcán Miravalles   COSTA RICA   ∇ 1481
ayo   Curubande   Miravalles   2028   San   Carlos
Liberia   ALAJUELA   Laguna de Arenal   Altamira   PARQUE NACIONAL TORTUGUERO
Sardinal   Bagaces   Volcán Arenal   Fortuna   HEREDIA
Filadelfia   Tilarán   1633   Venecia   Puerto Viejo
Portegolpe   Cañas   Quesada   PARQ. NAC. BRAULIO CARRILLO   Parismina   G
GUANACASTE   Juntas   Guápiles   Guápiles parismina   Parismina
intisiete   PENÍNSULA DE NICOYA   Miramar   Naranjo   VOLCÁN POÁS   Volcán Poás   Siquirres   Puerto Limón   10°
de Abril   Santa Cruz   San Antonio   Lagarto   Grecia   2704   Volcán Barva   2906   ∇ 2679
an   Nicoya   Mansión   San Ramón   CORD   Volcán Turrialba   Matina
Juanillo   Carrillo   Cerro Azul   Esparza   Alajuela   Heredia   3328   ∇ 47
1018   Lepanto   Palmares   San José   Guadalupe   Volcán Irazú 3432   H
Paquera   San Francisco   Golfo de   Puntarenas   Moravia   Turrialba   Juan Viñas   PUNTA CAHUITA   Portobelo   Colón   PANAMÁ
Cabuya   Nicoya   Desamparados   San Pedro   Tres Ríos   GUÁPILES   Puerto Viejo   Nombre de Dios   ∇ 97
CABO BLANCO   417 ∇   Parrita   Cartago   CARTAGO   Vesta   PUNTA MONA   Cerro Bruja   978
PUNTA JUDAS   Playa Bonita   Paraíso   Cerro Matama   PARQ. INTERNAC. DE LA AMISTAD   Sixaola   ESCLUSAS DE GATÚN   Nuevo Chagres   Palmas Bellas
Santa   San   CORDILLERA   2251   Suretka   Guabito   Lago   Cristóbal   Colón   Panamá   Cristóbal
María   Marcos   TALAMANCA   Amubri   Changuinola   ISLA COLÓN   ARCHIPIÉLAGO DE BOCAS DEL TORO   Gatún   Miguel de la Borda   Escobal   Gamboa
Cerro La Muerte   Piedra   Teribe   Bocas del Toro   Bastimentos   Paraíso   Lago Alajuela
Puntarenas   Cerro Chirripó   3491   3819   Coén   Almirante   Bahía de Almirante   ISLA BASTIMENTOS   ESCLUSAS DE MIRAFLORES   I
Quepos   San   Convento   Cerro Kámuk   3554   ISLA POPA   Bahía Azul   RODMAN NAVAL STATION   Balboa
Santidro   PARQ. NAC. MANUEL ANTONIO   José   Buenos   COSTA RICA   PANAMÁ   ISLA ESCUDO DE VERAGUAS   ISTMO   La Chorrera   PANAMÁ   Panamá
Dominical   Palmares   Aires   Guabito   ISLA CRISTÓBAL   Golfo de los   COLÓN   Taboga   Bahía de Panamá
Pottero   Cerro Pando   Cerro Fábrega   Chiriquí   Mosquitos   La Pintada   ISLA TABOGA   Capira
Bahía de   Boruca   Grande de   3335   Grande   Santa Catalina   Cerro Gaital   1173   Bejuco   PUNTA CHAME
Coronado   Palmar Sur   Térraba   BOCAS DEL TORO   o Calovebora   CERRO CHICU   COCLÉ   El Valle   ISLA OTOQUE
ISLA VIOLÍN   San Vito   Volcán Barú   Cerro Chorcha   Santa Fe   1764   La Pintada   Penonomé   Chame
∇ 3224   Rincón   Cerro   3475   2238   Cerro   Peña   CORDILLERA   Antón   San Carlos
Anguciana   PUNTARENAS   Golfito   Bajo Boquete   CENTRAL   Olá   Río Hato
PENÍNSULA DE OSA   1707   Volcán   Potrerillos   Cerro Chichu   La Concepción   CHIRIQUÍ   Penonomé
PARQ. NAC. CORCOVADO   Golfo   Boquerón   Blanca   Ola   Nata   Aguadulce   I
Cerro Tigre   782   Dulce   La Concepción   Dolega   Cañazas   Santa Fe   San Carlos
2331 ∇   Puerto Jiménez   David   Chichica   Tolé   San Francisco   Pocrí
CABO MATAPALO   Chiriquí   Boquerón del Monte   VERAGUAS   La Arena   Chitré
PUNTA BANCO   Divalá   Horconcitos   Las Lajas   Remedios   Santiago   Santa María
∇ 2891   Puerto Armuelles   Chiriquí Pedregal   ISLA BOCA BRAVA   Las Palmas   Santa María   Bahía de Parita
Bahía de   Chiriquí   San Pablo   La Mesa   La Arena   HERRERA   Monagrillo   8°
Charco Azul   Burica   ISLAS SECAS   Soná   Atalaya   Montijo   Ocú   Pesé   LOS SANTOS
Golfo de   Río de Jesús   Villa   J
PUNTA   Chiriquí   Golfo de
BURICA   Panamá

Kilometers |0   50   100   150   Km.

Statute Miles |0   50   100   150   Mi.

Scale 1:3,000,000

One centimeter represents 30 kilometers.
One inch represents approximately 47 miles.

Lambert Conformal Conic Projection

93

ATLANTIC

OCEAN

Sea

Sargasso

Tropic of Cancer

▽5486

SAMANA CAY

▽5420

MAYAGUANA

CAICOS ISLANDS

TURKS AND CAICOS ISLANDS
(U.K.)

NORTH CAICOS

MIDDLE CAICOS
Kew

PROVIDENCIALES
CAICOS
BANK
WEST CAICOS
EAST
CAICOS
TURKS
ISLANDS

▽6960

Grand
Turk

Turks Island Passage

SEAL
CAYS
Mouchoir Passage

Mouchoir Bank

SILVER BANK

▽2853

LITTLE
INAGUA

▽3877

GREAT INAGUA

NORTH EAST POINT

Lake
Rosa

Caicos Passage

NAVIDAD
BANK

Navidad Bank

▽8165

HAITI

HAÏTI

ÎLE DE LA TORTUE

Port-de-Paix
Cap-Haïtien

Monte Cristi
Puerto Plata

CABO ISABELA
CABO MACORÍS

CABO FRANCÉS VIEJO

▽3292

7433 ▽

Le Limbe
Manzanillo
Bay
Fort-Liberté
Yaque del Norte
Pico Diego de Ocampo
Bahía
Escocesa
Nagua

8605 ▽

SANS-SOUCI
LA CITADELLE
Gonaïves
Morne
Dajabón
1249

Mao
Santiago
Salcedo
CABO SAMANÁ

VIRGIN
ISLANDS

LEEWARD

HORSE SHOE REEF

SOMBRERO

Verrettes
Desdunes
Sabaneta
San Francisco
de Macorís
Bahía de Samaná

Sánchez
CABO
MACORÍS

ANGUILLA

Golfe de
la Gonâve

HISPANIOLA

Banhomme
Arbonito
1788
Comendador
Pico Duarte
3175
Bonao
2630

La Vega
Moca
Cotui

Sabana de La Mar
Miches
El Seibo

BRITISH
VIRGIN
ISLANDS

ANEGADA

DOG I.(U.K.)

The Valley
Marigot

ISLANDS

ÎLE DE
LA GONÂVE

178

Canal de Saint-Marc

Léogâne

San Juan

Hato
Mayor

Higüey

CABO
ENGAÑO

PUERTO RICO
(U.S.)

Aguadilla

ISLA DE
CULEBRA

VIRGIN
GORDA

TORTOLA

SAINT
THOMAS

Road Town
1172

SAINT MARTIN
Philipsburg
(Neth. Ant.)

ANTIGUA
AND
BARBUDA

BARBUDA

LESSER

Port-au-Prince

Morne
La Selle
2674

Lago
Enriquillo
(-40)
Neiba

Vicente Noble

Baní

Bajos de
Haina

Mayagüez

Utuado

CORDILLERA
CENTRAL

Arecibo

Manatí

Cerro
de Punta

Bayamón

SAN
JUAN

Caguas

Fajardo
Vieques

Humacao

ISLA DE VIEQUES

Charlotte
Amalie

SAINT JOHN

SAINT BARTHÉLEMY
(Guad.)

SAINT MARTIN
(Fr.) (Neth. Ant.)

SABA
(Neth. Ant.)

SAINT
EUSTATIUS
(Neth. Ant.)

SAINT CHRISTOPHER

ANGUILLA PASSAGE

LEEWARD

ANTIGUA

PENÍNSULA DE
BARAHONA

San
Cristóbal

San Pedro
de Macorís

Azua

PUNTA PALENQUE

San
Germán

Yauco

Ponce

Cayey

Cómo

Guayama

SAINT KITTS AND NEVIS

Basseterre

SAINT KITTS

Charlestown

NEVIS

REDONDA

Saint John's

ANTIGUA

ISLANDS

PASSAGE

▽5197

Bani

Pedernales

Barahona

CABO FALSO

CABO BEATA

ISLA BEATA

DOMINICAN REPUBLIC
REPÚBLICA DOMINICANA

La Romana

Bahía
de Yuma

ISLA SAONA

Canal de la Mona

PUNTA HIGÜERO

PUNTA
TUNA

CABO
ROJO

ISLA DE MONA

Christiansted

870

Frederiksted

SAINT CROIX

▽4096

MONTSERRAT
(U.K.)

Plymouth

GUADELOUPE PASSAGE

GRANDE-TERRE

Le Moule
LA DÉSIRADE

Pointe-à-Pitre
(Fr.)

Soufrière
Basse-Terre
1467

GUADELOUPE

BASSE-TERRE

MARIE GALANTE

Grand-Bourg

LES SAINTES

ANTILLES

▽2121

▽4200

DOMINICA

Morne
Diablotins
1433

Dominica Passage

Marigot

SEA

Roseau
Berekua

▽2560

MARTINIQUE PASSAGE

Martinique

Montagne
Pelée
1397

La Trinité

ISLA DE AVES
(Ven.)

▽603

Saint-Pierre

Le Lamentin

Fort-de-France

WINDWARD

ANTILLES

MARTINIQUE

Saint
Lucia
Channel

60°

▽5630

POINTE DU CAP

Castries

Mount Gimie
950

SAINT LUCIA

Vieux Fort

Saint
Vincent
Passage

▽5102

Soufrière
1234
Georgetown

Speightstown
Bathsheba

Mt. Hillaby 340

Kings
town

SAINT VINCENT

Bridgetown

BARBADOS

SAINT VINCENT
AND THE
GRENADINES

4120▽

BEQUIA

WINDWARD

GRENADINES

CANOUAN

CARRIACOU

▽4069

▽475

ARUBA
(Neth.)

NETHERLANDS ANTILLES
NEDERLANDSE ANTILLEN

LESSER

ANTILLES

Victoria

GRENADA

Oranjestad

CURAÇAO

BONAIRE

Kralendijk

Saint George's

ISLAS LAS AVES
(Ven.)

ISLA BLANQUILLA (Ven.)

▽570

Willemstad

ISLAS LOS ROQUES
(Ven.)

ISLA LA ORCHILA
(Ven.)

ISLAS LOS HERMANOS
(Ven.)

ISLAS LOS TESTIGOS
(Ven.)

Speyside

TOBAGO

PUNTA GALLINAS

PENÍNSULA DE
LA GUAJIRA

Bahía Honda

Punta Espada

PENÍNSULA
DE PARAGUANA

Pueblo Nuevo

Nueva Esparta

ISLA DE MARGARITA

ISLA LA TORTUGA
(Ven.)

▽1353

GALERA
POINT

TRINIDAD

Bahía Portete

Puerto Estrella

CABO SAN ROMÁN

Las Taques

Juangriego

Boca de Pozo

Porlamar

Río
Caribe

PENÍNSULA DE
PARIA

Punta
PIEDRAS

Scarborough

AND

Puerto Bolívar

Uribia

CABO DE LA VELA

Punta Espada

LA GUAJIRA

Punta Cardón

Punto Fijo

Golfete de
Coro

▽1902

Coro

Puerto Cumarebo

Punta Zamuro

San Juan de los Cayos

ISLA DE COCHE

ISLA CUBAGUA

Arama

PUNTA DE ARAYA

Araya

Golfo de
Cariaco

Cumaná

Carúpano

Güiria

San
Fernando

Río Claro

TRINIDAD

Port of Spain
Arima

Sangre Grande

Gulf of
Paria

SUCRE

El Pilar
Yaguaraparo

Maturin

Siparia

Princes Town

Galeota Point

AND

TOBAGO

Serpents Mouth

ISLA TOBÉJUBA

Riohacha

Manaure

Maicao

Albania

Nazaret

Sinamaica

San
Luis

La Vela
de Coro

Cabure

Capatárida

Dabajuro

▽18

Ensenada de
Calabozo
Paraguaipoa

Mene de Mauroa

Pedregal

Churuguara

Yaritagua

Yumare

Tucacas

Chichiriviche

PUNTA TUCACAS

PARQUE
NACIONAL
MORROCOY

Golfo
Triste

Puerto
Cabello

Morón

DISTRITO FEDERAL

Maiquetía

Caracas

Petare

Guarenas

MIRANDA

Río Chico

CABO CODERA

Carenero

Cúpira

Cumanacoa

Caripe

Carúpano

Casanay

Tunapuy

Yaguaraparo

Maturín

Jusepín

Uracoa

Barrancas

DELTA

AMACURO

Cúpira

COLOMBIA

VENEZUELA

Maracaibo

La Concepción

Santa
Rita

Cabimas

Ciudad
Ojeda

Cerro Cerrón
1990

Carora

Chivacoa

LARA

San Felipe

Chivacoa

Valencia

CARABOBO

Güigüe

Palo Negro

Guacara

Maracay

ARAGUA

Los Teques

Santa
Ana

San Juan de
los Morros

PARQUE
NACIONAL
HENRI PITTIER

Ocumare
del Tuy

Altagracia
de Orituco

Clarines

Barcelona

Puerto la Cruz

Pozuelos

Valle de
Guanape

ANZOÁTEGUI

Aragua de Maturín

Quiriquire

Caripito

Maturín

alledupar

Pico Cristóbal
Colón
5800

SERRANÍA DE PERIJÁ

Machiques

Mene Grande

El Tocuyo

Quíbor

Barquisimeto

Yaritagua

Tinaquillo

San Carlos

El Pao

Tinaco

Parapara

Valle de la Pascua

Santa María
de Ipire

Zaraza

Cantaura

Anaco

El Tigre

San José
de Guanipa

Tucupido

MONAGAS

Tigre

Temblador

GUÁRICO

▽250

La Ceiba

Bobures

CESAR

NORTE DE
SANTANDER

Cerro Mu
2610

TRUJILLO

Motatán

Trujillo

Valera

Biscucuy

PORTUGUESA

Acarigua

Araure

Ospino

Guanare

Turén

Guanarito

El Baúl

Calabozo

Camaguán

El Sombrero

Chaguaramas

El Socorro

El Cafetal

Cariaco

Pariaguán

Soledad

El Tigre

San Tomé

San José
de Unare

ZULIA

Altagracia

Lagunillas

San
Lorenzo

Bachaquero

La Ceiba

Valle del
Guárico

Sabaneta

Tucupita

ORINOCO

Caño Manamo

Barrancas

Curiapo

Kilometers
0   100   200   300   Km.

Statute Miles
0   100   200   300   Mi.

Scale 1:6,000,000

One centimeter represents 60 kilometers.
One inch represents approximately 95 miles.

Lambert Conformal Conic Projection

95

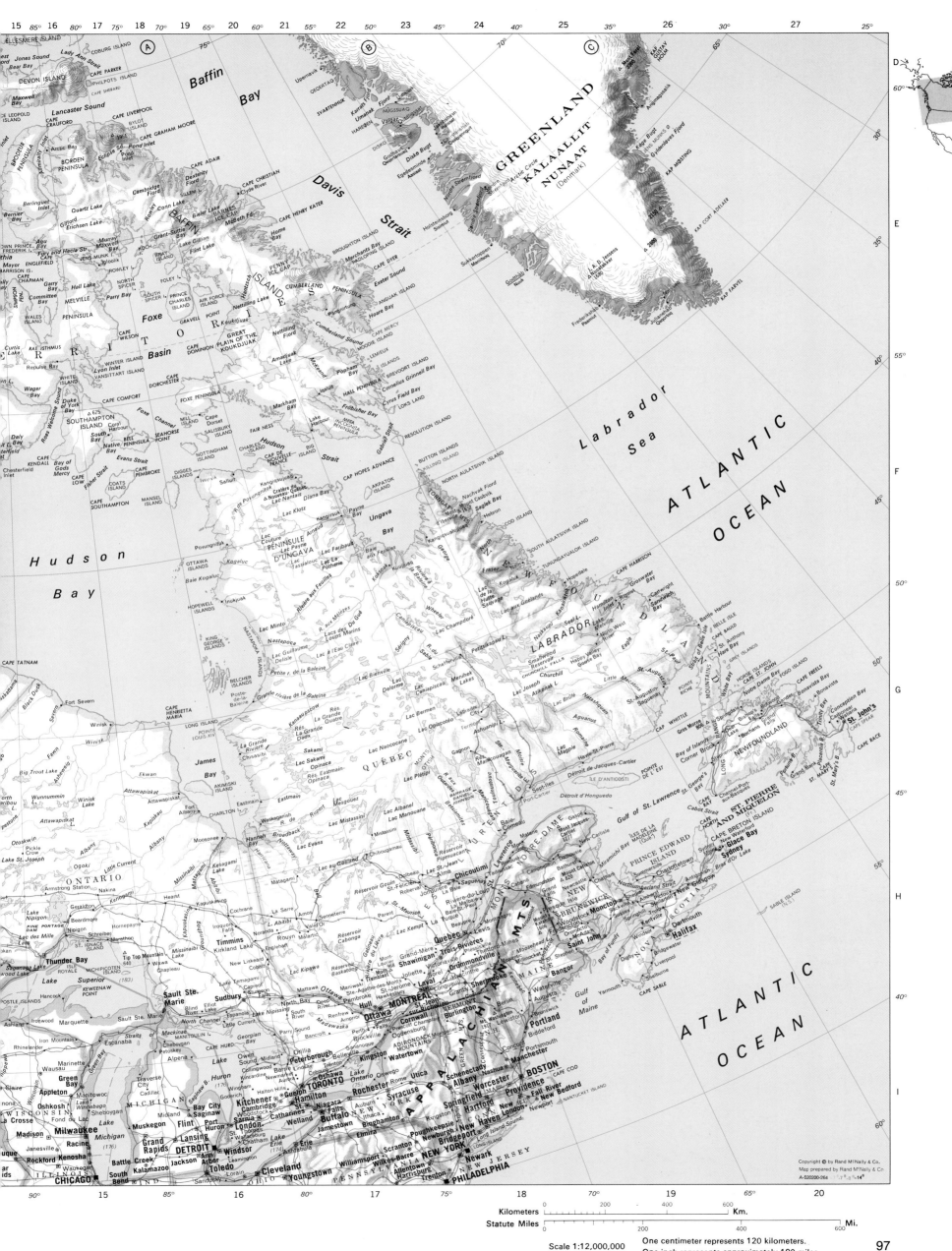

Kilometers

Statute Miles

Scale 1:12,000,000

One centimeter represents 120 kilometers.
One inch represents approximately 190 miles.

Lambert Conformal Conic Projection

Copyright © by Rand McNally & Co.
Map prepared by Rand McNally & Co
A-520200-264

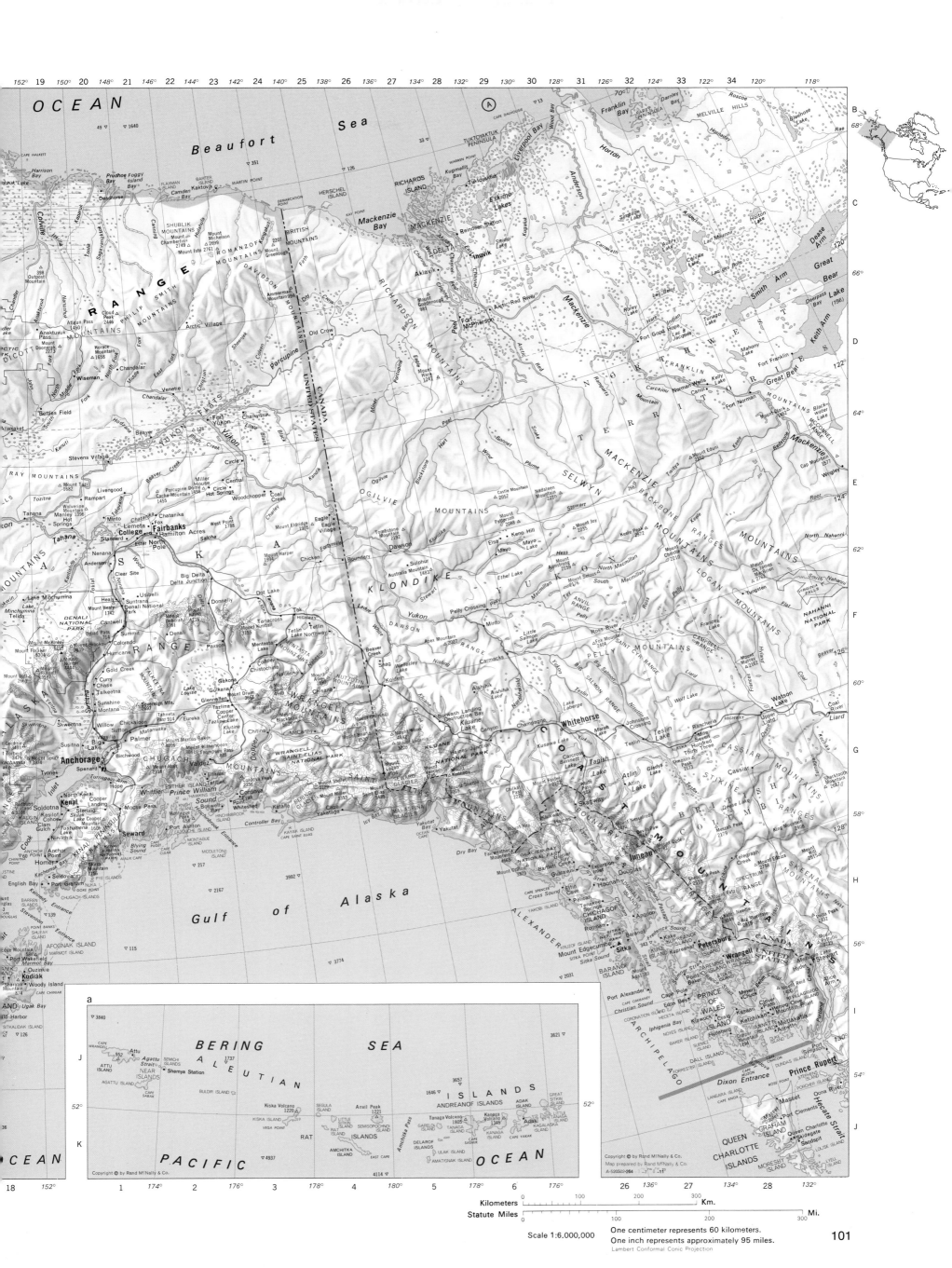

Kilometers
Statute Miles

Scale 1:6,000,000
One centimeter represents 60 kilometers.
One inch represents approximately 95 miles.
Lambert Conformal Conic Projection

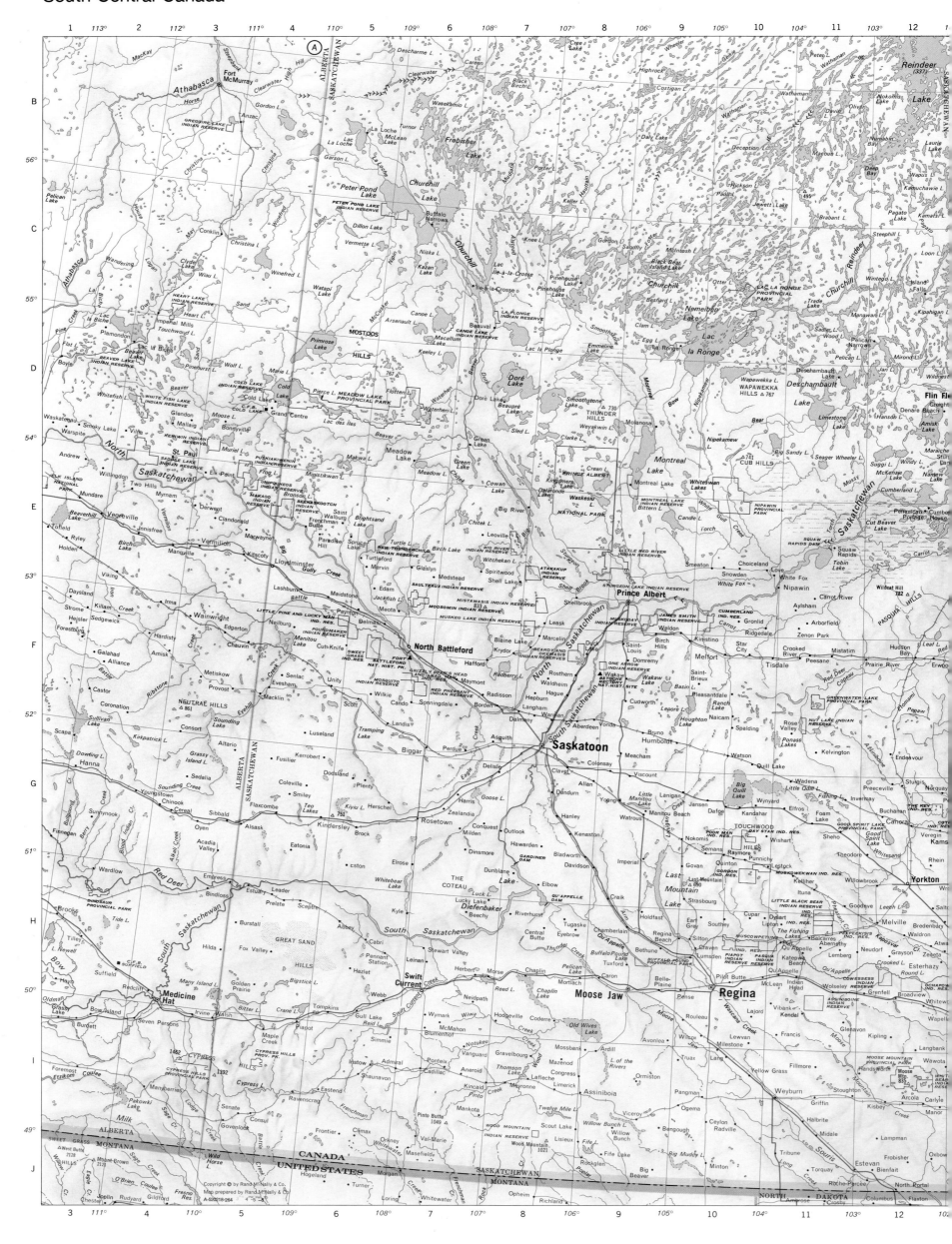

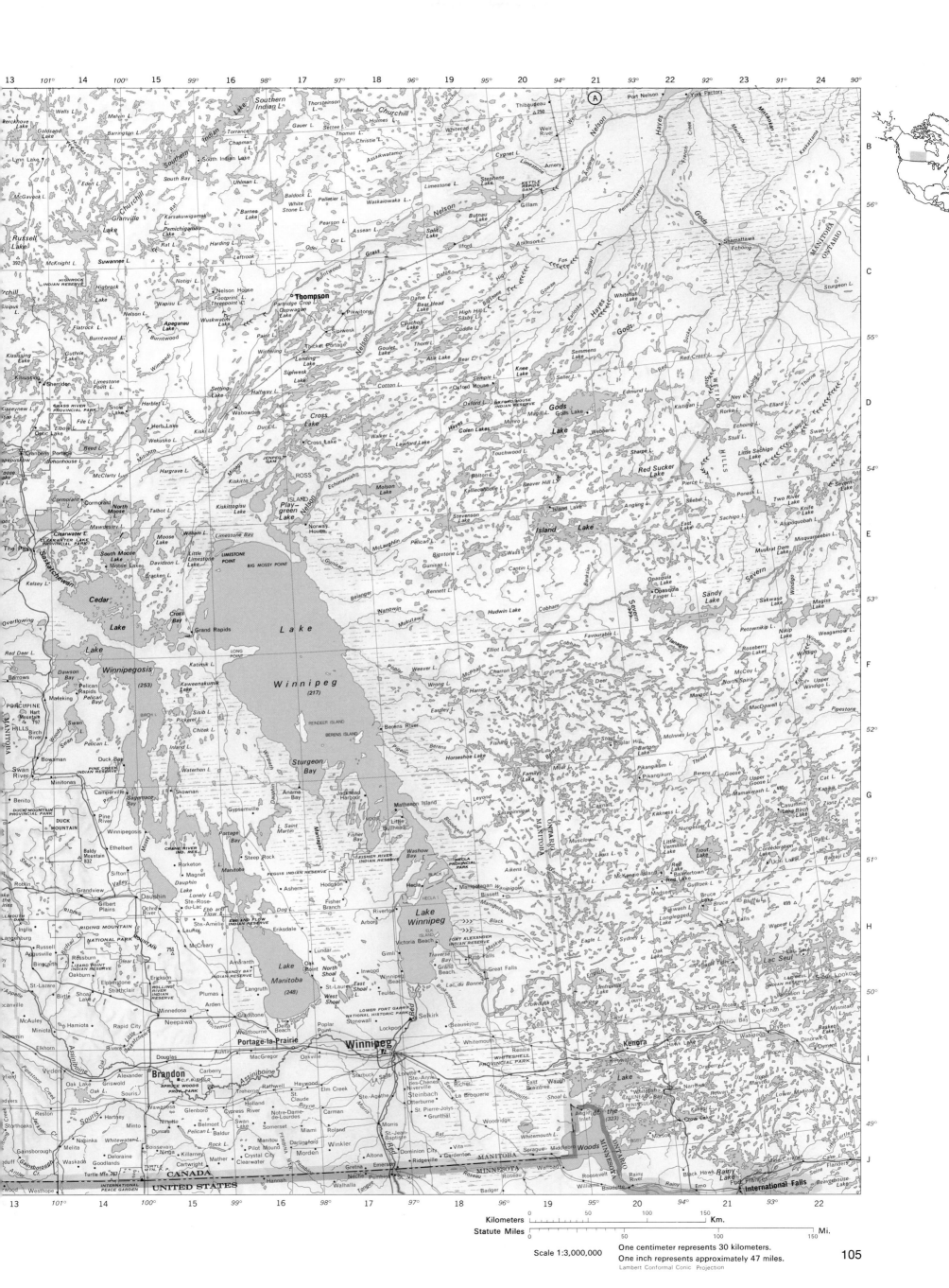

Scale 1:3,000,000

One centimeter represents 30 kilometers.
One inch represents approximately 47 miles.

Lambert Conformal Conic Projection

105

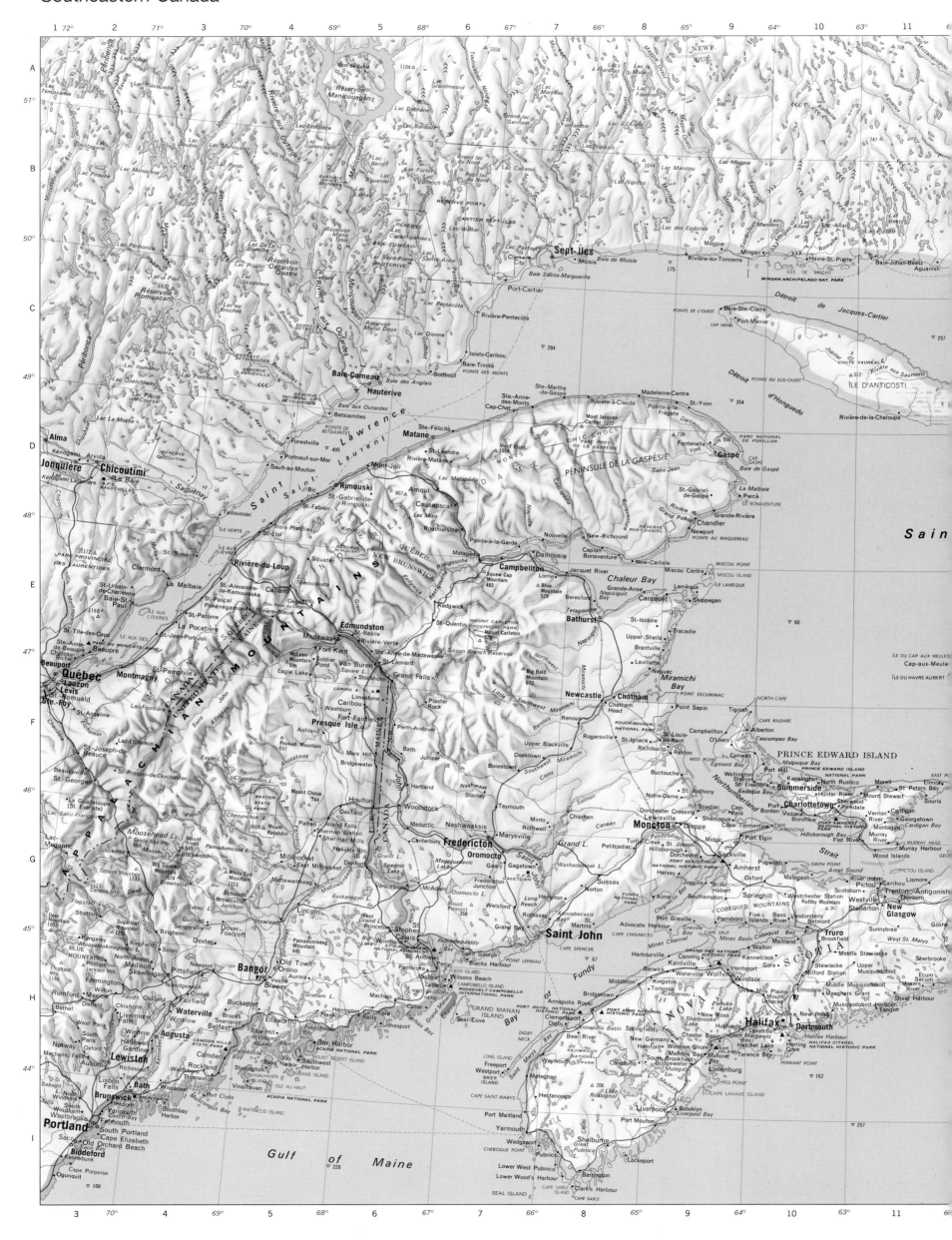

Map of Newfoundland and surrounding region, including Labrador Sea, Atlantic Ocean, Gulf of St. Lawrence, and Cape Breton Island.

107

Kilometers
Statute Miles

Scale 1:3,000,000

One centimeter represents 30 kilometers.
One inch represents approximately 47 miles.
Lambert Conformal Conic Projection

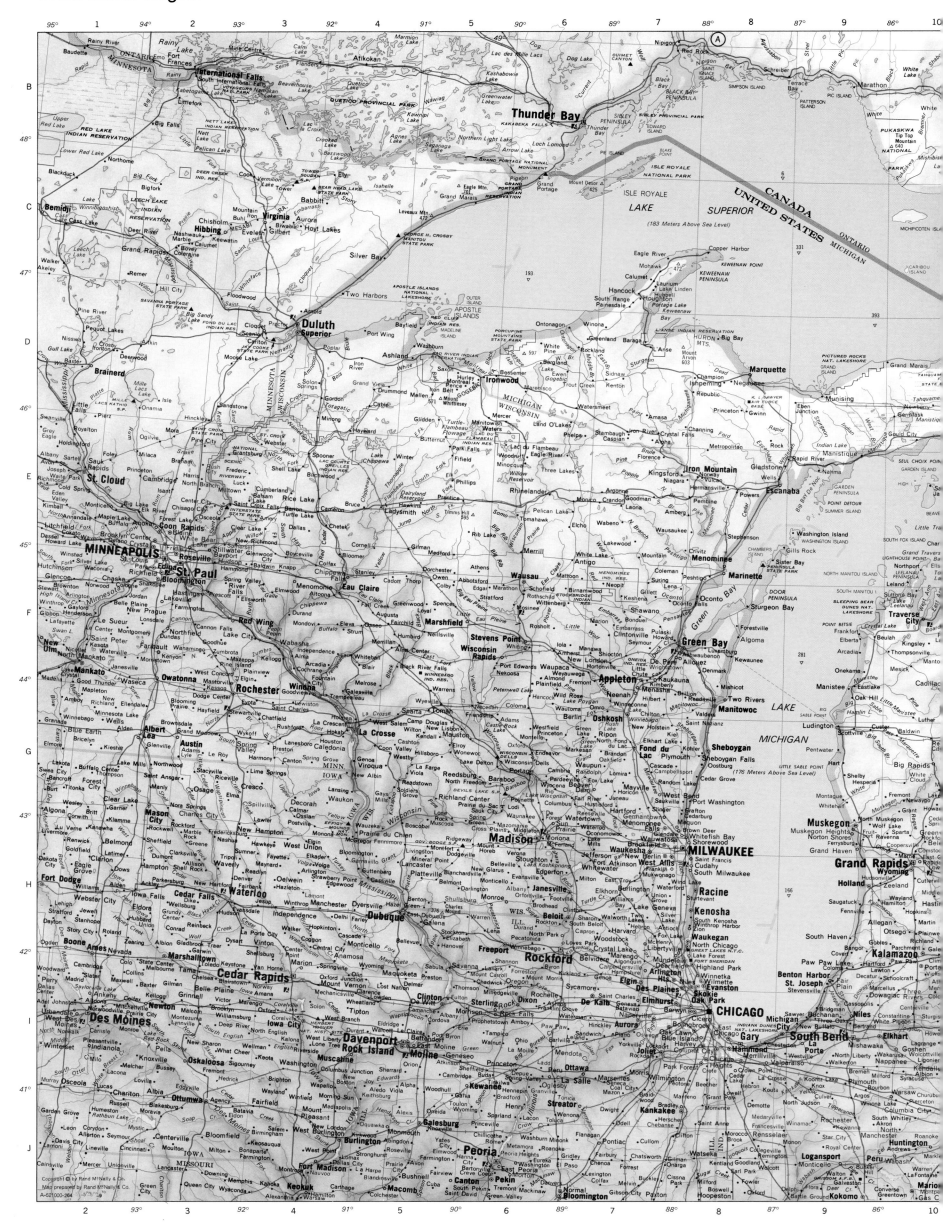

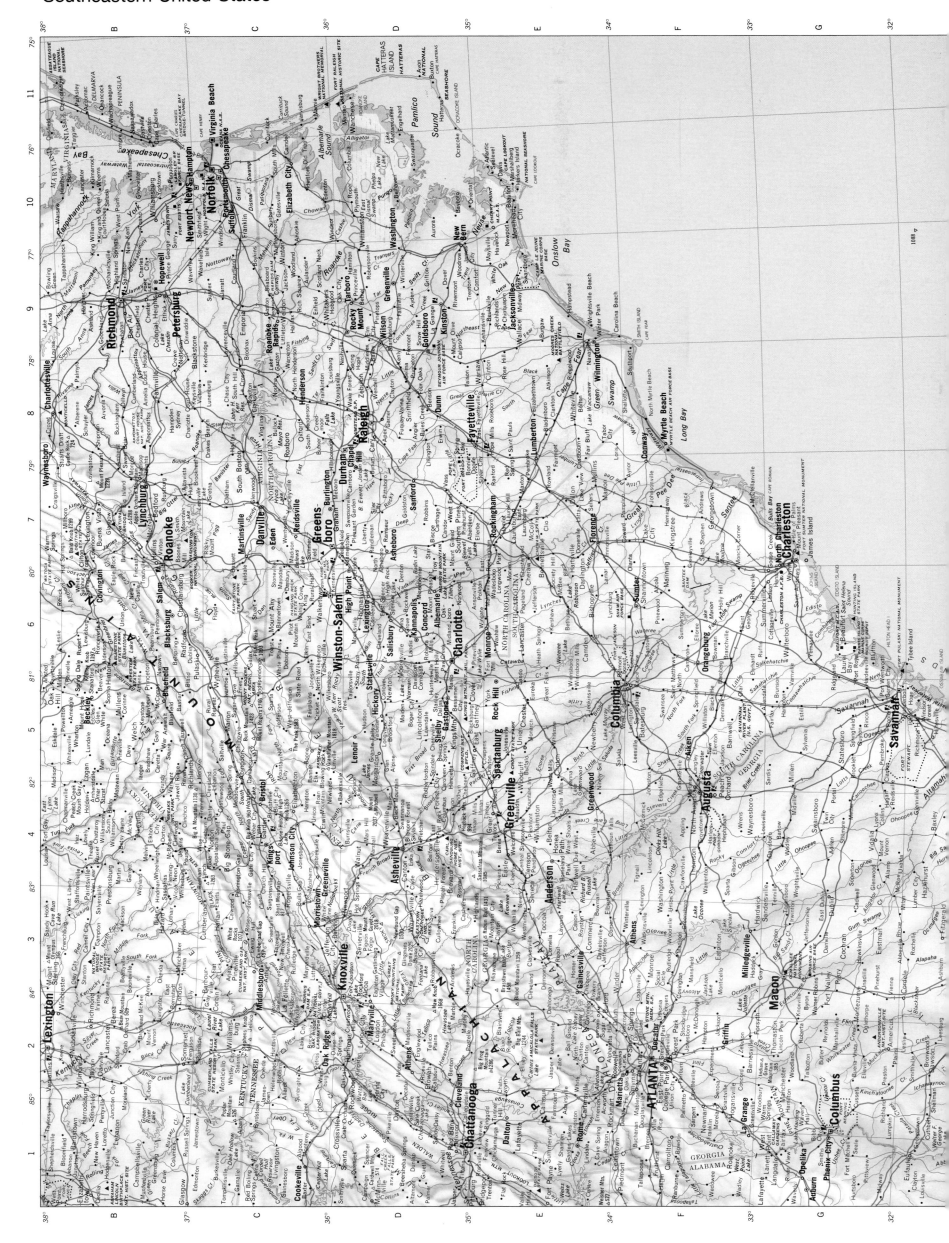

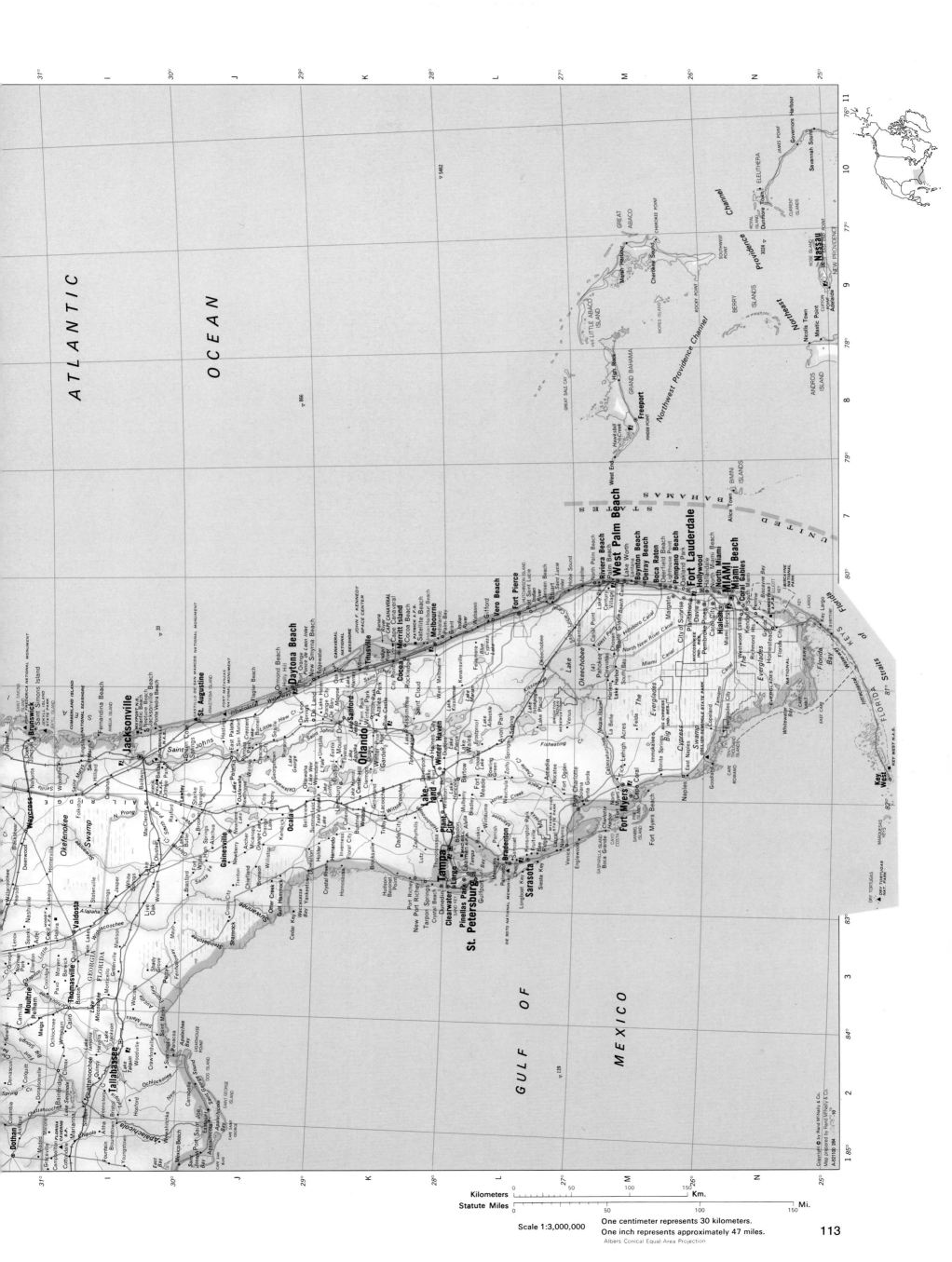

Kilometers
Statute Miles

Scale 1:3,000,000

One centimeter represents 30 kilometers.
One inch represents approximately 47 miles.
Albers Conical Equal-Area Projection

Kilometers

Statute Miles

Scale 1:3,000,000

One centimeter represents 30 kilometers.
One inch represents approximately 47 miles.
Albers Conical Equal-Area Projection

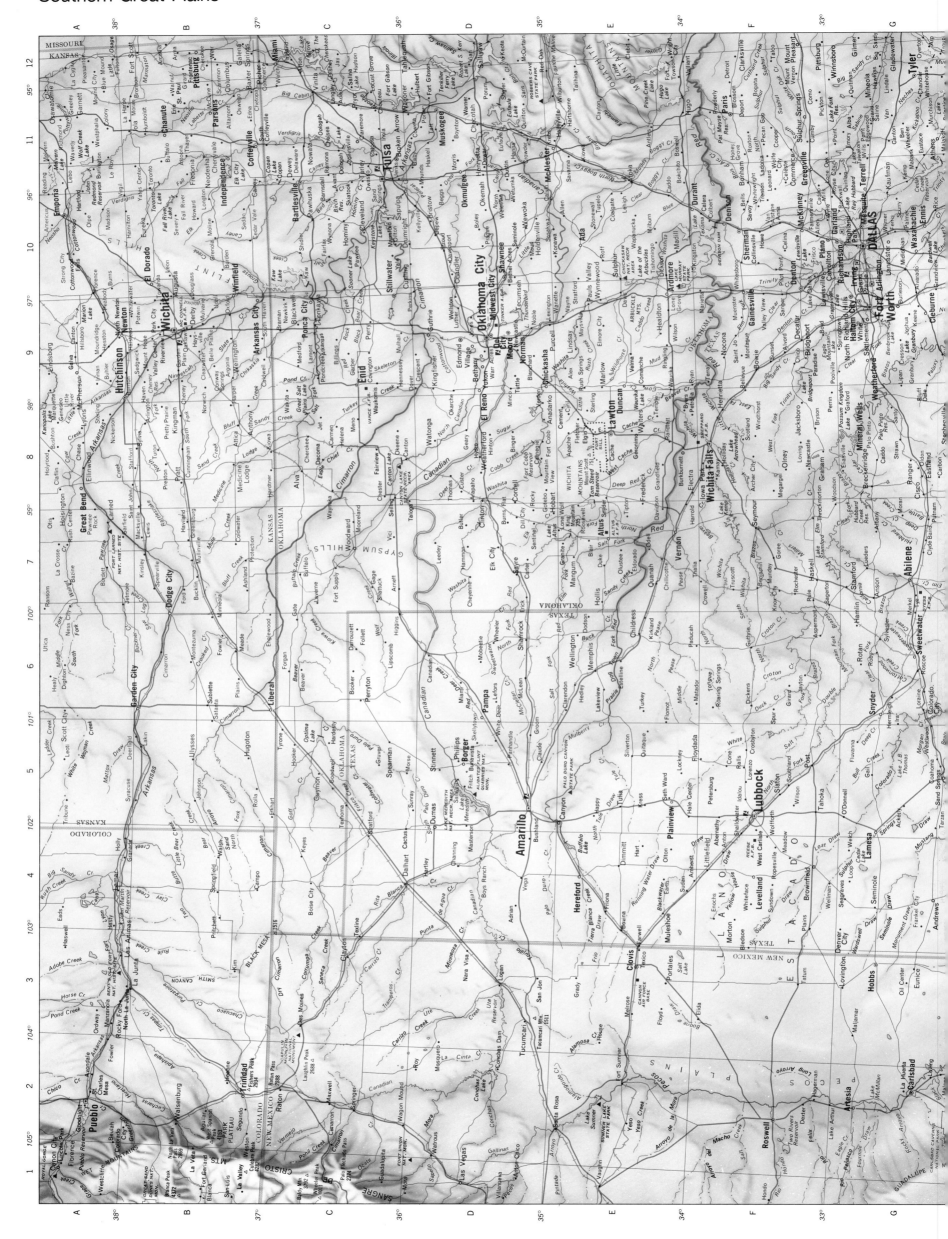

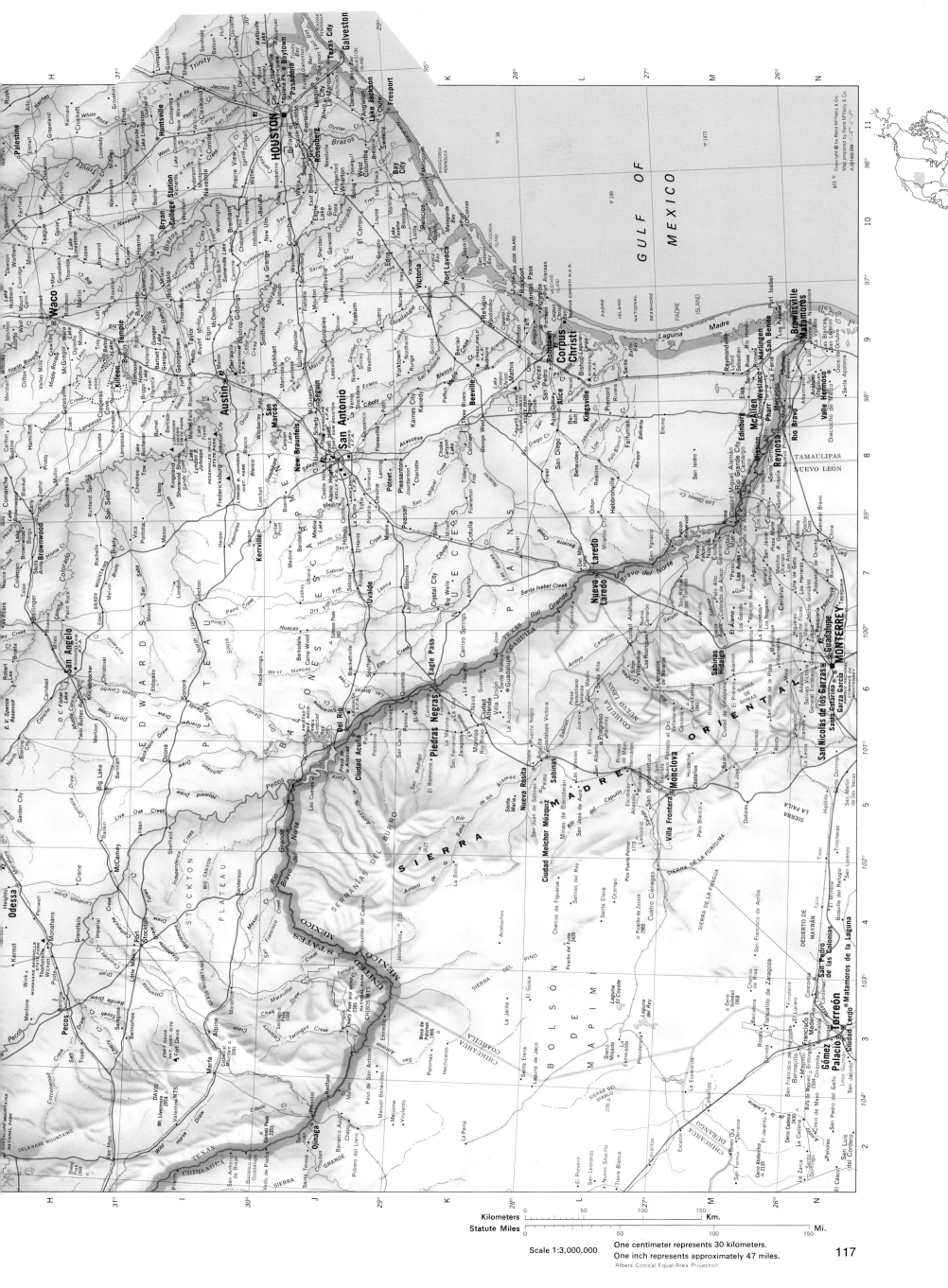

Kilometers

Statute Miles

One centimeter represents 30 kilometers.

One inch represents approximately 47 miles.

Scale 1:3,000,000

Albers Conical Equal-Area Projection

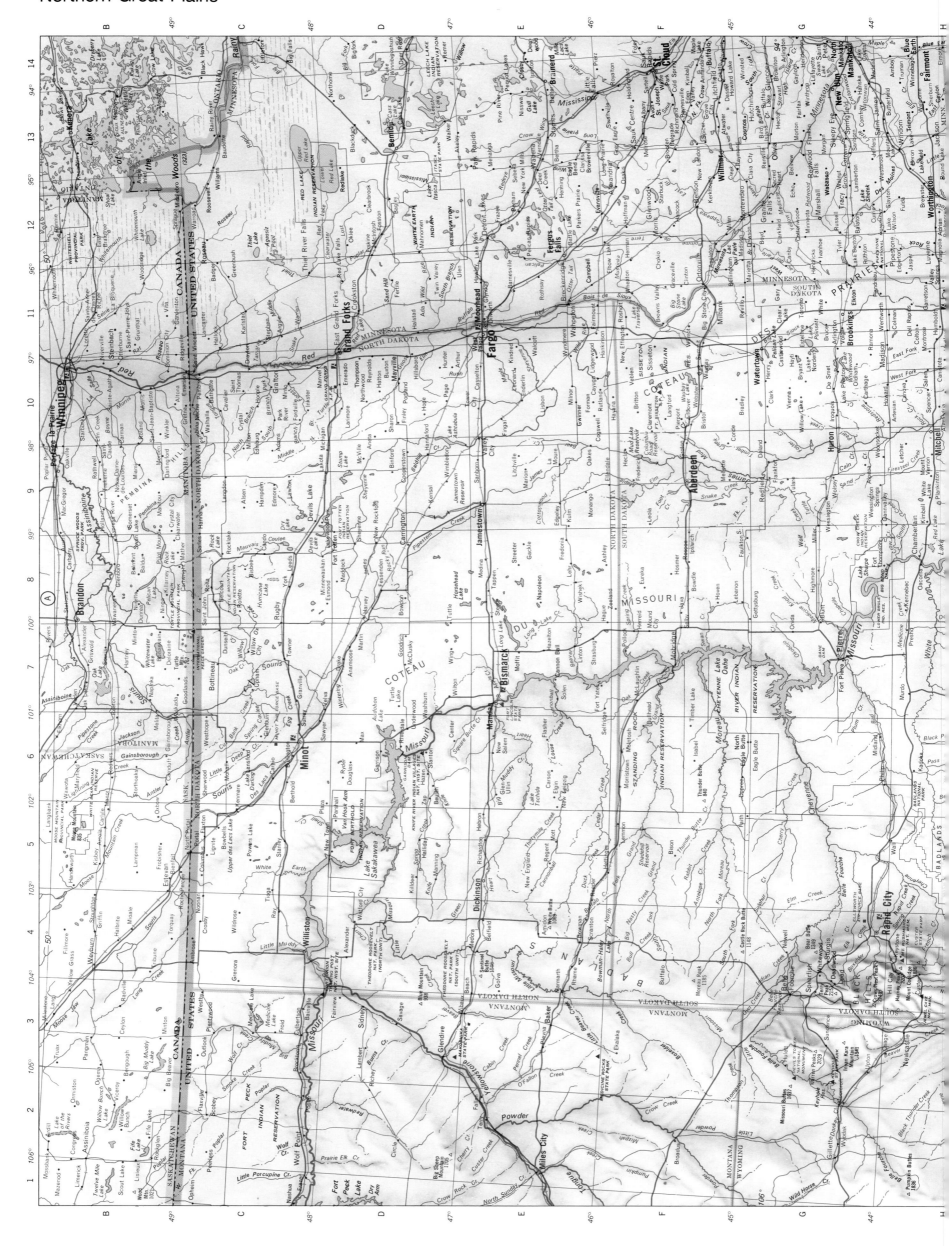

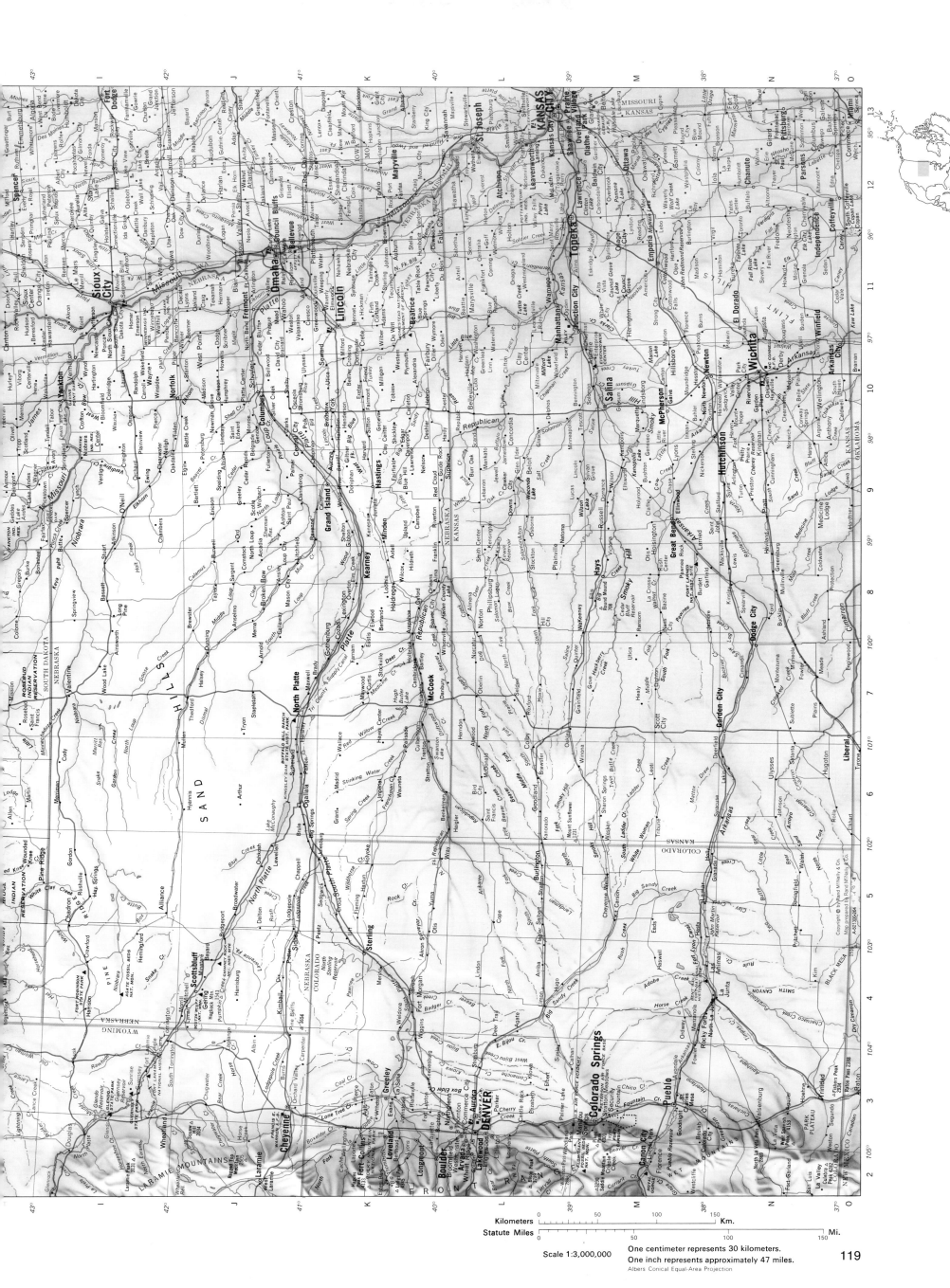

Kilometers

Statute Miles

Scale 1:3,000,000

One centimeter represents 30 kilometers.
One inch represents approximately 47 miles.

Albers Conical Equal-Area Projection

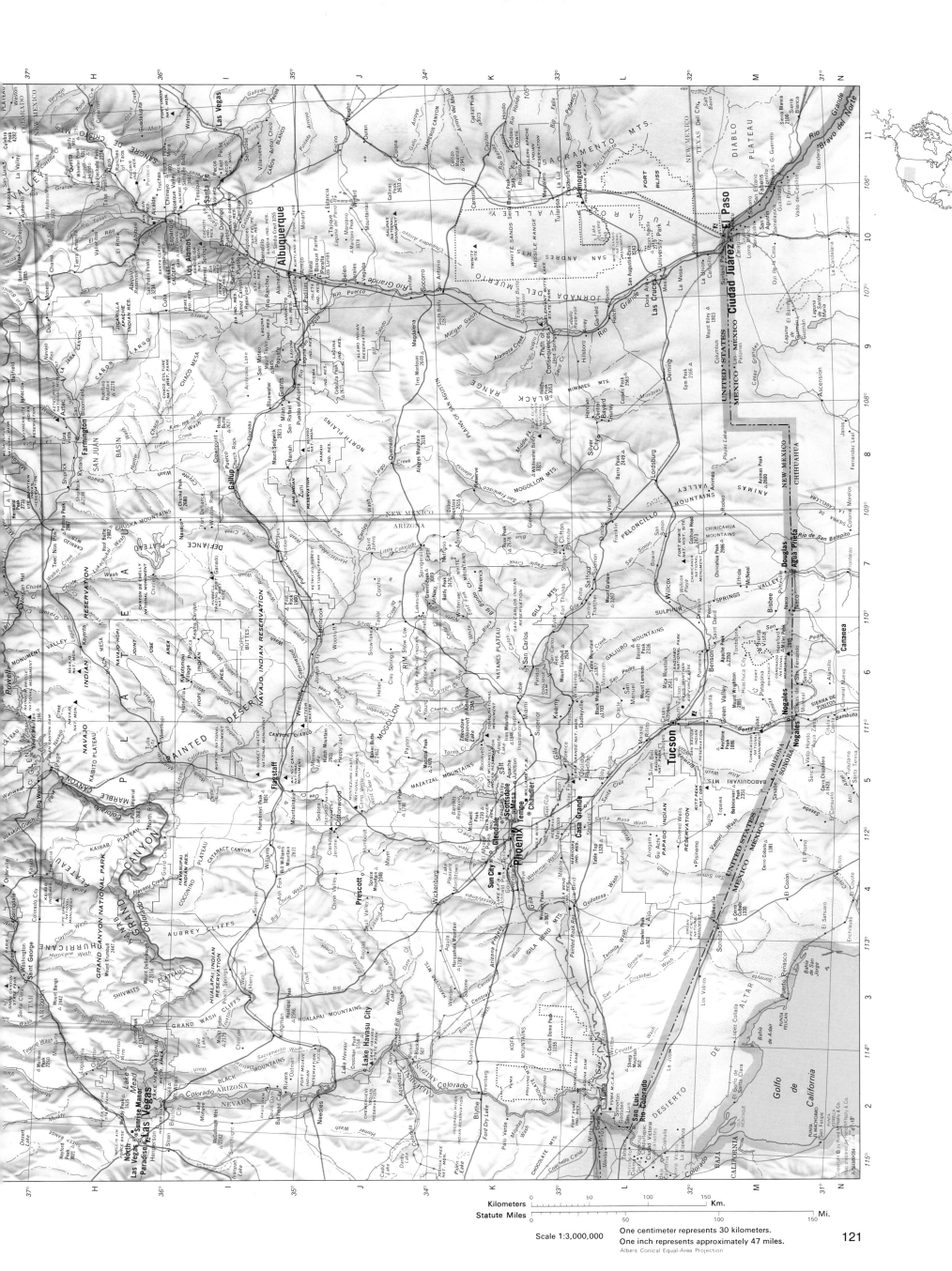

Kilometers |0 50 100 150| Km.

Statute Miles |0 50 100 150| Mi.

Scale 1:3,000,000

One centimeter represents 30 kilometers.

One inch represents approximately 47 miles.

Albers Conical Equal-Area Projection

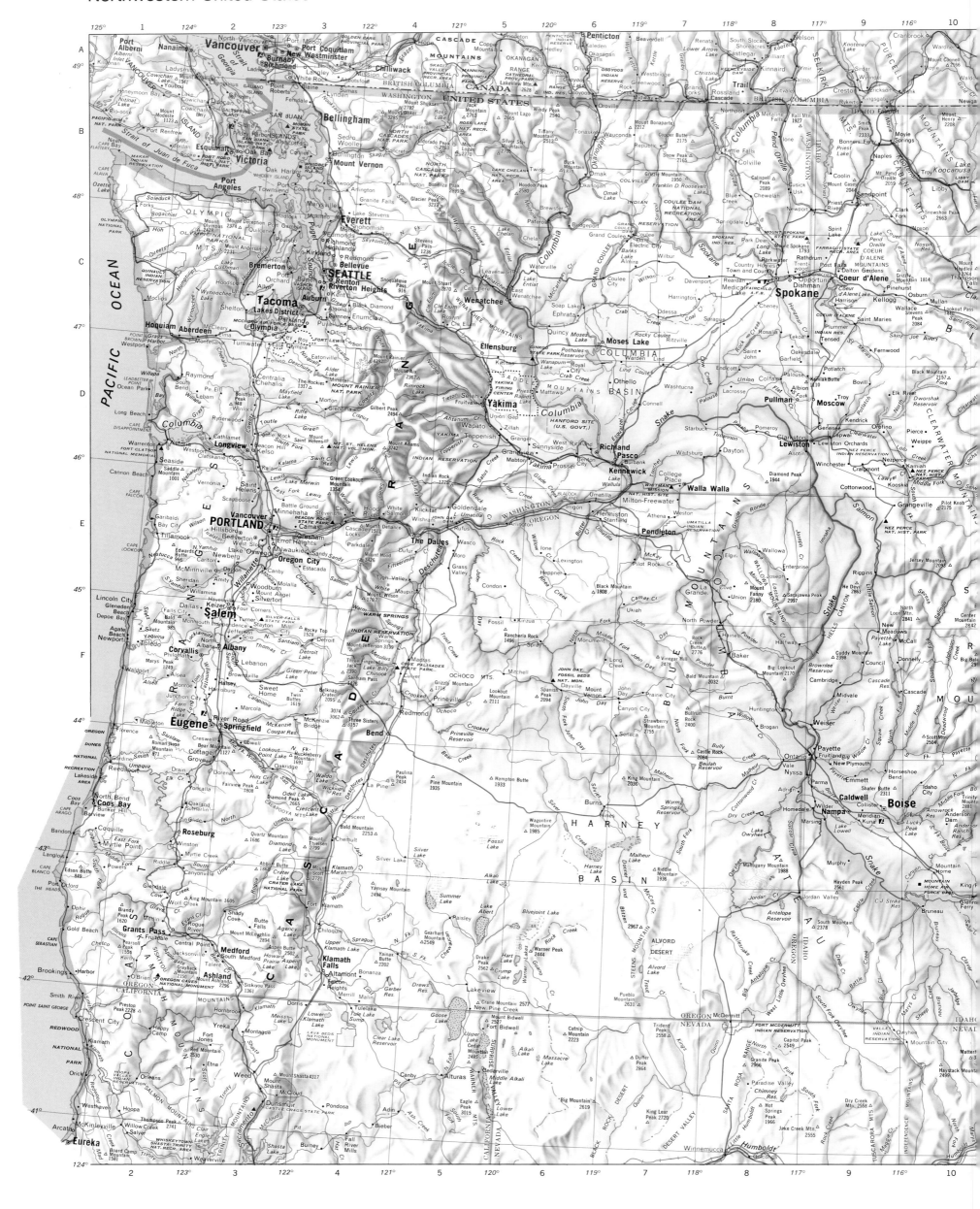

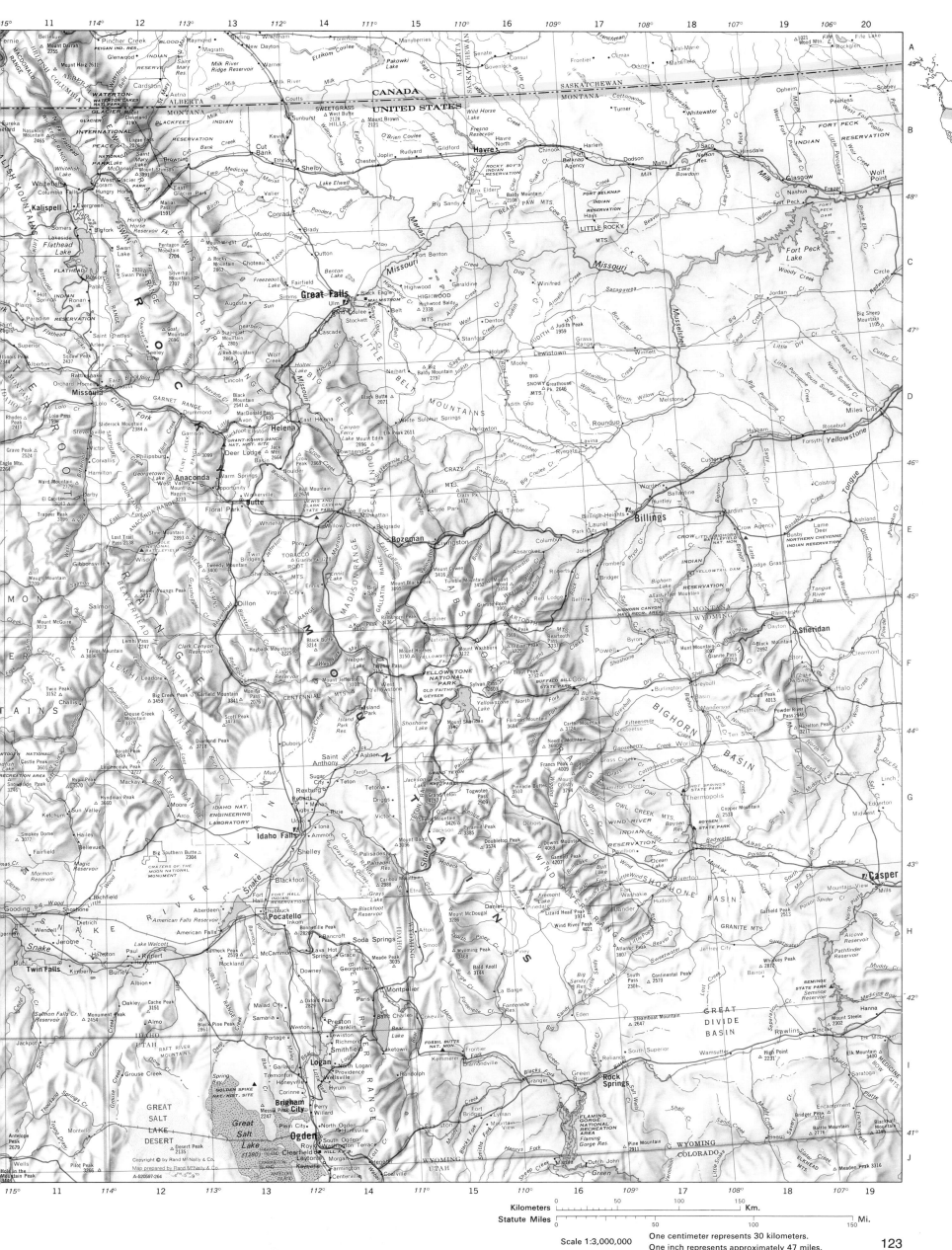

One centimeter represents 30 kilometers.
One inch represents approximately 47 miles.

Scale 1:3,000,000

Albers Conical Equal-Area Projection

123

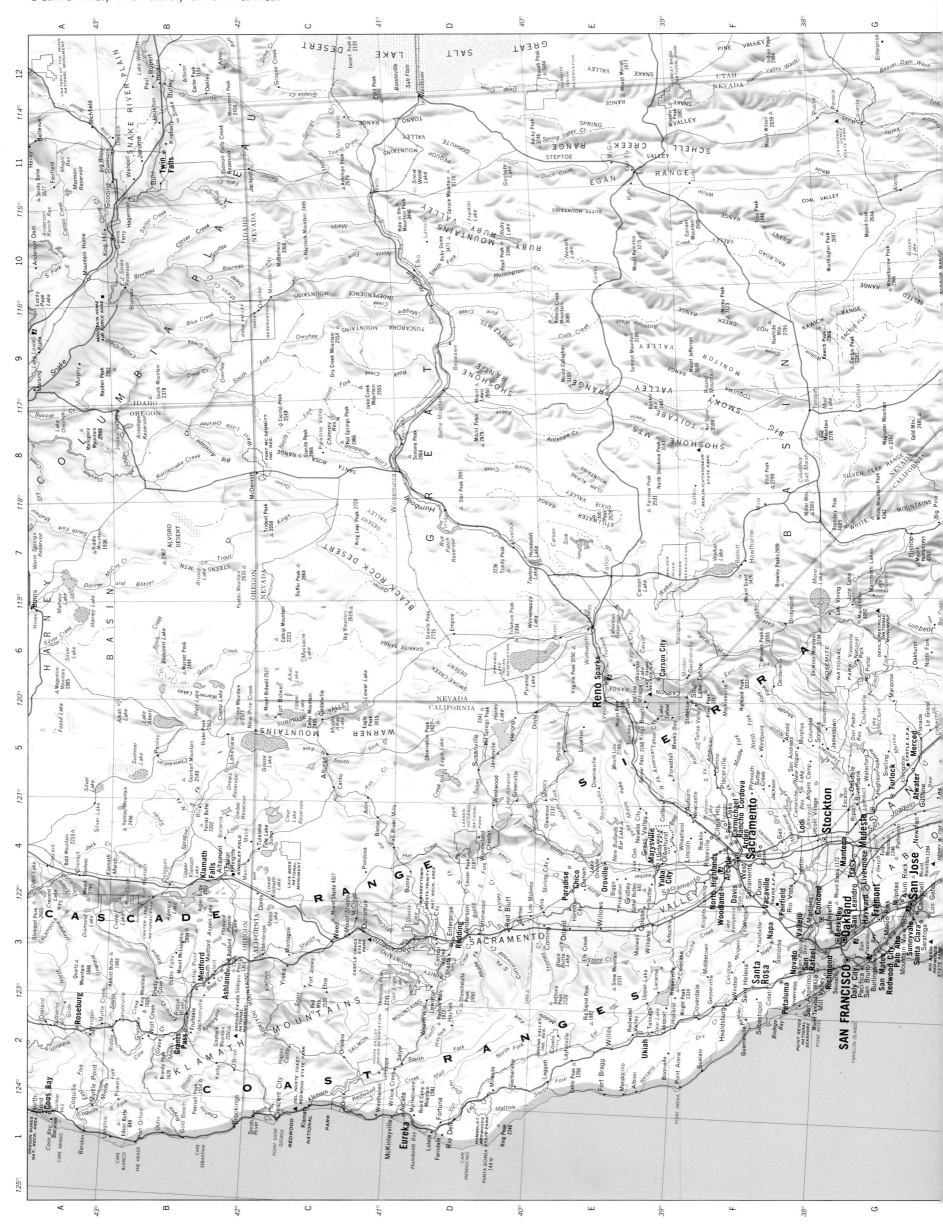

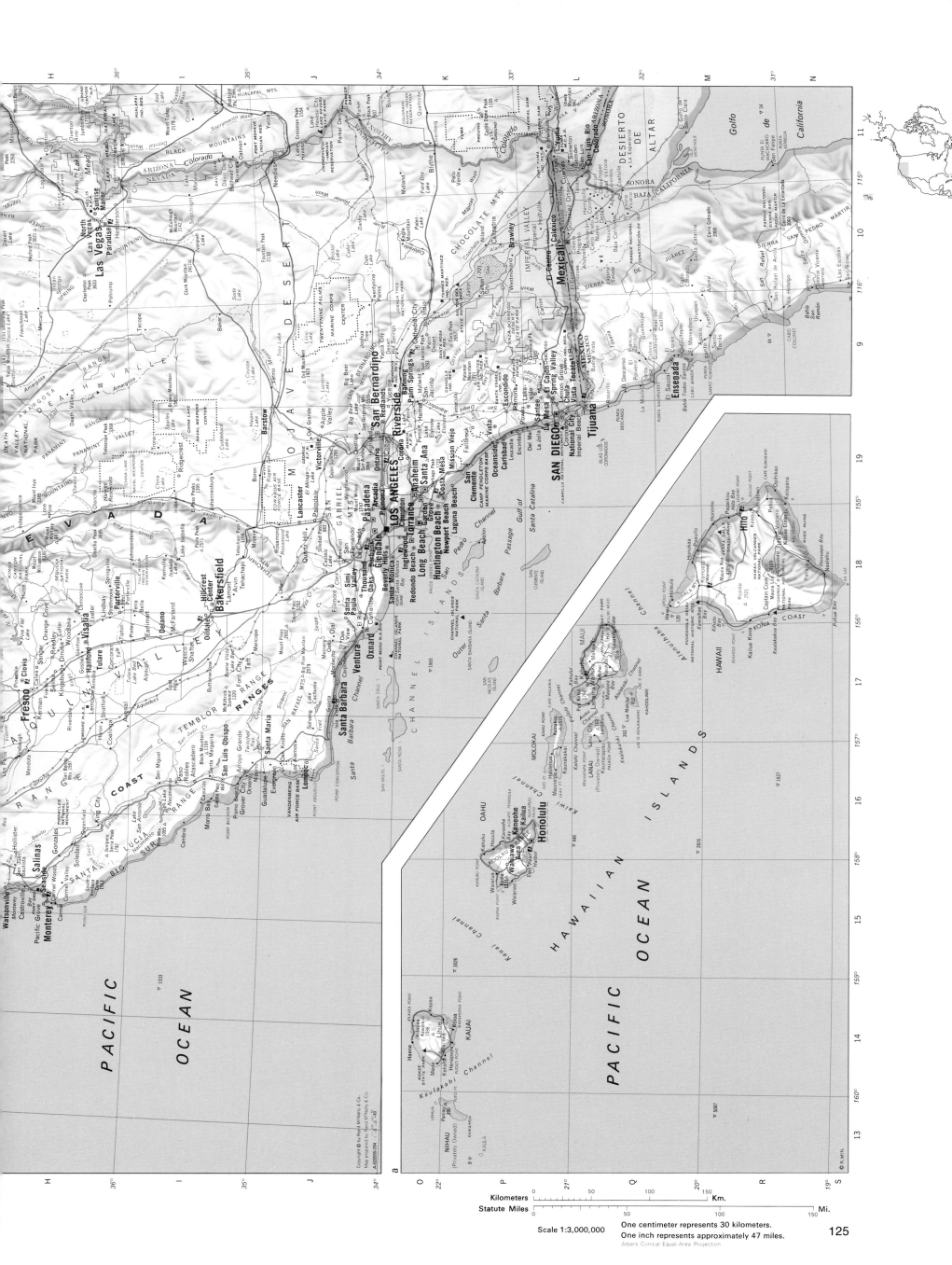

Kilometers

Statute Miles

Scale 1:3,000,000

One centimeter represents 30 kilometers.
One inch represents approximately 47 miles.
Albers Conical Equal-Area Projection

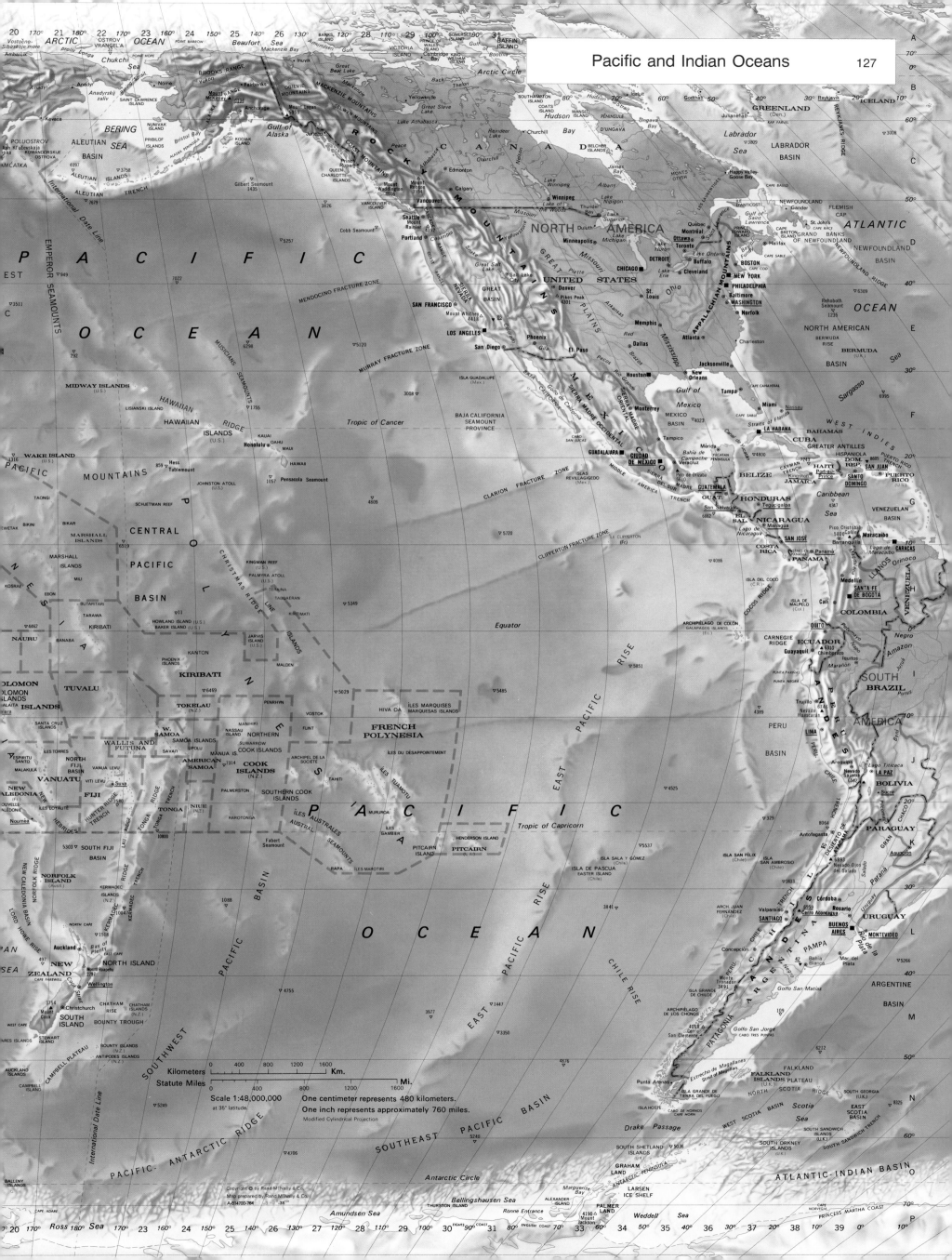

Index to World Reference Maps

Introduction to the Index

This universal index includes in a single alphabetical list over 52,000 names of features that appear on the reference maps. Each name is followed by the name of the country or continent in which it is located, a map-reference key and a page reference.

Names The names of cities appear in the index in regular type. The names of all other features appear in *italics*, followed by descriptive terms (hill, mtn., state) to indicate their nature.

Names that appear in shortened versions on the maps due to space limitations are spelled out in full in the index. The portions of these names omitted from the maps are enclosed in brackets — for example, Acapulco [de Juárez].

Abbreviations of names on the maps have been standardized as much as possible. Names that are abbreviated on the maps are generally spelled out in full in the index.

Country names and names of features that extend beyond the name of one country are followed by the name of the continent in which each is located. Country designations follow the names of all other places in the index. The locations of places in the United States, Canada, and the United Kingdom are further defined by abbreviations that indicate the state, province, or political division in which each is located.

All abbreviations used in the index are defined in the List of Abbreviations below.

Alphabetization Names are alphabetized in the order of the letters of the English alphabet. Spanish *ll* and *ch*, for example, are not treated as distinct letters. Furthermore, diacritical marks are disregarded in alphabetization — German or Scandinavian *ä* or *ö* are treated as *a* or *o*.

The names of physical features may appear inverted, since they are always alphabetized under the proper, not the generic, part of the name, thus: 'Gibraltar, Strait of'. Otherwise every entry, whether consisting of one word or more, is alphabetized as a single continuous entity. 'Lakeland', for example, appears after 'La Crosse' and before 'La Salle'. Names beginning with articles (Le Havre, Den Helder, Al Manşūrah) are not inverted. Names beginning 'St.', 'Ste.' and 'Sainte' are alphabetized as though spelled 'Saint'.

In the case of identical names, towns are listed first, then political divisions, then physical features. Entries that are completely identical are listed alphabetically by country name.

Map-Reference Keys and Page References The map-reference keys and page references are found in the last two columns of each entry.

Each map-reference key consists of a letter and number. The letters appear along the sides of the maps. Lowercase letters indicate reference to inset maps. Numbers appear across the tops and bottoms of the maps.

Map reference keys for point features, such as cities and mountain peaks, indicate the locations of the symbols. For extensive areal features, such as countries or mountain ranges, locations are given for the approximate centers of the features. Those for linear features, such as canals and rivers, are given for the locations of the names.

The page number generally refers to the main map for the country in which the feature is located. Page references to two-page maps always refer to the left-hand page.

List of Abbreviations

Afg.	Afghanistan	Cyp.	Cyprus	Kir.	Kiribati	N.J., U.S.	New Jersey, U.S.	*state*	state, republic, canton
Afr.	Africa	Czech.	Czech Republic	Ks., U.S.	Kansas, U.S.	N. Kor.	North Korea	St. Hel.	St. Helena
Ak., U.S.	Alaska, U.S.	D.C., U.S.	District of Columbia, U.S.	Kuw.	Kuwait	N.M., U.S.	New Mexico, U.S.	St. K./N	St. Kitts and Nevis
Al., U.S.	Alabama, U.S.			Ky., U.S.	Kentucky, U.S.	N. Mar. Is.	Northern Mariana Islands	St. Luc.	St. Lucia
Alb.	Albania	De., U.S.	Delaware, U.S.	Kyrg.	Kyrgyzstan			*stm.*	stream (river, creek)
Alg.	Algeria	Den.	Denmark	*l.*	lake, pond	Nmb.	Namibia	S. Tom./P.	Sao Tome and Principe
Alta., Can.	Alberta, Can.	*dep.*	dependency, colony	La., U.S.	Louisiana, U.S.	Nor.	Norway		
Am. Sam.	American Samoa	*depr.*	depression	Lat.	Latvia	Norf. I.	Norfolk Island	St. P./M.	St. Pierre and Miquelon
anch.	anchorage	*dept.*	department, district	Leb.	Lebanon	N.S., Can.	Nova Scotia, Can.		
And.	Andorra	*des.*	desert	Leso.	Lesotho	Nv., U.S.	Nevada, U.S.	*strt.*	strait, channel, sound
Ang.	Angola	Dji.	Djibouti	Lib.	Liberia	N.W. Ter., Can.	Northwest Territories, Can.		
Ant.	Antarctica	Dom.	Dominica	Liech.	Liechtenstein			St. Vin.	St. Vincent and the Grenadines
Antig.	Antigua and Barbuda	Dom. Rep.	Dominican Republic	Lith.	Lithuania	N.Y., U.S.	New York, U.S.		
		Ec.	Ecuador	Lux.	Luxembourg	N.Z.	New Zealand	Sur.	Suriname
Ar., U.S.	Arkansas, U.S.	El Sal.	El Salvador	Ma., U.S.	Massachusetts, U.S.	Oc.	Oceania	*sw.*	swamp, marsh
Arg.	Argentina	Eng., U.K.	England, U.K.			Oh., U.S.	Ohio, U.S.	Swaz.	Swaziland
Arm.	Armenia	Eq. Gui.	Equatorial Guinea	Mac.	Macedonia	Ok., U.S.	Oklahoma, U.S.	Swe.	Sweden
Aus.	Austria	Erit.	Eritrea	Madag.	Madagascar	Ont., Can.	Ontario, Can.	Switz.	Switzerland
Austl.	Australia	*est.*	estuary	Malay.	Malaysia	Or., U.S.	Oregon, U.S.	Tai.	Taiwan
Az., U.S.	Arizona, U.S.	Est.	Estonia	Mald.	Maldives	Pa., U.S.	Pennsylvania, U.S.	Taj.	Tajikistan
Azer.	Azerbaijan	Eth.	Ethiopia	Man., Can.	Manitoba, Can.	Pak.	Pakistan	Tan.	Tanzania
b.	bay, gulf, inlet, lagoon	Eur.	Europe	Marsh. Is.	Marshall Islands	Pan.	Panama	T./C. Is.	Turks and Caicos Islands
		Faer. Is.	Faeroe Islands	Mart.	Martinique	Pap. N. Gui.	Papua New Guinea		
Bah.	Bahamas	Falk. Is.	Falkland Islands	Maur.	Mauritania	Para.	Paraguay	*ter.*	territory
Bahr.	Bahrain	Fin.	Finland	May.	Mayotte	P.E.I., Can.	Prince Edward Island, Can.	Thai.	Thailand
Barb.	Barbados	Fl., U.S.	Florida, U.S.	Md., U.S.	Maryland, U.S.			Tn., U.S.	Tennessee, U.S.
B.C., Can.	British Columbia, Can.	*for.*	forest, moor	Me., U.S.	Maine, U.S.	*pen.*	peninsula	Tok.	Tokelau
		Fr.	France	Mex.	Mexico	Phil.	Philippines	Trin.	Trinidad and Tobago
Bdi.	Burundi	Fr. Gu.	French Guiana	Mi., U.S.	Michigan, U.S.	Pit.	Pitcairn		
Bel.	Belgium	Fr. Poly.	French Polynesia	Micron.	Federated States of Micronesia	*pl.*	plain, flat	Tun.	Tunisia
Bela.	Belarus	Ga., U.S.	Georgia, U.S.			*plat.*	plateau, highland	Tur.	Turkey
Ber.	Bermuda	Gam.	Gambia	Mid. Is.	Midway Islands	Pol.	Poland	Turk.	Turkmenistan
Bhu.	Bhutan	Gaza	Gaza Strip and Jericho Area	*mil.*	military installation	Port.	Portugal	Tx., U.S.	Texas, U.S.
B.I.O.T.	British Indian Ocean Territory			Mn., U.S.	Minnesota, U.S.	P.R.	Puerto Rico	U.A.E.	United Arab Emirates
		Geor.	Georgia	Mo., U.S.	Missouri, U.S.	*prov.*	province, region		
Bngl.	Bangladesh	Ger.	Germany	Mol.	Moldova	Que., Can.	Quebec, Can.	Ug.	Uganda
Bol.	Bolivia	Gib.	Gibraltar	Mon.	Monaco	*reg.*	physical region	U.K.	United Kingdom
Bos.	Bosnia and Herzegovina	Golan	Golan Heights	Mong.	Mongolia	*res.*	reservoir	Ukr.	Ukraine
		Grc.	Greece	Monts.	Montserrat	Reu.	Reunion	Ur.	Uruguay
Bots.	Botswana	Gren.	Grenada	Mor.	Morocco	*rf.*	reef, shoal	U.S.	United States
Braz.	Brazil	Grnld.	Greenland	Moz.	Mozambique	R.I., U.S.	Rhode Island, U.S.	Ut., U.S.	Utah, U.S.
Bru.	Brunei	Guad.	Guadeloupe	Mrts.	Mauritius	Rom.	Romania	Uzb.	Uzbekistan
Br. Vir. Is.	British Virgin Islands	Guat.	Guatemala	Ms., U.S.	Mississippi, U.S.	Rw.	Rwanda	Va., U.S.	Virginia, U.S.
Bul.	Bulgaria	Gui.	Guinea	Mt., U.S.	Montana, U.S.	S.A.	South America	*val.*	valley, watercourse
Burkina	Burkina Faso	Gui.-B.	Guinea-Bissau	*mth.*	river mouth or channel	S. Afr.	South Africa	Vat.	Vatican City
c.	cape, point	Guy.	Guyana			Sask., Can.	Saskatchewan, Can.	Ven.	Venezuela
Ca., U.S.	California, U.S.	Hi., U.S.	Hawaii, U.S.	*mtn.*	mountain			Viet.	Vietnam
Cam.	Cameroon	*hist.*	historic site, ruins	*mts.*	mountains	Sau. Ar.	Saudi Arabia	V.I.U.S.	Virgin Islands (U.S.)
Camb.	Cambodia	*hist. reg.*	historic region	Mwi.	Malawi	S.C., U.S.	South Carolina, U.S.	*vol.*	volcano
Can.	Canada	H.K.	Hong Kong	Mya.	Myanmar	*sci.*	scientific station	Vt., U.S.	Vermont, U.S.
Cay. Is.	Cayman Islands	Hond.	Honduras	N.A.	North America	Scot., U.K.	Scotland, U.K.	Wa., U.S.	Washington, U.S.
Cen. Afr. Rep.	Central African Republic	Hung.	Hungary	N.B., Can.	New Brunswick, Can.	S.D., U.S.	South Dakota, U.S.	Wal./F.	Wallis and Futuna
		i.	island			Sen.	Senegal	W.B.	West Bank
Christ. I.	Christmas Island	Ia., U.S.	Iowa, U.S.	N.C., U.S.	North Carolina, U.S.	Sey.	Seychelles	Wi., U.S.	Wisconsin, U.S.
C. Iv.	Cote d'Ivoire	Ice.	Iceland	N. Cal.	New Caledonia	Sing.	Singapore	W. Sah.	Western Sahara
clf.	cliff, escarpment	*ice*	ice feature, glacier	N. Cyp.	North Cyprus	S. Geor.	South Georgia	W. Sam.	Western Samoa
co.	county, parish	Id., U.S.	Idaho, U.S.	N.D., U.S.	North Dakota, U.S.	S. Kor.	South Korea	*wtfl.*	waterfall
Co., U.S.	Colorado, U.S.	Il., U.S.	Illinois, U.S.	Ne., U.S.	Nebraska, U.S.	S.L.	Sierra Leone	W.V., U.S.	West Virginia, U.S.
Col.	Colombia	In., U.S.	Indiana, U.S.	Neth.	Netherlands	Slo.	Slovenia	Wy., U.S.	Wyoming, U.S.
Com.	Comoros	Indon.	Indonesia	Neth. Ant.	Netherlands Antilles	Slov.	Slovakia	Yugo.	Yugoslavia
cont.	continent	I. of Man	Isle of Man	Newf., Can.	Newfoundland, Can.	S. Mar.	San Marino	Yukon, Can.	Yukon Territory, Can.
C.R.	Costa Rica	Ire.	Ireland	N.H., U.S.	New Hampshire, U.S.	Sol. Is.	Solomon Islands		
crat.	crater	*is.*	islands			Som.	Somalia	Zam.	Zambia
Cro.	Croatia	Isr.	Israel	Nic.	Nicaragua	Sp. N. Afr.	Spanish North Africa	Zimb.	Zimbabwe
Ct., U.S.	Connecticut, U.S.	Jam.	Jamaica	Nig.	Nigeria				
ctry.	country	Jord.	Jordan	N. Ire., U.K.	Northern Ireland, U.K.	Sri L.	Sri Lanka		
C.V.	Cape Verde	Kaz.	Kazakhstan						

Index

A

Name	Map Ref.	Page
Alcántara I, Embalse de, res., Spain	F5	16
Alcantarilla, Spain	H10	16
Alcantilado, Braz.	D2	79
Alcaudete, Spain	H7	16
Alcázar de San Juan, Spain	F8	16
Alcester, S.D., U.S.	H11	118
Alcira (Gigena), Arg.	G6	80
Alcoa, Tn., U.S.	D3	112
Alcobaça, Braz.	D9	79
Alcobaça, Port.	F3	16
Alcobaça, stm., Braz.	D9	79
Alcoi, Spain	G11	16
Alcolu, S.C., U.S.	F6	112
Alcorn, Ms., U.S.	K5	114
Alcorta, Arg.	G8	80
Alcoutim, Port.	H4	16
Alcovy, stm., Ga., U.S.	F3	112
Aldabra Island, i., Sey.	C9	58
Aldama, Mex.	C7	90
Aldama, Mex.	F10	90
Aldan, Russia	F17	28
Aldan, stm., Russia	F18	28
Aldanskoje nagorje, plat., Russia	F17	28
Aldeburgh, Eng., U.K.	I15	8
Alden, Ia., U.S.	H2	110
Alden, Mn., U.S.	G2	110
Alderney, i., Guernsey	L11	8
Aldershot, Eng., U.K.	J13	8
Alderson, W.V., U.S.	B6	112
Aledo, Il., U.S.	I5	110
Alefa, Eth.	L9	60
Aleg, Maur.	C3	64
Alegre, Braz.	F8	79
Alegre, stm., Braz.	F12	82
Alegres Mountain, mtn., N.M., U.S.	J8	120
Alegrete, Braz.	E11	80
Alejandro Roca, Arg.	G7	80
Alejandro Selkirk, Isla, i., Chile	H6	74
Alejo Ledesma, Arg.	G7	80
Alejsk, Russia	G8	28
Aleknagik, Ak., U.S.	G15	100
Aleksandro-Nevskij, Russia	H23	22
Aleksandrov, Russia	E21	22
Aleksandrov Gaj, Russia	G7	26
Aleksandrovskoje, Russia	E13	26
Aleksandrovsk-Sachalinskij, Russia	G20	28
Aleksejevka, Kaz.	G12	26
Aleksejevka, Russia	G5	26
Aleksejevsk, Russia	F13	28
Aleksin, Russia	G20	22
Aleksinac, Yugo.	F5	20
Alemania, Arg.	C6	80
Além Paraíba, Braz.	F7	79
Alençon, Fr.	D7	14
Alenquer, Braz.	D8	76
Alentejo, hist. reg., Port.	G3	16
Alenuihaha Channel, strt., Hi., U.S.	q17	125a
Aleppo see Ḥalab, Syria	C4	48
Aléria, Fr.	G4	18
Alert, N.T., Can.	A13	86
Alert Bay, B.C., Can.	G8	102
Alès, Fr.	H11	14
Alessandria, Italy	E3	18
Ålesund, Nor.	J10	6
Aletschhorn, mtn., Switz.	F9	13
Aleutian Islands, is., Ak., U.S.	J6	100
Aleutian Range, mts., Ak., U.S.	G17	100
Aleutian Trench	D3	86
Alevina, mys, c., Russia	F22	28
Alex, Ok., U.S.	E9	116
Alexander, Mb., Can.	I14	104
Alexander, N.D., U.S.	D4	118
Alexander Archipelago, is., Ak., U.S.	H27	100
Alexander Bay, S. Afr.	G3	66
Alexander City, Al., U.S.	J11	114
Alexander Indian Reserve, Ab., Can.	D21	102
Alexander Island, i., Ant.	C12	73
Alexandra, N.Z.	F2	72
Alexandra, stm., Austl.	B4	70
Alexandra Falls, wtfl, N.T., Can.	D9	96
Alexandretta see İskenderun, Tur.	C4	48
Alexandretta, Gulf of see İskenderun Körfezi, b., Tur.	H15	4
Alexandria, B.C., Can.	E12	102
Alexandria see Al-Iskandarīyah, Egypt	B5	60
Alexandria, In., U.S.	B11	114
Alexandria, Ky., U.S.	I2	108
Alexandria, La., U.S.	K4	114
Alexandria, Mn., U.S.	F12	118
Alexandria, Mo., U.S.	B5	114
Alexandria, Ne., U.S.	K10	118
Alexandria, On., Can.	B12	108
Alexandria, Rom.	F9	20
Alexandria, S.D., U.S.	H10	118
Alexandria, Tn., U.S.	F10	114
Alexandria, Va., U.S.	I9	108
Alexandria Bay, N.Y., U.S.	C11	108
Alexandrina, Lake, l., Austl.	J3	70
Alexandroúpolis, Grc.	I9	20
Alexis, Il., U.S.	I5	110
Alexis Creek, B.C., Can.	E11	102
Alexis Indian Reserve, Ab., Can.	D20	102
Alfaro, Spain	C10	16
Al-Fāshir, Sudan	K3	60
Al-Fashn, Egypt	C6	60
Al-Fāw, Iraq	G10	48
Al-Fayyūm, Egypt	C6	60
Alfeld, Ger.	D9	10
Alfenas, Braz.	F6	79
Al-Fifi, Sudan	L3	60
Alfiós, stm., Grc.	L5	20
Alföld, pl., Hung.	H20	10
Alfred, Me., U.S.	D16	108
Alfred, N.Y., U.S.	E9	108
Alfred, On., Can.	B12	108
Alga, Kaz.	H9	26
Ålgård, Nor.	L9	6
Al-Garef, Sudan	K8	60
Algarrobal, Chile	E3	80
Algarrobo, Arg.	J7	80
Algarrobo, Arg.	F4	80
Algarrobo, Chile	G3	80
Algarrobo del Águila, Arg.	I5	80
Algarve, hist. reg., Port.	H3	16
Algasovo, Russia	H24	22
Al-Gebir, Sudan	K5	60
Algeciras, Col.	F5	84
Algeciras, Spain	I6	16
Algemesí, Spain	F11	16
Algena, Erit.	I10	60
Alger, Oh., U.S.	G3	108
Algeria (Algérie), ctry., Afr.	C7	54
Al-Ghāṭ, Sau. Ar.	H8	48
Al-Ghawr, val., Asia	D5	50
Al-Ghayḍah, Yemen	F8	47
Al-Ghazālah, Sau. Ar.	H6	48
Alghero, Italy	I3	18
Al-Ghurayfah, Oman	B10	47
Al-Ghurdaqah, Egypt	D7	60
Algiers see El Djazaïr, Alg.	B12	62
Alginet, Spain	F11	16
Algodón, stm., Peru	I6	84
Algodones, N.M., U.S.	I10	120
Algoma, Wi., U.S.	F8	110
Algoma Mills, On., Can.	D13	110
Algona, Ia., U.S.	G1	110
Algona, Wa., U.S.	C3	122
Algonac, Mi., U.S.	H13	110
Algonquin, Il., U.S.	H7	110
Algood, Tn., U.S.	F11	114
Algorta, Spain	B8	16
Algorta, Ur.	G10	80
Al-Ḥadīthah, Iraq	D7	48
Al-Ḥadīthah, Sau. Ar.	E8	50
Al-Ḥajarah, reg., Asia	F8	48
Al Hajeb, Mor.	D8	62
Al-Ḥamād, pl., Sau. Ar.	E5	48
Alhama de Murcia, Spain	H10	16
Al-Ḥammām, Egypt	B5	60
Al-Ḥamrā', Sau. Ar.	C1	47
Al-Ḥarīq, Sau. Ar.	C5	47
Al-Harūj al-Aswad, hills, Libya	C4	56
Al-Ḥasakah, Syria	C6	48
Alhaurín el Grande, Spain	I7	16
Al-Ḥawātah, Sudan	K8	60
Al-Ḥawrah, Yemen	H5	47
Al-Ḥawṭah, Yemen	G6	47
Al-Ḥayy, Iraq	E9	48
Al-Ḥayyānīyah, Sau. Ar.	G7	48
Al-Ḥayz, Egypt	C5	60
Al-Ḥijāz, reg., Sau. Ar.	I5	48
Al-Ḥillah, Iraq	E8	48
Al-Ḥillah, Sudan	K4	60
Al-Hirmil, Leb.	D4	48
Al-Ḥiṣn, Jord.	D5	50
Al-Hoceïma, Mor.	A6	54
Al Hoceïma, Baie d', b., Afr.	J8	16
Alhucemas, Peñón de, i., Sp. N. Afr.	J8	16
Al-Ḥudaydah, Yemen	G3	47
Al-Hufūf, Sau. Ar.	B6	47
Al-Ḥulwah, Sau. Ar.	J9	48
Al-Humayshah, Yemen	H4	47
Al-Ḥuṣayḥiṣah, Sudan	J7	60
Al-Ḥuwaylizah, Golan	B5	50
Al-Ḥuwayyiṭ, Sau. Ar.	I6	48
'Alīābād, Iran	C13	48
Aliaga, Spain	E11	16
Aliákmon, stm., Grc.	I6	20
Aliákmonos, Tekhnití Límni, res., Grc.	I5	20
'Alī al-Gharbī, Iraq	E9	48
Alībāg, India	C2	46
Äli Bayramlı, Azer.	B10	48
Alibey, ozero, l., Ukr.	D14	20
Alibunar, Yugo.	D4	20
Alice, S. Afr.	I8	66
Alice, Tx., U.S.	L8	116
Alice Arm, B.C., Can.	B5	102
Alicedale, S. Afr.	I8	66
Alice Springs, Austl.	D6	68
Alice Town, Bah.	B5	94
Aliceville, Al., U.S.	I8	114
Alīgarh, India	G8	44
Alīgūdarz, Iran	E10	48
Alijos, Islas, is., Mex.	E2	90
Al-Ikhwān, is., Yemen	G5	42
Aliquippa, Pa., U.S.	G6	108
Al-'Irāq, Jord.	F5	50
Al-'Īsāwīyah, Sau. Ar.	F4	48
Al-Iskandarīyah (Alexandria), Egypt	B5	60
Al-Ismā'īlīyah, Egypt	B7	60
Aliwal North, S. Afr.	H8	66
Alix, Ab., Can.	E21	102
Al-Jabalayn, Sudan	K7	60
Al-Jadīdah, Egypt	E5	60
Al-Jafr, Jord.	H6	50
Al-Jaghbūb, Libya	C3	60
Al-Jawf, Libya	E2	60
Al-Jawf, Sau. Ar.	G5	48
Al-Jaylī, Sudan	I7	60
Al-Jazīrah, reg., Sudan	J7	60
Aljezur, Port.	H3	16
Al-Jifārah, Sau. Ar.	J8	48
Al-Jifārah (Jeffara), pl., Afr.	D16	62
Al-Jīzah, Egypt	B6	60
Al-Jubayl, Sau. Ar.	H10	48
Al-Jubayn, Sudan	K8	60
Al-Judayyidah, Jord.	E5	50
Al-Julaydah, well, Asia	G8	48
Al-Junaynah, Sudan	K2	60
Aljustrel, Port.	H3	16
Al-Kafr, Syria	C7	50
Alkali Creek, stm., Ab., Can.	G4	104
Alkali Lake, B.C., Can.	F12	102
Al-Kāmil, Oman	C11	47
Al-Karabah, Sudan	H7	60
Al-Karak, Jord.	F5	50
Al-Karnak, Egypt	E7	60
Al-Kawah, Sudan	K7	60
Al-Khabrā', Sau. Ar.	H7	48
Al-Khābūrah, Oman	C10	47
Al-Khalīl (Hebrón), W.B.	E4	50
Al-Khāliṣ, Iraq	E8	48
Al-Khandaq, Sudan	H6	60
Al-Khārijah, Egypt	E6	60
Al-Kharṭūm (Khartoum), Sudan	J7	60
Al-Kharṭūm Baḥrī, Sudan	J7	60
Al-Khaṣab, Oman	A10	47
Al-Khubar, Sau. Ar.	A7	47
Al-Khums, Libya	B3	56
Al-Khuraybah, Jord.	C5	50
Al-Khuraybah, Yemen	G6	47
Al-Khurmah, Sau. Ar.	D3	47
Al-Kidn, reg., Asia	C9	47
Alkmaar, Neth.	C6	12
Al-Kuntillah, Egypt	B8	60
Al-Kūt, Iraq	E8	48
Al-Kuwayt, Kuw.	G9	48
Allada, Benin	H11	64
Al-Lādhiqīyah (Latakia), Syria	D3	48
Al-Lagowa, Sudan	L5	60
Allahābād, India	H9	44
Allan, Sk., Can.	G8	104
Allanche, Fr.	G9	14
Allanmyo, Myan.	E3	40
'Allāq, Bi'r, well, Libya	E16	62
Allard, Lac, l., P.Q., Can.	B10	106
Allardt, Tn., U.S.	F12	114
Al-Layyah, Sudan	I8	60
Alldays, S. Afr.	D9	66
Allegan, Mi., U.S.	H10	110
Allegany, N.Y., U.S.	E8	108
Allegheny, stm., U.S.	G7	108
Allegheny Mountains, mts., U.S.	I6	108
Allegheny Plateau, plat., U.S.	G8	108
Allegheny Reservoir, res., U.S.	F8	108
Allemands, Lac Des, l., La., U.S.	M6	114
Allen, Arg.	J5	80
Allen, Ne., U.S.	I11	118
Allen, Ok., U.S.	E10	116
Allen, S.D., U.S.	H6	118
Allen, Tx., U.S.	F10	116
Allen, Mount, mtn., Ak., U.S.	E23	100
Allendale, Il., U.S.	D9	114
Allendale, S.C., U.S.	F5	112
Allende, Mex.	C9	90
Allenstein see Olsztyn, Pol.	B20	10
Allentown, Pa., U.S.	G11	108
Allentsteig, Aus.	G15	10
Alleppey, India	H4	46
Aller, stm., Ger.	C9	10
Allerton, Ia., U.S.	J2	110
Allgäu, reg., Ger.	H10	10
Allgäuer Alpen, mts., Eur.	E17	14
Alliance, Ab., Can.	E23	102
Alliance, Ne., U.S.	I5	118
Alliance, Oh., U.S.	G5	108
Al-Lidām, Sau. Ar.	D4	47
Allier, dept., Fr.	F9	14
Allier, stm., Fr.	F10	14
Alligator, stm., N.C., U.S.	D10	112
Allison, Ia., U.S.	H3	110
Alliston, On., Can.	F16	110
Al-Līth, Sau. Ar.	D2	47
Alloa, Scot., U.K.	E10	8
Allora, Austl.	G9	70
Allouez, Wi., U.S.	F7	110
Al-Luḥayyah, Yemen	G3	47
Allyn, Wa., U.S.	C3	122
Alma, Ar., U.S.	G2	114
Alma, Ga., U.S.	H4	112
Alma, Ks., U.S.	L11	118
Alma, Mi., U.S.	G11	110
Alma, N.B., Can.	G9	106
Alma, Ne., U.S.	K8	118
Alma, P.Q., Can.	D2	106
Alma, Wi., U.S.	F4	110
Alma-Ata see Alamty, Kaz.	I13	26
Alma Center, Wi., U.S.	F5	110
Almada, Port.	G2	16
Almadén, Spain	G7	16
Al-Madīnah (Medina), Sau. Ar.	B1	47
Al-Mafāzah, Sudan	K8	60
Al-Mafraq, Jord.	D6	50
Almafuerte, Arg.	G6	80
Almagro, Spain	G8	16
Al-Maḥallah al-Kubrā, Egypt	B6	60
Al-Maḥārīq, Egypt	E6	60
Al Mahbas, W. Sah.	G6	62
Al-Majma'ah, Sau. Ar.	I8	48
Al-Makhā' (Mocha), Yemen	H3	47
Almalyk, Uzb.	I11	26
Al-Manāmah, Bahr.	H11	48
Almansa, Spain	G10	16
Al-Manshāh, Egypt	D6	60
Al-Manṣūrah, Egypt	B6	60
Al-Manzilah, Egypt	F1	48
Almanzor, mtn., Spain	E6	16
Al-Marāghah, Egypt	D6	60
Al-Marj, Libya	B5	56
Almas, Pico das, mtn., Braz.	B8	79
Al-Masīd, Sudan	J7	60
Almassora, Spain	F11	16
Al-Matammah, Sudan	I7	60
Al-Maṭarīyah, Egypt	B7	60
Al-Matnah, Sudan	K8	60
Almaty (Alma-Ata), Kaz.	I13	26
Al-Mawṣil (Mosul), Iraq	C7	48
Al-Mayādīn, Syria	D6	48
Al-Mazār, Jord.	F5	50
Al-Mazra'ah, Jord.	F5	50
Almeida, Port.	E5	16
Almeirim, Port.	F3	16
Almelo, Neth.	D10	12
Almena, Ks., U.S.	L8	118
Almenara, Braz.	D8	79
Almendralejo, Spain	G5	16
Almería, Spain	I9	16
Almería, Golfo de, b., Spain	I9	16
Al'metjevsk, Russia	G8	26
Al-Midhnab, Sau. Ar.	I8	48
Al-Minyā, Egypt	C6	60
Almira, Wa., U.S.	C7	122
Almirante, Pan.	C1	84
Almirante, Bahía de, b., Pan.	H12	92
Almirante Latorre, Chile	E3	80
Al-Mismīyah, Syria	B6	50
Almo, Id., U.S.	H12	122
Almodôvar, Port.	H3	16
Almolonga, Guat.	C3	92
Almond, Wi., U.S.	F6	110
Almont, Mi., U.S.	H12	110
Almonte, On., Can.	E19	110
Almonte, Spain	H5	16
Almora, India	F8	44
Al-Mubarraz, Sau. Ar.	C5	47
Al-Mubarraz, Sau. Ar.	B6	47
Al-Mudawwarah, Jord.	G3	48
Al-Muglad, Sudan	L4	60
Al-Muḥarraq, Bahr.	H11	48
Al-Mukallā, Yemen	G6	47
Almuñécar, Spain	I8	16
Al-Musallamīyah, Sudan	J7	60
Al-Musayfirah, Syria	C6	50
Al-Musayjid, Sau. Ar.	B1	47
Al-Mutayn, Leb.	A5	50
Al-Muwayh, Sau. Ar.	C2	47
Al-Muwayliḥ, Sau. Ar.	H3	48
Alnwick, Eng., U.K.	F12	8
Aloândia, Braz.	D4	79
Aloja, Lat.	D7	22
Alor, Pulau, i., Indon.	G7	38
Alor Setar, Malay.	K6	40
Alosno, Spain	H4	16
Alost (Aalst), Bel.	G5	12
Alpachiri, Arg.	I7	80
Alpaugh, Ca., U.S.	I6	124
Alpena, Ar., U.S.	F3	114
Alpena, Mi., U.S.	E12	110
Alpena, S.D., U.S.	G9	118
Alpes-de-Haute-Provence, dept., Fr.	H13	14
Alpes-Maritimes, dept., Fr.	I14	14
Alpha, Austl.	D7	70
Alpha, Il., U.S.	I5	110
Alpha, Mi., U.S.	D7	110
Alpharetta, Ga., U.S.	E2	112
Alpine, Az., U.S.	K7	120
Alpine, Ca., U.S.	L9	124
Alpine, Tx., U.S.	I3	116
Alpine National Park, Austl.	K7	70
Alpinópolis, Braz.	F5	79
Alps, mts., Eur.	F10	4
Al-Qābil, Oman	C9	47
Al-Qaḍārif, Sudan	J8	60
Al-Qaḍīmah, Sau. Ar.	C1	47
Al-Qāhirah (Cairo), Egypt	B6	60
Al-Qaḥmah, Sau. Ar.	E2	47
Al-Qalībah, Sau. Ar.	G4	48
Al-Qāmishlī, Syria	C6	48
Al-Qanṭarah, Egypt	B7	60
Al-Qaryah ash-Sharqīyah, Libya	B3	56
Al-Qaṣr, Egypt	E5	60
Al-Qaṣr, Jord.	F5	50
Al-Qaṭīf, Sau. Ar.	A7	47
Al-Qaṭrānah, Jord.	F6	50
Al-Qaṭrūn, Libya	D3	56
Al-Qayṣūmah, Sau. Ar.	G9	48
Al-Qiṣfah, Jord.	C5	50
Al-Quds see Yerushalayim, Isr.	E4	50
Al-Qunayṭirah, Syria	B5	50
Al-Qunfudhah, Sau. Ar.	E2	47
Al-Qurnah, Iraq	F9	48
Al-Quṣaymah, Egypt	G2	50
Al-Quṣayr, Egypt	D8	60
Al-Qūṣīyah, Egypt	D6	60
Al-Quṭayfah, Syria	A7	50
Al-Quṭaynah, Sudan	J7	60
Al-Quway'īyah, Sau. Ar.	B4	47
Al-Quwaysī, Sudan	K8	60
Alsace, hist. reg., Fr.	D14	14
Alsask, Sk., Can.	G5	104
Alsea, Or., U.S.	F2	122
Alsea, stm., Or., U.S.	F2	122
Alsek, stm., N.A.	G25	100
Alsen, N.D., U.S.	C9	118
Alsfeld, Ger.	E9	10
Alsina, Arg.	G9	80
Alstead, stm., Sk., Can.	C7	104
Alsunga, Lat.	E4	22
Alta, Ia., U.S.	I12	118
Alta Gracia, Arg.	F6	80
Altagracia, Nic.	F9	92
Altagracia, Ven.	B7	84
Altagracia de Orituco, Ven.	C9	84
Altai, mts., Asia	H16	26
Altaj (Jesönbulag), Mong.	B6	30
Altaj, state, Russia	G15	26
Altamaha, stm., Ga., U.S.	H5	112
Altamira, Braz.	D8	76
Altamira, Chile	C4	80
Altamira, C.R.	G10	92
Altamont, Il., U.S.	C8	114
Altamont, Ks., U.S.	N12	118
Altamont, Or., U.S.	H4	122
Altamont, Tn., U.S.	G11	114
Altamura, Italy	I11	18
Altamura, Isla, i., Mex.	E5	90
Altar, Mex.	B4	90
Altar, stm., Mex.	B4	90
Altar, Desierto de, des., Mex.	B3	90
Altar de Los Sacrificios, hist., Guat.	I14	90
Altario, Ab., Can.	G4	104
Altata, Mex.	E6	90
Alta Verapaz, dept., Guat.	B4	92
Alta Vista, Ks., U.S.	M11	118
Altavista, Va., U.S.	B7	112
Altay, China	B4	30
Altay see Altaj, state, Russia	G15	26
Altdorf, Switz.	E10	13
Altenburg, Ger.	E12	10
Altha, Fl., U.S.	I1	112
Altheimer, Ar., U.S.	H5	114
Althofen, Aus.	I14	10
Altinópolis, Braz.	F5	79
Altiplano, plat., S.A.	H7	82
Altkirch, Fr.	E14	14
Altmark, reg., Ger.	C11	10
Altmühl, stm., Ger.	F10	10
Alto, Tx., U.S.	H11	116
Alto Araguaia, Braz.	D2	79
Alto Cedro, Cuba	D7	94
Alto Coité, Braz.	C1	79
Alto del Carmen, Chile	E3	80
Alto do Rio Doce, Braz.	F7	79
Alto Garças, Braz.	D2	79
Altomünster, Ger.	G11	10
Alton, Ia., U.S.	I11	118
Alton, Il., U.S.	D6	114
Alton, Ks., U.S.	L9	118
Alton, Mo., U.S.	F5	114
Alton, N.H., U.S.	D15	108
Altona, Mb., Can.	I17	104
Altoona, Al., U.S.	H10	114
Altoona, Ia., U.S.	I2	110
Altoona, Ks., U.S.	N12	118
Altoona, Pa., U.S.	G8	108
Altoona, Wi., U.S.	F4	110
Alto Paraguai, Braz.	F13	82
Alto Paraguay, dept., Para.	I12	82
Alto Paraíso de Goiás, Braz.	C5	79
Alto Paraná, dept., Para.	C11	80
Alto Parnaíba, Braz.	E9	76
Alto Purús, stm., Peru	D6	82
Alto Río Senguer, Arg.	F2	78
Alto Sucuriú, Braz.	E2	79
Altötting, Ger.	G12	10
Alto Yurua, stm., Peru	C5	82
Altstätten, Switz.	D12	13
Altuchovo, Russia	I17	22
Altunoluk, Tur.	J10	20
Altun Shan, mts., China	D4	30
Alturas, Ca., U.S.	C5	124
Altus, Ar., U.S.	G3	114
Altus, Ok., U.S.	E7	116
Al-'Ubaylah, Sau. Ar.	D7	47
Al-Ubayyiḍ, Sudan	K6	60
Al-'Udaysāt, Egypt	E7	60
Al-Uḍayyah, Sudan	K5	60
Aluk, Sudan	M4	60
Alūksne, Lat.	D10	22
Al-'Ulā, Sau. Ar.	H4	48
Aluminé, Lago, l., Arg.	J3	80
Alum Rock, Ca., U.S.	G4	124
Al-'Uqaylah, Libya	B4	56
Al-'Uqayr, Sau. Ar.	B7	47
Al-Uqṣur (Luxor), Egypt	E7	60
Al-'Uwaynāt, Libya	C3	56
Al-'Uyaynah, Sau. Ar.	B5	47
Alva, Ok., U.S.	C8	116
Alvarado, Mex.	H12	90
Alvarado, Tx., U.S.	G9	116
Alvarães, Braz.	I10	84
Álvaro Obregón, Presa, res., Mex.	D5	90
Alvdal, Nor.	J12	6
Alvear, Arg.	E10	80
Alvernia, Mount, hill, Bah.	B7	94
Alvesta, Swe.	M14	6
Alvin, Tx., U.S.	J11	116
Alvinópolis, Braz.	F7	79
Alvito, Port.	G4	16
Älvkarleby, Swe.	K15	6
Alvord, Tx., U.S.	F9	116
Älvros, Swe.	J14	6
Älvsborgs Län, co., Swe.	L13	6
Al-Wajh, Sau. Ar.	H4	48
Al-Wakrah, Qatar	I11	48
Alwar, India	G7	44
Al-Wāsiṭah, Egypt	C6	60
Al-Wazz, Sudan	J6	60
Alxa Zuoqi, China	D8	30
Alytus, Lith.	G7	22
Alzamaj, Russia	F11	28
Alzira (Alcira), Spain	F11	16
Amacuro, stm., S.A.	C12	84
Amadeus, Lake, l., Austl.	D6	68
Amadjuak Lake, l., N.T., Can.	C18	96
Amagansett, N.Y., U.S.	G14	108
Amagasaki, Japan	M10	36
Amagi, Japan	N5	36
Amagunze, Nig.	H13	64
Amahai, Indon.	F8	38
Amaichá del Valle, Arg.	D6	80
Amajac, stm., Mex.	G10	90
Amaka, stm., Nic.	C9	92
Amakusa-shotō, is., Japan	O5	36
Amakuso-Shimo-shima, i., Japan	O5	36
Åmål, Swe.	L13	6
Amalfi, Col.	D5	84
Amalfi, Italy	I9	18
Amaliás, Grc.	L5	20
Amambaí, Braz.	G1	79
Amambaí, stm., Braz.	G1	79
Amambay, dept., Para.	B10	80
Amami-Ō-shima, i., Japan	s4	37b
Amami-shotō, is., Japan	t3	37b
Amana, Ia., U.S.	I4	110
Amanã, stm., Braz.	J14	84
Amana, stm., Ven.	J13	94
Amaná, Lago, l., Braz.	I10	84
Amanda, Oh., U.S.	H4	108
Amapá, Braz.	C8	76
Amapala, Hond.	D7	92
Amapala, Punta de, c., El Sal.	D7	92
Amarante, Braz.	E10	76
Amaranth, Mb., Can.	H16	104
Amarapura, Myan.	D4	40
'Amārat Abū Sinn, Sudan	J8	60
Amares, Port.	D3	16
Amargosa, Braz.	B9	79
Amargosa, stm., U.S.	H9	124
Amargosa Range, mts., Ca., U.S.	H9	124
Amarillo, Tx., U.S.	D5	116
'Amar Jadīd, Sudan	J3	60
Amarkantak, India	G3	30
Amarnāth, India	C2	46
Amasa, Mi., U.S.	D7	110
Amasya, Tur.	G15	4
Amataurá, Braz.	I8	84
Amatikulu, S. Afr.	G10	66
Amatique, Bahía de, b., N.A.	B6	92
Amatitlán, Guat.	C4	92
Amatitlán, Lago de, l., Guat.	C4	92
Amazon (Solimões) (Amazonas), stm., S.A.	D7	76
Amazonas, state, Braz.	H10	84
Amazonas, dept., Col.	H7	84
Amazonas, dept., Peru	A2	82
Amazonas, ter., Ven.	F9	84
Ambakaka, Madag.	t22	67b
Ambāla, India	E7	44
Ambalanjanakomby, Madag.	p22	67b
Ambalavao, Madag.	r22	67b
Amba Maryam, Eth.	L10	60
Ambanja, Madag.	n23	67b
Ambar, Peru	D3	82
Ambararata, Madag.	o23	67b
Ambarčik, Russia	D24	28
Ambargasta, Salinas de, pl., Arg.	E6	80
Ambarnyj, Russia	I23	6
Ambato, Ec.	H3	84
Ambatofinandrahana, Madag.	r22	67b
Ambatolampy, Madag.	q22	67b
Ambatondrazaka, Madag.	p23	67b
Ámbelos, Ákra, c., Grc.	J7	20
Ambenja, Madag.	o22	67b
Amberg, Ger.	F11	10
Amberg, Wi., U.S.	E8	110
Ambergris Cay, i., Belize	H16	90
Ambérieu-en-Bugey, Fr.	G12	14
Ambert, Fr.	G10	14
Ambevongo, Madag.	o22	67b
Ambikāpur, India	I10	44
Ambilobe, Madag.	n23	67b
Ambinanindrano, Madag.	r23	67b
Ambivy, Madag.	r21	67b
Ambo, Peru	D3	82
Amboahangy, Madag.	t22	67b
Ambodifototra, Madag.	p23	67b
Ambodiriana, Madag.	p23	67b
Ambohidray, Madag.	q23	67b
Ambohimahamasina, Madag.	r22	67b
Amboise, Fr.	E7	14
Ambon, Indon.	F8	38
Ambondro, Madag.	t21	67b
Ambositra, Madag.	r22	67b
Ambovombe, Madag.	t22	67b
Amboy, Il., U.S.	I6	110
Amboy, Mn., U.S.	G1	110
Ambre, Cap d', c., Madag.	m23	67b
Ambridge, Pa., U.S.	G6	108
Ambrières, Fr.	D6	14
Ambriz, Ang.	C2	58
Ambrose, N.D., U.S.	C4	118
Ambrosia Lake, N.M., U.S.	I9	120
Ambunti, Pap. N. Gui.	F11	38
Amchitka Island, i., Ak., U.S.	k4	101a
'Amd, Yemen	G6	47
Amderma, Russia	D10	26
Amdo, China	E5	30
Ameagle, W.V., U.S.	B5	112
Ameca, Mex.	G7	90
Ameca, stm., Mex.	G7	90
Amecameca [de Juárez], Mex.	H10	90
Ameghino, Arg.	H7	80
Ameland, i., Neth.	B8	12
Amelia, Italy	G7	18
Amelia Court House, Va., U.S.	B9	112
Amelia Island, i., Fl., U.S.	I5	112
Āmer, India	G6	44
Americana, Braz.	G5	79
American Falls, Id., U.S.	H13	122
American Falls Reservoir, res., Id., U.S.	H13	122
American Fork, Ut., U.S.	D5	120
American Highland, plat., Ant.	C5	73
American Samoa, dep., Oc.	J22	126
Americus, Ga., U.S.	G2	112
Americus, Ks., U.S.	M11	118
Amersfoort, Neth.	D7	12
Amersfoort, S. Afr.	F9	66
Amery, Mb., Can.	B20	104
Amery, Wi., U.S.	E3	110
Amery Ice Shelf, Ant.	B5	73
Ames, Ia., U.S.	H2	110
Amesbury, Ma., U.S.	E16	108
Amet Sound, strt., N.S., Can.	G10	106
Ámfissa, Grc.	K6	20
Amga, Russia	E18	28
Amga, stm., Russia	E18	28
Amguema, stm., Russia	D27	28
Amguid, Alg.	G13	62
Amgun', stm., Russia	G19	28
Amherst, Ma., U.S.	E14	108
Amherst, N.S., Can.	G9	106
Amherst, N.Y., U.S.	E8	108
Amherst, Oh., U.S.	F4	108
Amherst, Tx., U.S.	E4	116
Amherst, Va., U.S.	B7	112
Amherst, Wi., U.S.	F6	110
Amherstburg, On., Can.	H12	110
Amherstdale, W.V., U.S.	J5	108
Amherstview, On., Can.	F19	110
Amidon, N.D., U.S.	E4	118
Amiens, Fr.	C9	14
Amili, China	F16	44
Amīndīvi Islands, is., India	G2	46
Aminga, Arg.	E5	80
Aminuis, Nmb.	D4	66
Amirante Islands, is., Sey.	C10	58
Amisk, Ab., Can.	E23	102
Amisk Lake, l., Sk., Can.	D12	104
Amistad, Parque Internacional de la, C.R.	H11	92
Amistad Reservoir (Presa de la Amistad), res., N.A.	J5	116
Amite, La., U.S.	L6	114
Amite, stm., La., U.S.	L6	114
Amity, Ar., U.S.	H3	114
Amity, Or., U.S.	E2	122
Amizmiz, Mor.	E6	62
'Amm-Adām, Sudan	I9	60
'Ammān, Jord.	E5	50
Ammarnäs, Swe.	I15	6
Ammon, Id., U.S.	G14	122
Ammonoosuc, stm., N.H., U.S.	C15	108
Amne Machin Shan see A'nyêmaqên Shan, mts., China	D6	30
Amnicon, stm., Wi., U.S.	D4	110
Amnok-kang (Yalu), stm., Asia	C13	32
Amo, stm., Asia	G13	44
Āmol, Iran	C12	48
Amolar, Braz.	H13	82
Amorgós, i., Grc.	M9	20
Amorinópolis, Braz.	D3	79
Amory, Ms., U.S.	I8	114
Amoy see Xiamen, China	K7	34
Ampanihy, Madag.	t21	67b
Amparihy, Madag.	s22	67b
Amparo, Braz.	G5	79
Ampato, Nevado, mtn., Peru	F6	82
Amper, Nig.	G14	64
Ampombiantambo, Madag.	n23	67b
Amposta, Spain	E12	16
Ampotaka, Madag.	t21	67b
Amqui, P.Q., Can.	D6	106
'Amrān, Yemen	G3	47
Amrāvati, India	J7	44
Amreli, India	J4	44
Amritsar, India	E6	44
Amroha, India	F8	44
Amsel, Alg.	I13	62
Åmsele, Swe.	I16	6
Amsteg, Switz.	E10	13
Amsterdam, Neth.	D6	12
Amsterdam, N.Y., U.S.	E12	108
Amsterdam, S. Afr.	F10	66
Amsterdam, Île, i., Afr.	L11	126
Amsterdam-Rijnkanaal, Neth.	E7	12
Amstetten, Aus.	G14	10
Am Timan, Chad	F5	56
Amubri, C.R.	H12	92
Amu-Darja, Turk.	C18	48
Amu Darya (Amudarja), stm., Asia	B2	44
Amundsen Gulf, b., N.T., Can.	B8	96
Amundsen-Scott, sci., Ant.	D10	73
Amundsen Sea, Ant.	C11	73
Amuntai, Indon.	F6	38
Amur (Heilong), stm., Asia	B14	30
Amurrio, Spain	I3	14
Amuzhong, China	E11	44
Amvrakikós Kólpos, b., Grc.	K4	20
Anabar, stm., Russia	C14	28
Anaco, Ven.	C10	84
Anacoco, La., U.S.	K3	114
Anaconda, Mt., U.S.	D13	122
Anacortes, Wa., U.S.	B3	122
Anadarko, Ok., U.S.	D8	116
Anadyr', Russia	E27	28
Anadyr', stm., Russia	E26	28
Anadyrskij zaliv, b., Russia	E28	28
Anadyrskoje ploskogorje, plat., Russia	D26	28
Anagni, Italy	H8	18
'Ānah, Iraq	D6	48
Anaheim, Ca., U.S.	K8	124
Anahim Lake, B.C., Can.	E9	102
Anáhuac, Mex.	D9	90
Anáhuac, Mex.	C6	90
Anahuac, Tx., U.S.	J12	116
Ānai Mudi, mtn., India	G4	46
Analalava, Madag.	o22	67b
Analapatsy, Madag.	t22	67b
Anamã, Braz.	I12	84
Anamã, Lago, l., Braz.	I12	84
Anama Bay, Mb., Can.	G16	104
Ana María, Golfo de, b., Cuba	D5	94
Anambas, Kepulauan, is., Indon.	M9	40
Anamoose, N.D., U.S.	D7	118
Anamosa, Ia., U.S.	H4	110
Anamu, stm., Braz.	G14	84
Anamur, Tur.	C2	48
Ānand, India	I5	44
Ananea, Peru	F7	82
Anantapur, India	E4	46
Anantnāg (Islāmābād), India	D6	44
Anan'yiv, Ukr.	B13	20
Anápolis, Braz.	D4	79
Anār, Iran	F13	48
Anārak, Iran	E12	48
Anār Darreh, Afg.	E16	48
Anastácio, Braz.	F1	79
Anastasia Island, i., Fl., U.S.	J5	112
'Anātā, W.B.	E4	50
Anatolikí Makedhonía kaí Thráki, prov., Grc.	H9	20
Añatuya, Arg.	E7	80
Anauá, stm., Braz.	G12	84
Anaurilândia, Braz.	G2	79
Anavilhanas, Arquipélago das, is., Braz.	I12	84
Anawalt, W.V., U.S.	B5	112
Anbanjing, China	C6	40
Anbu, China	L5	34
Anbyŏn, N. Kor.	D15	32
Ancash, dept., Peru	C3	82
Ancaster, On., Can.	G15	110
Ancasti, Arg.	E6	80
Ancasti, Sierra de, mts., Arg.	E6	80
Anchang, China	E9	34
Anchorage, Ak., U.S.	F20	100
Anchorena, Arg.	H6	80
Anchor Point, Ak., U.S.	G19	100
Anci (Langfang), China	D4	32
Ancien Goubéré, C.A.R.	O4	60
Anciferovo, Russia	C17	22
Ancón, Peru	D3	82
Ancona, Italy	F8	18
Ancón de Sardinas, Bahía de, b., S.A.	G3	84
Ancoraimes, Bol.	F7	82
Ancud, Chile	E2	78
Ancud, Golfo de, b., Chile	E2	78
Anda, China	B12	30
Andacollo, Arg.	I3	80
Andacollo, Chile	F3	80
Andahuaylas, Peru	E5	82
Andalgalá, Arg.	D5	80
Åndalsnes, Nor.	J10	6
Andalucía, state, Spain	H7	16
Andalusia, Al., U.S.	K10	114
Andaman Islands, is., India	H2	40
Andaman Sea, Asia	I3	40
Andamarca, Bol.	H8	82

Name — Map Ref. — Page

Andamarca, Peru D4 82
Andamooka, Austl. H2 70
Andapa, Madag. o23 67b
Andaraí, Braz. B8 79
Andaray, Peru F5 82
Andeer, Switz. E11 13
Andelot, Fr. D12 14
Andenes, Nor. G15 6
Andéranboukane, Mali D11 64
Andermatt, Switz. E10 13
Andernach, Ger. E7 10
Anderson, Al., U.S. H9 114
Anderson, Ca., U.S. D3 124
Anderson, In., U.S. B11 114
Anderson, Mo., U.S. F2 114
Anderson, S.C., U.S. E4 112
Anderson, Tx., U.S. I11 116
Anderson, stm., N.T., Can. B30 100
Anderson Dam, Id., U.S. G10 122
Anderson Lake, l., B.C., Can. G12 102
Andes, Col. E5 84
Andes, mts., S.A. G8 74
Andevoranto, Madag. q23 67b
Andhra Pradesh, state, India D5 46
Andikíthira, i., Grc. N7 20
Andimákhia, Grc. M11 20
Andīmeshk, Iran E10 48
Andirá, stm., Braz. I14 84
Andirá, Riozinho do, stm., Braz. C8 82
Andirlang, China B10 44
Ándissa, Grc. J9 20
Andižan, Uzb. I12 26
Andkhvoy, Afg. B1 44
Andoas, Peru I4 84
Andong, S. Kor. G16 32
Andorra, And. C13 16
Andorra, ctry., Eur. G8 4
Andover, Ma., U.S. E15 108
Andover, Me., U.S. C16 108
Andover, N.Y., U.S. E9 108
Andover, Oh., U.S. F6 108
Andover, S.D., U.S. F10 118
Andøya, i., Nor. G14 6
Andradina, Braz. F3 79
Andranopasy, Madag. r20 67b
Andranovory, Madag. s21 67b
Andreanof Islands, is., Ak., U.S. J6 100
Andreapol', Russia E15 22
Andrejevo, Russia F24 22
Andrew, Ab., Can. D22 102
Andrews, In., U.S. B11 114
Andrews, N.C., U.S. D3 112
Andrews, S.C., U.S. F7 112
Andrews, Tx., U.S. G4 116
Andria, Italy H11 18
Andriamena, Madag. p22 67b
Andriandampy, Madag. s21 67b
Andrijevica, Yugo. G3 20
Androka, Madag. t21 67b
Ándros, Grc. L8 20
Andros, i., Bah. B6 94
Ándros, i., Grc. L8 20
Androscoggin, stm., Me., U.S. C16 108
Andros Town, Bah. B6 94
Āndrott Island, i., India G2 46
Andrychów, Pol. F19 10
Andújar, Spain G7 16
Anécho, Togo H10 64
Anegada, i., Br. Vir. Is. E12 94
Anegada Passage, strt., N.A. E13 94
Anegam, Az., U.S. L4 120
Añelo, Arg. J4 80
Aneroid, Sk., Can. I7 104
Aneta, N.D., U.S. D10 118
Aneto, Pico de, mtn., Spain C12 16
Anfeng, China B9 34
Anfeng, China C9 34
Anfengqiao, China I7 34
Anfu, China H3 34
Angamos, Punta, c., Chile B3 80
Ang'angxi, China B11 30
Angao, China B1 34
Angara, stm., Russia F17 26
Angara-Débou, Benin F11 64
Angarbaka, Sudan M3 60
Angarsk, Russia G12 28
Angastaco, Arg. C5 80
Angatuba, Braz. G4 79
Ángel, Salto (Angel Falls), wtfl, Ven. E11 84
Ángel de la Guarda, Isla, i., Mex. C3 90
Angeles, Phil. n19 39b
Angel Falls see Ángel, Salto, wtfl, Ven. E11 84
Angelina, stm., Tx., U.S. K2 114
Angels Camp, Ca., U.S. F5 124
Angereb, stm., Afr. K9 60
Angermünde, Ger. B14 10
Angers, Fr. E6 14
Angerville, Fr. D9 14
Angical, Braz. B6 79
Angicos, Braz. E11 76
Angier, N.C., U.S. D8 112
Angijak Island, i., N.T., Can. C20 96
Angikuni Lake, l., N.T., Can. D13 96
Angkor Wat, hist., Camb. H7 40
Ângk Tasaôm, Camb. I8 40
Anglais, Baie des, b., P.Q., Can. C5 106
Angle Inlet, Mn., U.S. B12 118
Anglesey, i., Wales, U.K. H9 8
Angleton, Tx., U.S. J11 116
Angling, stm., Mb., Can. B21 104
Angling Lake, l., Mb., Can. E21 104
Angmagssalik, Grnld. C16 86
Angoche, Moz. E7 58
Angoche, Ilha, i., Moz. E7 58
Angol, Chile I2 80
Angola, In., U.S. A12 114
Angola, N.Y., U.S. E7 108
Angola, ctry., Afr. D3 58
Angoon, Ak., U.S. H27 100
Angora see Ankara, Tur. B2 48
Angoram, Pap. N. Gui. F11 38
Angostura, Mex. E5 90
Angostura, Presa de la, res., Mex. I13 90
Angoulême, Fr. G7 14
Angoumois, hist. reg., Fr. G6 14
Angra dos Reis, Braz. G6 79
Angren, Uzb. I12 26
Angualasto, Arg. F4 80
Anguciana, Cerro, mtn., C.R. I11 92
Anguilla, Ms., U.S. J6 114
Anguilla, dep., N.A. E13 94
Anguilla Cays, is., Bah. C5 94
Anguille, Cape, c., Nf., Can. E14 106
Anguo, China E3 32
Angus, On., Can. F16 110
Angusville, Mb., Can. H13 104
Angwin, Ca., U.S. F3 124
Anhai, China K7 34
Anhui (Anhwei), prov., China E10 30
Aniak, Ak., U.S. F15 100
Aniche, Fr. H3 12
Anicuns, Braz. D4 79
Anié, Togo H10 64
Animas, N.M., U.S. M8 120
Animas, stm., U.S. H9 120
Animas Peak, mtn., N.M., U.S. M8 120
Anina, Rom. D5 20
Anita, Ia., U.S. J13 118
Aniva, zaliv, b., Russia H20 28
Anivorano, Madag. q23 67b
Anjangaon, India B4 46
Anjār, India I4 44
ʿAnjar, Leb. A5 50
Anji, China E8 34
Anjiabe, Madag. n23 67b
Anjiang, China C5 32
Anjou, hist. reg., Fr. E6 14
Anju, N. Kor. D13 32
Ankang, China E8 30
Ankara, Tur. B2 48
Ankaratra, mts., Madag. q22 67b
Ankarimbelo, Madag. s22 67b
Ankasakasa, Madag. p21 67b
Ankavandra, Madag. q21 67b
Ankazoabo, Madag. s21 67b
Ankazobe, Madag. q22 67b
Ankazomiriotra, Madag. q22 67b
Ankeny, Ia., U.S. I2 110
Ankilimalinika, Madag. s20 67b
Ankisabe, Madag. q22 67b
Ankleshwar, India B2 46
Ankober, Eth. G8 56
Ankou, China J2 34
An'kovo, Russia E22 22
Ankpa, Nig. H13 64
Anliu, China L4 34
Anlu, China D2 34
Ann, Cape, c., Ant. B4 73
Anna, Il., U.S. E7 114
Anna, Tx., U.S. F10 116
Anna, Lake, res., Va., U.S. A9 112
Annaba (Bône), Alg. B14 62
Annaberg-Buchholz, Ger. E13 10
An-Nabk, Syria D4 48
An-Nafī, Sau. Ar. B3 47
An-Nafūd, des., Sau. Ar. G6 48
An-Najaf, Iraq F8 48
An-Nakhl, Egypt C7 60
Annamitique, Chaîne, mts., Asia F9 40
Annandale, Austl. C8 70
Annandale, Mn., U.S. E1 110
Annapolis, Md., U.S. I10 108
Annapolis Basin, b., N.S., Can. H8 106
Annapolis Royal, N.S., Can. H8 106
Annapūrṇa, mtn., Nepal F10 44
Ann Arbor, Mi., U.S. H12 110
Anna Regina, Guy. D13 84
An-Nāṣirīyah, Iraq F9 48
An-Nāṣirīyah, Syria A7 50
An-Nawfalāb, Sudan J7 60
Annecy, Fr. G13 14
Annemasse, Fr. F13 14
Annenskij Most, Russia A20 22
Annette, Ak., U.S. I29 100
An Nhon, Viet. H10 40
Anniston, Al., U.S. I11 114
Annobón, i., Eq. Gui. B1 58
Annonay, Fr. G11 14
An-Nuhūd, Sudan K5 60
An-Nuʿmānīyah, Iraq E8 48
Annville, Ky., U.S. B3 112
Annville, Pa., U.S. G10 108
Anoka, Mn., U.S. E2 110
Anopino, Russia F23 22
Anori, Braz. I12 84
Anorí, Col. D5 84
Anping, China D4 32
Anpu, China D11 40
Anqing, China E6 34
Anqiu, China G7 32
Ansbach, Ger. F10 10
Anse-d'Hainault, Haiti E7 94
Anselmo, Ne., U.S. J8 118
Anserma, Col. E5 84
Anshan, China B10 32
Anshun, China A8 40
Ansina, Ur. F11 80
Ansley, Ne., U.S. J8 118
Anson, Tx., U.S. G7 116
Ansŏng, S. Kor. F15 32
Ansongo, Mali D10 64
Ansonville, N.C., U.S. D6 112
Ansted, W.V., U.S. I5 108
Anta, Peru E5 82
Antabamba, Peru F5 82
Antalaha, Madag. o24 67b
Antalivtsi, Ukr. G22 10
Antalya, Tur. H14 4
Antalya Körfezi, b., Tur. H14 4
Antambohobe, Madag. s22 67b
Antanambao Manampotsy, Madag. q23 67b
Antananarivo, Madag. q22 67b
Antanetibe, Madag. q22 67b
Antanifotsy, Madag. q22 67b
Antarctica D5 73
Antarctic Peninsula, pen., Ant. B12 73
Antas, Rio das, stm., Braz. E13 80
Antelope Island, i., Ut., U.S. D4 120
Antelope Mine, Zimb. C9 66
Antelope Peak, mtn., Nv., U.S. C11 124
Antequera, Para. C10 80
Antequera, Spain H7 16
Antevamena, Madag. r21 67b
Anthon, Ia., U.S. I12 118
Anthony, Fl., U.S. J4 112
Anthony, Ks., U.S. N9 118
Anthony, N.M., U.S. L10 120
Anthony, Tx., U.S. M10 120
Anti-Atlas, mts., Mor. E6 62
Antibes, Fr. I14 14
Anticosti, Île d', i., P.Q., Can. C10 106
Antigo, Wi., U.S. E6 110
Antigonish, N.S., Can. G12 106
Antigua, i., Antig. F14 94
Antigua and Barbuda, ctry., N.A. F14 94
Antigua Guatemala, Guat. C4 92
Antiguo Morelos, Mex. F10 90
Anti-Lebanon see Sharqī, Al-Jabal ash-, mts., Asia A6 50
Antilla, Arg. D6 80
Antilla, Cuba D7 94
Antimony, Ut., U.S. F5 120
Antioch, Il., U.S. H7 110
Antioch see Hatay, Tur. C4 48
Antioquia, Col. D5 84
Antioquia, dept., Col. D5 84
Antipodes Islands, is., N.Z. M21 126
Antizana, vol., Ec. H3 84
Antler, stm., N.A. I13 104
Antlers, Ok., U.S. E11 116
Antofagasta, Chile B3 80
Antofagasta, prov., Chile B4 80
Antofagasta de la Sierra, Arg. D5 80
Antofalla, Salar de, pl., Arg. C5 80
Antofalla, Volcán, vol., Arg. C5 80
Antón, Pan. C2 84
Anton, Tx., U.S. F4 116
Anton Chico, N.M., U.S. I11 120
Antongila, Helodrano, b., Madag. o23 67b
Antonina, Braz. C14 80
Antonio Amaro, Mex. E7 90
Antônio Prado, Braz. E13 80
Antonito, Co., U.S. G10 120
Antón Lizardo, Punta, c., Mex. H12 90
Antopal', Bela. I7 22
Antou, China I7 34
Antrain, Fr. D5 14
Antrim, N. Ire., U.K. G7 8
Antrodoco, Italy G8 18
Antropovo, Russia C26 22
Antsalova, Madag. q21 67b
Antsenavolo, Madag. r23 67b
Antsiafabositra, Madag. p22 67b
Antsirabe, Madag. o23 67b
Antsirabe, Madag. q22 67b
Antsiranana, Madag. n23 67b
Antsla, Est. D9 22
Antsohihy, Madag. o22 67b
Antuševo, Russia B20 22
Antwerp see Antwerpen, Bel. F5 12
Antwerp, Oh., U.S. F2 108
Antwerpen (Anvers), Bel. F5 12
Antwerpen, prov., Bel. F6 12
Anugul, India B8 46
Anuradhapura, Sri L. H6 46
Anvers (Antwerpen), Bel. F5 12
Anvers Island, i., Ant. B12 73
Anvik, Ak., U.S. E14 100
Anvil Range, mts., Yk., Can. E28 100
Anxi, China C6 30
Anxi, China J7 34
Anxin, China E3 32
Anyama, C. Iv. I7 64
Anyang, China G2 32
A'nyêmaqên Shan, mts., China D6 30
Anyi, China G4 34
Anykščiai, Lith. F8 22
Anyox, B.C., Can. B5 102
Anyuan, China H2 34
Anzac, Ab., Can. B3 104
Anzaldo, Bol. G9 82
Anžero-Sudžensk, Russia F15 26
Anzhen, China D9 34
Anzhou, China E3 32
Anzin, Fr. B10 14
Anzio, Italy H7 18
Anzoátegui, state, Ven. C10 84
Anžu, ostrova, is., Russia B20 28
Aoga-shima, i., Japan E14 30
Aohan Qi (Xinhui), China A7 32
Aoji, N. Kor. A18 32
Aojiang, China H9 34
Aojiao, China L6 34
Aomori, Japan G15 36
Aóös (Vijosë), stm., Eur. J4 20
Aôral, Phnum, mtn., Camb. H8 40
Aosta, Italy D2 18
Aotou, China M3 34
Aouderas, Niger C14 64
Aouk, Bahr, stm., Afr. G5 56
Aoukâr, reg., Maur. B5 64
Aourou, Mali D4 64
Aozou, Chad D4 56
Apa, stm., S.A. B10 80
Apache, Ok., U.S. E8 116
Apache Junction, Az., U.S. K5 120
Apache Peak, mtn., Az., U.S. M6 120
Apalachicola, Fl., U.S. J2 112
Apalachicola, stm., Fl., U.S. I1 112
Apalachicola Bay, b., Fl., U.S. J1 112
Apanas, Laguna de, res., Nic. D9 92
Apaporis, stm., S.A. H7 84
Aparados da Serra, Parque Nacional de, Braz. E13 80
Aparri, Phil. I19 39b
Apaseo El Grande, Mex. G9 90
Apatin, Yugo. D2 20
Apatity, Russia D4 26
Apatzingán de la Constitución, Mex. H8 90
Apaxtla de Castrejón, Mex. H10 90
Apayacu, stm., Peru I6 84
Ape, Lat. D9 22
Apeganau Lake, l., Mb., Can. C15 104
Apeldoorn, Neth. D8 12
Apennines see Appennino, mts., Italy F7 18
Apex, N.C., U.S. D8 112
Apex Mountain, mtn., Yk., Can. E25 100
Api, mtn., Nepal F9 44
Apía, Col. E5 84
Apia, W. Sam. G1 2
Apiacá, stm., Braz. C13 82
Apiacás, Serra dos, plat., Braz. D13 82
Apiaí, Braz. C14 80
Apiaú, stm., Braz. F12 84
Apizaco, Mex. H10 90
Apizolaya, Mex. E8 90
Aplahoué, Benin H10 64
Aplao, Peru G5 82
Apo, Mount, mtn., Phil. D8 38
Apolakkiá, Grc. M11 20
Apolda, Ger. D11 10
Apolinario Saravia, Arg. C6 80
Apollo, Pa., U.S. G7 108
Apolo, Bol. F7 82
Apón, stm., Ven. B6 84
Aponguao, stm., Ven. E12 84
Apopa, El Sal. D5 92
Aporé, Braz. E2 79
Aporé, stm., Braz. E3 79
Apostle Islands, is., Wi., U.S. D5 110
Apóstoles, Arg. D11 80
Apostolove, Ukr. H4 26
Appalachia, Va., U.S. C4 112
Appalachian Mountains, mts., N.A. C11 98
Appennino (Apennines), mts., Italy F7 18
Appenzell, Switz. D11 13
Appenzell-Ausserrhoden, state, Switz. D11 13
Apple, stm., U.S. H5 110
Apple, stm., Wi., U.S. E3 110
Applegate, stm., Or., U.S. B2 124
Appleton, Mn., U.S. F11 118
Appleton, Wi., U.S. F7 110
Appleton City, Mo., U.S. D2 114
Apple Valley, Ca., U.S. J8 124
Appling, Ga., U.S. F4 112
Appomattox, Va., U.S. B8 112
Appomattox, stm., Va., U.S. B8 112
Aprelevka, Russia F20 22
Apt, Fr. I12 14
Apuaú, stm., Braz. I12 84
Apucarana, Braz. G3 79
Apure, state, Ven. D8 84
Apure, stm., Ven. D9 84
Apurímac, dept., Peru E5 82
Apurímac, stm., Peru E5 82
Apurito, Ven. D8 84
Aqaba, Gulf of, b. C8 60
ʿAqīq, Sudan H10 60
Aquidabã, stm., Braz. I13 82
Aquidabán, stm., Para. B10 80
Aquidauana, Braz. I14 82
Aquidauana, stm., Braz. I14 82
Aquila, Mex. H8 90
Aquila, Switz. E10 13
Aquiles Serdán, Mex. C7 90
Aquiles Serdán, Mex. E11 90
Aquilla, Tx., U.S. H9 116
Aquin, Haiti E8 94
Aquio, stm., Col. F9 84
Ara, India H11 44
Arab, Al., U.S. H10 114
ʿArab, Baḥr al-, stm., Sudan M4 60
Arab, Shatt al-, stm., Asia G10 48
ʿArab, Wādī al-, val., Jord. C5 50
ʿArabah, Wādī al- (HaʿArava), val., Asia G4 50
Arabako, prov., Spain C9 16
Arabelo, Ven. E10 84
Arabi, La., U.S. M6 114
Arabian Desert see Sharqīyah, Aṣ-Ṣaḥrā' ash-, des., Egypt D7 60
Arabian Gulf see Persian Gulf, b., Asia H11 48
Arabian Peninsula, pen., Asia G5 24
Arabian Sea H7 24
Araçá, stm., Braz. G11 84
Aracaju, Braz. F11 76
Aracataca, Col. B5 84
Aracati, Braz. D11 76
Araçatuba, Braz. F3 79
Aracena, Spain H5 16
Aracruz, Braz. E8 79
Araçuaí, Braz. D7 79
Araçuaí, stm., Braz. D7 79
Arad, Rom. C5 20
Arad, co., Rom. C5 20
Arada, Hond. C6 92
Arafura Sea I17 126
Aragarças, Braz. C2 79
Aragon, Ga., U.S. E1 112
Aragón, state, Spain D10 16
Aragón, stm., Spain C10 16
Aragua, state, Ven. B9 84
Araguacema, Braz. E9 76
Araguaçu, Braz. B4 79
Aragua de Barcelona, Ven. C10 84
Aragua de Maturín, Ven. C11 84
Araguaia, stm., Braz. E9 76
Araguaia, Braço Menor, stm., Braz. B3 79
Araguainha, Braz. D2 79
Araguao, Caño, mth., Ven. C12 84
Araguari, Braz. E4 79
Araguari, stm., Braz. C8 76
Araguari, stm., Braz. E4 79
Araguatins, Braz. E9 76
Arahal, Spain H6 16
Ârak, Alg. H12 62
Arāk, Iran D10 48
Arakan Yoma, mts., Myan. E3 40
Árakhthos, stm., Grc. J4 20
Aral Sea, Asia H10 26
Aral'sk, Kaz. H10 26
Aramac, Austl. D6 70
Aramac, stm., Austl. D6 70
Aramari, Braz. B9 79
Aramberri, Mex. E10 90
Arampampa, Bol. G8 82
Aramtalla, Sudan N5 60
Ārān, Iran D11 48
Aranda de Duero, Spain D8 16
Arandas, Mex. G8 90
Aranđelovac, Yugo. E4 20
Arandis, Nmb. D2 66
Arani, Bol. G9 82
Aran Islands, is., Ire. H4 8
Aranjuez, Spain E8 16
Aransas, stm., Tx., U.S. K9 116
Aransas Pass, Tx., U.S. L9 116
Aranyaprathet, Thai. H7 40
Arao, Japan O5 36
Araouane, Mali E6 54
Arapa, Laguna, l., Peru F6 82
Arapaho, Ok., U.S. D8 116
Arapahoe, Ne., U.S. K8 118
Arapey, Ur. F10 80
Arapey Chico, stm., Ur. F10 80
Arapey Grande, stm., Ur. F10 80
Arapiraca, Braz. E11 76
Arapkir, Tur. B5 48
Arapongas, Braz. G3 79
Arapoti, Braz. H4 79
ʿArʿar, Sau. Ar. F6 48
ʿArʿar, Wādī, val., Asia B11 60
Araranguá, Braz. E14 80
Araraquara, Braz. F4 79
Araras, Braz. G5 79
Ararat, Arm. B8 48
Ararat, Austl. K5 70
Ararat, Mount see Ağrı Dağı, mtn., Tur. B8 48
Ararirá, stm., Braz. H10 84
Araruama, Lagoa de, b., Braz. G7 79
Aras (Araz), stm., Asia B10 48
Áratos, Grc. H9 20
Aratuípe, Braz. B9 79
Arauã, stm., Braz. C9 82
Arauá, stm., Braz. A11 82
Arauá, stm., Braz. J10 84
Arauca, Col. D7 84
Arauca, dept., Col. D7 84
Arauca, stm., S.A. D9 84
Araucária, Braz. C14 80
Arauco, Chile I2 80
Arauco, Golfo de, b., Chile I2 80
Araújos, Braz. E6 79
Arauquita, Col. D7 84
Araure, Ven. C8 84
Arāvalli Range, mts., India H5 44
Araxá, Braz. E5 79
Araya, Ven. B10 84
Araya, Punta de, c., Ven. B10 84
Araz (Aras), stm., Asia B10 48
Arba Minch, Eth. N9 60
Arboga, Swe. L14 6
Arbois, Fr. F12 14
Arboledas, Arg. I8 80
Arboletes, Col. C4 84
Arbon, Switz. C11 13
Arborfield, Sk., Can. E11 104
Arborg, Mb., Can. H17 104
Arbroath, Scot., U.K. E11 8
Arbuckle, Ca., U.S. E3 124
Arc, Bayou des, stm., Ar., U.S. G5 114
Arcachon, Fr. H5 14
Arcade, Ca., U.S. J7 124
Arcade, N.Y., U.S. E8 108
Arcadia, Ca., U.S. J7 124
Arcadia, Fl., U.S. L5 112
Arcadia, Ia., U.S. I12 118
Arcadia, In., U.S. B10 114
Arcadia, Ks., U.S. N13 118
Arcadia, La., U.S. J4 114
Arcadia, Mi., U.S. F9 110
Arcadia, Mo., U.S. E6 114
Arcadia, Ne., U.S. J8 118
Arcadia, Pa., U.S. G8 108
Arcadia, S.C., U.S. E5 112
Arcadia, Wi., U.S. F4 110
Arcanum, Oh., U.S. H2 108
Arcas, Cayos, is., Mex. G14 90
Arcata, Ca., U.S. D1 124
Arcatao, El Sal. C6 92
Arc Dome, mtn., Nv., U.S. F8 124
Arcelia, Mex. H9 90
Archangel'sk, Russia E6 26
Archbold, Oh., U.S. F2 108
Archdale, N.C., U.S. D7 112
Archer, Fl., U.S. J4 112
Archer City, Tx., U.S. F8 116
Archidona, Spain H7 16
Archipovka, Russia E24 22
Arco, Id., U.S. G12 122
Arcola, Il., U.S. C8 114
Arcola, Ms., U.S. I6 114
Arcola, Sk., Can. I12 104
Arcos, Braz. F6 79
Arcos de la Frontera, Spain I6 16
Arcot, India F5 46
Arcoverde, Braz. E11 76
Arctic Bay, N.T., Can. B15 96
Arctic Ocean A1 86
Arctic Red, stm., N.T., Can. C28 100
Arctic Red River, N.T., Can. C28 100
Arctic Village, Ak., U.S. B22 100
Arctowski, sci., Ant. B1 73
Arcturus, Zimb. A10 66
Arda, stm., Eur. H9 20
Ardabīl, Iran B10 48
Ardahan, Tur. G16 4
Ardakān, Iran F12 48
Ardakān, Iran E12 48
Årdalstangen, Nor. K10 6
Ardatov, Russia F26 22
Ardèche, dept., Fr. H11 14
Arden, Ca., U.S. F4 124
Arden, Mb., Can. H15 104
Arden, Mount, mtn., Austl. I2 70
Ardennes, dept., Fr. C11 14
Ardennes, reg., Eur. E5 10
Ardestān, Iran E12 48
Ardila, stm., Eur. G4 16
Ardill, Sk., Can. I9 104
Ardino, Bul. H9 20
Ardlethan, Austl. J7 70
Ardmore, Al., U.S. H10 114
Ardmore, Ok., U.S. E9 116
Ardmore, Pa., U.S. G11 108
Ardoch, Austl. F6 70
Åre, Swe. J13 6
Areado, Braz. F5 79
Arecibo, P.R. E11 94
Areguá, Para. C10 80
Arèhausk, Bela. G13 22
Areia, Ribeirão da, stm., Braz. C6 79
Areia Branca, Braz. D11 76
Arena, Punta, c., Mex. F5 90
Arena de la Ventana, Punta, c., Mex. E5 90
Arenal, C.R. G10 92
Arenal, Laguna de, l., C.R. G10 92
Arenal, Volcán, vol., C.R. G10 92
Arenápolis, Braz. F13 82
Arenas, Cayo, i., Mex. F14 90
Arendal, Nor. L11 6
Arenillas, Ec. I2 84
Arenys de Mar, Spain D14 16
Arequipa, Peru G6 82
Arequipa, dept., Peru F5 82
Arequito, Arg. G8 80
Arès, Fr. H5 14
Arezzo, Italy F6 18
Argadargada, Austl. C2 70
Arganda, Spain E8 16
Arga-Sala, stm., Russia D13 28
Argelès-Gazost, Fr. I7 14
Argelès-sur-Mer, Fr. J10 14
Argenta, Il., U.S. C8 114
Argenta, Italy E6 18
Argentan, Fr. D6 14
Argentat, Fr. G8 14
Argentera, mtn., Italy E2 18
Argentia, Nf., Can. E20 106
Argentina, ctry., S.A. C4 78
Argentino, Lago, l., Arg. G2 78
Argenton-Château, Fr. F6 14
Argenton-sur-Creuse, Fr. F8 14
Argeș, co., Rom. E8 20
Argeș, stm., Rom. E9 20
Arghandāb, stm., Afg. D2 44
Argo, Sudan H6 60
Argolikós Kólpos, b., Grc. L6 20
Argonia, Ks., U.S. N10 118
Argonne, Wi., U.S. E7 110
Argonne, reg., Fr. C12 14
Árgos, Grc. L6 20
Argos, In., U.S. A10 114
Argostólion, Grc. K4 20
Argun' (Ergun), stm., Asia G16 28
Argyle, Mn., U.S. C11 118
Argyle, Lake, res., Austl. C5 68
Århus, Den. M12 6
Ariana, Tun. M5 18
Ariano Irpino, Italy H10 18
Ariari, stm., Col. F6 84
Arias, Arg. G7 80
Ariaú, Braz. I14 84
Aribinda, Burkina D9 64
Arica, Chile H6 82
Arica, Col. I7 84
Arichat, N.S., Can. G12 106
Arichuna, Ven. D9 84
Arid, Cape, c., Austl. F4 68
Ariège, dept., Fr. J8 14
Ariguaní, stm., Col. C6 84
Arīḥā (Jericho), Gaza E4 50
Arīḥā, Jord. F5 50
Arikaree, stm., U.S. L5 118
Arima, Trin. I14 94
Arinos, stm., Braz. D12 82
Ario de Rosales, Mex. H9 90
Ariogala, Lith. F6 22
Ariporo, stm., Col. D7 84
Aripuanã, Braz. C11 82
Aripuanã, stm., Braz. B11 82
Ariquemes, Braz. C10 82
Arisa, stm., Ven. D10 84
ʿArīsh, Wādī al-, val., Egypt B7 60
Arismendi, Ven. C8 84
Aristazabal Island, i., B.C., Can. E5 102
Ariton, Al., U.S. K11 114
Arivonimamo, Madag. q22 67b
Arizaro, Salar de, pl., Arg. C5 80
Arizgoiti, Spain B9 16
Arizona, Arg. H6 80
Arizona, state, U.S. E4 98
Arizpe, Mex. B4 90
Arjay, Ky., U.S. C3 112
Arjeplog, Swe. H15 6
Arjona, Col. B5 84
Arkadelphia, Ar., U.S. H3 114
Arkalyk, Kaz. G11 26
Arkansas, state, U.S. D8 98
Arkansas, stm., U.S. D8 98
Arkansas City, Ar., U.S. I5 114
Arkansas City, Ks., U.S. N10 118
Arkhangelsk see Archangel'sk, Russia E6 26
Arklow, Ire. I7 8
Arkoma, Ok., U.S. G2 114
Arkona, Kap, c., Ger. A13 10
Arkport, N.Y., U.S. E9 108
Arktičeskij, mys, c., Russia A11 28
Arktičeskogo Instituta, ostrova, is., Russia B14 26
Arlbergpass, Aus. D13 13
Arlberg-Tunnel, Aus. D13 13
Arlee, Mt., U.S. C11 122
Arles, Fr. I11 14
Arli, Burkina F10 64
Arlington, Ga., U.S. H2 112
Arlington, Ia., U.S. H4 110
Arlington, Ks., U.S. N9 118
Arlington, Ky., U.S. F7 114
Arlington, Mn., U.S. F1 110
Arlington, Ne., U.S. J11 118
Arlington, Oh., U.S. G3 108
Arlington, Or., U.S. E5 122
Arlington, S.D., U.S. G10 118
Arlington, Tn., U.S. G7 114
Arlington, Tx., U.S. G9 116
Arlington, Va., U.S. I9 108
Arlington, Vt., U.S. D13 108
Arlington, Wa., U.S. B3 122
Arlington Heights, Il., U.S. H8 110
Arlit, Niger B13 64
Arm, stm., Sk., Can. H9 104
Arma, Ks., U.S. N13 118
Armada, Mi., U.S. H13 110
Armageddon see Tel Megiddo, hist., Isr. C4 50
Armagh, N. Ire., U.K. G7 8
Armagnac, hist. reg., Fr. I7 14
Armant, Egypt E7 60
Armavir, Russia H6 26
Armazém, Braz. E14 80
Armenia, Col. E5 84
Armenia, ctry., Asia I6 26
Armentières, Fr. B9 14
Armería, Mex. H8 90
Armero, Col. E5 84
Armidale, Austl. H9 70
Armijo, N.M., U.S. I10 120
Armit Lake, l., N.T., Can. D14 96
Armona, Ca., U.S. H6 124
Armour, S.D., U.S. H9 118
Armstrong, Arg. G8 80
Armstrong, B.C., Can. G15 102
Armstrong, Ia., U.S. H13 118
Armstrong, Mo., U.S. C4 114
Armstrong, Mount, mtn., Yk., Can. E28 100
Armstrong Station, On., Can. F15 96
Arnaud, stm., P.Q., Can. E18 96
Arnaudville, La., U.S. L5 114
Arnay-le-Duc, Fr. E11 14
Arnedo, Spain C9 16
Årnes, Nor. K12 6
Arnett, Ok., U.S. C7 116
Arnhem, Neth. E8 12
Arnhem, Cape, c., Austl. B7 68
Arnhem Land, reg., Austl. B6 68
Árnissa, Grc. I5 20
Arno, stm., Italy F5 18
Arno Bay, Austl. I2 70
Arnold, Ca., U.S. F5 124
Arnold, Mn., U.S. D3 110
Arnold, Mo., U.S. D6 114
Arnold, Ne., U.S. J7 118
Arnolds Park, Ia., U.S. H12 118
Arnprior, On., Can. E19 110
Arnsberg, Ger. D8 10
Arnstadt, Ger. E10 10
Aro, stm., Ven. D10 84
Aroa, Ven. B8 84
Aroa, stm., Ven. B8 84
Aroab, Nmb. F4 66
Aroma, Sudan J9 60
Arona, Italy D3 18
Aroostook, stm., N.A. F5 106
Aros, stm., Mex. C5 90
Arosa, Switz. E12 13
Arp, Tx., U.S. G11 116
Arque, Bol. G8 82
Ar-Rabaḍ, Sau. Ar. K8 47
Ar-Radīsīyah Baḥrī, Egypt E7 60
Arraga, Arg. E6 80
Ar-Rahad, Sudan K6 60
Arraial do Cabo, Braz. G7 79
Arraias, Braz. B5 79
Arraias, stm., Braz. A1 79
Arraias, stm., Braz. B5 79
Ar-Ramādī, Iraq E7 48
Ar-Ramthā, Jord. C6 50
Arran, Island of, i., Scot., U.K. F8 8
Ar-Rank, Sudan L7 60
Ar-Raqqah, Syria D5 48
Arras, Fr. B9 14
Ar-Rāshidah, Egypt E5 60
Ar-Rass, Sau. Ar. I7 48
Ar-Rawḍah, Sau. Ar. H6 48
Ar-Rāwuk, Yemen G6 47
Ar-Rayyān, Qatar I11 48
Arrecife, Spain o27 17b
Arrecifes, Arg. H8 80
Arrey, N.M., U.S. L9 120
Arriaga, Mex. I13 90
Arriba, Co., U.S. L4 118
Ar-Rimāh, Sau. Ar. B5 47
Ar-Riyāḍ (Riyadh), Sau. Ar. B5 47
Arroio Grande, Braz. G12 80
Arrojado, stm., Braz. B6 79
Arronches, Port. F4 16
Arrowrock Reservoir, res., Id., U.S. G10 122
Arrowsmith, Mount, mtn., Austl. H4 70
Arrowwood, Ab., Can. G21 102
Arroyito, Arg. F7 80
Arroyo de la Luz, Spain F5 16
Arroyo Grande, Ca., U.S. I5 124
Arroyo Hondo, N.M., U.S. H11 120
Arroyo Seco, Arg. G8 80
Arroyos y Esteros, Para. C10 80
Ar-Ruʿat, Sudan K7 60
Ar-Rubʿ al-Khālī (Empty Quarter), des., Asia D7 47
Ar-Rukhaymīyah, well, Asia G8 48
Ar-Rumaythah, Iraq F8 48
Ar-Rummān, Jord. D5 50
Ar-Ruṣayfah, Jord. D6 50
Ar-Ruṣayriṣ, Sudan L8 60
Ar-Ruṭbah, Iraq E6 48
Ar-Ruways, Qatar H11 48
Arsenault Lake, l., Sk., Can. C6 104
Arsenjev, Russia I18 28
Arsenjevo, Russia H19 22
Árta, Grc. J4 20
Artašat, Arm. B8 48
Arteaga, Mex. H8 90
Artemisa, Cuba C3 94
Artémou, Maur. D3 64
Artenay, Fr. D8 14
Artesia, Ms., U.S. I8 114
Artesia, N.M., U.S. G2 116
Artesian, S.D., U.S. G10 118
Arth, Switz. D10 13
Arthabaska, P.Q., Can. A15 108

Name	Map Ref.	Page
Arthur, Il., U.S.	C8	114
Arthur, N.D., U.S.	D10	118
Arthur, Ne., U.S.	J6	118
Arthur, On., Can.	G15	110
Arthur, Tn., U.S.	C3	112
Arthur's Town, Bah.	B7	94
Artibonite, stm., Haiti	E8	94
Artigas, Ur.	F10	80
Artik, Arm.	A7	48
Artillery Lake, l., N.T., Can.	D11	96
Artois, hist. reg., Fr.	B9	14
Art'om, Russia	I18	28
Art'omovsk, Russia	G10	28
Art'omovskij, Russia	F10	26
Artsyz, Ukr.	C13	20
Artvin, Tur.	G16	4
Artyk, Russia	E21	28
Artyom, Azer.	A11	48
Aru, Kepulauan, is., Indon.	G9	38
Aruaddin, Erit.	I10	60
Aruanã, Braz.	C3	79
Aruba, dep., N.A.	H9	94
Arunāchal Pradesh, state, India	F16	44
Aruppukkottai, India	H5	46
Arusha, Tan.	B7	58
Aruwimi, stm., Zaire	H6	56
Arvada, Co., U.S.	E11	120
Arvajcheer, Mong.	B7	30
Arvi, India	B5	46
Arvida, P.Q., Can.	D2	106
Arvidsjaur, Swe.	I16	6
Arvika, Swe.	L13	6
Arvin, Ca., U.S.	I7	124
Arvon, Mount, mtn., Mi., U.S.	D7	110
Arvonia, Va., U.S.	B8	112
Arvorezinha, Braz.	E12	80
Arxan, China	H15	28
Arys', Kaz.	I11	26
Arzachena, Italy	H4	18
Arzamas, Russia	F6	26
Arziw, Alg.	C10	62
Aš, Czech Rep.	E12	10
Aša, Russia	F9	26
Asa, stm., Ven.	D11	84
Asab, Nmb.	E3	66
Asad, Buḥayrat al-, res., Syria	C5	48
Asahikawa, Japan	d17	36a
Asamankese, Ghana	I9	64
Asansol, India	I12	44
Asbest, Russia	F10	26
Asbestos, P.Q., Can.	B15	108
Asbury Park, N.J., U.S.	G12	108
Ascensión, Mex.	B6	90
Ascension, i., St. Hel.	I5	52
Aščhabad (Ashgabat), Turk.	J9	26
Aschach an der Donau, Aus.	A9	18
Aschaffenburg, Ger.	F9	10
Aschersleben, Ger.	D11	10
Ascoli Piceno, Italy	G8	18
Ascona, Switz.	F10	13
Ascope, Peru	B2	82
Ascotán, Chile	A4	80
Āseb, Erit.	H3	47
Åseda, Swe.	M14	6
Āsela, Eth.	N10	60
Åsele, Swe.	I15	6
Asendabo, Eth.	M9	60
Asenovgrad, Bul.	G8	20
Aşfūn al-Maṭā'inah, Egypt	E7	60
Ashburn, Ga., U.S.	H3	112
Ashburton, N.Z.	E3	72
Ashburton, stm., Austl.	D3	68
Ashcroft, B.C., Can.	G13	102
Ashdod, Isr.	E3	50
Ashdot Ya'aqov, Isr.	C5	50
Ashdown, Ar., U.S.	I2	114
Asheboro, N.C., U.S.	D7	112
Ashern, Mb., Can.	G16	104
Asherton, Tx., U.S.	K7	116
Asheville, N.C., U.S.	D4	112
Asheweig, stm., On., Can.	F15	96
Ash Flat, Ar., U.S.	F5	114
Ashford, Al., U.S.	K11	114
Ashford, Austl.	G9	70
Ash Fork, Az., U.S.	I4	120
Ash Grove, Mo., U.S.	E3	114
Ashibetsu, Japan	d17	36a
Ashikaga, Japan	K14	36
Ashkhabad see Aščhabad, Turk.	J9	26
Ashland, Al., U.S.	I11	114
Ashland, Il., U.S.	C6	114
Ashland, Ks., U.S.	N8	118
Ashland, Ky., U.S.	I4	108
Ashland, Mo., U.S.	D4	114
Ashland, Ms., U.S.	H7	114
Ashland, Mt., U.S.	E19	122
Ashland, Ne., U.S.	J11	118
Ashland, N.H., U.S.	D15	108
Ashland, Oh., U.S.	G4	108
Ashland, Or., U.S.	H3	122
Ashland, Pa., U.S.	G10	108
Ashland, Va., U.S.	B9	112
Ashland, Wi., U.S.	D5	110
Ashland, Mount, mtn., Or., U.S.	H3	122
Ashland City, Tn., U.S.	F9	114
Ashley, Il., U.S.	D7	114
Ashley, Mi., U.S.	G11	110
Ashley, N.D., U.S.	E8	118
Ashley, Oh., U.S.	G4	108
Ashmore, Il., U.S.	C8	114
Ashmore Islands, is., Austl.	B4	68
Ashmūn, Egypt	B6	60
Ashqelon, Isr.	E3	50
Ash-Shajarah, Jord.	C5	50
Ash-Shaqrā', Sau. Ar.	B4	47
Ash-Shāriqah (Sharjah), U.A.E.	B9	47
Ash-Sharmah, Sau. Ar.	G3	48
Ash-Shaṭrah, Iraq	F9	48
Ash-Shawbak, Jord.	G5	50
Ash-Shawmarah, Leb.	B4	50
Ash-Shiḥr, Yemen	G6	47
Ash-Shufayyah, Sau. Ar.	C1	47
Ash-Shumlul, Sau. Ar.	H9	48
Ash-Shuqayq, Sau. Ar.	F3	47
Ash-Shurayf, Sau. Ar.	I5	48
Ash-Shurayk, Sudan	H7	60
Ashtabula, Oh., U.S.	F6	108
Ashtabula, Lake, res., N.D., U.S.	D10	118
Ashton, Ia., U.S.	H12	118
Ashton, Id., U.S.	F14	122
Ashton, Il., U.S.	I6	110
Ashton, Ne., U.S.	J9	118
Ashton, S. Afr.	I5	66
Ashuanipi Lake, l., Nf., Can.	F19	96
Ashuelot, stm., N.H., U.S.	E14	108
Ashville, Al., U.S.	I10	114
Ashville, Oh., U.S.	H4	108
Ashwaubenon, Wi., U.S.	F7	110
Asi (Nahr al-'Āṣī), stm., Asia	C3	48
Asia	D11	24
Asia, Kepulauan, is., Indon.	E9	38
Asia Minor, hist. reg., Tur.	H14	4
Asilah, Mor.	C7	62
Asino, Russia	F9	28
Asipoquobah Lake, l., On., Can.	E23	104
Asipovičy, Bela.	H11	22
'Asīr, reg., Sau. Ar.	E2	47
Aşkale, Tur.	B6	48
Askham, S. Afr.	F5	66
Asmār, Afg.	C4	44
Asmara see Asmera, Erit.	E8	56
Asmera, Erit.	E8	56
Ašmjany, Bela.	G8	22
Asola, Italy	D5	18
Asosa, Eth.	F7	56
Asotin, Wa., U.S.	D8	122
Asp, Spain	G11	16
Aspang Markt, Aus.	H16	10
Aspen, Co., U.S.	E10	120
Aspen Butte, mtn., Or., U.S.	H3	122
Aspermont, Tx., U.S.	F6	116
Aspres-sur-Buëch, Fr.	H12	14
Aspy Bay, b., N.S., Can.	F13	106
Asquith, Sk., Can.	F7	104
As-Sa'ata, Sudan	K5	60
Aṣ-Ṣaff, Egypt	C6	60
As-Saffānīyah, Sau. Ar.	H10	48
Aṣ-Ṣāfī, Jord.	F4	50
Aṣ-Ṣāfiyah, Sudan	J6	60
Assaí, Braz.	G3	79
Assaikwatamo, stm., Mb., Can.	B18	104
'Assāl al-Ward, Syria	A6	50
As-Sallūm, Egypt	B3	60
As-Salṭ, Jord.	D5	50
Assam, state, India	G15	44
As-Samāwah, Iraq	F8	48
Aṣ-Ṣarīḥ, Jord.	C5	50
Assateague Island, i., U.S.	I11	108
Assean Lake, l., Mb., Can.	B18	104
Assekaifaf, Alg.	G15	62
Assenede, Bel.	F4	12
As-Sidr, Sau. Ar.	C1	47
Assiniboia, Sk., Can.	I9	104
Assiniboine, stm., Can.	I16	104
Assiniboine, Mount, mtn., Can.	G19	102
Assiniboine Indian Reserve, Sk., Can.	H11	104
Assinika, stm., Mb., Can.	F19	104
Assis, Braz.	G3	79
Assisi, Italy	F7	18
Assomada, C.V.	m17	64a
As-Sudd, reg., Sudan	N6	60
Aṣ-Ṣufayyah, Sudan	J8	60
As-Sulaymānīyah, Iraq	D8	48
As-Sulaymānīyah, Sau. Ar.	B5	47
As-Sulaymī, Sau. Ar.	H6	48
As-Sulayyil, Sau. Ar.	D4	47
As-Sumayḥ, Sudan	M4	60
Assumption, Il., U.S.	C7	114
Assumption Island, i., Sey.	C9	58
As-Suwaydā', Syria	C7	50
As-Suways (Suez), Egypt	C7	60
Astaffort, Fr.	H7	14
Āstāneh, Iran	C10	48
Āstāneh, Iran	E10	48
Astara, Azer.	J7	26
Āstārā, Iran	B10	48
Asti, Italy	E3	18
Astica, Arg.	F5	80
Astipálaia, Grc.	M10	20
Astipálaia, i., Grc.	M10	20
Astorga, Braz.	G3	79
Astorga, Spain	C5	16
Astoria, Il., U.S.	B6	114
Astoria, Or., U.S.	D2	122
Astrachan', Russia	H7	26
Astrašycki Haradok, Bela.	G10	22
Astroŭna, Bela.	F12	22
Asturias, state, Spain	B5	16
Asuka, sci., Ant.	C3	73
Asunción, Para.	C10	80
Asunción, Bahía, b., Mex.	D2	90
Asunción Mita, Guat.	C5	92
Asunción Nochixtlán, Mex.	I11	90
Asunga, Wādī, val., Afr.	K2	60
Asveja, Bela.	E11	22
Aswān, Egypt	E7	60
Aswān High Dam see 'Ālī, As-Sadd al-, Egypt	D7	60
Asyūṭ, Egypt	D6	60
Aszód, Hung.	H19	10
Atabapo, stm., S.A.	F9	84
Atacama, prov., Chile	D3	80
Atacama, Desierto de (Atacama Desert), des., Chile	A3	78
Atacama, Puna de, plat., S.A.	C5	80
Atacama, Salar de, pl., Chile	B4	80
Ataco, Col.	F5	84
Atacuari, stm., Peru	I7	84
Atakakup Indian Reserve, Sk., Can.	E8	104
Atakpamé, Togo	H10	64
Atalándi, Grc.	K7	20
Atalaya, Pan.	I14	92
Atalaya, Peru	D5	82
Atalaya, Cerro, mtn., Peru	E6	82
Atami, Japan	L14	36
Atâr, Maur.	A3	64
Atascadero, Ca., U.S.	I5	124
Atascosa, stm., Tx., U.S.	K8	116
Atasu, Kaz.	H12	26
Atauro, Pulau, i., Indon.	G8	38
Atbara ('Aṭbarah), stm., Afr.	I8	60
'Aṭbarah, Sudan	I7	60
'Aṭbarah (Atbara), stm., Afr.	E7	56
Atbasar, Kaz.	G11	26
Atchafalaya, stm., La., U.S.	L5	114
Atchafalaya Bay, b., La., U.S.	M5	114
Atchison, Ks., U.S.	L12	118
Atebubu, Ghana	H9	64
Ateca, Spain	D10	16
Atelchu, stm., Braz.	B1	79
Atenguillo, Mex.	G7	90
Ath (Aat), Bel.	G4	12
Athabasca, Ab., Can.	C21	102
Athabasca, stm., Ab., Can.	E10	96
Athabasca, Lake, l., Can.	E10	96
Athalmer, B.C., Can.	G18	102
Athapapuskow Lake, l., Mb., Can.	D13	104
Athārān Hazāri, Pak.	E5	44
Athena, Or., U.S.	E7	122
Athens, Al., U.S.	H10	114
Athens, Ga., U.S.	F3	112
Athens see Athínai, Grc.	L7	20
Athens, Il., U.S.	C7	114
Athens, La., U.S.	J3	114
Athens, Mi., U.S.	H10	110
Athens, N.Y., U.S.	E13	108
Athens, Oh., U.S.	H4	108
Athens, On., Can.	C11	108
Athens, Pa., U.S.	F10	108
Athens, Tn., U.S.	D2	112
Athens, Tx., U.S.	G11	116
Athens, Wi., U.S.	E5	110
Athens, W.V., U.S.	B5	112
Atherton, Austl.	A6	70
Athiémé, Benin	H10	64
Athínai (Athens), Grc.	L7	20
Athlone, Ire.	H6	8
Athok, Myan.	F3	40
Athol, Ma., U.S.	E14	108
Áthos, mtn., Grc.	I8	20
Ath-Thamad, Egypt	C8	60
Ati, Chad	F4	56
Atico, Peru	G5	82
Aticonipi, Lac, l., P.Q., Can.	A14	106
Atigun Pass, Ak., U.S.	B20	100
Atik Lake, l., Mb., Can.	C18	104
Atikokan, On., Can.	B4	110
Atikonak Lake, l., Nf., Can.	F20	96
Atimari, stm., Braz.	C8	82
Atiparaná, mth., Braz.	I9	84
Atiquizaya, El Sal.	D5	92
Atitlán, Lago de, l., Guat.	C3	92
Atitlán, Volcán, vol., Guat.	C3	92
Atka, Ak., U.S.	J7	100
Atka, Russia	E22	28
Atkarsk, Russia	G7	26
Atkins, Ar., U.S.	G4	114
Atkinson, Il., U.S.	I5	110
Atkinson, N.C., U.S.	E8	112
Atkinson, Ne., U.S.	I9	118
Atkinson Lake, l., Mb., Can.	C20	104
Atlanta, Ga., U.S.	F2	112
Atlanta, Il., U.S.	B7	114
Atlanta, Mi., U.S.	E11	110
Atlanta, Mo., U.S.	C4	114
Atlanta, Tx., U.S.	I2	114
Atlantic, Ia., U.S.	J12	118
Atlantic, N.C., U.S.	E10	112
Atlantic Beach, Fl., U.S.	I5	112
Atlantic City, N.J., U.S.	H12	108
Atlantic-Indian Ridge	N5	126
Atlántico, dept., Col.	B5	84
Atlantic Ocean	I11	128
Atlantic Peak, mtn., Wy., U.S.	H16	122
Atlántida, Ur.	H11	80
Atlántida, dept., Hond.	B7	92
Atlas Mountains, mts., Afr.	B6	54
Atlas Saharien, mts., Alg.	D11	62
Atlas Tellien, mts., Alg.	C11	62
Atlin, B.C., Can.	G28	100
Atlin Lake, l., Can.	G28	100
'Atlit, Isr.	C3	50
Atmore, Al., U.S.	K9	114
Atna Peak, mtn., B.C., Can.	D6	102
Atnarko, stm., B.C., Can.	E9	102
Atocha, Bol.	I8	82
Atoka, Ok., U.S.	E10	116
Atotonilco, Mex.	E8	90
Atoui, Khatt (Khaṭṭ Atoui), val., Afr.	J3	62
Atoyac, stm., Mex.	H10	90
Atoyac de Álvarez, Mex.	I9	90
Atoyaquillo, stm., Mex.	I11	90
Atrak (Atrek), l., Asia	C12	48
Atrato, stm., Col.	D4	84
Atrek (Atrak), stm., Asia	C12	48
Atri, Italy	G8	18
Atrisco, N.M., U.S.	J10	120
Aṭ-Ṭafīlah, Jord.	G5	50
Aṭ-Ṭā'if, Sau. Ar.	D2	47
At-Tāj, Libya	E2	60
At-Tall, Syria	A6	50
Attalla, Al., U.S.	H10	114
Attapu, Laos	G9	40
Attawapiskat, On., Can.	F16	96
Attawapiskat, stm., On., Can.	F16	96
Attawapiskat Lake, l., On., Can.	F15	96
Attica, In., U.S.	B9	114
Attica, Ks., U.S.	N9	118
Attica, N.Y., U.S.	E8	108
Attica, Oh., U.S.	F4	108
Attigny, Fr.	C11	14
Attikí, prov., Grc.	K7	20
Attikí, hist. reg., Grc.	K7	20
Attir, Sudan	N6	60
Attleboro, Ma., U.S.	F15	108
Attock, Pak.	D5	44
Attoyac, stm., Tx., U.S.	K2	114
Attu Island, i., Ak., U.S.	j1	101a
Aṭ-Ṭunayb, Jord.	E5	50
Aṭ-Ṭūr, Egypt	C7	60
Āttūr, India	G5	46
Aṭ-Ṭuwayshah, Sudan	K4	60
Aṭ-Ṭuwayyah, Sau. Ar.	H6	48
Atucatiquini, stm., Braz.	B7	82
Atucha, Arg.	G9	80
Atuel, stm., Arg.	H5	80
Atuel, Bañados del, sw., Arg.	I5	80
Atuntaqui, Ec.	G3	84
Atwater, Ca., U.S.	G5	124
Atwater, Mn., U.S.	F13	118
Atwater, Sk., Can.	H12	104
Atwood, Il., U.S.	C8	114
Atwood, Ks., U.S.	L6	118
Atwood, Tn., U.S.	G8	114
Atyrau, Kaz.	H8	26
Auari, stm., Braz.	F11	84
Aubagne, Fr.	I12	14
Aube, dept., Fr.	D11	14
Aube, stm., Fr.	D11	14
Aubigny-sur-Nère, Fr.	E9	14
Aubin, Fr.	H9	14
Aubrey Cliffs, clf, Az., U.S.	I3	120
Aubry Lake, l., N.T., Can.	C31	100
Auburn, Al., U.S.	J11	114
Auburn, Ca., U.S.	F4	124
Auburn, Il., U.S.	C7	114
Auburn, In., U.S.	A11	114
Auburn, Ky., U.S.	E10	114
Auburn, Ma., U.S.	E15	108
Auburn, Me., U.S.	C16	108
Auburn, Mi., U.S.	G11	110
Auburn, Ne., U.S.	K12	118
Auburn, N.Y., U.S.	E10	108
Auburn, Wa., U.S.	C3	122
Auburn, stm., Austl.	E9	70
Auburn Range, mts., Austl.	E9	70
Aubusson, Fr.	G9	14
Auca Mahuida, Arg.	I4	80
Auca Mahuida, Cerro, mtn., Arg.	I4	80
Aucará, Peru	F4	82
Auce, Lat.	E5	22
Auch, Fr.	I7	14
Aucilla, stm., U.S.	I3	112
Auckland, N.Z.	B5	72
Auckland Islands, is., N.Z.	N20	126
Aude, dept., Fr.	I9	14
Aude, stm., Fr.	I10	14
Audierne, Fr.	D2	14
Audincourt, Fr.	E13	14
Audubon, Ia., U.S.	J13	118
Aue, Ger.	E12	10
Augathella, Austl.	E7	70
Auglaize, stm., Oh., U.S.	F2	108
Au Gres, Mi., U.S.	F12	110
Au Gres, stm., Mi., U.S.	F12	110
Augsburg, Ger.	G10	10
Augšlīgatne, Lat.	D8	22
Augusta, Ar., U.S.	G5	114
Augusta, Austl.	F3	68
Augusta, Ga., U.S.	F4	112
Augusta, Il., U.S.	B6	114
Augusta, Italy	L10	18
Augusta, Ks., U.S.	N10	118
Augusta, Ky., U.S.	I2	108
Augusta, Me., U.S.	C17	108
Augusta, Mt., U.S.	C13	122
Augusta, Wi., U.S.	F4	110
Augustów, Pol.	B22	10
Auila, Ribeirão, stm., Braz.	B2	79
Aulander, N.C., U.S.	C9	112
Aulnay, Fr.	F6	14
Aulneau Peninsula, pen., On., Can.	I20	104
Ault, Co., U.S.	D12	120
Ault, Fr.	B8	14
Aumale, Fr.	C8	14
Auna, Nig.	F12	64
Auneau, Fr.	D8	14
Auob, stm., Afr.	F5	66
Aurangābād, India	C3	46
Auray, Fr.	E4	14
Aurelia, Ia., U.S.	I12	118
Aurès, Massif de l', mts., Alg.	C14	62
Aurich, Ger.	B7	10
Auriflama, Braz.	F3	79
Aurilândia, Braz.	D3	79
Aurillac, Fr.	H9	14
Aurora, Co., U.S.	E12	120
Aurora, Il., U.S.	I7	110
Aurora, In., U.S.	C12	114
Aurora, Mn., U.S.	C3	110
Aurora, Mo., U.S.	F3	114
Aurora, N.C., U.S.	D10	112
Aurora, Ne., U.S.	K9	118
Aurora, N.Y., U.S.	E10	108
Aurora, Oh., U.S.	F5	108
Aurora, On., Can.	F16	110
Aurora, Ut., U.S.	F5	120
Aurora, W.V., U.S.	H7	108
Aurora do Norte, Braz.	B5	79
Aurukun, Austl.	B8	68
Aus, Nmb.	F3	66
Au Sable, stm., Mi., U.S.	F12	110
Au Sable Forks, N.Y., U.S.	C13	108
Auschwitz see Oświęcim, Pol.	E19	10
Aust-Agder, co., Nor.	L10	6
Austin, In., U.S.	D11	114
Austin, Mb., Can.	I16	104
Austin, Mn., U.S.	G3	110
Austin, Nv., U.S.	E8	124
Austin, Pa., U.S.	F8	108
Austin, Tx., U.S.	I9	116
Austin Channel, strt., N.T., Can.	A12	96
Austinville, Va., U.S.	C6	112
Australes, Îles, is., Fr. Poly.	K24	126
Australia, ctry., Oc.	D7	68
Australia Mountain, mtn., Yk., Can.	E25	100
Australian Capital Territory, ter., Austl.	G9	68
Austria (Österreich), ctry., Eur.	F10	4
Autazes, Braz.	I13	84
Autlán de Navarro, Mex.	H7	90
Autun, Fr.	F11	14
Auvergne, hist. reg., Fr.	G9	14
Auxerre, Fr.	E10	14
Auxier, Ky., U.S.	B4	112
Auxi-le-Château, Fr.	B9	14
Auxonne, Fr.	E12	14
Auxvasse, Mo., U.S.	C5	114
Auyán Tepuy, mtn., Ven.	E11	84
Auzances, Fr.	F9	14
Auzangate, Nevado, mtn., Peru	E6	82
Ava, Il., U.S.	E7	114
Ava, Mo., U.S.	F4	114
Avaí, Braz.	G4	79
Avallon, Fr.	E10	14
Avalon, Ca., U.S.	K7	124
Avalon Peninsula, pen., Nf., Can.	E20	106
Ávalos, Mex.	C6	90
Avanos, Tur.	B3	48
Avant, Ok., U.S.	C10	116
Avaré, Braz.	G4	79
Avegbadje, mtn., Afr.	H10	64
Aveiro, Port.	E3	16
Avelgem, Bel.	G3	12
Avellaneda, Arg.	H9	80
Avellaneda, Arg.	E9	80
Avellino, Italy	I9	18
Avenal, Ca., U.S.	H5	124
Aversa, Italy	I9	18
Avery, Id., U.S.	C10	122
Avery, Tx., U.S.	I2	114
Avery Island, La., U.S.	M5	114
Aveyron, dept., Fr.	H9	14
Avezzano, Italy	G8	18
Aviemore, Scot., U.K.	D10	8
Avigliano, Italy	I10	18
Avignon, Fr.	I11	14
Ávila, Spain	E7	16
Ávila, prov., Spain	E7	16
Avilés, Spain	B6	16
Avis, Pa., U.S.	F9	108
Avispa, Cerro, mtn., Ven.	G10	84
Aviz, Port.	F4	16
Avoca, Ia., U.S.	J12	118
Avoca, N.Y., U.S.	E9	108
Avola, B.C., Can.	F15	102
Avola, Italy	M10	18
Avon, Il., U.S.	J5	110
Avon, Mn., U.S.	E1	110
Avon, Mt., U.S.	D13	122
Avon, N.C., U.S.	D11	112
Avon, N.Y., U.S.	E9	108
Avon, S.D., U.S.	H9	118
Avon, co., Eng., U.K.	J11	8
Avon, stm., Eng., U.K.	I12	8
Avon, stm., N.S., Can.	H9	106
Avondale, Az., U.S.	K4	120
Avondale, Co., U.S.	M3	118
Avon Downs, Austl.	C2	70
Avonlea, Sk., Can.	H9	104
Avonmore, Pa., U.S.	G7	108
Avon Park, Fl., U.S.	L5	112
Avontuur, S. Afr.	I6	66
Avranches, Fr.	D5	14
A'waj, Nahr al-, stm., Syria	B6	50
Awaji-shima, i., Japan	M9	36
'Awālī, Bahr.	H11	48
Awasa, Eth.	N10	60
Awash, Eth.	G9	56
Awash, stm., Eth.	M10	60
Awaso, Ghana	H8	64
Awbārī, Libya	C3	56
Awe, Nig.	G14	64
Awegyun, Myan.	H5	40
Awjilah, Libya	C5	56
Awled Djellal, Alg.	C13	62
Awlef, Alg.	G11	62
Aworo Kit, Sudan	L7	60
Axel Heiberg Island, i., N.T., Can.	B10	86
Axim, Ghana	I8	64
Axinim, Braz.	J13	84
Axiós (Vardar), stm., Eur.	I6	20
Axis, Al., U.S.	L8	114
Ax-les-Thermes, Fr.	J8	14
Axtell, Ks., U.S.	L11	118
Axtell, Ne., U.S.	K8	118
Ayabaca, Peru	J3	84
Ayabe, Japan	L10	36
Ayacucho, Arg.	I9	80
Ayacucho, Bol.	G10	82
Ayacucho, Peru	E4	82
Ayacucho, dept., Peru	E4	82
Ayamonte, Spain	H4	16
Ayangba, Nig.	H13	64
Ayapel, Col.	C5	84
Ayarza, Laguna de, l., Guat.	C4	92
Ayaviri, Peru	F6	82
Ayaviri, stm., Peru	F6	82
Ayden, N.C., U.S.	D9	112
Aydın, Tur.	L11	20
Ayer, Ma., U.S.	E15	108
Ayers Rock (Uluru), mtn., Austl.	E6	68
Ayeyarwady (Irrawaddy), stm., Myan.	F3	40
Ayía Paraskeví, Grc.	J10	20
Ayiássos, Grc.	J10	20
Áyion Óros, pen., Grc.	I8	20
Áyios Kírikos, Grc.	L10	20
Áyios Nikólaos, Grc.	N9	20
Ayíou Órous, Kólpos, b., Grc.	I8	20
Ayl, Jord.	H5	50
Aylmer, P.Q., Can.	B11	108
Aylmer, Mount, mtn., Ab., Can.	F19	102
Aylmer Lake, l., N.T., Can.	D11	96
Aylmer West, On., Can.	H15	110
Aylsham, Sk., Can.	E11	104
'Ayn Dār, Sau. Ar.	B6	47
Aynor, S.C., U.S.	F7	112
'Aynūnah, Sau. Ar.	G3	48
Ayo, Peru	F5	82
Ayo Ayo, Bol.	G7	82
Ayod, Sudan	M6	60
Ayom, Sudan	N5	60
'Ayoûn el 'Atroûs, Maur.	C5	64
Ayr, Austl.	B7	70
Ayr, On., Can.	G15	110
Ayr, Scot., U.K.	F9	8
'Aytā al-Fakhkhār, Leb.	A5	50
Ayu, Kepulauan, is., Indon.	E9	38
Ayutla, Mex.	G7	90
Ayutla de los Libres, Mex.	I10	90
Ayvacık, Tur.	J10	20
Ayvalık, Tur.	J10	20
Azacualpa, Hond.	C8	92
Azacualpa, Hond.	B6	92
Azalea Park, Fl., U.S.	K5	112
Azambuja, Port.	F3	16
Āzamgarh, India	G10	44
Azángaro, Peru	F6	82
Azángaro, stm., Peru	F6	82
Azaouagh, Vallée de l', val., Afr.	D11	64
Azapa, Quebrada de, stm., Chile	H6	82
Azar, val., Afr.	C12	64
Azare, Nig.	F15	64
Āzar Shahr, Iran	C8	48
Azaryčy, Bela.	I12	22
Azazga, Alg.	B13	62
Azeffâl, dunes, Afr.	J4	62
Azeffoun, Alg.	B13	62
Azemmour, Mor.	D6	62
Azerbaijan (Azărbaycan), ctry., Asia	I7	26
Azerbaydzan see Azerbaijan, ctry., Asia	I7	26
Azëry, Bela.	H7	22
Azezo, Eth.	K9	60
Azogues, Ec.	I3	84
Azores see Açores, is., Port.	k19	62a
Azoum, Bahr (Wādī 'Azūm), val., Afr.	K2	60
Azov, Russia	H5	26
Azov, Sea of, Eur.	H5	26
Azpeitia, Spain	B9	16
Azraq, Al-Baḥr al- see Blue Nile, stm., Afr.	K8	60
Azrou, Mor.	D8	62
Aztec, N.M., U.S.	H9	120
Aztec Peak, mtn., Az., U.S.	K6	120
Azua, Dom. Rep.	E9	94
Azuaga, Spain	G6	16
Azuay, prov., Ec.	I3	84
Azucena, Arg.	I9	80
Azuero, Península de, pen., Pan.	D2	84
Azul, Arg.	I9	80
Azul, Cerro, mtn., C.R.	H9	92
Azul, Cerro, mtn., Hond.	C6	92
Azur, Côte d', Fr.	I14	14
Azurduy, Bol.	H9	82
Azure Lake, l., B.C., Can.	E14	102
Az-Zabadānī, Syria	A6	50
Aẓ-Ẓahrān (Dhahran), Sau. Ar.	A7	47
Az-Zaqāzīq, Egypt	B6	60
Az-Zarqā', Jord.	D6	50
Az-Zāwiyah, Libya	B3	56
Az-Zaydīyah, Yemen	G3	47
Azzel Matti, Sebkha, pl., Alg.	H11	62
Az-Zilfī, Sau. Ar.	H8	48
Az-Zubayr, Iraq	F9	48

B

Name	Map Ref.	Page
Ba, stm., Viet.	H10	40
Baar, Switz.	D10	13
Baardheere, Som.	H9	56
Baarle-Hertog (Baerle-Duc), Bel.	F6	12
Baarle-Nassau, Bel.	F6	12
Baba, Ec.	H3	84
Babadağ, Tur.	L12	20
Babahoyo, Ec.	H3	84
Babailiqiao, China	C7	34
Babajevo, Russia	B18	22
Babana, Nig.	F11	64
Babanango, S. Afr.	G10	66
Babanūsah, Sudan	L4	60
Babar, Kepulauan, is., Indon.	G8	38
Babar, Pulau, i., Indon.	G8	38
Babbitt, Mn., U.S.	C4	110
Babbitt, Nv., U.S.	F7	124
Babel, Mont de, mtn., P.Q., Can.	A5	106
Bab el Mandeb see Mandeb, Bab el, strt.	H3	47
Babimost, Pol.	C15	10
Babina Greda, Cro.	D2	20
Babinda, Austl.	A6	70
Babine, B.C., Can.	B8	102
Babine, stm., B.C., Can.	B8	102
Babine Lake, l., B.C., Can.	C9	102
Babine Range, mts., B.C., Can.	B7	102
Babino, Russia	B14	22
Babino, Russia	B23	22
Babo, Indon.	F9	38
Bābol, Iran	C12	48
Bābol Sar, Iran	C12	48
Baboquivari Peak, mtn., Az., U.S.	M5	120
Babrujsk, Bela.	H12	22
Babuškin, Russia	G13	28
Babuyan Islands, is., Phil.	B7	38
Babynino, Russia	G18	22
Bacabal, Braz.	D10	76
Bacadéhuachi, Mex.	C5	90
Bacan, Pulau, i., Indon.	F8	38
Bacău, Rom.	C10	20
Bacău, co., Rom.	C10	20
Baccalieu Island, i., Nf., Can.	D21	106
Bac Can, Viet.	C8	40
Baccarat, Fr.	D13	14
Bacerac, Mex.	B5	90
Bac Giang, Viet.	D9	40
Bachaquero, Ven.	C7	84
Bacharden, Turk.	J9	26
Bachi, China	K4	34
Bachiniva, Mex.	C6	90
Bachmutovo, Russia	E17	22
Bachu, China	D2	30
Bachuma, Eth.	N8	60
Back, stm., N.T., Can.	C13	96
Bačka Palanka, Yugo.	D3	20
Bačka Topola, Yugo.	D3	20
Backbone Ranges, mts., N.T., Can.	E30	100
Backnang, Ger.	G9	10
Backstairs Passage, strt., Austl.	J2	70
Bac Lieu, Viet.	J8	40
Bac Ninh, Viet.	D9	40
Bacoachi, Mex.	B5	90
Bacolod, Phil.	C7	38
Baconton, Ga., U.S.	H2	112
Bacoor, Phil.	n19	39b
Bács-Kiskun, co., Hung.	I19	10
Bácum, Mex.	D4	90
Bad, stm., Mi., U.S.	G11	110
Bad, stm., S.D., U.S.	G6	118
Bad, stm., Wi., U.S.	D5	110
Badagara, India	G3	46
Badajia, China	B9	34
Badajós, stm., Braz.	I11	84
Badajós, Lago, l., Braz.	I11	84
Badajoz, Spain	G5	16
Badalona, Spain	D14	16
Bādāmi, India	E3	46
Badanah, Sau. Ar.	F6	48
Badaohao, China	B9	32
Badaohe, China	C10	32
Bad Aussee, Aus.	H13	10
Bad Axe, Mi., U.S.	G12	110
Bad Bevensen, Ger.	B10	10
Bad Brückenau, Ger.	E9	10
Baddeck, N.S., Can.	F13	106
Bad Doberan, Ger.	A11	10
Bad Dürkheim, Ger.	F8	10
Bad Dürrenberg, Ger.	D12	10
Badeggi, Nig.	G13	64
Badéguichéri, Niger	D12	64
Bad Ems, Ger.	E7	10
Baden, Erit.	I9	60
Baden, Switz.	D9	13
Baden-Baden, Ger.	G8	10
Badenweiler, Ger.	H7	10
Baden-Württemberg, state, Ger.	G8	10
Badgastein, Aus.	H13	10
Badger, Mn., U.S.	C11	118
Badger, Nf., Can.	D17	106
Bad Hall, Aus.	G14	10
Bad Harzburg, Ger.	D10	10
Bad Hersfeld, Ger.	E9	10
Bad Homburg [vor der Höhe], Ger.	E8	10
Badiraguato, Mex.	E6	90
Bad Kissingen, Ger.	E10	10
Bad Kreuznach, Ger.	F7	10
Badlands, hills, S.D., U.S.	H5	118
Badlands, hills, U.S.	E4	118
Badlands National Park, S.D., U.S.	H5	118
Bad Langensalza, Ger.	D10	10
Bad Lauterberg, Ger.	D10	10
Bad Leonfelden, Aus.	G14	10
Bad Mergentheim, Ger.	F9	10
Bad Muskau, Ger.	D14	10
Bad Nauheim, Ger.	E8	10
Bad Neustadt an der Saale, Ger.	E10	10
Bad Oeynhausen, Ger.	C8	10
Badogo, Mali	F5	64
Bad Oldesloe, Ger.	B10	10
Badou, China	G5	32
Badou, Togo	H10	64
Badoumbé, Mali	E4	64
Bad Pyrmont, Ger.	D9	10
Bad Ragaz, Switz.	D12	13
Bad Reichenhall, Ger.	H12	10
Badr Ḥunayn, Sau. Ar.	C1	47
Bad Salzuflen, Ger.	C8	10
Bad Salzungen, Ger.	E10	10
Bad Sankt Leonhard im Lavanttal, Aus.	I14	10
Bad Schwalbach, Ger.	E8	10
Bad Schwartau, Ger.	B10	10
Bad Segeberg, Ger.	B10	10
Bad Tölz, Ger.	H11	10
Badu, China	I8	34
Badulla, Sri L.	I6	46
Badupi, Myan.	D2	40
Bad Vöslau, Aus.	H16	10
Bad Waldsee, Ger.	H9	10
Bad Wildungen, Ger.	D9	10
Baediam, Maur.	D4	64
Baena, Spain	H7	16
Baependi, Braz.	F6	79
Baeza, Ec.	H4	84
Baezaeko, stm., B.C., Can.	E10	102
Bafatá, Gui.-B.	E2	64
Baffin Bay, b., N.A.	B13	86
Baffin Bay, b., Tx., U.S.	L9	116
Baffin Island, i., N.T., Can.	C18	96
Bafing, stm., Afr.	F4	54
Bafoulabé, Mali	E4	64
Bafoussam, Cam.	G9	54
Bāfq, Iran	F13	48
Bāft, Iran	G14	48
Bafwasende, Zaire	A5	58
Bagaces, C.R.	G9	92
Bagagem, stm., Braz.	C4	79
Bāgalkot, India	D3	46
Bagansiapiapi, Indon.	M6	40
Bağarası, Tur.	L11	20
Bagawi, Sudan	K8	60
Bagdad, Az., U.S.	J3	120
Bagdad, Fl., U.S.	L9	114
Bagdad see Baghdād, Iraq	E8	48
Bagdarin, Russia	G14	28
Bagé, Braz.	F11	80
Baggs, Wy., U.S.	I18	122
Baghdād, Iraq	E8	48
Bagheria, Italy	K8	18
Baghlān, Afg.	B3	44
Bagley, Mn., U.S.	D12	118
Bagnères-de-Bigorre, Fr.	I7	14
Bagnères-de-Luchon, Fr.	J7	14
Bagnols-sur-Cèze, Fr.	H11	14
Bago (Pegu), Myan.	F4	40
Bagoé, stm., Afr.	F6	64
Bagotville, Base des Forces canadiennes, mil., P.Q., Can.	D3	106
Bagrationovsk, Russia	G3	22
Baguio, Phil.	m19	39b
Bahamas, ctry., N.A.	D9	88
Bahār, Iran	D10	48
Baharampur, India	H13	44
Bahāwalnagar, Pak.	F5	44
Bahāwalpur, Pak.	F4	44

Name — Map Ref. — Page

Bahechuan, China C12 32
Bahia, state, Braz. B7 79
Bahía, Islas de la, is., Hond. A8 92
Bahía Azul, Pan. H13 92
Bahía Blanca, Arg. J7 80
Bahía Kino, Mex. C4 90
Bahir Dar, Eth. L9 60
Baḥrah, Sau. Ar. D1 47
Bahraich, India G9 44
Bahrain (Al-Baḥrayn), ctry., Asia D5 42
Baḥrayn, Khalīj al-, b., Asia B7 47
Bāhū Kalāt, Iran I16 48
Bahušèųsk, Bela. G13 22
Baï, Mali E8 64
Baia Mare, Rom. B7 20
Baía Rica, stm., Braz. E10 82
Baia Sprie, Rom. B7 20
Baicao, China B4 32
Baicheng, China B11 30
Baicheng, China C3 30
Baie-Comeau, P.Q., Can. C5 106
Baie-Comeau-Hauterive, Réserve, P.Q., Can. B5 106
Baie-des-Ha] Ha], P.Q., Can. B15 106
Baie-des-Moutons, P.Q., Can. B14 106
Baie-du-Renard, P.Q., Can. C12 106
Baie-Johan-Beetz, P.Q., Can. B11 106
Baie-Sainte-Claire, P.Q., Can. C9 106
Baie-Saint-Paul, P.Q., Can. E3 106
Baie-Trinité, P.Q., Can. C6 106
Baie Verte, Nf., Can. C17 106
Baigong, China K5 34
Baihebu, China C4 32
Baijian, China D3 32
Baiju, China B9 34
Baikal, Lake see Bajkal, ozero, l., Russia G13 28
Bailadores, Ven. C7 84
Baile, China D2 32
Baile Átha Cliath see Dublin, Ire. H7 8
Băile Govora, Rom. D8 20
Bailén, Spain G8 16
Băileşti, Rom. E7 20
Bailey, N.C., U.S. D8 112
Bailin, China H9 34
Bailique, Ilha, i., Braz. C9 76
Baillie, stm., N.T., Can. D11 96
Baillie Islands, is., N.T., Can. B7 96
Bailong, stm., China E7 30
Bailundo, Ang. D3 58
Baimaguan, China C4 32
Baimashi, China F7 34
Baimiaozi, China C8 32
Bainbridge, Ga., U.S. I2 112
Bainbridge, N.Y., U.S. E11 108
Bainbridge, Oh., U.S. H3 108
Bain-de-Bretagne, Fr. E5 14
Bainiqiao, China F3 34
Bains-les-Bains, Fr. D13 14
Bainville, Mt., U.S. C3 118
Baipu, China C9 34
Baiquan, China E11 34
Baird, Tx., U.S. G7 116
Baird, Mount, mtn., Id., U.S. G14 122
Bairin Zuoqi, China C10 30
Bairnsdale, Austl. K7 70
Bairoil, Wy., U.S. B9 120
Bairuopu, China G1 34
Baisha, China E10 40
Baishanji, China B5 34
Baishatan, China G9 32
Baishuifan, China E4 34
Baishuijiang, China E8 30
Baisogala, Lith. F6 22
Baitazi, China A8 32
Baitu, China D8 34
Baixa Grande, Braz. A8 79
Baixiang, China F2 32
Baiyin, China D7 30
Baizhongpu, China B3 34
Baja, Hung. I18 10
Baja, Punta, c., Mex. C2 90
Baja California, state, Mex. C2 90
Baja California, pen., Mex. C3 90
Baja California Sur, state, Mex. E4 90
Bajada del Agrio, Arg. J3 80
Bajanaul, Kaz. G13 26
Bajanchongor, Mong. B7 30
Bajánsenye, Hung. I16 10
Baja Verapaz, dept., Guat. B4 92
Bajdarackaja guba, b., Russia D11 26
Bajestān, Iran D15 48
Bajiazi, China B11 32
Bajimba, Mount, mtn., Austl. G10 70
Bajkal, ozero (Lake Baikal), l., Russia G13 28
Bajkal'skoje, Russia F13 28
Bajmak, Russia G9 26
Bajo Baudó, Col. E4 84
Bajo Boquete, Pan. C1 84
Bajos de Haina, Dom. Rep. E9 94
Bajram-Ali, Turk. J10 26
Bakebe, Cam. I14 64
Bakel, Sen. D3 64
Baker, Ca., U.S. I9 124
Baker, Fl., U.S. L10 114
Baker, La., U.S. L5 114
Baker, Mt., U.S. E3 118
Baker, Or., U.S. F8 122
Baker, Mount, mtn., Wa., U.S. B4 122
Baker Butte, mtn., Az., U.S. J5 120
Baker Creek, stm., B.C., Can. E12 102
Baker Island, i., Oc. H22 126
Baker Lake, N.T., Can. D13 96
Baker Lake, l., N.T., Can. D13 96
Bakersfield, Ca., U.S. I6 124
Bakersville, N.C., U.S. C4 112
Bākhtarān (Kermānshāh), Iran D9 48
Bakhtegān, Daryācheh-ye, l., Iran G13 48
Bakı (Baku), Azer. I7 26
Bakkagerði, Ice. B7 6a
Baklanka, Russia C23 22
Bako, Eth. O9 60
Bakony, mts., Hung. H17 10
Bakoy, stm., Afr. F5 54
Baku see Bakı, Azer. I7 26
Bakun, China D9 44
Bala, Sen. D3 64
Balâ, Tur. B2 48
Balabac Strait, strt., Asia D6 38
Ba'labakk, Leb. D4 48
Balabanovo, Russia F19 22
Balachna, Russia E26 22
Balad, Iraq D8 48
Bālāghāt, India J9 44
Balaguer, Spain D12 16
Balakirevo, Russia E21 22
Balaklava, Austl. J3 70
Balakovo, Russia G7 26
Balallan, Scot., U.K. C7 8
Bālā Morghāb, Afg. D17 48
Balāngīr, India B7 46
Balašicha, Russia F20 22
Balašov, Russia G6 26
Balassagyarmat, Hung. G19 10
Balāṭ, Egypt E5 60
Balatina, Mol. B11 20
Balaton, Mn., U.S. G12 118
Balaton, l., Hung. I17 10
Balayan, Phil. o19 39b
Balbieriškis, Lith. G6 22
Balbirini, Austl. C7 68
Balboa, Pan. I15 92
Balbriggan, Ire. H7 8
Balcanoona, Austl. H3 70
Balcarce, Arg. I9 80
Balcarres, Sk., Can. H11 104
Balchaš, Kaz. H12 26
Balchaš, ozero (Lake Balkhash), l., Kaz. H12 26
Balcones Escarpment, clf, Tx., U.S. J6 116
Balde, Arg. G5 80
Baldim, Braz. E7 79
Bald Knob, Ar., U.S. G5 114
Bald Mountain, mtn., Or., U.S. G4 122
Baldock Lake, l., Mb., Can. B17 104
Baldone, Lat. E7 22
Baldur, Mb., Can. I15 104
Baldwin, Fl., U.S. I5 112
Baldwin, La., U.S. M5 114
Baldwin, Mi., U.S. G10 110
Baldwin, Wi., U.S. F3 110
Baldwin City, Ks., U.S. M12 118
Baldwin Peninsula, pen., Ak., U.S. C13 100
Baldwinsville, N.Y., U.S. D10 108
Baldwinville, Ma., U.S. E14 108
Baldwyn, Ms., U.S. H8 114
Baldy Mountain, mtn., B.C., Can. F14 102
Baldy Mountain, mtn., Mb., Can. G14 104
Baldy Mountain, mtn., Mt., U.S. B16 122
Baldy Mountain, mtn., N.M., U.S. H11 120
Baldy Peak, mtn., Az., U.S. K7 120
Balearic Islands see Balears, Illes, is., Spain F15 16
Balears, state, Spain F15 16
Balears, Illes (Balearic Islands), is., Spain F15 16
Baleia, Ponta da, c., Braz. D9 79
Baleine, Grande rivière de la, stm., P.Q., Can. F18 96
Baleine, Petite rivière de la, stm., P.Q., Can. E18 96
Baleine, Rivière à la, stm., P.Q., Can. E19 96
Balej, Russia G15 28
Baler, Phil. n19 39b
Bāleshwar, India J12 44
Baléyara, Niger E11 64
Balfate, Hond. B8 92
Balfes Creek, Austl. C6 70
Balfour, N.C., U.S. D4 112
Bali, Laut (Bali Sea), Indon. G6 38
Bali, Selat, strt., Indon. G5 38
Balihan, China B6 32
Balıkesir, Tur. J11 20
Balikpapan, Indon. F6 38
Balimo, Pap. N. Gui. G11 38
Balin, China B11 30
Balingen, Ger. G8 10
Balintang Channel, strt., Phil. B7 38
Baliza, Braz. D2 79
Balkan Mountains see Stara Planina, mts., Eur. G8 20
Balkan Peninsula, pen., Eur. D9 52
Balkbrug, Neth. C9 12
Balkh, Afg. B2 44
Balkh, stm., Afg. B2 44
Balkhash, Lake see Balchaš, ozero, l., Kaz. H12 26
Ball, La., U.S. K4 114
Ballachulish, Scot., U.K. E8 8
Ballangen, Nor. G15 6
Ballantine, Mt., U.S. E17 122
Ballarat, Austl. K5 70
Ballé, Mali D5 64
Ballenas, Bahía de, b., Mex. D3 90
Balleny Islands, is., Ant. B8 73
Balleroy, Fr. C6 14
Ballesteros, Arg. G7 80
Balleza, Mex. D6 90
Balleza, stm., Mex. D6 90
Ball Ground, Ga., U.S. E2 112
Ballia, India H11 44
Ballina, Austl. G10 70
Ballina, Ire. G4 8
Ballinger, Tx., U.S. H7 116
Ballon, Fr. M14 8
Balls Pyramid, i., Austl. F11 68
Ballston Spa, N.Y., U.S. D13 108
Ballville, Oh., U.S. F3 108
Balmaceda, Chile F2 78
Balmertown, On., Can. G21 104
Balmorhea, Tx., U.S. I3 116
Balnearia, Arg. F7 80
Balonne, stm., Austl. F8 70
Bālotra, India H5 44
Balovale, Zam. D4 58
Baloži, Lat. E7 22
Balrāmpur, India G10 44
Balranald, Austl. J5 70
Balsam Lake, Wi., U.S. E3 110
Bálsamo, Braz. F2 79
Balsas, Braz. E9 76
Balsas, stm., Mex. H8 90
Balsas, Rio das, stm., Braz. E9 76
Balsas Sur, Mex. I10 90
Bal'šavik, Bela. I13 22
Balsthal, Switz. D8 13
Balta, Ukr. H3 26
Baltasar Brum, Ur. F10 80
Bălţi, Mol. F13 4
Baltic Sea, Eur. M16 6
Baltijsk, Russia G2 22
Baltijskaja kosa, spit, Eur. A19 10
Balṭīm, Egypt B6 60
Baltimore, Ire. J4 8
Baltimore, Md., U.S. H10 108
Baltimore, Oh., U.S. H4 108
Baltimore, S. Afr. D9 66
Baluarte, stm., Mex. F7 90
Balvi, Lat. D10 22
Balya, Tur. J11 20
Balykši, Kaz. H8 26
Balzac, Ab., Can. F20 102
Balzar, Ec. H3 84
Bam, Iran G15 48
Bama, China B9 40
Bamaga, Austl. B8 68
Bamaji Lake, l., On., Can. G23 104
Bamako, Mali E5 64
Bamba, Mali C9 64
Bambamarca, Peru B2 82
Bambana, stm., Nic. D11 92
Bambara Maoundé, Mali D8 64
Bambari, C.A.R. G5 56
Bambaroo, Austl. B7 70
Bamberg, Ger. F10 10
Bamberg, S.C., U.S. F5 112
Bambesi, Eth. M8 60
Bambezi, Zimb. C9 66
Bambuí, Braz. F6 79
Bamburral, stm., S.A. H12 82
Bam Co, l., China E14 44
Bamenda, Cam. I15 64
Bamfield, B.C., Can. I9 102
Bami, Turk. B14 48
Bamingui, stm., C.A.R. G4 56
Bampūr, Iran H16 48
Bamumo, China D15 44
Ba Na, Viet. G9 40
Banaba, i., Kir. I20 126
Banalia, Zaire A5 58
Banana, Zaire C2 58
Bananal, Ilha do, i., Braz. F8 76
Banana River, b., Fl., U.S. K6 112
Banarlı, Tur. H11 20
Banās, Ra's, c., Egypt F8 60
Banat, hist. reg., Eur. D4 20
Banbuji, China B5 34
Banco, Punta, c., C.R. I11 92
Bancroft, Ia., U.S. H13 118
Bancroft, Id., U.S. H14 122
Bancroft, Ne., U.S. I11 118
Bancroft, On., Can. E18 110
Bānda, India H9 44
Banda, Kepulauan, is., Indon. F8 38
Banda, Laut (Banda Sea), Indon. G8 38
Banda Aceh, Indon. L3 40
Bānda Dāūd Shāh, Pak. D4 44
Banda del Río Salí, Arg. D6 80
Bandama, stm., C. Iv. H7 64
Bandama Blanc, stm., C. Iv. G7 64
Bandama Rouge, stm., C. Iv. G6 64
Bandar see Machilīpatnam, India D6 46
Bandar Beheshtī, Iran I16 48
Bandar-e 'Abbās, Iran H14 48
Bandar-e Anzalī (Bandar-e Pahlavī), Iran C10 48
Bandar-e Būshehr, Iran G11 48
Bandar-e Deylam, Iran F11 48
Bandar-e Khomeynī (Bandar-e Shāhpūr), Iran F10 48
Bandar-e Lengeh, Iran H13 48
Bandar-e Māh Shahr, Iran F10 48
Bandar-e Rīg, Iran G11 48
Bandar-e Torkeman, Iran C13 48
Bandar Seri Begawan, Bru. E5 38
Banded Peak, mtn., Co., U.S. G10 120
Bandeira, Pico da, mtn., Braz. F8 79
Bandeirantes, Braz. B3 79
Bandeirantes, Braz. E1 79
Bandeirantes, Braz. G3 79
Bandera, Arg. E7 80
Bandera, Tx., U.S. J7 116
Bandera, Alto, mtn., Dom. Rep. E9 94
Banderas, Bahía de, b., Mex. G7 90
Bandiagara, Mali D8 64
Bandiantaolehai, China C7 30
Bandırma, Tur. I11 20
Bandon, Ire. J5 8
Bandon, Or., U.S. G1 122
Ban Don, Ao, b., Thai. J5 40
Bandula, Moz. B11 66
Bandundu, Zaire B3 58
Bandung, Indon. j13 39a
Bāneh, Iran D8 48
Banes, Cuba D7 94
Banff, Ab., Can. F19 102
Banff, Scot., U.K. D11 8
Banff National Park, Ab., Can. F18 102
Banfora, Burkina F7 64
Bangalore, India F4 46
Bangaon, India I13 44
Bangassou, C.A.R. H5 56
Banggai, Indon. F7 38
Banggai, Kepulauan, is., Indon. F7 38
Banghāzī, Libya B5 56
Bangil, Indon. j16 39a
Bangjang, Sudan L7 60
Bangjun, China D5 32
Bangka, Pulau, i., Indon. F4 38
Bangkalan, Indon. j16 39a
Bangkok see Krung Thep, Thai. H6 40
Bangladesh, ctry., Asia E13 42
Bang Mun Nak, Thai. F6 40
Bangolo, C. Iv. H6 64
Bangor, Me., U.S. C18 108
Bangor, Mi., U.S. H9 110
Bangor, N. Ire., U.K. G8 8
Bangor, Pa., U.S. G11 108
Bangor, Wales, U.K. H9 8
Bangs, Tx., U.S. H7 116
Bang Saphan, Thai. I5 40
Bangshi, China C10 32
Bangued, Phil. m19 39b
Bangui, C.A.R. H4 56
Bangweulu, Lake, l., Zam. D5 58
Ban Hin Heup, Laos E7 40
Ban Houayxay, Laos D6 40
Bani, Burkina D9 64
Baní, Dom. Rep. E9 94
Bani, stm., Mali E7 64
Baniachang, Bngl. H14 44
Banikoara, Benin F11 64
Banī Mazār, Egypt C6 60
Banī Suwayf, Egypt C6 60
Banī Walīd, Libya B3 56
Bāniyās, Golan B5 50
Banja Luka, Bos. E12 18
Banjarmasin, Indon. F5 38
Banjin, China C9 34
Banjul (Bathurst), Gam. E1 64
Bankas, Mali D8 64
Bankilaré, Niger D10 64
Banks, Al., U.S. K11 114
Banksian, stm., Can. E20 104
Banks Island, i., B.C., Can. D4 102
Banks Island, i., N.T., Can. B8 96
Banks Lake, res., Wa., U.S. C6 122
Banks Peninsula, pen., N.Z. E4 72
Banks Strait, strt., Austl. M8 70
Bānkura, India I12 44
Ban Mit, Laos E6 40
Bann, stm., N. Ire., U.K. G7 8
Ban Nahin, Laos E8 40
Ban Namnga, Laos D7 40
Banner Elk, N.C., U.S. C5 112
Bannertown, N.C., U.S. C6 112
Ban Ngam, Laos D8 40
Banning, Ca., U.S. K9 124
Bannock Peak, mtn., Id., U.S. H13 122
Bannu, Pak. D4 44
Banon, Fr. H12 14
Baños, Ec. H3 84
Baños, Peru D3 82
Ban Pakneun, Laos E6 40
Ban Pong, Thai. H5 40
Banpu, China A8 34
Banqiao, China E9 34
Banqiaoji, China C5 34
Banquan, China H6 32
Banshi, China J4 34
Banská Bystrica, Slvk. G19 10
Banská Štiavnica, Slvk. G18 10
Ban Songkhon, Laos F8 40
Bānswāra, India I6 44
Ban Thanoun, Laos E6 40
Bantry, Ire. J4 8
Ban Xènkhalôk, Laos E6 40
Banyak, Kepulauan, is., Indon. M4 40
Banyoles, Spain C14 16
Banzare Coast, Ant. B7 73
Banzi, China K6 34
Baode, China D9 30
Baoding, China E3 32
Baofeng, China B2 34
Bao Ha, Viet. C8 40
Baohekou, China C6 32
Baoji, China E8 30
Bao Lac, Viet. I9 40
Baonian, China D8 34
Baoquan, China G7 32
Baoshan, China D10 34
Baoshan, China B5 40
Baoting, China H8 30
Baotou, China C8 30
Baowei, China C9 40
Baoxinji, China C4 34
Baoying, China B8 34
Bāpatla, India E6 46
Bapaume, Fr. B9 14
Bapchule, Az., U.S. K5 120
Bāqa el Gharbīya, Isr. D4 50
Baqên, China E16 44
B'aqlīn, Leb. A5 50
Ba'qūbah, Iraq E8 48
Baquedano, Chile B4 80
Bar, Yugo. G3 20
Baraawe, Som. H9 56
Barabinsk, Russia F7 28
Barabinskaja step', pl., Russia F7 28
Baraboo, Wi., U.S. G6 110
Baraboo, stm., Wi., U.S. G6 110
Baraboulé, Burkina D9 64
Baracaju, stm., Braz. B3 79
Barachit, Erit. J10 60
Barachois Pond Provincial Park, Nf., Can. D15 106
Baracoa, Cuba D7 94
Baracoa, Hond. B7 92
Baradero, Arg. G9 80
Baradine, Austl. H8 70
Baraga, Mi., U.S. D7 110
Baragarh, India B7 46
Bārah, Sudan K6 60
Barahona, Dom. Rep. E9 94
Barak, Tur. C4 48
Baraka, val., Afr. E8 56
Barakaldo, Spain B9 16
Baralaba, Austl. E8 70
Baram, stm., Malay. E5 38
Barama, stm., Guy. D13 84
Baran', Bela. G13 22
Baranagar, India I13 44
Baranavičy, Bela. H9 22
Baranoa, Col. B5 84
Baranof Island, i., Ak., U.S. H27 100
Baranya, co., Hung. J18 10
Barão de Melgaço, Braz. G14 82
Baratang Island, i., India H2 40
Barataria, La., U.S. M6 114
Barataria Bay, b., La., U.S. M7 114
Barat Daya, Kepulauan, is., Indon. G8 38
Bar'atino, Russia G17 22
Barauana, stm., Braz. G12 84
Barauni, India H11 44
Baraut, India F7 44
Baravuḫa, Bela. F11 22
Baraya, Col. F5 84
Barbacena, Braz. F7 79
Barbacoas, Col. G3 84
Barbados, ctry., N.A. H15 94
Barbar, Sudan H7 60
Barbareta, Isla, i., Hond. A8 92
Barbas, Cap, c., W. Sah. I2 62
Barbastro, Spain C12 16
Barbate, Spain I6 16
Barbeau Peak, mtn., N.T., Can. A12 86
Barberena, Guat. C4 92
Barberton, Oh., U.S. F5 108
Barberton, S. Afr. E10 66
Barbezieux, Fr. G6 14
Barbil, India I11 44
Barbosa, Col. D5 84
Barbosa, Col. E6 84
Barboursville, W.V., U.S. I4 108
Barbourville, Ky., U.S. C3 112
Barbuda, i., Antig. F14 94
Barby, Ger. D11 10
Barcaldine, Austl. D6 70
Barcău (Berettyó), stm., Eur. B6 20
Barce see Al-Marj, Libya B5 56
Barcellona Pozzo di Gotto, Italy K10 18
Barcelona, Mex. D8 90
Barcelona, Spain D14 16
Barcelona, Ven. B10 84
Barcelos, Braz. H11 84
Barcin, Pol. C17 10
Barcoo, stm., Austl. E5 70
Barcs, Hung. J17 10
Barczewo, Pol. B20 10
Bärdä, Azer. A9 48
Barda del Medio, Arg. J4 80
Bardaï, Chad D4 56
Bardai, Sudan K1 60
Bardawīl, Sabkhat al-, sw., Egypt F2 48
Barddhamān, India I12 44
Bardejov, Slvk. F21 10
Bardi, Italy E4 18
Bardīyah, Libya B3 60
Bardo, Tun. M5 18
Bardonecchia, Italy D1 18
Bardoux, Lac, l., P.Q., Can. A6 106
Bardstown, Ky., U.S. E11 114
Bardu, Nor. G16 6
Bardufoss, Nor. G16 6
Bardwell, Ky., U.S. F7 114
Bareilly, India F8 44
Barents Sea, Eur. B4 24
Barentu, Erit. J9 60
Barfleur, Fr. C5 14
Barge, Eth. N9 60
Bargnop, Sudan M5 60
Barguzin, stm., Russia G14 28
Bar Harbor, Me., U.S. C18 108
Bari, Italy H11 18
Baria, stm., Ven. G9 84
Barichara, Col. D6 84
Barillas, Guat. B3 92
Barīm (Perim), i., Yemen H3 47
Barima, stm., S.A. C12 84
Barima-Waini, prov., Guy. D13 84
Barinas, Ven. C7 84
Barinas, state, Ven. C8 84
Baring, Cape, c., N.T., Can. B9 96
Barinitas, Ven. C7 84
Bāripada, India J12 44
Bariri, Braz. G4 79
Bārīs, Egypt E6 60
Barisāl, Bngl. I14 44
Barisan, Pegunungan, mts., Indon. F3 38
Barito, stm., Indon. F5 38
Barjols, Fr. I13 14
Bark, stm., Wi., U.S. H7 110
Barkal, Bngl. I15 44
Barkerville, B.C., Can. D13 102
Barkerville Historic Park, B.C., Can. D13 102
Barkley, Lake, res., U.S. F9 114
Barkley Sound, strt., B.C., Can. I9 102
Barkly East, S. Afr. H8 66
Barkly Tableland, plat., Austl. C7 68
Barkly West, S. Afr. G7 66
Barkol, China C5 30
Barksdale, Tx., U.S. J6 116
Bârlad, Rom. C11 20
Bar-le-Duc, Fr. D12 14
Barlee, Lake, l., Austl. E3 68
Barletta, Italy H11 18
Barling, Ar., U.S. G2 114
Barlow, Ky., U.S. E7 114
Bārmer, India H4 44
Barnard Castle, Eng., U.K. G15 8
Barnaul, Russia G14 26
Barn Bluff, mtn., Austl. M6 70
Barnegat, N.J., U.S. H12 108
Barnegat Bay, b., N.J., U.S. H12 108
Barnesboro, Pa., U.S. G8 108
Barnes Ice Cap, N.T., Can. B18 96
Barnes Lake, l., Mb., Can. B16 104
Barnesville, Ga., U.S. F2 112
Barnesville, Mn., U.S. E11 118
Barnesville, Oh., U.S. H5 108
Barnhart, Tx., U.S. H5 116
Barnsdall, Ok., U.S. C10 116
Barnstable, Ma., U.S. F16 108
Barnstaple, Eng., U.K. J9 8
Barnwell, Ab., Can. H22 102
Barnwell, S.C., U.S. F5 112
Baro, stm., Afr. G8 56
Barons, Ab., Can. G21 102
Barpeta, India G14 44
Barqa, China E9 44
Barqah (Cyrenaica), hist. reg., Libya C2 60
Barque Canada Reef, rf., Asia D5 38
Barques, Pointe aux, c., Mi., U.S. F13 110
Barquisimeto, Ven. B8 84
Barra, Braz. F10 76
Barra, Ponta da, c., Moz. D12 66
Barraba, Austl. H9 70
Barrackville, W.V., U.S. H6 108
Barra da Estiva, Braz. B8 79
Barra do Bugres, Braz. F13 82
Barra do Corda, Braz. E9 76
Barra do Cuanza, Ang. C2 58
Barra do Garças, Braz. C2 79
Barra do Mendes, Braz. A7 79
Barra do Piraí, Braz. G7 79
Barra do Ribeiro, Braz. F13 80
Barra Falsa, Ponta da, c., Moz. D12 66
Barrafranca, Italy L9 18
Barra Mansa, Braz. G6 79
Barranca, Peru D3 82
Barranca, Peru A3 82
Barrancabermeja, Col. D6 84
Barrancas, Col. B6 84
Barrancas, Ven. C7 84
Barrancas, Ven. C11 84
Barrancas, stm., Arg. I3 80
Barranqueras, Arg. D9 80
Barranquilla, Col. B5 84
Barras, Braz. D10 76
Barre, Vt., U.S. C14 108
Barreal, Arg. F4 80
Barreiras, Braz. B6 79
Barreirinha, Braz. I14 84
Barreiro, Port. G2 16
Barreiro, stm., Braz. C2 79
Barreiros, Braz. E11 76
Barren, stm., Ky., U.S. E10 114
Barren, Nosy, is., Madag. q20 67b
Barren Islands, is., Ak., U.S. G18 100
Barren River Lake, res., Ky., U.S. F10 114
Barretos, Braz. F4 79
Barrhead, Ab., Can. C20 102
Barrie, On., Can. F16 110
Barrière, B.C., Can. F14 102
Barrier Range, mts., Austl. H4 70
Barrington, N.S., Can. I8 106
Barrington Lake, l., Mb., Can. B14 104
Barringun, Austl. G6 70
Barrita Vieja, Guat. D4 92
Barro Alto, Braz. C4 79
Barron, Wi., U.S. E4 110
Barrow, Ak., U.S. A16 100
Barrow, Arg. J8 80
Barrow, Point, c., Ak., U.S. A16 100
Barrow Creek, Austl. D6 68
Barrow-in-Furness, Eng., U.K. G10 8
Barrow Island, i., Austl. D3 68
Barrows, Mb., Can. F13 104
Barrow Strait, strt., N.T., Can. B13 96
Barry, Il., U.S. C5 114
Barrys Bay, On., Can. E18 110
Barryton, Mi., U.S. G10 110
Bārsi, India C3 46
Barsinghausen, Ger. C9 10
Barstow, Ca., U.S. J8 124
Barstow, Tx., U.S. H3 116
Bar-sur-Aube, Fr. D11 14
Bar-sur-Seine, Fr. D11 14
Bartang, stm., Taj. A5 44
Barthélemy, Deo, Viet. E8 40
Bartholomew, Bayou, stm., U.S. I5 114
Bartica, Guy. D13 84
Bartle Frere, mtn., Austl. A6 70
Bartlesville, Ok., U.S. C11 116
Bartlett, Ne., U.S. J9 118
Bartlett, N.H., U.S. C15 108
Bartlett, Tn., U.S. G7 114
Bartlett, Tx., U.S. I9 116
Bartletts Harbour, Nf., Can. B16 106
Bartley, Ne., U.S. K7 118
Bartolomé de las Casas, Arg. C9 80
Bartolomeu Dias, Moz. C12 66
Barton, Vt., U.S. C14 108
Barton Lake, l., On., Can. F20 104
Barton-upon-Humber, Eng., U.K. H13 8
Bartonville, Il., U.S. J6 110
Bartoszyce, Pol. A20 10
Bartow, Fl., U.S. L5 112
Bartow, Ga., U.S. G4 112
Barú, Volcán, vol., Pan. I12 92
Baruun-Urt, Mong. B9 30
Barva, Volcán, vol., C.R. G10 92
Barview, Or., U.S. G1 122
Barwāni, India I6 44
Barwick, Ga., U.S. I3 112
Barwon, stm., Austl. G8 70
Barybino, Russia F20 22
Baryš, Russia G7 26
Barysaų, Bela. G11 22
Basacato del Este, Eq. Gui. J14 64
Basail, Arg. D9 80
Basankusu, Zaire A3 58
Basarabeasca, Mol. C12 20
Basarabi, Rom. E12 20
Basatongwula Shan, mtn., China D14 44
Basavilbaso, Arg. G9 80
Basco, Phil. A7 38
Bascuñán, Cabo, c., Chile E3 80
Basel (Bâle), Switz. C8 13
Basey, Phil. C8 38
Bashaw, Ab., Can. E22 102
Bashi Channel, strt., Asia G11 30
Bashkortostan see Baškirija, state, Russia G9 26
Basile, La., U.S. L4 114
Basilicata, prov., Italy I11 18
Basin, Mt., U.S. D13 122
Basin, Wy., U.S. F17 122
Basin Lake, l., Sk., Can. F9 104
Basīrhāt, India I13 44
Baskakovka, Russia G17 22
Basket Lake, l., On., Can. I22 104
Baškirija, state, Russia G9 26
Bašmakovo, Russia H26 22
Basoko, Zaire A4 58
Basque Lands see Euskal Herriko, state, Spain B9 16
Basra see Al-Başrah, Iraq F9 48
Bas-Rhin, dept., Fr. D14 14
Bassano, Ab., Can. G22 102
Bassano del Grappa, Italy D6 18
Bassari, Togo G10 64
Bassas da India, rf., Afr. F7 58
Bassecourt, Switz. D7 13
Bassein see Pathein, Myan. F3 40
Bassein, mth., Myan. F3 40
Basse-Terre, Guad. F14 94
Basseterre, St. K./N. F13 94
Basse-Terre, i., Guad. F14 94
Bassett, Ne., U.S. I8 118
Bassett, Va., U.S. C7 112
Bassett Peak, mtn., Az., U.S. L6 120
Basse-Yutz, Fr. J9 12
Bassfield, Ms., U.S. K7 114
Bass Harbor, Me., U.S. C18 108
Bassikounou, Maur. D7 64
Bassila, Benin G10 64
Bass River, N.S., Can. G10 106
Bass Strait, strt., Austl. L6 70
Basṭah, Jord. H5 50
Bastak, Iran H13 48
Bastelica, Fr. I24 15a
Basti, India G10 44
Bastia, Fr. J16 14
Bastian, Va., U.S. B5 112
Bastimentos, Pan. H12 92
Bastimentos, Isla, i., Pan. H12 92
Bastogne (Bastenaken), Bel. H8 12
Bastrop, La., U.S. J5 114
Bastrop, Tx., U.S. I9 116
Bastuträsk, Swe. I17 6
Basutoland see Lesotho, ctry., Afr. G5 58
Bata, Eq. Gui. A1 58
Bataan Peninsula, pen., Phil. n19 39b
Batabanó, Golfo de, b., Cuba C3 94
Bataguassu, Braz. F2 79
Bataiporã, Braz. G2 79
Batajsk, Russia H5 26
Batala, India E6 44
Batan, China A9 34
Batang, China E6 30
Batangas, Phil. o19 39b
Batan Islands, is., Phil. A7 38
Bátaszék, Hung. I18 10
Batatais, Braz. F5 79
Batavia, Arg. H6 80
Batavia, Ia., U.S. J3 110
Batavia, Il., U.S. I7 110
Batavia, N.Y., U.S. E8 108
Batavia, Oh., U.S. H2 108
Bătdâmbâng, Camb. H7 40
Bateckij, Russia C13 22
Batemans Bay, Austl. J9 70
Batesburg, S.C., U.S. F5 112
Batesville, Ar., U.S. G5 114
Batesville, In., U.S. C11 114
Batesville, Ms., U.S. H7 114
Batesville, Tx., U.S. K7 116
Bath, Eng., U.K. J11 8
Bath, Me., U.S. D17 108
Bath, N.B., Can. F6 106
Bath, N.Y., U.S. E9 108
Bathgate, N.D., U.S. C10 118
Bathinda, India E6 44
Bathsheba, Barb. H15 94
Bathurst, Austl. I8 70
Bathurst see Banjul, Gam. E1 64
Bathurst, N.B., Can. E8 106
Bathurst, S. Afr. I8 66
Bathurst, Cape, c., N.T., Can. B7 96
Bathurst Inlet, N.T., Can. C11 96
Bathurst Inlet, b., N.T., Can. C11 96
Bathurst Island, i., Austl. B6 68
Bathurst Island, i., N.T., Can. A12 96
Batia, Benin F10 64
Batié, Burkina G8 64
Bāṭin, Wādī al-, val., Asia G9 48
Batkanu, S.L. G3 64
Batlow, Austl. J8 70
Batman, Tur. C6 48
Batna, Alg. C14 62
Baṭn al-Ghūl, Jord. I5 50
Batoche Rectory National Historic Site, hist., Sk., Can. F8 104
Baton Rouge, La., U.S. L5 114
Batouri, Cam. H9 54
Batovi, Braz. C2 79
Baṭrā (Petra), hist., Jord. H4 50
Batson, Tx., U.S. I12 116
Batticaloa, Sri L. I6 46
Battle, stm., Can. F10 96
Battle Creek, Ia., U.S. I12 118
Battle Creek, Mi., U.S. H10 110
Battle Creek, Ne., U.S. J10 118
Battle Ground, In., U.S. B10 114
Battle Ground, Wa., U.S. E3 122
Battle Harbour, Nf., Can. F21 96
Battle Lake, Mn., U.S. E12 118
Battlement Mesa, mtn., Co., U.S. E8 120
Battle Mountain, Nv., U.S. D9 124
Battonya, Hung. I21 10
Batu, mtn., Eth. G8 56
Batu, Kepulauan, is., Indon. O5 40
Batumi, Geor. I6 26
Batu Pahat, Malay. N7 40
Baturité, Braz. D11 76
Bat Yam, Isr. D3 50

Name	Map Ref.	Page
Baubau, Indon.	G7	38
Baud, Fr.	E3	14
Baudette, Mn., U.S.	B1	110
Baudó, stm., Col.	E4	84
Bauld, Cape, c., Nf., Can.	A18	106
Baume-les-Dames, Fr.	E13	14
Baures, Bol.	E10	82
Baures, stm., Bol.	E10	82
Bauru, Braz.	G4	79
Baús, Braz.	E2	79
Bauska, Lat.	E7	22
Bautzen, Ger.	D14	10
Bauxite, Ar., U.S.	H4	114
Bavaria see Bayern, state, Ger.	F11	10
Bavispe, Mex.	B5	90
Bavispe, stm., Mex.	C5	90
Bavleny, Russia	E22	22
Bawdwin, Myan.	C4	40
Bawku, Ghana	F9	64
Baxian, China	D4	32
Baxley, Ga., U.S.	H4	112
Baxter, Ia., U.S.	I2	110
Baxter, Mn., U.S.	D1	110
Baxter, Tn., U.S.	F11	114
Baxter Springs, Ks., U.S.	N13	118
Baxterville, Ms., U.S.	K7	114
Bay, Ar., U.S.	G6	114
Bayamo, Cuba	D6	94
Bayamón, P.R.	E11	94
Bayan Har Shan, mts., China	E6	30
Bayano, Lago, res., Pan.	C3	84
Bayan Obo, China	C9	30
Bayard, Ia., U.S.	J13	118
Bayard, Ne., U.S.	J4	118
Bayard, N.M., U.S.	L8	120
Bayard, W.V., U.S.	H7	108
Bayboro, N.C., U.S.	D10	112
Bay Bulls, Nf., Can.	E21	106
Bayburt, Tur.	A6	48
Bay City, Mi., U.S.	G12	110
Bay City, Or., U.S.	E2	122
Bay City, Tx., U.S.	K11	116
Bay de Verde, Nf., Can.	D21	106
Baydhabo, Som.	H9	56
Bay du Nord, stm., Nf., Can.	E18	106
Bayerische Alpen, mts., Eur.	H11	10
Bayern, state, Ger.	F11	10
Bayeux, Fr.	C6	14
Bayfield, Co., U.S.	G9	120
Bayfield, Wi., U.S.	D5	110
Bayfield, Île, i., P.Q., Can.	A15	106
Bayiji, China	A6	34
Bayingzi, China	B8	32
Bay L'Argent, Nf., Can.	E19	106
Bay Minette, Al., U.S.	L9	114
Bayombong, Phil.	m19	39b
Bayon, Fr.	D13	14
Bayonne, Fr.	I5	14
Bayou Bodcau Reservoir, res., La., U.S.	J3	114
Bayou Cane, La., U.S.	M6	114
Bayou D'Arbonne Lake, res., La., U.S.	J4	114
Bayou La Batre, Al., U.S.	L8	114
Bayovar, Peru	A1	82
Bay Port, Mi., U.S.	G12	110
Bayport, Mn., U.S.	E3	110
Bayreuth, Ger.	F11	10
Bayrischzell, Ger.	H12	10
Bay Roberts, Nf., Can.	E20	106
Bayrūt (Beirut), Leb.	A5	50
Bay Saint Louis, Ms., U.S.	L7	114
Bay Shore, N.Y., U.S.	G13	108
Bayside, On., Can.	F18	110
Bay Springs, Ms., U.S.	K7	114
Bayt al-Faqīh, Yemen	G3	47
Bayt Jinn, Syria	B5	50
Bayt Lahm (Bethlehem), W.B.	E4	50
Bayt Mirī, Leb.	A5	50
Baytown, Tx., U.S.	J12	116
Bayzo, Niger	E12	64
Baza, Spain	H9	16
Bazaruto, Ilha do, i., Moz.	C12	66
Bazas, Fr.	H6	14
Bazdār, Pak.	G1	44
Bazi, China	K2	34
Bazine, Ks., U.S.	M8	118
Be, Nosy, i., Madag.	n23	67b
Beach, N.D., U.S.	E3	118
Beach Haven, N.J., U.S.	H12	108
Beachville, On., Can.	G15	110
Beacon, N.Y., U.S.	F13	108
Beacon Hill, Wa., U.S.	D3	122
Beaconsfield, Austl.	M7	70
Beagle Gulf, b., Austl.	B6	68
Beagle Reef, rf., Austl.	C4	68
Bealanana, Madag.	o23	67b
Beale, Cape, c., B.C., Can.	I9	102
Bear, stm., Ca., U.S.	E4	124
Bear, stm., Sk., Can.	D10	104
Bear, stm., U.S.	B5	120
Bear Bay, b., N.T., Can.	A15	96
Bear Cove, B.C., Can.	G7	102
Bearden, Ar., U.S.	I4	114
Beardmore, On., Can.	G15	96
Beardstown, Il., U.S.	B6	114
Beardy and Okemasis Indian Reserves, Sk., Can.	F8	104
Bear Head Lake, l., Mb., Can.	C18	104
Bear Island, i., Ant.	C11	73
Bear Island, i., Mb., Can.	D16	104
Bear Island see Bjørnøya, i., Nor.	B2	24
Bear Lake, B.C., Can.	A8	102
Bear Lake, l., Ab., Can.	B15	102
Bear Lake, l., B.C., Can.	A8	102
Bear Lake, l., Mb., Can.	C18	104
Bear Lake, l., U.S.	C5	120
Bear Mountain, mtn., Or., U.S.	G3	122
Béarn, hist. reg., Fr.	I6	14
Bear River, N.S., Can.	H8	106
Bear River Range, mts., U.S.	C5	120
Beartooth Pass, Wy., U.S.	F16	122
Bear Town, Ms., U.S.	K6	114
Beasain, Spain	B9	16
Beas de Segura, Spain	G9	16
Beata, Cabo, c., Dom. Rep.	F9	94
Beata, Isla, i., Dom. Rep.	F9	94
Beaton, B.C., Can.	G17	102
Beatrice, Al., U.S.	K9	114
Beatrice, Ne., U.S.	K11	118
Beatrice, Zimb.	B10	66
Beattie, Ks., U.S.	L11	118
Beatton, stm., B.C., Can.	E8	96
Beatty, Nv., U.S.	H9	124
Beattyville, Ky., U.S.	B3	112
Beaucaire, Fr.	I11	14
Beauce, reg., Fr.	D8	14
Beauceville, P.Q., Can.	A16	108
Beaudesert, Austl.	F10	70
Beaufort, N.C., U.S.	E10	112
Beaufort, S.C., U.S.	G6	112
Beaufort Sea, N.A.	B5	86
Beaufort West, S. Afr.	I6	66
Beaugency, Fr.	E8	14
Beauharnois, P.Q., Can.	B13	108
Beaumont, Ca., U.S.	K9	124
Beaumont, Fr.	C5	14
Beaumont, Ms., U.S.	K8	114
Beaumont, Nf., Can.	C18	106
Beaumont, Tx., U.S.	L2	114
Beaumont-sur-Sarthe, Fr.	D7	14
Beaune, Fr.	E11	14
Beauport, P.Q., Can.	F2	106
Beaupré, P.Q., Can.	E3	106
Beaupréau, Fr.	E5	14
Beaupré Lake, l., Sk., Can.	D7	104
Beaurepaire, Fr.	G12	14
Beauséjour, Mb., Can.	H18	104
Beauvais, Fr.	C9	14
Beauval, Sk., Can.	C7	104
Beauvoir-sur-Mer, Fr.	F4	14
Beaver, Ak., U.S.	C21	100
Beaver, Ok., U.S.	C6	116
Beaver, Pa., U.S.	G6	108
Beaver, Ut., U.S.	F4	120
Beaver, W.V., U.S.	B5	112
Beaver, stm., Can.	D7	96
Beaver, stm., Can.	D7	104
Beaver, stm., N.Y., U.S.	D11	108
Beaver, stm., Pa., U.S.	G6	108
Beaver, stm., Ut., U.S.	F4	120
Beaver City, Ne., U.S.	K8	118
Beaver Creek, Yk., Can.	E24	100
Beaver Crossing, Ne., U.S.	K10	118
Beaver Dam, Ky., U.S.	E10	114
Beaver Dam, Wi., U.S.	G7	110
Beaverdell, B.C., Can.	H15	102
Beaver Falls, Pa., U.S.	G6	108
Beaverhead, stm., Mt., U.S.	E13	122
Beaverhead Mountains, mts., U.S.	E12	122
Beaverhill Lake, l., Ab., Can.	D22	102
Beaver Hill Lake, l., Mb., Can.	D20	104
Beaver Island, i., Mi., U.S.	E10	110
Beaver Lake, l., Ab., Can.	C23	102
Beaver Lake, res., Ar., U.S.	F3	114
Beaver Lake Indian Reserve, Ab., Can.	C23	102
Beaverlodge, Ab., Can.	B15	102
Beaver Mountains, mts., Ak., U.S.	E16	100
Beaverton, Mi., U.S.	G11	110
Beaverton, On., Can.	F16	110
Beaverton, Or., U.S.	E3	122
Beāwar, India	G6	44
Beazley, Arg.	G5	80
Bebedouro, Braz.	F4	79
Bebeji, Nig.	F14	64
Becal, Mex.	G14	90
Bécancour, stm., P.Q., Can.	A15	108
Bečej, Yugo.	D4	20
Beceni, Rom.	D10	20
Becerro, Cayos, is., Hond.	B11	92
Béchar, Alg.	E9	62
Bechater, Tun.	L4	18
Bechyně, Czech Rep.	F14	10
Beckley, W.V., U.S.	J5	108
Beckum, Ger.	D8	10
Beckville, Tx., U.S.	J2	114
Becky Peak, mtn., Nv., U.S.	E11	124
Bédarieux, Fr.	I10	14
Bedele, Eth.	M9	60
Bedeque Bay, b., P.E., Can.	F10	106
Bedford, Ia., U.S.	K13	118
Bedford, In., U.S.	D10	114
Bedford, Ky., U.S.	D11	114
Bedford, Pa., U.S.	G8	108
Bedford, P.Q., Can.	B14	108
Bedford, Va., U.S.	B7	112
Bedfordshire, co., Eng., U.K.	I13	8
Bedias, Tx., U.S.	I11	116
Bednodemjanovsk, Russia	H26	22
Beebe, Ar., U.S.	G5	114
Beech, stm., Tn., U.S.	G8	114
Beech Creek, Ky., U.S.	E9	114
Beecher, Il., U.S.	I8	110
Beech Fork, stm., Ky., U.S.	E11	114
Beech Grove, In., U.S.	C10	114
Beechworth, Austl.	K7	70
Beechy, Sk., Can.	H7	104
Beecroft Head, c., Austl.	J9	70
Beemer, Ne., U.S.	J11	118
Beenleigh, Austl.	F10	70
Bee Ridge, Fl., U.S.	L4	112
Beersheba see Be'ér Sheva', Isr.	F3	50
Beersheba Springs, Tn., U.S.	G11	114
Be'ér Sheva' (Beersheba), Isr.	F3	50
Beestekraal, S. Afr.	E8	66
Beethoven Peninsula, pen., Ant.	C12	73
Beetz, Lac, l., P.Q., Can.	B11	106
Beeville, Tx., U.S.	K9	116
Befale, Zaire	A4	58
Befandriana, Madag.	o23	67b
Befasy, Madag.	r21	67b
Befotaka, Madag.	s22	67b
Bega, Austl.	K8	70
Bega (Begej), stm., Eur.	D5	20
Begej (Bega), stm., Eur.	D4	20
Beggs, Ok., U.S.	D10	116
Begičevskij, Russia	H21	22
Begoro, Ghana	H9	64
Begunicy, Russia	B12	22
Begusarai, India	H12	44
Behbahān, Iran	F11	48
Behshahr, Iran	C12	48
Bei, stm., China	K2	34
Bei'an, China	B12	30
Beida see Al-Baydā', Libya	B5	56
Beidaihe, China	D7	32
Beigi, Eth.	M8	60
Beihai, China	D10	40
Beijing (Peking), China	D4	32
Beijing Shi (Peking Shih), China	C10	30
Beikan, China	C10	34
Beiling, China	K4	34
Beinwil, Switz.	D8	13
Beipan, stm., China	F8	30
Beipiao, China	B8	32
Beiqi, China	C10	32
Beira, Moz.	B12	66
Beira Baixa, hist. reg., Port.	F4	16
Beira Litoral, hist. reg., Port.	E3	16
Beirut see Bayrūt, Leb.	A5	50
Beiseker, Ab., Can.	F21	102
Beishan, China	B10	40
Bei Shan, mts., China	C6	30
Beisu, China	E2	32
Beitang, China	D5	32
Beitbridge, Zimb.	D10	66
Beixinzhen, China	D10	34
Beizhen, China	B9	32
Beja, Port.	G4	16
Béja, Tun.	M4	18
Bejaïa (Bougie), Alg.	B13	62
Béjar, Spain	E6	16
Bejuco, Pan.	C3	84
Bejuma, Ven.	B8	84
Bekabad, Uzb.	I11	26
Bekdaš, Turk.	I8	26
Békés, Hung.	I21	10
Békés, co., Hung.	I20	10
Békéscsaba, Hung.	I21	10
Bekilli, Tur.	K13	20
Bekily, Madag.	t21	67b
Bekitro, Madag.	t21	67b
Bekkaria, Alg.	N3	18
Bekkevoort, Bel.	G6	12
Bekodoka, Madag.	p21	67b
Bekoji, Eth.	N10	60
Bela, India	H9	44
Bela, Pak.	G2	44
Bělaazěrsk, Bela.	I8	22
Belabolo, Sudan	M3	60
Bela Crkva, Yugo.	E5	20
Bel Air, Md., U.S.	H10	108
Belaja, stm., Russia	G9	26
Belaja Berëzka, Russia	I16	22
Bélanger, stm., Mb., Can.	E17	104
Bela Palanka, Yugo.	F6	20
Belarus, ctry., Eur.	E13	4
Belau see Palau, ctry., Oc.	E9	38
Belavenona, Madag.	t22	67b
Bela Vista, Braz.	B10	80
Bela Vista, Moz.	F11	66
Bela Vista de Goiás, Braz.	D4	79
Bela Vista do Paraíso, Braz.	G3	79
Belawan, Indon.	M5	40
Belbubulo, Sudan	M8	60
Belchatów, Pol.	D19	10
Belcher, La., U.S.	J3	114
Belcherāgh, Afg.	C1	44
Belcher Islands, is., N.T., Can.	E17	96
Belcourt, N.D., U.S.	C8	118
Belding, Mi., U.S.	G10	110
Beled Weyne, Som.	H10	56
Belém, Braz.	D9	76
Belén, Arg.	D5	80
Belén, Chile	H7	82
Belén, Col.	D6	84
Belén, Nic.	F9	92
Belen, N.M., U.S.	J10	120
Belén, Para.	B10	80
Belén, Ur.	F10	80
Belén, stm., Arg.	D5	80
Belén de Escobar, Arg.	H9	80
Belfast, Me., U.S.	C17	108
Belfast, N. Ire., U.K.	G8	8
Belfast, S. Afr.	E10	66
Belfield, N.D., U.S.	E4	118
Belfort, Fr.	E13	14
Belfry, Ky., U.S.	B4	112
Belfry, Mt., U.S.	E16	122
Belgaum, India	E3	46
Belgium, ctry., Eur.	E8	4
Belgorod, Russia	G5	26
Belgrade, Mn., U.S.	F12	118
Belgrade, Mt., U.S.	E14	122
Belgrade, Ne., U.S.	J9	118
Belgrade see Beograd, Yugo.	E4	20
Belhaven, N.C., U.S.	D10	112
Beli Drim, stm., Eur.	G4	20
Beli Manastir, Cro.	D2	20
Belington, W.V., U.S.	H7	108
Belitung, i., Indon.	F4	38
Belize, ctry., N.A.	I15	90
Belize, stm., Belize	I15	90
Belize City, Belize	I15	90
Belize Inlet, b., B.C., Can.	F7	102
Belknap Crater, crat., Or., U.S.	F4	122
Belkofski, Ak., U.S.	I13	100
Bell, stm., P.Q., Can.	G17	96
Bell, stm., Yk., Can.	C26	100
Bella Bella, B.C., Can.	E6	102
Bellac, Fr.	F8	14
Bella Coola, B.C., Can.	E8	102
Bella Coola, stm., B.C., Can.	E8	102
Bella Flor, Bol.	D8	82
Bellair, Fl., U.S.	I5	112
Bellaire, Mi., U.S.	F10	110
Bellaire, Oh., U.S.	G6	108
Bellaire, Tx., U.S.	J11	116
Bellamy, Al., U.S.	J8	114
Bellary, India	E4	46
Bella Unión, Ur.	F10	80
Bella Vista, Arg.	E9	80
Bella Vista, Arg.	D6	80
Bella Vista, Para.	B10	80
Bellavista, Peru	A1	82
Bellavista, Peru	B3	82
Belle, Mo., U.S.	D5	114
Bellé, Sen.	D3	64
Belle, W.V., U.S.	I5	108
Belle, stm., Mi., U.S.	H13	110
Belle Bay, b., Nf., Can.	E18	106
Bellefontaine, Oh., U.S.	G3	108
Bellefonte, Pa., U.S.	G9	108
Belle Fourche, S.D., U.S.	G4	118
Belle Fourche, stm., U.S.	G4	118
Bellegarde, Fr.	F12	14
Belle Glade, Fl., U.S.	M6	112
Belle-Île, i., Fr.	E3	14
Belle Isle, i., Nf., Can.	F21	96
Belle Isle, Strait of, strt., Nf., Can.	A17	106
Bellême, Fr.	D7	14
Belleoram, Nf., Can.	E18	106
Belle Plaine, Ia., U.S.	I3	110
Belle Plaine, Ks., U.S.	N10	118
Belle Plaine, Mn., U.S.	F2	110
Belle-Plaine, Sk., Can.	H9	104
Belleview, Fl., U.S.	J4	112
Belleville, Il., U.S.	D7	114
Belleville, Ks., U.S.	L10	118
Belleville, On., Can.	C9	108
Belleville, Pa., U.S.	G9	108
Belleville, Wi., U.S.	H6	110
Belleville-sur-Saône, Fr.	F11	14
Bellevue, Ab., Can.	H20	102
Bellevue, Ia., U.S.	H5	110
Bellevue, Id., U.S.	G11	122
Bellevue, Mi., U.S.	H10	110
Bellevue, Ne., U.S.	J12	118
Bellevue, Oh., U.S.	F4	108
Bellevue, Tx., U.S.	F8	116
Bellevue, Wa., U.S.	C3	122
Belley, Fr.	G12	14
Bellingen, Austl.	H10	70
Bellingham, Eng., U.K.	F11	8
Bellingham, Mn., U.S.	F11	118
Bellingham, Wa., U.S.	B3	122
Bellingshausen, sci., Ant.	B1	73
Bellingshausen Sea, Ant.	C11	73
Bellinzona, Switz.	F11	13
Bell Island, i., Nf., Can.	E21	106
Bell Island, i., Nf., Can.	B18	106
Bell Island Hot Springs, Ak., U.S.	B3	102
Bellmead, Tx., U.S.	H9	116
Bello, Col.	D5	84
Bellot Strait, strt., N.T., Can.	B14	96
Bellows Falls, Vt., U.S.	D14	108
Bell Peninsula, pen., N.T., Can.	D16	96
Bells, Tn., U.S.	G7	114
Bells, Tx., U.S.	F10	116
Bells Corners, On., Can.	B11	108
Belluno, Italy	C7	18
Bell Ville, Arg.	G7	80
Bellville, Oh., U.S.	G4	108
Bellville, Tx., U.S.	J10	116
Bellwood, Ne., U.S.	J10	118
Bellwood, Pa., U.S.	G8	108
Belly, stm., N.A.	H21	102
Belmond, Ia., U.S.	H2	110
Belmont, Mb., Can.	I15	104
Belmont, Ms., U.S.	H8	114
Belmont, N.H., U.S.	D15	108
Belmont, N.S., Can.	G10	106
Belmont, N.Y., U.S.	E8	108
Belmont, S. Afr.	G7	66
Belmont, S.C., U.S.	E5	112
Belmont, Wi., U.S.	H5	110
Belmonte, Braz.	C9	79
Belmonte, Port.	E4	16
Belmopan, Belize	I15	90
Belmullet, Ire.	G3	8
Belo, Madag.	q21	67b
Belogorsk, Russia	G17	28
Belo Horizonte, Braz.	E7	79
Beloit, Ks., U.S.	L9	118
Beloit, Wi., U.S.	H6	110
Beloje, ozero, l., Russia	A20	22
Beloje more (White Sea), Russia	D5	26
Belomorsk, Russia	E4	26
Belomorsko-Baltijskij kanal, Russia	I24	6
Beloomut, Russia	G22	22
Belorečensk, Russia	I5	26
Beloreck, Russia	G9	26
Belorussia see Belarus, ctry., Eur.	E13	4
Belot, Lac, l., N.T., Can.	C31	100
Belousovo, Russia	F19	22
Bel'ov, Russia	H19	22
Belo Vale, Braz.	F6	79
Belovo, Russia	G9	28
Beloz'orsk, Russia	A20	22
Belpre, Oh., U.S.	H5	108
Belspring, Va., U.S.	B6	112
Belt, Mt., U.S.	C15	122
Belton, Mo., U.S.	D2	114
Belton, S.C., U.S.	E4	112
Belton, Tx., U.S.	H9	116
Beltrán, Arg.	D6	80
Belucha, gora, mtn., Asia	H15	26
Belūr, India	G10	42
Belvès, Fr.	H8	14
Belvidere, Il., U.S.	H7	110
Belvidere, N.J., U.S.	G11	108
Belview, Mn., U.S.	G12	118
Belvís de la Jara, Spain	F7	16
Belyando, stm., Austl.	C7	70
Belyj, Russia	F15	22
Belyj, ostrov, i., Russia	C12	26
Belyje Berega, Russia	H17	22
Belyje Stolby, Russia	F20	22
Belyj Gorodok, Russia	E20	22
Belyj Luch, stm., Russia	D27	22
Belzoni, Ms., U.S.	I6	114
Bemarivo, Madag.	r21	67b
Bemavo, Madag.	r21	67b
Bembéréké, Benin	F11	64
Bement, Il., U.S.	C8	114
Bemidji, Mn., U.S.	C1	110
Bemis, Tn., U.S.	G8	114
Benāb, Iran	C9	48
Bena-Dibele, Zaire	B4	58
Benagerie, Austl.	H4	70
Benahmed, Mor.	D7	62
Benalla, Austl.	K6	70
Benares see Vārānasi, India	H10	44
Ben Arous, Tun.	B16	62
Benavente, Spain	C6	16
Benavides, Tx., U.S.	L8	116
Ben Badis, Alg.	K11	16
Ben Bolt, Tx., U.S.	L8	116
Bencubbin, Austl.	F3	68
Bend, Or., U.S.	F4	122
Bendaja, Lib.	H4	64
Bende, Nig.	I13	64
Bendemeer, Austl.	H9	70
Bendigo, Austl.	K6	70
Bendugu, S.L.	G4	64
Bēne, Lat.	E6	22
Bene Beraq, Isr.	D3	50
Benedito Leite, Braz.	E10	76
Benenitra, Madag.	s21	67b
Benešov, Czech Rep.	F14	10
Benevento, Italy	H9	18
Benfeld, Fr.	D14	14
Bengal, Bay of, b., Asia	J14	44
Ben Gardane, Tun.	D16	62
Bengbu, China	C6	34
Benghazi see Banghāzī, Libya	B5	56
Ben Giang, Viet.	G9	40
Bengkalis, Indon.	N7	40
Bengkulu, Indon.	F3	38
Bengough, Sk., Can.	I9	104
Benguela, Ang.	D2	58
Benguerir, Mor.	D7	62
Benham, Ky., U.S.	C4	112
Beni, Zaire	A5	58
Beni, dept., Bol.	E9	82
Beni, stm., Bol.	D9	82
Béni Abbas, Alg.	E9	62
Benicarló, Spain	E12	16
Benicito, stm., Bol.	D9	82
Benima, C.A.R.	O2	60
Beni-Mellal, Mor.	D7	62
Benin (Bénin), ctry., Afr.	G7	54
Benin, Bight of, Afr.	G7	54
Benin City, Nig.	H12	64
Beni Saf, Alg.	J10	16
Benissa, Spain	G12	16
Benito, Mb., Can.	G13	104
Benito Juárez, Arg.	I9	80
Benito Juárez, Presa, res., Mex.	I12	90
Benjakoni, Bela.	G8	22
Benjamin, Tx., U.S.	F7	116
Benjamín Aceval, Para.	C10	80
Benjamin Constant, Braz.	J7	84
Benjamín Hill, Mex.	B4	90
Benjamín Zorrilla, Arg.	J6	80
Benkelman, Ne., U.S.	K6	118
Benld, Il., U.S.	C7	114
Ben Lomond, Ca., U.S.	G3	124
Ben Mehidi, Alg.	M2	18
Benndale, Ms., U.S.	L8	114
Bennet, Ne., U.S.	K11	118
Bennetta, ostrov, i., Russia	B21	28
Bennett Lake, l., Can.	F27	100
Bennett Lake, l., Mb., Can.	E18	104
Bennettsville, S.C., U.S.	E7	112
Bennington, Ks., U.S.	L10	118
Bennington, Vt., U.S.	E13	108
Benniu, China	D8	34
Benoit, Ms., U.S.	I5	114
Benoni, S. Afr.	F9	66
Bénoué (Benue), stm., Afr.	G9	54
Benque Viejo del Carmen, Belize	I15	90
Bensheim, Ger.	F8	10
Ben-Slimane, Mor.	D7	62
Ben Smih, Alg.	M2	18
Benson, Az., U.S.	M6	120
Benson, Mn., U.S.	F12	118
Benson, N.C., U.S.	D8	112
Bentinck Island, i., Austl.	C7	68
Bentiu, Sudan	M5	60
Bentley, Ab., Can.	E20	102
Bento Gomes, stm., Braz.	G13	82
Bento Gonçalves, Braz.	E13	80
Benton, Ar., U.S.	H4	114
Benton, Il., U.S.	E8	114
Benton, Ky., U.S.	F8	114
Benton, La., U.S.	J3	114
Benton, Mo., U.S.	E7	114
Benton, Ms., U.S.	J6	114
Benton, Pa., U.S.	F10	108
Benton, Tn., U.S.	D2	112
Benton, Wi., U.S.	H5	110
Benton City, Wa., U.S.	D6	122
Bentong, Malay.	M6	40
Benton Harbor, Mi., U.S.	H9	110
Bentonia, Ms., U.S.	J6	114
Bentonville, Ar., U.S.	F2	114
Ben Tre, Viet.	I9	40
Benue (Bénoué), stm., Afr.	G8	54
Ben Wheeler, Tx., U.S.	G11	116
Benxi (Penhsi), China	B11	32
Beograd (Belgrade), Yugo.	E4	20
Beowawe, Nv., U.S.	D9	124
Beppu, Japan	N6	36
Bequia, i., St. Vin.	H14	94
Beramanja, Madag.	n23	67b
Berat, Alb.	I3	20
Berau, Teluk, b., Indon.	F9	38
Beravina, Madag.	q21	67b
Berazino, Bela.	H11	22
Berazino, Bela.	G11	22
Berbera, Som.	F10	56
Berbérati, C.A.R.	H4	56
Berbice, stm., Guy.	D14	84
Berchtesgaden, Ger.	H13	10
Berclair, Tx., U.S.	K9	116
Berdigest'ach, Russia	E17	28
Berdsk, Russia	G8	28
Berdyans'k, Ukr.	H5	26
Berdychiv, Ukr.	H3	26
Berea, Ky., U.S.	B2	112
Berea, Oh., U.S.	F5	108
Berea, S.C., U.S.	E4	112
Berehomet, Ukr.	A9	20
Berehove, Ukr.	G22	10
Berekua, Dom.	G14	94
Berendejevo, Russia	E22	22
Berens, stm., Can.	F18	104
Berens Island, i., Mb., Can.	F17	104
Berens River, Mb., Can.	F17	104
Beresford, N.B., Can.	E8	106
Beresford, S.D., U.S.	H11	118
Berettyó (Barcău), stm., Eur.	B5	20
Berevo, Madag.	q21	67b
Berezajka, Russia	D16	22
Berezniki, Russia	F9	26
Berezyne, Ukr.	C13	20
Berg, Nor.	G15	6
Berga, Spain	C13	16
Bergama, Tur.	J11	20
Bergamo, Italy	D4	18
Bergantín, Ven.	B10	84
Bergara, Spain	B9	16
Bergby, Swe.	K15	6
Bergen (Mons), Bel.	H4	12
Bergen, Neth.	C6	12
Bergen, Nor.	K9	6
Bergen, N.Y., U.S.	D9	108
Bergen aan Zee, Neth.	C6	12
Bergen [auf Rügen], Ger.	A13	10
Bergen op Zoom, Neth.	E5	12
Bergerac, Fr.	H7	14
Bergisch Gladbach, Ger.	E7	10
Bergland, Mi., U.S.	D6	110
Bergoo, W.V., U.S.	I6	108
Bergsche Maas, stm., Neth.	E6	12
Bergsjö, Swe.	K15	6
Berguent, Mor.	C9	62
Bergues, Fr.	B9	14
Berhala, Selat, strt., Indon.	O8	40
Beringa, ostrov, i., Russia	F25	28
Bering Glacier, Ak., U.S.	F23	100
Bering Sea	C2	86
Bering Strait, strt.	D10	100
Berja, Spain	I9	16
Berkane, Mor.	C9	62
Berkeley, Ca., U.S.	G3	124
Berkeley Springs, W.V., U.S.	H8	108
Berkner Island, i., Ant.	C1	73
Berkshire, co., Eng., U.K.	J12	8
Berkshire Hills, hills, Ma., U.S.	E13	108
Berlaimont, Fr.	B10	14
Berland, stm., Ab., Can.	C17	102
Berlin, Ger.	C13	10
Berlin, Md., U.S.	I11	108
Berlin, N.H., U.S.	C15	108
Berlin, N.J., U.S.	H12	108
Berlin, Pa., U.S.	H8	108
Berlin, S. Afr.	I8	66
Berlin, Wi., U.S.	G7	110
Berlin, Mount, mtn., Ant.	C10	73
Berlinguet Inlet, b., N.T., Can.	B15	96
Berlin Lake, res., Oh., U.S.	F5	108
Bermejillo, Mex.	E8	90
Bermejo, Arg.	F5	80
Bermejo, stm., Arg.	F5	80
Bermejo, stm., S.A.	C9	80
Bermejo, Paso del, S.A.	G3	80
Bermen, Lac, l., P.Q., Can.	F19	96
Bermeo, Spain	B9	16
Bermuda, dep., N.A.	B12	88
Bern (Berne), Switz.	E7	13
Bern (Berne), state, Switz.	E8	13
Bernalda, Italy	I11	18
Bernalillo, N.M., U.S.	I10	120
Bernasconi, Arg.	I7	80
Bernau bei Berlin, Ger.	C13	10
Bernay, Fr.	C7	14
Bernburg, Ger.	D11	10
Berne, In., U.S.	B12	114
Berner Alpen, mts., Switz.	F7	13
Bernice, La., U.S.	J4	114
Bernie, Mo., U.S.	F7	114
Bernier Bay, b., N.T., Can.	B15	96
Bernina, mts., Eur.	F12	13
Bernina, Passo del, Switz.	F13	13
Bernina, Piz, mtn., Eur.	F16	14
Beromünster, Switz.	H8	10
Berón de Astrada, Arg.	D10	80
Beroroha, Madag.	r21	67b
Beroun, Czech Rep.	F14	10
Berounka, stm., Czech Rep.	F13	10
Berovo, Mac.	H6	20
Ber'ozovo, Russia	E11	26
Berrechid, Mor.	D7	62
Berri, Austl.	J4	70
Berrigan, Austl.	J6	70
Berriyyane, Alg.	D12	62
Berry, Al., U.S.	I9	114
Berry, hist. reg., Fr.	E9	14
Berry Creek, stm., Ab., Can.	F23	102
Berryessa, Lake, res., Ca., U.S.	F3	124
Berry Islands, is., Bah.	B6	94
Berryville, Ar., U.S.	F3	114
Berseba, Nmb.	F3	66
Bersenbrück, Ger.	C7	10
Bershad', Ukr.	A13	20
Berté, Lac, l., P.Q., Can.	B5	106
Bertha, Mn., U.S.	E12	118
Berthold, N.D., U.S.	C6	118
Berthoud, Co., U.S.	D11	120
Berthoud Pass, Co., U.S.	E11	120
Bertoua, Cam.	H9	54
Bertram, Tx., U.S.	I8	116
Bertrand, Mi., U.S.	A10	114
Bertrand, Ne., U.S.	K8	118
Beruri, Braz.	I12	84
Berwick, La., U.S.	M5	114
Berwick, Me., U.S.	D16	108
Berwick, N.S., Can.	G9	106
Berwick, Pa., U.S.	F10	108
Berwick-upon-Tweed, Eng., U.K.	F11	8
Berwyn, Il., U.S.	I8	110
Besalampy, Madag.	p21	67b
Besançon, Fr.	E13	14
Bešankovičy, Bela.	F12	22
Besbes, Alg.	M2	18
Beskid Mountains, mts., Eur.	F20	10
Beskra, Alg.	C13	62
Besnard Lake, l., Sk., Can.	C8	104
Besni, Tur.	C4	48
Besor, Nahal, val., Asia	F2	50
Bessarabia, hist. reg., Mol.	C12	20
Besse, Nig.	F12	64
Bessemer, Al., U.S.	I10	114
Bessemer, Mi., U.S.	D5	110
Bessemer, Pa., U.S.	G6	108
Bessemer City, N.C., U.S.	D5	112
Best'ach, Russia	E17	28
Bestobe, Kaz.	G12	26
Betafo, Madag.	q22	67b
Betanzos, Bol.	H9	82
Betanzos, Spain	B3	16
Betaré Oya, Cam.	G9	54
Betbetti, Sudan	J3	60
Bete Hor, Eth.	L10	60
Bétera, Spain	F11	16
Bétérou, Benin	G11	64
Bet Guvrin, Isr.	E3	50
Bet Ha'arava, W.B.	E5	50
Bethal, S. Afr.	F9	66
Bethalto, Il., U.S.	D6	114
Bethanien, Nmb.	F3	66
Bethany, Il., U.S.	C8	114
Bethany, Mo., U.S.	B2	114
Bethany, Ok., U.S.	D9	116
Bethel, Ak., U.S.	F14	100
Bethel, Ct., U.S.	F13	108
Bethel, Me., U.S.	C16	108
Bethel, N.C., U.S.	D9	112
Bethel, Oh., U.S.	I2	108
Bethel Acres, Ok., U.S.	D9	116
Bethel Springs, Tn., U.S.	G8	114
Bethesda, Oh., U.S.	G5	108
Bethlehem, Pa., U.S.	G11	108
Bethlehem, S. Afr.	G9	66
Bethlehem see Bayt Lahm, W.B.	E4	50
Bethlehem, W.V., U.S.	G6	108
Béthune, Fr.	B9	14
Bethune, S.C., U.S.	E6	112
Bethune, Sk., Can.	H9	104
Betijoque, Ven.	C7	84
Betioky, Madag.	s21	67b
Betlica, Russia	G16	22
Betong, Thai.	L6	40
Betoota, Austl.	E4	70
Betpak-Dala, des., Kaz.	H12	26
Betroka, Madag.	s22	67b
Bet Sh'ean, Isr.	C5	50
Bet Shemesh, Isr.	E4	50
Betsiamites, P.Q., Can.	D5	106
Betsiamites, stm., P.Q., Can.	C4	106
Betsiamites, Barrage, P.Q., Can.	C4	106
Betsiamites, Pointe de, c., P.Q., Can.	D5	106
Betsiamites, Réserve indienne de, P.Q., Can.	C5	106
Betsiboka, stm., Madag.	p22	67b
Betsioky, Madag.	r21	67b
Betsy Layne, Ky., U.S.	B4	112
Bettendorf, Ia., U.S.	I5	110
Bettles Field, Ak., U.S.	C19	100
Betūl, India	J7	44
Betzdorf, Ger.	E7	10
Beulah, Co., U.S.	F12	120
Beulah, Mi., U.S.	F9	110
Beulah, Ms., U.S.	I6	114
Beulah, N.D., U.S.	D6	118
Beulaville, N.C., U.S.	E9	112
B. Everett Jordan Lake, res., N.C., U.S.	D7	112
Beverley, Austl.	F3	68
Beverley, Eng., U.K.	H13	8
Beverly, Ma., U.S.	E16	108
Beverly Hills, Ca., U.S.	J7	124
Beverly Lake, l., N.T., Can.	D12	96
Beverwijk, Neth.	D6	12
Bevier, Mo., U.S.	C4	114
Bexley, Oh., U.S.	H4	108
Beyçayın, Tur.	I10	20
Beylul, Erit.	H3	47
Beypazarı, Tur.	G14	4
Beyşehir Gölü, l., Tur.	H14	4
Bezaha, Madag.	s21	67b
Bežanicy, Russia	E12	22
Bezau, Aus.	H9	10
Bežeck, Russia	D19	22
Bezerra, stm., Braz.	B5	79
Béziers, Fr.	I10	14
Bezmein, Turk.	B15	48
Bhadrak, India	J12	44
Bhadrāvati, India	F3	46
Bhāg, Pak.	F2	44
Bhāgalpur, India	H12	44
Bhakkar, Pak.	E4	44
Bhaktapur, Nepal	G11	44
Bhamo, Myan.	B4	40
Bhandāra, India	J8	44
Bharatpur, India	G7	44
Bharatpur, Nepal	G11	44
Bharūch, India	J5	44
Bhātāpāra, India	B6	46
Bhātpāra, India	I13	44
Bhāvnagar, India	J5	44
Bhawānipatna, India	C7	46
Bhera, Pak.	D5	44
Bhilai, India	J9	44
Bhīlwāra, India	H6	44
Bhind, India	G8	44
Bhiwandi, India	C2	46
Bhiwāni, India	F7	44
Bhongīr, India	D5	46
Bhopāl, India	I7	44
Bhubaneshwar, India	J11	44
Bhuj, India	I3	44
Bhusāwal, India	J6	44
Bhutan (Druk-Yul), ctry., Asia	D13	42
Bia, stm., Afr.	H8	64
Biá, stm., Braz.	I9	84
Bia, Phou, mtn., Laos	E7	40
Biabo, stm., Peru	B3	82
Biafra, Bight of, Afr.	H8	54

Name	Map Ref.	Page
Bonaventure, P.Q., Can.	D8	106
Bonaventure, stm., P.Q., Can.	D8	106
Bonaventure, Île, i., P.Q., Can.	D9	106
Bonavista, Nf., Can.	D20	106
Bonavista, Cape, c., Nf., Can.	D20	106
Bonavista Bay, b., Nf., Can.	D20	106
Bond, Ms., U.S.	L7	114
Bondeno, Italy	E6	18
Bondo, Zaire	H5	56
Bondoukou, C. Iv.	G8	64
Bonduel, Wi., U.S.	F7	110
Bone, Teluk, b., Indon.	F7	38
Bonesteel, S.D., U.S.	H9	118
Bonete, Cerro, mtn., Arg.	D4	80
Bonete Chico, Cerro, mtn., Arg.	E4	80
Bonga, Eth.	N9	60
Bongak, Sudan	N7	60
Bongandanga, Zaire	A4	58
Bongo, Massif des, mts., C.A.R.	M2	60
Bongor, Chad	F4	56
Bongouanou, C. Iv.	H7	64
Bonham, Tx., U.S.	F10	116
Bonhomme, Morne, mtn., Haiti	E8	94
Bonifacio, Fr.	m24	15a
Bonifacio, Strait of, strt., Eur.	H4	18
Bonifay, Fl., U.S.	L11	114
Bonilla Island, i., B.C., Can.	D4	102
Bonita, La., U.S.	J5	114
Bonita Springs, Fl., U.S.	M5	112
Bonito, Braz.	I13	82
Bonito, stm., Braz.	D3	79
Bonito, Pico, mtn., Hond.	B8	92
Bonito, Rio, stm., N.M., U.S.	K11	120
Bonkoukou, Niger	D11	64
Bonn, Ger.	E7	10
Bonne Bay (Woody Point), Nf., Can.	C16	106
Bonne Bay, b., Nf., Can.	C16	106
Bonneia, Eth.	O9	60
Bonner, Mt., U.S.	D12	122
Bonners Ferry, Id., U.S.	B9	122
Bonnet, Lac du, l., Mb., Can.	H19	104
Bonnétable, Fr.	D7	14
Bonne Terre, Mo., U.S.	E6	114
Bonnet Plume, stm., Yk., Can.	D27	100
Bonneval, Fr.	D8	14
Bonneville, Fr.	F13	14
Bonneville Peak, mtn., Id., U.S.	H13	122
Bonneville Salt Flats, pl., Ut., U.S.	D3	120
Bonnie Doone, N.C., U.S.	D8	112
Bonnie Rock, Austl.	F3	68
Bonny, Nig.	I13	64
Bonnyville, Ab., Can.	C24	102
Bono, Ar., U.S.	G6	114
Bonorva, Italy	I3	18
Bon Secour, Al., U.S.	L9	114
Bonshaw, P.E., Can.	F10	106
Bonthe, S.L.	H3	64
Bontoc, Phil.	m19	39b
Bon Wier, Tx., U.S.	L3	114
Bonyhád, Hung.	I18	10
Booischot, Bel.	F6	12
Bookaloo, Austl.	H2	70
Book Cliffs, clf, U.S.	E7	120
Booker, Tx., U.S.	C6	116
Boola, Gui.	G5	64
Boom, Bel.	F5	12
Boomarra, Austl.	B4	70
Boomer, W.V., U.S.	I5	108
Boonah, Austl.	G10	70
Boone, Ia., U.S.	H2	110
Boone, N.C., U.S.	C5	112
Boone, stm., Ia., U.S.	H2	110
Boones Mill, Va., U.S.	B7	112
Booneville, Ar., U.S.	G3	114
Booneville, Ky., U.S.	B3	112
Booneville, Ms., U.S.	H8	114
Boonsboro, Md., U.S.	H9	108
Boonville, Ca., U.S.	E2	124
Boonville, In., U.S.	D9	114
Boonville, Mo., U.S.	D4	114
Boonville, N.Y., U.S.	D11	108
Boopi, stm., Bol.	G8	82
Boorama, Som.	G9	56
Boorindal, Austl.	H7	70
Boorowa, Austl.	J8	70
Boosaaso, Som.	F10	56
Bootahnie Indian Reserve, B.C., Can.	G13	102
Booth, Al., U.S.	J10	114
Boothbay Harbor, Me., U.S.	D17	108
Boothia, Gulf of, b., N.T., Can.	B14	96
Boothia Peninsula, pen., N.T., Can.	B14	96
Boothville, La., U.S.	M7	114
Booué, Gabon	B2	58
Bophuthatswana, hist. reg., S. Afr.	F7	66
Bopo, Nig.	H13	64
Boquerón, Pan.	I12	92
Boquerón, dept., Para.	B8	80
Boquilla, Presa de la, res., Mex.	D7	90
Boquillas del Carmen, Mex.	C8	90
Bor, Czech Rep.	F12	10
Bor, Russia	E27	22
Bor, Sudan	N6	60
Bor, Tur.	C3	48
Bor, Yugo.	E6	20
Boraha, Nosy, i., Madag.	p23	67b
Borah Peak, mtn., Id., U.S.	F12	122
Borås, Swe.	M13	6
Borāzjān, Iran	G11	48
Borba, Braz.	J13	84
Borba, Port.	G4	16
Borda, Cape, c., Austl.	J2	70
Bordeaux, Fr.	H6	14
Borden, Sk., Can.	F7	104
Borden Peninsula, pen., N.T., Can.	B16	96
Borders, prov., Scot., U.K.	F10	8
Bordertown, Austl.	K4	70
Borđeyri, Ice.	B3	6a
Bordighera, Italy	F2	18
Bordj Bou Arreridj, Alg.	B13	62
Bordj Menaïel, Alg.	B12	62
Bordj Omar Idriss, Alg.	F14	62
Bordj Sidi Toui, Tun.	D16	62
Boreda, Eth.	N9	60
Borgå (Porvoo), Fin.	K19	6
Borger, Tx., U.S.	D5	116
Borgholm, Swe.	M15	6
Borgne, Lake, b., La., U.S.	L7	114
Borgosesia, Italy	D3	18
Borinskoje, Russia	I22	22
Borisoglebsk, Russia	G6	26
Borisoglebskij, Russia	D22	22
Borja, Peru	J4	84
Borkavičy, Bela.	F11	22
Borken, Ger.	D6	10
Borkum, i., Ger.	B6	10
Borlänge, Swe.	K14	6
Bormes-les-Mimosas, Fr.	I13	14
Bormio, Italy	C5	18
Borna, Ger.	D13	10
Borneo (Kalimantan), i., Asia	N11	40
Bornholm, i., Den.	N14	6
Boro, stm., Sudan	M3	60
Borodarou, Benin	F11	64
Borodino, Russia	F18	22
Borodino, Ukr.	C13	20
Borogoncy, Russia	E18	28
Boromo, Burkina	F8	64
Boron, Ca., U.S.	J8	124
Borovičі, Russia	C16	22
Borovsk, Russia	F19	22
Borrachudo, stm., Braz.	E6	79
Borrazópolis, Braz.	G3	79
Borriana, Spain	F11	16
Borroloola, Austl.	C7	68
Borș, Rom.	B5	20
Borșa, Rom.	B8	20
Borsad, India	I5	44
Borsod-Abaúj-Zemplén, co., Hung.	G21	10
Borth, Wales, U.K.	I9	8
Bort-les-Orgues, Fr.	G9	14
Boruca, C.R.	H11	92
Borūjen, Iran	F11	48
Borūjerd, Iran	E10	48
Borz'a, Russia	G15	28
Bosa, Italy	I3	18
Bosanska Dubica, Bos.	D11	18
Bosanska Gradiška, Bos.	D12	18
Bosanski Novi, Bos.	D11	18
Bosanski Šamac, Bos.	D2	20
Bosavi, Mount, mtn., Pap. N. Gui.	G11	38
Boscobel, Wi., U.S.	G5	110
Bose, China	C9	40
Boshan, China	G5	32
Boshoek, S. Afr.	E8	66
Boshrūyeh, Iran	E14	48
Bosna, stm., Bos.	E13	18
Bosnia and Herzegovina, ctry., Eur.	G11	4
Bosporus see İstanbul Boğazı, strt., Tur.	H13	20
Bosque Farms, N.M., U.S.	J10	120
Bossangoa, C.A.R.	G4	56
Bossé Bangou, Niger	E10	64
Bossembélé, C.A.R.	G4	56
Bossier City, La., U.S.	J3	114
Bosso, Dallol, val., Niger	E11	64
Bosten Hu, l., China	C4	30
Boston, Eng., U.K.	I13	8
Boston, Ga., U.S.	I3	112
Boston, Ma., U.S.	E15	108
Boston Bar, B.C., Can.	H13	102
Boston Mountains, mts., Ar., U.S.	G3	114
Boswell, In., U.S.	B9	114
Boswell, Ok., U.S.	E11	116
Boswell, Pa., U.S.	G7	108
Bosworth, Mo., U.S.	C3	114
Botād, India	I4	44
Botany Bay, b., Austl.	I9	70
Boteti, stm., Bots.	C6	66
Botha's Hill, S. Afr.	G10	66
Bothaville, S. Afr.	F8	66
Bothnia, Gulf of, b., Eur.	J17	6
Bothwell, On., Can.	H14	110
Botija, Ilha da, i., Braz.	J11	84
Botkins, Oh., U.S.	G2	108
Botoșani, Rom.	B10	20
Botoșani, co., Rom.	B10	20
Botrange, mtn., Bel.	H9	12
Botro, C. Iv.	H7	64
Botswana, ctry., Afr.	F4	58
Bottenhavet (Selkämeri), b., Eur.	K16	6
Bottenviken (Perämeri), b., Eur.	I18	6
Bottineau, N.D., U.S.	C7	118
Botucatu, Braz.	G4	79
Botwood, Nf., Can.	C18	106
Bouaflé, C. Iv.	H7	64
Bou Ahmed, Mor.	J6	16
Bouaké, C. Iv.	H7	64
Bouandougou, C. Iv.	G7	64
Bouar, C.A.R.	G4	56
Bou Arada, Tun.	M4	18
Bouârfa, Mor.	D10	62
Bouaye, Fr.	E5	14
Bou Bernous, Alg.	G9	62
Bouchegouf, Alg.	M2	18
Boucher, stm., P.Q., Can.	C4	106
Boucher, Lac, l., P.Q., Can.	A14	106
Bouches-du-Rhône, dept., Fr.	I12	14
Boudry, Switz.	E6	13
Boufarik, Alg.	B12	62
Bou Ficha, Tun.	M5	18
Bougainville, i., Pap. N. Gui.	I19	126
Bougouni, Mali	F6	64
Bougouriba, stm., Burkina	F8	64
Bou Hadjar, Alg.	M3	18
Bou Hajar, Tun.	N5	18
Bouïra, Alg.	B12	62
Boujad, Mor.	D7	62
Boujdour, Cap, c., W. Sah.	G3	62
Bou Kadir, Alg.	B11	62
Bou Khadra, Alg.	N3	18
Boukombé, Benin	F10	64
Boularderie Island, i., N.S., Can.	F13	106
Boulder, Co., U.S.	D11	120
Boulder, Mt., U.S.	D13	122
Boulder, stm., Mt., U.S.	D13	122
Boulder City, Nv., U.S.	I11	124
Bouli, stm., Burkina	E9	64
Boulia, Austl.	D3	70
Boulogne-Billancourt, Fr.	D9	14
Boulogne-sur-Gesse, Fr.	I7	14
Boulogne-sur-Mer, Fr.	B8	14
Boulouba, C.A.R.	N2	60
Boulouli, Mali	D5	64
Boulsa, Burkina	E9	64
Bouly, Maur.	D4	64
Boumalne, Mor.	E8	62
Boûmdeïd, Maur.	C5	64
Bouna, C. Iv.	G8	64
Boundary, Ak., U.S.	D24	100
Boundary Peak, mtn., Nv., U.S.	G7	124
Boundary Ranges, mts., N.A.	G27	100
Bountiful, Ut., U.S.	D5	120
Bounty Islands, is., N.Z.	M21	126
Bouqteb, Alg.	C11	62
Boura, Mali	E7	64
Bourbeuse, stm., Mo., U.S.	D5	114
Bourbon, In., U.S.	A10	114
Bourbon, Mo., U.S.	D5	114
Bourbon-Lancy, Fr.	F10	14
Bourbonnais, hist. reg., Fr.	F9	14
Bourbonne-les-Bains, Fr.	E12	14
Bourem, Mali	C9	64
Bourg, La., U.S.	M6	114
Bourganeuf, Fr.	G8	14
Bourg-en-Bresse, Fr.	F12	14
Bourges, Fr.	E9	14
Bourget, On., Can.	B11	108
Bourgogne (Burgundy), hist. reg., Fr.	E11	14
Bourgogne, Canal de, Fr.	E11	14
Bourgoin, Fr.	G12	14
Bourg-Saint-Andéol, Fr.	H11	14
Bourg-Saint-Maurice, Fr.	G13	14
Bourke, Austl.	H6	70
Bourne, Eng., U.K.	I13	8
Bournemouth, Eng., U.K.	K12	8
Bourzanga, Burkina	E9	64
Bou Saâda, Alg.	C13	62
Bou Salem, Tun.	M3	18
Bouse, Az., U.S.	K2	120
Bou Smail, Alg.	B12	62
Boussac, Fr.	F9	14
Bousso, Chad	F4	56
Boussouma, Burkina	E9	64
Bouteldja, Alg.	M3	18
Boutilimit, Maur.	C2	64
Bouvetøya, i., Ant.	A3	73
Bouza, Niger	D13	64
Bou Zadjar, Alg.	J10	16
Bøverdal, Nor.	K11	6
Bovey, Mn., U.S.	C2	110
Bovill, Id., U.S.	D9	122
Bovina, Tx., U.S.	E4	116
Bovril, Arg.	F9	80
Bow, stm., Ab., Can.	G22	102
Bow, stm., Sk., Can.	D9	104
Bowang, China	D7	34
Bowbells, N.D., U.S.	C5	118
Bowden, Ab., Can.	F20	102
Bowdle, S.D., U.S.	F8	118
Bowdon, Ga., U.S.	F1	112
Bowdon, N.D., U.S.	D8	118
Bowen, Arg.	H5	80
Bowen, Austl.	C8	70
Bowen, Il., U.S.	B5	114
Bowie, Az., U.S.	L7	120
Bowie, Md., U.S.	H10	108
Bowie, Tx., U.S.	F9	116
Bow Island, Ab., Can.	I3	104
Bowling Green, Fl., U.S.	L5	112
Bowling Green, Ky., U.S.	F10	114
Bowling Green, Mo., U.S.	C5	114
Bowling Green, Oh., U.S.	F3	108
Bowling Green, Va., U.S.	A9	112
Bowling Green, Cape, c., Austl.	B7	70
Bowman, Ga., U.S.	E3	112
Bowman, N.D., U.S.	E4	118
Bowman, S.C., U.S.	F6	112
Bowman, Mount, mtn., B.C., Can.	F13	102
Bowmanville, On., Can.	G17	110
Bowral, Austl.	J9	70
Bowron, stm., B.C., Can.	D12	102
Bowron Lake Provincial Park, B.C., Can.	D13	102
Bowsman, Mb., Can.	F13	104
Box Elder, Mt., U.S.	B15	122
Boxey, Nf., Can.	E18	106
Boxey Point, c., Nf., Can.	E18	106
Boxian, China	B4	34
Boxmeer, Neth.	E8	12
Boxodoi, China	A3	32
Boxtel, Neth.	E7	12
Boyacá, dept., Col.	E6	84
Boyalık, Tur.	H12	20
Boyang, China	G5	34
Boyce, La., U.S.	K4	114
Boyceville, Wi., U.S.	E3	110
Boyd, Mn., U.S.	G12	118
Boyd, Tx., U.S.	F9	116
Boyd's Cove, Nf., Can.	C19	106
Boydton, Va., U.S.	C8	112
Boyer, stm., Ia., U.S.	J12	118
Boyertown, Pa., U.S.	G11	108
Boykins, Va., U.S.	C9	112
Boyle, Ab., Can.	C22	102
Boyle, Ire.	H5	8
Boyle, Ms., U.S.	I6	114
Boylston, Al., U.S.	J10	114
Boyne, stm., Austl.	E9	70
Boyne, stm., Ire.	H7	8
Boyne, stm., Mb., Can.	I16	104
Boyne City, Mi., U.S.	E10	110
Boynton, Ok., U.S.	D11	116
Boynton Beach, Fl., U.S.	M6	112
Boysen Reservoir, res., Wy., U.S.	G17	122
Boys Ranch, Tx., U.S.	D4	116
Boyuibe, Bol.	I10	82
Bozel, Fr.	G13	14
Bozeman, Mt., U.S.	E14	122
Bozen see Bolzano, Italy	C6	18
Bozhen, China	E4	32
Bozoum, C.A.R.	G4	56
Bozovici, Rom.	E5	20
Bra, Italy	E2	18
Brabant, prov., Bel.	G6	12
Brabant Island, i., Ant.	B12	73
Brabant Lake, l., Sk., Can.	B11	104
Brač, Otok, i., Cro.	F11	18
Bracciano, Italy	G7	18
Bracciano, Lago di, l., Italy	G7	18
Bracebridge, On., Can.	E16	110
Brackendale, B.C., Can.	H11	102
Bracken Lake, l., Mb., Can.	E15	104
Brackettville, Tx., U.S.	J6	116
Braço do Norte, Braz.	E14	80
Brad, Rom.	C6	20
Bradenton, Fl., U.S.	L4	112
Bradford, Ar., U.S.	G5	114
Bradford, Il., U.S.	I6	110
Bradford, Oh., U.S.	G2	108
Bradford, On., Can.	F16	110
Bradford, Pa., U.S.	F8	108
Bradford, Tn., U.S.	F8	114
Bradford, Vt., U.S.	D14	108
Bradley, Ar., U.S.	I3	114
Bradley, Fl., U.S.	L5	112
Bradley, Il., U.S.	I8	110
Bradley, S.D., U.S.	F10	118
Bradore-Bay, P.Q., Can.	A16	106
Bradshaw, Ne., U.S.	K10	118
Bradshaw, W.V., U.S.	B5	112
Brady, Mt., U.S.	B14	122
Brady, Ne., U.S.	J7	118
Brady, Tx., U.S.	H7	116
Braga, Port.	D3	16
Bragado, Arg.	H8	80
Bragança, Braz.	D9	76
Bragança, Port.	D5	16
Bragança Paulista, Braz.	G5	79
Braham, Mn., U.S.	E2	110
Brāhmanbāria, Bngl.	I14	44
Brāhmani, stm., India	J11	44
Brahmapur, India	C8	46
Brahmaputra (Yarlung), stm., Asia	G15	44
Braich y Pwll, c., Wales, U.K.	I9	8
Braidwood, Austl.	J8	70
Braidwood, Il., U.S.	I7	110
Brăila, Rom.	D11	20
Brăila, co., Rom.	D11	20
Brainard, Ne., U.S.	J10	118
Braine-l'Alleud (Eigenbrakel), Bel.	G5	12
Braine-le-Comte ('s-Gravenbrakel), Bel.	G5	12
Brainerd, Mn., U.S.	D1	110
Brake, Ger.	B8	10
Brakwater, Nmb.	D3	66
Bralorne, B.C., Can.	G12	102
Braman, Ok., U.S.	C9	116
Brampton, On., Can.	G16	110
Bramsche, Ger.	C7	10
Branch, Nf., Can.	F20	106
Branchville, S.C., U.S.	F6	112
Branco, stm., Braz.	I13	82
Branco, stm., Braz.	C7	82
Branco, stm., Braz.	C11	82
Branco, stm., Braz.	C9	82
Branco, stm., Braz.	C11	82
Branco, stm., Braz.	H12	84
Brandberg, mtn., Nmb.	C2	66
Brandbu, Nor.	K12	6
Brandenburg, Ger.	C12	10
Brandenburg, Ky., U.S.	D10	114
Brandenburg, state, Ger.	C13	10
Brand-Erbisdorf, Ger.	E13	10
Brandon, Fl., U.S.	L4	112
Brandon, Mb., Can.	I15	104
Brandon, Ms., U.S.	J7	114
Brandon, S.D., U.S.	H11	118
Brandon, Vt., U.S.	D13	108
Brandon, Wi., U.S.	G7	110
Brandsen, Arg.	H9	80
Brandvlei, S. Afr.	H5	66
Brandýs nad Labem, Czech Rep.	E14	10
Branford, Fl., U.S.	J4	112
Braniewo, Pol.	A19	10
Branquinho, stm., Braz.	A6	82
Bransby, Austl.	G5	70
Bransfield Strait, strt., Ant.	B12	73
Brańsk, Pol.	C22	10
Br'ansk, Russia	H17	22
Branson, Mo., U.S.	F3	114
Brantford, On., Can.	G15	110
Brant Lake, N.Y., U.S.	D13	108
Brantley, Al., U.S.	K10	114
Brantville, N.B., Can.	E9	106
Branxholme, Austl.	K4	70
Bras d'Or Lake, l., N.S., Can.	G13	106
Brasiléia, Braz.	D7	82
Brasília, Braz.	C5	79
Brasília, Parque Nacional de, Braz.	C4	79
Brasília de Minas, Braz.	D6	79
Brașov, Rom.	D9	20
Brașov, co., Rom.	D8	20
Brasstown Bald, mtn., Ga., U.S.	E3	112
Břasy, Czech Rep.	F13	10
Bratca, Rom.	C6	20
Bratislava, Slvk.	G17	10
Bratsk, Russia	F12	28
Bratskoje vodochranilišče, res., Russia	F18	26
Brattleboro, Vt., U.S.	E14	108
Braulio Carrillo, Parque Nacional, C.R.	G10	92
Braúnas, Braz.	E7	79
Braunau [am Inn], Aus.	G13	10
Braunschweig (Brunswick), Ger.	C10	10
Brava, i., C.V.	m16	64a
Brava, Costa, Spain	D15	16
Brava, Laguna, l., Arg.	E4	80
Brava, Punta, c., Ur.	H10	80
Brave, Pa., U.S.	H6	108
Bravicea, Mol.	B12	20
Bravo, Cerro, mtn., Bol.	G9	82
Bravo, Cerro, mtn., Peru	A2	82
Bravo del Norte (Rio Grande), stm., N.A.	F6	98
Brawley, Ca., U.S.	L10	124
Brawley Peaks, mts., Nv., U.S.	F7	124
Bray, Ire.	H7	8
Bray Island, i., N.T., Can.	C17	96
Braymer, Mo., U.S.	C3	114
Brazeau, stm., Ab., Can.	E18	102
Brazeau, Mount, mtn., Ab., Can.	E17	102
Brazeau Dam, Ab., Can.	E19	102
Brazil, In., U.S.	C9	114
Brazil, ctry., S.A.	F9	74
Brazoria, Tx., U.S.	J11	116
Brazos, stm., Tx., U.S.	J11	116
Brazzaville, Congo	B3	58
Brčko, Bos.	E2	20
Brea, Ca., U.S.	K8	124
Breadalbane, Austl.	D3	70
Breakenridge, Mount, mtn., B.C., Can.	H13	102
Brea Pozo, Arg.	E7	80
Breaux Bridge, La., U.S.	L5	114
Breaza, Rom.	D9	20
Brécey, Fr.	D5	14
Brechin, Scot., U.K.	E11	8
Breckenridge, Co., U.S.	E10	120
Breckenridge, Mi., U.S.	G11	110
Breckenridge, Mn., U.S.	E11	118
Breckenridge, Mo., U.S.	C3	114
Breckenridge, Tx., U.S.	G8	116
Břeclav, Czech Rep.	G16	10
Brecon, Wales, U.K.	J10	8
Breda, Ia., U.S.	I13	118
Breda, Neth.	E6	12
Bredasdorp, S. Afr.	J5	66
Bredenbury, Sk., Can.	H12	104
Breese, Il., U.S.	D7	114
Breezand, Neth.	C6	12
Bregenz, Aus.	H9	10
Bréhal, Fr.	D5	14
Breiđafjörđur, b., Ice.	B2	6a
Brejo, Braz.	D10	76
Brejões, Braz.	B9	79
Brekken, Nor.	J12	6
Brekstad, Nor.	J11	6
Bremen, Ger.	B8	10
Bremen, Ga., U.S.	F1	112
Bremen, In., U.S.	A10	114
Bremen, Oh., U.S.	H4	108
Bremerhaven, Ger.	B8	10
Bremerton, Wa., U.S.	C3	122
Bremervörde, Ger.	B9	10
Bremond, Tx., U.S.	H10	116
Brem River, B.C., Can.	G10	102
Brenham, Tx., U.S.	I10	116
Brenner Pass, Eur.	H11	10
Brent, Al., U.S.	J9	114
Brent, Fl., U.S.	L9	114
Brentwood, N.Y., U.S.	G13	108
Brentwood, Tn., U.S.	F10	114
Brescia, Italy	D8	18
Breslau see Wrocław, Pol.	D17	10
Bresse, reg., Fr.	F12	14
Bressuire, Fr.	F6	14
Brèst, Bela.	C23	10
Brest, Fr.	D2	14
Bretagne (Brittany), hist. reg., Fr.	D3	14
Breteuil, Fr.	C9	14
Breteuil-sur-Iton, Fr.	D7	14
Breton, Ab., Can.	D20	102
Breton Islands, is., La., U.S.	M7	114
Breton Sound, strt., La., U.S.	M7	114
Brett, Cape, c., N.Z.	A5	72
Bretten, Ger.	F8	10
Breu, Rio do, stm., Braz.	I9	84
Breukelen, Neth.	D7	12
Brevard, N.C., U.S.	D4	112
Breves, Braz.	D8	76
Brevoort Island, i., N.T., Can.	D20	96
Brewarrina, Austl.	G7	70
Brewer, Me., U.S.	C18	108
Brewster, Ks., U.S.	L6	118
Brewster, Mn., U.S.	H12	118
Brewster, Ne., U.S.	J8	118
Brewster, Oh., U.S.	G5	108
Brewster, Wa., U.S.	B6	122
Brewster, Kap, c., Grnld.	B17	86
Brewster, Lake, l., Austl.	I7	70
Brewton, Al., U.S.	K9	114
Brežice, Slvn.	D10	18
Brézina, Alg.	D11	62
Breznik, Bul.	G6	20
Bria, C.A.R.	N1	60
Brian Boru Peak, mtn., B.C., Can.	B7	102
Briançon, Fr.	H13	14
Brian Head, mtn., Ut., U.S.	G4	120
Briare, Fr.	E9	14
Bricelyn, Mn., U.S.	G2	110
Briceni, Mol.	A11	20
Briceville, Tn., U.S.	C2	112
Briçonnet, Lac, l., P.Q., Can.	A13	106
Bricquebec, Fr.	C5	14
Bridge, stm., B.C., Can.	G11	102
Bridge City, Tx., U.S.	L3	114
Bridge Lake, B.C., Can.	F14	102
Bridgeport, Al., U.S.	H11	114
Bridgeport, Ca., U.S.	F6	124
Bridgeport, Ct., U.S.	F13	108
Bridgeport, Il., U.S.	D9	114
Bridgeport, Mi., U.S.	G12	110
Bridgeport, Ne., U.S.	J4	118
Bridgeport, On., Can.	G15	110
Bridgeport, Tx., U.S.	F9	116
Bridgeport, Wa., U.S.	B6	122
Bridgeport, W.V., U.S.	H6	108
Bridgeport, Lake, res., Tx., U.S.	F9	116
Bridger, Mt., U.S.	E17	122
Bridge River Indian Reserve, B.C., Can.	G12	102
Bridgeton, N.J., U.S.	H11	108
Bridgetown, Austl.	F3	68
Bridgetown, Barb.	H15	94
Bridgetown, N.S., Can.	H8	106
Bridgeville, De., U.S.	I11	108
Bridgewater, Austl.	N7	70
Bridgewater, Ma., U.S.	F16	108
Bridgewater, N.S., Can.	H9	106
Bridgewater, S.D., U.S.	H10	118
Bridgewater, Va., U.S.	I8	108
Bridgman, Mi., U.S.	I9	110
Bridgton, Me., U.S.	C16	108
Bridgwater, Eng., U.K.	J10	8
Brie, reg., Fr.	D10	14
Briec, Fr.	D2	14
Brienne-le-Château, Fr.	D11	14
Brienz, Switz.	E9	13
Brienzersee, l., Switz.	E9	13
Brier Island, i., N.S., Can.	H7	106
Briey, Fr.	C12	14
Brig, Switz.	F9	13
Brig Bay, Nf., Can.	A17	106
Briggs, Tx., U.S.	I9	116
Brigham City, Ut., U.S.	C4	120
Bright, Austl.	K7	70
Brighton, Co., U.S.	E12	120
Brighton, Eng., U.K.	K13	8
Brighton, Ia., U.S.	I4	110
Brighton, Il., U.S.	C6	114
Brighton, Mi., U.S.	H12	110
Brighton, N.Y., U.S.	D9	108
Brighton, On., Can.	F18	110
Brighton Downs, Austl.	D4	70
Brightsand Lake, l., Sk., Can.	E6	104
Brignoles, Fr.	I13	14
Brigus, Nf., Can.	E20	106
Brikama, Gam.	E1	64
Brilhante, stm., Braz.	F1	79
Brilliant, Al., U.S.	H9	114
Brilliant, B.C., Can.	H17	102
Brillion, Wi., U.S.	F7	110
Brilon, Ger.	D8	10
Brindisi, Italy	I12	18
Brinje, Cro.	D10	18
Brinkley, Ar., U.S.	H5	114
Brion, Île, i., P.Q., Can.	E12	106
Brioude, Fr.	G10	14
Briouze, Fr.	D6	14
Brisbane, Austl.	F10	70
Bristol, Ct., U.S.	F14	108
Bristol, Eng., U.K.	J11	8
Bristol, Fl., U.S.	I2	112
Bristol, N.H., U.S.	D15	108
Bristol, Pa., U.S.	G12	108
Bristol, R.I., U.S.	F15	108
Bristol, S.D., U.S.	F10	118
Bristol, Tn., U.S.	C4	112
Bristol, Va., U.S.	C4	112
Bristol, Vt., U.S.	C13	108
Bristol Bay, b., Ak., U.S.	G15	100
Bristol Lake, l., Ca., U.S.	J10	124
Bristow, Ok., U.S.	D10	116
Britânia, Braz.	C3	79
Britannia Beach, B.C., Can.	H11	102
British Columbia, prov., Can.	F7	96
British Honduras see Belize, ctry., N.A.	I15	90
British Indian Ocean Territory, dep., Afr.	J8	24
British Mountains, mts., N.A.	B24	100
British Virgin Islands, dep., N.A.	E12	94
Brits, S. Afr.	E8	66
Britstown, S. Afr.	H6	66
Britt, Ia., U.S.	G2	110
Brittany see Bretagne, hist. reg., Fr.	D3	14
Britton, S.D., U.S.	F10	118
Brive-la-Gaillarde, Fr.	G8	14
Brixton, Austl.	D6	70
Brno, Czech Rep.	F16	10
Broa, Ensenada de la, b., Cuba	C3	94
Broad, stm., U.S.	E5	112
Broadalbin, N.Y., U.S.	D12	108
Broadback, stm., P.Q., Can.	F17	96
Broadford, Scot., U.K.	D8	8
Broad Sound, strt., Austl.	D8	70
Broad Sound Channel, strt., Austl.	D9	70
Broadus, Mt., U.S.	F2	118
Broadview, Sk., Can.	H12	104
Broadwater, Ne., U.S.	J5	118
Broadway, Va., U.S.	I8	108
Brocēni, Lat.	E5	22
Brochet, Mb., Can.	E12	96
Brochet, Lac au, l., P.Q., Can.	C4	106
Brock, Sk., Can.	G6	104
Brockport, N.Y., U.S.	D9	108
Brockton, Ma., U.S.	E15	108
Brockton, Mt., U.S.	C3	118
Brockville, On., Can.	C11	108
Brockway, Pa., U.S.	F8	108
Brocton, N.Y., U.S.	E7	108
Brodeur Peninsula, pen., N.T., Can.	B15	96
Brodhead, Ky., U.S.	B2	112
Brodhead, Wi., U.S.	H6	110
Brodnax, Va., U.S.	C8	112
Brodnica, Pol.	B19	10
Brogan, Or., U.S.	F8	122
Broken Arrow, Ok., U.S.	C11	116
Broken Bay, b., Austl.	I9	70
Broken Bow, Ne., U.S.	J8	118
Broken Bow, Ok., U.S.	H2	114
Broken Bow Lake, res., Ok., U.S.	H2	114
Brokenhead, stm., Mb., Can.	H18	104
Broken Hill, Austl.	H4	70
Brokopondo, Sur.	B8	76
Brokopondo Stuwmeer, res., Sur.	C7	76
Bromptonville, P.Q., Can.	B15	108
Bronlund Peak, mtn., B.C., Can.	E7	96
Bronnae, Bela.	I13	22
Bronnicy, Russia	F21	22
Bronson, Fl., U.S.	J4	112
Bronson, Ks., U.S.	N12	118
Bronson, Mi., U.S.	I10	110
Bronson, Tx., U.S.	K2	114
Bronson Lake, l., Sk., Can.	E5	104
Bronte, Italy	L9	18
Bronte, Tx., U.S.	H6	116
Bronwood, Ga., U.S.	H2	112
Brooch, Lac, l., P.Q., Can.	B6	106
Brook, In., U.S.	B9	114
Brookeland, Tx., U.S.	K2	114
Brooker, Fl., U.S.	J4	112
Brookfield, Mo., U.S.	C3	114
Brookfield, N.S., Can.	G10	106
Brookfield, Wi., U.S.	G7	110
Brookford, N.C., U.S.	D5	112
Brookhaven, Ms., U.S.	K6	114
Brookings, Or., U.S.	H1	122
Brookings, S.D., U.S.	G11	118
Brookland, Ar., U.S.	G6	114
Brooklet, Ga., U.S.	G5	112
Brooklyn, Ia., U.S.	I3	110
Brooklyn, Mi., U.S.	H11	110
Brooklyn, Ms., U.S.	K7	114
Brooklyn, N.S., Can.	H9	106
Brooklyn Center, Mn., U.S.	E2	110
Brookmere, B.C., Can.	H14	102
Brookneal, Va., U.S.	B8	112
Brookport, Il., U.S.	E8	114
Brooks, Ab., Can.	G23	102
Brooks, Me., U.S.	C17	108
Brooks, Mount, mtn., Ak., U.S.	E19	100
Brooks Bay, b., B.C., Can.	G7	102
Brookshire, Tx., U.S.	J11	116
Brooks Range, mts., Ak., U.S.	C16	100
Brooksville, Fl., U.S.	K4	112
Brooksville, Ky., U.S.	I2	108
Brooksville, Ms., U.S.	I8	114
Brookton, Austl.	F3	68
Brookville, In., U.S.	C11	114
Brookville, Pa., U.S.	F7	108
Brookville Lake, res., In., U.S.	C11	114
Broome, Austl.	C4	68
Broomfield, Co., U.S.	E11	120
Broons, Fr.	D4	14
Brooten, Mn., U.S.	F12	118
Brora, Scot., U.K.	C10	8
Brotas de Macaúbas, Braz.	B7	79
Brou, Fr.	D8	14
Broughton Island, i., N.T., Can.	C20	96
Broughty Ferry, Scot., U.K.	E11	8
Brouwersdam, Neth.	E4	12
Brouwershaven, Neth.	E4	12
Browerville, Mn., U.S.	E13	118
Brown City, Mi., U.S.	G13	110
Brown Deer, Wi., U.S.	G8	110
Browne Bay, b., N.T., Can.	B13	96
Brownfield, Tx., U.S.	F4	116
Browning, Mo., U.S.	B3	114
Browning, Mt., U.S.	B12	122
Browning Entrance, b., B.C., Can.	D4	102
Brown Lake, l., N.T., Can.	C14	96
Brownlee Reservoir, res., U.S.	F8	122
Brownsburg, In., U.S.	C10	114
Brownsburg, P.Q., Can.	B12	108
Brownsdale, Mn., U.S.	G3	110
Brownstown, Il., U.S.	D8	114
Brownstown, In., U.S.	D10	114
Browns Valley, Mn., U.S.	F11	118
Brownsville, Ky., U.S.	E10	114
Brownsville, La., U.S.	J4	114
Brownsville, Or., U.S.	F3	122
Brownsville, Pa., U.S.	G7	108
Brownsville, Tn., U.S.	G7	114
Brownsville, Tx., U.S.	N9	116
Brownton, Mn., U.S.	F1	110
Brownvale, Ab., Can.	A17	102
Brownville, Al., U.S.	I9	114
Brownville, Me., U.S.	B17	108
Brownville, Ne., U.S.	K12	118
Brownville Junction, Me., U.S.	B17	108
Brownwood, Tx., U.S.	H8	116
Browse Island, i., Austl.	B4	68
Broxton, Ga., U.S.	H4	112
Broža, Bela.	I12	22
Bruay-en-Artois, Fr.	B9	14
Bruce, Ms., U.S.	I7	114
Bruce, S.D., U.S.	G11	118
Bruce, Wi., U.S.	E4	110
Bruce, Mount, mtn., Austl.	D3	68
Bruce Lake, On., Can.	H21	104
Bruce Lake, l., On., Can.	H21	104
Bruce Mines, On., Can.	D12	110
Bruce Peninsula, pen., On., Can.	E14	110
Bruce Peninsula National Park, On., Can.	E14	110
Bruchsal, Ger.	F8	10
Bruck an der Mur, Aus.	H15	10
Bruderheim, Ab., Can.	D22	102
Bruges (Brugge), Bel.	F3	12
Brugg, Switz.	D9	13
Brugge (Bruges), Bel.	F3	12
Brugge-Gent, Kanaal, Bel.	F3	12
Brühl, Ger.	E6	10
Bruinisse, Neth.	E5	12
Bruin Point, mtn., Ut., U.S.	E6	120
Bruja, Cerro, mtn., Pan.	H15	92
Brule, Ne., U.S.	J6	118
Brule, stm., U.S.	E7	110
Brumadinho, Braz.	F6	79
Brumado, Braz.	C8	79
Brumath, Fr.	D14	14
Brundidge, Al., U.S.	K11	114
Bruneau, Id., U.S.	H10	122
Bruneau, stm., U.S.	H10	122
Brunei, ctry., Asia	E5	38
Brunette Island, i., Nf., Can.	E18	106
Bruno, Sk., Can.	F9	104
Brunson, S.C., U.S.	G5	112
Brunswick see Braunschweig, Ger.	C10	10
Brunswick, Ga., U.S.	H5	112

Name	Map Ref.	Page
Brunswick, Md., U.S.	H9	108
Brunswick, Me., U.S.	D17	108
Brunswick, Mo., U.S.	C3	114
Brunswick, Oh., U.S.	F5	108
Brunswick, Peninsula, pen., Chile	G2	78
Bruntál, Czech Rep.	F17	10
Brus, Laguna de, b., Hond.	B10	92
Brush, Co., U.S.	K4	118
Brus Laguna, Hond.	B10	92
Brusovo, Russia	D18	22
Brusque, Braz.	D14	80
Brussels see Bruxelles, Bel.	G5	12
Brussels, On., Can.	G14	110
Brusy, Pol.	B17	10
Bruthen, Austl.	K7	70
Bruxelles (Brussel) (Brussels), Bel.	G5	12
Bruyères, Fr.	D13	14
Bruzual, Ven.	C8	84
Bryan, Oh., U.S.	F2	108
Bryan, Tx., U.S.	I10	116
Bryansk see Br'ansk, Russia	H17	22
Bryant, Ar., U.S.	H4	114
Bryant, S.D., U.S.	G10	118
Bryce Canyon National Park, Ut., U.S.	G4	120
Bryson, P.Q., Can.	B10	108
Bryson, Tx., U.S.	F8	116
Bryson City, N.C., U.S.	D3	112
Brzeg, Pol.	E17	10
Brzesko, Pol.	F20	10
Brzeziny, Pol.	D19	10
Bsharrī, Leb.	D4	48
Bua Yai, Thai.	G7	40
Buba, Gui.-B.	F2	64
Bū Bānī, Jabal, mtn., Afr.	F3	60
Bubaque, Gui.-B.	F2	64
Būbiyān, i., Kuw.	G10	48
Bucaramanga, Col.	D6	84
Buccaneer Archipelago, is., Austl.	C4	68
Buccino, Italy	I10	18
Buchanan, Ga., U.S.	F1	112
Buchanan, Lib.	I4	64
Buchanan, Mi., U.S.	I9	110
Buchanan, Sk., Can.	G12	104
Buchanan, Va., U.S.	B7	112
Buchanan, Lake, l., Austl.	C6	70
Buchanan, Lake, res., Tx., U.S.	I8	116
Buchans, Nf., Can.	D17	106
Buchara, Uzb.	J10	26
Bucharest see București, Rom.	E10	20
Buchholz, Ger.	B9	10
Buchloe, Ger.	G10	10
Buchs, Switz.	D11	13
Buchy, Fr.	C8	14
Buckatunna, Ms., U.S.	K8	114
Bückeburg, Ger.	C9	10
Buckeye, Az., U.S.	K4	120
Buckeye Lake, Oh., U.S.	H4	108
Buckhannon, W.V., U.S.	I6	108
Buckhaven, Scot., U.K.	E10	8
Buckholts, Tx., U.S.	I9	116
Buckie, Scot., U.K.	D11	8
Buckingham, P.Q., Can.	B11	108
Buckingham, Va., U.S.	B8	112
Buckingham Bay, b., Austl.	B7	68
Buckinghamshire, co., Eng., U.K.	J13	8
Buck Lake, l., Ab., Can.	D20	102
Buckland, Ak., U.S.	D14	100
Bucklands, S. Afr.	G6	66
Buckley, Il., U.S.	J7	110
Buckley, Wa., U.S.	C3	122
Buckley, stm., Austl.	C3	70
Bucklin, Ks., U.S.	N8	118
Bucklin, Mo., U.S.	C4	114
Buckow, Ger.	C14	10
Bucksport, Me., U.S.	C18	108
Bucovăț, Mol.	B12	20
Buctouche, N.B., Can.	F9	106
Bucun, China	G5	32
București (Bucharest), Rom.	E10	20
București, co., Rom.	E10	20
Bucyrus, Oh., U.S.	G4	108
Buda, Il., U.S.	I6	110
Buda, Tx., U.S.	I9	116
Budalin, Myan.	C3	40
Budapest, Hung.	H19	10
Búdardalur, Ice.	B3	6a
Budaun, India	F8	44
Buddu, Sudan	L5	60
Bude, Ms., U.S.	K6	114
Büdingen, Ger.	E9	10
Búdir, Ice.	B7	6a
Budogošč', Russia	B15	22
Bud'onnovsk, Russia	I6	26
Budweis see České Budějovice, Czech Rep.	G14	10
Buea, Cam.	I14	64
Buena Esperanza, Arg.	H6	80
Buenaventura, Col.	F4	84
Buenaventura, Mex.	C6	90
Buena Vista, Bol.	G10	82
Buena Vista, Co., U.S.	F10	120
Buena Vista, Ga., U.S.	G2	112
Buena Vista, Ms., U.S.	I8	114
Buena Vista, Para.	D10	80
Buena Vista, Va., U.S.	B7	112
Buendia, Embalse de, res., Spain	E9	16
Buenópolis, Braz.	D6	79
Buenos Aires, Arg.	H9	80
Buenos Aires, Col.	F4	84
Buenos Aires, C.R.	H11	92
Buenos Aires, prov., Arg.	I8	80
Buenos Aires, Lago (Lago General Carrera), l., S.A.	F2	78
Buerarema, Braz.	C9	79
Buesaco, Col.	G4	84
Buffalo, Ks., U.S.	N12	118
Buffalo, Mn., U.S.	E2	110
Buffalo, Mo., U.S.	E3	114
Buffalo, N.Y., U.S.	E8	108
Buffalo, Oh., U.S.	H5	108
Buffalo, Ok., U.S.	C7	116
Buffalo, S.C., U.S.	E5	112
Buffalo, S.D., U.S.	F4	118
Buffalo, Tx., U.S.	H10	116
Buffalo, Wy., U.S.	F19	122
Buffalo, stm., Ar., U.S.	F4	114
Buffalo, stm., Can.	E10	96
Buffalo, stm., Mn., U.S.	D11	118
Buffalo, stm., Ms., U.S.	K5	114
Buffalo, stm., Tn., U.S.	G9	114
Buffalo, stm., Wi., U.S.	F4	110
Buffalo Center, Ia., U.S.	G2	110
Buffalo Lake, Mn., U.S.	G13	118
Buffalo Lake, l., Ab., Can.	E22	102
Buffalo Lake, l., N.T., Can.	D9	96
Buffalo Narrows, Sk., Can.	C6	104
Buffalo Pound Lake, l., Sk., Can.	H9	104
Buffalo Pound Provincial Park, Sk., Can.	H9	104
Buford, Ga., U.S.	E2	112
Bug, stm., Eur.	E12	4
Buga, Col.	F4	84
Buga, Nig.	G13	64
Bugalagrande, Col.	E4	84
Bugeat, Fr.	G8	14
Bugojno, Bos.	E12	18
Bugry, Russia	C18	22
Bugt, China	B11	30
Bugt, China	A8	32
Bugul'ma, Russia	G8	26
Buguruslan, Russia	G8	26
Buhera, Zimb.	B10	66
Buhl, Id., U.S.	H11	122
Buhl, Mn., U.S.	C3	110
Buhler, Ks., U.S.	M10	118
Buhuși, Rom.	C10	20
Builth Wells, Wales, U.K.	I10	8
Buin, Chile	G3	80
Buin, Piz, mtn., Eur.	E13	13
Buir Nuur, l., Asia	B10	30
Buj, Russia	C24	22
Bujalance, Spain	H7	16
Buji, China	D16	44
Bujnaksk, Russia	I7	26
Bujumbura, Bdi.	B5	58
Bukačača, Russia	G15	28
Bukama, Zaire	C5	58
Būkān, Iran	C9	48
Bukavu, Zaire	B5	58
Bukittinggi, Indon.	O6	40
Bukovina, hist. reg., Eur.	B9	20
Bülach, Switz.	C10	13
Bulan, Ky., U.S.	B3	112
Bulan, Phil.	o20	39b
Bulandshahr, India	F7	44
Būlāq, Egypt	E6	60
Bulawayo, Zimb.	C9	66
Buldibuyo, Peru	C3	82
Bulgan, Mong.	B5	30
Bulgan, Mong.	B7	30
Bulgaria (Bălgarija), ctry., Eur.	G13	4
Bulki, Eth.	N9	60
Bulkley, stm., B.C., Can.	C7	102
Bulkley Ranges, mts., B.C., Can.	C7	102
Bull, stm., B.C., Can.	H19	102
Bullard, Tx., U.S.	G11	116
Bullas, Spain	G10	16
Buller, Mount, mtn., Austl.	K7	70
Bullfinch, Austl.	F3	68
Bull Harbour, B.C., Can.	G7	102
Bullhead, S.D., U.S.	F6	118
Bullhead City, Az., U.S.	I2	120
Bull Mountain, mtn., Mt., U.S.	D13	122
Bullock, N.C., U.S.	C8	112
Bullock Creek, Austl.	A6	70
Bulloo, stm., Austl.	G5	70
Bullpound Creek, stm., Ab., Can.	F23	102
Bulls Gap, Tn., U.S.	C3	112
Bull Shoals, Ar., U.S.	F4	114
Bull Shoals Lake, res., U.S.	F4	114
Bulnes, Chile	I2	80
Bultfontein, S. Afr.	G8	66
Bulukumba, Indon.	G7	38
Bumba, Zaire	A4	58
Bumbuna, S.L.	G4	64
Bumpus, Mount, hill, N.T., Can.	C10	96
Buna, Tx., U.S.	L3	114
Bunavista, Tx., U.S.	D5	116
Bunbury, Austl.	F3	68
Bunceton, Mo., U.S.	D4	114
Bundaberg, Austl.	E10	70
Bünde, Ger.	C8	10
Būndi, India	H6	44
Bungo-suidō, strt., Japan	N7	36
Bunia, Zaire	A6	58
Bunker, Mo., U.S.	E5	114
Bunker Group, is., Austl.	D10	70
Bunker Hill, Il., U.S.	C7	114
Bunker Hill, In., U.S.	B10	114
Bunker Hill, Or., U.S.	G1	122
Bunker Hill, mtn., Nv., U.S.	E8	124
Bunkie, La., U.S.	L4	114
Bunnell, Fl., U.S.	J5	112
Buntok, Indon.	F5	38
Bünyan, Tur.	B3	48
Bunyola, Spain	F11	16
Bunza, Nig.	E11	64
Buon Me Thuot, Viet.	H10	40
Buor-Chaja, guba, b., Russia	C18	28
Buor-Chaja, mys, c., Russia	C18	28
Buqayq, Sau. Ar.	B6	47
Bura, Kenya	B7	58
Buram, Sudan	L3	60
Burang, China	E3	30
Buranhém, stm., Braz.	D9	79
Buras, La., U.S.	M7	114
Buraydah, Sau. Ar.	H7	48
Burbank, Ca., U.S.	J7	124
Burbank, Wa., U.S.	D6	122
Burcher, Austl.	I7	70
Burco, Som.	G10	56
Burdekin, stm., Austl.	B7	70
Burden, Ks., U.S.	N11	118
Burdett, Ab., Can.	H23	102
Burdett, Ks., U.S.	M8	118
Burdur, Tur.	H14	4
Bure, Eth.	L9	60
Bure, Eth.	M8	60
Bureinskij chrebet, mts., Russia	G18	28
Bureja, stm., Russia	G18	28
Büren, Ger.	D8	10
Burford, On., Can.	G15	110
Būr Fu'ād, Egypt	F2	48
Burgas, Bul.	G11	20
Burg [auf Fehmarn], Ger.	A11	10
Burgaw, N.C., U.S.	E9	112
Burg [bei Magdeburg], Ger.	C11	10
Burgdorf, Switz.	D8	13
Burgenland, state, Aus.	H16	10
Burgeo, Nf., Can.	E16	106
Burgersdorp, S. Afr.	H8	66
Burgess, Va., U.S.	B10	112
Burgettstown, Pa., U.S.	G6	108
Burgin, China	B4	30
Burgin, Ky., U.S.	E12	114
Burglengenfeld, Ger.	F12	10
Burgos, Mex.	E10	90
Burgos, Spain	C8	16
Burgos, prov., Spain	C8	16
Burgstädt, Ger.	E12	10
Burgundy see Bourgogne, hist. reg., Fr.	E11	14
Burhaniye, Tur.	J10	20
Burhānpur, India	J7	44
Buri, Braz.	G4	79
Burica, Punta, c., N.A.	I12	92
Burien, Wa., U.S.	C3	122
Burila Mare, Rom.	E6	20
Burin, Nf., Can.	E18	106
Burin Peninsula, pen., Nf., Can.	E18	106
Buri Ram, Thai.	G7	40
Buritama, Braz.	F3	79
Buriti, Braz.	D2	79
Buriti, stm., Braz.	E12	82
Buriti Alegre, Braz.	E4	79
Buritizeiro, Braz.	D6	79
Burj al-'Arab, Egypt	B5	60
Burjassot, Spain	F11	16
Burjatija, state, Russia	G20	26
Burkburnett, Tx., U.S.	E8	116
Burke, S.D., U.S.	H8	118
Burke, stm., Austl.	D3	70
Burke Channel, strt., B.C., Can.	E7	102
Burkesville, Ky., U.S.	F11	114
Burketown, Austl.	A3	70
Burkina Faso, ctry., Afr.	F6	54
Burleson, Tx., U.S.	G9	116
Burley, Id., U.S.	H12	122
Burlingame, Ca., U.S.	G3	124
Burlingame, Ks., U.S.	M12	118
Burlington, Co., U.S.	L5	118
Burlington, Ia., U.S.	J4	110
Burlington, Ks., U.S.	M12	118
Burlington, N.C., U.S.	C7	112
Burlington, N.D., U.S.	C6	118
Burlington, Nf., Can.	C17	106
Burlington, N.J., U.S.	G12	108
Burlington, On., Can.	G16	110
Burlington, Vt., U.S.	C13	108
Burlington, Wa., U.S.	B3	122
Burlington, Wi., U.S.	H7	110
Burlington, Wy., U.S.	F17	122
Burlington Junction, Mo., U.S.	B1	114
Burma see Myanmar, ctry., Asia	A2	38
Burmā, Tall, mtn., Jord.	G5	50
Burmakino, Russia	D23	22
Burnaby, B.C., Can.	H12	102
Burnaby Island, i., B.C., Can.	E3	102
Burnet, Tx., U.S.	I8	116
Burnett, stm., Austl.	E10	70
Burnett Bay, b., N.T., Can.	B8	96
Burney, Ca., U.S.	D4	124
Burnham, Pa., U.S.	G9	108
Burnie, Austl.	M6	70
Burnley, Eng., U.K.	H11	8
Burns, Ks., U.S.	M11	118
Burns, Or., U.S.	G6	122
Burns, Tn., U.S.	F9	114
Burns, Wy., U.S.	J3	118
Burns Flat, Ok., U.S.	D7	116
Burnside, Ky., U.S.	C2	112
Burnside, stm., N.T., Can.	C11	96
Burns Lake, B.C., Can.	C9	102
Burnsville, Al., U.S.	J10	114
Burnsville, Ms., U.S.	H8	114
Burnsville, N.C., U.S.	D4	112
Burnsville, W.V., U.S.	I6	108
Burnt, stm., Or., U.S.	F8	122
Burnt Islands, Nf., Can.	E15	106
Burnt Pond, l., Nf., Can.	D16	106
Burntwood, stm., Mb., Can.	C17	104
Burntwood Lake, l., Mb., Can.	C14	104
Burra, Austl.	I3	70
Burragorang, Lake, res., Austl.	I9	70
Burramurra, Austl.	C2	70
Burrendong Reservoir, res., Austl.	I8	70
Burrinjuck Reservoir, res., Austl.	J8	70
Burr Oak, Ks., U.S.	L9	118
Burro Burro, stm., Guy.	E13	84
Burro Peak, mtn., N.M., U.S.	L8	120
Burrton, Ks., U.S.	M10	118
Burruyacú, Arg.	D6	80
Burrwood, La., U.S.	N7	114
Bursa, Tur.	I13	20
Būr Safājah, Egypt	D7	60
Būr Sa'īd (Port Said), Egypt	B7	60
Burstall, Sk., Can.	H5	104
Būr Sūdān (Port Sudan), Sudan	H9	60
Burt, Ia., U.S.	H13	118
Būr Tawfīq, Egypt	G2	48
Burt Lake, l., Mi., U.S.	E11	110
Burton, B.C., Can.	H17	102
Burton, Mi., U.S.	G12	110
Burton, Tx., U.S.	I10	116
Burtundy, Austl.	I5	70
Buru, i., Indon.	F8	38
Burūm, Yemen	G6	47
Burundi, ctry., Afr.	B6	58
Burun-Šibertuj, gora, mtn., Russia	H13	28
Burwash, On., Can.	D15	110
Burwash Landing, Yk., Can.	F25	100
Burwell, Ne., U.S.	J8	118
Burwick, Scot., U.K.	C11	8
Buryatia see Burjatija, state, Russia	G14	28
Bury Saint Edmunds, Eng., U.K.	I14	8
Busby, Mt., U.S.	E19	122
Busca, Italy	E2	18
Bush, stm., S.C., U.S.	E5	112
Bushland, Tx., U.S.	D4	116
Bush Lot, Guy.	D14	84
Bushnell, Fl., U.S.	K4	112
Bushnell, Il., U.S.	J5	110
Bushton, Ks., U.S.	M9	118
Bushtyna, Ukr.	A7	20
Buskerud, co., Nor.	K11	6
Busko Zdrój, Pol.	E20	10
Buṣrā al-Ḥarīrī (Bosor), Syria	C6	50
Buṣrā ash-Shām, Syria	C6	50
Busselton, Austl.	F3	68
Bussey, Ia., U.S.	I3	110
Bussum, Neth.	D7	12
Bustamante, Mex.	D9	90
Buşteni, Rom.	D9	20
Busto Arsizio, Italy	D3	18
Busu-Djanoa, Zaire	A4	58
Bušuicha, Russia	B23	22
Buta, Zaire	H5	56
Butajira, Eth.	M10	60
Buta Ranquil, Arg.	I4	80
Butare, Rw.	B5	58
Bute Inlet, b., B.C., Can.	G10	102
Butera, Italy	L9	18
Butere, Kenya	A6	58
Butha Qi, China	B11	30
Butiá, Braz.	F13	80
Butler, Al., U.S.	J8	114
Butler, Ga., U.S.	G2	112
Butler, In., U.S.	A12	114
Butler, Mo., U.S.	D2	114
Butler, Oh., U.S.	G4	108
Butler, Ok., U.S.	D7	116
Butler, Pa., U.S.	G7	108
Butnau Lake, l., Mb., Can.	B19	104
Butner, N.C., U.S.	C8	112
Buton, Pulau, i., Indon.	G7	38
Butru, Austl.	C3	70
Butte, Mt., U.S.	D13	122
Butte, Ne., U.S.	I9	118
Butte Creek, stm., Ca., U.S.	E4	124
Butte du Lion, hist., Bel.	G5	12
Butte Falls, Or., U.S.	H3	122
Butterfield, Mn., U.S.	H13	118
Butternut, Wi., U.S.	D5	110
Butterworth, Malay.	L6	40
Butterworth, S. Afr.	I9	66
Buttle Lake, l., B.C., Can.	H9	102
Button Islands, is., N.T., Can.	D20	96
Buttonwillow, Ca., U.S.	I6	124
Butuan, Phil.	D8	38
Butylicy, Russia	F24	22
Butzbach, Ger.	E8	10
Bützow, Ger.	B11	10
Buurgplaatz, mtn., Lux.	H9	12
Buxtehude, Ger.	B9	10
Buxton, Guy.	D13	84
Buxton, N.C., U.S.	D11	112
Buxton, N.D., U.S.	D10	118
Buxton, S. Afr.	F7	66
Buxton, Mount, mtn., B.C., Can.	F7	102
Buxy, Fr.	F11	14
Buyo, C. Iv.	H6	64
Buzançais, Fr.	F8	14
Buzău, Rom.	D10	20
Buzău, co., Rom.	D10	20
Buzău, stm., Rom.	D11	20
Buzen, Japan	N6	36
Búzi, stm., Moz.	B12	66
Búzios, Ponta dos, c., Braz.	G8	79
Buzuluk, Russia	G8	26
Byam Channel, strt., N.T., Can.	A11	96
Byam Martin Channel, strt., N.T., Can.	A12	96
Byam Martin Island, i., N.T., Can.	A12	96
Bydgoszcz, Pol.	B18	10
Byelorussia see Belarus, ctry., Eur.	E13	4
Byers, Tx., U.S.	E8	116
Byesville, Oh., U.S.	H5	108
Bygdin, Nor.	K11	6
Byhalia, Ms., U.S.	H7	114
Bychau, Bela.	H13	22
Bykle, Nor.	L10	6
Bylas, Az., U.S.	K6	120
Bylot Island, i., N.T., Can.	B17	96
Byng Inlet, On., Can.	E15	110
Bynum, N.C., U.S.	D7	112
Byrdstown, Tn., U.S.	F11	114
Byron, Ga., U.S.	G3	112
Byron, Il., U.S.	H6	110
Byron, Wy., U.S.	F17	122
Byron, Cape, c., Austl.	G10	70
Byron Bay, Austl.	G10	70
Byrranga, gory, mts., Russia	B12	28
Bystřice, Czech Rep.	F14	10
Bystrzyca Kłodzka, Pol.	E16	10
Bytantaj, stm., Russia	D18	28
Bytkiv, Ukr.	A8	20
Bytom (Beuthen), Pol.	E18	10
Bytoš', Russia	H17	22
Bytów, Pol.	A17	10

C

Name	Map Ref.	Page
Ca, stm., Asia	E8	40
Caacupé, Para.	C10	80
Caaguazú, Para.	C10	80
Caaguazú, dept., Para.	C11	80
Caála, Ang.	D3	58
Caamaño Sound, strt., B.C., Can.	E5	102
Caapiranga, Braz.	I12	84
Caapucú, Para.	D10	80
Caarapó, Braz.	G1	79
Caazapá, Para.	D10	80
Caazapá, dept., Para.	D10	80
Cabaçal, stm., Braz.	F12	82
Cabaiguán, Cuba	C5	94
Cabaliana, Lago, l., Braz.	I12	84
Caballo Reservoir, res., N.M., U.S.	L9	120
Cabana, Peru	C2	82
Cabanaconde, Peru	F6	82
Cabanatuan, Phil.	n19	39b
Cabano, P.Q., Can.	E5	106
Cabeceiras, Braz.	C5	79
Cabedelo, Braz.	E12	76
Cabeza del Buey, Spain	G6	16
Cabezas, Bol.	H10	82
Cabildo, Arg.	J8	80
Cabildo, Chile	G3	80
Cabimas, Ven.	B7	84
Cabinda, Ang.	C2	58
Cabinda, dept., Ang.	C2	58
Cabixi, stm., Braz.	E11	82
Cable, Wi., U.S.	D4	110
Cabo, Braz.	E11	76
Cabo Frio, Braz.	G7	79
Cabo Gracias a Dios, Nic.	C11	92
Cabool, Mo., U.S.	E4	114
Caboolture, Austl.	F10	70
Cabora Bassa Dam, Moz.	E6	58
Caborca, Mex.	B3	90
Cabot, Ar., U.S.	H4	114
Cabot Strait, strt., Can.	E14	106
Cabra, Spain	H7	16
Cabramurra, Austl.	J8	70
Cabrera, stm., Col.	F5	84
Cabrera, Illa de, i., Spain	F14	16
Cabri, Sk., Can.	H6	104
Cabruta, Ven.	D9	84
Cabure, Ven.	B8	84
Cabuya, C.R.	H9	92
Cabuyal, C.R.	G9	92
Cabuyaro, Col.	E6	84
Caçador, Braz.	D13	80
Čačak, Yugo.	F4	20
Cacaohatán, Mex.	C2	92
Cacaoui, Lac, l., P.Q., Can.	B7	106
Caçapava, Braz.	G6	79
Caçapava do Sul, Braz.	F12	80
Cacapon, stm., W.V., U.S.	H8	108
Caccamo, Italy	L8	18
Cacequi, Braz.	E11	80
Cáceres, Braz.	G13	82
Cáceres, Col.	D5	84
Cáceres, Spain	F5	16
Čačersk, Bela.	I13	22
Čačevičy, Bela.	H12	22
Cacharí, Arg.	I9	80
Cache, Ok., U.S.	E8	116
Cache, stm., Il., U.S.	E7	114
Cache Creek, B.C., Can.	G13	102
Cache la Poudre, stm., Co., U.S.	D11	120
Cache Peak, mtn., Id., U.S.	H12	122
Cacheu, Gui.-B.	E1	64
Cachí, Arg.	C5	80
Cachimbo, Serra do, mts., Braz.	C13	82
Cachoeira Alta, Braz.	E3	79
Cachoeira de Goiás, Braz.	D3	79
Cachoeira do Sul, Braz.	F12	80
Cachoeiras de Macacu, Braz.	G7	79
Cachoeiro de Itapemirim, Braz.	F8	79
Cachuela Esperanza, Bol.	D9	82
Cacine, Gui.-B.	F2	64
Cacólo, Ang.	D3	58
Caconda, Ang.	D3	58
Cacra, Peru	E4	82
Cactus, Tx., U.S.	C4	116
Cactus Peak, mtn., Nv., U.S.	G9	124
Caçu, Braz.	E3	79
Caculé, Braz.	C7	79
Čadan, Russia	G16	26
Cadariri, stm., Braz.	B13	82
Caddo, Ok., U.S.	E10	116
Caddo, Tx., U.S.	G8	116
Caddo, stm., Ar., U.S.	H3	114
Caddo Lake, res., U.S.	J2	114
Caddo Mills, Tx., U.S.	F10	116
Cadereyta de Jiménez, Mex.	E9	90
Cadillac, Mi., U.S.	F10	110
Cadillac, Sk., Can.	I7	104
Cadiz, Ky., U.S.	F9	114
Cadiz, Oh., U.S.	G6	108
Cádiz, Spain	I5	16
Cádiz, Golfo de, b., Eur.	I4	16
Čadobec, stm., Russia	F11	28
Cadomin, Ab., Can.	D17	102
Cadott, Wi., U.S.	F4	110
Cadwell, Ga., U.S.	G3	112
Caen, Fr.	C6	14
Caernarfon, Wales, U.K.	H9	8
Cæsarea see Qesari, Ḥorbat, hist., Isr.	C3	50
Caetanópolis, Braz.	E6	79
Caeté, Braz.	E7	79
Caeté, stm., Braz.	C7	82
Caetité, Braz.	C7	79
Cafayate, Arg.	D6	80
Cafelândia do Leste, Braz.	D2	79
Cafuini, stm., Braz.	G14	84
Cagayan, stm., Phil.	I19	39b
Cagayan de Oro, Phil.	D7	38
Çağış, Tur.	J12	20
Cagli, Italy	F7	18
Cagliari, Italy	J4	18
Cagliari, Golfo di, b., Italy	J4	18
Cagnes, Fr.	I14	14
Čagoda, Russia	B18	22
Cagua, Ven.	B9	84
Caguán, stm., Col.	G5	84
Caguas, P.R.	E11	94
Cahaba, stm., Al., U.S.	J9	114
Cahabón, Guat.	B5	92
Cahabón, stm., Guat.	B5	92
Cahokia, Il., U.S.	D6	114
Cahors, Fr.	H8	14
Cahuinari, stm., Col.	H7	84
Cahuita, Punta, c., C.R.	H12	92
Cahul, Mol.	F13	4
Caí, stm., Braz.	E13	80
Caia, stm., Eur.	F4	16
Caiapó, stm., Braz.	D3	79
Caiapó, Serra do, mts., Braz.	D2	79
Caiapônia, Braz.	D3	79
Caibarién, Cuba	C5	94
Cai Bau, Dao, i., Viet.	D9	40
Caiçara, Braz.	C3	79
Caicara, Caño, stm., Ven.	D8	84
Caicara de Maturín, Ven.	C11	84
Caicara de Orinoco, Ven.	D9	84
Caicedonia, Col.	E5	84
Caicó, Braz.	E11	76
Caicos Islands, is., T./C. Is.	D9	94
Caicos Passage, strt., N.A.	C8	94
Caigou, China	B3	34
Cailloma, Peru	F6	82
Caimanera, Cuba	E7	94
Caine, stm., Bol.	G9	82
Cains, stm., N.B., Can.	F7	106
Cainsville, Mo., U.S.	B3	114
Caird Coast, Ant.	C2	73
Cairns, Austl.	A6	70
Cairns Lake, l., On., Can.	G20	104
Cairo see Al-Qāhirah, Egypt	B6	60
Cairo, Ga., U.S.	I2	112
Cairo, Il., U.S.	E7	114
Cairo, Ne., U.S.	J9	118
Cairo, W.V., U.S.	H5	108
Cairo Montenotte, Italy	E3	18
Cairu, Braz.	B9	79
Caiundo, Ang.	E3	58
Caixi, China	J5	34
Cajabamba, Ec.	H3	84
Cajabamba, Peru	B2	82
Cajacay, Peru	D3	82
Cajamarca, Peru	B2	82
Cajamarca, dept., Peru	B2	82
Cajatambo, Peru	D3	82
Cajàzeiras, Braz.	E11	76
Čajek, Kyrg.	I12	26
Čajkovskij, Russia	F8	26
Cajones, Cayos, rf., Hond.	A11	92
Cajon Summit, Ca., U.S.	J8	124
Cajuru, Braz.	F5	79
Čakeni, Ang.	A4	66
Čakovec, Cro.	C11	18
Cala, S. Afr.	H8	66
Calabar, Nig.	I14	64
Calabozo, Ven.	C9	84
Calabozo, Ensenada de, b., Ven.	B7	84
Calabria, prov., Italy	J11	18
Calahorra, Spain	C10	16
Calais, Fr.	B8	14
Calais, Me., U.S.	B19	108
Calais, Pas de (Strait of Dover), strt., Eur.	J15	8
Calalaste, Sierra de, mts., Arg.	C5	80
Calama, Chile	B4	80
Calamar, Col.	B5	84
Calamar, Col.	G6	84
Calamarca, Bol.	G7	82
Calamus, stm., Ne., U.S.	J8	118
Calapan, Phil.	o19	39b
Călărași, Mol.	B12	20
Călărași, Rom.	E11	20
Calarcá, Col.	E5	84
Calatayud, Spain	D10	16
Calau, Ger.	D13	10
Calaveras, stm., Ca., U.S.	F4	124
Calbayog, Phil.	C7	38
Calca, Peru	E6	82
Calcasieu, stm., La., U.S.	L4	114
Calcasieu Lake, l., La., U.S.	M3	114
Calceta, Ec.	H2	84
Calcha, Bol.	I8	82
Calchaquí, Arg.	E8	80
Calchaquí, stm., Arg.	C5	80
Calçoene, Braz.	C8	76
Calcutta, India	I13	44
Caldas, Braz.	F5	79
Caldas, Col.	D5	84
Caldas, dept., Col.	E5	84
Caldas Novas, Braz.	D4	79
Caldera, Chile	D3	80
Caldwell, Id., U.S.	G9	122
Caldwell, Ks., U.S.	N10	118
Caldwell, Oh., U.S.	H5	108
Caldwell, Tx., U.S.	I10	116
Caledon, stm., Afr.	H8	66
Caledonia, Belize	H15	90
Caledonia, Mn., U.S.	G4	110
Caledonia, Ms., U.S.	I8	114
Caledonia, N.S., Can.	H8	106
Caledonia, N.Y., U.S.	E9	108
Caledonia, Oh., U.S.	G4	108
Caledonia, On., Can.	G16	110
Calella, Spain	D14	16
Calera, Al., U.S.	I10	114
Calera, Ok., U.S.	F10	116
Calera, Spain	o23	17b
Caleta del Sebo, Spain	n27	17b
Caleufú, Arg.	H6	80
Calexico, Ca., U.S.	L10	124
Calfkiller, stm., Tn., U.S.	F11	114
Calfpasture, stm., Va., U.S.	I7	108
Calgary, Ab., Can.	F20	102
Calhan, Co., U.S.	L3	118
Calhoun, Al., U.S.	J10	114
Calhoun, Ga., U.S.	E2	112
Calhoun, Ky., U.S.	E9	114
Calhoun, Mo., U.S.	D3	114
Calhoun, Tn., U.S.	D2	112
Calhoun City, Ms., U.S.	I7	114
Calhoun Falls, S.C., U.S.	E4	112
Cali, Col.	F4	84
Calico Rock, Ar., U.S.	F4	114
Calicut, India	G3	46
Caliente, Nv., U.S.	G11	124
California, Mo., U.S.	D4	114
California, Pa., U.S.	G7	108
California, state, U.S.	D2	98
California, Golfo de, b., Mex.	D4	90
California Aqueduct, Ca., U.S.	H5	124
Cälilabad, Azer.	B10	48
Calilegua, Arg.	B6	80
Calimere, Point, c., India	G5	46
Calindó, stm., Braz.	C6	79
Calingasta, Arg.	F4	80
Calion, Ar., U.S.	I4	114
Calipatria, Ca., U.S.	K10	124
Calispell Peak, mtn., Wa., U.S.	B8	122
Calistoga, Ca., U.S.	F3	124
Calitri, Italy	I10	18
Callabonna, Lake, l., Austl.	G4	70
Callac, Fr.	D3	14
Callaghan, Mount, mtn., Nv., U.S.	E9	124
Callahan, Fl., U.S.	I5	112
Callander, On., Can.	D16	110
Callanmarca, Peru	E4	82
Callanna, Austl.	G2	70
Callao, Peru	E3	82
Callaway, Ne., U.S.	J8	118
Calliham, Tx., U.S.	K8	116
Calling Lake, Ab., Can.	B21	102
Calling Lake, l., Ab., Can.	B21	102
Callosa d'En Sarrià, Spain	G11	16
Callosa de Segura, Spain	G11	16
Calmar, Ab., Can.	D21	102
Calmar, Ia., U.S.	G4	110
Calobre, Pan.	I14	92
Caloosahatchee, stm., Fl., U.S.	M5	112
Caloundra, Austl.	F10	70
Calp, Spain	G12	16
Caltagirone, Italy	L9	18
Caltanissetta, Italy	L9	18
Calumet, Mi., U.S.	C7	110
Calumet, Mn., U.S.	C2	110
Calumet City, Il., U.S.	A9	114
Calunda, Ang.	D4	58
Caluula, Som.	F11	56
Calvados, dept., Fr.	C6	14
Calvert, Al., U.S.	K8	114
Calvert, Tx., U.S.	I10	116
Calvert Island, i., B.C., Can.	F6	102
Calvi, Fr.	I23	15a
Calvia, Spain	F14	16
Calvillo, Mex.	G8	90
Calvin, Ok., U.S.	E10	116
Calvinia, S. Afr.	H4	66
Calw, Ger.	G8	10
Calwa, Ca., U.S.	H6	124
Calypso, N.C., U.S.	D8	112
Calzada, Peru	B3	82
Camabatela, Ang.	C3	58
Camaçã, stm., Braz.	B8	82
Camaçari, Braz.	B9	79
Camacupa, Ang.	D3	58
Camaguán, Ven.	C9	84
Camagüey, Cuba	D6	94
Camaiore, Italy	F5	18
Camaiú, stm., Braz.	B12	82
Camajuaní, Cuba	C5	94
Camamu, Braz.	B9	79
Camaná, Peru	G5	82
Camaná, stm., Peru	G5	82
Camanaú, stm., Braz.	H12	84
Camanche, Ia., U.S.	I5	110
Camapuã, Braz.	E1	79
Camaquã, Braz.	F13	80
Camaquã, stm., Braz.	F12	80
Camará, Braz.	I11	84
Camararé, stm., Braz.	E12	82
Camarès, Fr.	I9	14
Camargo, Bol.	I9	82
Camargo, Mex.	D7	90
Camargue, reg., Fr.	I11	14
Camarillo, Ca., U.S.	J6	124
Camarón, Cabo, c., Hond.	A9	92
Camarones, Arg.	E3	78
Camas, Spain	H5	16
Ca Mau, Viet.	J8	40
Ca Mau, Mui, c., Viet.	J8	40
Cambados, Spain	C3	16
Cambará, Braz.	G3	79
Cambodia (Kâmpŭchéa), ctry., Asia	C4	38
Camboon, Austl.	E9	70
Camboriú, Braz.	D14	80
Cambrai, Fr.	B10	14
Cambria, Ca., U.S.	I4	124
Cambria, Wi., U.S.	G6	110
Cambria Ice Field, B.C., Can.	B5	102
Cambrian Mountains, mts., Wales, U.K.	I10	8
Cambridge, Eng., U.K.	I14	8
Cambridge, Ia., U.S.	I2	110
Cambridge, Id., U.S.	F9	122
Cambridge, Il., U.S.	I5	110
Cambridge, Ma., U.S.	E15	108
Cambridge, Md., U.S.	I10	108
Cambridge, Mn., U.S.	E2	110
Cambridge, Ne., U.S.	K7	118
Cambridge, N.Y., U.S.	D13	108
Cambridge, N.Z.	B5	72
Cambridge, Oh., U.S.	G5	108
Cambridge, On., Can.	G15	110
Cambridge Bay, N.T., Can.	C11	96
Cambridge City, In., U.S.	C11	114
Cambridge Fiord, N.T., Can.	B18	96
Cambridgeshire, co., Eng., U.K.	I13	8
Cambridge Springs, Pa., U.S.	F6	108
Cambriú, Ponta de, c., Braz.	C15	80
Cambuí, Braz.	G5	79
Cambundi-Catembo, Ang.	D3	58
Camden, Al., U.S.	K9	114
Camden, Ar., U.S.	I4	114
Camden, Austl.	J9	70
Camden, De., U.S.	H11	108
Camden, Me., U.S.	C17	108
Camden, Ms., U.S.	J7	114
Camden, N.C., U.S.	C10	112
Camden, N.J., U.S.	H11	108
Camden, N.Y., U.S.	D11	108
Camden, Oh., U.S.	H2	108
Camden, S.C., U.S.	E6	112
Camden, Tn., U.S.	F8	114
Camdenton, Mo., U.S.	D4	114
Camenca, Mol.	A12	20

Name	Map Ref.	Page
Clermont, P.Q., Can.	E3	106
Clermont-en-Argonne, Fr.	C12	14
Clermont-Ferrand, Fr.	G10	14
Cles, Italy	C6	18
Cleveland, Al., U.S.	I10	114
Cleveland, Ga., U.S.	E3	112
Cleveland, Ms., U.S.	I6	114
Cleveland, N.C., U.S.	D6	112
Cleveland, Oh., U.S.	F5	108
Cleveland, Ok., U.S.	C10	116
Cleveland, Tn., U.S.	G12	114
Cleveland, Tx., U.S.	I11	116
Cleveland, Va., U.S.	C4	112
Cleveland, Cape, c., Austl.	B7	70
Cleveland, Mount, mtn., Mt., U.S.	B12	122
Clevelândia, Braz.	D12	80
Clew Bay, b., Ire.	H4	8
Clewiston, Fl., U.S.	M6	112
Clifton, Az., U.S.	K7	120
Clifton, Il., U.S.	J8	110
Clifton, Ks., U.S.	L10	118
Clifton, Tn., U.S.	G9	114
Clifton, Tx., U.S.	H9	116
Clifton Forge, Va., U.S.	B7	112
Climax, Co., U.S.	E10	120
Climax, Ga., U.S.	I2	112
Climax, Mi., U.S.	H10	110
Climax, Sk., Can.	I6	104
Clinch, stm., U.S.	C3	112
Clinchco, Va., U.S.	B4	112
Clingmans Dome, mtn., U.S.	D3	112
Clinton, Al., U.S.	J8	114
Clinton, Ar., U.S.	G4	114
Clinton, B.C., Can.	F13	102
Clinton, Ct., U.S.	F14	108
Clinton, Ia., U.S.	I5	110
Clinton, Il., U.S.	B8	114
Clinton, In., U.S.	C9	114
Clinton, Ky., U.S.	F8	114
Clinton, La., U.S.	L5	114
Clinton, Ma., U.S.	E15	108
Clinton, Me., U.S.	C17	108
Clinton, Mi., U.S.	H12	110
Clinton, Mn., U.S.	F11	118
Clinton, Mo., U.S.	D3	114
Clinton, Ms., U.S.	J6	114
Clinton, N.C., U.S.	E8	112
Clinton, Ok., U.S.	D8	116
Clinton, On., Can.	G14	110
Clinton, S.C., U.S.	E5	112
Clinton, Tn., U.S.	C2	112
Clinton, Wi., U.S.	H7	110
Clinton, Cape, c., Austl.	D9	70
Clinton-Colden Lake, l., N.T., Can.	D11	96
Clinton Lake, res., Ks., U.S.	M12	118
Clintonville, Wi., U.S.	F7	110
Clintwood, Va., U.S.	B4	112
Clio, Al., U.S.	K11	114
Clio, Mi., U.S.	G12	110
Clio, S.C., U.S.	E7	112
Clipperton, Île, atoll, Oc.	F3	88
Clisson, Fr.	E5	14
Clodomira, Arg.	D6	80
Cloncurry, Austl.	C4	70
Cloncurry, stm., Austl.	B4	70
Clonmel, Ire.	I6	8
Cloppenburg, Ger.	C8	10
Cloquet, Mn., U.S.	D3	110
Cloquet, stm., Mn., U.S.	C3	110
Clorinda, Arg.	C10	80
Cloudcroft, N.M., U.S.	L11	120
Cloud Peak, mtn., Wy., U.S.	F18	122
Clover, S.C., U.S.	D5	112
Cloverdale, Al., U.S.	H9	114
Cloverdale, Ca., U.S.	F2	124
Cloverdale, In., U.S.	C10	114
Clover Pass, Ak., U.S.	I29	100
Cloverport, Ky., U.S.	E10	114
Clovis, Ca., U.S.	H6	124
Clovis, N.M., U.S.	E3	116
Cluj, co., Rom.	C7	20
Cluj-Napoca, Rom.	C7	20
Clunes, Austl.	K5	70
Cluny, Fr.	F11	14
Cluses, Fr.	F13	14
Clusone, Italy	D4	18
Clute, Tx., U.S.	J11	116
Clwyd, co., Wales, U.K.	H10	8
Clyde, Ab., Can.	C21	102
Clyde, Ks., U.S.	L10	118
Clyde, N.C., U.S.	D4	112
Clyde, N.Y., U.S.	D10	108
Clyde, Oh., U.S.	F4	108
Clyde, Tx., U.S.	G7	116
Clyde, stm., N.S., Can.	I8	106
Clyde, stm., Scot., U.K.	F10	8
Clyde, stm., Vt., U.S.	C14	108
Clyde, Firth of, est., Scot., U.K.	F8	8
Clyde Lake, l., Ab., Can.	B23	102
Clyde Park, Mt., U.S.	E15	122
Clyde River, N.T., Can.	B19	96
Clymer, Pa., U.S.	G7	108
Cna, stm., Russia	G25	22
Coachella, Ca., U.S.	K9	124
Coacoyole, Mex.	E6	90
Coahoma, Tx., U.S.	G5	116
Coahuila, state, Mex.	C8	90
Coal, stm., Can.	F31	100
Coal City, Il., U.S.	I7	110
Coalcomán de Matamoros, Mex.	H8	90
Coaldale, Ab., Can.	H22	102
Coal Fork, W.V., U.S.	I5	108
Coalgate, Ok., U.S.	E10	116
Coal Grove, Oh., U.S.	I4	108
Coal Harbour, B.C., Can.	G7	102
Coal Hill, Ar., U.S.	G3	114
Coalhurst, Ab., Can.	H22	102
Coalinga, Ca., U.S.	H5	124
Coalmont, B.C., Can.	H14	102
Coalport, Pa., U.S.	G8	108
Coal River, B.C., Can.	G31	100
Coalspur, Ab., Can.	D17	102
Coalville, Ut., U.S.	D5	120
Coamo, P.R.	E11	94
Coaraci, Braz.	C9	79
Coari, Braz.	J11	84
Coari, stm., Braz.	J11	84
Coari, Lago de, l., Braz.	J11	84
Coast Mountains, mts., N.A.	E6	96
Coast Ranges, mts., U.S.	C2	98
Coatán, stm., N.A.	C2	92
Coatbridge, Scot., U.K.	F9	8
Coatepeque, Guat.	C3	92
Coatepeque, Lago de, l., El Sal.	D5	92
Coatesville, Pa., U.S.	H11	108
Coaticook, P.Q., Can.	B15	108
Coats Island, i., N.T., Can.	D16	96
Coats Land, reg., Ant.	C2	73
Coatzacoalcos, Mex.	H12	90
Coayllo, Peru	E3	82
Cobá, hist., Mex.	G16	90
Cobadin, Rom.	E12	20
Coballo Cocha, Peru	I7	84
Cobalt, On., Can.	C16	110
Cobán, Guat.	B4	92
Cobar, Austl.	H6	70
Cobberas, Mount, mtn., Austl.	K8	70
Cobden, Il., U.S.	E7	114
Cobden, On., Can.	E19	110
Cobequid Bay, b., N.S., Can.	G10	106
Cobequid Mountains, mts., N.S., Can.	G9	106
Cobh, Ire.	J5	8
Cobham, stm., Can.	E20	104
Cobija, Bol.	D7	82
Cobija, Chile	B3	80
Cobleskill, N.Y., U.S.	E12	108
Cobourg, On., Can.	G17	110
Cobourg Peninsula, pen., Austl.	B6	68
Cobquecura, Chile	I2	80
Cobram, Austl.	J6	70
Cobre, stm., Pan.	I13	92
Cobre, Barranca del, val., Mex.	D6	90
Cóbuè, Moz.	D6	58
Coburg, Ger.	E10	10
Coburg Island, i., N.T., Can.	A17	96
Coca, stm., Ec.	H4	84
Cocachacra, Peru	G6	82
Cocentaina, Spain	G11	16
Cochabamba, Bol.	G8	82
Cochabamba, dept., Bol.	G9	82
Coche, Isla, i., Ven.	B11	84
Cochin, India	H4	46
Cochinos, Cayos, is., Hond.	B8	92
Cochise Head, mtn., Az., U.S.	L7	120
Cochran, Ga., U.S.	G3	112
Cochrane, Ab., Can.	F20	102
Cochrane, On., Can.	G16	96
Cochrane, Wi., U.S.	F4	110
Cochrane, stm., Can.	E12	96
Cochrane, Lago (Lago Pueyrredón), l., S.A.	F2	78
Cochranton, Pa., U.S.	F6	108
Cockburn Island, i., On., Can.	E12	110
Coclé, prov., Pan.	I14	92
Coclé del Norte, stm., Pan.	I14	92
Coco, stm., N.A.	G3	94
Coco, Cayo, i., Cuba	C5	94
Coco, Isla del, i., C.R.	G7	88
Cocoa, Fl., U.S.	K6	112
Cocoa Beach, Fl., U.S.	K6	112
Coco Channel, strt., Asia	C1	38
Coco Islands, is., Myan.	G2	40
Coconino Plateau, plat., Az., U.S.	I4	120
Cocorocuma, Cayos, rf., Hond.	B11	92
Cocos, Braz.	C6	79
Cocos (Keeling) Islands, dep., Oc.	K10	24
Cocuiza, stm., Ven.	B7	84
Cocula, Mex.	G8	90
Cod, Cape, pen., Ma., U.S.	F16	108
Codăeşti, Rom.	C11	20
Codajás, Braz.	I11	84
Codera, Cabo, c., Ven.	B10	84
Coderre, Sk., Can.	H8	104
Codesa, Ab., Can.	B16	102
Cod Island, i., Nf., Can.	E20	96
Codó, Braz.	D10	76
Codogno, Italy	D4	18
Codpa, Chile	H7	82
Codroy, Nf., Can.	E14	106
Codroy Pond, Nf., Can.	D15	106
Cody, Ne., U.S.	I6	118
Cody, Wy., U.S.	F16	122
Coeburn, Va., U.S.	C4	112
Coelemu, Chile	I2	80
Coen, Austl.	B8	68
Coén, stm., C.R.	H11	92
Coeroeni (Corentyne), stm., S.A.	F14	84
Coetivy Island, i., Sey.	C11	58
Coeur d'Alene, Id., U.S.	C9	122
Coeur d'Alene, stm., Id., U.S.	C9	122
Coeur d'Alene Lake, l., Id., U.S.	C9	122
Coevorden, Neth.	C10	12
Coffeen, Il., U.S.	C7	114
Coffeeville, Ms., U.S.	I7	114
Coffeyville, Ks., U.S.	N12	118
Coffin Bay, b., Austl.	F7	68
Coffs Harbour, Austl.	H10	70
Cofradía, Hond.	B6	92
Cofre de Perote, Cerro, mtn., Mex.	H11	90
Cofre de Perote, Parque Nacional, Mex.	H11	90
Coggon, Ia., U.S.	H4	110
Cognac, Fr.	G6	14
Cogolin, Fr.	I13	14
Cogoon, stm., Austl.	F8	70
Cogswell, N.D., U.S.	E10	118
Cohengu, stm., Peru	D5	82
Cohocton, stm., N.Y., U.S.	E9	108
Cohoe, Ak., U.S.	F19	100
Cohoes, N.Y., U.S.	E13	108
Cohuna, Austl.	J6	70
Coiba, Isla de, i., Pan.	D2	84
Coig, stm., Arg.	G2	78
Coihaique, Chile	F2	78
Coimbatore, India	G4	46
Coimbra, Braz.	F7	79
Coimbra, Braz.	H13	82
Coimbra, Port.	E3	16
Coin, Ia., U.S.	K12	118
Coín, Spain	I7	16
Coipasa, Lago, l., Bol.	H7	82
Coipasa, Salar de, pl., S.A.	H7	82
Čojbalsan, Mong.	B9	30
Cojedes, Ven.	C8	84
Cojedes, state, Ven.	C8	84
Cojutepeque, El Sal.	D6	92
Cokato, Mn., U.S.	E1	110
Cokeville, Wy., U.S.	H15	122
Colac, Austl.	L5	70
Colalao del Valle, Arg.	D6	80
Colatina, Braz.	E8	79
Colbeck, Cape, c., Ant.	C9	73
Colbert, Ok., U.S.	F10	116
Colborne, On., Can.	F18	110
Colbún, Chile	H3	80
Colby, Ks., U.S.	L6	118
Colby, Wi., U.S.	F5	110
Colca, Peru	E4	82
Colca, stm., Peru	F5	82
Colcamar, Peru	B3	82
Colchester, Ct., U.S.	F14	108
Colchester, Eng., U.K.	J14	8
Colchester, Il., U.S.	J5	110
Cold Bay, Ak., U.S.	I13	100
Cold Lake, Ab., Can.	D4	104
Cold Lake, l., Can.	D4	104
Cold Lake, Canadian Forces Base, mil., Ab., Can.	D4	104
Cold Lake Indian Reserve, Ab., Can.	D4	104
Cold Spring, Mn., U.S.	E1	110
Coldspring, Tx., U.S.	I11	116
Coldstream, Scot., U.K.	F11	8
Coldwater, Ks., U.S.	N8	118
Coldwater, Mi., U.S.	I10	110
Coldwater, Ms., U.S.	H7	114
Coldwater, Oh., U.S.	G2	108
Coldwater, stm., Ms., U.S.	H6	114
Coldwater Indian Reserve, B.C., Can.	G14	102
Colebrook, N.H., U.S.	C15	108
Cole Camp, Mo., U.S.	D3	114
Coleman, Ab., Can.	H20	102
Coleman, Fl., U.S.	K4	112
Coleman, Mi., U.S.	G11	110
Coleman, Tx., U.S.	H7	116
Coleman, Wi., U.S.	E7	110
Coleman, stm., Austl.	B8	68
Coleman, Lake, res., Tx., U.S.	G7	116
Colen Lakes, l., Mb., Can.	D19	104
Colenso, S. Afr.	G9	66
Coleraine, Austl.	K4	70
Coleraine, Mn., U.S.	C2	110
Coleridge, Ne., U.S.	I10	118
Coles, Ms., U.S.	K5	114
Coles, Punta, c., Peru	G6	82
Colesberg, S. Afr.	H7	66
Coleville, Sk., Can.	G5	104
Colfax, Ca., U.S.	E5	124
Colfax, Ia., U.S.	I2	110
Colfax, Il., U.S.	J7	110
Colfax, In., U.S.	B10	114
Colfax, La., U.S.	K4	114
Colfax, Wa., U.S.	D8	122
Colfax, Wi., U.S.	F4	110
Colhué Huapi, Lago, l., Arg.	F3	78
Colico, Italy	C4	18
Colima, Mex.	H8	90
Colima, state, Mex.	H8	90
Colima, Nevado de, mtn., Mex.	H8	90
Colimes, stm., Ec.	H2	84
Colina, Chile	G3	80
Colinas, Braz.	E10	76
Colinas, Braz.	C4	79
Colinet, Nf., Can.	E20	106
Colinton, Ab., Can.	C21	102
Collarenebri, Austl.	G8	70
Collbran, Co., U.S.	E9	120
College, Ak., U.S.	D21	100
Collegedale, Tn., U.S.	G11	114
College Park, Ga., U.S.	F2	112
College Place, Wa., U.S.	D7	122
College Station, Ar., U.S.	H4	114
College Station, Tx., U.S.	I10	116
Collegeville, In., U.S.	B9	114
Collerina, Austl.	G7	70
Colleymount, B.C., Can.	C8	102
Colleyville, Tx., U.S.	G9	116
Collie, Austl.	F3	68
Collier Bay, b., Austl.	C4	68
Collier Range National Park, Austl.	D3	68
Collierville, Tn., U.S.	G7	114
Collingwood, On., Can.	F15	110
Collins, Ga., U.S.	G4	112
Collins, Ia., U.S.	I2	110
Collins, Ms., U.S.	K7	114
Collins, stm., Tn., U.S.	G11	114
Collins Bay, On., Can.	F19	110
Collinston, La., U.S.	J5	114
Collinsville, Al., U.S.	H11	114
Collinsville, Austl.	C7	70
Collinsville, Ms., U.S.	J8	114
Collinsville, Ok., U.S.	C11	116
Collinsville, Tx., U.S.	F10	116
Collinwood, Tn., U.S.	G9	114
Collipulli, Chile	I2	80
Collister, Id., U.S.	G9	122
Colman, S.D., U.S.	H11	118
Colmar, Fr.	D14	14
Colmenar de Oreja, Spain	E8	16
Colmenar Viejo, Spain	E8	16
Colmeneros, Mex.	H9	90
Colmesneil, Tx., U.S.	L2	114
Colnett, Cabo, c., Mex.	B1	90
Colo, Ia., U.S.	H2	110
Cologne see Köln, Ger.	E6	10
Cologne, Mn., U.S.	F2	110
Cololo, Nevado, mtn., Bol.	F7	82
Coloma, Mi., U.S.	H9	110
Coloma, Wi., U.S.	F6	110
Colombey-les-Belles, Fr.	D12	14
Colômbia, Braz.	F4	79
Colombia, Col.	F5	84
Colombia, ctry., S.A.	C4	76
Colombo, Braz.	C14	80
Colombo, Sri L.	I5	46
Colome, S.D., U.S.	H8	118
Colón, Arg.	G8	80
Colón, Arg.	G9	80
Colón, Cuba	C4	94
Colon, Mi., U.S.	I10	110
Colón, Pan.	C3	84
Colón, Ur.	G11	80
Colón, prov., Pan.	I14	92
Colón, dept., Hond.	B9	92
Colón, Archipiélago de (Galapagos Islands), is., Ec.	j13	84a
Colón, Isla, i., Pan.	H12	92
Colón, Montañas de, mts., Hond.	C10	92
Colônia, stm., Braz.	C9	79
Colonia Alvear, Arg.	H5	80
Colonia Caroya, Arg.	F6	80
Colonia del Sacramento, Ur.	H10	80
Colonia Dora, Arg.	E7	80
Colonia Elisa, Arg.	D9	80
Colonia José Mármol, Arg.	D8	80
Colonia Lavalleja, Ur.	F10	80
Colonial Heights, Va., U.S.	B9	112
Colonias Unidas, Arg.	D9	80
Colonia Vicente Guerrero, Mex.	B1	90
Colonia Villafañe, Arg.	D9	80
Colonsay, Sk., Can.	G9	104
Colony, Ks., U.S.	M12	118
Colorada Grande, Salina, pl., Arg.	J7	80
Colorado, C.R.	G11	92
Colorado, Hond.	B7	92
Colorado, state, U.S.	D5	98
Colorado, stm., Arg.	J7	80
Colorado, stm., Braz.	E10	82
Colorado, stm., N.A.	M1	120
Colorado, stm., Tx., U.S.	J10	116
Colorado City, Az., U.S.	H4	120
Colorado City, Co., U.S.	G12	120
Colorado City, Tx., U.S.	G6	116
Colorado River Aqueduct, Ca., U.S.	K10	124
Colorado Springs, Co., U.S.	F12	120
Colotepec, stm., Mex.	J11	90
Colotlán, Mex.	F8	90
Colquechaca, Bol.	H8	82
Colquencha, Bol.	G7	82
Colquiri, Bol.	G8	82
Colquitt, Ga., U.S.	H2	112
Colstrip, Mt., U.S.	E19	122
Colt, Ar., U.S.	G6	114
Colta, Peru	F5	82
Coltauco, Chile	H3	80
Colton, Ca., U.S.	J8	124
Colton, S.D., U.S.	H11	118
Columbia, Al., U.S.	H1	112
Columbia, Ca., U.S.	F5	124
Columbia, Il., U.S.	D6	114
Columbia, Ky., U.S.	E11	114
Columbia, La., U.S.	J4	114
Columbia, Md., U.S.	H10	108
Columbia, Mo., U.S.	D4	114
Columbia, Ms., U.S.	K7	114
Columbia, N.C., U.S.	D10	112
Columbia, Pa., U.S.	G10	108
Columbia, S.C., U.S.	E5	112
Columbia, Tn., U.S.	G9	114
Columbia, stm., N.A.	G8	96
Columbia, Cape, c., N.T., Can.	A12	86
Columbia, Mount, mtn., Can.	E17	102
Columbia City, In., U.S.	A11	114
Columbia Falls, Me., U.S.	C19	108
Columbia Falls, Mt., U.S.	B11	122
Columbia Icefield, Can.	E17	102
Columbia Lake, l., B.C., Can.	G19	102
Columbia Lake Indian Reserve, B.C., Can.	G19	102
Columbia Mountains, mts., N.A.	D14	102
Columbiana, Al., U.S.	I10	114
Columbiana, Oh., U.S.	G6	108
Columbiaville, Mi., U.S.	G12	110
Columbus, Ga., U.S.	G2	112
Columbus, In., U.S.	C11	114
Columbus, Ks., U.S.	N13	118
Columbus, Ms., U.S.	I8	114
Columbus, Mt., U.S.	E16	122
Columbus, N.C., U.S.	D4	112
Columbus, N.D., U.S.	C5	118
Columbus, Ne., U.S.	J10	118
Columbus, N.M., U.S.	M9	120
Columbus, Oh., U.S.	H4	108
Columbus, Tx., U.S.	J10	116
Columbus, Wi., U.S.	G6	110
Columbus Grove, Oh., U.S.	G2	108
Columbus Junction, Ia., U.S.	I4	110
Columbus Point, c., Bah.	B7	94
Coluna, Braz.	E7	79
Colusa, Ca., U.S.	E3	124
Colville, Wa., U.S.	B8	122
Colville, stm., Ak., U.S.	B19	100
Colville, stm., Wa., U.S.	B8	122
Colville Lake, l., N.T., Can.	C31	100
Comacchio, Italy	E7	18
Comala, Mex.	H8	90
Comalapa, Guat.	C4	92
Comalapa, Nic.	E9	92
Comalcalco, Mex.	H13	90
Coman, Mount, mtn., Ant.	C12	73
Comanche, Ok., U.S.	E9	116
Comanche, Tx., U.S.	H8	116
Comandante Ferraz, sci., Ant.	B1	73
Comandante Fontana, Arg.	C9	80
Comandante Leal, Arg.	F6	80
Comandante Nicanor Otamendi, Arg.	J10	80
Comarapa, Bol.	G9	82
Comas, Peru	D4	82
Comayagua, Hond.	C7	92
Comayagua, dept., Hond.	C7	92
Comayagua, Montañas de, mts., Hond.	C7	92
Combahee, stm., S.C., U.S.	G6	112
Combarbalá, Chile	F3	80
Combeaufontaine, Fr.	E12	14
Combourg, Fr.	D5	14
Comboyne, Austl.	H10	70
Combronde, Fr.	G10	14
Come by Chance, Nf., Can.	E20	106
Comendador, Dom. Rep.	E9	94
Comendador Gomes, Braz.	E4	79
Comer, Ga., U.S.	E3	112
Comercinho, Braz.	D8	79
Comfort, N.C., U.S.	D9	112
Comfort, Tx., U.S.	J8	116
Comfort, Cape, c., N.T., Can.	C16	96
Comfrey, Mn., U.S.	G13	118
Comilla, Bngl.	I14	44
Comiso, Italy	M9	18
Comitan de Dominguez, Mex.	I13	90
Commentry, Fr.	F9	14
Commerce, Ga., U.S.	E3	112
Commerce, Ok., U.S.	C12	116
Commerce, Tx., U.S.	F11	116
Commerce City, Co., U.S.	E12	120
Commercy, Fr.	D12	14
Comminges, reg., Fr.	I7	14
Committee Bay, b., N.T., Can.	C15	96
Como, Italy	D4	18
Como, Ms., U.S.	H7	114
Como, Tx., U.S.	F11	116
Como, Lago di, l., Italy	C4	18
Comodoro Rivadavia, Arg.	F3	78
Comores, Archipel des, is., Afr.	D8	58
Comorin, Cape, c., India	H4	46
Comoros (Comores), ctry., Afr.	D8	58
Comox, B.C., Can.	H10	102
Comox, Canadian Forces Base, mil., B.C., Can.	H10	102
Compiègne, Fr.	C9	14
Compostela, Mex.	G7	90
Comprida, Ilha, i., Braz.	C15	80
Compton, Ca., U.S.	K7	124
Comrat, Mol.	C12	20
Comstock, Ne., U.S.	J8	118
Comstock, Tx., U.S.	J5	116
Comstock Park, Mi., U.S.	G10	110
Čona, stm., Russia	E13	28
Conakry, Gui.	G3	64
Conambo, stm., Ec.	H4	84
Conasauga, stm., U.S.	E2	112
Concarán, Arg.	G6	80
Concarneau, Fr.	E3	14
Conceição, Braz.	B12	82
Conceição, Cachoeira, wtfl, Braz.	C9	82
Conceição da Barra, Braz.	E9	79
Conceição das Alagoas, Braz.	E4	79
Conceição de Ipanema, Braz.	E8	79
Conceição do Almeida, Braz.	B9	79
Conceição do Araguaia, Braz.	E9	76
Conceição do Mato Dentro, Braz.	E7	79
Conceição do Maú, Braz.	F13	84
Conceição do Norte, Braz.	B5	79
Concepción, Arg.	E10	80
Concepción, Arg.	D6	80
Concepción, Bol.	D8	82
Concepción, Bol.	G10	82
Concepción, Chile	I2	80
Concepción, Col.	D6	84
Concepción, Para.	B10	80
Concepción, Peru	D4	82
Concepción, dept., Para.	B10	80
Concepción, Bahía, b., Mex.	D4	90
Concepción, Laguna, l., Bol.	G11	82
Concepción, Volcán, vol., Nic.	F9	92
Concepción de Ataco, El Sal.	D5	92
Concepción de la Sierra, Arg.	D11	80
Concepcíon del Oro, Mex.	E9	90
Concepción del Uruguay, Arg.	G9	80
Concepción Huista, Guat.	B3	92
Concepción Quezaltepeque, El Sal.	C6	92
Conception Bay, b., Nf., Can.	E20	106
Conception Bay, b., Nmb.	D2	66
Conchagua, El Sal.	D7	92
Conchagua, Volcán, vol., El Sal.	D7	92
Conchas, stm., N.M., U.S.	D2	116
Conchas Dam, N.M., U.S.	D2	116
Conche, Nf., Can.	B18	106
Conches-en-Ouche, Fr.	D7	14
Conchi, Chile	B4	80
Concho, Az., U.S.	J7	120
Concho, stm., Tx., U.S.	H7	116
Conchos, stm., Mex.	C7	90
Conchos, stm., Mex.	E10	90
Concise, Switz.	E6	13
Concón, Chile	G3	80
Concord, Ca., U.S.	G3	124
Concord, Ga., U.S.	F2	112
Concord, Mi., U.S.	H11	110
Concord, N.C., U.S.	D6	112
Concord, N.H., U.S.	D15	108
Concordia, Arg.	F9	80
Concórdia, Braz.	D12	80
Concórdia, Braz.	J9	84
Concordia, Ks., U.S.	L10	118
Concordia, Mex.	F6	90
Concordia, Mo., U.S.	D3	114
Concordia, Peru	J5	84
Concrete, Wa., U.S.	B4	122
Conde, Braz.	A10	79
Condé, Fr.	D6	14
Conde, S.D., U.S.	F9	118
Condega, Nic.	D8	92
Condeúba, Braz.	C8	79
Condobolin, Austl.	I7	70
Condom, Fr.	I7	14
Condon, Or., U.S.	E5	122
Condoto, Col.	E4	84
Cone, Tx., U.S.	F5	116
Conecuh, stm., U.S.	K10	114
Conegliano, Italy	D7	18
Conejos, Co., U.S.	G10	120
Conejos, stm., Co., U.S.	G10	120
Confederation Lake, l., On., Can.	G22	104
Confluence, Pa., U.S.	H7	108
Confolens, Fr.	F7	14
Confusion Bay, b., Nf., Can.	C18	106
Confuso, stm., Para.	C9	80
Congaree, stm., S.C., U.S.	F6	112
Congaz, Mol.	C12	20
Congo, ctry., Afr.	B3	58
Congo (Zaire) (Zaïre), stm., Afr.	C2	58
Congo Basin, Afr.	H9	52
Congress, Sk., Can.	I8	104
Coniston, On., Can.	D15	110
Conitaca, Mex.	E6	90
Conjeeveram see Kānchipuram, India	F5	46
Conklin, Ab., Can.	B23	102
Connaught, hist. reg., Ire.	H4	8
Conneaut, Oh., U.S.	F6	108
Conneautville, Pa., U.S.	F6	108
Connecticut, state, U.S.	C12	98
Connecticut, stm., U.S.	F14	108
Connell, Wa., U.S.	D7	122
Connell, Mount, mtn., B.C., Can.	H19	102
Connellsville, Pa., U.S.	G7	108
Connemara, reg., Ire.	H4	8
Connersville, In., U.S.	C11	114
Conn Lake, l., N.T., Can.	B18	96
Connors Range, mts., Austl.	C8	70
Cononaco, stm., Ec.	H4	84
Conorochite, stm., Ven.	F9	84
Conover, N.C., U.S.	D5	112
Conquest, Sk., Can.	G7	104
Conquista, Braz.	E5	79
Conrad, Ia., U.S.	H3	110
Conrad, Mt., U.S.	B14	122
Conroe, Tx., U.S.	I11	116
Conroe, Lake, res., Tx., U.S.	I11	116
Consecon, On., Can.	F18	110
Conselheiro Lafaiete, Braz.	F7	79
Conselheiro Pena, Braz.	E8	79
Consolación del Sur, Cuba	C3	94
Con Son, is., Viet.	J9	40
Consort, Ab., Can.	F4	104
Constance, Lake see Bodensee, l., Eur.	E16	14
Constanța, Rom.	E12	20
Constanța, co., Rom.	E12	20
Constantina, Spain	H6	16
Constantine see Qacentina, Alg.	B14	62
Constantine, Mi., U.S.	I10	110
Constantinople see İstanbul, Tur.	H12	20
Constitución, Chile	H2	80
Constitución, Ur.	F10	80
Consuegra, Spain	F8	16
Consul, Sk., Can.	I5	104
Contamana, Peru	B4	82
Contas, Rio de, stm., Braz.	C9	79
Contendas do Sincorá, Braz.	B8	79
Continental, Oh., U.S.	F2	108
Contraalmirante Cordero, Arg.	J4	80
Contratación, Col.	D6	84
Contumazá, Peru	B2	82
Contwoyto Lake, l., N.T., Can.	C10	96
Conty, Fr.	C9	14
Convención, Col.	C6	84
Convent, La., U.S.	L6	114
Convento, C.R.	H11	92
Conversano, Italy	I12	18
Converse, In., U.S.	B11	114
Convoy, Oh., U.S.	G2	108
Conway, Ar., U.S.	G4	114
Conway, Mo., U.S.	E4	114
Conway, N.C., U.S.	C9	112
Conway, N.H., U.S.	D15	108
Conway, P.E., Can.	F10	106
Conway, S.C., U.S.	F7	112
Conway Springs, Ks., U.S.	N10	118
Conyers, Ga., U.S.	F2	112
Cook, Mn., U.S.	C3	110
Cook, Ne., U.S.	K11	118
Cook, Cape, c., B.C., Can.	G7	102
Cook, Mount, mtn., N.Z.	E3	72
Cookes Peak, mtn., N.M., U.S.	L9	120
Cookeville, Tn., U.S.	F11	114
Cookhouse, S. Afr.	I7	66
Cooking Lake, l., Ab., Can.	D21	102
Cook Inlet, b., Ak., U.S.	F18	100
Cook Islands, dep., Oc.	J23	126
Cook's Harbour, Nf., Can.	A18	106
Cook Strait, strt., N.Z.	D5	72
Cooktown, Austl.	C9	68
Coolah, Austl.	H8	70
Coolamon, Austl.	J7	70
Coolangatta, Austl.	G10	70
Cooleemee, N.C., U.S.	D6	112
Coolgardie, Austl.	F4	68
Coolidge, Az., U.S.	L5	120
Coolidge, Ga., U.S.	H3	112
Coolidge, Tx., U.S.	H10	116
Coolin, Id., U.S.	B9	122
Cooma, Austl.	K8	70
Coonabarabran, Austl.	H8	70
Coonamble, Austl.	H8	70
Coonoor, India	G4	46
Coon Rapids, Ia., U.S.	J13	118
Coon Rapids, Mn., U.S.	E2	110
Coon Valley, Wi., U.S.	G4	110
Cooper, Tx., U.S.	F11	116
Cooper, Mount, mtn., B.C., Can.	G17	102
Cooper Creek, stm., Austl.	G3	70
Cooper Landing, Ak., U.S.	F20	100
Cooper Mountain, mtn., Ak., U.S.	F20	100
Cooper Road, La., U.S.	J3	114
Coopers, Al., U.S.	J10	114
Cooperstown, N.D., U.S.	D9	118
Cooperstown, N.Y., U.S.	E12	108
Coopersville, Mi., U.S.	G10	110
Cooroy, Austl.	F10	70
Coosa, stm., U.S.	J10	114
Coosawhatchie, stm., S.C., U.S.	G5	112
Coos Bay, Or., U.S.	G1	122
Coos Bay, b., Or., U.S.	G1	122
Cootamundra, Austl.	J8	70
Copacabana, Arg.	E5	80
Copacabana, Bol.	G7	82
Copainalá, Mex.	I13	90
Copán, Hond.	C5	92
Copan, Ok., U.S.	C11	116
Copán, dept., Hond.	C6	92
Copán, hist., Hond.	C5	92
Copatana, Braz.	I9	84
Cope, Co., U.S.	L5	118
Copeá, Paraná, mth., Braz.	I11	84
Copeau, stm., Sk., Can.	F11	104
Copeland, Fl., U.S.	N5	112
Copenhagen see København, Den.	N13	6
Copenhagen, N.Y., U.S.	D11	108
Copertino, Italy	I13	18
Copetonas, Arg.	J8	80
Copiapó, Chile	D3	80
Copiapó, stm., Chile	D3	80
Copley, Austl.	H3	70
Copparo, Italy	E6	18
Copper, stm., Ak., U.S.	F22	100
Copperas Cove, Tx., U.S.	H9	116
Copper Butte, mtn., Wa., U.S.	B7	122
Copper Canyon see Cobre, Barranca del, val., Mex.	D6	90
Copper Cliff, On., Can.	D14	110
Copper Harbor, Mi., U.S.	C8	110
Coppermine, N.T., Can.	C9	96
Coppermine, stm., N.T., Can.	C10	96
Copper Mountain, B.C., Can.	H14	102
Coppet, Switz.	F5	13
Copton Creek, stm., Ab., Can.	C15	102
Coquille, Or., U.S.	G1	122
Coquille, stm., Or., U.S.	G1	122
Coquimbo, Chile	E3	80
Coquimbo, prov., Chile	F3	80
Corabia, Rom.	F8	20
Coração de Jesus, Braz.	D6	79
Coração de Maria, Braz.	B9	79
Coracora, Peru	F5	82
Coral Gables, Fl., U.S.	N6	112
Coral Harbour, N.T., Can.	D16	96
Coralque, stm., Peru	G6	82
Coral Sea, Oc.	J19	126
Coral Sea Islands Territory, ter., Austl.	B9	70
Coralville, Ia., U.S.	I4	110
Coralville Lake, res., Ia., U.S.	I4	110
Coram, Mt., U.S.	B11	122
Corangamite, Lake, l., Austl.	L5	70
Corato, Italy	H11	18
Corbeil-Essonnes, Fr.	D9	14
Corbin, Ky., U.S.	C2	112
Corcoran, Ca., U.S.	H6	124
Corcovado, Golfo, b., Chile	E2	78
Corcovado, Parque Nacional, C.R.	I11	92
Corcovado, Volcán, vol., Chile	E2	78
Cordeiro, Braz.	G7	79
Cordele, Ga., U.S.	H3	112
Cordell, Ok., U.S.	D8	116
Cordell Hull Reservoir, res., Tn., U.S.	F11	114
Corder, Mo., U.S.	C3	114
Cordillera, dept., Para.	C10	80
Cordillo Downs, Austl.	F4	70
Cordisburgo, Braz.	E6	79
Córdoba, Arg.	F6	80
Córdoba, Mex.	H11	90
Córdoba, Spain	H7	16
Córdoba, prov., Arg.	F7	80
Córdoba, dept., Col.	C5	84
Cordova, Ak., U.S.	F22	100
Cordova, Al., U.S.	I9	114
Cordova, Il., U.S.	I5	110
Córdova, Peru	F4	82
Corentyne (Corantijn) (Coeroeni), stm., S.A.	E14	84
Corerepe, Mex.	E5	90
Corfu see Kérkira, Grc.	J3	20
Corfu see Kérkira, i., Grc.	J3	20
Coria, Spain	F5	16
Coria del Río, Spain	H5	16
Coribe, Braz.	B6	79
Corigliano Calabro, Italy	J11	18
Corinda, Austl.	A3	70
Corinne, Ut., U.S.	C4	120
Corinne, W.V., U.S.	B5	112
Corinth see Kórinthos, Grc.	L6	20
Corinth, Ms., U.S.	H8	114
Corinth, N.Y., U.S.	D13	108
Corinth, Gulf of see Korinthiakós Kólpos, b., Grc.	K6	20
Corinth Canal see Korínthou, Dhiórix, Grc.	L6	20
Corinto, Braz.	E6	79
Corinto, El Sal.	D7	92
Corinto, Nic.	E7	92
Coripata, Bol.	G8	82
Corire, Peru	G5	82
Coris, Peru	C3	82
Cork, Ire.	J5	8
Cork, co., Ire.	I5	8
Corlay, Fr.	D3	14
Corleone, Italy	L8	18
Çorlu, Tur.	H11	20
Čormeilles, Fr.	C7	14
Cormorant, Mb., Can.	D14	104

Name	Map Ref.	Page
Dike, Ia., U.S.	H3	110
Dikhil, Dji.	F9	56
Dikili, Tur.	J10	20
Dikodougou, C. Iv.	G7	64
Diksmuide (Dixmude), Bel.	F2	12
Dikson, Russia	C8	28
Dikwa, Nig.	F9	54
Dila, Eth.	N10	60
Dili, Indon.	G8	38
Dill City, Ok., U.S.	D7	116
Diller, Ne., U.S.	K11	118
Dilley, Tx., U.S.	K7	116
Dilling, Sudan	K5	60
Dillingen [an der Donau], Ger.	G10	10
Dillingham, Ak., U.S.	G15	100
Dillon, Co., U.S.	E10	120
Dillon, Mt., U.S.	E13	122
Dillon, S.C., U.S.	E7	112
Dillon, stm., Can.	C5	104
Dillon Lake, l., Sk., Can.	C5	104
Dillon Lake, res., Oh., U.S.	G4	108
Dillon Mountain, mtn., N.M., U.S.	K8	120
Dillwyn, Va., U.S.	B8	112
Dilly, Mali	D6	64
Dilolo, Zaire	D4	58
Dilworth, Mn., U.S.	E11	118
Dimāpur, India	H15	44
Dimashq (Damascus), Syria	A6	50
Dimboola, Austl.	K5	70
Dime, Eth.	N9	60
Dime Box, Tx., U.S.	I10	116
Dimitrovgrad, Bul.	G9	20
Dimitrovgrad, Russia	G7	26
Dimmitt, Tx., U.S.	E4	116
Dimona, Isr.	F4	50
Dinājpur, Bngl.	H13	44
Dinan, Fr.	D4	14
Dinant, Bel.	H6	12
Dinara (Dinaric Alps), mts., Eur.	F11	18
Dinard, Fr.	D4	14
Dinaric Alps see Dinara, mts., Eur.	F11	18
Dindar, Nahr ad- (Dinder), stm., Afr.	K8	60
Dindigul, India	G4	46
Dindima, Nig.	F15	64
Dingalan Bay, b., Phil.	n19	39b
Dinggyê, China	F4	30
Dinghai, China	E11	34
Dingle Bay, b., Ire.	I3	8
Dingnan, China	K3	34
Dingolfing, Ger.	G12	10
Dingshuzhen, China	D8	34
Dinguiraye, Gui.	F4	64
Dingwall, N.S., Can.	F13	106
Dingxi, China	D7	30
Dingxian, China	E2	32
Dingyuan, China	C6	34
Dinh Lap, Viet.	D9	40
Dinkelsbühl, Ger.	F10	10
Dinokwe, Bots.	D8	66
Dinorwic, On., Can.	I22	104
Dinorwic Lake, l., On., Can.	I22	104
Dinosaur, Co., U.S.	D7	120
Dinosaur Lake, res., B.C., Can.	B12	102
Dinosaur Provincial Park, Ab., Can.	G23	102
Dinsmore, Sk., Can.	G7	104
Dinuba, Ca., U.S.	H6	124
Dinwiddie, Va., U.S.	B9	112
Dioïla, Mali	E6	64
Diomede, Ak., U.S.	D10	100
Dionísio, Braz.	E7	79
Dionísio Cerqueira, Braz.	D12	80
Dionne, Lac, l., P.Q., Can.	C6	106
Diorama, Braz.	D3	79
Diouloulou, Sen.	E1	64
Dioundiou, Niger	E11	64
Dioura, Mali	D7	64
Diourbel, Sen.	D1	64
Dipkarpaz, N. Cyp.	D3	48
Dipolog, Phil.	D7	38
Dippoldiswalde, Ger.	E13	10
Dīr, Pak.	C4	44
Dire Dawa, Eth.	G9	56
Diriamba, Nic.	F8	92
Dirico, Ang.	A5	66
Diriomo, Nic.	F8	92
Dirj, Libya	E16	62
Dirk Hartog Island, i., Austl.	E2	68
Dirrah, Sudan	K4	60
Dirranbandi, Austl.	G8	70
Ḍirs, Sau. Ar.	E3	47
Dirty Devil, stm., Ut., U.S.	F6	120
Disappointment, Cape, c., S. Geor.	J11	74
Disappointment, Cape, c., Wa., U.S.	D1	122
Disappointment, Lake, l., Austl.	D4	68
Disaster Bay, b., Austl.	K9	70
Discovery Bay, b., Austl.	L4	70
Discovery Passage, strt., B.C., Can.	G9	102
Disentis, Switz.	E10	13
Dishman, Wa., U.S.	C8	122
Dishnā, Egypt	D7	60
Disko, i., Grnld.	C22	96
Dismal, stm., Ne., U.S.	J7	118
Dismal Lakes, l., N.T., Can.	C9	96
Disney, Ok., U.S.	C11	116
Disraeli, P.Q., Can.	B15	108
Dissimieux, Lac, l., P.Q., Can.	C4	106
Distrito Federal, dept., Braz.	C5	79
Distrito Federal, dept., Ven.	B9	84
Disūq, Egypt	B6	60
Diu, India	J4	44
Divalá, Pan.	I12	92
Divenskaja, Russia	B13	22
Divernon, Il., U.S.	C7	114
Divinhe, Moz.	C12	66
Divino, Braz.	F7	79
Divinópolis, Braz.	F6	79
Divisor, Serra do (Cordillera Ultraoriental), plat., S.A.	C5	82
Divnoje, Russia	H6	26
Divriği, Tur.	B5	48
Dix, Ne., U.S.	J4	118
Dix, stm., Ky., U.S.	B2	112
Dixfield, Me., U.S.	C16	108
Dixie Valley, val., Nv., U.S.	D7	124
Dixmude (Diksmuide), Bel.	F2	12
Dixon, Ca., U.S.	F4	124
Dixon, Il., U.S.	I6	110
Dixon, Ky., U.S.	E9	114
Dixon, Mo., U.S.	E4	114
Dixon, N.M., U.S.	H11	120
Dixon Entrance, strt., N.A.	C2	102
Dixons Mills, Al., U.S.	J9	114
Diyālā (Sīrvān), stm., Asia	E8	48
Diyarbakır, Tur.	C6	48
Dizhou, China	C9	40
Dja, stm., Afr.	H9	54
Djakarta see Jakarta, Indon.	j13	39a
Djamâa, Alg.	D13	62
Djambala, Congo	B2	58
Djanet, Alg.	H15	62
Djedi, Oued, val., Alg.	C13	62
Djema, C.A.R.	N3	60
Djemila, hist., Alg.	B13	62
Djénné, Mali	E7	64
Djérem, stm., Cam.	G9	54
Djibo, Burkina	D9	64
Djibouti, Dji.	F9	56
Djibouti, ctry., Afr.	F9	56
Djokupunda, Zaire	C4	58
Djougou, Benin	G10	64
Djúpivogur, Ice.	B6	6a
Djurås, Swe.	K14	6
Dmitrija Lapteva, proliv, strt., Russia	C20	28
Dmitrijevka, Russia	I23	22
Dmitrijev-L'govskij, Russia	I18	22
Dmitrov, Russia	E20	22
Dmitrovskij Pogost, Russia	F22	22
Dmitrovsk-Orlovskij, Russia	I18	22
Dnepropetrovsk see Dnipropetrovs'k, Ukr.	H4	26
Dnieper, stm., Eur.	H4	26
Dniprodzerzhyns'k, Ukr.	H4	26
Dnipropetrovs'k, Ukr.	H4	26
Dnister, stm., Eur.	F13	4
Dnistrovs'kyy lyman, l., Ukr.	C14	20
Dnjaprouska Buhski, kanal, Bela.	I7	22
Dno, Russia	D12	22
Doaktown, N.B., Can.	F7	106
Doany, Madag.	o23	67b
Doba, Chad	E4	56
Dobane, C.A.R.	N3	60
Dobbiaco, Italy	C7	18
Dobczyce, Pol.	F20	10
Dobele, Lat.	E6	22
Döbeln, Ger.	D13	10
Doberai, Jazirah, pen., Indon.	F9	38
Doboj, Bos.	E2	20
Dobr'anka, Russia	F9	26
Dobrič, Bul.	F11	20
Dobrinka, Russia	I23	22
Dobříš, Czech Rep.	F14	10
Dobromyl', Ukr.	F22	10
Dobrudžansko plato, plat., Bul.	F11	20
Dobruja, hist. reg., Eur.	E12	20
Dobruš, Bela.	I14	22
Dobson, N.C., U.S.	C6	112
Doce, stm., Braz.	E8	79
Doce, stm., Braz.	E3	79
Dock Junction, Ga., U.S.	H5	112
Doctor Arroyo, Mex.	F9	90
Doctor Cecilio Báez, Para.	C10	80
Doctor Pedro P. Peña, Para.	B7	80
Dod Ballāpur, India	F4	46
Doddridge, Ar., U.S.	I3	114
Doddsville, Ms., U.S.	I6	114
Dodecanese see Dhodhekánisos, is., Grc.	M10	20
Dodge, Ne., U.S.	J11	118
Dodge Center, Mn., U.S.	F3	110
Dodge City, Ks., U.S.	N7	118
Dodgeville, Wi., U.S.	H5	110
Dodola, Eth.	N10	60
Dodoma, Tan.	C7	58
Dodsland, Sk., Can.	G6	104
Dodson, La., U.S.	J4	114
Dodson, Mt., U.S.	B17	122
Dodson, Tx., U.S.	E6	116
Doe River, B.C., Can.	A14	102
Doerun, Ga., U.S.	H3	112
Doetinchem, Neth.	E9	12
Dogai Coring, l., China	C13	44
Dog Creek, B.C., Can.	F12	102
Dog Creek, stm., B.C., Can.	F12	102
Dog Island, i., Anguilla	E13	94
Dog Lake, l., Mb., Can.	G16	104
Dōgo, i., Japan	K8	36
Do Gonbadān, Iran	F11	48
Dogondoutchi, Niger	E12	64
Dogpound Creek, stm., Ab., Can.	F20	102
Doğubayazıt, Tur.	B8	48
Doha see Ad-Dawḥah, Qatar	B7	47
Doiran, Lake, l., Eur.	H6	20
Dois de Novembro, Cachoeira, wtfl, Braz.	C10	82
Dokka, Nor.	K12	6
Doksy, Czech Rep.	E14	10
Dokšycy, Bela.	G10	22
Doland, S.D., U.S.	G9	118
Dolbeau, P.Q., Can.	G18	96
Dol-de-Bretagne, Fr.	D5	14
Dole, Fr.	E12	14
Dolega, Pan.	C1	84
Dolgeville, N.Y., U.S.	D12	108
Dolgoje, Russia	I20	22
Dolgorukovo, Russia	I21	22
Dolinsk, Russia	H20	28
Dolisie, Congo	B2	58
Dolj, co., Rom.	E7	20
Dollard, b., Eur.	B11	12
Dolmatovskij, Russia	D25	22
Dolomites see Dolomiti, mts., Italy	C6	18
Dolomiti, mts., Italy	C6	18
Dolores, Arg.	I10	80
Dolores, Co., U.S.	G8	120
Dolores, Col.	F5	84
Dolores, Guat.	I15	90
Dolores, Ur.	G9	80
Dolores, Ven.	C8	84
Dolores, stm., U.S.	F8	120
Dolores Hidalgo, Mex.	G9	90
Dolphin and Union Strait, strt., N.T., Can.	C9	96
Dolzhak, Ukr.	A10	20
Dom Aquino, Braz.	C1	79
Domažlice, Czech Rep.	F12	10
Dombarovskij, Russia	G9	26
Dombås, Nor.	J11	6
Dombrád, Hung.	G21	10
Dom Cavati, Braz.	E7	79
Dome Creek, B.C., Can.	D13	102
Domeyko, Chile	E3	80
Domeyko, Cordillera, mts., Chile	B4	80
Domfront, Fr.	D6	14
Domiciano Ribeiro, Braz.	D5	79
Domíngo M. Irala, Para.	C11	80
Domingos Martins, Braz.	F8	79
Dominica, ctry., N.A.	G14	94
Dominical, C.R.	H11	92
Dominican Republic (República Dominicana), ctry., N.A.	E9	94
Dominica Passage, strt., N.A.	G14	94
Dominion, N.S., Can.	F13	106
Dominion, Cape, c., N.T., Can.	C18	96
Dominion City, Mb., Can.	I17	104
Dom Joaquim, Braz.	E7	79
Domo, Eth.	G10	56
Domodedovo, Russia	F20	22
Domodossola, Italy	C3	18
Domoni, Com.	I16	67a
Dom Pedrito, Braz.	F11	80
Domremy, Sk., Can.	F9	104
Dom Silvério, Braz.	F7	79
Domuyo, Volcán, vol., Arg.	I3	80
Don, stm., Russia	H6	26
Don, stm., Scot., U.K.	D11	8
Dona Ana, N.M., U.S.	L10	120
Donadeu, Arg.	D7	80
Donald, Austl.	K5	70
Donalda, Ab., Can.	E22	102
Donaldson, Ar., U.S.	H4	114
Donaldsonville, La., U.S.	L6	114
Donalsonville, Ga., U.S.	H2	112
Doñana, Parque Nacional de, Spain	H5	16
Donaueschingen, Ger.	H8	10
Donauwörth, Ger.	G10	10
Don Benito, Spain	G6	16
Doncaster, Eng., U.K.	H12	8
Dondo, Ang.	C2	58
Dondo, Moz.	B12	66
Dondra Head, c., Sri L.	J6	46
Dondușeni, Mol.	A11	20
Donegal, Ire.	G5	8
Donegal, co., Ire.	G5	8
Donegal Bay, b., Ire.	G5	8
Doneraile, S.C., U.S.	E7	112
Donets'k, Ukr.	H5	26
Dong, stm., China	L6	34
Donga, stm., Nig.	G15	64
Dong'an, China	B3	34
Dongara, Austl.	E2	68
Dongba, China	D8	34
Dongchuan, China	A7	40
Dongdaoan, China	E5	32
Dong'ezhen, China	G4	32
Dongfang (Basuo), China	E10	40
Dongfeng, China	A13	32
Donggu, China	I4	34
Dongguan, China	L2	34
Dongguanyingzi, China	B8	32
Donghai Dao, i., China	D11	40
Dong Hoi, Viet.	F9	40
Dongmen, China	G3	34
Dong Nai, stm., Viet.	I9	40
Dongshi, China	K7	34
Dongtai, China	C9	34
Dongting Hu, l., China	G1	34
Dongyang, China	F9	34
Dongzhi, China	E5	34
Donie, Tx., U.S.	H10	116
Doniphan, Mo., U.S.	F6	114
Doniphan, Ne., U.S.	K9	118
Donjek, stm., Yk., Can.	F25	100
Donji Vakuf, Bos.	E12	18
Don Matías, Col.	D5	84
Donna, Tx., U.S.	M8	116
Donnelly, Ab., Can.	B17	102
Donnelly, Id., U.S.	F9	122
Donner, La., U.S.	M6	114
Donner Pass, Ca., U.S.	E5	124
Donner und Blitzen, stm., Or., U.S.	G7	122
Donora, Pa., U.S.	G7	108
Donostia (San Sebastián), Spain	B10	16
Don Peninsula, pen., B.C., Can.	E6	102
Donskoj, Russia	H21	22
Donskoje, Russia	I22	22
Doolow, Som.	H9	56
Doomadgee, Austl.	A3	70
Doon, Ia., U.S.	H11	118
Doornik (Tournai), Bel.	G3	12
Door Peninsula, pen., Wi., U.S.	F8	110
Dora, Al., U.S.	I9	114
Doraville, Ga., U.S.	F2	112
Dorcheat, Bayou, stm., U.S.	I3	114
Dorchester, Eng., U.K.	K11	8
Dorchester, N.B., Can.	G9	106
Dorchester, Ne., U.S.	K10	118
Dorchester, On., Can.	H14	110
Dorchester, Wi., U.S.	E5	110
Dorchester, Cape, c., N.T., Can.	C17	96
Dorchester Crossing, N.B., Can.	F9	106
Dordogne, dept., Fr.	G7	14
Dordogne, stm., Fr.	H8	14
Dordrecht, Neth.	E6	12
Dordrecht, S. Afr.	H8	66
Doré, stm., Sk., Can.	D7	104
Doré Lake, Sk., Can.	D7	104
Doré Lake, l., Sk., Can.	D7	104
Dorena, Or., U.S.	G3	122
Dores do Indaiá, Braz.	E6	79
Dornach, Switz.	D8	13
Dornbirn, Aus.	H9	10
Doro, Mali	C9	64
Dorochovo, Russia	F19	22
Dorog, Hung.	H18	10
Dorogobuž, Russia	G16	22
Dorohoi, Rom.	B10	20
Dorrance, Ks., U.S.	M9	118
Dorre Island, i., Austl.	E2	68
Dorrigo, Austl.	H10	70
Dorris, Ca., U.S.	C4	124
Dorset, co., Eng., U.K.	K11	8
Dortmund, Ger.	D7	10
Dorton, Ky., U.S.	B4	112
Dörtyol, Tur.	C4	48
Do Rūd, Iran	E10	48
Doruma, Zaire	H6	56
Dos, Canal Numero, Arg.	I10	80
Dosatuj, Russia	G15	28
Dos Bahías, Cabo, c., Arg.	E3	78
Dosčatoje, Russia	F25	22
Dos Hermanas, Spain	H6	16
Dos Palos, Ca., U.S.	H5	124
Dos Quebradas, Col.	E5	84
Dossor, Kaz.	H8	26
Dothan, Al., U.S.	K11	114
Doting Cove, Nf., Can.	C20	106
Dotnuva, Lith.	F6	22
Douai, Fr.	B10	14
Douala, Cam.	I14	64
Douarnenez, Fr.	D2	14
Double, Lac, l., P.Q., Can.	B3	106
Double Island Point, c., Austl.	E10	70
Double Point, c., Austl.	A7	70
Double Springs, Al., U.S.	H9	114
Doubletop Peak, mtn., Wy., U.S.	G15	122
Doubs, dept., Fr.	E13	14
Doubs, stm., Eur.	E12	14
Doubs, Saut de, wtfl, Eur.	D6	13
Doudeville, Fr.	C7	14
Douentza, Mali	D8	64
Douglas, Ak., U.S.	G27	100
Douglas, Az., U.S.	M7	120
Douglas, Ga., U.S.	H4	112
Douglas, I. of Man	G9	8
Douglas, Mb., Can.	I15	104
Douglas, N.D., U.S.	D6	118
Douglas, Wy., U.S.	B11	120
Douglas, Cape, c., Ak., U.S.	G18	100
Douglas, Mount, mtn., Ak., U.S.	G18	100
Douglas Channel, strt., B.C., Can.	D5	102
Douglas Lake, B.C., Can.	G14	102
Douglas Lake, res., Tn., U.S.	C3	112
Douglas Lake Indian Reserve, B.C., Can.	G14	102
Douglass, Ks., U.S.	N10	118
Douglasville, Ga., U.S.	F2	112
Doulaincourt, Fr.	D12	14
Doulevant-le-Château, Fr.	D11	14
Doullens, Fr.	B9	14
Doumanaba, Mali	F7	64
Doura, Mali	E7	64
Dourada, Serra, plat., Braz.	B4	79
Dourados, Braz.	G1	79
Dourados, stm., Braz.	G1	79
Dourdan, Fr.	D9	14
Dourkoulé, Chad	J2	60
Douro (Duero), stm., Eur.	D4	16
Doushanhe, China	D3	34
Douz, Tun.	D15	62
Dove Creek, Co., U.S.	G8	120
Dover, Ar., U.S.	G3	114
Dover, Austl.	N7	70
Dover, De., U.S.	H11	108
Dover, Eng., U.K.	J15	8
Dover, Id., U.S.	B9	122
Dover, N.C., U.S.	D9	112
Dover, N.H., U.S.	D16	108
Dover, N.J., U.S.	G12	108
Dover, Oh., U.S.	G5	108
Dover, Ok., U.S.	D9	116
Dover, Tn., U.S.	F9	114
Dover, Strait of (Pas de Calais), strt., Eur.	J15	8
Dover-Foxcroft, Me., U.S.	B17	108
Dovre, Nor.	K11	6
Dovsk, Bela.	H13	22
Dowagiac, Mi., U.S.	I9	110
Dowagiac, stm., Mi., U.S.	H9	110
Dow City, Ia., U.S.	J12	118
Dowlatābād, Afg.	B2	44
Dowlatābād, Afg.	B1	44
Dowlat Yār, Afg.	C1	44
Dowling Lake, l., Ab., Can.	F22	102
Downey, Id., U.S.	H13	122
Downieville, Ca., U.S.	E5	124
Downing, Mo., U.S.	B4	114
Downingtown, Pa., U.S.	G11	108
Downs, Ks., U.S.	L9	118
Downs Mountain, mtn., Wy., U.S.	G16	122
Downsville, N.Y., U.S.	E12	108
Downton, Mount, mtn., B.C., Can.	E10	102
Downton Lake, l., B.C., Can.	G11	102
Dows, Ia., U.S.	H2	110
Dowshī, Afg.	C3	44
Doyle, Ca., U.S.	D5	124
Doyles, Nf., Can.	E14	106
Doylestown, Oh., U.S.	G5	108
Doylestown, Pa., U.S.	G11	108
Doyline, La., U.S.	J3	114
Dōzen, is., Japan	K8	36
Dozier, Al., U.S.	K10	114
Dra'a, Hamada du, des., Alg.	F7	62
Drâa, Oued, val., Afr.	F5	62
Dracena, Braz.	F3	79
Dracut, Ma., U.S.	E15	108
Drăgășani, Rom.	E8	20
Dragons Mouths, strt.	B12	84
Dragoon, Az., U.S.	L6	120
Draguignan, Fr.	I13	14
Drahičyn, Bela.	I8	22
Drain, Or., U.S.	G2	122
Drake, N.D., U.S.	D7	118
Drakensberg, mts., Afr.	F9	66
Drake Passage, strt.	J8	74
Drake Peak, mtn., Or., U.S.	H5	122
Drakesboro, Ky., U.S.	E9	114
Drakes Branch, Va., U.S.	C8	112
Dráma, Grc.	H8	20
Drammen, Nor.	L12	6
Drang, stm., Asia	H9	40
Draper, N.C., U.S.	C7	112
Draper, Ut., U.S.	D5	120
Drau (Drava) (Dráva), stm., Eur.	C8	18
Drava (Drau) (Dráva), stm., Eur.	D13	18
Drawno, Pol.	B15	10
Drayton, N.D., U.S.	C10	118
Drayton, S.C., U.S.	E5	112
Drayton Valley, Ab., Can.	D20	102
Drean, Alg.	M2	18
Drenthe, prov., Neth.	C10	12
Dresden, Ger.	D13	10
Dresden, Oh., U.S.	G4	108
Dresden, On., Can.	H13	110
Dresden, Tn., U.S.	F8	114
Drètun', Bela.	F12	22
Dreux, Fr.	D8	14
Drew, Ms., U.S.	I6	114
Driftpile, stm., Ab., Can.	B19	102
Drift Pile River Indian Reserve, Ab., Can.	B19	102
Driftwood, B.C., Can.	B8	102
Driftwood, stm., B.C., Can.	B8	102
Driftwood, stm., In., U.S.	C10	114
Driggs, Id., U.S.	G14	122
Drin, stm., Alb.	H3	20
Drina, stm., Eur.	E3	20
Drini i Zi, stm., Eur.	H4	20
Drinit, Gjiri i, b., Alb.	H3	20
Driscoll, Tx., U.S.	L9	116
Driskill Mountain, hill, La., U.S.	J4	114
Drobeta-Turnu Severin, Rom.	E6	20
Drochia, Mol.	A11	20
Drogheda, Ire.	H7	8
Drohiczyn, Pol.	C22	10
Drohobych, Ukr.	H2	26
Drôme, dept., Fr.	H12	14
Droskovo, Russia	I20	22
Druja, Bela.	F10	22
Drumheller, Ab., Can.	F22	102
Drummond, Mt., U.S.	D12	122
Drummond, Wi., U.S.	D4	110
Drummond Island, i., Mi., U.S.	D12	110
Drummond Range, mts., Austl.	E7	70
Drummondville, P.Q., Can.	B14	108
Drumright, Ok., U.S.	D10	116
Druskininkai, Lith.	G6	22
Družba, Kaz.	H14	26
Drvar, Bos.	E11	18
Dry Bay, b., Ak., U.S.	G25	100
Dryberry Lake, l., On., Can.	I21	104
Dry Cimarron, stm., U.S.	C3	116
Dry Creek Mountain, mtn., Nv., U.S.	C9	124
Dryden, On., Can.	I22	104
Dry Devils, stm., Tx., U.S.	J6	116
Dry Fork, stm., Mo., U.S.	E5	114
Dry Prong, La., U.S.	K4	114
Dry Ridge, Ky., U.S.	I2	108
Drysdale, stm., Austl.	C5	68
Drysdale River National Park, Austl.	B5	68
Dry Tortugas, is., Fl., U.S.	O4	112
Dschang, Cam.	I15	64
Du, Ghana	F9	64
Duarte, Pico, mtn., Dom. Rep.	E9	94
Duartina, Braz.	G4	79
Ḍubā, Sau. Ar.	H3	48
Dubach, La., U.S.	J4	114
Dubai see Dubayy, U.A.E.	B9	47
Dubăsari (Dubesar'), Mol.	B13	20
Dubăsari, Lacul, res., Mol.	B13	20
Dubawnt, stm., N.T., Can.	D12	96
Dubawnt Lake, l., N.T., Can.	D12	96
Dubayy (Dubai), U.A.E.	B9	47
Dubbo, Austl.	I8	70
Dübendorf, Switz.	D10	13
Dublin, Ga., U.S.	G4	112
Dublin (Baile Átha Cliath), Ire.	H7	8
Dublin, Tx., U.S.	G8	116
Dublin, Va., U.S.	B6	112
Dublin, co., Ire.	H7	8
Dubna, Russia	E20	22
Dubois, Id., U.S.	F13	122
Dubois, In., U.S.	D10	114
Du Bois, Ne., U.S.	K11	118
Du Bois, Pa., U.S.	F8	108
Dubois, Wy., U.S.	A7	120
Dubovka, Russia	H6	26
Dubréka, Gui.	G3	64
Dubrouna, Bela.	G13	22
Dubrovka, Russia	H16	22
Dubrovka, Russia	B13	22
Dubrovnik, Cro.	G2	20
Dubuque, Ia., U.S.	H5	110
Duchcov, Czech Rep.	E13	10
Duchesne, Ut., U.S.	D6	120
Duchesne, stm., Ut., U.S.	D6	120
Duchess, Austl.	C3	70
Duchovščina, Russia	F15	22
Duck, stm., Tn., U.S.	G9	114
Duck Bay, Mb., Can.	F14	104
Duck Hill, Ms., U.S.	I7	114
Duck Lake, Sk., Can.	F8	104
Duck Lake, l., Mb., Can.	D16	104
Duck Mountain, mtn., Mb., Can.	G13	104
Duck Mountain Provincial Park, Mb., Can.	G14	104
Duck Mountain Provincial Park, Sk., Can.	G13	104
Du Couedic, Cape, c., Austl.	K2	70
Duda, stm., Col.	F5	84
Dudelange, Lux.	J9	12
Duderstadt, Ger.	D10	10
Dudinka, Russia	D9	28
Dudleyville, Az., U.S.	L6	120
Dudorovskij, Russia	H18	22
Duékoué, C. Iv.	H6	64
Duerna, stm., Spain	C5	16
Duero (Douro), stm., Eur.	D5	16
Due West, S.C., U.S.	E4	112
Duffer Peak, mtn., Nv., U.S.	C7	124
Dufourspitze, mtn., Eur.	G14	14
Dufur, Or., U.S.	E4	122
Duga-Zapadnaja, mys, c., Russia	F21	28
Dugdemona, stm., La., U.S.	J4	114
Dugger, In., U.S.	C9	114
Dugi Otok, i., Cro.	E10	18
Du Gué, stm., P.Q., Can.	E18	96
Duhi, Sudan	N5	60
Duida, Cerro, mtn., Ven.	F10	84
Duisburg, Ger.	D6	10
Duitama, Col.	E6	84
Duiwelskloof, S. Afr.	D10	66
Dukambiya, Erit.	J9	60
Duke, Ok., U.S.	E7	116
Duke of York Bay, b., N.T., Can.	C16	96
Duk Fadiat, Sudan	N6	60
Duk Faiwil, Sudan	N6	60
Dukhān, Qatar	B7	47
Duki, Pak.	E3	44
Dukla Pass, Eur.	F21	10
Dūkštas, Lith.	F9	22
Duku, Nig.	F12	64
Dulan, China	D6	30
Dul'apino, Russia	D23	22
Dulce, N.M., U.S.	H10	120
Dulce, stm., Arg.	F7	80
Dulce, Golfo, b., C.R.	I11	92
Dulce Nombre de Culmí, Hond.	B9	92
Dul'durga, Russia	G14	28
Dulkaninna, Austl.	G3	70
Dulovka, Russia	D11	22
Dulovo, Bul.	F11	20
Duluth, Ga., U.S.	E2	112
Duluth, Mn., U.S.	D3	110
Duma, Bots.	B6	66
Dūmā, Syria	A6	50
Dumaguete, Phil.	D7	38
Dumaresq, stm., Austl.	G9	70
Dumaring, Indon.	E6	38
Dumas, Ar., U.S.	I5	114
Dumas, Tx., U.S.	D5	116
Ḍumayr, Syria	A7	50
Dumbarton, Scot., U.K.	F9	8
Dumei, China	K6	34
Dumfries, Scot., U.K.	F10	8
Dumfries and Galloway, prov., Scot., U.K.	F9	8
Duminiči, Russia	H18	22
Dumka, India	H12	44
Dumont, Ia., U.S.	H3	110
Dumraon, India	H11	44
Dumyāṭ, Egypt	B6	60
Dumyāṭ, Maṣabb, mth., Egypt	F1	48
Dunaföldvár, Hung.	I18	10
Dunaharaszti, Hung.	H19	10
Dunajec, stm., Eur.	E20	10
Dunakeszi, Hung.	H19	10
Dunaújváros, Hung.	I18	10
Dunbar, W.V., U.S.	I5	108
Dunblane, Sk., Can.	G8	104
Duncan, Az., U.S.	L7	120
Duncan, B.C., Can.	I11	102
Duncan, Ms., U.S.	H6	114
Duncan, Ok., U.S.	E9	116
Duncan, stm., B.C., Can.	G17	102
Duncan Lake, res., B.C., Can.	G18	102
Duncannon, Pa., U.S.	G9	108
Duncan Passage, strt., India	I2	40
Duncansby Head, c., Scot., U.K.	C10	8
Dundaga, Lat.	D5	22
Dundalk, Ire.	G7	8
Dundalk, Md., U.S.	H10	108
Dundalk, On., Can.	F15	110
Dundas, Mn., U.S.	F2	110
Dundas, On., Can.	G16	110
Dundas Island, i., B.C., Can.	C4	102
Dundas Peninsula, pen., N.T., Can.	B10	96
Dundee, Fl., U.S.	K5	112
Dundee, Mi., U.S.	I12	110
Dundee, Ms., U.S.	H6	114
Dundee, N.Y., U.S.	E10	108
Dundee, S. Afr.	G10	66
Dundee, Scot., U.K.	E11	8
Dundurn, Sk., Can.	G8	104
Dunedin, Fl., U.S.	K4	112
Dunedin, N.Z.	F3	72
Dunedoo, Austl.	I8	70
Dunfermline, Scot., U.K.	E10	8
Dungannon, Va., U.S.	C4	112
Dungas, Niger	E14	64
Dungog, Austl.	I9	70
Dungun, Malay.	L7	40
Dunhua, China	C12	30
Dunhuang, China	C5	30
Dunilovo, Russia	D21	22
Dunkerque, Fr.	A9	14
Dunkirk see Dunkerque, Fr.	A9	14
Dunkirk, In., U.S.	B11	114
Dunkirk, N.Y., U.S.	E7	108
Dunkirk, Oh., U.S.	G3	108
Dunkuj, Sudan	K7	60
Dunkwa, Ghana	I9	64
Dún Laoghaire, Ire.	H7	8
Dunlap, Ia., U.S.	J12	118
Dunlap, Tn., U.S.	G11	114
Dunleary see Dún Laoghaire, Ire.	H7	8
Dunmore, Pa., U.S.	F11	108
Dunmore Town, Bah.	B6	94
Dunn, N.C., U.S.	D8	112
Dunnellon, Fl., U.S.	J4	112
Dunning, Ne., U.S.	J7	118
Dunnville, On., Can.	H16	110
Dunqulah, Sudan	H6	60
Dunqulah al-Qadīmah, Sudan	H6	60
Dunqunāb, Sudan	G9	60
Dunrea, Mb., Can.	I15	104
Duns, Scot., U.K.	F11	8
Dunseith, N.D., U.S.	C7	118
Dunsmuir, Ca., U.S.	C3	124
Dunster, B.C., Can.	D15	102
Dun-sur-Auron, Fr.	F9	14
Dun-sur-Meuse, Fr.	C12	14
Dunville, Nf., Can.	E20	106
Duolun (Dolonnur), China	A4	32
Duolundabohuer, China	D15	44
Duomaer, China	E2	30
Duomula, China	E3	30
Duozhu, China	M3	34
Du Page, stm., Il., U.S.	I7	110
Dupnica, Bul.	G7	20
Dupree, S.D., U.S.	F6	118
Duque de Caxias, Braz.	G7	79
DuQuoin, Il., U.S.	E7	114
Durack Ranges, mts., Austl.	C5	68
Duran, N.M., U.S.	J11	120
Durance, stm., Fr.	I12	14
Durand, Il., U.S.	H6	110
Durand, Mi., U.S.	H12	110
Durand, Wi., U.S.	F4	110
Durango, Co., U.S.	G9	120
Durango, Mex.	E7	90
Durango, Spain	B9	16
Durango, state, Mex.	E7	90
Durant, Ia., U.S.	I5	110
Durant, Ms., U.S.	I7	114
Durant, Ok., U.S.	F10	116
Durazno, Ur.	G10	80
Durban, S. Afr.	G10	66
Durbe, Lat.	E4	22
Durbin, W.V., U.S.	I7	108
Đurđevac, Cro.	C12	18
Düren, Ger.	E6	10
Durg, India	J9	44
Durgāpur, India	I12	44
Durham, Ca., U.S.	E4	124
Durham, N.C., U.S.	D8	112
Durham, N.H., U.S.	D16	108
Durham, On., Can.	F15	110
Durham, co., Eng., U.K.	G12	8
Durham Heights, mtn., N.T., Can.	B8	96
Durlești, Mol.	B12	20
Durmitor, mtn., Yugo.	F3	20
Durness, Scot., U.K.	C9	8
Dürnkrut, Aus.	G16	10
Durrell, Nf., Can.	C19	106
Durrës, Alb.	H3	20
Dursunbey, Tur.	J12	20
D'Urville, Tanjung, c., Indon.	F10	38
D'Urville Island, i., N.Z.	D4	72
Dušak, Turk.	C16	48
Dušanbe, Taj.	J11	26
Dusetos, Lith.	F8	22
Dushan, China	B9	40
Dushanbe see Dušanbe, Taj.	J11	26
Dushanzi, China	C3	30
Dusheng, China	E4	32
Dushore, Pa., U.S.	F10	108
Duson, La., U.S.	L4	114
Düsseldorf, Ger.	D6	10
Dustin, Ok., U.S.	D10	116
Dutch Creek, stm., B.C., Can.	G18	102
Dutch Harbor, Ak., U.S.	J11	100
Dutch John, Ut., U.S.	D7	120
Dutlwe, Bots.	D6	66
Dutou, China	M4	34
Dutton, Mt., U.S.	C14	122
Dutton, On., Can.	H14	110
Dutton, stm., Austl.	C5	70
Dutton, Mount, mtn., Ut., U.S.	F4	120
Duyun, China	A9	40
Duze, China	F7	34
Dvinskaja guba, b., Russia	I26	6
Dvuch Cirkov, gora, mtn., Russia	D25	28
Dvůr Králové [nad Labem], Czech Rep.	E15	10
Dwārka, India	I3	44
Dwight, Il., U.S.	I7	110
Dworshak Reservoir, res., Id., U.S.	D10	122
Dyer, Tn., U.S.	F8	114
Dyer, Cape, c., N.T., Can.	C20	96
Dyersburg, Tn., U.S.	F7	114
Dyersville, Ia., U.S.	H4	110
Dyfed, co., Wales, U.K.	J9	8
Dyje (Thaya), stm., Eur.	G16	10
Dyment, On., Can.	I22	104
Dynów, Pol.	F22	10
Dysart, Ia., U.S.	H3	110
Dysart, Sk., Can.	H10	104
Dyviziya, Ukr.	D13	20
Džalal-Abad, Kyrg.	I12	26
Džalinda, Russia	G16	28
Džambejty, Kaz.	G8	26
Džanga, Turk.	A12	48
Džanybek, Kaz.	H7	26
Dzaoudzi, May.	I16	67a
Dzavchan, stm., Mong.	B5	30
Džebel, Turk.	B13	48
Dzemul, Mex.	G15	90
Dzeržinsk, Russia	E26	22
Dzeržinskoje, Kaz.	H14	26
Džetygara, Kaz.	G10	26
Dzhankoy, Ukr.	H4	26
Dzhuryn, Ukr.	A12	20
Dzibalchén, Mex.	H15	90
Dzibilchaltun, hist., Mex.	G15	90
Dzierżoniów (Reichenbach), Pol.	E16	10
Dzilam González, Mex.	G15	90
Dzioua, Alg.	D13	62
Dzisna, Bela.	F11	22
Dzitás, Mex.	G15	90
Dzitbalché, Mex.	G14	90
Dzivin, Bela.	J7	22
Džizak, Uzb.	I11	26
Dzjaržynsk, Bela.	H10	22
Dzjatlava, Bela.	H8	22

Name	Map Ref.	Page
Džugdžur, chrebet, mts., Russia	F19	28
Dzungarian Basin see Junggar Pendi, China	B4	30
Džungarskij Alatau, chrebet, mts., Asia	H8	28
Džusaly, Kaz.	H10	26
Džüün Charaa, Mong.	B8	30
Dzuunmod, Mong.	B8	30
Dzyhivka, Ukr.	A12	20
E		
Eads, Co., U.S.	M5	118
Eagar, Az., U.S.	J7	120
Eagle, Ak., U.S.	D24	100
Eagle, Co., U.S.	E10	120
Eagle, stm., Co., U.S.	E10	120
Eagle, stm., Nf., Can.	F21	96
Eagle, stm., Yk., Can.	C26	100
Eagle Bay, B.C., Can.	G15	102
Eagle Bend, Mn., U.S.	E12	118
Eagle Butte, S.D., U.S.	F6	118
Eagle Creek, stm., Sk., Can.	G7	104
Eagle Grove, Ia., U.S.	H2	110
Eaglehawk, Austl.	K6	70
Eagle Lake, Tx., U.S.	J10	116
Eagle Lake, l., B.C., Can.	F10	102
Eagle Lake, l., Ca., U.S.	D5	124
Eagle Lake, l., On., Can.	H20	104
Eagle Lake, l., On., Can.	I21	104
Eagle Mountain, Ca., U.S.	K10	124
Eagle Mountain, mtn., Id., U.S.	D10	122
Eagle Mountain, hill, Mn., U.S.	C5	110
Eagle Pass, Tx., U.S.	K6	116
Eagle Peak, mtn., Ca., U.S.	C5	124
Eagle River, Mi., U.S.	C7	110
Eagle River, Wi., U.S.	E6	110
Eagle Rock, Va., U.S.	B7	112
Eaglesham, Ab., Can.	B17	102
Eagleton Village, Tn., U.S.	D3	112
Eagletown, Ok., U.S.	H2	114
Eagle Village, Ak., U.S.	D24	100
Eardley Lake, l., Mb., Can.	F18	104
Ear Falls, On., Can.	H21	104
Earle, Ar., U.S.	G6	114
Earl Grey, Sk., Can.	H10	104
Earlham, Ia., U.S.	A2	114
Earlimart, Ca., U.S.	I6	124
Earlington, Ky., U.S.	E9	114
Earl Park, In., U.S.	B9	114
Earlville, Il., U.S.	I7	110
Earlville, N.Y., U.S.	E11	108
Early, Ia., U.S.	I12	118
Early, Tx., U.S.	H8	116
Earth, Tx., U.S.	E4	116
Easley, S.C., U.S.	E4	112
East Alton, Il., U.S.	D6	114
East-Angus, P.Q., Can.	B15	108
East Aurora, N.Y., U.S.	E8	108
East Bay, b., Tx., U.S.	J12	116
East Bend, N.C., U.S.	C6	112
East Berbice-Corentyne, prov., Guy.	E13	84
East Berlin, Pa., U.S.	H10	108
East Bernard, Tx., U.S.	J10	116
East Bernstadt, Ky., U.S.	B2	112
East Brady, Pa., U.S.	G7	108
East Braintree, Mb., Can.	I19	104
East Brewton, Al., U.S.	K9	114
East Caicos, i., T./C. Is.	D9	94
East Cape, c., N.Z.	B7	72
East Carbon, Ut., U.S.	E6	120
East Channel, mth., N.T., Can.	B28	100
East Chicago, In., U.S.	A9	114
East China Sea, Asia	r3	37b
East Coulee, Ab., Can.	F22	102
East Dublin, Ga., U.S.	G4	112
East Dubuque, Il., U.S.	H5	110
East Ely, Nv., U.S.	E11	124
Eastend, Sk., Can.	I6	104
Easter Island see Pascua, Isla de, i., Chile	G4	74
Eastern Cape, prov., S. Afr.	I8	66
Eastern Ghāts, mts., India	F5	46
East Falkland, i., Falk. Is.	G5	78
East Fayetteville, N.C., U.S.	D8	112
East Flat Rock, N.C., U.S.	D4	112
East Frisian Islands see Ostfriesische Inseln, is., Ger.	B7	10
East Gaffney, S.C., U.S.	D5	112
East Gallatin, stm., Mt., U.S.	E14	122
East Glacier Park, Mt., U.S.	B12	122
East Grand Forks, Mn., U.S.	D10	118
East Grand Rapids, Mi., U.S.	H10	110
East Greenwich, R.I., U.S.	F15	108
Easthampton, Ma., U.S.	E14	108
East Helena, Mt., U.S.	D14	122
East Jordan, Mi., U.S.	E10	110
East Kelowna, B.C., Can.	H15	102
East Kilbride, Scot., U.K.	F9	8
Eastlake, Mi., U.S.	F9	110
Eastlake, Oh., U.S.	F5	108
East Lake, l., On., Can.	E21	104
Eastland, Tx., U.S.	G8	116
East Lansing, Mi., U.S.	H11	110
East Laurinburg, N.C., U.S.	E7	112
East Liverpool, Oh., U.S.	G6	108
East London (Oos-Londen), S. Afr.	I8	66
East Lynn Lake, res., W.V., U.S.	I4	108
Eastmain, P.Q., Can.	F17	96
Eastmain, stm., P.Q., Can.	F17	96
Eastmain-Opinaca, Réservoir, res., P.Q., Can.	F17	96
Eastman, Ga., U.S.	G3	112
East Millinocket, Me., U.S.	B18	108
East Missoula, Mt., U.S.	D12	122
East Moline, Il., U.S.	I5	110
East Naples, Fl., U.S.	M5	112
East Nishnabotna, stm., Ia., U.S.	K12	118
East Olympia, Wa., U.S.	D3	122
Easton, Md., U.S.	I10	108
Easton, Pa., U.S.	G11	108
Eastover, S.C., U.S.	F6	112
East Palatka, Fl., U.S.	J5	112
East Palestine, Oh., U.S.	G6	108
East Pecos, N.M., U.S.	I11	120
East Peoria, Il., U.S.	J6	110
East Pine, B.C., Can.	B13	102
Eastpoint, Fl., U.S.	J2	112
East Point, Ga., U.S.	F2	112
East Point, c., P.E., Can.	F12	106
Eastport, Id., U.S.	A9	122
Eastport, Me., U.S.	C20	108
Eastport, Nf., Can.	D20	106
East Porterville, Ca., U.S.	H7	124
East Prairie, Mo., U.S.	F7	114
East Prairie, stm., Ab., Can.	B18	102
East Rockingham, N.C., U.S.	E7	112
East Saint Louis, Il., U.S.	D6	114
East Shoal Lake, l., Mb., Can.	H17	104
East Siberian Sea see Vostočno-Sibirskoje more, Russia	C23	28
East Spencer, N.C., U.S.	D6	112
East Stroudsburg, Pa., U.S.	G11	108
East Tawas, Mi., U.S.	F12	110
East Troy, Wi., U.S.	H7	110
Eastville, Va., U.S.	B11	112
East Wenatchee, Wa., U.S.	C5	122
East Wilmington, N.C., U.S.	E9	112
Eaton, Co., U.S.	D12	120
Eaton, In., U.S.	B11	114
Eaton, Oh., U.S.	H2	108
Eatonia, Sk., Can.	G5	104
Eaton Rapids, Mi., U.S.	H11	110
Eatonton, Ga., U.S.	F3	112
Eatonville, Wa., U.S.	D3	122
Eau Claire, Wi., U.S.	F4	110
Eau Claire, stm., Wi., U.S.	F4	110
Eau Claire, Lac à l', l., P.Q., Can.	E18	96
Eau Galle, stm., Wi., U.S.	F3	110
Eauze, Fr.	I7	14
Eban, Nig.	G12	64
Ebano, Mex.	F10	90
Ebb and Flow Indian Reserve, Mb., Can.	G15	104
Ebb and Flow Lake, l., Mb., Can.	G16	104
Ebbw Vale, Wales, U.K.	J10	8
Eben Junction, Mi., U.S.	D9	110
Ebensburg, Pa., U.S.	G8	108
Ebensee, Aus.	H13	10
Eberbach, Ger.	F8	10
Ebermannstadt, Ger.	F11	10
Eberndorf, Aus.	I14	10
Ebersbach, Ger.	D14	10
Ebersberg, Ger.	G11	10
Eberstein, Aus.	I14	10
Eberswalde-Finow, Ger.	C13	10
Ebetsu, Japan	d16	36a
Ebinur Hu, l., China	C3	30
Ebnat, Switz.	D11	13
Eboli, Italy	I10	18
Ebolowa, Cam.	H9	54
Ebony, Nmb.	D2	66
Ebro (Ebre), stm., Spain	E12	16
Ebro, Embalse del, res., Spain	B8	16
Eccles, W.V., U.S.	B5	112
Echaporã, Braz.	G3	79
Ech Cheliff (Orléansville), Alg.	B11	62
Echimamish, stm., Mb., Can.	D17	104
Echo, Mn., U.S.	G12	118
Echo Bay, N.T., Can.	C9	96
Echoing, stm., Can.	C23	104
Echoing Lake, l., On., Can.	D22	104
Echt, Neth.	F8	12
Echuca, Austl.	K6	70
Écija, Spain	H6	16
Eckernförde, Ger.	A9	10
Eckville, Ab., Can.	E20	102
Eclectic, Al., U.S.	J10	114
Eclipse Sound, strt., N.T., Can.	B17	96
Ečmiadzin, Arm.	I6	26
Écrins, Barre des, mtn., Fr.	H13	14
Ecru, Ms., U.S.	H7	114
Ecstall, stm., B.C., Can.	D5	102
Ecuador, ctry., S.A.	D3	76
Ecum Secum, N.S., Can.	H11	106
Ed, Erit.	H2	47
Edam, Neth.	C7	12
Edam, Sk., Can.	E6	104
Eddystone Point, c., Austl.	M8	70
Eddyville, Ia., U.S.	I3	110
Eddyville, Ky., U.S.	E8	114
Ede, Nig.	H12	64
Edéa, Cam.	H9	54
Edehon Lake, l., N.T., Can.	D13	96
Edéia, Braz.	D4	79
Edelény, Hung.	G20	10
Eden, Austl.	K8	70
Eden, Ms., U.S.	J6	114
Eden, Tx., U.S.	H7	116
Eden, Wy., U.S.	B7	120
Edenburg, S. Afr.	G7	66
Eden Lake, l., Mb., Can.	B14	104
Edenton, N.C., U.S.	C10	112
Eden Valley, Mn., U.S.	E1	110
Edenville, S. Afr.	F8	66
Edeowie, Austl.	H3	70
Eder, stm., Ger.	D8	10
Edfu see Idfū, Egypt	E7	60
Edgar, Ne., U.S.	K10	118
Edgar, Wi., U.S.	F6	110
Edgard, La., U.S.	L6	114
Edgartown, Ma., U.S.	F16	108
Edgefield, S.C., U.S.	F5	112
Edgeley, N.D., U.S.	E9	118
Edgemont, S.D., U.S.	H4	118
Edgeøya, i., Nor.	B3	24
Edgerton, Ab., Can.	F4	104
Edgerton, Mn., U.S.	H11	118
Edgerton, Oh., U.S.	F2	108
Edgerton, Wi., U.S.	H6	110
Edgerton, Wy., U.S.	A10	120
Edgewater, Al., U.S.	I10	114
Edgewater, Fl., U.S.	K6	112
Edgewood, B.C., Can.	H16	102
Edgewood, Ia., U.S.	H4	110
Edgewood, Il., U.S.	D8	114
Edgewood, Md., U.S.	H10	108
Edgewood, Tx., U.S.	G11	116
Édhessa, Grc.	I6	20
Edina, Mn., U.S.	F2	110
Edina, Mo., U.S.	B4	114
Edinboro, Pa., U.S.	F6	108
Edinburg, Il., U.S.	C7	114
Edinburg, In., U.S.	C11	114
Edinburg, Ms., U.S.	J7	114
Edinburg, N.D., U.S.	C10	118
Edinburg, Tx., U.S.	M8	116
Edinburg, Va., U.S.	I8	108
Edinburgh, Scot., U.K.	F10	8
Edinburgh, Arrecife, rf., Nic.	C12	92
Edinburgh Channel, strt., Nic.	C12	92
Edincik, Tur.	I11	20
Edirne, Tur.	H10	20
Edison, Ga., U.S.	H2	112
Edisto, stm., S.C., U.S.	G6	112
Edisto Island, i., S.C., U.S.	G6	112
Edith Cavell, Mount, mtn., Ab., Can.	E16	102
Edjeleh, Alg.	G15	62
Edmond, Ok., U.S.	D9	116
Edmonds, Wa., U.S.	C3	122
Edmonton, Ab., Can.	D21	102
Edmonton, Austl.	A6	70
Edmonton, Ky., U.S.	F11	114
Edmore, Mi., U.S.	G10	110
Edmore, N.D., U.S.	C9	118
Edmund Lake, l., Mb., Can.	D21	104
Edmundston, N.B., Can.	E5	106
Edna, Ks., U.S.	N12	118
Edna, Tx., U.S.	K10	116
Edna Bay, Ak., U.S.	I28	100
Edolo, Italy	C5	18
Edremit, Tur.	J11	20
Edsbro, Swe.	L16	6
Edsbyn, Swe.	K14	6
Edson, Ab., Can.	D18	102
Eduardo Castex, Arg.	H6	80
Eduni, Mount, mtn., N.T., Can.	D30	100
Edward, Lake, l., Afr.	B5	58
Edwards, Ms., U.S.	J6	114
Edwards, N.Y., U.S.	C11	108
Edwards, stm., Il., U.S.	I5	110
Edwards Plateau, plat., Tx., U.S.	I6	116
Edwardsville, Il., U.S.	D7	114
Edward VII Peninsula, pen., Ant.	C9	73
Edziza, Mount, mtn., B.C., Can.	H29	100
Eek, Ak., U.S.	F13	100
Eeklo, Bel.	F4	12
Eel, stm., Ca., U.S.	D1	124
Eel, stm., In., U.S.	B10	114
Eel, stm., In., U.S.	C9	114
Effingham, Il., U.S.	C8	114
Effingham, Ks., U.S.	L12	118
Ega, stm., Spain	C9	16
Egadi, Isole, is., Italy	L7	18
Egaña, Arg.	I9	80
Egan Range, mts., Nv., U.S.	E11	124
Eganville, On., Can.	E18	110
Egegik, Ak., U.S.	G16	100
Eger see Cheb, Czech Rep.	E12	10
Eger, Hung.	H20	10
Egeria Mountain, mtn., B.C., Can.	D4	102
Egersund, Nor.	L10	6
Eggenburg, Aus.	G15	10
Egg Harbor City, N.J., U.S.	H12	108
Egg Lake, l., Mb., Can.	D13	104
Egg Lake, l., Sk., Can.	C9	104
Egilsstaðir, Ice.	B6	6a
Egmont, Mount, mtn., N.Z.	C4	72
Egmont Bay, b., P.E., Can.	F9	106
Egremont, Ab., Can.	C21	102
Éguas, Rio das, stm., Braz.	B6	79
Egypt (Mişr), ctry., Afr.	C7	56
Ehrenberg, Az., U.S.	K2	120
Ehrhardt, S.C., U.S.	F5	112
Eibar, Spain	B9	16
Eichstätt, Ger.	G11	10
Eidsvåg, Nor.	J11	6
Eidsvold, Austl.	E9	70
Eifel, mts., Ger.	E6	10
Eiger, mtn., Switz.	E9	13
Eight Degree Channel, strt., Asia	I2	46
Eights Coast, Ant.	C11	73
Eighty Mile Beach, Austl.	C4	68
Eildon, Austl.	K6	70
Eildon, Lake, res., Austl.	K6	70
Eilenburg, Ger.	D12	10
Einasleigh, Austl.	B6	70
Einasleigh, stm., Austl.	A5	70
Einbeck, Ger.	D9	10
Eindhoven, Neth.	F7	12
Einsiedeln, Switz.	D10	13
Eiru, stm., Braz.	B6	82
Eirunepé, Braz.	B7	82
Eisden, Bel.	G8	12
Eisenach, Ger.	E10	10
Eisenberg, Ger.	E11	10
Eisenerz, Aus.	H14	10
Eisenhüttenstadt, Ger.	C14	10
Eisenkappel, Aus.	I14	10
Eisenstadt, Aus.	H16	10
Eišiškės, Lith.	G8	22
Eitorf, Ger.	E7	10
Eivissa, Spain	G13	16
Eivissa (Ibiza), i., Spain	G13	16
Ejea de los Caballeros, Spain	C10	16
Ejeda, Madag.	t21	67b
Ejido, Ven.	C7	84
Ejido Jaboncillos, Mex.	C8	90
Ejin Qi, China	C7	30
Ejutla de Crespo, Mex.	I11	90
Ekalaka, Mt., U.S.	F3	118
Eket, Nig.	I13	64
Ekibastuz, Kaz.	G7	28
Ekpoma, Nig.	H13	64
Eksjö, Swe.	M14	6
Ekwan, stm., On., Can.	F16	96
Ekwok, Ak., U.S.	G16	100
Ela, Myan.	E4	40
El Aaiún (La'youn), W. Sah.	G4	62
El Abiadh Sidi Cheikh, Alg.	D11	62
El Adeb Larache, Alg.	G15	62
El Adelanto, Guat.	C5	92
El Agreb, Alg.	E13	62
El Aguilar, Arg.	B6	80
Elaine, Ar., U.S.	H6	114
El Alamein see Al-'Alamayn, Egypt	B5	60
El Alia, Tun.	L5	18
El Alto, Arg.	E6	80
El Alto, Peru	J2	84
El Amparo de Apure, Ven.	D7	84
Elandsvlei, S. Afr.	I4	66
El Angel, Ec.	G4	84
El Aouinet, Alg.	N2	18
El Arco, Mex.	C3	90
El Aricha, Alg.	C10	62
El Aroussa, Tun.	M4	18
El Astillero, Spain	B8	16
Elat, Isr.	I3	50
El Ávila, Parque Nacional, Ven.	B9	84
Elazığ, Tur.	B5	48
Elba, Al., U.S.	K10	114
Elba, Isola d', i., Italy	G5	18
El Banco, Col.	C6	84
Elbasan, Alb.	H4	20
El Baúl, Ven.	C8	84
El Baúl, Cerro, mtn., Mex.	I9	90
El Baúl, Cerro, mtn., Mex.	I12	90
Elbe (Labe), stm., Eur.	B9	10
Elbert, Co., U.S.	L3	118
Elbert, Mount, mtn., Co., U.S.	E10	120
Elberta, Mi., U.S.	F9	110
Elberton, Ga., U.S.	E4	112
Elbeuf, Fr.	C8	14
El Beyyadh, Alg.	D11	62
Elbistan, Tur.	B4	48
Elbląg (Elbing), Pol.	A19	10
El Bluff, Nic.	F11	92
El-Borouj, Mor.	D7	62
El Boulaïda, Alg.	B12	62
Elbow, Sk., Can.	G8	104
Elbow, stm., Ab., Can.	G20	102
Elbow Cay, i., Bah.	C4	94
Elbow Lake, Mn., U.S.	F12	118
Elbow Lake, l., Mb., Can.	D14	104
El'brus, gora, mtn., Russia	I6	26
Elbrus, Mount see El'brus, gora, mtn., Russia	I6	26
El Cabezo, Arrecife, rf., Mex.	H12	90
El Caburé, Arg.	D7	80
El Caimanero, Laguna, b., Mex.	F6	90
El Cajon, Ca., U.S.	L9	124
El Cajón, Embalse, res., Hond.	B7	92
El Calafate, Arg.	G2	78
El Callao, Ven.	D12	84
El Calvario, Col.	E6	84
El Calvario, Ven.	C9	84
El Campo, Tx., U.S.	J10	116
El Capitan, mtn., Mt., U.S.	D11	122
El Carmen, Arg.	C6	80
El Cármen, Bol.	H12	82
El Carmen, Col.	C6	84
El Carmen, Peru	E3	82
El Carmen, stm., Mex.	B6	90
El Carmen de Bolívar, Col.	C5	84
El Carricito, Mex.	C8	90
El Carril, Arg.	C6	80
El Castillo de La Concepción, Nic.	F10	92
El Cedral, Guat.	A4	92
El Cedrito, Mex.	C9	90
El Centro, Ca., U.S.	L10	124
El Cerrito, Col.	F4	84
El Cerro, Bol.	G11	82
El Chile, Montaña, mtn., Hond.	C8	92
Elcho, Wi., U.S.	E6	110
El Chorrillo, Arg.	G5	80
El Cocuy, Col.	D6	84
El Colorado, Arg.	D9	80
El Cóndor, Cerro, mtn., Arg.	D4	80
El Congo, El Sal.	D5	92
El Corazón, Ec.	H3	84
El Corpus, Hond.	D7	92
El Coyote, stm., Mex.	B3	90
El Cozón, Mex.	B3	90
El Cuco, El Sal.	D6	92
El Cuervo, Laguna, l., Mex.	C7	90
Elda, Spain	G11	16
El Dátil, Mex.	B3	90
El Desemboque, Mex.	C3	90
El Desemboque, Mex.	B3	90
El'dikan, Russia	E19	28
El Diviso, Col.	G3	84
El Djazaïr (Algiers), Alg.	B12	62
El Djelfa, Alg.	C12	62
Eldon, Ia., U.S.	J3	110
Eldon, Mo., U.S.	D4	114
Eldora, Ia., U.S.	H2	110
El Dorado, Ar., U.S.	I4	114
Eldorado, Arg.	D11	80
Eldorado, Braz.	C14	80
Eldorado, Il., U.S.	E8	114
El Dorado, Ks., U.S.	N11	118
El Dorado, Mex.	E6	90
Eldorado, Ok., U.S.	E7	116
Eldorado, Tx., U.S.	I6	116
El Dorado, Ven.	D12	84
El Dorado Springs, Mo., U.S.	E2	114
Eldoret, Kenya	A7	58
Eldred, Pa., U.S.	F8	108
Eldridge, Ia., U.S.	I5	110
Eleanor, W.V., U.S.	I5	108
Electra, Tx., U.S.	E8	116
Electric City, Wa., U.S.	C6	122
Elefante, Isla del see Elephant Island, i., Ant.	B1	73
Elefantes, Rio dos (Olifants), stm., Afr.	E11	66
Elei, Wādī, val., Sudan	G8	60
Eleja, Lat.	E6	22
Elektrogorsk, Russia	F21	22
Elektrostal', Russia	F21	22
El Encanto, Col.	H6	84
El Encanto, Guat.	I15	90
Elephant Butte Reservoir, res., N.M., U.S.	K9	120
Elephant Island, i., Ant.	K9	74
El Estor, Guat.	B5	92
El Eulma, Alg.	B13	62
Eleuthera, i., Bah.	B6	94
Eleuthera Point, c., Bah.	B6	94
Eleva, Wi., U.S.	F4	110
Eleven Point, stm., U.S.	F5	114
Elevsís, Grc.	K7	20
El Fahs, Tun.	M4	18
Elfrida, Az., U.S.	M7	120
Elfros, Sk., Can.	G11	104
El Fuerte, Mex.	D5	90
El Galpón, Arg.	C6	80
El Ghazawet, Alg.	C10	62
Elgin, Ia., U.S.	H4	110
Elgin, Il., U.S.	H7	110
Elgin, Mn., U.S.	F3	110
Elgin, N.D., U.S.	E6	118
Elgin, Ne., U.S.	J9	118
Elgin, Ok., U.S.	E8	116
Elgin, Or., U.S.	E8	122
Elgin, Scot., U.K.	D10	8
Elgin, Tx., U.S.	I9	116
El Golfete, l., Guat.	B6	92
Elgon, Mount, mtn., Afr.	A6	58
El Grara, Alg.	D13	62
El Guaje, Mex.	D8	90
El Guaje, Laguna, l., Mex.	C8	90
El Guamo, Col.	B5	84
El Guapo, Ven.	B10	84
El Guayabo de Abajo, Mex.	D6	90
El Hadjar, Alg.	M2	18
El Hank, clf, Afr.	D5	54
El Haouaria, Tun.	L6	18
El Hierro, i., Spain	p22	17b
Elhovo, Bul.	G10	20
El Huecú, Arg.	I3	80
El Huisache, Mex.	F9	90
Eliasville, Tx., U.S.	G8	116
Elida, N.M., U.S.	F3	116
El Ídolo, Isla, i., Mex.	G11	90
El Idrissia, Alg.	C12	62
Elim, Ak., U.S.	D13	100
El Infiernillo, Canal, strt., Mex.	C3	90
Eliot, Me., U.S.	D16	108
Élisabethville see Lubumbashi, Zaire	D5	58
Elisenvaara, Russia	K21	6
Elista, Russia	H6	26
Elizabeth, Austl.	J3	70
Elizabeth, Co., U.S.	E12	120
Elizabeth, Il., U.S.	H5	110
Elizabeth, La., U.S.	L4	114
Elizabeth, N.J., U.S.	G12	108
Elizabeth, W.V., U.S.	H5	108
Elizabeth City, N.C., U.S.	C10	112
Elizabethton, Tn., U.S.	C4	112
Elizabethtown, Il., U.S.	E8	114
Elizabethtown, Ky., U.S.	E11	114
Elizabethtown, N.C., U.S.	E8	112
Elizabethtown, N.Y., U.S.	C13	108
Elizabethtown, Pa., U.S.	G10	108
El-Jadida (Mazagan), Mor.	D6	62
El Jaralito, Mex.	D7	90
El Jebel, Co., U.S.	E9	120
El-Jebha, Mor.	J7	16
El Jem, Tun.	N5	18
El Jícaro, stm., Nic.	D8	92
Ełk, Pol.	B22	10
Elk, stm., Ab., Can.	E19	102
Elk, stm., B.C., Can.	H19	102
Elk, stm., Co., U.S.	D10	120
Elk, stm., Ks., U.S.	N11	118
Elk, stm., Mn., U.S.	E2	110
Elk, stm., Mo., U.S.	F2	114
Elk, stm., U.S.	G10	114
Elk, stm., Wi., U.S.	E5	110
Elk, stm., W.V., U.S.	I5	108
Elkader, Ia., U.S.	H4	110
El Kantara, Tun.	D16	62
El-Karafab, Sudan	H6	60
Elk City, Ok., U.S.	D7	116
Elk Creek, Ca., U.S.	E3	124
El Kef, Tun.	M3	18
El-Kelâa-des-Srarhna, Mor.	D7	62
El Kerma, Alg.	J11	16
Elk Grove, Ca., U.S.	F4	124
Elkhart, In., U.S.	A11	114
Elkhart, Ks., U.S.	N6	118
Elkhart, Tx., U.S.	H11	116
Elkhart Lake, Wi., U.S.	G7	110
Elkhead Mountains, mts., Co., U.S.	D9	120
Elk Horn, Ia., U.S.	J12	118
Elkhorn, Mb., Can.	I13	104
Elkhorn, Wi., U.S.	H7	110
Elkhorn, stm., Ne., U.S.	J10	118
Elkhorn City, Ky., U.S.	B4	112
Elkhorn Mountain, mtn., B.C., Can.	H9	102
Elkin, N.C., U.S.	C6	112
Elkins, W.V., U.S.	I7	108
Elk Island, i., Mb., Can.	H18	104
Elk Island National Park, Ab., Can.	D22	102
Elkland, Pa., U.S.	F9	108
Elk Mountain, Wy., U.S.	C10	120
Elk Mountain, mtn., Wy., U.S.	C10	120
Elko, B.C., Can.	H19	102
Elko, Nv., U.S.	D10	124
El Kouif, Alg.	N3	18
Elk Point, Ab., Can.	D24	102
Elk Point, S.D., U.S.	I11	118
Elk Rapids, Mi., U.S.	F10	110
El Krib, Tun.	M4	18
Elk River, Id., U.S.	D9	122
Elk River, Mn., U.S.	E2	110
Elkton, Ky., U.S.	F9	114
Elkton, Md., U.S.	H11	108
Elkton, Mi., U.S.	G12	110
Elkton, S.D., U.S.	G11	118
Elkton, Va., U.S.	I8	108
Elkville, Il., U.S.	E7	114
Ellard Lake, l., On., Can.	D23	104
Ellaville, Ga., U.S.	G2	112
Ellef Ringnes Island, i., N.T., Can.	B9	86
Ellen, Mount, mtn., Ut., U.S.	F6	120
Ellendale, Mn., U.S.	G2	110
Ellendale, N.D., U.S.	E9	118
Ellensburg, Wa., U.S.	D5	122
Ellenton, Ga., U.S.	H3	112
Ellenville, N.Y., U.S.	F12	108
Ellerbe, N.C., U.S.	D7	112
Ellès, Tun.	N4	18
Ellesmere Island, i., N.T., Can.	A11	86
Ellettsville, In., U.S.	C10	114
Ellice, stm., N.T., Can.	C12	96
Ellice Islands see Tuvalu, ctry., Oc.	I21	126
Ellichpur see Achalpur, India	J7	44
Ellicott City, Md., U.S.	H10	108
Ellicottville, N.Y., U.S.	E8	108
Ellijay, Ga., U.S.	E2	112
El Limón de Teachi, Mex.	E6	90
Ellington, Mo., U.S.	E6	114
Ellinwood, Ks., U.S.	M9	118
Elliot, S. Afr.	H8	66
Elliotdale, S. Afr.	H9	66
Elliot Lake, On., Can.	D13	110
Elliot Lake, l., Mb., Can.	F19	104
Elliott, Ia., U.S.	J12	118
Elliott, Ms., U.S.	I7	114
Elliott Key, i., Fl., U.S.	N6	112
Ellis, Ks., U.S.	M8	118
Ellisras, S. Afr.	D8	66
Elliston, Mt., U.S.	D13	122
Elliston, Nf., Can.	D20	106
Ellisville, Ms., U.S.	K7	114
Ellore see Elūru, India	D6	46
Elloree, S.C., U.S.	F6	112
Ellsworth, Ks., U.S.	M9	118
Ellsworth, Me., U.S.	C18	108
Ellsworth, Mi., U.S.	E10	110
Ellsworth, Mn., U.S.	H11	118
Ellsworth, Wi., U.S.	F3	110
Ellsworth Land, reg., Ant.	C12	73
Ellsworth Mountains, mts., Ant.	C12	73
Ellwangen, Ger.	G10	10
Ellwood City, Pa., U.S.	G6	108
Elm, Switz.	E11	13
Elm, stm., N.D., U.S.	D10	118
Elm, stm., U.S.	F9	118
Elma, Ia., U.S.	G3	110
Elma, Wa., U.S.	C2	122
El Mahdia, Tun.	C16	62
El Malah, Alg.	J10	16
El Maneadero, Mex.	B1	90
El Manteco, Ven.	D11	84
El Marsa el Kebir, Alg.	C10	62
Elm City, N.C., U.S.	D9	112
Elm Creek, Mb., Can.	I16	104
Elm Creek, Ne., U.S.	K8	118
El Médano, Mex.	E4	90
El Menia, Alg.	E12	62
Elmer, N.J., U.S.	H11	108
El Mghayyar, Alg.	D13	62
Elmhurst, Il., U.S.	I8	110
El Milagro, Arg.	F6	80
El Miliyya, Alg.	B14	62
Elmina, Ghana	I9	64
Elmira, N.Y., U.S.	E10	108
Elmira, On., Can.	G15	110
Elmira, P.E., Can.	F11	106
El Mirage, Az., U.S.	K4	120
Elmira Heights, N.Y., U.S.	E10	108
El Mochito, Hond.	C6	92
El Mohammadia, Alg.	C11	62
El Molinillo, Spain	F7	16
El Monte, Chile	G3	80
Elmore, Austl.	K6	70
Elmore, Mn., U.S.	G1	110
Elmore, Oh., U.S.	F3	108
Elmore City, Ok., U.S.	E9	116
Elmsdale, N.S., Can.	H10	106
Elmshorn, Ger.	B9	10
Elm Springs, Ar., U.S.	F2	114
El Multe, Mex.	I14	90
Elmvale, On., Can.	F16	110
Elmwood, Il., U.S.	J6	110
Elmwood, Ne., U.S.	K11	118
Elmwood, Wi., U.S.	F3	110
Elne, Fr.	J9	14
El Negrito, Hond.	B7	92
El Nihuil, Arg.	H4	80
El Nopal, Cerro, mtn., Mex.	C6	90
Elnora, Ab., Can.	F21	102
Elnora, In., U.S.	D9	114
El Ocote, Cerro, mtn., Mex.	E6	90
Eloise, Fl., U.S.	L5	112
Elora, On., Can.	G15	110
Elora, Tn., U.S.	G10	114
El Oro, prov., Ec.	I3	84
Elortondo, Arg.	G8	80
Elorza, Ven.	D8	84
Eloy, Az., U.S.	L5	120
Eloy Alfaro, Ec.	I3	84
El Pacayal, Mex.	J13	90
El Palmar, Bol.	I10	82
El Palmar, Ven.	D12	84
El Palqui, Chile	F3	80
El Pao, Ven.	C11	84
El Pao, Ven.	C8	84
El Paraíso, Hond.	D8	92
El Paraíso, dept., Hond.	C8	92
El Paso, Il., U.S.	J6	110
El Paso, Spain	o23	17b
El Paso, Tx., U.S.	M10	120
El Peñuelo, Mex.	E9	90
El Perú, Ven.	D12	84
Elphinstone, Mb., Can.	H14	104
El Pilar, Ven.	B11	84
El Piñón, Col.	B5	84
El Pintado, Arg.	C8	80
El Piquete, Arg.	C6	80
El Pital, Cerro, mtn., N.A.	C5	92
El Portal, Ca., U.S.	G6	124
El Prat de Llobregat, Spain	D14	16
El Progreso, Guat.	C5	92
El Progreso, Hond.	B7	92
El Progreso, dept., Guat.	C4	92
El Puerto de Santa María, Spain	I5	16
El Puesto, Arg.	D5	80
El Qala, Alg.	B15	62
El Qoll, Alg.	B14	62
El Quebrachal, Arg.	C6	80
El Quelite, Mex.	F6	90
Elqui, stm., Chile	E3	80
El Rastro, Ven.	C9	84
El Real de Santa María, Pan.	C4	84
El Reno, Ok., U.S.	D9	116
El Rey, Parque Nacional, Arg.	C6	80
El Rio, Ca., U.S.	J6	124
El Rito, N.M., U.S.	H10	120
El Rito, stm., N.M., U.S.	H10	120
El Roble, Mesa, mtn., Mex.	B2	90
El Rom, Golan	B5	50
El Rosarito, Mex.	C2	90
Elrose, Sk., Can.	G6	104
Elroy, Wi., U.S.	G5	110
Elsa, Tx., U.S.	M9	116
Elsa, Yk., Can.	E27	100
El Salado, Chile	D3	80
El Salitre, Ec.	H3	84
El Salto, Mex.	F7	90
El Salvador, ctry., N.A.	D6	92
El Samán de Apure, Ven.	D8	84
El Sauz, Mex.	C6	90
El Sauzal, Mex.	B1	90
Elsberry, Mo., U.S.	C6	114
El Seibo, Dom. Rep.	E10	94
Elsie, Mi., U.S.	G11	110
Elsinore, Ut., U.S.	F4	120
Elsmere, De., U.S.	H11	108
El Socorro, Ven.	C10	84
El Sombrero, Ven.	C9	84
Elst, Neth.	E8	12
Elsterwerda, Ger.	D13	10
El Sueco, Mex.	C6	90
El Tagarete, Cerro, mtn., Mex.	D7	90
El Tajín, hist., Mex.	G11	90
El Tala, Arg.	D6	80
El Tamarindo, El Sal.	D7	92
El Tambo, Col.	G4	84
El Tarf, Alg.	M3	18
El Tecuán, Mex.	E6	90
El Tigre, Ven.	C10	84
El Tigre, Isla, i., Hond.	D7	92
Eltmann, Ger.	F10	10
El Tocuyo, Ven.	C8	84
El Tofo, Chile	E3	80
Elton, La., U.S.	L4	114
El Tránsito, Chile	E3	80
El Tránsito, El Sal.	D6	92
El Trébol, Arg.	G8	80
El Triunfo, Hond.	D7	92
El Triunfo, Mex.	F4	90
El Triunfo, Cerro, mtn., Mex.	B2	92
El Triunfo de la Cruz, Hond.	B7	92
El Tunal, Arg.	C6	80
El Turbio, Arg.	G2	78
Elūru, India	D6	46
Elva, Est.	C9	22
El Valle, Pan.	C2	84
Elvas, Port.	G4	16
El Vendrell, Spain	D13	16
El Viejo, Nic.	E7	92
El Vigía, Ven.	C7	84
El Vigía, Cerro, mtn., Mex.	G7	90
Elvins, Mo., U.S.	E6	114
Elvira, Arg.	H9	80
El Volcán, Chile	G3	80
El Wad, Alg.	D14	62
El Wanza, Alg.	C15	62
Elwell, Lake, res., Mt., U.S.	B14	122
Elwood, In., U.S.	B11	114
Elwood, Ks., U.S.	L13	118
Elwood, Ne., U.S.	K8	118
Elx, Spain	G11	16
Ely, Mn., U.S.	C4	110
Ely, Nv., U.S.	E11	124
El Yagual, Ven.	D8	84
Elyria, Oh., U.S.	F4	108
Emāmshahr (Shāhrūd), Iran	C13	48
Emas, Parque Nacional das, Braz.	E2	79
Emba, Kaz.	H9	26
Emba, stm., Kaz.	H9	26
Embarcación, Arg.	B6	80
Embarras, stm., Ab., Can.	D18	102
Embarras, stm., Il., U.S.	D9	114
Embarrass, Wi., U.S.	F7	110
Embarrass, stm., Mn., U.S.	C3	110
Embarrass, stm., Wi., U.S.	F7	110
Embreeville, Tn., U.S.	C4	112
Embrun, Fr.	H13	14
Embrun, On., Can.	B11	108
Emden, Ger.	B7	10
Emden, Il., U.S.	B7	114
Emelle, Al., U.S.	J8	114
Emerado, N.D., U.S.	D10	118
Emerald, Austl.	D8	70
Emerson, Ar., U.S.	I3	114
Emerson, Ga., U.S.	E2	112
Emerson, Ia., U.S.	J12	118
Emerson, Mb., Can.	I17	104
Emerson, Ne., U.S.	I11	118
Emery, S.D., U.S.	H10	118
Emery, Ut., U.S.	F5	120
Emet, Tur.	J13	20
Emiliano Zapata, Mex.	I14	90
Emiliano Zapata, Bahía, b., Mex.	H16	90
Emilia-Romagna, prov., Italy	E6	18
Emine, nos, c., Bul.	G11	20
Eminence, Ky., U.S.	D11	114
Eminence, Mo., U.S.	E5	114
Emlembe, mtn., Afr.	E10	66
Emlenton, Pa., U.S.	F7	108
Emmaus, Pa., U.S.	G11	108
Emmaville, Austl.	G9	70
Emmeline Lake, l., Sk., Can.	C8	104
Emmeloord, Neth.	C8	12
Emmen, Neth.	C10	12
Emmenbrücke, Switz.	D9	13
Emmendingen, Ger.	G7	10
Emmer-Compascuum, Neth.	C11	12

Name	Map Ref.	Page
Emmerich, Ger.	D6	10
Emmet, Ar., U.S.	I3	114
Emmetsburg, Ia., U.S.	H13	118
Emmett, Id., U.S.	G9	122
Emmigaṇūru, India	E4	46
Emmitsburg, Md., U.S.	H9	108
Emmonak, Ak., U.S.	E12	100
Emo, On., Can.	J21	104
Emory, Tx., U.S.	G11	116
Emory, stm., Tn., U.S.	C2	112
Emory Peak, mtn., Tx., U.S.	J3	116
Empalme, Mex.	D4	90
Empangeni, S. Afr.	G10	66
Empedrado, Arg.	D9	80
Empedrado, Chile	H2	80
Empire, La., U.S.	M7	114
Empire, Nv., U.S.	D6	124
Empoli, Italy	F5	18
Emporia, Ks., U.S.	M11	118
Emporia, Va., U.S.	C9	112
Emporium, Pa., U.S.	F8	108
Empress, Ab., Can.	H4	104
Empty Quarter see Ar-Rubʻ al-Khālī, des., Asia	D7	47
Ems, stm., Eur.	C7	10
Emsdetten, Ger.	C7	10
Emure-Ekiti, Nig.	H12	64
En (Inn), stm., Eur.	F17	14
Encampment, Wy., U.S.	C10	120
Encampment, stm., U.S.	C10	120
Encantado, Braz.	E13	80
Encarnación, Para.	D11	80
Encinal, Tx., U.S.	K7	116
Encinitas, Ca., U.S.	K8	124
Encino, N.M., U.S.	J11	120
Encino, Tx., U.S.	M8	116
Encontrados, Ven.	C6	84
Encounter Bay, b., Austl.	J3	70
Encruzilhada, Braz.	C8	79
Encruzilhada do Sul, Braz.	F12	80
Encs, Hung.	G21	10
Endako, B.C., Can.	C9	102
Endako, stm., B.C., Can.	C9	102
Ende, Indon.	G7	38
Endeavor, Wi., U.S.	G6	110
Endeavour, Sk., Can.	F12	104
Endeavour Strait, strt., Austl.	B8	68
Enderby, B.C., Can.	G15	102
Enderby Land, reg., Ant.	B4	73
Enderlin, N.D., U.S.	E10	118
Endicott, N.Y., U.S.	E10	108
Endicott, Wa., U.S.	D8	122
Endimari, stm., Braz.	C8	82
Endola, Nmb.	A2	66
Ene, stm., Peru	D4	82
Enewetak, atoll, Marsh. Is.	G20	126
Enez, Tur.	I10	20
Enfida, Tun.	M5	18
Enfield, N.C., U.S.	C9	112
Enfield, N.H., U.S.	D14	108
Engaño, Cabo, c., Dom. Rep.	E10	94
Engcobo, S. Afr.	H9	66
'En Gedi, Isr.	F4	50
Engelberg, Switz.	E9	13
Engelhard, N.C., U.S.	D11	112
Engel's, Russia	G7	26
Engen, B.C., Can.	C10	102
Engenho, Braz.	F13	82
'En Gev, Isr.	C5	50
Enggano, Pulau, i., Indon.	G3	38
England, Ar., U.S.	H5	114
England, ter., U.K.	I12	8
Englee, Nf., Can.	B17	106
Englefield, Cape, c., N.T., Can.	C15	96
Englehart, On., Can.	C16	110
Englewood, B.C., Can.	G8	102
Englewood, Co., U.S.	E12	120
Englewood, Fl., U.S.	M4	112
Englewood, Ks., U.S.	N8	118
Englewood, Tn., U.S.	D2	112
English, In., U.S.	D10	114
English, stm., Ia., U.S.	I4	110
English, stm., On., Can.	G14	96
English Bay, Ak., U.S.	G19	100
English Channel (La Manche), strt., Eur.	K12	8
English Coast, Ant.	C12	73
English Harbour West, Nf., Can.	E18	106
Énguera, Spain	G11	16
Engure, Lat.	D6	22
Engwilen, Switz.	C11	13
'En Harod, Isr.	C4	50
Enid, Ok., U.S.	C9	116
Enilda, Ab., Can.	B18	102
eNjesuthi, mtn., Afr.	G9	66
Enka, N.C., U.S.	D4	112
Enkhuizen, Neth.	C7	12
Enmedio, Cerro de, mtn., Mex.	H9	90
Enna, Italy	L9	18
Ennadai Lake, l., N.T., Can.	D12	96
Ennedi, plat., Chad	E5	56
Ennis, Mt., U.S.	E14	122
Ennis, Tx., U.S.	G10	116
Enniskillen, N. Ire., U.K.	G6	8
Enns, Aus.	G14	10
Enns, stm., Aus.	G14	10
Enochs, Tx., U.S.	F4	116
Enon, Oh., U.S.	H3	108
Enosburg Falls, Vt., U.S.	C14	108
Enrique Urien, Arg.	D8	80
Enriquillo, Dom. Rep.	F9	94
Enriquillo, Lago, l., Dom. Rep.	E9	94
Enschede, Neth.	D10	12
Ensenada, Arg.	H10	80
Ensenada, Mex.	B1	90
Enshi, China	E8	30
Entebbe, Ug.	A6	58
Enterprise, Al., U.S.	K11	114
Enterprise, Ca., U.S.	E4	124
Enterprise, Guy.	D13	84
Enterprise, Ks., U.S.	M10	118
Enterprise, Ms., U.S.	J8	114
Enterprise, Or., U.S.	E8	122
Enterprise, Ut., U.S.	G3	120
Entiat, stm., Wa., U.S.	C5	122
Entrée, Île d', i., P.Q., Can.	E12	106
Entre Rios, Bol.	I9	82
Entre Rios, Braz.	A9	79
Entre Ríos, prov., Arg.	F9	80
Entre Ríos, Cordillera, mts., Hond.	C9	92
Entre-Rios de Minas, Braz.	F6	79
Entroncamento, Port.	F3	16
Entwistle, Ab., Can.	D19	102
Enugu, Nig.	H13	64
Enumclaw, Wa., U.S.	C4	122
Envalira, Port d', Eur.	C13	16
Envermeu, Fr.	C8	14
Envigado, Col.	D5	84
Envira, Braz.	B6	82
Envira, stm., Braz.	B6	82
Eo, stm., Spain	B4	16
Eolia, Mo., U.S.	C5	114
Eolie, Isole, is., Italy	K9	18
Epe, Nig.	H11	64
Epecuén, Lago, l., Arg.	I7	80
Épéhy, Fr.	H3	12
Épernay, Fr.	C10	14
Epes, Al., U.S.	J8	114
Ephesus, hist., Tur.	L11	20
Ephraim, Ut., U.S.	E5	120
Ephrata, Pa., U.S.	G10	108
Ephrata, Wa., U.S.	C6	122
Épinal, Fr.	D13	14
Epirus see Ípeiros, hist. reg., Grc.	J4	20
Epokiro, Nmb.	C4	66
Epping, Eng., U.K.	J14	8
Epping, N.H., U.S.	D15	108
Epsom, Eng., U.K.	J13	8
Epukiro, stm., Afr.	C5	66
Eqlīd, Iran	F12	48
Equality, Il., U.S.	E8	114
Equatorial Guinea, ctry., Afr.	H8	54
Erath, La., U.S.	M4	114
Erciş, Tur.	B7	48
Erciyes Dağı, mtn., Tur.	B3	48
Érd, Hung.	H18	10
Erdaoliangzi, China	C7	32
Erdene, Mong.	C9	30
Erding, Ger.	G11	10
Erebato, stm., Ven.	E10	84
Erebus, Mount, mtn., Ant.	C8	73
Ereğli, Tur.	C3	48
Erenhot, China	C9	30
Erepecuru, Lago do, l., Braz.	H14	84
Eressós, Grc.	J9	20
Erétria, Grc.	K7	20
Erexim, Braz.	D12	80
Erfoud, Mor.	E8	62
Erft, stm., Ger.	D6	10
Erfurt, Ger.	E11	10
Erges (Erjas), stm., Eur.	F5	16
Ērgļi, Lat.	E8	22
Ergun (Argun'), stm., Asia	A11	30
Er Hai, l., China	B6	40
Erhlin, Tai.	L9	34
Eriba, Sudan	I9	60
Erice, Italy	K7	18
Erichsen Lake, l., N.T., Can.	B16	96
Erick, Ok., U.S.	D7	116
Erickson, B.C., Can.	H18	102
Erickson, Mb., Can.	H15	104
Ericson, Ne., U.S.	J9	118
Erie, Co., U.S.	D11	120
Erie, Il., U.S.	I5	110
Erie, Ks., U.S.	N12	118
Erie, Pa., U.S.	E6	108
Erie, Lake, l., N.A.	H15	110
Erie Canal see New York State Barge Canal, N.Y., U.S.	D10	108
Eriksdale, Mb., Can.	H16	104
Erimo-misaki, c., Japan	f18	36a
Erin, On., Can.	G15	110
Erin, Tn., U.S.	F9	114
Eritrea, ctry., Afr.	E8	56
Erjas (Erges), stm., Eur.	F5	16
Erjiazhen, China	C10	34
Erkelenz, Ger.	D6	10
Erkowit, Sudan	H9	60
Erlangen, Ger.	F11	10
Ermelo, Neth.	D8	12
Ermelo, S. Afr.	F9	66
Ermenek, Tur.	C2	48
Ermineskin Indian Reserve, Ab., Can.	E21	102
Ermoúpolis, Grc.	L8	20
Erne, Lower Lough, l., N. Ire., U.K.	G6	8
Erne, Upper Lough, l., Eur.	G6	8
Ernée, Fr.	D6	14
Erode, India	G4	46
Eromanga, Austl.	F5	70
Erongo, Nmb.	C2	66
Erota, Eritr.	I9	60
Er-Rachidia, Mor.	E8	62
Errol Heights, Or., U.S.	E3	122
Erskine, Mn., U.S.	D11	118
Erskine Inlet, b., N.T., Can.	A12	96
Erstein, Fr.	D14	14
Ertai, China	B5	30
Ertil', Russia	J23	22
Ertix (Irtyš), stm., Asia	H9	28
Ertuğrul, Tur.	J11	20
Erudina, Austl.	H3	70
Eruwa, Nig.	H11	64
Erval, Braz.	G12	80
Erval d'Oeste, Braz.	D13	80
Erwin, N.C., U.S.	D8	112
Erwin, Tn., U.S.	C4	112
Erwood, Sk., Can.	F12	104
Eryuan, China	A5	40
Erzgebirge (Krušné hory), mts., Eur.	E13	10
Erzin, Russia	G17	26
Erzincan, Tur.	B5	48
Erzurum, Tur.	B6	48
Esa'ala, Pap. N. Gui.	A10	68
Esashi, Japan	F15	36
Esashi, Japan	H16	36
Esbjerg, Den.	N11	6
Esca, stm., Spain	J5	14
Escalante, Ut., U.S.	G5	120
Escalante, stm., Ut., U.S.	G5	120
Escalante, stm., Ven.	C7	84
Escalante Desert, des., Ut., U.S.	G3	120
Escalon, Ca., U.S.	G5	124
Escalón, Mex.	D7	90
Escambia, stm., Fl., U.S.	L9	114
Escanaba, Mi., U.S.	E8	110
Escanaba, stm., Mi., U.S.	D8	110
Escárcega, Mex.	H14	90
Escarpada Point, c., Phil.	I20	39b
Escatawpa, stm., U.S.	L8	114
Escaut (Schelde), stm., Eur.	E3	10
Esch-sur-Alzette, Lux.	I8	12
Eschwege, Ger.	D10	10
Eschweiler, Ger.	E6	10
Escobal, Pan.	H15	92
Escobedo, Mex.	C8	90
Escocesa, Bahía, b., Dom. Rep.	E10	94
Escondido, Ca., U.S.	K8	124
Escondido, stm., Nic.	E11	92
Escudo de Veraguas, Isla, i., Pan.	H13	92
Escuinapa de Hidalgo, Mex.	F7	90
Escuintla, Guat.	C4	92
Escuintla, Mex.	J13	90
Escuintla, dept., Guat.	C3	92
Escuminac, Point, c., N.B., Can.	E9	106
Eşfahān (Isfahan), Iran	E11	48
Esfarāyen, Iran	C14	48
Eshkāshem, Afg.	B4	44
Eshowe, S. Afr.	G10	66
Esigodini, Zimb.	C9	66
Esk, Austl.	F10	70
Eskdale, W.V., U.S.	I5	108
Eskifjörđur, Ice.	B7	6a
Eskilstuna, Swe.	L15	6
Eskimo Lakes, l., N.T., Can.	B28	100
Eskimo Point, N.T., Can.	D14	96
Eskişehir, Tur.	H14	4
Eskridge, Ks., U.S.	M11	118
Esla, stm., Spain	C6	16
Eslāmābād, Iran	D9	48
Eslāmshahr, Iran	D11	48
Eşme, Tur.	K12	20
Esmeralda, Austl.	B5	70
Esmeralda, Cuba	D5	94
Esmeraldas, Ec.	G3	84
Esmeraldas, prov., Ec.	G3	84
Esmeraldas, stm., Ec.	G3	84
Esmond, N.D., U.S.	C8	118
Esneux, Bel.	G8	12
Espada, Punta, c., Col.	A7	84
Espalion, Fr.	H9	14
Espanola, N.M., U.S.	I10	120
Espanola, On., Can.	D14	110
Esparza, C.R.	H10	92
Espejo, Spain	H7	16
Espera Feliz, Braz.	F8	79
Esperança, Braz.	J8	84
Esperance, Austl.	F4	68
Esperance Bay, b., Austl.	F4	68
Esperanza, Arg.	F8	80
Esperanza, Mex.	D5	90
Esperanza Inlet, b., B.C., Can.	H8	102
Espinal, Col.	E5	84
Espinhaço, Serra do, mts., Braz.	C7	79
Espinho, Port.	D3	16
Espinillo, Arg.	C9	80
Espino, Ven.	C9	84
Espinosa, Braz.	C7	79
Espírito Santo, state, Braz.	E8	79
Espíritu Santo, Isla, i., Mex.	E4	90
Espita, Mex.	G15	90
Espoir, Bay d', b., Nf., Can.	E18	106
Espoo (Esbo), Fin.	K19	6
Es Port de Pollença, Spain	F15	16
Espumoso, Braz.	E12	80
Espungabera, Moz.	C11	66
Esquel, Arg.	E2	78
Esquimalt, B.C., Can.	I11	102
Esquina, Arg.	F9	80
Esquina Negra, Arg.	H9	80
Esquipulas, Guat.	C5	92
Esquipulas, Nic.	E9	92
Esquiú, Arg.	E6	80
Essaouira (Mogador), Mor.	E6	62
Es-Sekhira, Tun.	C16	62
Essen, Bel.	F5	12
Essen, Ger.	D7	10
Essequibo, stm., Guy.	E13	84
Essequibo Islands-West Demerara, prov., Guy.	D13	84
Es Sers, Tun.	M4	18
Essex, Ia., U.S.	K12	118
Essex, Md., U.S.	H10	108
Essex, Mo., U.S.	F7	114
Essex, On., Can.	H13	110
Essex, co., Eng., U.K.	J14	8
Essex Junction, Vt., U.S.	C13	108
Essexville, Mi., U.S.	G12	110
Esslingen, Ger.	G9	10
Es Smala es Souassi, Tun.	N5	18
Essonne, dept., Fr.	D9	14
Essoyes, Fr.	D11	14
Es-Suki, Sudan	K7	60
Est, Île de l', i., P.Q., Can.	E12	106
Est, Pointe de l', c., P.Q., Can.	C12	106
Estacada, Or., U.S.	E3	122
Estacado, Llano, pl., U.S.	F4	116
Estados, Isla de los, i., Arg.	G4	78
Eşṭahbān, Iran	G13	48
Estância, Braz.	F11	76
Estancia, N.M., U.S.	J10	120
Estanislao del Campo, Arg.	C8	80
Estanzuelas, El Sal.	D6	92
Estats, Pique d', mtn., Eur.	C13	16
Estcourt, S. Afr.	G9	66
Este, Italy	D6	18
Esteio, Braz.	E13	80
Estelí, Nic.	D8	92
Estelí, dept., Nic.	D8	92
Estella, Spain	C9	16
Estelline, S.D., U.S.	G11	118
Estelline, Tx., U.S.	E6	116
Estepa, Spain	H7	16
Estepona, Spain	I6	16
Esterhazy, Sk., Can.	H12	104
Esteros, Arg.	D7	80
Estes Park, Co., U.S.	D11	120
Este Sudeste, Cayos del, is., Col.	E13	92
Estevan, Sk., Can.	I12	104
Estevan Group, is., B.C., Can.	D5	102
Estevan Point, B.C., Can.	H8	102
Estherville, Ia., U.S.	H13	118
Estill, S.C., U.S.	F6	112
Estiva, Rio da, stm., Braz.	B6	79
Eston, Sk., Can.	G6	104
Estonia (Eesti), ctry., Eur.	C8	22
Estrela, Braz.	E13	80
Estrela, mtn., Port.	E4	16
Estrela do Norte, Braz.	B4	79
Estrela do Sul, Braz.	E5	79
Estremadura, hist. reg., Port.	F3	16
Estuary, Sk., Can.	H5	104
Esztergom, Hung.	H18	10
Étables, Fr.	D4	14
Etadunna, Austl.	G3	70
Etah, Grnld.	B12	86
Etah, India	G8	44
Étain, Fr.	C12	14
Étamamiou, stm., P.Q., Can.	B13	106
Étampes, Fr.	D9	14
Étaples, Fr.	B8	14
Etāwah, India	G8	44
Etchemin, stm., P.Q., Can.	F3	106
Etchojoa, Mex.	D5	90
Ethan, S.D., U.S.	H10	118
Ethel, Ms., U.S.	I7	114
Ethel, Mount, mtn., Co., U.S.	D10	120
Ethelbert, Mb., Can.	G14	104
Ethel Lake, l., Yk., Can.	E26	100
Ethiopia (Ityopiya), ctry., Afr.	G8	56
Ethridge, Mt., U.S.	B13	122
Ethridge, Tn., U.S.	G9	114
Etna, Ca., U.S.	C3	124
Etna, Wy., U.S.	A5	120
Etna, Monte, vol., Italy	L10	18
Etobicoke, On., Can.	G16	110
Etomami, stm., Sk., Can.	F12	104
Etosha Pan, pl., Nmb.	B3	66
Etowah, Tn., U.S.	D2	112
Etowah, stm., Ga., U.S.	E1	112
Étretat, Fr.	C7	14
Ettelbruck, Lux.	I9	12
Et Tîdra, i., Maur.	B1	64
Ettlingen, Ger.	G8	10
Ettrick, Va., U.S.	B9	112
Etzikom Coulee, stm., Ab., Can.	I3	104
Etzná, hist., Mex.	H14	90
Eu, Fr.	B8	14
Euchiniko, stm., B.C., Can.	D10	102
Eucla, Austl.	F5	68
Euclid, Oh., U.S.	F5	108
Eucumbene, Lake, res., Austl.	K8	70
Eudistes, Lac des, l., P.Q., Can.	B8	106
Eudora, Ar., U.S.	I5	114
Eudora, Ks., U.S.	M12	118
Eudunda, Austl.	J3	70
Eufaula, Al., U.S.	K11	114
Eufaula, Ok., U.S.	D11	116
Eufaula Lake, res., Ok., U.S.	D11	116
Eugene, Or., U.S.	F2	122
Eugenia, Punta, c., Mex.	D2	90
Eugenio Bustos, Arg.	G4	80
Eugowra, Austl.	I8	70
Eumungerie, Austl.	H8	70
Eunice, La., U.S.	L4	114
Eunice, N.M., U.S.	G3	116
Eupen, Bel.	G9	12
Euphrates (Firat) (Nahr al-Furāt), stm., Asia	F9	48
Eupora, Ms., U.S.	I7	114
Eure, dept., Fr.	C7	14
Eure, stm., Fr.	D8	14
Eure-et-Loir, dept., Fr.	D8	14
Eureka, Ca., U.S.	D1	124
Eureka, Il., U.S.	J6	110
Eureka, Ks., U.S.	N11	118
Eureka, Mt., U.S.	B10	122
Eureka, Nv., U.S.	E10	124
Eureka, S.C., U.S.	E5	112
Eureka, S.D., U.S.	F8	118
Eureka, Ut., U.S.	E4	120
Eureka Springs, Ar., U.S.	F3	114
Euroa, Austl.	K6	70
Europa, Île, i., Afr.	F8	58
Europa Point, c., Gib.	I6	16
Europe	C9	52
Europoort, Neth.	E5	12
Euskal Herriko, state, Spain	B9	16
Euskirchen, Ger.	E6	10
Eustace, Tx., U.S.	G10	116
Eustis, Fl., U.S.	K5	112
Eustis, Ne., U.S.	K7	118
Eutaw, Al., U.S.	J9	114
Eutsuk Lake, l., B.C., Can.	D8	102
Eva, Al., U.S.	H10	114
Evadale, Tx., U.S.	L2	114
Evans, Co., U.S.	D12	120
Evans, Lac, l., P.Q., Can.	F17	96
Evans, Mount, mtn., Co., U.S.	E11	120
Evansburg, Ab., Can.	D19	102
Evans City, Pa., U.S.	G6	108
Evansdale, Ia., U.S.	H3	110
Evans Head, c., Austl.	G10	70
Evans Strait, strt., N.T., Can.	D16	96
Evanston, Il., U.S.	H8	110
Evanston, Wy., U.S.	C6	120
Evansville, Il., U.S.	D7	114
Evansville, In., U.S.	E9	114
Evansville, Mn., U.S.	E12	118
Evansville, Wi., U.S.	H6	110
Evansville, Wy., U.S.	B10	120
Evant, Tx., U.S.	H8	116
Evart, Mi., U.S.	G10	110
Evarts, Ky., U.S.	C3	112
Eveleth, Mn., U.S.	C3	110
Evening Shade, Ar., U.S.	F5	114
Everard, Lake, l., Austl.	F7	68
Everard, Mount, mtn., B.C., Can.	F9	102
Everest, Ks., U.S.	L12	118
Everest, Mount (Qomolangma Feng), mtn., Asia	G12	44
Everett, Pa., U.S.	G8	108
Everett, Wa., U.S.	C3	122
Everglades, The, sw., Fl., U.S.	M6	112
Everglades City, Fl., U.S.	N5	112
Everglades National Park, Fl., U.S.	N6	112
Evergreen, Al., U.S.	K10	114
Evergreen, Ca., U.S.	I5	124
Evergreen, Mt., U.S.	B11	122
Everly, Ia., U.S.	H12	118
Everman, Volcán, vol., Mex.	H4	90
Evesham, Sk., Can.	F5	104
Évian-les-Bains, Fr.	F13	14
Evionnaz, Switz.	F7	13
Evisa, Fr.	G3	18
Évora, Port.	G4	16
Évreux, Fr.	C8	14
Évros (Marica) (Meriç), stm., Eur.	H10	20
Évry, Fr.	D9	14
Évvoia, i., Grc.	K7	20
Ewa, Hi., U.S.	p15	125a
Ewen, Mi., U.S.	D6	110
Ewing, Ne., U.S.	I9	118
Ewing, Va., U.S.	C3	112
Ewo, Congo	B2	58
Exaltación, Bol.	E9	82
Excelsior Mountain, mtn., Ca., U.S.	F6	124
Excelsior Springs, Mo., U.S.	C2	114
Exeter, Ca., U.S.	H6	124
Exeter, Eng., U.K.	K10	8
Exeter, Ne., U.S.	K10	118
Exeter, N.H., U.S.	E16	108
Exeter, On., Can.	G14	110
Exeter, stm., N.H., U.S.	D15	108
Exeter Sound, strt., N.T., Can.	C20	96
Exira, Ia., U.S.	J13	118
Exmore, Va., U.S.	B11	112
Exmouth, Austl.	D2	68
Exmouth, Eng., U.K.	K10	8
Exmouth Gulf, b., Austl.	D2	68
Expedition Range, mts., Austl.	E8	70
Experiment, Ga., U.S.	F2	112
Exploits, stm., Nf., Can.	D17	106
Exploits, Bay of, b., Nf., Can.	C18	106
Exploits Dam, Nf., Can.	D17	106
Exshaw, Ab., Can.	F19	102
Extremadura, state, Spain	F5	16
Exuma Cays, is., Bah.	B6	94
Exuma Sound, strt., Bah.	B6	94
Eyebrow, Sk., Can.	H8	104
Eyehill Creek, stm., Can.	F4	104
Eyl, Som.	G10	56
Eymoutiers, Fr.	G8	14
Eyota, Mn., U.S.	G3	110
Eyrarbakki, Ice.	C3	6a
Eyre, Austl.	F5	68
Eyre North, Lake, l., Austl.	G2	70
Eyre Peninsula, pen., Austl.	I1	70
Eyre South, Lake, l., Austl.	G2	70
Eysturoy, i., Faer. Is.	D8	6b
Ezine, Tur.	J10	20
Ezjaryšča, Bela.	F12	22

F

Name	Map Ref.	Page
Fabens, Tx., U.S.	M10	120
Faber Lake, l., N.T., Can.	D9	96
Fábrega, Cerro, mtn., Pan.	H12	92
Fabriano, Italy	F7	18
Facatativá, Col.	E5	84
Factoryville, Pa., U.S.	F11	108
Fada, Chad	E5	56
Fada Ngourma, Burkina	E10	64
Fadd, Hung.	I18	10
Faddeja, zaliv, b., Russia	B13	28
Fadit, Sudan	M7	60
Faenza, Italy	E6	18
Faeroe Islands (Føroyar), dep., Eur.	D8	6b
Fafa, Mali	D10	64
Fafakourou, Sen.	E2	64
Fafen, stm., Eth.	G9	56
Faga, stm., Burkina	E10	64
Făgăraş, Rom.	D8	20
Fagernes, Nor.	K11	6
Făget, Rom.	D6	20
Faguibine, Lac, l., Mali	C8	64
Fagurhólsmýri, Ice.	C5	6a
Faido, Switz.	F10	13
Fairbairn Reservoir, res., Austl.	D8	70
Fairbank, Ia., U.S.	H3	110
Fairbanks, Ak., U.S.	D21	100
Fairbanks, La., U.S.	L4	114
Fair Bluff, N.C., U.S.	E7	112
Fairborn, Oh., U.S.	H2	108
Fairburn, Ga., U.S.	F2	112
Fairbury, Il., U.S.	J7	110
Fairbury, Ne., U.S.	K10	118
Fairchance, Pa., U.S.	H7	108
Fairchild, Wi., U.S.	F5	110
Fairfax, Al., U.S.	J11	114
Fairfax, Mn., U.S.	G13	118
Fairfax, Mo., U.S.	B1	114
Fairfax, Ok., U.S.	C10	116
Fairfax, S.C., U.S.	G5	112
Fairfax, S.D., U.S.	H9	118
Fairfax, Va., U.S.	I9	108
Fairfax, Vt., U.S.	C13	108
Fairfield, Al., U.S.	I10	114
Fairfield, Ca., U.S.	F3	124
Fairfield, Ia., U.S.	I4	110
Fairfield, Id., U.S.	G11	122
Fairfield, Il., U.S.	D8	114
Fairfield, Me., U.S.	C17	108
Fairfield, Mt., U.S.	C14	122
Fairfield, Ne., U.S.	K9	118
Fairfield, Oh., U.S.	H2	108
Fairfield, Tx., U.S.	H10	116
Fairgrove, Mi., U.S.	G12	110
Fairhaven, Ma., U.S.	F16	108
Fair Haven, N.Y., U.S.	D10	108
Fair Haven, Vt., U.S.	D13	108
Fairhope, Al., U.S.	L9	114
Fairland, In., U.S.	C11	114
Fairland, Ok., U.S.	C12	116
Fairlie, N.Z.	F3	72
Fairmont, Mn., U.S.	H13	118
Fairmont, N.C., U.S.	E7	112
Fairmont, Ne., U.S.	K10	118
Fairmont, W.V., U.S.	H6	108
Fairmont Hot Springs, B.C., Can.	G19	102
Fairmount, Ga., U.S.	E2	112
Fairmount, Il., U.S.	B9	114
Fairmount, In., U.S.	B11	114
Fairmount, N.D., U.S.	E11	118
Fair Ness, c., N.T., Can.	D18	96
Fair Oaks, Ca., U.S.	F4	124
Fair Oaks, Ga., U.S.	F2	112
Fair Plain, Mi., U.S.	H9	110
Fairplains, N.C., U.S.	C5	112
Fairplay, Co., U.S.	E10	120
Fairview, Ab., Can.	A16	102
Fairview, Ga., U.S.	E1	112
Fairview, Il., U.S.	J5	110
Fairview, Ks., U.S.	L12	118
Fairview, Mi., U.S.	F11	110
Fairview, Mt., U.S.	D3	118
Fairview, Ok., U.S.	C8	116
Fairview, Tn., U.S.	G9	114
Fairview, Ut., U.S.	E5	120
Fairview, W.V., U.S.	H6	108
Fairview Park, In., U.S.	C9	114
Fairview Peak, mtn., Nv., U.S.	E7	124
Fairweather Mountain, mtn., N.A.	G26	100
Faisalabad, Pak.	E5	44
Faison, N.C., U.S.	D8	112
Faith, S.D., U.S.	F5	118
Faiyum see Al-Fayyūm, Egypt	C6	60
Faizābād, India	G10	44
Fajardo, P.R.	E12	94
Fakfak, Indon.	F9	38
Fakrinkotti, Sudan	H6	60
Faku, China	A11	32
Falaise, Fr.	D6	14
Falam, Myan.	C2	40
Falāvarjān, Iran	E11	48
Fălciu, Rom.	C12	20
Falcón, state, Ven.	B8	84
Falconara Marittima, Italy	F8	18
Falconbridge, On., Can.	D15	110
Falcon Heights, Or., U.S.	H4	122
Falcon Reservoir (Presa Falcón), res., N.A.	M7	116
Falémé, stm., Afr.	F4	54
Făleşti, Mol.	B11	20
Falfurrias, Tx., U.S.	L8	116
Falher, Ab., Can.	B17	102
Falkensee, Ger.	C13	10
Falkenstein, Ger.	E12	10
Falkirk, Scot., U.K.	E10	8
Falkland Islands, dep., S.A.	G5	78
Falkland Sound, strt., Falk. Is.	G5	78
Falkville, Al., U.S.	H10	114
Fall, stm., Ks., U.S.	N12	118
Fallais, Bel.	G7	12
Fallbrook, Ca., U.S.	K8	124
Fall Creek, Wi., U.S.	F4	110
Fallentimber Creek, stm., Ab., Can.	F19	102
Falling, stm., Va., U.S.	B8	112
Fallon, Mt., U.S.	E2	118
Fallon, Nv., U.S.	E7	124
Fall River, Ks., U.S.	N11	118
Fall River, Ma., U.S.	F15	108
Fall River, Wi., U.S.	G6	110
Fall River Mills, Ca., U.S.	C4	124
Falls City, Ne., U.S.	K12	118
Falls City, Or., U.S.	F2	122
Falls Creek, Pa., U.S.	F8	108
Falmouth, Eng., U.K.	K8	8
Falmouth, Jam.	E6	94
Falmouth, Ky., U.S.	I2	108
Falmouth, Ma., U.S.	F16	108
Falmouth, Me., U.S.	D16	108
Falmouth, Va., U.S.	I9	108
False Divi Point, c., India	E6	46
Falso, Cabo, c., Dom. Rep.	F9	94
Falso, Cabo, c., Hond.	B11	92
Falster, i., Den.	N12	6
Fălticeni, Rom.	B10	20
Falun, Swe.	K14	6
Famaillá, Arg.	D6	80
Famatina, Arg.	E5	80
Famatina, Sierra de, mts., Arg.	E5	80
Family Lake, l., Mb., Can.	G19	104
Fana, Mali	E6	64
Fanado, stm., Braz.	D7	79
Fanambana, Madag.	n24	67b
Fanchon, Pointe, c., Haiti	E7	94
Fanchuan, China	C8	34
Fandriana, Madag.	r22	67b
Fang, Thai.	E5	40
Fangak, Sudan	M6	60
Fangcheng, China	B1	34
Fangdao, China	H7	34
Fangxi, China	G3	34
Fanipal', Bela.	H10	22
Fanny, Mount, mtn., Or., U.S.	E8	122
Fanny Bay, B.C., Can.	H10	102
Fano, Italy	F8	18
Fan Si Pan, mtn., Viet.	C7	40
Fanxian, China	H3	32
Faraday, sci., Ant.	B12	73
Faradje, Zaire	H6	56
Faradofay, Madag.	t22	67b
Farafangana, Madag.	s22	67b
Farāh, Afg.	E17	48
Farahalana, Madag.	o24	67b
Farā'id, Jabal al-, mtn., Egypt	J3	48
Farallon Islands, is., Ca., U.S.	G2	124
Faramana, Burkina	E7	64
Faranah, Gui.	F4	64
Farasān, Jazā'ir, is., Sau. Ar.	F2	47
Faratsiho, Madag.	q22	67b
Farewell, Cape, c., N.Z.	D4	72
Fargo, N.D., U.S.	E11	118
Faribault, Mn., U.S.	F2	110
Faribault, Lac, l., P.Q., Can.	E18	96
Farīdkot, India	E6	44
Farīdpur, Bngl.	I13	44
Farīmān, Iran	D15	48
Farina, Il., U.S.	D8	114
Fāriskūr, Egypt	B6	60
Farley, Ia., U.S.	H4	110
Farmer City, Il., U.S.	B8	114
Farmersburg, In., U.S.	C9	114
Farmersville, Il., U.S.	C7	114
Farmersville, Tx., U.S.	F10	116
Farmerville, La., U.S.	J4	114
Farmington, Ia., U.S.	J4	110
Farmington, Il., U.S.	J5	110
Farmington, Me., U.S.	C16	108
Farmington, Mn., U.S.	F2	110
Farmington, Mo., U.S.	E6	114
Farmington, N.H., U.S.	D15	108
Farmington, N.M., U.S.	H8	120
Farmington, Ut., U.S.	D5	120
Far Mountain, mtn., B.C., Can.	E9	102
Farmville, N.C., U.S.	D9	112
Farmville, Va., U.S.	B8	112
Farnam, Ne., U.S.	K7	118
Farnham, P.Q., Can.	B14	108
Farnham, Mount, mtn., B.C., Can.	G18	102
Farnhamville, Ia., U.S.	I13	118
Faro, Braz.	I14	84
Faro, Port.	H4	16
Faro, stm., Afr.	G9	54
Farquhar Group, is., Sey.	D10	58
Farragut, Ia., U.S.	K12	118
Farrāshband, Iran	G12	48
Farrell, Pa., U.S.	F6	108
Farrukhābād, India	G8	44
Fārsī, Afg.	E17	48
Farsund, Nor.	L10	6
Fartak, Ra's, c., Yemen	G8	47
Farvel, Kap, c., Grnld.	E24	96
Farwell, Mi., U.S.	G11	110
Farwell, Tx., U.S.	I3	116
Fasā, Iran	G12	48
Fasano, Italy	I12	18
Fatehpur, India	G6	44
Fathai, Sudan	M6	60
Fathom Five National Marine Park, On., Can.	E14	110
Fatick, Sen.	D1	64
Fátima, Port.	F3	16
Fatoto, Gam.	E3	64
Fat'ož, Russia	I18	22
Faulkton, S.D., U.S.	F8	118
Faulquemont, Fr.	C13	14
Fauquier, B.C., Can.	H16	102
Fauske, Nor.	H14	6
Faust, Ab., Can.	B19	102
Fauvillers, Bel.	I8	12
Faux-Cap, Madag.	t21	67b
Favara, Italy	L8	18
Faverges, Fr.	G13	14
Favourable Lake, l., On., Can.	F21	104
Fawcett, Ab., Can.	C20	102
Fawcett Lake, l., Ab., Can.	B21	102
Fawn, stm., On., Can.	F15	96
Fawnie Nose, mtn., B.C., Can.	D9	102
Fawnie Range, mts., B.C., Can.	D10	102
Faxaflói, b., Ice.	B2	6a
Faxinal, Braz.	G3	79
Faxinal do Soturno, Braz.	E12	80
Faya, Chad	E4	56
Fayd, Sau. Ar.	H7	48
Fayette, Al., U.S.	I9	114
Fayette, Ia., U.S.	H4	110
Fayette, Mo., U.S.	C4	114
Fayette, Ms., U.S.	K5	114
Fayette, Oh., U.S.	F2	108
Fayetteville, Ar., U.S.	F2	114
Fayetteville, Ga., U.S.	F2	112
Fayetteville, N.C., U.S.	D8	112
Fayetteville, Tn., U.S.	G10	114
Fayetteville, W.V., U.S.	I5	108
Fayl-Billot, Fr.	E12	14
Fazenda de Cima, Braz.	F13	82
Fazenda Nova, Braz.	D3	79
Fāzilka, India	E6	44
Fāzilpur, Pak.	F4	44
Fazzān (Fezzan), hist. reg., Libya	C3	56
Fdérik, Maur.	I4	62
Fear, Cape, c., N.C., U.S.	F9	112
Feather, stm., Ca., U.S.	E4	124
Feathertop, Mount, mtn., Austl.	K7	70
Fécamp, Fr.	C7	14
Federación, Arg.	F10	80
Federal, Arg.	F9	80
Federalsburg, Md., U.S.	I11	108
Fehérgyarmat, Hung.	H22	10
Fehmarn, i., Ger.	A11	10
Fehmarnbelt, strt., Eur.	A11	10
Feia, Lagoa, b., Braz.	G8	79
Feijó, Braz.	C6	82
Feira, Zam.	E6	58
Feira de Santana, Braz.	B9	79
Feixiang, China	G2	32
Fejaj, Chott, sw., Tun.	D15	62
Fejér, co., Hung.	H18	10
Felanitx, Spain	F15	16
Felda, Fl., U.S.	M5	112
Feldbach, Aus.	I15	10
Feldkirch, Aus.	H9	10
Felhit, Erit.	I10	60
Feliciano, Arroyo, stm., Arg.	F9	80
Felix, Cape, c., N.T., Can.	C13	96
Felix, Rio, stm., N.M., U.S.	K11	120
Felixlândia, Braz.	E6	79
Felixstowe, Eng., U.K.	J15	8
Felixton, S. Afr.	G10	66
Félix U. Gómez, Mex.	C4	90
Fellbach, Ger.	G9	10

Name — Map Ref. — Page

Felletin, Fr. G9 14
Fellsmere, Fl., U.S. L6 112
Feltre, Italy C6 18
Femund, l., Nor. J12 6
Femundsenden, Nor. K12 6
Fen, stm., China D9 30
Fenelon Falls, On., Can. F17 110
Fengcheng, China C12 32
Fengcheng, China G4 34
Fengdu, China F8 30
Fengfeng, China G2 32
Fenghuanjing, China D6 34
Fengjia, China F9 32
Fenglin, Tai. L10 34
Fengxin, China G4 34
Fengyang, China E10 30
Fengyüan, Tai. K9 34
Fengzhen, China C9 30
Feni, Bngl. I14 44
Fennimore, Wi., U.S. H5 110
Fennville, Mi., U.S. H9 110
Fenoarivo Atsinanana, Madag. p23 67b
Fenshui'ao, China J3 34
Fenton, Mi., U.S. H12 110
Fentress, Tx., U.S. J9 116
Fenwick, W.V., U.S. I6 108
Fenyang, China D9 30
Feodosiya, Ukr. H5 26
Ferdinand, In., U.S. D10 114
Ferdows, Iran D15 48
Fergana, Uzb. I12 26
Fergus, On., Can. G15 110
Fergus Falls, Mn., U.S. E11 118
Ferguson, B.C., Can. G17 102
Ferguson, Ky., U.S. B2 112
Ferguson, Mo., U.S. D6 114
Fériana, Tun. C15 62
Ferkéssédougou, C. Iv. G7 64
Ferlo, Vallée du, val., Sen. D2 64
Fermo, Italy F8 18
Fermont, P.Q., Can. F19 96
Fernández, Arg. D7 80
Fernandina, Isla, i., Ec. j13 84a
Fernandina Beach, Fl., U.S. I5 112
Fernando de la Mora, Para. C10 80
Fernando de Noronha, Ilha, i., Braz. D12 76
Fernandópolis, Braz. F3 79
Fernando Póo see Bioko, i., Eq. Gui. J14 64
Fernán-Núñez, Spain H7 16
Ferndale, Ca., U.S. D1 124
Ferndale, Wa., U.S. B3 122
Fernie, B.C., Can. H19 102
Fernley, Nv., U.S. E6 124
Fern Park, Fl., U.S. K5 112
Fernwood, Id., U.S. C9 122
Ferolle Point, c., Nf., Can. A16 106
Ferrara, Italy E6 18
Ferreñafe, Peru B2 82
Ferreyra, Arg. F6 80
Ferriday, La., U.S. K5 114
Ferrières, Fr. D9 14
Ferris, Tx., U.S. G10 116
Ferro, stm., Braz. B1 79
Ferrol, Spain B3 16
Ferrol, Península de, pen., Peru C2 82
Ferron, Ut., U.S. E5 120
Ferros, Braz. E7 79
Ferryland, Nf., Can. E21 106
Ferrysburg, Mi., U.S. G9 110
Fertile, Mn., U.S. D11 118
Fès, Mor. C8 62
Feshi, Zaire C3 58
Fessenden, N.D., U.S. D8 118
Festus, Mo., U.S. D6 114
Fété Bowé, Sen. D3 64
Fetești, Rom. E11 20
Fethiye, Tur. M13 20
Feuchtwangen, Ger. F10 10
Feuet, Libya H16 62
Feuilles, Baie aux, b., P.Q., Can. E19 96
Feuilles, Rivière aux, stm., P.Q., Can. E18 96
Feyẕābād, Afg. B4 44
Fez see Fès, Mor. C8 62
Fiambalá, Arg. D5 80
Fianarantsoa, Madag. r22 67b
Fiantsonana, Madag. q22 67b
Fiche, Eth. M10 60
Fichtelberg, mtn., Ger. E12 10
Fichtelgebirge, mts., Eur. E11 10
Ficksburg, S. Afr. G8 66
Fidenza, Italy E5 18
Fidler Lake, l., Mb., Can. A18 104
Field, B.C., Can. F18 102
Fieldale, Va., U.S. C7 112
Fier, Alb. I3 20
Fiesch, Switz. F9 13
Fife, prov., Scot., U.K. E10 8
Fife Lake, Mi., U.S. F10 110
Fife Lake, Sk., Can. I9 104
Fife Lake, l., Sk., Can. I9 104
Fifield, Wi., U.S. E5 110
Figueira da Foz, Port. E3 16
Figueres, Spain C14 16
Figuig, Mor. D10 62
Fiji, ctry., Oc. J21 126
Filabusi, Zimb. C9 66
Filadelfia, C.R. G9 92
Filchner Ice Shelf, Ant. C1 73
File Lake, l., Mb., Can. D14 104
Filingué, Niger D11 64
Fillmore, Ca., U.S. J7 124
Fillmore, Sk., Can. I11 104
Fillmore, Ut., U.S. F4 120
Finale Ligure, Italy E3 18
Finarwa, Eth. K10 60
Fincastle, Va., U.S. B7 112
Findlay, Il., U.S. C8 114
Findlay, Oh., U.S. F3 108
Findlay, Mount, mtn., B.C., Can. G18 102
Fingal, N.D., U.S. E10 118
Finger Lake, l., On., Can. E21 104
Fíngoè, Moz. E6 58
Finistère, dept., Fr. D2 14
Finke, Austl. E6 68
Finke, stm., Austl. E7 68
Finland (Suomi), ctry., Eur. C13 4
Finland, Gulf of, b., Eur. L20 6
Finlay, stm., B.C., Can. E7 96
Finley, Austl. J6 70
Finley, N.D., U.S. D10 118
Finmoore, B.C., Can. D11 102
Finn, stm., Eur. G6 8
Finnegan, Ab., Can. F22 102
Finnmark, co., Nor. F19 6
Fins, Oman C11 47
Finsteraarhorn, mtn., Switz. E9 13
Finsterwalde, Ger. D13 10
Fiora, stm., Italy G6 18
Fīq, Golan C5 50
Firavitoba, Col. E6 84
Firebaugh, Ca., U.S. H5 124
Firenze (Florence), Italy F6 18
Firmat, Arg. G8 80
Firminópolis, Braz. D3 79
Firminy, Fr. G11 14
Firovo, Russia D16 22
Fīrozābād, India G8 44
Fīrozpur, India E6 44
Firth, Ne., U.S. K11 118
Firth, stm., N.A. B24 100
Fīrūzābād, Iran G12 48
Fīrūz Kūh, Iran D12 48
Fish, stm., Al., U.S. L9 114
Fish (Vis), stm., Nmb. F3 66
Fisher, Ar., U.S. G6 114
Fisher, Il., U.S. B8 114
Fisher, La., U.S. K3 114
Fisher, stm., Mb., Can. G17 104
Fisher, stm., Mt., U.S. B10 122
Fisher Bay, b., Mb., Can. G17 104
Fisher Branch, Mb., Can. G17 104
Fisher Channel, strt., B.C., Can. E7 102
Fisher River Indian Reserve, Mb., Can. G17 104
Fishers Island, i., N.Y., U.S. F15 108
Fisher Strait, strt., N.T., Can. D16 96
Fishing Creek, Md., U.S. I10 108
Fishing Lake, l., Mb., Can. F19 104
Fishing Lake, l., Sk., Can. G11 104
Fisk, Mo., U.S. F6 114
Fismes, Fr. C10 14
Fisterra, Cabo de, c., Spain C2 16
Fitchburg, Ma., U.S. E15 108
Fitzgerald, Ga., U.S. H3 112
Fitzgerald River National Park, Austl. F3 68
Fitz Hugh Sound, strt., B.C., Can. F7 102
Fitzroy, stm., Austl. C4 68
Fitzroy, stm., Austl. D9 70
Fitzroy, Monte (Cerro Chaltel), mtn., S.A. F2 78
Fitzroy Crossing, Austl. C5 68
Fiume see Rijeka, Cro. D9 18
Fiumicino, Italy H7 18
Five Islands, N.S., Can. G9 106
Five Points, N.M., U.S. I10 120
Fizi, Zaire B5 58
Fjällåsen, Swe. H17 6
Fkih-Ben-Salah, Mor. D7 62
Flagler, Co., U.S. L4 118
Flagler Beach, Fl., U.S. J5 112
Flagstaff, Az., U.S. I5 120
Flagstaff Lake, res., Me., U.S. B16 108
Flambeau, stm., Wi., U.S. E4 110
Flaming Gorge Reservoir, res., U.S. C7 120
Flanagan, Il., U.S. J7 110
Flanagan, stm., On., Can. F21 104
Flanders, On., Can. B3 110
Flanders (Flandre), hist. reg., Eur. G2 12
Flandes, Col. E5 84
Flandreau, S.D., U.S. G11 118
Flasher, N.D., U.S. E6 118
Flat, Tx., U.S. H9 116
Flat, stm., Mi., U.S. G10 110
Flat, stm., N.T., Can. F31 100
Flat Bay, Nf., Can. D15 106
Flatey, Ice. B2 6a
Flateyri, Ice. B2 6a
Flathead, stm., Mt., U.S. I20 102
Flathead Lake, l., Mt., U.S. C11 122
Flat Lake, l., Ab., Can. C22 102
Flat Lick, Ky., U.S. C3 112
Flatonia, Tx., U.S. J9 116
Flat River, Mo., U.S. E6 114
Flat River, P.E., Can. F11 106
Flat Rock, Al., U.S. H11 114
Flat Rock, Il., U.S. D9 114
Flatrock Lake, l., Mb., Can. C14 104
Flattery, Cape, c., Wa., U.S. B1 122
Flatwood, Al., U.S. J10 114
Flatwoods, Ky., U.S. I4 108
Flaxcombe, Sk., Can. G5 104
Flaxton, N.D., U.S. C5 118
Flaxville, Mt., U.S. C2 118
Fleetwood, Pa., U.S. G11 108
Fleming, Co., U.S. K5 118
Fleming-Neon, Ky., U.S. B4 112
Flemingsburg, Ky., U.S. I3 108
Flensburg, Ger. A9 10
Fletcher, N.C., U.S. D4 112
Fletcher, Ok., U.S. E8 116
Fletcher Pond, res., Mi., U.S. F12 110
Fleurance, Fr. I7 14
Fleur-de-Lys, Nf., Can. B17 106
Fleurier, Switz. E6 13
Flevoland, prov., Neth. D7 12
Flinders, stm., Austl. A4 70
Flinders Island, i., Austl. M8 70
Flinders Reefs, rf., Austl. A8 70
Flin Flon, Mb., Can. D13 104
Flint, Mi., U.S. G12 110
Flint, stm., Ga., U.S. I2 112
Flint, stm., Mi., U.S. G12 110
Flint, stm., U.S. H10 114
Flint Lake, l., N.T., Can. C18 96
Flintville, Tn., U.S. G10 114
Flippin, Ar., U.S. F4 114
Flisa, Nor. K13 6
Flize, Fr. C11 14
Flomaton, Al., U.S. K9 114
Flomot, Tx., U.S. E6 116
Floodwood, Mn., U.S. D3 110
Flora, Il., U.S. D8 114
Flora, In., U.S. B10 114
Flora, Ms., U.S. J6 114
Florac, Fr. H10 14
Florala, Al., U.S. K10 114
Floral City, Fl., U.S. K4 112
Floral Park, Mt., U.S. E13 122
Flora Vista, N.M., U.S. H8 120
Florence, Al., U.S. H9 114
Florence, Az., U.S. K5 120
Florence, Co., U.S. F11 120
Florence see Firenze, Italy F6 18
Florence, Ks., U.S. M11 118
Florence, Or., U.S. G1 122
Florence, S.C., U.S. E7 112
Florence, Tx., U.S. I9 116
Florence, Wi., U.S. E7 110
Florencia, Col. G5 84
Florencio Sánchez, Ur. G10 80
Flores, Braz. E11 76
Flores, i., Indon. G7 38
Flores, i., Port. k18 62a
Flores, Laut (Flores Sea), Indon. G7 38
Flores da Cunha, Braz. E13 80
Flores de Goiás, Braz. C5 79
Flores Island, i., B.C., Can. H8 102
Floresta Azul, Braz. C9 79
Florești, Mol. B12 20
Floresville, Tx., U.S. J8 116
Floriano, Braz. E10 76
Floriano Peixoto, Braz. C8 82
Florianópolis, Braz. D14 80
Florida, Col. F4 84
Florida, Cuba D5 94
Florida, Hond. B6 92
Florida, Peru A3 82
Florida, Ur. H10 80
Florida, state, U.S. F10 98
Florida, stm., Co., U.S. G9 120
Florida, Straits of, strt., N.A. B4 94
Florida Bay, b., Fl., U.S. N6 112
Floridablanca, Col. D6 84
Florida City, Fl., U.S. N6 112
Florida Keys, is., Fl., U.S. O5 112
Floridia, Italy L10 18
Florido, stm., Mex. D7 90
Florien, La., U.S. K3 114
Flórina, Grc. I5 20
Florissant, Mo., U.S. D6 114
Florø, Nor. K9 6
Flotten Lake, l., Sk., Can. D6 104
Flower's Cove, Nf., Can. A17 106
Flowery Branch, Ga., U.S. E3 112
Floyd, N.M., U.S. E3 116
Floyd, Va., U.S. C6 112
Floyd, stm., Ia., U.S. I11 118
Floydada, Tx., U.S. F5 116
Floyds Fork, stm., Ky., U.S. D11 114
Fluchthorn, mtn., Eur. E13 13
Flushing, Mi., U.S. G12 110
Fluvanna, Tx., U.S. G5 116
Fly, stm. m15 68a
Foam Lake, Sk., Can. G11 104
Foča, Bos. F2 20
Foça, Tur. K10 20
Focșani, Rom. D11 20
Fodě, C.A.R. O2 60
Fodécontea, Gui. F2 64
Foggaret el Arab, Alg. G12 62
Foggaret ez Zoua, Alg. G12 62
Foggia, Italy H10 18
Fogo, Nf., Can. C19 106
Fogo, i., C.V. m16 64a
Fogo, Cape, c., Nf., Can. C19 106
Fogo Island, i., Nf., Can. C19 106
Fogolawa, Nig. E14 64
Fohnsdorf, Aus. H14 10
Foix, Fr. J8 14
Foix, hist. reg., Fr. J8 14
Fokino, Russia H17 22
Folakara, Madag. q21 67b
Foley, Al., U.S. L9 114
Foley, Mn., U.S. E2 110
Foleyet, On., Can. B13 110
Foley Island, i., N.T., Can. C17 96
Foligno, Italy G7 18
Folkestone, Eng., U.K. J15 8
Folkston, Ga., U.S. I4 112
Follett, Tx., U.S. C6 116
Follonica, Italy G5 18
Follonica, Golfo di, b., Italy G5 18
Folsom, Ca., U.S. F4 124
Folsom Lake, res., Ca., U.S. F4 124
Fomboni, Com. I15 67a
Fonda, Ia., U.S. I13 118
Fonda, N.Y., U.S. E12 108
Fond du Lac, Sk., Can. E11 96
Fond du Lac, Wi., U.S. G7 110
Fond du Lac, stm., Sk., Can. E11 96
Fondi, Italy H8 18
Fondouk el Aouareb, Tun. N4 18
Fonni, Italy I4 18
Fonseca, Col. B6 84
Fonseca, Golfo de, b., N.A. D7 92
Fontainebleau, Fr. D9 14
Fontana, Arg. D9 80
Fontana, Ca., U.S. J8 124
Fontana Lake, res., N.C., U.S. D3 112
Fontanelle, Ia., U.S. J13 118
Fontarabie, Lac, l., P.Q., Can. A7 106
Fontas, stm., Can. E8 96
Fonte Boa, Braz. I9 84
Fonteneau, Lac, l., P.Q., Can. A12 106
Fontenelle, P.Q., Can. D9 106
Fontur, c., Ice. A6 6a
Fonyód, Hung. I17 10
Foochow see Fuzhou, China I8 34
Foothills, Ab., Can. D18 102
Footprint Lake, l., Mb., Can. C16 104
Footville, Wi., U.S. H6 110
Foraker, Mount, mtn., Ak., U.S. E19 100
Forbach, Fr. C13 14
Forbes, Austl. I8 70
Forbes, Mount, mtn., Ab., Can. F18 102
Forchheim, Ger. F11 10
Ford, Ks., U.S. N8 118
Ford, stm., Mi., U.S. D8 110
Ford City, Ca., U.S. I6 124
Ford City, Pa., U.S. G7 108
Ford Ranges, mts., Ant. C10 73
Fordsville, Ky., U.S. E10 114
Fordville, N.D., U.S. C10 118
Fordyce, Ar., U.S. I4 114
Forel, Mont, mtn., Grnld. C16 86
Foreman, Ar., U.S. I2 114
Foremost, Ab., Can. I3 104
Forest, Ms., U.S. J7 114
Forest, Oh., U.S. G3 108
Forest, On., Can. G13 110
Forest Acres, S.C., U.S. E6 112
Forestburg, Ab., Can. E22 102
Forest City, Ia., U.S. G2 110
Forest City, N.C., U.S. D5 112
Forest City, Pa., U.S. F11 108
Forest Grove, B.C., Can. F13 102
Foresthill, Ca., U.S. E5 124
Forest Home, Al., U.S. K10 114
Forest Lake, Mn., U.S. E3 110
Forest Park, Ga., U.S. F2 112
Forestville, P.Q., Can. D4 106
Forestville, Wi., U.S. F8 110
Forfar, Scot., U.K. E11 8
Forgan, Ok., U.S. C6 116
Forillon, Parc National de, P.Q., Can. D9 106
Forked Deer, stm., Tn., U.S. G7 114
Forks, Wa., U.S. C1 122
Forlì, Italy E7 18
Forman, N.D., U.S. E10 118
Formentera, i., Spain G13 16
Formia, Italy H8 18
Formiga, Braz. F6 79
Formosa, Arg. D9 80
Formosa, Braz. C5 79
Formosa, prov., Arg. C9 80
Formosa see Taiwan, ctry., Asia L9 34
Formosa, Serra, plat., Braz. D14 82
Formoso, stm., Braz. B6 79
Formoso, stm., Braz. E2 79
Forney, Tx., U.S. G10 116
Fornosovo, Russia B13 22
Forres, Arg. D7 80
Forrest, Austl. F5 68
Forrest, Il., U.S. J7 110
Forrest City, Ar., U.S. G6 114
Forreston, Il., U.S. H6 110
Forsan, Tx., U.S. G5 116
Forsayth, Austl. B5 70
Forst, Ger. D14 10
Forster, Austl. I10 70
Forsyth, Ga., U.S. F3 112
Forsyth, Mo., U.S. F3 114
Forsyth, Mt., U.S. D19 122
Forsyth Range, mts., Austl. D5 70
Fort Adams, Ms., U.S. K5 114
Fort Albany, On., Can. F16 96
Fort Alexander Indian Reserve, Mb., Can. H18 104
Fortaleza, Braz. D11 76
Fortaleza, stm., Peru D3 82
Fortaleza de Santa Teresa, hist., Ur. G12 80
Fortaleza do Ituxi, Braz. B8 82
Fort Amherst National Historic Park, P.E., Can. F10 106
Fort Anne National Historic Park, N.S., Can. H8 106
Fort Assiniboine, Ab., Can. C20 102
Fort Atkinson, Wi., U.S. H7 110
Fort Battleford National Historic Park, Sk., Can. F6 104
Fort Beaufort, S. Afr. I8 66
Fort Beauséjour National Historic Park, N.B., Can. G9 106
Fort Benton, Mt., U.S. C15 122
Fort Bidwell, Ca., U.S. C5 124
Fort Bragg, Ca., U.S. E2 124
Fort Branch, In., U.S. D9 114
Fort Bridger, Wy., U.S. C6 120
Fort Calhoun, Ne., U.S. J11 118
Fort-Carnot, Madag. r22 67b
Fort Chipewyan, Ab., Can. E10 96
Fort Cobb, Ok., U.S. D8 116
Fort Collins, Co., U.S. D11 120
Fort-Coulonge, P.Q., Can. B10 108
Fort Covington, N.Y., U.S. C12 108
Fort Davis, Al., U.S. J11 114
Fort Davis, Tx., U.S. I3 116
Fort Defiance, Az., U.S. I7 120
Fort-de-France, Mart. G14 94
Fort Deposit, Al., U.S. K10 114
Fort Dodge, Ia., U.S. H1 110
Fort Duchesne, Ut., U.S. D7 120
Forteau, Nf., Can. A17 106
Fort Edward, N.Y., U.S. D13 108
Fort Erie, On., Can. H17 110
Fortescue, stm., Austl. D3 68
Fortezza, Italy C6 18
Fort Fitzgerald, Ab., Can. E10 96
Fort Frances, On., Can. B2 110
Fort Franklin, N.T., Can. D33 100
Fort Fraser, B.C., Can. C10 102
Fort Gaines, Ga., U.S. H1 112
Fort Garland, Co., U.S. G11 120
Fort Gay, W.V., U.S. I4 108
Fort Gibson, Ok., U.S. D11 116
Fort Gibson Lake, res., Ok., U.S. C11 116
Fort Good Hope, N.T., Can. C30 100
Forth, Firth of, b., Scot., U.K. E11 8
Fort Hall, Id., U.S. G13 122
Fortin, Lac, l., P.Q., Can. B6 106
Fortín Ayacucho, Para. H12 82
Fortín Coroneles Sanchez, Para. H12 82
Fortín Florida, Para. I12 82
Fortín Garrapatal, Para. I11 82
Fortín Teniente Montanía, Para. B9 80
Fortín Uno, Arg. J6 80
Fort Jones, Ca., U.S. C3 124
Fort Klamath, Or., U.S. H4 122
Fort-Lamy see N'Djamena, Chad F4 56
Fort Laramie, Wy., U.S. B12 120
Fort Lauderdale, Fl., U.S. M6 112
Fort Liard, N.T., Can. D8 96
Fort-Liberté, Haiti E9 94
Fort Loramie, Oh., U.S. G2 108
Fort Loudoun Lake, res., Tn., U.S. D2 112
Fort Lupton, Co., U.S. D12 120
Fort Macleod, Ab., Can. H21 102
Fort Madison, Ia., U.S. J4 110
Fort McMurray, Ab., Can. B3 104
Fort McPherson, N.T., Can. C27 100
Fort Meade, Fl., U.S. L5 112
Fort Mill, S.C., U.S. D6 112
Fort Mitchell, Al., U.S. G1 112
Fort Morgan, Co., U.S. K4 118
Fort Myers, Fl., U.S. M5 112
Fort Myers Beach, Fl., U.S. M5 112
Fort Nelson, B.C., Can. E8 96
Fort Nelson, stm., B.C., Can. E8 96
Fort Norman, N.T., Can. D32 100
Fort Ogden, Fl., U.S. L5 112
Fort Payne, Al., U.S. H11 114
Fort Peck, Mt., U.S. B19 122
Fort Peck Lake, res., Mt., U.S. C19 122
Fort Pierce, Fl., U.S. L6 112
Fort Pierre, S.D., U.S. G7 118
Fort Plain, N.Y., U.S. E12 108
Fort Portal, Ug. A6 58
Fort Providence, N.T., Can. D9 96
Fort Qu'Appelle, Sk., Can. H11 104
Fort Recovery, Oh., U.S. G2 108
Fort Resolution, N.T., Can. D10 96
Fortress Mountain, mtn., Wy., U.S. F16 122
Fortress of Louisbourg National Historic Park, N.S., Can. G14 106
Fort Saint James, B.C., Can. C10 102
Fort Saint John, B.C., Can. A14 102
Fort Saskatchewan, Ab., Can. D21 102
Fort Scott, Ks., U.S. N13 118
Fort-Ševčenko, Kaz. I8 26
Fort Severn, On., Can. E15 96
Fort Simpson, N.T., Can. D8 96
Fort Smith, Ar., U.S. G2 114
Fort Smith, N.T., Can. D10 96
Fort Steele, B.C., Can. H19 102
Fort Stockton, Tx., U.S. I4 116
Fort Sumner, N.M., U.S. E2 116
Fort Supply, Ok., U.S. C7 116
Fort Thomas, Az., U.S. K7 120
Fort Thompson, S.D., U.S. G8 118
Fort Totten, N.D., U.S. D9 118
Fort Towson, Ok., U.S. E11 116
Fortuna, Arg. H6 80
Fortuna, Ca., U.S. D1 124
Fortuna, C.R. G10 92
Fortuna, Río de la, stm., Bol. G12 82
Fortuna Ledge (Marshall), Ak., U.S. F13 100
Fortune, Nf., Can. E18 106
Fortune Bay, b., Nf., Can. E18 106
Fortune Harbour, Nf., Can. C18 106
Fort Valley, Ga., U.S. G3 112
Fort Vermilion, Ab., Can. E9 96
Fortville, In., U.S. C11 114
Fort Walton Beach, Fl., U.S. L10 114
Fort Washakie, Wy., U.S. A8 120
Fort Wayne, In., U.S. A11 114
Fort Wellington, Guy. D14 84
Fort White, Fl., U.S. J4 112
Fort William see Thunder Bay, On., Can. B6 110
Fort William, Scot., U.K. E8 8
Fort Worth, Tx., U.S. G9 116
Fort Yates, N.D., U.S. E7 118
Fortymile, stm., N.A. D24 100
Fort Yukon, Ak., U.S. C22 100
Foshan, China L2 34
Fossano, Italy E2 18
Fossil, Or., U.S. F5 122
Fosston, Mn., U.S. D12 118
Foster, Austl. L7 70
Foster, stm., Sk., Can. C9 104
Foster, Mount, mtn., N.A. G27 100
Fosters, Al., U.S. I9 114
Fostoria, Oh., U.S. F3 108
Fouesnant, Fr. E2 14
Fougamou, Gabon B2 58
Fougères, Fr. D5 14
Fouke, Ar., U.S. I3 114
Foul Bay, b., Egypt J3 48
Foulpointe, Madag. p23 67b
Foulwind, Cape, c., N.Z. D3 72
Foumban, Cam. G9 54
Foumbouni, Com. k15 67a
Foum-el-Hisn, Mor. F6 62
Foum-Zguid, Mor. E7 62
Foundiougne, Sen. D1 64
Fountain, Co., U.S. M3 118
Fountain, Fl., U.S. I1 112
Fountain City, Wi., U.S. F4 110
Fountain Green, Ut., U.S. E5 120
Fountain Inn, S.C., U.S. E4 112
Fountain Peak, mtn., Ca., U.S. J10 124
Fountain Place, La., U.S. L5 114
Fourche LaFave, stm., Ar., U.S. H4 114
Fourche Maline, stm., Ok., U.S. E12 116
Fourchu, N.S., Can. G13 106
Four Corners, Or., U.S. F3 122
Fouriesburg, S. Afr. G9 66
Fourmies, Fr. B11 14
Four Mountains, Islands of, is., Ak., U.S. J9 100
Fournier, Lac, l., P.Q., Can. A8 106
Four Oaks, N.C., U.S. D8 112
Fouta Djalon, reg., Gui. F3 64
Foux, Cap à, c., Haiti E8 94
Foveaux Strait, strt., N.Z. G1 72
Fowler, Ca., U.S. H6 124
Fowler, Co., U.S. M3 118
Fowler, In., U.S. B9 114
Fowler, Ks., U.S. N7 118
Fowler, Mi., U.S. G11 110
Fowlerton, Tx., U.S. K8 116
Fowlerville, Mi., U.S. H11 110
Fowman, Iran C10 48
Fox, stm., Il., U.S. D8 114
Fox, stm., Mb., Can. C20 104
Fox, stm., U.S. B5 114
Fox, stm., Wi., U.S. F7 110
Foxe Basin, b., N.T., Can. C17 96
Foxe Channel, strt., N.T., Can. D16 96
Foxe Peninsula, pen., N.T., Can. D17 96
Fox Harbour, Nf., Can. E20 106
Fox Islands, is., Ak., U.S. J10 100
Fox Lake, Il., U.S. H7 110
Fox Lake, Wi., U.S. G7 110
Fox Mountain, mtn., Yk., Can. F28 100
Foxpark, Wy., U.S. C10 120
Fox Valley, Sk., Can. H5 104
Foxworth, Ms., U.S. K7 114
Foyle, Lough, b., Eur. F6 8
Foz do Cunene, Ang. E2 58
Foz do Iguaçu, Braz. C11 80
Foz do Jordão, Braz. C6 82
Foz Giraldo, Port. E4 16
Foziling, China D5 34
Fraga, Arg. G6 80
Fraile Muerto, Ur. G11 80
Framingham, Ma., U.S. E15 108
Frampol, Pol. E22 10
Franca, Braz. F5 79
Franca-Iosifa, Zeml'a (Franz Josef Land), is., Russia A6 24
Francavilla Fontana, Italy I12 18
France, ctry., Eur. F8 4
Frances, stm., Yk., Can. F30 100
Frances Lake, l., Yk., Can. F30 100
Francés Viejo, Cabo, c., Dom. Rep. E10 94
Francesville, In., U.S. B10 114
Franceville, Gabon B2 58
Franche-Comté, hist. reg., Fr. F12 14
Francia, Ur. G10 80
Francis, Sk., Can. H11 104
Francis Case, Lake, res., S.D., U.S. H8 118
Francisco Beltrão, Braz. D12 80
Francisco I. Madero, Mex. E8 90
Francisco I. Madero, Mex. E7 90
Francisco Morazán, dept., Hond. C7 92
Francisco Murguía, Mex. E8 90
Francisco Sá, Braz. D7 79
Francistown, Bots. C8 66
Francofonte, Italy L9 18
François, Nf., Can. E17 106
François, Lacs à, l., P.Q., Can. A8 106
François Lake, B.C., Can. C9 102
François Lake, l., B.C., Can. C9 102
Francs Peak, mtn., Wy., U.S. G16 122
Frangy, Fr. F12 14
Frankel City, Tx., U.S. G4 116
Frankenmuth, Mi., U.S. G12 110
Frankford, Mo., U.S. C5 114
Frankford, On., Can. F18 110
Frankfort, In., U.S. B10 114
Frankfort, Ks., U.S. L11 118
Frankfort, Ky., U.S. D12 114
Frankfort, Mi., U.S. F9 110
Frankfort, N.Y., U.S. D11 108
Frankfort, Oh., U.S. H3 108
Frankfort, S. Afr. F9 66
Frankfort, S. Afr. I8 66
Frankfort, S.D., U.S. G9 118
Frankfurt, Ger. C14 10
Frankfurt am Main, Ger. E8 10
Franklin, Az., U.S. L7 120
Franklin, Ga., U.S. F1 112
Franklin, Id., U.S. H14 122
Franklin, Il., U.S. C6 114
Franklin, In., U.S. C10 114
Franklin, Ky., U.S. F10 114
Franklin, La., U.S. M5 114
Franklin, Ma., U.S. E15 108
Franklin, Me., U.S. C18 108
Franklin, Mn., U.S. G13 118
Franklin, N.C., U.S. D3 112
Franklin, Ne., U.S. K9 118
Franklin, N.H., U.S. D15 108
Franklin, N.J., U.S. F12 108
Franklin, Oh., U.S. H2 108
Franklin, Pa., U.S. F7 108
Franklin, Tn., U.S. G10 114
Franklin, Tx., U.S. H10 116
Franklin, Va., U.S. C10 112
Franklin, Wi., U.S. H7 110
Franklin, W.V., U.S. I7 108
Franklin Bay, b., N.T., Can. C7 96
Franklin D. Roosevelt Lake, res., Wa., U.S. B7 122
Franklin Grove, Il., U.S. I6 110
Franklin Harbor, b., Austl. I2 70
Franklin Lake, l., N.T., Can. C13 96
Franklin Mountains, mts., N.T., Can. D31 100
Franklin Strait, strt., N.T., Can. B13 96
Franklinton, La., U.S. L6 114
Franklinton, N.C., U.S. C8 112
Franklinville, N.Y., U.S. E8 108
Frankston, Tx., U.S. G11 116
Frankton, In., U.S. B11 114
Frankville, Al., U.S. K8 114
Franz Josef Land see Franca Iosifa, Zeml'a, is., Russia A6 24
Frascati, Italy H7 18
Fraser, Co., U.S. E11 120
Fraser, stm., B.C., Can. G13 102
Fraser, stm., Co., U.S. D11 120
Fraser, stm., Nf., Can. E20 96
Fraserburg, S. Afr. H5 66
Fraser Island, i., Austl. E10 70
Fraser Lake, B.C., Can. C10 102
Fraser Lake, l., B.C., Can. C10 102
Fraser Plateau, plat., B.C., Can. E11 102
Frauenfeld, Switz. C10 13
Fray Bentos, Ur. G9 80
Fray Luis Beltrán, Arg. J6 80
Fray Marcos, Ur. H11 80
Frazee, Mn., U.S. E12 118
Frazer, Mt., U.S. B19 122
Fr'azino, Russia F21 22
Frederic, Wi., U.S. E3 110
Frederica, De., U.S. H11 108
Fredericia, Den. N11 6
Frederick, Md., U.S. H9 108
Frederick, Ok., U.S. E7 116
Frederick, S.D., U.S. F9 118
Frederick Reef, rf., Austl. C11 70
Fredericksburg, Ia., U.S. H3 110
Fredericksburg, Tx., U.S. I8 116
Fredericksburg, Va., U.S. I9 108
Fredericktown, Mo., U.S. E6 114
Fredericktown, Oh., U.S. G4 108
Frederico Westphalen, Braz. D12 80
Fredericton, N.B., Can. G7 106
Fredericton Junction, N.B., Can. G7 106
Frederikshavn, Den. M12 6
Frederiksted, V.I.U.S. F12 94
Frederik Willem IV Vallen, wtfl, Sur. F14 84
Fredonia, Az., U.S. H4 120
Fredonia, Col. E5 84
Fredonia, Ks., U.S. N12 118
Fredonia, N.D., U.S. E8 118
Fredonia, N.Y., U.S. E7 108
Fredrikstad, Nor. L12 6
Freeburg, Il., U.S. D7 114
Freeburg, Mo., U.S. D5 114
Freehold, N.J., U.S. G12 108
Freeland, Mi., U.S. G11 110
Freeland, Pa., U.S. F11 108
Freels, Cape, c., Nf., Can. C20 106
Freels, Cape, c., Nf., Can. F20 106
Freeman, S.D., U.S. H10 118
Freeman, stm., Ab., Can. C19 102
Freeport, Bah. A5 94
Freeport, Fl., U.S. L10 114
Freeport, Il., U.S. H6 110
Freeport, Me., U.S. D16 108
Freeport, N.S., Can. H7 106
Freeport, N.Y., U.S. G13 108
Freeport, Pa., U.S. G7 108
Freeport, Tx., U.S. K11 116
Freer, Tx., U.S. L8 116
Free State, prov., S. Afr. G8 66
Freetown, S.L. G3 64
Fregenal de la Sierra, Spain G5 16
Freiberg, Ger. E13 10
Freiburg [im Breisgau], Ger. H7 10
Freirina, Chile E3 80
Freising, Ger. G11 10
Freistadt, Aus. G14 10
Freital, Ger. D13 10
Fréjus, Fr. I13 14
Fremantle, Austl. F3 68
Fremont, Ca., U.S. G4 124
Fremont, Ia., U.S. I3 110
Fremont, In., U.S. A12 114
Fremont, Mi., U.S. G10 110
Fremont, N.C., U.S. D9 112
Fremont, Ne., U.S. J11 118
Fremont, Oh., U.S. F3 108
Fremont, Wi., U.S. F7 110
Fremont, stm., Ut., U.S. F6 120
French Broad, stm., U.S. D4 112
Frenchburg, Ky., U.S. B3 112
French Creek, stm., Mb., Can. B22 104
French Guiana (Guyane française), dep., S.A. C8 76
French Island, i., Austl. L6 70
French Lick, In., U.S. D10 114
Frenchman Bay, b., Me., U.S. C18 108
Frenchman Butte, Sk., Can. E5 104
Frenchmans Cap, mtn., Austl. N6 70
French Polynesia, dep., Oc. J25 126
Frenda, Alg. C11 62
Fresco, stm., Braz. E8 76
Freshfield, Mount, mtn., Can. F18 102
Fresne-Saint-Mamès, Fr. E12 14
Fresnes-en-Woëvre, Fr. C12 14
Fresnillo, Mex. F8 90
Fresno, Ca., U.S. H6 124
Fresno, Col. E5 84
Fresno, stm., Ca., U.S. H5 124
Fresno Reservoir, res., Mt., U.S. B16 122
Frewsburg, N.Y., U.S. E7 108
Freycinet Peninsula, pen., Austl. N8 70
Freyre, Arg. F7 80
Fria, Cape, c., Nmb. E2 58
Friant, Ca., U.S. H6 124
Friars Point, Ms., U.S. H6 114
Frías, Arg. E6 80
Frías, Peru A2 82
Fribourg (Freiburg), Switz. E7 13
Fribourg (Freiburg), state, Switz. E7 13
Friday Harbor, Wa., U.S. B2 122
Fridley, Mn., U.S. E2 110
Fridtjof Nansen, Mount, mtn., Ant. D9 73
Friedberg, Aus. H16 10
Friedberg, Ger. E8 10
Friedberg, Ger. G10 10
Friedland, Ger. B13 10
Friedrichshafen, Ger. H9 10
Friedrichsort, Ger. A10 10
Friedrichstadt, Ger. A9 10
Friend, Ne., U.S. K10 118
Friendship, N.Y., U.S. E8 108
Friendship, Tn., U.S. G7 114
Friendship, Wi., U.S. G6 110
Fries, Va., U.S. C6 112
Friesach, Aus. I14 10
Friesland, prov., Neth. B8 12
Friguia, Gui. E4 64

Name / Map Ref. / Page

Frío, stm., N.A. G10 92
Frio, stm., Tx., U.S. K8 116
Frio, Cabo, c., Braz. G7 79
Friona, Tx., U.S. E4 116
Frisco, Tx., U.S. F10 116
Frisco City, Al., U.S. K9 114
Frisian Islands, is., Eur. E9 4
Fritch, Tx., U.S. D5 116
Friuli-Venezia-Giulia, prov., Italy C7 18
Friza, proliv, strt., Russia H21 28
Frobisher, Sk., Can. I12 104
Frobisher Bay, b., N.T., Can. D19 96
Frobisher Lake, l., Sk., Can. B6 104
Frog Lake, l., Ab., Can. E4 104
Frohnleiten, Aus. H15 10
Froid, Mt., U.S. C3 118
Frolovo, Russia H6 26
Fromberg, Mt., U.S. E17 122
Frombork, Pol. A19 10
Frome, stm., Austl. G3 70
Frome, Lake, l., Austl. H3 70
Frontenac, Ks., U.S. N13 118
Frontera, Mex. D9 90
Frontera, Mex. H13 90
Frontier, Sk., Can. I6 104
Frontier, Wy., U.S. C6 120
Frontino, Col. D4 84
Frontino, Páramo, mtn., Col. D4 84
Front Range, mts., Co., U.S. D11 120
Front Royal, Va., U.S. I8 108
Frosinone, Italy H8 18
Frost, Tx., U.S. G10 116
Frostburg, Md., U.S. H8 108
Frostproof, Fl., U.S. L5 112
Frøya, i., Nor. J11 6
Fruges, Fr. B9 14
Fruita, Co., U.S. E8 120
Fruitdale, Al., U.S. K8 114
Fruitdale, Or., U.S. H2 122
Fruithurst, Al., U.S. I11 114
Fruitland, Id., U.S. F9 122
Fruitland, Md., U.S. I11 108
Fruitport, Mi., U.S. G9 110
Fruitvale, B.C., Can. H17 102
Fruitvale, Wa., U.S. D5 122
Fruitville, Fl., U.S. L4 112
Frunze see Biškek, Kyrg. I12 26
Frunzivka, Ukr. B13 20
Frutal, Braz. F4 79
Frutigen, Switz. E8 13
Frýdek-Místek, Czech Rep. F18 10
Fryeburg, Me., U.S. C16 108
Fryingpan, stm., Co., U.S. E10 120
Fuchang, China E2 34
Fuchū, Japan M8 36
Fuchun, stm., China F8 34
Fuding, China H9 34
Fuego, Volcán de, vol., Guat. C4 92
Fuencaliente de la Palma, Spain o23 17b
Fuensalida, Spain E7 16
Fuente de Cantos, Spain G5 16
Fuente de Oro, Col. F6 84
Fuentesaúco, Spain D6 16
Fuerte, stm., Mex. D5 90
Fuerte Olimpo, Para. I13 82
Fuerteventura, i., Spain o26 17b
Fufeng, China E8 30
Fuhe, China L2 34
Fuhu, China F7 34
Fuji, Japan L13 36
Fujian (Fukien), prov., China F10 30
Fujieda, Japan M13 36
Fujin, China B13 30
Fujinomiya, Japan L13 36
Fuji-san (Fujiyama), vol., Japan L13 36
Fujisawa, Japan L14 36
Fujiyama see Fuji-san, vol., Japan L13 36
Fuji-yoshida, Japan L13 36
Fukagawa, Japan d17 36a
Fukou, China I6 34
Fukuchiyama, Japan L9 36
Fukue-jima, i., Japan O3 36
Fukui, Japan K11 36
Fukuoka, Japan N5 36
Fukushima, Japan J15 36
Fukuyama, Japan M8 36
Fulacunda, Gui.-B. F2 64
Fūlādī, Kūh-e, mtn., Afg. C2 44
Fulda, Ger. E9 10
Fulda, Mn., U.S. H12 118
Fulda, stm., Ger. D9 10
Fulechang, China B8 40
Fuling, China F8 30
Fullerton, Ca., U.S. K8 124
Fullerton, Ne., U.S. J10 118
Fulpmes, Aus. H11 10
Fulton, Al., U.S. K9 114
Fulton, Ar., U.S. I3 114
Fulton, Il., U.S. I5 110
Fulton, Ks., U.S. M13 118
Fulton, Ky., U.S. F8 114
Fulton, Mo., U.S. D5 114
Fulton, Ms., U.S. H8 114
Fulton, N.Y., U.S. D10 108
Fulton, Tx., U.S. K9 116
Fulton, stm., B.C., Can. C8 102
Fultondale, Al., U.S. I10 114
Fumay, Fr. C11 14
Fumel, Fr. H7 14
Fumintun, China A14 32
Funabashi, Japan L14 36
Funchal, Port. m21 17a
Fundación, Col. B5 84
Fundy, Bay of, b., Can. H8 106
Fundy National Park, N.B., Can. G8 106
Funhalouro, Moz. D12 66
Funing, China B8 34
Funk Island, i., Nf., Can. C20 106
Funtua, Nig. F13 64
Funza, Col. E5 84
Fuqikou, China F6 34
Fuquay-Varina, N.C., U.S. D8 112
Furano, Japan d17 36a
Fūrg, Iran G13 48
Furmanov, Russia D24 22
Furnas, Represa de, res., Braz. F5 79
Furneaux Group, is., Austl. L8 70
Furnes (Veurne), Bel. F2 12
Furqlus, Syria D4 48
Fürstenfeldbruck, Ger. G11 10
Fürstenwalde, Ger. C14 10
Fürth, Ger. F10 10
Furth im Wald, Ger. F12 10
Furudal, Swe. K14 6
Furukawa, Japan I15 36
Furukawa, Japan K12 36
Fury and Hecla Strait, strt., N.T., Can. C15 96
Fusagasugá, Col. E5 84
Fushan, China D9 34
Fushuigang, China D2 34
Fushun, China B11 32
Fusilier, Sk., Can. G5 104
Fusui, China G8 30
Futianpu, China H1 34
Futuyu, China D2 32
Fuwah, Egypt B6 60
Fuxi, China J2 34
Fuxian, China D8 30
Fuxian (Wafangdian), China D10 32
Fuxian Hu, l., China B7 40
Fuxin, China A9 32
Fuyang, China C4 34
Fuyu, China B11 30
Fuzhai, China F9 34
Fuzhou, China G5 34
Fuzhou (Foochow), China I8 34
Fuzhuang, China I6 32
Füzuli, Azer. B9 48
Fyn, i., Den. N12 6

G

Gaalkacyo, Som. G10 56
Gabarus, N.S., Can. G13 106
Gabarus Bay, b., N.S., Can. G13 106
Gabas, stm., Fr. I6 14
Gabbs, Nv., U.S. F8 124
Gabela, Ang. D2 58
Gabès, Tun. D16 62
Gabès, Golfe de, b., Tun. C16 62
Gabiarra, Braz. D9 79
Gabir, Sudan M3 60
Gable Mountain, mtn., B.C., Can. C13 102
Gabon, ctry., Afr. B2 58
Gaborone, Bots. E7 66
Gabriel Strait, strt., N.T., Can. D19 96
Gabrovo, Bul. G9 20
Gacé, Fr. D7 14
Gachetá, Col. E6 84
Gachsārān, Iran F11 48
Gackle, N.D., U.S. E8 118
Gadag, India E3 46
Gadamai, Sudan I9 60
Gäddede, Swe. I14 6
Gadsden, Al., U.S. H10 114
Gadsden, Az., U.S. L2 120
Gaeta, Italy H8 18
Gaeta, Golfo di, b., Italy H8 18
Gaffney, S.C., U.S. D5 112
Gafour, Tun. M4 18
Gafsa, Tun. C15 62
Gagarin, Russia F18 22
Gage, Ok., U.S. C7 116
Gagetown, N.B., Can. G7 106
Gagetown, Canadian Forces Base, mil., N.B., Can. G7 106
Gaggenau, Ger. G8 10
Gaghamni, Sudan L5 60
Gagnoa, C. Iv. H7 64
Gagnon, P.Q., Can. F19 96
Gagra, Geor. I6 26
Gaibandha, Bngl. H13 44
Gail, Tx., U.S. G5 116
Gaillac, Fr. I8 14
Gaillard, Lac, l., P.Q., Can. B5 106
Gaillon, Fr. C8 14
Gainesboro, Tn., U.S. F11 114
Gainesville, Fl., U.S. J4 112
Gainesville, Ga., U.S. E3 112
Gainesville, Mo., U.S. F4 114
Gainesville, Tx., U.S. F9 116
Gainsborough, Sk., Can. I13 104
Gainsborough Creek, stm., Can. I13 104
Gairdner, Lake, l., Austl. F7 68
Gaital, Cerro, mtn., Pan. I14 92
Gaithersburg, Md., U.S. H9 108
Gaixian, China C10 32
Gajny, Russia E8 26
Gajutino, Russia C21 22
Galaassija, Uzb. B18 48
Galahad, Ab., Can. E23 102
Galán, Cerro, mtn., Arg. C5 80
Galapagos Islands see Colón, Archipiélago de, is., Ec. j13 84a
Galashiels, Scot., U.K. F11 8
Galaţi, Rom. D12 20
Galaţi, co., Rom. D11 20
Galatia, Il., U.S. E8 114
Galatina, Italy I13 18
Galax, Va., U.S. C6 112
Gáldar, Spain o25 17b
Galdhøpiggen, mtn., Nor. K11 6
Galeana, Mex. B6 90
Galeana, Mex. E9 90
Galela, Indon. E8 38
Galena, Ak., U.S. D16 100
Galena, Il., U.S. H5 110
Galena, Ks., U.S. N13 118
Galena, Mo., U.S. F3 114
Galena Park, Tx., U.S. J11 116
Galeota Point, c., Trin. I14 94
Galera, stm., Braz. F12 82
Galera, Punta, c., Ec. G2 84
Galera Point, c., Trin. I14 94
Galesburg, Il., U.S. J5 110
Galesburg, Mi., U.S. H10 110
Galesville, Wi., U.S. F4 110
Galeton, Pa., U.S. F9 108
Galheiros, Braz. B5 79
Galič, Russia C25 22
Galicia, state, Spain C3 16
Galicia, hist. reg., Eur. F12 4
Galilee, Lake, l., Austl. D6 70
Galilee, Sea of see Kinneret, Yam, l., Isr. C5 50
Galiléia, Braz. E8 79
Galion, Oh., U.S. G4 108
Galiuro Mountains, mts., Az., U.S. L6 120
Gallarate, Italy D3 18
Gallatin, Mo., U.S. C3 114
Gallatin, Tn., U.S. F10 114
Gallatin, stm., U.S. E14 122
Galle, Sri L. I6 46
Galliano, La., U.S. M6 114
Galliate, Italy D3 18
Gallinas, stm., N.M., U.S. D2 116
Gallinas, Punta, c., Col. A7 84
Gallinas Peak, mtn., N.M., U.S. J11 120
Gallipoli, Austl. B2 70
Gallipoli, Italy I12 18
Gallipoli see Gelibolu, Tur. I10 20
Gallipoli Peninsula see Gelibolu Yarımadası, pen., Tur. I10 20
Gallipolis, Oh., U.S. I4 108
Gällivare, Swe. H17 6
Galloway, Mull of, c., Scot., U.K. G9 8
Gallup, N.M., U.S. I8 120
Galougo, Mali E4 64
Galt, Ca., U.S. F4 124
Galtat Zemmour, W. Sah. H4 62
Galty Mountains, mts., Ire. I5 8
Galva, Ia., U.S. I12 118
Galva, Il., U.S. I5 110
Galva, Ks., U.S. M10 118
Galvarino, Chile J2 80
Galveston, In., U.S. B10 114
Galveston, Tx., U.S. J12 116
Galveston Bay, b., Tx., U.S. J12 116
Galveston Island, i., Tx., U.S. J12 116
Gálvez, Arg. G8 80
Galway, Ire. H4 8
Galway, co., Ire. H5 8
Galway Bay, b., Ire. H4 8
Gamagōri, Japan M12 36
Gamaliel, Ky., U.S. F11 114
Gamarra, Col. C6 84
Gambaga, Ghana F9 64
Gambela, Eth. M8 60
Gambell, Ak., U.S. E9 100
Gambia, ctry., Afr. F3 54
Gambia (Gambie), stm., Afr. F3 54
Gambi Atrash, Sudan L7 60
Gambier, Oh., U.S. G4 108
Gambier, Îles, is., Fr. Poly. K26 126
Gambo, Nf., Can. D19 106
Gamboa, Pan. C3 84
Gamboma, Congo B3 58
Gammon, stm., Can. G19 104
Gamoep, S. Afr. G4 66
Gamon, Sen. E3 64
Gan, stm., China A11 30
Gan, stm., China G4 34
Ganado, Az., U.S. I7 120
Ganado, Tx., U.S. J10 116
Gananoque, On., Can. F19 110
Ganāveh, Iran G11 48
Gäncä, Azer. I7 26
Gand (Gent), Bel. F4 12
Ganda, Ang. D2 58
Gandak (Nārāyani), stm., Asia G11 44
Gander, Nf., Can. D19 106
Gander, stm., Nf., Can. C19 106
Gander Bay, Nf., Can. C19 106
Gander Bay, b., Nf., Can. C19 106
Ganderkesee, Ger. B8 10
Gander Lake, l., Nf., Can. D19 106
Gāndhi Sāgar, res., India H6 44
Gandi, Nig. E12 64
Gandia, Spain G11 16
Gandu, Braz. B9 79
Ganfang, China G3 34
Gangānagar, India F5 44
Gangapur, India G7 44
Gangaw, Myan. C3 40
Gangdisê Shan, mts., China E9 44
Ganges, B.C., Can. I11 102
Ganges, Fr. I10 14
Ganges (Ganga) (Padma), stm., Asia I13 44
Ganghu, China D12 44
Gangi, Italy L9 18
Gangkou, China F4 34
Gangotri, India E8 44
Gangotri, India E8 44
Gangou, China C7 32
Gangoumen, China B4 32
Gang Ranch, B.C., Can. F12 102
Gangtok, India G13 44
Gangu, China E8 30
Gannett Peak, mtn., Wy., U.S. G16 122
Gannvalley, S.D., U.S. G9 118
Ganq, China B15 44
Gansu (Kansu), prov., China D7 30
Gantt, Al., U.S. K10 114
Ganxi, China G7 34
Ganzê, China E7 30
Ganzhou, China J3 34
Ganzo Azul, Peru C4 82
Gao, Mali C9 64
Gaobu, China H6 34
Gaocun, China F10 32
Gaohe, China M1 34
Gaokeng, China H2 34
Gaoling, China C5 32
Gaona, Arg. C6 80
Gaoqiaozhen, China C9 32
Gaoshan, China J8 34
Gaotan, China E6 34
Gaotingsi, China I1 34
Gaoua, Burkina F8 64
Gaoxinji, China A4 34
Gaoya, China G8 32
Gaoyou, China C8 34
Gaoyou Hu, l., China C8 34
Gap, Fr. H13 14
Gar, China E3 30
Garachiné, Pan. C3 84
Garagoa, Col. E6 84
Garanhuns, Braz. E11 76
Garara, Pap. N. Gui. A9 68
Garber, Ok., U.S. C9 116
Garberville, Ca., U.S. D2 124
Gârbovu, Rom. E7 20
Garça, Braz. G4 79
Garças, Rio das, stm., Braz. C2 79
Garcia, Mex. C5 90
García de Sola, Embalse de, res., Spain F6 16
Garcias, Braz. F2 79
Gard, dept., Fr. I11 14
Garda, Italy D5 18
Garda, Lago di, l., Italy D5 18
Gardelegen, Ger. C11 10
Garden City, Ga., U.S. G5 112
Garden City, Ks., U.S. N7 118
Garden City, Mo., U.S. D2 114
Garden City, Tx., U.S. H5 116
Gardendale, Al., U.S. I10 114
Garden Grove, Ca., U.S. K8 124
Garden Grove, Ia., U.S. J2 110
Garden Lakes, Ga., U.S. E1 112
Garden Peninsula, pen., Mi., U.S. E9 110
Garden Plain, Ks., U.S. N10 118
Garden Reach, India I13 44
Gardenton, Mb., Can. I18 104
Gardey, Arg. I9 80
Gardeyz, Afg. D3 44
Gardiner, Me., U.S. C17 108
Gardiner, Mt., U.S. E15 122
Gardiner, Or., U.S. G1 122
Gardiner Dam, Sk., Can. G8 104
Gardiners Bay, b., N.Y., U.S. F14 108
Gardner, Ks., U.S. M13 118
Gardner, Ma., U.S. E15 108
Gardner Canal, b., B.C., Can. D6 102
Gardnerville, Nv., U.S. F6 124
Gardone Val Trompia, Italy D5 18
Garešnica, Cro. D11 18
Garfield, Ks., U.S. M8 118
Garfield, N.M., U.S. L9 120
Garfield, Wa., U.S. C8 122
Garfield Mountain, mtn., Mt., U.S. F13 122
Gargouna, Mali D10 64
Gargždai, Lith. F4 22
Garibaldi, B.C., Can. H11 102
Garibaldi, Braz. E13 80
Garibaldi, Or., U.S. E2 122
Garibaldi, Mount, mtn., B.C., Can. H11 102
Garibaldi Provincial Park, B.C., Can. G12 102
Garies, S. Afr. H4 66
Garissa, Kenya B7 58
Garita Palmera, El Sal. D4 92
Garko, Nig. F14 64
Garland, Al., U.S. K10 114
Garland, Tx., U.S. G10 116
Garland, Ut., U.S. C4 120
Garlasco, Italy D3 18
Garliava, Lith. G6 22
Garlin, Fr. I6 14
Garm, Taj. J12 26
Garmisch-Partenkirchen, Ger. H11 10
Garnavillo, Ia., U.S. H4 110
Garner, Ia., U.S. G2 110
Garner, N.C., U.S. D8 112
Garnett, Ks., U.S. M12 118
Garnish, Nf., Can. E18 106
Garonne, stm., Eur. H6 14
Garoua, Cam. G9 54
Garretson, S.D., U.S. H11 118
Garrett, In., U.S. A11 114
Garrett, Ky., U.S. B4 112
Garrison, Mt., U.S. D13 122
Garrison, N.D., U.S. D6 118
Garrison, Tx., U.S. K2 114
Garrovillas, Spain F5 16
Garry Bay, b., N.T., Can. C15 96
Garry Lake, l., N.T., Can. C12 96
Garson, On., Can. D15 110
Garson Lake, l., Can. B4 104
Garub, Nmb. F3 66
Garut, Indon. j13 39a
Garwin, Ia., U.S. H3 110
Garwolin, Pol. D21 10
Garwood, Tx., U.S. J10 116
Gary, In., U.S. A9 114
Gary, S.D., U.S. G11 118
Gary, Tx., U.S. J2 114
Gary, W.V., U.S. B5 112
Garyarsa, China E9 44
Garza, Arg. E7 80
Garzón, Col. F5 84
Garzón, Ur. H11 80
Gas City, In., U.S. B11 114
Gascogne, hist. reg., Fr. H6 14
Gasconade, stm., Mo., U.S. D5 114
Gascoyne, stm., Austl. E2 68
Gash (Nahr al-Qāsh), stm., Afr. F8 56
Gashaka, Nig. G9 54
Gaspar, Braz. D14 80
Gaspard Creek, stm., B.C., Can. F12 102
Gaspé, P.Q., Can. D9 106
Gaspé, Baie de, b., P.Q., Can. D9 106
Gaspé, Cap, c., P.Q., Can. D9 106
Gaspé Peninsula see Gaspésie, Péninsule de la, pen., P.Q., Can. D8 106
Gaspereau Lake, l., N.S., Can. H9 106
Gaspésie, Parc Provincial de la, P.Q., Can. D8 106
Gaspésie, Péninsule de la, pen., P.Q., Can. D8 106
Gassaway, W.V., U.S. I6 108
Gaston, N.C., U.S. C9 112
Gaston, Lake, res., U.S. C8 112
Gastonia, N.C., U.S. D5 112
Gastre, Arg. E3 78
Gata, Cabo de, c., Spain I9 16
Gátas, Akrotírion, c., Cyp. D2 48
Gatčina, Russia B13 22
Gate, Ok., U.S. C6 116
Gate City, Va., U.S. C4 112
Gateshead, Eng., U.K. G12 8
Gateshead Island, i., N.T., Can. B12 96
Gatesville, N.C., U.S. C10 112
Gatesville, Tx., U.S. H9 116
Gateway, Co., U.S. F8 120
Gatineau, P.Q., Can. B11 108
Gatineau, stm., P.Q., Can. G17 96
Gatineau, Parc de la, P.Q., Can. B10 108
Gatlinburg, Tn., U.S. D3 112
Gattinara, Italy D3 18
Gatton, Austl. F10 70
Gatún, Esclusas de, Pan. H15 92
Gatún, Lago, res., Pan. H15 92
Gauer Lake, l., Mb., Can. A17 104
Gauley, stm., W.V., U.S. I5 108
Gauley Bridge, W.V., U.S. I5 108
Gaultois, Nf., Can. E18 106
Gaurīśaṅkar, mtn., Asia G12 44
Gause, Tx., U.S. I10 116
Gauteng, prov., S. Afr. F9 66
Gauting, Ger. G11 10
Gavà, Spain D14 16
Gávdhos, i., Grc. O8 20
Gavião, stm., Braz. C8 79
Gävle, Swe. K15 6
Gävleborgs Län, co., Swe. K15 6
Gavrilov-Jam, Russia D22 22
Gavrilov Posad, Russia E23 22
Gawler, Austl. J3 70
Gawler Ranges, mts., Austl. F7 68
Gaxun Nur, l., China C7 30
Gaya, India H11 44
Gaylord, Mi., U.S. E11 110
Gaylord, Mn., U.S. F1 110
Gayndah, Austl. E9 70
Gays Mills, Wi., U.S. G5 110
Gaza see Ghazzah, Gaza F3 48
Gaza Strip, hist. reg., Gaza F2 50
Gaziantep, Tur. C4 48
Gazimağusa (Famagusta), N. Cyp. D2 48
Gbangbatok, S.L. H3 64
Gbanhala, stm., Afr. G5 64
Gbarnga, Lib. H5 64
Gbongan, Nig. H12 64
Gcoverega, Bots. B7 66
Gdańsk (Danzig), Pol. A18 10
Gdansk, Gulf of, b., Eur. A19 10
Gdov, Russia C10 22
Gdyel, Alg. J11 16
Gdynia, Pol. A18 10
Gearhart Mountain, mtn., Or., U.S. H5 122
Geary, N.B., Can. G7 106
Geary, Ok., U.S. D8 116
Geba, stm., Afr. F4 54
Gebeit Mine, Sudan G9 60
Gebze, Tur. I13 20
Gecha, Eth. N8 60
Geddes, S.D., U.S. H9 118
Gedera, Isr. E3 50
Gediz, Tur. J13 20
Gedo, Eth. M9 60
Gedun, China H7 34
Geel, Bel. F7 12
Geelong, Austl. L6 70
Geesthacht, Ger. B10 10
Geeveston, Austl. N7 70
Gegong, China E6 34
Geiger, Al., U.S. J8 114
Geikie, stm., Sk., Can. E12 96
Geilo, Nor. K11 6
Geiranger, Nor. J10 6
Geislingen, Ger. G9 10
Geistown, Pa., U.S. G8 108
Gejiatun, China C7 32
Gejiu (Kokiu), China C7 40
Gela, Italy L9 18
Gelderland, prov., Neth. D8 12
Geldermalsen, Neth. E7 12
Geldrop, Neth. F8 12
Gelenbe, Tur. J11 20
Gelgaudiškis, Lith. F6 22
Gelibolu, Tur. I10 20
Gelibolu Yarımadası (Gallipoli Peninsula), pen., Tur. I10 20
Gelsenkirchen, Ger. D7 10
Geltsa, Eth. N9 60
Gemena, Zaire H4 56
Gemlik, Tur. I13 20
Gemsbok National Park, Bots. E5 66
Gemünden, Ger. E9 10
Gen, stm., China A11 30
Genale (Jubba), stm., Afr. G9 56
Gençay, Fr. F7 14
General, stm., C.R. H11 92
General Acha, Arg. I6 80
General Alvear, Arg. I8 80
General Alvear, Arg. H5 80
General Aquino, Para. C10 80
General Arenales, Arg. H8 80
General Belgrano, Arg. H9 80
General Bravo, Mex. E10 90
General Cabrera, Arg. G7 80
General Campos, Arg. F9 80
General Carneiro, Braz. C2 79
General Carrera, Lago (Lago Buenos Aires), l., S.A. F2 78
General Cepeda, Mex. E9 90
General Conesa, Arg. I10 80
General Daniel Cerri, Arg. J7 80
General Elizardo Aquino, Para. D10 80
General Enrique Martínez, Ur. G12 80
General Enrique Mosconi, Arg. B7 80
General Escobedo, Mex. E7 90
General Eugenio A. Garay, Para. C10 80
General Eugenio A. Garay, Para. I10 82
General Galarza, Arg. G9 80
General Güemes, Arg. C6 80
General Guido, Arg. I10 80
General José de San Martín, Arg. D9 80
General Juan José Ríos, Mex. E5 90
General Juan Madariaga, Arg. I10 80
General La Madrid, Arg. I8 80
General Lavalle, Arg. I10 80
General Leonidas Plaza Gutiérrez, Ec. I3 84
General Levalle, Arg. H7 80
General Manuel Belgrano, Cerro, mtn., Arg. E5 80
General O'Brien, Arg. H8 80
General Paz, Arg. H9 80
General Pico, Arg. H7 80
General Pinedo, Arg. D8 80
General Pinto, Arg. H8 80
General Pizarro, Arg. C6 80
General Roca, Arg. J5 80
General San Martín, Arg. H9 80
General San Martín, Arg. I7 80
General Santos, Phil. D8 38
General Terán, Mex. E10 90
General Viamonte (Los Toldos), Arg. H8 80
General Villegas, Arg. H7 80
Genesee, Id., U.S. D9 122
Genesee, stm., U.S. H18 110
Geneseo, Il., U.S. I5 110
Geneseo, Ks., U.S. M9 118
Geneseo, N.Y., U.S. E9 108
Geneva, Al., U.S. K11 114
Geneva, Il., U.S. I7 110
Geneva, In., U.S. B12 114
Geneva, Ne., U.S. K10 118
Geneva, N.Y., U.S. E9 108
Geneva, Oh., U.S. F6 108
Geneva see Genève, Switz. F13 14
Geneva, Lake, l., Eur. F13 14
Genève (Geneva), Switz. F5 13
Genève, state, Switz. F5 13
Genévriers, Île des, i., P.Q., Can. A15 106
Gengma, China C5 40
Genk, Bel. G8 12
Genlis, Fr. E12 14
Genoa, Il., U.S. H7 110
Genoa see Genova, Italy E3 18
Genoa, Ne., U.S. J10 118
Genoa, Oh., U.S. F3 108
Genoa, Wi., U.S. G4 110
Genova (Genoa), Italy E3 18
Genova, Golfo di, b., Italy E3 18
Genrijetty, ostrov, i., Russia B23 28
Gent (Gand), Bel. F4 12
Genthin, Ger. C12 10
Gentry, Ar., U.S. F2 114
Geographe Bay, b., Austl. F3 68
Geographe Channel, strt., Austl. D2 68
Geok-Tepe, Turk. B14 48
George, Ia., U.S. H11 118
George, S. Afr. I6 66
George, stm., P.Q., Can. E19 96
George, Cape, c., N.S., Can. G12 106
George, Lake, l., Austl. J8 70
George, Lake, l., Fl., U.S. J5 112
George, Lake, l., N.Y., U.S. D13 108
George, Lake, l., Ug. B6 58
Georges Bank E13 86
George Town, Austl. M7 70
George Town, Cay. Is. E4 94
Georgetown, Co., U.S. E11 120
Georgetown, De., U.S. I11 108
Georgetown, Fl., U.S. J5 112
Georgetown, Ga., U.S. H1 112
Georgetown, Gam. E2 64
Georgetown, Guy. D13 84
Georgetown, Id., U.S. H14 122
Georgetown, Il., U.S. C9 114
Georgetown, Ky., U.S. I2 108
George Town (Pinang), Malay. L6 40
Georgetown, Ms., U.S. K6 114
Georgetown, Oh., U.S. I3 108
Georgetown, P.E., Can. F11 106
Georgetown, S.C., U.S. F7 112
Georgetown, St. Vin. H14 94
Georgetown, Tx., U.S. I9 116
George V Coast, Ant. B7 73
George VI Sound, strt., Ant. C12 73
George West, Tx., U.S. K8 116
Georgia, ctry., Asia I6 26
Georgia, state, U.S. E10 98
Georgia, Strait of, strt., N.A. H11 102
Georgiana, Al., U.S. K10 114
Georgian Bay, b., On., Can. E14 110
Georgian Bay Islands National Park, On., Can. F16 110
Georgijevsk, Russia I6 26
Georgina, stm., Austl. D3 70
Gera, Ger. E12 10
Geral, Serra, clf, Braz. D14 80
Gerald, Mo., U.S. D5 114
Geral de Goiás, Serra, clf, Braz. B5 79
Geraldine, Mt., U.S. C15 122
Geraldton, Austl. E2 68
Geraldton, On., Can. G15 96
Gérardmer, Fr. D13 14
Gerber, Ca., U.S. D3 124
Gerdine, Mount, mtn., Ak., U.S. F18 100
Gereshk, Afg. E1 44
Gering, Ne., U.S. J4 118
Gerlachovský štít, mtn., Slvk. F20 10
Germain, Grand lac, l., P.Q., Can. A7 106
Germansen, Mount, mtn., B.C., Can. B10 102
Germansen Lake, l., B.C., Can. B10 102
Germansen Landing, B.C., Can. B10 102
Germantown, Il., U.S. D7 114
Germantown, Tn., U.S. G7 114
Germantown, Wi., U.S. G7 110
Germany (Deutschland), ctry., Eur. E9 4
Germfask, Mi., U.S. D10 110
Germiston, S. Afr. F9 66
Gernikao (Guernica), Spain B9 16
Geronimo, Ok., U.S. E8 116
Gers, dept., Fr. I7 14
Gerufa, Bots. B8 66
Gêrzê, China D11 44
Gesher HaZiw, Isr. B4 50
Getafe, Spain E8 16
Gettysburg, Pa., U.S. H9 108
Gettysburg, S.D., U.S. F8 118
Getulina, Braz. F4 79
Getúlio Vargas, Braz. D12 80
Gevgelija, Mac. H6 20
Gévora, stm., Eur. F4 16
Gex, Fr. F13 14
Geyikli, Tur. J10 20
Geyser, Mt., U.S. C15 122
Geyserville, Ca., U.S. F3 124
Ghaapplato, plat., S. Afr. F7 66
Ghadāmis, Libya E15 62
Ghāghara, stm., Asia G10 44
Ghana, ctry., Afr. G6 54
Ghanzi, Bots. C5 66
Ghanzi, dept., Bots. D6 66
Gharbi, Oued el, val., Alg. D11 62
Gharbīyah, Aş-Şahrā' al- (Western Desert), des., Egypt D4 60
Ghardaïa, Alg. D12 62
Ghardimaou, Tun. M3 18
Gharig, Sudan L4 60
Gharyān, Libya B3 56
Ghaşm, Syria C6 50
Ghāt, Libya H16 62
Ghātāl, India I12 44
Għawdex (Gozo), i., Malta M9 18
Ghawr ash-Sharqīyah, Qanāt al- (East Ghor Canal), Jord. D5 50
Ghayth, Wādī, val., Jord. G5 50
Ghazāl, Bahr al-, stm., Sudan M5 60
Ghazal, Bahr el, val., Chad F4 56
Ghāziābād, India F7 44
Ghāzīpur, India H10 44
Ghazlūna, Pak. E2 44
Ghaznī, Afg. D3 44
Ghazzah (Gaza), Gaza F3 48
Ghedi, Italy D5 18
Ghent see Gent, Bel. F4 12
Gheorgheni, Rom. C9 20
Gherla, Rom. B7 20
Ghilizane, Alg. C11 62
Ghisonaccia, Fr. I24 15a
Ghudāf, Wādī al-, val., Iraq E7 48
Ghūrīān, Afg. D16 48
Giant's Castle, mtn., Afr. G9 66
Giarre, Italy L10 18
Gibara, Cuba D6 94
Gibbon, Mn., U.S. F1 110
Gibbon, Ne., U.S. K9 118
Gibbons, Ab., Can. D21 102
Gibbonsville, Id., U.S. E12 122
Gibeon, Nmb. E3 66
Gibraleón, Spain H5 16
Gibraltar, Gib. I6 16
Gibraltar, dep., Eur. H6 4
Gibraltar, Strait of (Estrecho de Gibraltar), strt. J6 16
Gibsland, La., U.S. J3 114
Gibson, Ga., U.S. F4 112
Gibson City, Il., U.S. J7 110
Gibson Desert, des., Austl. D5 68
Gibsons, B.C., Can. H11 102
Gidami, Eth. M8 60
Gidda, Eth. M8 60
Giddings, Tx., U.S. I10 116
Gideon, Mo., U.S. F7 114
Gidole, Eth. O9 60
Gidrotorf, Russia E26 22
Gien, Fr. E9 14
Giessen, Ger. E8 10
Gifford, Fl., U.S. L5 112
Gifford, stm., N.T., Can. B16 96
Gifhorn, Ger. C10 10
Gifu, Japan L11 36
Gigantá, Sierra de la, mts., Mex. E4 90
Gigante, Col. F5 84
Gijón, Spain B6 16
Gila, stm., U.S. L2 120
Gila Bend, Az., U.S. L4 120
Gila Bend Mountains, mts., Az., U.S. K3 120
Gila Mountains, mts., Az., U.S. K7 120
Gilbert, La., U.S. J5 114
Gilbert, Mn., U.S. C3 110
Gilbert, stm., Austl. A4 70
Gilbert, Mount, mtn., B.C., Can. G10 102
Gilbertown, Al., U.S. K8 114
Gilbert Plains, Mb., Can. G14 104
Gilboa', Hare, hills, Asia D4 50
Gilbués, Braz. E9 76
Gildford, Mt., U.S. B15 122
Gilford Island, i., B.C., Can. G8 102
Gilgandra, Austl. H8 70
Gilgit, Pak. C6 44
Gilgit, stm., Pak. C5 44
Gil Island, i., B.C., Can. D5 102
Gillam, Mb., Can. B20 104
Gilles, Lake, l., Austl. I2 70
Gillespie, Il., U.S. C7 114
Gillett, Ar., U.S. H5 114
Gillett, Wi., U.S. F7 110
Gillette, Wy., U.S. G2 118
Gillian, Lake, l., N.T., Can. C17 96
Gills Rock, Wi., U.S. E8 110
Gilman, Ia., U.S. I3 110
Gilman, Il., U.S. J8 110
Gilman, Wi., U.S. E5 110
Gilmer, Tx., U.S. G12 116
Gilmore City, Ia., U.S. I13 118
Gilroy, Ca., U.S. G4 124

Name	Map Ref.	Page

Grea-Hale

Name	Map Ref.	Page
Great Namaqualand, hist. reg., Nmb.	E3	66
Great Nicobar, i., India	K2	40
Great Palm Island, i., Austl.	B7	70
Great Pee Dee, stm., S.C., U.S.	F7	112
Great Plain of the Koukdjuak, pl., N.T., Can.	C18	96
Great Plains, pl., N.A.	E9	86
Great Pubnico Lake, l., N.S., Can.	I8	106
Great Ruaha, stm., Tan.	C7	58
Great Sacandaga Lake, l., N.Y., U.S.	D12	108
Great Saint Bernard Pass see Grand-Saint-Bernard, Col du, Eur.	G7	13
Great Salt Lake, l., Ut., U.S.	C4	120
Great Salt Lake Desert, des., Ut., U.S.	D3	120
Great Sand Hills, hills, Sk., Can.	H5	104
Great Sandy Desert, des., Austl.	D4	68
Great Scarcies (Kolenté), stm., Afr.	G3	64
Great Slave Lake, l., N.T., Can.	D10	96
Great Smoky Mountains, mts., U.S.	D3	112
Great Smoky Mountains National Park, U.S.	D3	112
Great Victoria Desert, des., Austl.	E5	68
Great Wall, sci., Ant.	B1	73
Great Wall see Chang Cheng, hist., China	C4	32
Great Yarmouth, Eng., U.K.	I15	8
Great Zab (Büyükzap) (Az-Zāb al-Kabīr), stm., Asia	C7	48
Gréboun, mtn., Niger	A14	64
Grecia, C.R.	G10	92
Greco, Ur.	G10	80
Greece, N.Y., U.S.	D9	108
Greece (Ellás), ctry., Eur.	H12	4
Greeley, Co., U.S.	D12	120
Greeley, Ks., U.S.	M12	118
Greeley, Ne., U.S.	J9	118
Greeleyville, S.C., U.S.	F7	112
Green, stm., Il., U.S.	I6	110
Green, stm., Ky., U.S.	E9	114
Green, stm., N.B., Can.	E5	106
Green, stm., N.D., U.S.	D4	118
Green, stm., U.S.	F7	120
Green, stm., Wa., U.S.	C3	122
Greenacres, Wa., U.S.	C8	122
Green Bay, Wi., U.S.	F7	110
Green Bay, b., Nf., Can.	C18	106
Green Bay, b., U.S.	F8	110
Greenbrier, Ar., U.S.	G4	114
Green Brier, Tn., U.S.	F10	114
Greenbrier, stm., W.V., U.S.	J6	108
Greenburg, La., U.S.	L6	114
Greenbush, Mn., U.S.	C11	118
Greencastle, In., U.S.	C10	114
Greencastle, Pa., U.S.	H9	108
Green City, Mo., U.S.	B4	114
Green Cove Springs, Fl., U.S.	J5	112
Greendale, In., U.S.	C12	114
Greene, Ia., U.S.	H3	110
Greene, N.Y., U.S.	E11	108
Greeneville, Tn., U.S.	C4	112
Greenfield, Ca., U.S.	H4	124
Greenfield, Ia., U.S.	J13	118
Greenfield, Il., U.S.	C6	114
Greenfield, Ma., U.S.	E14	108
Greenfield, Mo., U.S.	E3	114
Greenfield, Oh., U.S.	H3	108
Greenfield, Tn., U.S.	F8	114
Green Forest, Ar., U.S.	F3	114
Green Head, c., Austl.	F2	68
Green Lake, Sk., Can.	D7	104
Green Lake, Wi., U.S.	G7	110
Green Lake, l., B.C., Can.	F13	102
Green Lake, l., Sk., Can.	D7	104
Greenland, Ar., U.S.	G2	114
Greenland, Mi., U.S.	D6	110
Greenland (Kalaallit Nunaat), dep., N.A.	B15	86
Greenland Sea	B20	86
Greenleaf, Ks., U.S.	L11	118
Green Mountains, mts., N.A.	D14	108
Green Peter Lake, res., Or., U.S.	F3	122
Green Pond, Al., U.S.	I9	114
Greenport, N.Y., U.S.	F14	108
Green River, Ut., U.S.	F6	120
Green River, Wy., U.S.	C7	120
Green River Lake, res., Ky., U.S.	E11	114
Greensboro, Al., U.S.	J9	114
Greensboro, Fl., U.S.	I2	112
Greensboro, Ga., U.S.	F3	112
Greensboro, Md., U.S.	I11	108
Greensboro, N.C., U.S.	C7	112
Greensburg, In., U.S.	C11	114
Greensburg, Ks., U.S.	N8	118
Greensburg, Ky., U.S.	E11	114
Greensburg, Pa., U.S.	G7	108
Greens Peak, mtn., Az., U.S.	J7	120
Greenspond, Nf., Can.	C20	106
Green Springs, Oh., U.S.	F3	108
Green Swamp, sw., N.C., U.S.	E8	112
Greentown, In., U.S.	B11	114
Greenup, Il., U.S.	C8	114
Greenup, Ky., U.S.	I4	108
Greenvale, Austl.	B6	70
Green Valley, Az., U.S.	M6	120
Green Valley, Il., U.S.	J6	110
Greenview, Il., U.S.	B7	114
Greenville, Al., U.S.	K10	114
Greenville, Ca., U.S.	D5	124
Greenville, Fl., U.S.	I3	112
Greenville, Ga., U.S.	F2	112
Greenville, Il., U.S.	D7	114
Greenville, Ky., U.S.	E9	114
Greenville, Lib.	I5	64
Greenville, Me., U.S.	B17	108
Greenville, Mi., U.S.	G10	110
Greenville, Mo., U.S.	E6	114
Greenville, Ms., U.S.	I5	114
Greenville, N.C., U.S.	D9	112
Greenville, N.H., U.S.	E15	108
Greenville, Oh., U.S.	G2	108
Greenville, Pa., U.S.	F6	108
Greenville, S.C., U.S.	E4	112
Greenville, Tx., U.S.	F10	116
Greenwater Lake Provincial Park, Sk., Can.	F11	104
Greenwich, Ct., U.S.	F13	108
Greenwich, N.Y., U.S.	D13	108
Greenwich, Oh., U.S.	F4	108
Greenwood, Ar., U.S.	G2	114
Greenwood, B.C., Can.	H16	102
Greenwood, In., U.S.	C10	114
Greenwood, Ms., U.S.	I6	114
Greenwood, Ne., U.S.	K11	118
Greenwood, S.C., U.S.	E4	112
Greenwood, Wi., U.S.	F5	110
Greenwood, Lake, res., S.C., U.S.	E4	112
Greer, S.C., U.S.	E4	112
Greers Ferry Lake, res., Ar., U.S.	G4	114
Gregoire Lake Indian Reserve, Ab., Can.	B3	104
Gregório, stm., Braz.	B6	82
Gregory, Mi., U.S.	H11	110
Gregory, S.D., U.S.	H8	118
Gregory, Tx., U.S.	L9	116
Gregory, stm., Austl.	B3	70
Gregory, Lake, l., Austl.	G3	70
Gregory Range, mts., Austl.	B5	70
Greifswald, Ger.	A13	10
Greiz, Ger.	E12	10
Grem'ačinsk, Russia	F9	26
Grenada, Ms., U.S.	I7	114
Grenada, ctry., N.A.	H14	94
Grenadines, is., N.A.	H14	94
Grenchen, Switz.	D7	13
Grenfell, Austl.	I8	70
Grenfell, Sk., Can.	H12	104
Grenoble, Fr.	G12	14
Grenola, Ks., U.S.	N11	118
Grenora, N.D., U.S.	C4	118
Grenville, Cape, c., Austl.	B8	68
Grenville Channel, strt., B.C., Can.	D5	102
Gréoux-les-Bains, Fr.	I12	14
Gresham, Or., U.S.	E3	122
Gresham Park, Ga., U.S.	F2	112
Gresik, Indon.	j16	39a
Gresten, Aus.	G15	10
Gretna, La., U.S.	M6	114
Gretna, Mb., Can.	I17	104
Gretna, Va., U.S.	C7	112
Greven, Ger.	C7	10
Grevená, Grc.	I5	20
Grevenbroich, Ger.	D6	10
Greville Bay, b., N.S., Can.	G9	106
Grey, stm., Nf., Can.	E17	106
Greybull, Wy., U.S.	F17	122
Greybull, stm., Wy., U.S.	F17	122
Grey Eagle, Mn., U.S.	E1	110
Grey Islands, is., Nf., Can.	B18	106
Greylock, Mount, mtn., Ma., U.S.	E13	108
Greymouth, N.Z.	E3	72
Grey Range, mts., Austl.	G5	70
Grey River, Nf., Can.	E16	106
Greys, stm., Wy., U.S.	G15	122
Greytown, S. Afr.	G10	66
Gribanovskij, Russia	G6	26
Gribbel Island, i., B.C., Can.	D5	102
Gridley, Ca., U.S.	E4	124
Gridley, Il., U.S.	J7	110
Griesbach, Ger.	G13	10
Griesheim, Ger.	F8	10
Griffin, Ga., U.S.	F2	112
Griffin, Sk., Can.	I11	104
Griffith, Austl.	J7	70
Griffith Island, i., N.T., Can.	B13	96
Grifton, N.C., U.S.	D9	112
Griggsville, Il., U.S.	C6	114
Grignan, Fr.	H11	14
Grigoriopol, Mol.	B13	20
Grijalva, stm., Mex.	I13	90
Grijalva (Cuilco), stm., N.A.	B3	92
Grim, Cape, c., Austl.	M6	70
Grimma, Ger.	D12	10
Grimsby, Eng., U.K.	H13	8
Grimsby, On., Can.	G16	110
Grimselpass, Switz.	E9	13
Grimshaw, Ab., Can.	A17	102
Grímsstaðir, Ice.	B5	6a
Grimstad, Nor.	L11	6
Grímsvötn, mtn., Ice.	B5	6a
Grindelwald, Switz.	E9	13
Grindstone Island see Cap-aux-Meules, P.Q., Can.	E12	106
Grinnell, Ia., U.S.	I3	110
Grinnell Peninsula, pen., N.T., Can.	A13	96
Gris-Nez, Cap, c., Fr.	B8	14
Griswold, Ia., U.S.	J12	118
Griswold, Mb., Can.	I14	104
Grizzly Bear Mountain, mtn., N.T., Can.	C8	96
Grizzly Bear's Head and Lead Man Indian Reserve, Sk., Can.	F6	104
Groais Island, i., Nf., Can.	B18	106
Grobiņa, Lat.	E4	22
Groblersdal, S. Afr.	E9	66
Groblershoop, S. Afr.	G5	66
Grodków, Pol.	E17	10
Grodzisk Mazowiecki, Pol.	C20	10
Groede, Neth.	F4	12
Groenlo, Neth.	D10	12
Groesbeck, Tx., U.S.	H10	116
Groesbeek, Neth.	E8	12
Groix, Fr.	E3	14
Grójec, Pol.	D20	10
Grombalia, Tun.	M5	18
Gronau, Ger.	C7	10
Groningen, Neth.	B10	12
Groningen, prov., Neth.	B10	12
Gronlid, Sk., Can.	E10	104
Groom, Tx., U.S.	D5	116
Groot-Brakrivier, S. Afr.	I5	66
Groote Eylandt, i., Austl.	B7	68
Grootfontein, Nmb.	B4	66
Groot Karasberge, mts., Nmb.	F4	66
Groot-Kei, stm., S. Afr.	I9	66
Groot Laagte, stm., Afr.	C5	66
Groot-Marico, S. Afr.	E8	66
Groot-Vis, stm., S. Afr.	I8	66
Gros Mécatina, Cap du, c., P.Q., Can.	B14	106
Gros Morne, mtn., Nf., Can.	C16	106
Gros Morne National Park, Nf., Can.	C16	106
Grosse Île, La, i., P.Q., Can.	E12	106
Grossenhain, Ger.	D13	10
Grosse Pointe, Mi., U.S.	H13	110
Großer Bärensee, l., N.T., Can.	C8	96
Grosseto, Italy	G6	18
Gross-Gerau, Ger.	F8	10
Grossglockner, mtn., Aus.	H12	10
Grosshöchstetten, Switz.	E8	13
Grossräschen, Ger.	D14	10
Gros Ventre, stm., Wy., U.S.	G15	122
Groswater Bay, b., Nf., Can.	F21	96
Groton, Ct., U.S.	F14	108
Groton, N.Y., U.S.	E10	108
Groton, S.D., U.S.	F9	118
Grottaglie, Italy	I12	18
Grottoes, Va., U.S.	I8	108
Grouard Mission, Ab., Can.	B18	102
Groundbirch, B.C., Can.	B14	102
Groundhog, stm., On., Can.	G16	96
Grove, Ok., U.S.	C12	116
Grove City, Mn., U.S.	F13	118
Grove City, Oh., U.S.	H3	108
Grove City, Pa., U.S.	F6	108
Grove Hill, Al., U.S.	K9	114
Groveland, Fl., U.S.	K5	112
Grover City, Ca., U.S.	I5	124
Groves, Tx., U.S.	M3	114
Groveton, N.H., U.S.	C15	108
Groveton, Tx., U.S.	H11	116
Grovetown, Ga., U.S.	F4	112
Groznyj, Russia	I7	26
Grudziądz, Pol.	B18	10
Gruetli-Laager, Tn., U.S.	G11	114
Gruitrode, Bel.	F8	12
Grulla, Tx., U.S.	M8	116
Grünau, Nmb.	F4	66
Grünau [im Almtal], Aus.	H13	10
Grundy, Va., U.S.	B4	112
Grundy Center, Ia., U.S.	H3	110
Grunthal, Mb., Can.	I18	104
Gruver, Tx., U.S.	C5	116
Gruziya see Georgia, ctry., Asia	I6	26
Grybów, Pol.	F20	10
Gryfice, Pol.	B15	10
Gstaad, Switz.	F7	13
Guabito, Pan.	H12	92
Guacanayabo, Golfo de, b., Cuba	D6	94
Guacara, Ven.	B9	84
Guacarí, Col.	F4	84
Gu Achi, Az., U.S.	L4	120
Guachiría, stm., Col.	E7	84
Guachochi, Mex.	D6	90
Guaçuí, Braz.	F8	79
Guadalajara, Mex.	G8	90
Guadalajara, Spain	E8	16
Guadalcanal, i., Sol. Is.	I20	126
Guadalén, stm., Spain	G8	16
Guadalén, Embalse de, res., Spain	G8	16
Guadalmena, stm., Spain	G9	16
Guadalquivir, stm., Spain	H6	16
Guadalupe, Bol.	H9	82
Guadalupe, Ca., U.S.	J5	124
Guadalupe, Col.	F5	84
Guadalupe, C.R.	H10	92
Guadalupe, Mex.	E9	90
Guadalupe, Mex.	F8	90
Guadalupe, Peru	B2	82
Guadalupe, stm., Tx., U.S.	K9	116
Guadalupe [Bravos], Mex.	B6	90
Guadalupe Mountains National Park, Tx., U.S.	H2	116
Guadalupe Peak, mtn., Tx., U.S.	H2	116
Guadalupe Victoria, Mex.	E7	90
Guadalupita, N.M., U.S.	H11	120
Guadarrama, Sierra de, mts., Spain	E7	16
Guadeloupe, dep., N.A.	F14	94
Guadeloupe Passage, strt., N.A.	F14	94
Guadiana, stm., Eur.	H4	16
Guadix, Spain	H8	16
Guaíba, Braz.	F13	80
Guaíba, est., Braz.	F13	80
Guaihe, China	B1	34
Guaimaca, Hond.	C8	92
Guaimoreto, Laguna de, b., Hond.	B9	92
Guainía, dept., Col.	F8	84
Guainía, stm., S.A.	F9	84
Guaiquinima, Cerro, mtn., Ven.	E11	84
Guaíra, Braz.	F4	79
Guaíra, Braz.	C11	80
Guairá, dept., Para.	C10	80
Guáitara, stm., Col.	G4	84
Guajaba, Cayo, i., Cuba	D6	94
Guajará-Mirim, Braz.	D9	82
Gualaca, Pan.	C1	84
Gualaceo, Ec.	I3	84
Gualala, Ca., U.S.	F2	124
Gualán, Guat.	B5	92
Gualaquiza, Ec.	I3	84
Gualdo Tadino, Italy	F7	18
Gualeguay, Arg.	G9	80
Gualeguay, stm., Arg.	G9	80
Gualeguaychú, Arg.	G9	80
Gualicho, Salina del, pl., Arg.	E3	78
Guam, dep., Oc.	G18	126
Guamal, Col.	F6	84
Guamal, Col.	C5	84
Guamini, Arg.	I7	80
Guamo, Col.	E5	84
Guamote, Ec.	H3	84
Guamúchil, Mex.	E5	90
Guamués, stm., Col.	G4	84
Guanacaste, prov., C.R.	G9	92
Guanacaste, Cordillera de, mts., C.R.	G9	92
Guanacaste, Parque Nacional, C.R.	G9	92
Guanacaure, Cerro, mtn., Hond.	D7	92
Guanaceví, Mex.	E7	90
Guanache, stm., Peru	B4	82
Guanahacabibes, Golfo de, b., Cuba	C2	94
Guanaja, Hond.	A9	92
Guanaja, Isla de, i., Hond.	A9	92
Guanajay, Cuba	C3	94
Guanajuato, Mex.	G9	90
Guanajuato, state, Mex.	G9	90
Guanambi, Braz.	C7	79
Guanaparo, Caño, stm., Ven.	C8	84
Guañape, Islas, is., Peru	C2	82
Guanare, Ven.	C8	84
Guanare, stm., Ven.	C8	84
Guanarito, Ven.	C8	84
Guanay, Bol.	F8	82
Guanay, Cerro, mtn., Ven.	E9	84
Guanbuqiao, China	F3	34
Guandacol, Arg.	E4	80
Guandanghu, China	E2	34
Guandian, China	C7	34
Guane, Cuba	C2	94
Guang'an, China	E8	30
Guangde, China	E8	34
Guangdong (Kwangtung), prov., China	G9	30
Guanghua, China	E9	30
Guangnan, China	G8	30
Guangrao, China	F6	32
Guangxi Zhuangzu Zizhiqu (Kwangsi Chuang), prov., China	G8	30
Guangyuan, China	E8	30
Guangzhou (Canton), China	L2	34
Guanhães, Braz.	E7	79
Guanipa, stm., Ven.	C11	84
Guankou, China	E4	34
Guano, Ec.	H3	84
Guanqian, China	E5	34
Guanqiaopu, China	D1	34
Guanta, Ven.	B10	84
Guantánamo, Cuba	D7	94
Guantao (Nanguantao), China	G3	32
Guantou, China	G9	34
Guanxian, China	E7	30
Guanyintang, China	D1	34
Guanzhuang, China	F2	32
Guanzhuang, China	C3	34
Guapí, Col.	F4	84
Guapiara, Braz.	H4	79
Guápiles, C.R.	G11	92
Guaporé, Braz.	E13	80
Guaporé (Itenes), stm., S.A.	E10	82
Guaqui, Bol.	G7	82
Guará, stm., Braz.	B6	79
Guarabira, Braz.	E11	76
Guaraçaí, Braz.	F3	79
Guaraci, Braz.	F4	79
Guaraciaba, Braz.	D7	79
Guaramirim, Braz.	D14	80
Guaranda, Ec.	H3	84
Guaraniaçu, Braz.	C12	80
Guarani das Missões, Braz.	E11	80
Guarani de Goiás, Braz.	B5	79
Guarapari, Braz.	F8	79
Guarapuava, Braz.	C13	80
Guaraqueçaba, Braz.	C14	80
Guararé, Pan.	D2	84
Guaratinguetá, Braz.	G6	79
Guaratuba, Braz.	C14	80
Guarda, Port.	E4	16
Guardafui, Cape see Gwardafuy, Gees, c., Som.	F11	56
Guardavalle, Italy	K11	18
Guardia Escolta, Arg.	E7	80
Guardiagrele, Italy	G9	18
Guardo, Spain	C7	16
Guareña, Spain	G5	16
Guarenas, Ven.	B9	84
Guariba, stm., Braz.	C11	82
Guarico, Ven.	C8	84
Guárico, state, Ven.	C9	84
Guárico, stm., Ven.	C9	84
Guárico, Embalse del, res., Ven.	C9	84
Guariquito, stm., Ven.	D9	84
Guarizama, Hond.	C8	92
Guarulhos, Braz.	G5	79
Guasare, stm., Ven.	B6	84
Guasave, Mex.	E5	90
Guasdualito, Ven.	D7	84
Guasipati, Ven.	D12	84
Guastalla, Italy	E5	18
Guastatoya, Guat.	C4	92
Guatajiagua, El Sal.	D6	92
Guatemala, Guat.	C4	92
Guatemala, dept., Guat.	C4	92
Guatemala, ctry., N.A.	E6	88
Guateque, Col.	E6	84
Guatimozín, Arg.	G7	80
Guatopo, Parque Nacional, Ven.	C9	84
Guatraché, Arg.	I7	80
Guaviare, ter., Col.	F6	84
Guaviare, stm., Col.	F8	84
Guaxupé, Braz.	F5	79
Guayabal, Cuba	D6	94
Guayabal, Ven.	C9	84
Guayabero, stm., Col.	F6	84
Guayacán, Chile	E3	80
Guayama, P.R.	F11	94
Guayambre, stm., Hond.	C8	92
Guayape, Hond.	C8	92
Guayape, stm., Hond.	C9	92
Guayapo, stm., Ven.	E9	84
Guayaquil, Ec.	D3	76
Guayaquil, Golfo de, b., S.A.	I2	84
Guayaramerín, Bol.	D9	82
Guayas, prov., Ec.	H2	84
Guayas, stm., Col.	G5	84
Guayas, stm., Ec.	I3	84
Guayatayoc, Laguna de, l., Arg.	B6	80
Guaycora, Mex.	C5	90
Guaymas, Mex.	D4	90
Guayquiraró, stm., Arg.	F9	80
Guayuriba, stm., Col.	F6	84
Guazacapán, Guat.	C4	92
Guazapares, Mex.	D5	90
Guazárachi, Mex.	D6	90
Guba, Eth.	L8	60
Gubacha, Russia	F9	26
Gubbio, Italy	F7	18
Guben, Ger.	D14	10
Gubin, Pol.	D14	10
Gubkin, Russia	G5	26
Gucheng, China	C7	34
Güdalür, India	H4	46
Gudermes, Russia	I7	26
Gudiyāttam, India	F5	46
Güdür, India	E5	46
Guebwiller, Fr.	E14	14
Güéjar, stm., Col.	F6	84
Guelma, Alg.	B14	62
Guelph, On., Can.	G15	110
Guéméné-sur-Scorff, Fr.	D3	14
Guené, Benin	F11	64
Guérande, Fr.	E4	14
Guercif, Mor.	C9	62
Güere, stm., Ven.	C10	84
Guéréda, Chad	J2	60
Guéret, Fr.	F8	14
Guerneville, Ca., U.S.	F2	124
Guernsey, Wy., U.S.	B12	120
Guernsey, dep., Eur.	F7	4
Guerrero, Mex.	C6	90
Guerrero, state, Mex.	I9	90
Guerzim, Alg.	F10	62
Guessou-Sud, Benin	F11	64
Gueydan, La., U.S.	L4	114
Gugang, China	G2	34
Guge, mtn., Eth.	N9	60
Guia, Braz.	F13	82
Guía de Isora, Spain	o24	17b
Guia Lopes da Laguna, Braz.	I13	82
Guibes, Nmb.	F3	66
Güicán, Col.	D6	84
Guichen, Fr.	E5	14
Guichón, Ur.	G10	80
Guidan Roumji, Niger	E13	64
Guide, China	D7	30
Guide Rock, Ne., U.S.	K9	118
Guidigri, Niger	E14	64
Guidimouni, Niger	E14	64
Guiding, China	A9	40
Guifuji, China	H9	34
Guiglo, C. Iv.	H6	64
Güija, Lago de, l., N.A.	C5	92
Guildford, Eng., U.K.	J13	8
Guildhall, Vt., U.S.	C15	108
Guilford, Me., U.S.	B17	108
Guilin (Kweilin), China	B11	40
Guillaume-Delisle, Lac, l., P.Q., Can.	E17	96
Guillaumes, Fr.	H13	14
Güimar, Spain	o24	17b
Guimarães, Port.	D3	16
Guin, Al., U.S.	I9	114
Guinea (Guinée), ctry., Afr.	F4	54
Guinea, Gulf of, b., Afr.	H7	52
Guinea-Bissau (Guiné-Bissau), ctry., Afr.	F3	54
Guinecourt, Lac, l., P.Q., Can.	B4	106
Güines, Cuba	C3	94
Guînes, Fr.	B8	14
Guingamp, Fr.	D3	14
Güinope, Hond.	D8	92
Guiones, Punta, c., C.R.	H9	92
Guiping, China	C11	40
Guir, Hammada du, des., Afr.	E9	62
Guir, Oued, val., Afr.	E9	62
Güira de Melena, Cuba	C3	94
Guiraí, stm., Braz.	G2	79
Guiratinga, Braz.	D2	79
Güiria, Ven.	B11	84
Guiricema, Braz.	F7	79
Güisisil, mtn., Nic.	E8	92
Guita Koulouba, C.A.R.	O2	60
Guitou, China	K2	34
Guîtres, Fr.	G6	14
Guiuan, Phil.	C8	38
Guixi, China	G6	34
Guixian, China	C10	40
Guiyang (Kweiyang), China	A9	40
Güiza, stm., Col.	G3	84
Guizhou (Kweichow), prov., China	F8	30
Gujarāt, state, India	I4	44
Gujrānwāla, Pak.	D6	44
Gujrāt, Pak.	D6	44
Gulbarga, India	D4	46
Gulbene, Lat.	D9	22
Guledagudda, India	D3	46
Guleitou, China	L6	34
Gulf Hammock, Fl., U.S.	J4	112
Gulfport, Fl., U.S.	L4	112
Gulfport, Ms., U.S.	L7	114
Gulf Shores, Al., U.S.	L9	114
Gulgong, Austl.	I8	70
Gulistan, Pak.	E2	44
Gulistan, Uzb.	I11	26
Gull Lake, Sk., Can.	H6	104
Gull Lake, l., Ab., Can.	E21	102
Gull Lake, l., On., Can.	G23	104
Gullrock Lake, l., On., Can.	H21	104
Güllük, Tur.	L11	20
Gulnam, Sudan	N5	60
Gülpınar, Tur.	J10	20
Guluy, Erit.	J9	60
Gumal (Gowmal), stm., Asia	D3	44
Gumare, Bots.	B6	66
Gumiao, China	C2	34
Gummersbach, Ger.	D7	10
Gummi, Nig.	E12	64
Gümüşhane, Tur.	A5	48
Guna, India	H7	44
Gundagai, Austl.	J8	70
Gungu, Zaire	C3	58
Gunisao, stm., Mb., Can.	E17	104
Gunisao Lake, l., Mb., Can.	E18	104
Gunnar, Sk., Can.	E11	96
Gunnbjørn Fjeld, mtn., Grnld.	C17	86
Gunnedah, Austl.	H9	70
Gunnison, Co., U.S.	F10	120
Gunnison, Ut., U.S.	E5	120
Gunnison, stm., Co., U.S.	F8	120
Guntakal, India	E4	46
Guntersville, Al., U.S.	H10	114
Guntersville Lake, res., Al., U.S.	H10	114
Guntūr, India	D6	46
Gunungsitoli, Indon.	N4	40
Gunzenhausen, Ger.	F10	10
Guojiazhen, China	C4	34
Guozhuang, China	H5	32
Gupei, China	I5	32
Guraferda, Eth.	N8	60
Gura Galbenei, Mol.	C12	20
Gurara, stm., Nig.	G13	64
Gurdāspur, India	D6	44
Gurdon, Ar., U.S.	I3	114
Güre, Tur.	K13	20
Gurgueia, stm., Braz.	E10	76
Guri, Embalse de, res., Ven.	D11	84
Gurjevsk, Russia	G3	22
Gurjevsk, Russia	G15	26
Gurupá, Braz.	D8	76
Gurupi, Braz.	F9	76
Gurupi, stm., Braz.	D9	76
Gusau, Nig.	E13	64
Gus'-Chrustal'nyj, Russia	F23	22
Gusev, Russia	G5	22
Gusevskij, Russia	F23	22
Gushanzi, China	C8	32
Gushi, China	C4	34
Gushikawa, Japan	u2	37b
Gusino, Russia	G14	22
Gusinoozersk, Russia	G13	28
Guspini, Italy	J3	18
Gustavus, Ak., U.S.	G27	100
Gustine, Ca., U.S.	G5	124
Gustine, Tx., U.S.	H8	116
Güstrow, Ger.	B12	10
Gus'-Železnyj, Russia	F24	22
Gütersloh, Ger.	D8	10
Guthrie, Ky., U.S.	F9	114
Guthrie, Ok., U.S.	D9	116
Guthrie, Tx., U.S.	F6	116
Guthrie Center, Ia., U.S.	J13	118
Guthrie Lake, l., Mb., Can.	C14	104
Gutian, China	I7	34
Gutierrez, Bol.	H10	82
Gutiérrez Zamora, Mex.	G11	90
Guttenberg, Ia., U.S.	H4	110
Gutu, Zimb.	B10	66
Guwāhāti, India	G14	44
Guxian, China	F9	32
Guxiansi, China	C5	34
Guyana, ctry., S.A.	B7	76
Guyandotte, stm., W.V., U.S.	I4	108
Guyi, China	J7	34
Guymon, Ok., U.S.	C5	116
Guyot, Mount, mtn., U.S.	D3	112
Guyra, Austl.	H9	70
Guysborough, N.S., Can.	G12	106
Guyton, Ga., U.S.	G5	112
Guyuan, China	D8	30
Guzar, Uzb.	J11	26
Guzhu, China	I5	34
Guzmán, Laguna, l., Mex.	B6	90
Gvardejsk, Russia	G4	22
Gwa, Myan.	F3	40
Gwadabawa, Nig.	E12	64
Gwādar, Pak.	I17	48
Gwai, Zimb.	B8	66
Gwāl Haidarzai, Pak.	E3	44
Gwalior, India	G8	44
Gwanda, Zimb.	C9	66
Gwandu, Nig.	E12	64
Gwardafuy, Gees, c., Som.	F11	56
Gwātar Bay, b., Asia	I16	48
Gwent, co., Wales, U.K.	J11	8
Gweru, Zimb.	B9	66
Gweta, Bots.	C7	66
Gwinn, Mi., U.S.	D8	110
Gwinner, N.D., U.S.	E10	118
Gwynedd, co., Wales, U.K.	H9	8
Gy, Fr.	E12	14
Gyangzê, China	F4	30
Gyaring Co, l., China	E13	44
Gyaring Hu, l., China	E6	30
Gydanskaja guba, b., Russia	C13	26
Gydanskij poluostrov, pen., Russia	C13	26
Gyirong, China	F11	44
Gym Peak, mtn., N.M., U.S.	L9	120
Gympie, Austl.	F10	70
Gyobingauk, Myan.	E3	40
Gyoma, Hung.	I20	10
Gyöngyös, Hung.	H19	10
Győr, Hung.	H17	10
Győr-Moson-Sopron, co., Hung.	H17	10
Gypsum, Co., U.S.	E10	120
Gypsum, Ks., U.S.	M10	118
Gypsum Point, c., N.T., Can.	D10	96
Gypsumville, Mb., Can.	G16	104
Gyula, Hung.	I21	10

H

Name	Map Ref.	Page
Haag in Oberbayern, Ger.	G12	10
Haalenberg, Nmb.	F2	66
Haaltert, Bel.	G5	12
Haapajärvi, Fin.	J19	6
Haapamäki, Fin.	J19	6
Haapsalu, Est.	C6	22
Ha'Arava (Wādī al-Jayb), val., Asia	H4	50
Ha'Arava (Wādī al-'Arabah), val., Asia	G4	50
Haarlem, Neth.	D6	12
Ḩabarūt, Yemen	F8	47
Ḩabbān, Yemen	G5	47
Ḩabbūsh, Leb.	B4	50
Habermehl Peak, mtn., Ant.	C3	73
Habiganj, Bngl.	H14	44
Habomai-shotō see Malaja Kuril'skaja Gr'ada, is., Russia	d21	36a
Hache, Lac la, l., B.C., Can.	F13	102
Hachijō-jima, i., Japan	E14	30
Hachinohe, Japan	G16	36
Hachiōji, Japan	L14	36
Hacienda Miravalles, C.R.	G9	92
Hacienda Murciélago, C.R.	G9	92
Hackberry, Az., U.S.	I3	120
Hackberry, La., U.S.	M3	114
Hackensack, N.J., U.S.	G12	108
Hackett, Ar., U.S.	G2	114
Hackettstown, N.J., U.S.	G12	108
Hackleburg, Al., U.S.	H9	114
Hadaliya, Sudan	I9	60
Ḩadd, Ra's al-, c., Oman	C11	47
Haddam, Ks., U.S.	L10	118
Haddington, Scot., U.K.	F11	8
Haddock, Ga., U.S.	F3	112
Hadejia, Nig.	E14	64
Hadejia, stm., Nig.	E14	64
Ḩadera, Isr.	D3	50
Ḩadera, stm., Asia	D3	50
Hadley Bay, b., N.T., Can.	B11	96
Hadlock, Wa., U.S.	B3	122
Ha Dong, Viet.	D8	40
Ḩaḑramawt, reg., Yemen	G6	47
Hadzilavičy, Bela.	H13	22
Haeju, N. Kor.	E13	32
Haenam, S. Kor.	I14	32
Hafford, Sk., Can.	F7	104
Haffouz, Tun.	N4	18
Hafirat al-'Ayda, Sau. Ar.	H5	48
Hafnarfjörður, Ice.	B3	6a
Haft Gel, Iran	F10	48
Hagan, Ga., U.S.	G5	112
Hagen, Ger.	D7	10
Hagensborg, B.C., Can.	E8	102
Hagere Hiywet, Eth.	M9	60
Hagere Selam, Eth.	N10	60
Hagerman, Id., U.S.	H11	122
Hagerman, N.M., U.S.	F2	116
Hagerstown, In., U.S.	C11	114
Hagerstown, Md., U.S.	H9	108
Hagersville, On., Can.	H15	110
Hagetmau, Fr.	I6	14
Haggin, Mount, mtn., Mt., U.S.	D12	122
Ha Giang, Viet.	C8	40
Hagondange, Fr.	C13	14
Hague, N.D., U.S.	E8	118
Hague, Sk., Can.	F8	104
Hague, Cap de la, c., Fr.	C5	14
Haguenau, Fr.	D14	14
Hagues Peak, mtn., Co., U.S.	D11	120
Hahaïa, Com.	k15	67a
Hahira, Ga., U.S.	I3	112
Haian Shanmo, mts., Tai.	L10	34
Haicheng, China	C10	32
Haïdra, Tun.	N3	18
Hai Duong, Viet.	D9	40
Haifa see Hefa, Isr.	C4	50
Haifeng, China	M4	34
Haig, Austl.	F5	68
Haig, Mount, mtn., Can.	H20	102
Haigler, Ne., U.S.	K6	118
Haikang (Leizhou), China	D11	40
Haikou, China	D11	40
Hā'il, Sau. Ar.	H6	48
Hailākāndi, India	H15	44
Hailar, China	B10	30
Hailar, stm., China	B11	30
Hailey, Id., U.S.	G11	122
Haileybury, On., Can.	C16	110
Haileyville, Ok., U.S.	E11	116
Hailong (Meihekou), China	A13	32
Hailun, China	B12	30
Haimen, China	G10	34
Haimen, China	L5	34
Hainan, prov., China	H8	30
Hainan Dao, i., China	E10	40
Hainaut, prov., Bel.	G4	12
Hainaut, hist. reg., Eur.	H4	12
Haines, Ak., U.S.	G27	100
Haines City, Fl., U.S.	K5	112
Haines Junction, Yk., Can.	F26	100
Hainfeld, Aus.	G15	10
Hai Phong, Viet.	D9	40
Haiti (Haïti), ctry., N.A.	E8	94
Haitou, China	I7	32
Haiyaopu, China	A6	40
Haizhou, China	A8	34
Hajdú-Bihar, co., Hung.	H21	10
Hajdúböszörmény, Hung.	H21	10
Hajdúnánás, Hung.	H21	10
Hajeb el Ayoun, Tun.	N4	18
Haji Langar, China	C8	44
Hājīpur, India	H11	44
Ḩajjah, Yemen	G3	47
Hajnówka, Pol.	C23	10
Ḩakīm, Abyār al-, well, Libya	B2	60
Hakkâri, Tur.	C7	48
Hakodate, Japan	f15	36a
Hakui, Japan	K11	36
Halab (Aleppo), Syria	C4	48
Halabjah, Iraq	D8	48
Halachó, Mex.	G14	90
Halā'ib, Egypt	F9	60
Halaula, Hi., U.S.	q18	125a
Halawa, Cape, c., Hi., U.S.	p17	125a
Halawotekale, China	B14	44
Halberstadt, Ger.	D11	10
Halbrite, Sk., Can.	I11	104
Haldwāni, India	F8	44
Hale, Mo., U.S.	C3	114
Haleakala Crater, crat., Hi., U.S.	q17	125a
Haleakala National Park, Hi., U.S.	q17	125a

Name	Map Ref.	Page
Hale Center, Tx., U.S.	E5	116
Haleyville, Al., U.S.	H9	114
Halfmoon Bay, B.C., Can.	H11	102
Halfway, Md., U.S.	H9	108
Halfway, Or., U.S.	F8	122
Halfway, stm., B.C., Can.	E8	96
Halfway Lake, l., Mb., Can.	C16	104
Haliburton, On., Can.	E17	110
Halifax, Austl.	B7	70
Halifax, N.C., U.S.	C9	112
Halifax, N.S., Can.	H10	106
Halifax, Va., U.S.	C8	112
Halifax, Canadian Forces Base, mil., N.S., Can.	H10	106
Halifax Bay, b., Austl.	B7	70
Halifax Citadel National Historic Park, N.S., Can.	H10	106
Halifax Harbour, b., N.S., Can.	H10	106
Hallam Peak, mtn., B.C., Can.	E16	102
Hallandale, Fl., U.S.	N6	112
Hallands Län, co., Swe.	M13	6
Halla-san, mtn., S. Kor.	E12	30
Halle (Hal), Bel.	G5	12
Halle, Ger.	D11	10
Hallein, Aus.	H13	10
Hallettsville, Tx., U.S.	J10	116
Halliday, N.D., U.S.	D5	118
Hall in Tirol, Aus.	H11	10
Hall Lake, l., N.T., Can.	C16	96
Hällnäs, Swe.	I16	6
Hallock, Mn., U.S.	C11	118
Hallowell, Me., U.S.	C17	108
Hall Peninsula, pen., N.T., Can.	D19	96
Halls, Tn., U.S.	G7	114
Hallsberg, Swe.	L14	6
Halls Creek, Austl.	C5	68
Hallstavik, Swe.	K16	6
Hallstead, Pa., U.S.	F11	108
Hallsville, Mo., U.S.	C4	114
Hallsville, Tx., U.S.	J2	114
Halma, Bel.	H7	12
Halmahera, i., Indon.	E8	38
Halmahera, Laut (Halmahera Sea), Indon.	F8	38
Halmstad, Swe.	M13	6
Halsey, Ne., U.S.	J7	118
Halsey, Or., U.S.	F2	122
Hälsingborg see Helsingborg, Swe.	M13	6
Halstad, Mn., U.S.	D11	118
Halstead, Ks., U.S.	M10	118
Haltern, Ger.	D7	10
Haltiatunturi, mtn., Eur.	G17	6
Haltom City, Tx., U.S.	G9	116
Halton Hills, On., Can.	G16	110
Halvorson, Mount, mtn., B.C., Can.	D14	102
Hamad, Sudan	J7	60
Hamada, Japan	M7	36
Hamadān, Iran	D10	48
Ḩamāh, Syria	D4	48
Hamale, Ghana	F8	64
Hamamatsu, Japan	M12	36
Hamar, Nor.	K12	6
Ḩamāṭah, Jabal, mtn., Egypt	I3	48
Hamber Provincial Park, B.C., Can.	E17	102
Hamburg, Ar., U.S.	I5	114
Hamburg, Ger.	B9	10
Hamburg, Ia., U.S.	K12	118
Hamburg, N.J., U.S.	F12	108
Hamburg, N.Y., U.S.	E8	108
Hamburg, Pa., U.S.	G11	108
Ḩamdānah, Sau. Ar.	E2	47
Hamden, Ct., U.S.	F14	108
Hamden, Oh., U.S.	H4	108
Hämeen lääni, prov., Fin.	K19	6
Hämeenlinna, Fin.	K19	6
Hameln, Ger.	C9	10
Hamersley Range, mts., Austl.	D3	68
Hamersley Range National Park, Austl.	D3	68
Hamhŭng, N. Kor.	D15	32
Hami, China	C5	30
Hamilton, Al., U.S.	H9	114
Hamilton, Austl.	K5	70
Hamilton, Ber.	B12	88
Hamilton, Ga., U.S.	G2	112
Hamilton, Il., U.S.	J4	110
Hamilton, Ks., U.S.	N11	118
Hamilton, Mi., U.S.	H9	110
Hamilton, Mo., U.S.	C3	114
Hamilton, Mt., U.S.	D11	122
Hamilton, N.C., U.S.	D9	112
Hamilton, N.Y., U.S.	E11	108
Hamilton, N.Z.	B5	72
Hamilton, Oh., U.S.	H2	108
Hamilton, On., Can.	G16	110
Hamilton, Scot., U.K.	F9	8
Hamilton, Tx., U.S.	H8	116
Hamilton, stm., Austl.	D4	70
Hamilton, Mount, mtn., Nv., U.S.	E10	124
Hamilton City, Ca., U.S.	E3	124
Hamilton Creek Indian Reserve, B.C., Can.	G14	102
Hamilton Dome, Wy., U.S.	A8	120
Hamilton Hotel, Austl.	D4	70
Hamilton Inlet, b., Nf., Can.	F21	96
Hamilton Sound, strt., Nf., Can.	C19	106
Hamina, Fin.	K20	6
Hamiota, Mb., Can.	H14	104
Ḩāmir, Wādī, val., Asia	F7	48
Hamīrpur, India	H9	44
Hamlet, N.C., U.S.	E7	112
Hamlin, Tx., U.S.	G6	116
Hamlin, W.V., U.S.	I4	108
Hamm, Ger.	D7	10
Hammamet, Alg.	N2	18
Hammamet, Tun.	M5	18
Hammamet, Golfe de, b., Tun.	M5	18
Hammam Lif, Tun.	M5	18
Ḩammār, Hawr al-, l., Iraq	F9	48
Hamme, Bel.	F5	12
Hammerdal, Swe.	J14	6
Hammerfest, Nor.	F18	6
Hammon, Ok., U.S.	D7	116
Hammond, In., U.S.	A9	114
Hammond, La., U.S.	L6	114
Hammond, Wi., U.S.	F3	110
Hammondsport, N.Y., U.S.	E9	108
Hammonton, N.J., U.S.	H12	108
Hamoyet, Jabal, mtn., Afr.	I10	60
Hampden, Me., U.S.	C18	108
Hampden, N.D., U.S.	C9	118
Hampden, Nf., Can.	C17	106
Hampden Sydney, Va., U.S.	B8	112
Hampshire, Il., U.S.	H7	110
Hampshire, co., Eng., U.K.	J12	8
Hampstead, N.C., U.S.	E9	112
Hampton, Ar., U.S.	I4	114
Hampton, Fl., U.S.	J4	112
Hampton, Ga., U.S.	F2	112
Hampton, Ia., U.S.	H2	110
Hampton, N.B., Can.	G8	106
Hampton, Ne., U.S.	K10	118
Hampton, N.H., U.S.	E16	108
Hampton, N.J., U.S.	G12	108
Hampton, S.C., U.S.	G5	112
Hampton, Tn., U.S.	C4	112
Hampton, Va., U.S.	B10	112
Hampton Bays, N.Y., U.S.	G14	108
Hampton Butte, mtn., Or., U.S.	G5	122
Hamra, As Saquia al, val., W. Sah.	G4	62
Hams Fork, stm., Wy., U.S.	C6	120
Hamyang, S. Kor.	H15	32
Han, stm., China	E9	30
Hana, Hi., U.S.	q18	125a
Hanahan, S.C., U.S.	G6	112
Hanamaki, Japan	H16	36
Hanapepe, Hi., U.S.	p14	125a
Hanau, Ger.	E8	10
Hanbury, stm., N.T., Can.	D11	96
Hancavičy, Bela.	I9	22
Hâncești, Mol.	C12	20
Hanceville, Al., U.S.	H10	114
Hanceville, B.C., Can.	F11	102
Hancheng, China	D9	30
Hancock, Md., U.S.	H8	108
Hancock, Mi., U.S.	C7	110
Hancock, Mn., U.S.	F12	118
Hancock, N.Y., U.S.	F11	108
Hancock, Wi., U.S.	F6	110
Handa, Japan	M11	36
Handa, Som.	F11	56
Handan, China	G2	32
Handsworth, Sk., Can.	I11	104
Handub, Sudan	H9	60
HaNegev (Negev Desert), reg., Isr.	G3	50
Haney, B.C., Can.	H12	102
Hanford, Ca., U.S.	H6	124
Han'gang, China	I2	32
Han-gang, stm., Asia	F14	32
Hangchow see Hangzhou, China	E9	34
Hanggin Houqi, China	C8	30
Hanggin Qi, China	D8	30
Hangö (Hanko), Fin.	L18	6
Hangu, China	D5	32
Hangu, Pak.	D4	44
Hangzhou (Hangchow), China	E9	34
Hangzhou Wan (Hangchow Bay), b., China	E10	34
Hani, Tur.	B6	48
Hanīsh, is., Yemen	H3	47
Hanita, Isr.	B4	50
Hanjiang, China	J8	34
Hankey, S. Afr.	I7	66
Hankinson, N.D., U.S.	E11	118
Hanko see Hangö, Fin.	D12	4
Hankow see Wuhan, China	E3	34
Hanley, Sk., Can.	G8	104
Hanmer, On., Can.	D15	110
Hanna, Ab., Can.	F23	102
Hanna, Ok., U.S.	D11	116
Hanna, Wy., U.S.	C10	120
Hanna City, Il., U.S.	J6	110
Hannaford, N.D., U.S.	D9	118
Hannah, N.D., U.S.	C9	118
Hannah Bay, b., On., Can.	F17	96
Hannibal, Mo., U.S.	C5	114
Hannover, Ger.	C9	10
Ha Noi, Viet.	D8	40
Hanover see Hannover, Ger.	C9	10
Hanover, Il., U.S.	H5	110
Hanover, In., U.S.	D11	114
Hanover, Ks., U.S.	L11	118
Hanover, N.H., U.S.	D14	108
Hanover, N.M., U.S.	L8	120
Hanover, On., Can.	F14	110
Hanover, Pa., U.S.	H10	108
Hanover, Va., U.S.	B9	112
Hansard, B.C., Can.	C13	102
Hānsi, India	F6	44
Hanska, Mn., U.S.	G13	118
Hanson Lake, l., Sk., Can.	D12	104
Hant's Harbour, Nf., Can.	D20	106
Hantsport, N.S., Can.	H9	106
Hantzsch, stm., N.T., Can.	C18	96
Hanumangarh, India	F6	44
Hanušovice, Czech Rep.	E16	10
Hanwood, Austl.	J7	70
Hanzhong, China	E8	30
Hanzhuang, China	I5	32
Haohekou, China	G1	34
Hāora, India	I13	44
Hapeville, Ga., U.S.	F2	112
Happy, Tx., U.S.	E5	116
Happy Camp, Ca., U.S.	C2	124
Happy Jack, Az., U.S.	J5	120
Happy Valley-Goose Bay, Nf., Can.	F20	96
Hāpur, India	F7	44
Haquira, Peru	F5	82
Harad, Sau. Ar.	B6	47
Harad, Jabal al-, mtn., Jord.	I5	50
Haradok, Bela.	F12	22
Haradzeja, Bela.	H9	22
Haradzišča, Bela.	H9	22
Harany, Bela.	F12	22
Harare (Salisbury), Zimb.	B10	66
Ḩarash, Bi'r al-, well, Libya	E2	60
Harbavičy, Bela.	H13	22
Harbin, China	B12	30
Harbor, Or., U.S.	H1	122
Harbor Beach, Mi., U.S.	G13	110
Harbor Springs, Mi., U.S.	E11	110
Harbour Breton, Nf., Can.	E18	106
Harbour Buffett, Nf., Can.	E19	106
Harbour Deep, Nf., Can.	B17	106
Harbour Grace, Nf., Can.	E20	106
Harbourville, N.S., Can.	G9	106
Harcuvar Mountains, mts., Az., U.S.	K3	120
Harda, India	I7	44
Hardangerfjorden, Nor.	K10	6
Hardeeville, S.C., U.S.	G5	112
Harderwijk, Neth.	D8	12
Hardesty, Ok., U.S.	C5	116
Hardin, Il., U.S.	C6	114
Hardin, Mt., U.S.	E18	122
Harding, S. Afr.	H9	66
Harding Lake, l., Mb., Can.	B16	104
Hardinsburg, Ky., U.S.	E10	114
Hardisty, Ab., Can.	E23	102
Hardisty Lake, l., N.T., Can.	D9	96
Hardoi, India	G9	44
Hardtner, Ks., U.S.	N9	118
Hardwick, Ga., U.S.	F3	112
Hardwick, Vt., U.S.	C14	108
Hardwood, La., U.S.	L5	114
Hardy, Ar., U.S.	F5	114
Hardy, Ne., U.S.	K10	118
Hardy Bay, b., N.T., Can.	A9	96
Hare, Mount, mtn., Yk., Can.	C26	100
Hare Bay, Nf., Can.	D19	106
Hare Bay, b., Nf., Can.	A18	106
Hare Indian, stm., N.T., Can.	C31	100
Harer, Eth.	G9	56
Hareto, Eth.	M9	60
Hargeysa, Som.	G9	56
Harghita, co., Rom.	C9	20
Hargrave, stm., Mb., Can.	D15	104
Hargrave Lake, l., Mb., Can.	D15	104
Har Hu, l., China	D6	30
Hari, stm., Indon.	F3	38
Haría, Spain	n27	17b
Haridwār, India	F8	44
Harihar, India	E3	46
Haringvliet, strt., Neth.	E5	12
Harīrūd (Tedžen), stm., Asia	C16	48
Harkers Island, N.C., U.S.	E10	112
Harlan, Ia., U.S.	J12	118
Harlan, Ky., U.S.	C3	112
Harlan County Lake, res., Ne., U.S.	K8	118
Harlem, Fl., U.S.	M6	112
Harlem, Ga., U.S.	F4	112
Harlem, Mt., U.S.	B17	122
Harlingen, Neth.	B7	12
Harlingen, Tx., U.S.	M9	116
Harlowton, Mt., U.S.	D16	122
Harman, W.V., U.S.	I7	108
Harmanli, Bul.	H9	20
Harmony, In., U.S.	C9	114
Harmony, Mn., U.S.	G3	110
Harney Peak, mtn., S.D., U.S.	H4	118
Härnösand, Swe.	J15	6
Haro, Spain	C9	16
Haro, Cabo, c., Mex.	D4	90
Harper, Ks., U.S.	N9	118
Harper, Lib.	I6	64
Harper, Tx., U.S.	I7	116
Harqin Qi (Jinshan), China	B6	32
Harrān al-'Awāmid, Syria	B7	50
Harrell, Ar., U.S.	I4	114
Harricana, stm., Can.	F17	96
Harriman, Tn., U.S.	D2	112
Harrington, De., U.S.	I11	108
Harrington, Me., U.S.	C19	108
Harrington, Wa., U.S.	C7	122
Harris, Mn., U.S.	E3	110
Harris, Sk., Can.	G7	104
Harrisburg, Ar., U.S.	G6	114
Harrisburg, Il., U.S.	E8	114
Harrisburg, Ne., U.S.	J4	118
Harrisburg, Or., U.S.	F2	122
Harrisburg, Pa., U.S.	G10	108
Harrismith, S. Afr.	G9	66
Harrison, Ar., U.S.	F3	114
Harrison, Id., U.S.	C9	122
Harrison, Mi., U.S.	F11	110
Harrison, Ne., U.S.	I4	118
Harrison, Cape, c., Nf., Can.	F21	96
Harrisonburg, La., U.S.	K5	114
Harrisonburg, Va., U.S.	I8	108
Harrison Islands, is., N.T., Can.	C14	96
Harrison Lake, l., B.C., Can.	H13	102
Harrisonville, Mo., U.S.	D2	114
Harriston, Ms., U.S.	K5	114
Harriston, On., Can.	G15	110
Harrisville, Mi., U.S.	F12	110
Harrisville, N.Y., U.S.	C11	108
Harrisville, W.V., U.S.	H5	108
Harrodsburg, Ky., U.S.	E12	114
Harrogate, Eng., U.K.	G12	8
Harrold, Tx., U.S.	E7	116
Harrop Lake, l., Mb., Can.	F19	104
Harrow, On., Can.	H13	110
Harrowsmith, On., Can.	F19	110
Harry S. Truman Reservoir, res., Mo., U.S.	D3	114
Harsīn, Iran	D9	48
Hart, Mi., U.S.	G9	110
Hart, Tx., U.S.	E4	116
Hart, stm., Yk., Can.	D26	100
Hart, Lake, l., Austl.	H2	70
Hartberg, Aus.	H15	10
Hartford, Al., U.S.	K11	114
Hartford, Ar., U.S.	G2	114
Hartford, Ct., U.S.	F14	108
Hartford, Ks., U.S.	M12	118
Hartford, Ky., U.S.	E9	114
Hartford, Mi., U.S.	H9	110
Hartford, S.D., U.S.	H11	118
Hartford City, In., U.S.	B11	114
Hartington, Ne., U.S.	I10	118
Hartland, Me., U.S.	C17	108
Hartland, N.B., Can.	F6	106
Hartlepool, Eng., U.K.	G12	8
Hartley, Ia., U.S.	H12	118
Hartley, Tx., U.S.	D4	116
Hartley Bay, B.C., Can.	D5	102
Hart Mountain, mtn., Mb., Can.	F13	104
Hartney, Mb., Can.	I14	104
Harts, stm., S. Afr.	G7	66
Hartselle, Al., U.S.	H10	114
Hartshorne, Ok., U.S.	E11	116
Hartsville, S.C., U.S.	E6	112
Hartsville, Tn., U.S.	F10	114
Hartville, Mo., U.S.	E4	114
Hartwell, Ga., U.S.	E4	112
Hartwell Lake, res., U.S.	E4	112
Harvard, Il., U.S.	H7	110
Harvard, Ne., U.S.	K9	118
Harvey, Il., U.S.	I8	110
Harvey, N.B., Can.	G9	106
Harvey, N.D., U.S.	D8	118
Harwich, Eng., U.K.	J15	8
Haryāna, state, India	F7	44
Harz, mts., Ger.	D10	10
Ḩaṣāh, Bi'r al-, well, Sudan	J3	48
Hasan Kīādeh, Iran	C10	48
Ḩāṣbānī, Nahr al-, stm., Asia	B5	50
Hasenkamp, Arg.	F9	80
Hashā', Jabal al-, mtn., Yemen	H4	47
Hāsilpur, Pak.	F5	44
Haskell, Ok., U.S.	D11	116
Haskell, Tx., U.S.	F7	116
Haskovo, Bul.	H9	20
Hasperos Canyon, val., N.M., U.S.	K11	120
Hassan, India	F4	46
Hasselt, Bel.	G7	12
Hassi Bel Guebbour, Alg.	F14	62
Hassi el Ghella, Alg.	J10	16
Hassi Mameche, Alg.	J12	16
Hassi Messaoud, Alg.	E13	62
Hassi Zehana, Alg.	J11	16
Hässleholm, Swe.	M13	6
Hastings, Eng., U.K.	K14	8
Hastings, Fl., U.S.	J5	112
Hastings, Mi., U.S.	H10	110
Hastings, Mn., U.S.	F3	110
Hastings, Ne., U.S.	K9	118
Hastings, N.Z.	C6	72
Hastings, On., Can.	F18	110
Hasty, Co., U.S.	M5	118
Haswell, Co., U.S.	M4	118
Hatay, Tur.	C4	48
Hatch, N.M., U.S.	L9	120
Hatch, Ut., U.S.	G4	120
Hatchet Lake, N.S., Can.	H10	106
Hatchie, stm., U.S.	G7	114
Hatfield, Ar., U.S.	H2	114
Hatfield, Ma., U.S.	E14	108
Hāthras, India	G8	44
Ha Tien, Viet.	I8	40
Ha Tinh, Viet.	E8	40
Hato Mayor [del Rey], Dom. Rep.	E10	94
Hatteras, N.C., U.S.	D11	112
Hatteras, Cape, c., N.C., U.S.	D11	112
Hatteras Island, i., N.C., U.S.	D11	112
Hattiesburg, Ms., U.S.	K7	114
Hatton, Al., U.S.	H9	114
Hatton, N.D., U.S.	D10	118
Hatvan, Hung.	H19	10
Hat Yai, Thai.	K6	40
Haubstadt, In., U.S.	D9	114
Hauge, Nor.	L10	6
Haugesund, Nor.	L9	6
Haugsdorf, Aus.	G16	10
Haultain, stm., Sk., Can.	B8	104
Hauraki Gulf, b., N.Z.	B5	72
Haut Atlas, mts., Mor.	E7	62
Haute-Corse, dept., Fr.	I24	15a
Haute-Garonne, dept., Fr.	I8	14
Haute-Loire, dept., Fr.	G10	14
Haute-Marne, dept., Fr.	D12	14
Hauterive, P.Q., Can.	C5	106
Hautes-Alpes, dept., Fr.	H13	14
Haute-Saône, dept., Fr.	E13	14
Haute-Savoie, dept., Fr.	F13	14
Hautes Fagnes, mts., Eur.	E6	10
Hautes-Pyrénées, dept., Fr.	I7	14
Haute-Vienne, dept., Fr.	G8	14
Haut-Folin, mtn., Fr.	E11	14
Hautmont, Fr.	B10	14
Haut-Rhin, dept., Fr.	E14	14
Hauula, Hi., U.S.	p16	125a
Havana, Ar., U.S.	G3	114
Havana see La Habana, Cuba	C3	94
Havana, Fl., U.S.	I2	112
Havana, Il., U.S.	B6	114
Havana, N.D., U.S.	F10	118
Havasu, Lake, res., U.S.	J2	120
Havelock, N.C., U.S.	E10	112
Havelock, On., Can.	F18	110
Haven, Ks., U.S.	N10	118
Haverhill, Ma., U.S.	E15	108
Hāveri, India	E3	46
Haviland, Ks., U.S.	N8	118
Havířov, Czech Rep.	F18	10
Havlíčkův Brod, Czech Rep.	F15	10
Havre, Mt., U.S.	B16	122
Havre-Aubert, P.Q., Can.	E12	106
Havre Aubert, Île du, i., P.Q., Can.	E12	106
Havre aux Maisons, Île du, i., P.Q., Can.	E12	106
Havre de Grace, Md., U.S.	H10	108
Havre North, Mt., U.S.	B16	122
Havre-Saint-Pierre, P.Q., Can.	B10	106
Havsa, Tur.	H10	20
Haw, stm., N.C., U.S.	D7	112
Hawaii, state, U.S.	q16	125a
Hawaii, i., Hi., U.S.	r18	125a
Hawaiian Islands, is., Hi., U.S.	q16	125a
Hawaiian Ridge	F22	126
Hawaii Volcanoes National Park, Hi., U.S.	r18	125a
Hawarden, Ia., U.S.	I11	118
Hawarden, Sk., Can.	G8	104
Hawea, Lake, l., N.Z.	F2	72
Hawera, N.Z.	C5	72
Hawesville, Ky., U.S.	E10	114
Hawi, Hi., U.S.	q18	125a
Hawick, Scot., U.K.	F11	8
Hawke, Cape, c., Austl.	I10	70
Hawke Bay, b., N.Z.	C6	72
Hawker, Austl.	H3	70
Hawkes, Mount, mtn., Ant.	D1	73
Hawkesbury, On., Can.	B12	108
Hawkesbury Island, i., B.C., Can.	D5	102
Hawkins, Tx., U.S.	G11	116
Hawkins, Wi., U.S.	E5	110
Hawkinsville, Ga., U.S.	G3	112
Hawk Junction, On., Can.	B11	110
Hawk Lake, On., Can.	I21	104
Hawksbill, mtn., Va., U.S.	I8	108
Hawks Nest Point, c., Bah.	B7	94
Hawley, Mn., U.S.	E11	118
Hawley, Pa., U.S.	F11	108
Hawthorne, Fl., U.S.	J4	112
Hawthorne, Nv., U.S.	F7	124
Ḩawwārah, Jord.	C5	50
Hawza, W. Sah.	G5	62
Hawzen, Eth.	K10	60
Haxtun, Co., U.S.	K5	118
Hay, Austl.	J6	70
Hay, stm., Austl.	D2	70
Hay, stm., Can.	E9	96
Hay, stm., Wi., U.S.	E3	110
Hay, Cape, c., N.T., Can.	B10	96
Hay, Mount, mtn., N.A.	G26	100
Hayange, Fr.	C13	14
Haybān, Sudan	L6	60
Hayden, Az., U.S.	K6	120
Hayden, Co., U.S.	D9	120
Haydenville, Oh., U.S.	H4	108
Hayes, La., U.S.	L4	114
Hayes, stm., Mb., Can.	B22	104
Hayes, stm., N.T., Can.	C14	96
Hayes, Mount, mtn., Ak., U.S.	E21	100
Hayes Center, Ne., U.S.	K6	118
Hayesville, N.C., U.S.	D3	112
Hayesville, Or., U.S.	F3	122
Hayfield, Mn., U.S.	G3	110
Hayfork, Ca., U.S.	D2	124
Haykota, Erit.	J9	60
Hay Lakes, Ab., Can.	D21	102
Haymana, Tur.	B2	48
Haynes, Ar., U.S.	H6	114
Haynesville, La., U.S.	J3	114
Hayneville, Al., U.S.	J10	114
Hay River, N.T., Can.	D9	96
Hays, Ab., Can.	G23	102
Hays, Ks., U.S.	M8	118
Hays, Mt., U.S.	C17	122
Hay Springs, Ne., U.S.	I5	118
Haystack Mountain, mtn., Nv., U.S.	C10	124
Haysville, Ks., U.S.	N10	118
Hayti, Mo., U.S.	F7	114
Hayti, S.D., U.S.	G10	118
Hayvoron, Ukr.	A13	20
Hayward, Ca., U.S.	G3	124
Hayward, Wi., U.S.	D4	110
Haywood, Mb., Can.	I16	104
Hazard, Ky., U.S.	B3	112
Hazārībāg, India	I11	44
Hazebrouck, Fr.	B9	14
Hazel, stm., Va., U.S.	I9	108
Hazel Green, Wi., U.S.	H5	110
Hazelton, B.C., Can.	B7	102
Hazelton, Id., U.S.	H11	122
Hazelton, N.D., U.S.	E7	118
Hazelton Mountains, mts., B.C., Can.	C6	102
Hazelwood, N.C., U.S.	D3	112
Hazen, Ar., U.S.	H5	114
Hazen, N.D., U.S.	D6	118
Hazlehurst, Ga., U.S.	H4	112
Hazlehurst, Ms., U.S.	K6	114
Hazlet, Sk., Can.	H6	104
Hazleton, Ia., U.S.	H4	110
Hazleton, Pa., U.S.	G11	108
Ḩaẓor HaGelilit, Isr.	C5	50
Head Bay d'Espoir, Nf., Can.	E18	106
Headland, Al., U.S.	K11	114
Headley, Mount, mtn., Mt., U.S.	C10	122
Healdsburg, Ca., U.S.	F3	124
Healdton, Ok., U.S.	E9	116
Healesville, Austl.	K6	70
Healy, Ak., U.S.	E20	100
Healy, Ks., U.S.	M7	118
Heany Junction, Zimb.	C9	66
Heard Island, i., Austl.	N11	126
Hearne, Tx., U.S.	I10	116
Hearst, On., Can.	G16	96
Hearst Island, i., Ant.	B12	73
Heart, stm., Ab., Can.	A17	102
Heart, stm., N.D., U.S.	E6	118
Heart Lake, l., Ab., Can.	B23	102
Heart Lake Indian Reserve, Ab., Can.	B23	102
Heart's Content, Nf., Can.	E20	106
Heath, stm., S.A.	E7	82
Heath, Pointe, c., P.Q., Can.	C12	106
Heathcote, Austl.	K6	70
Heath Springs, S.C., U.S.	E6	112
Heathsville, Va., U.S.	B10	112
Heavener, Ok., U.S.	H2	114
Hebbronville, Tx., U.S.	L8	116
Hebei (Hopeh), prov., China	D10	30
Heber, Az., U.S.	J6	120
Heber, Ca., U.S.	L10	124
Heber City, Ut., U.S.	D5	120
Heber Springs, Ar., U.S.	G4	114
Hebi, China	H2	32
Hebrides, is., Scot., U.K.	D6	4
Hebron, Il., U.S.	H7	110
Hebron, In., U.S.	A9	114
Hebron, Md., U.S.	I11	108
Hebron, N.D., U.S.	E5	118
Hebron, Ne., U.S.	K10	118
Hebron, Nf., Can.	E20	96
Hebron see Al-Khalīl, W.B.	E4	50
Hebu, China	H4	34
Hecate Strait, strt., B.C., Can.	D3	102
Hecelchakán, Mex.	G14	90
Hechi, China	B10	40
Hechingen, Ger.	G8	10
Hechuan, China	E8	30
Hecla, Mb., Can.	G18	104
Hecla, S.D., U.S.	F9	118
Hecla Island, i., Mb., Can.	G18	104
Hecla Provincial Park, Mb., Can.	G18	104
Hectanooga, N.S., Can.	H7	106
Hector, Mn., U.S.	G13	118
Hédé, Fr.	D5	14
He Devil, mtn., Id., U.S.	E9	122
Hedian, China	C3	34
Hedley, B.C., Can.	H14	102
Hedley, Tx., U.S.	E6	116
Hedmark, co., Nor.	K12	6
Hedrick, Ia., U.S.	I3	110
Heerenveen, Neth.	C8	12
Heerlen, Neth.	G8	12
Ḩefa (Haifa), Isr.	C4	50
Hefei, China	D6	34
Heflin, Al., U.S.	I11	114
Hegang, China	B13	30
Heho, Myan.	D4	40
Heichengzi, China	A9	32
Heide, Ger.	A9	10
Heidelberg, Ger.	F8	10
Heidelberg, Ms., U.S.	K8	114
Heidelberg, S. Afr.	J5	66
Heidelberg, S. Afr.	F9	66
Heidenheim, Ger.	F10	10
Heidenreichstein, Aus.	G15	10
Heilbad Heiligenstadt, Ger.	D10	10
Heilbron, S. Afr.	F8	66
Heilbronn, Ger.	F9	10
Heilin, China	H6	32
Heilong (Amur), stm., Asia	A12	30
Heilongjiang (Heilungkiang), prov., China	B12	30
Heimaey, i., Ice.	C3	6a
Heirnkut, Myan.	H16	44
Heishan, China	B10	32
Heishantou, China	A13	32
Heisler, Ab., Can.	E22	102
Hejian, China	E4	32
Hekla, vol., Ice.	C4	6a
Hekou, China	C7	40
Hel, Pol.	A18	10
Helen, Mount, mtn., Austl.	C4	70
Helena, Ar., U.S.	H6	114
Helena, Mt., U.S.	D13	122
Helena, Ok., U.S.	C8	116
Helensburgh, Scot., U.K.	E9	8
Helgoland, i., Ger.	A7	10
Helgoländer Bucht, b., Ger.	A8	10
Heliuji, China	B5	34
Hellertown, Pa., U.S.	G11	108
Hellín, Spain	G10	16
Hell Point, c., N.S., Can.	H9	106
Hells Canyon, val., U.S.	E9	122
Hells Gate, val., B.C., Can.	H13	102
Hell-Ville, Madag.	n23	67b
Helmand, stm., Asia	D1	44
Helmcken Falls, wtfl, B.C., Can.	F14	102
Helmond, Neth.	F8	12
Helmstedt, Ger.	C11	10
Helper, Ut., U.S.	E6	120
Helsingborg, Swe.	M13	6
Helsingfors see Helsinki, Fin.	K19	6
Helsingør (Elsinore), Den.	M13	6
Helsinki (Helsingfors), Fin.	K19	6
Helska, Mierzeja, spit, Pol.	A18	10
Helvecia, Arg.	F8	80
Hemau, Ger.	F11	10
Hemel Hempstead, Eng., U.K.	J13	8
Hemet, Ca., U.S.	K9	124
Hemford, N.S., Can.	H9	106
Hemingford, Ne., U.S.	I4	118
Hemingway, S.C., U.S.	F7	112
Hemphill, Tx., U.S.	K3	114
Hempstead, Tx., U.S.	I10	116
Hemujing, China	F3	32
Henan (Honan), prov., China	E9	30
Henderson, Arg.	I8	80
Henderson, Ky., U.S.	E9	114
Henderson, Mn., U.S.	F2	110
Henderson, N.C., U.S.	C8	112
Henderson, Ne., U.S.	K10	118
Henderson, Nv., U.S.	H11	124
Henderson, Tn., U.S.	G8	114
Henderson, Tx., U.S.	J2	114
Henderson Island, i., Pit.	K27	126
Hendersonville, N.C., U.S.	D4	112
Hendersonville, Tn., U.S.	F10	114
Hendījān, Iran	F10	48
Hendricks, Mn., U.S.	G11	118
Hendricks, W.V., U.S.	H7	108
Henefer, Ut., U.S.	C5	120
Hengdaohe, China	A11	32
Hengelo, Neth.	D10	12
Henggang, China	F4	34
Hengshan, China	D8	30
Hengshan, China	H1	34
Hengshui, China	F3	32
Hengxian, China	C10	40
Hengyang, China	F9	30
Henlopen, Cape, c., De., U.S.	I11	108
Hennaya, Alg.	K10	16
Hennebont, Fr.	E3	14
Hennef, Ger.	E7	10
Hennenman, S. Afr.	F8	66
Hennepin, Il., U.S.	I6	110
Hennessey, Ok., U.S.	C9	116
Henniker, N.H., U.S.	D15	108
Henning, Mn., U.S.	E12	118
Henning, Tn., U.S.	G7	114
Henri, Cap, c., P.Q., Can.	C9	106
Henri-Chapelle (Hendrik-Kapelle), Bel.	G8	12
Henrietta, N.C., U.S.	D5	112
Henrietta, N.Y., U.S.	D9	108
Henrietta, Tx., U.S.	F8	116
Henrietta Maria, Cape, c., On., Can.	E16	96
Henri Pittier, Parque Nacional, Ven.	B9	84
Henry, Il., U.S.	I6	110
Henry, S.D., U.S.	G10	118
Henry, Cape, c., Va., U.S.	C10	112
Henry, Mount, mtn., Mt., U.S.	B10	122
Henryetta, Ok., U.S.	D11	116
Henry Kater, Cape, c., N.T., Can.	C19	96
Henrys Fork, stm., U.S.	C6	120
Hensall, On., Can.	G14	110
Hensley, Ar., U.S.	H4	114
Hentiesbaai, Nmb.	D2	66
Henty, Austl.	J7	70
Henzada, Myan.	F3	40
Hepburn, Sk., Can.	F8	104
Hephzibah, Ga., U.S.	F4	112
Heping, China	K3	34
Heppenheim, Ger.	F8	10
Heppner, Or., U.S.	E6	122
Hepu (Lianzhou), China	D10	40
Heqiao, China	D8	34
Herāt, Afg.	D17	48
Hérault, dept., Fr.	I10	14
Herbert, Sk., Can.	H7	104
Herbert, stm., Austl.	B6	70
Herberton, Austl.	A6	70
Herbignac, Fr.	E4	14
Herb Lake, Mb., Can.	D15	104
Herblet Lake, l., Mb., Can.	D15	104
Herceg-Novi, Yugo.	G2	20
Herculaneum, Mo., U.S.	D6	114
Hércules, Mex.	C8	90
Heredia, C.R.	G10	92
Heredia, prov., C.R.	G10	92
Hereford, Az., U.S.	M6	120
Hereford, Tx., U.S.	E4	116
Hereford and Worcester, co., Eng., U.K.	I11	8
Herencia, Spain	F8	16
Herentals, Bel.	F6	12
Herford, Ger.	C8	10
Hergla, Tun.	M5	18
Herington, Ks., U.S.	M11	118
Herisau, Switz.	D11	13
Herkimer, N.Y., U.S.	D12	108
Herleshausen, Ger.	D10	10
Herlong, Ca., U.S.	D5	124
Herman, Mn., U.S.	F11	118
Herman, Ne., U.S.	J11	118
Hermann, Mo., U.S.	D5	114
Hermansville, Mi., U.S.	E8	110
Hermanus, S. Afr.	J4	66
Hermanville, Ms., U.S.	K6	114
Hermiston, Or., U.S.	E6	122
Hermitage, Ar., U.S.	I4	114
Hermitage, Mo., U.S.	E3	114
Hermitage, Nf., Can.	E18	106
Hermitage Bay, b., Nf., Can.	E17	106
Hermleigh, Tx., U.S.	G6	116
Hermon, Mount see Shaykh, Jabal ash-, mtn., Asia	B5	50
Hermosillo, Mex.	C4	90
Hermoso, Cerro, mtn., Ec.	H3	84
Hernád, stm., Eur.	G21	10
Hernandarias, Para.	C11	80
Hernando, Arg.	G7	80
Hernando, Fl., U.S.	K4	112
Hernando, Ms., U.S.	H7	114
Herndon, Ks., U.S.	L7	118
Herndon, Pa., U.S.	G10	108
Heroica Zitácuaro, Mex.	H9	90
Heron Island, i., Austl.	D9	70
Heron Lake, Mn., U.S.	H12	118
Herradura, Arg.	D9	80
Herreid, S.D., U.S.	F7	118
Herrera, Arg.	E7	80
Herrera, prov., Pan.	I14	92
Herrick Creek, stm., B.C., Can.	C13	102
Herrin, Il., U.S.	E7	114
Herring Cove, Ak., U.S.	I29	100
Herring Cove, N.S., Can.	H10	106
Herschel, Sk., Can.	G6	104
Herschel Island, i., Yk., Can.	B25	100
Herscher, Il., U.S.	I7	110
Hershey, Ne., U.S.	J6	118
Hershey, Pa., U.S.	G10	108
Herstal, Bel.	G8	12
Hertford, N.C., U.S.	C10	112
Hertfordshire, co., Eng., U.K.	J13	8
Hervey Bay, b., Austl.	E10	70
Herzberg, Ger.	D13	10
Herzberg [am Harz], Ger.	D10	10
Herzliyya, Isr.	D3	50
Hesdin, Fr.	B9	14
Heshangqiao, China	A2	34
Heshi, China	J7	34
Heshuijian, China	E5	34
Hesperia, Mi., U.S.	G9	110
Hesperus Mountain, mtn., Co., U.S.	G8	120
Hess, stm., Yk., Can.	E28	100
Hessen, state, Ger.	E9	10
Hesston, Ks., U.S.	M10	118
Hetang, China	I8	34
Hetch Hetchy Aqueduct, Ca., U.S.	G4	124
Hetou, China	K2	34
Hettinger, N.D., U.S.	E5	118
Hettstedt, Ger.	D11	10
Hetupu, China	E5	34
Heuvelton, N.Y., U.S.	C11	108
Heves, Hung.	H20	10
Heves, co., Hung.	H20	10
Ḩevron, Naḩal, val., Asia	F3	50
Hexi, China	K6	34
Hexian, China	G9	30
Heyang, China	H6	32
Heyburn, Id., U.S.	H12	122
Heywood, Austl.	L4	70
Heyworth, Il., U.S.	B8	114
Heze (Caozhou), China	F9	32
Hezhen, China	F8	34
Hialeah, Fl., U.S.	N6	112
Hiawassee, Ga., U.S.	E3	112

Name	Map Ref.	Page
Hiawatha, Ks., U.S.	L12	118
Hiawatha, Ut., U.S.	E5	120
Hibbing, Mn., U.S.	C3	110
Hibbs, Point, c., Austl.	N6	70
Hibernia Reef, rf., Austl.	B4	68
Hickman, Ky., U.S.	F7	114
Hickman, Ne., U.S.	K11	118
Hickman's Harbour, Nf., Can.	D20	106
Hickory, Ms., U.S.	J7	114
Hickory, N.C., U.S.	D5	112
Hickory Flat, Ms., U.S.	H7	114
Hicks, Point, c., Austl.	K8	70
Hickson Lake, l., Sk., Can.	B10	104
Hicksville, Oh., U.S.	F2	108
Hico, Tx., U.S.	H8	116
Hidalgo, Mex.	D10	90
Hidalgo, Mex.	E9	90
Hidalgo, Mex.	E10	90
Hidalgo, Mex.	F8	90
Hidalgo, state, Mex.	G10	90
Hidalgo del Parral, Mex.	D7	90
Hida-sammyaku, mts., Japan	K12	36
Hidrolândia, Braz.	D4	79
Hidrolina, Braz.	C4	79
Hieflau, Aus.	H14	10
Higashine, Japan	I15	36
Higashiōsaka, Japan	M10	36
Higbee, Mo., U.S.	C4	114
Higgins, Tx., U.S.	C6	116
Higginsville, Mo., U.S.	C3	114
High Bar Indian Reserve, B.C., Can.	F13	102
High Hill, stm., Can.	B4	104
High Hill, stm., Mb., Can.	C20	104
High Hill Lake, l., Mb., Can.	C19	104
Highland, Ca., U.S.	J8	124
Highland, Il., U.S.	D7	114
Highland, In., U.S.	A9	114
Highland, Ks., U.S.	L12	118
Highland, prov., Scot., U.K.	D8	8
Highland Home, Al., U.S.	K10	114
Highland Park, Il., U.S.	H8	110
Highland Park, Tx., U.S.	G10	116
Highlands, N.C., U.S.	D3	112
Highlands, N.J., U.S.	G13	108
Highlands, Tx., U.S.	J11	116
Highland Springs, Va., U.S.	B9	112
Highmore, S.D., U.S.	G8	118
High Point, N.C., U.S.	D6	112
High Point, mtn., N.J., U.S.	F12	108
High Prairie, Ab., Can.	B18	102
High River, Ab., Can.	G21	102
Highrock Indian Reserve, Mb., Can.	C14	104
Highrock Lake, l., Mb., Can.	C14	104
Highrock Lake, l., Sk., Can.	A9	104
High Rock Lake, res., N.C., U.S.	D6	112
High Springs, Fl., U.S.	J4	112
Hightstown, N.J., U.S.	G12	108
Highwood, Mt., U.S.	C15	122
Highwood, stm., Ab., Can.	G20	102
High Wycombe, Eng., U.K.	J13	8
Higuera de Abuya, Mex.	E6	90
Higuera de Zaragoza, Mex.	E5	90
Higüero, Punta, c., P.R.	E11	94
Higüey, Dom. Rep.	E10	94
Higuito, stm., Hond.	C6	92
Hiiumaa, i., Est.	C5	22
Hikone, Japan	L11	36
Hilbert, Wi., U.S.	F7	110
Hilda, Ab., Can.	H4	104
Hildburghausen, Ger.	E10	10
Hildesheim, Ger.	C9	10
Hildreth, Ne., U.S.	K8	118
Hillaby, Mount, mtn., Barb.	H15	94
Hill Bank, Belize	I15	90
Hill City, Ks., U.S.	L8	118
Hill City, Mn., U.S.	D2	110
Hill City, S.D., U.S.	H4	118
Hillcrest Center, Ca., U.S.	I7	124
Hillcrest Mines, Ab., Can.	H20	102
Hilli, Bngl.	H13	44
Hilliard, Fl., U.S.	I5	112
Hill Island Lake, l., N.T., Can.	D11	96
Hillister, Tx., U.S.	L2	114
Hillman, Mi., U.S.	E12	110
Hills, Mn., U.S.	H11	118
Hillsboro, Il., U.S.	C7	114
Hillsboro, Ks., U.S.	M10	118
Hillsboro, Mo., U.S.	D6	114
Hillsboro, N.D., U.S.	D10	118
Hillsboro, N.H., U.S.	D15	108
Hillsboro, N.M., U.S.	L9	120
Hillsboro, Oh., U.S.	H3	108
Hillsboro, Or., U.S.	E3	122
Hillsboro, Tx., U.S.	G9	116
Hillsboro, Wi., U.S.	G5	110
Hillsboro Canal, Fl., U.S.	M6	112
Hillsborough, N.B., Can.	G9	106
Hillsborough, N.C., U.S.	C7	112
Hillsborough, stm., Fl., U.S.	K4	112
Hillsborough, Cape, c., Austl.	C8	70
Hillsborough Bay, b., P.E., Can.	F10	106
Hillsdale, Mi., U.S.	I11	110
Hillsdale Lake, res., Ks., U.S.	M13	118
Hillston, Austl.	I6	70
Hillsville, Va., U.S.	C6	112
Hilo, Hi., U.S.	r18	125a
Hilo Bay, b., Hi., U.S.	r18	125a
Hilton, N.Y., U.S.	D9	108
Hilton Head Island, i., S.C., U.S.	G6	112
Hilversum, Neth.	D7	12
Hima, Ky., U.S.	B3	112
Himāchal Pradesh, state, India	E7	44
Himalayas, mts., Asia	F11	44
Himeji, Japan	M9	36
Himi, Japan	K11	36
Ḥimṣ (Homs), Syria	D4	48
Hinche, Haiti	E8	94
Hinchinbrook Entrance, strt., Ak., U.S.	F21	100
Hinchinbrook Island, i., Ak., U.S.	F21	100
Hinchinbrook Island, i., Austl.	B7	70
Hinckley, Il., U.S.	I7	110
Hinckley, Mn., U.S.	D3	110
Hinckley, Ut., U.S.	E4	120
Hindaun, India	G7	44
Hindman, Ky., U.S.	B4	112
Hindmarsh, Lake, l., Austl.	K4	70
Hinds Lake, l., Nf., Can.	D17	106
Hindu Kush, mts., Asia	B4	44
Hindupur, India	F4	46
Hines, Or., U.S.	G6	122
Hines Creek, Ab., Can.	A16	102
Hines Creek, stm., Ab., Can.	A16	102
Hinesville, Ga., U.S.	H5	112
Hinganghāt, India	B5	46
Hingham, Ma., U.S.	E16	108
Hingol, stm., Pak.	H1	44
Hingoli, India	C4	46
Hınıs, Tur.	B6	48
Hinnøya, i., Nor.	G14	6
Hinojosa del Duque, Spain	G6	16
Hinsdale, Mt., U.S.	B18	122
Hinsdale, N.H., U.S.	E14	108
Hinterrhein, stm., Switz.	E11	13
Hinton, Ab., Can.	D17	102
Hinton, Ok., U.S.	D8	116
Hinton, W.V., U.S.	B6	112
Hipólito, Mex.	E9	90
Hipólito Yrigoyen, Arg.	G5	80
Hirado, Japan	N4	36
Hīrākud Reservoir, res., India	B7	46
Hiram, Me., U.S.	D16	108
Hirata, Japan	L7	36
Hiratsuka, Japan	L14	36
Hirhafok, Alg.	I13	62
Ḥirjillah, Syria	B6	50
Hirosaki, Japan	G15	36
Hiroshima, Japan	M7	36
Hirson, Fr.	C11	14
Hisār, India	F6	44
Ḥisbān, Jord.	E5	50
Ḥiṣn al-Qarn, Yemen	G6	47
Hispaniola, i., N.A.	E9	94
Hita, Japan	N5	36
Hitachi, Japan	K15	36
Hitchcock, Tx., U.S.	J11	116
Hitchins, Ky., U.S.	I4	108
Hitoyoshi, Japan	O5	36
Hitra, i., Nor.	J11	6
Hiva Oa, i., Fr. Poly.	I26	126
Hiwannee, Ms., U.S.	K8	114
Hiwassee, stm., U.S.	D2	112
Hixon, B.C., Can.	D12	102
Hixson, Tn., U.S.	G11	114
Hkakabo Razi, mtn., Myan.	F6	30
Hkok (Kok), stm., Asia	D5	40
Hlatikulu, Swaz.	F10	66
Hlegu, Myan.	F4	40
Hlinsko, Czech Rep.	F15	10
Hlobane, S. Afr.	F10	66
Hlohovec, Slvk.	G17	10
Hluboká nad Vltavou, Czech Rep.	F14	10
Hlučín, Czech Rep.	F18	10
Hluša, Bela.	H11	22
Hlusk, Bela.	I11	22
Hlyboka, Ukr.	A9	20
Hlybokae, Bela.	F10	22
Hmawbi, Myan.	F4	40
Ho, Ghana	H10	64
Hoa Binh, Viet.	D8	40
Hoare Bay, b., N.T., Can.	C20	96
Hoback, stm., Wy., U.S.	G15	122
Hobart, Austl.	N7	70
Hobart, Ok., U.S.	D7	116
Hobbs, N.M., U.S.	G3	116
Hobe Sound, Fl., U.S.	L6	112
Hobgood, N.C., U.S.	C9	112
Hobo, Col.	F5	84
Hoboken, Bel.	F5	12
Hobson, Mt., U.S.	C16	122
Hobson Lake, l., B.C., Can.	E14	102
Hobyo, Som.	G10	56
Hochalmspitze, mtn., Aus.	H13	10
Ho Chi Minh City see Thanh Pho Ho Chi Minh, Viet.	I9	40
Hochkönig, mtn., Aus.	H13	10
Höchstadt an der Aisch, Ger.	F10	10
Ḥocimsk, Bela.	H15	22
Hockenheim, Ger.	F8	10
Hocking, stm., Oh., U.S.	H5	108
Hodeida see Al-Ḥudaydah, Yemen	G3	47
Hodge, La., U.S.	J4	114
Hodgenville, Ky., U.S.	E11	114
Hodges Hill, hill, Nf., Can.	C18	106
Hodgeville, Sk., Can.	H8	104
Hodgson, Mb., Can.	G17	104
Hódmezővásárhely, Hung.	I20	10
Hodna, Chott el, l., Alg.	C13	62
Hodonín, Czech Rep.	G17	10
Hoehne, Co., U.S.	N3	118
Hoek van Holland, Neth.	E5	12
Hoeryŏng, N. Kor.	A17	32
Hoeyang, N. Kor.	E15	32
Hof, Ger.	E11	10
Hof, Ice.	B6	6a
Hoffman, Mn., U.S.	F12	118
Hofmeyr, S. Afr.	H7	66
Höfn, Ice.	B6	6a
Hofors, Swe.	K15	6
Hōfu, Japan	M6	36
Hofuf see Al-Hufūf, Sau. Ar.	I10	48
Hogansville, Ga., U.S.	F2	112
Hoggar see Ahaggar, mts., Alg.	I13	62
Högsby, Swe.	M15	6
Hoh, stm., Wa., U.S.	C1	122
Hohenau, Para.	D11	80
Hohenau an der March, Aus.	G16	10
Hohenthurn, Aus.	I13	10
Hohenwald, Tn., U.S.	G9	114
Hoher Dachstein, mtn., Aus.	H13	10
Hohe Tauern, mts., Aus.	H12	10
Hohhot, China	C9	30
Hohoe, Ghana	H10	64
Hoh Xil Shan, mts., China	C13	44
Hoi An, Viet.	G10	40
Hoisington, Ks., U.S.	M9	118
Hojāi, India	G15	44
Hokah, Mn., U.S.	G4	110
Hokes Bluff, Al., U.S.	I11	114
Hokitika, N.Z.	E3	72
Hokkaidō, i., Japan	d17	36a
Holberg, B.C., Can.	G6	102
Holbrook, Austl.	J7	70
Holbrook, Az., U.S.	J6	120
Holbrook, Ne., U.S.	K7	118
Holden, Ab., Can.	D22	102
Holden, Mo., U.S.	D3	114
Holden, Ut., U.S.	E4	120
Holden, W.V., U.S.	J4	108
Holdenville, Ok., U.S.	D10	116
Holder, Fl., U.S.	K4	112
Holdfast, Sk., Can.	H9	104
Holdingford, Mn., U.S.	E1	110
Holdrege, Ne., U.S.	K8	118
Hole in the Mountain Peak, mtn., Nv., U.S.	D10	124
Holgate, Oh., U.S.	F2	108
Holguín, Cuba	D6	94
Holíč, Slvk.	G17	10
Hollabrunn, Aus.	G16	10
Holladay, Ut., U.S.	D5	120
Holland, Mb., Can.	I16	104
Holland, Mi., U.S.	H9	110
Holland, Tx., U.S.	I9	116
Holland see Netherlands, ctry., Eur.	E9	4
Hollandale, Ms., U.S.	I6	114
Hollandsbird Island, i., Nmb.	E2	66
Hollandsch Diep, strt., Neth.	E5	12
Holley, N.Y., U.S.	D8	108
Holliday, Tx., U.S.	F8	116
Hollidaysburg, Pa., U.S.	G8	108
Hollins, Va., U.S.	B7	112
Hollis, Ok., U.S.	E7	116
Hollister, Ca., U.S.	H4	124
Hollow Rock, Tn., U.S.	F8	114
Holly, Co., U.S.	M5	118
Holly Grove, Ar., U.S.	H5	114
Holly Hill, Fl., U.S.	J5	112
Holly Hill, S.C., U.S.	F6	112
Holly Springs, Ms., U.S.	H7	114
Hollywood, Fl., U.S.	M6	112
Holman, N.T., Can.	B9	96
Holmen, Wi., U.S.	G4	110
Holmes, Mount, mtn., Wy., U.S.	F15	122
Holmes Lake, l., Mb., Can.	A18	104
Holmestrand, Nor.	L12	6
Holmia, Guy.	E13	84
Holod, Rom.	C6	20
Holoit, Punta, c., Mex.	G15	90
Ḥolon, Isr.	D3	50
Holoog, Nmb.	F3	66
Holovanivs'k, Ukr.	A14	20
Holstebro, Den.	M11	6
Holstein, Ia., U.S.	I12	118
Holston, stm., Tn., U.S.	C3	112
Holston High Knob, mtn., Tn., U.S.	C4	112
Holt, Al., U.S.	I9	114
Holt, Fl., U.S.	L10	114
Holt, Mi., U.S.	H11	110
Holton, Ks., U.S.	L12	118
Holts Summit, Mo., U.S.	D4	114
Holtville, Ca., U.S.	L10	124
Holy Cross, Ak., U.S.	E15	100
Holy Cross Mountain, mtn., B.C., Can.	D14	102
Holyoke, Co., U.S.	K5	118
Holyoke, Ma., U.S.	E14	108
Holyrood, Ks., U.S.	M9	118
Holzkirchen, Ger.	H11	10
Holzminden, Ger.	D9	10
Homalin, Myan.	B3	40
Homathko, stm., B.C., Can.	F10	102
Homathko Icefield, B.C., Can.	F10	102
Homberg, Ger.	D9	10
Hombori Tondo, mtn., Mali	D9	64
Hombre Muerto, Salar del, pl., Arg.	C5	80
Homburg see Bad Homburg vor der Höhe, Ger.	E8	10
Homburg, Ger.	F7	10
Home Bay, b., N.T., Can.	C19	96
Homedale, Id., U.S.	G9	122
Home Hill, Austl.	B7	70
Homel', Bela.	I14	22
Homeland Park, S.C., U.S.	E4	112
Homer, Ak., U.S.	G19	100
Homer, Ga., U.S.	E3	112
Homer, La., U.S.	J3	114
Homer, Mi., U.S.	H11	110
Homer, Ne., U.S.	I11	118
Homer, N.Y., U.S.	E10	108
Homer City, Pa., U.S.	G7	108
Homerville, Ga., U.S.	H4	112
Homestead, Fl., U.S.	N6	112
Homewood, Al., U.S.	I10	114
Hominy, Ok., U.S.	C10	116
Homochitto, stm., Ms., U.S.	K5	114
Homosassa, Fl., U.S.	K4	112
Homs see Al-Khums, Libya	B3	56
Homs see Ḥimṣ, Syria	D4	48
Honaker, Va., U.S.	B5	112
Honan see Henan, prov., China	E9	30
Honaz, Tur.	L13	20
Honda, Col.	E5	84
Honda, Bahía, b., Col.	A7	84
Hondeklipbaai, S. Afr.	H3	66
Hondo, Ab., Can.	B20	102
Hondo, N.M., U.S.	K11	120
Hondo, Tx., U.S.	J7	116
Hondo, stm., N.A.	H15	90
Hondo, Rio, stm., N.M., U.S.	F2	116
Hondsrug, hills, Neth.	C10	12
Honduras, ctry., N.A.	B8	92
Honduras, Cabo de, c., Hond.	A8	92
Honduras, Gulf of, b., N.A.	E7	88
Honduras, Port, b., Belize	A6	92
Honea Path, S.C., U.S.	E4	112
Hønefoss, Nor.	K12	6
Honesdale, Pa., U.S.	F11	108
Honey Grove, Tx., U.S.	F11	116
Honey Lake, l., Ca., U.S.	D5	124
Honeyville, Ut., U.S.	C4	120
Honfleur, Fr.	C7	14
Hong see Red, stm., Asia	C8	40
Hon Gai, Viet.	D9	40
Hong'an, China	D3	34
Hongch'ŏn, S. Kor.	F15	32
Hongcun, China	H5	34
Honghu, China	F2	34
Hongjiang, China	F8	30
Hong Kong, dep., Asia	G9	30
Honglai, China	J7	34
Hongliuyuan, China	C6	30
Honglu, China	J8	34
Hongmendu, China	A7	40
Hong Ngu, Viet.	I8	40
Hongshi, China	B7	32
Hongshui, stm., China	C10	40
Hongshuyangzi, China	C4	32
Hongsŏng, S. Kor.	G14	32
Hongtong, China	D9	30
Honguedo, Détroit d', strt., P.Q., Can.	C10	106
Hongwŏn, N. Kor.	C15	32
Hongxingqiao, China	E8	34
Hongyang, China	L5	34
Hongze Hu, l., China	B7	34
Honiara, Sol. Is.	I19	126
Honokaa, Hi., U.S.	q18	125a
Honolulu, Hi., U.S.	p16	125a
Honomu, Hi., U.S.	r18	125a
Hon Quan, Viet.	I9	40
Honshū, i., Japan	K13	36
Hood, stm., N.T., Can.	C10	96
Hood, Mount, mtn., Or., U.S.	E4	122
Hood Canal, b., Wa., U.S.	C2	122
Hoodoo Peak, mtn., Wa., U.S.	B5	122
Hood Point, c., Austl.	F3	68
Hood River, Or., U.S.	E4	122
Hoodsport, Wa., U.S.	C2	122
Hoods Range, mts., Austl.	G6	70
Hooker, Ok., U.S.	C5	116
Hookina, Austl.	H3	70
Hook Island, i., Austl.	C8	70
Hooks, Tx., U.S.	I2	114
Hoolehua, Hi., U.S.	p16	125a
Hoonah, Ak., U.S.	G27	100
Hoopa, Ca., U.S.	C2	124
Hooper, Ne., U.S.	J11	118
Hooper Bay, Ak., U.S.	F11	100
Hoopeston, Il., U.S.	J8	110
Hooping Harbour, Nf., Can.	B17	106
Hoople, N.D., U.S.	C10	118
Hoosick Falls, N.Y., U.S.	E13	108
Hoover Dam, U.S.	H2	120
Hooversville, Pa., U.S.	G8	108
Hopatcong, N.J., U.S.	G12	108
Hope, Ar., U.S.	I3	114
Hope, B.C., Can.	H13	102
Hope, In., U.S.	C11	114
Hope, N.D., U.S.	D10	118
Hope, Point, c., Ak., U.S.	B11	100
Hopedale, Il., U.S.	B7	114
Hopedale, La., U.S.	M7	114
Hopedale, Nf., Can.	E20	96
Hopefield, S. Afr.	I4	66
Hope Island, i., B.C., Can.	G7	102
Hopelchén, Mex.	H15	90
Hope Mills, N.C., U.S.	E8	112
Hopes Advance, Cap, c., P.Q., Can.	D19	96
Hopetoun, Austl.	F4	68
Hopetoun, Austl.	J5	70
Hopetown, S. Afr.	G7	66
Hope Valley, R.I., U.S.	F15	108
Hopewell, Va., U.S.	B9	112
Hopewell Islands, is., N.T., Can.	E17	96
Hopkins, Mi., U.S.	H10	110
Hopkins, Mo., U.S.	B2	114
Hopkinsville, Ky., U.S.	F9	114
Hopkinton, Ia., U.S.	H4	110
Hopland, Ca., U.S.	F2	124
Hopólito Bouchard, Arg.	H7	80
Hopwood, Mount, mtn., Austl.	C6	70
Hoquiam, Wa., U.S.	D2	122
Horancia, Eth.	N10	60
Horatio, Ar., U.S.	I2	114
Horconcitos, Pan.	I12	92
Hordaland, co., Nor.	K10	6
Horezu, Rom.	D7	20
Horgen, Switz.	D10	13
Horicon, Wi., U.S.	G7	110
Horizontina, Braz.	D11	80
Horki, Bela.	G13	22
Horlick Mountains, mts., Ant.	D10	73
Horlivka, Ukr.	H5	26
Hormuz, Strait of, strt., Asia	H14	48
Horn, Aus.	G15	10
Horn, c., Ice.	A2	6a
Horn, stm., N.T., Can.	D9	96
Horn, Cape see Hornos, Cabo de, c., Chile	H3	78
Hornaday, stm., N.T., Can.	B33	100
Hornbeak, Tn., U.S.	F7	114
Hornbeck, La., U.S.	K3	114
Hornbrook, Ca., U.S.	C3	124
Hornby Bay, b., N.T., Can.	C9	96
Hornell, N.Y., U.S.	E9	108
Hornepayne, On., Can.	G16	96
Horn Island, i., Ms., U.S.	L8	114
Hornito, Cerro, mtn., Pan.	I12	92
Horn Lake, Ms., U.S.	H6	114
Hornos, Cabo de (Cape Horn), c., Chile	H3	78
Horn Plateau, plat., N.T., Can.	D9	96
Horodenka, Ukr.	A9	20
Horodkivka, Ukr.	A12	20
Horodne, Ukr.	D12	20
Horqin Youyi Qianqi, China	B11	30
Horqueta, Para.	B10	80
Horse, stm., Ab., Can.	B3	104
Horse Cave, Ky., U.S.	E11	114
Horse Creek, Wy., U.S.	C11	120
Horsefly, B.C., Can.	E13	102
Horsefly Lake, l., B.C., Can.	E14	102
Horseheads, N.Y., U.S.	E10	108
Horse Islands, is., Nf., Can.	B18	106
Horsens, Den.	N11	6
Horseshoe Bend, Ar., U.S.	F5	114
Horseshoe Bend, Id., U.S.	G9	122
Horseshoe Lake, l., Mb., Can.	F19	104
Horse Shoe Reef, rf., Br. Vir. Is.	E12	94
Horsham, Austl.	K5	70
Horsham, Eng., U.K.	J13	8
Horst, Neth.	F9	12
Horton, Ks., U.S.	L12	118
Horton, stm., N.T., Can.	B31	100
Horton Lake, l., N.T., Can.	C33	100
Hortonville, Wi., U.S.	F7	110
Hosaina, Eth.	N9	60
Hoséré Vokré, mtn., Cam.	G9	54
Hosford, Fl., U.S.	I2	112
Hoshangābād, India	I7	44
Hoshiārpur, India	E6	44
Hosmer, B.C., Can.	H20	102
Hosmer, S.D., U.S.	F8	118
Hospers, Ia., U.S.	H12	118
Hospet, India	E4	46
Hossegor, Fr.	I5	14
Hosston, La., U.S.	J3	114
Hosta Butte, mtn., N.M., U.S.	I8	120
Hoste, Isla, i., Chile	H3	78
Hot, Thai.	E5	40
Hotan, China	D2	30
Hotan, stm., China	D3	30
Hotazel, S. Afr.	F6	66
Hotchkiss, Co., U.S.	F9	120
Hotevilla, Az., U.S.	I6	120
Hotham Inlet, b., Ak., U.S.	C14	100
Hot Springs, Mt., U.S.	C11	122
Hot Springs, N.C., U.S.	D4	112
Hot Springs see Truth or Consequences, N.M., U.S.	K9	120
Hot Springs, S.D., U.S.	H4	118
Hot Springs, Va., U.S.	B7	112
Hot Springs National Park, Ar., U.S.	H3	114
Hot Sulphur Springs, Co., U.S.	D10	120
Hottah Lake, l., N.T., Can.	C9	96
Hottentotbaai, b., Nmb.	F2	66
Houbao, China	B13	32
Houdan, Fr.	D8	14
Houghton, Mi., U.S.	C7	110
Houghton, N.Y., U.S.	E8	108
Houghton Lake, Mi., U.S.	F11	110
Houghton Lake, l., Mi., U.S.	F11	110
Houghton Lake, l., Sk., Can.	F9	104
Houjie, China	M2	34
Houlka, Ms., U.S.	H7	114
Houlton, Me., U.S.	A19	108
Houma, China	D9	30
Houma, La., U.S.	M6	114
Houndé, Burkina	F8	64
Housatonic, Ma., U.S.	E13	108
House, N.M., U.S.	E3	116
House, stm., Ab., Can.	C2	104
Houston, B.C., Can.	C8	102
Houston, Mn., U.S.	G4	110
Houston, Mo., U.S.	E5	114
Houston, Ms., U.S.	I8	114
Houston, Tx., U.S.	J11	116
Houston, stm., La., U.S.	L3	114
Houston, Lake, res., Tx., U.S.	J11	116
Houtman Abrolhos, is., Austl.	E2	68
Houtzdale, Pa., U.S.	G8	108
Houxijie, China	G7	34
Houxinqiu, China	A10	32
Hoven, S.D., U.S.	F8	118
Howar, Wādī (Ouadi Howa), val., Afr.	I3	60
Howard, Austl.	E10	70
Howard, Ks., U.S.	N11	118
Howard, Pa., U.S.	F9	108
Howard, S.D., U.S.	G10	118
Howard, Wi., U.S.	F7	110
Howard City, Mi., U.S.	G10	110
Howard Lake, Mn., U.S.	E1	110
Howe, In., U.S.	A11	114
Howe, Tx., U.S.	F10	116
Howe, Cape, c., Austl.	K8	70
Howeke, Lib.	I6	64
Howell, Mi., U.S.	H12	110
Howells, Ne., U.S.	J10	118
Howe Sound, strt., B.C., Can.	H11	102
Howick, S. Afr.	G10	66
Howitt, Mount, mtn., Austl.	K7	70
Howland, Me., U.S.	B18	108
Howland Island, i., Oc.	H22	126
Howley, Nf., Can.	C16	106
Howley, Mount, mtn., Nf., Can.	D15	106
Howse Peak, mtn., Can.	F18	102
Howser, B.C., Can.	G18	102
Howson Peak, mtn., B.C., Can.	C7	102
Hoxie, Ar., U.S.	F6	114
Hoxie, Ks., U.S.	L7	118
Höxter, Ger.	D9	10
Høyanger, Nor.	K10	6
Hoyerswerda, Ger.	D14	10
Hoyleton, Il., U.S.	D7	114
Hoyt Lakes, Mn., U.S.	C3	110
Hradec Králové, Czech Rep.	E15	10
Hrandzičy, Bela.	H6	22
Hranice, Czech Rep.	F17	10
Hrodna, Bela.	H6	22
Hron, stm., Slvk.	G18	10
Hronov, Czech Rep.	E16	10
Hrubieszów, Pol.	E23	10
Hrynyavka, Ukr.	B8	20
Hsihu, Tai.	L9	34
Hsilo, Tai.	L9	34
Hsinchu, Tai.	K9	34
Hsinchuang, Tai.	J10	34
Hsinhua, Tai.	L9	34
Hsintien, Tai.	K10	34
Hsipaw, Myan.	C4	40
Hsüehchia, Tai.	L9	34
Hua'an, China	J6	34
Huacaña, Peru	F4	82
Huacaraje, Bol.	E10	82
Huachacalla, Bol.	H7	82
Huacheng, China	K4	34
Huachi, Laguna, l., Bol.	F10	82
Huacho, Peru	D3	82
Huachón, Peru	D4	82
Huachos, Peru	E4	82
Huachuca City, Az., U.S.	M6	120
Huaco, Arg.	F4	80
Huacrachuco, Peru	C3	82
Huadian, China	C12	30
Hua Hin, Thai.	H5	40
Huai, stm., China	C6	34
Huai'an, China	B8	34
Huaibin, China	C4	34
Huaide, China	C11	30
Huailai, China	C3	32
Huaillati, Peru	F5	82
Huainan, China	C6	34
Huaining, China	E5	34
Huaitunas, Lagunas, l., Bol.	E8	82
Huaiyang, China	B3	34
Huaiyuan, China	C6	34
Huajuapan de León, Mex.	I11	90
Huakou, China	J6	34
Hualahuises, Mex.	E10	90
Hualalai, vol., Hi., U.S.	r18	125a
Hualañé, Chile	H3	80
Hualapai Peak, mtn., Az., U.S.	I3	120
Hualfín, Arg.	D5	80
Hualgayoc, Peru	B2	82
Hualien, Tai.	L10	34
Huallaga, stm., Peru	A4	82
Huallanca, Peru	C3	82
Huallanca, Peru	C3	82
Huallayabamba, stm., Peru	B3	82
Huamanquiquia, Peru	E4	82
Huambo (Nova Lisboa), Ang.	D3	58
Huambos, Peru	B2	82
Huancabamba, Peru	D4	82
Huancabamba, Peru	A2	82
Huancané, Peru	F7	82
Huancapi, Peru	E4	82
Huancarama, Peru	E5	82
Huancarqui, Peru	G5	82
Huancavelica, Peru	E4	82
Huancavelica, dept., Peru	E4	82
Huancaybamba, Peru	C3	82
Huancayo, Peru	E4	82
Huanchaca, Bol.	I8	82
Huanchaca, Serranía de, mts., S.A.	F11	82
Huando, Peru	E4	82
Huang, stm., Asia	F6	40
Huang (Yellow), stm., China	D10	30
Huang'an, China	H3	32
Huangbai, China	B14	32
Huangchuan, China	C4	34
Huangdu, China	D10	34
Huanggang, China	E3	34
Huangguoshu, China	A8	40
Huanghua, China	E5	32
Huangkeng, China	H6	34
Huangling, China	D8	30
Huangmao, China	G3	34
Huangnihe, China	D6	34
Huangqi, China	I8	34
Huangqiao, China	C9	34
Huangshapu, China	J1	34
Huangshatuo, China	B10	32
Huangshi, China	E4	34
Huangshiguan, China	I4	34
Huangtankou, China	G7	34
Huangtianfan, China	F9	34
Huangtugang, China	D4	34
Huanguelén, Arg.	I8	80
Huangyan, China	G10	34
Huangyuan, China	D7	30
Huangzhuang, China	A1	34
Huanjiang, China	B10	40
Huanta, Peru	E4	82
Huántar, Peru	C3	82
Huánuco, Peru	C3	82
Huánuco, dept., Peru	C4	82
Huanuni, Bol.	H8	82
Huanxi, China	I2	34
Huanzo, Cordillera de, mts., Peru	F5	82
Huapí, Serranías, mts., Nic.	E10	92
Huara, Chile	H7	82
Huaral, Peru	D3	82
Huaráz, Peru	C3	82
Huari, Peru	C3	82
Huariaca, Peru	D3	82
Huaribamba, Peru	E4	82
Huarina, Bol.	G7	82
Huarmey, Peru	D2	82
Huarochirí, Peru	E3	82
Huarocondo, Peru	E5	82
Huasaga, stm., S.A.	I4	84
Huascarán, Nevado, mtn., Peru	C3	82
Huasco, Chile	E3	80
Huasco, stm., Chile	E3	80
Huashan, China	I4	32
Huashi, China	D9	34
Huatabampo, Mex.	D5	90
Huatong, China	C9	32
Huauchinango, Mex.	G10	90
Huaura, Peru	D3	82
Huaura, stm., Peru	D3	82
Huautla, Mex.	H11	90
Huaxian, China	L2	34
Huayllay, Peru	D3	82
Huayna Potosí, Nevado, mtn., Bol.	G7	82
Huaytará, Peru	E4	82
Huayuanzui, China	B7	34
Huayunca, Nevado, mtn., Peru	F5	82
Huayuri, Pampa de, pl., Peru	F4	82
Huazhou, China	D11	40
Hubbard, Ia., U.S.	H2	110
Hubbard, Tx., U.S.	H10	116
Hubbard Creek Reservoir, res., Tx., U.S.	G7	116
Hubbard Lake, l., Mi., U.S.	F12	110
Hubbards, N.S., Can.	H9	106
Hubbell, Mi., U.S.	C7	110
Hubei (Hupeh), prov., China	E9	30
Huberdeau, P.Q., Can.	B12	108
Hubli-Dhārwār, India	E3	46
Huch'ang, N. Kor.	B15	32
Huchi, China	D6	34
Huddersfield, Eng., U.K.	H12	8
Hūdī, Sudan	I8	60
Hudiksvall, Swe.	K15	6
Hudson, Ia., U.S.	H3	110
Hudson, Ma., U.S.	E15	108
Hudson, Mi., U.S.	I11	110
Hudson, N.C., U.S.	D5	112
Hudson, N.H., U.S.	E15	108
Hudson, N.Y., U.S.	E13	108
Hudson, Oh., U.S.	F5	108
Hudson, S.D., U.S.	H11	118
Hudson, Wi., U.S.	F3	110
Hudson, Wy., U.S.	B8	120
Hudson, stm., U.S.	F12	108
Hudson, Lake, res., Ok., U.S.	C11	116
Hudson Bay, Sk., Can.	F12	104
Hudson Bay, b., Can.	D15	96
Hudson-Bayonet Point, Fl., U.S.	K4	112
Hudson Falls, N.Y., U.S.	D13	108
Hudson Hope, B.C., Can.	A13	102
Hudson Strait, strt., Can.	D18	96
Hudsonville, Mi., U.S.	H10	110
Hudwin Lake, l., Mb., Can.	E19	104
Hue, Viet.	F9	40
Huehuetán, Mex.	B2	92
Huehuetenango, Guat.	B3	92
Huehuetenango, dept., Guat.	B3	92
Huejutla de Reyes, Mex.	G10	90
Huelgoat, Fr.	D3	14
Huelva, Spain	H5	16
Huenque, stm., Peru	G7	82
Huentelauquén, Chile	F3	80
Huércal-Overa, Spain	H10	16
Huerfano, stm., Co., U.S.	M3	118
Huerfano Mountain, mtn., N.M., U.S.	H9	120
Huerva, stm., Spain	D10	16
Huesca, Spain	C11	16
Huéscar, Spain	H9	16
Huetamo de Núñez, Mex.	H9	90
Hueytown, Al., U.S.	I10	114
Huggins, Mount, mtn., Ant.	C8	73
Hugh Butler Lake, res., Ne., U.S.	K7	118
Hughenden, Austl.	C6	70
Hughes, Ak., U.S.	C17	100
Hughes, Ar., U.S.	H6	114
Hughes, stm., Mb., Can.	B14	104
Hughes Springs, Tx., U.S.	I2	114
Hughesville, Pa., U.S.	F10	108
Hugh Keenleyside Dam, B.C., Can.	H17	102
Hughson, Ca., U.S.	G5	124
Hugh Town, Eng., U.K.	L7	8
Hugli, stm., India	J12	44
Hugo, Co., U.S.	L4	118
Hugo, Ok., U.S.	E11	116
Hugoton, Ks., U.S.	N6	118
Hugou, China	B6	34
Huichang, China	J4	34
Huichapan, Mex.	G10	90
Hŭich'ŏn, N. Kor.	C14	32
Huicungo, Peru	B3	82
Huidong, China	A7	40
Huila, dept., Col.	F5	84
Huila, Nevado del, mtn., Col.	F4	84
Huili, China	A7	40
Huillapima, Arg.	E6	80
Huilong, China	K2	34
Huimin, China	F5	32
Huinan (Chaoyang), China	A14	32
Huínaymarca, Lago, l., S.A.	G7	82
Huinca Renancó, Arg.	H6	80
Huisduinen, Neth.	C6	12
Huiting, China	I4	32
Huitzo, Mex.	I11	90
Huitzuco de los Figueroa, Mex.	H10	90
Huixtla, Mex.	J13	90
Huiyang, China	A5	38
Huize, China	A7	40
Huizen, Neth.	D7	12
Huizhou, China	L3	34
Hukeng, China	H3	34
Ḥukūmah, Sudan	K9	60
Hukuntsi, Bots.	E5	66
Hulan, China	B12	30
Hulan Ergi, China	B11	30
Hulbert, Mi., U.S.	D10	110
Hulbert, Ok., U.S.	G1	114
Hulett, Wy., U.S.	G3	118
Hulin, China	B13	30
Hull see Kingston upon Hull, Eng., U.K.	H13	8
Hull, Ia., U.S.	H11	118
Hull, Il., U.S.	C5	114
Hull, P.Q., Can.	B11	108
Hull, Tx., U.S.	I12	116
Hulun Nur, l., China	B10	30
Ḥulwān, Egypt	C6	60
Huma, China	A12	30
Huma, stm., China	A11	30
Humacao, P.R.	E12	94
Humahuaca, Arg.	B6	80
Humaitá, Braz.	B10	82
Humaitá, Para.	D9	80
Humaitá, stm., Braz.	C5	82
Humansdorp, S. Afr.	J7	66
Humansville, Mo., U.S.	E3	114
Humayingzi, China	B4	32
Humbe, Ang.	E2	58
Humber, stm., Eng., U.K.	H13	8
Humberside, co., Eng., U.K.	H13	8
Humbird, Wi., U.S.	F5	110
Humboldt, Az., U.S.	J4	120
Humboldt, Ia., U.S.	I13	118
Humboldt, Il., U.S.	C8	114
Humboldt, Ks., U.S.	N12	118
Humboldt, Ne., U.S.	K12	118
Humboldt, S.D., U.S.	H10	118

Name — Map Ref. — Page

Humboldt, Sk., Can. F9 104
Humboldt, Tn., U.S. G8 114
Humboldt, stm., Nv., U.S. D7 124
Hume, Ca., U.S. H7 124
Hume, Lake, res., Austl. K7 70
Humeburn, Austl. F6 70
Humenné, Slvk. G21 10
Humeston, Ia., U.S. J2 110
Humphrey, Ar., U.S. H5 114
Humphrey, Ne., U.S. J10 118
Humphreys, Mount, mtn., Ca., U.S. G7 124
Humphreys Peak, mtn., Az., U.S. I5 120
Humptulips, stm., Wa., U.S. C2 122
Humpty Doo, Austl. B6 68
Humuya, stm., Hond. C7 92
Húnaflói, b., Ice. B3 6a
Hunan, prov., China F9 30
Hunchun, China A18 32
Hundred, W.V., U.S. H6 108
Hunedoara, Rom. D6 20
Hunedoara, co., Rom. D6 20
Hünfeld, Ger. E9 10
Hungary (Magyarország), ctry., Eur. F12 4
Hungerford, Tx., U.S. J10 116
Hŭngnam, N. Kor. D15 32
Hungry Horse, Mt., U.S. B11 122
Hungry Horse Reservoir, res., Mt., U.S. B12 122
Hung Yen, Viet. D9 40
Huningue, Fr. E14 14
Hunjiang (Badaojiang), China B14 32
Ḥunkurāb, Ra's, c., Egypt I3 48
Hunlen Falls, wtfl, B.C., Can. E9 102
Hunsberge, mts., Nmb. F3 66
Hunsrück, mts., Ger. F6 10
Hunter, N.D., U.S. D10 118
Hunter, Mount, mtn., Ak., U.S. E19 100
Hunter Island, i., Austl. M6 70
Hunter Island, i., B.C., Can. F6 102
Hunter River, P.E., Can. F10 106
Hunters Road, Zimb. B9 66
Huntersville, N.C., U.S. D6 112
Huntingburg, In., U.S. D10 114
Huntingdon, Pa., U.S. G8 108
Huntingdon, P.Q., Can. B12 108
Huntingdon, Tn., U.S. F8 114
Huntington, In., U.S. B11 114
Huntington, N.Y., U.S. G13 108
Huntington, Or., U.S. F8 122
Huntington, Tx., U.S. K2 114
Huntington, Ut., U.S. E6 120
Huntington, W.V., U.S. I4 108
Huntington Beach, Ca., U.S. K8 124
Huntland, Tn., U.S. G10 114
Huntley, Mt., U.S. E17 122
Huntly, N.Z. B5 72
Hunt Mountain, mtn., Wy., U.S. F18 122
Huntsville, Al., U.S. H10 114
Huntsville, Ar., U.S. F3 114
Huntsville, Mo., U.S. C4 114
Huntsville, On., Can. E16 110
Huntsville, Tn., U.S. C2 112
Huntsville, Tx., U.S. I11 116
Huntsville, Ut., U.S. C5 120
Hunucmá, Mex. G15 90
Hunyani, stm., Afr. E6 58
Hunyuan, China D1 32
Huon Gulf, b., Pap. N. Gui. m16 68a
Huonville, Austl. N7 70
Huoqiu, China C5 34
Huotong, China I8 34
Hupeh see Hubei, prov., China E9 30
Ḥuraymilā, Sau. Ar. B5 47
Hurd, Cape, c., On., Can. E14 110
Hure Qi, China A9 32
Huriel, Fr. F9 14
Hurley, Ms., U.S. L8 114
Hurley, N.M., U.S. L8 120
Hurley, S.D., U.S. H10 118
Hurley, Wi., U.S. D5 110
Hurlock, Md., U.S. I11 108
Huron, Ca., U.S. H5 124
Huron, Oh., U.S. F4 108
Huron, S.D., U.S. G9 118
Huron, stm., Mi., U.S. H12 110
Huron, Lake, l., N.A. F13 110
Hurricane, Ut., U.S. G3 120
Hurricane, W.V., U.S. I4 108
Hurricane Cliffs, clf, U.S. H3 120
Hurstbridge, Austl. K6 70
Hurt, Va., U.S. B7 112
Hurtado, stm., Chile F3 80
Hurtsboro, Al., U.S. J11 114
Húsavík, Faer. Is. E8 6b
Húsavík, Ice. A5 6a
Husheib, Sudan J8 60
Hushiha, China C4 32
Huși, Rom. C12 20
Huslia, Ak., U.S. D16 100
Hussar, Ab., Can. F22 102
Hustisford, Wi., U.S. G7 110
Husum, Ger. A9 10
Husum, Swe. J16 6
Hutanopan, Indon. N5 40
Hutchinson, Ks., U.S. M10 118
Hutchinson, Mn., U.S. F1 110
Hutchinson, S. Afr. H6 66
Hutouya, China F7 32
Hutsonville, Il., U.S. C9 114
Hutte Sauvage, Lac de la, l., P.Q., Can. E20 96
Huttig, Ar., U.S. I4 114
Hutto, Tx., U.S. I9 116
Huttwil, Switz. D8 13
Huwei, Tai. L9 34
Ḥuwwārah, W.B. D4 50
Huxford, Al., U.S. K9 114
Huxley, Ab., Can. F21 102
Huyangzhen, China C1 34
Hūzgān, Iran F10 48
Huzhou, China E9 34
Hvannadalshnúkur, mtn., Ice. B5 6a
Hvar, Cro. F11 18
Hvar, Otok, i., Cro. F11 18
Hveragerði, Ice. B3 6a
Hvizdets', Ukr. A9 20
Hvolsvöllur, Ice. C3 6a
Hwange, Zimb. B8 66
Hwang Ho see Huang, stm., China D10 30
Hwangju, N. Kor. E13 32
Hyannis, Ma., U.S. F16 108
Hyannis, Ne., U.S. I6 118
Hyattville, Wy., U.S. F18 122
Hyco, stm., U.S. C8 112
Hydaburg, Ak., U.S. I28 100
Hyden, Austl. F3 68
Hyden, Ky., U.S. B3 112
Hyde Park, Guy. D13 84
Hyde Park, N.Y., U.S. F13 108
Hyde Park, Vt., U.S. C14 108
Hyderābād, India D5 46
Hyderābād, Pak. H3 44
Hydra see Ídhra, i., Grc. L7 20
Hydraulic, B.C., Can. E13 102
Hydro, Ok., U.S. D8 116
Hydrographers Passage, strt., Austl. C8 70
Hyères, Fr. I13 14
Hyères, Îles d', is., Fr. B18 16
Hyesan, N. Kor. B16 32
Hyland, stm., Can. F30 100
Hymaya, stm., Mex. E6 90
Hymera, In., U.S. C9 114
Hyndman, Pa., U.S. H8 108
Hyndman Peak, mtn., Id., U.S. G11 122
Hyŏpch'ŏn, S. Kor. H16 32
Hyrra Banda, C.A.R. O2 60
Hyrum, Ut., U.S. C5 120
Hysham, Mt., U.S. D18 122
Hythe, Ab., Can. B15 102

I

Iacanga, Braz. F4 79
Iaciara, Braz. C5 79
Iaco (Yaco), stm., S.A. C7 82
Iaçu, Braz. B8 79
Iaeger, W.V., U.S. B5 112
Ialomița, co., Rom. E11 20
Ialomița, stm., Rom. E11 20
Ianakafy, Madag. s21 67b
Iapó, stm., Braz. C13 80
Iapu, Braz. E7 79
Iargara, Mol. C12 20
Iași, Rom. B11 20
Iași, co., Rom. B11 20
Iauaretê, Braz. G8 84
Ibadan, Nig. H11 64
Ibagué, Col. E5 84
Ibaiti, Braz. G3 79
Ibans, Laguna de, b., Hond. B10 92
Ibapah Peak, mtn., Ut., U.S. E3 120
Ibarra, Ec. G3 84
Ibarreta, Arg. C9 80
Ibb, Yemen G4 47
Ibbenbüren, Ger. C7 10
Iberia, Mo., U.S. D4 114
Ibérico, Sistema, mts., Spain D9 16
Iberville, Mont d' (Mount Caubvick), mtn., Can. E20 96
Ibeto, Nig. F12 64
Ibiá, Braz. E5 79
Ibicaraí, Braz. C9 79
Ibicuí, Braz. C9 79
Ibicuí, stm., Braz. E10 80
Ibicuy, Arg. G9 80
Ibiquera, Braz. B8 79
Ibiraci, Braz. F5 79
Ibiraçu, Braz. E8 79
Ibirama, Braz. D14 80
Ibirapuã, Braz. D8 79
Ibirapuitã, stm., Braz. F11 80
Ibirataia, Braz. C9 79
Ibirubá, Braz. E12 80
Ibitiara, Braz. B7 79
Ibitinga, Braz. F4 79
Ibo, Moz. D8 58
Ibotirama, Braz. B7 79
'Ibrī, Oman C10 47
Ibshawāy, Egypt C6 60
Ibusuki, Japan P5 36
Ica, Peru F4 82
Ica, dept., Peru F4 82
Ica, stm., Peru F4 82
Içá (Putumayo), stm., S.A. I8 84
Icabarú, stm., Ven. E11 84
Icamaquã, stm., Braz. E11 80
Içana, Braz. G9 84
Içana (Isana), stm., S.A. G9 84
Icaño, Arg. E6 80
Icaño, Arg. E7 80
Iceberg Pass, Co., U.S. D11 120
İçel, Tur. C3 48
Iceland (Ísland), ctry., Eur. B4 4
Icém, Braz. F4 79
Ice Mountain, mtn., B.C., Can. C13 102
Ichaikaronji, India D3 46
Ichikawa, Japan L14 36
Ichilo, stm., Bol. G9 82
Ichinomiya, Japan L11 36
Ichinoseki, Japan I16 36
Ichkeul, Lac, l., Tun. L4 18
Ichoa, stm., Bol. F9 82
Ichoca, Bol. G8 82
Ich'on, N. Kor. E14 32
Ich'ŏn, S. Kor. F15 32
Ičinskaja Sopka, vulkan, vol., Russia F23 28
Icó, Braz. E11 76
Iconha, Braz. F8 79
Icy Bay, b., Ak., U.S. F24 100
Ida, Mi., U.S. I12 110
Idabel, Ok., U.S. I2 114
Ida Grove, Ia., U.S. I12 118
Idah, Nig. H13 64
Idaho, state, U.S. C4 98
Idaho City, Id., U.S. G10 122
Idaho Falls, Id., U.S. G13 122
Idaho Springs, Co., U.S. E11 120
Idalou, Tx., U.S. F5 116
Idanre, Nig. H12 64
Idāppādi, India G4 46
Idar-Oberstein, Ger. F7 10
Idelès, Alg. I13 62
Idfū, Egypt E7 60
Ídhi Óros, mtn., Grc. N8 20
Ídhra (Hydra), i., Grc. L7 20
Idi, Indon. L4 40
Idiofa, Zaire C3 58
Idlib, Syria D4 48
Idoûkâl-n-Taghès, mtn., Niger C14 64
Idre, Swe. K13 6
Idrica, Russia E11 22
Idrija, Slvn. C9 18
Idutywa, S. Afr. I9 66
Idyllwild, Ca., U.S. K9 124
Iecava, Lat. E7 22
Iepê, Braz. G3 79
Ieper (Ypres), Bel. G2 12
Ierisós, Grc. I7 20
Ife, Nig. H12 64
Iferouâne, Niger B14 64
Ifni, hist. reg., Mor. F5 62
Ifôghas, Adrar des, mts., Afr. E7 54
Ifon-Oshogbo, Nig. H12 64
Igal, Hung. I17 10
Iganna, Nig. H11 64
Igaporã, Braz. B7 79
Igara Paraná, stm., Col. H6 84
Igarka, Russia D9 28
Igbasa-Odo, Nig. H11 64
Iğdır, Tur. B8 48
Igharghar, Oued, val., Afr. J14 62
Igizyar, China A7 44
Iglesia, Arg. F4 80
Iglesias, Italy J3 18
Igli, Alg. E9 62
Igloolik, N.T., Can. C16 96
Ignacio, Co., U.S. G9 120
Ignacio Zaragoza, Mex. C6 90
Ignalina, Lith. F9 22
Ignaței, Mol. B12 20
İğneada, Tur. H11 20
Iguaçu, stm., S.A. C12 80
Iguaçu, Cataratas do (Iguassu Falls), wtfl, S.A. C11 80
Iguaí, Braz. C8 79
Iguala, Mex. H10 90
Igualada, Spain D13 16
Iguana, stm., Ven. C10 84
Iguape, Braz. C15 80
Iguassu Falls see Iguaçu, Cataratas do, wtfl, S.A. C11 80
Iguatemi, Braz. G1 79
Iguatemi, stm., Braz. G1 79
Iguatu, Braz. E11 76
Iguazú, Parque Nacional, S.A. C11 80
Iguéla, Gabon B1 58
Iguîdi, 'Erg, dunes, Afr. C5 54
Igžej, Russia G12 28
Iheya-shima, i., Japan t2 37b
Ihiala, Nig. I13 64
Ihosy, Madag. s22 67b
Ihtiman, Bul. G7 20
Iida, Japan L12 36
Iisaku, Est. B10 22
Ii-shima, i., Japan F12 30
Iiyama, Japan K13 36
Iizuka, Japan N5 36
Ijâfene, des., Afr. D5 54
Ijaji, Eth. M9 60
Ijebu-Igbo, Nig. H12 64
IJmuiden, Neth. D6 12
IJssel, stm., Neth. C8 12
IJsselmeer (Zuiderzee), Neth. C7 12
IJsselstein, Neth. D7 12
Ijuí, Braz. E12 80
Ijuí, stm., Braz. E11 80
Ikalamavony, Madag. r22 67b
Ikang, Nig. I14 64
Ikaría, i., Grc. L10 20
Ikeja, Nig. H11 64
Ikela, Zaire B4 58
Ikirun, Nig. H12 64
Ikot Ekpene, Nig. I13 64
Ikša, Russia E20 22
Ilabaya, Peru G6 82
Ilagan, Phil. m19 39b
Ilaka, Madag. q23 67b
Īlām, Iran E9 48
Ilām, Nepal G12 44
Ilan, Tai. K10 34
Ilanskij, Russia F17 26
Ilanz, Switz. E11 13
Ilaro, Nig. H11 64
Iława, Pol. B19 10
Ilbenge, Russia E16 28
Île-à-la-Crosse, Sk., Can. C7 104
Île-à-la-Crosse, Lac, l., Sk., Can. C7 104
Ilebo, Zaire B4 58
Île-de-France, hist. reg., Fr. C9 14
Ilek, stm., Asia G8 26
Îles, Lac des, l., Sk., Can. D5 104
Ilesha, Nig. H12 64
Ilesha Ibarida, Nig. G11 64
Ilford, Mb., Can. B19 104
Ilfracombe, Austl. D6 70
Ilhabela, Braz. G6 79
Ilha Grande, Baía da, b., Braz. G6 79
Ilhéus, Braz. C9 79
Ili, stm., Asia H12 26
Iliamna, Ak., U.S. G17 100
Iliamna Lake, l., Ak., U.S. G17 100
Ilicínia, Braz. F6 79
Iliff, Co., U.S. K4 118
Iligan, Phil. D7 38
Ilimsk, Russia F12 28
Ilinza, mtn., Ec. H3 84
Ilion, N.Y., U.S. D11 108
Ilizi, Alg. G15 62
Iljinskij, Russia K23 6
Iljinskij, Russia H20 28
Iljinskoje, Russia D21 22
Iljinskoje, Russia E20 22
Iljinskoje-Chovanskoje, Russia E22 22
Ilkal, India E4 46
Il'kino, Russia F24 22
Illampu, Nevado, mtn., Bol. F7 82
Illapel, Chile F3 80
Ille-et-Vilaine, dept., Fr. D5 14
Illéla, Niger D12 64
Iller, stm., Ger. H10 10
Illescas, Mex. F8 90
Illescas, Spain E8 16
Illiers, Fr. D8 14
Illimani, Nevado, mtn., Bol. G8 82
Illimo, Peru B2 82
Illinois, state, U.S. D9 98
Illinois, stm., Il., U.S. I6 110
Illinois, stm., Or., U.S. H2 122
Illinois, stm., U.S. F2 114
Illinois Peak, mtn., U.S. C10 122
Illiopolis, Il., U.S. C7 114
Il'men', ozero, l., Russia C14 22
Ilo, Peru G6 82
Ilobasco, El Sal. D6 92
Iloilo, Phil. C7 38
Ilopango, Lago de, l., El Sal. D5 92
Ilora, Nig. H11 64
Ilorin, Nig. G12 64
Ilūkste, Lat. F9 22
Ilwaki, Indon. G8 38
Imabari, Japan M8 36
Imabu, stm., Braz. H14 84
Imandra, ozero, l., Russia H23 6
Imari, Japan N4 36
Imaruí, Braz. E14 80
Imaruí, Lagoa do, b., Braz. E14 80
Imatra, Fin. K21 6
Imbabura, prov., Ec. G3 84
Imbituba, Braz. E14 80
Imbituva, Braz. C13 80
Imboden, Ar., U.S. F5 114
Imeni Babuškina, Russia B26 22
Imeni C'urupy, Russia F21 22
Imeni Vorovskogo, Russia F24 22
Imeni Žel'abova, Russia C19 22
Imerimandroso, Madag. p23 67b
Imi, Eth. G9 56
Imías, Cuba D7 94
Imilac, Chile C4 80
Imi-n'Tanout, Mor. E6 62
İmişli, Azer. B10 48
Imjin-gang, stm., Asia F14 32
Imlay, Nv., U.S. D7 124
Imlay City, Mi., U.S. G12 110
Immingham Dock, Eng., U.K. H13 8
Immokalee, Fl., U.S. M5 112
Imola, Italy E6 18
Imotski, Cro. F12 18
Imperatriz, Braz. E9 76
Imperia, Italy F3 18
Imperial, Ca., U.S. L10 124
Imperial, Ne., U.S. K6 118
Imperial, Peru E3 82
Imperial, Sk., Can. G9 104
Imperial, Tx., U.S. H4 116
Imperial, stm., Chile J2 80
Imperial Beach, Ca., U.S. L8 124
Imperial Mills, Ab., Can. B23 102
Imperial Valley, val., Ca., U.S. L10 124
Impfondo, Congo A3 58
Imphāl, India H15 44
Impilachti, Russia K22 6
Imsil, S. Kor. H15 32
Imuris, Mex. B4 90
Ina, Il., U.S. D8 114
Ina, Japan L12 36
Inambari, stm., Peru E7 82
In Amguel, Alg. I13 62
In Amnas, Alg. F15 62
Iñapari, Peru D7 82
In'aptuk, gora, mtn., Russia F14 28
Inari, Fin. G20 6
Inarijärvi, l., Fin. G20 6
Inauini, stm., Braz. C8 82
Inawashiro-ko, l., Japan J15 36
In Belbel, Alg. G11 62
Inca, Spain F14 16
Inca de Oro, Chile D4 80
Incaguasi, Chile E3 80
İncesu, Tur. B3 48
Inch'ŏn, S. Kor. F14 32
Incline Village, Nv., U.S. E6 124
Incomáti (Komati), stm., Afr. E11 66
Indaiá, stm., Braz. E6 79
Inda Silase, Eth. J10 60
Indaw, Myan. C3 40
Indé, Mex. E7 90
Independence, Ca., U.S. H7 124
Independence, Ia., U.S. H4 110
Independence, Ks., U.S. N12 118
Independence, Ky., U.S. I2 108
Independence, La., U.S. L6 114
Independence, Mo., U.S. C2 114
Independence, Or., U.S. F2 122
Independence, Va., U.S. C5 112
Independence, Wi., U.S. F4 110
Independence, stm., N.Y., U.S. D11 108
Independence Mountains, mts., Nv., U.S. C9 124
Independencia, Bol. G8 82
Independencia, Isla, i., Peru F3 82
India (Bhārat), ctry., Asia E10 42
Indialantic, Fl., U.S. K6 112
Indian, stm., Mi., U.S. D9 110
Indiana, Pa., U.S. G7 108
Indiana, state, U.S. C9 98
Indiana Dunes National Lakeshore, In., U.S. A9 114
Indianapolis, In., U.S. C10 114
Indian Brook, N.S., Can. F13 106
Indian Church, Belize I15 90
Indian Head, Sk., Can. H11 104
Indian Lake, N.Y., U.S. D12 108
Indian Ocean J11 126
Indianola, Ia., U.S. I2 110
Indianola, Ms., U.S. I6 114
Indianola, Ne., U.S. K7 118
Indianópolis, Braz. E5 79
Indian Peak, mtn., Ut., U.S. F3 120
Indian Peak, mtn., Wy., U.S. F16 122
Indian River, Mi., U.S. E11 110
Indian River, b., Fl., U.S. K6 112
Indian Springs, Nv., U.S. H10 124
Indiantown, Fl., U.S. L6 112
Indiaporã, Braz. E3 79
Indibir, Eth. M9 60
Indigirka, stm., Russia D21 28
Indio, Ca., U.S. K9 124
Indio, stm., Nic. F10 92
Indio, stm., Pan. H14 92
Indira Gandhi Canal, India F5 44
Indispensable Reefs, rf., Sol. Is. B12 68
Indochina, reg., Asia B3 38
Indonesia, ctry., Asia G7 38
Indore, India I6 44
Indragiri, stm., Indon. O7 40
Indrāvati, stm., India C6 46
Indre, dept., Fr. F8 14
Indre-et-Loire, dept., Fr. E7 14
Indura, Bela. H6 22
Indus, stm., Asia H2 44
Industry, Il., U.S. B6 114
Industry, Tx., U.S. J10 116
Indwe, S. Afr. H8 66
İnece, Tur. H11 20
In Ecker, Alg. H13 62
İnegöl, Tur. I13 20
Inez, Ky., U.S. B4 112
Inez, Tx., U.S. K10 116
Inferior, Laguna, b., Mex. I12 90
Infiernillo, Presa del, res., Mex. H9 90
Ingal, Niger C13 64
Ingelheim, Ger. F8 10
Ingelmunster, Bel. G3 12
Ingende, Zaire B3 58
Ingeniero Luiggi, Arg. H6 80
Ingeniero Luis A. Huergo, Arg. J5 80
Ingeniero White, Arg. J7 80
Ingenio La Esperanza, Arg. C6 80
Ingenio Santa Ana, Arg. D6 80
Ingersoll, On., Can. G15 110
Ingham, Austl. B7 70
Ingleside, Tx., U.S. L9 116
Inglewood, Austl. G9 70
Inglewood, Ca., U.S. K7 124
Inglis, Mb., Can. H13 104
Ingoda, stm., Russia G14 28
Ingolstadt, Ger. G11 10
Ingonish, N.S., Can. F13 106
Ingornachoix Bay, b., Nf., Can. B16 106
Ingrāj Bāzār, India H13 44
Ingram, Tx., U.S. I7 116
In Guezzam, Alg. B12 64
Ingwiller, Fr. D14 14
Inhaca, Ilha da, i., Moz. F11 66
Inhafenga, Moz. C11 66
Inhambane, Moz. D12 66
Inhambupe, Braz. A9 79
Inhaminga, Moz. B12 66
Inhanduí, stm., Braz. F1 79
Inhapim, Braz. E7 79
Inharrime, Moz. E12 66
Inhaúma, Braz. E6 79
Inhumas, Braz. D4 79
Inimutaba, Braz. E6 79
Inírida, stm., Col. F8 84
Inisa, Nig. H12 64
Inishmore, i., Ire. H4 8
Injibara, Eth. L9 60
Injune, Austl. E8 70
Inkom, Id., U.S. H13 122
Inkster, N.D., U.S. C10 118
Inland Lake, l., Mb., Can. F15 104
Inland Sea see Seto-naikai, Japan M7 36
Inle Lake, l., Myan. D4 40
Inman, Ks., U.S. M10 118
Inman, S.C., U.S. D4 112
Inman Mills, S.C., U.S. D4 112
Inn (En), stm., Eur. D20 14
Innamincka, Austl. F4 70
Inner Channel, strt., Belize I15 90
Inner Hebrides, is., Scot., U.K. E7 8
Inner Mongolia see Nei Monggol Zizhiqu, prov., China C10 30
Innertkirchen, Switz. E9 13
Innisfail, Ab., Can. E21 102
Innisfail, Austl. A7 70
Innisfree, Ab., Can. D23 102
Innsbruck, Aus. H11 10
Inocência, Braz. E3 79
Inola, Ok., U.S. C11 116
Inongo, Zaire B3 58
Inowrocław, Pol. C18 10
In Rhar, Alg. G11 62
In Salah, Alg. G12 62
Ińsko, Pol. B15 10
Inspiration, Az., U.S. K6 120
Instow, Sk., Can. I6 104
Inta, Russia D10 26
Intendente Alvear, Arg. H7 80
İntepe, Tur. I10 20
Interlaken, Switz. E8 13
Interlândia, Braz. D4 79
International Falls, Mn., U.S. B2 110
Inthanon, Doi, mtn., Thai. E5 40
Intibucá, Hond. C6 92
Intibucá, dept., Hond. C6 92
Intipucá, El Sal. D6 92
Intiyaco, Arg. E8 80
Intracoastal Waterway, U.S. H5 112
Intracoastal Waterway, U.S. K10 116
Intuto, Peru I5 84
Inukjuak, P.Q., Can. E17 96
Inuvik, N.T., Can. B28 100
Inuya, stm., Peru D5 82
Invercargill, N.Z. G2 72
Inverell, Austl. G9 70
Invergordon, Scot., U.K. D9 8
Invermay, Sk., Can. G11 104
Invermere, B.C., Can. G18 102
Inverness, Ca., U.S. F3 124
Inverness, Fl., U.S. K4 112
Inverness, Ms., U.S. I6 114
Inverness, N.S., Can. F12 106
Inverness, Scot., U.K. D9 8
Investigator Group, is., Austl. F6 68
Investigator Strait, strt., Austl. J2 70
Inwood, Ia., U.S. H11 118
Inwood, Mb., Can. H17 104
Inyangani, mtn., Zimb. B11 66
Inyantue, Zimb. B8 66
Inyati, Zimb. B9 66
Inyokern, Ca., U.S. I8 124
Inywa, Myan. C4 40
Inza, Russia G7 26
Inzana Lake, l., B.C., Can. C10 102
Inžavino, Russia I25 22
Ioánnina, Grc. J4 20
Iō-jima (Iwo Jima), i., Japan F18 126
Iola, Ks., U.S. N12 118
Iola, Wi., U.S. F6 110
Iolotan', Turk. J10 26
Iona, Id., U.S. G14 122
Iona, N.S., Can. G13 106
Ione, Ca., U.S. F5 124
Ione, Or., U.S. E6 122
Ione, Wa., U.S. B8 122
Ionia, Mi., U.S. H10 110
Ionian Islands see Iónioi Nísoi, is., Grc. K4 20
Ionian Sea, Eur. H11 4
Iónioi Nísoi, prov., Grc. K4 20
Iónioi Nísoi, is., Grc. K4 20
Íos, i., Grc. M9 20
Iosegun, stm., Ab., Can. C18 102
Iosegun Lake, Ab., Can. C18 102
Iota, La., U.S. L4 114
Iowa, La., U.S. L3 114
Iowa, state, U.S. C8 98
Iowa, stm., Ia., U.S. I4 110
Iowa City, Ia., U.S. I4 110
Iowa Falls, Ia., U.S. H2 110
Iowa Park, Tx., U.S. F8 116
Ipameri, Braz. D4 79
Ipatinga, Braz. E7 79
Ipava, Il., U.S. B6 114
Ípeiros, hist. reg., Grc. J4 20
Ipel' (Ipoly), stm., Eur. G19 10
Ipiales, Col. G4 84
Ipiaú, Braz. C9 79
Ipirá, Braz. B9 79
Ipiranga, Braz. C13 80
Ípiros, prov., Grc. J4 20
Ipita, Bol. H10 82
Ipixuna, stm., Braz. B5 82
Ipixuna, stm., Braz. B10 82
Ipixuna, stm., Braz. B10 82
Ipoh, Malay. L6 40
Ipoly (Ipel'), stm., Eur. G18 10
Iporá, Braz. D3 79
Iporã, Braz. G2 79
Ipoti-Ekiti, Nig. H12 64
Ipswich, Austl. F10 70
Ipswich, Eng., U.K. I15 8
Ipswich, Ma., U.S. E16 108
Ipswich, S.D., U.S. F8 118
Ipu, Braz. D10 76
Ipupiara, Braz. A7 79
Iqaluit, N.T., Can. D19 96
Iquique, Chile I6 82
Iquitos, Peru I6 84
Ira, Tx., U.S. G5 116
Iraan, Tx., U.S. I5 116
Iracajá, Cachoeira do, wtfl, Braz. D9 82
Iraí, Braz. D12 80
Iráklion, Grc. N9 20
Iran (Īrān), ctry., Asia C5 42
Iran, Pegunungan, mts., Asia E5 38
Īrānshahr, Iran H16 48
Irapa, Ven. B11 84
Irapuato, Mex. G9 90
Iraq (Al-'Irāq), ctry., Asia C3 42
Irará, Braz. B9 79
Irati, Braz. C13 80
Irazú, Volcán, vol., C.R. H11 92
Irbeni väin (Irbes jūras šaurums), strt., Eur. D5 22
Irbes jūras šaurums (Irbeni väin), strt., Eur. D5 22
Irbid, Jord. C5 50
Irbīl, Iraq C8 48
Irbit, Russia F10 26
Ireland (Éire), ctry., Eur. E6 4
Irene, S. Afr. E9 66
Irene, S.D., U.S. H10 118
Ireng (Maú), stm., S.A. E13 84
Ireton, Ia., U.S. I11 118
Irgiz, Kaz. H10 26
Iri, S. Kor. H14 32
Iriba, Chad J2 60
Irîgui, reg., Afr. C7 64
Iringa, Tan. C7 58
Iriona, Hond. B9 92
Iriri, stm., Braz. D8 76
Irish, Mount, mtn., Nv., U.S. G10 124
Irish Sea, Eur. H8 8
Irkutsk, Russia G12 28
Irma, Ab., Can. E23 102
Iron Belt, Wi., U.S. D5 110
Iron Bridge, On., Can. D12 110
Iron City, Tn., U.S. G9 114
Iron Creek, stm., Ab., Can. E23 102
Irondale, Al., U.S. I10 114
Irondale, Mo., U.S. E6 114
Irondequoit, N.Y., U.S. D9 108
Iron Gate, val., Eur. E6 20
Iron Gate Reservoir, res., Eur. E6 20
Iron Knob, Austl. I2 70
Iron Mountain, Mi., U.S. E7 110
Iron Mountains, mts., U.S. C5 112
Iron Range, Austl. B8 68
Iron River, Mi., U.S. D7 110
Iron River, Wi., U.S. D4 110
Ironton, Mn., U.S. D2 110
Ironton, Mo., U.S. E6 114
Ironton, Oh., U.S. I4 108
Ironwood, Mi., U.S. D5 110
Iroquois, On., Can. C11 108
Iroquois, S.D., U.S. G10 118
Iroquois, stm., U.S. J8 110
Iroquois Falls, On., Can. B15 110
Irrawaddy see Ayeyarwady, stm., Myan. F3 40
Irricana, Ab., Can. F21 102
Irrigon, Or., U.S. E6 122
Irshava, Ukr. A7 20
Irtysh (Irtyš) (Ertix), stm., Asia E11 26
Irtyšsk, Kaz. G13 26
Irumu, Zaire A5 58
Irún, Spain B10 16
Irupana, Bol. G8 82
Irurzun, Spain C10 16
Irú Tepuy, mtn., Ven. E12 84
Irvine, Ab., Can. I4 104
Irvine, Ky., U.S. B3 112
Irvine, Scot., U.K. F9 8
Irvines Landing, B.C., Can. H10 102
Irving, Il., U.S. C7 114
Irving, Tx., U.S. G10 116
Irvington, Ky., U.S. E10 114
Irwinton, Ga., U.S. G3 112
Isaac, stm., Austl. D8 70
Isaac Lake, l., B.C., Can. D14 102
Isabel, S.D., U.S. F6 118
Isabela, Phil. D7 38
Isabela, Cabo, c., Dom. Rep. E9 94
Isabela, Isla, i., Ec. j13 84a
Isabela, Isla, i., Mex. G7 90
Isabelia, Cordillera, mts., Nic. D9 92
Isabelle, stm., Mn., U.S. C4 110
Isaccea, Rom. D12 20
Ísafjörður, Ice. A2 6a
Isahaya, Japan O5 36
Īsa Khel, Pak. D4 44
Ișalnița, Rom. E7 20
Isana (Içana), stm., S.A. G8 84
Isanti, Mn., U.S. E2 110
Isar, stm., Eur. G11 10
Isara, Nig. H11 64
Ischia, Italy I8 18
Ischia, Isola d', i., Italy I8 18
Iscuandé, stm., Col. F4 84
Ise (Uji-yamada), Japan M11 36
Iseo, Lago d', l., Italy D5 18
Isère, dept., Fr. G12 14
Isère, stm., Fr. G12 14
Iserlohn, Ger. D7 10
Isernia, Italy H9 18
Isesaki, Japan K14 36
Iset', stm., Russia F11 26
Iseyin, Nig. H11 64
Isherton, Guy. F13 84
Ishinomaki, Japan I16 36
Ishioka, Japan K15 36
Ishpeming, Mi., U.S. D8 110
Isigny, Fr. C5 14
Isil'kul', Russia G12 26
Išim, Russia F11 26
Išim, stm., Asia F12 26
Išimbaj, Russia G9 26
Isiolo, Kenya A7 58
Isipingo, S. Afr. G10 66
Isiro, Zaire H6 56
Isisford, Austl. E6 70
Iskăr, stm., Bul. F8 20
Iskăr, Jazovir, res., Bul. G7 20
İskele, N. Cyp. D2 48
İskenderun, Tur. C4 48
İskenderun Körfezi, b., Tur. H15 4
Iskitim, Russia G8 28
Iskut, stm., B.C., Can. H29 100
Isla, Mex. H12 90
Isla, Salar de la, pl., Chile C4 80
Isla Cristina, Spain H4 16
Isla de Maipo, Chile G3 80
Islāmābād, Pak. D5 44
Islāmkot, Pak. H4 44
Islāmpur, India D3 46
Isla Mujeres, Mex. G16 90
Island, Ky., U.S. E9 114
Island Falls, Me., U.S. A18 108
Island Falls, Sk., Can. C12 104
Island Lagoon, l., Austl. H2 70
Island Lake, Mb., Can. E20 104
Island Lake, l., Mb., Can. E20 104
Island Park, Id., U.S. F14 122
Island Park Reservoir, res., Id., U.S. F14 122
Island Pond, Vt., U.S. C15 108
Island Pond, l., Nf., Can. D17 106
Islands, Bay of, b., Nf., Can. C15 106
Isla Patrulla, Ur. G11 80
Islas de la Bahía, dept., Hond. A8 92
Isla Verde, Arg. G7 80
Isla Vista, Ca., U.S. J6 124
Islay, i., Scot., U.K. F7 8
Islay, Punta, c., Peru G5 82
Isle, Mn., U.S. D2 110
Isle-aux-Morts, Nf., Can. E15 106
Isle of Hope, Ga., U.S. H5 112
Isle of Man, dep., Eur. E7 4
Isle of Palms, S.C., U.S. G7 112
Isle of Wight, Va., U.S. C10 112
Isle of Wight, co., Eng., U.K. K12 8
Isle Royale National Park, Mi., U.S. B7 110
Islesboro Island, i., Me., U.S. C18 108
Isleta, N.M., U.S. J10 120
Isleton, Ca., U.S. F4 124
Islets-Caribou, P.Q., Can. C6 106
Islón, Chile E3 80
Ismael Cortinas, Ur. G10 80
Ismailia see Al-Ismā'īlīyah, Egypt B7 60
İsmailli, Tur. K11 20
Isnā, Egypt E7 60
Isojoki, Fin. J17 6
Isola, Ms., U.S. I6 114
Isone, Switz. F10 13
Isparta, Tur. H14 4
İspir, Tur. A6 48
Israel (Yisra'el), ctry., Asia C2 42
Israel, stm., N.H., U.S. C15 108
Issano, Guy. E13 84
Issoire, Fr. G10 14
Issoudun, Fr. F9 14
Is-sur-Tille, Fr. E12 14

Name	Map Ref.	Page
Issyk-Kul' (Rybačje), Kyrg.	I13	26
Issyk-Kul', ozero, l., Kyrg.	I13	26
İstanbul, Tur.	H12	20
İstanbul Boğazı (Bosporus), strt., Tur.	H13	20
Istmina, Col.	E4	84
Isto, Mount, mtn., Ak., U.S.	B23	100
Istokpoga, Lake, l., Fl., U.S.	L5	112
Istra, Russia	F19	22
Istra, pen., Eur.	D8	18
Istria see Istra, pen., Eur.	D8	18
Itá, Para.	C10	80
Itabaiana, Braz.	E11	76
Itabaiana, Braz.	F11	76
Itabapoana, Braz.	F8	79
Itaberá, Braz.	G4	79
Itaberaba, Braz.	B8	79
Itaberaí, Braz.	D4	79
Itabira, Braz.	E7	79
Itabuna, Braz.	C9	79
Itacambiruçu, stm., Braz.	D7	79
Itacaré, Braz.	C9	79
Itacoatiara, Braz.	I13	84
Itacurubí del Rosario, Para.	C10	80
Itaeté, Braz.	B8	79
Itagi, Braz.	C8	79
Itaguaçu, Braz.	E8	79
Itaguajé, Braz.	G3	79
Itaguara, Braz.	F6	79
Itaguari, stm., Braz.	C6	79
Itaguaru, Braz.	C4	79
Itagüí, Col.	D5	84
Itaí, Braz.	G4	79
Itá-Ibaté, Arg.	D10	80
Itaiópolis, Braz.	D14	80
Itaituba, Braz.	D7	76
Itajá, Braz.	E3	79
Itajaí, Braz.	D14	80
Itajaí do Sul, stm., Braz.	D14	80
Itajubá, Braz.	G6	79
Itaju do Colônia, Braz.	C9	79
Itajuípe, Braz.	C9	79
Italy, Tx., U.S.	G10	116
Italy (Italia), ctry., Eur.	G10	4
Itamaraju, Braz.	D9	79
Itamarandiba, Braz.	D7	79
Itamarandiba, stm., Braz.	D7	79
Itamari, Braz.	B9	79
Itambacuri, Braz.	E8	79
Itambé, Braz.	C8	79
Itami, Japan	M10	36
Itanhaém, Braz.	H5	79
Itanhauã, stm., Braz.	A9	82
Itanhém, Braz.	D8	79
Itanhomi, Braz.	E8	79
Itaobim, Braz.	D8	79
Itapaci, Braz.	C4	79
Itapagipe, Braz.	E4	79
Itaparaná, stm., Braz.	B10	82
Itaparica, Ilha de, i., Braz.	B9	79
Itapaya, Bol.	G8	82
Itapé, Braz.	C9	79
Itapebi, Braz.	C9	79
Itapecerica, Braz.	F6	79
Itapecuru-Mirim, Braz.	D10	76
Itapemirim, Braz.	F8	79
Itaperuna, Braz.	F8	79
Itapetinga, Braz.	C8	79
Itapetininga, Braz.	G4	79
Itapetininga, stm., Braz.	G5	79
Itapeva, Braz.	G4	79
Itapicuru, stm., Braz.	D10	76
Itapicuru, stm., Braz.	F11	76
Itapira, Braz.	G5	79
Itapiranga, Braz.	D12	80
Itapiranga, Braz.	I13	84
Itapirapuã, Braz.	C3	79
Itapitanga, Braz.	C9	79
Itápolis, Braz.	F4	79
Itaporã, Braz.	G1	79
Itaporanga, Braz.	G4	79
Itapúa, dept., Para.	D11	80
Itapuranga, Braz.	C4	79
Itaquaí, stm., Braz.	J7	84
Itaquara, Braz.	B9	79
Itaquari, Braz.	F8	79
Itaqui, Braz.	E10	80
Itaquyry, Para.	C11	80
Itarantim, Braz.	C8	79
Itararé, Braz.	H4	79
Itārsi, India	I7	44
Itarumã, Braz.	E3	79
Itasca, Tx., U.S.	G9	116
Itasca, Lake, l., Mn., U.S.	D12	118
Itata, stm., Chile	I2	80
Itatí, Arg.	D9	80
Itatiaia, Parque Nacional do, Braz.	G6	79
Itatinga, Braz.	G4	79
Itaúna, Braz.	F6	79
Itenes (Guaporé), stm., S.A.	E10	82
Ithaca, Mi., U.S.	G11	110
Ithaca, N.Y., U.S.	E10	108
Itháki, Grc.	K4	20
Itháki, i., Grc.	K4	20
Itinga, Braz.	D8	79
Itinga, stm., Braz.	D8	79
Itiquira, Braz.	D1	79
Itirapina, Braz.	G5	79
Itiruçu, Braz.	B8	79
Itō, Japan	M14	36
Itoigawa, Japan	J12	36
Itomamo, Lac, l., P.Q., Can.	C3	106
Itonamas, stm., Bol.	E9	82
Itororó, Braz.	C8	79
Iṭsā, Egypt	C6	60
Itta Bena, Ms., U.S.	I6	114
Itú, Braz.	G5	79
Itu, stm., Braz.	E11	80
Ituaçu, Braz.	B8	79
Ituango, Col.	D5	84
Ituberá, Braz.	B9	79
Itucumã, stm., Braz.	B7	82
Itueta, Braz.	E8	79
Ituí, stm., Braz.	J7	84
Ituim, stm., Braz.	E13	80
Ituiutaba, Braz.	E4	79
Itumbiara, Braz.	E4	79
Ituna, Sk., Can.	G11	104
Ituni, Guy.	E13	84
Ituporanga, Braz.	D14	80
Iturama, Braz.	E3	79
Iturbe, Para.	D10	80
Iturbide, Mex.	H15	90
Iturup, ostrov (Etorofu-tō), i., Russia	c22	36a
Ituverava, Braz.	F5	79
Ituxi, stm., Braz.	B9	82
Ituzaingó, Arg.	D10	80
Itzehoe, Ger.	B9	10
Iṷe, Bela.	H8	22
Iuka, Ms., U.S.	H8	114
Iúna, Braz.	F8	79
Iva, S.C., U.S.	E4	112
Ivacėvičy, Bela.	I8	22
Ivahona, Madag.	s22	67b
Ivaí, stm., Braz.	G2	79
Ivaiporã, Braz.	C13	80
Ivanava, Bela.	I8	22
Ivane-Puste, Ukr.	A10	20
Ivangorod, Russia	B11	22
Ivangrad, Yugo.	G3	20
Ivanhoe, Austl.	I6	70
Ivanhoe, Ca., U.S.	H6	124
Ivanhoe, Mn., U.S.	G11	118
Ivanhoe, Va., U.S.	C6	112
Ivan'kovo, Russia	G20	22
Ivan'kovskij, Russia	E23	22
Ivan'kovskoje vodochranilišče, res., Russia	E19	22
Ivano-Frankivs'k, Ukr.	H2	26
Ivanovo, Russia	D23	22
Ivato, Madag.	r22	67b
Ivatuba, Braz.	G2	79
Ivdel', Russia	E10	26
Ivinheima, stm., Braz.	G2	79
Ivjanec, Bela.	H9	22
Ivón, stm., Bol.	D8	82
Ivorogbo, Nig.	I13	64
Ivory Coast see Cote d'Ivoire, ctry., Afr.	G5	54
Ivory Coast, C. Iv.	I7	64
Ivrea, Italy	D2	18
İvrindi, Tur.	J11	20
Ivujivik, P.Q., Can.	D17	96
Iwaki (Taira), Japan	J15	36
Iwakuni, Japan	M7	36
Iwamizawa, Japan	d16	36a
Iwanai, Japan	e15	36a
Iwo, Nig.	H12	64
Iwo Jima see Iō-jima, i., Japan	F18	126
Iwŏn, N. Kor.	C16	32
Ixcán, stm., N.A.	B3	92
Ixchiguán, Guat.	B3	92
Ixiamas, Bol.	E7	82
Iximché, hist., Guat.	C4	92
Ixmiquilpan, Mex.	G10	90
Ixopo, S. Afr.	H10	66
Ixtahuacán, Guat.	B3	92
Ixtapa, Mex.	I9	90
Ixtepec, Mex.	I12	90
Ixtlán de Juárez, Mex.	I11	90
Ixtlán del Río, Mex.	G7	90
'Iyāl Bakhīt, Sudan	K5	60
Iyo-mishima, Japan	N8	36
Izabal, Guat.	B5	92
Izabal, dept., Guat.	B5	92
Izabal, Lago de, l., Guat.	B5	92
Īzad Khvāst, Iran	F12	48
Izalco, El Sal.	D5	92
Izamal, Mex.	G15	90
Izapa, hist., Mex.	J13	90
'Izbat Abū Ṣuql, Egypt	F1	50
Izberbaš, Russia	I7	26
Izbica, Pol.	A17	10
Izd'oškovo, Russia	F16	22
Izegem, Bel.	G3	12
Īzeh, Iran	F10	48
Iževsk, Russia	F8	26
Izkī, Oman	C10	47
Ižma, stm., Russia	E8	26
Izmalkovo, Russia	I20	22
Izmajil, Ukr.	H3	26
İzmir (Smyrna), Tur.	K11	20
İzmit, Tur.	G13	4
Iznájar, Embalse de, res., Spain	H7	16
Izoplit, Russia	E19	22
Izopo, Punta, c., Hond.	B7	92
Izozog, Bañados del, sw., Bol.	H10	82
Izra', Syria	C6	50
Izsák, Hung.	I19	10
Iztaccíhuatl, Volcán, vol., Mex.	H10	90
Iztaccíhuatl y Popocatépetl, Parques Nacionales, Mex.	H10	90
Iztapa, Guat.	D4	92
Izucar de Matamoros, Mex.	H10	90
Izuhara, Japan	M4	36
Izumi, Japan	O5	36
Izumi, Japan	M10	36
Izumi, Japan	I15	36
Izumo, Japan	L7	36
Izu-shotō, is., Japan	E15	30
Izvestij CIK, ostrova, is., Russia	B14	26
Izyum, Ukr.	H5	26

J

Name	Map Ref.	Page
Jaba, Eth.	N8	60
Jabal al-Awliyā', Sudan	J7	60
Jabalpur, India	I8	44
Jabālyah, Gaza	E2	50
Jabiru, Austl.	B6	68
Jabjabah, Wādī, val., Afr.	G7	60
Jablah, Syria	D3	48
Jablonec nad Nisou, Czech Rep.	E15	10
Jabłonka, Pol.	F19	10
Jablonovyj chrebet, mts., Russia	G14	28
Jaboatão, Braz.	E11	76
Jaborandi, Braz.	F4	79
Jaboticabal, Braz.	F4	79
Jabung, Tanjung, c., Indon.	O8	40
Jaca, Spain	C11	16
Jacala, Mex.	G10	90
Jacaleapa, Hond.	C8	92
Jacaltenango, Guat.	B3	92
Jacaraci, Braz.	C7	79
Jacaré, stm., Braz.	B8	79
Jacaré, stm., Braz.	B10	82
Jacareí, Braz.	G6	79
Jacarezinho, Braz.	G4	79
Jaceel, val., Som.	F11	56
Jáchal, stm., Arg.	F4	80
Jachroma, Russia	E20	22
Jaciara, Braz.	C1	79
Jacinto, Braz.	D8	79
Jacinto Aráuz, Arg.	J7	80
Jacinto City, Tx., U.S.	J11	116
Jacinto Machado, Braz.	E14	80
Jaciparaná, Braz.	C9	82
Jaciparaná, stm., Braz.	D9	82
Jackfish Lake, l., Sk., Can.	E6	104
Jackhead Harbour, Mb., Can.	G17	104
Jackman, Me., U.S.	B16	108
Jack Mountain, mtn., Wa., U.S.	B5	122
Jackpot, Nv., U.S.	C11	124
Jacksboro, Tn., U.S.	C2	112
Jacksboro, Tx., U.S.	F8	116
Jacks Fork, stm., Mo., U.S.	E5	114
Jackson, Al., U.S.	K9	114
Jackson, Ca., U.S.	F5	124
Jackson, Ga., U.S.	F3	112
Jackson, Ky., U.S.	B3	112
Jackson, La., U.S.	L5	114
Jackson, Mi., U.S.	H11	110
Jackson, Mn., U.S.	H13	118
Jackson, Mo., U.S.	E7	114
Jackson, Ms., U.S.	J6	114
Jackson, N.C., U.S.	C9	112
Jackson, Oh., U.S.	H4	108
Jackson, S.C., U.S.	F5	112
Jackson, Tn., U.S.	G8	114
Jackson, Wy., U.S.	A6	120
Jackson, Mount, mtn., Ant.	C12	73
Jackson Center, Oh., U.S.	G2	108
Jackson Creek, stm., Can.	I13	104
Jackson Lake, l., Wy., U.S.	G15	122
Jackson's Arm, Nf., Can.	C17	106
Jacksonville, Al., U.S.	I11	114
Jacksonville, Ar., U.S.	H4	114
Jacksonville, Fl., U.S.	I5	112
Jacksonville, Il., U.S.	C6	114
Jacksonville, N.C., U.S.	E9	112
Jacksonville, Or., U.S.	H3	122
Jacksonville, Tx., U.S.	H11	116
Jacksonville Beach, Fl., U.S.	I5	112
Jacmel, Haiti	E8	94
Jaco, Mex.	D7	90
Jacobābād, Pak.	F3	44
Jacobina, Braz.	F10	76
Jacobsdal, S. Afr.	G7	66
Jacques, Lac à, l., N.T., Can.	C31	100
Jacques-Cartier, Détroit de, strt., P.Q., Can.	C10	106
Jacques-Cartier, Mont, mtn., P.Q., Can.	D8	106
Jacquet River, N.B., Can.	E7	106
Jacqueville, C. Iv.	I7	64
Jacuba, stm., Braz.	E2	79
Jacuí, stm., Braz.	F12	80
Jacuípe, stm., Braz.	B9	79
Jacumba, Ca., U.S.	L9	124
Jacupiranga, Braz.	C14	80
Jaén, Peru	A2	82
Jaén, Spain	H8	16
Jāfarābād, India	B1	46
Jaffa, Cape, c., Austl.	K3	70
Jaffa, Tel Aviv- see Tel Aviv-Yafo, Isr.	D3	50
Jaffna, Sri L.	H6	46
Jaffrey, N.H., U.S.	E14	108
Jafr, Qā'al-, depr., Jord.	H6	50
Jagādhri, India	E7	44
Jagdalpur, India	C7	46
Jagersfontein, S. Afr.	G7	66
Jagodnoje, Russia	E21	28
Jagraon, India	E6	44
Jagtiāl, India	C5	46
Jaguaquara, Braz.	B9	79
Jaguarão, Braz.	G12	80
Jaguarão (Yaguarón), stm., S.A.	G12	80
Jaguari, Braz.	E11	80
Jaguariaíva, Braz.	C14	80
Jaguaribe, stm., Braz.	E11	76
Jaguaripe, Braz.	B9	79
Jaguaruna, Braz.	E14	80
Jagüé, Arg.	E4	80
Jagüey Grande, Cuba	C4	94
Jahānābād, India	H11	44
Jahrom, Iran	G12	48
Jailolo, Indon.	E8	38
Jaipur, India	G6	44
Jaisalmer, India	G4	44
Jaja, Russia	F15	26
Jājapur, India	J12	44
Jajce, Bos.	E12	18
Jakarta, Indon.	j13	39a
Jake Creek Mountain, mtn., Nv., U.S.	C9	124
Jakobstad (Pietarsaari), Fin.	J18	6
Jakša, Russia	E9	26
Jakutija, state, Russia	D18	28
Jakutsk, Russia	E17	28
Jal, N.M., U.S.	G3	116
Jalālābād, Afg.	C4	44
Jalāmīd, Sau. Ar.	B10	60
Jalán, stm., Hond.	C8	92
Jalandhar, India	E6	44
Jalapa, Guat.	C5	92
Jalapa, Nic.	D8	92
Jalapa, dept., Guat.	C5	92
Jālgaon, India	J6	44
Jalisco, state, Mex.	G7	90
Jalizava, Bela.	H12	22
Jālna, India	C3	46
Jālor, India	H5	44
Jalostotitlán, Mex.	G8	90
Jalpa, Mex.	G8	90
Jalpāiguri, India	G13	44
Jalpan, Mex.	G10	90
Jaltepec, stm., Mex.	I12	90
Jalūlā', Iraq	D8	48
Jalutorovsk, Russia	F11	26
Jamaame, Som.	A8	58
Jamaica, ctry., N.A.	E6	94
Jamaica Channel, strt., N.A.	E7	94
Jamal, poluostrov, pen., Russia	C12	26
Jamālpur, Bngl.	H13	44
Jamālpur, India	H12	44
Jamantau, gora, mtn., Russia	G9	26
Jamanxim, stm., Braz.	A13	82
Jamari, stm., Braz.	C10	82
Jamarovka, Russia	G14	28
Jambelí, Canal de, strt., Ec.	I2	84
Jambi, Indon.	F3	38
Jambol, Bul.	G10	20
James, stm., Ab., Can.	F20	102
James, stm., Mo., U.S.	E3	114
James, stm., U.S.	H10	118
James, stm., Va., U.S.	B9	112
James Bay, b., Can.	F16	96
James City, N.C., U.S.	D9	112
James Craik, Arg.	G7	80
James Island, S.C., U.S.	G7	112
Jamesport, Mo., U.S.	C3	114
James Ross, Cape, c., N.T., Can.	B10	96
James Ross Strait, strt., N.T., Can.	C13	96
James Smith Indian Reserve, Sk., Can.	E10	104
Jamestown, Austl.	I3	70
Jamestown, Ca., U.S.	G5	124
Jamestown, Ks., U.S.	L10	118
Jamestown, Ky., U.S.	F11	114
Jamestown, N.C., U.S.	D7	112
Jamestown, N.D., U.S.	E9	118
Jamestown, N.Y., U.S.	E7	108
Jamestown, Oh., U.S.	H3	108
Jamestown, S. Afr.	H8	66
Jamestown, Tn., U.S.	F12	114
Jamestown Reservoir, res., N.D., U.S.	D9	118
Jaminauá, stm., Braz.	C6	82
Jamkhandi, India	D3	46
Jamm, Russia	C11	22
Jammu, India	D6	44
Jammu and Kashmīr, dep., Asia	C10	42
Jamnagar, India	I4	44
Jamsah, Egypt	D7	60
Jamshedpur, India	I12	44
Jamsk, Russia	F22	28
Jämtlands Län, co., Swe.	J13	6
Jamūi, India	H12	44
Jamuna, stm., Bngl.	H13	44
Jamundí, Col.	F4	84
Jana, stm., Russia	C19	28
Janauacá, Lago, l., Braz.	I12	84
Janaúba, Braz.	C7	79
Janaucu, Ilha, i., Braz.	C8	76
Janavičy, Bela.	F13	22
Jand, Pak.	D5	44
Jandaia, Braz.	D3	79
Jandaia do Sul, Braz.	G3	79
Jandaq, Iran	D13	48
Jandiāla, India	E6	44
Jandiatuba, stm., Braz.	J8	84
Janeiro, Rio de, stm., Braz.	A6	79
Janesville, Ca., U.S.	D5	124
Janesville, Mn., U.S.	F2	110
Janesville, Wi., U.S.	H6	110
Jangijul', Uzb.	I11	26
Jangīpur, India	H13	44
Janīn, W.B.	D4	50
Janjina, Madag.	r21	67b
Jan Kempdorp (Andalusia), S. Afr.	F7	66
Jan Lake, l., Sk., Can.	D12	104
Jan Mayen, i., Nor.	B19	86
Janos, Mex.	B5	90
Jánoshalma, Hung.	I19	10
Jánosháza, Hung.	H17	10
Jansen, Sk., Can.	G10	104
Janskij zaliv, b., Russia	C19	28
Jantarnyj, Russia	G2	22
Januária, Braz.	C6	79
Janzé, Fr.	E5	14
Jaora, India	I6	44
Japan (Nihon), ctry., Asia	D14	30
Japan, Sea of (Nihon-kai), Asia	K7	36
Japim, Braz.	B5	82
Japurá, Braz.	H9	84
Japurá (Caquetá), stm., S.A.	H8	84
Jaqué, Pan.	D3	84
Jaquí, Peru	F4	82
Jarābulus, Syria	C5	48
Jarad, Sau. Ar.	E2	47
Jaraguá, Braz.	C4	79
Jaraguá do Sul, Braz.	D14	80
Jaraíz de la Vera, Spain	E6	16
Jarales, N.M., U.S.	J10	120
Jarama, stm., Spain	E8	16
Jaramānah, Syria	B6	50
Jaransk, Russia	F7	26
Jarash, Jord.	D5	50
Jarbidge, stm., U.S.	H10	122
Jarcevo, Russia	F15	22
Jardim, Braz.	I13	82
Jardín América, Arg.	D11	80
Jardine River National Park, Austl.	B8	68
Jardines de la Reina, Archipiélago de los, is., Cuba	D5	94
Jardinópolis, Braz.	F5	79
Jaredi, Nig.	E12	64
Jarensk, Russia	E7	26
Jargeau, Fr.	E9	14
Jari, stm., Braz.	A10	82
Jari, Lago, l., Braz.	J11	84
Jaridih, India	I12	44
Jarnac, Fr.	G6	14
Jarocin, Pol.	D17	10
Jaroměř, Czech Rep.	E15	10
Jaroslavl', Russia	D22	22
Jarosław, Pol.	E22	10
Jarratt, Va., U.S.	C9	112
Jarreau, La., U.S.	L5	114
Jaru, Braz.	D10	82
Jaru, stm., Braz.	D10	82
Järva-Jaani, Est.	B8	22
Järvenpää, Fin.	K19	6
Jarvie, Ab., Can.	C21	102
Jarvis, On., Can.	H15	110
Jarvisburg, N.C., U.S.	C11	112
Jarvis Island, i., Oc.	I23	126
Jaša Tomić, Yugo.	D4	20
Jasikan, Ghana	H10	64
Jāsk, Iran	I14	48
Jasło, Pol.	F21	10
Jasnogorsk, Russia	G20	22
Jason Islands, is., Falk. Is.	G4	78
Jasonville, In., U.S.	C9	114
Jasper, Ab., Can.	E16	102
Jasper, Al., U.S.	I9	114
Jasper, Ar., U.S.	F3	114
Jasper, Fl., U.S.	I4	112
Jasper, Ga., U.S.	E2	112
Jasper, In., U.S.	D10	114
Jasper, Mn., U.S.	H11	118
Jasper, Mo., U.S.	E2	114
Jasper, Tn., U.S.	G11	114
Jasper, Tx., U.S.	L3	114
Jasper Lake, l., Ab., Can.	D16	102
Jasper National Park, Ab., Can.	E17	102
Jászapáti, Hung.	H20	10
Jászberény, Hung.	H19	10
Jász-Nagykun-Szolnok, co., Hung.	H20	10
Jataí, Braz.	D3	79
Jatapu, stm., Braz.	H13	84
Jataté, stm., Mex.	I14	90
Jatni, India	J11	44
Jatobá, stm., Braz.	B1	79
Jaú, Braz.	G4	79
Jaú, stm., Braz.	H12	84
Jauaperi, stm., Braz.	H12	84
Jauja, Peru	D4	82
Jaungulbene, Lat.	D9	22
Jaunjelgava, Lat.	E8	22
Jaunpiebalga, Lat.	D9	22
Jaunpur, India	H10	44
Jaupaci, Braz.	D3	79
Jauquara, stm., Braz.	F13	82
Jauru, stm., Braz.	E1	79
Jauru, stm., Braz.	G13	82
Java, S.D., U.S.	F8	118
Java see Jawa, i., Indon.	j15	39a
Javari (Yavarí), stm., S.A.	D4	76
Javas, Russia	G25	22
Java Sea see Jawa, Laut, Indon.	G5	38
Java Trench	J11	24
Jawa (Java), i., Indon.	j15	39a
Jawa, Laut (Java Sea), Indon.	G5	38
Jawbar, Syria	A6	50
Jawor, Pol.	D16	10
Jaworzno, Pol.	E19	10
Jay, Fl., U.S.	L9	114
Jay, Ok., U.S.	C12	116
Jaya, Puncak, mtn., Indon.	F10	38
Jayanca, Peru	B2	82
Jayapura (Sukarnapura), Indon.	F11	38
Jayb, Wādī al- (Ha'Arava), val., Asia	H4	50
Jaynes, Az., U.S.	L5	120
Jaypur, India	C7	46
Jayton, Tx., U.S.	F6	116
Jažėlbicy, Russia	C15	22
Jeanerette, La., U.S.	M5	114
Jebba, Nig.	G12	64
Jebeniana, Tun.	C16	62
Jeberos, Peru	A3	82
Jechegnadzor, Arm.	B8	48
Jeddore Lake, res., Nf., Can.	D18	106
Jędrzejów, Pol.	E20	10
Jefawa, Sudan	L2	60
Jeffara (Al-Jifārah), pl., Afr.	D16	62
Jeffers, Mn., U.S.	G12	118
Jefferson, Ga., U.S.	E3	112
Jefferson, Ia., U.S.	I13	118
Jefferson, N.C., U.S.	C5	112
Jefferson, Oh., U.S.	F6	108
Jefferson, Or., U.S.	F2	122
Jefferson, S.C., U.S.	E6	112
Jefferson, S.D., U.S.	I11	118
Jefferson, Tx., U.S.	J2	114
Jefferson, Wi., U.S.	G7	110
Jefferson, stm., Mt., U.S.	E13	122
Jefferson, Mount, mtn., Nv., U.S.	F9	124
Jefferson, Mount, mtn., Or., U.S.	F4	122
Jefferson, Mount, mtn., U.S.	F14	122
Jefferson City, Mo., U.S.	D4	114
Jefferson City, Tn., U.S.	C3	112
Jeffersonton, Va., U.S.	I9	108
Jeffersontown, Ky., U.S.	D11	114
Jeffersonville, Ga., U.S.	G3	112
Jeffersonville, In., U.S.	D11	114
Jeffersonville, Oh., U.S.	H3	108
Jeffrey City, Wy., U.S.	B9	120
Jefimovskij, Russia	L24	6
Jefremov, Russia	G5	26
Jega, Nig.	E12	64
Jegenstorf, Switz.	D8	13
Jegorjevsk, Russia	F22	22
Jejsk, Russia	H5	26
Jēkabpils, Lat.	E8	22
Jekaterinburg, Russia	F10	26
Jekateriny, proliv, strt., Russia	I21	28
Jekimoviči, Russia	G16	22
Jekyll Island, i., Ga., U.S.	H5	112
Jelabuga, Russia	F8	26
Jelancy, Russia	G13	28
Jel'cy, Russia	E16	22
Jelec, Russia	I21	22
Jelenia Góra (Hirschberg), Pol.	E15	10
Jelenskij, Russia	H18	22
Jelgava, Lat.	E6	22
Jelizarovo, Russia	C27	22
Jelizavety, mys, c., Russia	G20	28
Jellico, Tn., U.S.	C2	112
Jelm Mountain, mtn., Wy., U.S.	C11	120
Jel'n'a, Russia	G16	22
Jelnat', Russia	D25	22
Jeloguj, stm., Russia	E15	26
Jelšava, Slvk.	G20	10
Jemanželinsk, Russia	G10	26
Jember, Indon.	G5	38
Jemca, Russia	J27	6
Jemez, stm., N.M., U.S.	I10	120
Jemez Springs, N.M., U.S.	I10	120
Jemmal, Tun.	N5	18
Jena, Ger.	E11	10
Jena, La., U.S.	K4	114
Jenašimskij Polkan, gora, mtn., Russia	F16	26
Jenbach, Aus.	H11	10
Jendouba (Souk el Arba), Tun.	M3	18
Jenisej (Yenisey), stm., Russia	D15	26
Jenisejsk, Russia	F10	28
Jenisejskij kr'až, mts., Russia	F16	26
Jenisejskij zaliv, b., Russia	C8	28
Jenkins, Ky., U.S.	B4	112
Jenkinsville, S.C., U.S.	E5	112
Jenkintown, Pa., U.S.	G11	108
Jenks, Ok., U.S.	C11	116
Jennersdorf, Aus.	I16	10
Jennings, Fl., U.S.	I3	112
Jennings, La., U.S.	L4	114
Jenpeg Dam, Mb., Can.	D16	104
Jensen, Ut., U.S.	D7	120
Jensen Beach, Fl., U.S.	L6	112
Jens Munk Island, i., N.T., Can.	C17	96
Jeparit, Austl.	K4	70
Jepelacio, Peru	B3	82
Jepifan', Russia	H21	22
Jequeri, Braz.	F7	79
Jequetepeque, stm., Peru	B2	82
Jequié, Braz.	B8	79
Jequitaí, Braz.	D6	79
Jequitinhonha, Braz.	D8	79
Jequitinhonha, stm., Braz.	D9	79
Jerada, Mor.	C9	62
Jeradou, Tun.	M5	18
Jerba, Île de, i., Tun.	D16	62
Jerécuaro, Mex.	G9	90
Jérémie, Haiti	E7	94
Jeremoabo, Braz.	F11	76
Jerevan, Arm.	I6	26
Jerez de García Salinas, Mex.	F8	90
Jerez de la Frontera, Spain	I5	16
Jerez de los Caballeros, Spain	G5	16
Jergeni, hills, Russia	H6	26
Jericho see Arīḥā, Gaza	E4	50
Jericó, Col.	E5	84
Jerid, Chott, sw., Tun.	D15	62
Jerilderie, Austl.	J6	70
Jerimoth Hill, hill, R.I., U.S.	F15	108
Jermiš', Russia	G25	22
Jermolajevo (Kumertau), Russia	G9	26
Jermolino, Russia	F19	22
Jeroaquara, Braz.	C3	79
Jerofej Pavlovič, Russia	G16	28
Jerome, Az., U.S.	J4	120
Jerome, Id., U.S.	H11	122
Jersey, dep., Eur.	F7	4
Jersey City, N.J., U.S.	G12	108
Jersey Mountain, mtn., Id., U.S.	E10	122
Jersey Shore, Pa., U.S.	F9	108
Jerseyville, Il., U.S.	C6	114
Jeršov, Russia	G7	26
Jerusalem see Yerushalayim, Isr.	E4	50
Jervis, Cape, c., Austl.	J3	70
Jervis Bay, b., Austl.	J9	70
Jervis Inlet, b., B.C., Can.	H10	102
Jesenice, Czech Rep.	E13	10
Jesi, Italy	F8	18
Jesil', Kaz.	G11	26
Jessentuki, Russia	I6	26
Jessore, Bngl.	I13	44
Jessup, Pa., U.S.	F11	108
Jesup, Ga., U.S.	H5	112
Jesup, Ia., U.S.	H3	110
Jesús, Para.	D11	80
Jesús Carranza, Mex.	I12	90
Jesús de Otoro, Hond.	C7	92
Jesús María, Arg.	F6	80
Jesús María, Mex.	E6	90
Jesús María, stm., Mex.	F7	90
Jesús Menéndez, Cuba	D6	94
Jet, Ok., U.S.	C8	116
Jetmore, Ks., U.S.	M8	118
Jetpur, India	J4	44
Jette, Bel.	G5	12
Jeumont, Fr.	B11	14
Jeune Landing, B.C., Can.	G7	102
Jever, Ger.	B7	10
Jewell, Ia., U.S.	H2	110
Jewell, Ks., U.S.	L9	118
Jewell Ridge, Va., U.S.	B5	112
Jewett, Il., U.S.	C8	114
Jewett, Tx., U.S.	H10	116
Jewett City, Ct., U.S.	F15	108
Jewett Lake, l., Sk., Can.	B10	104
Jezerce, mtn., Alb.	G3	20
Jeziorany, Pol.	B20	10
Jhābua, India	I6	44
Jhālāwār, India	H7	44
Jhal Jhao, Pak.	G1	44
Jhang Sadar, Pak.	E5	44
Jhānsi, India	H8	44
Jharia, India	I12	44
Jhārsuguda, India	B8	46
Jhelum, Pak.	D5	44
Jhelum, stm., Asia	E5	44
Jhok Rind, Pak.	E4	44
Jhunjhunūn, India	F6	44
Jiaban, China	B9	40
Jiading, China	D10	34
Jiāganj, India	H13	44
Jiakou, China	E8	34
Jiali, China	E5	30
Jialing, stm., China	E8	30
Jialou, China	C2	34
Jiamusi, China	B13	30
Ji'an, China	H3	34
Jianchang, China	B12	32
Jianchuan, China	A5	40
Jiangbeixu, China	I4	34
Jiangbianzhai, China	C6	40
Jiangcun, China	G6	34
Jiangdihe, China	B6	40
Jiangduo, China	C9	34
Jianggezhuang, China	D7	32
Jiangji, China	C4	34
Jiangjin, China	F8	30
Jiangkou, China	G9	30
Jiangkou, China	H7	34
Jiangkouji, China	C5	34
Jiangliadian, China	A5	32
Jiangmen, China	M2	34
Jiangsu (Kiangsu), prov., China	E10	30
Jiangtun, China	B10	32
Jiangxi (Kiangsi), prov., China	F10	30
Jiangxiang, China	C6	34
Jiangyin, China	D9	34
Jiangzhasiji, China	E13	44
Jianli, China	F1	34
Jianning, China	I5	34
Jian'ou, China	H7	34
Jianshan, China	F9	34
Jianshui, China	C7	40
Jiantouji, China	I5	32
Jiaohe, China	C12	30
Jiaomei, China	K6	34
Jiaoshanhe, China	F1	34
Jiaoxian, China	G7	32
Jiaozuo, China	D9	30
Jiashan, China	C7	34
Jiashun Hu, l., China	C12	44
Jiawang, China	A6	34
Jiaxian, China	B2	34
Jiaxing, China	E9	34
Jiayu, China	F2	34
Jiazi, China	M5	34
Jibiya, Nig.	E13	64
Jiboa, stm., El Sal.	D5	92
Jicarón, Isla, i., Pan.	D2	84
Jicatuyo, stm., Hond.	C6	92
Jiddah (Jeddah), Sau. Ar.	D1	47
Jidingxilin, China	D15	44
Jiedong, China	I2	34
Jiehe, China	H5	32
Jieji, China	B7	34
Jiepai, China	E8	34
Jiesheng, China	M4	34
Jieshou, China	B4	34
Jieshou, China	B8	34
Jieyang, China	L5	34
Jieznas, Lith.	G7	22
Jigongzhen, China	A4	34
Jiguaní, Cuba	D6	94
Jiguanshan, China	A12	32
Jigüey, Bahía de, b., Cuba	C5	94
*Jihlava, Czech Rep.	F15	10
Jijel, Alg.	B13	62
Jijiadianzi, China	H6	32
Jikawo, Eth.	M7	60
Jikawo, stm., Afr.	M8	60
Jilib, Som.	A8	58
Jili Hu, l., China	B4	30
Jilin, China	C12	30
Jilin (Kirin), prov., China	C12	30
Jill, Kediet ej, mtn., Maur.	I4	62
Jima, Eth.	N9	60
Jimbolia, Rom.	D4	20
Jiménez, Mex.	C9	90
Jiménez, Mex.	D7	90
Jiménez del Téul, Mex.	F7	90
Jimo, China	G8	32
Jim Thorpe, Pa., U.S.	G11	108
Jin (Gam), stm., Asia	C8	40
Jināḥ, Egypt	E6	60
Jinan (Tsinan), China	G4	32
Jinbang, China	J7	34
Jincheng, China	D9	30
Jīnd, India	F7	44
Jindřichův Hradec, Czech Rep.	F15	10
Jingangtou, China	H2	34
Jingcheng, China	K6	34
Jingdezhen (Kingtechen), China	F6	34
Jinggang, China	G1	34
Jinggangshan (Ciping), China	I3	34
Jinghai, China	E4	32
Jinghaiwei, China	G10	32
Jinghong, China	C6	40
Jingning, China	H8	34
Jingoutun, China	B5	32
Jingxi, China	C9	40
Jingxian, China	F4	32
Jingyu, China	A14	32
Jingzhi, China	G7	32
Jinhua, China	F8	34
Jining, China	C9	30
Jining, China	H4	32
Jinja, Ug.	A6	58
Jinjiang, China	A6	40
Jinjing, China	G2	34
Jinkeng, China	H6	34
Jinkou, China	G8	32
Jinlingzhen, China	G6	32
Jinmu Jiao, c., China	H8	30
Jinning, China	B7	40
Jinotega, Nic.	D8	92
Jinotega, dept., Nic.	D9	92
Jinotepe, Nic.	F8	92
Jinping, China	A10	40
Jinrui, China	H3	34
Jinsha, stm., China	F6	30
Jinshan, China	E10	34
Jinshi, China	F9	30
Jintian, China	H3	34
Jinxi, China	C8	32
Jinxian, China	D9	32
Jinyun, China	G9	34
Jinzhaizhen, China	D4	34
Jinzhou (Chinchou), China	B9	32
Ji-Paraná, Braz.	D11	82
Jipijapa, Ec.	H2	84
Jiquilisco, El Sal.	D6	92
Jiquilisco, Bahía de, b., El Sal.	D6	92
Jiquiriçá, stm., Braz.	B8	79

Name	Map Ref.	Page
Jirāfī, Wādī al- (Nahal Paran), val.	I3	50
Jirbān, Sudan	L6	60
Jirjā, Egypt	D6	60
Jirkov, Czech Rep.	E13	10
Jīroft, Iran	G14	48
Jisr ash-Shughūr, Syria	D4	48
Jitan, China	K4	34
Jitaúna, Braz.	C9	79
Jiu, stm., Rom.	F7	20
Jiubao, China	J4	34
Jiucheng, China	E5	32
Jiuguan, China	F9	32
Jiuhu, China	F5	32
Jiuhuaxian, China	L2	34
Jiujiang, China	F4	34
Jiukou, China	E1	34
Jiulian Shan, mts., China	K3	34
Jiuling Shan, mts., China	G3	34
Jiulong, China	K1	34
Jiumianyang, China	E2	34
Jiuningyang, China	J6	34
Jiuquan, China	D6	30
Jiushangshui, China	B3	34
Jiutai, China	C12	30
Jiuxian, China	B2	34
Jiuxiangcheng, China	B3	34
Jixi, China	B13	30
Jixian, China	H2	32
Jixian, China	C5	32
Jixingji, China	C5	34
Jiyang, China	G5	32
Jīzān, Sau. Ar.	F3	47
Joaçaba, Braz.	D13	80
Joaíma, Braz.	D8	79
Joanna, S.C., U.S.	E5	112
João Neiva, Braz.	E8	79
João Pessoa, Braz.	E12	76
João Pinheiro, Braz.	D5	79
Joaquim Távora, Braz.	G4	79
Joaquin, Tx., U.S.	K2	114
Joaquín V. González, Arg.	C6	80
Job Peak, mtn., Nv., U.S.	E7	124
Jocolí, Arg.	G4	80
Jocón, Hond.	B8	92
Jocoro, El Sal.	D6	92
Jocotán, Guat.	C5	92
Jódar, Spain	H8	16
Jodhpur, India	G5	44
Joe Batt's Arm, Nf., Can.	C19	106
Joensuu, Fin.	J21	6
Joetsu, Japan	J13	36
Joffre, Mount, mtn., Can.	G19	102
Jõgeva, Est.	C9	22
Jog Falls, wtfl, India	E3	46
Joggins, N.S., Can.	G9	106
Jogui, stm., Braz.	G1	79
Johannesburg, Ca., U.S.	I8	124
Johannesburg, S. Afr.	F9	66
John Day, Or., U.S.	F7	122
John Day, stm., Or., U.S.	E5	122
John H. Kerr Reservoir, res., U.S.	C8	112
John Martin Reservoir, res., Co., U.S.	M4	118
John o' Groats, Scot., U.K.	C10	8
John Redmond Reservoir, res., Ks., U.S.	M12	118
Johnson, Ar., U.S.	F2	114
Johnson, Ks., U.S.	N6	118
Johnson, Ne., U.S.	K12	118
Johnson, Vt., U.S.	C14	108
Johnsonburg, Pa., U.S.	F8	108
Johnson City, N.Y., U.S.	E11	108
Johnson City, Tn., U.S.	C4	112
Johnson City, Tx., U.S.	I8	116
Johnsondale, Ca., U.S.	I7	124
Johnsons Crossing, Yk., Can.	F28	100
Johnsonville, S.C., U.S.	F7	112
Johnston, Ia., U.S.	I2	110
Johnston, S.C., U.S.	F5	112
Johnston Atoll, atoll, Oc.	G23	126
Johnston City, Il., U.S.	E8	114
Johnstone Strait, strt., B.C., Can.	G8	102
Johnstown, Co., U.S.	D12	120
Johnstown, N.Y., U.S.	D12	108
Johnstown, Oh., U.S.	G4	108
Johnstown, Pa., U.S.	G8	108
Johor Baharu, Malay.	N7	40
Joigny, Fr.	E10	14
Joiner, Ar., U.S.	G6	114
Joinvile, Braz.	D14	80
Joinville, Fr.	D12	14
Joinville Island, i., Ant.	B1	73
Jokkmokk, Swe.	H16	6
Jolārpettai, India	F5	46
Jolfā, Iran	B8	48
Joliet, Il., U.S.	I7	110
Joliet, Mt., U.S.	E17	122
Joliette, P.Q., Can.	A13	108
Jolo, Phil.	D7	38
Jomda, China	E6	30
Jonava, Lith.	F7	22
Jones, Ok., U.S.	D9	116
Jonesboro, Ar., U.S.	G6	114
Jonesboro, Ga., U.S.	F2	112
Jonesboro, Il., U.S.	E7	114
Jonesboro, In., U.S.	B11	114
Jonesboro, La., U.S.	J4	114
Jonesboro, Tn., U.S.	C4	112
Jonesburg, Mo., U.S.	D5	114
Jones Mill, Ar., U.S.	H4	114
Jonesport, Me., U.S.	C19	108
Jones Sound, strt., N.T., Can.	A15	96
Jonestown, Ms., U.S.	H6	114
Jonesville, La., U.S.	K5	114
Jonesville, Mi., U.S.	I11	110
Jonesville, N.C., U.S.	C6	112
Jonesville, S.C., U.S.	E5	112
Jonesville, Va., U.S.	C3	112
Joniškėlis, Lith.	E7	22
Joniškis, Lith.	E6	22
Jönköping, Swe.	M14	6
Jonquière, P.Q., Can.	D2	106
Jonuta, Mex.	H13	90
Joplin, Mo., U.S.	E2	114
Joplin, Mt., U.S.	B15	122
Joppa, Il., U.S.	E8	114
Jordan, Mn., U.S.	F2	110
Jordan, Mt., U.S.	C19	122
Jordan, N.Y., U.S.	D10	108
Jordan (Al-Urdun), ctry., Asia	C2	42
Jordan (Nahr al-Urdun) (HaYarden), stm., Asia	E5	50
Jordan, stm., Ut., U.S.	D5	120
Jordânia, Braz.	C8	79
Jordanów, Pol.	F19	10
Jordan Valley, Or., U.S.	H8	122
Jordão, stm., Braz.	C13	80
Jordet, Nor.	K13	6
Jorhāt, India	G16	44
Jornado del Muerto, des., N.M., U.S.	K10	120
Jos, Nig.	G14	64
José Batlle y Ordóñez, Ur.	G11	80
José Bonifácio, Braz.	F4	79
José Francisco Vergara, Chile	B4	80
Joselândia, Braz.	G13	82
José Pedro Varela, Ur.	G11	80
Joseph, Or., U.S.	E8	122
Joseph, Lac, l., Nf., Can.	F19	96
Joseph Bonaparte Gulf, b., Austl.	B5	68
Joseph City, Az., U.S.	J6	120
Joshua, Tx., U.S.	G9	116
Joshua Tree, Ca., U.S.	J9	124
Joškar-Ola, Russia	F7	26
Josselin, Fr.	E4	14
Joubertina, S. Afr.	I6	66
Jourdanton, Tx., U.S.	K8	116
Jovellanos, Cuba	C4	94
Joviânia, Braz.	D4	79
Jowhar, Som.	H10	56
Joy, Il., U.S.	I5	110
Joy, Mount, mtn., Yk., Can.	E28	100
Joyce, La., U.S.	K4	114
Józefów, Pol.	C21	10
J. Percy Priest Lake, res., Tn., U.S.	F10	114
Juami, stm., Braz.	H9	84
Juan Aldama, Mex.	E8	90
Juan B. Arruabarrena, Arg.	F9	80
Juan Bautista Alberdi, Arg.	D6	80
Juan de Fuca, Strait of, strt., N.A.	I10	102
Juan de Mena, Para.	C10	80
Juan de Nova, Île, i., Afr.	E8	58
Juan E. Barra, Arg.	I8	80
Juan Eugenio, Mex.	E8	90
Juan Fernández, Archipiélago, is., Chile	C1	78
Juangriego, Ven.	B11	84
Juan Guerra, Peru	B3	82
Juan Jorba, Arg.	G6	80
Juan José Castelli, Arg.	C8	80
Juán José Perez, Bol.	F7	82
Juanjuí, Peru	B3	82
Juan L. Lacaze, Ur.	H10	80
Juan N. Fernández, Arg.	J9	80
Juan Perez Sound, strt., B.C., Can.	E3	102
Juan Viñas, C.R.	H11	92
Juárez, Mex.	D9	90
Juárez, Mex.	B5	90
Juárez see Ciudad Juárez, Mex.	B6	90
Juárez, Sierra de, mts., Mex.	B2	90
Juatinga, Ponta de, c., Braz.	G6	79
Juàzeiro, Braz.	E10	76
Juazeiro do Norte, Braz.	E11	76
Jūbā, Sudan	H7	56
Juba, stm., Braz.	F12	82
Jūbāl, Maḍīq, strt., Egypt	D7	60
Jubal, Strait of see Jūbāl, Maḍīq, strt., Egypt	D7	60
Jubaysho, Eth.	O9	60
Jubayt, Sudan	H9	60
Jubba (Genale), stm., Afr.	H9	56
Jubbah, Sau. Ar.	G6	48
Jubilee Lake, l., Nf., Can.	D18	106
Jubones, stm., Ec.	I3	84
Juby, Cap, c., Mor.	G4	62
Júcar (Xúquer), stm., Spain	F10	16
Juçara, Braz.	C3	79
Júcaro, Cuba	D5	94
Juchipila, Mex.	G8	90
Juchitán de Zaragoza, Mex.	I12	90
Juchnov, Russia	G18	22
Jucuapa, El Sal.	D6	92
Jucurucu, stm., Braz.	D9	79
Judaea, hist. reg., Asia	E4	50
Judas, Punta, c., C.R.	H10	92
Jude Island, i., Nf., Can.	E19	106
Judenburg, Aus.	H14	10
Judique, N.S., Can.	G12	106
Judith, stm., Mt., U.S.	C16	122
Judith Gap, Mt., U.S.	D16	122
Judith Mountains, mts., Mt., U.S.	C16	122
Judson, S.C., U.S.	E4	112
Judsonia, Ar., U.S.	G5	114
Juexi, China	F10	34
Jufari, stm., Braz.	H11	84
Jugon, Fr.	D4	14
Juhā, Sau. Ar.	F3	47
Juhavičy, Bela.	E11	22
Juidongshan, China	L6	34
Juigalpa, Nic.	E9	92
Juína, stm., Braz.	E12	82
Juiz de Fora, Braz.	F7	79
Jujuy, prov., Arg.	B5	80
Jukagirskoje ploskogorje, plat., Russia	D23	28
Julesburg, Co., U.S.	K5	118
Juli, Peru	G7	82
Juliaca, Peru	F6	82
Julia Creek, Austl.	C4	70
Julianakanaal, Neth.	F8	12
Julian Alps, mts., Eur.	C8	18
Juliana Top, mtn., Sur.	F14	84
Julianehåb (Qaqortoq), Grnld.	D23	96
Jülich, Ger.	E6	10
Julimes, Mex.	C7	90
Júlio de Castilhos, Braz.	E12	80
Julu, China	F3	32
Juma, Russia	I23	6
Jumay, Volcán, vol., Guat.	C5	92
Jumbilla, Peru	A3	82
Jumboo, Som.	B8	58
Jumentos Cays, is., Bah.	C7	94
Jumet, Bel.	H5	12
Jumilla, Spain	G10	16
Jump, stm., Wi., U.S.	E5	110
Jūnāgadh, India	J4	44
Junaynah, Ra's al-, mtn., Egypt	G2	48
Junction, Tx., U.S.	I7	116
Junction, Ut., U.S.	F4	120
Junction City, Ar., U.S.	I4	114
Junction City, Ks., U.S.	L11	118
Junction City, Ky., U.S.	E12	114
Junction City, Or., U.S.	F2	122
Jundiaí, Braz.	G5	79
Jundiaí do Sul, Braz.	G3	79
Juneau, Ak., U.S.	G27	100
Juneau, Wi., U.S.	G7	110
Junee, Austl.	J7	70
June Lake, Ca., U.S.	G6	124
Jungar Qi, China	D9	30
Jungfrau, mtn., Switz.	E8	13
Junggar Pendi, China	B4	30
Jungshāhi, Pak.	H2	44
Juniata, Ne., U.S.	K9	118
Juniata, stm., Pa., U.S.	G9	108
Junín, Arg.	H8	80
Junín, Ec.	H2	84
Junín, Peru	D3	82
Junín, dept., Peru	D4	82
Junín, Lago de, l., Peru	D3	82
Junior, W.V., U.S.	I7	108
Juniper, N.B., Can.	F6	106
Juniville, Fr.	C11	14
Junqueirópolis, Braz.	F3	79
Juntas, C.R.	G9	92
Junxian, China	E9	30
Juparanã, Lagoa, l., Braz.	E8	79
Jupilingo, stm., Guat.	C5	92
Jupiter, Fl., U.S.	M6	112
Jupiter, stm., P.Q., Can.	C10	106
Juquiá, Braz.	C15	80
Juquiá, Ponta do, c., Braz.	C15	80
Jur, stm., Sudan	M5	60
Jura, state, Switz.	D7	13
Jura, dept., Fr.	F12	14
Jura, mts., Eur.	F13	14
Jura, i., Scot., U.K.	E8	8
Juraciški, Bela.	G8	22
Juramento, Braz.	D7	79
Jurbarkas, Lith.	F5	22
Jurf ad-Darāwīsh, Jord.	G5	50
Jurga, Russia	F8	28
Jurjevec, Russia	D26	22
Jurjev-Pol'skij, Russia	E22	22
Jūrmala, Lat.	E6	22
Jurty, Russia	F17	26
Juruá, Braz.	I9	84
Juruá, stm., S.A.	D5	76
Juruá-mirim, stm., Braz.	C5	82
Juruena, stm., Braz.	B12	82
Jurupari, stm., Braz.	C7	82
Jur'uzan', Russia	G9	26
Juscelândia, Braz.	C3	79
Jusepín, Ven.	C11	84
Juskatla, B.C., Can.	D2	102
Jussey, Fr.	E12	14
Justiniano Posse, Arg.	G7	80
Justo Daract, Arg.	G6	80
Jutaí, Braz.	A7	82
Jutaí, stm., Braz.	D5	76
Jüterbog, Ger.	D13	10
Juti, Braz.	G1	79
Jutiapa, Guat.	C5	92
Jutiapa, dept., Guat.	C5	92
Juticalpa, Hond.	C8	92
Jutiquile, Hond.	C8	92
Jutland see Jylland, pen., Den.	M11	6
Juva, Fin.	K20	6
Juventud, Isla de la (Isla de Pinos), i., Cuba	D3	94
Juxi, China	H8	34
Juža, Russia	E25	22
Južno-Sachalinsk, Russia	H20	28
Južno-Ural'sk, Russia	G10	26
Južnyj, mys, c., Russia	F23	28
Jwayyā, Leb.	B4	50
Jylland, reg., Den.	M11	6
Jyväskylä, Fin.	J19	6

K

Name	Map Ref.	Page
K2 (Qogir Feng), mtn., Asia	C7	44
Kaachka, Turk.	C15	48
Kaala, mtn., Hi., U.S.	p15	125a
Kaapstad see Cape Town, S. Afr.	I4	66
Kabah, hist., Mex.	G15	90
Kabale, Ug.	B5	58
Kabalega Falls, wtfl, Ug.	H7	56
Kabalo, Zaire	C5	58
Kabambare, Zaire	B5	58
Kabba, Nig.	H13	64
Kabetogama Lake, l., Mn., U.S.	B3	110
Kabinda, Zaire	C4	58
Kabīr Kūh, mts., Iran	E9	48
Kabkābīyah, Sudan	K3	60
Kabna, Sudan	H7	60
Kābol, Afg.	C3	44
Kābol, stm., Asia	C4	44
Kabompo, stm., Zam.	D4	58
Kabongo, Zaire	C5	58
Kabot, Gui.	F2	64
Kabou, Togo	G10	64
Kabr, Sudan	L4	60
Kābul see Kābol, Afg.	C3	44
Kaburuang, Pulau, i., Indon.	E8	38
Kabwe (Broken Hill), Zam.	D5	58
Kačanik, Yugo.	G5	20
Kačerginė, Lith.	G6	22
Kachchh, Gulf of, b., India	I3	44
Kachemak Bay, b., Ak., U.S.	G19	100
Kachisi, Eth.	M9	60
K'achta, Russia	G13	28
Kačug, Russia	G13	28
Kadaiyanallūr, India	H4	46
Kadanai (Kadaney), stm., Asia	E2	44
Kadaney (Kadanai), stm., Asia	E2	44
Kadan Kyun, i., Myan.	H5	40
Kade, Ghana	H9	64
Kadéï, stm., Afr.	H4	56
Kadi, India	I5	44
Kadiana, Mali	F6	64
Kadina, Austl.	I2	70
Kadiri, India	E5	46
Kadirli, Tur.	C4	48
Kadja, Ouadi (Wādī Kaja), val., Afr.	L3	60
Kadnikov, Russia	B23	22
Kadnikovskij, Russia	A23	22
Kado, Nig.	H14	64
Kadodo, Sudan	L5	60
Kadoka, S.D., U.S.	H6	118
Kadom, Russia	G25	22
Kadoma, Zimb.	B9	66
Kaduj, Russia	B20	22
Kaduna, Nig.	F13	64
Kaduna, stm., Nig.	G12	64
Kāduqlī, Sudan	L5	60
Kadyj, Russia	D26	22
Kadykčan, Russia	E21	28
Kadžerom, Russia	E9	26
Kaech'ŏn, N. Kor.	D13	32
Kaédi, Maur.	C3	64
Kaegudeck Lake, l., Nf., Can.	D18	106
Kaena Point, c., Hi., U.S.	p15	125a
Kaesŏng, N. Kor.	F14	32
Kāf, Sau. Ar.	F4	48
Kafan, Arm.	B9	48
Kafanchan, Nig.	G14	64
Kaffraria, hist. reg., S. Afr.	H9	66
Kaffrine, Sen.	D2	64
Kafia Kingi, Sudan	M3	60
Kafin Madaki, Nig.	F14	64
Kafirévs, Ákra, c., Grc.	K8	20
Kafr ad-Dawwār, Egypt	B6	60
Kafr ash-Shaykh, Egypt	B6	60
Kafue, stm., Zam.	E5	58
Kagan, Uzb.	J10	26
Kagaznagar, India	C5	46
Kagelike, China	B12	44
Kagera, stm., Afr.	B6	58
Kağızman, Tur.	A7	48
Kagmar, Sudan	J6	60
Kagoshima, Japan	P5	36
Kagoshima-wan, b., Japan	P5	36
Kahayan, stm., Indon.	F5	38
Kahemba, Zaire	C3	58
Kahnūj, Iran	H14	48
Kahoka, Mo., U.S.	B5	114
Kahoolawe, i., Hi., U.S.	q17	125a
Kahramanmaraş, Tur.	C4	48
Kahuku, Hi., U.S.	p16	125a
Kahuku Point, c., Hi., U.S.	p16	125a
Kahului, Hi., U.S.	q17	125a
Kahului Bay, b., Hi., U.S.	q17	125a
Kai, Kepulauan, is., Indon.	G9	38
Kaiama, Nig.	G11	64
Kaiapoi, N.Z.	E4	72
Kaibab Plateau, plat., Az., U.S.	H4	120
Kaibito Plateau, plat., Az., U.S.	H5	120
Kaidu, stm., China	C4	30
Kaieteur Fall, wtfl, Guy.	E13	84
Kaifeng, China	I2	32
Kaikoura, N.Z.	E4	72
Kailahun, S.L.	G4	64
Kaili, China	A9	40
Kailu, China	C11	30
Kailua, Hi., U.S.	p16	125a
Kailua Kona, Hi., U.S.	r18	125a
Kaimanawa Mountains, mts., N.Z.	C5	72
Kainan, Japan	M10	36
Kaipara Harbour, b., N.Z.	B5	72
Kaiping, China	G9	30
Kairāna, India	F7	44
Kairouan, Tun.	N5	18
Kaiserslautern, Ger.	F7	10
Kaishantun, China	A17	32
Kaišiadorys, Lith.	G7	22
Kaitangata, N.Z.	G2	72
Kaithal, India	F7	44
Kaituma, stm., Guy.	D13	84
Kaiwi Channel, strt., Hi., U.S.	p16	125a
Kaiyuan, China	A12	32
Kaja, Wādī (Ouadi Kadja), val., Afr.	L3	60
Kajaani, Fin.	I20	6
Kajang, Malay.	M6	40
Kajnar, Kaz.	H13	26
Kaka, C.A.R.	N4	60
Kākā, Sudan	L7	60
Kakadu National Park, Austl.	B6	68
Kakagi Lake, l., On., Can.	I21	104
Kakamas, S. Afr.	G5	66
Kake, Ak., U.S.	H28	100
Kakegawa, Japan	M13	36
Kakhovs'ke vodoskhovyshche, res., Ukr.	H4	26
Kākināda, India	D7	46
Kakisa Lake, l., N.T., Can.	D9	96
Kako, stm., Guy.	E12	84
Kakoaka, Bots.	B7	66
Kakogawa, Japan	M9	36
Kaktovik, Ak., U.S.	A23	100
Kakwa, stm., Ab., Can.	C15	102
Kalaa Kebira, Tun.	N5	18
Kalaallit Nunaat see Greenland, dep., N.A.	B15	86
Kalaa Sghira, Tun.	N5	18
Kālābagh, Pak.	D4	44
Kalabo, Zam.	D4	58
Kalač, Russia	G6	26
Kalačinsk, Russia	F12	26
Kalač-na-Donu, Russia	H6	26
Kaladan, stm., Asia	D2	40
Ka Lae, c., Hi., U.S.	s18	125a
Kalagwe, Myan.	C4	40
Kalahari Desert, des., Afr.	E5	66
Kalai-Chumb, Taj.	A4	44
Kalai-Mor, Turk.	D17	48
Kalajoki, Fin.	I18	6
Kalakamate, Bots.	C8	66
Kalām, Pak.	C5	44
Kalama, Wa., U.S.	D3	122
Kalámai, Grc.	L6	20
Kalamalka Lake, l., B.C., Can.	G15	102
Kalamazoo, Mi., U.S.	H10	110
Kalamazoo, stm., Mi., U.S.	H9	110
Kalapana, Hi., U.S.	r19	125a
Kalasin, Thai.	F7	40
Kalašnikovo, Russia	D18	22
Kalāt, Pak.	F2	44
Kalaw, Myan.	D4	40
Kal'azin, Russia	D20	22
Kalb, Ra's al-, c., Yemen	G6	47
Kalbā', U.A.E.	B10	47
Kalbarri, Austl.	E2	68
Kale, Tur.	L12	20
Kaleden, B.C., Can.	H15	102
Kalemie (Albertville), Zaire	C5	58
Kalemyo, Myan.	C3	40
Kaletwa, Myan.	D2	40
Kalevala, Russia	D4	26
Kalewa, Myan.	C3	40
Kálfafell, Ice.	C5	6a
Kalgan see Zhangjiakou, China	C2	32
Kalgoorlie-Boulder, Austl.	F4	68
Kali, Mali	E4	64
Kaliakra, nos, c., Bul.	F12	20
Kalibo, Phil.	C7	38
Kalima, Zaire	B5	58
Kalimantan see Borneo, i., Asia	E5	38
Kálimnos, Grc.	M10	20
Kālimpang, India	G13	44
Kalinin see Tver', Russia	E18	22
Kaliningrad (Königsberg), Russia	G3	22
Kalinkavičy, Bela.	I12	22
Kalinovik, Bos.	F2	20
Kalispell, Mt., U.S.	B11	122
Kalisz, Pol.	D18	10
Kalkaska, Mi., U.S.	F10	110
Kalkfontein, Bots.	D5	66
Kallaste, Est.	C10	22
Kallavesi, l., Fin.	J20	6
Kalliecahoolie Lake, l., Mb., Can.	D19	104
Kallnach, Switz.	D7	13
Kalmar, Swe.	M15	6
Kalmykia see Kalmykija, state, Russia	H7	26
Kalmykija, state, Russia	H7	26
Kālna, India	I13	44
Kalnciems, Lat.	E6	22
Kālol, India	I5	44
Kalomo, Zam.	E5	58
Kalona, Ia., U.S.	I4	110
Kalone Peak, mtn., B.C., Can.	E8	102
Kalpeni Island, i., India	G2	46
Kalskag, Ak., U.S.	F14	100
Kaltag, Ak., U.S.	D15	100
Kaltan, Russia	G15	26
Kaluga, Russia	G19	22
Kalundborg, Den.	N12	6
Kałuszyn, Pol.	C21	10
Kalutara, Sri L.	I5	46
Kalvarija, Lith.	G6	22
Kalyān, India	C2	46
Kama, stm., Russia	F8	26
Kamaishi, Japan	H16	36
Kamakou, mtn., Hi., U.S.	p17	125a
Kamakura, Japan	L14	36
Kamamaung, Myan.	F4	40
Kamanjab, Nmb.	B2	66
Kamarān, i., Yemen	G3	47
Kamarang, stm., S.A.	E12	84
Kamas, Ut., U.S.	D5	120
Kamatsi Lake, l., Sk., Can.	B12	104
Kamay, Tx., U.S.	F8	116
Kamba, Nig.	F11	64
Kambam, India	H4	46
Kambar, Pak.	G3	44
Kambarka, Russia	F8	26
Kambia, S.L.	G3	64
Kamčatka, poluostrov (Kamchatka), pen., Russia	F24	28
Kamčatskij zaliv, b., Russia	F24	28
Kamchatka see Kamčatka, poluostrov, pen., Russia	F24	28
Kâmchay Méa, Camb.	I8	40
Kamčija, stm., Bul.	F11	20
Kamen', Bela.	F11	22
Kamen', gora, mtn., Russia	D16	26
Kamenjak, Rt, c., Cro.	E8	18
Kamenka, Russia	G6	26
Kamen'-na-Obi, Russia	G8	28
Kamennogorsk, Russia	K21	6
Kamensk-Ural'skij, Russia	F10	26
Kameškovo, Russia	E24	22
Kāmet, mtn., Asia	E8	44
Kamiah, Id., U.S.	D9	122
Kamienna Góra, Pol.	E16	10
Kamieńsk, Pol.	D19	10
Kamilukuak Lake, l., N.T., Can.	D12	96
Kamina, Zaire	C5	58
Kaminak Lake, l., N.T., Can.	D13	96
Kaminaljuyú, hist., Guat.	C4	92
Kaminoyama, Japan	I15	36
Kaminskij, Russia	D24	22
Kaminuriak Lake, l., N.T., Can.	D13	96
Kamishak Bay, b., Ak., U.S.	G18	100
Kamisunagawa, Japan	d17	36a
Kamjanec, Bela.	I6	22
Kamloops, B.C., Can.	G14	102
Kamloops Indian Reserve, B.C., Can.	G14	102
Kamloops Lake, l., B.C., Can.	G14	102
Kamo, Arm.	A8	48
Kamoa Mountains, mts., Guy.	G13	84
Kampala, Ug.	A6	58
Kampar, Malay.	L6	40
Kampar, stm., Indon.	N7	40
Kampen, Neth.	C8	12
Kamphaeng Phet, Thai.	F5	40
Kamp'o, S. Kor.	H17	32
Kâmpóng Cham, Camb.	H8	40
Kâmpóng Chhnăng, Camb.	H8	40
Kâmpóng Saôm, Camb.	I7	40
Kâmpóng Saôm, Chhâk, b., Camb.	I7	40
Kâmpóng Thum, Camb.	H8	40
Kâmpôt, Camb.	I8	40
Kampsville, Il., U.S.	C6	114
Kâmpŭchéa see Cambodia, ctry., Asia	C4	38
Kamsack, Sk., Can.	G13	104
Kamskoje vodochranilišče, res., Russia	F9	26
Kāmthi, India	B5	46
Kamuchawie Lake, l., Can.	B12	104
Kamuela (Waimea), Hi., U.S.	q18	125a
Kámuk, Cerro, mtn., C.R.	H11	92
Kam'yanets'-Podil's'kyy, Ukr.	H3	26
Kamyšin, Russia	G7	26
Kamyšlov, Russia	F10	26
Kanaaupscow, stm., P.Q., Can.	F17	96
Kanab, Ut., U.S.	G4	120
Kanab Plateau, plat., U.S.	H4	120
Kanafis, Sudan	M3	60
Kanaga Volcano, vol., Ak., U.S.	K6	100
Kanairiktok, stm., Nf., Can.	F20	96
Kananaskis, stm., Ab., Can.	G19	102
Kananga (Luluabourg), Zaire	C4	58
Kanarraville, Ut., U.S.	G3	120
Kanaš, Russia	F7	26
Kanawha, Ia., U.S.	H2	110
Kanawha, stm., W.V., U.S.	I4	108
Kanazawa, Japan	K11	36
Kanchanaburi, Thai.	G5	40
Kānchenjunga, mtn., Asia	G13	44
Kānchipuram, India	F5	46
Kandahar, Sk., Can.	G10	104
Kandalakša, Russia	D4	26
Kandalakšskaja guba, b., Russia	H23	6
Kandangan, Indon.	F6	38
Kandava, Lat.	D5	22
Kandersteg, Switz.	E8	13
Kandi, Benin	F11	64
Kandi, India	I13	44
Kandiāro, Pak.	G3	44
Kandik, stm., N.A.	D24	100
Kandos, Austl.	I8	70
Kandrāch, Pak.	H1	44
Kandy, Sri L.	I6	46
Kane, Il., U.S.	C6	114
Kane, Pa., U.S.	F8	108
Kaneohe, Hi., U.S.	p16	125a
Kaneohe Bay, b., Hi., U.S.	p16	125a
Kang, Bots.	D6	66
Kangal, Tur.	B4	48
Kangalassy, Russia	E17	28
Kangar, Malay.	K6	40
Kangaroo Island, i., Austl.	J2	70
Kangāvar, Iran	D9	48
Kangding, China	E7	30
Kangdong, N. Kor.	D14	32
Kangean, Kepulauan, is., Indon.	G6	38
Kanggye, N. Kor.	C14	32
Kanghwa, S. Kor.	F14	32
Kanghwa-man, b., S. Kor.	F14	32
Kangiqsualujjuaq, P.Q., Can.	E19	96
Kangiqsujuaq, P.Q., Can.	D18	96
Kangirsuk, P.Q., Can.	D18	96
Kangjin, S. Kor.	I14	32
Kangnichumike, China	D9	44
Kangnŭng, S. Kor.	F16	32
Kango, Gabon	A2	58
Kangping, China	A11	32
Kangrinboqê Feng, mtn., China	E9	44
Kangshan, Tai.	M9	34
Kangsŏ, N. Kor.	E13	32
Kangto, mtn., Asia	G15	44
Kangyidaung, Myan.	F3	40
Kani, Myan.	C3	40
Kaniama, Zaire	C4	58
Kanin, poluostrov, pen., Russia	D7	26
Kanin Nos, mys, c., Russia	D6	26
Kaniva, Austl.	K4	70
Kanjiža, Yugo.	C4	20
Kankakee, Il., U.S.	I8	110
Kankakee, stm., U.S.	A8	114
Kankan, Gui.	F5	64
Kankéla, Mali	F6	64
Kankossa, Maur.	D4	64
Kanmaw Kyun, i., Myan.	I5	40
Kannapolis, N.C., U.S.	D6	112
Kannauj, India	G8	44
Kano, Nig.	E14	64
Kanonji, Japan	M8	36
Kanopolis, Ks., U.S.	M9	118
Kanorado, Ks., U.S.	L5	118
Kanosh, Ut., U.S.	F4	120
Kanoya, Japan	P5	36
Kānpur, India	G9	44
Kansas, Il., U.S.	C9	114
Kansas, state, U.S.	D7	98
Kansas, stm., Ks., U.S.	L11	118
Kansas City, Ks., U.S.	L13	118
Kansas City, Mo., U.S.	C2	114
Kansau, Myan.	C2	40
Kanshan, China	E9	34
Kansk, Russia	F11	28
Kansu see Gansu, prov., China	D7	30
Kant, Kyrg.	I12	26
Kantang, Thai.	K5	40
Kantché, Niger	E14	64
Kantishna, stm., Ak., U.S.	D19	100
Kantō-sanchi, mts., Japan	K13	36
Kantunilkin, Mex.	G16	90
Kanuku Mountains, mts., Guy.	F13	84
Kanuma, Japan	K14	36
Kanus, Nmb.	F4	66
Kan'utino, Russia	F16	22
Kanye, Bots.	E7	66
Kanyu, Bots.	C7	66
Kaohsiung, Tai.	M9	34
Kaohsiunghsien, Tai.	M9	34
Kaoko Veld, plat., Nmb.	B1	66
Kaolack, Sen.	D1	64
Kaoma, Zam.	D4	58
Kaoshanpu, China	E3	34
Kapaa, Hi., U.S.	o14	125a
Kapadvanj, India	I5	44
Kapanga, Zaire	C4	58
Kapčagaj, Kaz.	I13	26
Kapčagajskoje vodochranilišče, res., Kaz.	I13	26
Kapcèvičy, Bela.	I11	22
Kapfenberg, Aus.	H15	10
Kapikik Lake, l., On., Can.	G23	104
Kapiskau, stm., On., Can.	F16	96
Kaplan, La., U.S.	M4	114
Kapoe, Thai.	J5	40
Kaposvár, Hung.	I17	10
Kaposvar Creek, stm., Sk., Can.	H12	104
Kappeln, Ger.	A9	10
Kapps, Nmb.	D3	66
Kaprun, Aus.	H12	10
Kapsan, N. Kor.	B16	32
Kapuas, stm., Indon.	F4	38
Kapuas Hulu, Pegunungan, mts., Asia	E5	38
Kapunda, Austl.	J3	70
Kapūrthala, India	E6	44
Kapuskasing, On., Can.	G16	96
Kapuskasing, stm., On., Can.	G16	96
Kapuvár, Hung.	H17	10
Kapyl', Bela.	H10	22
Kara, stm., Afr.	G10	64
Kara-Balta, Kyrg.	I12	26
Karabanovo, Russia	E21	22
Karabaš, Russia	F10	26
Karabekaul, Turk.	B18	48
Kara-Bogaz-Gol, zaliv, b., Turk.	I8	26
Karabük, Tur.	G14	4
Karacabey, Tur.	I12	20
Karacadağ, Tur.	H11	20
Karačev, Russia	H18	22
Karāchi, Pak.	H2	44
Karād, India	D3	46
Karaganda, Kaz.	H12	26
Karaginskij, ostrov, i., Russia	F24	28
Karaginskij zaliv, b., Russia	F24	28
Karagoš, gora, mtn., Russia	G15	26
Kāraikāl, India	G5	46
Kāraikkudi, India	G5	46
Karaj, Iran	D11	48
Karakax, stm., China	B8	44
Karakelong, Pulau, i., Indon.	E8	38
Karakol (Prževal'sk), Kyrg.	I13	26
Karakoram Pass, Asia	C7	44
Karakoram Range, mts., Asia	C7	44
Karakoro, stm., Afr.	D4	64
Karakumskij kanal, Turk.	C16	48
Karakumy, des., Turk.	J9	26
Karaman, Tur.	L13	20
Karaman, Tur.	C2	48
Karamay, China	B3	30
Karamea Bight, N.Z.	D3	72
Karamürsel, Tur.	I13	20
Karamyševo, Russia	D11	22
Kāranja, India	B4	46
Karapınar, Tur.	C2	48
Karasburg, Nmb.	G4	66
Kara Sea see Karskoje more, Russia	C11	26
Karasjok, Nor.	G19	6
Karasu, stm., Tur.	B5	48
Karasuk, Russia	G7	28
Karatau, Kaz.	I12	26
Karatau, chrebet, mts., Kaz.	I12	26
Karaton, Kaz.	H8	26
Karatsu, Japan	N4	36
Karauli, India	G7	44
Karawang, Indon.	j13	39a
Karawang, Tanjung, c., Indon.	i13	39a
Karawanken, mts., Eur.	C9	18
Karaye, Nig.	F14	64
Karažal, Kaz.	H12	26
Karbalā', Iraq	E8	48
Karcag, Hung.	H20	10
Kardhítsa, Grc.	J5	20
Kärdla, Est.	B5	22
Kardymovo, Russia	G15	22
Kărdžali, Bul.	H9	20
Karelia see Karelija, state, Russia	E4	26
Karelia, hist. reg., Eur.	J22	6
Karèličy, Bela.	H9	22
Karelija, state, Russia	E4	26
Karesuando, Swe.	G18	6
Kargopol', Russia	E5	26
Karia-ba-Mohammed, Mor.	C8	62
Kariba, Zimb.	E5	58
Kariba, Lake, res., Afr.	E5	58
Karibib, Nmb.	C2	66
Karigasniemi, Fin.	G19	6
Karimata, Kepulauan, is., Indon.	F4	38
Karimata, Selat (Karimata Strait), strt., Indon.	F4	38
Karīmnagar, India	C5	46
Karimunjawa, Kepulauan, is., Indon.	G5	38
Karin, Som.	F10	56
Karis (Karjaa), Fin.	K18	6
Karisimbi, Volcan, vol., Afr.	B5	58
Kariya, Japan	M11	36
Kārīz, Iran	D16	48
Karkaralinsk, Kaz.	H13	26
Karl-Marx-Stadt see Chemnitz, Ger.	E12	10
Karloske, stm., Mb., Can.	C20	104
Karlovac, Cro.	D10	18
Karlovo, Bul.	G8	20
Karlovy Vary, Czech Rep.	E12	10
Karlsborg, Swe.	I18	6
Karlskoga, Swe.	L14	6
Karlskrona, Swe.	M14	6
Karlsruhe, Ger.	F8	10
Karlstad, Mn., U.S.	C11	118

Name	Map Ref.	Page
Karlstadt, Ger.	F9	10
Karma, Niger	E10	64
Karmah, Sudan	H6	60
Karmel, Har (Mount Carmel), mtn., Isr.	C4	50
Karmiyya, Isr.	E3	50
Karnack, Tx., U.S.	J2	114
Karnak see Al-Karnak, Egypt	E7	60
Karnak, Il., U.S.	E8	114
Karnāl, India	F7	44
Karṇālī, stm., Asia	F9	44
Karnātaka, state, India	E3	46
Karnes City, Tx., U.S.	K9	116
Karnobat, Bul.	G10	20
Kärnten, state, Aus.	I13	10
Karonga, Mwi.	C6	58
Karora, Sudan	I10	60
Kárpathos, i., Grc.	N11	20
Karpenísion, Grc.	K5	20
Karpinsk, Russia	F10	26
Karpogory, Russia	E6	26
Karratha, Austl.	D3	68
Kars, Tur.	A7	48
Karsakpaj, Kaz.	H11	26
Karsakuwigamak Lake, l., Mb., Can.	B15	104
Kärsämäki, Fin.	J19	6
Kārsava, Lat.	E10	22
Karši, Uzb.	J11	26
Karsin, Pol.	B17	10
Karskije Vorota, proliv, strt., Russia	C9	26
Karskoje more (Kara Sea), Russia	C11	26
Kartaly, Russia	G10	26
Karthaus, Pa., U.S.	F8	108
Kartuzy, Pol.	A18	10
Karukuwisa, Nmb.	B4	66
Karūr, India	G5	46
Karviná, Czech Rep.	F18	10
Kārwār, India	E3	46
Karymskoje, Russia	G14	28
Kas, Sudan	K3	60
Kasaan, Ak., U.S.	I28	100
Kasai (Cassai), stm., Afr.	B3	58
Kasaji, Zaire	D4	58
Kasama, Zam.	D6	58
Kasan, Uzb.	B18	48
Kasane, Bots.	A7	66
Kasanga, Tan.	C6	58
Kasaoka, Japan	M8	36
Kāsaragod, India	F3	46
Kasba Lake, l., N.T., Can.	D12	96
Kasba-Tadla, Mor.	D7	62
Kascjukouka, Bela.	I13	22
Kascjukovičy, Bela.	H15	22
Kaseda, Japan	P5	36
Kasempa, Zam.	D5	58
Kasenga, Zaire	D5	58
Kasese, Zaire	B5	58
Kāsganj, India	G8	44
Kāshān, Iran	K8	26
Kashgar see Kashi, China	D2	30
Kashi, China	D2	30
Kashihara, Japan	M10	36
Kashima, Japan	N5	36
Kāshīpur, India	F8	44
Kashiwazaki, Japan	J13	36
Kāshmar, Iran	D15	48
Kashmir see Jammu and Kashmīr, dep., Asia	C10	42
Kashmor, Pak.	F3	44
Kashunuk, stm., Ak., U.S.	F12	100
Kasigluk, Ak., U.S.	F13	100
Kasimov, Russia	G24	22
Kašin, Russia	D20	22
Kasinka, Bots.	B7	66
Kašira, Russia	G21	22
Kasiruta, Pulau, i., Indon.	F8	38
Kaskaskia, stm., Il., U.S.	D7	114
Kaskattama, stm., Mb., Can.	E14	96
Kaskö (Kaskinen), Fin.	J17	6
Kasli, Russia	F10	26
Kaslo, B.C., Can.	H18	102
Kasn'a, Russia	F17	22
Kasongo, Zaire	B5	58
Kasongo-Lunda, Zaire	C3	58
Kásos, i., Grc.	N10	20
Kasota, Mn., U.S.	F2	110
Kaspijsk, Russia	I7	26
Kaspijskij, Russia	H7	26
Kasr, Ra's, c., Afr.	H10	60
Kassalā, Sudan	J9	60
Kassándra, pen., Grc.	I7	20
Kassándras, Kólpos, b., Grc.	I7	20
Kassel, Ger.	D9	10
Kasserine, Tun.	C15	62
Kassikaityu, stm., Guy.	G13	84
Kassinger, Sudan	H6	60
Kasson, Mn., U.S.	F3	110
Kastamonu, Tur.	G14	4
Kastoría, Grc.	I5	20
Kastrávion, Tekhnití Límni, res., Grc.	K5	20
Kasūr, Pak.	E6	44
Kataeregi, Nig.	G13	64
Katahdin, Mount, mtn., Me., U.S.	B18	108
Katanga, hist. reg., Zaire	D5	58
Katanga, stm., Russia	F12	28
Katanning, Austl.	F3	68
Katchall Island, i., India	K2	40
Katélé, Mali	F7	64
Katepwa Beach, Sk., Can.	H11	104
Kateríni, Grc.	I6	20
Kates Needle, mtn., N.A.	H28	100
Katha, Myan.	B4	40
Katherine, Austl.	B6	68
Kāthiāwār Peninsula, pen., India	I4	44
Kāṭhmāṇḍau, Nepal	G11	44
Kathrabbā, Jord.	F5	50
Katihār, India	F4	30
Katimik Lake, l., Mb., Can.	F15	104
Katiola, C. Iv.	G7	64
Katmandu see Kāṭhmāṇḍau, Nepal	G11	44
Katoomba, Austl.	I9	70
Katoúna, Grc.	K5	20
Katowice, Pol.	E19	10
Kātrīnā, Jabal, mtn., Egypt	C7	60
Katsepe, Madag.	o22	67b
Katsina, Nig.	E13	64
Katsina Ala, Nig.	H14	64
Katsina Ala, stm., Afr.	G8	54
Katsuta, Japan	K15	36
Katsuura, Japan	L15	36
Katsuyama, Japan	K11	36
Kattakurgan, Uzb.	J11	26
Kattaviá, Grc.	N11	20
Kattegat, strt., Eur.	M12	6
Katun', stm., Russia	G9	28
Katunki, Russia	E26	22
Kātwa, India	I13	44
Katwijk aan Zee, Neth.	D5	12
Katyn, Russia	G14	22
Kauai, i., Hi., U.S.	o14	125a
Kauai Channel, strt., Hi., U.S.	p15	125a
Kau Desert, des., Hi., U.S.	r18	125a
Kaufbeuren, Ger.	H10	10
Kaufman, Tx., U.S.	G10	116
Kaukauna, Wi., U.S.	F7	110
Kaukau Veld, plat., Afr.	B5	66
Kauliranta, Fin.	H18	6
Kaumalapau, Hi., U.S.	q17	125a
Kaunakakai, Hi., U.S.	p16	125a
Kaunas, Lith.	G6	22
Kaura Namoda, Nig.	E13	64
Kauru, Nig.	F14	64
Kaustinen, Fin.	J18	6
Kautokeino, Nor.	G18	6
Kavacık, Tur.	J12	20
Kavajë, Alb.	H3	20
Kavála, Grc.	I8	20
Kavalerovo, Russia	I19	28
Kāvali, India	E5	46
Kavaratti Island, i., India	G2	46
Kāveri, stm., India	G5	46
Kāveri Falls, wtfl, India	F4	46
Kaverino, Russia	G24	22
Kavieng, Pap. N. Gui.	k17	68a
Kavimba, Bots.	B7	66
Kavīr, Dasht-e, des., Iran	D13	48
Kaw, Ok., U.S.	C10	116
Kawagoe, Japan	L14	36
Kawaguchi, Japan	L14	36
Kawaihae Bay, b., Hi., U.S.	q18	125a
Kawaikini, mtn., Hi., U.S.	o14	125a
Kawambwa, Zam.	C5	58
Kawara Débé, Niger	E11	64
Kawasaki, Japan	L14	36
Kawdut, Myan.	G4	40
Kaweenakumik Lake, l., Mb., Can.	F15	104
Kawich Peak, mtn., Nv., U.S.	G9	124
Kaw Lake, res., Ok., U.S.	C10	116
Kawludo, Myan.	E4	40
Kawm Umbū, Egypt	E7	60
Kawthaung, Myan.	J5	40
Kaxgar, stm., China	D2	30
Kaya, Burkina	E9	64
Kayak Island, i., Ak., U.S.	G22	100
Kayan, Myan.	F4	40
Kayan, stm., Indon.	E6	38
Kāyankulam, India	H4	46
Kaycee, Wy., U.S.	A10	120
Kayenta, Az., U.S.	H6	120
Kayes, Congo	B2	58
Kayes, Mali	D4	64
Kay Point, c., Yk., Can.	B25	100
Kayser Gebergte, mts., Sur.	F14	84
Kayseri, Tur.	B3	48
Kaysville, Ut., U.S.	C5	120
Kazachskij melkosopočnik, hills, Kaz.	H12	26
Kazačinskoje, Russia	F16	26
Kazakhstan, ctry., Asia	H11	26
Kazaki, Russia	I21	22
Kazakstan see Kazakhstan, ctry., Asia	H11	26
Kazalinsk, Kaz.	H10	26
Kazan', Russia	F7	26
Kazan, stm., N.T., Can.	D13	96
Kazandžik, Turk.	J9	26
Kazanlăk, Bul.	G9	20
Kazan Lake, l., Sk., Can.	C6	104
Kazanovka, Russia	H21	22
Kazbek, gora, mtn.	I6	26
Kāzerūn, Iran	G11	48
Kazimierza Wielka, Pol.	E20	10
Kazincbarcika, Hung.	G20	10
Kazinka, Russia	I22	22
Kazloŭščyna, Bela.	H8	22
Kazlų Rūda, Lith.	G6	22
Kazungula, Zam.	A7	66
Kazym, stm., Russia	E5	28
Kazyr, stm., Russia	G17	26
Kcynia, Pol.	B17	10
Kdyně, Czech Rep.	F13	10
Kéa, i., Grc.	L8	20
Keaau, Hi., U.S.	r18	125a
Keahole Point, c., Hi., U.S.	r17	125a
Kealakekua Bay, b., Hi., U.S.	r18	125a
Keams Canyon, Az., U.S.	I6	120
Kearney, Mo., U.S.	C2	114
Kearney, Ne., U.S.	K8	118
Kearns, Ut., U.S.	D5	120
Kearny, Az., U.S.	K6	120
Kebeiti, China	B8	44
Kébémer, Sen.	D1	64
Kebili, Tun.	D15	62
Kebnekaise, mtn., Swe.	H16	6
Kebri Dehar, Eth.	G9	56
Kecel, Hung.	I19	10
Kech, stm., Pak.	H17	48
Kechika, stm., B.C., Can.	E7	96
Kecskemét, Hung.	I19	10
Kėdainiai, Lith.	F7	22
Kedgwick, N.B., Can.	E6	106
Kedgwick, stm., Can.	E6	106
Kediri, Indon.	j16	39a
Kédougou, Sen.	E3	64
Kedrikí Makedhonía, prov., Grc.	I7	20
Kędzierzyn Kozle, Pol.	E18	10
Keefers, B.C., Can.	G13	102
Keele, stm., N.T., Can.	D31	100
Keele Peak, mtn., Yk., Can.	E29	100
Keeley Lake, l., Sk., Can.	D6	104
Keeling Islands see Cocos Islands, dep., Oc.	K10	24
Keels, Nf., Can.	D20	106
Keene, Ky., U.S.	B2	112
Keene, N.H., U.S.	E14	108
Keene, Tx., U.S.	G9	116
Keenesburg, Co., U.S.	D12	120
Keerbergen, Bel.	F6	12
Keeseville, N.Y., U.S.	C13	108
Keetmanshoop, Nmb.	F4	66
Keewatin, Mn., U.S.	C2	110
Keewatin, On., Can.	I20	104
Kefallinía, i., Grc.	K4	20
Kefar Blum, Isr.	B5	50
Kefar 'Eẕyon, W.B.	E4	50
Kefar Naḥum (Capernaum), hist., Isr.	C5	50
Kefar Sava, Isr.	D3	50
Keffi, Nig.	G13	64
Keffin Hausa, Nig.	E14	64
Keflavík, Ice.	B2	6a
Keftya, Eth.	K9	60
Ke Ga, Mui, c., Viet.	H10	40
Kégashka, P.Q., Can.	B12	106
Kégashka, Lac, l., P.Q., Can.	B12	106
Keg River, Ab., Can.	E9	96
Kegums, Lat.	E7	22
Kehiwin Indian Reserve, Ab., Can.	C24	102
Kehra, Est.	B8	22
Ke-hsi Mānsām, Myan.	D4	40
Keila, Est.	B7	22
Keimoes, S. Afr.	G5	66
Keiser, Ar., U.S.	G6	114
Keith, Scot., U.K.	D11	8
Keith Arm, b., N.T., Can.	C8	96
Keithley Creek, B.C., Can.	E13	102
Keithsburg, Il., U.S.	I5	110
Keizer, Or., U.S.	F2	122
Kejimkujik National Park, N.S., Can.	H8	106
Kekaha, Hi., U.S.	p14	125a
Kékes, mtn., Hung.	H20	10
Kekexili, China	D5	30
Kelafo, Eth.	G9	56
Kelang, Malay.	M6	40
Kelantan, stm., Malay.	L7	40
Kelegou, China	B6	32
Kelibia, Tun.	M6	18
Kellerberrin, Austl.	F3	68
Keller Lake, l., N.T., Can.	D8	96
Keller Lake, l., Sk., Can.	B8	104
Kellett, Cape, c., N.T., Can.	B7	96
Kelleys Island, i., Oh., U.S.	F4	108
Kelliher, Sk., Can.	G11	104
Kellogg, Ia., U.S.	I3	110
Kellogg, Id., U.S.	C9	122
Kellogg, Mn., U.S.	F4	110
Kelly Lake, l., N.T., Can.	D31	100
Kellyville, Ok., U.S.	D10	116
Kelmė, Lith.	F5	22
Kel'mentsi, Ukr.	A10	20
Kelmet, Erit.	I10	60
Kelo, Chad	G4	56
Kelolokan, Indon.	E6	38
Kelowna, B.C., Can.	H15	102
Kelsey Bay, B.C., Can.	G9	102
Kelsey Lake, l., Mb., Can.	E13	104
Kelseyville, Ca., U.S.	F3	124
Kelso, Wa., U.S.	D3	122
Keluang, Malay.	M7	40
Kelvington, Sk., Can.	F11	104
Kem', Russia	E4	26
Kemah, Tx., U.S.	J11	116
Kemalpaşa, Tur.	K11	20
Kemano, B.C., Can.	D7	102
Kemer Barajı, res., Tur.	L12	20
Kemerovo, Russia	F9	28
Kemi, Fin.	I19	6
Kemijärvi, Fin.	H20	6
Kemijoki, stm., Fin.	H19	6
Kemmerer, Wy., U.S.	C6	120
Kemnath, Ger.	F11	10
Kemp, Tx., U.S.	G10	116
Kemp, Lake, res., Tx., U.S.	F7	116
Kemparana, Mali	E7	64
Kempele, Fin.	I19	6
Kempner, Tx., U.S.	H8	116
Kemps Bay, Bah.	B6	94
Kempsey, Austl.	H10	70
Kempt, Lac, l., P.Q., Can.	G18	96
Kempten [Allgäu], Ger.	H10	10
Kemptville, On., Can.	B11	108
Kenai, Ak., U.S.	F19	100
Kenai Peninsula, pen., Ak., U.S.	G19	100
Kenansville, Fl., U.S.	L6	112
Kenansville, N.C., U.S.	E9	112
Kenaston, Sk., Can.	G8	104
Kenbridge, Va., U.S.	C8	112
Kendal, S. Afr.	F9	66
Kendal, Sk., Can.	H11	104
Kendall, Fl., U.S.	N6	112
Kendall, Wi., U.S.	G5	110
Kendall, Cape, c., N.T., Can.	D15	96
Kendallville, In., U.S.	A11	114
Kendari, Indon.	F7	38
Kendrāparha, India	J12	44
Kendrick, Fl., U.S.	J4	112
Kendrick, Id., U.S.	D9	122
Kenedy, Tx., U.S.	K9	116
Kenema, S.L.	H4	64
Kenesaw, Ne., U.S.	K9	118
Kenge, Zaire	B3	58
Kengtian, China	J8	34
Kēng Tung, Myan.	D5	40
Kenhardt, S. Afr.	G5	66
Kenilworth, Ut., U.S.	E6	120
Kenitra, Mor.	C7	62
Kenly, N.C., U.S.	D8	112
Kenmare, N.D., U.S.	C5	118
Kennard, Tx., U.S.	H11	116
Kennebec, S.D., U.S.	H8	118
Kennebec, stm., Me., U.S.	C17	108
Kennebecasis Bay, b., N.B., Can.	G8	106
Kennebunk, Me., U.S.	D16	108
Kennedy, Al., U.S.	I9	114
Kennedy, Zimb.	B8	66
Kennedy, Cape see Canaveral, Cape, c., Fl., U.S.	K6	112
Kennedy, Mount, mtn., B.C., Can.	G9	102
Kennedy, Mount, mtn., Yk., Can.	F25	100
Kennedy Entrance, strt., Ak., U.S.	G18	100
Kennedy Lake, l., B.C., Can.	H9	102
Kenner, La., U.S.	M6	114
Kennetcook, N.S., Can.	G10	106
Kennett, Mo., U.S.	F6	114
Kennett Square, Pa., U.S.	H11	108
Kennewick, Wa., U.S.	D6	122
Kenney Dam, B.C., Can.	D10	102
Kenn Reef, rf., Austl.	D11	68
Kénogami, P.Q., Can.	D2	106
Kenogami, stm., On., Can.	G15	96
Kénogami, Lac, l., P.Q., Can.	D2	106
Keno Hill, Yk., Can.	E27	100
Kenora, On., Can.	I20	104
Kenosha, Wi., U.S.	H8	110
Kenova, W.V., U.S.	I4	108
Kensal, N.D., U.S.	D9	118
Kensett, Ar., U.S.	G5	114
Kensington, Ks., U.S.	L8	118
Kensington, P.E., Can.	F10	106
Kensington Park, Fl., U.S.	L4	112
Kent, Oh., U.S.	F5	108
Kent, S.L.	G3	64
Kent, Wa., U.S.	C3	122
Kent, co., Eng., U.K.	J14	8
Kentau, Kaz.	I11	26
Kent Group, is., Austl.	L7	70
Kentland, In., U.S.	B9	114
Kenton, Mi., U.S.	D7	110
Kenton, Oh., U.S.	G3	108
Kenton, Tn., U.S.	F7	114
Kent Peninsula, pen., N.T., Can.	C11	96
Kentucky, state, U.S.	D9	98
Kentucky, stm., Ky., U.S.	D11	114
Kentucky Lake, res., U.S.	F8	114
Kentville, N.S., Can.	G9	106
Kentwood, La., U.S.	L6	114
Kenya, ctry., Afr.	B7	58
Kenya, Mount see Kirinyaga, mtn., Kenya	B7	58
Kenyon, Mn., U.S.	F3	110
Keokea, Hi., U.S.	q17	125a
Keokuk, Ia., U.S.	J4	110
Keo Neua, Col de, Asia	E8	40
Keosauqua, Ia., U.S.	J4	110
Keota, Ia., U.S.	I4	110
Keota, Ok., U.S.	D12	116
Kępice, Pol.	A16	10
Kępno, Pol.	D17	10
Keppel Bay, b., Austl.	D9	70
Kequan, China	G2	32
Kerala, state, India	G4	46
Kerang, Austl.	J5	70
Kerby, Or., U.S.	H2	122
Kerch, Ukr.	H5	26
Keremeos, B.C., Can.	H15	102
Keren, Erit.	J10	60
Kerend, Iran	D9	48
Kerens, Tx., U.S.	G10	116
Keret', ozero, l., Russia	I23	6
Kerewan, Gam.	E1	64
Kerguélen, Îles, is., Afr.	M10	126
Kericho, Kenya	B7	58
Keri Kera, Sudan	K7	60
Kerinci, Gunung, mtn., Indon.	F3	38
Keriya, stm., China	B9	44
Kerkebet, Erit.	I9	60
Kerkenna, Îles, is., Tun.	C16	62
Kerkhoven, Mn., U.S.	F12	118
Kerki, Turk.	J11	26
Kérkira (Corfu), Grc.	J3	20
Kérkira (Corfu), i., Grc.	J3	20
Kerkrade, Neth.	G9	12
Kermadec Islands, is., N.Z.	K22	126
Kerman, Ca., U.S.	H5	124
Kermān, Iran	F14	48
Kermit, Tx., U.S.	H3	116
Kermode, Mount, mtn., B.C., Can.	E3	102
Kern, stm., Ca., U.S.	I7	124
Kernersville, N.C., U.S.	C6	112
Kernville, Ca., U.S.	I7	124
Kérou, Benin	F11	64
Kerrobert, Sk., Can.	G5	104
Kerrville, Tx., U.S.	I7	116
Kerry, co., Ire.	I4	8
Kershaw, S.C., U.S.	E6	112
Kersley, B.C., Can.	E12	102
Kerulen (Cherlen) (Herlen), stm., Asia	B10	30
Kerzaz, Alg.	F10	62
Kerzers, Switz.	E7	13
Kesagami Lake, l., On., Can.	F16	96
Keşan, Tur.	I10	20
Kesennuma, Japan	I16	36
Keshena, Wi., U.S.	F7	110
Keshendeh, Afg.	B2	44
Keshod, India	J4	44
Keskin, Tur.	B2	48
Keski-Suomen lääni, prov., Fin.	J19	6
Keskozero, Russia	K23	6
Kes'ma, Russia	C20	22
Kesova Gora, Russia	D20	22
Kesra, Tun.	N4	18
Kesten'ga, Russia	I22	6
Keszthely, Hung.	I17	10
Ket', stm., Russia	F8	28
Keta, Ghana	I10	64
Keta, ozero, l., Russia	D10	28
Ketama, Mor.	K7	16
Ketang, China	M4	34
Ketchikan, Ak., U.S.	I29	100
Ketchum, Id., U.S.	G11	122
Kete Krachi, Ghana	H9	64
Kétou, Benin	H11	64
Kętrzyn (Rastenburg), Pol.	A21	10
Kettering, Eng., U.K.	I13	8
Kettering, Oh., U.S.	H2	108
Kettle, stm., Mb., Can.	B20	104
Kettle, stm., Mn., U.S.	D3	110
Kettle, stm., N.A.	I16	102
Kettle Falls, Wa., U.S.	B7	122
Kettle Rapids Dam, Mb., Can.	B20	104
Keuka Lake, l., N.Y., U.S.	E9	108
Kevin, Mt., U.S.	B14	122
Kew, T./C. Is.	D8	94
Kewanee, Il., U.S.	I6	110
Kewanna, In., U.S.	A10	114
Kewaunee, Wi., U.S.	F8	110
Keweenaw Bay, b., Mi., U.S.	C7	110
Keweenaw Peninsula, pen., Mi., U.S.	C7	110
Keweenaw Point, c., Mi., U.S.	C8	110
Keya Paha, stm., U.S.	I8	118
Keyes, Ok., U.S.	C4	116
Key Largo, Fl., U.S.	N6	112
Key Largo, i., Fl., U.S.	N6	112
Keyser, W.V., U.S.	H8	108
Keystone, Ia., U.S.	I3	110
Keystone, S.D., U.S.	H4	118
Keystone, W.V., U.S.	B5	112
Keystone Lake, res., Ok., U.S.	C10	116
Keysville, Va., U.S.	B8	112
Keytesville, Mo., U.S.	C4	114
Key West, Fl., U.S.	O5	112
Kežmarok, Slvk.	F20	10
Kgalagadi, dept., Bots.	E5	66
Kgatleng, dept., Bots.	E8	66
Khābūr, Nahr al-, stm., Asia	D6	48
Khadki (Kirkee), India	C2	46
Khairpur, Pak.	G3	44
Khajrāho, India	H8	44
Khakassia see Chakasija, state, Russia	G15	26
Khakhea, Bots.	E6	66
Khalkhalah, Syria	B7	50
Khalkidhikí, hist. reg., Grc.	I7	20
Khalkís, Grc.	K7	20
Khalūf, Oman	D11	47
Khambhāliya, India	I3	44
Khambhāt, India	I5	44
Khambhāt, Gulf of, b., India	J5	44
Khāmgaon, India	B4	46
Khamir, Yemen	F3	47
Khamīs Mushayṭ, Sau. Ar.	E3	47
Khamkeut, Laos	E8	40
Khammam, India	D6	46
Khānābād, Afg.	B3	44
Khān al-Baghdādī, Iraq	E7	48
Khānaqīn, Iraq	D8	48
Khancoban, Austl.	K8	70
Khandwa, India	J7	44
Khānewāl, Pak.	E4	44
Khāngarh, Pak.	F4	44
Khaniá, Grc.	N8	20
Khānpur, Pak.	F4	44
Khān Yūnus, Gaza	F2	50
Kharagpur, India	I12	44
Kharānoq, Iran	E13	48
Kharg Island see Khārk, Jazīreh-ye, i., Iran	G11	48
Khargon, India	J6	44
Khāriān Cantonment, Pak.	D5	44
Kharkiv (Kharkov), Ukr.	G5	26
Kharkov see Kharkiv, Ukr.	G5	26
Khartoum see Al-Kharṭūm, Sudan	J7	60
Khartoum North see Al-Kharṭūm Baḥrī, Sudan	J7	60
Khartum see Al-Kharṭūm, Sudan	J7	60
Khasebake, Bots.	C7	66
Khāsh, Afg.	F17	48
Khāsh, Iran	G16	48
Khashm al-Qirbah, Sudan	J8	60
Khatt, Oued al, val., W. Sah.	G4	62
Khawsa, Myan.	G4	40
Khemis, Alg.	B12	62
Khemmarat, Thai.	F8	40
Khenchla, Alg.	C14	62
Khenifra, Mor.	D8	62
Kherrata, Alg.	B13	62
Kherson, Ukr.	H4	26
Khíos, Grc.	K10	20
Khíos (Chios), i., Grc.	K10	20
Khirbat 'Awwād, Syria	D7	50
Khlong Thom, Thai.	K5	40
Khmel'nyts'kyy, Ukr.	H3	26
Kholm, Afg.	B2	44
Khomeyn, Iran	E11	48
Khomeynīshahr, Iran	E11	48
Khomodimo, Bots.	D6	66
Khon Kaen, Thai.	F7	40
Khóra, Grc.	L5	20
Khorramābād, Iran	E10	48
Khorramshahr, Iran	F10	48
Khossanto, Sen.	E4	64
Khotyn, Ukr.	A10	20
Khouribga, Mor.	D7	62
Khowst, Afg.	D3	44
Khuff, Sau. Ar.	B4	47
Khugaung, Myan.	A5	40
Khuis, Bots.	F5	66
Khu Khan, Thai.	G8	40
Khulna, Bngl.	I13	44
Khūnjerāb Pass, Asia	B6	44
Khurai, India	H8	44
Khurīyā Murīyā, Jazā'ir, is., Oman	F10	47
Khurja, India	F7	44
Khust, Ukr.	H2	26
Khuzdār, Pak.	G2	44
Khvāf, Iran	D16	48
Khvor, Iran	E13	48
Khvormūj, Iran	G11	48
Khvoy, Iran	B8	48
Khwae Noi, stm., Thai.	G5	40
Khyber Pass, Asia	C4	44
Khyriv, Ukr.	F22	10
Kiama, Austl.	J9	70
Kiamichi, stm., Ok., U.S.	E11	116
Kiana, Ak., U.S.	C14	100
Kiangarow, Mount, mtn., Austl.	F9	70
Kiangsi see Jiangxi, prov., China	F10	30
Kiangsu see Jiangsu, prov., China	E10	30
Kibangou, Congo	B2	58
Kibombo, Zaire	B5	58
Kibre Mengist, Eth.	O10	60
Kičevo, Mac.	H4	20
Kickapoo, stm., Wi., U.S.	G5	110
Kicking Horse Pass, Can.	F18	102
Kidal, Mali	B10	64
Kidira, Sen.	D3	64
Kiel, Ger.	A10	10
Kiel, Wi., U.S.	G7	110
Kiel Canal see Nord-Ostsee-Kanal, Ger.	A9	10
Kielce, Pol.	E20	10
Kieler Bucht, b., Ger.	A10	10
Kiester, Mn., U.S.	G2	110
Kiev see Kyyiv, Ukr.	G4	26
Kiffa, Maur.	C4	64
Kifisiá, Grc.	K7	20
Kifrī, Iraq	D8	48
Kigali, Rw.	B6	58
Kigille, Sudan	M8	60
Kigoma, Tan.	B5	58
Kihei, Hi., U.S.	q17	125a
Kihniö, Fin.	J18	6
Kihnu, i., Est.	C7	22
Kii-suidō, strt., Japan	N9	36
Kikerino, Russia	B12	22
Kikerk Lake, l., N.T., Can.	C10	96
Kikinda, Yugo.	D4	20
Kikládhes (Cyclades), is., Grc.	L9	20
Kikori, Pap. N. Gui.	G11	38
Kikwit, Zaire	C3	58
Kilambé, Cerro, mtn., Nic.	D9	92
Kilauea, Hi., U.S.	o14	125a
Kilauea Crater, crat., Hi., U.S.	r18	125a
Kilchu, N. Kor.	C17	32
Kilcoy, Austl.	F10	70
Kildare, Ire.	H7	8
Kildare, co., Ire.	H7	8
Kildare, Cape, c., P.E., Can.	F10	106
Kil'din, ostrov, i., Russia	G24	6
Kil'dinstroj, Russia	G23	6
Kildonan, B.C., Can.	H9	102
Kilgore, Tx., U.S.	J2	114
Kilian Island, i., N.T., Can.	B11	96
Kilibo, Benin	G11	64
Kilikollūr, India	H4	46
Kilimanjaro, mtn., Tan.	B7	58
Kilimavony, Madag.	s20	67b
Kilingi-Nõmme, Est.	C7	22
Kilis, Tur.	C4	48
Kiliya, Ukr.	D13	20
Kilkenny, Ire.	I6	8
Kilkenny, co., Ire.	I6	8
Kilkís, Grc.	H6	20
Killaloe, Ire.	I5	8
Killaloe Station, On., Can.	E18	110
Killam, Ab., Can.	E23	102
Killarney, Ire.	I4	8
Killarney, Mb., Can.	I15	104
Killarney, On., Can.	E14	110
Killbuck, Oh., U.S.	G5	108
Killdeer, N.D., U.S.	D5	118
Killeen, Tx., U.S.	H9	116
Killen, Al., U.S.	H9	114
Killington Peak, mtn., Vt., U.S.	D14	108
Killiniq Island, i., Can.	D20	96
Killinkoski, Fin.	J18	6
Kilmarnock, Scot., U.K.	F9	8
Kilmarnock, Va., U.S.	B10	112
Kilmichael, Ms., U.S.	I7	114
Kilomines, Zaire	A6	58
Kilosa, Tan.	C7	58
Kilpisjärvi, Fin.	G17	6
Kilrush, Ire.	I4	8
Kilttān Island, i., India	G2	46
Kilwa, Zaire	C5	58
Kim, Co., U.S.	N4	118
Kim, stm., Cam.	G9	54
Kimba, Austl.	I2	70
Kimball, Mn., U.S.	E1	110
Kimball, Ne., U.S.	J4	118
Kimball, S.D., U.S.	H9	118
Kimberley, B.C., Can.	H19	102
Kimberley, S. Afr.	G7	66
Kimberley Plateau, plat., Austl.	C5	68
Kimberling City, Mo., U.S.	F3	114
Kimberly, Id., U.S.	H11	122
Kimberly, Wi., U.S.	F7	110
Kimch'aek (Sŏngjin), N. Kor.	C17	32
Kimch'ŏn, S. Kor.	G16	32
Kimito (Kemiö), Fin.	K18	6
Kimiwan Lake, l., Ab., Can.	B18	102
Kimje, S. Kor.	H14	32
Kimovsk, Russia	H21	22
Kimry, Russia	E20	22
Kimsquit, B.C., Can.	E8	102
Kinabalu, Gunong, mtn., Malay.	D6	38
Kinbasket Lake, res., B.C., Can.	F17	102
Kincaid, Il., U.S.	C7	114
Kincaid, Sk., Can.	I7	104
Kincardine, On., Can.	F14	110
Kincolith, B.C., Can.	B5	102
Kindberg, Aus.	H15	10
Kinde, Mi., U.S.	G13	110
Kinder, La., U.S.	L4	114
Kindersley, Sk., Can.	G5	104
Kindia, Gui.	F3	64
Kindred, N.D., U.S.	E10	118
Kindu, Zaire	B5	58
Kinel', Russia	G8	26
Kinešma, Russia	D25	22
King, N.C., U.S.	C6	112
King and Queen Court House, Va., U.S.	B10	112
Kingaroy, Austl.	F9	70
King City, Ca., U.S.	H4	124
King City, Mo., U.S.	B2	114
King City, On., Can.	G16	110
King Cove, Ak., U.S.	I13	100
Kingfield, Me., U.S.	C16	108
Kingfisher, Ok., U.S.	D9	116
King George, Va., U.S.	I9	108
King George, Mount, mtn., B.C., Can.	G19	102
King George Island, i., Ant.	B1	73
King George Islands, is., N.T., Can.	E17	96
King Hill, Id., U.S.	G10	122
Kingisepp, Russia	B11	22
King Island, i., Austl.	L6	70
King Island, i., B.C., Can.	E7	102
King Lear Peak, mtn., Nv., U.S.	C7	124
King Leopold Ranges, mts., Austl.	C5	68
Kingman, Az., U.S.	I2	120
Kingman, Ks., U.S.	N9	118
Kingman Reef, rf., Oc.	H23	126
King Mountain, mtn., B.C., Can.	G30	100
King Mountain, mtn., Or., U.S.	G7	122
Kings, Ms., U.S.	J6	114
Kings, stm., Ar., U.S.	F3	114
Kings, stm., Ca., U.S.	H6	124
Kings, stm., Nv., U.S.	C7	124
King Salmon, Ak., U.S.	G16	100
Kings Beach, Ca., U.S.	E5	124
Kingsburg, Ca., U.S.	H6	124
Kings Canyon National Park, Ca., U.S.	H7	124
Kingscote, Austl.	J2	70
Kingsford, Mi., U.S.	E7	110
Kingsgate, B.C., Can.	H18	102
Kingsland, Ar., U.S.	I4	114
Kingsland, Ga., U.S.	I5	112
Kingsland, Tx., U.S.	I8	116
Kingsley, Ia., U.S.	I12	118
Kingsley, Mi., U.S.	F10	110
King's Lynn, Eng., U.K.	I14	8
Kingsmere Lake, l., Sk., Can.	D8	104
Kings Mountain, N.C., U.S.	D5	112
King Solomon's Mines see Mikhrot Shelomo Hamelekh, hist., Isr.	I3	50
King Sound, strt., Austl.	C4	68
Kings Peak, mtn., Ut., U.S.	D6	120
King's Point, Nf., Can.	C17	106
Kingsport, Tn., U.S.	C4	112
Kingston, Ga., U.S.	E2	112
Kingston, Jam.	E6	94
Kingston, Ma., U.S.	F16	108
Kingston, Mo., U.S.	C2	114
Kingston, N.S., Can.	H9	106
Kingston, N.Y., U.S.	F13	108
Kingston, N.Z.	F2	72
Kingston, Oh., U.S.	H4	108
Kingston, Ok., U.S.	F10	116
Kingston, On., Can.	F19	110
Kingston, Pa., U.S.	F11	108
Kingston, Tn., U.S.	D2	112
Kingston Southeast, Austl.	K3	70
Kingston upon Hull, Eng., U.K.	H13	8
Kingstown, St. Vin.	H14	94
Kingstree, S.C., U.S.	F7	112
Kingsville, On., Can.	H13	110
Kingsville, Tx., U.S.	L9	116
King William, Va., U.S.	B9	112
King William Island, i., N.T., Can.	C13	96
King William's Town, S. Afr.	I8	66
Kingwood, W.V., U.S.	H7	108
Kinistino, Sk., Can.	F9	104
Kinkony, Lac, l., Madag.	p21	67b
Kinmundy, Il., U.S.	D8	114
Kinnaird, B.C., Can.	H17	102
Kinnaird Head, c., Scot., U.K.	D11	8
Kinneret, Yam (Sea of Galilee), l., Isr.	C5	50
Kinsale, Old Head of, c., Ire.	J5	8
Kinshasa (Léopoldville), Zaire	B3	58
Kinsley, Ks., U.S.	N8	118
Kinsman, Oh., U.S.	F6	108
Kinston, Al., U.S.	K10	114
Kinston, N.C., U.S.	D9	112
Kintampo, Ghana	G9	64
Kintyre, pen., Scot., U.K.	F8	8
Kintyre, Mull of, c., Scot., U.K.	F8	8
Kinuseo Falls, wtfl, B.C., Can.	C13	102
Kinuso, Ab., Can.	B19	102
Kinyeti, mtn., Sudan	H7	56
Kinzua, Or., U.S.	F5	122
Kiowa, Co., U.S.	L3	118
Kiowa, Ks., U.S.	N9	118
Kiowa, Ok., U.S.	E11	116
Kipahigan Lake, l., Can.	C12	104
Kipengere Range, mts., Tan.	C6	58
Kipling, Sk., Can.	H12	104
Kipnuk, Ak., U.S.	G12	100
Kipushi, Zaire	D5	58
Kirane, Mali	D4	64
Kiraŭsk, Bela.	H12	22
Kirazlı, Tur.	I10	20
Kirbyville, Tx., U.S.	L3	114
Kirchberg, Ger.	F9	10
Kirchheimbolanden, Ger.	F8	10
Kirchmöser, Ger.	C12	10
Kirchschlag in der Buckligen Welt, Aus.	H16	10
Kirejevsk, Russia	H20	22
Kirenga, stm., Russia	F13	28
Kirensk, Russia	F13	28
Kirghizia see Kyrgyzstan, ctry., Asia	I13	26
Kirgizskij chrebet, mts., Asia	I12	26
Kiri, Zaire	B3	58
Kiribati, ctry., Oc.	I22	126
Kırıkhan, Tur.	C4	48
Kırıkkale, Tur.	B2	48
Kirillov, Russia	B21	22
Kirillovskoje, Russia	A12	22
Kirin see Jilin, China	C12	30
Kirin see Jilin, prov., China	C12	30
Kirinyaga, mtn., Kenya	B7	58
Kiriši, Russia	B15	22

Name	Map Ref.	Page
Kiriwina Islands, is., Pap. N. Gui.	A10	68
Kırkağaç, Tur.	J11	20
Kirkcaldy, Scot., U.K.	E10	8
Kirkcudbright, Scot., U.K.	G9	8
Kirkenes, Nor.	G22	6
Kirkjubæjarklaustur, Ice.	C4	6a
Kirkland, Il., U.S.	H7	110
Kirkland, Tx., U.S.	E6	116
Kirkland, Wa., U.S.	C3	122
Kirkland Lake, On., Can.	B15	110
Kırklareli, Tur.	H11	20
Kirklin, In., U.S.	B10	114
Kirkness Lake, l., On., Can.	G21	104
Kirkpatrick, Mount, mtn., Ant.	D8	73
Kirkpatrick Lake, l., Ab., Can.	F23	102
Kirksville, Mo., U.S.	B4	114
Kirkūk, Iraq	D8	48
Kirkwall, Scot., U.K.	C11	8
Kirkwood, Il., U.S.	J5	110
Kirkwood, Mo., U.S.	D6	114
Kirkwood, S. Afr.	I7	66
Kirov, Russia	G17	22
Kirov, Russia	F7	26
Kirovakan, Arm.	I6	26
Kirovgrad, Russia	F10	26
Kirovohrad, Ukr.	H4	26
Kirovsk, Russia	B14	22
Kirovsk, Russia	D4	26
Kirovskij, Kaz.	I13	26
Kirs, Russia	F8	26
Kirsanov, Russia	I25	22
Kırşehir, Tur.	B3	48
Kīrthar Range, mts., Pak.	G2	44
Kirtland, N.M., U.S.	H8	120
Kiruna, Swe.	H17	6
Kirwin, Ks., U.S.	L8	118
Kiryū, Japan	K14	36
Kiržač, Russia	E21	22
Kisa, Swe.	M14	6
Kisangani (Stanleyville), Zaire	A5	58
Kisarazu, Japan	L14	36
Kisbey, Sk., Can.	I12	104
Kisel'ovsk, Russia	G9	28
Kishanganj, India	G12	44
Kishangarh Bās, India	G6	44
Kishi, Nig.	G11	64
Kishikas, stm., On., Can.	F23	104
Kishinev see Chişinău, Mol.	B12	20
Kishiwada, Japan	M10	36
Kishorganj, Bngl.	H14	44
Kisii, Kenya	B6	58
Kiska Island, i., Ak., U.S.	j3	101a
Kiskatinaw, stm., B.C., Can.	B14	102
Kiski Lake, l., Mb., Can.	D16	104
Kiskittogisu Lake, l., Mb., Can.	D16	104
Kiskitto Lake, l., Mb., Can.	D16	104
Kiskunfélegyháza, Hung.	I19	10
Kiskunhalas, Hung.	I19	10
Kiskunmajsa, Hung.	I19	10
Kislovodsk, Russia	I6	26
Kismaayo, Som.	B8	58
Kiso-sammyaku, mts., Japan	L12	36
Kispiox, B.C., Can.	B7	102
Kispiox, stm., B.C., Can.	B7	102
Kispiox Mountain, mtn., B.C., Can.	B7	102
Kisseynew Lake, l., Can.	D13	104
Kissidougou, Gui.	G4	64
Kissimmee, Fl., U.S.	K5	112
Kissimmee, stm., Fl., U.S.	L6	112
Kissimmee, Lake, l., Fl., U.S.	L5	112
Kississing, Mb., Can.	C13	104
Kississing Lake, l., Mb., Can.	C13	104
Kistigan Lake, l., Mb., Can.	D22	104
Kisújszállás, Hung.	H20	10
Kisumu, Kenya	B6	58
Kisvárda, Hung.	G22	10
Kita, Mali	E5	64
Kita-Daitō-jima, i., Japan	F13	30
Kitaibaraki, Japan	K15	36
Kitakata, Japan	J14	36
Kitakyūshū, Japan	N5	36
Kitale, Kenya	A7	58
Kitami, Japan	d18	36a
Kitami-sanchi, mts., Japan	c17	36a
Kit Carson, Co., U.S.	M5	118
Kitchener, On., Can.	G15	110
Kiteiyab, Sudan	I7	60
Kíthira, Grc.	M7	20
Kíthira, i., Grc.	M6	20
Kíthnos, i., Grc.	L8	20
Kitimat, B.C., Can.	C6	102
Kitimat, stm., B.C., Can.	C6	102
Kitimat Ranges, mts., B.C., Can.	D5	102
Kitlope, stm., B.C., Can.	D7	102
Kitlope Lake, l., B.C., Can.	D7	102
Kitscoty, Ab., Can.	E4	104
Kitsman', Ukr.	A9	20
Kittanning, Pa., U.S.	G7	108
Kittery, Me., U.S.	D16	108
Kittilä, Fin.	H19	6
Kittitas, Wa., U.S.	D5	122
Kitui, Kenya	B7	58
Kitwanga, B.C., Can.	B6	102
Kitwangar Indian Reserve, B.C., Can.	B6	102
Kitwe, Zam.	D5	58
Kitwitwi, Nmb.	A4	66
Kitzbühel, Aus.	H12	10
Kitzingen, Ger.	F10	10
Kiukiang see Jiujiang, China	F4	34
Kiviõli, Est.	B9	22
Kivu, Lac, l., Afr.	B5	58
Kıyıköy, Tur.	H12	20
Kiyiu Lake, l., Sk., Can.	G6	104
Kizel, Russia	F9	26
Kızıl, stm., Tur.	A2	48
Kızıltepe, Tur.	C6	48
Kizl'ar, Russia	I7	26
Kizyl-Arvat, Turk.	J9	26
Kizyl-Atrek, Turk.	J8	26
Kizyl-Su, Turk.	B12	48
Kjustendil, Bul.	G6	20
Kladanj, Bos.	E2	20
Kladno, Czech Rep.	E14	10
Klagenfurt, Aus.	I14	10
Klahoose Indian Reserve, B.C., Can.	G10	102
Klaipėda (Memel), Lith.	F4	22
Klaksvík, Faer. Is.	D8	6b
Klamath, Ca., U.S.	C1	124
Klamath, stm., U.S.	C1	124
Klamath Falls, Or., U.S.	H4	122
Klamath Mountains, mts., U.S.	B2	124
Klangpi, Myan.	C2	40
Klarälven, stm., Eur.	K13	6
Klatovy, Czech Rep.	F13	10
Klawer, S. Afr.	H4	66
Klawock, Ak., U.S.	I28	100
Kl'az'ma, stm., Russia	E25	22
Kleck, Bela.	H9	22
Kleena Kleene, B.C., Can.	F10	102
Klemme, Ia., U.S.	G2	110
Klemtu, B.C., Can.	E6	102
Klerksdorp, S. Afr.	F8	66
Klet', mtn., Czech Rep.	G14	10
Kletn'a, Russia	H16	22
Kleve, Ger.	D6	10
Kličau̯, Bela.	H12	22
Klickitat, Wa., U.S.	E4	122
Klickitat, stm., Wa., U.S.	E4	122
Klimavičy, Bela.	H14	22
Klimovo, Russia	I15	22
Klimovsk, Russia	F20	22
Klin, Russia	E19	22
Klinaklini, stm., B.C., Can.	F9	102
Klincy, Russia	I15	22
Klipplaat, S. Afr.	I7	66
Klishkivtsi, Ukr.	A10	20
Kljascicy, Bela.	F11	22
Kłobuck, Pol.	E18	10
Kłodzko, Pol.	E16	10
Klondike, hist. reg., Yk., Can.	E25	100
Klondike, stm., Yk., Can.	D26	100
Klosterneuburg, Aus.	G16	10
Klosters, Switz.	E12	13
Kloten, Switz.	D10	13
Klotz, Lac, l., P.Q., Can.	D18	96
Klötze, Ger.	C11	10
Klouto, Togo	H10	64
Kluane, stm., Yk., Can.	F25	100
Kluane Lake, l., Yk., Can.	F25	100
Kluane National Park, Yk., Can.	F25	100
Kl'učevskaja Sopka, vulkan, vol., Russia	F24	28
Kl'uči, Russia	F24	28
Kluczbork, Pol.	E18	10
Klukwan, Ak., U.S.	G27	100
Knapp, Wi., U.S.	F3	110
Knäred, Swe.	M13	6
Kn'ažji Gory, Russia	E18	22
Kneehills Creek, stm., Ab., Can.	F21	102
Knee Lake, l., Mb., Can.	C20	104
Knee Lake, l., Sk., Can.	C7	104
Knevicy, Russia	D15	22
Kneža, Bul.	F8	20
Knić, Yugo.	F4	20
Knickerbocker, Tx., U.S.	H6	116
Knife, stm., N.D., U.S.	D6	118
Knife Lake, l., On., Can.	E23	104
Knight Inlet, b., B.C., Can.	G9	102
Knights Landing, Ca., U.S.	F4	124
Knightstown, In., U.S.	C11	114
Knik Arm, b., Ak., U.S.	F20	100
Knin, Cro.	E11	18
Knippa, Tx., U.S.	J7	116
Knittelfeld, Aus.	H14	10
Knob Noster, Mo., U.S.	D3	114
Knokke-Heist, Bel.	F3	12
Knox, In., U.S.	A10	114
Knox, Pa., U.S.	F7	108
Knox, Cape, c., B.C., Can.	C1	102
Knox City, Tx., U.S.	F7	116
Knox Coast, Ant.	B6	73
Knoxville, Ga., U.S.	G3	112
Knoxville, Ia., U.S.	I2	110
Knoxville, Il., U.S.	J5	110
Knoxville, Tn., U.S.	D3	112
Knysna, S. Afr.	J6	66
Knyszyn, Pol.	B22	10
Kobar Sink, depr., Eth.	F9	56
Kobayashi, Japan	P5	36
Kōbe, Japan	M10	36
København (Copenhagen), Den.	N13	6
Koblenz, Ger.	E7	10
Koboža, Russia	C18	22
Kobrinskoje, Russia	B13	22
Kobryn, Bela.	I7	22
Kobuk, Ak., U.S.	C16	100
Kobylin, Pol.	D17	10
Kočani, Mac.	H6	20
Kočečum, stm., Russia	D12	28
Kočetovka, Russia	I23	22
Kočevje, Slvn.	D9	18
Kŏch'ang, S. Kor.	H14	32
Koch Bihār, India	G13	44
Kōchi, Japan	N8	36
Koch Island, i., N.T., Can.	C17	96
Kochma, Russia	E24	22
Kodaikānal, India	G4	46
Kodāri, Nepal	G11	44
Kodiak, Ak., U.S.	H18	100
Kodiak Island, i., Ak., U.S.	H18	100
Kodino, Russia	J26	6
Kodok, Sudan	M7	60
Kodyma, Ukr.	A13	20
Koekelare, Bel.	F2	12
Koersel, Bel.	F7	12
Koes, Nmb.	E4	66
Köflach, Aus.	H15	10
Koforidua, Ghana	H9	64
Kōfu, Japan	L13	36
Koga, Japan	K14	36
Kogaluc, stm., P.Q., Can.	E17	96
Kogaluc, Baie, b., P.Q., Can.	E17	96
Kogaluk, stm., Nf., Can.	E20	96
Kogan, Austl.	F9	70
Køge, Den.	N13	6
Kogoni, Mali	D6	64
Koh̨anava, Bela.	G13	22
Kohāt, Pak.	D4	44
Kohila, Est.	B7	22
Kohīma, India	H16	44
Kohler, Wi., U.S.	G8	110
Kohtla-Järve, Est.	B10	22
Kohŭng, S. Kor.	I15	32
Kohunlich, hist., Mex.	H15	90
Koidern, Yk., Can.	F24	100
Koidu, S.L.	G4	64
Koigi, Est.	C8	22
Koimbani, Com.	k15	67a
Kojgorodok, Russia	E8	26
Kojŏ, N. Kor.	E15	32
Kok (Hkok), stm., Asia	D5	40
Kokand, Uzb.	I12	26
Kokanee Glacier Provincial Park, B.C., Can.	H17	102
Kokčetav, Kaz.	G11	26
Koki, Sen.	D2	64
Kokka, Sudan	G6	60
Kokkola (Karleby), Fin.	J18	6
Koknese, Lat.	E8	22
Koko, Nig.	F12	64
Kokoda, Pap. N. Gui.	A9	68
Kokomo, In., U.S.	B10	114
Kokomo, Ms., U.S.	K6	114
Kokong, Bots.	E6	66
Koko Nor see Qinghai Hu, l., China	D7	30
Kokopo, Pap. N. Gui.	k17	68a
Kokorevka, Russia	I17	22
Kokšaalatau, chrebet, mts., Asia	I13	26
Koksan, N. Kor.	E14	32
Koksoak, stm., P.Q., Can.	E19	96
Koksŏng, S. Kor.	H15	32
Kokstad, S. Afr.	H9	66
Kola, Russia	G23	6
Kolahun, Lib.	G4	64
Kola Peninsula see Kol'skij poluostrov, pen., Russia	D5	26
Kolār, India	F5	46
Kolār Gold Fields, India	F5	46
Kolárovo, Slvk.	H18	10
Kolbio, Kenya	B8	58
Kolchozabad, Taj.	B3	44
Kol'čugino, Russia	E22	22
Kolda, Sen.	E2	64
Kolenté (Great Scarcies), stm., Afr.	G3	64
Kolgujev, ostrov, i., Russia	D7	26
Kolhāpur, India	D3	46
Kolia, C. Iv.	G6	64
Koliba (Corubal), stm., Afr.	E3	64
Koliganek, Ak., U.S.	G16	100
Kolimbine, stm., Afr.	D4	64
Kolín, Czech Rep.	E15	10
Kolisne, Ukr.	C13	20
Kolka, Lat.	D5	22
Kolkasrags, c., Lat.	D5	22
Kollegāl, India	F4	46
Köln (Cologne), Ger.	E6	10
Kolno, Pol.	B21	10
Kolo, Niger	E11	64
Koło, Pol.	C18	10
Koloa, Hi., U.S.	p14	125a
Kolobovo, Russia	E24	22
Kołobrzeg, Pol.	A15	10
Kolodn'a, Russia	G15	22
Kologriv, Russia	C27	22
Koloko, Burkina	F7	64
Kolomna, Russia	F21	22
Kolomyya, Ukr.	H3	26
Kolpaševo, Russia	F8	28
Kolpino, Russia	B13	22
Kolpny, Russia	I20	22
Kol'skij poluostrov (Kola Peninsula), pen., Russia	D5	26
Kol'ubakino, Russia	F19	22
Kolwezi, Zaire	D5	58
Kolyma, stm., Russia	D23	28
Kolymskaja nizmennost', pl., Russia	D22	28
Koma, Eth.	M9	60
Komadugu Gana, stm., Nig.	F9	54
Komadugu Yobe, stm., Afr.	F9	54
Komandorskije ostrova, is., Russia	F25	28
Komariči, Russia	I17	22
Komárno, Slvk.	H18	10
Komarnyky, Ukr.	F23	10
Komárom, Hung.	H18	10
Komárom-Esztergom, co., Hung.	H18	10
Komarovo, Russia	C16	22
Komati (Incomáti), stm., Afr.	E10	66
Komatipoort, S. Afr.	E10	66
Komatsu, Japan	K11	36
Komatsushima, Japan	M9	36
Kombone, Cam.	I14	64
Komi, state, Russia	E8	26
Komin Yanga, Burkina	F10	64
Komló, Hung.	I18	10
Kommunizma, pik, mtn., Taj.	J12	26
Komodo, Pulau, i., Indon.	G6	38
Komoé, stm., Afr.	G6	54
Komotiní, Grc.	H9	20
Komsomolec, Kaz.	G10	26
Komsomolec, ostrov, i., Russia	A17	26
Komsomolec, zaliv, b., Kaz.	H8	26
Komsomol'sk, Russia	D23	22
Komsomol'sk, Turk.	B17	48
Komsomol'sk-na-Amure, Russia	G19	28
Komsomol'skoj Pravdy, ostrova, is., Russia	B13	28
Kona, Mali	D8	64
Kona Coast, Hi., U.S.	r18	125a
Konakovo, Russia	E19	22
Konakpınar, Tur.	J11	20
Konar, stm., Asia	C4	44
Konārak, India	K12	44
Konawa, Ok., U.S.	E10	116
Konch, India	H8	44
Konda, stm., Russia	E5	28
Kondoa, Tan.	B7	58
Kondopoga, Russia	E4	26
Kondratjevo, Russia	A11	22
Kondrovo, Russia	G18	22
Kondūz, Afg.	B3	44
Konfara, Gui.	F5	64
Kông, stm., Asia	H9	40
Kongcheng, China	D6	34
Kongfang, China	H5	34
Kongju, S. Kor.	G15	32
Konglong, China	F4	34
Kongolo, Zaire	C5	58
Kongor, Sudan	N6	60
Kongsvinger, Nor.	K13	6
Kongur Shan, mtn., China	D2	30
Kongzhen, China	D8	34
Konice, Czech Rep.	F16	10
Königswinter, Ger.	E7	10
Konin, Pol.	C18	10
Köniz, Switz.	E7	13
Konjic, Bos.	F1	20
Könkämäälven, stm., Eur.	G17	6
Kon'-Kolodez', Russia	I22	22
Konkouré, stm., Gui.	F3	64
Konnur, India	D3	46
Konoša, Russia	E6	26
Konotop, Ukr.	G4	26
Kon'ovo, Russia	J26	6
Konqi, stm., China	C4	30
Końskie, Pol.	D20	10
Konstantinovskij, Russia	D22	22
Konstanz, Ger.	H9	10
Kontagora, Nig.	F12	64
Kontejevo, Russia	C24	22
Kontich, Bel.	F5	12
Kontiomäki, Fin.	I21	6
Kontseba, Ukr.	A13	20
Kon Tum, Viet.	G10	40
Kontum, Plateau du, plat., Viet.	H10	40
Konya, Tur.	C2	48
Konza, Kenya	B7	58
Konžakovskij Kamen', gora, mtn., Russia	F9	26
Koocanusa, Lake, res., N.A.	B10	122
Koolamarra, Austl.	C4	70
Koolau Range, mts., Hi., U.S.	p15	125a
Kooloonong, Austl.	J5	70
Koondrook, Austl.	J6	70
Koontz Lake, In., U.S.	A10	114
Koosharem, Ut., U.S.	F5	120
Kooskia, Id., U.S.	D10	122
Koossa, Gui.	G5	64
Kootenai (Kootenay), stm., N.A.	I18	102
Kootenay (Kootenai), stm., N.A.	H17	102
Kootenay Indian Reserve, B.C., Can.	H19	102
Kootenay Lake, l., B.C., Can.	H18	102
Kootenay National Park, B.C., Can.	F18	102
Kootjieskolk, S. Afr.	H5	66
Kopargaon, India	C3	46
Kópasker, Ice.	A5	6a
Kopejsk, Russia	F10	26
Koper, Slvn.	D8	18
Kopetdag, chrebet, mts., Asia	C15	48
Koppal, India	E4	46
Kopparbergs Län, co., Swe.	K14	6
Koprivnica, Cro.	C11	18
Kopt'ovo, Russia	E23	22
Kopys', Bela.	G13	22
Korab (Maja e Korabit), mtn., Eur.	H4	20
Korabit, Maja e (Korab), mtn., Eur.	H4	20
Korablino, Russia	H23	22
Kor'akskaja Sopka, vulkan, vol., Russia	G23	28
Korāput, India	C7	46
Korba, Tun.	M5	18
Korbach, Ger.	D8	10
Korbous, Tun.	M5	18
Korçë, Alb.	I4	20
Korčula, Otok, i., Cro.	G11	18
Kord Kūy, Iran	C13	48
Korea, North, ctry., Asia	C12	30
Korea, South, ctry., Asia	D12	30
Korea Bay, b., Asia	E11	32
Korea Strait, strt., Asia	I16	32
Korekozevo, Russia	G19	22
Korfovskij, Russia	H19	28
Korgus, Sudan	H7	60
Korhogo, C. Iv.	G7	64
Korinthiakós Kólpos (Gulf of Corinth), b., Grc.	K6	20
Kórinthos (Corinth), Grc.	L6	20
Korínthou, Dhiórix, Grc.	L6	20
Kōriyama, Japan	J15	36
Korkino, Russia	G10	26
Korla, China	C4	30
Korneuburg, Aus.	G16	10
Koro, Mali	D8	64
Korogwe, Tan.	C7	58
Koroit, Austl.	L5	70
Koroleve, Ukr.	A7	20
Koróni, Grc.	M5	20
Koronowo, Pol.	B17	10
Körös, stm., Hung.	I21	10
Korosten', Ukr.	G3	26
Korotovo, Russia	C20	22
Korpilahti, Fin.	J19	6
Korpo (Korppoo), Fin.	K17	6
Korsakov, Russia	H20	28
Korsør, Den.	N12	6
Korsze, Pol.	A21	10
Kortrijk (Courtrai), Bel.	G3	12
Koruçam Burnu, c., N. Cyp.	D2	48
Korumburra, Austl.	L6	70
Koryŏng, S. Kor.	H16	32
Kos, Grc.	M11	20
Kos (Cos), i., Grc.	M11	20
Kosa, Eth.	N9	60
Kosa, Russia	F8	26
Koš-Agač, Russia	G15	26
Kosaja Gora, Russia	G20	22
Koščagyl, Kaz.	H8	26
Kościan, Pol.	C16	10
Kościerzyna, Pol.	A18	10
Kosciusko, Ms., U.S.	I7	114
Kosciusko, Mount, mtn., Austl.	K8	70
Kosciusko National Park, Austl.	K8	70
Koshikijima-rettō, is., Japan	P4	36
Koshkonong, Mo., U.S.	F5	114
Košice, Slvk.	G21	10
Kosiv, Ukr.	A9	20
Köşk, Tur.	L12	20
Koskaecodde Lake, l., Nf., Can.	D18	106
Koski, Fin.	K18	6
Koslan, Russia	E7	26
Kosmynino, Russia	D23	22
Kosŏng, N. Kor.	E16	32
Kosovo-Metohija, prov., Yugo.	G5	20
Kosovska Mitrovica, Yugo.	G4	20
Kosse, Tx., U.S.	H10	116
Koster, S. Afr.	E8	66
Kosterevo, Russia	F22	22
Kostroma, Russia	D23	22
Kostroma, stm., Russia	C23	22
Kostryzhivka, Ukr.	A9	20
Kostrzyn, Pol.	C14	10
Kostyantynivka, Ukr.	H5	26
Koszalin (Köslin), Pol.	A16	10
Kőszeg, Hung.	H16	10
Kota, India	H6	44
Kota Baharu, Malay.	K7	40
Kotabaru, Indon.	F6	38
Kotabumi, Indon.	F3	38
Kotadabok, Indon.	O8	40
Kotcho Lake, l., B.C., Can.	E8	96
Kotel'nič, Russia	F7	26
Kotel'nikovo, Russia	H6	26
Kotel'nyj, ostrov, i., Russia	B19	28
Köthen, Ger.	D11	10
Kotka, Fin.	K20	6
Kot Kapūra, India	E6	44
Kotlas, Russia	E7	26
Kotli, Pak.	D5	44
Kotlin, ostrov, i., Russia	A12	22
Kotly, Russia	B11	22
Koton-Karifi, Nig.	G13	64
Kotonkoro, Nig.	F12	64
Kotor, Yugo.	G2	20
Kotoriba, Cro.	C11	18
Kotorovo, Russia	G24	22
Kotouba, C. Iv.	G8	64
Kotovsk, Russia	I24	22
Kotovs'k, Ukr.	H3	26
Kottagūdem, India	D6	46
Kottayam, India	H4	46
Kotto, stm., C.A.R.	G5	56
Kotuj, stm., Russia	C12	28
Kotzebue, Ak., U.S.	C13	100
Kotzebue Sound, strt., Ak., U.S.	C13	100
Kötzting, Ger.	F12	10
Kou'an, China	C8	34
Kouandé, Benin	F10	64
Kouchibouguac National Park, N.B., Can.	F8	106
Koudougou, Burkina	E8	64
Kouéré, Burkina	F8	64
Koukdjuak, stm., N.T., Can.	C18	96
Koulamoutou, Gabon	B2	58
Koulikoro, Mali	E6	64
Koulouguidi, Mali	E4	64
Koulountou, stm., Afr.	E3	64
Koumbakara, Sen.	E2	64
Koumbal, C.A.R.	M2	60
Koumpentoum, Sen.	E2	64
Koumra, Chad	G4	56
Koundara, Gui.	E3	64
Koungheul, Sen.	E2	64
Kounradskij, Kaz.	H13	26
Kountze, Tx., U.S.	L2	114
Koupéla, Burkina	E9	64
Kouroukoto, Mali	E4	64
Kouroussa, Gui.	F5	54
Koussanar, Sen.	E2	64
Koussané, Mali	D4	64
Koussane, Sen.	D3	64
Koussi, Emi, mtn., Chad	E4	56
Koussili, Mali	E4	64
Koutia Ba, Sen.	D2	64
Koutiala, Mali	E7	64
Kouto, C. Iv.	G6	64
Koutou, China	E2	32
Kouts, In., U.S.	A9	114
Kovarskas, Lith.	F7	22
Kovdor, Russia	H22	6
Kovel', Ukr.	G2	26
Kovernino, Russia	D26	22
Kovilpatti, India	H4	46
Kovrov, Russia	F6	26
Kovvur, India	D6	46
Kowalewo Pomorskie, Pol.	B18	10
Kowŏn, N. Kor.	D15	32
Koyna Reservoir, res., India	D2	46
Koyuk, Ak., U.S.	D14	100
Koyukuk, Ak., U.S.	D16	100
Koyukuk, stm., Ak., U.S.	D17	100
Kozan, Tur.	C3	48
Kozáni, Grc.	I5	20
Kozel'sk, Russia	G18	22
Kozlov Béreg, Russia	C10	22
Kozlovo, Russia	E19	22
Kpandae, Ghana	G9	64
Kpandu, Ghana	H10	64
Kra, Isthmus of, Asia	I5	40
Krabi, Thai.	J5	40
Krâchéh, Camb.	H9	40
Kragerø, Nor.	L11	6
Kragujevac, Yugo.	E4	20
Krajenka, Pol.	B17	10
Krajina, reg., Cro.	D10	18
Krakatoa see Rakata, Pulau, i., Indon.	j12	39a
Krâkôr, Camb.	H8	40
Kraków, Pol.	E19	10
Kralendijk, Neth. Ant.	H10	94
Kraljevo, Yugo.	F4	20
Kralovice, Czech Rep.	F13	10
Kramators'k, Ukr.	H5	26
Kranj, Slvn.	C9	18
Kranzberg, Nmb.	C2	66
Kraskino, Russia	A18	32
Krāslava, Lat.	F10	22
Krasnae, Bela.	G10	22
Krasnaja Gorbatka, Russia	F24	22
Krasnaja Gorka, Russia	E26	22
Krasnaja Zar'a, Russia	I20	22
Kraśnik, Pol.	E22	10
Krasni Okny, Ukr.	B13	20
Krasnoarmejsk, Russia	E21	22
Krasnodar, Russia	H5	26
Krasnofarfornyj, Russia	B14	22
Krasnogorsk, Russia	F20	22
Krasnogorsk, Russia	H20	28
Krasnoil's'k, Ukr.	A9	20
Krasnojarsk, Russia	F10	28
Krasnojarskoje vodochranilišče, res., Russia	F16	26
Krasnoje Echo, Russia	F23	22
Krasnoje-na-Volge, Russia	D24	22
Krasnoje Selo, Russia	B13	22
Krasnoje Znam'a, Turk.	C17	48
Krasnokamsk, Russia	F9	26
Krasnolesje, Russia	G5	22
Krasnoslobodsk, Russia	H6	26
Krasnoturjinsk, Russia	F10	26
Krasnoufimsk, Russia	F9	26
Krasnoural'sk, Russia	F10	26
Krasnovišersk, Russia	E9	26
Krasnovodsk, Turk.	I8	26
Krasnovodskij poluostrov, pen., Turk.	A12	48
Krasnovodskij zaliv, b., Turk.	B12	48
Krasnozavodsk, Russia	E21	22
Krasnoznamenskoje, Kaz.	G11	26
Krasnoz'orskoje, Russia	G13	26
Krasnyj Bogatyr', Russia	E24	22
Krasnyj Cholm, Russia	C20	22
Krasnyje Tkači, Russia	D22	22
Krasnyj Kut, Russia	G7	26
Krasnyj Luč, Russia	D13	22
Krasnyj Okt'abr', Russia	E21	22
Krasnyj Profintern, Russia	D23	22
Krasnyj Rog, Russia	I16	22
Krasnyj Tkač, Russia	F22	22
Krasnystaw, Pol.	E23	10
Krasnyy Luch, Ukr.	H5	26
Kraszna (Crasna), stm., Eur.	A6	20
Krebs, Ok., U.S.	E11	116
Krečetovo, Russia	K26	6
Krečevicy, Russia	C14	22
Krefeld, Ger.	D6	10
Kremastón, Tekhnití Límni, res., Grc.	K5	20
Kremenchuk, Ukr.	H4	26
Kremenchuts'ke vodoskhovyshche, res., Ukr.	H4	26
Kremmling, Co., U.S.	D10	120
Krems an der Donau, Aus.	G15	10
Kress, Tx., U.S.	E5	116
Kresta, zaliv, b., Russia	D28	28
Krestcy, Russia	C15	22
Kretinga, Lith.	F4	22
Kribi, Cam.	H8	54
Kriens, Switz.	D9	13
Kriljon, mys, c., Russia	b17	36a
Křimice, Czech Rep.	F13	10
Krishna, stm., India	D5	46
Krishnagiri, India	F5	46
Krishnanagar, India	I13	44
Krishnarāja Sāgara, res., India	F4	46
Kristdala, Swe.	M15	6
Kristiansand, Nor.	L11	6
Kristianstad, Swe.	M14	6
Kristiansund, Nor.	J10	6
Kristineberg, Swe.	I16	6
Kríti, prov., Grc.	N8	20
Kríti (Crete), i., Grc.	N8	20
Kritikón Pélagos (Sea of Crete), Grc.	N8	20
Kriva Palanka, Mac.	G6	20
Krivodol, Bul.	F7	20
Križevci, Cro.	C11	18
Krk, Otok, i., Cro.	D9	18
Krnov, Czech Rep.	E17	10
Krobia, Pol.	D16	10
Krokek, Swe.	L15	6
Kroken, Nor.	I14	6
Krokowa, Pol.	A18	10
Krombi Pits, Bots.	B7	66
Kroměříž, Czech Rep.	F17	10
Kromy, Russia	I18	22
Krŏng Kaôh Kŏng, Camb.	I7	40
Krŏng Kêb, Camb.	I8	40
Kronobergs Län, co., Swe.	M14	6
Kronoby (Kruunupyy), Fin.	J18	6
Kronockaja Sopka, vulkan, vol., Russia	G24	28
Kronockij zaliv, b., Russia	G24	28
Kronštadt, Russia	B12	22
Kroonstad, S. Afr.	F8	66
Kropotkin, Russia	H6	26
Krosno, Pol.	F21	10
Krotoszyn, Pol.	D17	10
Krotz Springs, La., U.S.	L5	114
Kr'učkovo, Russia	D18	22
Krugersdorp, S. Afr.	F8	66
Kruidfontein, S. Afr.	I5	66
Kruisfontein, S. Afr.	J7	66
Krukira, Laguna de, b., Nic.	D11	92
Kr'ukovo, Russia	F20	22
Kruleu̯ščyna, Bela.	F10	22
Krumbach [Schwaben], Ger.	G10	10
Krung Thep (Bangkok), Thai.	H6	40
Krupka, Czech Rep.	E13	10
Krupki, Bela.	G12	22
Kruševac, Yugo.	F5	20
Kruševo, Mac.	H5	20
Krušné hory (Erzgebirge), mts., Eur.	B19	14
Kruszwica, Pol.	C18	10
Krutoje, Russia	I20	22
Kruzenšterna, proliv, strt., Russia	H22	28
Kruzof Island, i., Ak., U.S.	H27	100
Kryčau̯, Bela.	H14	22
Krydor, Sk., Can.	F7	104
Kryms'kyy pivostriv (Crimean Peninsula), pen., Ukr.	H4	26
Krynica, Pol.	F20	10
Krynychne, Ukr.	D12	20
Kryve Ozero, Ukr.	B14	20
Kryvičy, Bela.	G10	22
Kryvyy Rih (Krivoy Rog), Ukr.	H4	26
Kryzhopil', Ukr.	A12	20
Ksar Chellala, Alg.	C12	62
Ksar el Barka, Maur.	B3	64
Ksar-el-Kebir, Mor.	J6	16
Ksar-el-Seghir, Mor.	J6	16
Ksar Hellal, Tun.	N5	18
Ksenjevka, Russia	G15	28
Ksour, Monts des, mts., Alg.	D10	62
Ksour Essaf, Tun.	N6	18
Kuala Kangsar, Malay.	L6	40
Kualakapuas, Indon.	F5	38
Kuala Lipis, Malay.	L7	40
Kuala Lumpur, Malay.	M6	40
Kuala Pilah, Malay.	M7	40
Kuala Terengganu, Malay.	L7	40
Kuancheng, China	C6	32
Kuantan, Malay.	M7	40
Kuban', stm., Russia	H5	26
Kubbum, Sudan	L2	60
Kubenskoje, Russia	B22	22
Kubenskoje, ozero, l., Russia	B22	22
Kučevo, Yugo.	E5	20
Kuchāman, India	G6	44
Kuching, Malay.	N11	40
Kuçovë, Alb.	I3	20
Kudirkos Naumiestis, Lith.	G5	22
Kudus, Indon.	j15	39a
Kudymkar, Russia	F8	26
Kuee Ruins, hist., Hi., U.S.	r18	125a
Kufstein, Aus.	H12	10
Kugaluk, stm., N.T., Can.	B29	100
Kugmallit Bay, b., N.T., Can.	B28	100
Kūhdasht, Iran	E9	48
Kūhpāyeh, Iran	E12	48
Kuidesu, China	B7	32
Kuidou, China	J7	34
Kuiseb, stm., S. Afr.	D2	66
Kuito, Ang.	D3	58
Kuiu Island, i., Ak., U.S.	H27	100
Kujang, N. Kor.	D14	32
Kujbyšev see Samara, Russia	G8	26
Kujbyšev, Russia	F13	26
Kujbyševskij, Uzb.	J11	26
Kujbyševskoje vodochranilišče, res., Russia	G7	26
Kujman', Russia	I22	22
Kukalaya, stm., Nic.	D11	92
Kukawa, Nig.	F9	54
Kukkola, Fin.	I19	6
Kula, Yugo.	D3	20
Kul'ab, Taj.	J11	26
Kula Kangri, mtn., Bhu.	F14	44
Kulākh, Sau. Ar.	D2	47
Kulautuva, Lith.	G6	22
Kulaykilī, Sudan	L3	60
Kuldīga, Lat.	E4	22
Kule, Bots.	D5	66
Kulebaki, Russia	F25	22
Kulikovo, Russia	I22	22
Kulim, Malay.	L6	40
Kulm, N.D., U.S.	E9	118
Kulmbach, Ger.	E11	10
Kuloj, Russia	E6	26
Kulongshan, China	B4	32
Kulotino, Russia	C16	22
Kul'sary, Kaz.	H8	26
Kulti, India	I12	44
Kulumadau, Pap. N. Gui.	A10	68
Kulundinskaja step', pl., Asia	G7	28
Kuma, stm., Russia	I7	26
Kumagaya, Japan	K14	36
Kumajri, Arm.	I6	26
Kumamoto, Japan	O5	36
Kumanovo, Mac.	G5	20
Kumārapālaiyam, India	G4	46
Kumasi, Ghana	H9	64
Kumba, Cam.	I14	64
Kumbakonam, India	G5	46
Kumba Pits, Bots.	B7	66
Kŭmch'ŏn, N. Kor.	E14	32
Kum-Dag, Turk.	J8	26
Kume-jima, i., Japan	u1	37b
Kŭmhwa, S. Kor.	E15	32
Kumla, Swe.	L14	6
Kumo, Nig.	F9	54
Kumukahi, Cape, c., Hi., U.S.	r19	125a
Kumukuli, China	B13	44
Kumzār, Oman	A10	47
Kuna, Id., U.S.	G9	122
Kunašir, ostrov (Kunashiri-tō), i., Russia	c21	36a
Kunchhā, Nepal	F11	44
Kunda, Est.	B9	22
Kundar, stm., Asia	E3	44
Kunene, prov., Nmb.	B2	66
Kunene (Cunene), stm., Afr.	E2	58
Kunghit Island, i., B.C., Can.	E3	102
Kungrad, Uzb.	I9	26
Kungsbacka, Swe.	M13	6
Kungur, Russia	F9	26
Kunhegyes, Hung.	H20	10
Kunja, Russia	E13	22
Kunjāh, Pak.	D5	44
Kunlong, Myan.	C5	40
Kunlun Shan, mts., China	B12	44
Kunming, China	B7	40
Kunsan, S. Kor.	H14	32
Kunshan, China	D9	34
Kunszentmárton, Hung.	I20	10
Kuntair, Gam.	E1	64
Kuntaur, Gam.	E2	64
Kunting, China	F10	34
Kununurra, Austl.	C5	68
Kunwi, S. Kor.	G16	32
Kuokegan, China	B13	44
Kuopio, Fin.	J20	6
Kuopion lääni, prov., Fin.	J20	6
Kupang, Indon.	H7	38
Kupanskoje, Russia	E21	22
Kupino, Russia	G7	28

Name	Map Ref.	Page
Kupiškis, Lith.	F7	22
Küplü, Tur.	H10	20
Kupreanof Island, i., Ak., U.S.	H28	100
Kup'yans'k, Ukr.	H5	26
Kuqa, China	C3	30
Kür, stm., Asia	B10	48
Kurashiki, Japan	M8	36
Kuraymah, Sudan	H6	60
Kurayyimah, Jord.	D5	50
Kurba, Russia	D22	22
Kürdämir, Azer.	A10	48
Kür dili, spit, Azer.	B10	48
Kurdistan, hist. reg., Asia	B4	42
Kure, Japan	M7	36
Kurejka, stm., Russia	D9	28
Kuresaare, Est.	C5	22
Kurgan, Russia	F11	26
Kurgan-T'ube, Taj.	J11	26
Kuria Muria Islands see Khurīyā Murīyā, is., Oman	F10	47
Kuridala, Austl.	C4	70
Kurīgrām, Bngl.	H13	44
Kuril Islands see Kuril'skije ostrova, is., Russia	H22	28
Kuril'skije ostrova (Kuril Islands), is., Russia	H22	28
Kuril Strait see Pervyj Kuril'skij proliv, strt., Russia	G23	28
Kuril Trench	D19	126
Kurinwás, stm., Nic.	E11	92
Kurkino, Russia	H21	22
Kurlovskij, Russia	F23	22
Kurmuk, Sudan	L8	60
Kurnool, India	E5	46
Kurort Schmalkalden, Ger.	E10	10
Kurovskoje, Russia	F21	22
Kurow, N.Z.	F3	72
Kuršėnai, Lith.	E5	22
Kursk, Russia	G5	26
Kuršskaja kosa, spit, Eur.	F4	22
Kuršskij zaliv (Kuršių marios), b., Eur.	F3	22
Kūrtī, Sudan	H6	60
Kurtistown, Hi., U.S.	r18	125a
Kuru, Sudan	N4	60
Kuruman, S. Afr.	F6	66
Kuruman, stm., S. Afr.	F5	66
Kurumanheuwels, hills, S. Afr.	F6	66
Kurume, Japan	N5	36
Kurumkan, Russia	G14	28
Kurun, stm., Afr.	O8	60
Kurunegala, Sri L.	I6	46
Kurzeme, hist. reg., Lat.	E5	22
Kusa, Russia	F9	26
Kušalino, Russia	D19	22
Kusawa Lake, l., Yk., Can.	F26	100
Kusel, Ger.	F7	10
Kushaka, Nig.	F13	64
Kushiro, Japan	e19	36a
Kushnytsya, Ukr.	A7	20
Kushtia, Bngl.	I13	44
Kushui, China	C5	30
Kuška, Turk.	J10	26
Kuška, stm., Asia	C17	48
Kuskokwim, stm., Ak., U.S.	F14	100
Kuskokwim Mountains, mts., Ak., U.S.	E16	100
Kušmurun, Kaz.	G10	26
Küsnacht, Switz.	D10	13
Kusŏng, N. Kor.	D13	32
Kussharo-ko, l., Japan	d19	36a
Küssnacht am Rigi, Switz.	D9	13
Kustanaj, Kaz.	G10	26
Kustar'ovka, Russia	G25	22
Kūstī, Sudan	K7	60
Kušva, Russia	F9	26
Kut, Ko, i., Thai.	I7	40
Kuta, Nig.	G13	64
Kütahya, Tur.	H13	4
Kutaisi, Geor.	I6	26
Kutch, Rann of (Rann of Kachchh), reg., Asia	H4	44
Kutina, Cro.	D11	18
Kutná Hora, Czech Rep.	F15	10
Kutno, Pol.	C19	10
Kutse Game Reserve, Bots.	D7	66
Kuttura, Fin.	G20	6
Kuttusoja, Fin.	H21	6
Kutu, Zaire	B3	58
Kutum, Sudan	J3	60
Kuty, Ukr.	A9	20
Kutztown, Pa., U.S.	G11	108
Kuujjuaq, P.Q., Can.	E19	96
Kuusamo, Fin.	I21	6
Kuusankoski, Fin.	K20	6
Kuvandyk, Russia	G9	26
Kuvango, Ang.	D3	58
Kuvšinovo, Russia	D17	22
Kuwait see Al-Kuwayt, Kuw.	G9	48
Kuwait (Al-Kuwayt), ctry., Asia	D4	42
Kuwana, Japan	L11	36
Kuwayt, Jūn al- (Kuwait Bay), b., Kuw.	G10	48
Kuybyshev see Samara, Russia	G8	26
Küysanjaq, Iraq	C8	48
Kuyuwini, stm., Guy.	F13	84
Kuženkino, Russia	D16	22
Kuzneck, Russia	G7	26
Kuzneckij Alatau, mts., Russia	G9	28
Kvaløy, i., Nor.	G16	6
Kwai see Khwae Noi, stm., Thai.	G5	40
Kwajok, Sudan	M4	60
Kwakoegron, Sur.	B7	76
Kwando (Cuando), stm., Afr.	E4	58
Kwangchow see Guangzhou, China	L2	34
Kwangju, S. Kor.	H14	32
Kwango (Cuango), stm., Afr.	B3	58
Kwangtung see Guangdong, prov., China	G9	30
Kwangyang, S. Kor.	I15	32
Kwazulu see KwaZulu-Natal, prov., S. Afr.	G10	66
KwaZulu-Natal, prov., S. Afr.	G10	66
Kwekwe, Zimb.	B9	66
Kweneng, dept., Bots.	E7	66
Kwenge, stm., Afr.	C3	58
Kwethluk, Ak., U.S.	F14	100
Kwidzyn, Pol.	B18	10
Kwigillingok, Ak., U.S.	G13	100
Kwilu (Cuilo), stm., Afr.	B3	58
Kwitaro, stm., Guy.	F13	84
Kwolla, Nig.	G14	64
Kyabra, Austl.	F5	70
Kyabram, Austl.	K6	70
Kyaiklat, Myan.	F3	40
Kyaikto, Myan.	F4	40
Kyaukhnyat, Myan.	E4	40
Kyaukpyu, Myan.	E2	40
Kyaukse, Myan.	D4	40
Kyauktaw, Myan.	D2	40
Kyaunggon, Myan.	F3	40
Kybartai, Lith.	G5	22
Kyeikdon, Myan.	F5	40
Kyindwe, Myan.	D2	40
Kykotsmovi Village, Az., U.S.	I6	120
Kyle, S.D., U.S.	H5	118
Kyle, Sk., Can.	H6	104
Kyle, Tx., U.S.	J9	116
Kyle of Lochalsh, Scot., U.K.	D8	8
Kymen lääni, prov., Fin.	K20	6
Kyneton, Austl.	K6	70
Kyoga, Lake, l., Ug.	A6	58
Kyogle, Austl.	G10	70
Kyŏnggi-man, b., Asia	F13	32
Kyŏngju, S. Kor.	H17	32
Kyŏngsan, S. Kor.	H16	32
Kyŏngsŏng, N. Kor.	B17	32
Kyŏngwŏn, N. Kor.	A18	32
Kyōto, Japan	L10	36
Kyren, Russia	G12	28
Kyrgyzstan, ctry., Asia	I13	26
Kyritz, Ger.	C12	10
Kyštovka, Russia	F13	26
Kyštym, Russia	F10	26
Kyunhla, Myan.	C3	40
Kyuquot, B.C., Can.	G7	102
Kyuquot Sound, strt., B.C., Can.	G7	102
Kyūshū, i., Japan	O5	36
Kywebwe, Myan.	E4	40
Kywong, Austl.	J7	70
Kyyiv (Kiev), Ukr.	G4	26
Kyyivs'ke vodoskhovyshche, res., Ukr.	G4	26
Kyyjärvi, Fin.	J19	6
Kyzyl, Russia	G10	28
Kyzyl-Kija, Kyrg.	I12	26
Kyzylkum, des., Asia	I10	26
Kzyl-Orda, Kaz.	I11	26
Kzyltu, Kaz.	G12	26

L

Name	Map Ref.	Page
Laa an der Thaya, Aus.	G16	10
La Aguja, Cabo de, c., Col.	B5	84
La Alcarria, reg., Spain	E9	16
La Algaba, Spain	H5	16
La Antigua, Salina, pl., Arg.	E5	80
La Araucanía, prov., Chile	J2	80
La Arena, Pan.	J14	92
Laas Caanood, Som.	G10	56
La Ascención, Mex.	E10	90
La Asunción, Ven.	B11	84
La Atravesada, Loma, hill, Mex.	C3	90
Laau Point, c., Hi., U.S.	p16	125a
La Babia, Mex.	C8	90
Labadieville, La., U.S.	M6	114
La Baie, P.Q., Can.	D3	106
La Banda, Arg.	D6	80
La Bandera, Cerro, mtn., Mex.	E7	90
La Bañeza, Spain	C6	16
La Barca, Mex.	G8	90
La Barge, Wy., U.S.	B6	120
La Barra, Nic.	E11	92
La Barrita, Guat.	C3	92
La Baule-Escoublac, Fr.	E4	14
Labé, Gui.	F3	64
Labe (Elbe), stm., Eur.	B9	10
La Belle, Fl., U.S.	M5	112
La Belle, Mo., U.S.	B5	114
Labelle, P.Q., Can.	A12	108
Laberge, Lake, l., Yk., Can.	F27	100
La Biche, stm., Ab., Can.	B22	102
Labin, Cro.	D9	18
Labinsk, Russia	I6	26
La Bisbal, Spain	D15	16
La Blanca Grande, Laguna, l., Arg.	J7	80
Labná, hist., Mex.	G15	90
Laboe, Ger.	A10	10
Laborde, Arg.	G7	80
Labouheyre, Fr.	H6	14
Laboulaye, Arg.	H7	80
Labrador, reg., Nf., Can.	F20	96
Labrador City, Nf., Can.	F19	96
Labrador Sea, N.A.	E22	96
Lábrea, Braz.	B9	82
Labrieville, Réserve, P.Q., Can.	C4	106
Labrit, Fr.	H6	14
La Broquerie, Mb., Can.	I18	104
Labutta, Myan.	F3	40
Labytnangi, Russia	D11	26
Lača, ozero, l., Russia	K26	6
Laca Jahuira, stm., Bol.	H8	82
La Cal, stm., Bol.	G12	82
Lac-Allard, P.Q., Can.	B10	106
La Campana, Spain	H6	16
La Canada, Ca., U.S.	J7	124
La Candelaria, Arg.	D6	80
Lacantún, stm., Mex.	I14	90
La Capelle [-en-Thierache], Fr.	C10	14
Lacapelle-Marival, Fr.	H8	14
La Carlota, Arg.	G7	80
La Carolina, Spain	G8	16
Lacaune, Fr.	I9	14
Laccadive Islands see Lakshadweep, is., India	G2	46
Lac du Flambeau, Wi., U.S.	E6	110
La Ceiba, Hond.	B8	92
La Ceiba, Ven.	C7	84
La Center, Ky., U.S.	E8	114
Lac-Etchemin, P.Q., Can.	F3	106
Lacey, Wa., U.S.	C3	122
Lac-Frontière, P.Q., Can.	F3	106
La Chambre, Fr.	G13	14
La Chapelle-d'Angillon, Fr.	E9	14
La Chartre-sur-le-Loir, Fr.	E7	14
La Châtaigneraie, Fr.	F6	14
La Chaux-de-Fonds, Switz.	D6	13
Lachay, Punta, c., Peru	D3	82
Lachdenpochja, Russia	K22	6
Lachen, Switz.	D10	13
Lachhmangarh Sīkar, India	G6	44
Lachine, P.Q., Can.	B13	108
Lachkaltsap Indian Reserve, B.C., Can.	B5	102
Lachlan, stm., Austl.	J6	70
La Chorrera, Col.	H6	84
La Chorrera, Pan.	C3	84
L'achovskije ostrova, is., Russia	C20	28
Lachute, P.Q., Can.	B12	108
La Ciénaga, Arg.	D5	80
La Ciotat, Fr.	I12	14
La Citadelle, hist., Haiti	E8	94
La Ciudad, Mex.	F7	90
Lackawanna, N.Y., U.S.	E8	108
Lac la Biche, Ab., Can.	C23	102
Lac la Hache, B.C., Can.	F13	102
Lac la Ronge Provincial Park, Sk., Can.	C10	104
Laclede, Id., U.S.	I18	102
Laclede, Mo., U.S.	C3	114
La Clotilde, Arg.	D8	80
Lac-Mégantic, P.Q., Can.	B16	108
La Cocha, Arg.	D6	80
La Colorada, Mex.	C4	90
La Coma, Mex.	E10	90
Lacombe, Ab., Can.	E21	102
Lacombe, La., U.S.	L7	114
Lacon, Il., U.S.	I6	110
Lacona, Ia., U.S.	I2	110
La Concepción, Pan.	C1	84
La Concepción, Ven.	B7	84
Laconia, N.H., U.S.	D15	108
La Conner, Wa., U.S.	B3	122
La Consulta, Arg.	G4	80
Lacoochee, Fl., U.S.	K4	112
La Coste, Tx., U.S.	J8	116
Lac qui Parle, stm., Mn., U.S.	G11	118
La Crescent, Mn., U.S.	G4	110
La Crosse, In., U.S.	A10	114
La Crosse, Ks., U.S.	M8	118
La Crosse, Va., U.S.	C8	112
Lacrosse, Wa., U.S.	D8	122
La Crosse, Wi., U.S.	G4	110
La Crosse, stm., Wi., U.S.	G4	110
La Cruz, Arg.	E10	80
La Cruz, Col.	G4	84
La Cruz, C.R.	F9	92
La Cruz, Ur.	G10	80
La Cruz, Cerro, mtn., Mex.	I9	90
La Cruz de Río Grande, Nic.	D10	92
Lac Seul, On., Can.	H22	104
Lac Seul Indian Reserve, On., Can.	H22	104
La Cuesta, C.R.	I12	92
La Cumbre, Arg.	F6	80
La Cygne, Ks., U.S.	M13	118
Ladainha, Braz.	D8	79
Ladākh Range, mts., Asia	C7	44
Ladário, Braz.	H13	82
Ladd, Il., U.S.	I6	110
Laddonia, Mo., U.S.	C5	114
La Désirade, i., Guad.	F14	94
La Digue, i., Sey.	B11	58
Ladismith, S. Afr.	I5	66
Lādīz, Iran	G16	48
Lādnūn, India	G6	44
Ladoga, In., U.S.	C10	114
Ladoga, Lake see Ladožskoje ozero, l., Russia	E4	26
Ladonia, Tx., U.S.	F11	116
La Dorada, Col.	E5	84
La Dormida, Arg.	G5	80
Ladožskoje Ozero, Russia	A14	22
Ladožskoje ozero (Lake Ladoga), l., Russia	E4	26
Ladson, S.C., U.S.	G6	112
Ladue, stm., N.A.	E24	100
Laduškin, Russia	G3	22
Ladva-Vetka, Russia	K24	6
L'ady, Russia	C11	22
Lady Ann Strait, strt., N.T., Can.	A16	96
Ladybrand, S. Afr.	G8	66
Lady Elliot Island, i., Austl.	E10	70
Ladysmith, B.C., Can.	I11	102
Ladysmith, S. Afr.	G9	66
Ladysmith, Wi., U.S.	E4	110
Lae, Pap. N. Gui.	m16	68a
La Encantada, Mex.	E9	90
La Esmeralda, Mex.	D8	90
La Esmeralda, Para.	B7	80
La Esmeralda, Ven.	F10	84
La Esperanza, Cuba	C3	94
La Esperanza, Hond.	C6	92
La Estrella, Bol.	G10	82
La Falda, Arg.	F6	80
La Farge, Wi., U.S.	G5	110
Lafayette, Al., U.S.	J11	114
Lafayette, Ca., U.S.	G3	124
Lafayette, Co., U.S.	L2	118
Lafayette, Ga., U.S.	E1	112
Lafayette, In., U.S.	B10	114
Lafayette, La., U.S.	L4	114
Lafayette, Mn., U.S.	F1	110
Lafayette, Tn., U.S.	F10	114
La Fé, Cuba	D3	94
La Fère, Fr.	C10	14
La Feria, Tx., U.S.	M9	116
La Ferté-Bernard, Fr.	D7	14
La Ferté-Gaucher, Fr.	D10	14
La Ferté-Macé, Fr.	D6	14
La Ferté-Saint-Aubin, Fr.	E8	14
Lafia, Nig.	G14	64
La Flèche, Fr.	E6	14
Lafleche, Sk., Can.	I8	104
La Florida, Guat.	I14	90
Lafnitz, stm., Eur.	H16	10
La Follette, Tn., U.S.	C2	112
La Fontaine, In., U.S.	B11	114
Lafourche, Bayou, stm., La., U.S.	M6	114
La Fragua, Arg.	D6	80
La Francia, Arg.	F7	80
La Fría, Ven.	C6	84
La Galite, i., Tun.	L3	18
La Gallareta, Arg.	E8	80
Lagangzong, China	F14	44
Lagarto, C.R.	G10	92
Lagawe, Phil.	m19	39b
Lage, China	F11	44
Lågen, stm., Nor.	K11	6
Lågen, stm., Nor.	K12	6
Lages, Braz.	D13	80
Lage Zwaluwe, Neth.	E6	12
Laghouat, Alg.	D12	62
La Gleize, Bel.	H8	12
La Gloria, Col.	C6	84
Lagoa da Prata, Braz.	F6	79
Lagoa Formosa, Braz.	E5	79
Lagoa Santa, Braz.	E7	79
Lagoa Vermelha, Braz.	E13	80
Lagolândia, Braz.	C4	79
La Gomera, i., Spain	o23	17b
Lagos, Nig.	H11	64
Lagos, Port.	H3	16
Lagos de Moreno, Mex.	G9	90
La Gouèra, W. Sah.	J2	62
La Goulette, Tun.	M5	18
La Grand'Combe, Fr.	H11	14
La Grande, Or., U.S.	E7	122
La Grande Deux, Réservoir, res., P.Q., Can.	F17	96
La Grande Quatre, Réservoir, res., P.Q., Can.	F18	96
La Grange, Austl.	C4	68
La Grange, Ga., U.S.	F1	112
Lagrange, In., U.S.	A11	114
La Grange, Ky., U.S.	D11	114
La Grange, Mo., U.S.	B5	114
La Grange, N.C., U.S.	D9	112
La Grange, Tx., U.S.	J10	116
Lagrange, Wy., U.S.	J3	118
La Gran Sabana, pl., Ven.	E12	84
La Grita, Ven.	C7	84
Lagu, China	A6	40
La Guadeloupe (Saint-Évariste), P.Q., Can.	B16	108
La Guajira, dept., Col.	B6	84
La Guajira, Península de, pen., S.A.	A7	84
La Guardia, Arg.	E6	80
La Guardia, Bol.	G10	82
La Guerche-de-Bretagne, Fr.	E5	14
La Guerche-sur-l'Aubois, Fr.	F9	14
Laguna, Braz.	E14	80
Laguna, N.M., U.S.	I9	120
Laguna, Ilha da, i., Braz.	D8	76
Laguna Beach, Ca., U.S.	K8	124
Laguna Larga, Arg.	F7	80
Laguna Limpia, Arg.	D9	80
Laguna Paiva, Arg.	F8	80
Lagunas, Peru	A4	82
Lagunas de Chacagua, Parque Nacional, Mex.	I11	90
Lagunas de Montebello, Parque Nacional, Mex.	A3	92
Lagunillas, Bol.	H10	82
Lagunillas, Ven.	C7	84
Lagunillás, Laguna, l., Peru	F6	82
Laguntara, b., Hond.	B10	92
La Habana (Havana), Cuba	C3	94
Lahaina, Hi., U.S.	q17	125a
La Harpe, Il., U.S.	J5	110
La Harpe, Ks., U.S.	N12	118
Lahat, Indon.	F3	38
LaHave, stm., N.S., Can.	H9	106
La Haye-du-Puits, Fr.	C5	14
La Higuera, Chile	E3	80
Lahij, Yemen	H4	47
Lāhījān, Iran	C11	48
Lahnstein, Ger.	E7	10
Lahojsk, Bela.	G10	22
Lahontan Reservoir, res., Nv., U.S.	E6	124
Lahore, Pak.	E6	44
La Horqueta, Col.	F6	84
Lahr, Ger.	G7	10
Lahri, Pak.	F3	44
Lahti, Fin.	K19	6
La Huaca, Peru	A1	82
La Huacana, Mex.	H9	90
La Huerta, N.M., U.S.	G2	116
Lahva, Bela.	I10	22
Laibin, China	C10	40
Lai Chau, Viet.	C7	40
L'Aigle, Fr.	D7	14
Laifang, China	J5	34
Laignes, Fr.	E11	14
La Independencia, Bahía de, b., Peru	F3	82
Laingsburg, Mi., U.S.	H11	110
Laingsburg, S. Afr.	I5	66
La Inmaculada, Mex.	C4	90
Laird Hill, Tx., U.S.	J2	114
Laishan, China	F9	32
Laishui, China	D3	32
Laiwu, China	G5	32
Laiyang, China	G8	32
Laizhou Wan (Laichow Bay), b., China	F7	32
Laja, stm., Chile	I3	80
Laja, Laguna de la, l., Chile	I3	80
Laja, Salto del, wtfl, Chile	I3	80
La Jalca, Peru	B3	82
La Jara, Co., U.S.	G11	120
La Jara Canyon, val., N.M., U.S.	H9	120
Lajas, Cuba	C4	94
Laje, Braz.	B9	79
Lajeado, Braz.	E13	80
Lajes, Braz.	E11	76
Lajinha, Braz.	F8	79
La Jolla, Ca., U.S.	L8	124
Lajord, Sk., Can.	H10	104
Lajosmizse, Hung.	H19	10
La Joya, Peru	G6	82
La Junta, Co., U.S.	N4	118
Lakamané, Mali	D5	64
Lake, Ms., U.S.	J7	114
Lake Alfred, Fl., U.S.	K5	112
Lake Andes, S.D., U.S.	H9	118
Lake Arthur, La., U.S.	L4	114
Lake Arthur, N.M., U.S.	G2	116
Lake Benton, Mn., U.S.	G11	118
Lake Brownwood, Tx., U.S.	H7	116
Lake Butler, Fl., U.S.	I4	112
Lake Cargelligo, Austl.	I7	70
Lake Carmel, N.Y., U.S.	F13	108
Lake Charles, La., U.S.	L3	114
Lake City, Ar., U.S.	G6	114
Lake City, Co., U.S.	F9	120
Lake City, Fl., U.S.	I4	112
Lake City, Ia., U.S.	I13	118
Lake City, Mi., U.S.	F10	110
Lake City, Mn., U.S.	F3	110
Lake City, Pa., U.S.	E6	108
Lake City, S.C., U.S.	F7	112
Lake City, Tn., U.S.	C2	112
Lake Cowichan, B.C., Can.	I10	102
Lake Crystal, Mn., U.S.	F1	110
Lake Dallas, Tx., U.S.	F9	116
Lake Delton, Wi., U.S.	G6	110
Lake Elsinore, Ca., U.S.	K8	124
Lakefield, Mn., U.S.	H12	118
Lakefield, On., Can.	F17	110
Lakefield National Park, Austl.	C8	68
Lake Forest, Fl., U.S.	N6	112
Lake Forest, Il., U.S.	H8	110
Lake Fork, stm., Ut., U.S.	D6	120
Lake Geneva, Wi., U.S.	H7	110
Lake George, N.Y., U.S.	D13	108
Lake Harbor, Fl., U.S.	M6	112
Lake Harbour, N.T., Can.	D19	96
Lake Havasu City, Az., U.S.	J2	120
Lake Helen, Fl., U.S.	K5	112
Lakehurst, N.J., U.S.	G12	108
Lake Isabella, Ca., U.S.	I7	124
Lake Jackson, Tx., U.S.	J11	116
Lakeland, Fl., U.S.	K5	112
Lakeland, Ga., U.S.	H3	112
Lake Linden, Mi., U.S.	C7	110
Lake Louise, Ab., Can.	F18	102
Lake Mills, Ia., U.S.	G2	110
Lake Mills, Wi., U.S.	G7	110
Lakemont, Pa., U.S.	G8	108
Lake Nash, Austl.	C2	70
Lake Norden, S.D., U.S.	G10	118
Lake Odessa, Mi., U.S.	H10	110
Lake Oswego, Or., U.S.	E3	122
Lake Ozark, Mo., U.S.	D3	114
Lake Park, Fl., U.S.	M6	112
Lake Park, Ia., U.S.	H12	118
Lake Park, Mn., U.S.	E11	118
Lake Placid, Fl., U.S.	L5	112
Lake Placid, N.Y., U.S.	C13	108
Lake Pleasant, N.Y., U.S.	D12	108
Lakeport, Ca., U.S.	E3	124
Lakeport, Mi., U.S.	G13	110
Lake Preston, S.D., U.S.	G10	118
Lake Providence, La., U.S.	J5	114
Lakes District, Wa., U.S.	C3	122
Lakeshore, Ms., U.S.	L7	114
Lakeside, Az., U.S.	J7	120
Lakeside, Ca., U.S.	L9	124
Lakeside, Mt., U.S.	B11	122
Lakeside, N.S., Can.	H10	106
Lakeside, Or., U.S.	G1	122
Lake Stevens, Wa., U.S.	B3	122
Laketown, Ut., U.S.	C5	120
Lake View, Ar., U.S.	H6	114
Lakeview, Ga., U.S.	E1	112
Lake View, Ia., U.S.	I12	118
Lakeview, Mi., U.S.	H10	110
Lakeview, Mi., U.S.	G10	110
Lake View, N.Y., U.S.	E8	108
Lakeview, Oh., U.S.	G3	108
Lakeview, Or., U.S.	H5	122
Lake View, S.C., U.S.	E7	112
Lakeview, Tx., U.S.	M3	114
Lakeview, Tx., U.S.	E6	116
Lakeview Mountain, mtn., B.C., Can.	H14	102
Lake Village, Ar., U.S.	I5	114
Lakeville, Mn., U.S.	F2	110
Lake Wales, Fl., U.S.	L5	112
Lake Wilson, Mn., U.S.	H12	118
Lakewood, Co., U.S.	E11	120
Lakewood, N.J., U.S.	G12	108
Lakewood, N.Y., U.S.	E7	108
Lakewood, Oh., U.S.	F5	108
Lakewood, Wi., U.S.	E7	110
Lakewood Park, N.D., U.S.	C9	118
Lake Worth, Fl., U.S.	M6	112
Lakhīmpur, India	G9	44
Lakhish, val., Asia	E3	50
Lakin, Ks., U.S.	N6	118
Lakinsk, Russia	E22	22
Lakonikós Kólpos, b., Grc.	M6	20
Lakota, Ia., U.S.	H13	118
Lakota, N.D., U.S.	C9	118
Lakshadweep, ter., India	H2	46
Lakshadweep, is., India	G2	46
Lakshadweep Sea, Asia	H3	46
La Lajilla, Mex.	D10	90
L'Albufera, l., Spain	F11	16
La Leonesa, Arg.	D9	80
Lalibela, Eth.	K10	60
La Libertad, El Sal.	D5	92
La Libertad, Guat.	I14	90
La Libertad, Hond.	C7	92
La Libertad, Nic.	E9	92
La Libertad, dept., Peru	B2	82
La Ligua, Chile	G3	80
La Lima, Hond.	B7	92
La Línea, Spain	I6	16
Lalitpur, India	H8	44
Lālmanir Hāt, Bngl.	H13	44
La Loche, Sk., Can.	B5	104
La Loche, stm., Sk., Can.	B5	104
La Loche, Lac, l., Sk., Can.	B5	104
La Loupe, Fr.	D8	14
Lalupon, Nig.	H12	64
La Luz, Mex.	E11	90
La Luz, Nic.	D10	92
La Luz, N.M., U.S.	L11	120
Lama, ozero, l., Russia	D16	26
La Macarena, Serranía de, mts., Col.	F6	84
La Maddalena, Italy	H4	18
La Madrid, Arg.	D6	80
Lamadong, China	C7	32
La Malbaie, P.Q., Can.	E3	106
Lamaline, Nf., Can.	F18	106
La Mancha, reg., Spain	G8	16
Lamar, Co., U.S.	M5	118
Lamar, Mo., U.S.	E2	114
Lamar, S.C., U.S.	E6	112
Lamar, stm., Wy., U.S.	F16	122
Lamarche, Fr.	D12	14
La Mariscala, Ur.	H11	80
Lamarque, Arg.	J6	80
La Marque, Tx., U.S.	J12	116
La Marsa, Tun.	M5	18
Lamas, Peru	B3	82
La Masica, Hond.	B7	92
Lamastre, Fr.	H11	14
Lamballe, Fr.	D4	14
Lambaréné, Gabon	B2	58
Lambari, stm., Braz.	F6	79
Lambayeque, Peru	B2	82
Lambayeque, dept., Peru	B1	82
Lambayeque, stm., Peru	B2	82
Lambert, Ms., U.S.	H6	114
Lambert, Mt., U.S.	D3	118
Lambert Glacier, Ant.	C5	73
Lamberton, Mn., U.S.	G12	118
Lambert's Bay, S. Afr.	I4	66
Lambertville, N.J., U.S.	G12	108
Lambeth, On., Can.	H14	110
Lambomakondro, Madag.	s21	67b
Lambrama, Peru	E5	82
Lambton, Cape, c., N.T., Can.	B8	96
Lame Deer, Mt., U.S.	E19	122
La Media Luna, Arrecifes de, rf., Hond.	B12	92
La Mendieta, Arg.	C6	80
Lamèque, N.B., Can.	E9	106
Lamèque, Île, i., N.B., Can.	E9	106
La Merced, Arg.	E6	80
La Merced, Arg.	C6	80
La Merced, Peru	D4	82
La Mesa, Ca., U.S.	L8	124
La Mesa, N.M., U.S.	L10	120
La Mesa, Pan.	I13	92
Lamesa, Tx., U.S.	G5	116
Lamía, Grc.	K6	20
L'amin, stm., Russia	E12	26
Lamine, stm., Mo., U.S.	D4	114
Lamming Mills, B.C., Can.	D14	102
La Moille, Il., U.S.	I6	110
Lamoille, Nv., U.S.	D10	124
Lamoille, stm., Vt., U.S.	C14	108
La Moine, stm., Il., U.S.	B6	114
Lamon Bay, b., Phil.	n19	39b
Lamoni, Ia., U.S.	J2	110
Lamont, Ab., Can.	D22	102
Lamont, Ca., U.S.	I7	124
Lamont, Ia., U.S.	H4	110
Lamont, Ok., U.S.	C9	116
La Monte, Mo., U.S.	D3	114
La Mosquitia, hist. reg., Hond.	B11	92
La Mothe, Lac, res., P.Q., Can.	D2	106
La Mothe-Achard, Fr.	F5	14
Lamotte-Beuvron, Fr.	E9	14
La Moure, N.D., U.S.	E9	118
Lampa, Peru	F6	82
Lampang, Thai.	E5	40
Lampasas, Tx., U.S.	H8	116
Lampasas, stm., Tx., U.S.	H8	116
Lampazos de Naranjo, Mex.	D9	90
Lampedusa, Isola di, i., Italy	N7	18
Lamphun, Thai.	E5	40
Lampman, Sk., Can.	I12	104
Lamud, Peru	B3	82
La Muerte, Cerro, mtn., C.R.	H11	92
Lana, Italy	C6	18
Lanai, i., Hi., U.S.	q17	125a
Lanai City, Hi., U.S.	q17	125a
Lanalhue, Lago, l., Chile	I2	80
Lanark, Il., U.S.	H6	110
Lanark, On., Can.	E19	110
Lanbi Kyun, i., Myan.	I5	40
Lancashire, co., Eng., U.K.	H11	8
Lancaster, Ca., U.S.	J7	124
Lancaster, Eng., U.K.	G11	8
Lancaster, Ky., U.S.	B2	112
Lancaster, Mn., U.S.	C11	118
Lancaster, Mo., U.S.	B4	114
Lancaster, N.H., U.S.	C15	108
Lancaster, N.Y., U.S.	E8	108
Lancaster, Oh., U.S.	H4	108
Lancaster, On., Can.	B12	108
Lancaster, Pa., U.S.	G10	108
Lancaster, S.C., U.S.	E6	112
Lancaster, Tx., U.S.	G10	116
Lancaster, Va., U.S.	B10	112
Lancaster, Wi., U.S.	H5	110
Lancaster Sound, strt., N.T., Can.	B16	96
Lance Creek, Wy., U.S.	A12	120
Lanchyn, Ukr.	A8	20
Lanciano, Italy	G9	18
Lancones, Peru	J2	84
Lancun, China	G8	32
Łańcut, Pol.	E22	10
Lancy, Switz.	F5	13
Landau, Ger.	F8	10
Landau an der Isar, Ger.	G12	10
Landeck, Aus.	H10	10
Landen, Bel.	G7	12
Lander, Wy., U.S.	B8	120
Landerneau, Fr.	D2	14
Landes, dept., Fr.	H6	14
Landete, Spain	F10	16
Landing Lake, l., Mb., Can.	C17	104
Landis, N.C., U.S.	D6	112
Landis, Sk., Can.	F6	104
Landivisiau, Fr.	D2	14
Lando, S.C., U.S.	E5	112
Land O'Lakes, Wi., U.S.	D6	110
Landquart, Switz.	E12	13
Landrum, S.C., U.S.	D4	112
Landsberg [am Lech], Ger.	G10	10
Land's End, c., Eng., U.K.	K8	8
Landshut, Ger.	G12	10
Landskrona, Swe.	N13	6
La Negra, Chile	B3	80
Lanesboro, Mn., U.S.	G4	110
Lanett, Al., U.S.	J11	114
Lanezi Lake, l., B.C., Can.	D14	102
Lang, Sk., Can.	I10	104
Langano, Lake, l., Eth.	N10	60
Langara Island, i., B.C., Can.	C1	102
Langarūd, Iran	C11	48
Langbank, Sk., Can.	H12	104
Lang Bay, B.C., Can.	H10	102
Langdale, Al., U.S.	G1	112
Langdon, N.D., U.S.	C9	118
Langeac, Fr.	G10	14
Langeais, Fr.	E7	14
Langenburg, Sk., Can.	H13	104
Langenhagen, Ger.	C9	10
Langenthal, Switz.	D8	13
Langford, S.D., U.S.	F10	118
Langham, Sk., Can.	F8	104
Langholm, Scot., U.K.	F10	8
Langley, B.C., Can.	H12	102
Langley, Ok., U.S.	C11	116
Langley, S.C., U.S.	F5	112
Langlo, stm., Austl.	E6	70
Langlois, Or., U.S.	H1	122
Langnau, Switz.	E8	13
Langogne, Fr.	H10	14
Langon, Fr.	H6	14
Langøya, i., Nor.	G14	6
Langqiao, China	E7	34
Langreo, Spain	B6	16
Langres, Fr.	E12	14
Langruth, Mb., Can.	H16	104
Langsa, Indon.	L4	40
Lang Son, Viet.	D9	40
Langtian, China	J2	34
Langue, Hond.	D7	92
Languedoc, hist. reg., Fr.	I9	14
Langui Layo, Laguna de, l., Peru	F6	82
L'Anguille, stm., Ar., U.S.	G6	114
Langxi, China	D8	34
Langzhong, China	E8	30
Lanigan, Sk., Can.	G9	104
Lanigan Creek, stm., Sk., Can.	G9	104
Länkäran, Azer.	J7	26
Lankou, China	L4	34
Lannemezan, Fr.	I7	14
Lannilis, Fr.	D2	14
Lannion, Fr.	D3	14
L'Annonciation, P.Q., Can.	A12	108
Lanquín, Guat.	B5	92
L'Anse, Mi., U.S.	D7	110
L'Anse-aux-Meadows National Historic Park, Nf., Can.	A18	106
Lansford, N.D., U.S.	C6	118
Lansing, Ia., U.S.	G4	110
Lansing, Ks., U.S.	L13	118
Lansing, Mi., U.S.	E2	108
Lanslebourg, Fr.	G13	14
Lantana, Fl., U.S.	M6	112
Lantang, China	L3	34
Lantau Island, i., H.K.	M2	34
Lantsch, Switz.	E12	13
Lanusei, Italy	J4	18
Lanxi, China	F8	34
Lanzarote, i., Spain	n27	17b
Lanzhou, China	D7	30
Laoag, Phil.	l19	39b
Lao Cai, Viet.	C7	40
Laochang, China	B8	40
Laoge, China	C8	34
Laoha, stm., China	A7	32
Laois, co., Ire.	I6	8
Laojie, China	B5	40
La Oliva, Spain	o27	17b
Laon, Fr.	C10	14
Laona, Wi., U.S.	E7	110
La Orchila, Isla, i., Ven.	B10	84
La Orotava, Spain	o24	17b
La Oroya, Peru	D4	82
Laos (Lao), ctry., Asia	B3	38
Laoxinkou, China	E1	34
Laoyingpan, China	I4	34
Laozishan, China	B7	34
Lapa, Braz.	C14	80
Lapalisse, Fr.	F10	14
La Palma, Col.	E5	84
La Palma, El Sal.	C5	92
La Palma, Pan.	C3	84
La Palma, Pan.	D2	84
La Palma, i., Spain	o23	17b
La Palma del Condado, Spain	H5	16
La Paloma, Ur.	H11	80
La Pampa, prov., Arg.	I5	80
La Paragua, Ven.	D11	84
La Pasión, Río de, stm., Guat.	I14	90
La Paz, Arg.	F9	80
La Paz, Arg.	G4	80
La Paz, Bol.	G7	82
La Paz, Col.	B6	84
La Paz, Hond.	C7	92
La Paz, Mex.	E4	90
La Paz, Mex.	F9	90
La Paz, Ur.	H10	80
La Paz, dept., Bol.	F7	82
La Paz, dept., Hond.	C7	92
La Paz, Bahía de, b., Mex.	E4	90
La Paz, Río de, stm., Bol.	G8	82
La Paz Centro, Nic.	E8	92
La Pedrera, Col.	H8	84
Lapeer, Mi., U.S.	G12	110
La Perla, Mex.	C7	90
La Perouse Strait (Sōya-kaikyō), strt., Asia	b17	36a
La Pesca, Mex.	F11	90
La Piedad de Cabadas, Mex.	G8	90
La Pine, Or., U.S.	G4	122

Name	Map Ref.	Page
Libyan Desert see Lībīyah, Aṣ-Ṣaḥrā' al-, des., Afr.	D6	56
Libyan Plateau see Aḍ-Ḍiffah, plat., Afr.	B3	60
Licancábur, Volcán, vol., S.A.	J8	82
Licantén, Chile	H2	80
Licata, Italy	L8	18
Lice, Tur.	B6	48
Lichinga, Moz.	D7	58
Lichoslavl', Russia	D18	22
Lichtenfels, Ger.	E11	10
Lichuan, China	H5	34
Lickershamn, Swe.	M16	6
Licking, Mo., U.S.	E5	114
Licking, stm., Ky., U.S.	I2	108
Lida, Bela.	H8	22
Lidao, China	F10	32
Liddon Gulf, b., N.T., Can.	A10	96
Liden, Swe.	J15	6
Lidesi, China	B4	34
Lidgerwood, N.D., U.S.	E10	118
Lídice, Pan.	C3	84
Lidköping, Swe.	L13	6
Lidzbark, Pol.	B19	10
Lidzbark Warmiński, Pol.	A20	10
Liechtenstein, ctry., Eur.	F9	4
Liège (Luik), Bel.	G8	12
Liège, prov., Bel.	G8	12
Liegnitz see Legnica, Pol.	D16	10
Lielvārde, Lat.	E7	22
Lienz, Aus.	I12	10
Liepāja, Lat.	E4	22
Lier (Lierre), Bel.	F6	12
Lierre (Lier), Bel.	F6	12
Lieshout, Neth.	E8	12
Liestal, Switz.	D8	13
Liévin, Fr.	B9	14
Lièvre, Rivière du, stm., P.Q., Can.	B11	108
Lièvres, Île aux, i., P.Q., Can.	E4	106
Liezen, Aus.	H14	10
Liffré, Fr.	D5	14
Lighthouse Point, Fl., U.S.	M6	112
Lighthouse Point, c., Mi., U.S.	E10	110
Lighthouse Reef, rf., Belize	I16	90
Lightning Creek, stm., Sk., Can.	I13	104
Lignières, Fr.	F9	14
Lignite, N.D., U.S.	C5	118
Ligny-en-Barrois, Fr.	D12	14
Ligonha, stm., Moz.	E7	58
Ligonier, In., U.S.	A11	114
Ligonier, Pa., U.S.	G7	108
Ligui, Mex.	E4	90
Liguria, prov., Italy	E3	18
Ligurian Sea, Eur.	F4	18
Lihue, Hi., U.S.	p14	125a
Lihula, Est.	C6	22
Lijia, China	F6	32
Lijiang, China	F7	30
Lijiawobao, China	B10	32
Likasi (Jadotville), Zaire	D5	58
Likely, B.C., Can.	E13	102
Likino-Dulevo, Russia	F21	22
Liknes, Nor.	L10	6
Likoma Island, i., Mwi.	D6	58
Likou, China	F6	34
Likus, stm., Nic.	C11	92
Lilbourn, Mo., U.S.	F7	114
L'Île-Rousse, Fr.	J15	14
Lilienfeld, Aus.	G15	10
Liling, China	H2	34
Lille, Fr.	B10	14
Lillebonne, Fr.	C7	14
Lillehammer, Nor.	K12	6
Lillers, Fr.	B9	14
Lillesand, Nor.	L11	6
Lillestrøm, Nor.	L12	6
Lillington, N.C., U.S.	D8	112
Lillooet, B.C., Can.	G13	102
Lillooet, stm., B.C., Can.	H12	102
Lillooet Lake, l., B.C., Can.	G12	102
Lilongwe, Mwi.	D6	58
Lilo Viejo, Arg.	D7	80
Liloy, Phil.	D7	38
Lily, Ky., U.S.	B2	112
Lilydale, Austl.	M7	70
Lima, Mt., U.S.	F13	122
Lima, N.Y., U.S.	E9	108
Lima, Oh., U.S.	G2	108
Lima, Para.	B10	80
Lima, Peru	E3	82
Lima, dept., Peru	D3	82
Lima (Limia), stm., Eur.	D3	16
Limache, Chile	G3	80
Limanowa, Pol.	F20	10
Limarí, stm., Chile	F3	80
Limay, stm., Arg.	J4	80
Limay Mahuida, Arg.	I5	80
Limbani, Peru	F7	82
Limbaži, Lat.	D7	22
Līmbdi, India	I4	44
Limbe, Cam.	I14	64
Limburg, prov., Bel.	G7	12
Limburg, prov., Neth.	F8	12
Limburg an der Lahn, Ger.	E8	10
Limeira, Braz.	G5	79
Limen, China	H8	34
Limerick, Ire.	I5	8
Limerick, Sk., Can.	I8	104
Limerick, co., Ire.	I5	8
Lime Springs, Ia., U.S.	G3	110
Limestone, stm., Mb., Can.	B20	104
Limestone Bay, b., Mb., Can.	E16	104
Limestone Lake, l., Mb., Can.	B18	104
Limestone Lake, l., Sk., Can.	D11	104
Limestone Point, pen., Mb., Can.	E16	104
Limestone Point Lake, l., Mb., Can.	C14	104
Limfjorden, strt., Den.	M11	6
Limia (Lima), stm., Eur.	D3	16
Liminka, Fin.	I19	6
Limmen Bight, Austl.	B7	68
Límnos, i., Grc.	J9	20
Limoges, Fr.	G8	14
Limogne, Fr.	H8	14
Limon, Co., U.S.	L4	118
Limón, Hond.	B9	92
Limón, prov., C.R.	H11	92
Limoux, Fr.	I9	14
Limpopo, stm., Afr.	E11	66
Limu, China	B11	40
Linachamari, Russia	G22	6
Līnah, Sau. Ar.	G7	48
Lin'an, China	E8	34
Linares, Chile	H3	80
Linares, Col.	G4	84
Linares, Mex.	E10	90
Linares, Spain	G8	16
Lincang, China	C7	40
Linch, Wy., U.S.	A10	120
Lincoln, Ar., U.S.	G2	114
Lincoln, Arg.	H8	80
Lincoln, Ca., U.S.	F4	124
Lincoln, Eng., U.K.	H13	8
Lincoln, Il., U.S.	B7	114
Lincoln, Ks., U.S.	L9	118
Lincoln, Me., U.S.	B18	108
Lincoln, Mi., U.S.	F12	110
Lincoln, Mo., U.S.	D3	114
Lincoln, Mt., U.S.	D13	122
Lincoln, Ne., U.S.	K11	118
Lincoln, N.H., U.S.	C15	108
Lincoln, Mount, mtn., Co., U.S.	E10	120
Lincoln City, Or., U.S.	F1	122
Lincoln Park, Co., U.S.	F11	120
Lincoln Park, Ga., U.S.	G2	112
Lincoln Park, Mi., U.S.	H12	110
Lincoln Sea, N.A.	A14	86
Lincolnshire, co., Eng., U.K.	H13	8
Lincolnton, Ga., U.S.	F4	112
Lincolnton, N.C., U.S.	D5	112
Lincoln Village, Ca., U.S.	F4	124
Lind, Wa., U.S.	D7	122
Linda, Ca., U.S.	E4	124
Linda, Russia	E27	22
Lindale, Ga., U.S.	E1	112
Lindale, Tx., U.S.	G11	116
Lindau, Ger.	H9	10
Linde, stm., Russia	D16	28
Linden, Al., U.S.	J9	114
Linden, Guy.	D13	84
Linden, In., U.S.	B10	114
Linden, Mi., U.S.	H12	110
Linden, Tn., U.S.	G9	114
Linden, Tx., U.S.	I2	114
Lindi, Tan.	D7	58
Lindley, S. Afr.	G8	66
Lindon, Co., U.S.	L4	118
Lindong, China	I7	34
Lindsay, Ca., U.S.	H6	124
Lindsay, Ne., U.S.	J10	118
Lindsay, Ok., U.S.	E9	116
Lindsay, On., Can.	F17	110
Lindsborg, Ks., U.S.	M10	118
Line Islands, is., Oc.	H24	126
Linesville, Pa., U.S.	F6	108
Lineville, Al., U.S.	I11	114
Lineville, Ia., U.S.	J2	110
Linfen, China	D9	30
Linganamakki Reservoir, res., India	F3	46
Lingao, China	E10	40
Lingayen, Phil.	m19	39b
Lingbi, China	B6	34
Lingen, Ger.	C7	10
Lingfengwei, China	K4	34
Lingga, Kepulauan, is., Indon.	O8	40
Lingga, Pulau, i., Indon.	O8	40
Linghu, China	E9	34
Lingle, Wy., U.S.	B12	120
Lingling, China	A11	40
Linglongta, China	C7	32
Lingqiu, China	D2	32
Lingshan, China	G8	32
Lingshui, China	E11	40
Linguère, Sen.	D2	64
Lingxiazhu, China	F8	34
Lingyuan, China	B7	32
Linh, Ngoc, mtn., Viet.	G9	40
Linhai, China	G10	34
Linhares, Braz.	E8	79
Linhe, China	C8	30
Linhuaiguan, China	C6	34
Linjiang, China	B14	32
Linjianghu, China	G6	34
Linköping, Swe.	L14	6
Linkou, China	B13	30
Linksmakalnis, Lith.	G6	22
Linkuva, Lith.	E6	22
Linn, Ks., U.S.	L10	118
Linn, Mo., U.S.	D5	114
Linnancang, China	D5	32
Linqing, China	G3	32
Linqu, China	G6	32
Linquan, China	B4	34
Linru, China	A1	34
Linruzhen, China	A1	34
Lins, Braz.	F4	79
Linshanhe, China	E3	34
Lintao, China	D7	30
Linthal, Switz.	E11	13
Linton, In., U.S.	C9	114
Linton, N.D., U.S.	E7	118
Linville, N.C., U.S.	C5	112
Linxi, China	C10	30
Linxia, China	D7	30
Linxiang, China	F2	34
Linyanti, Nmb.	B7	66
Linyanti, stm., Afr.	B7	66
Linyi, China	H6	32
Linying, China	B2	34
Linz, Aus.	G14	10
Linzhai, China	K4	34
Linzikou, China	G1	34
Lion, Golfe du, b., Fr.	I11	14
Lipan, Tx., U.S.	G8	116
Lipari, Isola, i., Italy	K9	18
Lipcani, Mol.	A10	20
Lipeck, Russia	I22	22
Lipetsk see Lipeck, Russia	I22	22
Lipez, Cerro, mtn., Bol.	I8	82
Lipin Bor, Russia	A20	22
Lipki, Russia	H20	22
Lipno, Pol.	C19	10
Lipno, údolní nádrž, res., Czech Rep.	G14	10
Lipova, Rom.	C5	20
Lippe, stm., Ger.	D8	10
Lippstadt, Ger.	D8	10
Lipscomb, Tx., U.S.	C6	116
Lipton, Sk., Can.	H11	104
Liptovský Mikuláš, Slvk.	F19	10
Liptrap, Cape, c., Austl.	L6	70
Lira, Ug.	H7	56
Lircay, Peru	E4	82
Liren, China	B7	34
Lisala, Zaire	A4	58
Lisboa (Lisbon), Port.	G2	16
Lisbon, N.D., U.S.	E10	118
Lisbon, N.H., U.S.	C15	108
Lisbon, Oh., U.S.	G6	108
Lisbon see Lisboa, Port.	G2	16
Lisbon Falls, Me., U.S.	D16	108
Lisburn, N. Ire., U.K.	G7	8
Lisburne, Cape, c., Ak., U.S.	B11	100
Lishe, China	F10	34
Lishui, China	G8	34
Lisieux, Fr.	C7	14
Lisieux, Sk., Can.	I9	104
Liski (Georgiu-Dež), Russia	G5	26
L'Isle Jourdain, Fr.	F7	14
L'Isle-sur-le-Doubs, Fr.	E13	14
Lisman, Al., U.S.	J8	114
Lismore, Austl.	G10	70
Lismore, N.S., Can.	G11	106
Lišov, Czech Rep.	F14	10
Listowel, On., Can.	G15	110
Lita, China	H5	34
Litang, China	E7	30
Litang, China	G8	30
Litang, stm., China	F7	30
Litchfield, Il., U.S.	C7	114
Litchfield, Mi., U.S.	H11	110
Litchfield, Mn., U.S.	E1	110
Litchfield, Ne., U.S.	J8	118
Litchfield Park, Az., U.S.	K4	120
Litchville, N.D., U.S.	E9	118
Lithgow, Austl.	I9	70
Líthinon, Ákra, c., Grc.	O8	20
Lithonia, Ga., U.S.	F2	112
Lithuania (Lietuva), ctry., Eur.	F6	22
Litian, China	I3	34
Lititz, Pa., U.S.	G10	108
Litoměřice, Czech Rep.	E14	10
Litomyšl, Czech Rep.	F16	10
Litovko, Russia	H19	28
Little, stm., Al., U.S.	H11	114
Little, stm., Ga., U.S.	F4	112
Little, stm., Ky., U.S.	F9	114
Little, stm., La., U.S.	K4	114
Little, stm., Ok., U.S.	D10	116
Little, stm., S.C., U.S.	E5	112
Little, stm., Tn., U.S.	D3	112
Little, stm., U.S.	I2	114
Little Abaco, i., Bah.	A6	94
Little Andaman, i., India	I2	40
Little Arkansas, stm., Ks., U.S.	M9	118
Little Bay, Nf., Can.	E15	106
Little Bay Islands, Nf., Can.	C18	106
Little Bear, stm., Ut., U.S.	C5	120
Little Belt Mountains, mts., Mt., U.S.	D15	122
Little Bighorn, stm., U.S.	E18	122
Little Bitterroot, stm., Mt., U.S.	C11	122
Little Black Bear Indian Reserve, Sk., Can.	G11	104
Little Blackfoot, stm., Mt., U.S.	D13	122
Little Blue, stm., U.S.	L11	118
Little Bow, stm., Ab., Can.	G21	102
Little Buffalo, stm., Can.	D10	96
Little Bullhead, Mb., Can.	G18	104
Little Catalina, Nf., Can.	D20	106
Little Cayman, i., Cay. Is.	E4	94
Little Cedar, stm., U.S.	G3	110
Little Churchill, stm., Mb., Can.	A19	104
Little Chute, Wi., U.S.	F7	110
Little Colorado, stm., Az., U.S.	I5	120
Little Cottonwood, stm., Mn., U.S.	G13	118
Little Current, On., Can.	E14	110
Little Current, stm., On., Can.	F15	96
Little Deschutes, stm., Or., U.S.	G4	122
Little Desert, des., Austl.	K4	70
Little Diomede Island, i., Ak., U.S.	D10	100
Little Eau Pleine, stm., Wi., U.S.	F5	110
Little Exuma, i., Bah.	C7	94
Little Falls, Mn., U.S.	E1	110
Little Falls, N.Y., U.S.	D12	108
Littlefield, Tx., U.S.	F4	116
Littlefork, Mn., U.S.	B2	110
Little Fork, stm., Mn., U.S.	B2	110
Little Fort, B.C., Can.	F14	102
Little Harbour Deep, Nf., Can.	B17	106
Little Humboldt, stm., Nv., U.S.	C8	124
Little Inagua, i., Bah.	D8	94
Little Juniata, stm., Pa., U.S.	G8	108
Little Kanawha, stm., W.V., U.S.	H5	108
Little Lake, l., La., U.S.	M6	114
Little Limestone Lake, l., Mb., Can.	E15	104
Little Manitou Lake, l., Sk., Can.	G9	104
Little Mecatina, stm., Can.	F20	96
Little Mexico, Tx., U.S.	I4	116
Little Missouri, stm., Ar., U.S.	I3	114
Little Missouri, stm., U.S.	D4	118
Little Muddy, stm., Il., U.S.	E7	114
Little Muddy, stm., N.D., U.S.	C4	118
Little Nemaha, stm., Ne., U.S.	K11	118
Little Nicobar, i., India	K2	40
Little Osage, stm., U.S.	D2	114
Little Pee Dee, stm., S.C., U.S.	F7	112
Little Pine and Lucky Man Indian Reserve, Sk., Can.	F5	104
Little Platte, stm., Mo., U.S.	C2	114
Little Powder, stm., U.S.	G2	118
Little Quill Lake, l., Sk., Can.	G10	104
Little Rann of Kachchh, pl., India	I4	44
Little Red, stm., Ar., U.S.	G5	114
Little Red Deer, stm., Ab., Can.	F20	102
Little Red River Indian Reserve, Sk., Can.	E9	104
Little River, Ks., U.S.	M9	118
Little Rock, Ar., U.S.	H4	114
Little Rock, Ia., U.S.	H12	118
Little Sable Point, c., Mi., U.S.	G9	110
Little Sac, stm., Mo., U.S.	E3	114
Little Sachigo Lake, l., On., Can.	D22	104
Little Saint Bernard Pass see Petit-Saint-Bernard, Col du, Eur.	G13	14
Little Salkehatchie, stm., S.C., U.S.	F6	112
Little Salmon Lake, l., Yk., Can.	E27	100
Little Sandy, stm., Ky., U.S.	I3	108
Little Saskatchewan, stm., Mb., Can.	H14	104
Little Scarcies, stm., Afr.	G4	54
Little Sioux, stm., U.S.	I12	118
Little Smoky, stm., Ab., Can.	B17	102
Little Snake, stm., U.S.	D8	120
Little Southwest Miramichi, stm., N.B., Can.	F7	106
Littlestown, Pa., U.S.	H9	108
Little Tallapoosa, stm., U.S.	F1	112
Little Tennessee, stm., U.S.	D2	112
Littleton, Co., U.S.	E11	120
Littleton, N.C., U.S.	C9	112
Littleton, N.H., U.S.	C15	108
Littleton, W.V., U.S.	H6	108
Little Traverse Bay, b., Mi., U.S.	E10	110
Little Turtle, stm., On., Can.	J22	104
Little Valley, N.Y., U.S.	E8	108
Little Vermilion Lake, l., On., Can.	G21	104
Little Wabash, stm., Il., U.S.	D8	114
Little Washita, stm., Ok., U.S.	E8	116
Little White, stm., S.D., U.S.	H6	118
Little White Mountain, mtn., B.C., Can.	H15	102
Little Wolf, stm., Wi., U.S.	F6	110
Little Wood, stm., Id., U.S.	G11	122
Little Zab (Zāb-e Kūchek) (Az-Zāb aṣ-Ṣaghīr), stm., Asia	D7	48
Litvínov, Czech Rep.	E13	10
Liuchen, China	C11	40
Liucheng, China	B10	40
Liucura, Chile	J3	80
Liudaogou, China	B15	32
Liufangling, China	E3	34
Liuguan, China	F2	34
Liuhe, China	A13	32
Liuhe, China	C7	34
Liujia, China	B9	40
Liujiadu, China	C9	34
Liujiahe, China	C2	34
Liuku, China	B5	40
Liulongtai, China	B8	32
Liuquan, China	I5	32
Liurenba, China	F3	34
Liushilipu, China	C4	34
Liushuigou, China	D1	34
Liutai, China	B1	32
Liuwanglou, China	I4	32
Liuyang, China	G2	34
Liuyuan, China	G2	32
Liuzhou, China	B10	40
Liuzhuang, China	B9	34
Līvāni, Lat.	E9	22
Lively, On., Can.	D14	110
Live Oak, Ca., U.S.	E4	124
Live Oak, Fl., U.S.	I4	112
Livermore, Ca., U.S.	G4	124
Livermore, Ia., U.S.	H1	110
Livermore, Ky., U.S.	E9	114
Livermore Falls, Me., U.S.	C16	108
Liverpool, Eng., U.K.	H11	8
Liverpool, N.S., Can.	H9	106
Liverpool, Pa., U.S.	G10	108
Liverpool, Cape, c., N.T., Can.	B17	96
Liverpool Bay, b., N.S., Can.	H9	106
Liverpool Bay, b., N.T., Can.	B29	100
Livingston, Al., U.S.	J8	114
Livingston, Ca., U.S.	G5	124
Lívingston, Guat.	B6	92
Livingston, Il., U.S.	D7	114
Livingston, Ky., U.S.	B2	112
Livingston, La., U.S.	L6	114
Livingston, Mt., U.S.	E15	122
Livingston, Tn., U.S.	F11	114
Livingston, Tx., U.S.	I12	116
Livingston, Wi., U.S.	H5	110
Livingstone, Zam.	A7	66
Livingstone, Chutes de, wtfl, Afr.	B2	58
Livingstone, Lake, res., Tx., U.S.	I11	116
Livingstone Falls see Livingstone, Chutes de, wtfl, Afr.	B2	58
Livingstone Mountains, mts., N.Z.	F2	72
Livingstonia, Mwi.	D6	58
Livingston Island, i., Ant.	B12	73
Livingston Manor, N.Y., U.S.	F12	108
Livno, Bos.	F12	18
Livny, Russia	I20	22
Livonia, La., U.S.	L5	114
Livonia, Mi., U.S.	H12	110
Livonia, N.Y., U.S.	E9	108
Livorno (Leghorn), Italy	F5	18
Livramento do Brumado, Braz.	B8	79
Lixi, China	F3	34
Lixian, China	E3	32
Lixing, China	B4	34
Liyang, China	D8	34
Liyuanbao, China	J1	34
Liyujiang, China	J2	34
Lizard Head Peak, mtn., Wy., U.S.	H16	122
Lizard Point, c., Eng., U.K.	L8	8
Lizard Point Indian Reserve, Mb., Can.	H14	104
Lizhu, China	F9	34
Ljahavičy, Bela.	H9	22
Ljasnaja, Bela.	I8	22
Ljuban', Bela.	I10	22
Ljubča, Bela.	H9	22
Ljubija, Bos.	E11	18
Ljubljana, Slvn.	C9	18
Ljubuški, Bos.	F12	18
Ljungby, Swe.	M13	6
Ljusdal, Swe.	K15	6
Ljusina, Bela.	I9	22
Llaima, Volcán, vol., Chile	J3	80
Llamara, Salar de, pl., Chile	I7	82
Llancanelo, Laguna, l., Arg.	H4	80
Llandrindod Wells, Wales, U.K.	I10	8
Llangefni, Wales, U.K.	H9	8
Llangollen, Wales, U.K.	I10	8
Llanidloes, Wales, U.K.	I10	8
Llano, Tx., U.S.	I8	116
Llano, stm., Tx., U.S.	I8	116
Llanos, pl., S.A.	E7	84
Llanwrtyd Wells, Wales, U.K.	I10	8
Llata, Peru	C3	82
Lleida, Spain	D12	16
Llera de Canales, Mex.	F10	90
Lleulleu, Lago, l., Chile	J2	80
Llica, Bol.	H7	82
Llico, Chile	H2	80
Lliria, Spain	F11	16
Llorona, Punta, c., C.R.	I11	92
Lloydminster, Sk., Can.	E4	104
Lloyds, stm., Nf., Can.	D16	106
Llucmajor, Spain	F14	16
Llullaillaco, Volcán, vol., S.A.	C4	80
Llusco, Peru	F5	82
Lluta, stm., Chile	H7	82
Lo (Panlong), stm., Asia	C8	40
Loa, Ut., U.S.	F5	120
Loa, stm., Chile	I7	82
Loami, Il., U.S.	C7	114
Loanda, Braz.	G2	79
Loange (Luangue), stm., Afr.	C3	58
Lobanovo, Russia	H21	22
Lobatse, Bots.	E7	66
Lobaye, stm., C.A.R.	H4	56
Lobelville, Tn., U.S.	G9	114
Lobería, Arg.	J9	80
Lobito, Ang.	D2	58
Lobitos, Peru	J2	84
Lobn'a, Russia	E20	22
Lobos, Arg.	H9	80
Lobos, Cay, i., Bah.	C6	94
Lobos, Isla, i., Mex.	D4	90
Lobos, Punta, c., Chile	I6	82
Lobos de Afuera, Islas, is., Peru	B1	82
Lobos de Tierra, Isla, i., Peru	B1	82
Locarno, Switz.	F10	13
Loches, Fr.	E8	14
Lochmaben, Scot., U.K.	F10	8
Lock, Austl.	I1	70
Lockeport, N.S., Can.	I8	106
Lockerbie, Scot., U.K.	F10	8
Lockesburg, Ar., U.S.	I2	114
Lockhart, Austl.	J7	70
Lockhart, Tx., U.S.	J9	116
Lock Haven, Pa., U.S.	F9	108
Lockney, Tx., U.S.	E5	116
Löcknitz, Ger.	B14	10
Lockport, Il., U.S.	I7	110
Lockport, La., U.S.	M6	114
Lockport, Mb., Can.	H18	104
Lockport, N.Y., U.S.	D8	108
Lockwood, Mo., U.S.	E3	114
Loc Ninh, Viet.	I9	40
Locri, Italy	K11	18
Locroja, Peru	E4	82
Locumba, Peru	G6	82
Locumba, stm., Peru	G6	82
Locust Fork, stm., Al., U.S.	H10	114
Locust Grove, Ok., U.S.	C11	116
Lod (Lydda), Isr.	E3	50
Lodejnoje Pole, Russia	A16	22
Lodève, Fr.	I10	14
Lodge Grass, Mt., U.S.	E18	122
Lodgepole, Ab., Can.	D19	102
Lodgepole, Ne., U.S.	J5	118
Lodi, Ca., U.S.	F4	124
Lodi, Italy	D4	18
Lodi, Oh., U.S.	F4	108
Lodi, Wi., U.S.	G6	110
Lodja, Zaire	B4	58
Lodwar, Kenya	H8	56
Łódź, Pol.	D19	10
Loei, Thai.	F6	40
Loeriesfontein, S. Afr.	H4	66
Lofa, stm., Afr.	G4	54
Lofoten, is., Nor.	G13	6
Loga, Niger	E11	64
Logan, Ia., U.S.	J12	118
Logan, Ks., U.S.	L8	118
Logan, N.M., U.S.	D3	116
Logan, Oh., U.S.	H4	108
Logan, Ut., U.S.	C5	120
Logan, W.V., U.S.	J5	108
Logan, stm., Ab., Can.	B23	102
Logan, stm., Ut., U.S.	C5	120
Logan, Mount, mtn., Yk., Can.	F24	100
Logandale, Nv., U.S.	H11	124
Logan Martin Lake, res., Al., U.S.	I10	114
Logan Mountains, mts., Yk., Can.	E30	100
Logan Pass, Mt., U.S.	B12	122
Logansport, In., U.S.	B10	114
Logansport, La., U.S.	K3	114
Loganville, Ga., U.S.	F3	112
Logone, stm., Afr.	F4	56
Logroño, Spain	C9	16
Løgstør, Den.	M11	6
Lohiniva, Fin.	H19	6
Lohit, stm., Asia	G16	44
Lohja, Fin.	K19	6
Lohne, Ger.	C8	10
Lohr, Ger.	E9	10
Lohrville, Ia., U.S.	I13	118
Loi, stm., Asia	D6	40
Loi-kaw, Myan.	E4	40
Loimaa, Fin.	K18	6
Loire, dept., Fr.	G11	14
Loire, stm., Fr.	E5	14
Loire-Atlantique, dept., Fr.	E5	14
Loiret, dept., Fr.	D9	14
Loir-et-Cher, dept., Fr.	E8	14
Loja, Ec.	I3	84
Loja, Spain	H7	16
Loja, prov., Ec.	J3	84
Lokandu, Zaire	B5	58
Lokan tekojärvi, res., Fin.	H20	6
Lökbatan, Azer.	A10	48
Lokka, Fin.	H20	6
Løkken, Den.	M11	6
Lokn'a, Russia	E13	22
Loko, Nig.	G13	64
Lokoja, Nig.	H13	64
Lokolama, Zaire	B3	58
Lokossa, Benin	H10	64
Lokot', Russia	I17	22
Loks Land, i., N.T., Can.	D20	96
Lol, Sudan	N5	60
Lol, stm., Sudan	M4	60
Lola, Gui.	H5	64
Loleta, Ca., U.S.	D1	124
Lolita, Tx., U.S.	K10	116
Lolo, Mt., U.S.	D11	122
Lolo Pass, U.S.	D11	122
Lolotique, El Sal.	D6	92
Lom, Bul.	F7	20
Lom, Russia	D22	22
Lom, stm., Afr.	G9	54
Loma, Eth.	N9	60
Lomas de Zamora, Arg.	H9	80
Lomax, Il., U.S.	J4	110
Lombardia, prov., Italy	D4	18
Lomblen, Pulau, i., Indon.	G7	38
Lombok, i., Indon.	G6	38
Lomé, Togo	H10	64
Lomela, Zaire	B4	58
Lometa, Tx., U.S.	H8	116
Lomira, Wi., U.S.	G7	110
Lo Miranda, Chile	H3	80
Lommel, Bel.	F7	12
Lomond, Ab., Can.	G22	102
Lomond, Loch, l., N.S., Can.	G13	106
Lomond, Loch, l., Scot., U.K.	E9	8
Lomonosov, Russia	B12	22
Lomonosovka, Kaz.	G11	26
Lompoc, Ca., U.S.	J5	124
Lom Sak, Thai.	F6	40
Łomża, Pol.	B22	10
Lonaconing, Md., U.S.	H8	108
Loncoche, Chile	D2	78
Loncopué, Arg.	J3	80
Londinières, Fr.	C8	14
London, Eng., U.K.	J13	8
London, Ky., U.S.	B2	112
London, Oh., U.S.	H3	108
London, On., Can.	H14	110
London, Tx., U.S.	I7	116
Londonderry (Derry), N. Ire., U.K.	F6	8
Londonderry, N.S., Can.	G10	106
Londonderry, Cape, c., Austl.	B5	68
Londres, Arg.	D5	80
Londrina, Braz.	G3	79
Lone Grove, Ok., U.S.	E9	116
Lonely Lake, l., Mb., Can.	G15	104
Lone Mountain, mtn., Nv., U.S.	F8	124
Lone Oak, Ky., U.S.	E8	114
Lone Oak, Tx., U.S.	F11	116
Lone Pine, Ca., U.S.	H7	124
Lone Rock, Wi., U.S.	G5	110
Lone Star, Tx., U.S.	J2	114
Lone Tree, Ia., U.S.	I4	110
Lone Wolf, Ok., U.S.	E7	116
Longa, stm., Ang.	D2	58
Longa, proliv, strt., Russia	C27	28
Long'an, China	B10	40
Longaví, Chile	H3	80
Long Bay, b., U.S.	F8	112
Long Beach, Ca., U.S.	K7	124
Long Beach, Ms., U.S.	L7	114
Long Beach, N.Y., U.S.	G13	108
Long Beach, Wa., U.S.	D1	122
Longboat Key, Fl., U.S.	L4	112
Long Branch, N.J., U.S.	G13	108
Long Branch, stm., Mo., U.S.	C4	114
Long Cay, i., Bah.	C7	94
Longchang, China	F8	30
Longchuan, China	K4	34
Longchuan (Shweli), stm., Asia	B4	40
Long Creek, Or., U.S.	F6	122
Long Creek, stm., N.A.	I11	104
Longcun, China	L4	34
Longdou, China	H6	34
Longeau, Fr.	E12	14
Longford, Austl.	L7	70
Longford, co., Ire.	H6	8
Long Harbour, Nf., Can.	E20	106
Long Harbour, b., Nf., Can.	E18	106
Longhua, China	B5	32
Long Island, i., Austl.	D8	70
Long Island, i., Bah.	C7	94
Long Island, i., Nf., Can.	E19	106
Long Island, i., N.S., Can.	H7	106
Long Island, i., N.T., Can.	F17	96
Long Island, i., N.Y., U.S.	G14	108
Long Island Sound, strt., U.S.	F14	108
Longitudinal, Valle, val., Chile	H3	80
Longjiang, China	B11	30
Longjin, China	G5	34
Longka, China	D8	44
Longkangji, China	B5	34
Longkou, China	D11	30
Longkou, China	I4	34
Long Lake, N.Y., U.S.	D12	108
Long Lake, l., N.D., U.S.	E7	118
Longleaf, La., U.S.	K4	114
Long Leaf Park, N.C., U.S.	E9	112
Longlegged Lake, l., On., Can.	H20	104
Longli, China	F8	30
Longling, China	B5	40
Longmeadow, Ma., U.S.	E14	108
Longmensuo, China	C3	32
Longming, China	C9	40
Longmont, Co., U.S.	D11	120
Longnan, China	K3	34
Longnawan, Indon.	E5	38
Longny, Fr.	M14	8
Long Pine, Ne., U.S.	I8	118
Long Point, c., Nf., Can.	D15	106
Long Point, c., N.S., Can.	F13	106
Long Point, pen., Mb., Can.	E16	104
Long Point, pen., On., Can.	H15	110
Long Prairie, Mn., U.S.	F13	118
Long Prairie, stm., Mn., U.S.	E13	118
Longquan, China	G8	34
Longquanguan, China	E1	32
Long Range Mountains, mts., Nf., Can.	D16	106
Longreach, Austl.	D6	70
Long Reach, b., N.B., Can.	G7	106
Long-Sault, On., Can.	B12	108
Longshansuo, China	E10	34
Longsheng, China	B11	40
Longs Peak, mtn., Co., U.S.	D11	120
Longtian, China	J8	34
Long Tom, stm., Or., U.S.	F2	122
Longton, Ks., U.S.	N11	118
Longtoupu, China	H2	34
Longueuil, P.Q., Can.	B13	108
Longuyon, Fr.	C12	14
Longview, Ab., Can.	G20	102
Longview, N.C., U.S.	D5	112
Longview, Tx., U.S.	J2	114
Longview, Wa., U.S.	D3	122
Longwangmiao, China	G3	32
Longwood Park, N.C., U.S.	E7	112
Longworth, B.C., Can.	D13	102
Longwy, Fr.	C12	14
Longxi, China	E7	30
Long Xuyen, Viet.	I8	40
Longyan, China	J6	34
Longyuanba, China	K3	34
Longzhou, China	C9	40
Lonigo, Italy	D6	18
Löningen, Ger.	C7	10
Lonoke, Ar., U.S.	H5	114
Lonsdale, Mn., U.S.	F2	110
Lons-le-Saunier, Fr.	F12	14
Lonton, Myan.	B4	40
Lontra, Ribeirão da, stm., Braz.	F2	79
Loogootee, In., U.S.	D10	114
Looking Glass, stm., Mi., U.S.	H11	110
Lookout, Cape, c., N.C., U.S.	E10	112
Lookout Mountain, mtn., Or., U.S.	F5	122
Lookout Mountain, mtn., U.S.	H11	114
Lookout Pass, U.S.	C10	122
Lookout Ridge, mts., Ak., U.S.	B15	100
Loomis, Ne., U.S.	K8	118
Loon, stm., Mb., Can.	B13	104
Loon Lake, l., Can.	C12	104
Loon op Zand, Neth.	E7	12
Loop, Tx., U.S.	G4	116
Lop, China	B9	44
Lopar'ovo, Russia	C25	22
Lopatina, gora, mtn., Russia	G20	28
Lopatka, mys, c., Russia	G23	28
Lop Buri, Thai.	G6	40
López, Mex.	D7	90
Lopez, Cap, c., Gabon	B1	58
Lop Nur (Lop Nor), l., China	C5	30
Łopuszno, Pol.	E20	10
Lora, stm., Ven.	C6	84
Lora, Hāmūn-i-, l., Asia	F1	44
Lora del Río, Spain	H6	16
Lorain, Oh., U.S.	F4	108
Loraine, Tx., U.S.	G6	116
Lorca, Spain	H10	16
Lord Howe Island, i., Austl.	F11	68
Lord Mayor Bay, b., N.T., Can.	C14	96
Lordsburg, N.M., U.S.	L8	120
Loreauville, La., U.S.	L5	114
Loreley, Ger.	E7	10
Lorena, Braz.	G6	79
Lorenzo, Tx., U.S.	F5	116
Lorenzo Geyres (Queguay), Ur.	G10	80
Loreto, Arg.	D10	80
Loreto, Bol.	F9	82
Loreto, Braz.	E9	76
Loreto, Mex.	D4	90
Loreto, Mex.	F9	90
Loreto, Para.	B10	80
Loreto, dept., Peru	I5	84
Loreto Mocagua, Col.	I7	84
Lorette, Mb., Can.	I18	104
Loretto, Ky., U.S.	E11	114
Loretto, Tn., U.S.	G9	114
Lorica, Col.	C5	84
Lorient, Fr.	E3	14
L'Orignal, On., Can.	B12	108

Name	Map Ref.	Page
Mahākālī (Sārda), stm., Asia	F9	44
Mahakam, stm., Indon.	E6	38
Mahalatswe, Bots.	D8	66
Maḥallāt, Iran	E11	48
Mahanoro, Madag.	q23	67b
Mahanoy City, Pa., U.S.	G10	108
Mahārāshtra, state, India	C3	46
Maha Sarakham, Thai.	F7	40
Mahasoa, Madag.	s22	67b
Mahasolo, Madag.	q22	67b
Mahates, Col.	B5	84
Mahatsinjo, Madag.	r21	67b
Maḥaṭṭat al-Ḥafīf, Jord.	D8	50
Mahbūbnagar, India	D4	46
Mahd adh-Dhahab, Sau. Ar.	C2	47
Mahdia, Tun.	N6	18
Mahe, India	G3	46
Mahébourg, Mrts.	v18	67c
Mahé Island, i., Sey.	B11	58
Mahendra Giri, mtn., India	C8	46
Mahesāna, India	I5	44
Mahia Peninsula, pen., N.Z.	C7	72
Mahilëu, Bela.	H13	22
Mahnomen, Mn., U.S.	D12	118
Mahoba, India	H8	44
Mahomet, Il., U.S.	B8	114
Mahone Bay, N.S., Can.	H9	106
Mahone Bay, b., N.S., Can.	H9	106
Mahony Lake, l., N.T., Can.	D32	100
Mahood Falls, B.C., Can.	F14	102
Mahood Lake, l., B.C., Can.	F14	102
Mahres, Tun.	C16	62
Mahuva, India	B1	46
Mai Aini, Erit.	J10	60
Maicao, Col.	B6	84
Maîche, Fr.	E13	14
Maici, stm., Braz.	B11	82
Maicuru, stm., Braz.	D8	76
Maiden, N.C., U.S.	D5	112
Maidenhead, Eng., U.K.	J13	8
Maidstone, Eng., U.K.	J14	8
Maidstone, Sk., Can.	E5	104
Maiduguri, Nig.	F9	54
Maienfeld, Switz.	D12	13
Maigatari, Nig.	E14	64
Maignelay, Fr.	C9	14
Maillezais, Fr.	F6	14
Mai Mefales, Erit.	J10	60
Main, stm., Ger.	F9	10
Main Channel, strt., On., Can.	E14	110
Mai-Ndombe, Lac, l., Zaire	B3	58
Maine, hist. reg., Fr.	D6	14
Maine, state, U.S.	B13	98
Maine, Gulf of, b., N.A.	C13	98
Maine-et-Loire, dept., Fr.	E6	14
Mainhardt, Ger.	F9	10
Mainland, i., Scot., U.K.	B10	8
Mainland, i., Scot., U.K.	A12	8
Mainpuri, India	G8	44
Maintenon, Fr.	D8	14
Maintirano, Madag.	q21	67b
Main Topsail, mtn., Nf., Can.	C17	106
Mainz, Ger.	E8	10
Maio, i., C.V.	m17	64a
Maipo, stm., Chile	G3	80
Maipo, Volcán, vol., S.A.	H4	80
Maipú, Arg.	I10	80
Maipú, Arg.	G4	80
Maipú, Chile	G3	80
Maiquetía, Ven.	B9	84
Mairipotaba, Braz.	D4	79
Maitengwe, Bots.	C8	66
Maitengwe, stm., Afr.	C8	66
Maitland, Austl.	J2	70
Maitland, Austl.	I9	70
Maitland, N.S., Can.	G10	106
Maíz, stm., Nic.	F10	92
Maíz, Islas del, is., Nic.	E11	92
Maizuru, Japan	L10	36
Maja, stm., Russia	F18	28
Majagual, Col.	C5	84
Majari, stm., Braz.	F12	84
Majé, Braz.	G7	79
Maji, Eth.	N8	60
Majia, China	C7	34
Majie, China	B7	40
Majja, Russia	E18	28
Majkain, Kaz.	G13	26
Majkop, Russia	I6	26
Majorca see Mallorca, i., Spain	F15	16
Maka, Sen.	E2	64
Makabana, Congo	B2	58
Makalamabedi, Bots.	C6	66
Makallé, Arg.	D9	80
Makālu, mtn., Asia	G12	44
Makanza, Zaire	A3	58
Makaoo Indian Reserve, Ab., Can.	E4	104
Makarjev, Russia	D26	22
Makarov, Russia	H20	28
Makarska, Cro.	F12	18
Makasar, Selat (Makassar Strait), strt., Indon.	F6	38
Makassar Strait see Makasar, Selat, strt., Indon.	F6	38
Makat, Kaz.	H8	26
Makawao, Hi., U.S.	q17	125a
Makeni, S.L.	G3	64
Makeyevka see Makiyivka, Ukr.	H5	26
Makgadikgadi, pl., Bots.	C7	66
Makgadikgadi Pans Game Reserve, Bots.	C7	66
Makhfar al-Quwayrah, Jord.	I4	50
Makhfar Ramn, Jord.	I4	50
Makhrūq, Wādī al-, val., Asia	F7	50
Makindu, Kenya	B7	58
Makinsk, Kaz.	G12	26
M'akiševo, Russia	E11	22
M'akit, Russia	E22	28
Makiyivka, Ukr.	H5	26
Makkah (Mecca), Sau. Ar.	D1	47
Makó, Hung.	I20	10
Makokou, Gabon	A2	58
Makoua, Congo	A3	58
Makrāna, India	G6	44
Makran Coast, Asia	I16	48
M'aksa, Russia	C21	22
Maksaticha, Russia	D18	22
Makthar, Tun.	N4	18
Mākū, Iran	B8	48
Makumbi, Zaire	C4	58
Makung (P'enghu), Tai.	L8	34
Makurdi, Nig.	H14	64
Makwa Lake, l., Sk., Can.	D5	104
Makwassie, S. Afr.	F8	66
Mal, Maur.	C3	64
Mala, Peru	E3	82
Mala, stm., Peru	E3	82
Mala, Punta, c., Pan.	D3	84
Malabang, Phil.	D7	38
Malabar Coast, India	F3	46
Malabo, Eq. Gui.	J14	64
Malacacheta, Braz.	D7	79
Malacca, Strait of, strt., Asia	M6	40
Malacky, Slvk.	G17	10
Malad, stm., U.S.	C4	120
Malad City, Id., U.S.	H13	122
Maladzečna, Bela.	G9	22
Málaga, Col.	D6	84
Malaga, N.M., U.S.	G2	116
Málaga, Spain	I7	16
Malagash, N.S., Can.	G10	106
Malagasy Republic see Madagascar, ctry., Afr.	E9	58
Malagón, Spain	F8	16
Malaimbandy, Madag.	r21	67b
Malaja Kuril'skaja Gr'ada (Habomai-Shotō), is., Russia	d21	36a
Malaja Višera, Russia	C15	22
Malakāl, Sudan	M6	60
Malakoff, Tx., U.S.	G10	116
Malān, Myan.	B4	40
Malang, Indon.	j16	39a
Malanggwā, Nepal	G11	44
Malanje, Ang.	C3	58
Malanville, Benin	F11	64
Malanzán, Arg.	F5	80
Mälaren, l., Swe.	L15	6
Malargüe, Arg.	H4	80
Malaspina Glacier, Ak., U.S.	G24	100
Malaspina Strait, strt., B.C., Can.	H10	102
Malatya, Tur.	B5	48
Malaut, India	E6	44
Malawi, ctry., Afr.	D6	58
Malawi, Lake see Nyasa, Lake, l., Afr.	D6	58
Malaybalay, Phil.	D8	38
Malāyer, Iran	D10	48
Malay Peninsula, pen., Asia	K6	40
Malay Reef, rf., Austl.	A8	70
Malaysia, ctry., Asia	E3	38
Malazgirt, Tur.	B7	48
Malbaie, stm., P.Q., Can.	E3	106
Malbaie, La, b., P.Q., Can.	D9	106
Malbork, Pol.	A19	10
Malbrán, Arg.	E7	80
Malcolm, Austl.	E4	68
Malcolm Island, i., B.C., Can.	G7	102
Malcom, Ia., U.S.	I3	110
Maldegem, Bel.	F3	12
Malden, Mo., U.S.	F7	114
Maldive Islands, is., Mald.	I2	46
Maldives, ctry., Asia	I8	24
Maldonado, Ur.	H11	80
Malé, Italy	C5	18
Male', Mald.	I8	24
Maléa, Ákra, c., Grc.	M7	20
Mālegaon, India	B3	46
Malek, Sudan	N6	60
Malek Sīāh, Kūh-e, mtn., Asia	G16	48
Malema, Moz.	D7	58
Malen'ga, Russia	J25	6
Māler Kotla, India	E6	44
Malesherbes, Fr.	D9	14
Malestroit, Fr.	E4	14
Malha Wells, Sudan	J4	60
Malheur, stm., Or., U.S.	G8	122
Malheur Lake, l., Or., U.S.	G7	122
Mali, ctry., Afr.	E6	54
Mali, stm., Myan.	A4	40
Maligne, stm., Ab., Can.	E17	102
Maligne Lake, l., Ab., Can.	E17	102
Malik, Wādī al-, val., Sudan	I6	60
Mali Kyun, i., Myan.	H5	40
Malin, Or., U.S.	H4	122
Malinalco, hist., Mex.	H10	90
Malinaltepec, Mex.	I10	90
Malines (Mechelen), Bel.	F5	12
Malin Head, c., Ire.	F6	8
Maliwun, Myan.	I5	40
Maljamar, N.M., U.S.	G3	116
Malka, Russia	G23	28
Malkāpur, India	B4	46
Malkara, Tur.	I10	20
Mallāḥ, Syria	C7	50
Mallaig, Ab., Can.	C23	102
Mallaig, Scot., U.K.	D8	8
Mallala, Austl.	J3	70
Mallaoua, Niger	E14	64
Mallawī, Egypt	D6	60
Mallery Lake, l., N.T., Can.	D13	96
Mallet, Braz.	C13	80
Malligasta, Arg.	E5	80
Mallnitz, Aus.	I13	10
Mallorca, i., Spain	F15	16
Mallow, Ire.	I5	8
Malmédy, Bel.	H9	12
Malmesbury, S. Afr.	I4	66
Malmö, Swe.	N13	6
Malmöhus Län, co., Swe.	N13	6
Maloarchangel'sk, Russia	I19	22
Maloja, Switz.	F12	13
Malojaroslavec, Russia	F19	22
Maloje Kozino, Russia	E26	22
Maloje Skuratovo, Russia	H20	22
Malolos, Phil.	n19	39b
Malone, Fl., U.S.	I1	112
Malone, N.Y., U.S.	C12	108
Malonga, Zaire	D4	58
Małopolska, reg., Pol.	E21	10
Malošujka, Russia	E5	26
Måløy, Nor.	K9	6
Malpaisillo, Nic.	E8	92
Malpas, Austl.	J4	70
Malpelo, Isla de, i., Col.	C2	76
Malpeque Bay, b., P.E., Can.	F10	106
Malta, Lat.	E10	22
Malta, Mt., U.S.	B18	122
Malta, Oh., U.S.	H5	108
Malta, ctry., Eur.	H10	4
Malta, i., Malta	N9	18
Malta Channel, strt., Eur.	M9	18
Maltahöhe, Nmb.	E3	66
Maltepe, Tur.	I11	20
Maluku (Moluccas), is., Indon.	F8	38
Maluku, Laut (Molucca Sea), Indon.	F7	38
Malumfashi, Nig.	F13	64
Malvern, Ar., U.S.	H4	114
Malvern, Ia., U.S.	J12	118
Malvern, Oh., U.S.	G5	108
Malvinas, Arg.	E9	80
Malwal, Sudan	M6	60
Malý Dunaj, stm., Slvk.	H17	10
Malyj, ostrov, i., Russia	A11	22
Malyj An'uj, stm., Russia	D24	28
Malyj Jenisej, stm., Russia	G11	28
Malyj Tajmyr, ostrov, i., Russia	B13	28
Malyj T'uters, ostrov, i., Russia	B9	22
Malyj Uzen', stm., Eur.	H7	26
Malyševo, Russia	D18	22
Mamakwash Lake, l., On., Can.	G22	104
Mamara, Peru	F5	82
Mambaí, Braz.	C5	79
Mamberamo, stm., Indon.	F10	38
Mambéré, stm., C.A.R.	H4	56
Ma-Me-O Beach, Ab., Can.	E21	102
Mamers, Fr.	D7	14
Mamfe, Cam.	G8	54
Mamiá, Lago, l., Braz.	J11	84
Mamie, N.C., U.S.	C11	112
Mamiña, Chile	I7	82
Mammoth, Az., U.S.	L6	120
Mammoth, W.V., U.S.	I5	108
Mammoth Cave National Park, Ky., U.S.	E10	114
Mammoth Lakes, Ca., U.S.	G7	124
Mammoth Spring, Ar., U.S.	F5	114
Mamonovo, Russia	G2	22
Mamoré, stm., S.A.	D9	82
Mamori, Lago, l., Braz.	I12	84
Mamoriá, stm., Braz.	B8	82
Mamou, Gui.	F3	64
Mamou, La., U.S.	L4	114
Mamoutzou, May.	I16	67a
Mampikony, Madag.	p22	67b
Mamry, Jezioro, l., Pol.	A21	10
Mamuchi, China	H6	32
Ma'mūn, Sudan	K2	60
Mamuno, Bots.	D5	66
Mamuru, stm., Braz.	I14	84
Man, C. Iv.	H6	64
Man, W.V., U.S.	B5	112
Mana, Hi., U.S.	o14	125a
Mana, stm., Fr. Gu.	B8	76
Manabí, prov., Ec.	H2	84
Manacacías, stm., Col.	F6	84
Manacapuru, Braz.	I12	84
Manacor, Spain	F15	16
Manado, Indon.	E7	38
Managua, Nic.	E8	92
Managua, dept., Nic.	E8	92
Managua, Lago de, l., Nic.	E8	92
Manakara, Madag.	s23	67b
Manāli, India	D7	44
Manama see Al-Manāmah, Bahr.	H11	48
Manambato, Madag.	n23	67b
Manambolosy, Madag.	p23	67b
Mánamo, Caño, mth., Ven.	C11	84
Mananara, Madag.	p23	67b
Mananjary, Madag.	r23	67b
Manantenina, Madag.	t22	67b
Manapiare, stm., Ven.	E9	84
Manapire, stm., Ven.	C9	84
Manaquiri, Lago, l., Braz.	I12	84
Manaravolo, Madag.	s21	67b
Manas, China	C4	30
Manās, stm., Asia	G14	44
Manas Hu, l., China	B4	30
Manāslu, mtn., Nepal	F11	44
Manasquan, N.J., U.S.	G12	108
Manassa, Co., U.S.	G11	120
Manassas, Va., U.S.	I9	108
Manatí, Col.	B5	84
Manatí, P.R.	E11	94
Manaung, Myan.	E2	40
Manaus, Braz.	I12	84
Manawa, Wi., U.S.	F7	110
Manawan Lake, l., Sk., Can.	C11	104
Manbij, Syria	C4	48
Mancelona, Mi., U.S.	F10	110
Mancha Real, Spain	H8	16
Manche, dept., Fr.	C5	14
Manchester, Ct., U.S.	F14	108
Manchester, Eng., U.K.	H11	8
Manchester, Ga., U.S.	G2	112
Manchester, Ia., U.S.	H4	110
Manchester, Ky., U.S.	B3	112
Manchester, Ma., U.S.	E16	108
Manchester, Mi., U.S.	H11	110
Manchester, N.H., U.S.	E15	108
Manchester, Oh., U.S.	I3	108
Manchester, Tn., U.S.	G10	114
Manchester, Vt., U.S.	D13	108
Manchón, Guat.	C2	92
Manchuria, hist. reg., China	B12	30
Máncora, Peru	J2	84
Mancos, Co., U.S.	G8	120
Mancos, stm., U.S.	G8	120
Mandabe, Madag.	r21	67b
Mandaguari, Braz.	G3	79
Mandal, Nor.	L10	6
Mandala, Puncak, mtn., Indon.	F11	38
Mandalay, Myan.	C4	40
Mandalgov', Mong.	B8	30
Mandalī, Iraq	E8	48
Mandan, N.D., U.S.	E7	118
Mandara Mountains, mts., Afr.	F9	54
Mandas, Italy	J4	18
Mandeb, Bab el, strt.	H3	47
Mandel, Afg.	E16	48
Manderson, Wy., U.S.	F18	122
Mandeville, Jam.	E6	94
Mandeville, La., U.S.	L6	114
Mandi, India	E7	44
Mandiana, Gui.	F5	64
Mandimba, Moz.	D7	58
Mandioli, Pulau, i., Indon.	F8	38
Mandioré, Lagoa, l., S.A.	H13	82
Mandla, India	A6	46
Mandoto, Madag.	q22	67b
Mandouri, Togo	F10	64
Mandra, Pak.	D5	44
Mandritsara, Madag.	o23	67b
Mandronarivo, Madag.	r21	67b
Mandsaur, India	H6	44
Manduria, Italy	I12	18
Māndvi, India	I3	44
Mandya, India	F4	46
Manfalūṭ, Egypt	D6	60
Manfredonia, Italy	H10	18
Manfredonia, Golfo di, b., Italy	H11	18
Manga, Braz.	C7	79
Manga, Burkina	F9	64
Mangabeiras, Chapada das, hills, Braz.	F9	76
Mangalagiri, India	D6	46
Mangalore, India	F3	46
Mangaoka, Madag.	n23	67b
Mangchang, China	F8	30
Mange, China	D10	44
Mange, S.L.	G3	64
Mangham, La., U.S.	J5	114
Manglares, Cabo, c., Col.	G3	84
Mangochi, Mwi.	D7	58
Mangoky, stm., Madag.	r21	67b
Mangole, Pulau, i., Indon.	F8	38
Mangoupa, C.A.R.	O3	60
Mangrol, India	J4	44
Mangrove Cay, i., Bah.	B6	94
Mangueira, Lagoa, b., Braz.	G12	80
Mangueirinha, Braz.	C12	80
Mangulile, Hond.	B8	92
Mangum, Ok., U.S.	E7	116
Mangya, China	D5	30
Manhattan, Ks., U.S.	L11	118
Manhattan, Mt., U.S.	E14	122
Manhuaçu, Braz.	F7	79
Manhuaçu, stm., Braz.	E8	79
Manhumirim, Braz.	F8	79
Maniago, Italy	C7	18
Maniamba, Moz.	D7	58
Manic Deux, Réservoir, res., P.Q., Can.	C5	106
Manicoré, Braz.	A11	82
Manicoré, stm., Braz.	B11	82
Manicouagan, stm., P.Q., Can.	C5	106
Manicouagan, Réservoir, res., P.Q., Can.	A5	106
Manic Trois, Réservoir, res., P.Q., Can.	B5	106
Manignan, C. Iv.	F6	64
Manigotagan, Mb., Can.	G18	104
Manigotagan, stm., Can.	H19	104
Manila, Ar., U.S.	G6	114
Manila, Phil.	n19	39b
Manila, Ut., U.S.	D7	120
Manila Bay, b., Phil.	n19	39b
Manilla, Austl.	H9	70
Manilla, Ia., U.S.	J12	118
Manily, Russia	E25	28
Manimpé, Mali	D7	64
Manino, Russia	H17	22
Manipur, state, India	H15	44
Manipur, stm., Asia	C2	40
Manisa, Tur.	K11	20
Manissauá-Miçu, stm., Braz.	A1	79
Manistee, Mi., U.S.	F9	110
Manistee, stm., Mi., U.S.	F9	110
Manistique, Mi., U.S.	E9	110
Manistique, stm., Mi., U.S.	D9	110
Manito, Il., U.S.	B7	114
Manitoba, prov., Can.	D17	104
Manitoba, Lake, l., Mb., Can.	H16	104
Manitou, Mb., Can.	I16	104
Manitou, stm., On., Can.	I21	104
Manitou, stm., P.Q., Can.	B8	106
Manitou, Lac, l., P.Q., Can.	B10	106
Manitou, Lac, l., P.Q., Can.	B8	106
Manitou Beach, Sk., Can.	G9	104
Manitou Lake, l., Sk., Can.	F5	104
Manitoulin Island, i., On., Can.	E13	110
Manitou Springs, Co., U.S.	F12	120
Manitowaning, On., Can.	E14	110
Manitowish Waters, Wi., U.S.	D6	110
Manitowoc, Wi., U.S.	F8	110
Manitowoc, stm., Wi., U.S.	F7	110
Maniwaki, P.Q., Can.	A11	108
Manizales, Col.	E5	84
Manja, Madag.	r21	67b
Manjacaze, Moz.	E11	66
Manjakandriana, Madag.	q22	67b
Manjimup, Austl.	F3	68
Mankato, Ks., U.S.	L9	118
Mankato, Mn., U.S.	F2	110
Mankayane, Swaz.	F10	66
Mankota, Sk., Can.	I7	104
Manlleu, Spain	C14	16
Manly, Ia., U.S.	G2	110
Manmād, India	B3	46
Mannahill, Austl.	I3	70
Mannar, Gulf of, b., Asia	H5	46
Mannārgudi, India	G5	46
Männedorf, Switz.	D10	13
Mannford, Ok., U.S.	C10	116
Mannheim, Ger.	F8	10
Manni, China	C12	44
Manning, Ia., U.S.	J12	118
Manning, N.D., U.S.	D5	118
Manning, S.C., U.S.	F6	112
Mannington, W.V., U.S.	H6	108
Mannum, Austl.	J3	70
Mannville, Ab., Can.	D23	102
Mano, stm., Afr.	H4	64
Manoa, Bol.	C9	82
Manoel Ribas, Braz.	C13	80
Manokotak, Ak., U.S.	G15	100
Manombo, Madag.	s20	67b
Manono, Zaire	C5	58
Manor, Sk., Can.	I12	104
Manor, Tx., U.S.	I9	116
Manosque, Fr.	I12	14
Manouane, stm., P.Q., Can.	B3	106
Manouane, Lac, l., P.Q., Can.	B3	106
Manouanis, stm., P.Q., Can.	A3	106
Manouanis, Lac, l., P.Q., Can.	B3	106
Manp'o, N. Kor.	B14	32
Manresa, Spain	D13	16
Mānsa, India	F6	44
Mansa, Zam.	D5	58
Mansel Island, i., N.T., Can.	D17	96
Mansfield, Ar., U.S.	G2	114
Mansfield, Austl.	K7	70
Mansfield, Ga., U.S.	F3	112
Mansfield, Il., U.S.	B8	114
Mansfield, La., U.S.	J3	114
Mansfield, Ma., U.S.	E15	108
Mansfield, Mo., U.S.	E4	114
Mansfield, Oh., U.S.	G4	108
Mansfield, Pa., U.S.	F9	108
Mansfield, Tx., U.S.	G9	116
Mansfield, Mount, mtn., Vt., U.S.	C14	108
Mansión, C.R.	G9	92
Mansle, Fr.	G7	14
Manso, stm., Braz.	F13	82
Manson, Ia., U.S.	I13	118
Manson, stm., B.C., Can.	B11	102
Manson Creek, B.C., Can.	B10	102
Mansura see Al-Manṣūrah, Egypt	B6	60
Mansura, La., U.S.	K4	114
Manta, Ec.	H2	84
Manta, Bahía de, b., Ec.	H2	84
Mantagao, stm., Mb., Can.	G17	104
Mantaro, stm., Peru	E4	82
Manteca, Ca., U.S.	G4	124
Mantecal, Ven.	D8	84
Manteno, Il., U.S.	I8	110
Manteo, N.C., U.S.	D11	112
Mantes-la-Jolie, Fr.	D8	14
Manti, Ut., U.S.	E5	120
Mantiqueira, Serra da, mts., Braz.	G6	79
Manton, Mi., U.S.	F10	110
Mantorville, Mn., U.S.	F3	110
Mantos Blancos, Chile	B3	80
Mantova, Italy	D5	18
Mantua, Cuba	C2	94
Mantua see Mantova, Italy	D5	18
Mantua, Oh., U.S.	F5	108
Manturovo, Russia	C27	22
Mäntyharju, Fin.	K20	6
Manu, Peru	E6	82
Manú, stm., Peru	E6	82
Manua Islands, is., Am. Sam.	J23	126
Manuel, Mex.	F10	90
Manuel Antonio, Parque Nacional, C.R.	H10	92
Manuel Benavides, Mex.	C8	90
Manuel Derqui, Arg.	D9	80
Manuel Urbano, Braz.	C7	82
Manuripe (Mamuripi), stm., S.A.	D8	82
Manuripi, stm., Bol.	E8	82
Manus Island, i., Pap. N. Gui.	k16	68a
Manvel, N.D., U.S.	C10	118
Many, La., U.S.	K3	114
Manyana, Bots.	D5	66
Manyara, Lake, l., Tan.	B7	58
Manyberries, Ab., Can.	I4	104
Manyč, stm., Russia	H6	26
Many Island Lake, l., Can.	H4	104
Manzanares, Spain	F8	16
Manzanillo, Cuba	D6	94
Manzanillo, Mex.	H7	90
Manzanillo, Punta, c., Pan.	H15	92
Manzanillo Bay, b., N.A.	E9	94
Manzano, N.M., U.S.	J10	120
Manzanola, Co., U.S.	M4	118
Manzano Peak, mtn., N.M., U.S.	J10	120
Manzhouli, China	B10	30
Manzini, Swaz.	F10	66
Mao, Chad	F4	56
Mao, Dom. Rep.	E9	94
Maó, Spain	F16	16
Maoke, Pegunungan, mts., Indon.	F10	38
Maoming, China	G9	30
Maouri, Dallol, val., Niger	E11	64
Mapari, stm., Braz.	I9	84
Mapastepec, Mex.	J13	90
Mapia, Kepulauan, is., Indon.	E9	38
Mapimí, Mex.	E8	90
Mapimí, Bolsón de, des., Mex.	D8	90
Maping, China	D2	34
Mapinhane, Moz.	D12	66
Mapire, Ven.	D10	84
Mapiri, Bol.	F7	82
Mapiri, stm., Bol.	D8	82
Mapixari, Ilha, i., Braz.	I10	84
Maple, stm., Ia., U.S.	I12	118
Maple, stm., Mi., U.S.	G11	110
Maple, stm., Mn., U.S.	G1	110
Maple, stm., N.D., U.S.	E10	118
Maple, stm., U.S.	F9	118
Maple Creek, Sk., Can.	I5	104
Maple Lake, Mn., U.S.	E1	110
Maple Mount, Ky., U.S.	E9	114
Maplesville, Al., U.S.	J10	114
Mapleton, Ia., U.S.	I12	118
Mapleton, Mn., U.S.	G2	110
Mapleton, Or., U.S.	F2	122
Mapleton, Ut., U.S.	D5	120
Mapuera, stm., Braz.	H14	84
Mapulanguene, Moz.	E11	66
Maputo, Moz.	E11	66
Maputo, stm., Afr.	F11	66
Maqna, Sau. Ar.	G3	48
Maquela do Zombo, Ang.	C3	58
Maquereau, Pointe au, c., P.Q., Can.	D9	106
Maquilaú, stm., Braz.	G11	84
Maquinchao, Arg.	E3	78
Maquoketa, Ia., U.S.	H5	110
Maqucketa, stm., Ia., U.S.	H5	110
Mar, Serra do, clf, Braz.	C14	80
Mara, Peru	F5	82
Mara, stm., Afr.	B6	58
Maraã, Braz.	H10	84
Marabá, Braz.	E9	76
Maracá, Ilha de, i., Braz.	F12	84
Maracaí, Braz.	G3	79
Maracaibo, Ven.	B7	84
Maracaibo, Lago de, l., Ven.	C7	84
Maracaju, Braz.	F1	79
Maracaju, Serra de, hills, S.A.	F1	79
Maracanã, stm., Braz.	C12	82
Maracás, Braz.	B8	79
Maracay, Ven.	B9	84
Marādah, Libya	C4	56
Maradi, Niger	E13	64
Maradi, Goulbin, stm., Afr.	E13	64
Marāgheh, Iran	C9	48
Maragogipe, Braz.	B9	79
Marahuaca, Cerro, mtn., Ven.	F10	84
Maraiche Lake, l., Sk., Can.	D12	104
Marais des Cygnes, stm., U.S.	D1	114
Marajó, Baía de, b., Braz.	D9	76
Marajó, Ilha de, i., Braz.	D9	76
Marakabei, Leso.	G9	66
Maralal, Kenya	A7	58
Maralaleng, Bots.	E6	66
Marampa, S.L.	G3	64
Maramureș, co., Rom.	B8	20
Maran, Malay.	M7	40
Marana, Az., U.S.	L5	120
Marand, Iran	B8	48
Marangani, Peru	F6	82
Maranguape, Braz.	D11	76
Maranhão, stm., Braz.	C4	79
Maranoa, stm., Austl.	E9	68
Marañón, stm., Peru	D3	76
Marapanim, Braz.	D9	76
Marapi, stm., Braz.	G14	84
Maras, Peru	E5	82
Marathon, Austl.	C5	70
Marathón, Grc.	K7	20
Marathon, N.Y., U.S.	E10	108
Marathon, On., Can.	B9	110
Marathon, Tx., U.S.	I3	116
Marathon, Wi., U.S.	F6	110
Maraú, Braz.	C9	79
Marau, Braz.	E12	80
Marauiá, stm., Braz.	H10	84
Maravilha, Braz.	D12	80
Maravillas, Mex.	D7	90
Marawī, Sudan	H6	60
Marayes, Arg.	F5	80
Marbach, Switz.	E8	13
Marbella, Spain	I7	16
Marble, Mn., U.S.	C2	110
Marble, N.C., U.S.	D3	112
Marble Bar, Austl.	D3	68
Marble Canyon, val., Az., U.S.	H5	120
Marble Falls, Tx., U.S.	I8	116
Marble Hall, S. Afr.	E9	66
Marblehead, Oh., U.S.	F4	108
Marble Hill, Mo., U.S.	E7	114
Marble Rock, Ia., U.S.	H3	110
Marburg, Ger.	E8	10
Marcala, Hond.	C6	92
Marcali, Hung.	I17	10
Marcaria, Italy	D5	18
Marceau, Lac, l., P.Q., Can.	A7	106
Marcelin, Sk., Can.	F8	104
Marceline, Mo., U.S.	C4	114
Marcelino Ramos, Braz.	D13	80
Marcellus, Mi., U.S.	H10	110
March (Morava), stm., Eur.	G16	10
Marcha, stm., Russia	E15	28
Marche, prov., Italy	F8	18
Marche, hist. reg., Fr.	F8	14
Marche-en-Famenne, Bel.	H7	12
Marchegg, Aus.	G16	10
Marchena, Spain	H6	16
Mar Chiquita, Laguna, b., Arg.	I10	80
Mar Chiquita, Laguna, l., Arg.	F7	80
Marcigny, Fr.	F11	14
Marcola, Or., U.S.	F3	122
Marcona, Peru	F4	82
Marcos Juárez, Arg.	G7	80
Marcos Paz, Arg.	H9	80
Marcus, Ia., U.S.	I12	118
Marcus Baker, Mount, mtn., Ak., U.S.	F21	100
Marcy, Mount, mtn., N.Y., U.S.	C13	108
Mardān, Pak.	C5	44
Mardarivka, Ukr.	B13	20
Mar del Plata, Arg.	J10	80
Mardin, Tur.	C6	48
Marea de Portillo, Cuba	E6	94
Marechal Cândido Rondon, Braz.	C11	80
Marechal Taumaturgo, Braz.	C5	82
Mareeba, Austl.	A6	70
Marengo, Ia., U.S.	I3	110
Marengo, Il., U.S.	H7	110
Marengo, In., U.S.	D10	114
Marenisco, Mi., U.S.	D6	110
Marfa, Tx., U.S.	I2	116
Margaree, N.S., Can.	F12	106
Margaree Harbour, N.S., Can.	F12	106
Margaret Bay, B.C., Can.	F7	102
Margaretville, N.Y., U.S.	E12	108
Margarita, Isla de, i., Ven.	B10	84
Margarita Belén, Arg.	D9	80
Margate, Eng., U.K.	J15	8
Margate, Fl., U.S.	M6	112
Margate, S. Afr.	H10	66
Margate City, N.J., U.S.	H12	108
Margecany, Slvk.	G21	10
Margherita Peak, mtn., Afr.	A5	58
Marghī, Afg.	C2	44
Margilan, Uzb.	I12	26
Margos, Peru	D3	82
Margot Lake, l., On., Can.	F21	104
Māragow, Dasht-e, des., Afg.	F17	48
Marguerite Bay, b., Ant.	B12	73
Marhanets', Ukr.	H4	26
María Cleofas, Isla, i., Mex.	G6	90
María Elena, Chile	B4	80
Maria Gail, Aus.	I13	10
María Ignacia (Vela), Arg.	I9	80
Maria Island, i., Austl.	N8	70
María la Baja, Col.	C5	84
María Madre, Isla, i., Mex.	G6	90
María Magdalena, Isla, i., Mex.	G6	90
Mariana, Braz.	F7	79
Mariana Islands, is., Oc.	G18	126
Mariana Trench	G18	126
Mariāni, India	G16	44
Marian Lake, l., N.T., Can.	D9	96
Marianna, Ar., U.S.	H6	114
Marianna, Fl., U.S.	I1	112
Mariano I. Loza, Arg.	E9	80
Mariano Moreno, Arg.	J3	80
Mariánské Lázně, Czech Rep.	F12	10
Marias, stm., Mt., U.S.	B15	122
Marías, Islas, is., Mex.	G6	90
Marias Pass, Mt., U.S.	B12	122
María Teresa, Arg.	H8	80
Mariato, Punta, c., Pan.	D2	84
Mā'rib, Yemen	G4	47
Maribor, Slvn.	C10	18
Marica (Évros) (Meriç), stm., Eur.	H10	20
Marico, stm., Afr.	E8	66
Maricopa, Az., U.S.	K4	120
Maricopa, Ca., U.S.	I6	124
Maricunga, Salar de, pl., Chile	D4	80
Marié, stm., Braz.	H9	84
Marie Byrd Land, reg., Ant.	C10	73
Marie-Galante, i., Guad.	G14	94
Mariehamn, Fin.	K16	6
Mari El see Marij El, state, Russia	F7	26
Marie Lake, l., Ab., Can.	D4	104
Marienbad see Mariánské Lázně, Czech Rep.	F12	10
Marienburg see Malbork, Pol.	A19	10
Mariental, Nmb.	E3	66
Marienville, Pa., U.S.	F7	108
Maries, stm., Mo., U.S.	D4	114
Mariestad, Swe.	L13	6
Marieta, stm., Ven.	E9	84
Marietta, Ga., U.S.	F2	112
Marietta, Mn., U.S.	F11	118
Marietta, Oh., U.S.	H5	108
Marietta, Ok., U.S.	F9	116
Marieville, P.Q., Can.	B13	108
Mariga, stm., Nig.	F13	64
Marignane, Fr.	I12	14
Marigot, Dom.	G14	94
Marigot, Guad.	E13	94
Mariinsk, Russia	F9	28
Marijampole, Lith.	G6	22
Marij El, state, Russia	F7	26
Marikana, S. Afr.	E8	66
Marília, Braz.	G4	79
Marimari, stm., Braz.	J13	84
Marimba, Ang.	C3	58
Marín, Spain	C3	16
Marina di Ravenna, Italy	E7	18
Marina Fall, wtfl, Guy.	E13	84
Mar'ina Horka, Bela.	H11	22
Marine City, Mi., U.S.	H13	110
Marinette, Wi., U.S.	E8	110
Maringá, Braz.	G3	79
Maringouin, La., U.S.	L5	114
Marínguè, Moz.	A12	66
Marion, Al., U.S.	J9	114
Marion, Ar., U.S.	G6	114
Marion, Ia., U.S.	H4	110
Marion, Il., U.S.	E8	114
Marion, In., U.S.	B11	114
Marion, Ks., U.S.	M10	118
Marion, Ky., U.S.	E8	114
Marion, La., U.S.	J4	114
Marion, Mi., U.S.	F10	110
Marion, Ms., U.S.	J8	114
Marion, N.C., U.S.	D4	112
Marion, N.D., U.S.	E9	118
Marion, Oh., U.S.	G3	108
Marion, S.C., U.S.	E7	112
Marion, S.D., U.S.	H10	118
Marion, Va., U.S.	C5	112
Marion, Wi., U.S.	F7	110
Marion, Lake, res., S.C., U.S.	F6	112
Marion Junction, Al., U.S.	J9	114
Marion Lake, res., Ks., U.S.	M10	118
Marion Reef, rf., Austl.	B10	70
Marionville, Mo., U.S.	E3	114
Mariópolis, Braz.	D12	80
Maripa, Ven.	D10	84
Mariposa, Ca., U.S.	G6	124
Mariquita, Col.	E5	84
Mariscal Estigarribia, Para.	B8	80
Marissa, Il., U.S.	D7	114
Maritime Alps, mts., Eur.	H14	14
Maritime Atlas see Atlas Tellien, mts., Alg.	C11	62
Mariupol' (Ždanov), Ukr.	H5	26
Mariusa, Caño, mth., Ven.	C12	84
Marīvān, Iran	D9	48
Märjamaa, Est.	C7	22
Marjinsko, Russia	C11	22
Marka, Som.	H9	56
Markala, Mali	E6	64
Markdale, On., Can.	F15	110
Marked Tree, Ar., U.S.	G6	114
Markesan, Wi., U.S.	G7	110
Markham, On., Can.	G16	110
Markham, Tx., U.S.	K10	116
Markham, Mount, mtn., Ant.	D8	73

Name	Map Ref.	Page
Markham Bay, b., N.T., Can.	D18	96
Markle, In., U.S.	B11	114
Markleeville, Ca., U.S.	F6	124
Markovo, Russia	D23	22
Markovo, Russia	E26	28
Marks, Ms., U.S.	H6	114
Marks, Russia	G7	26
Marksville, La., U.S.	K4	114
Marktheidenfeld, Ger.	F9	10
Marktoberdorf, Ger.	H10	10
Marktredwitz, Ger.	E12	10
Mark Twain Lake, res., Mo., U.S.	C5	114
Markundi, Sudan	L2	60
Marlboro, Ab., Can.	D18	102
Marlboro, N.Y., U.S.	F13	108
Marlborough, Austl.	D8	70
Marlborough, Eng., U.K.	J12	8
Marlborough, Guy.	D13	84
Marlborough, Ma., U.S.	E15	108
Marle, Fr.	C10	14
Marlette, Mi., U.S.	G12	110
Marlin, Tx., U.S.	H10	116
Marlinton, W.V., U.S.	I6	108
Marlow, Ok., U.S.	E9	116
Marmaduke, Ar., U.S.	F6	114
Marmande, Fr.	H7	14
Marmara Denizi (Sea of Marmara), Tur.	I12	20
Marmara Ereğlisi, Tur.	I11	20
Marmaris, Tur.	M12	20
Marmarth, N.D., U.S.	E4	118
Marmaton, stm., U.S.	E2	114
Marmelos, Braz.	B11	82
Marmelos, Rio dos, stm., Braz.	B11	82
Marmet, W.V., U.S.	I5	108
Marmora, On., Can.	F18	110
Mar Muerto, Laguna, b., Mex.	I12	90
Marnay, Fr.	E12	14
Marne, Mi., U.S.	G10	110
Marne, dept., Fr.	D11	14
Marne, stm., Fr.	C10	14
Marne au Rhin, Canal de la, Fr.	D13	14
Maroa, Il., U.S.	B8	114
Maroa, Ven.	F9	84
Maroala, Madag.	o22	67b
Maroantsetra, Madag.	o23	67b
Maroelaboom, Nmb.	B4	66
Marolambo, Madag.	r23	67b
Maromme, Fr.	C8	14
Maromokotro, mtn., Madag.	o23	67b
Marondera, Zimb.	B10	66
Maroni, stm., S.A.	C8	76
Maros (Mureș), stm., Eur.	C4	20
Maroseranana, Madag.	q23	67b
Maroua, Cam.	F9	54
Marovato, Madag.	o23	67b
Marovoay, Madag.	p22	67b
Marquand, Mo., U.S.	E6	114
Marquesas Islands see Marquises, Îles, is., Fr. Poly.	I26	126
Marquesas Keys, is., Fl., U.S.	O4	112
Marquette, Ks., U.S.	M10	118
Marquette, Mi., U.S.	D8	110
Marquise, Fr.	B8	14
Marquises, Îles (Marquesas Islands), is., Fr. Poly.	I26	126
Marrah, Jabal, mtn., Sudan	K3	60
Marrakech, Mor.	E6	62
Marrawah, Austl.	M6	70
Marree, Austl.	G3	70
Marrero, La., U.S.	M6	114
Marromeu, Moz.	B12	66
Mars, Pa., U.S.	G6	108
Marsā al-Burayqah, Libya	B4	56
Marsabit, Kenya	H8	56
Marsala, Italy	L7	18
Marsā Maṭrūḥ, Egypt	B4	60
Marsden, Austl.	I7	70
Marseille, Fr.	I12	14
Marseille-en-Beauvaisis, Fr.	C8	14
Marseilles, Il., U.S.	I7	110
Marshall, Ar., U.S.	G4	114
Marshall, Il., U.S.	C9	114
Marshall, Lib.	H4	64
Marshall, Mi., U.S.	H11	110
Marshall, Mn., U.S.	G12	118
Marshall, Mo., U.S.	C3	114
Marshall, N.C., U.S.	D4	112
Marshall, Tx., U.S.	J2	114
Marshall, Va., U.S.	I9	108
Marshallberg, N.C., U.S.	E10	112
Marshall Islands, ctry., Oc.	H20	126
Marshalltown, Ia., U.S.	H3	110
Marshallville, Ga., U.S.	G3	112
Marshfield, Mo., U.S.	E4	114
Marshfield, Wi., U.S.	F5	110
Marsh Harbour, Bah.	A6	94
Mars Hill, N.C., U.S.	D4	112
Marsh Island, i., La., U.S.	M5	114
Marsh Lake, l., Yk., Can.	F27	100
Marsh Peak, mtn., Ut., U.S.	D7	120
Marshville, N.C., U.S.	E6	112
Marsing, Id., U.S.	G9	122
Mart, Tx., U.S.	H10	116
Martaban, Myan.	F4	40
Martaban, Gulf of, b., Myan.	F4	40
Martapura, Indon.	F5	38
Marten Mountain, mtn., Ab., Can.	B20	102
Marte R. Gómez, Presa, res., Mex.	D10	90
Martha's Vineyard, i., Ma., U.S.	F16	108
Martí, Cuba	D6	94
Martigny, Switz.	F7	13
Martigues, Fr.	I12	14
Martil, Mor.	J6	16
Martin, Ky., U.S.	B4	112
Martin, Mi., U.S.	H10	110
Martin, N.D., U.S.	D7	118
Martin, S.D., U.S.	H6	118
Martin, Slvk.	F18	10
Martin, Tn., U.S.	F8	114
Martina Franca, Italy	I12	18
Martindale, Tx., U.S.	J9	116
Martinez, Ca., U.S.	F3	124
Martinez, Ga., U.S.	F4	112
Martínez de la Torre, Mex.	G11	90
Martinho Campos, Braz.	E6	79
Martinique, dep., N.A.	G14	94
Martinique Passage, strt., N.A.	G14	94
Martin Lake, res., Al., U.S.	J11	114
Martinniemi, Fin.	I19	6
Martinsberg, Aus.	G15	10
Martinsburg, Pa., U.S.	G8	108
Martinsburg, W.V., U.S.	H9	108
Martins Ferry, Oh., U.S.	G6	108
Martinsville, Il., U.S.	C9	114
Martinsville, In., U.S.	C10	114
Martinsville, Va., U.S.	C7	112
Martin Vaz, Ilhas, is., Braz.	G12	74
Martisovo, Russia	E14	22
Martos, Spain	H8	16
Martre, Lac la, l., N.T., Can.	D9	96
Martti, Fin.	H21	6
Maru, Nig.	E13	64
Marugame, Japan	M8	36
Marula, Zimb.	C9	66
Marunga, Ang.	A5	66
Marungu, mts., Zaire	C5	58
Ma'rūt, Afg.	E2	44
Marv Dasht, Iran	G12	48
Marvejols, Fr.	H10	14
Marvell, Ar., U.S.	H6	114
Marvine, Mount, mtn., Ut., U.S.	F5	120
Marwayne, Ab., Can.	E4	104
Mary, Turk.	J10	26
Maryborough, Austl.	E10	70
Maryborough, Austl.	K5	70
Marydale, S. Afr.	G6	66
Maryfield, Sk., Can.	I13	104
Mary Kathleen, Austl.	C3	70
Maryland, state, U.S.	D11	98
Maryneal, Tx., U.S.	G6	116
Marys, stm., Nv., U.S.	C10	124
Marystown, Nf., Can.	E18	106
Marysvale, Ut., U.S.	F4	120
Marysville, B.C., Can.	H19	102
Marysville, Ca., U.S.	E4	124
Marysville, Ks., U.S.	L11	118
Marysville, Mi., U.S.	H13	110
Marysville, N.B., Can.	G7	106
Marysville, Oh., U.S.	G3	108
Marysville, Pa., U.S.	G10	108
Marysville, Wa., U.S.	B3	122
Maryville, Mo., U.S.	B2	114
Maryville, Tn., U.S.	D3	112
Marzagão, Braz.	D4	79
Marzo, Punta, c., Col.	D4	84
Marzūq, Libya	C3	56
Marzūq, Ṣaḥrā', des., Libya	D3	56
Masachapa, Nic.	F8	92
Masada see Meẕada, Ḥorvot, hist., Isr.	F4	50
Masagua, Guat.	C4	92
Masai Steppe, plat., Tan.	B7	58
Masaka, Ug.	B6	58
Masallı, Azer.	B10	48
Masan, S. Kor.	H16	32
Masasi, Tan.	D7	58
Masatepe, Nic.	F8	92
Masaya, Nic.	F8	92
Masaya, dept., Nic.	E8	92
Masbate, Phil.	C7	38
Mascarene Islands, is., Afr.	F11	58
Mascasín, Arg.	F5	80
Mascot, Tn., U.S.	C3	112
Mascota, Mex.	G7	90
Mascoutah, Il., U.S.	D7	114
Masefield, Sk., Can.	I7	104
Maseru, Leso.	G8	66
Mashaba Mountains, mts., Zimb.	B10	66
Mashābih, i., Sau. Ar.	I4	48
Mashar, Sudan	M4	60
Mashhad, Iran	C15	48
Mashīz, Iran	G14	48
Māshkel, Hāmūn-i-, l., Pak.	G17	48
Māshkel, Rūd-i- (Māshkīd), stm., Asia	G17	48
Mashra'ur-Raqq, Sudan	M5	60
Masi Manimba, Zaire	B3	58
Maṣīrah, Khalīj, b., Oman	E11	47
Masisea, Peru	C4	82
Masjed-e Soleymān, Iran	F10	48
Mask, Lough, l., Ire.	H4	8
Maska, Nig.	F13	64
Maskanah, Syria	C5	48
Maskin, Oman	C10	47
Maskwa, stm., Mb., Can.	H19	104
Masoala, Madag.	o24	67b
Masoala, Cap, c., Madag.	o24	67b
Masoala, Presqu'île de, pen., Madag.	o24	67b
Masoarivo, Madag.	q21	67b
Masomeloka, Madag.	r23	67b
Mason, Mi., U.S.	H11	110
Mason, Oh., U.S.	H2	108
Mason, Tn., U.S.	G7	114
Mason, Tx., U.S.	I7	116
Mason, W.V., U.S.	H4	108
Mason City, Ia., U.S.	G2	110
Mason City, Il., U.S.	B7	114
Mason City, Ne., U.S.	J8	118
Masqaṭ (Muscat), Oman	C11	47
Massa, Italy	E5	18
Massachusetts, state, U.S.	C12	98
Massachusetts Bay, b., Ma., U.S.	E16	108
Massafra, Italy	I12	18
Massa Marittima, Italy	F5	18
Massangena, Moz.	C11	66
Massarosa, Italy	F5	18
Massena, Ia., U.S.	J13	118
Massena, N.Y., U.S.	C12	108
Massenya, Chad	F4	56
Masset, B.C., Can.	C2	102
Masset Inlet, b., B.C., Can.	D2	102
Masseube, Fr.	I7	14
Massey, On., Can.	D13	110
Massillon, Oh., U.S.	G5	108
Massina, reg., Mali	D7	64
Massinga, Moz.	D12	66
Massive, Mount, mtn., Co., U.S.	E10	120
Mastābah, Sau. Ar.	D1	47
Maştağa, Azer.	I8	26
Masterson, Tx., U.S.	D5	116
Masterton, N.Z.	D5	72
Mastok, Bela.	H13	22
Mastung, Pak.	F2	44
Mastūrah, Sau. Ar.	C1	47
Masty, Bela.	H7	22
Masuda, Japan	M6	36
Masvingo, Zimb.	C10	66
Matachewan, On., Can.	C15	110
Matacuni, stm., Ven.	F10	84
Mata de São João, Braz.	B9	79
Matadi, Zaire	C2	58
Matador, Tx., U.S.	E6	116
Matagalpa, Nic.	E9	92
Matagalpa, dept., Nic.	E9	92
Matagami, P.Q., Can.	G17	96
Matagorda, Tx., U.S.	K11	116
Matagorda Bay, b., Tx., U.S.	K10	116
Matagorda Island, i., Tx., U.S.	K10	116
Matale, Sri L.	I6	46
Matam, Sen.	D3	64
Matama, Cerro, mtn., C.R.	H11	92
Matamoras, Pa., U.S.	F12	108
Matamoros, Mex.	E11	90
Matamoros, Mex.	E8	90
Matane, P.Q., Can.	D6	106
Matanuska, stm., Ak., U.S.	F20	100
Matanzas, Cuba	C4	94
Matanzas, Mex.	G9	90
Matapalo, Cabo, c., C.R.	I11	92
Matape, stm., Mex.	C4	90
Matapédia, P.Q., Can.	E7	106
Matapédia, Lac, l., P.Q., Can.	D6	106
Mataquito, stm., Chile	H3	80
Matará, Peru	B2	82
Matara, Sri L.	J6	46
Mataram, Indon.	G6	38
Matarani, Peru	G5	82
Mataró, Spain	D14	16
Matatiele, S. Afr.	H9	66
Matauá, stm., Braz.	B11	82
Mateare, Nic.	E8	92
Matehuala, Mex.	F9	90
Matera, Italy	I11	18
Mátészalka, Hung.	H22	10
Mateur, Tun.	L4	18
Matewan, W.V., U.S.	B4	112
Mather, Mb., Can.	I15	104
Mather, Pa., U.S.	H6	108
Matheson, On., Can.	B15	110
Matheson Island, Mb., Can.	G18	104
Mathews, Va., U.S.	B10	112
Mathis, Tx., U.S.	K9	116
Mathura, India	G7	44
Matiacoali, Burkina	E10	64
Matias Barbosa, Braz.	F7	79
Matías Romero, Mex.	I12	90
Matícora, stm., Ven.	B7	84
Matignon, Fr.	D4	14
Matiguás, Nic.	E9	92
Matipó, Braz.	F7	79
Matiyure, stm., Ven.	D8	84
Matlamanyane, Bots.	B7	66
M'atlevo, Russia	G18	22
Matmata, Tun.	D15	62
Mato, stm., Ven.	D10	84
Mato, Cerro, mtn., Ven.	D10	84
Matočkin Šar, proliv, strt., Russia	C8	26
Mato Grosso, state, Braz.	D13	82
Mato Grosso, Planalto do, plat., Braz.	G7	76
Matonipi, stm., P.Q., Can.	A4	106
Matopo Hills, hills, Zimb.	C9	66
Matos, stm., Bol.	F9	82
Matosinhos, Port.	D3	16
Matou, Tai.	L9	34
Matoury, Fr. Gu.	C8	76
Matouying, China	D6	32
Mato Verde, Braz.	C7	79
Matozinhos, Braz.	E6	79
Maṭraḥ, Oman	C11	47
Matrei in Osttirol, Aus.	H12	10
Matru, S.L.	H3	64
Matsapha, Swaz.	F10	66
Matsudo, Japan	L14	36
Matsue, Japan	L8	36
Matsumae, Japan	F15	36
Matsumoto, Japan	K12	36
Matsu Tao, i., Tai.	I8	34
Matsuyama, Japan	N7	36
Mattagami, stm., On., Can.	F16	96
Mattagami Heights, On., Can.	B14	110
Mattawa, On., Can.	D17	110
Mattawa, Wa., U.S.	D6	122
Mattawamkeag, Me., U.S.	B18	108
Mattawamkeag, stm., Me., U.S.	B18	108
Matterhorn, mtn., Eur.	G14	14
Matterhorn, mtn., Nv., U.S.	C10	124
Mattersburg, Aus.	H16	10
Matthews Ridge, Guy.	D12	84
Matthew Town, Bah.	D8	94
Maṭṭī, Sabkhat, l., Asia	J12	48
Mattighofen, Aus.	G13	10
Mattoon, Il., U.S.	C8	114
Mattoon, Wi., U.S.	E6	110
Mattydale, N.Y., U.S.	D10	108
Matuba, Moz.	E11	66
Matucana, Peru	D3	82
Maturín, Ven.	C11	84
Maturino, Russia	B20	22
Matutina, Braz.	E6	79
Maú (Ireng), stm., S.A.	E13	84
Maúa, Moz.	D7	58
Maubeuge, Fr.	B10	14
Maud, Ok., U.S.	D10	116
Maud, Tx., U.S.	I2	114
Maude, Austl.	J6	70
Maués, Braz.	I14	84
Maués, stm., Braz.	I14	84
Maui, i., Hi., U.S.	q17	125a
Mauldin, S.C., U.S.	E4	112
Maule, prov., Chile	H2	80
Maule, stm., Chile	H2	80
Maule, Laguna del, l., Chile	I3	80
Mauléon, Fr.	F6	14
Maumee, Oh., U.S.	F3	108
Maumee, stm., U.S.	F2	108
Maun, Bots.	C6	66
Mauna Kea, vol., Hi., U.S.	r18	125a
Maunaloa, Hi., U.S.	p16	125a
Mauna Loa, vol., Hi., U.S.	r18	125a
Maunath Bhanjan, India	H10	44
Maunatlala, Bots.	D8	66
Maungdaw, Myan.	D2	40
Maunoir, Lac, l., N.T., Can.	C32	100
Maupin, Or., U.S.	E4	122
Mau Rānīpur, India	H8	44
Maure-de-Bretagne, Fr.	E5	14
Maurepas, Lake, l., La., U.S.	L6	114
Mauri, stm., Bol.	G7	82
Mauriac, Fr.	G9	14
Mauritania (Mauritanie), ctry., Afr.	D4	54
Mauritius, ctry., Afr.	F11	58
Mauritius, i., Mrts.	v18	67c
Mauron, Fr.	D4	14
Maury Channel, strt., N.T., Can.	A13	96
Mauston, Wi., U.S.	G5	110
Mauterndorf, Aus.	H13	10
Mauthausen, Aus.	G14	10
Mauvezin, Fr.	I7	14
Mavaca, stm., Ven.	F10	84
Maverick, Az., U.S.	K7	120
Mavinga, Ang.	E4	58
Mawchi, Myan.	E4	40
Maw-daung Pass, Asia	I5	40
Mawdesley Lake, l., Mb., Can.	D14	104
Mawkhi, Myan.	F5	40
Mawlaik, Myan.	C3	40
Mawlamyine (Moulmein), Myan.	F4	40
Maw Taung, mtn., Asia	I5	40
Max, N.D., U.S.	D6	118
Maxcanú, Mex.	G15	90
Maxixe, Moz.	D12	66
Maxton, N.C., U.S.	E7	112
Maxville, On., Can.	B12	108
Maxwell, Ca., U.S.	E3	124
Maxwell, Ia., U.S.	I2	110
Maxwell, Ne., U.S.	J7	118
Maxwell, N.M., U.S.	C2	116
Maxwell Bay, b., N.T., Can.	B15	96
May, Tx., U.S.	H8	116
May, stm., Ab., Can.	B23	102
May, Cape, pen., N.J., U.S.	I12	108
May, Mount, mtn., Ab., Can.	C15	102
Mayaguana, i., Bah.	C8	94
Mayaguana Passage, strt., Bah.	C8	94
Mayagüez, P.R.	E11	94
Mayaky, Ukr.	C14	20
Mayales, Punta, c., Nic.	F9	92
Maya Mountains, mts., N.A.	I15	90
Mayapan, hist., Mex.	G15	90
Mayarí, Cuba	D7	94
Maybeury, W.V., U.S.	B5	112
Maybole, Scot., U.K.	F9	8
Mayenne, Fr.	M13	8
Mayenne, dept., Fr.	D6	14
Mayer, Az., U.S.	J4	120
Mayersville, Ms., U.S.	J5	114
Mayerthorpe, Ab., Can.	D19	102
Mayfield, Ky., U.S.	F8	114
Mayfield, Ut., U.S.	E5	120
Mayflower, Ar., U.S.	H4	114
May Inlet, b., N.T., Can.	A12	96
May Jirgui, Niger	E14	64
Maymont, Sk., Can.	F7	104
Maymyo, Myan.	C4	40
Maynard, Ia., U.S.	H4	110
Maynardville, Tn., U.S.	C3	112
Mayne, stm., Austl.	D4	70
Mayo, Fl., U.S.	I3	112
Mayo, Yk., Can.	E27	100
Mayo, co., Ire.	H4	8
Mayo, stm., Col.	G4	84
Mayo, stm., Mex.	D5	90
Mayo, stm., Peru	B3	82
Mayodan, N.C., U.S.	C7	112
Mayo Lake, l., Yk., Can.	E27	100
Mayon Volcano, vol., Phil.	o20	39b
Mayor Buratovich, Arg.	J7	80
Mayor Pablo Lagerenza, Para.	H11	82
Mayotte, dep., Afr.	D9	58
May Pen, Jam.	F6	94
Mayrhofen, Aus.	H11	10
Mays Landing, N.J., U.S.	H12	108
Maysville, Ky., U.S.	I3	108
Maysville, Mo., U.S.	C2	114
Maysville, N.C., U.S.	E9	112
Maysville, Ok., U.S.	E9	116
Mayumba, Gabon	B2	58
Māyūram, India	G5	46
Mayville, Mi., U.S.	G12	110
Mayville, N.D., U.S.	D10	118
Mayville, N.Y., U.S.	E7	108
Mayville, Wi., U.S.	G7	110
Maywood, Ne., U.S.	K7	118
Maza, Arg.	I7	80
Mazabuka, Zam.	E5	58
Mazagan see El-Jadida, Mor.	D6	62
Mazagão, Braz.	D8	76
Mazamet, Fr.	I9	14
Mazán, stm., Peru	I6	84
Mazār, Jabal, mtn., Asia	A6	50
Mazara del Vallo, Italy	L7	18
Mazār-e Sharīf, Afg.	B2	44
Mazaruni, stm., Guy.	E13	84
Mazatenango, Guat.	C3	92
Mazatlán, Mex.	F6	90
Mazatzal Peak, mtn., Az., U.S.	J5	120
Mažeikiai, Lith.	E5	22
Mazenod, Sk., Can.	I8	104
Mazeppa, Mn., U.S.	F3	110
Mazhuang, China	C3	34
Mazirbe, Lat.	D5	22
Mazoe, stm., Afr.	E6	58
Mazomanie, Wi., U.S.	G6	110
Mazon, Il., U.S.	I7	110
Mazsalaca, Lat.	D8	22
Mazunga, Zimb.	C9	66
Mazury, reg., Pol.	B20	10
Mazyr, Bela.	G3	26
Mbabane, Swaz.	F10	66
Mbacké, Sen.	D2	64
Mbage, C.A.R.	O3	60
Mbaïki, C.A.R.	H4	56
Mbala, Zam.	C6	58
Mbale, Ug.	A6	58
Mbalmayo, Cam.	H9	54
Mbamba Bay, Tan.	D6	58
Mbandaka (Coquilhatville), Zaire	A3	58
Mbanga, Cam.	I14	64
M'banza Congo, Ang.	C2	58
Mbanza-Ngungu, Zaire	C2	58
Mbarara, Ug.	B6	58
Mbari, stm., C.A.R.	G5	56
Mbashe, stm., S. Afr.	I9	66
M'bengué, C. Iv.	F7	64
Mbeya, Tan.	C6	58
Mbinda, Congo	B2	58
Mbini, Eq. Gui.	H8	54
Mbomou (Bomu), stm., Afr.	H5	56
Mbonge, Cam.	I14	64
Mboro, Sudan	N5	60
Mbour, Sen.	D1	64
Mbout, Maur.	C3	64
Mbuji-Mayi (Bakwanga), Zaire	C4	58
Mburucuyá, Arg.	E9	80
McAdam, N.B., Can.	G6	106
McAdoo, Pa., U.S.	G11	108
McAlester, Ok., U.S.	E11	116
McAllen, Tx., U.S.	M8	116
McArthur, Oh., U.S.	H4	108
McAuley, Mb., Can.	H13	104
McBain, Mi., U.S.	F10	110
McBee, S.C., U.S.	E6	112
McBeth Fjord, N.T., Can.	C19	96
McBride, B.C., Can.	D14	102
McCall, Id., U.S.	F9	122
McCall Creek, Ms., U.S.	K6	114
McCallum, Nf., Can.	E17	106
McCamey, Tx., U.S.	H4	116
McCammon, Id., U.S.	H13	122
McCauley Island, i., B.C., Can.	D4	102
McCaysville, Ga., U.S.	E2	112
McClarty Lake, l., Mb., Can.	D14	104
McCleary, Wa., U.S.	C2	122
McClellanville, S.C., U.S.	F7	112
McClintock, Mount, mtn., Ant.	D8	73
McCloud, Ca., U.S.	C3	124
McClure, Il., U.S.	E7	114
McClure, Pa., U.S.	G9	108
McClusky, N.D., U.S.	D7	118
McColl, S.C., U.S.	E7	112
McComas, W.V., U.S.	B5	112
McComb, Ms., U.S.	K6	114
McComb, Oh., U.S.	F3	108
McConaughy, Lake, res., Ne., U.S.	J6	118
McConnell Range, mts., N.T., Can.	E33	100
McConnellsburg, Pa., U.S.	H9	108
McConnelsville, Oh., U.S.	H5	108
McCook, Ne., U.S.	K7	118
McCormick, S.C., U.S.	F4	112
McCoy Lake, l., On., Can.	F22	104
McCreary, Mb., Can.	H15	104
McCrory, Ar., U.S.	G5	114
McCune, Ks., U.S.	N12	118
McCurtain, Ok., U.S.	D12	116
McCusker, stm., Sk., Can.	C5	104
McDade, Tx., U.S.	I9	116
McDavid, Fl., U.S.	L9	114
McDermitt, Nv., U.S.	C8	124
McDermott, Oh., U.S.	I3	108
McDonald, Ks., U.S.	L6	118
McDonough, Ga., U.S.	F2	112
Mcensk, Russia	H19	22
McEwen, Tn., U.S.	F9	114
McFadden, Wy., U.S.	C10	120
McFarland, Ca., U.S.	I6	124
McFarland, Wi., U.S.	G6	110
McGavock Lake, l., Mb., Can.	B13	104
McGehee, Ar., U.S.	I5	114
McGill, Nv., U.S.	E11	124
McGrath, Ak., U.S.	E17	100
McGraw, N.Y., U.S.	E10	108
McGregor, Ia., U.S.	G4	110
McGregor, Tx., U.S.	H9	116
McGregor, stm., B.C., Can.	C13	102
McGregor Lake, l., Ab., Can.	G22	102
McGregor Range, mts., Austl.	F5	70
McHenry, Il., U.S.	H7	110
McHenry, Ms., U.S.	L7	114
Mchinji, Mwi.	D6	58
McInnes Lake, l., On., Can.	F21	104
McIntosh, Al., U.S.	K8	114
McIntosh, Mn., U.S.	D12	118
McIntosh, S.D., U.S.	F6	118
McIntosh Lake, l., Sk., Can.	C9	104
McIntyre Bay, b., B.C., Can.	C3	102
McKeand, stm., N.T., Can.	D19	96
McKee, Ky., U.S.	B3	112
McKeesport, Pa., U.S.	G7	108
McKenzie, Al., U.S.	K10	114
McKenzie, Tn., U.S.	F8	114
McKenzie Bridge, Or., U.S.	F3	122
McKenzie Island, On., Can.	G21	104
McKenzie Lake, l., Sk., Can.	D12	104
McKinley, Mount, mtn., Ak., U.S.	E19	100
McKinleyville, Ca., U.S.	D1	124
McKinney, Tx., U.S.	F10	116
McKnight Lake, l., Mb., Can.	B13	104
McLain, Ms., U.S.	K8	114
McLaughlin, S.D., U.S.	F7	118
McLaughlin, stm., Mb., Can.	E18	104
McLaurin, Ms., U.S.	K7	114
McLean, Il., U.S.	B7	114
McLean, Sk., Can.	H10	104
McLean, Tx., U.S.	D6	116
McLean Lake, l., Sk., Can.	B5	104
McLeansboro, Il., U.S.	D8	114
McLennan, Ab., Can.	B18	102
McLeod, stm., Ab., Can.	D19	102
McLeod Bay, b., N.T., Can.	D10	96
McLeod Lake, B.C., Can.	C11	102
M'Clintock Channel, strt., N.T., Can.	B12	96
McLoughlin, Mount, mtn., Or., U.S.	H3	122
McLoughlin Bay, b., N.T., Can.	C13	96
McLouth, Ks., U.S.	L12	118
McLure, B.C., Can.	F14	102
M'Clure Strait, strt., N.T., Can.	B9	96
McMahon, Sk., Can.	H7	104
McMillan, Lake, res., N.M., U.S.	G2	116
McMinnville, Or., U.S.	E2	122
McMinnville, Tn., U.S.	G11	114
McMurdo, sci., Ant.	C8	73
McMurdo Sound, strt., Ant.	C8	73
McNary, Az., U.S.	J7	120
McNeil, Ar., U.S.	I3	114
McNeil, Mount, mtn., B.C., Can.	C4	102
McNeill, Ms., U.S.	L7	114
McPhail, stm., Mb., Can.	F19	104
McPherson, Ks., U.S.	M10	118
McPherson Range, mts., Austl.	G10	70
McQueeney, Tx., U.S.	J8	116
McRae, Ar., U.S.	G5	114
McRae, Ga., U.S.	G4	112
McRoberts, Ky., U.S.	B4	112
McVeigh, Ky., U.S.	B4	112
McVille, N.D., U.S.	D9	118
McWilliams, Al., U.S.	K9	114
M'Daourouch, Alg.	M2	18
Meacham, Sk., Can.	F9	104
Mead, Ne., U.S.	J11	118
Mead, Lake, res., U.S.	H2	120
Meade, Ks., U.S.	N7	118
Meaden Peak, mtn., Co., U.S.	D9	120
Meadow, Tx., U.S.	F4	116
Meadow, Ut., U.S.	F4	120
Meadow Lake, Sk., Can.	D6	104
Meadow Lake, l., Sk., Can.	D6	104
Meadow Lake Provincial Park, Sk., Can.	D5	104
Meadowview, Va., U.S.	C5	112
Meadville, Mo., U.S.	C3	114
Meadville, Ms., U.S.	K6	114
Meadville, Pa., U.S.	F6	108
Meaford, On., Can.	F15	110
Meaghers Grant, N.S., Can.	H10	106
Méan, Bel.	H7	12
Meana, Turk.	C16	48
Meandarra, Austl.	F8	70
Meander River, Ab., Can.	E9	96
Meath, co., Ire.	H7	8
Meath, hist. reg., Ire.	H6	8
Meaux, Fr.	D9	14
Mebane, N.C., U.S.	C7	112
Mecaya, stm., Col.	G5	84
Mecca see Makkah, Sau. Ar.	D1	47
Mechanic Falls, Me., U.S.	C16	108
Mechanicsburg, Oh., U.S.	G3	108
Mechanicsville, Ia., U.S.	I4	110
Mechanicsville, Va., U.S.	B9	112
Mechanicville, N.Y., U.S.	E13	108
Mechelen (Malines), Bel.	F5	12
Mechita, Arg.	H8	80
Mechra Safsaf, Mor.	K9	16
Mechriyya, Alg.	D10	62
Mechroha, Alg.	M2	18
Mecklenburg, hist. reg., Ger.	B12	10
Mecklenburger Bucht, b., Ger.	A11	10
Mecklenburg-Vorpommern, state, Ger.	B12	10
Meda, Port.	E4	16
Medan, Indon.	M5	40
Médanos, Arg.	J7	80
Medanosa, Punta, c., Arg.	F3	78
Medaryville, In., U.S.	A10	114
Mede, Italy	D3	18
Medeiros Neto, Braz.	D8	79
Medellín, Col.	D5	84
Médenine, Tun.	D16	62
Mederdra, Maur.	C2	64
Medford, Ok., U.S.	C9	116
Medford, Or., U.S.	H3	122
Medford, Wi., U.S.	E5	110
Medgidia, Rom.	E12	20
Mediapolis, Ia., U.S.	I4	110
Mediaș, Rom.	C8	20
Medical Lake, Wa., U.S.	C8	122
Medicina, Italy	E6	18
Medicine Bow, Wy., U.S.	C10	120
Medicine Bow, stm., Wy., U.S.	B10	120
Medicine Bow Mountains, mts., U.S.	C10	120
Medicine Bow Peak, mtn., Wy., U.S.	C10	120
Medicine Hat, Ab., Can.	H4	104
Medicine Lake, Mt., U.S.	C3	118
Medicine Lodge, Ks., U.S.	N9	118
Medicine Lodge, stm., U.S.	B8	116
Medina, Braz.	D8	79
Medina, N.D., U.S.	E8	118
Medina, N.Y., U.S.	D8	108
Medina, Oh., U.S.	F5	108
Medina see Al-Madīnah, Sau. Ar.	B1	47
Medina, Tx., U.S.	J7	116
Medina, stm., Tx., U.S.	J8	116
Medina del Campo, Spain	D7	16
Medininkai, Lith.	G8	22
Medinīpur, India	I12	44
Medio, Punta, c., Chile	D3	80
Mediterranean Sea	E9	52
Medjerda, Monts de la, mts., Afr.	M3	18
Mednogorsk, Russia	G9	26
Mednoje, Russia	E18	22
Mednyj, ostrov, i., Russia	G25	28
Médoc, reg., Fr.	G6	14
Medora, In., U.S.	D10	114
Medora, N.D., U.S.	E4	118
Médouneu, Gabon	A2	58
Medstead, Sk., Can.	E6	104
Meductic, N.B., Can.	F6	106
Medveđa, Yugo.	G5	20
Medvedevskoje, Russia	C18	22
Medvedica, stm., Russia	G6	26
Medvežjegorsk, Russia	E4	26
Medvežji ostrova, is., Russia	C24	28
Medway, stm., N.S., Can.	H9	106
Medyn', Russia	G18	22
Meekatharra, Austl.	E3	68
Meeker, Co., U.S.	D9	120
Meeks Bay, Ca., U.S.	E5	124
Meelpaeg Lake, res., Nf., Can.	D17	106
Meer, Bel.	F6	12
Meerane, Ger.	E12	10
Meerut, India	F7	44
Meeteetse, Wy., U.S.	F17	122
Mega, Eth.	H8	56
Mégantic, Lac, l., P.Q., Can.	B16	108
Mégara, Grc.	K7	20
Megargel, Tx., U.S.	F8	116
Meghālaya, state, India	H14	44
Meghna, stm., Bngl.	H14	44
Mehadia, Rom.	E6	20
Mehar, Pak.	G2	44
Mehdia, Alg.	C11	62
Mehedinți, co., Rom.	E6	20
Meherrin, stm., U.S.	C9	112
Mehrān, Iran	E9	48
Meia Ponte, Rio da, stm., Braz.	D4	79
Meigs, Ga., U.S.	H2	112
Meiktila, Myan.	D3	40
Meilie, China	I6	34
Meiners Oaks, Ca., U.S.	J6	124
Meiningen, Ger.	E10	10
Meiringen, Switz.	E9	13
Meissen, Ger.	D13	10
Meixian, China	K5	34
Meiyino, Sudan	N8	60
Meizhai, China	B10	40
Mejerda, Oued (Oued Medjerda), stm., Afr.	M4	18
Mejez el Bab, Tun.	M4	18
Mejicanos, El Sal.	D5	92
Mejillones, Chile	B3	80
Mejillones, Península, pen., Chile	B3	80
Mejillones del Sur, Bahía de, b., Chile	B3	80
Mékambo, Gabon	A2	58
Mekele, Eth.	K10	60
Meknès, Mor.	D8	62
Mekong, stm., Asia	H8	40
Mekoryuk, Ak., U.S.	F11	100
Mékrou, stm., Afr.	F7	54
Melado, stm., Chile	H3	80
Melaka, Malay.	M7	40
Melanesia, is., Oc.	I19	126
Melbourne, Ar., U.S.	F5	114
Melbourne, Austl.	K6	70
Melbourne, Fl., U.S.	K6	112
Melbourne, Ia., U.S.	I2	110
Melbourne Island, i., N.T., Can.	C12	96
Melby House, Scot., U.K.	A12	8
Melcher, Ia., U.S.	I2	110
Melchor Múzquiz, Mex.	D9	90
Meldorf, Ger.	A9	10
Meldrum Bay, On., Can.	E12	110
Meldrum Creek, B.C., Can.	E12	102
Melechovo, Russia	E24	22
Melegnano, Italy	D4	18
Melenki, Russia	F24	22
Meleuz, Russia	G9	26
Mélèzes, Rivière aux, stm., P.Q., Can.	E18	96
Melfi, Chad	F4	56
Melfi, Italy	H10	18
Melfort, Sk., Can.	F10	104
Melgaço, Port.	C3	16
Melgar, Col.	E5	84
Melghir, Chott, l., Alg.	C14	62
Melhus, Nor.	J12	6
Meli, stm., Afr.	G4	64
Meliane, Oued, stm., Tun.	M5	18
Melide, Switz.	G10	13
Melilla, Sp. N. Afr.	C9	62
Melincué, Arg.	G8	80
Melipilla, Chile	G3	80
Melita, Mb., Can.	I13	104
Melitopol', Ukr.	F15	4
Mellègue, Oued, stm., Afr.	M3	18
Mellen, Wi., U.S.	D5	110
Mellette, S.D., U.S.	F9	118
Mělník, Czech Rep.	E14	10
Mel'nytsya-Podil's'ka, Ukr.	A10	20
Melo, Ur.	G11	80
Melo, stm., Para.	I12	82
Melong, Cam.	I14	64
Melos see Mílos, i., Grc.	M8	20
Melrose, Mn., U.S.	F13	118
Melrose, N.M., U.S.	E3	116
Melrose, Wi., U.S.	F5	110
Melstone, Mt., U.S.	D18	122
Melton Mowbray, Eng., U.K.	I13	8
Melúa, Col.	F6	84
Melun, Fr.	D9	14
Melun, Myan.	D2	40
Melvern, Ks., U.S.	M12	118
Melville, La., U.S.	L5	114
Melville, Sk., Can.	H12	104
Melville, Détroit de see Viscount Melville Sound, strt., N.T., Can.	B11	96
Melville, Lake, l., Nf., Can.	F21	96
Melville Bugt, b., Grnld.	B13	86
Melville Hills, hills, N.T., Can.	B33	100
Melville Island, i., Austl.	B6	68
Melville Island, i., N.T., Can.	B8	86
Melville Peninsula, pen., N.T., Can.	C16	96

Name	Map Ref.	Page
Melville Sound, strt., N.T., Can.	C11	96
Melvin, Il., U.S.	J7	110
Melvin, Ky., U.S.	B4	112
Melvin, Tx., U.S.	H7	116
Melvin, Lough, l., Eur.	G5	8
Melvin Lake, l., Mb., Can.	A14	104
Melyana, Alg.	B12	62
Melzo, Italy	D4	18
Memel, S. Afr.	F9	66
Memel see Nemunas, stm., Eur.	F6	22
Memmingen, Ger.	H10	10
Memo, stm., Ven.	C9	84
Mémót, Camb.	I9	40
Mempawah, Indon.	N10	40
Memphis, Fl., U.S.	L4	112
Memphis, Mi., U.S.	H13	110
Memphis, Mo., U.S.	B4	114
Memphis, Tn., U.S.	G6	114
Memphis, Tx., U.S.	E6	116
Memphremagog, Lake, l., N.A.	B14	108
Mena, Ar., U.S.	H2	114
Menahga, Mn., U.S.	E12	118
Ménaka, Mali	D11	64
Menaldum, Neth.	B8	12
Menan, Id., U.S.	G14	122
Menard, Tx., U.S.	I7	116
Menasha, Wi., U.S.	F7	110
Menawashei, Sudan	K3	60
Mendawai, stm., Indon.	F5	38
Mende, Fr.	H10	14
Mendenhall, Ms., U.S.	K7	114
Méndez, Mex.	E10	90
Mendi, Eth.	M8	60
Mendi, Pap. N. Gui.	G11	38
Mendocino, Ca., U.S.	E2	124
Mendocino, Cape, c., Ca., U.S.	D1	124
Mendon, Il., U.S.	B5	114
Mendon, Mi., U.S.	H10	110
Mendota, Ca., U.S.	H5	124
Mendota, Il., U.S.	I6	110
Mendoza, Arg.	G4	80
Mendoza, Peru	B3	82
Mendoza, prov., Arg.	H4	80
Mendoza, stm., Arg.	G4	80
Ménéac, Fr.	D4	14
Mene de Mauroa, Ven.	B7	84
Mene Grande, Ven.	C7	84
Menemen, Tur.	K11	20
Menen (Menin), Bel.	G3	12
Menfi, Italy	L7	18
Mengcheng, China	E10	30
Menggala, Indon.	F4	38
Menggu, China	A7	40
Menghai, China	C6	40
Mengla, China	D6	40
Mengzhi, China	B5	40
Mengzi, China	C7	40
Menihek Lakes, l., Nf., Can.	F19	96
Menindee, Austl.	I5	70
Menindee Lake, l., Austl.	I5	70
Menlo Park, Ca., U.S.	G3	124
Menno, S.D., U.S.	H10	118
Meno, Ok., U.S.	C8	116
Menominee, Mi., U.S.	E8	110
Menominee, stm., U.S.	E8	110
Menomonee Falls, Wi., U.S.	G7	110
Menomonie, Wi., U.S.	F4	110
Menongue, Ang.	D3	58
Menorca, i., Spain	F16	16
Mens, Fr.	H12	14
Mentasta Mountains, mts., Ak., U.S.	E23	100
Mentawai, Kepulauan, is., Indon.	F2	38
Mentawai, Selat, strt., Indon.	F3	38
Menton, Fr.	I14	14
Mentone, Tx., U.S.	H3	116
Mentor, Oh., U.S.	F5	108
Menzel Bourguiba, Tun.	L4	18
Menzel Bou Zelfa, Tun.	M5	18
Menzel Djemil, Tun.	L4	18
Menzel Temime, Tun.	M5	18
Menzies, Austl.	E4	68
Menzies, Mount, mtn., Ant.	C5	73
Meoqui, Mex.	C7	90
Meota, Sk., Can.	E6	104
Meppel, Neth.	C9	12
Meppen, Ger.	C7	10
Meqerghane, Sebkha, pl., Alg.	G11	62
Mequon, Wi., U.S.	G8	110
Mer, Fr.	E8	14
Meramec, stm., Mo., U.S.	D5	114
Merano (Meran), Italy	C6	18
Merasheen, Nf., Can.	E19	106
Merasheen Island, i., Nf., Can.	E19	106
Merate, Italy	D4	18
Merauke, Indon.	G11	38
Mercaderes, Col.	G4	84
Mercāra, India	F3	46
Merced, Ca., U.S.	G5	124
Merced, stm., Ca., U.S.	G5	124
Mercedario, Cerro, mtn., Arg.	F3	80
Mercedes, Arg.	H9	80
Mercedes, Arg.	E9	80
Mercedes, Arg.	G6	80
Mercedes, Tx., U.S.	M9	116
Mercedes, Ur.	G9	80
Mercer, Mo., U.S.	B3	114
Mercer, Pa., U.S.	F6	108
Mercer, Wi., U.S.	D5	110
Mercersburg, Pa., U.S.	H9	108
Merchants Bay, b., N.T., Can.	C20	96
Merchtem, Bel.	G5	12
Mercoal, Ab., Can.	D17	102
Mercury, Nv., U.S.	H10	124
Mercy, Cape, c., N.T., Can.	D20	96
Mercy Bay, b., N.T., Can.	B9	96
Meredith, N.H., U.S.	D15	108
Meredith, Lake, res., Tx., U.S.	D5	116
Meredosia, Il., U.S.	C6	114
Mereeg, Som.	H10	56
Merenkurkku (Norra Kvarken), strt., Eur.	J17	6
Merevari, stm., Ven.	E10	84
Merewa, Eth.	N9	60
Mergui (Myeik), Myan.	H5	40
Mergui Archipelago, is., Myan.	H5	40
Meriç (Marica) (Évros), stm., Eur.	H10	20
Mérida, Mex.	G15	90
Mérida, Spain	G5	16
Mérida, Ven.	C7	84
Mérida, state, Ven.	C7	84
Mérida, Cordillera de, mts., Ven.	C7	84
Meriden, Ct., U.S.	F14	108
Meridian, Ga., U.S.	H5	112
Meridian, Id., U.S.	G9	122
Meridian, Ms., U.S.	J8	114
Meridian, Tx., U.S.	H9	116
Meridianville, Al., U.S.	H10	114
Mérignac, Fr.	H6	14
Merigold, Ms., U.S.	I6	114
Merimbula, Austl.	K8	70
Merín, Laguna (Lagoa Mirim), b., S.A.	G12	80
Merino, Co., U.S.	K4	118
Merinos, Ur.	G10	80
Merkel, Tx., U.S.	G6	116
Merkendorf, Ger.	F10	10
Merkinė, Lith.	G7	22
Merkulavičy, Bela.	I13	22
Merlin, On., Can.	H13	110
Merlin, Or., U.S.	H2	122
Merlo, Arg.	G6	80
Merna, Ne., U.S.	J8	118
Mernye, Hung.	I17	10
Meron, Hare, mtn., Isr.	C4	50
Merredin, Austl.	F3	68
Merrickville, On., Can.	C11	108
Merrill, Ia., U.S.	I11	118
Merrill, Mi., U.S.	G11	110
Merrill, Or., U.S.	H4	122
Merrill, Wi., U.S.	E6	110
Merrillan, Wi., U.S.	F5	110
Merrillville, In., U.S.	A9	114
Merrimack, stm., U.S.	D15	108
Merriman, Ne., U.S.	I6	118
Merritt, B.C., Can.	G14	102
Merritt Island, Fl., U.S.	K6	112
Merriwa, Austl.	I9	70
Mer Rouge, La., U.S.	J5	114
Merryville, La., U.S.	L3	114
Mersch, Lux.	I9	12
Merseburg, Ger.	D11	10
Mersey, stm., Austl.	M7	70
Mersey, stm., N.S., Can.	H9	106
Mersing, Malay.	M7	40
Mērsrags, Lat.	D6	22
Merthyr Tydfil, Wales, U.K.	J10	8
Mértola, Port.	H4	16
Mertzon, Tx., U.S.	H6	116
Méru, Fr.	C9	14
Meru, Kenya	A7	58
Meru, Mount, mtn., Tan.	B7	58
Mervin, Sk., Can.	E6	104
Mëry, Bela.	F10	22
Méry, Fr.	D10	14
Merzig, Ger.	F6	10
Mesa, Az., U.S.	K5	120
Mesa, stm., Spain	D10	16
Mesabi Range, hills, Mn., U.S.	C3	110
Mesagne, Italy	I12	18
Mesa Mountain, mtn., Co., U.S.	G10	120
Mesa Verde National Park, Co., U.S.	G8	120
Mescalero, N.M., U.S.	K11	120
Meschede, Ger.	D8	10
Meščovsk, Russia	G18	22
Mesfinto, Eth.	K9	60
Mesgouez, Lac, l., P.Q., Can.	F17	96
Meshgīn Shahr, Iran	B9	48
Mesick, Mi., U.S.	F10	110
Mesilinka, stm., B.C., Can.	A10	102
Mesilla, N.M., U.S.	L10	120
Meskiana, Alg.	C14	62
Meslay-du-Maine, Fr.	E6	14
Mesocco, Switz.	F11	13
Mesolóngion, Grc.	K5	20
Mesopotamia, hist. reg., Asia	D8	48
Mesquita, Braz.	E7	79
Mesquite, Nv., U.S.	H11	124
Mesquite, Tx., U.S.	G10	116
Messalo, stm., Moz.	D7	58
Messina, Italy	K10	18
Messina, S. Afr.	D10	66
Messina, Stretto di, strt., Italy	K10	18
Messíni, Grc.	L6	20
Messiniakós Kólpos, b., Grc.	M6	20
Messix Peak, mtn., Ut., U.S.	C4	120
Messojacha, stm., Russia	D13	26
Mestá, Grc.	K9	20
Mesta (Néstos), stm., Eur.	H7	20
Mestasa, Mor.	C8	62
Mestghanem, Alg.	C11	62
Mestre, Italy	D7	18
Meszah Peak, mtn., B.C., Can.	G29	100
Meta, dept., Col.	F6	84
Meta, stm., S.A.	D9	84
Meta Incognita Peninsula, pen., N.T., Can.	D19	96
Metairie, La., U.S.	M6	114
Metaline Falls, Wa., U.S.	B8	122
Metamora, Il., U.S.	J6	110
Metán, Arg.	C6	80
Metapán, El Sal.	C5	92
Meteghan, N.S., Can.	H7	106
Metema, Eth.	K9	60
Meteor Crater, crat., Az., U.S.	I5	120
Methóni, Grc.	M5	20
Methow, stm., Wa., U.S.	B5	122
Metiskow, Ab., Can.	F4	104
Metković, Cro.	F12	18
Metlakatla, Ak., U.S.	I29	100
Metlakatla, B.C., Can.	C4	102
Metlaoui, Tun.	C15	62
Metlatonoc, Mex.	I10	90
Meto, Bayou, stm., Ar., U.S.	H5	114
Metolius, stm., Or., U.S.	F4	122
Metropolis, Il., U.S.	E8	114
Metropolitan, Mi., U.S.	D8	110
Metsematluku, Bots.	E7	66
Metter, Ga., U.S.	G4	112
Mettuppālaiyam, India	G4	46
Mettūr, India	G4	46
Metu, Eth.	M8	60
Metulla, Isr.	B5	50
Metz, Fr.	C13	14
Meulan, Fr.	C8	14
Meureudu, Indon.	L4	40
Meurthe, stm., Fr.	D13	14
Meurthe-et-Moselle, dept., Fr.	D13	14
Meuse, dept., Fr.	D12	14
Meuse (Maas), stm., Eur.	E5	10
Meuselwitz, Ger.	D12	10
Mexia, Tx., U.S.	H10	116
Mexiana, Ilha, i., Braz.	D9	76
Mexicali, Mex.	A2	90
Mexican Hat, Ut., U.S.	G7	120
Mexico, Me., U.S.	C16	108
Mexico, Mo., U.S.	C5	114
Mexico, N.Y., U.S.	D10	108
México, state, Mex.	H10	90
Mexico (México), ctry., N.A.	F9	90
Mexico, Gulf of, b., N.A.	C6	88
Mexico Beach, Fl., U.S.	J1	112
Mexico City see Ciudad de México, Mex.	H10	90
Meximieux, Fr.	G12	14
Meycauayan, Phil.	n19	39b
Meyers Chuck, Ak., U.S.	I28	100
Meyersdale, Pa., U.S.	H7	108
Meyísti, i., Grc.	H13	4
Meymac, Fr.	G9	14
Meymaneh, Afg.	C1	44
Meymeh, stm., Asia	E9	48
Meyrargues, Fr.	I12	14
Meyronne, Sk., Can.	I8	104
Meẕada, Ḥorvot (Masada), hist., Isr.	F4	50
Mezapa, Hond.	B7	92
Mezcala, Mex.	I10	90
Mezcalapa, stm., Mex.	I13	90
Meždurečensk, Russia	G9	28
Mèze, Fr.	I10	14
Mezen', Russia	D6	26
Mezen', stm., Russia	D6	26
Meziadin Lake, l., B.C., Can.	A5	102
Mézin, Fr.	H7	14
Mezinovskij, Russia	F23	22
Mezőberény, Hung.	I21	10
Mezőcsát, Hung.	H20	10
Mezőkovácsháza, Hung.	I20	10
Mezőkövesd, Hung.	H20	10
Mezőtúr, Hung.	H20	10
Mezquital, Mex.	F7	90
Mezquital, stm., Mex.	F7	90
Mglin, Russia	H15	22
M'Goun, Irhil, mtn., Mor.	E7	62
Mhow, India	I6	44
Miahuatlán de Porfirio Díaz, Mex.	I11	90
Miajadas, Spain	F6	16
Miami, Az., U.S.	K6	120
Miami, Fl., U.S.	N6	112
Miami, Mb., Can.	I16	104
Miami, Ok., U.S.	C12	116
Miami, Tx., U.S.	D6	116
Miami Beach, Fl., U.S.	N6	112
Miami Canal, Fl., U.S.	M6	112
Miamisburg, Oh., U.S.	H2	108
Miami Springs, Fl., U.S.	N6	112
Mīāndoāb, Iran	C9	48
Miandrivazo, Madag.	q21	67b
Mīāneh, Iran	C9	48
Miangas, Pulau, i., Indon.	D8	38
Mianhu, China	L5	34
Miānwāli, Pak.	D4	44
Mianyang, China	E7	30
Mianyang, China	E2	34
Miaoli, Tai.	K9	34
Miarinavaratra, Madag.	r22	67b
Miass, Russia	G10	26
Miastko, Pol.	A17	10
Micanopy, Fl., U.S.	J4	112
Micaúne, Moz.	B13	66
Michajlov, Russia	G22	22
Michajlovka, Russia	G6	26
Michaud, Point, c., N.S., Can.	G13	106
Micheal Peak, mtn., B.C., Can.	D8	102
Michel, B.C., Can.	H20	102
Miches, Dom. Rep.	E10	94
Michigamme, stm., Mi., U.S.	D7	110
Michigan, N.D., U.S.	C9	118
Michigan, state, U.S.	C9	98
Michigan, Lake, l., U.S.	F8	110
Michigan Center, Mi., U.S.	H11	110
Michigan City, In., U.S.	A10	114
Michipicoten Island, i., On., Can.	C10	110
Michnevo, Russia	F20	22
Michoacán, state, Mex.	H9	90
Mico, stm., Nic.	E10	92
Mico, Montañas del, mts., Guat.	B6	92
Micronesia, is., Oc.	G19	126
Micronesia, Federated States of, ctry., Oc.	H19	126
Mičurinsk, Russia	I23	22
Midale, Sk., Can.	I11	104
Midar, Mor.	C9	62
Mid-Atlantic Ridge	F9	128
Middelburg, Neth.	E4	12
Middelburg, S. Afr.	H7	66
Middelburg, S. Afr.	E9	66
Middelfart, Den.	N11	6
Middelharnis, Neth.	E5	12
Middelpos, S. Afr.	H5	66
Middelwater, S. Afr.	D10	66
Middenmeer, Neth.	C7	12
Middle, stm., B.C., Can.	B9	102
Middle, stm., Ia., U.S.	A2	114
Middle America Trench	H10	86
Middle Andaman, i., India	H2	40
Middle-Bay, P.Q., Can.	A16	106
Middleboro, Ma., U.S.	F16	108
Middlebourne, W.V., U.S.	H6	108
Middlebro, Mb., Can.	I19	104
Middle Brook, Nf., Can.	D19	106
Middleburg, N.Y., U.S.	E12	108
Middleburg, Pa., U.S.	G9	108
Middlebury, Vt., U.S.	C13	108
Middle Caicos, i., T./C. Is.	D9	94
Middle Channel, mth., N.T., Can.	B27	100
Middle Fabius, stm., Mo., U.S.	C4	114
Middlefield, Oh., U.S.	F5	108
Middle Loup, stm., Ne., U.S.	J8	118
Middle Musquodoboit, N.S., Can.	G10	106
Middle Point, Oh., U.S.	G2	108
Middleport, Oh., U.S.	H4	108
Middlesboro, Ky., U.S.	C3	112
Middlesbrough, Eng., U.K.	G12	8
Middlesex, Belize	I15	90
Middlesex, N.C., U.S.	D8	112
Middle Stewiacke, N.S., Can.	G10	106
Middleton, Mi., U.S.	G11	110
Middleton, N.S., Can.	H8	106
Middleton, Tn., U.S.	G8	114
Middleton, Wi., U.S.	G6	110
Middleton Island, i., Ak., U.S.	G21	100
Middletown, Ca., U.S.	F3	124
Middletown, Ct., U.S.	F14	108
Middletown, De., U.S.	H11	108
Middletown, Il., U.S.	B7	114
Middletown, In., U.S.	B11	114
Middletown, Ky., U.S.	D11	114
Middletown, Md., U.S.	H9	108
Middletown, N.Y., U.S.	F12	108
Middletown, Oh., U.S.	H2	108
Middletown, Pa., U.S.	G10	108
Middletown, R.I., U.S.	F15	108
Middletown, Va., U.S.	H8	108
Middleville, Mi., U.S.	H10	110
Midelt, Mor.	D8	62
Midgic, N.B., Can.	G9	106
Mid Glamorgan, co., Wales, U.K.	J10	8
Midi, Canal du, Fr.	I9	14
Midi de Bigorre, Pic du, mtn., Fr.	J7	14
Midland, Ca., U.S.	K11	124
Midland, Mi., U.S.	G11	110
Midland, N.C., U.S.	D6	112
Midland, On., Can.	F16	110
Midland, S.D., U.S.	G6	118
Midland, Tx., U.S.	H4	116
Midlothian, Tx., U.S.	G10	116
Midnapore, Ab., Can.	G20	102
Midongy Sud, Madag.	s22	67b
Miduzhen, China	B6	40
Midvale, Id., U.S.	F9	122
Midville, Ga., U.S.	G4	112
Midway, Al., U.S.	J11	114
Midway, B.C., Can.	H16	102
Midway, Ky., U.S.	I2	108
Midway, Tx., U.S.	H11	116
Midway, Ut., U.S.	D5	120
Midway Islands, dep., Oc.	F22	126
Midway Park, N.C., U.S.	E9	112
Midwest, Wy., U.S.	A10	120
Midwest City, Ok., U.S.	D9	116
Midyat, Tur.	C6	48
Midžor (Midžur), mtn., Eur.	F6	20
Miechów, Pol.	E20	10
Międzychód, Pol.	C15	10
Międzyrzec Podlaski, Pol.	C22	10
Międzyrzecz, Pol.	C15	10
Miélan, Fr.	I7	14
Mielec, Pol.	E21	10
Mier, Mex.	D10	90
Miercurea-Ciuc, Rom.	C9	20
Mieres, Spain	B6	16
Mier y Noriega, Mex.	F9	90
Miesbach, Ger.	H11	10
Mifflinburg, Pa., U.S.	G9	108
Migdal, Isr.	C5	50
Miguel Alemán, Presa, res., Mex.	H11	90
Miguel Auza, Mex.	E8	90
Miguel de la Borda, Pan.	H14	92
Miguel Hidalgo, Presa, res., Mex.	D5	90
Miguelópolis, Braz.	F4	79
Miguel Riglos, Arg.	I7	80
Miḫanavičy, Bela.	H10	22
Mihara, Japan	M8	36
Mijdaḥah, Yemen	G6	47
Mikaševičy, Bela.	I10	22
Mikhrot Shelomo Hamelekh (Timna') (King Solomon's Mines), hist., Isr.	I3	50
Mikkeli, Fin.	K20	6
Mikkelin lääni, prov., Fin.	J20	6
Mikkwa, stm., Ab., Can.	E10	96
Mikołajki, Pol.	B21	10
Mikołów, Pol.	E18	10
Míkonos, Grc.	L9	20
Mikun', Russia	E8	26
Milaca, Mn., U.S.	E2	110
Milagro, Ec.	I3	84
Milan, Ga., U.S.	G3	112
Milan, In., U.S.	C11	114
Milan see Milano, Italy	D4	18
Milan, Mi., U.S.	H12	110
Milan, Mn., U.S.	F12	118
Milan, Mo., U.S.	B3	114
Milan, N.M., U.S.	I9	120
Milan, Tn., U.S.	G8	114
Milano (Milan), Italy	D4	18
Milano, Tx., U.S.	I10	116
Milanoa, Madag.	n23	67b
Milazzo, Italy	K10	18
Milbank, S.D., U.S.	F11	118
Milbanke Sound, strt., B.C., Can.	E6	102
Milburn, Ok., U.S.	E10	116
Milden, Sk., Can.	G7	104
Mildmay, On., Can.	F14	110
Mildred, Pa., U.S.	F10	108
Mildura, Austl.	J5	70
Mile, China	B7	40
Miles, Austl.	F9	70
Miles, Tx., U.S.	H6	116
Miles City, Mt., U.S.	D20	122
Mile Seven Hundred Thirty Three, Yk., Can.	F29	100
Milestone, Sk., Can.	H10	104
Milevsko, Czech Rep.	F14	10
Milford, Ct., U.S.	F13	108
Milford, De., U.S.	I11	108
Milford, Ia., U.S.	H12	118
Milford, Il., U.S.	J8	110
Milford, In., U.S.	A11	114
Milford, Ma., U.S.	E15	108
Milford, Me., U.S.	C18	108
Milford, Mi., U.S.	H12	110
Milford, N.H., U.S.	E15	108
Milford, N.J., U.S.	G11	108
Milford, Pa., U.S.	F12	108
Milford, Ut., U.S.	F3	120
Milford Center, Oh., U.S.	G3	108
Milford Haven, Wales, U.K.	J8	8
Milford Station, N.S., Can.	G10	106
Milḥ, Baḥr al-, l., Iraq	E7	48
Milicz, Pol.	D17	10
Milk, stm., N.A.	B19	122
Mil'kovo, Russia	G23	28
Milk River, Ab., Can.	H22	102
Milk River Ridge Reservoir, res., Ab., Can.	H22	102
Millard, Ne., U.S.	J11	118
Millau, Fr.	H10	14
Millboro, Va., U.S.	B7	112
Millbrook, N.Y., U.S.	F13	108
Millbrook, On., Can.	F17	110
Mill City, Or., U.S.	F3	122
Millcreek, Pa., U.S.	E6	108
Millcreek, Ut., U.S.	D5	120
Mill Creek, W.V., U.S.	I7	108
Milledgeville, Ga., U.S.	F3	112
Milledgeville, Il., U.S.	I6	110
Mille Lacs, Lac des, l., On., Can.	B5	110
Mille Lacs Lake, l., Mn., U.S.	D2	110
Millen, Ga., U.S.	G5	112
Miller, Mo., U.S.	E3	114
Miller, S.D., U.S.	G9	118
Miller Mountain, mtn., Nv., U.S.	F7	124
Millerovo, Russia	H6	26
Miller Peak, mtn., Az., U.S.	M6	120
Millersburg, Ky., U.S.	I2	108
Millersburg, Mi., U.S.	E11	110
Millersburg, Oh., U.S.	G5	108
Millersburg, Pa., U.S.	G10	108
Millers Ferry, Al., U.S.	J9	114
Millersport, Oh., U.S.	H4	108
Millersville, Pa., U.S.	H10	108
Millerton, N.Y., U.S.	F13	108
Millertown, Nf., Can.	D17	106
Millertown Junction, Nf., Can.	C17	106
Millet, Ab., Can.	D21	102
Millett, Tx., U.S.	K7	116
Millevaches, Plateau de, plat., Fr.	G9	14
Mill Hall, Pa., U.S.	F9	108
Millicent, Austl.	K4	70
Milligan, Fl., U.S.	L10	114
Milligan, Ne., U.S.	K10	118
Millington, Mi., U.S.	G12	110
Millington, Tn., U.S.	G7	114
Millinocket, Me., U.S.	B18	108
Mill Island, i., N.T., Can.	D17	96
Millmerran, Austl.	F9	70
Millport, Al., U.S.	I8	114
Millry, Al., U.S.	K8	114
Mills, Wy., U.S.	B10	120
Mills Lake, l., N.T., Can.	D9	96
Millstatt, Aus.	I13	10
Millstream Chichester National Park, Austl.	D3	68
Milltown, In., U.S.	D10	114
Milltown, Mt., U.S.	D12	122
Milltown, Wi., U.S.	E3	110
Mill Valley, Ca., U.S.	G3	124
Millville, N.J., U.S.	H11	108
Millwood, Va., U.S.	H8	108
Millwood Lake, res., Ar., U.S.	I2	114
Milne Bay, b., Pap. N. Gui.	B10	68
Milnor, N.D., U.S.	E10	118
Milo, Ab., Can.	G22	102
Milo, Ia., U.S.	I2	110
Milo, Me., U.S.	B18	108
Mílos, Grc.	M8	20
Mílos, i., Grc.	M8	20
Miloslavskoje, Russia	H22	22
Milparinka, Austl.	G4	70
Milpitas, Ca., U.S.	G4	124
Milroy, In., U.S.	C11	114
Milroy, Pa., U.S.	G9	108
Miltenberg, Ger.	F9	10
Milton, De., U.S.	I11	108
Milton, Fl., U.S.	L9	114
Milton, Ia., U.S.	J3	110
Milton, N.D., U.S.	C9	118
Milton, N.Z.	G2	72
Milton, On., Can.	G16	110
Milton, Pa., U.S.	F10	108
Milton, Vt., U.S.	C13	108
Milton, Wi., U.S.	H7	110
Milton, W.V., U.S.	I4	108
Milton-Freewater, Or., U.S.	E7	122
Miltonvale, Ks., U.S.	L10	118
Milverton, On., Can.	G15	110
Milwaukee, Wi., U.S.	G8	110
Milwaukee, stm., Wi., U.S.	G7	110
Milwaukie, Or., U.S.	E3	122
Mim, Ghana	H8	64
Mimbres, stm., N.M., U.S.	L9	120
Mimoso, Braz.	C4	79
Mimoso, Braz.	G14	82
Mimoso do Sul, Braz.	F8	79
Mims, Fl., U.S.	K6	112
Min, stm., China	E7	30
Min, stm., China	I7	34
Mina, Nv., U.S.	F7	124
Mīnāb, Iran	H14	48
Mina El Limón, Nic.	E8	92
Minago, stm., Mb., Can.	D16	104
Minahasa, pen., Indon.	E7	38
Minamata, Japan	O5	36
Minami-Daitō-jima, i., Japan	F13	30
Mina Pirquitas, Arg.	B5	80
Minas, Cuba	D6	94
Minas, Ur.	H11	80
Minas, Sierra de las, mts., Guat.	B5	92
Minas Basin, b., N.S., Can.	G9	106
Minas Channel, strt., N.S., Can.	G9	106
Minas de Barroterán, Mex.	D9	90
Minas de Corrales, Ur.	F11	80
Minas de Matahambre, Cuba	C3	94
Minas de Oro, Hond.	C7	92
Minas Gerais, state, Braz.	E6	79
Minas Novas, Braz.	D7	79
Minatare, Ne., U.S.	J4	118
Minatitlán, Mex.	I12	90
Minbu, Myan.	D3	40
Minco, Ok., U.S.	D9	116
Mindanao, i., Phil.	D8	38
Mindelo, C.V.	k16	64a
Mindemoya, On., Can.	E13	110
Minden, Ger.	C8	10
Minden, La., U.S.	J3	114
Minden, Ne., U.S.	K9	118
Minden, Nv., U.S.	F6	124
Minden, On., Can.	F17	110
Minden, W.V., U.S.	J5	108
Minden City, Mi., U.S.	G13	110
Mindenmines, Mo., U.S.	E2	114
Mindon, Myan.	E3	40
Mindoro, i., Phil.	C7	38
Mindoro Strait, strt., Phil.	C7	38
Mine Centre, On., Can.	B3	110
Mineiros, Braz.	D2	79
Mineola, Tx., U.S.	G11	116
Miner, stm., Yk., Can.	C25	100
Mineral, Wa., U.S.	D3	122
Mineral de Cucharas, Mex.	F7	90
Mineral'nyje Vody, Russia	I6	26
Mineral Point, Wi., U.S.	H5	110
Mineral Springs, Ar., U.S.	I3	114
Mineral Wells, Tx., U.S.	G8	116
Minersville, Pa., U.S.	G10	108
Minersville, Ut., U.S.	F4	120
Minerva, Oh., U.S.	G5	108
Minervino Murge, Italy	H11	18
Mineville, N.Y., U.S.	C13	108
Minfeng, China	D3	30
Mingäçevir, Azer.	I7	26
Mingan, P.Q., Can.	B9	106
Mingan, stm., P.Q., Can.	B10	106
Mingan, Îles de, is., P.Q., Can.	B10	106
Mingan Archipelago National Park, P.Q., Can.	B10	106
Mingela, Austl.	B7	70
Minggang, China	C3	34
Mingo Junction, Oh., U.S.	G6	108
Minhang, China	D10	34
Minhla, Myan.	F3	40
Minho, hist. reg., Port.	D3	16
Minho (Miño), stm., Eur.	D3	16
Minhou, China	I8	34
Minicoy Island, i., India	H2	46
Minier, Il., U.S.	B7	114
Minīn, Syria	A6	50
Miniota, Mb., Can.	H13	104
Ministikwan Lake, l., Sk., Can.	D5	104
Minitonas, Mb., Can.	F13	104
Minjar, Russia	F9	26
Min'kovo, Russia	B26	22
Minlaton, Austl.	J2	70
Minle, China	D7	30
Minna, Nig.	G13	64
Minneapolis, Ks., U.S.	L10	118
Minneapolis, Mn., U.S.	F2	110
Minnedosa, Mb., Can.	H15	104
Minnehaha, Wa., U.S.	E3	122
Minneola, Ks., U.S.	N7	118
Minneota, Mn., U.S.	G12	118
Minnesota, state, U.S.	B8	98
Minnesota, stm., Mn., U.S.	F2	110
Minnesota Lake, Mn., U.S.	G2	110
Minnewanka, Lake, l., Ab., Can.	F19	102
Minnewaukan, N.D., U.S.	C8	118
Minnitaki Lake, l., On., Can.	I22	104
Mino, Japan	L11	36
Miño (Minho), stm., Eur.	D3	16
Minocqua, Wi., U.S.	E6	110
Minong, Wi., U.S.	D4	110
Minonk, Il., U.S.	J6	110
Minot, N.D., U.S.	C6	118
Minsk, Bela.	H10	22
Mińsk Mazowiecki, Pol.	C21	10
Minster, Oh., U.S.	G2	108
Mintaka Pass, Asia	B6	44
Minto, Ak., U.S.	D20	100
Minto, Mb., Can.	I14	104
Minto, N.B., Can.	F7	106
Minto, N.D., U.S.	C10	118
Minto, Yk., Can.	E26	100
Minto, Lac, l., P.Q., Can.	E17	96
Minto Inlet, b., N.T., Can.	B9	96
Minton, Sk., Can.	I10	104
Minturn, Co., U.S.	E10	120
Minturno, Italy	H8	18
Minusinsk, Russia	G10	28
Minxian, China	E7	30
Minya see Al-Minyā, Egypt	C6	60
Minya Konka see Gongga Shan, mtn., China	F7	30
Mio, Mi., U.S.	F11	110
Mir, Bela.	H9	22
Mira, Port.	E3	16
Mira, stm., Col.	G3	84
Mira, stm., N.S., Can.	G13	106
Mira Bay, b., N.S., Can.	F14	106
Miracema do Tocantins, Braz.	E9	76
Mirador, Braz.	E10	76
Miradouro, Braz.	F7	79
Miraflores, Arg.	E6	80
Miraflores, Col.	E6	84
Miraflores, Col.	G6	84
Miraflores, Esclusas de, Pan.	I15	92
Mīrah, Wādī al-, val., Asia	B11	60
Miraj, India	D3	46
Miramar, Arg.	J10	80
Miramar, Arg.	F7	80
Miramar, C.R.	G10	92
Miramas, Fr.	I12	14
Miramichi Bay, b., N.B., Can.	E9	106
Miranda, Braz.	I13	82
Miranda, Ca., U.S.	D2	124
Miranda, Col.	F4	84
Miranda, state, Ven.	B9	84
Miranda, stm., Braz.	H13	82
Miranda de Ebro, Spain	C9	16
Miranda do Douro, Port.	D5	16
Mirande, Fr.	I7	14
Mirandela, Port.	D4	16
Mirando City, Tx., U.S.	L7	116
Mirandola, Italy	E6	18
Mirante do Paranapanema, Braz.	G3	79
Mirapuxi, stm., Braz.	B3	79
Mira Taglio, Italy	D7	18
Miravalles, Volcán, vol., C.R.	G9	92
Mirbāṭ, Oman	F9	47
Mirebeau-sur-Bèze, Fr.	E12	14
Mirecourt, Fr.	D13	14
Miri, Malay.	E5	38
Miriam Vale, Austl.	E9	70
Mirim, Lagoa (Laguna Merín), b., S.A.	G12	80
Miriñay, stm., Arg.	E10	80
Miritiparaná, stm., Col.	H7	84
Mīrjāveh, Iran	G16	48
Mirnyj, Russia	E14	28
Mirnyy, sci., Ant.	B6	73
Mirond Lake, l., Sk., Can.	C12	104
Mirow, Ger.	B12	10
Mīrpur, Pak.	D5	44
Mīrpur Khās, Pak.	H3	44
Mirria, Niger	E14	64
Mirror, Ab., Can.	E21	102
Mirzāpur, India	H10	44
Misāḥah, Bi'r, well, Egypt	F4	60
Misantla, Mex.	H11	90
Miscou Centre, N.B., Can.	E9	106
Miscou Island, i., N.B., Can.	E9	106
Miscou Point, c., N.B., Can.	D9	106
Misenheimer, N.C., U.S.	D6	112
Mishagua, stm., Peru	D5	82
Mishan, China	B13	30
Mishawaka, In., U.S.	A10	114
Mishbiḥ, Jabal, mtn., Egypt	J3	48
Mishicot, Wi., U.S.	F8	110
Misikan, China	C13	44
Misilmeri, Italy	K8	18
Misiones, prov., Arg.	D11	80
Misiones, dept., Para.	D10	80
Misión San Francisco de Laishí, Arg.	D9	80
Misión San Vicente, Mex.	B1	90
Miskī, Sudan	J3	60
Miskito Channel, strt., Nic.	C11	92
Miskitos, Cayos, is., Nic.	C12	92
Miskitos Reef, rf., Nic.	C12	92
Miskolc, Hung.	G20	10
Mislata, Spain	A10	62
Misool, Pulau, i., Indon.	F9	38
Misquamaebin Lake, l., On., Can.	E23	104
Misrātah, Libya	B4	56
Missinaibi, stm., On., Can.	F16	96
Missinaibi Lake, l., On., Can.	B12	110
Mission, S.D., U.S.	H7	118
Mission, Tx., U.S.	M8	116
Mission City, B.C., Can.	H12	102
Mississauga, On., Can.	G16	110
Mississinewa, stm., U.S.	B11	114
Mississippi, state, U.S.	E9	98
Mississippi, stm., U.S.	E8	98
Mississippi Delta, La., U.S.	M7	114
Mississippi Sound, strt., U.S.	L8	114
Mississippi State, Ms., U.S.	I8	114
Missoula, Mt., U.S.	D12	122
Missouri, state, U.S.	D8	98
Missouri, stm., U.S.	C7	98
Missouri Valley, Ia., U.S.	J12	118
Mistaken Point, c., Nf., Can.	F20	106
Mistanipisipou, stm., P.Q., Can.	A11	106
Mistassibi, stm., P.Q., Can.	G18	96
Mistassibi Nord-Est, stm., P.Q., Can.	B2	106
Mistassini, P.Q., Can.	F18	96
Mistassini, Lac, l., P.Q., Can.	F18	96
Mistatim, Sk., Can.	F11	104
Mistawasis Indian Reserve, Sk., Can.	E8	104
Mistelbach, Aus.	G16	10
Misterbianco, Italy	L10	18
Misterei, Sudan	K2	60
Misti, Volcán, vol., Peru	G6	82
Mistikokan, stm., Mb., Can.	B23	104
Mistretta, Italy	L9	18
Mita, Punta, c., Mex.	G7	90
Mitchell, Austl.	F7	70
Mitchell, In., U.S.	D10	114
Mitchell, Ne., U.S.	J4	118
Mitchell, On., Can.	G14	110
Mitchell, Or., U.S.	F5	122
Mitchell, S.D., U.S.	H9	118
Mitchell, stm., Austl.	K7	70
Mitchell, Lake, res., Al., U.S.	J10	114
Mitchell, Mount, mtn., N.C., U.S.	D4	112
Mitchell Lake, l., B.C., Can.	E14	102
Mitchellville, Ia., U.S.	I2	110
Mitilíni, Grc.	J10	20
Mitis, Lac, l., P.Q., Can.	D6	106
Mitishto, stm., Mb., Can.	D15	104
Mitla, hist., Mex.	I11	90
Mito, Japan	K15	36
Mitsamiouli, Com.	k15	67a
Mitsinjo, Madag.	p21	67b

Name — Map Ref. — Page

Mitsio, Nosy, i., Madag. n23 67b
Mitsiwa (Massawa), Erit. J10 60
Mittellandkanal, Ger. C9 10
Mittenwald, Ger. H11 10
Mittersill, Aus. H12 10
Mitú, Col. G7 84
Mitumba, Monts, mts., Zaire B5 58
Mitwaba, Zaire C5 58
Mitzic, Gabon A2 58
Miura, Japan L14 36
Mixco Viejo, hist., Guat. C4 92
Miyake-jima, i., Japan M14 36
Miyako, Japan H16 36
Miyakonojō, Japan P6 36
Miyazaki, Japan P6 36
Miyazu, Japan L10 36
Miyun, China C4 32
Mizan Teferi, Eth. N8 60
Mizdah, Libya B3 56
Mize, Ms., U.S. K7 114
Mizen Head, c., Ire. J4 8
Mizhhir'ya, Ukr. A7 20
Mizoram, state, India I15 44
Mizpé Ramon, Isr. G3 50
Mizque, Bol. G9 82
Mizque, stm., Bol. H9 82
Mjadzel, Bela. G9 22
Mjøsa, l., Nor. K12 6
Mladá Boleslav, Czech Rep. E14 10
Mladenovac, Yugo. E4 20
Mlanje Peak see Sapitwa, mtn., Mwi. E7 58
Mława, Pol. B20 10
Mmabatho, S. Afr. E7 66
Mmadinare, Bots. C8 66
Mo, Nor. H14 6
Mo, stm., Afr. G10 64
Moa, stm., Afr. G4 54
Moa, stm., Braz. B5 82
Moab, Ut., U.S. F7 120
Moaco, stm., Braz. C7 82
Moa Island, i., Austl. B8 68
Moama, Austl. K6 70
Moanda, Gabon B2 58
Moar Lake, l., Can. F19 104
Mobara, Japan L15 36
Mobaye, C.A.R. H5 56
Mobeetie, Tx., U.S. D6 116
Moberly, Mo., U.S. C4 114
Moberly, stm., B.C., Can. A13 102
Moberly Lake, B.C., Can. B13 102
Moberly Lake, l., B.C., Can. B13 102
Mobile, Al., U.S. L8 114
Mobile, Az., U.S. K4 120
Mobile, stm., Al., U.S. L8 114
Mobile Bay, b., Al., U.S. L8 114
Mobridge, S.D., U.S. F7 118
Moca, Dom. Rep. E9 94
Mocal, stm., N.A. C6 92
Moçambique, Moz. E8 58
Mocanal, Spain p23 17b
Mocha see Al-Makhā', Yemen H3 47
Mocha, Isla, i., Chile J2 80
Moche, stm., Peru C2 82
Moche, hist., Peru C2 82
Mochudi, Bots. E8 66
Mocímboa da Praia, Moz. D8 58
Mocksville, N.C., U.S. D6 112
Moclips, Wa., U.S. C1 122
Môco, Serra do, mtn., Ang. D3 58
Mocoa, Col. G4 84
Mococa, Braz. F5 79
Mocoduene, Moz. D12 66
Mocoretá, Arg. F10 80
Mocorito, Mex. E6 90
Moctezuma, Mex. C5 90
Moctezuma, stm., Mex. C5 90
Moctezuma, stm., Mex. G10 90
Mocuba, Moz. E7 58
Modane, Fr. G13 14
Modderrivier, S. Afr. G7 66
Modena, Italy E5 18
Modesto, Ca., U.S. G5 124
Modica, Italy M9 18
Mödling, Aus. G16 10
Moe, Austl. L7 70
Moeda, Braz. F6 79
Moema, Braz. E6 79
Moengo, Sur. B8 76
Moenkopi, Az., U.S. H5 120
Moffit, N.D., U.S. E7 118
Moga, India E6 44
Mogadiscio see Muqdisho, Som. H10 56
Mogadishu see Muqdisho, Som. H10 56
Mogán, Spain p25 17b
Mogapinyana, Bots. D8 66
Mogaung, Myan. B4 40
Mogincual, Moz. E8 58
Mogliano Veneto, Italy D7 18
Mogoča, Russia G15 28
Mogogh, Sudan M6 60
Mogok, Myan. C4 40
Mogollon Rim, clf, Az., U.S. J6 120
Mogotes, Col. D6 84
Mogotón, mtn., N.A. D8 92
Moguer, Spain H5 16
Mogzon, Russia G14 28
Mohács, Hung. J18 10
Mohall, N.D., U.S. C6 118
Mohammedia (Fedala), Mor. D7 62
Mohave, Lake, res., U.S. I11 124
Mohawk, Mi., U.S. C7 110
Mohawk, stm., N.Y., U.S. E12 108
Mohe, China A11 30
Moho, stm., Belize A6 92
Mohyliv-Podil's'kyy, Ukr. H3 26
Moinești, Rom. C10 20
Moiporá, Braz. D3 79
Mõisaküla, Est. C8 22
Moisés Ville, Arg. F8 80
Moisie, P.Q., Can. B7 106
Moisie, stm., P.Q., Can. F19 96
Moisie, Baie de, b., P.Q., Can. B8 106
Moissac, Fr. H8 14
Moitaco, Ven. C10 84
Mojana, Brazo, mth., Col. C5 84
Mojave, Ca., U.S. I7 124
Mojave Desert, des., Ca., U.S. J8 124
Mojicuaçu, stm., Braz. F5 79
Mojimirim, Braz. G5 79
Mojjero, stm., Russia D12 28
Mojo, Eth. M10 60
Mojynty, Kaz. H12 26
Mokāma, India H11 44
Mokelumne, stm., Ca., U.S. F4 124
Moknine, Tun. N5 18
Mokp'o, S. Kor. I14 32
Mokrisset, Mor. K6 16
Mokša, stm., Russia G24 22
Mokwa, Nig. G12 64
Mol, Bel. F7 12
Mola di Bari, Italy H12 18
Molalla, Or., U.S. E3 122
Molanosa, Sk., Can. D9 104
Moldau see Vltava, stm., Czech Rep. F14 10
Moldavia, hist. reg., Rom. B11 20
Moldavia see Moldova, ctry., Eur. F13 4

Molde, Nor. J10 6
Moldova, ctry., Eur. F13 4
Moldoveanu, Vârful, mtn., Rom. D8 20
Môle, Cap du, c., Haiti E8 94
Molega Lake, l., N.S., Can. H9 106
Molepolole, Bots. E7 66
Molėtai, Lith. F8 22
Molfetta, Italy H11 18
Molina, Chile H3 80
Molina de Segura, Spain G10 16
Moline, Il., U.S. I5 110
Moline, Ks., U.S. N11 118
Molino, Fl., U.S. L9 114
Molinos, Arg. C5 80
Molins de Rei, Spain D14 16
Molise, prov., Italy H9 18
Mollendo, Peru G5 82
Mollepata, Peru E5 82
Mölln, Ger. B10 10
Mölndal, Swe. M13 6
Moločnoje, Russia B22 22
Mologa, stm., Russia C19 22
Molokai, i., Hi., U.S. p16 125a
Molong, Austl. I8 70
Molopo, stm., Afr. F5 66
Molotov see Perm', Russia F9 26
Molou, Chad K1 60
Molsheim, Fr. D14 14
Molson Lake, l., Mb., Can. D18 104
Molteno, S. Afr. H8 66
Moluccas see Maluku, is., Indon. F8 38
Molucca Sea see Maluku, Laut, Indon. F7 38
Moma, Moz. E7 58
Moma, stm., Russia D20 28
Momanga, Nmb. B5 66
Mombachito, Cerro, mtn., Nic. E9 92
Mombacho, Volcán, vol., Nic. F9 92
Mombasa, Kenya B7 58
Mombetsu, Japan c18 36a
Momence, Il., U.S. I8 110
Momotombo, Volcán, vol., Nic. E8 92
Mompós, Col. C5 84
Mona, Ut., U.S. E5 120
Mona, Canal de la, strt., N.A. E11 94
Mona, Isla de, i., P.R. E11 94
Mona, Punta, c., C.R. H12 92
Monaca, Pa., U.S. G6 108
Monaco, ctry., Eur. G9 4
Monadnock Mountain, mtn., N.H., U.S. E14 108
Monagas, state, Ven. C11 84
Monaghan, co., Ire. G6 8
Monagrillo, Pan. D2 84
Monahans, Tx., U.S. H4 116
Monango, N.D., U.S. E9 118
Monarch, S.C., U.S. E5 112
Monarch Mountain, mtn., B.C., Can. F9 102
Monarch Pass, Co., U.S. F10 120
Monashee Mountains, mts., B.C., Can. F16 102
Monashee Provincial Park, B.C., Can. G16 102
Monastir see Bitola, Mac. H5 20
Monastir, Tun. N5 18
Monastyrščina, Russia G14 22
Moncalieri, Italy D2 18
Monção, Braz. D9 76
Mončegorsk, Russia D4 26
Mönchengladbach, Ger. D6 10
Moncks Corner, S.C., U.S. F6 112
Monclova, Mex. D9 90
Moncontour, Fr. D4 14
Moncoutant, Fr. F6 14
Moncton, N.B., Can. F9 106
Mondaí, Braz. D12 80
Monday, stm., Para. C11 80
Mondoro, Mali D9 64
Mondoubleau, Fr. E7 14
Mondovi, Wi., U.S. F4 110
Mondragone, Italy H8 18
Monero, N.M., U.S. H10 120
Moneron, ostrov, i., Russia a16 36a
Monessen, Pa., U.S. G7 108
Monesterio, Spain G5 16
Monett, Mo., U.S. F3 114
Monette, Ar., U.S. G6 114
Monfalcone, Italy D8 18
Monflanquin, Fr. H7 14
Monforte, Port. F4 16
Monforte de Lemos, Spain C4 16
Mongaguá, Braz. H5 79
Mongalla, Sudan G7 56
Mong Cai, Viet. D9 40
Monger, Îles, is., P.Q., Can. A15 106
Mongers Lake, l., Austl. E3 68
Möng Hsat, Myan. D5 40
Möng Mit, Myan. C4 40
Mongo, Chad F4 56
Mongo, stm., Afr. G4 64
Mongol Altajn nuruu, mts., Asia H16 26
Mongolia (Mongol Ard Uls), ctry., Asia B8 30
Mongororo, Chad K2 60
Möng Pai, Myan. E4 40
Mongu, Zam. E4 58
Möng Yawng, Myan. D6 40
Monheim, Ger. G10 10
Monico, Wi., U.S. E6 110
Monida Pass, U.S. F13 122
Monino, Russia F21 22
Moniquirá, Col. E6 84
Monistrol-sur-Loire, Fr. G11 14
Monitor Range, mts., Nv., U.S. F9 124
Monitor Valley, val., Nv., U.S. F9 124
Monkey River, Belize A6 92
Mońki, Pol. B22 10
Monkira, Austl. E4 70
Monmouth, Il., U.S. J5 110
Monmouth, Or., U.S. F2 122
Monmouth Mountain, mtn., B.C., Can. F11 102
Mono, stm., Afr. G7 54
Mono, Caño, stm., Col. E8 84
Mono, Punta, c., Nic. F11 92
Mono Lake, l., Ca., U.S. F7 124
Monon, In., U.S. B10 114
Monona, Ia., U.S. G4 110
Monona, Wi., U.S. G6 110
Monongahela, stm., U.S. H7 108
Monopoli, Italy I12 18
Monòver, Spain G11 16
Monreale, Italy K8 18
Monroe, Ga., U.S. F3 112
Monroe, Ia., U.S. I2 110
Monroe, La., U.S. J4 114
Monroe, Mi., U.S. I12 110
Monroe, N.C., U.S. E6 112
Monroe, Ne., U.S. J10 118
Monroe, N.Y., U.S. F12 108
Monroe, Or., U.S. F2 122
Monroe, Ut., U.S. F4 120
Monroe, Va., U.S. B7 112
Monroe, Wa., U.S. C4 122

Monroe, Wi., U.S. H6 110
Monroe City, In., U.S. D9 114
Monroe City, Mo., U.S. C5 114
Monroe Lake, res., In., U.S. C10 114
Monroeville, Al., U.S. K9 114
Monroeville, In., U.S. B12 114
Monroeville, Oh., U.S. F4 108
Monroeville, Pa., U.S. G7 108
Monrovia, Lib. H4 64
Mons (Bergen), Bel. H4 12
Monsefú, Peru B2 82
Monselice, Italy D6 18
Monson, Me., U.S. B17 108
Montabaur, Ger. E7 10
Montagnana, Italy D6 18
Montagu, S. Afr. I5 66
Montague, Ca., U.S. C3 124
Montague, Mi., U.S. G9 110
Montague, P.E., Can. F11 106
Montague, Tx., U.S. F9 116
Montague, Isla, i., Mex. B2 90
Montague Island, i., Ak., U.S. F21 100
Montagu Island, i., S. Geor. A2 73
Montaigu, Fr. F5 14
Montalcino, Italy F6 18
Montalegre, Port. D4 16
Montana, Bul. F7 20
Montana, Switz. F7 13
Montana, state, U.S. B4 98
Montana Indian Reserve, Ab., Can. E21 102
Montargis, Fr. D9 14
Montauban, Fr. H8 14
Montauk, N.Y., U.S. F15 108
Montauk Point, c., N.Y., U.S. F15 108
Montbard, Fr. E11 14
Montbarrey, Fr. E12 14
Montbéliard, Fr. E13 14
Mont Belvieu, Tx., U.S. J12 116
Mont Blanc, Tunnel du, Eur. G6 13
Montbrison, Fr. G11 14
Montbron, Fr. G7 14
Montceau [-les-Mines], Fr. F11 14
Montcevelles, Lac, l., P.Q., Can. A13 106
Montchanin, Fr. F11 14
Montclair, Ca., U.S. J8 124
Montclair, N.J., U.S. G12 108
Mont-de-Marsan, Fr. I6 14
Montdidier, Fr. C9 14
Monte, Laguna del, l., Arg. I7 80
Monteagle, Tn., U.S. G11 114
Monteagudo, Bol. H10 82
Monte Albán, hist., Mex. I11 90
Monte Alegre, Braz. D8 76
Monte Alegre de Goiás, Braz. B5 79
Monte Alegre de Minas, Braz. E4 79
Monte Azul, Braz. C7 79
Monte Azul Paulista, Braz. F4 79
Montebello, P.Q., Can. B12 108
Monte Bello Islands, is., Austl. D3 68
Monte Buey, Arg. G7 80
Montecarlo, Arg. D11 80
Monte Caseros, Arg. F10 80
Montecassino, Abbazia di, Italy H8 18
Montecatini-Terme, Italy F5 18
Montecillos, Cordillera de, mts., Hond. C7 92
Montecito, Ca., U.S. J6 124
Monte Comán, Arg. H5 80
Monte Creek, B.C., Can. G15 102
Monte Cristi, Dom. Rep. E9 94
Montecristi, Ec. H2 84
Monte Cristo, Bol. F11 82
Monte Escobedo, Mex. F8 90
Montego Bay, Jam. E6 94
Monte Grande, Chile F3 80
Montegut, La., U.S. M6 114
Monteith, Mount, mtn., B.C., Can. B12 102
Montelíbano, Col. C5 84
Montélimar, Fr. H11 14
Montelindo, stm., Para. B9 80
Montellano, Spain H6 16
Montello, Nv., U.S. C11 124
Montello, Wi., U.S. G6 110
Monte Maíz, Arg. G7 80
Montemorelos, Mex. E10 90
Montemor-o-Novo, Port. G3 16
Montemor-o-Velho, Port. E3 16
Montendre, Fr. G6 14
Montenegro, Braz. E13 80
Montenegro see Crna Gora, state, Yugo. G2 20
Monte Pascoal, Parque Nacional de, Braz. D9 79
Monte Patria, Chile F3 80
Montepuez, Moz. D7 58
Montepulciano, Italy F6 18
Monte Quemado, Arg. C7 80
Montereau-Faut-Yonne, Fr. D9 14
Monterey, Ca., U.S. H4 124
Monterey, Tn., U.S. F11 114
Monterey, Va., U.S. I7 108
Monterey Bay, b., Ca., U.S. H4 124
Montería, Col. C5 84
Montero, Bol. G10 82
Monteros, Arg. D6 80
Monterotondo, Italy G7 18
Monterrey, Mex. E9 90
Montesano, Italy I10 18
Montesano, Wa., U.S. D2 122
Monte Sant'Angelo, Italy H10 18
Montesarchio, Italy H9 18
Montes Claros, Braz. D7 79
Montevallo, Al., U.S. I10 114
Montevarchi, Italy F6 18
Montevideo, Mn., U.S. G12 118
Montevideo, Ur. H10 80
Monte Vista, Co., U.S. G10 120
Montezuma, Ga., U.S. G2 112
Montezuma, Ia., U.S. I3 110
Montezuma, In., U.S. C9 114
Montezuma, Ks., U.S. N7 118
Montfort, Fr. D5 14
Montfort, Wi., U.S. H5 110
Montgomery, Al., U.S. J10 114
Montgomery, La., U.S. K4 114
Montgomery, Mn., U.S. F2 110
Montgomery, Pa., U.S. F10 108
Montgomery, Tx., U.S. I11 116
Montgomery, W.V., U.S. I5 108
Montgomery City, Mo., U.S. D5 114
Monthermé, Fr. C11 14
Monthey, Switz. F6 13
Monthois, Fr. C11 14
Monticello, Ar., U.S. I5 114
Monticello, Fl., U.S. I3 112
Monticello, Ga., U.S. F3 112
Monticello, Ia., U.S. H4 110
Monticello, Il., U.S. B8 114
Monticello, In., U.S. B10 114
Monticello, Ky., U.S. F12 114
Monticello, Mn., U.S. E2 110
Monticello, Mo., U.S. B5 114
Monticello, Ms., U.S. K6 114
Monticello, N.Y., U.S. F12 108
Monticello, Ut., U.S. G7 120

Monticello, Wi., U.S. H6 110
Montichiari, Italy D5 18
Montignac, Fr. G8 14
Montigny-le-Roi, Fr. D12 14
Montigny-sur-Aube, Fr. E11 14
Montijo, Pan. D2 84
Montijo, Port. G3 16
Montijo, Spain G5 16
Montijo, Golfo de, b., Pan. D2 84
Montilla, Spain H7 16
Montividiu, Braz. D3 79
Montivilliers, Fr. C7 14
Mont-Joli, P.Q., Can. D5 106
Mont-Laurier, P.Q., Can. G17 96
Mont-Louis, Fr. J9 14
Montluçon, Fr. F9 14
Montluel, Fr. G12 14
Montmagny, P.Q., Can. F3 106
Montmédy, Fr. C12 14
Montmirail, Fr. D10 14
Montmorency see Beauport, P.Q., Can. F2 106
Montmorency, stm., P.Q., Can. E2 106
Montmorillon, Fr. F7 14
Monto, Austl. E9 70
Montoro, Spain G7 16
Montour Falls, N.Y., U.S. E10 108
Montoursville, Pa., U.S. F10 108
Montpelier, Id., U.S. H14 122
Montpelier, In., U.S. G1 108
Montpelier, Ms., U.S. I8 114
Montpelier, Oh., U.S. F2 108
Montpelier, Vt., U.S. C14 108
Montpellier, Fr. I10 14
Montpon-Ménesterol, Fr. G7 14
Montréal, P.Q., Can. B13 108
Montreal, Wi., U.S. D5 110
Montreal, stm., Sk., Can. D9 104
Montreal Lake, Sk., Can. D9 104
Montreal Lake, l., Sk., Can. D9 104
Montreal Lake Indian Reserve, Sk., Can. D9 104
Montreuil, Fr. B8 14
Montreux, Switz. F6 13
Montrevel [-en-Bresse], Fr. F12 14
Montrose, Co., U.S. F9 120
Montrose, Ia., U.S. J4 110
Montrose, Mi., U.S. G12 110
Montrose, Pa., U.S. F11 108
Montrose, Scot., U.K. E11 8
Montrose, S.D., U.S. H10 118
Montross, Va., U.S. I10 108
Monts, Pointe des, c., P.Q., Can. C6 106
Mont-Sainte-Anne, Parc du, P.Q., Can. E3 106
Mont-Saint-Michel see Le Mont-Saint-Michel, Fr. D5 14
Montserrat, dep., N.A. F13 94
Montvale, Va., U.S. B7 112
Monument, Or., U.S. F6 122
Monument Peak, mtn., Id., U.S. H11 122
Monument Valley, val., U.S. G6 120
Monywa, Myan. C3 40
Monza, Italy D4 18
Monzón, Peru C3 82
Monzón, Spain D12 16
Moodie Island, i., N.T., Can. D19 96
Moody, Tx., U.S. H9 116
Mooirivier, S. Afr. G9 66
Mookane, Bots. E7 66
Moolawatana, Austl. G3 70
Moonie, stm., Austl. F8 70
Moonta, Austl. J2 70
Moora, Austl. F3 68
Moorcroft, Wy., U.S. G3 118
Moore, Id., U.S. G12 122
Moore, Mt., U.S. D16 122
Moore, Ok., U.S. D9 116
Moore, Tx., U.S. J7 116
Moore, Lake, l., Austl. E3 68
Moorefield, W.V., U.S. H8 108
Moore Haven, Fl., U.S. M5 112
Mooreland, Ok., U.S. C7 116
Mooresville, In., U.S. C10 114
Mooresville, N.C., U.S. D6 112
Moorhead, Mn., U.S. E11 118
Moorhead, Ms., U.S. I6 114
Mooringsport, La., U.S. J3 114
Moornanyah Lake, l., Austl. I5 70
Moorreesburg, S. Afr. I4 66
Moosburg, Ger. G11 10
Moosehead Lake, l., Me., U.S. B17 108
Moose Heights, B.C., Can. D12 102
Moose Island, i., Mb., Can. G17 104
Moose Jaw, Sk., Can. H9 104
Moose Jaw, stm., Sk., Can. H9 104
Moose Lake, Mb., Can. E14 104
Moose Lake, Mn., U.S. D3 110
Moose Lake, l., Ab., Can. C24 102
Moose Lake, l., Mb., Can. E15 104
Mooselookmeguntic Lake, l., Me., U.S. C16 108
Moose Mountain, mtn., Sk., Can. I12 104
Moose Mountain Creek, stm., Sk., Can. H11 104
Moose Mountain Provincial Park, Sk., Can. I12 104
Moose Pass, Ak., U.S. F20 100
Moosomin, Sk., Can. H13 104
Moosomin Indian Reserve, Sk., Can. E6 104
Moosonee, On., Can. F16 96
Mopane, S. Afr. D9 66
Mopipi, Bots. C7 66
Mopti, Mali D7 64
Moquegua, Peru G6 82
Moquegua, dept., Peru G6 82
Mór, Hung. H18 10
Mora, Mn., U.S. E2 110
Mora, N.M., U.S. I11 120
Mora, Spain F8 16
Mora, Swe. K14 6
Mora, stm., N.M., U.S. H11 120
Morādābād, India F8 44
Morada Nova de Minas, Braz. E6 79
Moradel, Montaña de, mtn., Hond. B8 92
Mora de Rubielos, Spain E11 16
Morafenobe, Madag. p21 67b
Mórahalom, Hung. I19 10
Mor'akovskij Zaton, Russia F14 26
Moraleda, Canal, strt., Chile E2 78
Morales, Guat. B6 92
Morales, Peru B3 82
Morales, Laguna, b., Mex. F11 90
Moran, Ks., U.S. N12 118
Moran, Mi., U.S. E11 110
Moran, Tx., U.S. G7 116
Morant Bay, Jam. F6 94
Morant Cays, is., Jam. F7 94
Morant Point, c., Jam. F6 94
Moratalla, Spain G10 16
Moratuwa, Sri L. I5 46
Morava, hist. reg., Czech Rep. F17 10
Morava (March), stm., Eur. G16 10
Moravia, C.R. H11 92
Moravia, Ia., U.S. J3 110

Moravia, N.Y., U.S. E10 108
Moravia see Morava, hist. reg., Czech Rep. F17 10
Morawhanna, Guy. C13 84
Moraya, Bol. I9 82
Moray Firth, est., Scot., U.K. D10 8
Morazán, Guat. C4 92
Morazán, Hond. B7 92
Morbegno, Italy C4 18
Morbi, India I4 44
Morbihan, dept., Fr. E4 14
Morcenx, Fr. H6 14
Morden, Mb., Can. I16 104
Mordovija, state, Russia G6 26
Mordovo, Russia I23 22
Mordves, Russia G21 22
Mordvinia see Mordovija, state, Russia G6 26
Moreau, stm., S.D., U.S. F6 118
Moreauville, La., U.S. K5 114
Moree, Austl. G8 70
Morée, Fr. E8 14
Morehead, Ky., U.S. I3 108
Morehead City, N.C., U.S. E10 112
Morehouse, Mo., U.S. F7 114
Moreland, Ga., U.S. F2 112
Moreland, Ky., U.S. E12 114
Morelia, Mex. H9 90
Morell, P.E., Can. F11 106
Morelos, Mex. D6 90
Morelos, state, Mex. H10 90
Moremi Wildlife Reserve, Bots. B6 66
Morena, India G8 44
Morena, Sierra, mts., Spain G6 16
Morenci, Az., U.S. K7 120
Morenci, Mi., U.S. I11 110
Moreno, Bahía, b., Chile B3 80
Møre og Romsdal, co., Nor. J10 6
Moresby Island, i., B.C., Can. E3 102
Mores Island, i., Bah. A6 94
Moresnet, Bel. G8 12
Moreton Island, i., Austl. F10 70
Moreuil, Fr. C9 14
Morez, Fr. F13 14
Morgan, Ga., U.S. H2 112
Morgan, Mn., U.S. G13 118
Morgan, Tx., U.S. G9 116
Morgan, Ut., U.S. C5 120
Morgan City, Al., U.S. H10 114
Morgan City, La., U.S. M5 114
Morganfield, Ky., U.S. E9 114
Morgan Hill, Ca., U.S. G4 124
Morganito, Ven. E9 84
Morganton, N.C., U.S. D5 112
Morgantown, In., U.S. C10 114
Morgantown, Ky., U.S. E10 114
Morgantown, Ms., U.S. K5 114
Morgantown, Ms., U.S. K7 114
Morgantown, W.V., U.S. H7 108
Morganza, La., U.S. L5 114
Morgenzon, S. Afr. F9 66
Morghāb (Murgab), stm., Asia B16 48
Moriah, Mount, mtn., Nv., U.S. E11 124
Moriarty, N.M., U.S. J10 120
Moribaya, Gui. G5 64
Morice, stm., B.C., Can. C7 102
Morice Lake, l., B.C., Can. C7 102
Morichal Largo, stm., Ven. C11 84
Moriki, Nig. E13 64
Moringen, Ger. D9 10
Morino, Russia D13 22
Morinville, Ab., Can. D21 102
Morioka, Japan H16 36
Morisset, Austl. I9 70
Morkill, stm., B.C., Can. D14 102
Morkiny Gory, Russia D19 22
Morkoka, stm., Russia D14 28
Morlaix, Fr. D3 14
Morley, Mi., U.S. G10 110
Mormal', Bela. I12 22
Morney, Austl. E4 70
Morning Sun, Ia., U.S. I4 110
Mornington, Austl. L6 70
Mornington, Isla, i., Chile F1 78
Mornington Island, i., Austl. A3 70
Moro, Or., U.S. E5 122
Moro, stm., Afr. H4 64
Morobe, Pap. N. Gui. m16 68a
Morocco, In., U.S. B9 114
Morocco (Al-Magreb), ctry., Afr. B5 54
Morococala, Bol. H8 82
Morococha, Peru D3 82
Morogoro, Tan. C7 58
Moro Gulf, b., Phil. D7 38
Moroleón, Mex. G9 90
Morombe, Madag. r20 67b
Morón, Arg. H9 80
Morón, Cuba C5 94
Mörön, Mong. B7 30
Morón, Ven. B8 84
Morona, stm., Peru I4 84
Morona-Santiago, prov., Ec. I3 84
Morondava, Madag. r21 67b
Morón de la Frontera, Spain H6 16
Moroni, Com. k15 67a
Moroni, Ut., U.S. E5 120
Morotai, i., Indon. E8 38
Morozovsk, Russia H6 26
Morrill, Ne., U.S. J4 118
Morrilton, Ar., U.S. G4 114
Morrin, Ab., Can. F22 102
Morrinhos, Braz. D4 79
Morrinsville, N.Z. B5 72
Morris, Il., U.S. I7 110
Morris, Mb., Can. I17 104
Morris, Mn., U.S. F12 118
Morris, Ok., U.S. D11 116
Morris, stm., Mb., Can. I17 104
Morrisburg, On., Can. C11 108
Morris Jesup, Kap, c., Grnld. A16 86
Morrison, Arg. G7 80
Morrison, Il., U.S. I6 110
Morrisonville, Il., U.S. C7 114
Morristown, Az., U.S. K4 120
Morristown, In., U.S. C11 114
Morristown, Mn., U.S. F2 110
Morristown, S.D., U.S. F6 118
Morristown, Tn., U.S. C3 112
Morrisville, N.Y., U.S. E11 108
Morrisville, Pa., U.S. G12 108
Morrisville, Vt., U.S. C14 108
Morrito, Nic. F9 92
Morro, Ec. I2 84
Morro, Punta, c., Mex. H14 90
Morro Bay, Ca., U.S. I5 124
Morro del Jable, Spain o26 17b
Morro do Chapéu, Braz. F10 76
Morropón, Peru A1 82
Morrosquillo, Golfo de, b., Col. C5 84
Morrow, La., U.S. L4 114
Morrumbene, Moz. D12 66
Moršansk, Russia H24 22
Morse, La., U.S. L4 114
Morse, Sk., Can. H7 104
Morse, Tx., U.S. C5 116
Morson, On., Can. I20 104

Mortagne, Fr. D7 14
Mortagne-sur-Sèvre, Fr. E6 14
Mortain, Fr. D6 14
Mortara, Italy D3 18
Morteau, Fr. E13 14
Morteros, Arg. F7 80
Mortes, Rio das, stm., Braz. B3 79
Mortesoro, Sudan L8 60
Mortlach, Sk., Can. H8 104
Mortlake, Austl. L5 70
Morton, Il., U.S. J6 110
Morton, Mn., U.S. G13 118
Morton, Ms., U.S. J7 114
Morton, Tx., U.S. F4 116
Morton, Wa., U.S. D3 122
Mortons Gap, Ky., U.S. E9 114
Moruya, Austl. J9 70
Morven, Austl. F7 70
Morven, Ga., U.S. I3 112
Morven, N.C., U.S. E6 112
Morwell, Austl. L7 70
Morženga, Russia B23 22
Mosal'sk, Russia G17 22
Moščnyj, ostrov, i., Russia A10 22
Moscow, Id., U.S. D9 122
Moscow see Moskva, Russia F20 22
Mosel (Moselle), stm., Eur. C13 14
Moselle, Ms., U.S. K7 114
Moselle, dept., Fr. D13 14
Moselle (Mosel), stm., Eur. D13 14
Mosers River, N.S., Can. H11 106
Moses Lake, Wa., U.S. C6 122
Moses Point, Ak., U.S. D13 100
Mosetse, Bots. C8 66
Moshanpu, China F1 34
Moshaweng, stm., S. Afr. F6 66
Mosheim, Tn., U.S. C4 112
Moshi, Tan. B7 58
Mosina, Pol. C16 10
Mosinee, Wi., U.S. F6 110
Mosjøen, Nor. I13 6
Moskva (Moscow), Russia F20 22
Moskva, stm., Russia F21 22
Moskvy, kanal imeni, Russia E20 22
Mošok, Russia F24 22
Mosolovo, Russia G23 22
Mosomane, Bots. E8 66
Mosonmagyaróvár, Hung. H17 10
Mosopa, Bots. E7 66
Mosquera, Col. F3 84
Mosquero, N.M., U.S. D3 116
Mosquito, Punta, c., Pan. C4 84
Mosquito, Riacho, stm., Para. B9 80
Mosquito Creek Lake, res., Oh., U.S. F6 108
Mosquito Indian Reserve, Sk., Can. F6 104
Mosquitos, Costa de, hist. reg., Nic. D11 92
Mosquitos, Golfo de los, b., Pan. H13 92
Moss, Nor. L12 6
Mossaka, Congo B3 58
Mossâmedes, Braz. D3 79
Mossbank, Sk., Can. I9 104
Mosselbaai, S. Afr. J6 66
Mossendjo, Congo B2 58
Mossleigh, Ab., Can. G21 102
Mossoró, Braz. E11 76
Moss Point, Ms., U.S. L8 114
Moss Vale, Austl. J9 70
Mossy, stm., Mb., Can. G15 104
Mossy, stm., Sk., Can. D11 104
Most, Czech Rep. E13 10
Mosta, Russia E25 22
Mostar, Bos. F12 18
Mostardas, Braz. F13 80
Mostoos Hills, hills, Sk., Can. C5 104
Mostys'ka, Ukr. F23 10
Mosul see Al-Mawṣil, Iraq C7 48
Mota, Eth. L9 60
Motagua, stm., N.A. B6 92
Motala, Swe. L14 6
Motatán, Ven. C7 84
Motherwell, Scot., U.K. F9 8
Motihāri, India G11 44
Motloutse, Bots. C8 66
Motozintla de Mendoza, Mex. J13 90
Motril, Spain I8 16
Motru, Rom. E7 20
Mott, N.D., U.S. E5 118
Mottola, Italy I12 18
Motueka, N.Z. D4 72
Motul [de Felipe Carrillo Puerto], Mex. G15 90
Motupe, Peru B2 82
Mouaskar, Alg. C11 62
Mouchoir Passage, strt., N.A. D9 94
Moudjéria, Maur. C3 64
Moudon, Switz. E6 13
Mouila, Gabon B2 58
Mouit, Maur. C3 64
Mouka, C.A.R. N1 60
Moulamein, Austl. J6 70
Moulay-Idriss, Mor. C8 62
Moulins, Fr. F10 14
Moulins-la-Marche, Fr. D7 14
Moulmein see Mawlamyine, Myan. F4 40
Moulmeingyun, Myan. F3 40
Moulouya, Oued, stm., Mor. C9 62
Moulton, Al., U.S. H9 114
Moulton, Ia., U.S. J3 110
Moulton, Tx., U.S. J9 116
Moultrie, Ga., U.S. H3 112
Moultrie, Lake, res., S.C., U.S. F6 112
Mound Bayou, Ms., U.S. I6 114
Mound City, Il., U.S. E7 114
Mound City, Ks., U.S. M13 118
Mound City, Mo., U.S. B1 114
Mound City, S.D., U.S. F7 118
Moundou, Chad G4 56
Moundridge, Ks., U.S. M10 118
Mounds, Il., U.S. E7 114
Mounds, Ok., U.S. D10 116
Moundsville, W.V., U.S. H6 108
Moundville, Al., U.S. J9 114
Mounlapamôk, Laos G8 40
Mountain, Wi., U.S. E7 110
Mountain, stm., N.T., Can. D30 100
Mountainair, N.M., U.S. J10 120
Mountainaire, Az., U.S. I5 120
Mountain Brook, Al., U.S. I10 114
Mountain City, Ga., U.S. E3 112
Mountain City, Nv., U.S. C10 124
Mountain City, Tn., U.S. C5 112
Mountain Creek, Al., U.S. J10 114
Mountain Grove, Mo., U.S. E4 114
Mountain Home, Ar., U.S. F4 114
Mountain Home, Id., U.S. G10 122
Mountain Iron, Mn., U.S. C3 110
Mountain Lake, Mn., U.S. H13 118
Mountain Nile (Baḥr al-Jabal), stm., Sudan M6 60
Mountain Park, Ab., Can. E17 102
Mountain Pine, Ar., U.S. H3 114
Mountain Point, Ak., U.S. I29 100
Mountain View, Ar., U.S. G4 114

Name	Map Ref.	Page
Mountain View, Ca., U.S.	G3	124
Mountain View, Mo., U.S.	F5	114
Mountain View, Ok., U.S.	D8	116
Mountain View, Wy., U.S.	C6	120
Mountain View, Wy., U.S.	B10	120
Mountain Village, Ak., U.S.	E13	100
Mount Airy, Md., U.S.	H9	108
Mount Airy, N.C., U.S.	C6	112
Mount Alida, S. Afr.	G10	66
Mount Angel, Or., U.S.	E3	122
Mount Assiniboine Provincial Park, B.C., Can.	G19	102
Mount Ayr, Ia., U.S.	K13	118
Mount Barker, Austl.	F3	68
Mount Barker, Austl.	J3	70
Mount Brydges, On., Can.	H14	110
Mount Calm, Tx., U.S.	H10	116
Mount Carleton Provincial Park, N.B., Can.	E7	106
Mount Carmel, Il., U.S.	D9	114
Mount Carmel, Nf., Can.	E20	106
Mount Carmel, Pa., U.S.	G10	108
Mount Carroll, Il., U.S.	H6	110
Mount Clare, W.V., U.S.	H6	108
Mount Clemens, Mi., U.S.	H13	110
Mount Currie Indian Reserve, B.C., Can.	G12	102
Mount Desert Island, i., Me., U.S.	C18	108
Mount Dora, Fl., U.S.	K5	112
Mount Edgecumbe, Ak., U.S.	H27	100
Mount Enterprise, Tx., U.S.	K2	114
Mount Forest, On., Can.	G15	110
Mount Gambier, Austl.	K4	70
Mount Garnet, Austl.	A6	70
Mount Gay, W.V., U.S.	J4	108
Mount Gilead, N.C., U.S.	D6	112
Mount Gilead, Oh., U.S.	G4	108
Mount Hagen, Pap. N. Gui.	G11	38
Mount Holly, N.C., U.S.	D5	112
Mount Holly Springs, Pa., U.S.	G9	108
Mount Hope, Austl.	J1	70
Mount Hope, Ks., U.S.	N10	118
Mount Hope, W.V., U.S.	J5	108
Mount Horeb, Wi., U.S.	G6	110
Mount Ida, Ar., U.S.	H3	114
Mount Isa, Austl.	C3	70
Mount Jackson, Va., U.S.	I8	108
Mount Jewett, Pa., U.S.	F8	108
Mount Juliet, Tn., U.S.	F10	114
Mount Kisco, N.Y., U.S.	F13	108
Mount Lebanon, Pa., U.S.	G6	108
Mount Magnet, Austl.	E3	68
Mount Manara, Austl.	I5	70
Mount Morgan, Austl.	D9	70
Mount Morris, Il., U.S.	H6	110
Mount Morris, Mi., U.S.	G12	110
Mount Morris, N.Y., U.S.	E9	108
Mount Mulligan, Austl.	A6	70
Mount Olive, Il., U.S.	C7	114
Mount Olive, Ms., U.S.	K7	114
Mount Olive, N.C., U.S.	D8	112
Mount Olivet, Ky., U.S.	I2	108
Mount Orab, Oh., U.S.	H3	108
Mount Perry, Austl.	E9	70
Mount Pleasant, Ia., U.S.	J4	110
Mount Pleasant, Mi., U.S.	G11	110
Mount Pleasant, N.C., U.S.	D6	112
Mount Pleasant, On., Can.	G15	110
Mount Pleasant, Pa., U.S.	G7	108
Mount Pleasant, S.C., U.S.	G7	112
Mount Pleasant, Tn., U.S.	G9	114
Mount Pleasant, Tx., U.S.	F12	116
Mount Pleasant, Ut., U.S.	E5	120
Mount Pulaski, Il., U.S.	B7	114
Mount Rainier National Park, Wa., U.S.	D4	122
Mount Revelstoke National Park, B.C., Can.	F16	102
Mount Robson Provincial Park, B.C., Can.	E15	102
Mount Savage, Md., U.S.	H8	108
Mount Seymour Provincial Park, B.C., Can.	H12	102
Mount Shasta, Ca., U.S.	C3	124
Mount Sterling, Il., U.S.	C6	114
Mount Sterling, Ky., U.S.	A3	112
Mount Sterling, Oh., U.S.	H3	108
Mount Stewart, P.E., Can.	F11	106
Mount Stewart, S. Afr.	I7	66
Mount Surprise, Austl.	B6	70
Mount Uniacke, N.S., Can.	H10	106
Mount Union, Pa., U.S.	G9	108
Mount Vernon, Al., U.S.	K8	114
Mount Vernon, Ga., U.S.	G4	112
Mount Vernon, Ia., U.S.	I4	110
Mount Vernon, Il., U.S.	D8	114
Mount Vernon, In., U.S.	E9	114
Mount Vernon, Ky., U.S.	B2	112
Mount Vernon, Mo., U.S.	E3	114
Mount Vernon, Oh., U.S.	G4	108
Mount Vernon, Or., U.S.	F6	122
Mount Vernon, S.D., U.S.	H9	118
Mount Vernon, Tx., U.S.	F11	116
Mount Vernon, Wa., U.S.	B3	122
Mount Victory, Oh., U.S.	G3	108
Mount Wolf, Pa., U.S.	G10	108
Moura, Austl.	E8	70
Moura, Braz.	H12	84
Moura, Port.	G4	16
Mourdi, Dépression du, depr., Chad	E5	56
Mourdiah, Mali	D6	64
Mourne Mountains, mts., N. Ire., U.K.	G7	8
Moussoro, Chad	F4	56
Moutier, Switz.	D7	13
Moûtiers, Fr.	G13	14
Mouzon, Fr.	C12	14
Moville, Ia., U.S.	I11	118
Moville, Ire.	F6	8
Moweaqua, Il., U.S.	C7	114
Moya, Com.	I16	67a
Moya, Peru	E4	82
Moyahua, Mex.	G8	90
Moyamba, S.L.	G3	64
Moyen Atlas, mts., Mor.	D8	62
Moyeuvre-Grande, Fr.	C13	14
Moyie, B.C., Can.	H19	102
Moyie Springs, Id., U.S.	B9	122
Moyobamba, Peru	B3	82
Moyogalpa, Nic.	F9	92
Moyuta, Volcán, vol., Guat.	C4	92
Možajsk, Russia	F19	22
Mozambique (Moçambique), ctry., Afr.	E7	58
Mozambique Channel, strt., Afr.	E8	58
Mozarlândia, Braz.	C3	79
Mozdok, Russia	I6	26
Možga, Russia	F8	26
Mphoengs, Zimb.	C8	66
Mpika, Zam.	D6	58
Mpraeso, Ghana	H9	64
Mpumalanga, prov., S. Afr.	E10	66
Mpwapwa, Tan.	C7	58
Mqanduli, S. Afr.	H9	66
Mrągowo, Pol.	B21	10
M'Ramani, Com.	I16	67a
Mrkopalj, Cro.	D9	18
M'Saken, Tun.	N5	18
Mscislaŭ, Bela.	G14	22
M'Sila, Alg.	C13	62
Mšinskaja, Russia	B12	22
Msta, Russia	D17	22
Msta, stm., Russia	C14	22
Mstera, Russia	E24	22
Mszczonów, Pol.	D20	10
Mtamvuna, stm., S. Afr.	H9	66
Mtwara, Tan.	D8	58
Mu, Cerro, mtn., S.A.	C6	84
Muanda, Zaire	C2	58
Muang Hôngsa, Laos	E6	40
Muang Huang, Laos	E7	40
Muang Khammouan, Laos	F8	40
Muang Khi, Laos	E6	40
Muang Không, Laos	G8	40
Muang Khôngxédôn, Laos	G8	40
Muang Long, Laos	D6	40
Muang Ngoy, Laos	D7	40
Muang Ou Nua, Laos	C6	40
Muang Ou Tai, Laos	C6	40
Muang Pak-Lay, Laos	E6	40
Muang Pakxan, Laos	E7	40
Muang Phiang, Laos	E6	40
Muang Phoun, Laos	E7	40
Muang Sing, Laos	D6	40
Muang Souy, Laos	E7	40
Muang Thadua, Laos	E6	40
Muang Vangviang, Laos	E7	40
Muang Vapi, Laos	G8	40
Muang Xaignabouri, Laos	E6	40
Muang Xay, Laos	D6	40
Muang Xépôn, Laos	F9	40
Muang Xon, Laos	D7	40
Muang You, Laos	E7	40
Muar (Bandar Maharani), Malay.	M7	40
Muarasiberut, Indon.	F2	38
Mucajaí, stm., Braz.	F12	84
Muchanovo, Russia	E21	22
Muchinga Mountains, mts., Zam.	D6	58
Muchtolovo, Russia	F26	22
Muckadilla, Austl.	F8	70
Mučkapskij, Russia	J25	22
Muconda, Ang.	D4	58
Mucuchíes, Ven.	C7	84
Mucugê, Braz.	B8	79
Mucuim, stm., Braz.	B9	82
Muçum, Braz.	E13	80
Mucupia, Moz.	B13	66
Mucupina, Monte, mtn., Hond.	B8	92
Mucur, Tur.	B3	48
Mucuri, Braz.	E9	79
Mucuri, stm., Braz.	E9	79
Mucusso, Ang.	B5	66
Mud, stm., Ky., U.S.	E10	114
Mud, stm., W.V., U.S.	I4	108
Mudan, stm., China	B12	30
Mudanjiang, China	C12	30
Muddy, stm., Nv., U.S.	H11	124
Mudgee, Austl.	I8	70
Mudjatik, stm., Sk., Can.	B7	104
Mudjuga, Russia	J26	6
Mudon, Myan.	F4	40
Mudu, China	D9	34
Muelle de los Bueyes, Nic.	E10	92
Muenster, Tx., U.S.	F9	116
Muerto, stm., Arg.	B7	80
Mufulira, Zam.	D5	58
Mu Gia, Deo, Asia	F8	40
Muğla, Tur.	L12	20
Mugron, Fr.	I6	14
Muḥammad, Ra's, c., Egypt	D8	60
Muḥammad Qawl, Sudan	G9	60
Mühlacker, Ger.	G8	10
Mühldorf, Ger.	G12	10
Mühlhausen, Ger.	D10	10
Mühlig-Hofmann Mountains, mts., Ant.	C3	73
Muhu, i., Est.	C6	22
Muhu väin, strt., Est.	C6	22
Muiron Islands, is., Austl.	D2	68
Muisne, Ec.	G2	84
Mujang-ni, S. Kor.	H14	32
Mujezerskij, Russia	J22	6
Mujnak, Uzb.	I9	26
Muju, S. Kor.	G15	32
Mukacheve, Ukr.	H2	26
Mukah, Malay.	E5	38
Mukdahan, Thai.	F8	40
Mukden see Shenyang, China	B11	32
Mukilteo, Wa., U.S.	C3	122
Mukry, Turk.	J11	26
Muktsar, India	E6	44
Mukutawa, stm., Mb., Can.	E18	104
Mukwonago, Wi., U.S.	H7	110
Mula, Spain	G10	16
Mulanje, Mwi.	E7	58
Mulas, Punta de, c., Cuba	D7	94
Mulatos, Mex.	C5	90
Mulberry, Ar., U.S.	G2	114
Mulberry, Fl., U.S.	L5	112
Mulberry, In., U.S.	B10	114
Mulberry, stm., Ar., U.S.	G3	114
Mulberry Fork, stm., Al., U.S.	I9	114
Mulchatna, stm., Ak., U.S.	F17	100
Mulchén, Chile	I2	80
Mulde, stm., Ger.	D12	10
Muldoon, Tx., U.S.	J9	116
Muldraugh, Ky., U.S.	E11	114
Muldrow, Ok., U.S.	G2	114
Mule, Lac la, l., P.Q., Can.	A8	106
Mulegé, Mex.	D3	90
Mulegns, Switz.	E12	13
Muleshoe, Tx., U.S.	E4	116
Mulgowie, Austl.	F10	70
Mulgrave, N.S., Can.	G12	106
Mulhacén, mtn., Spain	H8	16
Mulhall, Ok., U.S.	C9	116
Mulhouse, Fr.	E14	14
Mull, Island of, i., Scot., U.K.	E7	8
Mullan, Id., U.S.	C10	122
Mullen, Ne., U.S.	I6	118
Mullengudgery, Austl.	H7	70
Mullens, W.V., U.S.	B5	112
Muller, Pegunungan, mts., Indon.	E5	38
Mullett Lake, l., Mi., U.S.	E11	110
Mullewa, Austl.	E3	68
Mullica, stm., N.J., U.S.	H12	108
Mulligan, stm., Austl.	D3	70
Mullin, Tx., U.S.	H8	116
Mullingar, Ire.	H6	8
Mullins, S.C., U.S.	E7	112
Mullinville, Ks., U.S.	N8	118
Mullumbimby, Austl.	G10	70
Multān, Pak.	E4	44
Mulvane, Ks., U.S.	N10	118
Mulyah Mountain, mtn., Austl.	H6	70
Mumbwa, Zam.	D5	58
Mumford, Tx., U.S.	I10	116
Mumu, Sudan	K2	60
Mumungwe, Bots.	C8	66
Mun, stm., Thai.	G8	40
Muna, Mex.	G15	90
Munā, Sau. Ar.	D1	47
Muna, stm., Russia	D15	28
Münchberg, Ger.	E11	10
München (Munich), Ger.	G11	10
München-Gladbach see Mönchengladbach, Ger.	D6	10
Münchenstein, Switz.	C8	13
Munchique, Cerro, mtn., Col.	F4	84
Munch'ŏn, N. Kor.	D15	32
Muncie, In., U.S.	B11	114
Muncy, Pa., U.S.	F10	108
Mundare, Ab., Can.	D22	102
Munday, Tx., U.S.	F7	116
Mundelein, Il., U.S.	H7	110
Münden, Ger.	D9	10
Mundo Novo, Braz.	A8	79
Mundubbera, Austl.	E9	70
Munene, Zimb.	C10	66
Munford, Tn., U.S.	G7	114
Munfordville, Ky., U.S.	E11	114
Mungallala, Austl.	F7	70
Mungbere, Zaire	H6	56
Munger, India	H12	44
Mungindi, Austl.	G8	70
Munhango, Ang.	D3	58
Munich see München, Ger.	G11	10
Munising, Mi., U.S.	D9	110
Muniz Freire, Braz.	F8	79
Munku-Sardyk, gora, mtn., Asia	G12	28
Munro Lake, l., Mb., Can.	D19	104
Munsan, S. Kor.	F14	32
Münsingen, Switz.	E8	13
Munson, Ab., Can.	F22	102
Munsons Corners, N.Y., U.S.	E10	108
Munster, Ger.	C10	10
Münster, Ger.	D7	10
Munster, Fr.	D14	14
Munster, hist. reg., Ire.	I5	8
Munuscong Lake, l., N.A.	D11	110
Muong Saiapoun, Laos	E6	40
Muonio, Fin.	H18	6
Muqayshiṭ, i., U.A.E.	B8	47
Muqdisho (Mogadishu), Som.	H10	56
Muqi, China	B12	32
Muqui, Braz.	F8	79
Mur (Mura), stm., Eur.	I15	10
Mura (Mur), stm., Eur.	I16	10
Muradiye, Tur.	B7	48
Murakami, Japan	I14	36
Muraši, Russia	F7	26
Murat, stm., Tur.	B5	48
Muravjovo, Russia	E17	22
Murča, Port.	D4	16
Mūrcheh Khvort, Iran	E11	48
Murchison, Austl.	K6	70
Murchison, Tx., U.S.	G11	116
Murchison, stm., Austl.	E3	68
Murchison, Mount, mtn., N.Z.	E3	72
Murchison Falls see Kabalega Falls, wtfl, Ug.	H7	56
Murcia, Spain	H10	16
Murcia, state, Spain	G10	16
Murciélago, Islas, is., C.R.	G9	92
Murdo, S.D., U.S.	H7	118
Mureck, Aus.	I15	10
Mureș, co., Rom.	C8	20
Mureș (Maros), stm., Eur.	C5	20
Muret, Fr.	I8	14
Murfreesboro, Ar., U.S.	H3	114
Murfreesboro, N.C., U.S.	C9	112
Murfreesboro, Tn., U.S.	G10	114
Murgab, Taj.	J12	26
Murgab (Morghāb), stm., Asia	B16	48
Murgha Kibzai, Pak.	E3	44
Murgon, Austl.	F9	70
Muri, Switz.	E7	13
Muriaé, Braz.	F7	79
Muriaé, stm., Braz.	F8	79
Muriel Lake, l., Ab., Can.	C24	102
Müritz, l., Ger.	B12	10
Murmansk, Russia	D4	26
Murmino, Russia	G23	22
Murnei, Sudan	K2	60
Murom, Russia	F25	22
Muroran, Japan	e15	36a
Muroto, Japan	N9	36
Murphy, Id., U.S.	G9	122
Murphy, N.C., U.S.	D2	112
Murphy Lake, l., B.C., Can.	E13	102
Murphys, Ca., U.S.	F5	124
Murphysboro, Il., U.S.	E7	114
Murray, Ia., U.S.	I2	110
Murray, Ky., U.S.	F8	114
Murray, Ut., U.S.	D5	120
Murray, stm., Austl.	J3	70
Murray, stm., B.C., Can.	B13	102
Murray, Lake, l., Pap. N. Gui.	G11	38
Murray, Lake, res., S.C., U.S.	E5	112
Murray, Mount, mtn., Yk., Can.	F30	100
Murray Bay see La Malbaie, P.Q., Can.	E3	106
Murray Bridge, Austl.	J3	70
Murray City, Oh., U.S.	H4	108
Murray Harbour, P.E., Can.	F11	106
Murray Head, c., P.E., Can.	F11	106
Murray Maxwell Bay, b., N.T., Can.	B16	96
Murray River, P.E., Can.	F11	106
Murraysburg, S. Afr.	H6	66
Murrayville, Il., U.S.	C6	114
Murree, Pak.	D5	44
Murrhardt, Ger.	G9	10
Murrí, stm., Col.	D4	84
Murrumbidgee, stm., Austl.	J6	70
Murrumburrah, Austl.	J8	70
Murrurundi, Austl.	H9	70
Murska Sobota, Slvn.	C11	18
Murtajāpur, India	B4	46
Murten, Switz.	E7	13
Murtle Lake, l., B.C., Can.	E15	102
Murtoa, Austl.	K5	70
Murtosa, Port.	E3	16
Muru, stm., Braz.	C6	82
Murud, Gunong, mtn., Malay.	E6	38
Murupara, N.Z.	C6	72
Murutinga, Braz.	I13	84
Murwāra, India	I9	44
Murwillumbah, Austl.	G10	70
Mürzzuschlag, Aus.	H15	10
Muş, Tur.	B6	48
Mūsā, Jabal (Mount Sinai), mtn., Egypt	C7	60
Musaid, Libya	B3	60
Musala, mtn., Bul.	G7	20
Musan, N. Kor.	A17	32
Musandam Peninsula, pen., Oman	A10	47
Mūsā Qal'eh, Afg.	D1	44
Musay'īd, Qatar	D11	56
Muscat see Masqaṭ, Oman	C11	47
Muscatatuck, stm., In., U.S.	D10	114
Muscatine, Ia., U.S.	I4	110
Mus-Chaja, gora, mtn., Russia	E20	28
Muscle Shoals, Al., U.S.	H9	114
Musclow, Mount, mtn., B.C., Can.	D7	102
Musclow Lake, l., On., Can.	G20	104
Muscoda, Wi., U.S.	G5	110
Muscowpetung Indian Reserve, Sk., Can.	H10	104
Müsgebi, Tur.	L11	20
Musgrave, Austl.	B8	68
Musgravetown, Nf., Can.	D20	106
Mushandike Sanctuary, Zimb.	C10	66
Mushie, Zaire	B3	58
Mushin, Nig.	H11	64
Muskeg, stm., Ab., Can.	D16	102
Muskeg Lake Indian Reserve, Sk., Can.	F8	104
Muskegon, Mi., U.S.	G9	110
Muskegon, stm., Mi., U.S.	D1	108
Muskegon Heights, Mi., U.S.	G9	110
Muskingum, stm., Oh., U.S.	H5	108
Muskoday Indian Reserve, Sk., Can.	E9	104
Muskogee, Ok., U.S.	D11	116
Muskowekwan Indian Reserve, Sk., Can.	G10	104
Muskrat Dam Lake, l., On., Can.	E23	104
Muskwa, stm., B.C., Can.	E8	96
Muskwa Lake, l., Ab., Can.	A20	102
Muslimbāgh, Pak.	E2	44
Musoma, Tan.	B6	58
Musquanousse, Lac, l., P.Q., Can.	B12	106
Musquaro, Lac, l., P.Q., Can.	B12	106
Musquodoboit Harbour, N.S., Can.	H10	106
Musselshell, stm., Mt., U.S.	C18	122
Mussomeli, Italy	L8	18
Mussuma, Ang.	D4	58
Mustafakemalpaşa, Tur.	I12	20
Mustang Island, i., Tx., U.S.	L10	116
Mustinka, stm., Mn., U.S.	F11	118
Mustla, Est.	C8	22
Mustvee, Est.	C9	22
Muswellbrook, Austl.	I9	70
Mūt, Egypt	E5	60
Mut, Tur.	C2	48
Mutá, Ponta do, c., Braz.	B9	79
Mutambara, Zimb.	B11	66
Mutare, Zimb.	B11	66
Mutlu (Rezovska), stm., Eur.	H11	20
Mutsamudu, Com.	I16	67a
Mutsu, Japan	F16	36
Mutsu-wan, b., Japan	F15	36
Muttaburra, Austl.	D6	70
Muttenz, Switz.	C8	13
Mutuípe, Braz.	B9	79
Mutum, Braz.	E8	79
Mutum, stm., Braz.	J8	84
Mutunópolis, Braz.	B4	79
Muxima, Ang.	C2	58
Muymano, stm., S.A.	D7	82
Muy Muy, Nic.	E9	92
Muyua Island, i., Pap. N. Gui.	A10	68
Muyumba, Zaire	C5	58
Muzaffarābād, Pak.	C5	44
Muzaffarnagar, India	F7	44
Muzaffarpur, India	G11	44
Muzat, stm., China	C3	30
Muztag, mtn., China	B9	44
Muztag, mtn., China	B12	44
Mvolo, Sudan	N5	60
Mvuma, Zimb.	B10	66
Mwali (Mohéli), i., Com.	I15	67a
Mwanza, Tan.	B6	58
Mweka, Zaire	B4	58
Mwenezi, Zimb.	C10	66
Mweru, Lake, l., Afr.	C5	58
Mwinilunga, Zam.	D4	58
Myaing, Myan.	D3	40
Myanaung, Myan.	E3	40
Myanmar (Burma), ctry., Asia	A2	38
Myaungmya, Myan.	F3	40
Myebon, Myan.	D2	40
Myerstown, Pa., U.S.	G10	108
Myingyan, Myan.	D3	40
Myitkyinā, Myan.	B4	40
Myittha, Myan.	D4	40
Myjava, Slvk.	G17	10
Mykolayiv, Ukr.	H4	26
Mykolayivka, Ukr.	C13	20
Myllymäki, Fin.	J19	6
Mymensingh, Bngl.	H14	44
Mynämäki, Fin.	K18	6
Mynfontein, S. Afr.	H6	66
Myrnam, Ab., Can.	D23	102
Myrskylä (Mörskom), Fin.	K19	6
Myrtle Beach, S.C., U.S.	F8	112
Myrtle Creek, Or., U.S.	G2	122
Myrtle Grove, Fl., U.S.	L9	114
Myrtle Point, Or., U.S.	G1	122
Myrtletowne, Ca., U.S.	D1	124
Myski, Russia	G9	28
Myškino, Russia	D21	22
Myślenice, Pol.	F19	10
Mysłowice, Pol.	E19	10
Mysore, India	F4	46
Mystic, Ct., U.S.	F15	108
Mystic, Ia., U.S.	J3	110
Myszków, Pol.	E19	10
Myt, Russia	E25	22
My Tho, Viet.	I9	40
Mytišči, Russia	F20	22
Myton, Ut., U.S.	D6	120
Mzimba, Mwi.	D6	58
Mzimvubu, stm., S. Afr.	H9	66
Mzuzu, Mwi.	D6	58
N		
Na (Tengtiao), stm., Asia	C7	40
Naalehu, Hi., U.S.	r18	125a
Naas, Ire.	H7	8
Nabā, Jabal an- (Mount Nebo), mtn., Jord.	E5	50
Nabalat Al-Ḥajanah, Sudan	K5	60
Nabburg, Ger.	F12	10
Naberežnyje Čelny, Russia	F8	26
Nabesna, Ak., U.S.	E23	100
Nabeul, Tun.	M5	18
Nābha, India	E7	44
Nabileque, stm., Braz.	I13	82
Nabī Shu'ayb, Jabal an-, mtn., Yemen	G3	47
Nabisipi, stm., P.Q., Can.	B11	106
Nabogame, Mex.	D6	90
Naboomspruit, S. Afr.	E9	66
Nabq, Egypt	C8	60
Nābulus, W.B.	D4	50
Nacala-Velha, Moz.	D8	58
Nacaome, Hond.	D7	92
Naches, stm., Wa., U.S.	D4	122
Náchod, Czech Rep.	E16	10
Nachodka, Russia	I18	28
Nachvak Fiord, Nf., Can.	E20	96
Nacimiento, Chile	I2	80
Naco, Az., U.S.	M7	120
Naco, Mex.	B5	90
Nacogdoches, Tx., U.S.	K2	114
Nácori Chico, Mex.	C5	90
Nacozari de García, Mex.	B5	90
Ñacunday, Para.	D11	80
Nadaleen Mountain, mtn., Yk., Can.	D28	100
Naden Harbour, b., B.C., Can.	C2	102
Nadiād, India	I5	44
Nădlac, Rom.	C4	20
Nador, Mor.	C9	62
Nadvirna, Ukr.	A8	20
Nadvoicy, Russia	J24	6
Nadym, Russia	D12	26
Nadym, stm., Russia	D12	26
Nafadji, Sen.	E4	64
Näfels, Switz.	D11	13
Nafī, Sau. Ar.	I7	48
Naga, Phil.	o20	39b
Nâga, Kreb en, clf, Afr.	I7	62
Naga Hills, mts., Asia	B3	40
Nāgāland, state, India	H16	44
Nagano, Japan	K13	36
Nagaoka, Japan	J13	36
Nagaon, India	G15	44
Nāgappattinam, India	G5	46
Nāgārjuna Sāgar, res., India	D5	46
Nagarote, Nic.	E8	92
Nagar Pārkar, Pak.	H4	44
Nagasaki, Japan	O4	36
Nāgaur, India	G5	44
Nagda, India	I6	44
Nāgercoil, India	H4	46
Nagīna, India	F8	44
Nagold, Ger.	G8	10
Nagorno-Karabakh, hist. reg., Azer.	A9	48
Nagornyj, Russia	F16	28
Nagoya, Japan	L11	36
Nāgpur, India	J8	44
Nagqu, China	E5	30
Nagua, Dom. Rep.	E10	94
Nagyatád, Hung.	I17	10
Nagybajom, Hung.	I17	10
Nagyecsed, Hung.	H22	10
Nagykálló, Hung.	H21	10
Nagykanizsa, Hung.	I17	10
Nagykőrös, Hung.	H19	10
Naha, Japan	u2	37b
Nāhan, India	E7	44
Nahang (Nihing), stm., Asia	H17	48
Nahanni National Park, N.T., Can.	F31	100
Nahariyya, Isr.	B4	50
Nahāvand, Iran	D10	48
Nahe, China	B11	30
Nahirne, Ukr.	D12	20
Nahma, Mi., U.S.	E9	110
Nahualate, stm., Guat.	C3	92
Nahuel Huapí, Lago, l., Arg.	E2	78
Nahunta, Ga., U.S.	H5	112
Naica, Mex.	D7	90
Naicam, Sk., Can.	F10	104
Naikoon Provincial Park, B.C., Can.	D3	102
Nailin, China	B7	32
Nā'īn, Iran	E12	48
Nain, Nf., Can.	E20	96
Naini Tāl, India	F8	44
Nairn, La., U.S.	M7	114
Nairobi, Kenya	B7	58
Naissaar, i., Est.	B7	22
Naivasha, Kenya	B7	58
Najafābād, Iran	E11	48
Najasa, stm., Cuba	D6	94
Nájera, Spain	C9	16
Naj'Ḥammādī, Egypt	D7	60
Najībābād, India	F8	44
Najin, N. Kor.	A18	32
Najstenjarvi, Russia	J23	6
Naju, S. Kor.	H14	32
Nakadōri-shima, i., Japan	O4	36
Nakaminato, Japan	K15	36
Nakano-shima, i., Japan	r4	37b
Nakape, Sudan	O5	60
Nakatsu, Japan	N6	36
Nakfa, Erit.	I10	60
Nakhon Nayok, Thai.	G6	40
Nakhon Pathom, Thai.	H6	40
Nakhon Phanom, Thai.	F8	40
Nakhon Ratchasima, Thai.	G7	40
Nakhon Sawan, Thai.	G6	40
Nakhon Si Thammarat, Thai.	J5	40
Nakina, On., Can.	F15	96
Nakło nad Notecią, Pol.	B17	10
Naknek, Ak., U.S.	G16	100
Nakskov, Den.	N12	6
Nakuru, Kenya	B7	58
Nakusp, B.C., Can.	G17	102
Nalajch, Mong.	B8	30
Nālanda, India	H11	44
Nal'čik, Russia	I6	26
Nalgonda, India	D5	46
Nālūt, Libya	E16	62
Nam, stm., Asia	D5	40
Namaacha, Moz.	E11	66
Namak, Daryācheh-ye, l., Iran	D11	48
Namakan Lake, l., N.A.	B3	110
Namaksār, Kowl-e, l., Asia	D18	48
Namangan, Uzb.	I12	26
Namapa, Moz.	D7	58
Namatanai, Pap. N. Gui.	k17	68a
Nambour, Austl.	F10	70
Nambucca Heads, Austl.	H10	70
Nam Can, Viet.	J8	40
Nam Co, l., China	E14	44
Nam Dinh, Viet.	D9	40
Namekagon, stm., Wi., U.S.	D3	110
Namen (Namur), Bel.	H6	12
Namew Lake, l., Can.	D13	104
Namhkam, Myan.	C4	40
Namib Desert, des., Nmb.	D2	66
Namibe, Ang.	E2	58
Namibia, ctry., Afr.	F3	58
Namjagbarwa Feng, mtn., China	F16	44
Namoi, stm., Austl.	H8	70
Namounou, Burkina	F10	64
Nampa, Ab., Can.	A17	102
Nampa, Id., U.S.	G9	122
Nampawng, Myan.	C4	40
Namp'o, N. Kor.	E13	32
Nampula, Moz.	E7	58
Namsang, Myan.	D4	40
Namsos, Nor.	I12	6
Namtu, Myan.	A2	38
Namu, B.C., Can.	F7	102
Namur (Namen), Bel.	H6	12
Namur, prov., Bel.	H6	12
Namutoni, Nmb.	B3	66
Namwŏn, S. Kor.	H15	32
Namyang, N. Kor.	A17	32
Namyit Island, i., Asia	C5	38
Namysłów, Pol.	D17	10
Nan, Thai.	E6	40
Nan, stm., Thai.	F6	40
Nanaimo, B.C., Can.	H11	102
Nanam, N. Kor.	B17	32
Nanango, Austl.	F10	70
Nanao, Japan	J11	36
Nanay, stm., Peru	I6	84
Nanchang, China	G4	34
Nancheng, China	H5	34
Nanchong, China	E8	30
Nancowry Island, i., India	K2	40
Nancun, China	G8	32
Nancy, Fr.	D13	14
Nanda Devi, mtn., India	E8	44
Nandaime, Nic.	F8	92
Nānded, India	C4	46
Nanding, stm., Asia	C5	40
N'andoma, Russia	E6	26
Nandu, stm., China	E11	40
Nandurbār, India	J6	44
Nandyāl, India	E5	46
Nanga Parbat, mtn., Pak.	C6	44
Nangin, Myan.	I5	40
Nangnim, N. Kor.	C15	32
Nangola, Mali	E6	64
Nang Rong, Thai.	G7	40
Nanika Lake, l., B.C., Can.	D7	102
Nanjangūd, India	F4	46
Nanjiang, China	C9	34
Nanjing (Nanking), China	C7	34
Nankang, China	J3	34
Nanking see Nanjing, China	C7	34
Nankou, China	I6	34
Nan Ling, mts., China	J2	34
Nanlinqiao, China	F3	34
Nannine, Austl.	E3	68
Nanning, China	C10	40
Nanowin, stm., Mb., Can.	E18	104
Nanpi, China	E4	32
Nanping, China	I7	34
Nanpu, China	D6	32
Nansa, stm., Spain	B7	16
Nansei-shotō (Ryukyu Islands), is., Japan	s4	37b
Nanshan see Qilian Shan, mts., China	D6	30
Nanshan Island, i., Asia	C6	38
Nant, Fr.	H10	14
Nantais, Lac, l., P.Q., Can.	D18	96
Nantang, China	I4	34
Nantes, Fr.	E5	14
Nanticoke, Pa., U.S.	F10	108
Nanticoke, stm., U.S.	I11	108
Nanton, Ab., Can.	G21	102
Nantong, China	C9	34
Nant'ou, Tai.	L9	34
Nantua, Fr.	F12	14
Nantucket, Ma., U.S.	F16	108
Nantucket Island, i., Ma., U.S.	F16	108
Nantucket Sound, strt., Ma., U.S.	F16	108
Nanty Glo, Pa., U.S.	G8	108
Nanuque, Braz.	D8	79
Nanwan, China	C2	34
Nanxiang, China	D10	34
Nanxiong, China	J3	34
Nanyang, China	B1	34
Nanzhao, China	B1	34
Naococane, Lac, l., P.Q., Can.	F18	96
Não-me-Toque, Braz.	E12	80
Naosap Lake, l., Mb., Can.	D13	104
Náousa, Grc.	I6	20
Napa, Ca., U.S.	F3	124
Napakiak, Ak., U.S.	F14	100
Napanee, On., Can.	F19	110
Napaskiak, Ak., U.S.	F14	100
Napè, Laos	E8	40
Napenay, Arg.	D8	80
Naperville, Il., U.S.	I7	110
Napetipi, stm., Can.	A15	106
Napier, N.Z.	C6	72
Napier, S. Afr.	J4	66
Napier Mountains, mts., Ant.	B4	73
Napinka, Mb., Can.	I14	104
Naples, Fl., U.S.	M5	112
Naples, Id., U.S.	B9	122
Naples see Napoli, Italy	I9	18
Naples, N.Y., U.S.	E9	108
Naples, Tx., U.S.	I2	114
Napo, prov., Ec.	H4	84
Napo, stm., S.A.	I6	84
Napoleon, N.D., U.S.	E8	118
Napoleon, Oh., U.S.	F2	108
Napoleonville, La., U.S.	M5	114
Napoli (Naples), Italy	I9	18
Nappanee, In., U.S.	A10	114
Naqādah, Egypt	E7	60
Naqadeh, Iran	C8	48
Nara, Japan	M10	36
Nara, Mali	D6	64
Naracoorte, Austl.	K4	70
Naradhan, Austl.	I7	70
Naramata, B.C., Can.	H15	102
Naranjal, Ec.	I3	84
Naranjito, Hond.	C6	92
Naranjo, C.R.	G10	92
Naranjo, stm., Guat.	C3	92
Narasapur, India	D6	46
Narasaraopet, India	D6	46
Narathiwat, Thai.	K6	40
Nara Visa, N.M., U.S.	D3	116
Nārāyanganj, Bngl.	I14	44
Nārāyaṇi (Gandak), stm., Asia	G11	44
Nārāyanpet, India	D4	46
Narbonne, Fr.	I10	14
Narcosli Creek, stm., B.C., Can.	E12	102
Nardò, Italy	I13	18
Nare, stm., Col.	D5	84
Nares Strait, strt., N.A.	A13	86
Narew, stm., Eur.	C21	10
Narinda, Baie de, b., Madag.	o22	67b
Nariño, dept., Col.	G3	84
Narita, Japan	L15	36
Nar'jan-Mar, Russia	D8	26
Narmada, stm., India	J5	44
Nārnaul, India	F7	44
Narni, Italy	G7	18
Naro, Italy	L8	18
Narodnaja, gora, mtn., Russia	D10	26
Naro-Fominsk, Russia	F19	22
Narol, Pol.	E23	10
Narooma, Austl.	K9	70
Narrabri, Austl.	H8	70
Narran, stm., Austl.	G7	70
Narrandera, Austl.	J7	70
Narraway, stm., Can.	C14	102
Narrogin, Austl.	F3	68
Narromine, Austl.	I8	70
Narrows, Va., U.S.	B6	112
Narsimhapur, India	I8	44
Narsīpatnam, India	D7	46
Narva, Est.	B11	22
Narva, stm., Eur.	B10	22
Narva laht (Narvskij zaliv), b., Eur.	B10	22
Narvik, Nor.	G15	6
Narvskij zaliv (Narva laht), b., Eur.	B10	22
Narvskoje vodochranilišče, res., Eur.	B11	22
Naryn, Kyrg.	I13	26
Naryn, stm., Asia	I12	26
Naryškino, Russia	I18	22
Na San, Thai.	J5	40
Nasarawa, Nig.	G13	64
Naschel, Arg.	G6	80
Nash, Tx., U.S.	I2	114

Name — Map Ref. — Page

Nishio, Japan M12 36
Niska Lake, l., Sk., Can. C6 104
Nisling, stm., Yk., Can. E25 100
Nisqually, stm., Wa., U.S. D3 122
Nisswa, Mn., U.S. D1 110
Nistru (Dnister), stm., Eur. H3 26
Nisutlin, stm., Yk., Can. F28 100
Niterói, Braz. G7 79
Nithi River, B.C., Can. C9 102
Nitinat Lake, l., B.C., Can. I10 102
Nitra, Slvk. G18 10
Nitro, W.V., U.S. I5 108
Niubu, China D6 34
Niue, dep., Oc. K23 126
Niut, Gunung, mtn., Indon. N10 40
Niutuo, China D4 32
Niuzhuang, China C10 32
Nive, stm., Austl. E7 70
Nivelles (Nijvel), Bel. G5 12
Nivernais, hist. reg., Fr. E10 14
Niverville, Mb., Can. I17 104
Nivskij, Russia H23 6
Nixa, Mo., U.S. E3 114
Nixon, Nv., U.S. E6 124
Nixon, Tx., U.S. J9 116
Nizāmābād, India C5 46
Nizām Sāgar, res., India C4 46
Nizhyn, Ukr. G4 26
Nizip, Tur. C4 48
Nízke Tatry, mts., Slvk. G19 10
Nižn'aja Pojma, Russia F11 28
Nižn'aja Tunguska, stm., Russia E10 28
Nižn'aja Tura, Russia F9 26
Nižneudinsk, Russia G11 28
Nižnevartovsk, Russia E13 26
Nižnij Novgorod (Gor'kij), Russia E27 22
Nižnij P'andž, Taj. J11 26
Nižnij Tagil, Russia F9 26
Nizwā, Oman C10 47
Nizzana, Isr. G2 50
Njasviž, Bela. H9 22
Njazidja (Grande Comore), i., Com. k15 67a
Njombe, Tan. C6 58
Nkhata Bay, Mwi. D6 58
Nkhotakota, Mwi. D6 58
Nkongsamba, Cam. H8 54
Nkurenkuru, Nmb. A4 66
Nmai, stm., Myan. B4 40
Noākhāli, Bngl. I14 44
Noatak, Ak., U.S. C13 100
Nobeoka, Japan O6 36
Noble, Il., U.S. D8 114
Noble, Ok., U.S. D9 116
Noblesville, In., U.S. B10 114
Noboribetsu, Japan e16 36a
Nobres, Braz. F13 82
Nobsa, Col. E6 84
Nocatee, Fl., U.S. L5 112
Nocera [Inferiore], Italy I9 18
Noci, Italy I12 18
Nockatunga, Austl. F5 70
Nocona, Tx., U.S. F9 116
Nocupétaro, Mex. H9 90
Nodaway, stm., U.S. B1 114
Noel, Mo., U.S. F2 114
Noetinger, Arg. G7 80
Nogales, Az., U.S. M6 120
Nogales, Chile G3 80
Nogales, Mex. B4 90
Nogara, Eth. K9 60
Nogaro, Fr. I6 14
Nōgata, Japan N5 36
Nogent-le-Rotrou, Fr. D7 14
Noginsk, Russia F21 22
Nogoa, stm., Austl. D7 70
Nogoyá, Arg. G9 80
Nógrád, co., Hung. H19 10
Noirmoutier, Île de, i., Fr. E4 14
Nokaneng, Bots. B6 66
Nokomis, Fl., U.S. L4 112
Nokomis, Il., U.S. C7 114
Nokomis, Sk., Can. G9 104
Nokomis Lake, l., Sk., Can. B11 104
Nola, Italy I9 18
Nolichucky, stm., U.S. C3 112
Nolin, stm., Ky., U.S. E10 114
Nolin Lake, res., Ky., U.S. E10 114
Nolinsk, Russia F7 26
Nombre de Dios, Mex. F7 90
Nombre de Dios, Pan. C3 84
Nombre de Dios, Cordillera, mts., Hond. B8 92
Nome, Ak., U.S. D12 100
Nomgon, Mong. C8 30
Nominingue, P.Q., Can. A11 108
Nonacho Lake, l., N.T., Can. D11 96
Nondalton, Ak., U.S. F17 100
Nondweni, S. Afr. G10 66
Nong'an, China C12 30
Nong Khai, Thai. F7 40
Nongoma, S. Afr. F10 66
Nono, Eth. M9 60
Nonoai, Braz. D12 80
Nonoava, Mex. D6 90
Nonogasta, Arg. E5 80
Nonsan, S. Kor. G15 32
Nonthaburi, Thai. H6 40
Nontron, Fr. G7 14
Nooksack, stm., Wa., U.S. B3 122
Noonan, N.D., U.S. C4 118
Noord-Brabant, prov., Neth. E6 12
Noord-Holland, prov., Neth. C6 12
Noordoewer, Nmb. G3 66
Noordoostpolder, reg., Neth. C8 12
Noordwijk aan Zee, Neth. D5 12
Noordzeekanaal, Neth. D5 12
Noorvik, Ak., U.S. C14 100
Nootka Island, i., B.C., Can. H8 102
Nootka Sound, strt., B.C., Can. H8 102
Nóqui, Ang. C2 58
Norah, i., Erit. E9 56
Noralee, B.C., Can. D8 102
Nora Springs, Ia., U.S. G2 110
Norberto de la Riestra, Arg. H9 80
Norborne, Mo., U.S. C3 114
Norcatur, Ks., U.S. L7 118
Norcia, Italy G8 18
Norcross, Ga., U.S. F2 112
Nord, dept., Fr. B10 14
Nord, Grand lac du, l., P.Q., Can. B6 106
Nord, Petit lac du, l., P.Q., Can. B6 106
Nordaustlandet, i., Nor. B3 24
Nordegg, Ab., Can. E18 102
Nordegg, stm., Ab., Can. E19 102
Norden, Ger. B7 10
Nordenham, Ger. B8 10
Nordenšel'da, archipelag, is., Russia B11 28
Nordenskiold, stm., Yk., Can. F26 100
Norderstedt, Ger. B10 10
Nordhausen, Ger. D10 10
Nordheim, Tx., U.S. K9 116
Nordhorn, Ger. C7 10
Nordkapp, c., Nor. F19 6
Nordland, co., Nor. H14 6
Nördlingen, Ger. G10 10
Nordostrundingen, c., Grnld. A18 86
Nord-Ostsee-Kanal, Ger. A9 10
Nordreisa, Nor. G17 6
Nordrhein-Westfalen, state, Ger. D7 10
Nord-Trøndelag, co., Nor. I12 6
Nore, Nor. K11 6
Norfolk, Ne., U.S. I10 118
Norfolk, Va., U.S. C10 112
Norfolk, co., Eng., U.K. I15 8
Norfolk Island, dep., Oc. K20 126
Norfork Lake, res., U.S. F4 114
Noril'sk, Russia D9 28
Norlina, N.C., U.S. C8 112
Normal, Al., U.S. H10 114
Normal, Il., U.S. J7 110
Norman, Ar., U.S. H3 114
Norman, Ok., U.S. D9 116
Norman, stm., Austl. B4 70
Norman, Lake, res., N.C., U.S. D6 112
Normandie, hist. reg., Fr. D6 14
Normandie, Collines de, hills, Fr. D6 14
Normandy see Normandie, hist. reg., Fr. D6 14
Normangee, Tx., U.S. H10 116
Norman Park, Ga., U.S. H3 112
Normanton, Austl. A4 70
Norman Wells, N.T., Can. D31 100
Norogachi, Mex. D6 90
Norphlet, Ar., U.S. I4 114
Norquay, Sk., Can. G12 104
Norra Kvarken (Merenkurkku), strt., Eur. J17 6
Norrbottens Län, co., Swe. H16 6
Norridgewock, Me., U.S. C17 108
Norris, Tn., U.S. C2 112
Norris Arm, Nf., Can. C18 106
Norris City, Il., U.S. E8 114
Norris Lake, res., Tn., U.S. C3 112
Norris Point, Nf., Can. C16 106
Norristown, Pa., U.S. G11 108
Norrköping, Swe. L15 6
Norrtälje, Swe. L16 6
Norseman, Austl. F4 68
Norsk, Russia G17 28
Norte, Canal do, strt., Braz. C8 76
Norte, Serra do, plat., Braz. D12 82
Norte de Santander, state, Col. J8 94
Norte de Santander, dept., Col. C6 84
Nortelândia, Braz. F13 82
North, S.C., U.S. F5 112
North, stm., Al., U.S. I9 114
North, stm., Ia., U.S. I2 110
North, stm., Nf., Can. E20 96
North, Cape, c., N.S., Can. E13 106
North Adams, Ma., U.S. E13 108
North Adams, Mi., U.S. I11 110
North Albany, Or., U.S. F2 122
Northam, Austl. F3 68
North America E8 86
Northampton, Austl. E2 68
Northampton, Eng., U.K. I13 8
Northampton, Ma., U.S. E14 108
Northampton, Pa., U.S. G11 108
Northamptonshire, co., Eng., U.K. I13 8
North Andaman, i., India H2 40
North Anna, stm., Va., U.S. B9 112
North Anson, Me., U.S. C17 108
North Asheboro, N.C., U.S. D7 112
North Atlanta, Ga., U.S. F2 112
North Augusta, S.C., U.S. F5 112
North Aulatsivik Island, i., Nf., Can. E20 96
North Baltimore, Oh., U.S. F3 108
North Battleford, Sk., Can. F6 104
North Bay, On., Can. D16 110
North Bend, B.C., Can. H13 102
North Bend, Ne., U.S. J11 118
North Bend, Or., U.S. G1 122
North Bennington, Vt., U.S. E13 108
North Berwick, Me., U.S. D16 108
North Berwick, Scot., U.K. E11 8
North Bourke, Austl. H6 70
North Branch, Mi., U.S. G12 110
North Branch, Mn., U.S. E3 110
North Caicos, i., T./C. Is. D9 94
North Canadian, stm., Ok., U.S. D10 116
North Canton, Ga., U.S. E2 112
North Canton, Oh., U.S. G5 108
North Cape see Nordkapp, c., Nor. F19 6
North Cape, c., N.Z. A4 72
North Cape, c., P.E., Can. E9 106
North Caribou Lake, l., On., Can. F14 96
North Carolina, state, U.S. D11 98
North Cascades National Park, Wa., U.S. B4 122
North Channel, strt., On., Can. D12 110
North Channel, strt., U.K. F8 8
North Charleston, S.C., U.S. G7 112
North Chicago, Il., U.S. H8 110
North College Hill, Oh., U.S. H2 108
North Collins, N.Y., U.S. E8 108
North Conway, N.H., U.S. C15 108
North Creek, N.Y., U.S. D13 108
North Crossett, Ar., U.S. I5 114
North Dakota, state, U.S. B6 98
North East, Md., U.S. H11 108
North East, Pa., U.S. E7 108
North-East, dept., Bots. C8 66
North East Point, c., Bah. D8 94
North East Point, c., Bah. C8 94
Northeast Providence Channel, strt., Bah. B6 94
Northeim, Ger. D10 10
North English, Ia., U.S. I3 110
Northern, prov., S. Afr. D9 66
Northern Arm, Nf., Can. C18 106
Northern Cape, prov., S. Afr. G5 66
Northern Dvina see Severnaja Dvina, stm., Russia E6 26
Northern Indian Lake, l., Mb., Can. E13 96
Northern Ireland, ter., U.K. G7 8
Northern Mariana Islands, dep., Oc. G19 126
Northern Territory, ter., Austl. C6 68
North Fabius, stm., U.S. B4 114
Northfield, Ma., U.S. E14 108
Northfield, Mn., U.S. F2 110
Northfield, Vt., U.S. C14 108
North Flinders Range, mts., Austl. H3 70
North Fond du Lac, Wi., U.S. G7 110
North Foreland, c., Eng., U.K. J15 8
North Fork, Ca., U.S. G6 124
North Fork, stm., U.S. F4 114
North Fort Myers, Fl., U.S. M5 112
North Freedom, Wi., U.S. G6 110
North Frisian Islands, is., Eur. A8 10
Northglenn, Co., U.S. E12 120
North Gulfport, Ms., U.S. L7 114
North Henderson, N.C., U.S. C8 112
North Henik Lake, l., N.T., Can. D13 96
North Hero, Vt., U.S. C13 108
North Highlands, Ca., U.S. F4 124
North Island, i., N.Z. B4 72
North Judson, In., U.S. A10 114
North Kenai, Ak., U.S. F19 100
North Kingsville, Oh., U.S. F6 108
North Knife Lake, l., Mb., Can. E13 96
North La Junta, Co., U.S. N4 118
North Lakhimpur, India G16 44
North Las Vegas, Nv., U.S. H10 124
North La Veta Pass, Co., U.S. G11 120
North Liberty, In., U.S. A10 114
North Little Rock, Ar., U.S. H4 114
North Logan, Ut., U.S. C5 120
North Loon Mountain, mtn., Id., U.S. E10 122
North Loup, Ne., U.S. J9 118
North Loup, stm., Ne., U.S. J9 118
North Macmillan, stm., Yk., Can. E28 100
North Magnetic Pole B9 86
North Mamm Peak, mtn., Co., U.S. E9 120
North Manchester, In., U.S. A11 114
North Manitou Island, i., Mi., U.S. E9 110
North Mankato, Mn., U.S. F1 110
North Miami, Fl., U.S. N6 112
North Miami Beach, Fl., U.S. N6 112
North Moose Lake, l., Mb., Can. D14 104
North Muskegon, Mi., U.S. G9 110
North Myrtle Beach, S.C., U.S. F8 112
North Nahanni, stm., N.T., Can. E32 100
North New River Canal, Fl., U.S. M6 112
North Newton, Ks., U.S. M10 118
North Ogden, Ut., U.S. C5 120
Northome, Mn., U.S. C1 110
North Ossetia see Severnaja Osetija, state, Russia I6 26
North Palisade, mtn., Ca., U.S. G7 124
North Palm Beach, Fl., U.S. M6 112
North Park, Il., U.S. H6 110
North Platte, Ne., U.S. J7 118
North Platte, stm., U.S. C6 98
North Pole, Ak., U.S. D21 100
North Pole A4 86
Northport, Al., U.S. I9 114
Northport, Mi., U.S. E10 110
Northport, Wa., U.S. B8 122
North Portal, Sk., Can. I12 104
North Powder, Or., U.S. E8 122
North Ram, stm., Ab., Can. E18 102
North Rhine-Westphalia see Nordrhein-Westfalen, state, Ger. D7 10
North Richland Hills, Tx., U.S. G9 116
North Rim, Az., U.S. H4 120
North Rustico, P.E., Can. F10 106
North Salt Lake, Ut., U.S. D5 120
North Santiam, stm., Or., U.S. F3 122
North Saskatchewan, stm., Can. F10 96
North Sea, Eur. D8 4
North Shoal Lake, l., Mb., Can. H17 104
North Siberian Lowland see Severo-Sibirskaja nizmennost', pl., Russia C18 26
North Solitary Island, i., Austl. G10 70
North Spicer Island, i., N.T., Can. C17 96
North Spirit Lake, l., On., Can. F22 104
North Spot, i., Belize A6 92
North Stradbroke Island, i., Austl. F10 70
North Sydney, N.S., Can. F13 106
North Taranaki Bight, N.Z. C5 72
North Terre Haute, In., U.S. C9 114
North Thompson, stm., B.C., Can. G14 102
North Troy, Vt., U.S. C14 108
North Tunica, Ms., U.S. H6 114
North Twin Lake, l., Nf., Can. C18 106
North Uist, i., Scot., U.K. D6 8
Northumberland, co., Eng., U.K. F11 8
Northumberland Isles, is., Austl. C9 70
Northumberland Strait, strt., Can. F9 106
North Vancouver, B.C., Can. H11 102
North Vernon, In., U.S. C11 114
Northville, N.Y., U.S. D12 108
North Wabasca Lake, l., Ab., Can. A21 102
North-West, prov., S. Afr. F7 66
North West Cape, c., Austl. D2 68
Northwest Gander, stm., Nf., Can. D18 106
Northwest Miramichi, stm., N.B., Can. E7 106
Northwest Providence Channel, strt., Bah. A5 94
North West River, Nf., Can. F20 96
Northwest Territories, prov., Can. C12 96
North Wilkesboro, N.C., U.S. C5 112
North Windham, Me., U.S. D16 108
Northwood, Ia., U.S. G2 110
Northwood, N.D., U.S. D10 118
North Yamhill, stm., Or., U.S. E2 122
North York, On., Can. G16 110
North Yorkshire, co., Eng., U.K. G12 8
North Zulch, Tx., U.S. I10 116
Norton, Ks., U.S. L8 118
Norton, N.B., Can. G8 106
Norton, Va., U.S. C4 112
Norton Shores, Mi., U.S. G9 110
Norton Sound, strt., Ak., U.S. E12 100
Nortonville, Ks., U.S. L12 118
Nortorf, Ger. A9 10
Norvegia, Cape, c., Ant. C2 73
Norwalk, Ct., U.S. F13 108
Norwalk, Ia., U.S. I2 110
Norwalk, Oh., U.S. F4 108
Norway, Ia., U.S. I4 110
Norway, Me., U.S. C16 108
Norway, Mi., U.S. E8 110
Norway (Norge), ctry., Eur. C10 4
Norway Bay, b., N.T., Can. B12 96
Norway House, Mb., Can. E17 104
Norwegian Sea, Eur. C1 24
Norwich, Ct., U.S. F14 108
Norwich, Eng., U.K. I15 8
Norwich, Ks., U.S. N10 118
Norwich, N.Y., U.S. E11 108
Norwich, On., Can. H15 110
Norwood, Co., U.S. F8 120
Norwood, Ma., U.S. E15 108
Norwood, Mn., U.S. F2 110
Norwood, N.C., U.S. D6 112
Norwood, N.Y., U.S. C12 108
Norwood, Oh., U.S. H2 108
Norwood, On., Can. F18 110
Norwoodville, Ia., U.S. I2 110
Nose Creek, stm., Ab., Can. C15 102
Noshiro, Japan G15 36
Nosop (Nossob), stm., Afr. E5 66
Nossa Senhora do Livramento, Braz. F13 82
Nossob (Nosop), stm., Afr. E5 66
Nosy Varika, Madag. r23 67b
Notasulga, Al., U.S. J11 114
Notch Hill, B.C., Can. G15 102
Notch Peak, mtn., Ut., U.S. E3 120
Noteć, stm., Pol. C15 10
Notigi Lake, l., Mb., Can. C15 104
Notikewin, stm., Ab., Can. E9 96
Nótion Aiyaíon, prov., Grc. L9 20
Noto, Italy M10 18
Notodden, Nor. L11 6
Noto-hantō, pen., Japan J11 36
Notozero, ozero, l., Russia H23 6
Notre-Dame, N.B., Can. F9 106
Notre-Dame, Monts, mts., P.Q., Can. D5 106
Notre Dame Bay, b., Nf., Can. C18 106
Notre-Dame-de-Lourdes, Mb., Can. I16 104
Notre-Dame-du-Laus, P.Q., Can. A11 108
Notrees, Tx., U.S. H4 116
Nottawasaga Bay, b., On., Can. F15 110
Nottaway, stm., P.Q., Can. F17 96
Nottingham, Eng., U.K. I12 8
Nottingham Island, i., N.T., Can. D17 96
Nottinghamshire, co., Eng., U.K. H12 8
Nottoway, Va., U.S. B8 112
Nottoway, stm., Va., U.S. C10 112
Notukeu Creek, stm., Sk., Can. I7 104
Nouâdhibou, Maur. J2 62
Nouâdhibou, Râs, c., Afr. J2 62
Nouakchott, Maur. B2 64
Nouâmghâr, Maur. B1 64
Nouméa, N. Cal. K20 126
Nouna, Burkina E8 64
Noupoort, S. Afr. H7 66
Nouveau-Québec, Cratère du, crat., P.Q., Can. D18 96
Nouvelle, P.Q., Can. D7 106
Nouvelle, stm., P.Q., Can. D7 106
Nouvelle-France, Cap de, c., P.Q., Can. D18 96
Nova América, Braz. C4 79
Nova Andradina, Braz. G2 79
Nova Caipemba, Ang. C2 58
Nova Era, Braz. E7 79
Nova Esperança, Braz. G2 79
Nova Friburgo, Braz. G7 79
Nova Gradiška, Cro. D12 18
Nova Granada, Braz. F4 79
Nova Iguaçu, Braz. G7 79
Nova Ivanivka, Ukr. D13 20
Nova Kazanka, Kaz. H7 26
Novaja Ladoga, Russia A15 22
Novaja Sibir', ostrov, i., Russia B21 28
Novaja Zeml'a, is., Russia C9 26
Nova Kakhovka, Ukr. H4 26
Nova Lamego, Gui.-B. E2 64
Nova Lima, Braz. E7 79
Nova Mambone, Moz. C12 66
Nova Olinda do Norte, Braz. I13 84
Nova Ponte, Braz. E5 79
Nova Prata, Braz. E13 80
Novara, Italy D3 18
Nova Roma, Braz. B5 79
Nova Scotia, prov., Can. G20 96
Nova Sofala, Moz. C12 66
Novato, Ca., U.S. F3 124
Nova Varoš, Yugo. F3 20
Nova Venécia, Braz. E8 79
Nova Vida, Braz. D10 82
Nova Vida, Cachoeira, wtfl, Braz. C10 82
Nova Zagora, Bul. G10 20
Novelda, Spain G11 16
Nové Zámky, Slvk. H18 10
Novgorod, Russia C14 22
Novi Bečej, Yugo. D4 20
Novice, Tx., U.S. H7 116
Novigrad, Cro. E10 18
Novi Ligure, Italy E3 18
Novinger, Mo., U.S. B4 114
Novi Pazar, Bul. F11 20
Novi Pazar, Yugo. F4 20
Novi Sad, Yugo. D3 20
Novki, Russia E24 22
Novl'anka, Russia F24 22
Novlenskoje, Russia B22 22
Novo, stm., Braz. A6 82
Nôvo Acôrdo, Braz. B5 79
Novoaltajsk, Russia G8 28
Novoanninskij, Russia G6 26
Novo Aripuanã, Braz. J12 84
Novo Brasil, Braz. D3 79
Novočerkassk, Russia H6 26
Novo Cruzeiro, Braz. D8 79
Novodugino, Russia F17 22
Novodvinsk, Russia E6 26
Novo Hamburgo, Braz. E13 80
Novo Horizonte, Braz. F4 79
Novohrad-Volyns'kyy, Ukr. G3 26
Novoizborsk, Russia D10 22
Novoje Leušino, Russia E23 22
Novokaširsk, Russia G21 22
Novokazalinsk, Kaz. H10 26
Novokujbyševsk, Russia G7 26
Novokuzneck, Russia G9 28
Novol'vovsk, Russia H21 22
Novo Mesto, Slvn. D10 18
Novomoskovsk, Russia G21 22
Novomoskovs'k, Ukr. H5 26
Novopetrovskoje, Russia F19 22
Novopiscovo, Russia D24 22
Novorossijsk, Russia I5 26
Novorybnoje, Russia C13 28
Novoržev, Russia D12 22
Novošachtinsk, Russia H5 26
Novoselytsya, Ukr. A10 20
Novosibirsk, Russia F8 28
Novosibirskije ostrova, is., Russia B20 28
Novosibirskoje vodochranilišče, res., Russia G14 26
Novosil', Russia I20 22
Novosil's'ke, Ukr. D12 20
Novosokol'niki, Russia E13 22
Novos'olki, Russia G22 22
Novotroick, Russia G9 26
Novouzensk, Russia G7 26
Novov'atsk, Russia F7 26
Novov'azniki, Russia E25 22
Novovolyns'k, Ukr. G2 26
Novozavidovskij, Russia E19 22
Novozybkov, Russia I14 22
Novska, Cro. D11 18
Nový Bohumín, Czech Rep. F18 10
Nový Jičín, Czech Rep. F18 10
Novyj Nekouz, Russia D21 22
Novyj Ropsk, Russia I15 22
Nowa Ruda, Pol. E16 10
Nowa Sól (Neusalz), Pol. D15 10
Nowata, Ok., U.S. C11 116
Nowitna, stm., Ak., U.S. D17 100
Nowogród, Pol. H4 22
Nowogrodziec, Pol. D15 10
Nowood, stm., Wy., U.S. F18 122
Nowra, Austl. J9 70
Nowshāk, mtn., Asia B4 44
Nowshera, Pak. C4 44
Nowy Dwór Mazowiecki, Pol. C20 10
Nowy Sącz, Pol. F20 10
Nowy Targ, Pol. F20 10
Noxapater, Ms., U.S. J7 114
Noxen, Pa., U.S. F10 108
Noxon, Mt., U.S. B10 122
Noxubee, stm., U.S. I8 114
Noyon, Fr. C10 14
N'Riquinha, Ang. E4 58
Nsanje, Mwi. E7 58
Nsawam, Ghana I9 64
Nsukka, Nig. H13 64
Ntakat, Maur. C4 64
Ntem, stm., Afr. H9 54
N'Tsaoueni, Com. k15 67a
Ntwetwe Pan, pl., Bots. C7 66
Nuanetsi, stm., Afr. C10 66
Nuanli, China C6 40
Nūbah, Jibāl an-, mts., Sudan L6 60
Nubian Desert, des., Sudan G8 60
Ñuble, stm., Chile I3 80
Nucet, Rom. C6 20
Nuchatlitz Inlet, b., B.C., Can. H8 102
N'uchča, Russia E7 26
Nucla, Co., U.S. F8 120
Nucuray, stm., Peru J5 84
Nueces, stm., Tx., U.S. L9 116
Nueltin Lake, l., Can. D13 96
Nuestra Señora de Talavera, Arg. C7 80
Nueva, Isla, i., Chile H3 78
Nueva Antioquia, Col. D8 84
Nueva Asunción, dept., Para. I11 82
Nueva Ciudad Guerrero, Mex. D10 90
Nueva Concepción, El Sal. C5 92
Nueva Esparta, state, Ven. B10 84
Nueva Francia, Arg. E6 80
Nueva Galia, Arg. H6 80
Nueva Germania, Para. B10 80
Nueva Gerona, Cuba D3 94
Nueva Helvecia, Ur. H10 80
Nueva Imperial, Chile J2 80
Nueva Italia de Ruiz, Mex. H8 90
Nueva Ocotepeque, Hond. C5 92
Nueva Palmira, Ur. G9 80
Nueva Rosita, Mex. D9 90
Nueva San Salvador, El Sal. D5 92
Nueva Segovia, dept., Nic. D8 92
Nueva Venecia, Guat. C3 92
Nueve, Canal Numero, Arg. I9 80
Nueve de Julio, Arg. H8 80
Nuevitas, Cuba D6 94
Nuevo, Bajo, Col. G5 94
Nuevo, Cayo, i., Mex. G13 90
Nuevo Berlín, Ur. G9 80
Nuevo Casas Grandes, Mex. B6 90
Nuevo Chagres, Pan. H14 92
Nuevo Delicias, Mex. D8 90
Nuevo Laredo, Mex. D10 90
Nuevo León, state, Mex. D9 90
Nuevo Progreso, Mex. H13 90
Nuevo Rocafuerte, Ec. H5 84
Nuia, Est. C8 22
Nuits-Saint-Georges, Fr. E11 14
N'uja, stm., Russia E14 28
N'uk, ozero, l., Russia I22 6
Nukey Bluff, clf, Austl. I1 70
Nukus, Uzb. I9 26
Nulato, Ak., U.S. D15 100
Nullagine, Austl. D4 68
Nullarbor National Park, Austl. F6 68
Nullarbor Plain, pl., Austl. F5 68
Numabin Bay, b., Sk., Can. B11 104
Numazu, Japan L13 36
Numurkah, Austl. K6 70
Nunapitchuk, Ak., U.S. F13 100
Nunda, N.Y., U.S. E9 108
Nungesser Lake, l., On., Can. G21 104
Nunivak Island, i., Ak., U.S. F11 100
Nunjiang, China B12 30
Nunkini, Mex. G14 90
Nunnelly, Tn., U.S. G9 114
Nuomin, stm., China B11 30
Nuon, stm., Afr. H5 64
Nuoro, Italy I4 18
Nuquí, Col. E4 84
Nura, stm., Kaz. G12 26
N'urba, Russia E15 28
Nürburgring, Ger. H10 12
Nurek, Taj. A3 44
Nuremberg see Nürnberg, Ger. F11 10
Nürnberg (Nuremberg), Ger. F11 10
Nurri, Italy J4 18
Nurri, Mount, hill, Austl. H7 70
Nursery, Tx., U.S. K9 116
Nürtingen, Ger. G9 10
Nūsah, Yemen G5 47
Nusaybin, Tur. C6 48
Nu Shan, mts., China F6 30
Nushki, Pak. F2 44
Nut Lake Indian Reserve, Sk., Can. F11 104
Nutrioso, Az., U.S. K7 120
Nuttby Mountain, hill, N.S., Can. G10 106
Nutter Fort, W.V., U.S. H6 108
Nuwaybi' al-Muzayyinah, Egypt C8 60
Nuwerus, S. Afr. H4 66
Nxainxai, Bots. B5 66
Nxai Pan National Park, Bots. B7 66
Nxaunxau, Bots. B5 66
Nyaake, Lib. I6 64
Nyabing, Austl. F3 68
Nyack, N.Y., U.S. F13 108
Nyah West, Austl. J5 70
Nyainqêntanglha Shan, mts., China E13 44
Nyakrom, Ghana I9 64
Nyala, Sudan K3 60
Nyamandhlovu, Zimb. B9 66
Nyamina, Mali E6 64
Nyamlell, Sudan M4 60
Nyanza, Rw. B5 58
Nyasa, Lake (Lake Malawi), l., Afr. D6 58
Nyasaland see Malawi, ctry., Afr. D6 58
Nyaunglebin, Myan. F4 40
Nybergsund, Nor. K13 6
Nyiel, Sudan N6 60
Nyíradony, Hung. H21 10
Nyírbátor, Hung. H22 10
Nyíregyháza, Hung. H21 10
Nykøbing, Den. M11 6
Nykøbing, Den. N12 6
Nyköping, Swe. L15 6
Nylstroom, S. Afr. E9 66
Nymburk, Czech Rep. E15 10
Nynäshamn, Swe. L15 6
Nyngan, Austl. H7 70
Nyon, Switz. F5 13
Nyong, stm., Cam. H9 54
Nýrsko, Czech Rep. F13 10
Nysa, Pol. E17 10
Nysa Łużycka (Neisse), stm., Eur. D14 10
Nyssa, Or., U.S. G9 122
Nytva, Russia F9 26
Nyzhankovychi, Ukr. F22 10
Nzébéla, Gui. G5 64
Nzérékoré, Gui. H5 64
N'zeto, Ang. C2 58
Nzi, stm., C. Iv. H7 64
Nzwani (Anjouan), i., Com. I16 67a

O

Oacoma, S.D., U.S. H8 118
Oahe, Lake, res., U.S. F7 118
Oahu, i., Hi., U.S. p15 125a
Oak, stm., Mb., Can. I14 104
Oakbank, Austl. I4 70
Oak Bay, B.C., Can. I11 102
Oak Bluffs, Ma., U.S. F16 108
Oakboro, N.C., U.S. D6 112
Oakburn, Mb., Can. H14 104
Oak City, N.C., U.S. D9 112
Oak City, Ut., U.S. E4 120
Oak Creek, Co., U.S. D10 120
Oak Creek, stm., Az., U.S. J5 120
Oakdale, Ca., U.S. G5 124
Oakdale, La., U.S. L4 114
Oakdale, Ne., U.S. I10 118
Oakdale, Tn., U.S. D2 112
Oakes, N.D., U.S. E9 118
Oakesdale, Wa., U.S. C8 122
Oakey, Austl. F9 70
Oakfield, Me., U.S. A18 108
Oakfield, N.Y., U.S. D8 108
Oakfield, Wi., U.S. G7 110
Oak Grove, La., U.S. J5 114
Oak Harbor, Wa., U.S. B3 122
Oak Hill, Fl., U.S. K6 112
Oak Hill, Mi., U.S. F9 110
Oak Hill, Oh., U.S. I4 108
Oak Hill, W.V., U.S. J5 108
Oakhurst, Ca., U.S. G6 124
Oakhurst, Tx., U.S. I11 116
Oak Island, i., N.S., Can. H9 106
Oak Knolls, Ca., U.S. J5 124
Oak Lake, Mb., Can. I14 104
Oak Lake, l., Mb., Can. I14 104
Oak Lake, l., On., Can. H21 104
Oakland, Ca., U.S. G3 124
Oakland, Ia., U.S. J12 118
Oakland, Il., U.S. C8 114
Oakland, Md., U.S. H7 108
Oakland, Me., U.S. C17 108
Oakland, Ms., U.S. H7 114
Oakland, Ne., U.S. J11 118
Oakland, Or., U.S. G2 122
Oakland City, In., U.S. D9 114
Oakland Park, Fl., U.S. M6 112
Oak Lawn, Il., U.S. I8 110
Oaklawn, Ks., U.S. N10 118
Oakley, Id., U.S. H12 122
Oakley, Ks., U.S. L7 118
Oakman, Al., U.S. I9 114
Oak Park, Il., U.S. I8 110
Oak Point, Mb., Can. H16 104
Oakridge, Or., U.S. G3 122
Oak Ridge, Tn., U.S. C2 112
Oaktown, In., U.S. D9 114
Oak View, Ca., U.S. J6 124
Oakville, Mb., Can. I17 104
Oakville, On., Can. G16 110
Oakwood, Oh., U.S. F2 108
Oakwood, Tx., U.S. H11 116
Oamaru, N.Z. F3 72
Oancea, Rom. D12 20
Oatlands, Austl. N7 70
Oatman, Az., U.S. I2 120
Oaxaca, state, Mex. I11 90
Oaxaca [de Juárez], Mex. I11 90
Ob', stm., Russia D11 26
Obal', Bela. F12 22
Obama, Japan L10 36
Oban, Austl. C3 70
Oban, Nig. I14 64
Oban, Scot., U.K. E8 8
O Barco de Valdeorras, Spain C5 16
Obed, Ab., Can. D17 102
Obed, stm., Tn., U.S. C2 112
Obeliai, Lith. F8 22
Oberá, Arg. D11 80
Oberdrauburg, Aus. I12 10
Obergurgl, Aus. I11 10
Oberhausen, Ger. D6 10
Oberlin, Ks., U.S. L7 118
Oberlin, La., U.S. L4 114
Oberlin, Oh., U.S. F4 108
Obernai, Fr. D14 14
Obernburg am Main, Ger. F9 10
Oberon, Austl. I8 70
Oberösterreich, state, Aus. G13 10
Oberpullendorf, Aus. H16 10
Obertyn, Ukr. A9 20
Oberursel, Ger. E8 10
Obervellach, Aus. I13 10
Oberwart, Aus. H16 10
Obi, Nig. G14 64
Obi, Kepulauan, is., Indon. F8 38
Obiaruku, Nig. I13 64
Óbidos, Braz. D7 76
Obihiro, Japan e18 36a
Obilatu, Pulau, i., Indon. F8 38
Obing, Ger. G12 10
Obion, Tn., U.S. F7 114
Obion, stm., Tn., U.S. F7 114
Oblong, Il., U.S. C9 114
Oblučje, Russia H18 28
Obninsk, Russia F19 22
Obock, Dji. F9 56
Oborniki, Pol. C16 10
Oboz'orskij, Russia J27 6
O'Brien, Or., U.S. H2 122

Name | Map Ref. | Page

Obščij Syrt, mtn., Eur. G8 26
Observatory Inlet, b., B.C., Can. B5 102
Obskaja guba, b., Russia D12 26
Obuasi, Ghana H9 64
Obuchova, Russia E15 22
Obžericha, Russia D25 22
Ocala, Fl., U.S. J4 112
Ocallí, Peru B2 82
Ocamo, stm., Ven. F10 84
Ocampo, Mex. C5 90
Ocampo, Mex. D8 90
Ocaña, Col. C6 84
Occidental, Cordillera, mts., Col. E4 84
Occidental, Cordillera, mts., Peru C3 82
Oceana, W.V., U.S. B5 112
Ocean Cape, c., Ak., U.S. G25 100
Ocean City, Md., U.S. I11 108
Ocean City, N.J., U.S. H12 108
Ocean Falls, B.C., Can. E7 102
Oceano, Ca., U.S. I5 124
Ocean Park, Wa., U.S. D1 122
Oceanside, Ca., U.S. K8 124
Ocean Springs, Ms., U.S. L8 114
Ocha, Russia G20 28
Ochapowace Indian Reserve, Sk., Can. H12 104
Ocheyedan, Ia., U.S. H12 118
O'Chiese Indian Reserve, Ab., Can. E19 102
Ochlocknee, Ga., U.S. I2 112
Ochlockonee, stm., U.S. I2 112
Ocho Rios, Jam. E6 94
Ochota, stm., Russia F20 28
Ochotsk, Russia F20 28
Ochre River, Mb., Can. G15 104
Ochsenfurt, Ger. F10 10
Ochvat, Russia E15 22
Ocilla, Ga., U.S. H3 112
Ocmulgee, stm., Ga., U.S. H3 112
Ocnița, Mol. A11 20
Ocoa, Bahía de, b., Dom. Rep. E9 94
Ocoee, Fl., U.S. K5 112
Ocoee (Toccoa), stm., U.S. D2 112
Ocoña, Peru G5 82
Ocoña, stm., Peru G5 82
Oconee, stm., Ga., U.S. G4 112
Ocongate, Peru E6 82
Oconomowoc, Wi., U.S. G7 110
Oconto, Wi., U.S. F8 110
Oconto, stm., Wi., U.S. F7 110
Oconto Falls, Wi., U.S. F7 110
Ocós, Guat. C2 92
Ocosingo, Mex. I13 90
Ocotal, Nic. D8 92
Ocotepeque, dept., Hond. C5 92
Ocotlán, Mex. G8 90
Ocotlán de Morelos, Mex. I11 90
Ocozocoautla [de Espinosa], Mex. I13 90
Ocracoke, N.C., U.S. D11 112
Ocracoke Island, i., N.C., U.S. D11 112
Ocros, Peru D3 82
Ocú, Pan. J14 92
Ocumare del Tuy, Ven. B9 84
Ocuri, Bol. H9 82
Ocussi, Indon. A4 68
Oda, Ghana I9 64
Oda, Jabal, mtn., Sudan G9 60
Odanakumadona, Bots. C7 66
Ōdate, Japan G15 36
Odawara, Japan L14 36
Odda, Nor. K10 6
Odebolt, Ia., U.S. I12 118
Odei, stm., Mb., Can. B17 104
Odell, Il., U.S. I7 110
Odell, Ne., U.S. K11 118
Odell, Tx., U.S. E7 116
Odem, Tx., U.S. L9 116
Ödemiş, Tur. K11 20
Odendaalsrus, S. Afr. F8 66
Odense, Den. N12 6
Oder (Odra), stm., Eur. C14 10
Oderberg, Ger. C14 10
Oderzo, Italy D7 18
Odesa (Odessa), Ukr. H4 26
Odessa, Mo., U.S. D3 114
Odessa, On., Can. F19 110
Odessa, Tx., U.S. H4 116
Odessa see Odesa, Ukr. H4 26
Odessa, Wa., U.S. C7 122
Odesskoje, Russia G12 26
Odiakwe, Bots. C7 66
Odīb, Wādī, val., Sudan I5 64
Odienné, C. Iv. G6 64
Odin, Mount, mtn., B.C., Can. G16 102
Odincovo, Russia F20 22
Odojev, Russia H19 22
Odon, In., U.S. D10 114
O'Donnell, Tx., U.S. G5 116
Odorheiu Secuiesc, Rom. C9 20
Odum, Ga., U.S. H4 112
Odzi, Zimb. B11 66
Oebisfelde, Ger. C11 10
Oeiras, Braz. E10 76
Oelde, Ger. D8 10
Oelsnitz, Ger. E12 10
Oelwein, Ia., U.S. H4 110
Oesterdam, Neth. F5 12
Oettingen in Bayern, Ger. G10 10
Oetz, Aus. H10 10
O'Fallon, Mo., U.S. D6 114
Ofaqim, Isr. F3 50
Offa, Nig. G12 64
Offaly, co., Ire. H6 8
Offenbach, Ger. E8 10
Offenburg, Ger. G7 10
Oficina Alemania, Chile C4 80
Oficina Alianza, Chile I7 82
Oficina Chile, Chile C4 80
Oficina Pedro de Valdivia, Chile B4 80
Oficina Victoria, Chile I7 82
Ōfunato, Japan H16 36
Oga, Japan H14 36
Ogaden, reg., Afr. G9 56
Ōgaki, Japan L11 36
Ogallala, Ne., U.S. J6 118
Ogbomosho, Nig. G12 64
Ogden, Ia., U.S. H1 110
Ogden, Ks., U.S. L11 118
Ogden, Ut., U.S. C5 120
Ogden, Mount, mtn., N.A. G28 100
Ogdensburg, N.Y., U.S. C11 108
Ogeechee, stm., Ga., U.S. G5 112
Ogema, Sk., Can. I10 104
Ogilvie, Mn., U.S. E2 110
Ogilvie, stm., Yk., Can. D25 100
Ogilvie Mountains, mts., Yk., Can. D25 100
Oglesby, Il., U.S. I6 110
Oglesby, Tx., U.S. H9 116
Oglethorpe, Ga., U.S. G2 112
Oglio, stm., Italy D5 18
Ogmore, Austl. D8 70
Ognon, stm., Fr. E12 14
Ogoja, Nig. H14 64
Ogoki, stm., On., Can. F15 96
Ogooué, stm., Afr. B1 58
Ogr, Sudan K4 60
Ogre, Lat. E7 22
O Grove, Spain C3 16
Ogulin, Cro. D10 18
Ogunquit, Me., U.S. D16 108
Ogurčinskij, ostrov, i., Turk. B12 48
Oğuzeli, Tur. C4 48
Ogwashi-Uku, Nig. H13 64
Ohanet, Alg. F15 62
Ōhara, Japan L15 36
O'Higgins, Lago (Lago San Martín), l., S.A. F2 78
Ohio, Il., U.S. I6 110
Ohio, state, U.S. C10 98
Ohio, stm., U.S. D9 98
Ohio City, Oh., U.S. G2 108
Ohře, stm., Eur. E13 10
Ohrid, Mac. H4 20
Ohrid, Lake, l., Eur. H4 20
Öhringen, Ger. F9 10
Ohuira, Bahía, b., Mex. E5 90
Oiapoque, Braz. C8 76
Oiapoque (Oyapock), stm., S.A. C8 76
Oies, Île aux, i., P.Q., Can. E3 106
Oil Center, N.M., U.S. G3 116
Oil City, La., U.S. J3 114
Oil City, Pa., U.S. F7 108
Oil Creek, stm., Pa., U.S. F7 108
Oildale, Ca., U.S. I6 124
Oilton, Ok., U.S. C10 116
Oilton, Tx., U.S. L8 116
Oil Trough, Ar., U.S. G5 114
Oise, dept., Fr. C9 14
Oise, stm., Eur. C9 14
Oisemont, Fr. C8 14
Ōita, Japan N6 36
Ojai, Ca., U.S. J6 124
Ojat', stm., Russia A16 22
Ojinaga, Mex. C7 90
Ojocaliente, Mex. F8 90
Ojo del Carrizo, Mex. C7 90
Ojo de Liebre, Laguna, b., Mex. D2 90
Ojos del Salado, Nevado, mtn., S.A. D4 80
Ojos Negros, Mex. B1 90
Oju, Nig. H14 64
Oka, stm., Russia F24 22
Oka, stm., Russia G12 28
Okahandja, Nmb. C3 66
Okanagan (Okanogan), stm., N.A. H15 102
Okanagan Centre, B.C., Can. G15 102
Okanagan Falls, B.C., Can. H15 102
Okanagan Indian Reserve, B.C., Can. G15 102
Okanagan Lake, l., B.C., Can. G15 102
Okanagan Landing, B.C., Can. G15 102
Okanagan Mountain Provincial Park, B.C., Can. H15 102
Okanagan Range (Okanogan Range), mts., N.A. H14 102
Okanogan, Wa., U.S. B6 122
Okanogan (Okanagan), stm., N.A. I15 102
Okaputa, Nmb. C3 66
Okāra, Pak. E5 44
Okarche, Ok., U.S. D9 116
Okaukuejo, Nmb. B2 66
Okavango (Cubango), stm., Afr. E3 58
Okavango Delta, Bots. B6 66
Okawville, Il., U.S. D7 114
Okaya, Japan K13 36
Okayama, Japan M8 36
Okazaki, Japan M12 36
Okeechobee, Fl., U.S. L6 112
Okeechobee, Lake, l., Fl., U.S. M6 112
Okeene, Ok., U.S. C8 116
Okefenokee Swamp, sw., U.S. I4 112
Okeigbo, Nig. H12 64
Okemah, Ok., U.S. D10 116
Okemos, Mi., U.S. H11 110
Okene, Nig. H13 64
Oke-Ode, Nig. G12 64
Okhotsk, Sea of, Asia c19 36a
Okhtyrka, Ukr. G4 26
Okiep, S. Afr. G3 66
Okinawa, Japan u2 37b
Okinawa-jima, i., Japan u2 37b
Okinawa-shotō, is., Japan u2 37b
Okino-Daitō-jima, i., Japan G13 30
Okino-Erabu-shima, i., Japan t3 37b
Okino-Tori-shima (Parece Vela), i., Japan G14 30
Oki-shotō, is., Japan K6 36
Okladnevo, Russia C16 22
Oklahoma, state, U.S. D7 98
Oklahoma City, Ok., U.S. D9 116
Oklawaha, Fl., U.S. J5 112
Oklee, Mn., U.S. D12 118
Okmulgee, Ok., U.S. D10 116
Okolona, Ar., U.S. I3 114
Okolona, Ky., U.S. D11 114
Okolona, Ms., U.S. H8 114
Okombahe, Nmb. C2 66
Okotoks, Ab., Can. G21 102
Okpara, stm., Afr. H11 64
Okrika, Nig. I13 64
Okt'abr', Russia D20 22
Okt'abr'skij, Russia D23 22
Okt'abr'skij, Russia C27 22
Okt'abr'skij, Russia G21 22
Okt'abr'skij, Russia G8 26
Okt'abr'skoje, Russia I22 22
Okt'abr'skoj Revol'ucii, ostrov, i., Russia B17 26
Okulovka, Russia C16 22
Okushiri-tō, i., Japan e14 36a
Okuta, Nig. G11 64
Okwa (Chapman's), stm., Afr. D5 66
Okwoga, Nig. H13 64
Ola, Ar., U.S. G3 114
Olá, Pan. I14 92
Ólafsfjördur, Ice. A4 6a
Olancha, Ca., U.S. H7 124
Olancha Peak, mtn., Ca., U.S. H7 124
Olanchito, Hond. B8 92
Olancho, dept., Hond. C9 92
Öland, i., Swe. M15 6
Olanta, S.C., U.S. F7 112
Olar, S.C., U.S. F5 112
Olary, Austl. I4 70
Olascoaga, Arg. H8 80
Olathe, Co., U.S. F9 120
Olathe, Ks., U.S. M13 118
Olavarría, Arg. I8 80
Oława, Pol. E17 10
Olbia, Italy I4 18
Olca, Volcán, vol., S.A. I7 82
Olcott, N.Y., U.S. D8 108
Old Bahama Channel, strt., N.A. C5 94
Old Crow, Yk., Can. C25 100
Old Crow, stm., N.A. B24 100
Olden, Tx., U.S. G8 116
Oldenburg, hist. reg., Ger. B8 10
Oldenburg [in Holstein], Ger. A10 10
Oldenzaal, Neth. D10 12
Old Faithful Geyser, well, Wy., U.S. F15 122
Old Forge, N.Y., U.S. D12 108
Old Forge, Pa., U.S. F11 108
Old Fort Mountain, mtn., B.C., Can. B8 102
Oldham, S.D., U.S. G10 118
Old Harbor, Ak., U.S. H18 100
Old Hickory Lake, res., Tn., U.S. F10 114
Oldman, stm., Ab., Can. H23 102
Old Man Mountain, mtn., Nf., Can. C16 106
Oldmeldrum, Scot., U.K. D11 8
Old Orchard Beach, Me., U.S. D16 108
Old Perlican, Nf., Can. D20 106
Olds, Ab., Can. F20 102
Old Saybrook, Ct., U.S. F14 108
Old Tate, Bots. C8 66
Old Town, Me., U.S. C18 108
Old Trap, N.C., U.S. C10 112
Old Wives Lake, l., Sk., Can. H8 104
Olean, N.Y., U.S. E8 108
O'Leary, P.E., Can. F9 106
Olecko, Pol. A22 10
Oleksandriya, Ukr. H4 26
Olen, Bel. F6 12
Ølen, Nor. L9 6
Olenegorsk, Russia D4 26
Olenij, ostrov, i., Russia C13 26
Olenino, Russia E16 22
Olen'ok, stm., Russia C16 28
Olen'okskij zaliv, b., Russia C16 28
Oléron, Île d', i., Fr. G5 14
Oleśnica, Pol. D17 10
Olesno, Pol. E18 10
Ol'ga, Russia I19 28
Ölgij, Mong. B4 30
Olhão, Port. H4 16
Ol'hopil', Ukr. A13 20
Oli, stm., Afr. G12 64
Olifants (Rio dos Elefantes), stm., Afr. E10 66
Ólimbos, mtn., Cyp. D2 48
Ólimbos, Óros (Mount Olympus), mtn., Grc. I6 20
Olímpia, Braz. F4 79
Olin, Ia., U.S. I4 110
Olinalá, Mex. I10 90
Olinda, Braz. E12 76
Olio, Austl. C5 70
Oliva, Arg. G7 80
Oliva, Spain G11 16
Oliva de la Frontera, Spain G5 16
Olivares, Cerro de, mtn., S.A. F4 80
Olive Branch, Ms., U.S. H7 114
Olive Hill, Ky., U.S. I3 108
Olivehurst, Ca., U.S. E4 124
Oliveira, Braz. F6 79
Oliveira dos Brejinhos, Braz. B7 79
Olivenza, Spain G4 16
Oliver, B.C., Can. H15 102
Oliver Lake, l., Sk., Can. B11 104
Oliver Springs, Tn., U.S. C2 112
Olivet, Mi., U.S. H11 110
Olivet, S.D., U.S. H10 118
Olivia, Mn., U.S. G13 118
Olla, La., U.S. K4 114
Ollagüe, Chile I7 82
Ollagüe, Volcán, vol., S.A. I7 82
Ollantaitambo, Peru E5 82
Olmos, Peru A2 82
Olney, Il., U.S. D8 114
Olney, Tx., U.S. F8 116
Ol'okma, stm., Russia F16 28
Ol'okminsk, Russia E16 28
Olomane, stm., P.Q., Can. A13 106
Olomega, Laguna, l., El Sal. D6 92
Olomouc, Czech Rep. F17 10
Olonec, Russia E4 26
Olongapo, Phil. n19 39b
Oloron-Sainte-Marie, Fr. I6 14
Olot, Spain C14 16
Olov'annaja, Russia G15 28
Olpe, Ger. D7 10
Olpe, Ks., U.S. M11 118
Olsztyn (Allenstein), Pol. B20 10
Olsztynek, Pol. B20 10
Olt, co., Rom. E8 20
Olt, stm., Rom. F8 20
Olta, Arg. F5 80
Olten, Switz. D8 13
Oltenița, Rom. E10 20
Olton, Tx., U.S. E4 116
Oltu, Tur. A6 48
Oluan Pi, c., Tai. N9 34
Olukonda, Nmb. B3 66
Olustee, Fl., U.S. I4 112
Olustee, Ok., U.S. E7 116
Ol'utorskij, mys, c., Russia F26 28
Ol'utorskij zaliv, b., Russia E25 28
Olvera, Spain I6 16
Olympia, Wa., U.S. C3 122
Olympic Mountains, mts., Wa., U.S. C2 122
Olympic National Park, Wa., U.S. C2 122
Olympus, Mount see Ólimbos, Óros, mtn., Grc. I6 20
Olympus, Mount, mtn., Wa., U.S. C2 122
Om', stm., Russia F7 28
Omagh, N. Ire., U.K. G6 8
Omaguas, Peru J6 84
Omaha, Ne., U.S. J12 118
Omaha, Tx., U.S. I2 114
Omaheke, prov., Nmb. C4 66
Omak, Wa., U.S. B6 122
Oman ('Umān), ctry., Asia E6 42
Oman, Gulf of, b., Asia B10 47
Omar, W.V., U.S. B5 112
Omarama, N.Z. F2 72
Omaruru, Nmb. C2 66
Omas, Peru E3 82
Omatako, stm., Nmb. B5 66
Omate, Peru G6 82
Ombombo, Nmb. B1 66
Omboué, Gabon B1 58
Omčak, Russia E21 28
Omdurman see Umm Durmān, Sudan J7 60
Omega, Ga., U.S. H3 112
Omegna, Italy D3 18
Omemee, On., Can. F17 110
Omeo, Austl. K7 70
Ometepe, Isla de, i., Nic. F9 92
Ometepec, Mex. I10 90
Om Hajer, Erit. J9 60
Omineca, stm., B.C., Can. B10 102
Omineca Mountains, mts., B.C., Can. B9 102
Ōmiya, Japan L14 36
Ommaney, Cape, c., Ak., U.S. H27 100
Ommanney Bay, b., N.T., Can. B12 96
Omo, stm., Afr. G8 56
Omoa, Bahía de, b., N.A. B6 92
Omoloj, stm., Russia C18 28
Omolon, stm., Russia D23 28
Omro, Wi., U.S. F7 110
Omsk, Russia F6 28
Omsukčan, Russia E23 28
Omu-Aran, Nig. G12 64
Ōmuta, Japan N5 36
Omutninsk, Russia F8 26
On, Viet. D9 40
Onabas, Mex. C5 90
Onaga, Ks., U.S. L11 118
Onamia, Mn., U.S. D2 110
Onancock, Va., U.S. B11 112
Onarga, Il., U.S. J7 110
Onatchiway, Lac, l., P.Q., Can. C2 106
Onawa, Ia., U.S. I11 118
Onaway, Mi., U.S. E11 110
Oncativo, Arg. F7 80
Once, Canal Numero, Arg. I9 80
Onda, Spain F11 16
Ondangwa, Nmb. A3 66
Ondas, Rio de, stm., Braz. B6 79
Onderdijk, Neth. C7 12
Ondjiva, Ang. E3 58
Ondo, Nig. H12 64
Öndörchaan, Mong. B9 30
Ondozero, ozero, l., Russia J23 6
One Arrow Indian Reserve, Sk., Can. F8 104
Oneco, Fl., U.S. L4 112
Onega, Russia E5 26
Onega, stm., Russia J26 6
Onega, Lake see Onežskoje ozero, l., Russia E5 26
One Hundred and Two, stm., Mo., U.S. C2 114
One Hundred Fifty Mile House, B.C., Can. E13 102
One Hundred Mile House, B.C., Can. F13 102
Oneida, Il., U.S. I5 110
Oneida, Ky., U.S. B3 112
Oneida, N.Y., U.S. D11 108
Oneida, Tn., U.S. C2 112
Oneida Lake, l., N.Y., U.S. D11 108
O'Neill, Ne., U.S. I9 118
Onekama, Mi., U.S. F9 110
Onekotan, ostrov, i., Russia H22 28
Oneonta, Al., U.S. I10 114
Oneonta, N.Y., U.S. E11 108
Onești, Rom. C10 20
Onežskaja guba, b., Russia I25 6
Onežskij poluostrov, pen., Russia I25 6
Onežskoje ozero, l., Russia E5 26
Ongjin, N. Kor. F13 32
Ongole, India E6 46
Onida, S.D., U.S. G7 118
Onistagane, Lac, l., P.Q., Can. B2 106
Onitsha, Nig. H13 64
Ōno, Japan L11 36
Onoda, Japan N6 36
Onomichi, Japan M8 36
Onon, stm., Asia A9 30
Onoto, Ven. C10 84
Onoway, Ab., Can. D20 102
Onseepkans, S. Afr. G4 66
Onset, Ma., U.S. F16 108
Onslow, Austl. D3 68
Onslow Bay, b., N.C., U.S. E9 112
Ontario, Ca., U.S. J8 124
Ontario, Oh., U.S. G4 108
Ontario, Or., U.S. F9 122
Ontario, prov., Can. F15 96
Ontario, Lake, l., N.A. G18 110
Ontinyent (Onteniente), Spain G11 16
Ontonagon, Mi., U.S. D6 110
Ontonagon, stm., Mi., U.S. D6 110
Onverwacht, Sur. B7 76
Ŏnyang, S. Kor. G15 32
Oodnadatta, Austl. E7 68
Ooldea, Austl. F6 68
Oolitic, In., U.S. D10 114
Oologah, Ok., U.S. C11 116
Oologah Lake, res., Ok., U.S. C11 116
Oona River, B.C., Can. D4 102
Oostburg, Wi., U.S. G8 110
Oostelijk Flevoland, reg., Neth. C8 12
Oostende (Ostende), Bel. F2 12
Oosterend, Neth. B6 12
Oosterhout, Neth. E6 12
Oosterschelde, b., Neth. E4 12
Oosterscheldedam, Neth. E4 12
Oosterwolde, Neth. C9 12
Oostflakkee, Neth. E5 12
Oost-Vlaanderen, prov., Bel. G4 12
Oostvleteren, Bel. G2 12
Ootsa Lake, B.C., Can. D8 102
Ootsa Lake, l., B.C., Can. D8 102
Ootsi, Bots. E7 66
Opala, Zaire B4 58
Opalaca, Cordillera, mts., Hond. C6 92
Oparino, Russia F7 26
Opasquia, On., Can. E21 104
Opasquia Lake, l., On., Can. E21 104
Opatów, Pol. E21 10
Opava, Czech Rep. F17 10
Opava, stm., Eur. E17 10
Opelika, Al., U.S. J11 114
Opelousas, La., U.S. L4 114
Opheim, Mt., U.S. B19 122
Ophir, Or., U.S. H1 122
Opihikao, Hi., U.S. r19 125a
Opinaca, stm., P.Q., Can. F17 96
Opiscotéo, Lac, l., P.Q., Can. F19 96
Opobo, Nig. I13 64
Opočka, Russia E11 22
Opoczno, Pol. D20 10
Opole (Oppeln), Pol. E17 10
Opononо, Lake, l., Nmb. B2 66
Oporto see Porto, Port. D3 16
Opotiki, N.Z. B6 72
Opp, Al., U.S. K10 114
Oppland, co., Nor. K11 6
Opportunity, Mt., U.S. D13 122
Opportunity, Wa., U.S. C8 122
Opsa, Bela. F10 22
Optic Lake, Mb., Can. D13 104
Opuwo, Nmb. B1 66
Oquawka, Il., U.S. J5 110
Ora, Italy C6 18
Oracle, Az., U.S. L6 120
Oradea, Rom. B5 20
Orai, India H8 44
Oran see Wahran, Alg. A6 54
Oran, Mo., U.S. E7 114
Orange, Austl. I8 70
Orange, Fr. H11 14
Orange, Ma., U.S. E14 108
Orange, Tx., U.S. L3 114
Orange, Va., U.S. I8 108
Orange (Oranje), stm., Afr. G4 66
Orange, Cabo, c., Braz. C8 76
Orangeburg, S.C., U.S. F6 112
Orange City, Fl., U.S. K5 112
Orange City, Ia., U.S. H11 118
Orange Cove, Ca., U.S. H6 124
Orange Grove, Tx., U.S. L9 116
Orange Lake, Fl., U.S. J4 112
Orange Park, Fl., U.S. I5 112
Orangeville, On., Can. G15 110
Orangeville, Ut., U.S. E5 120
Orange Walk, Belize H15 90
Oranienburg, Ger. C13 10
Oranjefontein, S. Afr. D8 66
Oranjemund, Nmb. G3 66
Oranjerivier, S. Afr. G7 66
Oranjestad, Aruba H9 94
Or 'Aqiva, Isr. C3 50
Orarak, Sudan N7 60
Orăștie, Rom. D7 20
Oravais (Oravainen), Fin. J18 6
Orbe, Switz. E6 13
Orbetello, Italy G6 18
Orbisonia, Pa., U.S. G9 108
Orbost, Austl. K8 70
Orcadas, sci., Ant. B1 73
Orcera, Spain G9 16
Orchard, Ne., U.S. I9 118
Orchard City, Co., U.S. F9 120
Orchard Homes, Mt., U.S. D11 122
Orchard Mesa, Co., U.S. E8 120
Orchard Park, N.Y., U.S. E8 108
Orchard Valley, Wy., U.S. C12 120
Orchies, Fr. B10 14
Orchon, stm., Mong. B7 30
Ord, Ne., U.S. J9 118
Ord, stm., Austl. C5 68
Ord, Mount, mtn., Austl. C5 68
Orderville, Ut., U.S. G4 120
Ordoqui, Arg. H8 80
Ordu, Tur. G15 4
Ordway, Co., U.S. M4 118
Ore, Nig. H12 64
Örebro, Swe. L14 6
Orechovo-Zujevo, Russia F21 22
Ore City, Tx., U.S. J2 114
Oredež, Russia C13 22
Oregon, Il., U.S. H6 110
Oregon, Mo., U.S. C1 114
Oregon, Oh., U.S. F3 108
Oregon, state, U.S. C2 98
Oregon City, Or., U.S. E3 122
Orel, Russia I19 22
Orellana, Peru B4 82
Orem, Ut., U.S. D5 120
Orenburg, Russia G9 26
Örencik, Tur. J13 20
Orense, Arg. J9 80
Orestes Pereyra, Mex. D7 90
Orestiás, Grc. H10 20
Orfanoú, Kólpos, b., Grc. I7 20
Orfordville, Wi., U.S. H6 110
Organ Needle, mtn., N.M., U.S. L10 120
Orgelet, Fr. F12 14
Orgtrud, Russia E23 22
Orgūn, Afg. D3 44
Orhaniar, Tur. J11 20
Orhei, Mol. B12 20
Orica, Hond. C8 92
Orichuna, stm., Ven. D8 84
Orick, Ca., U.S. C1 124
Orient, Ia., U.S. J13 118
Oriental, N.C., U.S. D10 112
Oriental, Cordillera, mts., Col. E6 84
Oriental, Cordillera, mts., Peru C4 82
Oriente, Arg. J8 80
Orillia, On., Can. F16 110
Orinduik, Guy. E12 84
Orinoco, stm., S.A. C11 84
Orinoco, Delta del, Ven. C12 84
Oriola (Orihuela), Spain G11 16
Orion, Il., U.S. I5 110
Oripää, Fin. K18 6
Oriskany, N.Y., U.S. D11 108
Orissa, state, India B7 46
Orissaare, Est. C6 22
Oristano, Italy J3 18
Orituco, stm., Ven. C9 84
Oriximiná, Braz. D7 76
Orizaba, Mex. H11 90
Orizaba, Pico de (Volcán Citlaltépetl), vol., Mex. H11 90
Orizona, Braz. D4 79
Orkney, S. Afr. F8 66
Orkney, Sk., Can. I7 104
Orkney, prov., Scot., U.K. B10 8
Orkney Islands, is., Scot., U.K. B10 8
Orland, Ca., U.S. E3 124
Orlândia, Braz. F5 79
Orlando, Fl., U.S. K5 112
Orléanais, hist. reg., Fr. E8 14
Orleans, Ca., U.S. C2 124
Orléans, Fr. E8 14
Orleans, In., U.S. D10 114
Orleans, Ma., U.S. F17 108
Orleans, Ne., U.S. K8 118
Orléans, On., Can. B11 108
Orleans, Vt., U.S. C14 108
Orléans, Île d', i., P.Q., Can. F3 106
Orlová, Czech Rep. F18 10
Ormāra, Pak. I18 48
Ormiston, Sk., Can. I9 104
Ormoc, Phil. C7 38
Ormond Beach, Fl., U.S. J5 112
Ornans, Fr. E13 14
Orne, dept., Fr. D7 14
Orne, stm., Fr. D6 14
Örnsköldsvik, Swe. J16 6
Oro, N. Kor. C15 32
Orocué, Col. E7 84
Orocuina, Hond. D7 92
Orodara, Burkina F7 64
Orofino, Id., U.S. D9 122
Oro Grande, Ca., U.S. J8 124
Oromocto, N.B., Can. G7 106
Oromocto Lake, l., N.B., Can. G7 106
Oron, Nig. I14 64
Orono, Me., U.S. C18 108
Orono, On., Can. G17 110
Oronoque, stm., Guy. F14 84
Orosháza, Hung. I20 10
Orosí, Volcán, vol., C.R. G9 92
Oroville, Ca., U.S. E4 124
Oroville, Wa., U.S. B6 122
Oroville, Lake, res., Ca., U.S. E4 124
Orrick, Mo., U.S. C2 114
Orrin, N.D., U.S. C7 118
Orr Lake, l., Mb., Can. B17 104
Orroroo, Austl. I3 70
Orrs Island, Me., U.S. D17 108
Orrville, Al., U.S. J9 114
Orrville, Oh., U.S. G5 108
Orša, Bela. G13 22
Orsières, Switz. F7 13
Orsk, Russia G9 26
Orta Nova, Italy H10 18
Ortega, Col. F5 84
Ortegal, Cabo, c., Spain B4 16
Orteguaza, stm., Col. G5 84
Orthez, Fr. I6 14
Orthon, stm., Bol. D8 82
Orting, Wa., U.S. C3 122
Ortisei, Italy C6 18
Ortiz, Mex. C4 90
Ortiz, Ven. C9 84
Ortles (Ortler), mtn., Italy E14 13
Ortona, Italy G9 18
Ortonville, Mn., U.S. F11 118
Orūmīyeh (Reżā'īyeh), Iran C8 48
Oruro, Bol. G8 82
Oruro, dept., Bol. H8 82
Orvieto, Italy G7 18
Orwell, Oh., U.S. F6 108
Orxon, stm., China B10 30
Or Yehuda, Isr. D3 50
Orzinuovi, Italy D4 18
Orzola, Spain n27 17b
Orzysz, Pol. B21 10
Oš, Kyrg. I12 26
Osa, Península de, pen., C.R. I11 92
Osage, Ia., U.S. G3 110
Osage, Wy., U.S. H3 118
Osage, stm., Mo., U.S. D4 114
Osage Beach, Mo., U.S. D4 114
Osage City, Ks., U.S. M12 118
Ōsaka, Japan M10 36
Ōsaka-wan, b., Japan M10 36
Osakis, Mn., U.S. F12 118
Osan, S. Kor. F15 32
Osawatomie, Ks., U.S. M13 118
Osborne, Ks., U.S. L9 118
Osburn, Id., U.S. C10 122
Oscar Peak, mtn., B.C., Can. C5 102
Osceola, Ar., U.S. G7 114
Osceola, Ia., U.S. I2 110
Osceola, Mo., U.S. D3 114
Osceola, Ne., U.S. J10 118
Osceola, Wi., U.S. E3 110
Osceola Mills, Pa., U.S. G8 108
Oschatz, Ger. D13 10
Oschersleben, Ger. C11 10
Oscoda, Mi., U.S. F12 110
Osgood, In., U.S. C11 114
O'Shanassy, stm., Austl. B3 70
Oshawa, On., Can. G17 110
Oshigambo, Nmb. A3 66
Ō-shima, i., Japan M14 36
Ō-shima, i., Japan f14 36a
Oshkosh, Ne., U.S. J5 118
Oshkosh, Wi., U.S. F7 110
Oshnovīyeh, Iran C8 48
Oshogbo, Nig. H12 64
Oshwe, Zaire B3 58
Osi, Nig. G12 64
Osich'ŏn-ni, N. Kor. B16 32
Osijek, Cro. D2 20
Osilinka, stm., B.C., Can. A10 102
Osimo, Italy F8 18
Osinniki, Russia G9 28
Osire, Nmb. C3 66
Oskaloosa, Ia., U.S. I3 110
Oskaloosa, Ks., U.S. L12 118
Oskarshamn, Swe. M15 6
Oskū, Iran C9 48
Oslo, Nor. L12 6
Osmānābād, India C4 46
Osmaniye, Tur. C4 48
Osmond, Ne., U.S. I10 118
Osmore, stm., Peru G6 82
Osnabrück, Ger. C8 10
Osório Fonseca, Braz. I13 84
Osorno, Chile E2 78
Osoyoos, B.C., Can. H15 102
Osoyoos Indian Reserve, B.C., Can. H15 102
Osoyoos Lake, l., N.A. H15 102
Ospino, Ven. C8 84
Ospwagan Lake, l., Mb., Can. C16 104
Ossa, Mount, mtn., Austl. M7 70
Ossabaw Island, i., Ga., U.S. H5 112
Osse, stm., Nig. H12 64
Osseo, Wi., U.S. F4 110
Ossian, Ia., U.S. G4 110
Ossian, In., U.S. B11 114
Ossining, N.Y., U.S. F13 108
Ossipee, N.H., U.S. D15 108
Ossora, Russia F24 28
Ošta, Russia K24 6
Ostaškov, Russia D16 22
Ostende (Oostende), Bel. F2 12
Osterburg, Ger. C11 10
Östergötlands Län, co., Swe. L14 6
Osterholz-Scharmbeck, Ger. B8 10
Osterode, Ger. D10 10
Östersund, Swe. J14 6
Osterwieck, Ger. D10 10
Østfold, co., Nor. L12 6
Ostfriesische Inseln, is., Ger. B7 10
Ostfriesland, hist. reg., Ger. B7 10
Ost'or, Russia G15 22
Ostrava, Czech Rep. F18 10
Ostróda, Pol. B19 10
Ostrogožsk, Russia G5 26
Ostrołęka, Pol. B21 10
Ostrov, Czech Rep. E12 10
Ostrov, Russia D11 22
Ostrov, i., Slvk. H17 10
Ostrovskoje, Russia D25 22
Ostrowiec Świętokrzyski, Pol. E21 10
Ostrów Mazowiecka, Pol. C21 10
Ostrów Wielkopolski, Pol. D17 10
Ostrzeszów, Pol. D17 10
Ostúa, stm., N.A. C5 92
Ostuni, Italy I12 18
Ōsumi-kaikyō, strt., Japan Q5 36
Ōsumi-shotō, is., Japan q5 37b
Osuna, Spain H6 16
Osvaldo Cruz, Braz. F3 79
Oswego, Il., U.S. I7 110
Oswego, Ks., U.S. N12 118
Oswego, N.Y., U.S. D10 108
Oswego, stm., N.Y., U.S. D10 108
Oświęcim, Pol. E19 10
Osyka, Ms., U.S. K6 114
Otaci, Mol. A11 20
Otaki, N.Z. D5 72
Otanmäki, Fin. I20 6
Otaru, Japan d16 36a
Otava, Fin. K20 6
Otava, stm., Czech Rep. F13 10
Otavalo, Ec. G3 84
Otavi, Nmb. B3 66
Otepää, Est. C9 22
Oteros, stm., Mex. D5 90
Othello, Wa., U.S. D6 122
Óthris, Óros, mts., Grc. J6 20
Oti, stm., Afr. G7 54
Otinapa, Mex. E7 90
Otis, Co., U.S. K5 118
Otis, Ks., U.S. M8 118
Otish, Monts, mts., P.Q., Can. F18 96
Otjimbingue, Nmb. D3 66
Otjiwarongo, Nmb. C3 66
Otočac, Cro. E10 18
Otoque, Isla, i., Pan. I15 92

Name | Map Ref. | Page

Otoro, stm., Hond. C6 92
Otoskwin, stm., On., Can. F14 96
Otra, stm., Nor. L10 6
Otradnyj, Russia G8 26
Otranto, Italy I13 18
Otranto, Strait of, strt., Eur. I2 20
Otsego, Mi., U.S. H10 110
Otselic, stm., N.Y., U.S. E11 108
Ōtsu, Japan L10 36
Otta, Nor. K11 6
Ottawa, Il., U.S. I7 110
Ottawa, Ks., U.S. M12 118
Ottawa, Oh., U.S. F2 108
Ottawa, On., Can. B11 108
Ottawa, stm., Can. G17 96
Ottawa Islands, is., N.T., Can. E16 96
Otterburne, Mb., Can. I17 104
Otter Creek, Fl., U.S. J4 112
Otter Lake, Mi., U.S. G12 110
Otter-Lake, P.Q., Can. B10 108
Otter Lake, l., Sk., Can. C10 104
Otter Tail, stm., Mn., U.S. E11 118
Otterville, Mo., U.S. D3 114
Ottoville, Oh., U.S. G2 108
Ottumwa, Ia., U.S. I3 110
Ottweiler, Ger. F7 10
Otu, Nig. G11 64
Otumpa, Arg. D7 80
Otuquis, Bañados de, sw., Bol. H12 82
Oturkpo, Nig. H14 64
Otway, Cape, c., Austl. L5 70
Otwock, Pol. C21 10
Otyniya, Ukr. A8 20
Ötztaler Alpen, mts., Eur. C5 18
Ou, stm., China J2 34
Ou, stm., Laos D7 40
Ouachita, stm., U.S. K5 114
Ouachita, Lake, res., Ar., U.S. H3 114
Ouachita Mountains, mts., U.S. H2 114
Ouadâne, Maur. J5 62
Ouadda, C.A.R. M2 60
Ouagadougou, Burkina E9 64
Ouahigouya, Burkina E8 64
Ouaka, stm., C.A.R. G5 56
Oualâta, Maur. C6 64
Oualé, stm., Afr. F10 64
Oualidia, Mor. D6 62
Ouallam, Niger D11 64
Ouallene, Alg. H11 62
Ouanda Djallé, C.A.R. M2 60
Ouaninou, C. Iv. G6 64
Ouan Taredert, Alg. G15 62
Ouarâne, reg., Maur. A4 64
Ouarkziz, Jbel, mts., Afr. F6 62
Ouarzazate, Mor. E7 62
Ouassoulou, stm., Afr. F5 64
Ouatcha, Niger E14 64
Oubangui (Ubangi), stm., Afr. H8 52
Oud-Beijerland, Neth. E5 12
Ouddorp, Neth. F4 12
Oudenaarde (Audenarde), Bel. G4 12
Oude Pekela, Neth. B10 12
Oudtshoorn, S. Afr. I6 66
Oudyoumoudi, Burkina D9 64
Oued Cheham, Alg. M2 18
Oued Meliz, Tun. M3 18
Oued Tlelat, Alg. J11 16
Oued Zarga, Tun. M4 18
Oued-Zem, Mor. D7 62
Ouémé, stm., Benin H11 64
Ouenza, Alg. N3 18
Ouessant, Île d' (Ushant), i., Fr. D1 14
Ouesso, Congo A3 58
Ouest, Pointe de l', c., P.Q., Can. C9 106
Ouezzane, Mor. C8 62
Ouham, stm., Afr. G4 56
Ouidah, Benin H11 64
Ouistreham, Fr. C6 14
Oujda, Mor. C10 62
Oulainen, Fin. I19 6
Oulu, Fin. I19 6
Oulujärvi, l., Fin. I20 6
Oulujoki, stm., Fin. I20 6
Oulun lääni, prov., Fin. I20 6
Oum-Chalouba, Chad E5 56
Oum El Bouagui, Alg. C14 62
Oum er Rbia, Oued, stm., Mor. D7 62
Ounara, Mor. E6 62
Ounianga Kébir, Chad E5 56
Ouray, Co., U.S. F9 120
Ouray, Mount, mtn., Co., U.S. F10 120
Ourense, Spain C4 16
Ourinhos, Braz. G4 79
Ouro, Paraná do, stm., Braz. C6 82
Ouro Fino, Braz. G5 79
Ouro Preto, Braz. F7 79
Ouro Preto, stm., Braz. D9 82
Oursi, Burkina D9 64
Ourthe, stm., Bel. H8 12
Ōu-sammyaku, mts., Japan I15 36
Ouse, stm., Eng., U.K. H12 8
Outaouais, Rivière des see Ottawa, stm., Can. G17 96
Outardes, Baie aux, b., P.Q., Can. C5 106
Outardes, Rivière aux, stm., P.Q., Can. C5 106
Outardes Quatre, Réservoir, res., P.Q., Can. C4 106
Outardes Trois, Barrage, P.Q., Can. C5 106
Outer Hebrides, is., Scot., U.K. D6 8
Outer Island, i., Wi., U.S. C5 110
Outjo, Nmb. C3 66
Outlook, Mt., U.S. C3 118
Outlook, Sk., Can. G7 104
Ouvidor, Braz. E5 79
Ouyen, Austl. J5 70
Ouzouer-le-Marché, Fr. E8 14
Ouzzal, Oued i-n-, val., Alg. J12 62
Ovalle, Chile F3 80
Ovamboland, hist. reg., Nmb. A3 66
Ovana, Cerro, mtn., Ven. E9 84
Ovejas, Col. C5 84
Overbrook, Ks., U.S. M12 118
Overflakkee, i., Neth. E5 12
Overflowing, stm., Can. E13 104
Overhalla, Nor. I12 6
Overijssel, prov., Neth. D9 12
Overland Park, Ks., U.S. M13 118
Overpelt, Bel. F7 12
Overton, Ne., U.S. K8 118
Overton, Nv., U.S. H11 124
Overton, Tx., U.S. G12 116
Övertorneå, Swe. H18 6
Ovett, Ms., U.S. K7 114
Ovid, Mi., U.S. G11 110
Ovid, N.Y., U.S. E10 108
Oviedo, Spain B6 16
Ovino, Russia B16 22
Ovstug, Russia H16 22
Owando, Congo B3 58
Owasso, Ok., U.S. C11 116
Owatonna, Mn., U.S. F2 110
Owbeh, Afg. D17 48
Owego, N.Y., U.S. E10 108
Owen, Wi., U.S. F5 110
Owensboro, Ky., U.S. E9 114
Owens Lake, l., Ca., U.S. H8 124
Owen Sound, On., Can. F15 110
Owen Stanley Range, mts., Pap. N. Gui. m16 68a
Owensville, In., U.S. D9 114
Owensville, Mo., U.S. D5 114
Owenton, Ky., U.S. D12 114
Owerri, Nig. I13 64
Owikeno Lake, l., B.C., Can. F7 102
Owingsville, Ky., U.S. I3 108
Owl, stm., Ab., Can. B23 102
Owl, stm., Mb., Can. E14 96
Owl Creek Mountains, mts., Wy., U.S. G17 122
Owo, Nig. H12 64
Owosso, Mi., U.S. H11 110
Owyhee, Nv., U.S. C9 124
Owyhee, stm., U.S. G8 122
Owyhee, Lake, res., Or., U.S. G8 122
Oxapampa, Peru D4 82
Oxbow, Sk., Can. I12 104
Oxford, Al., U.S. I11 114
Oxford, Eng., U.K. J12 8
Oxford, Ia., U.S. I4 110
Oxford, In., U.S. B9 114
Oxford, Ks., U.S. N10 118
Oxford, Md., U.S. I10 108
Oxford, Me., U.S. C16 108
Oxford, Mi., U.S. H12 110
Oxford, Ms., U.S. H7 114
Oxford, N.C., U.S. C8 112
Oxford, Ne., U.S. K8 118
Oxford, N.S., Can. G10 106
Oxford, N.Y., U.S. E11 108
Oxford, Oh., U.S. H2 108
Oxford, Pa., U.S. H11 108
Oxford, Wi., U.S. G6 110
Oxford House, Mb., Can. D19 104
Oxford House Indian Reserve, Mb., Can. D19 104
Oxford Junction, Ia., U.S. I5 110
Oxford Lake, l., Mb., Can. D19 104
Oxfordshire, co., Eng., U.K. J12 8
Oxkutzcab, Mex. G15 90
Oxley, Austl. J6 70
Oxnard, Ca., U.S. J6 124
Oyama, B.C., Can. G15 102
Oyama, Japan K14 36
Oyem, Gabon A2 58
Oyen, Ab., Can. G4 104
Oyo, Nig. H11 64
Oyón, Peru D3 82
Oyonnax, Fr. F12 14
Oyotún, Peru B2 82
Ozamiz, Phil. D7 38
Ozark, Al., U.S. K11 114
Ozark, Ar., U.S. G3 114
Ozark, Mo., U.S. E3 114
Ozark Plateau, plat., U.S. F3 114
Ozark Reservoir, res., Ar., U.S. G2 114
Ozarks, Lake of the, res., Mo., U.S. D4 114
Ózd, Hung. G20 10
Oželerje, Russia G21 22
Ozernovskij, Russia G23 28
Ozery, Russia G21 22
Ozieri, Italy I4 18
Ozimek, Pol. E18 10
Ozona, Tx., U.S. I5 116
Ozorków, Pol. D19 10
Oz'ornyj, Russia D23 22
Ozubulu, Nig. I13 64
Ozuluama, Mex. G11 90

P

Paarl, S. Afr. I4 66
Paauilo, Hi., U.S. q18 125a
Pabellones, Ensenada, b., Mex. E6 90
Pabianice, Pol. D19 10
Pablo, Mt., U.S. C11 122
Pābna, Bngl. H13 44
Pabradė, Lith. G8 22
Pacaás Novos, stm., Braz. D9 82
Pacaás Novos, Serra dos, mts., Braz. D10 82
Pacaembu, Braz. F3 79
Pacaltsdorp, S. Afr. J6 66
Pacarán, Peru E3 82
Pacaraos, Peru D3 82
Pacasmayo, Peru B2 82
Pace, Fl., U.S. L9 114
Pace, Ms., U.S. I6 114
Pachacamac, hist., Peru E3 82
Pachino, Italy M10 18
Pachitea, stm., Peru C4 82
Pachiza, Peru B3 82
Pachmarhi, India I8 44
Pacho, Col. E5 84
Pachuca [de Soto], Mex. G10 90
Pacific, B.C., Can. C6 102
Pacific, Mo., U.S. D6 114
Pacifica, Ca., U.S. G3 124
Pacific Grove, Ca., U.S. H4 124
Pacific Ocean J24 126
Pacific Ranges, mts., B.C., Can. F8 102
Pacific Rim National Park, B.C., Can. I9 102
Paclión, Peru D3 82
Pacohuaras, stm., Bol. D8 82
Pacolet, stm., S.C., U.S. E5 112
Pacolet Mills, S.C., U.S. E5 112
Pacora, Pan. C3 84
Pacquet, Nf., Can. C18 106
Pacuare, stm., C.R. G11 92
Pacuí, stm., Braz. D6 79
Pacuneiro, stm., Braz. B2 79
Padamo, stm., Ven. F10 84
Padang, Indon. O6 40
Padang Endau, Malay. M7 40
Padangpanjang, Indon. O6 40
Padangsidempuan, Indon. N5 40
Padauari, stm., Braz. G10 84
Padcaya, Bol. I9 82
Paddle, stm., Ab., Can. C20 102
Paddle Prairie, Ab., Can. E9 96
Paden City, W.V., U.S. H6 108
Paderborn, Ger. D8 10
Padilla, Bol. H9 82
Padloping Island, i., N.T., Can. C20 96
Padova, Italy D6 18
Padre Bernardo, Braz. C4 79
Padre Island, i., Tx., U.S. L9 116
Padre Paraíso, Braz. D8 79
Padsville, Bela. F10 22
Padua see Padova, Italy D6 18
Paducah, Ky., U.S. E8 114
Paducah, Tx., U.S. E6 116
Paektu-san, mtn., Asia A16 32
Páez, stm., Col. F4 84
Pafúri, Moz. D10 66
Pag, Cro. E10 18
Pag, Otok, i., Cro. E10 18
Pagadian, Phil. D7 38
Pagai Selatan, Pulau, i., Indon. F3 38
Pagai Utara, Pulau, i., Indon. F3 38
Pagan, Myan. D3 40
Pagancillo, Arg. E4 80
Pagasitikós Kólpos, b., Grc. J6 20
Pagato, stm., Sk., Can. B12 104
Pagato Lake, l., Sk., Can. B12 104
Page, Az., U.S. H5 120
Page, N.D., U.S. D10 118
Pagėgiai, Lith. F4 22
Pageland, S.C., U.S. E6 112
Pagoda Peak, mtn., Co., U.S. D9 120
Pagoda Point, c., Myan. G3 40
Pagon, Bukit, mtn., Asia E6 38
Pagosa Springs, Co., U.S. G9 120
Pagouda, Togo G10 64
Paguate, N.M., U.S. I9 120
Pahala, Hi., U.S. r18 125a
Pahang, stm., Malay. M7 40
Páhara, Laguna, b., Nic. C11 92
Pahoa, Hi., U.S. r19 125a
Pahokee, Fl., U.S. M6 112
Pahost, Bela. H12 22
Pahraničny, Bela. H6 22
Pahrump, Nv., U.S. H10 124
Pahvant Range, mts., Ut., U.S. F4 120
Pai, stm., Asia E5 40
Paico, Peru F5 82
Paide, Est. C8 22
Paige, Tx., U.S. I9 116
Paignton, Eng., U.K. K10 8
Paiguano, Chile F3 80
Paiján, Peru B2 82
Päijänne, l., Fin. K19 6
Paila, stm., Bol. G10 82
Pailin, Camb. H7 40
Pailitas, Col. C6 84
Paimpol, Fr. D3 14
Painesdale, Mi., U.S. C7 110
Painesville, Oh., U.S. F5 108
Paint, stm., Mi., U.S. D7 110
Painted Desert, des., Az., U.S. I5 120
Painted Rock Reservoir, res., Az., U.S. K4 120
Paint Lake, l., Mb., Can. C17 104
Paint Rock, Tx., U.S. H7 116
Paint Rock, stm., Al., U.S. H10 114
Paintsville, Ky., U.S. B4 112
Paisley, Or., U.S. H5 122
Paisley, Scot., U.K. F9 8
Paita, Peru A1 82
Paita, Bahía de, b., Peru A1 82
Paizhou, China E2 34
Pajala, Swe. H18 6
Paján, Ec. H2 84
Pájara, Spain o26 17b
Pajjer, gora, mtn., Russia D10 26
Pakaraima Mountains, mts., S.A. E12 84
Pak Ban, Laos D7 40
Pakch'ŏn, N. Kor. D13 32
Pakeng, Sudan N6 60
Pakhoi see Beihai, China G8 30
Pakistan (Pākistān), ctry., Asia C9 42
Pakokku, Myan. D3 40
Pakouabo, C. Iv. H7 64
Pakowki Lake, l., Ab., Can. I4 104
Pākpattan, Pak. E5 44
Pak Phanang, Thai. J6 40
Pak Phraek, Thai. J6 40
Pakrac, Cro. D12 18
Pakruojis, Lith. F6 22
Paks, Hung. I18 10
P'akupur, stm., Russia E7 28
Pakwash Lake, l., On., Can. H21 104
Pakxé, Laos G8 40
Pala, Chad G3 56
Palacca Point, c., Bah. D8 94
Palacios, Tx., U.S. K10 116
Palacios, stm., Bol. G10 82
Palagonia, Italy L9 18
Palagruža, Otoci, is., Cro. G11 18
Pālakollu, India D6 46
Palamós, Spain D15 16
Palana, Russia F23 28
Palanga, Lith. F4 22
Palangkaraya, Indon. F5 38
Pālanpur, India H5 44
Palapye, Bots. D8 66
Palatka, Fl., U.S. J5 112
Palatka, Russia E22 28
Palau, ctry., Oc. H17 126
Palauk, Myan. H5 40
Palawan, i., Phil. D6 38
Pālayankottai, India H4 46
Palca, Bol. G8 82
Palca, Peru D4 82
Palcamayo, Peru D4 82
Pal'co, Russia H17 22
Paldiski, Est. B7 22
Palech, Russia E24 22
Palembang, Indon. F3 38
Palena, Italy H9 18
Palencia, Spain C7 16
Palenque, Mex. I14 90
Palenque, hist., Mex. I13 90
Palenque, Punta, c., Dom. Rep. E9 94
Palermo, Col. F5 84
Palermo, Italy K8 18
Palermo, Ur. G11 80
Palestina, Braz. F4 79
Palestine, Ar., U.S. H6 114
Palestine, Il., U.S. C9 114
Palestine, Tx., U.S. H11 116
Palestine, hist. reg., Asia D4 50
Palestine, Lake, res., Tx., U.S. G11 116
Palestrina, Italy H7 18
Paletwa, Myan. D2 40
Pālghāt, India G4 46
Pāli, India H5 44
Palin, Guat. C4 92
Palisade, Co., U.S. E8 120
Palisade, Ne., U.S. K6 118
Palisades, Id., U.S. G14 122
Palisades Reservoir, res., U.S. G14 122
Paliseul, Bel. I7 12
Pālitāna, India B1 46
Palivere, Est. C6 22
Palizada, Mex. H13 90
Palk Bay, b., Asia H5 46
Palk Strait, strt., Asia H5 46
Palla Bianca (Weisskugel), mtn., Eur. E14 13
Pallasca, Peru C2 82
Palling, B.C., Can. C9 102
Palliser, Cape, c., N.Z. D5 72
Palma, Braz. F7 79
Palma, Moz. D8 58
P'al'ma, Russia J24 6
Palma, stm., Braz. B5 79
Palma del Río, Spain H6 16
Palma [de Mallorca], Spain F14 16
Palma di Montechiaro, Italy L8 18
Palmar, stm., Ven. B6 84
Palmar Camp, Belize I15 90
Palmar de los Sepúlveda, Mex. E6 90
Palmar de Varela, Col. B5 84
Palmares, Braz. E11 76
Palmares, C.R. G10 92
Palmares do Sul, Braz. F13 80
Palmarito, Ven. D7 84
Palmar Sur, C.R. I11 92
Palmas, Braz. F9 76
Palmas, Braz. D12 80
Palmas Bellas, Pan. C2 84
Palmas de Monte Alto, Braz. C7 79
Palma Soriano, Cuba D6 94
Palm Bay, Fl., U.S. K6 112
Palm Beach, Fl., U.S. M6 112
Palmdale, Ca., U.S. J7 124
Palm Desert, Ca., U.S. K9 124
Palmeira, Braz. C13 80
Palmeira, C.V. k17 64a
Palmeira das Missões, Braz. D12 80
Palmeira d'Oeste, Braz. F3 79
Palmeiras, Braz. B8 79
Palmeiras, stm., Braz. C3 79
Palmelo, Braz. D4 79
Palmer, Ak., U.S. F20 100
Palmer, Ma., U.S. E14 108
Palmer, Ms., U.S. K7 114
Palmer, Ne., U.S. J9 118
Palmer, Tn., U.S. G11 114
Palmer, Tx., U.S. G10 116
Palmer, sci., Ant. B12 73
Palmer Lake, Co., U.S. F12 120
Palmer Land, reg., Ant. C12 73
Palmerston, N.Z. F3 72
Palmerston, On., Can. G15 110
Palmerston, Cape, c., Austl. C8 70
Palmerston North, N.Z. D5 72
Palmerton, Pa., U.S. G11 108
Palmetto, Fl., U.S. L4 112
Palmetto, Ga., U.S. F2 112
Palmetto, La., U.S. L5 114
Palmi, Italy K10 18
Palminópolis, Braz. D3 79
Palmira, Arg. G4 80
Palmira, Col. F4 84
Palmira, Cuba C4 94
Palmira, Ec. I3 84
Palmitas, Ur. G10 80
Palmitos, Braz. D12 80
Palm Springs, Ca., U.S. K9 124
Palmyra, Il., U.S. C7 114
Palmyra, Mo., U.S. C5 114
Palmyra, N.Y., U.S. D9 108
Palmyra, Pa., U.S. G10 108
Palmyra see Tudmur, Syria D5 48
Palmyra, Va., U.S. B8 112
Palmyra, hist., Syria D5 48
Palmyra Atoll, atoll, Oc. H23 126
Palo Alto, Ca., U.S. G3 124
Palo Flechado Pass, N.M., U.S. H11 120
Paloich, Sudan L7 60
Palomar Mountain, mtn., Ca., U.S. K9 124
Palomas Viejo, Mex. B6 90
Palo Negro, Ven. B9 84
Palo Pinto, Tx., U.S. G8 116
Palopo, Indon. F7 38
Palora, stm., Ec. H3 84
Palos see Palos de la Frontera, Spain H5 16
Palos, Cabo de, c., Spain H11 16
Palo Santo, Arg. C9 80
Palos de la Frontera, Spain H5 16
Palouse, Wa., U.S. D8 122
Palouse, stm., U.S. D7 122
Palo Verde, Ca., U.S. K11 124
Palo Verde, Parque Nacional, C.R. G9 92
Palpa, Peru F4 82
Palpalá, Arg. C6 80
Palu, Indon. F6 38
Palwal, India F7 44
Pama, Burkina F10 64
Pāmban Island, i., India H5 46
Pambeguwa, Nig. F14 64
Pamekasan, Indon. j16 39a
Pamiers, Fr. I8 14
Pamir, mts., Asia B5 44
Pamlico, stm., N.C., U.S. D10 112
Pamlico Sound, strt., N.C., U.S. D11 112
Pampa, Tx., U.S. D6 116
Pampã, stm., Braz. D8 79
Pampa, reg., Arg. I6 80
Pampa Almirón, Arg. D9 80
Pampacolca, Peru F5 82
Pampa del Chañar, Arg. F4 80
Pampa del Indio, Arg. D9 80
Pampa del Infierno, Arg. D8 80
Pampa de los Guanacos, Arg. D8 80
Pampa Grande, Bol. H9 82
Pampas, Peru E4 82
Pampas, stm., Peru E5 82
Pamplico, S.C., U.S. F7 112
Pamplona, Col. D6 84
Pamplona (Iruña), Spain C10 16
Pampoenpoort, S. Afr. H6 66
Pamunkey, stm., Va., U.S. B9 112
Pana, Il., U.S. C7 114
Panabá, Mex. G15 90
Panaca, Nv., U.S. G11 124
Panacea, Fl., U.S. I2 112
Panaji (Panjim), India E2 46
Panamá, Braz. E4 79
Panama, Il., U.S. C7 114
Panama, Ok., U.S. G2 114
Panamá, Pan. C3 84
Panamá, prov., Pan. I15 92
Panama (Panamá), ctry., N.A. G8 88
Panamá, Bahía de, b., Pan. C3 84
Panamá, Canal de, Pan. H15 92
Panamá, Golfo de, b., Pan. C3 84
Panamá, Istmo de, Pan. C2 84
Panama City, Fl., U.S. L11 114
Panamá Vieja, hist., Pan. H15 92
Panambi, Braz. E12 80
Panamint Range, mts., Ca., U.S. H8 124
Panao, Peru C3 82
Pančevo, Yugo. E4 20
Pandamatenga, Bots. B7 66
Pan de Azúcar, Ur. H11 80
Pandėlys, Lith. E8 22
Pandharpur, India D3 46
Pāndhurna, India B5 46
Pando, dept., Bol. D8 82
P'andž (Panj), stm., Asia A4 44
Panevėžys, Lith. F7 22
Panfang, China H4 34
Panfilov, Kaz. I14 26
Pangala, Congo B2 58
Pangalanes, Canal des, Madag. q23 67b
Pangani, Tan. C7 58
Pangburn, Ar., U.S. G5 114
Pangfou see Bengbu, China E10 30
Pangi, Zaire B5 58
Pangkalanbuun, Indon. F5 38
Pangkalpinang, Indon. F4 38
Pangman, Sk., Can. I10 104
Pangnirtung, N.T., Can. C19 96
Pangong Tso, l., Asia D8 44
Panguitch, Ut., U.S. G4 120
Panhandle, Tx., U.S. D5 116
Panino, Russia E17 22
Pānīpat, India F7 44
Panj (P'andž), stm., Asia B4 44
Panjāb, Afg. C2 44
Panjgūr, Pak. H18 48
Panjim see Panaji, India E2 46
Pankshin, Nig. G14 64
Panlong (Lo), stm., Asia C8 40
P'anmunjŏm, N. Kor. F14 32
Panna, India H9 44
Pannawonica, Austl. D3 68
Panola, Al., U.S. K10 114
Panora, Ia., U.S. J13 118
Panorama, Braz. F3 79
Pansik, Rápido, wtfl., N.A. C9 92
Pantelleria, Isola di, i., Italy M7 18
Pantha, Myan. C3 40
Pánuco, Mex. F10 90
Pánuco, stm., Mex. G10 90
Panuke Lake, l., N.S., Can. H9 106
Panxian, China B8 40
Panxidu, China H3 32
Panyam, Nig. G14 64
Panyang, Sudan L5 60
Panyu, China M2 34
Panzós, Guat. B5 92
Pao, stm., Ven. C8 84
Pao, stm., Ven. C10 84
Paola, Italy J11 18
Paola, Ks., U.S. M13 118
Paoli, In., U.S. D10 114
Paonia, Co., U.S. F9 120
Paotow see Baotou, China C8 30
P'aozero, ozero, l., Russia H22 6
Paozi, China A10 32
Pápa, Hung. H17 10
Papagaio, stm., Braz. I11 84
Papagayo, Golfo de, b., C.R. G9 92
Papaikou, Hi., U.S. r18 125a
Papantla [de Olarte], Mex. G11 90
Papenburg, Ger. B7 10
Papilė, Lith. E5 22
Papillion, Ne., U.S. J11 118
Papineau-Labelle, Réserve, P.Q., Can. B11 108
Paposo, Chile C3 80
Papua, Gulf of, b., Pap. N. Gui. m15 68a
Papua New Guinea, ctry., Oc. m15 68a
Papudo, Chile G3 80
Papun, Myan. E4 40
Papunáua, stm., Col. G7 84
Papurí, stm., S.A. G7 84
Paquera, C.R. H10 92
Pará, state, Braz. B13 82
Pará, stm., Braz. D9 76
Pará, stm., Braz. E6 79
Paraburdoo, Austl. D3 68
Paracari, stm., Braz. A13 82
Paracas, Bahía de, b., Peru E3 82
Paracas, Península de, pen., Peru E3 82
Paracatu, Braz. D5 79
Paracatu, stm., Braz. D6 79
Paracatu, stm., Braz. D6 79
Paracel Islands see Xisha Qundao, is., China B5 38
Parachilna, Austl. H3 70
Paracho de Verduzco, Mex. H8 90
Parachute, Co., U.S. E8 120
Paraćin, Yugo. F5 20
Parád, Hung. H20 10
Parada, Punta, c., Peru F4 82
Paradas, Spain H6 16
Paradise, Ca., U.S. E4 124
Paradise, Guy. D14 84
Paradise, Mt., U.S. C11 122
Paradise, Nv., U.S. H10 124
Paradise, Tx., U.S. F9 116
Paradise Hill, Sk., Can. E5 104
Paradise Valley, Az., U.S. K5 120
Paradise Valley, Nv., U.S. C8 124
Parado, stm., Braz. D14 82
Paragonah, Ut., U.S. G4 120
Paragould, Ar., U.S. F6 114
Paraguá, stm., Bol. E11 82
Paragua, stm., Ven. D11 84
Paraguaçu, stm., Braz. B9 79
Paraguaçu Paulista, Braz. G3 79
Paraguaipoa, Ven. B7 84
Paraguaná, Península de, pen., Ven. B8 84
Paraguarí, Para. C10 80
Paraguarí, dept., Para. D10 80
Paraguay, ctry., S.A. G9 74
Paraguay (Paraguai), stm., S.A. G9 74
Paraíba do Sul, stm., Braz. F7 79
Paraíso, Braz. E2 79
Paraíso, C.R. H11 92
Paraíso, Mex. H13 90
Paraíso, Pan. C3 84
Paraíso do Norte, Braz. G2 79
Paraisópolis, Braz. G6 79
Paraitinga, stm., Braz. G6 79
Parakou, Benin G11 64
Paramakkudi, India H5 46
Paramaribo, Sur. E14 76
Paramirim, Braz. B7 79
Paramirim, stm., Braz. B7 79
Paramonga, Peru D3 82
Paramušir, ostrov, i., Russia G23 28
Paran, Naḥal (Wādī al-Jirāfī), val. H3 50
Paraná, Arg. F8 80
Paranã, Braz. B5 79
Paraná, state, Braz. C13 80
Paranã, stm., Braz. B5 79
Paraná, stm., S.A. G9 80
Paranaguá, Braz. C14 80
Paranaguá, Baía de, b., Braz. C14 80
Paranaíba, Braz. E3 79
Paranaíba, stm., Braz. E3 79
Paranaíta, stm., Braz. C13 82
Paranam, Sur. B7 76
Paranapanema, stm., Braz. G3 79
Paranapiacaba, Serra do, mts., Braz. C14 80
Paranavaí, Braz. G2 79
Parângu Mare, Vârful, mtn., Rom. D7 20
Paranhos, Braz. G1 79
Paranoá, Lago do, l., Braz. C5 79
Paraopeba, Braz. E6 79
Parapara, Ven. C9 84
Parapetí, stm., Bol. H10 82
Paras, Peru E4 82
Paratinga, Braz. B7 79
Parauari, stm., Braz. J13 84
Paraúna, Braz. D3 79
Paray-le-Monial, Fr. F11 14
Pārbati, stm., India H7 44
Pārbatipur, Bngl. H13 44
Parbhani, India C4 46
Parchment, Mi., U.S. H10 110
Parczew, Pol. D22 10
Pardeeville, Wi., U.S. G6 110
Pardes Hanna-Karkur, Isr. D3 50
Pardo, stm., Braz. C6 79
Pardo, stm., Braz. F4 79
Pardo, stm., Braz. G4 79
Pardo, stm., Braz. C9 79
Pardo, stm., Braz. F2 79
Pardo, stm., Braz. E12 80
Pardubice, Czech Rep. E15 10
Parèčča, Bela. H7 22
Parecis, Braz. F13 82
Parecis, stm., Braz. E13 82
Parecis, Chapada dos, mts., Braz. F12 82
Paredón, Mex. E9 90
Paren', stm., Russia E24 28
Parent, P.Q., Can. G18 96
Parepare, Indon. F6 38
Parera, Arg. H6 80
Parfino, Russia D14 22
Paria, stm., U.S. H5 120
Paria, Gulf of, b. B11 84
Paria, Península de, pen., Ven. B11 84
Pariaguán, Ven. C10 84
Pariaman, Indon. O6 40
Pariamanu, stm., Peru E6 82
Paricutín, vol., Mex. H8 90
Parida, Isla, i., Pan. I12 92
Parika, Guy. D13 84
Parima, stm., Braz. F11 84
Parima, Sierra, mts., S.A. F10 84
Pariñas, Punta, c., Peru J2 84
Parintins, Braz. I14 84
Pariquera-Açu, Braz. C15 80
Paris, Ar., U.S. G3 114
Paris, Fr. D9 14
Paris, Id., U.S. H14 122
Paris, Il., U.S. C9 114
Paris, Ky., U.S. I2 108
Paris, Me., U.S. C16 108
Paris, Mo., U.S. C4 114
Paris, On., Can. G15 110
Paris, Tn., U.S. F8 114
Paris, Tx., U.S. F11 116
Parismina, C.R. G11 92
Parismina, stm., C.R. G11 92
Parita, Bahía de, b., Pan. I14 92
Parit Buntar, Malay. L6 40
Park, stm., N.D., U.S. C10 118
Parkano, Fin. J18 6
Park City, Ks., U.S. N10 118
Park City, Mt., U.S. E17 122
Park City, Ut., U.S. D5 120
Parkdale, Or., U.S. E4 122
Parkdale, P.E., Can. F10 106
Parker, Az., U.S. J2 120
Parker, Co., U.S. L3 118
Parker, Fl., U.S. L11 114
Parker, S.D., U.S. H10 118
Parker, Cape, c., N.T., Can. A17 96
Parker City, In., U.S. B11 114
Parker Dam, Ca., U.S. J11 124
Parkersburg, Ia., U.S. H3 110
Parkersburg, Il., U.S. D8 114
Parkersburg, W.V., U.S. H5 108
Parkers Prairie, Mn., U.S. E12 118
Parkes, Austl. I8 70
Park Falls, Wi., U.S. E5 110
Park Forest, Il., U.S. I8 110
Parkhill, On., Can. G14 110
Parkin, Ar., U.S. G6 114
Parkland, Wa., U.S. C3 122
Park Range, mts., Co., U.S. D10 120
Park Rapids, Mn., U.S. E12 118
Park River, N.D., U.S. C10 118
Parkrose, Or., U.S. E3 122
Parksley, Va., U.S. B11 112
Parkston, S.D., U.S. H10 118
Parksville, B.C., Can. H10 102
Parkville, Md., U.S. H10 108
Parkville, Mo., U.S. C2 114
Parkwater, Wa., U.S. C8 122
Parla, Spain E8 16
Parlākimidi, India C8 46
Parle, Lac qui, l., Mn., U.S. F11 118
Parli, India C4 46
Parma, Id., U.S. G9 122
Parma, Italy E5 18
Parma, Mo., U.S. F7 114
Parma, Oh., U.S. F5 108
Parnaguá, Braz. F10 76
Parnaíba, Braz. D10 76
Parnaíba, stm., Braz. D10 76
Parnassós, mtn., Grc. K6 20
Pärnu, Est. C7 22
Pärnu-Jaagupi, Est. C7 22
Paro, Bhu. G13 44
Paromaj, Russia G20 28
Paroo, stm., Austl. H5 70
Páros, i., Grc. L9 20
Parowan, Ut., U.S. G4 120
Parpaillon, mts., Fr. H13 14
Parpan, Switz. E12 13
Parral, Chile I3 80
Parral see Hidalgo del Parral, Mex. D7 90
Parral, stm., Mex. D7 90
Parramatta, Austl. I9 70
Parras de la Fuente, Mex. E8 90
Parrish, Al., U.S. I9 114
Parrish, Fl., U.S. L4 112
Parrita, C.R. H10 92
Parrita, stm., C.R. H10 92
Parrsboro, N.S., Can. G9 106
Parry, Cape, c., N.T., Can. B8 96
Parry, Mount, mtn., B.C., Can. E6 102
Parry Bay, b., N.T., Can. C16 96
Parry Channel, strt., N.T., Can. B9 86
Parry Peninsula, pen., N.T., Can. B32 100
Parry Sound, On., Can. E15 110
Parsberg, Ger. F11 10
Parseierspitze, mtn., Aus. D13 13
Parshall, N.D., U.S. D5 118
Parsnip, stm., B.C., Can. C12 102
Parsons, Ks., U.S. N12 118
Parsons, Tn., U.S. G8 114
Parsons, W.V., U.S. H7 108
Parson's Pond, Nf., Can. B16 106
Parsons Pond, l., Nf., Can. B16 106
Pārsti, Est. C8 22
Partanna, Italy L7 18
Parthenay, Fr. F6 14
Partinico, Italy K8 18
Partizansk, Russia I18 28
Partridge Crop Lake, l., Mb., Can. C17 104
Partridge Point, c., Nf., Can. B17 106
Paru, stm., Braz. D8 76
Parú, stm., Ven. E10 84
Paru de Oeste, stm., Braz. D7 76
Paruro, Peru E6 82
Pārvatīpuram, India C7 46
Paryang, China E10 44
Paryčy, Bela. I12 22

Port-Pusk

Name — Map Ref. — Page

Port-Cartier Sept-Îles, Réserve, P.Q., Can. B6 106
Port Chalmers, N.Z. F3 72
Port Charlotte, Fl., U.S. M4 112
Port Chester, N.Y., U.S. F13 108
Port Clements, B.C., Can. D2 102
Port Clinton, Oh., U.S. F4 108
Port Clyde, Me., U.S. D17 108
Port Colborne, On., Can. H16 110
Port Coquitlam, B.C., Can. H12 102
Port Credit, On., Can. G16 110
Port-Daniel, Réserve, P.Q., Can. D9 106
Port-de-Paix, Haiti E8 94
Port Dickson, Malay. M6 40
Port Dover, On., Can. H15 110
Porte Crayon, Mount, mtn., W.V., U.S. I7 108
Port Edward, B.C., Can. C4 102
Port Edward, S. Afr. H10 66
Port Edwards, Wi., U.S. F6 110
Portegolpe, C.R. G9 92
Porteirinha, Braz. C7 79
Portel, Braz. D8 76
Port Elgin, N.B., Can. F9 106
Port Elgin, On., Can. F14 110
Port Elizabeth, S. Afr. I7 66
Port-en-Bessin, Fr. C6 14
Porter, Ok., U.S. D11 116
Porter, Tx., U.S. I11 116
Porter Lake, l., Sk., Can. B7 104
Porterville, Ca., U.S. H6 124
Porterville, Ms., U.S. J8 114
Port Essington, B.C., Can. C5 102
Portete, Bahía, b., Col. A6 84
Port Fairy, Austl. L5 70
Port Gamble, Wa., U.S. C3 122
Port Gentil, Gabon B1 58
Port Germein, Austl. I3 70
Port Gibson, Ms., U.S. K6 114
Port Graham, Ak., U.S. G19 100
Port Greville, N.S., Can. G9 106
Port Harcourt, Nig. I13 64
Port Hardy, B.C., Can. G7 102
Port Hawkesbury, N.S., Can. G12 106
Port Hedland, Austl. D3 68
Port Henry, N.Y., U.S. C13 108
Port Hill, P.E., Can. F10 106
Port Hood, N.S., Can. F12 106
Port Hope, Mi., U.S. G13 110
Port Hope, On., Can. G17 110
Port Howe, Bah. B7 94
Port Huron, Mi., U.S. H13 110
Port-İliç, Azer. B10 48
Portimão, Port. H3 16
Port Isabel, Tx., U.S. M9 116
Port Jervis, N.Y., U.S. F12 108
Port Kembla, Austl. J9 70
Portland, Ar., U.S. I5 114
Portland, Austl. I9 70
Portland, Austl. L4 70
Portland, In., U.S. B12 114
Portland, Me., U.S. D16 108
Portland, Mi., U.S. H11 110
Portland, N.D., U.S. D10 118
Portland, Or., U.S. E3 122
Portland, Tn., U.S. F10 114
Portland, Tx., U.S. L9 116
Portland, Bill of, c., Eng., U.K. K11 8
Portland, Cape, c., Austl. M7 70
Portland Bay, b., Austl. L4 70
Portland Bight, Jam. F6 94
Portland Canal, b., N.A. B4 102
Portland Creek Pond, l., Nf., Can. B16 106
Portland Inlet, b., B.C., Can. C4 102
Portland Point, c., Jam. F6 94
Port Laoise, Ire. H6 8
Port Lavaca, Tx., U.S. K10 116
Port Leyden, N.Y., U.S. D11 108
Port Lincoln, Austl. J1 70
Port Lions, Ak., U.S. H18 100
Port Loko, S.L. G3 64
Port-Louis, Fr. E3 14
Port Louis, Mrts. v18 67c
Port Macquarie, Austl. H10 70
Port Maitland, N.S., Can. I7 106
Port Maria, Jam. E6 94
Port McNeill, B.C., Can. G7 102
Port McNicoll, On., Can. F16 110
Port Mellon, B.C., Can. H11 102
Port-Menier, P.Q., Can. C9 106
Port Moody, B.C., Can. H12 102
Port Moresby, Pap. N. Gui. m16 68a
Port Morien, N.S., Can. F14 106
Port Mouton, N.S., Can. I9 106
Port Neches, Tx., U.S. M3 114
Port Nelson, Mb., Can. A22 104
Portneuf, stm., Id., U.S. H13 122
Portneuf, stm., P.Q., Can. D4 106
Portneuf, Lac, l., P.Q., Can. C3 106
Portneuf-sur-Mer, P.Q., Can. D4 106
Port Neville, B.C., Can. G8 102
Port Nolloth, S. Afr. G3 66
Port Norris, N.J., U.S. H11 108
Porto, Port. D3 16
Porto Acre, Braz. C8 82
Porto Alegre, Braz. F13 80
Porto Amboim, Ang. D2 58
Porto Belo, Braz. D14 80
Portobelo, Pan. C3 84
Port O'Connor, Tx., U.S. K10 116
Porto de Moz, Braz. D8 76
Porto de Pedras, Braz. E11 76
Porto Empedocle, Italy L8 18
Porto Esperança, Braz. H13 82
Porto Esperidião, Braz. F12 82
Porto Farina, Tun. L5 18
Porto Feliz, Braz. G5 79
Porto Ferreira, Braz. F5 79
Port of Spain, Trin. I14 94
Portogruaro, Italy D7 18
Porto Inglês, C.V. m17 64a
Portola, Ca., U.S. E5 124
Porto Lucena, Braz. D11 80
Pörtom (Pirttikylä), Fin. J17 6
Porto Mendes, Braz. C11 80
Porto Murtinho, Braz. I13 82
Porto Nacional, Braz. F9 76
Porto-Novo, Benin H11 64
Port Orange, Fl., U.S. J6 112
Port Orchard, Wa., U.S. C3 122
Porto Recanati, Italy F8 18
Port Orford, Or., U.S. H1 122
Porto San Giorgio, Italy F8 18
Porto Santo, i., Port. I21 17a
Porto São José, Braz. G2 79
Porto Seguro, Braz. D9 79
Porto-Séguro, Togo H10 64
Porto Torres, Italy I3 18
Porto União, Braz. D13 80
Porto Válter, Braz. C5 82
Porto-Vecchio, Fr. m24 15a
Porto Velho, Braz. C10 82
Portoviejo, Ec. H2 84
Port Perry, On., Can. F17 110
Port Phillip Bay, b., Austl. L6 70
Port Pirie, Austl. I3 70
Port Rexton, Nf., Can. D20 106
Port Richey, Fl., U.S. K4 112
Port Rowan, On., Can. H15 110
Port Royal, Pa., U.S. G9 108
Port Royal, S.C., U.S. G6 112
Port Royal National Historic Park, N.S., Can. H8 106
Port Said see Būr Sa'īd, Egypt B7 60
Port Saint Joe, Fl., U.S. J1 112
Port Saint Johns, S. Afr. H9 66
Port Saint Lucie, Fl., U.S. L6 112
Port-Saint-Servan, P.Q., Can. A15 106
Port Sanilac, Mi., U.S. G13 110
Port Saunders, Nf., Can. B16 106
Portsea, Austl. L6 70
Port Shepstone, S. Afr. H10 66
Portsmouth, Eng., U.K. K12 8
Portsmouth, N.H., U.S. D16 108
Portsmouth, Oh., U.S. I4 108
Portsmouth, Va., U.S. C10 112
Portsoy, Scot., U.K. D11 8
Port Stanley, On., Can. H14 110
Port Sudan see Būr Sūdān, Sudan H9 60
Port Sulphur, La., U.S. M7 114
Port Talbot, Wales, U.K. J10 8
Port Taufiq see Būr Tawfīq, Egypt G2 48
Porttipahdan tekojärvi, res., Fin. G20 6
Port Townsend, Wa., U.S. B3 122
Portugal, ctry., Eur. H6 4
Portugal, Cachoeira, wtfl, Braz. C9 82
Portugal Cove South, Nf., Can. F20 106
Portugalete, Spain B8 16
Portuguesa, state, Ven. C8 84
Portuguesa, stm., Ven. C9 84
Portuguese Guinea see Guinea-Bissau, ctry., Afr. F3 54
Port Union, Nf., Can. D20 106
Port-Vendres, Fr. J10 14
Portville, N.Y., U.S. E8 108
Port Wakefield, Ak., U.S. G18 100
Port Wakefield, Austl. J3 70
Port Washington, Wi., U.S. G8 110
Port Wentworth, Ga., U.S. G5 112
Port Wing, Wi., U.S. D4 110
Porum, Ok., U.S. D11 116
Porvenir, Chile G2 78
Porvenir, Mex. B7 90
Porzuna, Spain F7 16
Posada, Italy I4 18
Posadas, Arg. D11 80
Posadas, Spain H6 16
Poschiavo, Switz. F13 13
Pošechon'e, Russia C22 22
Posen, Mi., U.S. E12 110
Posen see Poznań, Pol. C16 10
Positano, Italy I9 18
Posjet, Russia I18 28
Posse, Braz. C5 79
Possession Islands, is., Ant. C8 73
Pössneck, Ger. E11 10
Possum Kingdom Lake, res., Tx., U.S. G8 116
Post, Tx., U.S. F5 116
Poste-de-la-Baleine, P.Q., Can. E17 96
Postelle, Tn., U.S. D2 112
Poste Ramartina, Madag. q21 67b
Post Falls, Id., U.S. C9 122
Postojna, Slvn. D9 18
P'ostraja Dresva, Russia E23 28
Postrevalle, Bol. H10 82
Postville, Ia., U.S. G4 110
Pótam, Mex. D4 90
Potaro, stm., Guy. E13 84
Potaro Landing, Guy. E13 84
Poté, Braz. D8 79
Poteau, Ok., U.S. G2 114
Poteau, stm., U.S. G2 114
Poteet, Tx., U.S. J8 116
Potenza, Italy I10 18
Potes, Spain B7 16
Potgietersrus, S. Afr. E9 66
Poth, Tx., U.S. J8 116
Potholes Reservoir, res., Wa., U.S. C6 122
Poti, Geor. I6 26
Poti, stm., Braz. E10 76
Potiraguá, Braz. C9 79
Potirendaba, Braz. F4 79
Potiskum, Nig. F9 54
Potlatch, Id., U.S. D9 122
Potomac, Il., U.S. B9 114
Potomac, stm., U.S. I10 108
Potomac Heights, Md., U.S. I9 108
Potosí, Bol. H9 82
Potosi, Mo., U.S. E6 114
Potosí, dept., Bol. I8 82
Potrerillos, Chile D4 80
Potrerillos, Hond. B7 92
Potrerillos Arriba, Pan. I12 92
Potrero, C.R. G9 92
Potrero Grande, C.R. H11 92
Potro, Cerro del, mtn., S.A. E4 80
Potsdam, Ger. C13 10
Potsdam, N.Y., U.S. C12 108
Potter, Ne., U.S. J4 118
Potterville, Mi., U.S. H11 110
Potts Camp, Ms., U.S. H7 114
Pottstown, Pa., U.S. G11 108
Pottsville, Pa., U.S. G10 108
Potwin, Ks., U.S. N10 118
P'otzu, Tai. L9 34
Pouancé, Fr. E5 14
Pouce-Coupe, B.C., Can. B14 102
Pouce Coupé, stm., Can. A15 102
Pouch Cove, Nf., Can. E21 106
Poughkeepsie, N.Y., U.S. F13 108
Poulan, Ga., U.S. H3 112
Poulin-de-Courval, Lac, l., P.Q., Can. D3 106
Poulsbo, Wa., U.S. C3 122
Poultney, Vt., U.S. D13 108
Poŭn, S. Kor. G15 32
Pound, Va., U.S. B4 112
Poundmaker Indian Reserve, Sk., Can. F5 104
Pouso Alegre, Braz. G6 79
Pouso Redondo, Braz. D14 80
Poŭthĭsăt, Camb. H7 40
Považská Bystrica, Slvk. F18 10
Povenec, Russia J24 6
Póvoa de Varzim, Port. D3 16
Povorino, Russia G6 26
Povungnituk, P.Q., Can. D17 96
Povungnituk, Rivière de, stm., P.Q., Can. D18 96
Powassan, On., Can. D16 110
Poway, Ca., U.S. L8 124
Powder, stm., Or., U.S. F8 122
Powder, stm., U.S. B5 98
Powderly, Ky., U.S. E9 114
Powderly, Tx., U.S. F11 116
Powell, Wy., U.S. F17 122
Powell, stm., U.S. C3 112
Powell, Lake, res., U.S. G6 120
Powell, Mount, mtn., Co., U.S. E10 120
Powellhurst, Or., U.S. E3 122
Powell Lake, l., B.C., Can. G10 102
Powell River, B.C., Can. H10 102
Powellton, W.V., U.S. I5 108
Powers, Mi., U.S. E8 110
Powers, Or., U.S. H1 122
Powers Lake, N.D., U.S. C5 118
Powhatan, La., U.S. K3 114
Powhatan, Va., U.S. B9 112
Powhatan Point, Oh., U.S. H6 108
Powys, co., Wales, U.K. I10 8
Poxoréo, Braz. C1 79
Poyang Hu, l., China F5 34
Poyen, Ar., U.S. H4 114
Poygan, Lake, l., Wi., U.S. F7 110
Poynette, Wi., U.S. G6 110
Požarevac, Yugo. E5 20
Poza Rica, Mex. G11 90
Poznań, Pol. C16 10
Pozo Almonte, Chile I7 82
Pozoblanco, Spain G7 16
Pozo Colorado, Para. B9 80
Pozo del Molle, Arg. G7 80
Pozo del Tigre, Arg. C8 80
Pozo Hondo, Arg. D6 80
Pozo Negro, Spain o27 17b
Pozuelo de Alarcón, Spain E8 16
Pozuelos, Ven. B10 84
Pozuelos, Laguna, l., Arg. B6 80
Pozuzo, Peru D4 82
Pozuzo, stm., Peru C4 82
Pozzallo, Italy M9 18
Pozzuoli, Italy I9 18
Prachin Buri, Thai. G6 40
Prachuap Khiri Khan, Thai. I5 40
Pradera, Col. F4 84
Prades, Fr. J9 14
Prado, Braz. D9 79
Prados, Braz. F6 79
Prague see Praha, Czech Rep. E14 10
Prague, Ne., U.S. J11 118
Prague, Ok., U.S. D10 116
Praha (Prague), Czech Rep. E14 10
Prahova, co., Rom. D10 20
Praia, C.V. m17 64a
Praia Grande, Braz. E14 80
Prainha Nova, Braz. B11 82
Prairie, stm., Mn., U.S. C2 110
Prairie, stm., Wi., U.S. E6 110
Prairie City, Ia., U.S. I2 110
Prairie City, Il., U.S. J5 110
Prairie City, Or., U.S. F7 122
Prairie du Chien, Wi., U.S. G4 110
Prairie du Sac, Wi., U.S. G6 110
Prairie Grove, Ar., U.S. G2 114
Prairie River, Sk., Can. F11 104
Prairies, Lake of the, res., Can. G13 104
Prairie View, Tx., U.S. I11 116
Prairie Village, Ks., U.S. M13 118
Prampram, Ghana I10 64
Pran Buri, Thai. H5 40
Praslin, Lac, l., P.Q., Can. B4 106
Praslin Island, i., Sey. B11 58
Prata, Braz. E4 79
Prata, Rio da, stm., Braz. D5 79
Prata, Rio da, stm., Braz. E4 79
Pratāpgarh, India H6 44
Pratápolis, Braz. F5 79
Pratas Island see Tungsha Tao, i., Tai. G10 30
Pratinha, Braz. E5 79
Prato, Italy F6 18
Pratt, Ks., U.S. N9 118
Prattsburg, N.Y., U.S. E9 108
Prattville, Al., U.S. J10 114
Pratudão, stm., Braz. B6 79
Pravdinsk, Russia G4 22
Pravdinsk, Russia E26 22
Pravdinskij, Russia E20 22
Praya, Indon. G6 38
Pr'aža, Russia K23 6
Prečistoje, Russia F15 22
Prečistoje, Russia C23 22
Preda, Switz. E12 13
Predazzo, Italy C6 18
Predeal, Rom. D9 20
Predeşti, Rom. E7 20
Predlitz [-Turrach], Aus. H13 10
Preeceville, Sk., Can. G12 104
Pré-en-Pail, Fr. D6 14
Preetz, Ger. A10 10
Pregarten, Aus. G14 10
Pregol'a, stm., Russia G4 22
Pregonero, Ven. C7 84
Preila, Lith. F4 22
Preiļi, Lat. E9 22
Prelate, Sk., Can. H5 104
Premnitz, Ger. C12 10
Premont, Tx., U.S. L8 116
Prentice, Wi., U.S. E5 110
Prentiss, Ms., U.S. K7 114
Prenzlau, Ger. B13 10
Preparis Island, i., Myan. G2 40
Preparis North Channel, strt., Myan. G3 40
Preparis South Channel, strt., Myan. G3 40
Přerov, Czech Rep. F17 10
Prescott, Ar., U.S. I3 114
Prescott, Az., U.S. J4 120
Prescott, On., Can. C11 108
Prescott, Wi., U.S. F3 110
Prescott Island, i., N.T., Can. B13 96
Preševo, Yugo. G5 20
Presho, S.D., U.S. H7 118
Presidencia de la Plaza, Arg. D9 80
Presidencia Roca, Arg. D9 80
Presidencia Roque Sáenz Peña, Arg. D8 80
Presidente Epitácio, Braz. F2 79
Presidente Getúlio, Braz. D14 80
Presidente Hayes, dept., Para. C9 80
Presidente Olegário, Braz. E5 79
Presidente Prudente, Braz. G3 79
Presidente Venceslau, Braz. F3 79
Presidio, Tx., U.S. J2 116
Presidio, stm., Mex. F7 90
Prešov, Slvk. F21 10
Prespa, Lake, l., Eur. I5 20
Presque Isle, pen., Pa., U.S. E6 108
Preston, Eng., U.K. H11 8
Preston, Ga., U.S. G2 112
Preston, Ia., U.S. H5 110
Preston, Id., U.S. H14 122
Preston, Ks., U.S. N9 118
Preston, Mn., U.S. G3 110
Prestonsburg, Ky., U.S. B4 112
Prestville, Ab., Can. B16 102
Prestwick, Scot., U.K. F9 8
Preto, stm., Braz. B4 79
Preto, stm., Braz. D5 79
Preto, stm., Braz. E3 79
Preto, stm., Braz. F4 79
Preto, stm., Braz. C10 82
Preto, stm., Braz. H10 84
Preto do Igapó-açu, stm., Braz. J12 84
Pretoria, S. Afr. E9 66
Pretty Prairie, Ks., U.S. N9 118
Préveza, Grc. K4 20
Prey Vêng, Camb. I8 40
Pribilof Islands, is., Ak., U.S. H9 100
Priboj, Yugo. F3 20
Příbram, Czech Rep. F14 10
Price, Tx., U.S. J2 114
Price, Ut., U.S. E6 120
Price, stm., Ut., U.S. E6 120
Price Island, i., B.C., Can. E6 102
Prichard, Al., U.S. L8 114
Priddy, Tx., U.S. H8 116
Priego de Córdoba, Spain H7 16
Priekule, Lat. E4 22
Priekule, Lith. F4 22
Prienai, Lith. G6 22
Prieska, S. Afr. G6 66
Priest, stm., Id., U.S. B9 122
Priest Lake, l., Id., U.S. B9 122
Priestley, Mount, mtn., B.C., Can. B6 102
Priest River, Id., U.S. B9 122
Prievidza, Slvk. G18 10
Prijedor, Bos. E11 18
Prijutovo, Russia G8 26
Prikaspijskaja nizmennost', pl. H7 26
Prilep, Mac. H5 20
Priluki, Ukr. G4 26
Primeiro de Maio, Braz. G3 79
Primera, Tx., U.S. M9 116
Primero, stm., Arg. F7 80
Primghar, Ia., U.S. H12 118
Primorje [Warnicken], Russia G3 22
Primorsk, Russia G3 22
Primorsk, Russia A11 22
Primrose Lake, l., Can. D5 104
Prince Albert, S. Afr. I6 66
Prince Albert, Sk., Can. E9 104
Prince Albert Mountains, mts., Ant. C8 73
Prince Albert National Park, Sk., Can. D8 104
Prince Albert Sound, strt., N.T., Can. B9 96
Prince Charles Island, i., N.T., Can. C17 96
Prince Charles Mountains, mts., Ant. C5 73
Prince Edward Island, prov., Can. G20 96
Prince Edward Island National Park, P.E., Can. F10 106
Prince Edward Islands, is., S. Afr. M7 126
Prince Frederick, Md., U.S. I10 108
Prince George, B.C., Can. D12 102
Prince George, Va., U.S. B9 112
Prince Leopold Island, i., N.T., Can. B15 96
Prince of Wales, Cape, c., Ak., U.S. D10 100
Prince of Wales Island, i., Ak., U.S. I28 100
Prince of Wales Island, i., Austl. B8 68
Prince of Wales Island, i., N.T., Can. B13 96
Prince of Wales Strait, strt., N.T., Can. B9 96
Prince Olav Coast, Ant. B4 73
Prince Patrick Island, i., N.T., Can. B8 86
Prince Regent Inlet, b., N.T., Can. B14 96
Prince Rupert, B.C., Can. C4 102
Princess Anne, Md., U.S. I11 108
Princess Astrid Coast, Ant. C3 73
Princess Martha Coast, Ant. C2 73
Princess Ragnhild Coast, Ant. C3 73
Princess Royal Channel, strt., B.C., Can. D6 102
Princess Royal Island, i., B.C., Can. E6 102
Princes Town, Trin. I14 94
Princeton, B.C., Can. H14 102
Princeton, Ca., U.S. E3 124
Princeton, Il., U.S. I6 110
Princeton, In., U.S. D9 114
Princeton, Ky., U.S. E9 114
Princeton, Me., U.S. B19 108
Princeton, Mi., U.S. D8 110
Princeton, Mn., U.S. E2 110
Princeton, Mo., U.S. B3 114
Princeton, N.C., U.S. D8 112
Princeton, Nf., Can. D20 106
Princeton, N.J., U.S. G12 108
Princeton, Wi., U.S. G6 110
Princeton, W.V., U.S. B5 112
Princeville, Il., U.S. J6 110
Princeville, N.C., U.S. D9 112
Princeville, P.Q., Can. A15 108
Prince William Sound, strt., Ak., U.S. F21 100
Príncipe, i., S. Tom./P. A1 58
Principe Channel, strt., B.C., Can. D4 102
Príncipe da Beira, Braz. E9 82
Prineville, Or., U.S. F5 122
Prinzapolka, Nic. D11 92
Prinzapolka, stm., Nic. D11 92
Prior, Cabo, c., Spain B3 16
Prioz'orsk, Russia K22 6
Pripet Marshes see Polesje, reg., Eur. G3 26
Priština, Yugo. G5 20
Pritchett, Co., U.S. N5 118
Pritzwalk, Ger. B12 10
Privas, Fr. H11 14
Priverno, Italy H8 18
Privolžsk, Russia D24 22
Privolžskaja vozvyšennost', plat., Russia G7 26
Privolžskij, Russia G7 26
Prizren, Yugo. G4 20
Prizzi, Italy L8 18
Prnjavor, Bos. E12 18
Probolinggo, Indon. j16 39a
Probstzella, Ger. E11 10
Procter, B.C., Can. H18 102
Proctor, Mn., U.S. D3 110
Proctor, Vt., U.S. D13 108
Proddatūr, India E5 46
Progreso, Mex. G15 90
Progreso, Ur. H10 80
Project City, Ca., U.S. D3 124
Prokopjevsk, Russia G9 28
Prokuplje, Yugo. F5 20
Proletarij, Russia C14 22
Proletarskij, Russia F20 22
Prome (Pyè), Myan. E3 40
Promissão, Braz. F4 79
Promontogno, Switz. F12 13
Pronsk, Russia G22 22
Prophet, stm., B.C., Can. E8 96
Prophetstown, Il., U.S. I6 110
Propriá, Braz. F11 76
Propriano, Fr. m23 15a
Proserpine, Austl. C8 70
Prospect, Oh., U.S. G3 108
Prosser, Wa., U.S. D6 122
Prostějov, Czech Rep. F17 10
Proston, Austl. F9 70
Protection, Ks., U.S. N8 118
Protem, S. Afr. J5 66
Protville, Tun. M5 18
Provadija, Bul. F11 20
Provencal, La., U.S. K3 114
Provence, hist. reg., Fr. I13 14
Providence, Ky., U.S. E9 114
Providence, R.I., U.S. F15 108
Providence, Ut., U.S. C5 120
Providence, Cape, c., N.Z. F1 72
Providence Island, i., Sey. C10 58
Providencia, Isla de, i., Col. H4 94
Providenciales, i., T./C. Is. D8 94
Providenija, Russia E29 28
Provincetown, Ma., U.S. E16 108
Provins, Fr. D10 14
Provo, Ut., U.S. D5 120
Provo, stm., Ut., U.S. D5 120
Provost, Ab., Can. F4 104
Prudentópolis, Braz. C13 80
Prudhoe Bay, b., Ak., U.S. A20 100
Prudhoe Island, i., Austl. C8 70
Prudnik, Pol. E17 10
Prüm, Ger. E6 10
Pruszków, Pol. C20 10
Prut, stm., Eur. D12 20
Prutz, Aus. H10 10
Pružany, Bela. I7 22
Prydz Bay, b., Ant. B5 73
Pryor, Ok., U.S. C11 116
Prypjac', stm., Eur. G3 26
Przasnysz, Pol. B20 10
Przedbórz, Pol. D19 10
Przemyśl, Pol. F22 10
Przeworsk, Pol. E22 10
Pskov, Russia D11 22
Pskovskoje ozero, l., Eur. C11 22
Pszczyna, Pol. F18 10
Ptarmigan, Cape, c., N.T., Can. B9 96
Ptolemaís, Grc. I5 20
Ptuj, Slvn. C10 18
Puán, Arg. I7 80
Puan, S. Kor. H14 32
Pubnico, N.S., Can. I8 106
Pucallpa, Peru C4 82
Pucara, Bol. H9 82
Pucarani, Bol. G7 82
Puccha, stm., Peru C3 82
Pučež, Russia E26 22
Pucheng, China H7 34
Pucheta, Arg. E10 80
Puck, Pol. A18 10
Pudding, stm., Or., U.S. E3 122
Pudops Dam, Nf., Can. D17 106
Pudož, Russia E5 26
Puduari, stm., Braz. I12 84
Puduhe, China B7 40
Pudukkottai, India G5 46
Puebla, state, Mex. H10 90
Puebla [de Zaragoza], Mex. H10 90
Pueblo, Co., U.S. F12 120
Pueblo Libertador, Arg. F9 80
Pueblo Nuevo, Col. C5 84
Pueblo Nuevo, Nic. D8 92
Pueblo Nuevo, Ven. B8 84
Pueblo Nuevo Tiquisate, Guat. C3 92
Pueblo of Acoma, N.M., U.S. I9 120
Puebloviejo, Ec. H3 84
Pueblo Viejo, Laguna, b., Mex. F11 90
Pueblo Yaqui, Mex. D4 90
Puelches, Arg. J6 80
Puente Alto, Chile G3 80
Puente Genil, Spain H7 16
Puerco, stm., U.S. I7 120
Puerco, Rio, stm., N.M., U.S. J10 120
Puerto Acosta, Bol. F7 82
Puerto Adela, Para. C11 80
Puerto Aisén, Chile F2 78
Puerto Alegre, Bol. E11 82
Puerto Ángel, Mex. J11 90
Puerto Arista, Mex. J13 90
Puerto Armuelles, Pan. C1 84
Puerto Asís, Col. G4 84
Puerto Ayacucho, Ven. E9 84
Puerto Bahía Negra, Para. I12 82
Puerto Baquerizo Moreno, Ec. j14 84a
Puerto Barrios, Guat. B6 92
Puerto Bermejo, Arg. D9 80
Puerto Bermúdez, Peru D4 82
Puerto Berrío, Col. D5 84
Puerto Bolívar, Ec. I3 84
Puerto Boyacá, Col. E5 84
Puerto Busch, Bol. I13 82
Puerto Cabello, Ven. B8 84
Puerto Cabezas, Nic. C11 92
Puerto Carreño, Col. D9 84
Puerto Casado, Para. B10 80
Puerto Castilla, Hond. A8 92
Puerto Chicama, Peru B2 82
Puerto Colombia, Col. B5 84
Puerto Cortés, Hond. B7 92
Puerto Cumarebo, Ven. B8 84
Puerto de Eten, Peru B2 82
Puerto de la Cruz, Spain o24 17b
Puerto Delicia, Arg. D11 80
Puerto de Lomas, Peru F4 82
Puerto Delón, Hond. C9 92
Puerto del Rosario, Spain o27 17b
Puerto El Triunfo, El Sal. D6 92
Puerto Escondido, Mex. J11 90
Puerto Esperanza, Arg. D11 80
Puerto Fonciere, Para. B10 80
Puerto Francisco de Orellana, Ec. H4 84
Puerto Guaraní, Para. I13 82
Puerto Heath, Bol. E7 82
Puerto Iguazú, Arg. C11 80
Puerto Inírida, Col. F9 84
Puerto Jiménez, C.R. I11 92
Puerto Juárez, Mex. G16 90
Puerto la Cruz, Ven. B10 84
Puerto Leda, Para. I12 82
Puerto Leguízamo, Col. H5 84
Puerto Lempira, Hond. B11 92
Puerto Libertad, Arg. C11 80
Puerto Libertad, Mex. C3 90
Puerto Limón, Col. F6 84
Puerto Limón, C.R. G11 92
Puertollano, Spain G7 16
Puerto López, Col. E6 84
Puerto Madero, Mex. C2 92
Puerto Maldonado, Peru E7 82
Puerto Manatí, Cuba D6 94
Puerto Mihanovich, Para. I13 82
Puerto Montt, Chile E2 78
Puerto Morazán, Nic. E7 92
Puerto Morelos, Mex. G16 90
Puerto Nariño, Col. E9 84
Puerto Natales, Chile G2 78
Puerto Padre, Cuba D6 94
Puerto Páez, Ven. D9 84
Puerto Peñasco, Mex. B3 90
Puerto Pilón, Pan. H15 92
Puerto Pinasco, Para. B10 80
Puerto Piray, Arg. D11 80
Puerto Píritu, Ven. B10 84
Puerto Plata, Dom. Rep. E9 94
Puerto Portillo, Peru C5 82
Puerto Princesa, Phil. D6 38
Puerto Real, Spain I5 16
Puerto Rico, Arg. D11 80
Puerto Rico, Bol. D8 82
Puerto Rico, Col. G5 84
Puerto Rico, dep., N.A. E11 94
Puerto Rico Trench G13 86
Puerto Rondón, Col. D7 84
Puerto Saavedra, Chile J2 80
Puerto Salgar, Col. E5 84
Puerto Sandino, Nic. E8 92
Puerto San José, Guat. D4 92
Puerto San Julián, Arg. F3 78
Puerto Santa Cruz, Arg. G3 78
Puerto Sastre, Para. B10 80
Puerto Siles, Bol. E9 82
Puerto Suarez, Bol. H13 82
Puerto Supe, Peru D3 82
Puerto Tejada, Col. F4 84
Puerto Tolosa, Col. H5 84
Puerto Umbría, Col. G4 84
Puerto Vallarta, Mex. G7 90
Puerto Varas, Chile E2 78
Puerto Victoria, Arg. D11 80
Puerto Victoria, Peru C4 82
Puerto Viejo, C.R. G11 92
Puerto Viejo, C.R. H12 92
Puerto Villamil, Ec. j13 84a
Puerto Villamizar, Col. C6 84
Puerto Villarroel, Bol. G9 82
Puerto Wilches, Col. D6 84
Puerto Ybapobó, Para. B10 80
Pueyrredón, Lago (Lago Cochrane), l., S.A. F2 78
Pugačov, Russia G7 26
Puget Sound, strt., Wa., U.S. C3 122
Puget-Théniers, Fr. I13 14
Puglia, prov., Italy I11 18
Pugwash, N.S., Can. G10 106
Puhavičy, Bela. H11 22
Puica, Peru F5 82
Puigcerdá, Spain C13 16
Puigmal, mtn., Eur. C14 16
Puinahua, Canal de, mth., Peru A4 82
Pujehun, S.L. H4 64
Pujiang, China F8 34
Pujilí, Ec. H3 84
Pukch'ang, N. Kor. D14 32
Pukch'ŏng, N. Kor. C16 32
Pukeashun Mountain, mtn., B.C., Can. F15 102
Pukekohe, N.Z. B5 72
Pukhan-gang, stm., Asia F15 32
Pukou, China C7 34
Puksoozero, Russia J27 6
Pula, Cro. E8 18
Pulacayo, Bol. I8 82
Púlar, Cerro, mtn., Chile C4 80
Pulaski, N.Y., U.S. D10 108
Pulaski, Tn., U.S. G9 114
Pulaski, Va., U.S. B6 112
Pulaski, Wi., U.S. F7 110
Puławy, Pol. D21 10
Pulgaon, India B5 46
Puli, Tai. L9 34
Puliyangudi, India H4 46
Pullman, Wa., U.S. D8 122
Púllo, Peru F5 82
Pully, Switz. E6 13
Pulog, Mount, mtn., Phil. m19 39b
Pulsano, Italy I12 18
Pułtusk, Pol. C21 10
Puná, Isla, i., Ec. I2 84
Punakha, Bhu. G13 44
Punata, Bol. G9 82
Pūnch, India D6 44
Punchaw, B.C., Can. D11 102
Punduga, Russia A23 22
Pune (Poona), India C2 46
Púngoè, stm., Afr. B11 66
P'ungsan, N. Kor. C16 32
Punia, Zaire B5 58
Punilla, Sierra de la, mts., Arg. E4 80
Puning, China L5 34
Punitaqui, Chile F3 80
Punjab, state, India E6 44
Punnichy, Sk., Can. G10 104
Puno, Peru F6 82
Puno, dept., Peru F6 82
Punta, Cerro de, mtn., P.R. E11 94
Punta Alta, Arg. J7 80
Punta Arenas, Chile G2 78
Punta Banda, Cabo, c., Mex. B1 90
Punta Cardón, Ven. B7 84
Punta Colnett, Mex. B1 90
Punta de Bombón, Peru G6 82
Punta de Díaz, Chile E3 80
Punta del Cobre, Chile D3 80
Punta del Este, Ur. H11 80
Punta de los Llanos, Arg. F5 80
Punta de Mata, Ven. C11 84
Punta de Piedras, Ven. B10 84
Punta Gorda, Belize I15 90
Punta Gorda, Fl., U.S. M4 112
Punta Gorda, Nic. F11 92
Punta Gorda, stm., Nic. F11 92
Punta Gorda, Bahía de, b., Nic. F11 92
Punta Negra, Salar de, pl., Chile C4 80
Punta Prieta, Mex. C2 90
Puntarenas, C.R. H10 92
Puntarenas, prov., C.R. I11 92
Puntas del Sauce, Ur. G10 80
Punto Fijo, Ven. B7 84
Puntzi Lake, l., B.C., Can. E10 102
Punxsutawney, Pa., U.S. G8 108
Puolanka, Fin. I20 6
Puqi, China F9 30
Puquio, Peru F4 82
Pur, stm., Russia D7 28
Puracé, Volcán, vol., Col. F4 84
Purcell, Ok., U.S. D9 116
Purcell Mountains, mts., N.A. G18 102
Purcellville, Va., U.S. H9 108
Purdy, Mo., U.S. F3 114
Purgatoire, stm., Co., U.S. N4 118
Puri, India K11 44
Purificación, Col. F5 84
Purificación, Mex. H7 90
Purificación, stm., Mex. E10 90
Purikari neem, c., Est. B8 22
Purmerend, Neth. C6 12
Pūrnia, India H12 44
Purros, Nmb. B1 66
Puruí, stm., Braz. H8 84
Puruliya, India I12 44
Puruni, stm., Guy. D13 84
Purus (Purús), stm., S.A. D6 76
Purvis, Ms., U.S. K7 114
Purwakarta, Indon. j13 39a
Purwokerto, Indon. j14 39a
Pusan, S. Kor. H17 32
Pushkar, India G6 44
Pushthrough, Nf., Can. E17 106
Puskiakiwenin Indian Reserve, Ab., Can. E4 104
Puškin, Russia B13 22
Puškino, Russia E20 22
Puškinskije Gory, Russia D11 22

Name	Map Ref.	Page
Puskwaskau, stm., Ab., Can.	B17	102
Püspökladány, Hung.	H21	10
Püssi, Est.	B10	22
Pustoška, Russia	E12	22
Putaendo, Chile	G3	80
Putao, Myan.	G17	44
Put'atino, Russia	G24	22
Putian, China	J8	34
Putina, Peru	F7	82
Puting, Tanjung, c., Indon.	F5	38
Putnam, Ct., U.S.	F15	108
Putnam, Tx., U.S.	G7	116
Putney, Ga., U.S.	H2	112
Putney, Vt., U.S.	E14	108
Putorana, plato, plat., Russia	D17	26
Putre, Chile	H7	82
Puttalam, Sri L.	H5	46
Puttgarden, Ger.	A11	10
Putú, Chile	H2	80
Putumayo, ter., Col.	G4	84
Putumayo (Içá), stm., S.A.	I7	84
Putuo, China	F11	34
Putyla, Ukr.	A9	20
Pu'uhonua o Honaunau National Historical Park, Hi., U.S.	r18	125a
Puukohola National Historic Site, hist., Hi., U.S.	q18	125a
Puula, l., Fin.	K20	6
Puumala, Fin.	K21	6
Puurmani, Est.	C9	22
Puxi, China	J8	34
Puxico, Mo., U.S.	F6	114
Puyallup, Wa., U.S.	C3	122
Puyallup, stm., Wa., U.S.	D3	122
Puyang, China	H2	32
Puyango (Tumbes), stm., S.A.	I3	84
Puy-de-Dôme, dept., Fr.	G10	14
Puylaurens, Fr.	I9	14
Puyo, Ec.	H4	84
Puyŏ, S. Kor.	G14	32
Pweto, Zaire	C5	58
Pyapon, Myan.	F3	40
Pyaye, Myan.	E3	40
Pye Islands, is., Ak., U.S.	G19	100
Pyhäjoki, Fin.	I19	6
Pyhäselkä, l., Fin.	J21	6
Pyinmana, Myan.	E4	40
Pymatuning Reservoir, res., U.S.	F6	108
Pyŏktong, N. Kor.	C13	32
Pyŏlch'ang-ni, N. Kor.	D14	32
P'yŏngch'ang, S. Kor.	F16	32
P'yŏngsan, N. Kor.	E14	32
P'yŏngt'aek, S. Kor.	F15	32
P'yŏngyang, N. Kor.	D13	32
Pyote, Tx., U.S.	H3	116
Pyramid Lake, l., Nv., U.S.	D6	124
Pyrenees, mts., Eur.	C13	16
Pyrénées-Atlantiques, dept., Fr.	I6	14
Pyrénées-Orientales, dept., Fr.	J9	14
Pyrzyce, Pol.	B14	10
Pytalovo, Russia	D10	22
Pyu, Myan.	E4	40
Pyuntaza, Myan.	F4	40

Q

Name	Map Ref.	Page
Qacentina (Constantine), Alg.	B14	62
Qā'emshahr, Iran	C12	48
Qā'en, Iran	E15	48
Qaidam Pendi, China	B16	44
Qalāt, Afg.	D2	44
Qal'at ash-Shaqīf (Beaufort Castle), hist., Leb.	B5	50
Qal'at Bīshah, Sau. Ar.	D3	47
Qal'at Şāliḩ, Iraq	F9	48
Qal'at Sukkar, Iraq	F9	48
Qal'eh-ye Now, Afg.	C2	44
Qallābāt, Sudan	K9	60
Qalqīlya, W.B.	D3	50
Qamar, Ghubbat al-, b., Yemen	F8	47
Qamdo, China	E6	30
Qānā, Leb.	B4	50
Qanā, Sau. Ar.	H6	48
Qandahār, Afg.	E1	44
Qandala, Som.	F10	56
Qantur, Sudan	M3	60
Qārah, Sau. Ar.	G6	48
Qardho, Som.	G10	56
Qarqan, stm., China	D4	30
Qārūn, Birkat, l., Egypt	C6	60
Qāsh, Nahr al- (Gash), stm., Afr.	E8	56
Qaşr al-Farāfirah, Egypt	D4	60
Qasr el-Boukhari, Alg.	C12	62
Qaşr-e Shīrīn, Iran	D8	48
Qa'ṭabah, Yemen	H4	47
Qaṭanā, Syria	B6	50
Qatar (Qaṭar), ctry., Asia	D5	42
Qattara Depression see Qaṭṭārah, Munkhafaḍ al-, depr., Egypt	B4	60
Qaṭṭārah, Munkhafaḍ al- (Qattara Depression), depr., Egypt	B4	60
Qazımämmäd, Azer.	I7	26
Qazvīn, Iran	C11	48
Qesari, Ḥorbat (Cæsarea), hist., Isr.	C3	50
Qeshm, Iran	H14	48
Qeshm, Jazīreh-ye, i., Iran	H13	48
Qetura, Isr.	I4	50
Qezel Owzan, stm., Iran	C10	48
Qianfang, China	G5	34
Qianqi, China	H9	34
Qianyang, China	F9	30
Qiaogou, China	C4	34
Qiddīsah Kātrīnā, Dayr al- (Monastery of Saint Catherine), Egypt	G3	48
Qidong, China	D10	34
Qidu, China	E6	34
Qiemo, China	A11	44
Qifṭ (Coptos), Egypt	D7	60
Qijiang, China	F8	30
Qijiawan, China	E3	34
Qila Lādgasht, Pak.	H17	48
Qilian Shan, mtn., China	D6	30
Qilian Shan, mts., China	D6	30
Qimen, China	J2	34
Qinā, Egypt	D7	60
Qinā, Wādī, val., Egypt	H2	48
Qingchengzi, China	C11	32
Qingdao (Tsingtao), China	G8	32
Qinghai (Tsinghai), prov., China	D6	30
Qinghai Hu, l., China	D7	30
Qinghezhen, China	F5	32
Qingjiang, China	G4	34
Qingjiang, China	B8	34
Qinglian, China	K1	34
Qinglong, China	B8	40
Qingpu, China	D10	34
Qingshan, China	E3	34
Qingshui, stm., China	D8	30
Qingshui, stm., China	F8	30
Qingtang, China	K2	34
Qingyang, China	D8	30
Qingyangzhen, China	D9	34
Qingyuan, China	G8	30
Qingyuan, China	L2	34
Qingzhou, China	L5	34
Qinhuangdao (Chinwangtao), China	D7	32
Qin Ling, mts., China	E8	30
Qinzhou, China	D10	40
Qionglai, China	E7	30
Qiongzhong, China	E10	40
Qiongzhou Haixia, strt., China	D11	40
Qipanshan, China	A5	32
Qiqian, China	A11	30
Qiqihar (Tsitsihar), China	B11	30
Qiryat Ata, Isr.	C4	50
Qiryat Bialik, Isr.	C4	50
Qiryat Gat, Isr.	E3	50
Qiryat Mal'akhi, Isr.	E3	50
Qiryat Motzkin, Isr.	C4	50
Qiryat Ono, Isr.	D3	50
Qiryat Shemona, Isr.	B5	50
Qiryat Yam, Isr.	C4	50
Qishn, Yemen	G7	47
Qishon, stm., Asia	C4	50
Qishuyan, China	D9	34
Qitai, China	C4	30
Qiyang, China	A11	40
Qnadsa, Alg.	E9	62
Qogir Feng (K2), mtn., Asia	C7	44
Qom, Iran	D11	48
Qomsheh, Iran	E11	48
Qondūz, Afg.	J11	26
Qondūz, stm., Afg.	B3	44
Qonggyai, China	F5	30
Qorveh, Iran	D9	48
Quabbin Reservoir, res., Ma., U.S.	E14	108
Quadra Island, i., B.C., Can.	G9	102
Quadros, Lagoa dos, b., Braz.	E13	80
Quakenbrück, Ger.	C7	10
Quakertown, Pa., U.S.	G11	108
Qualicum Beach, B.C., Can.	H10	102
Quanah, Tx., U.S.	E7	116
Quangang, China	G4	34
Quang Ngai, Viet.	G10	40
Quang Trach, Viet.	F9	40
Quantico, Va., U.S.	I9	108
Quanzhou (Chuanchou), China	K7	34
Qu'Appelle, Sk., Can.	H11	104
Qu'Appelle, stm., Can.	H13	104
Qu'Appelle Dam, Sk., Can.	G8	104
Quaraí, Braz.	F10	80
Quaraí, stm., S.A.	F10	80
Quarryville, Pa., U.S.	H10	108
Quartu Sant'Elena, Italy	J4	18
Quartz Hill, Ca., U.S.	J7	124
Quartz Lake, l., N.T., Can.	B16	96
Quartz Mountain, mtn., Or., U.S.	G3	122
Quartzsite, Az., U.S.	K2	120
Quatsino Sound, strt., B.C., Can.	G7	102
Quba, Azer.	I7	26
Qūchān, Iran	C15	48
Queanbeyan, Austl.	J8	70
Québec, P.Q., Can.	F2	106
Québec, prov., Can.	F18	96
Quebeck, Tn., U.S.	G11	114
Quebra-Anzol, stm., Braz.	E5	79
Quebracho, Ur.	F10	80
Quedas, Moz.	B11	66
Quedlinburg, Ger.	D11	10
Queen Alexandra Range, mts., Ant.	D8	73
Queen Bess, Mount, mtn., B.C., Can.	F10	102
Queen Charlotte, B.C., Can.	D2	102
Queen Charlotte Islands, is., B.C., Can.	D2	102
Queen Charlotte Mountains, mts., B.C., Can.	D2	102
Queen Charlotte Sound, strt., B.C., Can.	F5	102
Queen Charlotte Strait, strt., B.C., Can.	G7	102
Queen City, Mo., U.S.	B4	114
Queen City, Tx., U.S.	I2	114
Queen Elizabeth Islands, is., N.T., Can.	B9	86
Queen Mary Coast, Ant.	B6	73
Queen Maud Gulf, b., N.T., Can.	C12	96
Queen Maud Land, reg., Ant.	C3	73
Queen Maud Mountains, mts., Ant.	D9	73
Queens Channel, strt., N.T., Can.	A13	96
Queenscliff, Austl.	L6	70
Queensland, state, Austl.	D9	68
Queensport, N.S., Can.	G12	106
Queens Sound, strt., B.C., Can.	F6	102
Queenstown, Austl.	N6	70
Queenstown, Guy.	D13	84
Queenstown, N.Z.	F2	72
Queenstown, S. Afr.	H8	66
Queguay Grande, stm., Ur.	G10	80
Queimados, Braz.	G7	79
Quelimane, Moz.	A13	66
Quemado, N.M., U.S.	J8	120
Quemado, Tx., U.S.	K6	116
Quemado, Punta de, c., Cuba	D7	94
Quemado de Güines, Cuba	C4	94
Quemoy see Chinmen Tao, i., Tai.	K7	34
Quemú Quemú, Arg.	I7	80
Quepos, C.R.	H10	92
Quequén, Arg.	J9	80
Querary, stm., Col.	G7	84
Quercy, hist. reg., Fr.	H8	14
Querecotillo, Peru	A1	82
Querétaro, Mex.	G9	90
Querétaro, state, Mex.	G10	90
Querobabi, Mex.	B4	90
Quesada, C.R.	G10	92
Quesada, Spain	H8	16
Queshan, China	C3	34
Quesnel, B.C., Can.	E12	102
Quesnel, stm., B.C., Can.	E12	102
Quesnel Lake, l., B.C., Can.	E13	102
Questa, N.M., U.S.	H11	120
Quetta, Pak.	E2	44
Quettehou, Fr.	C5	14
Quetzaltenango, Guat.	C3	92
Quetzaltenango, dept., Guat.	C3	92
Quevedo, Ec.	H3	84
Quezaltepeque, El Sal.	D5	92
Quezaltepeque, Guat.	C5	92
Quezon City, Phil.	n19	39b
Qufu, China	H5	32
Quibdó, Col.	E4	84
Quiberon, Fr.	E3	14
Quíbor, Ven.	C8	84
Quiches, Peru	C3	82
Quiindy, Para.	C10	80
Quila, Mex.	E6	90
Quilalí, Nic.	D8	92
Quilcene, Wa., U.S.	C3	122
Quilimarí, Chile	G3	80
Quilino, Arg.	F6	80
Quillabamba, Peru	E5	82
Quillacollo, Bol.	G8	82
Quillagua, Chile	I7	82
Quillan, Fr.	J9	14
Quill Lake, Sk., Can.	F10	104
Quillota, Chile	G3	80
Quilon, India	H4	46
Quilpie, Austl.	F6	70
Quilpué, Chile	G3	80
Quimarí, Alto de, mtn., Col.	C4	84
Quimbaya, Col.	E5	84
Quimby, Ia., U.S.	I12	118
Quime, Bol.	G8	82
Quimilí, Arg.	D7	80
Quimper, Fr.	D2	14
Quimperlé, Fr.	E3	14
Quinault, stm., Wa., U.S.	C2	122
Quince Mil, Peru	E6	82
Quinches, Peru	E3	82
Quincy, Ca., U.S.	E5	124
Quincy, Fl., U.S.	I2	112
Quincy, Il., U.S.	C5	114
Quincy, Ma., U.S.	E15	108
Quincy, Mi., U.S.	I11	110
Quincy, Wa., U.S.	C6	122
Quindío, dept., Col.	E5	84
Quines, Arg.	G6	80
Quinga, Moz.	E8	58
Quinhagak, Ak., U.S.	G14	100
Qui Nhon, Viet.	H10	40
Quinlan, Tx., U.S.	G10	116
Quinn, stm., Nv., U.S.	C7	124
Quintanar de la Orden, Spain	F8	16
Quintana Roo, state, Mex.	H15	90
Quinte, Bay of, b., On., Can.	F18	110
Quinter, Ks., U.S.	L7	118
Quintero, Chile	G3	80
Quintette Mountain, mtn., B.C., Can.	C14	102
Quintin, Fr.	D4	14
Quinto, stm., Arg.	H6	80
Quinto de Noviembre, Presa, El Sal.	D6	92
Quinton, Ok., U.S.	D11	116
Quinton, Sk., Can.	G10	104
Quiriguá, hist., Guat.	B5	92
Quirihue, Chile	I2	80
Quirindi, Austl.	H9	70
Quirinópolis, Braz.	E3	79
Quiriquire, Ven.	C11	84
Quiroga, Mex.	H9	90
Quiroga, Spain	C4	16
Quirós, Arg.	E6	80
Quirpon Island, i., Nf., Can.	A18	106
Quissanga, Moz.	D8	58
Quitaque, Tx., U.S.	E5	116
Quitilipi, Arg.	D8	80
Quitman, Ga., U.S.	I3	112
Quitman, Ms., U.S.	J8	114
Quitman, Tx., U.S.	G11	116
Quito, Ec.	H3	84
Quivilla, Peru	C3	82
Quixadá, Braz.	D11	76
Quixito, stm., Braz.	J7	84
Qujiang, China	K2	34
Qujing, China	B7	40
Qulin, Mo., U.S.	F6	114
Qumar, stm., China	D5	30
Qumarlêb, China	E6	30
Quoich, stm., N.T., Can.	D14	96
Quorn, Austl.	I3	70
Qurayyāt, Oman	C11	47
Qurdūd, Sudan	L5	60
Qūş, Egypt	E7	60
Quthing, Leso.	H8	66
Quxi, China	L5	34
Quxian, China	G7	34
Quyon, P.Q., Can.	B10	108
Quyquyó, Para.	D10	80
Quzhou, China	G2	32

R

Name	Map Ref.	Page
Raab (Rába), stm., Eur.	H15	10
Raahe, Fin.	I19	6
Raalte, Neth.	D9	12
Ra'ananna, Isr.	D3	50
Raasiku, Est.	B8	22
Raba, Indon.	G6	38
Rába (Raab), stm., Eur.	H17	10
Rabak, Sudan	K7	60
Rabat (Victoria), Malta	M9	18
Rabat, Mor.	C7	62
Rabaul, Pap. N. Gui.	k17	68a
Rabbit Ears Pass, Co., U.S.	D10	120
Rābigh, Sau. Ar.	C1	47
Rabinal, Guat.	B4	92
Rabka, Pol.	F19	10
Rabkavi Banhatti, India	D3	46
Râbniţa (Rybnica), Mol.	B13	20
Raboćeostrovsk, Russia	I24	6
Rabyānah, Şaḩrā', des., Libya	D5	56
Raccoon, stm., Ia., U.S.	A3	114
Race, Cape, c., Nf., Can.	F20	106
Raceland, La., U.S.	M6	114
Race Point, c., Ma., U.S.	E16	108
Rach'a, Russia	A13	22
Rach Gia, Viet.	I8	40
Racibórz (Ratibor), Pol.	E18	10
Racine, Wi., U.S.	H8	110
Ráckeve, Hung.	H18	10
Radaškovičy, Bela.	G10	22
Rădăuţi, Rom.	B9	20
Radcliff, Ky., U.S.	E11	114
Radeberg, Ger.	D13	10
Radebeul, Ger.	D13	10
Rades, Tun.	B16	62
Radford, Va., U.S.	B6	112
Rādhanpur, India	I4	44
Radisson, Sk., Can.	F7	104
Radium Hot Springs, B.C., Can.	G18	102
Radofinnikovo, Russia	B13	22
Radolfzell, Ger.	H8	10
Radom, Pol.	D21	10
Radomsko, Pol.	D19	10
Radoviš, Mac.	H6	20
Radun', Bela.	G8	22
Radviliškis, Lith.	F6	22
Radville, Sk., Can.	I10	104
Raḍwā, Jabal, mtn., Sau. Ar.	E10	60
Radway, Ab., Can.	C22	102
Rae, N.T., Can.	D9	96
Rae, stm., N.T., Can.	C9	96
Rāe Bareli, India	G9	44
Raeford, N.C., U.S.	E7	112
Rae Isthmus, N.T., Can.	C15	96
Rae Strait, strt., N.T., Can.	C13	96
Raetihi, N.Z.	C5	72
Rafaela, Arg.	F8	80
Rafaḥ, Gaza	F2	50
Raffadali, Italy	L8	18
Rafḩā', Sau. Ar.	G7	48
Rafsanjān, Iran	F14	48
Raft, stm., U.S.	H12	122
Raft River Mountains, mts., Ut., U.S.	C3	120
Rafz, Switz.	C10	13
Raga, Sudan	M3	60
Ragged Island, i., Bah.	C7	94
Ragged Island Range, is., Bah.	C7	94
Ragland, Al., U.S.	I10	114
Ragusa, Italy	M9	18
Raguva, Lith.	F7	22
Rahačou, Bela.	H13	22
Rahad, Nahr ar-, stm., Afr.	F8	56
Rahad al-Bardī, Sudan	L2	60
Rahīmyār Khān, Pak.	F4	44
Rahway, N.J., U.S.	G12	108
Rāichūr, India	D4	46
Raiford, Fl., U.S.	I4	112
Raiganj, India	H13	44
Raigarh, India	J10	44
Railton, Austl.	M7	70
Rainbow Falls, wtfl, B.C., Can.	E15	102
Rainelle, W.V., U.S.	J6	108
Rainier, Mount, mtn., Wa., U.S.	D4	122
Rainy, stm., Mi., U.S.	E11	110
Rainy, stm., N.A.	J20	104
Rainy Lake, l., N.A.	B2	110
Rainy River, On., Can.	B1	110
Raipur, India	J9	44
Ra'īs, Sau. Ar.	C1	47
Raisin, stm., Mi., U.S.	I12	110
Raití, Nic.	C9	92
Rājahmundry, India	D6	46
Rajāj, Sudan	L3	60
Rajang, stm., Malay.	E5	38
Rājapālaiyam, India	H4	46
Rājasthān, state, India	G5	44
Rajčichinsk, Russia	H17	28
Rajka, Hung.	G17	10
Rājkot, India	I4	44
Rāj Nāndgaon, India	J9	44
Rājpipla, India	B2	46
Rājshāhi, Bngl.	H13	44
Rakamaz, Hung.	G21	10
Rakaposhi, mtn., Pak.	B6	44
Rakata, Pulau, i., Indon.	j12	39a
Rakhiv, Ukr.	A8	20
Rakops, Bots.	C7	66
Rakovník, Czech Rep.	E13	10
Rakvere, Est.	B9	22
Raleigh, Ms., U.S.	J7	114
Raleigh, N.C., U.S.	D8	112
Raleigh, Nf., Can.	A18	106
Ralls, Tx., U.S.	F5	116
Ralston, Ne., U.S.	J11	118
Ralston, Pa., U.S.	F10	108
Ram, stm., Ab., Can.	E19	102
Rama, Isr.	C4	50
Rama, Nic.	E10	92
Rama, stm., Nic.	F10	92
Ramacca, Italy	L9	18
Ramah, N.M., U.S.	I8	120
Rām Allāh, W.B.	E4	50
Rāmanāthapuram, India	H5	46
Ramasucha, Russia	I16	22
Ramat Gan, Isr.	D3	50
Ramat HaSharon, Isr.	D3	50
Ramathlabama, Bots.	E7	66
Rambervillers, Fr.	D13	14
Rambouillet, Fr.	D8	14
Ramea, Nf., Can.	E16	106
Ramea Islands, is., Nf., Can.	E16	106
Ramenskoje, Russia	F21	22
Ramer, Al., U.S.	J10	114
Rameški, Russia	D19	22
Rāmeswaram, India	H5	46
Rāmhormoz, Iran	F10	48
Ramingstein, Aus.	H13	10
Ramiriquí, Col.	E6	84
Ramla, Isr.	E3	50
Ramlu, mtn., Afr.	F9	56
Ramm, Jabal, mtn., Jord.	I4	50
Râmnicu Sărat, Rom.	D11	20
Râmnicu Vâlcea, Rom.	D8	20
Ramona, Ca., U.S.	K9	124
Ramona, Ok., U.S.	C11	116
Ramona, S.D., U.S.	G10	118
Ramos, Mex.	F9	90
Ramos, stm., Mex.	E7	90
Ramot, Golan	C5	50
Ramotswa, Bots.	E7	66
Rampart, Ak., U.S.	D19	100
Ramparts, stm., N.T., Can.	D29	100
Rāmpur, India	F8	44
Rāmpur Hāt, India	H12	44
Ramree Island, i., Myan.	E2	40
Ramseur, N.C., U.S.	D7	112
Ramsey, Il., U.S.	C7	114
Ramsey, I. of Man	G9	8
Rāmshīr, Iran	F10	48
Ramu, stm., Pap. N. Gui.	m16	68a
Ramygala, Lith.	F7	22
Rānāghāt, India	I13	44
Ranburne, Al., U.S.	I11	114
Rancagua, Chile	H3	80
Rance, stm., Fr.	D4	14
Rancevo, Russia	E17	22
Rancharia, Braz.	G3	79
Rancheria, Yk., Can.	F29	100
Ranchería, stm., Col.	B6	84
Ranches of Taos, N.M., U.S.	H11	120
Ranchester, Wy., U.S.	F18	122
Rānchi, India	I11	44
Ranchillos, Arg.	D6	80
Ranch Lake, l., Sk., Can.	F10	104
Rancho Cordova, Ca., U.S.	F4	124
Rancul, Arg.	H6	80
Randers, Den.	M12	6
Randleman, N.C., U.S.	D7	112
Randlett, Ok., U.S.	E8	116
Randolph, Az., U.S.	L5	120
Randolph, Me., U.S.	C17	108
Randolph, Ne., U.S.	I10	118
Randolph, N.Y., U.S.	E8	108
Randolph, Ut., U.S.	C5	120
Randolph, Vt., U.S.	D14	108
Randolph, Wi., U.S.	G6	110
Random Island, i., Nf., Can.	D20	106
Random Lake, Wi., U.S.	G8	110
Råneå, Swe.	I18	6
Rāngāmāti, Bngl.	I15	44
Range Indian Reserve, B.C., Can.	H15	102
Rangeley, Me., U.S.	C16	108
Rangely, Co., U.S.	D8	120
Ranger, Tx., U.S.	G8	116
Rangoon see Yangon, Myan.	B2	38
Rangpur, Bngl.	H13	44
Ranguana Cay, i., Belize	A6	92
Ranguana Entrance, strt., Belize	A6	92
Rānībennur, India	E3	46
Rānīganj, India	I12	44
Rānikhet, India	F8	44
Ranken, stm., Austl.	C2	70
Ranken Store, Austl.	B2	70
Rankin, Il., U.S.	B9	114
Rankin, Tx., U.S.	H5	116
Rankin Inlet, N.T., Can.	D14	96
Ranlo, N.C., U.S.	D5	112
Ranohira, Madag.	s21	67b
Ranomafana, Madag.	t22	67b
Ranong, Thai.	J5	40
Ranopiso, Madag.	t22	67b
Ranotsara Nord, Madag.	s22	67b
Ransom, Ks., U.S.	M8	118
Ranson, W.V., U.S.	H9	108
Rantauprapat, Indon.	M5	40
Rantekombola, Bulu, mtn., Indon.	F7	38
Rantoul, Il., U.S.	B8	114
Ranua, Fin.	I20	6
Ranwanalenaus, Bots.	B6	66
Raoping, China	L6	34
Raoul, Ga., U.S.	E3	112
Rapa, Ponta do, c., Braz.	D14	80
Rapallo, Italy	E4	18
Rapel, stm., Chile	G3	80
Rapelli, Arg.	D6	80
Rapid, stm., Mi., U.S.	D8	110
Rapid, stm., Mn., U.S.	B1	110
Rapidan, stm., Va., U.S.	I9	108
Rapid City, Mb., Can.	H14	104
Rapid City, Mi., U.S.	F10	110
Rapid City, S.D., U.S.	G4	118
Rapid River, Mi., U.S.	E9	110
Räpina, Est.	C10	22
Rapla, Est.	B7	22
Rappahannock, stm., Va., U.S.	B10	112
Rapperswil, Switz.	D10	13
Rāpti, stm., Asia	G10	44
Rapulo, stm., Bol.	F8	82
Raron, Switz.	F8	13
Rasa, Punta, c., Arg.	I10	80
Ra's al-'Ayn, Syria	C6	48
Ra's al-Khaymah, U.A.E.	B9	47
Ra's an-Naqb, Egypt	I3	50
Ra's an-Naqb, Jord.	H4	50
Râşcani, Mol.	B11	20
Raşcov, Mol.	B12	20
Ras Dashen Terara, mtn., Eth.	K10	60
Raseiniai, Lith.	F6	22
Râs el Aïoun, Alg.	N3	18
Ras el Ma, Alg.	C10	62
Rashād, Sudan	L6	60
Rashīd, Egypt	B6	60
Rasht, Iran	C10	48
Rāsipuram, India	G5	46
Raška, Yugo.	F4	20
Rasony, Bela.	F11	22
Rass Jebel, Tun.	L5	18
Rasskazovo, Russia	I24	22
Rassua, ostrov, i., Russia	H22	28
Ra's Tannūrah, Sau. Ar.	H11	48
Rastatt, Ger.	G8	10
Rastede, Ger.	B8	10
Rasūl, Pak.	D5	44
Rat, stm., Mb., Can.	I18	104
Rat, stm., Mb., Can.	B15	104
Ratamka, Bela.	H10	22
Ratangarh, India	F6	44
Rätansbyn, Swe.	J14	6
Rāth, India	H8	44
Rathbun Lake, res., Ia., U.S.	J2	110
Rathdrum, Id., U.S.	C9	122
Rathenow, Ger.	C12	10
Rathwell, Mb., Can.	I16	104
Rat Islands, is., Ak., U.S.	k4	101a
Rat Lake, l., Mb., Can.	B15	104
Ratlām, India	I6	44
Ratnāgiri, India	D2	46
Ratnapura, Sri L.	I6	46
Raton, N.M., U.S.	C2	116
Raton Pass, N.M., U.S.	O3	118
Rattlesnake, Mt., U.S.	D12	122
Rattling Brook, Nf., Can.	C17	106
Ratz, Mount, mtn., B.C., Can.	H28	100
Ratzeburg, Ger.	B10	10
Raub, Malay.	M6	40
Rauch, Arg.	I9	80
Raul Soares, Braz.	F7	79
Rauma, Fin.	K17	6
Raurkela, India	I11	44
Ravanusa, Italy	L8	18
Rāvar, Iran	F14	48
Ravelo, Bol.	H9	82
Raven, Va., U.S.	B5	112
Ravena, N.Y., U.S.	E13	108
Ravenna, Italy	E7	18
Ravenna, Ky., U.S.	B3	112
Ravenna, Mi., U.S.	G10	110
Ravenna, Ne., U.S.	J9	118
Ravenna, Oh., U.S.	F5	108
Ravensburg, Ger.	H9	10
Ravenscrag, Sk., Can.	I5	104
Ravenshoe, Austl.	A6	70
Ravensthorpe, Austl.	F4	68
Ravenswood, W.V., U.S.	I5	108
Rāvi, stm., Asia	E5	44
Ravnina, Turk.	C17	48
Rāwalpindi, Pak.	D5	44
Rawa Mazowiecka, Pol.	D20	10
Rāwāndūz, Iraq	C8	48
Rawdon, P.Q., Can.	A13	108
Rawicz, Pol.	D16	10
Rawlinna, Austl.	F5	68
Rawlins, Wy., U.S.	C9	120
Rawson, Arg.	E3	78
Rawson, Arg.	H8	80
Raxāul, India	G11	44
Ray, N.D., U.S.	C4	118
Ray, Cape, c., Nf., Can.	E14	106
Raya, Bukit, mtn., Indon.	F5	38
Rāyadurg, India	E4	46
Raymond, Ab., Can.	H22	102
Raymond, Il., U.S.	C7	114
Raymond, Mn., U.S.	F12	118
Raymond, Ms., U.S.	J6	114
Raymond, Wa., U.S.	D2	122
Raymond Terrace, Austl.	I9	70
Raymondville, Tx., U.S.	M9	116
Raymore, Sk., Can.	G10	104
Rayne, La., U.S.	L4	114
Rayón, Mex.	C4	90
Rayones, Mex.	E9	90
Rayong, Thai.	H6	40
Raytown, Mo., U.S.	C2	114
Rayville, La., U.S.	J5	114
Razan, Iran	D10	48
R'azan', Russia	G22	22
R'azancevo, Russia	E22	22
Ražanj, Yugo.	F5	20
Razdan, Arm.	A8	48
Razdil'na, Ukr.	C14	20
Răzeni, Mol.	C12	20
Razgrad, Bul.	F10	20
Razorback Mountain, mtn., B.C., Can.	F10	102
R'ažsk, Russia	H23	22
Ré, Île de, i., Fr.	F5	14
Reading, Eng., U.K.	J13	8
Reading, Ks., U.S.	M12	118
Reading, Mi., U.S.	I11	110
Reading, Oh., U.S.	H2	108
Reading, Pa., U.S.	G11	108
Readlyn, Ia., U.S.	H3	110
Readstown, Wi., U.S.	G5	110
Real, Cordillera, mts., S.A.	H9	82
Real, Estero, stm., Nic.	E7	92
Real del Padre, Arg.	H5	80
Realicó, Arg.	H6	80
Realitos, Tx., U.S.	L8	116
Reardan, Wa., U.S.	C8	122
Reata, Mex.	D9	90
Reay, Scot., U.K.	C10	8
Reboly, Russia	J22	6
Rebouças, Braz.	C13	80
Rebun-tō, i., Japan	b16	36a
Recalde, Arg.	I8	80
Recanati, Italy	F8	18
Rečane, Russia	E14	22
Recherche, Archipelago of the, is., Austl.	F4	68
Recife, Braz.	E12	76
Recinto, Chile	I3	80
Recklinghausen, Ger.	D7	10
Reconquista, Arg.	E9	80
Recreio, Braz.	F7	79
Recreo, Arg.	E6	80
Rector, Ar., U.S.	F6	114
Recuay, Peru	C3	82
Rèčyca, Bela.	I13	22
Red (Hong) (Yuan), stm., Asia	C8	40
Red, stm., Ky., U.S.	B3	112
Red, stm., N.A.	B7	98
Red, stm., N.M., U.S.	H11	120
Red, stm., U.S.	E8	98
Red, stm., Wi., U.S.	E7	110
Redange, Lux.	I8	12
Red Bank, N.J., U.S.	G12	108
Red Bank, Tn., U.S.	G11	114
Red Banks, Ms., U.S.	H7	114
Red Bay, Al., U.S.	H8	114
Redbay, Fl., U.S.	L11	114
Red Bay, Nf., Can.	A17	106
Redberry Lake, l., Sk., Can.	F7	104
Red Bluff, Ca., U.S.	D3	124
Red Bluff Reservoir, res., U.S.	B8	90
Red Boiling Springs, Tn., U.S.	F11	114
Red Bud, Il., U.S.	D7	114
Red Cedar, stm., Mi., U.S.	H11	110
Red Cedar, stm., Wi., U.S.	E4	110
Redcliff, Ab., Can.	H4	104
Red Cliff, Co., U.S.	E10	120
Redcliff, Zimb.	B9	66
Redcliffe, Austl.	F10	70
Red Cliffs, Austl.	J5	70
Red Cloud, Ne., U.S.	K9	118
Red Cross Lake, l., Mb., Can.	C22	104
Red Deer, Ab., Can.	E21	102
Red Deer, stm., Can.	F12	104
Red Deer Lake, l., Ab., Can.	E21	102
Red Deer Lake, l., Mb., Can.	F13	104
Red Devil, Ak., U.S.	F16	100
Redding, Ca., U.S.	D3	124
Redeye, stm., Mn., U.S.	E12	118
Redfield, Ia., U.S.	J13	118
Redfield, S.D., U.S.	G9	118
Redford, Tx., U.S.	J2	116
Red Hook, N.Y., U.S.	F13	108
Red Indian Lake, l., Nf., Can.	D17	106
Red Island, i., Nf., Can.	E19	106
Redkey, In., U.S.	B11	114
Redkino, Russia	E19	22
Redlake, Mn., U.S.	D12	118
Red Lake, On., Can.	G21	104
Red Lake, l., On., Can.	G20	104
Red Lake, stm., Mn., U.S.	D11	118
Red Lake Falls, Mn., U.S.	D11	118
Red Lake Road, On., Can.	I21	104
Redlands, Ca., U.S.	J8	124
Redlands, Co., U.S.	E8	120
Redlands, S. Afr.	G6	66
Red Level, Al., U.S.	K10	114
Red Lick, Ms., U.S.	K6	114
Red Lion, Pa., U.S.	H10	108
Red Lodge, Mt., U.S.	E16	122
Redmond, Or., U.S.	F4	122
Redmond, Ut., U.S.	E5	120
Redmond, Wa., U.S.	C3	122
Red Mountain, mtn., Ca., U.S.	C2	124
Red Mountain Pass, Co., U.S.	G9	120
Red Oak, Ia., U.S.	J12	118
Red Oak, Ok., U.S.	E11	116
Redon, Fr.	E4	14
Redonda, i., Antig.	F13	94
Redonda Islands, is., B.C., Can.	G10	102
Redondo, Port.	G4	16
Redondo Beach, Ca., U.S.	K7	124
Red Pass, B.C., Can.	E16	102
Red Pheasant Indian Reserve, Sk., Can.	F6	104
Red Rock, B.C., Can.	D12	102
Red Rock, On., Can.	B7	110
Red Rock, stm., Mt., U.S.	F13	122
Red Rock, Lake, res., Ia., U.S.	I2	110
Red Sea	D8	56
Red Springs, N.C., U.S.	E7	112
Redstone, B.C., Can.	E11	102
Redstone, stm., N.T., Can.	E32	100
Red Sucker, stm., Mb., Can.	C22	104
Red Sucker Lake, l., Mb., Can.	D21	104
Redvers, Sk., Can.	I13	104
Redwater, Ab., Can.	D21	102
Redwater, stm., Mt., U.S.	D2	118
Redwillow, stm., Can.	B15	102
Red Wing, Mn., U.S.	F3	110
Redwood, stm., Mn., U.S.	G12	118
Redwood City, Ca., U.S.	G3	124
Redwood Falls, Mn., U.S.	G12	118
Redwood National Park, Ca., U.S.	C1	124
Redwood Valley, Ca., U.S.	E2	124
Ree, Lough, l., Ire.	H5	8
Reed City, Mi., U.S.	G10	110
Reeder, N.D., U.S.	E5	118
Reed Lake, l., Mb., Can.	D14	104
Reed Lake, l., Sk., Can.	H7	104
Reedley, Ca., U.S.	H6	124
Reedsburg, Wi., U.S.	G5	110
Reeds Peak, mtn., N.M., U.S.	K9	120
Reedsport, Or., U.S.	G1	122
Reedsville, Wi., U.S.	F8	110
Reefton, N.Z.	E3	72
Reelfoot Lake, l., Tn., U.S.	F7	114
Reese, Mi., U.S.	G12	110
Reese, stm., Nv., U.S.	D8	124
Reeseville, Wi., U.S.	G7	110
Reform, Al., U.S.	I8	114
Refuge Cove, B.C., Can.	G10	102
Refugio, Tx., U.S.	K9	116
Regaïa, Mor.	J6	16
Regência, Braz.	E9	79
Regensburg, Ger.	F12	10
Regent, N.D., U.S.	E5	118
Reggâne, Alg.	G11	62
Reggello, Italy	F6	18
Reggio di Calabria, Italy	K10	18
Reggio nell'Emilia, Italy	E5	18

Name — Map Ref. — Page

Name | Map Ref. | Page

Sanjō, Japan J13 36
San Joaquín, Bol. E9 82
San Joaquín, Para. C10 80
San Joaquín, stm., Bol. E10 82
San Joaquin, stm., Ca., U.S. G4 124
San Joaquin Valley, val., Ca., U.S. H5 124
San Jon, N.M., U.S. D3 116
San Jorge, Arg. F8 80
San Jorge, El Sal. D6 92
San Jorge, Nic. F9 92
San Jorge, stm., Col. C5 84
San Jorge, Bahía, b., Mex. B3 90
San Jorge, Golfo, b., Arg. F3 78
San José, Arg. D11 80
San Jose, Ca., U.S. G4 124
San José, C.R. H10 92
San Jose, Il., U.S. B7 114
San Jose, N.M., U.S. I11 120
San José, Para. C10 80
San Jose, Phil. n19 39b
San José, prov., C.R. H11 92
San Jose, stm., B.C., Can. F13 102
San José, Isla, i., Mex. E4 90
San José, Isla, i., Pan. C3 84
San Jose, Rio, stm., N.M., U.S. J9 120
San José Batuc, Mex. C5 90
San José Buena Vista, Guat. D4 92
San José de Bácum, Mex. D4 90
San José de Chiquitos, Bol. G11 82
San José de Copán, Hond. C6 92
San José de Feliciano, Arg. F9 80
San José de Guanipa, Ven. C10 84
San José de Guaribe, Ven. C10 84
San José de Jáchal, Arg. F4 80
San José de la Esquina, Arg. G8 80
San José de las Lajas, Cuba C3 94
San José de las Raíces, Mex. E9 90
San José del Cabo, Mex. F5 90
San José del Guaviare, Col. F6 84
San José de los Molinos, Peru E4 82
San José de Mayo, Ur. H10 80
San José de Ocuné, Col. E7 84
San José de Sisa, Peru B3 82
San José de Tiznados, Ven. C9 84
San Jose Island, i., Tx., U.S. K10 116
San Juan, Arg. F4 80
San Juan, Guat. B6 92
San Juan, Peru F4 82
San Juan, P.R. E11 94
San Juan, prov., Arg. F4 80
San Juan, stm., Arg. G5 80
San Juan, stm., Col. E4 84
San Juan, stm., Mex. E10 90
San Juan, stm., N.A. G10 92
San Juan, stm., Peru E4 82
San Juan, stm., S.A. G3 84
San Juan, stm., U.S. G6 120
San Juan, stm., Ven. B11 84
San Juan, Pico, mtn., Cuba D4 94
San Juan Bautista, Ca., U.S. H4 124
San Juan Bautista, Para. D10 80
San Juan Cotzal, Guat. B3 92
San Juan de Abajo, Mex. G7 90
San Juan de Colón, Ven. C6 84
San Juan de Guadalupe, Mex. E8 90
San Juan de la Maguana, Dom. Rep. E9 94
San Juan del César, Col. B6 84
San Juan del Norte, Nic. G11 92
San Juan del Oro, stm., Bol. I9 82
San Juan de los Cayos, Ven. B8 84
San Juan de los Morros, Ven. C9 84
San Juan del Río, Mex. E7 90
San Juan del Río, Mex. G9 90
San Juan del Sur, Nic. F9 92
San Juan de Micay, stm., Col. F4 84
San Juan de Payara, Ven. D9 84
San Juan Evangelista, Mex. I12 90
San Juanico, Mex. D3 90
San Juanillo, C.R. G9 92
San Juan Islands, is., Wa., U.S. B3 122
San Juanito, Isla, i., Mex. G6 90
San Juan Mountains, mts., Co., U.S. G9 120
San Juan Nepomuceno, Col. C5 84
San Juan Nepomuceno, Para. D11 80
San Juan Sacatepéquez, Guat. C4 92
San Juan Teotihuacán, Mex. H10 90
San Justo, Arg. F8 80
Sankarani, stm., Afr. F5 64
Sankosh, stm., Asia G14 44
Sankt Aegyd am Neuwalde, Aus. H15 10
Sankt Anton [am Arlberg], Aus. H10 10
Sankt Gallen, Aus. H14 10
Sankt Gallen, Switz. D11 13
Sankt Gallen, state, Switz. D11 13
Sankt Gilgen, Aus. H13 10
Sankt Goar, Ger. E7 10
Sankt Goarshausen, Ger. E7 10
Sankt Ingbert, Ger. F7 10
Sankt Johann im Pongau, Aus. H13 10
Sankt Johann in Tirol, Aus. H12 10
Sankt Moritz, Switz. E12 13
Sankt Niklaus, Switz. F8 13
Sankt Paul [im Lavanttal], Aus. I14 10
Sankt-Peterburg (Saint Petersburg), Russia B13 22
Sankt Peter-Ording, Ger. A8 10
Sankt Pölten, Aus. G15 10
Sankt Valentin, Aus. G14 10
Sankt Veit an der Glan, Aus. I14 10
Sankt Vith (Saint-Vith), Bel. H9 12
Sankt Wendel, Ger. F7 10
San Lázaro, Para. B10 80
San Lázaro, Cabo, c., Mex. E3 90
San Leandro, Ca., U.S. G3 124
Sanlicheng, China D3 34
Şanlıurfa, Tur. C5 48
San Lope, Col. D7 84
San Lorenzo, Arg. E9 80
San Lorenzo, Arg. G8 80
San Lorenzo, Bol. I9 82
San Lorenzo, Ec. G3 84
San Lorenzo, Hond. D7 92
San Lorenzo, Mex. E8 90
San Lorenzo, Nic. E9 92
San Lorenzo, Ven. C7 84
San Lorenzo, stm., Mex. E6 90
San Lorenzo, Bahía de, b., Hond. D7 92
San Lorenzo, Cabo, c., Ec. H2 84
San Lorenzo, Isla, i., Mex. C3 90
San Lorenzo, Isla, i., Peru E3 82
San Lorenzo de El Escorial, Spain E7 16
Sanlúcar de Barrameda, Spain I5 16
Sanlúcar la Mayor, Spain H5 16
San Lucas, Bol. I9 82
San Lucas, Ec. I3 84
San Lucas, Mex. F5 90
San Lucas, Cabo, c., Mex. F5 90
San Luis, Arg. G5 80
San Luis, Az., U.S. L5 120
San Luis, Co., U.S. G11 120
San Luis, Cuba D7 94
San Luis, Guat. A5 92
San Luis, Ven. B8 84
San Luis, prov., Arg. H5 80
San Luis, Laguna, l., Bol. E9 82
San Luis, Sierra de, mts., Arg. G6 80
San Luis de la Paz, Mex. G9 90
San Luis del Cordero, Mex. E7 90
San Luis del Palmar, Arg. D9 80
San Luis Gonzaga, Mex. E4 90
San Luis Gonzaga, Bahía, b., Mex. C2 90
San Luis Jilotepeque, Guat. C5 92
San Luis Obispo, Ca., U.S. I5 124
San Luis Peak, mtn., Co., U.S. G10 120
San Luis Potosí, Mex. F9 90
San Luis Potosí, state, Mex. F9 90
San Luis Reservoir, res., Ca., U.S. G4 124
San Luis Río Colorado, Mex. A2 90
San Luis Valley, val., Co., U.S. G10 120
Sanluri, Italy J3 18
San Manuel, Arg. I9 80
San Manuel, Az., U.S. L6 120
San Marcial, stm., Mex. C4 90
San Marcos, Chile F3 80
San Marcos, Col. C5 84
San Marcos, C.R. H10 92
San Marcos, El Sal. D5 92
San Marcos, Guat. C3 92
San Marcos, Hond. C6 92
San Marcos, Hond. B6 92
San Marcos, Mex. I10 90
San Marcos, Tx., U.S. J9 116
San Marcos, dept., Guat. B3 92
San Marcos, stm., Tx., U.S. J9 116
San Marcos, Isla, i., Mex. D3 90
San Marcos de Colón, Hond. D8 92
San Marino, S. Mar. F7 18
San Marino, ctry., Eur. G10 4
San Martín, Arg. E6 80
San Martín, Arg. G4 80
San Martín, Col. F6 84
San Martín, dept., Peru B3 82
San Martín, stm., Bol. D8 82
San Martín, stm., Bol. E10 82
San Martín, Lago (Lago O'Higgins), l., S.A. F2 78
San Martín de los Andes, Arg. E2 78
San Martín Texmelucan, Mex. H10 90
San Mateo, Ca., U.S. G3 124
San Mateo, Fl., U.S. J5 112
San Mateo, N.M., U.S. I9 120
San Mateo, Ven. C10 84
San Mateo Ixtatán, Guat. B3 92
San Matías, Bol. G12 82
San Matías, Golfo, b., Arg. E4 78
Sanmenxia, China E9 30
San Miguel, Arg. E10 80
San Miguel, Bol. G11 82
San Miguel, Ca., U.S. I5 124
San Miguel, Ec. H3 84
San Miguel, El Sal. D6 92
San Miguel, Mex. C9 90
San Miguel, Pan. C3 84
San Miguel, Peru E5 82
San Miguel, Spain o24 17b
San Miguel, stm., Bol. F10 82
San Miguel, stm., Co., U.S. F8 120
San Miguel (Cuilco), stm., N.A. B2 92
San Miguel, stm., S.A. H11 82
San Miguel, Cerro, hill, Bol. H11 82
San Miguel, Golfo de, b., Pan. C3 84
San Miguel, Volcán de, vol., El Sal. D6 92
San Miguel de Allende, Mex. G9 90
San Miguel de Cruces, Mex. E7 90
San Miguel del Monte, Arg. H9 80
San Miguel de Pallaques, Peru B2 82
San Miguel de Salcedo, Ec. H3 84
San Miguel de Tucumán, Arg. D6 80
San Miguel el Alto, Mex. G8 90
San Miguelito, Nic. F10 92
San Miguel Ixtahuacán, Guat. B3 92
San Miniato, Italy F5 18
Sannār, Sudan K7 60
Sannicandro Garganico, Italy H10 18
San Nicolás, Hond. B6 92
San Nicolás, Peru F4 82
San Nicolás, Spain p25 17b
San Nicolás, stm., Mex. H7 90
San Nicolás de los Arroyos, Arg. G8 80
San Nicolás de los Garza, Mex. E9 90
San Nicolas Island, i., Ca., U.S. K6 124
Sânnicolau Mare, Rom. C4 20
Sannikova, proliv, strt., Russia C20 28
Sanniquellie, Lib. H5 64
Sano, Japan K14 36
Sañogasta, Arg. E5 80
Sanok, Pol. F22 10
San Onofre, Col. C5 84
San Pablo, Col. G4 84
San Pablo, Phil. n19 39b
San Pablo, stm., Bol. F10 82
San Pablo, stm., Pan. I13 92
San Pablo Bay, b., Ca., U.S. F3 124
San Pedro, Arg. G9 80
San Pedro, Arg. C6 80
San Pedro, Arg. D6 80
San Pedro, Chile A4 80
San Pedro, Chile G3 80
San Pédro, C. Iv. I6 64
San Pedro, Col. C5 84
San Pedro, C.R. H10 92
San Pedro, Para. C10 80
San Pedro, Tx., U.S. L9 116
San Pedro, Ven. C7 84
San Pedro, dept., Para. C10 80
San Pedro, stm., Mex. B5 90
San Pedro, stm., N.A. I14 90
San Pedro, stm., N.A. L6 120
San Pedro, Punta, c., Chile C3 80
San Pedro, Volcán, vol., Chile A4 80
San Pedro Ayampuc, Guat. C4 92
San Pedro Carchá, Guat. B4 92
San Pedro Channel, strt., Ca., U.S. K7 124
San Pedro de Atacama, Chile B4 80
San Pedro de Buena Vista, Bol. H9 82
San Pedro de Curahuara, Bol. G7 82
San Pedro de la Cueva, Mex. C5 90
San Pedro de las Colonias, Mex. E8 90
San Pedro del Gallo, Mex. E7 90
San Pedro de Lloc, Peru B2 82
San Pedro del Norte, Nic. D10 92
San Pedro del Paraná, Para. D10 80
San Pedro de Macorís, Dom. Rep. E10 94
San Pedro Peaks, mts., N.M., U.S. H10 120
San Pedro Pinula, Guat. C5 92
San Pedro Pochutla, Mex. J11 90
San Pedro Sacatepéquez, Guat. C3 92
San Pedro Sula, Hond. B6 92
San Pedro Tabasco, Mex. I14 90
San Pelayo, Col. C5 84
San Pitch, stm., Ut., U.S. E5 120
Sanpoil, stm., Wa., U.S. B7 122
San Quintín, Cabo, c., Mex. B1 90
San Rafael, Arg. H4 80
San Rafael, Ca., U.S. G3 124
San Rafael, Chile H3 80
San Rafael, Mex. E9 90
San Rafael, N.M., U.S. I9 120
San Rafael, Ven. B7 84
San Rafael, stm., Bol. H12 82
San Rafael, stm., Ut., U.S. F6 120
San Rafael del Norte, Nic. D8 92
San Rafael del Sur, Nic. F8 92
San Rafael Desert, des., Ut., U.S. F6 120
San Rafael Oriente, El Sal. D6 92
San Rafael Swell, plat., Ut., U.S. F6 120
San Rafael Tasajera, El Sal. D6 92
San Ramón, Arg. D6 80
San Ramón, Bol. E9 82
San Ramón, C.R. G10 92
San Ramón, Hond. C10 92
San Ramón, Peru D4 82
San Ramón, Ur. H11 80
San Ramón de la Nueva Orán, Arg. B6 80
Sanrao, China L5 34
San Remo, Italy F2 18
San Román, stm., Guat. A4 92
San Román, Cabo, c., Ven. A7 84
San Roque, Arg. E9 80
San Roque, Arg. F4 80
San Roque, Spain I6 16
San Roque, Punta, c., Mex. D2 90
San Saba, Tx., U.S. H8 116
San Saba, stm., Tx., U.S. I7 116
San Salvador, Arg. E10 80
San Salvador, Arg. F9 80
San Salvador, Arg. D10 80
San Salvador, El Sal. D5 92
San Salvador (Watling Island), i., Bah. B7 94
San Salvador, Volcán de, vol., El Sal. D5 92
San Salvador de Jujuy, Arg. C6 80
Sansanné-Mango, Togo F10 64
San Sebastián, El Sal. D6 92
San Sebastián, Guat. C3 92
San Sebastián, Hond. C6 92
San Sebastián de la Gomera, Spain o23 17b
San Sebastián de Yalí, Nic. D8 92
Sansepolcro, Italy F7 18
San Severo, Italy H10 18
Sanshui, China L1 34
San Simon, Az., U.S. L7 120
San Simon, stm., Az., U.S. L7 120
San Simón, stm., Bol. E10 82
Sanso, Mali F6 64
San Solano, Arg. F6 80
Sans-Souci, hist., Haiti E8 94
Santa, Peru C2 82
Santa, stm., Peru C2 82
Santa, Isla del, i., Peru C2 82
Santa Adélia, Braz. F4 79
Santa Albertina, Braz. F3 79
Santa Ana, Arg. D11 80
Santa Ana, Bol. E9 82
Santa Ana, Bol. H12 82
Santa Ana, Ca., U.S. K8 124
Santa Ana, Col. C5 84
Santa Ana, Ec. H2 84
Santa Ana, El Sal. D5 92
Santa Ana, Mex. E9 90
Santa Ana, Mex. B4 90
Santa Ana, Ven. C10 84
Santa Ana, Volcán de, vol., El Sal. D5 92
Santa Ana del Alto Beni, Bol. F8 82
Santa Anna, Tx., U.S. H7 116
Santa Barbara, Ca., U.S. J6 124
Santa Bárbara, Chile I2 80
Santa Barbara, Col. E5 84
Santa Bárbara, Hond. C6 92
Santa Bárbara, Mex. D7 90
Santa Bárbara, Ven. F9 84
Santa Bárbara, Ven. D7 84
Santa Bárbara, dept., Hond. B6 92
Santa Bárbara, stm., Bol. G11 82
Santa Barbara Channel, strt., Ca., U.S. J5 124
Santa Bárbara do Sul, Braz. E12 80
Santa Catalina, Arg. A5 80
Santa Catalina, Gulf of, b., Ca., U.S. L7 124
Santa Catalina, Isla, i., Mex. E4 90
Santa Catalina Island, i., Ca., U.S. K7 124
Santa Catalina o Calovébora, Pan. I13 92
Santa Catarina, Mex. E9 90
Santa Catarina, state, Braz. D13 80
Santa Catarina, Ilha de, i., Braz. D14 80
Santa Cecília, Braz. D13 80
Santa Clara, Ca., U.S. G4 124
Santa Clara, Col. I8 84
Santa Clara, Cuba C5 94
Santa Clara, Mex. C6 90
Santa Clara, Ut., U.S. G3 120
Santa Clara, stm., Ut., U.S. G3 120
Santa Clara de Olimar, Ur. G11 80
Santa Clotilde, Peru I6 84
Santa Coloma de Farners, Spain D14 16
Santa Comba Dão, Port. E3 16
Santa Cruz, Braz. E8 79
Santa Cruz, Ca., U.S. H3 124
Santa Cruz, Chile H3 80
Santa Cruz, C.R. G9 92
Santa Cruz, Peru B2 82
Santa Cruz, Phil. n19 39b
Santa Cruz, Phil. o20 39b
Santa Cruz, Port. m21 17a
Santa Cruz, Ven. C7 84
Santa Cruz, dept., Bol. G11 82
Santa Cruz, stm., Arg. G2 78
Santa Cruz, stm., N.A. L5 120
Santa Cruz, Isla, i., Ec. j13 84a
Santa Cruz, Sierra de, mts., Guat. B5 92
Santa Cruz Cabrália, Braz. D9 79
Santa Cruz de Goiás, Braz. D4 79
Santa Cruz de la Palma, Spain o23 17b
Santa Cruz de la Sierra, Bol. G10 82
Santa Cruz del Quiché, Guat. B3 92
Santa Cruz del Sur, Cuba D5 94
Santa Cruz de Tenerife, Spain o24 17b
Santa Cruz de Tenerife, prov., Spain o23 17b
Santa Cruz do Rio Pardo, Braz. G4 79
Santa Cruz do Sul, Braz. E12 80
Santa Cruz Island, i., Ca., U.S. J6 124
Santa Cruz Islands, is., Sol. Is. J20 126
Santa Elena, Arg. F9 80
Santa Elena, Ec. I2 84
Santa Elena, El Sal. D6 92
Santa Elena, Mex. D8 90
Santa Elena, stm., Bol. G8 82
Santa Elena, Bahía de, b., Ec. I2 84
Santa Elena, Cabo, c., C.R. G9 92
Santa Elena, Golfo de, b., C.R. G9 92
Santa Elena, Punta, c., Ec. I2 84
Santa Elena de Uairén, Ven. E12 84
Santa Eulalia, Guat. B3 92
Santa Eulària del Riu, Spain G13 16
Santa Fe, Arg. F8 80
Santa Fé, Braz. C3 79
Santa Fé, Braz. G3 79
Santa Fe, Hond. B8 92
Santa Fe, N.M., U.S. I11 120
Santa Fé, Pan. I13 92
Santa Fe, Spain H8 16
Santa Fe, prov., Arg. F8 80
Santa Fe, stm., N.M., U.S. I10 120
Santa Fe Baldy, mtn., N.M., U.S. I11 120
Santa Fe de Bogotá, Col. E5 84
Santa Fé do Sul, Braz. F3 79
Santa Filomena, Braz. E9 76
Santa Helena de Goiás, Braz. D3 79
Santai, China E8 30
Santa Inês, Braz. B9 79
Santa Inés, Bahía, b., Mex. D4 90
Santa Inés, Isla, i., Chile G2 78
Santa Isabel, Arg. I5 80
Santa Isabel, Arg. G8 80
Santa Isabel, Ec. I3 84
Santa Isabel, i., Sol. Is. I19 126
Santa Isabel, stm., Guat. B5 92
Santa Isabel de Sihuas, Peru G5 82
Santa Juliana, Braz. E5 79
Santa Lucía, Arg. E9 80
Santa Lucía, Arg. F4 80
Santa Lucía, Cuba D6 94
Santa Lucía, Ur. H10 80
Santa Lucía, Ven. C8 84
Santa Lucía Cotzumalguapa, Guat. C3 92
Santa Lucia Range, mts., Ca., U.S. H4 124
Santa Luzia, i., C.V. E2 54
Santa Magdalena, Arg. H7 80
Santa Margarita, Ca., U.S. I5 124
Santa Margarita, Isla, i., Mex. E4 90
Santa Margherita Ligure, Italy E4 18
Santa María, Arg. D5 80
Santa Maria, Braz. E12 80
Santa Maria, Ca., U.S. J5 124
Santa María, C.R. H11 92
Santa Maria, C.V. k17 64a
Santa María, Pan. I14 92
Santa Maria, Switz. F11 13
Santa Maria, Switz. E13 13
Santa Maria, stm., Braz. F11 80
Santa Maria, stm., Braz. A11 80
Santa María, stm., Mex. B6 90
Santa María, stm., Mex. G10 90
Santa María, stm., Pan. I14 92
Santa María, Bahía, b., Mex. E5 90
Santa María, Cabo, c., Ur. H11 80
Santa Maria, Cabo de, c., Ang. D2 58
Santa Maria, Cape, c., Bah. C7 94
Santa María, Isla, i., Chile I2 80
Santa María, Isla, i., Ec. j13 84a
Santa María, Laguna, l., Mex. B6 90
Santa María, Volcán, vol., Guat. C3 92
Santa Maria Asunción Tlaxiaco, Mex. I11 90
Santa Maria Capua Vetere, Italy H9 18
Santa María Colotepec, Mex. J11 90
Santa Maria da Vitória, Braz. B6 79
Santa María de Huazamota, Mex. F7 90
Santa María de Ipire, Ven. C10 84
Santa Maria de Itabira, Braz. E7 79
Santa María del Oro, Mex. E7 90
Santa María del Río, Mex. G9 90
Santa María de Mohovano, Mex. D8 90
Santa Maria di Leuca, Capo, c., Italy J13 18
Santa Maria do Suaçuí, Braz. E7 79
Santa María Madalena, Braz. F7 79
Santa-Maria-Siché, Fr. m23 15a
Santa Marinella, Italy G6 18
Santa Marta, Col. B5 84
Santa Marta, Guat. D3 92
Santa Marta, Cerro, mtn., Mex. H12 90
Santa Marta, Ciénaga Grande, b., Col. B5 84
Santa Marta Grande, Cabo de, c., Braz. E14 80
Santa Monica, Ca., U.S. J7 124
Santa Monica Bay, b., Ca., U.S. K7 124
Santana, Braz. B6 79
Santana, Port. m21 17a
Santana, stm., Braz. E3 79
Santana, Coxilha de, hills, S.A. F11 80
Santana da Boa Vista, Braz. F12 80
Santana do Livramento, Braz. F11 80
Santander, Col. F4 84
Santander, Spain B8 16
Santander, dept., Col. D6 84
Santander Jiménez, Mex. E10 90
Santanilla, Islas, is., Hond. F3 94
Sant Antoni de Portmany, Spain G13 16
Santa Paula, Ca., U.S. J6 124
Santaquin, Ut., U.S. E5 120
Santarém, Braz. D8 76
Santarém, Port. F3 16
Santaren Channel, strt., Bah. C5 94
Santa Rita, Col. G6 84
Santa Rita, Hond. B7 92
Santa Rita, Mex. C4 90
Santa Rita, Ven. B7 84
Santa Rita de Catuna, Arg. F5 80
Santa Rita do Araguaia, Braz. D2 79
Santa Rita do Weil, Braz. I8 84
Santa Rosa, Arg. I6 80
Santa Rosa, Arg. B6 80
Santa Rosa, Bol. F8 82
Santa Rosa, Bol. D8 82
Santa Rosa, Bol. G10 82
Santa Rosa, Braz. C5 79
Santa Rosa, Braz. D11 80
Santa Rosa, Ca., U.S. F3 124
Santa Rosa, Col. F8 84
Santa Rosa, C.R. G9 92
Santa Rosa, Ec. I3 84
Santa Rosa, N.M., U.S. E2 116
Santa Rosa, Para. D10 80
Santa Rosa, Para. I11 82
Santa Rosa, Tx., U.S. M9 116
Santa Rosa, Ven. C8 84
Santa Rosa, dept., Guat. C4 92
Santa Rosa, Parque Nacional, C.R. G9 92
Santa Rosa Beach, Fl., U.S. L10 114
Santa Rosa de Aguán, Hond. B9 92
Santa Rosa de Amanadona, Ven. G9 84
Santa Rosa de Cabal, Col. E5 84
Santa Rosa [de Copán], Hond. C6 92
Santa Rosa del Conlara, Arg. G6 80
Santa Rosa de Leales, Arg. D6 80
Santa Rosa de Lima, El Sal. D7 92
Santa Rosa del Palmar, Bol. G10 82
Santa Rosa de Osos, Col. D5 84
Santa Rosa de Río Primero, Arg. F7 80
Santa Rosa de Sucumbíos, Ec. G4 84
Santa Rosa de Viterbo, Col. E6 84
Santa Rosa Island, i., Ca., U.S. K5 124
Santa Rosa Island, i., Fl., U.S. L10 114
Santa Rosalía, Mex. D3 90
Santa Rosalía, Ven. C8 84
Santa Rosa Range, mts., Nv., U.S. C8 124
Šantarskije ostrova, is., Russia F19 28
Santa Sylvina, Arg. D8 80
Santa Teresa, Braz. E8 79
Santa Teresa, Mex. E11 90
Santa Teresa, stm., Braz. B4 79
Santa Teresa, Embalse de, res., Spain E6 16
Santa Tereza de Goiás, Braz. B4 79
Santa Uxía, Spain C2 16
Santa Vitória, Braz. E3 79
Santa Vitória do Palmar, Braz. G12 80
Santa Ynez, stm., Ca., U.S. J5 124
Sant Carles de la Ràpita, Spain E12 16
Santee, Ca., U.S. L9 124
Santee, stm., S.C., U.S. F7 112
Sant Feliu de Guíxols, Spain D15 16
Santhià, Italy D3 18
Santiago, Bol. H12 82
Santiago, Braz. E11 80
Santiago, Chile G3 80
Santiago, Mex. F5 90
Santiago, Pan. C2 84
Santiago, Para. D10 80
Santiago, Peru F4 82
Santiago, i., C.V. m17 64a
Santiago, stm., Mex. E7 90
Santiago, stm., S.A. I4 84
Santiago, Cerro, mtn., Pan. I13 92
Santiago, Isla, i., Ec. j13 84a
Santiago, Serranía de, mts., Bol. H12 82
Santiago Atitlán, Guat. C3 92
Santiago Choapan, Mex. I12 90
Santiago de Cao, Peru B2 82
Santiago de Chocorvos, Peru E4 82
Santiago de Chuco, Peru C2 82
Santiago de Compostela, Spain C3 16
Santiago de Cuba, Cuba D7 94
Santiago de Huari, Bol. H8 82
Santiago de Huata, Bol. G7 82
Santiago del Estero, Arg. D6 80
Santiago del Estero, prov., Arg. E7 80
Santiago de los Caballeros, Dom. Rep. E9 94
Santiago de Machaca, Bol. G7 82
Santiago de Méndez, Ec. I3 84
Santiago Ixcuintla, Mex. G7 90
Santiago Jamiltepec, Mex. I11 90
Santiago Larre, Arg. H9 80
Santiago Papasquiaro, Mex. E7 90
Santiaguillo, Laguna, l., Mex. E7 90
Santiam Pass, Or., U.S. F4 122
San Timoteo, Ven. C7 84
Säntis, mtn., Switz. D11 13
Sant Jordi, Golf de, b., Spain E13 16
Santo, Tx., U.S. G8 116
Santo Amaro, Braz. B9 79
Santo Anastácio, Braz. F3 79
Santo André, Braz. G5 79
Santo Ângelo, Braz. E11 80
Santo Antão, i., C.V. k16 64a
Santo António, S. Tom./P. A1 58
Santo Antônio, stm., Braz. E6 79
Santo Antônio da Patrulha, Braz. E13 80
Santo Antônio de Jesus, Braz. B9 79
Santo Antônio de Pádua, Braz. F7 79
Santo Antônio do Amparo, Braz. F6 79
Santo Antônio do Içá, Braz. I9 84
Santo Antônio do Leverger, Braz. F13 82
Santo Antônio do Rio Verde, Braz. D5 79
Santo Antônio do Sudoeste, Braz. D12 80
Santo Augusto, Braz. D12 80
Santo Corazón, Bol. G12 82
Santo Domingo, Dom. Rep. E10 94
Santo Domingo, Mex. E3 90
Santo Domingo, Nic. E9 92
Santo Domingo, stm., Mex. A3 92
Santo Domingo de los Colorados, Ec. H3 84
Santo Domingo Pueblo, N.M., U.S. I10 120
Santo Domingo Tehuantepec, Mex. I12 90
Santo Domingo Zanatepec, Mex. I12 90
Santo Estêvão, Braz. B9 79
San Tomé, Ven. C10 84
Santoña, Spain B8 16
Santo Onofre, stm., Braz. B7 79
Santorini see Thíra, i., Grc. M9 20
Santos, Braz. G5 79
Santos Dumont, Braz. F7 79
Santos Tomás del Norte, Nic. D8 92
Santo Tomás, Col. B5 84
Santo Tomás, Mex. B1 90
Santo Tomás, Nic. E9 92
Santo Tomás, Peru B3 82
Santo Tomás, Peru F5 82
Santo Tomás, stm., Peru F5 82
Santo Tomás, Punta, c., Mex. B1 90
Santo Tomé, Arg. E10 80
Santo Tomé, Arg. F8 80
Santuario de Quillacas, Bol. H8 82
Santunying, China C6 32
San Ubaldo, Nic. F9 92
San Vicente, Arg. E6 80
San Vicente, El Sal. D6 92
San Vicente, Volcán de, vol., El Sal. D6 92
San Vicente de Cañete, Peru E3 82
San Vicente de Chucurí, Col. D6 84
San Vicente del Caguán, Col. F5 84
San Vicente de Tagua-Tagua, Chile H3 80
San Vincenzo, Italy F5 18
San Vito, C.R. I12 92
San Vito, Italy J4 18
San Vito dei Normanni, Italy I12 18
San Ygnacio, Tx., U.S. L7 116
Sanyuan, China E8 30
Sanza Pombo, Ang. C3 58
Sanzha, China B2 32
São Benedito, stm., Braz. C13 82
São Bento, Braz. D10 76
São Bento do Sul, Braz. D14 80
São Borja, Braz. E10 80
São Caetano do Sul, Braz. G5 79
São Carlos, Braz. G5 79
São Cristóvão, Braz. F11 76
São Domingos, Braz. B5 79
São Domingos, Braz. D12 80
São Domingos, Gui.-B. E1 64
São Domingos, stm., Braz. B5 79
São Domingos, stm., Braz. E3 79
São Domingos, stm., Braz. E9 82
São Felipe, Braz. C8 79
São Filipe, C.V. m16 64a
São Francisco, Braz. C6 79
São Francisco, stm., Braz. E11 76
São Francisco, stm., Braz. C8 79
São Francisco, Baía de, b., Braz. D14 80
São Francisco, Ilha de, i., Braz. D14 80
São Francisco de Assis, Braz. E11 80
São Francisco de Goiás, Braz. C4 79
São Francisco de Paula, Braz. E13 80
São Francisco do Sul, Braz. D14 80
São Gabriel, Braz. F11 80
São Gabriel da Palha, Braz. E8 79
São Gabriel de Goiás, Braz. C5 79
São Gonçalo do Abaeté, Braz. E6 79
São Gonçalo do Sapucaí, Braz. F6 79
São Gonçalo dos Campos, Braz. B9 79
Sao Hill, Tan. C7 58
São Jerônimo, Braz. E13 80
São Jerônimo, Serra de, plat., Braz. D1 79
São Jerônimo da Serra, Braz. G3 79
São João, stm., Braz. B3 79
São João da Barra, Braz. F8 79
São João da Boa Vista, Braz. F5 79
São João D'Aliança, Braz. C5 79
São João da Madeira, Port. E3 16
São João da Ponte, Braz. C6 79
São João del-Rei, Braz. F6 79
São João do Araguaia, Braz. E9 76
São João do Paraíso, Braz. C7 79
São João Evangelista, Braz. E7 79
São Joaquim, Braz. E14 80
São Joaquim, Parque Nacional de, Braz. E14 80
São Joaquim da Barra, Braz. F5 79
São José, Braz. D14 80
São José, stm., Braz. E8 79
São José de Anauá, Braz. G12 84
São José do Cedro, Braz. D12 80
São José do Norte, Braz. G12 80
São José do Rio Preto, Braz. F4 79
São José dos Campos, Braz. G6 79
São José dos Pinhais, Braz. C14 80
São Leopoldo, Braz. E13 80
São Lourenço, Braz. G6 79
São Lourenço, Pantanal de, sw., Braz. G13 82
São Lourenço do Oeste, Braz. D12 80
São Lourenço do Sul, Braz. F13 80
São Luís, Braz. D10 76
São Luís de Montes Belos, Braz. D3 79
São Luís Gonzaga, Braz. E11 80
São Manuel, Braz. G4 79
São Manuel, stm., Braz. C13 82

Name	Map Ref.	Page
São Marcos, stm., Braz.	D5	79
São Mateus, Braz.	E9	79
São Mateus, Braço Norte, stm., Braz.	E8	79
São Mateus do Sul, Braz.	C13	80
São Miguel, i., Port.	m21	62a
São Miguel, stm., Braz.	D8	79
São Miguel do Araguaia, Braz.	B3	79
São Miguel d'Oeste, Braz.	D12	80
Saona, Isla, i., Dom. Rep.	E10	94
Saône, stm., Fr.	F11	14
Saône-et-Loire, dept., Fr.	F11	14
São Nicolau, i., C.V.	k16	64a
São Paulo, Braz.	G5	79
São Paulo, state, Braz.	G4	79
São Paulo de Olivença, Braz.	I8	84
São Pedro, Braz.	E3	79
São Pedro, stm., Braz.	D8	79
São Pedro do Sul, Braz.	E11	80
São Pedro do Sul, Port.	E3	16
São Raimundo Nonato, Braz.	E10	76
São Romão, Braz.	D6	79
São Roque, Braz.	G5	79
São Roque, Cabo de, c., Braz.	E11	76
São Sebastião, Braz.	G6	79
São Sebastião, Ilha de, i., Braz.	G6	79
São Sebastião, Ponta, c., Moz.	D12	66
São Sebastião do Maranhão, Braz.	E7	79
São Sebastião do Paraíso, Braz.	F5	79
São Sebastião do Rio Claro, Braz.	C3	79
São Sepé, Braz.	F12	80
São Simão, Braz.	E3	79
São Simão, Braz.	F5	79
São Tiago, Braz.	F6	79
São Timóteo, Braz.	B7	79
São Tomé, S. Tom./P.	A1	58
São Tomé, i., S. Tom./P.	A1	58
São Tomé, stm., Braz.	C13	82
São Tomé, Cabo de, c., Braz.	F8	79
Sao Tome and Principe (São Tomé e Principe), ctry., Afr.	A1	58
Saoura, Oued, val., Alg.	F10	62
São Vicente, Braz.	G5	79
São Vicente, i., C.V.	k16	64a
São Vicente, Cabo de (Cape Saint Vincent), c., Port.	H2	16
São Vicente de Minas, Braz.	F6	79
Sapé, Braz.	E11	76
Sapele, Nig.	I12	64
Sapello, stm., N.M., U.S.	I11	120
Sapelo Island, i., Ga., U.S.	H5	112
Şaphane, Tur.	J13	20
Šapitwa, mtn., Mwi.	E7	58
Šapki, Russia	B14	22
Sa Pobla, Spain	F15	16
Sapodilla Cays, i., Belize	A6	92
Saponé, Burkina	E9	64
Saposoa, Peru	B3	82
Sapožok, Russia	H23	22
Sapporo, Japan	d16	36a
Sapri, Italy	I10	18
Saptakośī, stm., Nepal	G12	44
Sapulpa, Ok., U.S.	D10	116
Sāqiat al-ʿAbd, Sudan	G6	60
Saqqez, Iran	C9	48
Saquena, Peru	A5	82
Saquisilí, Ec.	H3	84
Sarāb, Iran	C9	48
Saraburi, Thai.	G6	40
Saracura, stm., Braz.	B8	79
Saragosa, Tx., U.S.	H3	116
Saragossa see Zaragoza, Spain	D11	16
Saraguro, Ec.	I3	84
Sarai, Russia	H24	22
Sarajevo, Bos.	F2	20
Sarakhs, Iran	C16	48
Saraland, Al., U.S.	L8	114
Saran', Kaz.	H12	26
Saranac, Mi., U.S.	H10	110
Saranac, stm., N.Y., U.S.	C13	108
Saranac Lake, N.Y., U.S.	C12	108
Sarandi, Braz.	D12	80
Sarandí del Yi, Ur.	G11	80
Sarandí Grande, Ur.	G10	80
Saransk, Russia	G7	26
Sarapiquí, stm., C.R.	G11	92
Sarapul, Russia	F8	26
Sarare, Ven.	C8	84
Sara Sara, Nevado, mtn., Peru	F5	82
Sarasota, Fl., U.S.	L4	112
Šarašova, Bela.	I7	22
Sarata, Ukr.	C13	20
Saratoga, Ca., U.S.	G3	124
Saratoga, Tx., U.S.	I12	116
Saratoga, Wy., U.S.	C10	120
Saratoga Springs, N.Y., U.S.	D13	108
Saratov, Russia	G7	26
Saratovskoje vodochranilišče, res., Russia	G7	26
Saraurcu, mtn., Ec.	H4	84
Saravan, Laos	G9	40
Sarawak, hist. reg., Malay.	E5	38
Saraya, Gui.	F4	64
Sarayköy, Tur.	L12	20
Sarbāz, Iran	H16	48
Sárbogárd, Hung.	I18	10
Sarcee Indian Reserve, Ab., Can.	G20	102
Sarcoxie, Mo., U.S.	E2	114
Sārda (Mahākālī), stm., Asia	F9	44
Sardārshahr, India	F6	44
Sardegna, prov., Italy	I4	18
Sardegna (Sardinia), i., Italy	I4	18
Sardinal, C.R.	G9	92
Sardinata, Col.	C6	84
Sardinia see Sardegna, i., Italy	I4	18
Sardis, Al., U.S.	J10	114
Sardis, Ga., U.S.	G5	112
Sardis, Ms., U.S.	H7	114
Sardis, Tn., U.S.	G8	114
Sardis Lake, res., Ms., U.S.	H7	114
Sar-e Pol, Afg.	B1	44
Sarepta, La., U.S.	J3	114
Sargans, Switz.	D11	13
Sargasso Sea	B8	74
Sargent, Ga., U.S.	F2	112
Sargent, Ne., U.S.	J8	118
Sargodha, Pak.	D5	44
Sarh, Chad	G4	56
Sārī, Iran	C12	48
Saric, Mex.	B4	90
Şārif, Yemen	F7	47
Sarıkamış, Tur.	A7	48
Sarina, Austl.	C8	70
Sariñena, Spain	D11	16
Sarīr, Libya	D2	60
Sarita, Tx., U.S.	B9	116
Şariwŏn, N. Kor.	E13	32
Šarja, Russia	F7	26
Sark, i., Guernsey	L11	8
Şarkad, Hung.	I21	10
Šarkaųščyna, Bela.	F10	22
Şarkışla, Tur.	B4	48
Şarköy, Tur.	I11	20
Šarlauk, Turk.	B13	48
Sarles, N.D., U.S.	C9	118
Sármellék, Hung.	I17	10
Sarmiento de Gamboa, Cerro, mtn., Chile	G2	78
Särna, Swe.	K13	6
Sarnen, Switz.	E9	13
Sarnia, On., Can.	H13	110
Sarno, Italy	I9	18
Saron, S. Afr.	I4	66
Saronikós Kólpos, b., Grc.	L7	20
Saronno, Italy	D4	18
Sárospatak, Hung.	G21	10
Sarpsborg, Nor.	L12	6
Sarralbe, Fr.	C14	14
Sarrebourg, Fr.	D14	14
Sarreguemines, Fr.	C14	14
Sarre-Union, Fr.	D14	14
Sarro, Mali	E7	64
Sarstoon (Sarstún), stm., N.A.	B5	92
Sarstún (Sarstoon), stm., N.A.	B5	92
Sartang, stm., Russia	D18	28
Sartell, Mn., U.S.	E1	110
Sartène, Fr.	H3	18
Sarthe, dept., Fr.	D7	14
Sartilly, Fr.	D5	14
Saruhanlı, Tur.	K11	20
Sarūr, Oman	C11	47
Sárvár, Hung.	H16	10
Sarvestān, Iran	G12	48
Saryg-Sep, Russia	G17	26
Sarykol'skij chrebet, mts., Asia	A6	44
Saryozek, Kaz.	I13	26
Sarysu, stm., Kaz.	H11	26
Sary-Taš, Kyrg.	J12	26
Sarzana, Italy	E4	18
Sasaginnigak Lake, l., Mb., Can.	G19	104
Sasakwa, Ok., U.S.	E10	116
Sāsarām, India	H11	44
Sásd, Hung.	I18	10
Sasebo, Japan	N4	36
Saskatchewan, prov., Can.	F11	96
Saskatchewan, stm., Can.	E13	104
Saskatoon, Sk., Can.	F8	104
Saslaya, Cerro, mtn., Nic.	H2	94
Sasnovy Bor, Bela.	I12	22
Sasolburg, S. Afr.	F8	66
Sasovo, Russia	G24	22
Saspamco, Tx., U.S.	J8	116
Sassafras, Ky., U.S.	B3	112
Sassafras Mountain, mtn., U.S.	D4	112
Sassandra, C. Iv.	I6	64
Sassandra, stm., C. Iv.	I6	64
Sassari, Italy	I3	18
Sassoferrato, Italy	F7	18
Sasso Marconi, Italy	E6	18
S'as'stroj, Russia	A15	22
Sassuolo, Italy	E5	18
Sastown, Lib.	I5	64
Sastre, Arg.	F8	80
Sasyk, ozero, l., Ukr.	D13	20
Şatah Mountain, mtn., B.C., Can.	E10	102
Šatalovo, Russia	G15	22
Sata-misaki, c., Japan	Q5	36
Satanta, Ks., U.S.	N7	118
Sātāra, India	D2	46
Satara, S. Afr.	E10	66
Satélite, Mex.	B6	90
Satellite Beach, Fl., U.S.	K6	112
Satipo, Peru	D4	82
Satīt (Tekeze), stm., Afr.	J9	60
Satka, Russia	F9	26
Satna, India	H9	44
Sátoraljaújhely, Hung.	G21	10
Sātpura Range, mts., India	J7	44
Satsuma, Al., U.S.	L8	114
Satsunan-shotō, is., Japan	r4	37b
Sattahip, Thai.	H6	40
Satthwa, Myan.	F3	40
Satu Mare, Rom.	B6	20
Satu Mare, co., Rom.	B6	20
Şatun, Thai.	K6	40
Šatura, Russia	F22	22
Şaturnino M. Laspiur, Arg.	F7	80
Šaturtorf, Russia	F22	22
Sauce, Arg.	F9	80
Sauce, Peru	B3	82
Sauce, Ur.	H10	80
Sauce Corto, Arroyo, stm., Arg.	I8	80
Saucier, Ms., U.S.	L7	114
Saucillo, Mex.	C7	90
Sauda, Nor.	L10	6
Saudi Arabia (Al-ʿArabīyah as-Suʿūdīyah), ctry., Asia	D4	42
Sauer (Sûre), stm., Eur.	I10	12
Saueruiná, stm., Braz.	E12	82
Sauê-Uiná, stm., Braz.	E12	82
Saugatuck, Mi., U.S.	H9	110
Saugerties, N.Y., U.S.	E13	108
Saugstad, Mount, mtn., B.C., Can.	E8	102
Saujil, Arg.	E5	80
Sauk, stm., Mn., U.S.	E1	110
Sauk Centre, Mn., U.S.	F13	118
Sauk City, Wi., U.S.	G6	110
Sauk Rapids, Mn., U.S.	E1	110
Saukville, Wi., U.S.	G8	110
Saül, Fr. Gu.	C8	76
Saulgau, Ger.	G9	10
Saulieu, Fr.	E11	14
Saulkrasti, Lat.	D7	22
Sault-au-Mouton, P.Q., Can.	D4	106
Sault aux Cochons, Rivière du, stm., P.Q., Can.	D4	106
Saulteaux, stm., Ab., Can.	C20	102
Saulteaux Indian Reserve, Sk., Can.	E6	104
Sault Sainte Marie, Mi., U.S.	D11	110
Sault Sainte Marie, On., Can.	D11	110
Saumarez Reef, rf., Austl.	C10	70
Saumons, Riviére aux, stm., P.Q., Can.	C11	106
Saumur, Fr.	E6	14
Saunders Island, i., S. Geor.	J12	74
Sauquoit, N.Y., U.S.	D11	108
Saurimo, Ang.	C4	58
Sausalito, Ca., U.S.	G3	124
Sauveterre-de-Béarn, Fr.	I6	14
Sauvo, Fin.	K18	6
Sava, Italy	I12	18
Sava, stm., Eur.	F11	4
Savage, Md., U.S.	H10	108
Savage, Mt., U.S.	D3	118
Savai'i, i., W. Sam.	J22	126
Savalou, Benin	H10	64
Savane, stm., P.Q., Can.	A2	106
Savanna, Il., U.S.	H5	110
Savanna, Ok., U.S.	E11	116
Savannah, Ga., U.S.	G5	112
Savannah, Mo., U.S.	C2	114
Savannah, Tn., U.S.	G8	114
Savannah, stm., U.S.	G5	112
Savannakhét, Laos	F8	40
Savanna-la-Mar, Jam.	E5	94
Savé, Benin	G11	64
Save (Sabi), stm., Afr.	C12	66
Sāveh, Iran	D11	48
Savelli, Italy	J11	18
Saverdun, Fr.	I8	14
Saverne, Fr.	D14	14
Savigliano, Italy	E2	18
Savino, Russia	E24	22
Şavinskij, Russia	J27	6
Šavnik, Yugo.	G3	20
Savognin, Switz.	E12	13
Savoie, dept., Fr.	G13	14
Savona, B.C., Can.	G14	102
Savona, Italy	E3	18
Savoonga, Ak., U.S.	E9	100
Savoy, Tx., U.S.	F10	116
Savran', Ukr.	A14	20
Savu Sea see Sawu, Laut, Indon.	G7	38
Sawahlunto, Indon.	O6	40
Sawāi Mādhopur, India	H7	44
Sawākin, Sudan	H9	60
Sawankhalok, Thai.	F5	40
Sawatch Range, mts., Co., U.S.	E10	120
Sawdā', Jabal, mtn., Sau. Ar.	E3	47
Sawdā', Jabal as-, hills, Libya	C4	56
Sawdā', Qurnat as-, mtn., Leb.	D4	48
Sawdirī, Sudan	J5	60
Sawhāj, Egypt	D6	60
Sawknah, Libya	C4	56
Şawqirah, Ghubbat, b., Oman	E10	47
Sawu, Laut (Savu Sea), Indon.	G7	38
Sawu, Pulau, i., Indon.	H7	38
Sawyer, Mi., U.S.	I9	110
Sawyer, N.D., U.S.	C6	118
Sawyers Hill, hill, Nf., Can.	E20	106
Saxby, stm., Austl.	B4	70
Saxis, Va., U.S.	B11	112
Saxon, Switz.	F7	13
Saxon, Wi., U.S.	D5	110
Saxony see Sachsen, state, Ger.	C9	10
Saxton, Pa., U.S.	G8	108
Say, Niger	E11	64
Sayán, Peru	D3	82
Sayan Mountains (Sajany), mts., Asia	G11	28
Sayaxché, Guat.	I14	90
Saybrook, Il., U.S.	B8	114
Şaydā (Sidon), Leb.	A4	50
Sayḥūt, Yemen	G7	47
Sayil, hist., Mex.	G15	90
Saylorville Lake, res., Ia., U.S.	I2	110
Saylūn, Khirbat (Shiloh), hist., W.B.	D4	50
Sayre, Ok., U.S.	D7	116
Sayre, Pa., U.S.	F10	108
Sayreville, N.J., U.S.	G12	108
Sayula, Mex.	H8	90
Sayward, B.C., Can.	G9	102
Saywūn, Yemen	G6	47
Şazonovo, Russia	B18	22
Šazud, Taj.	B5	44
Sba, Alg.	F10	62
Sbeïtla, Tun.	N4	18
Sbiba, Tun.	N4	18
Scafell Pikes, mtn., Eng., U.K.	G10	8
Scalea, Italy	J10	18
Scammon, Ks., U.S.	N13	118
Scandia, Ks., U.S.	L10	118
Scanlon, Mn., U.S.	D3	110
Scapa, Ab., Can.	F23	102
Scapa Flow, b., Scot., U.K.	C10	8
Scapegoat Mountain, mtn., Mt., U.S.	C13	122
Ščapino, Russia	F23	28
Scappoose, Or., U.S.	E3	122
Scarborough, Eng., U.K.	G13	8
Scarborough, On., Can.	G16	110
Scarborough, Trin.	I14	94
Scatarie Island, i., N.S., Can.	G14	106
Şcawfell Island, i., Austl.	C8	70
Ščelkovo, Russia	F21	22
Şceptre, Sk., Can.	H5	104
Ščerbinka, Russia	F20	22
Schaerbeek (Schaarbeek), Bel.	G5	12
Schaffhausen, Switz.	C10	13
Schaffhausen, state, Switz.	C10	13
Schaller, Ia., U.S.	I12	118
Schärding, Aus.	G13	10
Schefferville, P.Q., Can.	F19	96
Scheibbs, Aus.	G15	10
Scheinfeld, Ger.	F10	10
Schelde (Escaut), stm., Eur.	D4	10
Schenectady, N.Y., U.S.	E13	108
Schertz, Tx., U.S.	J8	116
Schesslitz, Ger.	F11	10
Scheveningen, Neth.	D5	12
Schiedam, Neth.	E5	12
Schiermonnikoog, Neth.	B9	12
Schiermonnikoog, i., Neth.	B9	12
Schiltigheim, Fr.	D14	14
Schio, Italy	D6	18
Schipbeek, stm., Eur.	D9	12
Schkeuditz, Ger.	D12	10
Schladming, Aus.	H13	10
Schlater, Ms., U.S.	I6	114
Schleswig, Ger.	A9	10
Schleswig, Ia., U.S.	I12	118
Schleswig-Holstein, state, Ger.	A9	10
Schleusingen, Ger.	E10	10
Schlieren, Switz.	D9	13
Schlitz, Ger.	E9	10
Schlüchtern, Ger.	E9	10
Schmidmühlen, Ger.	F11	10
Schmölln, Ger.	E12	10
Schneverdingen, Ger.	B9	10
Schodn'a, Russia	F20	22
Schofield, Wi., U.S.	F6	110
Schoharie, N.Y., U.S.	E12	108
Schönebeck, Ger.	C11	10
Schongau, Ger.	H10	10
Schoolcraft, Mi., U.S.	H10	110
Schopfheim, Ger.	H7	10
Schorndorf, Ger.	G9	10
Schouten Island, i., Austl.	N8	70
Schouwen, i., Neth.	E4	12
Schramberg, Ger.	G8	10
Schreiber, On., Can.	B8	110
Schriever, La., U.S.	M6	114
Schroffenstein, mtn., Nmb.	F4	66
Schulenburg, Tx., U.S.	J10	116
Schultz Lake, l., N.T., Can.	D13	96
Schumacher, On., Can.	B14	110
Schüpfheim, Switz.	E9	13
Schuyler, Ne., U.S.	J10	118
Schuyler, Va., U.S.	B8	112
Schuylkill, stm., Pa., U.S.	G11	108
Schuylkill Haven, Pa., U.S.	G10	108
Schwabach, Ger.	F11	10
Schwaben, hist. reg., Ger.	G10	10
Schwäbische Alb, mts., Ger.	G9	10
Schwäbisch Gmünd, Ger.	G9	10
Schwäbisch Hall, Ger.	F9	10
Schwabmünchen, Ger.	G10	10
Schwanden, Switz.	D11	13
Schwandorf, Ger.	F12	10
Schwaner, Pegunungan, mts., Indon.	F5	38
Schwarzach im Pongau, Aus.	H13	10
Schwarzenburg, Switz.	E7	13
Schwarzwald (Black Forest), mts., Ger.	G8	10
Schwaz, Aus.	H11	10
Schwedt, Ger.	B14	10
Schweinfurt, Ger.	E10	10
Schweizer Nationalpark, Switz.	E13	13
Schwerin, Ger.	B11	10
Schwyz, Switz.	D10	13
Schwyz, state, Switz.	D10	13
Sciacca, Italy	L8	18
Scicli, Italy	M9	18
Scilla, Italy	K10	18
Scilly, Isles of, is., Eng., U.K.	L7	8
Scio, Oh., U.S.	G5	108
Scio, Or., U.S.	F3	122
Scioto, stm., Oh., U.S.	I3	108
Scipio, Ut., U.S.	E4	120
Şcobey, Mt., U.S.	B20	122
Ščokino, Russia	G20	22
Scone, Austl.	I9	70
Scooba, Ms., U.S.	J8	114
Scordia, Italy	L9	18
Scotia, Ne., U.S.	J9	118
Scotia, N.Y., U.S.	E13	108
Scotia Sea	A1	73
Scotland, On., Can.	G15	110
Scotland, S.D., U.S.	H10	118
Scotland, Tx., U.S.	F8	116
Scotland, ter., U.K.	D9	8
Scotland Neck, N.C., U.S.	C9	112
Scotlandville, La., U.S.	L5	114
Scotsburn, N.S., Can.	G11	106
Scott, Ms., U.S.	I5	114
Scott, Sk., Can.	F6	104
Scott, stm., Ca., U.S.	C3	124
Scott, Cape, c., B.C., Can.	G6	102
Scott, Mount, mtn., Or., U.S.	H3	122
Scott Base, sci., Ant.	C8	73
Scottburgh, S. Afr.	H10	66
Scott City, Ks., U.S.	M7	118
Scott City, Mo., U.S.	E7	114
Scottdale, Pa., U.S.	G7	108
Scott Islands, is., B.C., Can.	G6	102
Scott Mountain, mtn., Id., U.S.	F10	122
Scott Reef, rf., Austl.	B4	68
Scottsbluff, Ne., U.S.	J4	118
Scottsboro, Al., U.S.	H10	114
Scottsburg, In., U.S.	D11	114
Scottsdale, Austl.	M7	70
Scottsdale, Az., U.S.	K5	120
Scotts Hill, Tn., U.S.	G8	114
Scottsville, Ky., U.S.	F10	114
Scottville, Mi., U.S.	G9	110
Scout Lake, Sk., Can.	I8	104
Scranton, Ia., U.S.	I13	118
Scranton, N.D., U.S.	E4	118
Scranton, Pa., U.S.	F11	108
Screven, Ga., U.S.	H4	112
Şcribner, Ne., U.S.	J11	118
Ščučinsk, Kaz.	G12	26
Ščučyn, Bela.	H7	22
Scuol (Schuls), Switz.	E13	13
Scurry, Tx., U.S.	G10	116
Scutari, Lake, l., Eur.	G3	20
Seabird Island Indian Reserve, B.C., Can.	H13	102
Seaboard, N.C., U.S.	C9	112
Seadrift, Tx., U.S.	K10	116
Seaford, De., U.S.	I11	108
Seaforth, On., Can.	G14	110
Seager Wheeler Lake, l., Sk., Can.	D11	104
Seagraves, Tx., U.S.	G4	116
Seahorse Point, c., N.T., Can.	D16	96
Sea Islands, is., U.S.	I5	112
Sea Isle City, N.J., U.S.	H12	108
Seal, stm., Mb., Can.	E13	96
Sea Lake, Austl.	J5	70
Seal Cays, is., T./C. Is.	D9	94
Seal Cove, N.B., Can.	H7	106
Seal Cove, Nf., Can.	C17	106
Seale, Al., U.S.	J11	114
Sealevel, N.C., U.S.	E10	112
Seal Island, i., N.S., Can.	I7	106
Seal Lake, l., Nf., Can.	F20	96
Sealy, Tx., U.S.	J10	116
Seara, Braz.	D12	80
Searchlight, Nv., U.S.	I11	124
Searcy, Ar., U.S.	G5	114
Searsport, Me., U.S.	C18	108
Seaside, Ca., U.S.	H4	124
Seaside, Or., U.S.	E2	122
Seaside Park, N.J., U.S.	H12	108
Seattle, Wa., U.S.	C3	122
Seattle, Mount, mtn., N.A.	F25	100
Sébaco, Nic.	E8	92
Sebago Lake, l., Me., U.S.	D16	108
Sebakwe Recreational Area, Zimb.	B10	66
Šebalino, Russia	G15	26
Sebastian, Tx., U.S.	M9	116
Sebastián Vizcaíno, Bahía, b., Mex.	C2	90
Sebastopol, Ca., U.S.	F3	124
Sebastopol, Ms., U.S.	J7	114
Sebderat, Erit.	J9	60
Sebeka, Mn., U.S.	E12	118
Seberi, Braz.	D12	80
Sebeş, Rom.	D7	20
Sebes Körös (Crişul Repede), stm., Eur.	B5	20
Sebewaing, Mi., U.S.	G12	110
Sebež, Russia	E11	22
Şebinkarahisar, Tur.	A5	48
Šebiş, Rom.	C6	20
Sebnitz, Ger.	E14	10
Sebree, Ky., U.S.	E9	114
Sebring, Fl., U.S.	L5	112
Secas, Islas, is., Pan.	J12	92
Sechelt, B.C., Can.	H11	102
Sechura, Peru	A1	82
Sechura, Bahía de, b., Peru	A1	82
Sechura, Desierto de, des., Peru	A1	82
Seclantas, Arg.	C5	80
Seco, stm., Arg.	B7	80
Sečovce, Slvk.	G21	10
Section, Al., U.S.	H11	114
Sécure, stm., Bol.	F9	82
Security, Co., U.S.	M3	118
Seda, China	E7	30
Seda, Lat.	D8	22
Seda, Lith.	E5	22
Sedalia, Ab., Can.	G4	104
Sedalia, Mo., U.S.	D3	114
Sedan, Fr.	C11	14
Sedan, Ks., U.S.	N11	118
Sedano, Spain	C8	16
Sedel'nikovo, Russia	F13	26
Sederot, Isr.	E3	50
Sedgefield, N.C., U.S.	D6	112
Sedgewick, Ab., Can.	E23	102
Sedgwick, Co., U.S.	K5	118
Sedgwick, Ks., U.S.	N10	118
Sedgwick, Mount, mtn., N.M., U.S.	I8	120
Sedini, Italy	I3	18
Sedlčany, Czech Rep.	F14	10
Sedom (Sodom), hist., Isr.	F4	50
Sedona, Az., U.S.	J5	120
Sedot Yam, Isr.	D3	50
Sedova, pik, mtn., Russia	C8	26
Sedrata, Alg.	M2	18
Şedro Woolley, Wa., U.S.	B3	122
Šeduva, Lith.	F6	22
Seeberg, Switz.	D8	13
Seeber Lake, l., On., Can.	E21	104
Seefeld in Tirol, Aus.	H11	10
Seehausen, Ger.	C11	10
Seeheim, Nmb.	F3	66
Seeis, Nmb.	D3	66
Seekaskootch Indian Reserve, Sk., Can.	E5	104
Seeley Lake, Mt., U.S.	C12	122
Seelow, Ger.	C14	10
Seelyville, In., U.S.	C9	114
Seengen, Switz.	D9	13
Sées, Fr.	D7	14
Seesen, Ger.	D10	10
Sefadu, S.L.	G4	64
Sefar, hist., Alg.	H15	62
Sefare, Bots.	D8	66
Sefīd Ābeh, Iran	F16	48
Sefrou, Mor.	D8	62
Segamat, Malay.	M7	40
Şegarcea, Rom.	E7	20
Şegbana, Benin	F11	64
Segbwema, S.L.	G4	64
Segeža, Russia	E4	26
Segni, Italy	H8	18
Segorbe, Spain	F11	16
Ségou, Mali	E6	64
Segovia, Col.	D5	84
Segovia, Spain	E7	16
Segozero, ozero, l., Russia	J23	6
Segre, stm., Eur.	D12	16
Séguédine, Niger	D9	54
Séguéla, C. Iv.	H6	64
Séguéla, Mali	D6	64
Seguí, Arg.	F8	80
Seguin, Tx., U.S.	J9	116
Segundo, Co., U.S.	N3	118
Segundo, stm., Arg.	F7	80
Segura, Port.	F5	16
Segura, stm., Spain	G11	16
Sehithwa, Bots.	C6	66
Seia, Port.	E4	16
Seibert, Co., U.S.	L5	118
Seiling, Ok., U.S.	C8	116
Seilo, Sudan	K2	60
Sein, Île de, i., Fr.	D2	14
Seinäjoki, Fin.	J18	6
Seine, stm., Fr.	C7	14
Seine, stm., Mb., Can.	I18	104
Seine, stm., On., Can.	B3	110
Seine, Baie de la, b., Fr.	C6	14
Seine-et-Marne, dept., Fr.	D10	14
Seine-Maritime, dept., Fr.	C8	14
Seixal, Port.	G2	16
Sejm, stm., Eur.	G4	26
Sejmčan, Russia	E22	28
Seke, Eth.	M10	60
Šeki, Azer.	I7	26
Šeki, Japan	L11	36
Seki, Tur.	M13	20
Sekoma, Bots.	E6	66
Sekondi-Takoradi, Ghana	I9	64
Şekota, Eth.	K10	60
Šeksna, Russia	B21	22
Šelagskij, mys, c., Russia	C26	28
Selah, Wa., U.S.	D5	122
Selaru, Pulau, i., Indon.	G9	38
Selatan, Tanjung, c., Indon.	F5	38
Selawik, Ak., U.S.	C14	100
Selayar, Pulau, i., Indon.	G7	38
Selb, Ger.	E12	10
Selbu, Nor.	J12	6
Selby, S.D., U.S.	F7	118
Selbyville, De., U.S.	I11	108
Sel'co, Russia	H17	22
Selden, Ks., U.S.	L7	118
Seldovia, Ak., U.S.	G19	100
Selebi Phikwe, Bots.	D8	66
Selenga (Selenge), stm., Asia	G19	26
Selenge (Selenga), stm., Asia	B7	30
Selenn'ach, stm., Russia	D20	28
Sélestat, Fr.	D14	14
Selezn'ovo, Russia	A11	22
Selfridge, N.D., U.S.	E7	118
Sélibaby, Maur.	D3	64
Šelichova, zaliv, b., Russia	F23	28
Seliger, ozero, l., Russia	D16	22
Seligman, Az., U.S.	I4	120
Seligman, Mo., U.S.	F3	114
Selinsgrove, Pa., U.S.	G10	108
Selišče, Russia	E16	22
Seližarovo, Russia	E16	22
Selje, Nor.	J9	6
Seljord, Nor.	L11	6
Selkirk, Mb., Can.	H18	104
Selkirk, Scot., U.K.	F11	8
Selkirk Mountains, mts., N.A.	F16	102
Seller Lake, l., Mb., Can.	C20	104
Sellers, S.C., U.S.	E7	112
Sellersburg, In., U.S.	D11	114
Sells, Az., U.S.	M5	120
Selm, Ger.	D7	10
Selma, Al., U.S.	J9	114
Selma, Ca., U.S.	H6	124
Selma, N.C., U.S.	D8	112
Selmer, Tn., U.S.	G8	114
Selmont, Al., U.S.	J9	114
Selous, Mount, mtn., Yk., Can.	E28	100
Seltz, Fr.	D15	14
Selva, Arg.	E7	80
Selvas, for., Braz.	E6	76
Selwyn, Austl.	C4	70
Selwyn, Mount, mtn., B.C., Can.	B11	102
Selwyn Lake, l., Can.	E12	96
Selwyn Mountains, mts., Can.	D28	100
Selwyn Range, mts., Austl.	C4	70
Seman, stm., Alb.	I3	20
Semans, Sk., Can.	G10	104
Semarang, Indon.	j15	39a
Semenivka, Ukr.	I15	22
Semeru, Gunung, mtn., Indon.	k16	39a
Semežava, Bela.	I10	22
Semibratovo, Russia	D22	22
Seminary, Ms., U.S.	K7	114
Seminoe Reservoir, res., Wy., U.S.	B10	120
Seminole, Ok., U.S.	D10	116
Seminole, Tx., U.S.	G4	116
Seminole, Lake, res., U.S.	I2	112
Semipalatinsk, Kaz.	G8	28
Semmens Lake, l., Mb., Can.	C20	104
Semnān, Iran	D12	48
Şemois, stm., Eur.	I7	12
Šemonaicha, Kaz.	G14	26
Sem'onov, Russia	F6	26
Semple Lake, l., Mb., Can.	C19	104
Semporna, Malay.	E6	38
Semuliki, stm., Afr.	A5	58
Semur-en-Auxois, Fr.	E11	14
Sena, Bol.	D8	82
Sena, Moz.	E7	58
Senador Canedo, Braz.	D4	79
Senador Firmino, Braz.	F7	79
Senador Pompeu, Braz.	E11	76
Senahú, Guat.	B5	92
Sena Madureira, Braz.	C7	82
Senanga, Zam.	E4	58
Senate, Sk., Can.	I5	104
Senath, Mo., U.S.	F6	114
Senatobia, Ms., U.S.	H7	114
Sendafa, Eth.	M10	60
Sendai, Japan	I15	36
Sêndo, China	E15	44
Seneca, Il., U.S.	I7	110
Seneca, Ks., U.S.	L11	118
Seneca, Mo., U.S.	F2	114
Seneca, Or., U.S.	F7	122
Seneca, S.C., U.S.	E4	112
Seneca Falls, N.Y., U.S.	E10	108
Seneca Lake, l., N.Y., U.S.	E10	108
Senegal (Sénégal), ctry., Afr.	F4	54
Sénégal, stm., Afr.	E4	54
Senekal, S. Afr.	G8	66
Senftenberg, Ger.	D14	10
Sengés, Braz.	H4	79
Senhor do Bonfim, Braz.	F10	76
Senica, Slvk.	G17	10
Senigallia, Italy	F8	18
Senise, Italy	I11	18
Senj, Cro.	E9	18
Şenja, i., Nor.	G15	6
Šenkursk, Russia	E6	26
Senlac, Sk., Can.	F5	104
Senlis, Fr.	C9	14
Senmonorom, Camb.	H9	40
Sennori, Italy	I3	18
Senoia, Ga., U.S.	F2	112
Senqu see Orange, stm., Afr.	G4	66
Sens, Fr.	D10	14
Sensuntepeque, El Sal.	D6	92
Senta, Yugo.	D4	20
Sentinel, Ok., U.S.	D7	116
Sentinel Peak, mtn., B.C., Can.	C13	102
Seo de Urgel, Spain	C13	16
Seoni, India	I8	44
Seoul see Sŏul, S. Kor.	F14	32
Sepatini, stm., Braz.	B9	82
Sepetiba, Baía de, b., Braz.	G7	79
Sepik, stm., Pap. N. Gui.	k15	68a
Sępólno Krajeńskie, Pol.	B17	10
Sepopa, Bots.	B6	66
Sepoti, stm., Braz.	B11	82
Sepotuba, stm., Braz.	F13	82
Sept-Îles (Seven Islands), P.Q., Can.	B7	106
Sepulga, stm., Al., U.S.	K10	114
Sequatchie, stm., Tn., U.S.	D1	112
Sequeros, Spain	E5	16
Sequim, Wa., U.S.	B2	122
Sequoia National Park, Ca., U.S.	H7	124
Šerabad, Uzb.	B2	44
Serachs, Turk.	C16	48
Serafimovič, Russia	H6	26
Seraidi, Alg.	M2	18
Seraing, Bel.	G7	12
Seram (Ceram), i., Indon.	F8	38
Seram, Laut (Ceram Sea), Indon.	F8	38
Serang, Indon.	j13	39a
Serbia see Srbija, state, Yugo.	F4	20
Serdobsk, Russia	G6	26
Serebr'anyje Prudy, Russia	G21	22
Sered', Slvk.	G17	10
Seredejskij, Russia	G18	22
Seredina-Buda, Ukr.	I17	22
Seredžius, Lith.	F6	22
Seremban, Malay.	M6	40
Serengeti Plain, pl., Tan.	B6	58
Serenje, Zam.	D6	58
Seret (Siret), stm., Eur.	A9	20
Sergeant Bluff, Ia., U.S.	I11	118
Sergeja Kirova, ostrova, is., Russia	B15	26
Sergejevka, Russia	I18	28
Sergijev Posad, Russia	E21	22
Seria, Bru.	E5	38
Serian, Malay.	N11	40
Sérifos, i., Grc.	L8	20
Sérigny, stm., P.Q., Can.	E19	96
Şerkhe, Cerro, mtn., Bol.	G7	82
Šerlovaja Gora, Russia	G15	28
Sermata, Pulau, i., Indon.	G8	38
Serodino, Arg.	G8	80
Serov, Russia	F10	26
Serowe, Bots.	D8	66
Serpa, Port.	H4	16
Serpent, Rivière au, stm., P.Q., Can.	C2	106
Serpents Mouth, strt.	C12	84
Serpuchov, Russia	G20	22
Serra, Braz.	F8	79
Serra de Outes, Spain	C3	16
Serra do Navio, Braz.	C8	76
Serra do Salitre, Braz.	E5	79
Sérrai, Grc.	H7	20
Serrana, Braz.	F5	79
Serrânia, Braz.	F5	79
Serranópolis, Braz.	E2	79
Serra Talhada, Braz.	E11	76
Serrezuela, Arg.	F6	80
Serrinha, Braz.	F11	76
Serro, Braz.	E7	79
Sersale, Italy	J11	18
Sertânia, Braz.	E11	76
Seruini, stm., Braz.	C8	82
Serule, Bots.	C8	66
Sêrxü, China	E6	30
Sesfontein, Nmb.	B1	66
Sesheke, Zam.	E4	58
Seskar, ostrov, i., Russia	A11	22
Sessa Aurunca, Italy	H8	18
Sestao, Spain	B8	16
Sestri Levante, Italy	E4	18
Şestroreck, Russia	A12	22
Šešupe, stm., Eur.	G5	22
Setana, Japan	e14	36a
Sète, Fr.	I10	14
Sete Barras, Braz.	C15	80
Sete de Setembro, stm., Braz.	B2	79
Sete Lagoas, Braz.	E6	79

Name	Map Ref.	Page

Name | Map Ref. | Page

Sparta, Il., U.S. D7 114
Sparta, Ky., U.S. D12 114
Sparta, Mi., U.S. G10 110
Sparta, N.C., U.S. C5 112
Sparta, N.J., U.S. F12 108
Sparta, Tn., U.S. G11 114
Sparta, Wi., U.S. G5 110
Spartanburg, S.C., U.S. E5 112
Spárti (Sparta), Grc. L6 20
Spartivento, Capo, c., Italy K3 18
Spartivento, Capo, c., Italy L11 18
Spas-Demensk, Russia G17 22
Spas-Klepiki, Russia F23 22
Spassk-Dal'nij, Russia I18 28
Spátha, Ákra, c., Grc. N7 20
Spear, Cape, c., Nf., Can. E21 106
Spearfish, S.D., U.S. G4 118
Spearman, Tx., U.S. C5 116
Spearville, Ks., U.S. N8 118
Spectrum Range, mts., B.C., Can. H29 100
Spednic Lake, l., N.A. G6 106
Speedway, In., U.S. C10 114
Speightstown, Barb. H15 94
Spello, Italy G7 18
Spenard, Ak., U.S. F20 100
Spence Bay, N.T., Can. C14 96
Spencer, Ia., U.S. H12 118
Spencer, In., U.S. C10 114
Spencer, Ma., U.S. E15 108
Spencer, N.C., U.S. D6 112
Spencer, Ne., U.S. I9 118
Spencer, S.D., U.S. H10 118
Spencer, Tn., U.S. G11 114
Spencer, Wi., U.S. F5 110
Spencer, W.V., U.S. I5 108
Spencer, Cape, c., Austl. J2 70
Spencer, Cape, c., N.B., Can. G8 106
Spencer Gulf, b., Austl. J2 70
Spencerville, Oh., U.S. G2 108
Spences Bridge, B.C., Can. G13 102
Spenser Mountains, mts., N.Z. E4 72
Sperryville, Va., U.S. I8 108
Speyer, Ger. F8 10
Speyside, Trin. I14 94
Spezia see La Spezia, Italy E4 18
Spicer, Mn., U.S. F13 118
Spickard, Mo., U.S. B3 114
Spiez, Switz. E8 13
Spijkenisse, Neth. F5 12
Spillimacheen, stm., B.C., Can. F18 102
Spillville, Ia., U.S. G4 110
Spinazzola, Italy I11 18
Spincourt, Fr. C12 14
Spindale, N.C., U.S. D5 112
Spirit Lake, Ia., U.S. H12 118
Spirit Lake, Id., U.S. C9 122
Spirit River, Ab., Can. B16 102
Spiritwood, Sk., Can. E7 104
Spiro, Ok., U.S. G2 114
Spirovo, Russia D17 22
Spišská Nová Ves, Slvk. G20 10
Spitsbergen, i., Nor. B2 24
Spittal an der Drau, Aus. I13 10
Spitz, Aus. G15 10
Split, Cro. F11 18
Split, Cape, c., N.S., Can. G9 106
Split Lake, l., Mb., Can. B18 104
Spluga, Passo della (Splügenpass), Eur. E11 13
Splügen, Switz. E11 13
Spofford, Tx., U.S. J6 116
Špogi, Lat. E9 22
Spokane, Wa., U.S. C8 122
Spokane, stm., U.S. C7 122
Spoleto, Italy G7 18
Spoon, stm., Il., U.S. B6 114
Spooner, Wi., U.S. E4 110
Spornoje, Russia E22 28
Spotsylvania, Va., U.S. I9 108
Sprague, Mb., Can. I19 104
Sprague, Wa., U.S. C8 122
Sprague, stm., Or., U.S. H4 122
Spratly Islands, is., Asia D5 38
Spray, Or., U.S. F6 122
Spray Lakes Reservoir, res., Ab., Can. G19 102
Spremberg, Ger. D14 10
Spring, stm., Ar., U.S. F5 114
Spring, stm., U.S. E3 114
Springbok, S. Afr. G3 66
Spring City, Tn., U.S. D2 112
Spring City, Ut., U.S. E5 120
Springdale, Ar., U.S. F2 114
Springdale, Nf., Can. C17 106
Springdale, S.C., U.S. F5 112
Springdale, Ut., U.S. G4 120
Springdale, Wa., U.S. B8 122
Spring Dale, W.V., U.S. B6 112
Springe, Ger. C9 10
Springer, N.M., U.S. C2 116
Springerville, Az., U.S. J7 120
Springfield, Co., U.S. N5 118
Springfield, Fl., U.S. L11 114
Springfield, Ga., U.S. G5 112
Springfield, Il., U.S. C7 114
Springfield, Ky., U.S. E11 114
Springfield, Ma., U.S. E14 108
Springfield, Mn., U.S. G13 118
Springfield, Mo., U.S. E3 114
Springfield, N.S., Can. H9 106
Springfield, Oh., U.S. H3 108
Springfield, Or., U.S. F2 122
Springfield, S.C., U.S. F5 112
Springfield, S.D., U.S. I10 118
Springfield, Tn., U.S. F10 114
Springfield, Vt., U.S. D14 108
Springfontein, S. Afr. H7 66
Spring Garden, Guy. D13 84
Spring Glen, Ut., U.S. E6 120
Spring Green, Wi., U.S. G5 110
Spring Grove, Mn., U.S. G4 110
Spring Grove, Pa., U.S. H10 108
Springhill, La., U.S. I3 114
Springhill, N.S., Can. G9 106
Spring Hill, Tn., U.S. G10 114
Spring Hope, N.C., U.S. D8 112
Springhouse, B.C., Can. F12 102
Spring Lake, N.C., U.S. D8 112
Spring Mountains, mts., Nv., U.S. H10 124
Springs, S. Afr. F9 66
Springsure, Austl. E8 70
Springtown, Tx., U.S. G9 116
Springvale, Austl. D4 70
Springvale, Me., U.S. D16 108
Spring Valley, Ca., U.S. L9 124
Spring Valley, Il., U.S. I6 110
Spring Valley, Mn., U.S. G3 110
Spring Valley, N.Y., U.S. F12 108
Spring Valley, Wi., U.S. F3 110
Springview, Ne., U.S. I8 118
Springville, Al., U.S. I10 114
Springville, Ca., U.S. H7 124
Springville, Ia., U.S. H4 110
Springville, N.Y., U.S. E8 108
Springville, Ut., U.S. D5 120
Sproat Lake, l., B.C., Can. H9 102
Spruce, stm., Sk., Can. E9 104
Spruce Brook, Nf., Can. D15 106
Spruce Grove, Ab., Can. D21 102
Spruce Knob, mtn., W.V., U.S. I7 108
Spruce Lake, Sk., Can. E5 104
Spruce Mountain, mtn., Az., U.S. J4 120
Spruce Mountain, mtn., Nv., U.S. D11 124
Spruce Pine, Al., U.S. H9 114
Spruce Pine, N.C., U.S. D4 112
Spruce Woods Provincial Park, Mb., Can. I15 104
Spur, Tx., U.S. F6 116
Spurfield, Ab., Can. B20 102
Spurger, Tx., U.S. L2 114
Spuzzum, B.C., Can. H13 102
Spy Hill, Sk., Can. H13 104
Squally Channel, strt., B.C., Can. D5 102
Squamish, B.C., Can. H11 102
Squamish, stm., B.C., Can. G11 102
Squatec, P.Q., Can. E5 106
Squaw Cap Mountain, mtn., N.B., Can. E7 106
Squaw Peak, mtn., Mt., U.S. C11 122
Squaw Rapids, Sk., Can. E11 104
Squaw Rapids Dam, Sk., Can. E11 104
Squilax, B.C., Can. G15 102
Squinzano, Italy I13 18
Squire, W.V., U.S. B5 112
Srbija (Serbia), state, Yugo. F4 20
Srbobran, Yugo. D3 20
Sredinnyj chrebet, mts., Russia F24 28
Sredna Gora, mts., Bul. G8 20
Sredneje Kujto, ozero, l., Russia I22 6
Srednekolymsk, Russia D22 28
Srednerusskaja vozvyšennost', plat., Russia G5 26
Srednesibirskoje ploskogorje, plat., Russia D13 28
Śrem, Pol. C17 10
Srê Moăt, Camb. H9 40
Sremska Mitrovica, Yugo. E3 20
Sremski Karlovci, Yugo. D3 20
Sretensk, Russia G15 28
Sri Jayawardenepura (Kotte), Sri L. I5 46
Srīkākulam, India C7 46
Sri Kālahasti, India F5 46
Sri Lanka, ctry., Asia H11 42
Srīnagar, India C6 44
Srīrampur, India C3 46
Srīrangam, India G5 46
Srīvilliputtūr, India H4 46
Środa Wielkopolski, Pol. C17 10
Staaten, stm., Austl. C8 68
Staaten River National Park, Austl. C8 68
Stacyville, Ia., U.S. G3 110
Stade, Ger. B9 10
Staden, Bel. G3 12
Stadl-Paura, Aus. G13 10
Stadskanaal, Neth. B10 12
Staffelstein, Ger. E11 10
Stafford, Eng., U.K. I11 8
Stafford, Ks., U.S. N9 118
Stafford, Va., U.S. I9 108
Staffordshire, co., Eng., U.K. I11 8
Stafford Springs, Ct., U.S. F14 108
Staicele, Lat. D7 22
Staines, Eng., U.K. J13 8
Stakhanov, Ukr. H5 26
Stalden, Switz. F8 13
Stalheim, Nor. K10 6
Stalingrad see Volgograd, Russia H6 26
Stalowa Wola, Pol. E22 10
Stambaugh, Mi., U.S. D7 110
Stamford, Austl. C5 70
Stamford, Ct., U.S. F13 108
Stamford, N.Y., U.S. E12 108
Stamford, Tx., U.S. G7 116
Stamford, Lake, res., Tx., U.S. F7 116
Stamps, Ar., U.S. I3 114
Stanaford, W.V., U.S. J5 108
Stanardsville, Va., U.S. I8 108
Stanberry, Mo., U.S. B2 114
Standard, Ab., Can. F22 102
Standard, Ak., U.S. D20 100
Standerton, S. Afr. F9 66
Standish, Mi., U.S. G12 110
Stanfield, Az., U.S. L5 120
Stanfield, Or., U.S. E6 122
Stanford, Ky., U.S. B2 112
Stanford, Mt., U.S. C15 122
Stanhope, Ia., U.S. H2 110
Stanislaus, stm., Ca., U.S. G5 124
Stanley, Falk. Is. G5 78
Stanley, N.B., Can. F7 106
Stanley, N.C., U.S. D5 112
Stanley, N.D., U.S. C5 118
Stanley, Va., U.S. I8 108
Stanley, Wi., U.S. F5 110
Stanley Reservoir, res., India G4 46
Stanleyville see Kisangani, Zaire A5 58
Stanovoj chrebet, mts., Russia F17 28
Stanovoje nagorje (Stanovoy Mountains), mts., Russia F14 28
Stans, Switz. E9 13
Stanthorpe, Austl. G9 70
Stanton, Ia., U.S. J12 118
Stanton, Ky., U.S. B3 112
Stanton, Mi., U.S. G10 110
Stanton, N.D., U.S. D6 118
Stanton, Ne., U.S. J10 118
Stanton, Tn., U.S. G7 114
Stanton, Tx., U.S. G5 116
Stantonsburg, N.C., U.S. D9 112
Stanwood, Wa., U.S. B3 122
Staples, Mn., U.S. E13 118
Stapleton, Al., U.S. L9 114
Stapleton, Ne., U.S. J7 118
Star, Ms., U.S. J6 114
Star, N.C., U.S. D7 112
Stará Boleslav, Czech Rep. E14 10
Starachowice, Pol. D21 10
Staraja Russa, Russia C14 22
Staraja Toropa, Russia E14 22
Staraja Vičuga, Russia D24 22
Stara Pazova, Yugo. E4 20
Stara Planina (Balkan Mountains), mts., Eur. G8 20
Stara Ushytsya, Ukr. A11 20
Stara Zagora, Bul. G9 20
Starbuck, Mb., Can. I17 104
Starbuck, Mn., U.S. F12 118
Starbuck, Wa., U.S. D7 122
Star City, Ar., U.S. I5 114
Star City, In., U.S. B10 114
Star City, Sk., Can. F10 104
Stargard Szczeciński (Stargard in Pommern), Pol. B15 10
Stargo, Az., U.S. K7 120
Starica, Russia E17 22
Stari Popylyukhy, Ukr. A12 20
Starke, Fl., U.S. J4 112
Starkville, Ms., U.S. I8 114
Starnberg, Ger. G11 10
Starnberger See, l., Ger. H11 10
Starobin, Bela. I10 22
Starodub, Russia I15 22
Starogard Gdański, Pol. B18 10
Staroje Sjalo, Bela. F12 22
Staroje Ustje, Russia H24 22
Starokozache, Ukr. C13 20
Staroseslavino, Russia H23 22
Starožilovo, Russia G22 22
Staryja Darohi, Bela. H11 22
Staryj Oskol, Russia G5 26
Staryy Sambir, Ukr. F22 10
Stassfurt, Ger. D11 10
Staszów, Pol. E21 10
State Center, Ia., U.S. H2 110
State College, Pa., U.S. G9 108
State Line, Ms., U.S. K8 114
Stateline, Nv., U.S. F6 124
Statenville, Ga., U.S. I3 112
State Road, N.C., U.S. C6 112
Statesboro, Ga., U.S. G5 112
Statesville, N.C., U.S. D6 112
Staunton, Il., U.S. C7 114
Staunton, Va., U.S. I7 108
Stavanger, Nor. L9 6
Stave Lake, l., B.C., Can. H12 102
Stavely, Ab., Can. G21 102
Stavne, Ukr. G22 10
Stavropol', Russia H6 26
Stawell, Austl. K5 70
Stawell, stm., Austl. C5 70
Stawiszyn, Pol. D18 10
Stayner, On., Can. F15 110
Stayton, Or., U.S. F3 122
Steamboat Mountain, mtn., Wy., U.S. C8 120
Steamboat Springs, Co., U.S. D10 120
Stearns, Ky., U.S. C2 112
Stebbins, Ak., U.S. E13 100
Steckborn, Switz. C10 13
Steele, Mo., U.S. F7 114
Steele, N.D., U.S. E8 118
Steeleville, Il., U.S. D7 114
Steelville, Mo., U.S. E5 114
Steepbank, stm., Ab., Can. B3 104
Steephill Lake, l., Sk., Can. C11 104
Steep Rock, Mb., Can. G16 104
Stefanie, Lake see Chew Bahir, l., Afr. H8 56
Stefansson Island, i., N.T., Can. B11 96
Steffisburg, Switz. E8 13
Steiermark, state, Aus. H15 10
Stein, Switz. C8 13
Steinach, Aus. H11 10
Steinbach, Mb., Can. I18 104
Steinhausen, Nmb. C4 66
Steinkjer, Nor. I12 6
Steksovo, Russia F26 22
Stella, Ne., U.S. K12 118
Stellaquo Indian Reserve, B.C., Can. C10 102
Stellarton, N.S., Can. G11 106
Stellenbosch, S. Afr. I4 66
Stenay, Fr. C12 14
Stendal, Ger. C11 10
Stende, Lat. D5 22
Stephen, Mn., U.S. C11 118
Stephens, Ar., U.S. I3 114
Stephens, Port, b., Austl. I10 70
Stephens City, Va., U.S. H8 108
Stephens Island, i., B.C., Can. C4 102
Stephens Lake, res., Mb., Can. B19 104
Stephenson, Mi., U.S. E8 110
Stephenville, Nf., Can. D15 106
Stephenville, Tx., U.S. G8 116
Stephenville Crossing, Nf., Can. D15 106
Stepn'ak, Kaz. G12 26
Stereá Ellás, prov., Grc. K7 20
Sterkstroom, S. Afr. H8 66
Sterling, Ak., U.S. F19 100
Sterling, Co., U.S. K4 118
Sterling, Il., U.S. I6 110
Sterling, Ks., U.S. M9 118
Sterling, Mi., U.S. F11 110
Sterling, Ne., U.S. K11 118
Sterling, Ok., U.S. E8 116
Sterling City, Tx., U.S. H6 116
Sterlington, La., U.S. J4 114
Sterlitamak, Russia G9 26
Stettin see Szczecin, Pol. B14 10
Stettler, Ab., Can. E22 102
Steubenville, Oh., U.S. G6 108
Stevenson, Al., U.S. H11 114
Stevenson, Wa., U.S. E4 122
Stevenson Lake, l., Mb., Can. E18 104
Stevens Pass, Wa., U.S. C4 122
Stevens Point, Wi., U.S. F6 110
Stevens Village, Ak., U.S. C20 100
Stevensville, Mi., U.S. H9 110
Stevensville, Mt., U.S. D11 122
Stewardson, Il., U.S. C8 114
Stewart, B.C., Can. B5 102
Stewart, Mn., U.S. F1 110
Stewart, stm., Yk., Can. E25 100
Stewart Island, i., N.Z. G1 72
Stewarton, Scot., U.K. F9 8
Stewartstown, Pa., U.S. H10 108
Stewartsville, Mo., U.S. C2 114
Stewart Valley, Sk., Can. H7 104
Stewartville, Mn., U.S. G3 110
Stewiacke, N.S., Can. G10 106
Steynsburg, S. Afr. H7 66
Steyr, Aus. G14 10
Steytlerville, S. Afr. I7 66
Stickney, S.D., U.S. H9 118
Stif, Alg. B13 62
Stigler, Ok., U.S. D11 116
Stikine, stm., N.A. H29 100
Stikine Ranges, mts., B.C., Can. G29 100
Stilbaai, S. Afr. J5 66
Stilfontein, S. Afr. F8 66
Stilís, Grc. K6 20
Still, Alg. C13 62
Stillhouse Hollow Lake, res., Tx., U.S. H9 116
Stillmore, Ga., U.S. G4 112
Stillwater, B.C., Can. H10 102
Stillwater, Mn., U.S. E3 110
Stillwater, Ok., U.S. C9 116
Stillwater, stm., Mt., U.S. E16 122
Stillwell, Ok., U.S. G2 114
Stimson, Mount, mtn., Mt., U.S. B12 122
Stînca-Costești, Lacul, res., Eur. B11 20
Stinking Water Creek, stm., Ne., U.S. K6 118
Stinnett, Tx., U.S. D5 116
Štip, Mac. H6 20
Stirling, Ab., Can. H22 102
Stirling, On., Can. F18 110
Stirling, Scot., U.K. E10 8
Stirling City, Ca., U.S. E4 124
Stirrat, W.V., U.S. B4 112
Stittsville, On., Can. E20 110
Stockach, Ger. H9 10
Stöckalp, Switz. E9 13
Stockbridge, Ga., U.S. F2 112
Stockbridge, Mi., U.S. H11 110
Stockdale, Tx., U.S. J9 116
Stockerau, Aus. G16 10
Stockett, Mt., U.S. C14 122
Stockholm, Swe. L16 6
Stockton, Al., U.S. L9 114
Stockton, Ca., U.S. G4 124
Stockton, Il., U.S. H5 110
Stockton, Ks., U.S. L8 118
Stockton, Mo., U.S. E3 114
Stockton, Ut., U.S. D4 120
Stockton [-on-Tees], Eng., U.K. G12 8
Stockton Plateau, plat., Tx., U.S. I4 116
Stockton Reservoir, res., Mo., U.S. E3 114
Stockton Springs, Me., U.S. C18 108
Stockville, Ne., U.S. K7 118
Stodolišče, Russia G15 22
Stœng Tréng, Camb. H8 40
Stoke-on-Trent, Eng., U.K. H11 8
Stolac, Bos. F12 18
Stolberg, Ger. E6 10
Stolbovoj, ostrov, i., Russia C19 28
Stolp see Słupsk, Pol. A17 10
Stoneboro, Pa., U.S. F6 108
Stonefort, Il., U.S. E8 114
Stone Harbor, N.J., U.S. H12 108
Stonehenge, Austl. E5 70
Stone Indian Reserve, B.C., Can. F11 102
Stone Mountain, Ga., U.S. F2 112
Stoner, B.C., Can. D12 102
Stoneville, N.C., U.S. C7 112
Stonewall, La., U.S. J3 114
Stonewall, Mb., Can. H17 104
Stonewall, Ms., U.S. J8 114
Stonewall, Ok., U.S. E10 116
Stoney Creek, On., Can. G16 110
Stonington, Il., U.S. C7 114
Stonington, Me., U.S. C18 108
Stony, stm., Mn., U.S. C4 110
Stony Creek Indian Reserve, B.C., Can. D10 102
Stony Indian Reserve, Ab., Can. F20 102
Stony Lake, l., Mb., Can. E13 96
Stony Plain, Ab., Can. D20 102
Stony Plain Indian Reserve, Ab., Can. D21 102
Stony Point, Mi., U.S. I12 110
Stony Point, N.C., U.S. D5 112
Stony Rapids, Sk., Can. E11 96
Storby, Fin. K16 6
Storkerson Bay, b., N.T., Can. B8 96
Storkerson Peninsula, pen., N.T., Can. B11 96
Storlien, Swe. J13 6
Storm Bay, b., Austl. N7 70
Storm Lake, Ia., U.S. I12 118
Stormsrivier, S. Afr. I6 66
Stornoway, Scot., U.K. C7 8
Storozhynets', Ukr. A9 20
Storrs, Ct., U.S. F14 108
Storthoaks, Sk., Can. I13 104
Storuman, Swe. I15 6
Story, Wy., U.S. F19 122
Story City, Ia., U.S. H2 110
Stoubcy, Bela. H9 22
Stoughton, Ma., U.S. E15 108
Stoughton, Sk., Can. I11 104
Stoughton, Wi., U.S. H6 110
Stout Lake, l., On., Can. F20 104
Stover, Mo., U.S. D4 114
Stow, Oh., U.S. F5 108
Stowe, Vt., U.S. C14 108
Stowell, Tx., U.S. M2 114
Stoyoma Mountain, mtn., B.C., Can. H13 102
Stradella, Italy D4 18
Stradzečy, Bela. J6 22
Strahan, Austl. N6 70
Strakonice, Czech Rep. F13 10
Stralsund, Ger. A13 10
Strand, S. Afr. J4 66
Strangford Lough, l., N. Ire., U.K. G8 8
Stranraer, Scot., U.K. G8 8
Strasbourg, Fr. D14 14
Strasbourg, Sk., Can. G10 104
Strasburg, Co., U.S. L3 118
Strasburg, N.D., U.S. E7 118
Strasburg, Oh., U.S. G5 108
Strasburg, Pa., U.S. H10 108
Strasburg, Va., U.S. I8 108
Stratford, Ca., U.S. H6 124
Stratford, Ct., U.S. F13 108
Stratford, Ia., U.S. H2 110
Stratford, N.Z. C5 72
Stratford, Ok., U.S. E10 116
Stratford, On., Can. G15 110
Stratford, Tx., U.S. C4 116
Stratford, Wi., U.S. F5 110
Stratford-upon-Avon, Eng., U.K. I12 8
Strathalbyn, Austl. J3 70
Strathclair, Mb., Can. H14 104
Strathclyde, prov., Scot., U.K. F8 8
Strathcona Provincial Park, B.C., Can. H9 102
Strathlorne, N.S., Can. F12 106
Strathmore, Ab., Can. F21 102
Strathmore, Ca., U.S. H6 124
Strathroy, On., Can. H14 110
Stratton, Co., U.S. L5 118
Stratton, Me., U.S. B16 108
Stratton, Ne., U.S. K6 118
Straubing, Ger. G12 10
Strausberg, Ger. C13 10
Strawberry, stm., Ar., U.S. F5 114
Strawberry, stm., Ut., U.S. D6 120
Strawberry Mountain, mtn., Or., U.S. F7 122
Strawberry Point, Ia., U.S. H4 110
Strawn, Tx., U.S. G8 116
Streatham, B.C., Can. D8 102
Streator, Il., U.S. I7 110
Streeter, N.D., U.S. E8 118
Streetman, Tx., U.S. H10 116
Streetsboro, Oh., U.S. F5 108
Streetsville, On., Can. G16 110
Strel'na, Russia B13 22
Strenči, Lat. D8 22
Stresa, Italy D3 18
Strèšyn, Bela. I13 22
Streymoy, i., Faer. Is. D8 6b
Strickland, stm., Pap. N. Gui. m15 68a
Strimón (Struma), stm., Eur. I7 20
Strobel, Arg. G8 80
Strogonof Point, c., Ak., U.S. H15 100
Stromboli, Isola, i., Italy K10 18
Strome, Ab., Can. E22 102
Stromeferry, Scot., U.K. D8 8
Stromness, Scot., U.K. C10 8
Stromsburg, Ne., U.S. J10 118
Strömsund, Swe. J14 6
Strong, Ar., U.S. I4 114
Strong, stm., Ms., U.S. J7 114
Strong City, Ks., U.S. M11 118
Stronghurst, Il., U.S. J5 110
Stroud, Austl. I9 70
Stroud, Ok., U.S. D10 116
Stroudsburg, Pa., U.S. G11 108
Struer, Den. M11 6
Struga, Mac. H4 20
Strugi-Krasnyje, Russia C12 22
Strum, Wi., U.S. F4 110
Struma (Strimón), stm., Eur. H7 20
Strumica, Mac. H6 20
Strunino, Russia E21 22
Struthers, Oh., U.S. F6 108
Stryker, Oh., U.S. F2 108
Stryy, Ukr. H2 26
Strzegom, Pol. E16 10
Strzelce Opolskie, Pol. E18 10
Strzelecki Creek, stm., Austl. G4 70
Strzelecki Desert, des., Austl. F4 70
Strzelin, Pol. E17 10
Stuart, Fl., U.S. L6 112
Stuart, Ia., U.S. J13 118
Stuart, Ne., U.S. I8 118
Stuart, Va., U.S. C6 112
Stuart, stm., B.C., Can. C10 102
Stuart Lake, l., B.C., Can. C10 102
Stuarts Draft, Va., U.S. A7 112
Studen Kladenec, Jazovir, res., Bul. H9 20
Stuie, B.C., Can. E8 102
Stull, stm., Can. D22 104
Stull Lake, l., Can. D22 104
Stupart, stm., Mb., Can. C21 104
Stupino, Russia G21 22
Sturgeon, Mo., U.S. C4 114
Sturgeon, stm., Mi., U.S. E11 110
Sturgeon, stm., Sk., Can. E8 104
Sturgeon Bay, Wi., U.S. F8 110
Sturgeon Bay, b., Mb., Can. F17 104
Sturgeon Falls, On., Can. D16 110
Sturgeon Lake, l., Ab., Can. B17 102
Sturgeon Lake, l., On., Can. C24 104
Sturgeon Lake Indian Reserve, Ab., Can. B17 102
Sturgeon Lake Indian Reserve, Sk., Can. E8 104
Sturgeon Landing, Sk., Can. D13 104
Sturgis, Ky., U.S. E9 114
Sturgis, Mi., U.S. I10 110
Sturgis, Ms., U.S. I7 114
Sturgis, S.D., U.S. G4 118
Sturgis, Sk., Can. G12 104
Sturtevant, Wi., U.S. H8 110
Sturt National Park, Austl. G4 70
Sturt Stony Desert, des., Austl. G4 70
Stutterheim, S. Afr. I8 66
Stuttgart, Ar., U.S. H5 114
Stuttgart, Ger. G9 10
Stykkishólmur, Ice. B2 6a
Styx, stm., Al., U.S. L9 114
Šu, Kaz. I12 26
Suaçuí Grande, stm., Braz. E7 79
Suaita, Col. D6 84
Suakin Archipelago, is., Sudan H10 60
Su'ao, China J8 34
Suapure, stm., Ven. D9 84
Suaqui Grande, Mex. C5 90
Subačius, Lith. F7 22
Subansiri, stm., Asia F16 44
Subarnarekha, stm., India I12 44
Subate, Lat. E8 22
Subiaco, Italy H8 18
Sublette, Ks., U.S. N7 118
Subotica, Yugo. C3 20
Suca, Eth. N10 60
Sucarnoochee, stm., U.S. J8 114
Suceava, Rom. B10 20
Suceava, co., Rom. B9 20
Sucha [Beskidzka], Pol. F19 10
Süchbaatar, Mong. A8 30
Suchiapa, stm., Mex. I13 90
Súchil, Mex. F8 90
Suchiniči, Russia G18 22
Suchitepéquez, dept., Guat. C3 92
Suchitoto, El Sal. D5 92
Suchodol'skij, Russia H21 22
Suchona, stm., Russia E6 26
Suchotinka, Russia I24 22
Suchou see Suzhou, China E11 30
Suchoverkovo, Russia E18 22
Suchumi, Geor. I6 26
Sucio, stm., Col. D4 84
Sucker Creek Indian Reserve, Ab., Can. B18 102
Sucre, Bol. H9 82
Sucre, Col. C5 84
Sucre, Ec. H2 84
Sucre, state, Ven. B11 84
Sucre, dept., Col. C5 84
Sucúa, Ec. I3 84
Sucuaro, Col. E8 84
Sucunduri, stm., Braz. B12 82
Sucuriú, stm., Braz. F3 79
Sud, Canal du, strt., Haiti E8 94
Suda, Russia B20 22
Sudan, Tx., U.S. E4 116
Sudan (As-Sūdān), ctry., Afr. E7 56
Sudan, reg., Afr. F9 54
Sudañez, Bol. H9 82
Sudbury, On., Can. D14 110
Suddie, Guy. D13 84
Sudeten see Sudety, mts., Eur. E16 10
Sudety, mts., Eur. E16 10
Sudislavl', Russia D24 22
Sudogda, Russia F23 22
Süd-Orkney-Inseln, is., S. Geor. B1 73
Sud-Ouest, Pointe du, c., P.Q., Can. C10 106
Südpol, Ant. D4 73
Süd-Shetland-Inseln, is., S. Geor. B1 73
Suđuroy, i., Faer. Is. E8 6b
Sue, stm., Sudan N5 60
Sueca, Spain F11 16
Suez see As-Suways, Egypt C7 60
Suez, Gulf of see Suways, Khalīj as-, b., Egypt C7 60
Suez Canal see Suways, Qanāt as-, Egypt C7 60
Şufaynah, Sau. Ar. C2 47
Suffield, Ab., Can. H3 104
Suffield, Canadian Forces Base, mil., Ab., Can. H3 104
Suffolk, Va., U.S. C10 112
Suffolk, co., Eng., U.K. I15 8
Sufu see Kashi, China D2 30
Sugar, stm., N.H., U.S. D14 108
Sugar, stm., U.S. H6 110
Sugar City, Id., U.S. G14 122
Sugarcreek, Pa., U.S. F7 108
Sugar Grove, Va., U.S. C5 112
Sugar Hill, Ga., U.S. E2 112
Sugar Island, i., Mi., U.S. D11 110
Sugar Land, Tx., U.S. J11 116
Sugarloaf Mountain, mtn., Me., U.S. B16 108
Sugarloaf Point, c., Austl. I10 70
Suggi Lake, l., Sk., Can. D12 104
Sugoj, stm., Russia E23 28
Şuḩār, Oman B10 47
Suhl, Ger. E10 10
Suhr, Switz. D9 13
Suiá-Miçu, stm., Braz. A2 79
Suichuan, China I3 34
Suide, China D9 30
Suifenhe, China C13 30
Suihua, China B12 30
Suining, China E8 30
Suipacha, Arg. H9 80
Suiping, China B2 34
Suippes, Fr. C11 14
Suixian, China D2 34
Suiyangdian, China C1 34
Suizhong, China C8 32
Šuja, Russia K24 6
Šuja, Russia E24 22
Sujāngarh, India G6 44
Sujiatun, China B11 32
Sukabumi, Indon. j13 39a
Sukagawa, Japan J15 36
Sukch'ŏn, N. Kor. D13 32
Sukhothai, Thai. F5 40
Sukkozero, Russia E4 26
Sukkur, Pak. G3 44
Sukumo, Japan O7 36
Sukunka, stm., B.C., Can. B13 102
Sul, Baía, b., Braz. D14 80
Sul, Canal do, strt., Braz. D9 76
Sula, Kepulauan, is., Indon. F8 38
Sulaco, stm., Hond. B7 92
Sulaimān Range, mts., Pak. F3 44
Sulawesi (Celebes), i., Indon. F7 38
Sulaymān, Birak (Solomon's Pools), hist., W.B. E4 50
Sulechów, Pol. C15 10
Sulejówek, Pol. C21 10
Sulima, S.L. H4 64
Sulingen, Ger. C8 10
Sulitelma, mtn., Eur. H15 6
Sullana, Peru A1 82
Sulligent, Al., U.S. I8 114
Sullivan, Il., U.S. C8 114
Sullivan, In., U.S. C9 114
Sullivan, Mo., U.S. D5 114
Sullivan Lake, l., Ab., Can. E23 102
Sully, Fr. E9 14
Sulmona, Italy G8 18
Sulphur, La., U.S. L3 114
Sulphur, Ok., U.S. E10 116
Sulphur, Yk., Can. E25 100
Sulphur, stm., Ab., Can. D16 102
Sulphur, stm., U.S. I2 114
Sulphur Springs, Tx., U.S. F11 116
Sulphur Springs Valley, val., Az., U.S. M7 120
Sultan, Wa., U.S. C4 122
Sultānpur, India G10 44
Sulu Archipelago, is., Phil. D7 38
Sululta, Eth. M10 60
Sulūq, Libya B5 56
Sulu Sea, Asia D6 38
Sulzbach-Rosenberg, Ger. F11 10
Sumampa, Arg. E7 80
Sumas, Wa., U.S. A3 122
Sumatera (Sumatra), i., Indon. F3 38
Sumatra see Sumatera, i., Indon. F3 38
Sumayḩ, Sudan K6 60
Sumba, Faer. Is. E8 6b
Sumba, i., Indon. G7 38
Sumbawa, i., Indon. G6 38
Sumbawa Besar, Indon. G6 38
Sumbawanga, Tan. C6 58
Sumbay, Peru F6 82
Sumbe, Ang. D2 58
Sümber, Mong. B8 30
Sumbilla, Spain B10 16
Sumbuya, S.L. H4 64
Sümeg, Hung. I17 10
Šumen, Bul. F10 20
Sumenep, Indon. j16 39a
Šumerl'a, Russia F7 26
Šumicha, Russia F10 26
Šumilina, Bela. F12 22
Sumisu-jima, i., Japan E15 30
Sumiswald, Switz. D8 13
Summerfield, Fl., U.S. J4 112
Summerfield, N.C., U.S. C7 112
Summerford, Nf., Can. C19 106
Summerland, B.C., Can. H15 102
Summerside, P.E., Can. F10 106
Summersville, Mo., U.S. E5 114
Summersville, W.V., U.S. I6 108
Summerton, S.C., U.S. F6 112
Summertown, Tn., U.S. G9 114
Summerville, Ga., U.S. E1 112
Summerville, S.C., U.S. F6 112
Summit, Ms., U.S. K6 114
Summit, S.D., U.S. F10 118
Summit Lake, B.C., Can. C12 102
Summit Mountain, mtn., Nv., U.S. E9 124
Summit Peak, mtn., Co., U.S. G10 120
Sumner, Ia., U.S. H3 110
Sumner, Ms., U.S. I6 114
Sumner, Wa., U.S. C3 122
Sumoto, Japan M9 36
Šumperk, Czech Rep. F16 10
Sumprabum, Myan. A4 40
Sumqayıt, Azer. I7 26
Sumrall, Ms., U.S. K7 114
Šumšu, ostrov, i., Russia G23 28
Sumter, S.C., U.S. F6 112
Sumy, Ukr. G4 26
Sumzom, China F17 44
Sun, stm., Mt., U.S. C13 122
Suna, stm., Russia J23 6
Sunan, N. Kor. D13 32
Sunbright, Tn., U.S. C2 112
Sunburst, Mt., U.S. B14 122
Sunbury, Austl. K6 70
Sunbury, N.C., U.S. C10 112
Sunbury, Oh., U.S. G4 108
Sunbury, Pa., U.S. G10 108
Sunchales, Arg. F8 80
Sunch'ang, S. Kor. H15 32
Sunchild Indian Reserve, Ab., Can. E19 102
Suncho Corral, Arg. D7 80
Sunch'ŏn, N. Kor. D13 32
Sunch'ŏn, S. Kor. I15 32
Sun City, Az., U.S. K4 120
Suncook, N.H., U.S. D15 108
Suncook, stm., N.H., U.S. D15 108
Sunda, Selat, strt., Indon. G4 38
Sundance, Wy., U.S. G3 118
Sundarbans, reg., Asia J13 44
Sunda Strait see Sunda, Selat, strt., Indon. G4 38
Sundown, Tx., U.S. F4 116
Sundre, Ab., Can. F20 102

Name	Map Ref.	Page
Sundridge, On., Can.	E16	110
Sundsvall, Swe.	J15	6
Sunflower, Ms., U.S.	I6	114
Sunflower, Mount, mtn., Ks., U.S.	L5	118
Sungaipenuh, Indon.	F3	38
Sungai Petani, Malay.	L6	40
Sunjiabu, China	E7	34
Sunjikāy, Sudan	K5	60
Sunland Park, N.M., U.S.	L10	120
Sunnybrae, N.S., Can.	G11	106
Sunnynook, Ab., Can.	F23	102
Sunnyside, Nf., Can.	E20	106
Sunnyside, Ut., U.S.	E6	120
Sunnyside, Wa., U.S.	D5	122
Sunnyslope, Ab., Can.	F21	102
Sunnyvale, Ca., U.S.	G3	124
Sun Prairie, Wi., U.S.	G6	110
Sunray, Tx., U.S.	C5	116
Sunrise, Wy., U.S.	B12	120
Sunrise Manor, Nv., U.S.	H10	124
Sunset, La., U.S.	L4	114
Sunset, Tx., U.S.	F9	116
Sunset Country, reg., Austl.	J4	70
Sunset Heights, Tx., U.S.	H4	116
Sunset Prairie, B.C., Can.	B14	102
Sunshine, Austl.	K6	70
Suntrana, Ak., U.S.	E20	100
Suntu, Eth.	M9	60
Sun Valley, Id., U.S.	G11	122
Sunwapta, stm., Ab., Can.	E17	102
Sunyani, Ghana	H8	64
Sunzom, China	F6	30
Suojarvi, Russia	J23	6
Suonenjoki, Fin.	J20	6
Supachuy, Bol.	H9	82
Supamo, stm., Ven.	D11	84
Supe, Eth.	M8	60
Superior, Az., U.S.	K5	120
Superior, Mt., U.S.	C11	122
Superior, Ne., U.S.	K9	118
Superior, Wi., U.S.	D3	110
Superior, Laguna, b., Mex.	I12	90
Superior, Lake, l., N.A.	C8	110
Suphan Buri, Thai.	G6	40
Suponevo, Russia	H17	22
Sup'ung-chŏsuji, res., Asia	C13	32
Sūq ash-Shuyūkh, Iraq	F9	48
Suq'at al-Jamal, Sudan	K4	60
Suqian, China	B7	34
Sūq Suwayq, Sau. Ar.	I5	48
Suquṭrā (Socotra), i., Yemen	G5	42
Ṣūr (Tyre), Leb.	B4	50
Ṣūr, Oman	C11	47
Sura, stm., Russia	G7	26
Surabaya, Indon.	j16	39a
Surakarta, Indon.	j15	39a
Sūrat, India	J5	44
Surat Thani (Ban Don), Thai.	J5	40
Suraž, Bela.	F13	22
Suraž, Russia	H15	22
Surdulica, Yugo.	G6	20
Sûre (Sauer), stm., Eur.	I9	12
Surendranagar, India	I4	44
Suretka, C.R.	H12	92
Surf City, N.J., U.S.	H12	108
Surfers Paradise, Austl.	G10	70
Surgoinsville, Tn., U.S.	C4	112
Surgut, Russia	E6	28
Suriāpet, India	D5	46
Surigao, Phil.	D8	38
Surin, Thai.	G7	40
Suriname, ctry., S.A.	C7	76
Suring, Wi., U.S.	F7	110
Sūrmaq, Iran	F12	48
Surprise, Az., U.S.	K4	120
Surprise Valley, val., U.S.	C5	124
Surrency, Ga., U.S.	H4	112
Surrey, N.D., U.S.	C6	118
Surrey, co., Eng., U.K.	J13	8
Surry, Va., U.S.	B10	112
Sursee, Switz.	D9	13
Surt, Libya	B4	56
Surt, Khalīj, b., Libya	B4	56
Surtsey, i., Ice.	C3	6a
Sürüç, Tur.	C5	48
Surumu, stm., Braz.	F12	84
Susa, Italy	D2	18
Susaki, Japan	N8	36
Susanino, Russia	C24	22
Susanville, Ca., U.S.	D5	124
Ṣusch, Switz.	E13	13
Šušenskoje, Russia	G16	26
Sušice, Czech Rep.	F13	10
Susitna, Ak., U.S.	F19	100
Susitna, stm., Ak., U.S.	E19	100
Susoh, Indon.	M4	40
Susquehanna, Pa., U.S.	F11	108
Susquehanna, stm., U.S.	H10	108
Susques, Arg.	B5	80
Sussex, N.B., Can.	G8	106
Sussex, N.J., U.S.	F12	108
Sussex, Va., U.S.	C9	112
Susuman, Russia	E21	28
Susurluk, Tur.	J12	20
Susuzmüsellim, Tur.	H11	20
Sutherland, Ia., U.S.	I12	118
Sutherland, Ne., U.S.	J6	118
Sutherland, S. Afr.	I5	66
Sutherland, stm., B.C., Can.	C9	102
Sutherlin, Or., U.S.	G2	122
Sutlej (Satluj) (Langqên), stm., Asia	F4	44
Sutter, Ca., U.S.	E4	124
Sutter Creek, Ca., U.S.	F5	124
Sutton, Ak., U.S.	F20	100
Sutton, Ne., U.S.	K10	118
Sutton, W.V., U.S.	I6	108
Sutton in Ashfield, Eng., U.K.	H12	8
Suttons Bay, Mi., U.S.	F10	110
Sutton West, On., Can.	F16	110
Suttor, stm., Austl.	C7	70
Suurbraak, S. Afr.	J5	66
Suure-Jaani, Est.	C8	22
Suva, Fiji	J21	126
Suvainiškis, Lith.	E8	22
Suvorov, Russia	G19	22
Suvorove, Ukr.	D12	20
Suwa, Erit.	G2	47
Suwa, Japan	K13	36
Suwałki, Pol.	A22	10
Suwannee, stm., U.S.	J3	112
Suwannee Lake, l., Mb., Can.	B14	104
Suwanose-jima, i., Japan	r4	37b
Ṣuwaylih, Jord.	D5	50
Suways, Khalīj as- (Gulf of Suez), b., Egypt	C7	60
Suways, Qanāt as- (Suez Canal), Egypt	C7	60
Suwŏn, S. Kor.	F15	32
Suxi, China	F9	34
Suxian, China	B5	34
Suyo, Peru	J2	84
Suzak, Kaz.	I11	26
Suzdal', Russia	E23	22
Suzhou (Soochow), China	D9	34
Suzigou, China	C11	32
Suzuka, Japan	M11	36
Svalbard, is., Nor.	B2	24
Svalyava, Ukr.	A6	20
Svappavaara, Swe.	H17	6
Svataj, Russia	D22	28
Sv'atoj Nos, mys, c., Russia	G26	6
Sv'atoj Nos, mys, c., Russia	C20	28
Svay Riĕng, Camb.	I8	40
Svėdasai, Lith.	F8	22
Svelgen, Nor.	K9	6
Svelvik, Nor.	L12	6
Ṣven', Russia	H17	22
Švenčionėliai, Lith.	F9	22
Švenčionys, Lith.	F9	22
Sverdlovsk see Jekaterinburg, Russia	F10	26
Sverdlovs'k, Ukr.	H5	26
Sverdrup, ostrov, i., Russia	C13	26
Svetlahorsk, Bela.	I12	22
Svetlogorsk, Russia	G3	22
Svetlograd, Russia	H6	26
Svetlyj, Russia	G3	22
Svetogorsk, Russia	K21	6
Svilajnac, Yugo.	E5	20
Svilengrad, Bul.	H10	20
Svindal, Nor.	L10	6
Svir, Bela.	G9	22
Svir', stm., Russia	A16	22
Svirica, Russia	A15	22
Svirsk, Russia	G12	28
Svir'stroj, Russia	A16	22
Svislač, Bela.	H7	22
Svištov, Bul.	F9	20
Svobodnyj, Russia	G17	28
Svolvær, Nor.	G14	6
Swain Reefs, rf., Austl.	C10	70
Swainsboro, Ga., U.S.	G4	112
Swakop, stm., Nmb.	D2	66
Swakopmund, Nmb.	D2	66
Swan, stm., Ab., Can.	B19	102
Swan, stm., Can.	F14	104
Swan, stm., Mn., U.S.	C2	110
Swan, stm., Mt., U.S.	C12	122
Swanee see Suwannee, stm., U.S.	J3	112
Swan Hill, Austl.	J5	70
Swan Hills, Ab., Can.	C19	102
Swan Hills, hills, Ab., Can.	C19	102
Swan Islands see Santanilla, Islas, is., Hond.	F3	94
Swan Lake, Mb., Can.	I16	104
Swan Lake, Mt., U.S.	C12	122
Swan Lake, l., Mb., Can.	F14	104
Swan Lake, l., On., Can.	D23	104
Swannanoa, N.C., U.S.	D4	112
Swanquarter, N.C., U.S.	D10	112
Swan Range, mts., Mt., U.S.	C12	122
Swan River, Mb., Can.	F13	104
Swansboro, N.C., U.S.	E9	112
Swansea, Austl.	N8	70
Swansea, S.C., U.S.	F5	112
Swansea, Wales, U.K.	J10	8
Swanton, Oh., U.S.	F3	108
Swanton, Vt., U.S.	C13	108
Swanville, Mn., U.S.	E1	110
Swartz Creek, Mi., U.S.	H12	110
Swarzędz, Pol.	C17	10
Swasey Peak, mtn., Ut., U.S.	E3	120
Swatow see Shantou, China	L5	34
Swaziland, ctry., Afr.	G6	58
Swea City, Ia., U.S.	H13	118
Sweden (Sverige), ctry., Eur.	C11	4
Swedish Knoll, mtn., Ut., U.S.	E5	120
Swedru, Ghana	I9	64
Sweeny, Tx., U.S.	J11	116
Sweet Briar, Va., U.S.	B7	112
Sweet Grass Indian Reserve, Sk., Can.	F6	104
Sweet Home, Or., U.S.	F3	122
Sweet Home, Tx., U.S.	J9	116
Sweet Springs, Mo., U.S.	D3	114
Sweetwater, Tn., U.S.	D2	112
Sweetwater, Tx., U.S.	G6	116
Sweetwater, stm., Wy., U.S.	H18	122
Swellendam, S. Afr.	J5	66
Ṣwepsonville, N.C., U.S.	C7	112
Świdnica (Schweidnitz), Pol.	E16	10
Świdnik, Pol.	D22	10
Świdwin, Pol.	B15	10
Świebodzice, Pol.	E16	10
Świebodzin, Pol.	C15	10
Świecie, Pol.	B18	10
Swift Current, Sk., Can.	H7	104
Swift Current Creek, stm., Sk., Can.	H7	104
Swifton, Ar., U.S.	G5	114
Swilly, Lough, b., Ire.	F6	8
Swinburne, Cape, c., N.T., Can.	B13	96
Swindle Island, i., B.C., Can.	E6	102
Ṣwindon, Eng., U.K.	J12	8
Świnoujście (Swinemünde), Pol.	B14	10
Switzerland, ctry., Eur.	F9	4
Swords Range, mts., Austl.	C4	70
Sycamore, Ga., U.S.	H3	112
Sycamore, Il., U.S.	I7	110
Sycamore, Oh., U.S.	G3	108
Sycan, stm., Or., U.S.	H4	122
Syčovka, Russia	F17	22
Sydenham, On., Can.	F19	110
Sydney, Austl.	I9	70
Sydney, N.S., Can.	F13	106
Sydney Lake, l., On., Can.	H20	104
Sydney Mines, N.S., Can.	F13	106
Syke, Ger.	C8	10
Sykesville, Md., U.S.	H10	108
Sykesville, Pa., U.S.	F8	108
Syktyvkar, Russia	E8	26
Sylacauga, Al., U.S.	I10	114
Sylhet, Bngl.	H14	44
Sylt, i., Ger.	A8	10
Sylva, N.C., U.S.	D3	112
Sylvan Grove, Ks., U.S.	L9	118
Sylvan Hills, Ar., U.S.	H4	114
Sylvania, Ga., U.S.	G5	112
Sylvania, Oh., U.S.	F3	108
Sylvan Lake, Ab., Can.	E20	102
Sylvan Lake, l., Ab., Can.	E20	102
Sylvester, Ga., U.S.	H3	112
Sylvester, Tx., U.S.	G6	116
Sylvester, Mount, hill, Nf., Can.	D18	106
Ṣylvia, Ks., U.S.	N9	118
Šymkent, Kaz.	I11	26
Synevir, Ukr.	A7	20
Syntul, Russia	F24	22
Syracuse, In., U.S.	A11	114
Syracuse see Siracusa, Italy	L10	18
Syracuse, Ks., U.S.	N6	118
Syracuse, Ne., U.S.	K11	118
Syracuse, N.Y., U.S.	D10	108
Syrdarja, Uzb.	I11	26
Syr Darya (Syrdar'ja), stm., Asia	H10	26
Syria (Sūrīyah), ctry., Asia	B2	42
Syriam, Myan.	F4	40
Ṣyrskij, Russia	I22	22
Šyščycy, Bela.	H10	22
Sysert', Russia	F10	26
Syzran', Russia	G7	26
Szabolcs-Szatmár-Bereg, co., Hung.	G22	10
Szamos (Someş), stm., Eur.	B6	20
Szamotuły, Pol.	C16	10
Szarvas, Hung.	I20	10
Szczeciński, Zalew, b., Eur.	B14	10
Szczecin (Stettin), Pol.	B14	10
Szczecinek (Neustettin), Pol.	B16	10
Szczuczyn, Pol.	B22	10
Szczytno, Pol.	B21	10
Szechwan see Sichuan, prov., China	E7	30
Szécsény, Hung.	G19	10
Szeged, Hung.	I20	10
Szeghalom, Hung.	H21	10
Székesfehérvár, Hung.	H18	10
Szekszárd, Hung.	I18	10
Szentendre, Hung.	H19	10
Szentes, Hung.	I20	10
Szentgotthárd, Hung.	I16	10
Szerencs, Hung.	G21	10
Szob, Hung.	H18	10
Szolnok, Hung.	H20	10
Szombathely, Hung.	H16	10
Szprotawa, Pol.	D15	10
Szubin, Pol.	B17	10
T		
Tabacal, Arg.	B6	80
Tabaco, Phil.	o20	39b
Tabacundo, Ec.	G3	84
Tabalosos, Peru	B3	82
Tabarka, Tun.	M3	18
Ṭabas, Iran	E14	48
Tabasará, stm., Pan.	I13	92
Tabasco, state, Mex.	I13	90
Ṭabas Masīnā, Iran	E16	48
Tabatinga, stm., Braz.	D7	79
Tabelbala, Alg.	C6	54
Taber, Ab., Can.	H22	102
Tabla, Niger	E11	64
Table Bay, b., S. Afr.	I4	66
Table Mountain, mtn., Nf., Can.	E14	106
Table Rock, Ne., U.S.	K11	118
Table Rock Lake, res., U.S.	F3	114
Tabligbo, Togo	H10	64
Taboco, stm., Braz.	I14	82
Taboga, Pan.	I15	92
Tábor, Czech Rep.	F14	10
Tabor, Ia., U.S.	K12	118
Tabor, S.D., U.S.	I10	118
Tabora, Tan.	C6	58
Tabor City, N.C., U.S.	E8	112
Tabou, C. Iv.	I6	64
Tabrīz, Iran	B9	48
Tabūk, Sau. Ar.	G4	48
Tacámbaro de Codallos, Mex.	H9	90
Tacaná, Guat.	B2	92
Tacaná, Volcán, vol., N.A.	B2	92
Tacañitas, Arg.	E7	80
Taché, Lac, l., N.T., Can.	D8	96
Tacheng, China	B3	30
Tachiataš, Uzb.	I9	26
Tachie, stm., B.C., Can.	C10	102
Tachikawa, Japan	L14	36
Táchira, state, Ven.	D6	84
Tachov, Czech Rep.	F12	10
Tachtamygda, Russia	G16	28
Taciuã, Lago, stm., Braz.	J12	84
Tacna, Az., U.S.	L3	120
Tacna, Peru	H6	82
Tacna, dept., Peru	G6	82
Tacoma, Wa., U.S.	C3	122
Taconic Range, mts., U.S.	E13	108
Taco Pozo, Arg.	C7	80
Tacotalpa, stm., Mex.	I13	90
Tacuarembó, Ur.	F11	80
Tacuarembó, stm., Ur.	F11	80
Tacuarí, stm., Ur.	G11	80
Tacuatí, Para.	B10	80
Tacuparé, Cachoeira, wtfl, Braz.	A14	82
Tacutu (Takutu), stm., S.A.	F12	84
Tademaït, Plateau du, plat., Alg.	F12	62
Tādepallegūdem, India	D6	46
Tadía, Ciénaga de, l., Col.	D4	84
Tadjemout, Alg.	H12	62
Tadjoura, Dji.	F9	56
Tadoule Lake, l., Mb., Can.	E13	96
Tadoussac, P.Q., Can.	D4	106
Tādpatri, India	E5	46
Tadzhikistan see Tajikistan, ctry., Asia	J12	26
T'aebaek-sanmaek, mts., Asia	F16	32
Taech'ŏn, S. Kor.	G14	32
Taedong, N. Kor.	D13	32
Taegu, S. Kor.	H16	32
Taegwan, N. Kor.	C13	32
T'aein, S. Kor.	H14	32
Taejŏn, S. Kor.	G15	32
Ta'erwan, China	D2	34
Tafalla, Spain	C10	16
Ṭafas, Syria	C6	50
Tafassâsset, Oued, val., Afr.	D8	54
Tafiré, C. Iv.	G7	64
Tafí Viejo, Arg.	D6	80
Tafraoute, Mor.	F6	62
Taft, Ca., U.S.	I6	124
Taft, Ok., U.S.	D11	116
Taft, Tx., U.S.	L9	116
Taganrog, Russia	H5	26
Tagawa, Japan	N5	36
Tagaytay, Phil.	n19	39b
Taghit, Alg.	E9	62
Tagish Lake, l., Can.	G27	100
Taguatinga, Braz.	B5	79
Taguke, China	D11	44
Tagula Island, i., Pap. N. Gui.	B10	68
Tagus (Tejo) (Tajo), stm., Eur.	F3	16
Tah, Sebkha, l., Afr.	G4	62
Tahakopa, N.Z.	G2	72
Tahala, Mor.	C8	62
Tahanaoute, Mor.	E7	62
Tahart, Alg.	I13	62
Tahat, mtn., Alg.	I13	62
Tahifet, Alg.	I13	62
Tahiryuak Lake, l., N.T., Can.	B10	96
Tahiti, i., Fr. Poly.	J25	126
Tahkuna nina, c., Est.	B5	22
Tāhlāb (Ṭālāb), stm., Asia	G17	48
Tahlequah, Ok., U.S.	D12	116
Tahoe, Lake, l., U.S.	E5	124
Tahoe City, Ca., U.S.	E5	124
Tahoe Lake, l., N.T., Can.	B11	96
Tahoe Valley, Ca., U.S.	F5	124
Tahoka, Tx., U.S.	F5	116
Tahoua, Niger	D12	64
Tahquamenon, stm., Mi., U.S.	D10	110
Tahsis, B.C., Can.	H8	102
Ṭahṭā, Egypt	D6	60
Tahtsa Lake, l., B.C., Can.	D7	102
Tahtsa Peak, mtn., B.C., Can.	D7	102
Tahuamanu, stm., S.A.	D7	82
Tahuna, Indon.	E8	38
Tai'an, China	G5	32
Taibai Shan, mtn., China	D2	32
T'aichung, Tai.	K9	34
Taif see Aṭ-Ṭā'if, Sau. Ar.	D2	47
Taihang Shan, mts., China	D9	30
Taihape, N.Z.	C5	72
Taihe, China	B4	34
Tai Hu, l., China	D9	34
Taijiang, China	A10	40
Taikkyi, Myan.	F3	40
Tailai, China	B11	30
Tailem Bend, Austl.	J3	70
T'ainan, Tai.	L9	34
Taínaron, Ákra, c., Grc.	M6	20
Taining, China	I6	34
Taiobeiras, Braz.	C7	79
T'aipei, Tai.	J10	34
T'aipeihsien, Tai.	J10	34
Taiping, China	M2	34
Taiping, Malay.	L6	40
Taishun, China	H8	34
Taitao, Península de, pen., Chile	F1	78
Taitouying, China	C7	32
T'aitung, Tai.	M10	34
Taiwan (T'aiwan), ctry., Asia	G11	30
Taiwan Strait, strt., Asia	K8	34
Taixian, China	C9	34
Taixing, China	C9	34
Ṭaiyiba, Isr.	D4	50
Taiyuan, China	D9	30
Taizhou, China	C8	34
Ta'izz, Yemen	H4	47
Tajerouine, Tun.	N3	18
Tajga, Russia	F9	28
Tajgonos, mys, c., Russia	E24	28
Tajikistan, ctry., Asia	J12	26
Tajimi, Japan	L12	36
Tajique, N.M., U.S.	J10	120
Tajitos, Mex.	B3	90
Tajmura, stm., Russia	E17	26
Tajmyr, ozero, l., Russia	C18	26
Tajmyr, poluostrov, pen., Russia	B18	26
Tajšet, Russia	F11	28
Tajumulco, Volcán, vol., Guat.	B3	92
Tak, Thai.	F5	40
Takāb, Iran	C9	48
Takachu, Bots.	D5	66
Takahashi, Japan	M8	36
Takahe, Mount, mtn., Ant.	C11	73
Takaka, N.Z.	D4	72
Takakkaw Falls, wtfl, B.C., Can.	F18	102
Takamatsu, Japan	M9	36
Takaoka, Japan	K12	36
Takapuna, N.Z.	B5	72
Takasaki, Japan	K14	36
Takatsuki, Japan	M10	36
Takayama, Japan	K12	36
Takefu, Japan	L11	36
Takenake, China	C9	44
Takengon, Indon.	L4	40
Take-shima, i., Japan	q5	37b
Take-shima (Tok-to), is., Asia	J6	36
Tākestān, Iran	C10	48
Takêv, Camb.	I8	40
Takhli, Thai.	G6	40
Takijuk Lake, l., N.T., Can.	C10	96
Takikawa, Japan	d16	36a
Takla Lake, l., B.C., Can.	B9	102
Takla Landing, B.C., Can.	B9	102
Taklimakan Shamo, des., China	D3	30
Takrouna, Tun.	M5	18
Taku, stm., N.A.	G28	100
Takua Pa, Thai.	J5	40
Taku Glacier, Ak., U.S.	G27	100
Takum, Nig.	H14	64
Takutu (Tacutu), stm., S.A.	F13	84
Takysie Lake, B.C., Can.	D9	102
Tala, Mex.	G8	90
Tala, Ur.	H11	80
Talačyn, Bela.	G12	22
Talagang, Pak.	D5	44
Talagante, Chile	G3	80
Talamanca, Cordillera de, mts., C.R.	H11	92
Talara, Peru	J2	84
Talas, Kyrg.	I12	26
Talasea, Pap. N. Gui.	m17	68a
Talata Mafara, Nig.	E13	64
Talaud, Kepulauan, is., Indon.	E8	38
Talavera de la Reina, Spain	F7	16
Talawdī, Sudan	L6	60
Talbot Lake, l., Mb., Can.	D15	104
Talbotton, Ga., U.S.	G2	112
Talbragar, stm., Austl.	I8	70
Talca, Chile	H3	80
Talcahuano, Chile	I2	80
Talchichitle, Isla, i., Mex.	E5	90
Talco, Tx., U.S.	F11	116
Taldom, Russia	E20	22
Taldykorgan, Kaz.	H13	26
Talent, Or., U.S.	H3	122
Tālesh, Iran	C10	48
Talgar, Kaz.	I13	26
Taliabu, Pulau, i., Indon.	F7	38
Talica, Russia	F10	26
Talickij Čamlyk, Russia	I23	22
Talihina, Ok., U.S.	E11	116
Taliouine, Mor.	E7	62
Tali Post, Sudan	O6	60
Talish Mountains (Kūhhā-ye Ṭavālesh), mts., Asia	B10	48
Tal'ka, Bela.	H11	22
Talkeetna, Ak., U.S.	E19	100
Talladega, Al., U.S.	I10	114
Tall 'Afar, Iraq	C7	48
Tallah, Egypt	C6	60
Tallahassee, Fl., U.S.	I2	112
Tallahatchie, stm., Ms., U.S.	I6	114
Tallangatta, Austl.	K7	70
Tallapoosa, Ga., U.S.	F1	112
Tallapoosa, stm., U.S.	J10	114
Tallassee, Al., U.S.	J11	114
Tallinn, Est.	B7	22
Tall Kalakh, Syria	D4	48
Tallmadge, Oh., U.S.	F5	108
Tallula, Il., U.S.	C7	114
Tallulah, La., U.S.	J5	114
Talmage, Ca., U.S.	E2	124
Talmage, Ne., U.S.	K11	118
Tal'menka, Russia	G14	26
Talmont, Fr.	F5	14
Talo, mtn., Eth.	L9	60
Taloga, Ok., U.S.	C8	116
Talpa, Tx., U.S.	H7	116
Talsi, Lat.	D5	22
Taltal, Chile	C3	80
Taltapin Lake, l., B.C., Can.	C9	102
Taltson, stm., N.T., Can.	D10	96
Talwood, Austl.	G8	70
Tama, Arg.	F5	80
Tama, Ia., U.S.	I3	110
Tamacuarí, Pico, mtn., S.A.	G10	84
Tamadjert, Alg.	H14	62
Tamalameque, Col.	C6	84
Tamale, Ghana	G9	64
Tamana, Japan	O5	36
Tamaná, Cerro, mtn., Col.	E4	84
Tamanaco, stm., Ven.	C10	84
Tamaniquá, Braz.	I10	84
Tamano, Japan	M8	36
Tamanquaré, Ilha, i., Braz.	H10	84
Tamapatz, Mex.	G10	90
Tamaqua, Pa., U.S.	G11	108
Tamar, stm., Austl.	M7	70
Támara, Col.	E6	84
Tamarac, stm., Mn., U.S.	C10	118
Tamaroa, Il., U.S.	D7	114
Tamarugal, Pampa del, pl., Chile	I7	82
Tamási, Hung.	I18	10
Tamaské, Niger	D12	64
Tamaulipas, state, Mex.	F10	90
Tamaya, stm., Peru	C4	82
Tamazula, Mex.	E6	90
Tamazula de Gordiano, Mex.	H8	90
Tamazulapan del Progreso, Mex.	I11	90
Tamazunchale, Mex.	G10	90
Tambacounda, Sen.	E3	64
Tamba Dabatou, Gui.	F4	64
Tāmbaram, India	F6	46
Tambelan, Kepulauan, is., Indon.	N9	40
Tamberías, Arg.	F4	80
Tambo, Austl.	E7	70
Tambo, Peru	E4	82
Tambo, stm., Austl.	K7	70
Tambo, stm., Peru	G6	82
Tambo, stm., Peru	D5	82
Tamboara, Braz.	G2	79
Tambo Grande, Peru	A1	82
Tambohorano, Madag.	p20	67b
Tambopata, stm., S.A.	E7	82
Tambor, C.R.	H9	92
Tamboritha, Mount, mtn., Austl.	K7	70
Tamboryacu, stm., Peru	H5	84
Tambov, Russia	I24	22
Tambura, Sudan	O4	60
Tamchaket, Maur.	C4	64
Tame, Col.	D7	84
Tameapa, Mex.	E6	90
Tameghza, Tun.	C14	62
Tamel Aike, Arg.	F2	78
Tamelelt, Mor.	E7	62
Tamenghest, Alg.	I13	62
Tamenghest, Oued, val., Alg.	I11	62
Tamiahua, Mex.	G11	90
Tamiahua, Laguna de, b., Mex.	G11	90
Tamiami Canal, Fl., U.S.	N5	112
Tamil Nādu, state, India	G5	46
Tamiš (Timiş), stm., Eur.	D4	20
Tamitatoala, stm., Braz.	B2	79
Tam Ky, Viet.	G10	40
Tamms, Il., U.S.	E7	114
Tamnum, Yemen	G7	47
Tampa, Fl., U.S.	L4	112
Tampa Bay, b., Fl., U.S.	L4	112
Tampaón, stm., Mex.	G10	90
Tampere, Fin.	K18	6
Tampico, Il., U.S.	I6	110
Tampico, Mex.	F11	90
Tampin, Malay.	M7	40
Tam Quan, Viet.	G10	40
Tamri, Mor.	E6	62
Tamsagbulag, Mong.	B10	30
Tamsalu, Est.	B9	22
Tamshiyacu, Peru	J6	84
Tamsweg, Aus.	H13	10
Tamworth, Austl.	H9	70
Tamyang, S. Kor.	H14	32
Tana, Chile	H7	82
Tana (Teno), stm., Eur.	F20	6
Tana, Lake, l., Eth.	K9	60
Tanabe, Japan	N10	36
Tanabi, Braz.	F4	79
Tanacross, Ak., U.S.	E23	100
Tanahbala, Pulau, i., Indon.	O5	40
Tanahmasa, Pulau, i., Indon.	O5	40
Tanami Desert, des., Austl.	C5	68
Tan An, Viet.	I9	40
Tanana, Ak., U.S.	D18	100
Tanana, stm., Ak., U.S.	D19	100
Tananarive see Antananarivo, Madag.	q22	67b
Tancheng, China	I6	32
Tanchoj, Russia	G13	28
Tanch'ŏn, N. Kor.	C16	32
Tancítaro, Pico de, mtn., Mex.	H8	90
Tānda, India	G10	44
Tandaltī, Sudan	K6	60
Tandil, Arg.	I9	80
Tandou Lake, l., Austl.	I5	70
Tanega-shima, i., Japan	q6	37b
Tan Emellel, Alg.	G15	62
Taneytown, Md., U.S.	H9	108
Tanezrouft, des., Afr.	D6	54
Tanga, Tan.	C7	58
Tangail, Bngl.	H13	44
Tangainony, Madag.	s22	67b
Tangalla, Sri L.	I6	46
Tanganyika, Lake, l., Afr.	C5	58
Tangarana, stm., Peru	I5	84
Tangcun, China	J2	34
Tanger (Tangier), Mor.	C8	62
Tangermünde, Ger.	C11	10
Tanggou, China	B7	34
Tanggu, China	D5	32
Tanggula Shan, mts., China	D13	44
Tangier see Tanger, Mor.	C8	62
Tangier, N.S., Can.	H11	106
Tangier, Va., U.S.	B11	112
Tangipahoa, stm., U.S.	K6	114
Tangjiagou, China	E6	34
Tangjin, S. Kor.	G14	32
Tangra Yumco, l., China	E12	44
Tangsanying, China	B5	32
Tangshan, China	D6	32
Tanguiéta, Benin	F10	64
Tangxian, China	E2	32
Tanimbar, Kepulauan, is., Indon.	G9	38
Taninges, Fr.	F13	14
Tanjiafang, China	G6	32
Tanjiang, China	K5	34
Tanjungbalai, Indon.	M5	40
Tanjungpandan, Indon.	F4	38
Tanjungpinang, Indon.	N8	40
Tanjungselor, Indon.	E6	38
Tānk, Pak.	D4	44
Tan Kena, Alg.	G15	62
Tännàs, Swe.	J13	6
Tanner, Al., U.S.	H10	114
Tanner, Mount, mtn., B.C., Can.	H16	102
Tannu-Ola, chrebet, mts., Asia	G10	28
Tannūrah, Ra's, c., Sau. Ar.	H11	48
Tano, stm., Afr.	I8	64
Tânout, Niger	D14	64
Tanquinho, Braz.	A9	79
Tanshui, Tai.	J10	34
Tánsin, Isla de, i., Hond.	B11	92
Tánsin, Laguna de, b., Hond.	B11	92
Ṭanṭā, Egypt	B6	60
Tan-Tan, Mor.	F5	62
Tantoyuca, Mex.	G10	90
Tanuku, India	D6	46
Tanyang, S. Kor.	G16	32
Tanzania, ctry., Afr.	C6	58
Tao, stm., China	E7	30
Taochong, China	D7	34
Tao'er, stm., China	B11	30
Taolakepa, China	D11	44
Taoling, China	E7	34
Taormina, Italy	L10	18
Taos, Mo., U.S.	D4	114
Taos, N.M., U.S.	H11	120
Taos Pueblo, N.M., U.S.	H11	120
Taoudenni, Mali	I8	62
Taounate, Mor.	C8	62
Taoura, Alg.	M3	18
Taourirt, Mor.	C9	62
Taoussa, Mali	C9	64
Taoyuan, China	J6	34
Tapa, Est.	B8	22
Tapacari, Bol.	G8	82
Tapachula, Mex.	J13	90
Tapah, Malay.	L6	40
Tapaje, stm., Col.	F3	84
Tapajós, stm., Braz.	D7	76
Tapalqué, Arg.	I8	80
Tapanahony, stm., Sur.	C7	76
Tapauá, Braz.	A10	82
Tapauá, stm., Braz.	A9	82
Tapejara, Braz.	E12	80
Tapera, Braz.	E12	80
Taperas, Bol.	G11	82
Taperoá, Braz.	B9	79
Tapes, Braz.	F13	80
Tapeta, Lib.	H5	64
Taphan Hin, Thai.	F6	40
Tāpi, stm., India	B2	46
Tapiche, stm., Peru	A5	82
Taping (Daying), stm., Asia	B4	40
Tapiraí, Braz.	E5	79
Tāplejungg, Nepal	G12	44
Tapoa, stm., Afr.	E11	64
Tapolca, Hung.	I17	10
Tappahannock, Va., U.S.	B10	112
Tappen, N.D., U.S.	E8	118
Tappi-zaki, c., Japan	F15	36
Tappo, Ghana	F8	64
Tapurucuara, Braz.	H10	84
Taqāṭu' Hayyā, Sudan	H9	60
Taquara, Braz.	E13	80
Taquaras, Ponta das, c., Braz.	D14	80
Taquari, Braz.	D2	79
Taquari, Braz.	E13	80
Taquari, stm., Braz.	E13	80
Taquari, stm., Braz.	H13	82
Taquari, Pantanal do, sw., Braz.	H13	82
Taquaritinga, Braz.	F4	79
Taquaruçu, stm., Braz.	F2	79
Tar, stm., N.C., U.S.	D9	112
Tara, Austl.	F9	70
Tara, Russia	F6	28
Taraba, stm., Nig.	G9	54
Tarabine, Oued ti-n-, val., Afr.	J14	62
Tarabuco, Bol.	H9	82
Ṭarābulus (Tripoli), Leb.	D3	48
Ṭarābulus (Tripoli), Libya	B3	56
Ṭarābulus (Tripolitania), hist. reg., Libya	B3	56
Taraclia, Mol.	D12	20
Tarago, Austl.	J8	70
Taraira (Traíra), stm., S.A.	H8	84
Tarakan, Indon.	E6	38
Taranaki, Mount see Egmont, Mount, mtn., N.Z.	C4	72
Tarancón, Spain	E8	16
Taranto, Italy	I12	18
Taranto, Golfo di, b., Italy	I12	18
Tarapacá, Col.	I8	84
Tarapoto, Peru	B3	82
Taraquá, Braz.	G8	84
Tarare, Fr.	G11	14
Tarariras, Ur.	H10	80
Tarāsa Dwīp, i., India	J2	40
Tarascon, Fr.	J8	14
Tarascon, Fr.	I11	14
Tarat, Alg.	G15	62
Tarata, Bol.	G8	82
Tarata, Peru	G6	82
Tarauacá, Braz.	C6	82
Tarauacá, stm., Braz.	B6	82
Tarawa, atoll, Kir.	H21	126
Tarawera, N.Z.	C6	72
Tarazona, Spain	D10	16
Tarazona de la Mancha, Spain	F10	16
Tarbagataj, chrebet, mts., Asia	H8	28
Tarbes, Fr.	I7	14
Tarboro, N.C., U.S.	D9	112
Tarbū, Libya	C4	56
Tarcento, Italy	C8	18
Tarcoola, Austl.	F6	68
Tardajos, Spain	C8	16
Tardoki-Jani, gora, mtn., Russia	H19	28
Taree, Austl.	H10	70
Tärendö, Swe.	H18	6
Tarentum, Pa., U.S.	G7	108
Ṭarfā', Ra's aṭ-, c., Sau. Ar.	F3	47
Ṭarfā', Wādī aṭ-, val., Egypt	G1	48
Tarfaya, Mor.	G4	62
Targhee Pass, U.S.	F14	122
Tărgovište, Bul.	F10	20
Târgovişte, Rom.	E9	20
Târgu Bujor, Rom.	D11	20
Târgu Cărbuneşti, Rom.	E7	20
Targuist, Mor.	C8	62
Târgu Jiu, Rom.	D7	20
Târgu Mureş, Rom.	C8	20
Târgu-Neamţ, Rom.	B10	20
Târgu Ocna, Rom.	C10	20
Târguşor, Rom.	E12	20
Tarhjijt, Mor.	F6	62
Tarhūnah, Libya	B3	56
Tari, Pap. N. Gui.	G11	38
Táriba, Ven.	D6	84
Tarifa, Spain	I6	16
Tarifa, Punta de, c., Spain	I6	16
Tarija, Bol.	I9	82
Tarija, dept., Bol.	I9	82
Tarīm, Yemen	F6	47
Tarim, stm., China	C3	30
Tarim Pendi, China	A9	44
Taritatu, stm., Indon.	F10	38
Tarka, Niger	D13	64
Tarkastad, S. Afr.	I8	66
Tarkio, Mo., U.S.	B1	114
Tarkio, stm., U.S.	K12	118
Tarkwa, Ghana	I9	64
Tarlac, Phil.	n19	39b
Tarm, Den.	N11	6
Tarma, Peru	D4	82
Tarn, dept., Fr.	I9	14
Tärnaby, Swe.	I14	6

Name | Map Ref. | Page

Târnăveni, Rom. C8 20
Tarn-et-Garonne, dept., Fr. H8 14
Tarnobrzeg, Pol. E21 10
Tarnów, Pol. E21 10
Tarnowskie Góry, Pol. E18 10
Taroom, Austl. E8 70
Taroudant, Mor. E6 62
Tarpon Springs, Fl., U.S. K4 112
Tarqui, Peru H5 84
Tarra, stm., Ven. C6 84
Tarrafal, C.V. k16 64a
Tarrafal, C.V. m17 64a
Tarragona, Spain D13 16
Tarraleah, Austl. N7 70
Tarrant City, Al., U.S. I10 114
Tàrrega, Spain D13 16
Tarsus, Tur. C3 48
Tartagal, Arg. B7 80
Tartagal, Arg. E9 80
Tartu, Est. C9 22
Ţarţūs, Syria D3 48
Tarumirim, Braz. E8 79
Tarusa, Russia G20 22
Tarutung, Indon. M5 40
Tarutyne, Ukr. C13 20
Tarvisio, Italy C8 18
Tarvo, stm., S.A. F11 82
Tarzan, Tx., U.S. G5 116
Tašauz, Turk. I9 26
Tasejeva, stm., Russia F16 26
Tasejevo, Russia F16 26
Taseko, stm., B.C., Can. F11 102
Taseko Lakes, l., B.C., Can. F11 102
Taseko Mountain, mtn., B.C., Can. F11 102
Tashi Gang Dzong, Bhu. G14 44
Ţashk, Daryācheh-ye, l., Iran G12 48
Tashkent see Taškent, Uzb. I11 26
Tasikmalaya, Indon. j14 39a
Taškent, Uzb. I11 26
Taškepri, Turk. J10 26
Tasman Bay, b., N.Z. D4 72
Tasmania, state, Austl. H9 68
Tasmania, i., Austl. N7 70
Tasman Peninsula, pen., Austl. N7 70
Tasman Sea, Oc. L19 126
Tăşnad, Rom. B6 20
Tassara, Niger C12 64
Tassialouc, Lac, l., P.Q., Can. E18 96
Taštagol, Russia G9 28
Tastiota, Mex. C4 90
Tata, Hung. H18 10
T'at'a, vulkan, vol., Russia c21 36a
Tatabánya, Hung. H18 10
Tataouine, Tun. D16 62
Tatarbunary, Ukr. D13 20
Tatarija, state, Russia F8 26
Tatarka, Bela. H11 22
Tatarlar, Tur. H10 20
Tatarsk, Russia F7 28
Tatarskij proliv, strt., Russia H20 28
Tatarstan see Tatarija, state, Russia F8 26
Tatar Strait see Tatarskij proliv, strt., Russia H20 28
Tate, Ga., U.S. E2 112
Tate, stm., Austl. A6 70
Tathlina Lake, l., N.T., Can. D9 96
Tatitlek, Ak., U.S. F21 100
Tatla Lake, B.C., Can. F10 102
Tatla Lake, l., B.C., Can. F10 102
Tatlayoko Lake, B.C., Can. F10 102
Tatlayoko Lake, l., B.C., Can. F10 102
Tatlow, Mount, mtn., B.C., Can. F11 102
Tatnam, Cape, c., Mb., Can. E14 96
Tatrang, China A11 44
Tatta, Pak. H2 44
Tatuk Lake, l., B.C., Can. D10 102
Tatum, N.M., U.S. F3 116
Tatum, Tx., U.S. J2 114
Tatvan, Tur. B7 48
Taubaté, Braz. G6 79
Tauberbischofsheim, Ger. F9 10
Taučik, Kaz. I8 26
Tauini, stm., Braz. G13 84
Taulabé, Hond. C7 92
Taumarunui, N.Z. C5 72
Taum Sauk Mountain, mtn., Mo., U.S. E6 114
Taunay, Braz. I13 82
Taung, S. Afr. F7 66
Taungdwingyi, Myan. D3 40
Taunggyi, Myan. D4 40
Taungup, Myan. E3 40
Taunton, Eng., U.K. J10 8
Taunton, Ma., U.S. F15 108
Taupo, N.Z. C6 72
Taupo, Lake, l., N.Z. C5 72
Tauragė, Lith. F5 22
Tauranga, N.Z. B6 72
Taurianova, Italy K11 18
Tauripampa, Peru E3 82
Taurisma, Peru F5 82
Tauroa Point, c., N.Z. A4 72
Taurus Mountains see Toros Dağları, mts., Tur. H14 4
Tauste, Spain D10 16
Tavaí, Para. D11 80
Tavanasa, Switz. E11 13
Tavares, Fl., U.S. K5 112
Tavda, Russia F11 26
Tavda, stm., Russia F10 26
Tavernes de la Valldigna, Spain F11 16
Tavernier, Fl., U.S. N6 112
Tavira, Port. H4 16
Tavistock, On., Can. G15 110
Tavolžan, Kaz. G13 26
Tavor, Har (Mount Tabor), mtn., Isr. C4 50
Tavoy see Dawei, Myan. G5 40
Tavşanlı, Tur. J13 20
Tawakoni, Lake, res., Tx., U.S. G10 116
Tawas City, Mi., U.S. F12 110
Ţawīlah, Juzur, is., Egypt H2 48
Ţawkar, Sudan H9 60
Taxco de Alarcón, Mex. H10 90
Taxisco, Guat. C4 92
Taxkorgan, China D2 30
Tay, stm., Scot., U.K. E10 8
Tay, stm., Yk., Can. E28 100
Tayabamba, Peru C3 82
Taylor, Ar., U.S. I3 114
Taylor, Az., U.S. J6 120
Taylor, B.C., Can. A14 102
Taylor, Ne., U.S. J8 118
Taylor, Tx., U.S. I9 116
Taylor, Mount, mtn., N.M., U.S. I9 120
Taylors, S.C., U.S. E4 112
Taylorsville, In., U.S. C11 114
Taylorsville, Ky., U.S. D11 114
Taylorsville, Ms., U.S. K7 114
Taylorsville, N.C., U.S. D5 112
Taylorville, Il., U.S. C7 114
Taymā', Sau. Ar. H5 48
Taymouth, N.B., Can. F7 106
Taymyr Peninsula see Tajmyr, poluostrov, pen., Russia B12 28
Tay Ninh, Viet. I9 40
Tayoltita, Mex. E7 90
Tayside, prov., Scot., U.K. E10 8
Taytay, Phil. C6 38
Tayyārah, Sudan K6 60
Taz, stm., Russia D8 28
Taza, Mor. C8 62
Tazenakht, Mor. E7 62
Tazewell, Tn., U.S. C3 112
Tazewell, Va., U.S. B5 112
Tazin, stm., Can. D10 96
Tazin Lake, l., Sk., Can. E11 96
Tazovskaja guba, b., Russia D7 28
Tazovskij poluostrov, pen., Russia D13 26
Tazrouk, Alg. I14 62
Tazumal, hist., El Sal. D5 92
Tazungdām, Myan. F17 44
Tbessa, Alg. C15 62
Tbilisi, Geor. I6 26
Tchamba, Togo G10 64
Tchaourou, Benin G11 64
Tchefuncta, stm., La., U.S. L6 114
Tchentlo Lake, l., B.C., Can. B9 102
Tchériba, Burkina E8 64
Tchesinkut Lake, l., B.C., Can. C9 102
Tchetti, Benin H10 64
Tchibanga, Gabon B2 58
Tchin-Tabáradene, Niger D12 64
Tchula, Ms., U.S. I6 114
Tczew, Pol. A18 10
Teá, stm., Braz. H10 84
Teaca, Rom. C8 20
Teacapan, Mex. F7 90
Teague, Tx., U.S. H10 116
Te Anau, Lake, l., N.Z. F1 72
Teano, Italy H9 18
Teapa, Mex. I13 90
Te Awamutu, N.Z. C5 72
Teba, Spain I7 16
Tebicuary, stm., Para. D10 80
Tebicuary-Mí, stm., Para. D10 80
Tebingtinggi, Indon. M5 40
Tebingtinggi, Pulau, i., Indon. N7 40
Tébourba, Tun. M4 18
Téboursouk, Tun. M4 18
Tecalitlán, Mex. H8 90
Tecamachalco, Mex. H11 90
Tecate, Mex. A1 90
Teche, Bayou, stm., La., U.S. L5 114
Techirghiol, Rom. E12 20
Techlé, W. Sah. J3 62
Tecklenburg, Ger. C7 10
Tecomán, Mex. H8 90
Tecopa, Ca., U.S. I9 124
Tecpan de Galeana, Mex. I9 90
Tecpán Guatemala, Guat. C3 92
Tecuala, Mex. F7 90
Tecuamburro, Volcán, vol., Guat. C4 92
Tecuci, Rom. D11 20
Tecumseh, Mi., U.S. H12 110
Tecumseh, Ne., U.S. K11 118
Tecumseh, Ok., U.S. D10 116
Tedžen, Turk. J10 26
Tedžen (Harīrūd), stm., Asia C16 48
Teec Nos Pos, Az., U.S. H7 120
Teeli, Russia G16 26
Tees, stm., Eng., U.K. G12 8
Teesside see Middlesbrough, Eng., U.K. G12 8
Teeswater, On., Can. F14 110
Tefé, Braz. I10 84
Tefé, stm., Braz. D5 76
Tefé, Lago, l., Braz. I10 84
Tegal, Indon. j14 39a
Tegelen, Neth. F9 12
Tegernsee, Ger. H11 10
Tegina, Nig. F13 64
Tegucigalpa, Hond. C7 92
Teguise, Spain n27 17b
Tehachapi, Ca., U.S. I7 124
Tehachapi Pass, Ca., U.S. I7 124
Tehamiyam, Sudan H9 60
Tehek Lake, l., N.T., Can. D13 96
Téhini, C. Iv. G8 64
Tehrān, Iran D11 48
Tehrathum, Nepal G12 44
Tehuacán, Mex. H11 90
Tehuantepec, Golfo de, b., Mex. J12 90
Tehuantepec, Istmo de, Mex. I12 90
Teide, Pico del, mtn., Spain o24 17b
Teixeira Pinto, Gui.-B. E3 64
Teixeira Soares, Braz. C13 80
Tejamén, Mex. E7 90
Tejkovo, Russia E23 22
Tejo see Tagus, stm., Eur. F3 16
Tejupan, Punta, c., Mex. H8 90
Tejupilco de Hidalgo, Mex. H9 90
Tekamah, Ne., U.S. J11 118
Tekapo, Lake, l., N.Z. E3 72
Tekax, Mex. G15 90
Tekeli, Kaz. I13 26
Tekeze, stm., Afr. F8 56
Tekirdağ, Tur. I11 20
Tekoa, Wa., U.S. C8 122
Tekonsha, Mi., U.S. H11 110
Te Kuiti, N.Z. C5 72
Tela, Hond. B7 92
Tela, Bahía de, b., Hond. B7 92
Télagh, Alg. C10 62
Tel Aviv-Yafo, Isr. D3 50
Telde, Spain o25 17b
Telefomin, Pap. N. Gui. G11 38
Telegraph Cove, B.C., Can. G8 102
Telegraph Creek, B.C., Can. H29 100
Telemark, co., Nor. L11 6
Telembí, stm., Col. G4 84
Telén, Arg. H6 80
Telenești, Mol. B12 20
Teleorman, co., Rom. F8 20
Telertheba, Djebel, mtn., Alg. H14 62
Telescope Peak, mtn., Ca., U.S. H8 124
Telfs, Aus. H11 10
Telica, stm., Hond. C8 92
Telica, Volcán, vol., Nic. E8 92
Telkwa, B.C., Can. C7 102
Telkwa, stm., B.C., Can. C7 102
Tell City, In., U.S. E10 114
Teller, Ak., U.S. D11 100
Tellicherry, India G3 46
Tellico, stm., U.S. D2 112
Tellico Plains, Tn., U.S. D2 112
Tello, Col. F5 84
Telluride, Co., U.S. G9 120
Tel Megiddo (Armageddon), hist., Isr. C4 50
Tel Mond, Isr. D3 50
Telok Anson, Malay. L6 40
Teloloapan, Mex. H10 90
Telpaneca, Nic. D8 92
Telšiai, Lith. F5 22
Telti, Italy I4 18
Teltow, Ger. C13 10
Tema, Ghana I10 64
Temagami, Lake, l., On., Can. C15 110
Temax, Mex. G15 90
Tembenči, stm., Russia D11 28
Temblador, Ven. C11 84
Tembleque, Spain F8 16
Temecula, Ca., U.S. K8 124
Temera, Mor. D7 62
Temirtau, Kaz. G12 26
Témiscamie, Lac, l., P.Q., Can. A1 106
Témiscouata, Lac, l., P.Q., Can. E5 106
Temora, Austl. J7 70
Temosachic, Mex. C6 90
Tempe, Az., U.S. K5 120
Temperance, Mi., U.S. I12 110
Tempio Pausania, Italy I4 18
Tempisque, stm., C.R. G9 92
Temple, Ok., U.S. E8 116
Temple, Tx., U.S. H9 116
Templeton, stm., Austl. C3 70
Templin, Ger. B13 10
Tempoal, stm., Mex. G10 90
Tempoal de Sánchez, Mex. G10 90
Tempy, Russia E20 22
Temr'uk, Russia H5 26
Temuco, Chile J2 80
Tena, Ec. H4 84
Tenabo, Mex. G14 90
Tenaha, Tx., U.S. K2 114
Tenakee Springs, Ak., U.S. H27 100
Tenāli, India D6 46
Tenasserim, Myan. H5 40
Tendaho, Eth. F9 56
Tende, Col de, Eur. H14 14
Ten Degree Channel, strt., India J2 40
Tenente Marques, stm., Braz. D11 82
Tenente Portela, Braz. D12 80
Ténéré, des., Niger E9 54
Tenerife, i., Spain o24 17b
Ténès, Alg. B11 62
Teng'aopu, China B10 32
Tengchong, China B5 40
Tenggara, Nusa (Lesser Sunda Islands), is., Indon. G7 38
Tengiz, ozero, l., Kaz. G11 26
Tengtian, China H4 34
Tengtiao (Na), stm., Asia C7 40
Tengxian, China H5 32
Tenente Rodolfo Marsh, sci., Ant. B1 73
Tenino, Wa., U.S. D3 122
Tenkāsi, India H4 46
Tenke, Zaire D5 58
Tenkiller Ferry Lake, res., Ok., U.S. D11 116
Tenkodogo, Burkina F9 64
Ten Mile Lake, l., Nf., Can. A17 106
Tennant Creek, Austl. C6 68
Tennessee, state, U.S. D9 98
Tennessee, stm., U.S. D9 98
Tennille, Ga., U.S. G4 112
Teno, Chile H3 80
Teno (Tana), stm., Eur. F20 6
Tenosique, Mex. I14 90
Tenryū, Japan M12 36
Tensas, stm., La., U.S. K5 114
Tensed, Id., U.S. C9 122
Ten Sleep, Wy., U.S. F18 122
Tenterfield, Austl. G10 70
Ten Thousand Islands, is., Fl., U.S. N5 112
Teocaltiche, Mex. G8 90
Teodelina, Arg. H8 80
Teófilo Otoni, Braz. D8 79
Teo Lakes, l., Sk., Can. G5 104
Teotihuacán, hist., Mex. H10 90
Tepalcatepec, Mex. H8 90
Tepeaca, Mex. H11 90
Tepehuanes, Mex. E7 90
Tepehuanes, stm., Mex. E7 90
Tepeji de Ocampo, Mex. H10 90
Tepelenë, Alb. I4 20
Tepi, Eth. N8 60
Tepic, Mex. G7 90
Teplice, Czech Rep. E13 10
Teplovo, Russia F25 22
Tepoca, Bahía, b., Mex. B3 90
Tepoca, Punta, c., Mex. C3 90
Tepopa, Cabo, c., Mex. C3 90
Téra, Niger D10 64
Tera, stm., Spain D6 16
Teramo, Italy G8 18
Terang, Austl. L5 70
Terborg, Neth. E9 12
Terbuny, Russia I21 22
Terceira, i., Port. k21 62a
Tercero, stm., Arg. G7 80
Tereida, Sudan L6 60
Terek, stm., Russia I7 26
Terence Bay, N.S., Can. H10 106
Terenino, Russia G16 22
Terenos, Braz. F1 79
Teresina, Braz. E10 76
Teresópolis, Braz. G7 79
Terespol, Pol. C23 10
Teresva, Ukr. A7 20
Terhorne, Neth. B8 12
Teribe, stm., N.A. H12 92
Terlingua, Tx., U.S. J3 116
Termas de Río Hondo, Arg. D6 80
Termez, Uzb. J11 26
Termini Imerese, Italy L8 18
Términos, Laguna de, b., Mex. H14 90
Termoli, Italy G10 18
Ternate, Indon. E8 38
Ternberg, Aus. H14 10
Ternej, Russia H19 28
Terneuzen, Neth. F4 12
Terni, Italy G7 18
Ternivka, Ukr. A13 20
Ternopil', Ukr. H3 26
Teror, Spain o25 17b
Terpenija, mys, c., Russia H20 28
Terpenija, zaliv, b., Russia H20 28
Terra Alta, W.V., U.S. H7 108
Terra Bella, Ca., U.S. I6 124
Terrace, B.C., Can. C6 102
Terrace Bay, On., Can. B8 110
Terracina, Italy H8 18
Terral, Ok., U.S. F9 116
Terralba, Italy J3 18
Terra Nova Lake, l., Nf., Can. D19 106
Terra Nova National Park, Nf., Can. D20 106
Terra Rica, Braz. G2 79
Terra Roxa, Braz. C12 80
Terra Santa, Braz. I14 84
Terrassa, Spain D14 16
Terrebonne Bay, b., La., U.S. M6 114
Terre Haute, In., U.S. C9 114
Terrell, Tx., U.S. G10 116
Terrell Hills, Tx., U.S. J8 116
Terrenceville, Nf., Can. E19 106
Terror Point, c., B.C., Can. D5 102
Terry, Ms., U.S. J6 114
Terry, Mt., U.S. E2 118
Terry Peak, mtn., S.D., U.S. G4 118
Terschelling, i., Neth. B7 12
Teruel, Col. F5 84
Teruel, Spain E10 16
Terzaghi Dam, B.C., Can. G12 102
Teša, Russia F25 22
Tesalia, Col. F5 84
Tešanj, Bos. E2 20
Tes-Chem (Tesijn), stm., Asia A5 30
Tescott, Ks., U.S. L10 118
Teseney, Erit. J9 60
Tesijn (Tes-Chem), stm., Asia B6 30
Teslić, Bos. E1 20
Teslin, Yk., Can. F28 100
Teslin, stm., Can. F27 100
Teslin Lake, l., Can. F28 100
Tesouras, stm., Braz. C3 79
Tesouro, Braz. D2 79
Tessala, Monts du, mts., Alg. J11 16
Tessalit, Mali A10 64
Tessaoua, Niger E13 64
Tessenderlo, Bel. F7 12
Tessy-sur-Vire, Fr. D5 14
Testour, Tun. M4 18
Tesuque, N.M., U.S. I11 120
Tetachuck Lake, l., B.C., Can. D9 102
Tetagouche, stm., N.B., Can. E8 106
Tete, Moz. E6 58
Tête-à-la-Baleine, P.Q., Can. B14 106
Tête-Jaune-Cache, B.C., Can. E15 102
Tétépisca, Lac, l., P.Q., Can. A4 106
Teterow, Ger. B12 10
Tetlin, Ak., U.S. E23 100
Tetlin Lake, l., Ak., U.S. E23 100
Teton, Id., U.S. G14 122
Teton, stm., Mt., U.S. C14 122
Tetonia, Id., U.S. G14 122
Teton Range, mts., Wy., U.S. G15 122
Tétouan, Mor. C8 62
Tetovo, Mac. G4 20
Teuco, stm., Arg. C8 80
Teulada, Italy K3 18
Teulada, Capo, c., Italy K3 18
Teúl de González Ortega, Mex. G8 90
Tėuli, Bela. I7 22
Teulon, Mb., Can. H17 104
Teutopolis, Il., U.S. C8 114
Teuva, Fin. J17 6
Tevere (Tiber), stm., Italy G7 18
Teverya (Tiberias), Isr. C5 50
Texada Island, i., B.C., Can. H10 102
Texarkana, Ar., U.S. I2 114
Texarkana, Tx., U.S. I2 114
Texas, Austl. G9 70
Texas, state, U.S. E7 98
Texas City, Tx., U.S. J12 116
Texel, i., Neth. B6 12
Texhoma, Ok., U.S. C5 116
Texico, N.M., U.S. E3 116
Texline, Tx., U.S. C3 116
Texoma, Lake, res., U.S. F10 116
Teyateyaneng, Leso. G8 66
Teywarah, Afg. D1 44
Teziutlán, Mex. H11 90
Tezpur, India G15 44
Tezzeron Lake, l., B.C., Can. C10 102
Tha-anne, stm., N.T., Can. D13 96
Thabana-Ntlenyana, mtn., Leso. G9 66
Thabazimbi, S. Afr. E8 66
Thai Binh, Viet. D9 40
Thailand (Prathet Thai), ctry., Asia B3 38
Thailand, Gulf of, b., Asia I6 40
Thai Nguyen, Viet. D8 40
Thal, Pak. D4 44
Thala, Tun. N3 18
Thalfang, Ger. F6 10
Thalia, Tx., U.S. F7 116
Thalwil, Switz. D10 13
Thamar, Jabal, mtn., Yemen H4 47
Thames, N.Z. B5 72
Thames, stm., Eng., U.K. J12 8
Thamesford, On., Can. G14 110
Thamesville, On., Can. H14 110
Thāna, India C2 46
Thanbyuzayat, Myan. G4 40
Thang Binh, Viet. G10 40
Thanh Hoa, Viet. E8 40
Thanh Pho Ho Chi Minh (Saigon), Viet. I9 40
Thanjāvūr, India G5 46
Thann, Fr. E14 14
Thar Desert (Great Indian Desert), des., Asia F4 44
Thargomindah, Austl. G5 70
Thar Nhom, Sudan N6 60
Tharrawaddy, Myan. F3 40
Thásos, i., Grc. I8 20
Thatcher, Az., U.S. L7 120
Thaton, Myan. F4 40
Thaungdut, Myan. B3 40
Thaungyin, stm., Asia F5 40
Thaya (Dyje), stm., Eur. G15 10
Thayer, Ks., U.S. N12 118
Thayer, Mo., U.S. F5 114
Thayetmyo, Myan. E3 40
Thazi, Myan. D4 40
Thealka, Ky., U.S. B4 112
Thebes see Thívai, Grc. K7 20
Thebes, Il., U.S. E7 114
Thebes, hist., Egypt E7 60
The Coteau, hills, Sk., Can. G7 104
The Dalles, Or., U.S. E4 122
Thedford, Ne., U.S. J7 118
The English Company's Islands, is., Austl. B7 68
The Fens, reg., Eng., U.K. I14 8
The Fishing Lakes, l., Sk., Can. H11 104
The Flat Tops, mts., Co., U.S. D9 120
The Hague see 's-Gravenhage, Neth. E5 12
The Key Indian Reserve, Sk., Can. G12 104
The Little Minch, strt., Scot., U.K. D7 8
Thelon, stm., N.T., Can. D12 96
The Lynd, Austl. B6 70
The Minch, strt., Scot., U.K. C8 8
Thenia, Alg. B12 62
Theniet el Hadd, Alg. C12 62
Theodore, Al., U.S. L8 114
Theodore, Austl. E9 70
Theodore, Sk., Can. G12 104
Theodore Roosevelt Lake, res., Az., U.S. K5 120
Theólogos, Grc. I8 20
The Pas, Mb., Can. E13 104
The Rajah, mtn., Ab., Can. D16 102
The Rand see Witwatersrant, reg., S. Afr. E8 66
Theresa, N.Y., U.S. C11 108
Thermaïkós Kólpos, b., Grc. I6 20
Thermopílai (Thermopylae), hist., Grc. K6 20
Thermopolis, Wy., U.S. A8 120
Thermopylae see Thermopílai, hist., Grc. K6 20
The Rock, Austl. J7 70
Thesiger Bay, b., N.T., Can. B8 96
The Sound, strt., Eur. N13 6
Thessalía, hist. reg., Grc. J6 20
Thessalía, prov., Grc. J6 20
Thessalon, On., Can. D12 110
Thessaloníki (Salonika), Grc. I6 20
Thetford-Mines, P.Q., Can. A15 108
The Valley, Anguilla E13 94
The Wash, b., Eng., U.K. I14 8
Thibaudeau, Mb., Can. A20 104
Thibodaux, La., U.S. M6 114
Thicket Portage, Mb., Can. C17 104
Thief, stm., Mn., U.S. C11 118
Thief River Falls, Mn., U.S. C11 118
Thielsen, Mount, mtn., Or., U.S. G3 122
Thiene, Italy D6 18
Thiers, Fr. G10 14
Thiès, Sen. D1 64
Thiesi, Italy I3 18
Thika, Kenya B7 58
Thimphu, Bhu. G13 44
Thingvellir, Ice. B3 6a
Thingvellir National Park, Ice. B3 6a
Thionville, Fr. C13 14
Thíra (Santorini), i., Grc. M9 20
Thiruvārūr, India G5 46
Thistle Island, i., Austl. J2 70
Thívai (Thebes), Grc. K7 20
Thlewiaza, stm., N.T., Can. D13 96
Thoa, stm., N.T., Can. D11 96
Thohoyandou, S. Afr. D10 66
Thoi Binh, Viet. J8 40
Thomas, Ok., U.S. D8 116
Thomas, W.V., U.S. H7 108
Thomasboro, Il., U.S. B8 114
Thomas Lake, l., Mb., Can. A18 104
Thomaston, Al., U.S. J9 114
Thomaston, Ct., U.S. F13 108
Thomaston, Ga., U.S. G2 112
Thomaston, Me., U.S. C17 108
Thomasville, Al., U.S. K9 114
Thomasville, Ga., U.S. I3 112
Thomasville, N.C., U.S. D6 112
Thom Lake, l., Mb., Can. C18 104
Thomlinson, Mount, mtn., B.C., Can. B7 102
Thompson, Ia., U.S. G2 110
Thompson, Mb., Can. C17 104
Thompson, stm., B.C., Can. G13 102
Thompson, stm., U.S. C3 114
Thompson Falls, Mt., U.S. C10 122
Thompson Pass, Ak., U.S. F22 100
Thompsonville, Mi., U.S. F10 110
Thomsen, stm., N.T., Can. B9 96
Thomson, Ga., U.S. F4 112
Thomson, Il., U.S. I5 110
Thomson, stm., Austl. E5 70
Thomson Lake, res., Sk., Can. I8 104
Thon Buri, Thai. H6 40
Thongwa, Myan. F4 40
Thonon-les-Bains, Fr. F13 14
Thonotosassa, Fl., U.S. K4 112
Thonze, Myan. F3 40
Thorburn, N.S., Can. G11 106
Thoreau, N.M., U.S. I8 120
Thorhild, Ab., Can. C21 102
Thorial, Sudan M5 60
Thornapple, stm., Wi., U.S. E4 110
Thornbury, On., Can. F15 110
Thorndale, Tx., U.S. I9 116
Thorne, stm., On., Can. D23 104
Thornton, Ar., U.S. I4 114
Thornton, Co., U.S. E12 120
Thornton, Tx., U.S. H10 116
Thorntonville, Tx., U.S. H4 116
Thorp, Wi., U.S. F5 110
Thorsby, Ab., Can. D20 102
Thorsby, Al., U.S. J10 114
Thorsteinson Lake, l., Mb., Can. A17 104
Thouars, Fr. F6 14
Thousand Lake Mountain, mtn., Ut., U.S. F5 120
Thousand Oaks, Ca., U.S. J7 124
Thrace, hist. reg., Eur. H10 20
Thrakikón Pélagos, Grc. I8 20
Three Fingered Jack, mtn., Or., U.S. F4 122
Three Forks, Mt., U.S. E14 122
Three Hills, Ab., Can. F21 102
Three Hummock Island, i., Austl. M6 70
Three Lakes, Wi., U.S. E6 110
Three Mile Plains, N.S., Can. H9 106
Three Oaks, Mi., U.S. I9 110
Three Pagodas Pass, Asia G5 40
Threepoint Lake, l., Mb., Can. C16 104
Three Rivers, Mi., U.S. I10 110
Three Rivers, Tx., U.S. K8 116
Three Sisters, S. Afr. H6 66
Three Sisters, mtn., Or., U.S. F4 122
Three Springs, Austl. E3 68
Throat, stm., On., Can. G21 104
Throckmorton, Tx., U.S. F7 116
Thu Dau Mot, Viet. I9 40
Thule, Grnld. B13 86
Thun, Switz. E8 13
Thunder Bay, On., Can. B6 110
Thunder Bay, b., Mi., U.S. F12 110
Thunder Bay, b., On., Can. B6 110
Thunder Bay, stm., Mi., U.S. E12 110
Thunderbolt, Ga., U.S. G5 112
Thunder Creek, stm., Sk., Can. H8 104
Thunder Hills, hills, Sk., Can. D8 104
Thunersee, l., Switz. E8 13
Thung Song, Thai. J5 40
Thur, stm., Switz. C10 13
Thurgau, state, Switz. C11 13
Thüringen, state, Ger. D11 10
Thüringer Wald, mts., Ger. E10 10
Thurmont, Md., U.S. H9 108
Thursday Island, Austl. B8 68
Thurso, Scot., U.K. C10 8
Thurston Island, i., Ant. C11 73
Thusis, Switz. E11 13
Thwaites Iceberg Tongue, Ant. C11 73
Thyolo, Mwi. E7 58
Tía Juana, Ven. B7 84
Tianchang, China C8 34
Tiandong, China C9 40
Tianfanjie, China F5 34
Tianjiazhen, China F4 34
Tianjin (Tientsin), China D5 32
Tianjin Shi, China D10 30
Tianjun, China D6 30
Tianlin, China B9 40
Tianmen, China E2 34
Tianshui, China E8 30
Tiantai, China F10 34
Tiantou, China I4 34
Tianxiyang, China I7 34
Tianzhu, China D7 30
Tianzhuang, China J2 34
Tibaji, Braz. C13 80
Tibaji, stm., Braz. B13 80
Tibasti, Sarīr, des., Libya D4 56
Tibbie, Al., U.S. K8 114
Tibe, Eth. M9 60
Tiber see Tevere, stm., Italy G7 18
Tibesti, mts., Chad D4 56
Tibet see Xizang Zizhiqu, prov., China E3 30
Tibiri, Niger E13 64
Tibooburra, Austl. G5 70
Tiburón, Cabo, c. C4 84
Tiburón, Isla, i., Mex. C3 90
Tiča, Jazovir, res., Bul. F10 20
Tice, Fl., U.S. M5 112
Tīchīt, Maur. B5 64
Tichmenevo, Russia C21 22
Tichoreck, Russia H6 26
Tichvin, Russia B16 22
Ticino, state, Switz. F10 13
Ticino, stm., Eur. D3 18
Tickfaw, La., U.S. L6 114
Tickfaw, stm., U.S. L6 114
Ticonderoga, N.Y., U.S. D13 108
Ticul, Mex. G15 90
Tide Lake, l., Ab., Can. H3 104
Tidikelt, pl., Alg. G11 62
Tidioute, Pa., U.S. F7 108
Tidjikja, Maur. B4 64
Tidore, Indon. E8 38
Tiekou, China F9 32
Tieli, China B12 30
Tieling, China A11 32
Tielt, Bel. F3 12
Tielutou, China H4 34
Tiémé, C. Iv. G6 64
T'ienchung, Tai. L9 34
Tien Shan, mts., Asia C3 30
Tientsin see Tianjin, China D5 32
Tie Plant, Ms., U.S. I7 114
Tierra Amarilla, Chile D3 80
Tierra Amarilla, N.M., U.S. H10 120
Tierra Blanca, Mex. H11 90
Tierra del Fuego, Isla Grande de, i., S.A. G3 78
Tierralta, Col. C4 84
Tieshanguan, China L2 34
Tietê, Braz. G5 79
Tietê, stm., Braz. F3 79
Tif, Alg. G11 62
Tiffany Mountain, mtn., Wa., U.S. B6 122
Tiffin, Oh., U.S. F3 108
Tifton, Ga., U.S. H3 112
Tiftona, Tn., U.S. D1 112
Tighennif, Alg. C11 62
Tighina (Bender), Mol. F13 4
Tigil', Russia F23 28
Tiglid, Mor. F5 62
Tignall, Ga., U.S. F4 112
Tignish, P.E., Can. F9 106
Tigre, Col. F8 84
Tigre, stm., Peru J5 84
Tigre, stm., Ven. C11 84
Tigre, Cerro, mtn., C.R. I11 92
Tigris (Dicle) (Dijlah), stm., Asia F9 48
Tiguabos, Cuba D7 94
Tiguentourine, Alg. G15 62
Tihāmah, pl., Asia H4 48
Tihert, Alg. C11 62
Tihuatlán, Mex. G11 90
Tijamuchi, stm., Bol. F9 82
Tijesno, Cro. F10 18
Tijuana, Mex. A1 90
Tijucas, Braz. D14 80
Tijucas do Sul, Braz. C14 80
Tijuco, stm., Braz. E4 79
Tikal, hist., Guat. I15 90
Tiko, Cam. I14 64
Tikrīt, Iraq D7 48
Tikša, Russia I23 6
Tikšeozero, ozero, l., Russia H22 6
Tilarán, C.R. G10 92
Tilbalakan, Laguna, b., Hond. B10 92
Tilburg, Neth. E7 12
Tilbury, On., Can. H13 110
Tilcara, Arg. B6 80
Tilden, Il., U.S. D7 114
Tilden, Ne., U.S. I10 118
Tilden, Tx., U.S. K8 116
Tilemsès, Niger D12 64
Tilemsi, Vallée du, val., Mali B10 64
Tilhar, India G8 44
Tilimsen, Alg. C10 62
Tilisarao, Arg. G6 80
Tillaberi, Niger D10 64
Tillamook, Or., U.S. E2 122
Tillanchāng Dwīp, i., India J2 40
Tilley, Ab., Can. G23 102
Tillia, Niger C12 64
Tillmans Corner, Al., U.S. L8 114
Tillson, N.Y., U.S. F12 108
Tillsonburg, On., Can. H15 110
Tilpa, Austl. H6 70
Tilrhemt, Alg. D12 62
Tilton, Il., U.S. B9 114
Tilton, N.H., U.S. D15 108
Tiltonsville, Oh., U.S. G6 108
Timā, Egypt D6 60
Timaná, Col. G5 84
Timane, stm., Para. I12 82
Timanskij kr'až, mtn., Russia D7 26
Timaru, N.Z. F3 72
Timbedgha, Maur. C6 64
Timber Lake, S.D., U.S. F6 118
Timbío, Col. F4 84
Timbó, Braz. D14 80
Timbo, Lib. I5 64
Timboon, Austl. L5 70
Timbuktu see Tombouctou, Mali C8 64
Timétrine, Mali B9 64
Timeu Creek, stm., Ab., Can. C20 102
Timgad, hist., Alg. C14 62
Timimoun, Alg. F11 62
Timinar, Sudan H6 60
Timir'azevskij, Russia F14 26
Timirist, Râs, c., Maur. B1 64
Timiș, co., Rom. D5 20
Timiș (Tamiš), stm., Eur. D5 20
Timișoara, Rom. D5 20
Timmendorfer Strand, Ger. A10 10
Timmins, On., Can. B14 110
Timmonsville, S.C., U.S. E7 112
Timms Hill, hill, Wi., U.S. E5 110
Timor, i., Indon. G8 38
Timor Sea J16 126
Timotes, Ven. C7 84
Timoudi, Alg. F10 62

Name — Map Ref. — Page

Utique, Tun. L5 18
Uto, Japan O5 36
Utopia, Tx., U.S. J7 116
Utorgoš, Russia C13 22
Utrecht, Neth. D7 12
Utrecht, S. Afr. F10 66
Utrecht, prov., Neth. D7 12
Utrera, Spain H6 16
Utsunomiya, Japan K14 36
Uttaradit, Thai. F6 40
Uttar Pradesh, state, India G9 44
Utuado, P.R. E11 94
Uudenmaan lääni, prov., Fin. K19 6
Uusikaupunki (Nystad), Fin. K17 6
Uvá, Braz. C3 79
Uvá, stm., Col. F8 84
Uvalda, Ga., U.S. F3 112
Uvalde, Tx., U.S. J7 116
Uvaravičy, Bela. I13 22
Uvarovka, Russia F18 22
Uvarovo, Russia J25 22
Uvat, Russia F11 26
Uvinza, Tan. C6 58
Uvira, Zaire B5 58
Uvs nuur, l., Asia A5 30
Uwajima, Japan N7 36
Uwayl, Sudan M4 60
'Uwaynāt, Jabal al-, mtn., Afr. D5 56
Uxbridge, On., Can. F16 110
Uxmal, hist., Mex. G15 90
Uyuni, Bol. I8 82
Uyuni, Salar de, pl., Bol. I8 82
Užava, Lat. D4 22
Uzbekistan, ctry., Asia I10 26
Uzboj, stm., Turk. B13 48
Uzda, Bela. H10 22
Uzdin, Yugo. D4 20
Uzhhorod, Ukr. H2 26
Užice, Yugo. F3 20
Uzlovaja, Russia H21 22
Uzunköprü, Tur. H10 20
Užur, Russia F9 28
Užventis, Lith. F5 22

V

Vääksy, Fin. K19 6
Vaala, Fin. I20 6
Vaalserberg, mtn., Neth. G9 12
Vaalwater, S. Afr. E9 66
Vaanta (Vanda), Fin. K19 6
Vaasa (Vasa), Fin. J17 6
Vaasan lääni, prov., Fin. J18 6
Vabalninkas, Lith. F7 22
Vabkent, Uzb. A18 48
Vác, Hung. H19 10
Vaca, Bol. H10 82
Vača, Russia F25 22
Vacacaí, stm., Braz. F11 80
Vacaria, Braz. E13 80
Vacaria, stm., Braz. D7 79
Vacaria, stm., Braz. F1 79
Vacaville, Ca., U.S. F4 124
Vaccarès, Étang de, b., Fr. I11 14
Vach, stm., Russia E7 28
Vache, Île à, i., Haiti E8 94
Vachš, stm., Taj. J11 26
Vacoas, Mrts. v18 67c
Vadino, Russia F16 22
Vadodara, India I5 44
Vado Ligure, Italy E3 18
Vaduz, Liech. E16 14
Vaga, stm., Russia E6 26
Vagaj, Russia F11 26
Vågåmo, Nor. K11 6
Vágar, i., Faer. Is. D8 6b
Váh, stm., Slvk. G17 10
Vaiden, Ms., U.S. I7 114
Vaihingen, Ger. G8 10
Väike-Maarja, Est. B9 22
Vail, Co., U.S. E10 120
Vail, Ia., U.S. I12 118
Vailly-sur-Aisne, Fr. C10 14
Vaiņode, Lat. E4 22
Vajgač, ostrov, i., Russia C9 26
Valais (Wallis), state, Switz. F7 13
Valašské Meziříčí, Czech Rep. F17 10
Valatie, N.Y., U.S. E13 108
Vâlcea, co., Rom. E8 20
Valcheta, Arg. E3 78
Valdagno, Italy D6 18
Valdai Hills see Valdajskaja vozvyšennost', hills, Russia D15 22
Valdaj, Russia D16 22
Valdajskaja vozvyšennost', hills, Russia D16 22
Valdelândia, Braz. C3 79
Valdemārpils, Lat. D5 22
Valdepeñas, Spain G8 16
Valders, Wi., U.S. F8 110
Valdés, Península, pen., Arg. E4 78
Val-des-Bois, P.Q., Can. B11 108
Valdese, N.C., U.S. D5 112
Valdez, Ak., U.S. F21 100
Valdéz, Ec. G3 84
Val-d'Isère, Fr. G13 14
Valdivia, Chile D2 78
Valdivia, Col. D5 84
Valdobbiadene, Italy D7 18
Val-d'Oise, dept., Fr. C9 14
Valdosta, Ga., U.S. I3 112
Vale, Or., U.S. G8 122
Valemount, B.C., Can. E15 102
Valença, Braz. B9 79
Valença, Braz. G7 79
Valença, Port. C3 16
Valençay, Fr. E8 14
Valence, Fr. H11 14
Valencia, Hond. C9 92
València, Spain F11 16
Valencia, Ven. B8 84
València, prov., Spain F11 16
València, Golf de, b., Spain F12 16
Valencia, Lago de, l., Ven. B9 84
Valencia de Alcántata, Spain F4 16
Valenciennes, Fr. B10 14
Valentine, Ne., U.S. I7 118
Valentine, Tx., U.S. I2 116
Valenza, Italy D3 18
Valera, Ven. C7 84
Valga, Est. D9 22
Valiente, Península, pen., Pan. C2 84
Valiente, Punta, c., Pan. H13 92
Valier, Il., U.S. D7 114
Valier, Mt., U.S. B13 122
Valjevo, Yugo. E3 20
Valka, Lat. D9 22
Valkininkas, Lith. G7 22
Valladolid, Ec. J3 84
Valladolid, Mex. G15 90
Valladolid, Spain D7 16
Valldal, Nor. J10 6
Valle, Lat. E7 22
Valle, Spain B7 16
Valle, dept., Hond. D7 92
Vallecitos, N.M., U.S. H10 120
Valle d'Aosta, prov., Italy D2 18
Valle de Guanape, Ven. C10 84
Valle de la Pascua, Ven. C9 84
Valle del Cauca, dept., Col. F4 84
Valle de Olivos, Mex. D6 90
Valle de Santiago, Mex. G9 90
Valle de Zaragoza, Mex. D7 90
Valledupar, Col. B6 84
Valle Edén, Ur. F10 80
Vallegrande, Bol. H9 82
Valle Hermoso, Arg. F6 80
Valle Hermoso, Mex. E11 90
Vallehermoso, Spain o23 17b
Vallejo, Ca., U.S. F3 124
Vallenar, Chile E3 80
Valles Caldera, crat., N.M., U.S. I10 120
Valletta, Malta N9 18
Valley, Al., U.S. J11 114
Valley, Ne., U.S. J11 118
Valley, stm., Mb., Can. G14 104
Valley Bend, W.V., U.S. I7 108
Valley Center, Ks., U.S. N10 118
Valley City, N.D., U.S. E10 118
Valley Falls, Ks., U.S. L12 118
Valley Farms, Az., U.S. L5 120
Valleyfield, Nf., Can. C20 106
Valley Head, Al., U.S. H11 114
Valley Head, W.V., U.S. I6 108
Valley Mills, Tx., U.S. H9 116
Valley of the Kings, hist., Egypt E7 60
Valley Springs, S.D., U.S. H11 118
Valley Station, Ky., U.S. D11 114
Valleyview, Ab., Can. B17 102
Valley View, Tx., U.S. F9 116
Valliant, Ok., U.S. E11 116
Vallimanca, Arroyo, stm., Arg. H8 80
Vallorbe, Switz. E5 13
Valls, Spain D13 16
Val-Marie, Sk., Can. I7 104
Valmaseda, Spain B8 16
Valmeyer, Il., U.S. D6 114
Valmiera, Lat. D8 22
Valognes, Fr. C5 14
Valongo, Port. D3 16
Valožyn, Bela. G9 22
Vālpārai, India G4 46
Valparaíso, Braz. F3 79
Valparaíso, Chile G3 80
Valparaiso, Fl., U.S. L10 114
Valparaiso, In., U.S. A9 114
Valparaiso, Ne., U.S. J11 118
Valparaíso, prov., Chile G3 80
Valréas, Fr. H11 14
Vals, Tanjung, c., Indon. G10 38
Valsbaai, b., S. Afr. J4 66
Valsetz, Or., U.S. F2 122
Valtimo, Fin. J21 6
Valujki, Russia G5 26
Valverde del Camino, Spain H5 16
Van, Tur. B7 48
Van, Tx., U.S. G11 116
Van Alstyne, Tx., U.S. F10 116
Vananda, B.C., Can. H10 102
Van Buren, Ar., U.S. G2 114
Van Buren, Mo., U.S. F5 114
Vanč, Taj. J12 26
Vanceboro, Me., U.S. B19 108
Vanceburg, Ky., U.S. I3 108
Vancleave, Ms., U.S. L8 114
Vancouver, B.C., Can. H11 102
Vancouver, Wa., U.S. E3 122
Vancouver, Cape, c., Ak., U.S. F12 100
Vancouver, Cape, c., Austl. G3 68
Vancouver, Mount, mtn., N.A. F25 100
Vancouver Island, i., B.C., Can. H9 102
Vancouver Island Ranges, mts., B.C., Can. H9 102
Vandalia, Il., U.S. D7 114
Vandalia, Mo., U.S. C5 114
Vandalia, Oh., U.S. H2 108
Vandekerckhove Lake, l., Mb., Can. A13 104
Vanderbijlpark, S. Afr. F8 66
Vanderbilt, Mi., U.S. E11 110
Vanderbilt, Tx., U.S. K10 116
Vandergrift, Pa., U.S. G7 108
Vanderhoof, B.C., Can. C10 102
Vanderlin Island, i., Austl. C7 68
Vandervoort, Ar., U.S. H2 114
Van Diemen Gulf, b., Austl. B6 68
Vändra, Est. C8 22
Vanegas, Mex. F9 90
Vänern, l., Swe. L13 6
Vänersborg, Swe. L13 6
Vangaindrano, Madag. s22 67b
Van Gölü, l., Tur. B7 48
Vangsnes, Nor. K10 6
Vanguard, Sk., Can. I7 104
Van Horn, Tx., U.S. H2 116
Van Horne, Ia., U.S. H3 110
Vanier, On., Can. B11 108
Vanimo, Pap. N. Gui. F11 38
Vanino, Russia H20 28
Vāniyambādi, India F5 46
Vankleek Hill, On., Can. B12 108
Van Lear, Ky., U.S. B4 112
Vanndale, Ar., U.S. G6 114
Vannes, Fr. E4 14
Van Ninh, Viet. H10 40
Van Rees, Pegunungan, mts., Indon. F10 38
Vanrhynsdorp, S. Afr. H4 66
Vansant, Va., U.S. B4 112
Vansittart Island, i., N.T., Can. C16 96
Vanskoje, Russia C19 22
Vanstadensrus, S. Afr. G8 66
Vanua Levu, i., Fiji J21 126
Vanuatu, ctry., Oc. J20 126
Van Vleck, Tx., U.S. J11 116
Van Wert, Oh., U.S. G2 108
Vanzylsrus, S. Afr. F6 66
Vapnyarka, Ukr. A12 20
Var, dept., Fr. I13 14
Var, stm., Fr. I13 14
Varakļāni, Lat. E9 22
Varallo, Italy D3 18
Vārānasi (Benares), India H10 44
Varangerfjorden, Nor. G22 6
Varangerhalvøya, pen., Nor. F21 6
Varapaeva, Bela. F10 22
Varaždin, Cro. C11 18
Varazze, Italy E3 18
Varberg, Swe. M13 6
Vardaman, Ms., U.S. I7 114
Vardar (Axiós), stm., Eur. H6 20
Vardø, Nor. F22 6
Varegovo, Russia D22 22
Varel, Ger. B8 10
Varela, Arg. H5 80
Varėna, Lith. G7 22
Vareš, Bos. E2 20
Varese, Italy D3 18
Vârfurile, Rom. C6 20
Varginha, Braz. F6 79
Varjão, Braz. D4 79
Varkaus, Fin. J20 6
Värmlands Län, co., Swe. L13 6
Varna, Bul. F11 20
Värnamo, Swe. M14 6
Varnsdorf, Czech Rep. E14 10
Varnville, S.C., U.S. G5 112
Várpalota, Hung. H18 10
Värska, Est. D10 22
Vârtopu, Rom. E7 20
Várzea, Rio da, stm., Braz. D12 80
Várzea da Palma, Braz. D6 79
Várzea Grande, Braz. F13 82
Varzeão, Braz. C14 80
Vas, co., Hung. H16 10
Vasalemma, Est. B7 22
Vashkivtsi, Ukr. A11 20
Vashkivtsi, Ukr. A9 20
Vasilevičy, Bela. I12 22
Vasiliká, Grc. I7 20
Vasiljevskij Moch, Russia D18 22
Vasiljevskoje, Russia E24 22
Vaskelovo, Russia A13 22
Vaslui, Rom. C11 20
Vaslui, co., Rom. C11 20
Vass, N.C., U.S. D7 112
Vassar, Mi., U.S. G12 110
Västerås, Swe. L15 6
Västerbottens Län, co., Swe. I15 6
Västernorrlands Län, co., Swe. J15 6
Västervik, Swe. M15 6
Västmanlands Län, co., Swe. L15 6
Vasto, Italy G9 18
Vas'ugan, stm., Russia F13 26
Vas'uganje, sw., Russia F7 28
Vasvár, Hung. H16 10
Vatan, Fr. E8 14
Vatican City (Città del Vaticano), ctry., Eur. H7 18
V'atka, stm., Russia F8 26
Vatnajökull, Ice. B5 6a
Vatneyri, Ice. B2 6a
Vatomandry, Madag. q23 67b
Vatra Dornei, Rom. B9 20
V'atskije Pol'any, Russia F8 26
Vättern, l., Swe. L14 6
Vaucluse, dept., Fr. I12 14
Vaucouleurs, Fr. D12 14
Vaud, state, Switz. E6 13
Vaughan, On., Can. G16 110
Vaughn, N.M., U.S. J11 120
Vaukavysk, Bela. H7 22
Vaupés, ter., Col. G7 84
Vaupés (Uaupés), stm., S.A. G7 84
Vauréal, Chute, wtfl, P.Q., Can. C11 106
Vauvert, Fr. I11 14
Vauxhall, Ab., Can. G22 102
Vavatenina, Madag. p23 67b
Vavoua, C. Iv. H6 64
Växjö, Swe. M14 6
Vazante, Braz. E5 79
Vazante Grande, stm., Braz. H13 82
V'azemskij, Russia H18 28
V'az'ma, Russia F17 22
V'azniki, Russia E25 22
Veazie, Me., U.S. C18 108
Veblen, S.D., U.S. F10 118
Vecht, stm., Eur. C9 12
Vechta, Ger. C8 10
Vecsés, Hung. H19 10
Vedea, Rom. E8 20
Vedia, Arg. H8 80
Veedersburg, In., U.S. B9 114
Veendam, Neth. B10 12
Veenendaal, Neth. D8 12
Vega, Tx., U.S. D4 116
Veghel, Neth. E8 12
Vegreville, Ab., Can. D22 102
Veguita, N.M., U.S. J10 120
Veinticinco de Mayo, Arg. H8 80
Veinticinco de Mayo, Arg. H4 80
Veinticinco de Mayo, Ur. H10 80
Veintiocho de Mayo, Ec. I3 84
Veintisiete de Abril, C.R. G9 92
Veisiejai, Lith. G6 22
Vejer de la Frontera, Spain I6 16
Vejle, Den. N11 6
Velardeña, Mex. E8 90
Velas, Cabo, c., C.R. G9 92
Velázquez, Ur. H11 80
Velddrif, S. Afr. I4 66
Velden, Ger. G12 10
Veldhoven, Neth. F7 12
Velet'ma, Russia F25 22
Vélez, Col. D6 84
Velez de la Gomera, Peñón de, i., Sp. N. Afr. J7 16
Vélez-Málaga, Spain I7 16
Vel'gija, Russia C16 22
Velhas, Rio das, stm., Braz. D6 79
Velikaja, stm., Russia E26 28
Velika Morava, stm., Yugo. E5 20
Velika Plana, Yugo. E5 20
Velikije Luki, Russia E13 22
Velikij Ust'ug, Russia E7 26
Velikodvorskij, Russia F23 22
Veliko Gradište, Yugo. E5 20
Velikoje, Russia D22 22
Veliko Tărnovo, Bul. F9 20
Vélingara, Sen. F4 54
Veliž, Russia F14 22
Velletri, Italy H7 18
Vellore, India F5 46
Velma, Ok., U.S. E9 116
Velp, Neth. D8 12
Vel'sk, Russia E6 26
Velten, Ger. C13 10
Velva, N.D., U.S. C7 118
Velyka Koshnytsya, Ukr. A12 20
Velyka Mykhaylivka, Ukr. B13 20
Velyki Luchky, Ukr. A6 20
Velykoploske, Ukr. B13 20
Velykyy Bereznyy, Ukr. G22 10
Velykyy Bychkiv, Ukr. B8 20
Venaco, Fr. G4 18
Venadillo, Col. E5 84
Venado, Isla del, i., Nic. F11 92
Venado Tuerto, Arg. G8 80
Venâncio Aires, Braz. E12 80
Vence, Fr. I14 14
Venceslau Braz, Braz. G4 79
Venda, hist. reg., S. Afr. D10 66
Venda Nova, Port. D4 16
Vendas Novas, Port. G3 16
Vendée, dept., Fr. F5 14
Vendeuvre-sur-Barse, Fr. D11 14
Vendôme, Fr. E8 14
Vendychany, Ukr. A11 20
Venecia, C.R. G10 92
Veneto, prov., Italy G18 14
Venev, Russia G21 22
Venezia (Venice), Italy D7 18
Venezuela, ctry., S.A. B5 76
Venezuela, Golfo de, b., S.A. B7 84
Vengerovo, Russia F13 26
Veniaminof, Mount, mtn., Ak., U.S. H15 100
Venice, Fl., U.S. L4 112
Venice see Venezia, Italy D7 18
Venice, La., U.S. M7 114
Venice, Gulf of, b., Eur. D8 18
Vénissieux, Fr. G11 14
Venlo, Neth. F9 12
Venosa, Italy I10 18
Vent, Aus. I10 10
Ventanas, Ec. H3 84
Ventersdorp, S. Afr. F8 66
Venterstad, S. Afr. H7 66
Ventimiglia, Italy F2 18
Ventspils, Lat. D4 22
Ventuari, stm., Ven. E9 84
Ventura, Ca., U.S. J6 124
Venus, Fl., U.S. L5 112
Venustiano Carranza, Mex. I13 90
Venustiano Carranza, Mex. H8 90
Venustiano Carranza, Bahía, b., Mex. H16 90
Venustiano Carranza, Presa, res., Mex. D9 90
Vera, Arg. E8 80
Veracruz, state, Mex. H12 90
Veracruz [Llave], Mex. H11 90
Veraguas, prov., Pan. I13 92
Veramejki, Bela. H14 22
Veranópolis, Braz. E13 80
Verāval, India J4 44
Verbania, Italy D3 18
Verbilki, Russia E20 22
Verbovskij, Russia F25 22
Vercelli, Italy D3 18
Vercel [-Villedieu-le-Camp], Fr. E13 14
Verchn'aja Inta, Russia D10 26
Verchn'aja Salda, Russia F10 26
Verchn'aja Tajmyra, stm., Russia C11 28
Verchn'aja Troica, Russia D20 22
Verchn'aja Tura, Russia F9 26
Verchnedneprovskij, Russia G16 22
Verchnemulomskoje vodochranilišče, res., Russia G22 6
Verchnevil'ujsk, Russia E16 28
Verchnij Baskunčak, Russia H7 26
Verchnij Ufalej, Russia F10 26
Verchojansk, Russia D18 28
Verchojanskij chrebet, mts., Russia D17 28
Verchoturje, Russia F10 26
Verchovje, Russia I20 22
Vercors, reg., Fr. H12 14
Verde, stm., Az., U.S. K5 120
Verde, stm., Braz. C4 79
Verde, stm., Braz. D5 79
Verde, stm., Braz. D3 79
Verde, stm., Braz. E3 79
Verde, stm., Braz. E4 79
Verde, stm., Braz. F2 79
Verde, stm., Braz. E13 82
Verde, stm., Braz. E12 82
Verde, stm., Mex. G8 90
Verde, stm., Para. B9 80
Verde, stm., S.A. F11 82
Verde, Arroyo, stm., Bol. E8 82
Verde, Cape, c., Bah. C7 94
Verde Grande, stm., Braz. C7 79
Verden, Ger. C9 10
Verden, Ok., U.S. D8 116
Verde Pequeno, stm., Braz. C7 79
Verdi, Nv., U.S. E6 124
Verdigre, Ne., U.S. I9 118
Verdigris, stm., U.S. C11 116
Verdinho, stm., Braz. D3 79
Verdon, Ne., U.S. K12 118
Verdun, Fr. I8 14
Verdun, P.Q., Can. B13 108
Verdun-sur-le-Doubs, Fr. F12 14
Verdun-sur-Meuse, Fr. C12 14
Vereeniging, S. Afr. F8 66
Veregin, Sk., Can. G12 104
Vereja, Russia F19 22
Vereščagino, Russia F8 26
Vergara, Ur. G12 80
Vergennes, Vt., U.S. C13 108
Verhnjadzvinsk, Bela. F10 22
Verín, Spain D4 16
Veriora, Est. C10 22
Veríssimo, Braz. E4 79
Verkhovyna, Ukr. A8 20
Verkhoyansk see Verchojansk, Russia D18 28
Vermejo, stm., N.M., U.S. H12 120
Vermelho, stm., Braz. C3 79
Vermette Lake, l., Sk., Can. C5 104
Vermilion, Ab., Can. D24 102
Vermilion, Oh., U.S. F4 108
Vermilion, stm., Ab., Can. E3 104
Vermilion, stm., Il., U.S. I7 110
Vermilion, stm., La., U.S. M4 114
Vermilion, stm., Mn., U.S. B3 110
Vermilion Bay, On., Can. I21 104
Vermilion Bay, b., La., U.S. M4 114
Vermilion Lake, l., Mn., U.S. C3 110
Vermilion Lake, l., On., Can. H22 104
Vermilion Pass, Can. F18 102
Vermillion, S.D., U.S. I11 118
Vermillion, stm., S.D., U.S. H11 118
Vermont, Il., U.S. B6 114
Vermont, state, U.S. C12 98
Vernal, Ut., U.S. D7 120
Vernayaz, Switz. F7 13
Verndale, Mn., U.S. E12 118
Verner, On., Can. D15 110
Verneuil, Fr. D7 14
Vernon, Al., U.S. I8 114
Vernon, B.C., Can. G15 102
Vernon, Ct., U.S. F14 108
Vernon, Fl., U.S. L11 114
Vernon, Fr. C8 14
Vernon, In., U.S. D11 114
Vernon, Tx., U.S. E7 116
Vernon, Ut., U.S. D4 120
Vernonia, Or., U.S. E2 122
Vernon River, P.E., Can. F11 106
Verny, Fr. C13 14
Vero Beach, Fl., U.S. L6 112
Véroia, Grc. I6 20
Verona, Italy D6 18
Verona, Ms., U.S. H8 114
Verona, On., Can. F19 110
Verona, Wi., U.S. H6 110
Verónica, Arg. H10 80
Verrettes, Haiti E8 94
Versailles, Fr. D9 14
Versailles, Il., U.S. C6 114
Versailles, In., U.S. C11 114
Versailles, Ky., U.S. D12 114
Versailles, Mo., U.S. D4 114
Versailles, Oh., U.S. G2 108
Veršino-Darasunskij, Russia G15 28
Vert, Cap, c., Sen. D1 64
Verte, Île, i., P.Q., Can. D4 106
Vertientes, Cuba D5 94
Vertou, Fr. E5 14
Verviers, Bel. G8 12
Vervins, Fr. C10 14
Vescovato, Fr. G4 18
Vesjegonsk, Russia C20 22
Vesoul, Fr. E13 14
Vespasiano, Braz. E7 79
Vesta, C.R. H11 92
Vest-Agder, co., Nor. L10 6
Vestavia Hills, Al., U.S. I10 114
Vesterålen, is., Nor. G14 6
Vestfjorden, Nor. H14 6
Vestfold, co., Nor. L12 6
Vestmannaeyjar, Ice. C3 6a
Vesuvio, vol., Italy I9 18
Vesuvius see Vesuvio, vol., Italy I9 18
Veszprém, Hung. H17 10
Veszprém, co., Hung. H17 10
Vésztő, Hung. I21 10
Vetluga, Russia F7 26
Vetralla, Italy G7 18
Vetrișoaia, Rom. C12 20
Vetryna, Bela. F11 22
Vetschau, Ger. D14 10
Veurne (Furnes), Bel. F2 12
Vevay, In., U.S. D11 114
Vevey, Switz. F6 13
Vézelise, Fr. D13 14
Viacha, Bol. G7 82
Viadana, Italy E5 18
Viadutos, Braz. D12 80
Viale, Arg. F8 80
Viamão, Braz. F13 80
Viamonte, Arg. G7 80
Vian, Ok., U.S. D12 116
Viana, Braz. D9 76
Viana do Alentejo, Port. G3 16
Viana do Castelo, Port. D3 16
Viangchan (Vientiane), Laos F7 40
Viangphoukha, Laos D6 40
Viareggio, Italy F5 18
Vibank, Sk., Can. H11 104
Viborg, Den. M11 6
Viborg, S.D., U.S. H10 118
Vibo Valentia, Italy K11 18
Vibraye, Fr. D7 14
Viburnum, Mo., U.S. E5 114
Vic (Vich), Spain D14 16
Vícam, Mex. D4 90
Vicco, Ky., U.S. B3 112
Vicebsk, Bela. F13 22
Vic-en-Bigorre, Fr. I7 14
Vicente Guerrero, Mex. F8 90
Vicente López, Arg. H9 80
Vicente Noble, Dom. Rep. E9 94
Vicenza, Italy D6 18
Viceroy, Sk., Can. I9 104
Vichada, dept., Col. E8 84
Vichada, stm., Col. E8 84
Vichadero, Ur. F11 80
Vichigasta, Arg. E5 80
Vichuquén, Chile H2 80
Vichy, Fr. F10 14
Vici, Ok., U.S. C7 116
Vicksburg, Mi., U.S. H10 110
Vicksburg, Ms., U.S. J6 114
Vico, Fr. I23 15a
Viçosa, Braz. F7 79
Victor, Ia., U.S. I3 110
Victor, Id., U.S. G14 122
Victor, Mt., U.S. D11 122
Victor, Lac, l., P.Q., Can. B12 106
Victor Harbor, Austl. J3 70
Victoria, Arg. G8 80
Victoria, B.C., Can. I11 102
Victoria, Chile J2 80
Victoria, Gren. H14 94
Victoria (Xianggang), H.K. M3 34
Victoria, Ks., U.S. M8 118
Victoria, Malay. D6 38
Victoria, P.E., Can. F10 106
Victoria, Sey. B11 58
Victoria, Tx., U.S. K9 116
Victoria, Va., U.S. C8 112
Victoria, state, Austl. G9 68
Victoria, stm., Austl. C6 68
Victoria, stm., Nf., Can. D17 106
Victoria, Lake, l., Afr. B6 58
Victoria, Lake, l., Austl. I4 70
Victoria, Mount, mtn., Myan. D2 40
Victoria, Mount, mtn., Pap. N. Gui. A9 68
Victoria Beach, Mb., Can. H18 104
Victoria Falls, Zimb. A7 66
Victoria Falls, wtfl, Afr. A7 66
Victoria Harbour, On., Can. F16 110
Victoria Island, i., N.T., Can. B10 96
Victoria Lake, res., Nf., Can. D16 106
Victoria Land, reg., Ant. C8 73
Victoria Nile, stm., Ug. H7 56
Victoria Peak, mtn., B.C., Can. G8 102
Victoria Peak, mtn., Belize I15 90
Victoria River Downs, Austl. C6 68
Victoria Strait, strt., N.T., Can. C12 96
Victoriaville, P.Q., Can. A15 108
Victoria West, S. Afr. H6 66
Victorica, Arg. I6 80
Victorino, Ven. F9 84
Victorino de la Plaza, Arg. I7 80
Victorville, Ca., U.S. J8 124
Vičuga, Russia D24 22
Vicuña, Chile F3 80
Vicuña Mackenna, Arg. G6 80
Vidalia, Ga., U.S. G4 112
Vidalia, La., U.S. K5 114
Vidal Ramos, Braz. D14 80
Vidauban, Fr. I13 14
Videira, Braz. D13 80
Vidigueira, Port. G4 16
Vidin, Bul. F6 20
Vidisha, India I7 44
Vidlica, Russia K23 6
Vidor, Tx., U.S. L2 114
Vidzeme, hist. reg., Lat. D8 22
Vidzy, Bela. F9 22
Viechtach, Ger. F12 10
Viedma, Arg. E4 78
Viedma, Lago, l., Arg. F2 78
Viejo, Cerro, mtn., Peru J3 84
Viekšniai, Lith. E5 22
Vielha, Spain C12 16
Vienna see Wien, Aus. G16 10
Vienna, Ga., U.S. G3 112
Vienna, Il., U.S. E8 114
Vienna, Md., U.S. I11 108
Vienna, Mo., U.S. D5 114
Vienna, S.D., U.S. G10 118
Vienna, W.V., U.S. H5 108
Vienne, Fr. G11 14
Vienne, dept., Fr. F7 14
Vienne, stm., Fr. E7 14
Vientiane see Viangchan, Laos F7 40
Vieques, P.R. E12 94
Vieques, Isla de, i., P.R. E12 94
Vierfontein, S. Afr. F8 66
Vierwaldstättersee, l., Switz. D9 13
Vierzon, Fr. E9 14
Viesca, Mex. E8 90
Viesīte, Lat. E8 22
Vieste, Italy H11 18
Vietnam, ctry., Asia B4 38
Viet Tri, Viet. D8 40
Vieux-Fort, P.Q., Can. A16 106
Vieux Fort, St. Luc. H14 94
Vievis, Lith. G7 22
Vieytes, Arg. H10 80
Vigan, Phil. m19 39b
Vigeland, Nor. L10 6
Vigevano, Italy D3 18
Vigneulles-lès-Hattonchâtel, Fr. D12 14
Vignola, Italy E6 18
Vigo, Spain C3 16
Vihowa, Pak. E4 44
Viitasaari, Fin. J19 6
Vijāpur, India I5 44
Vijayawāda, India D6 46
Vijosë (Aóös), stm., Eur. I4 20
Viking, Ab., Can. D23 102
Vikna, i., Nor. C10 4
Vikno, Ukr. A9 20
Vikramasingapuram, India H4 46
Vila da Ribeira Brava, C.V. k16 64a
Vila de Manica, Moz. B11 66
Vila do Bispo, Port. H3 16
Vila Fontes, Moz. A12 66
Vilafranca del Penedès, Spain D13 16
Vila Gomes da Costa, Moz. E11 66
Viļaka, Lat. D10 22
Vilama, Laguna de, l., Arg. B5 80
Vila Machado, Moz. B12 66
Vilanculos, Moz. D12 66
Viļāni, Lat. E9 22
Vila Nova de Foz Côa, Port. D4 16
Vila Nova de Gaia, Port. D3 16
Vilanova i la Geltrú, Spain D13 16
Vila Novo de Ourém, Port. F3 16
Vila Paiva de Andrada, Moz. B12 66
Vila Real, Port. D4 16
Vila Real de Santo António, Port. H4 16
Vilar Formoso, Port. E5 16
Vila Velha, Braz. F8 79
Vila Velha de Ródão, Port. F4 16
Vila Verde, Port. D3 16
Vil'che, Ukr. F22 10
Vilejka, Bela. G9 22
Vilelas, Arg. D7 80
Vilhelmina, Swe. I15 6
Vilhena, Braz. E11 82
Viljandi, Est. C8 22
Viljoenskroon, S. Afr. F8 66
Vilkaviškis, Lith. G6 22
Vil'kickogo, ostrov, i., Russia C13 26
Vil'kickogo, proliv, strt., Russia B18 26
Vilkija, Lith. F6 22
Villa Abecia, Bol. I9 82
Villa Aberastain, Arg. F4 80
Villa Alemana, Chile G3 80
Villa Ana, Arg. E9 80
Villa Ángela, Arg. D8 80
Villa Atamisqui, Arg. E7 80
Villa Atuel, Arg. H5 80
Villa Bella, Bol. D9 82
Villa Berthet, Arg. D8 80
Villa Bruzual, Ven. C8 84
Villa Cañás, Arg. H8 80
Villacañas, Spain F8 16
Villa Carlos Paz, Arg. F6 80
Villacarrillo, Spain G8 16
Villa Castelli, Arg. E4 80
Villach, Aus. I13 10
Villacidro, Italy J3 18
Villa Comaltitlan, Mex. B2 92
Villa Concepción del Tío, Arg. F7 80
Villa Constitución, Arg. G8 80
Villada, Spain C7 16
Villa de Arista, Mex. F9 90
Villa de Arriaga, Mex. G9 90
Villa de Cos, Mex. F8 90
Villa de Cura, Ven. B9 84
Villa del Carmen, Arg. G6 80
Villa del Rosario, Arg. F7 80
Villa del Rosario, Arg. F10 80
Villa de María, Arg. E7 80
Villa de Nova Sintra, C.V. m16 64a
Villa de San Antonio, Hond. C7 92
Villa de San Francisco, Hond. C8 92
Villa de Soto, Arg. F6 80
Villadiego, Spain C7 16
Villa Dolores, Arg. F6 80
Villa Elisa, Arg. G9 80
Villa Flores, Mex. I13 90
Villa Florida, Para. D10 80
Villafranca de los Barros, Spain G5 16
Villafranca di Verona, Italy D5 18
Village, Ok., U.S. D9 116
Villa General Roca, Arg. G5 80
Villagrán, Mex. E10 90
Villa Grove, Il., U.S. C8 114
Villaguay, Arg. F9 80
Villa Guerrero, Mex. H10 90
Villa Guillermina, Arg. E9 80
Villa Hayes, Para. C10 80
Villahermosa, Mex. I13 90
Villa Hernandarias, Arg. F9 80
Villa Hidalgo, Mex. G8 90
Villa Huidobro, Arg. H6 80
Villaines-la-Juhel, Fr. D6 14
Villa Insurgentes, Mex. E4 90
Villa Iris, Arg. J7 80
Villa Juárez, Mex. D5 90
Villa Krause, Arg. F4 80
Villa Larca, Arg. G6 80
Villaldama, Mex. D9 90
Villalonga, Arg. D4 78
Villa Mainero, Mex. E10 90
Villa María, Arg. G7 80
Villa María Grande, Arg. F9 80
Villa Martín, Bol. I8 82
Villa Matoque, Arg. C7 80
Villa Mazán, Arg. E5 80
Villa Media Agua, Arg. F4 80
Villa Mercedes, Arg. F4 80
Villamontes, Bol. I10 82
Villa Nueva, Arg. G7 80
Villa Nueva, Arg. G4 80
Villanueva, Col. B6 84
Villa Nueva, Guat. C4 92
Villanueva, Hond. B6 92
Villanueva, Mex. F8 90
Villa Nueva, Nic. E8 92
Villanueva, N.M., U.S. I11 120
Villanueva de Córdoba, Spain G7 16
Villanueva de la Serana, Spain G6 16
Villanueva del Río y Minas, Spain H6 16
Villa Ocampo, Arg. E9 80
Villa Ojo de Agua, Arg. E7 80
Villa Oliva, Para. D10 80
Villa Oropeza, Bol. H9 82
Villapinzón, Col. E6 84
Villa Quinteros, Arg. D6 80
Villa Ramírez, Arg. G8 80
Villarcayo, Spain C8 16
Villa Regina, Arg. J5 80
Villa Reynolds, Arg. G6 80
Villa Rica, Ga., U.S. F2 112
Villa Rivero, Bol. G9 82
Villarrica, Chile D2 78
Villarrica, Col. F5 84
Villarrica, Para. C10 80
Villarrobledo, Spain F9 16
Villas, N.J., U.S. H12 108

Name | Map Ref. | Page

Wilson, stm., Or., U.S. E2 122
Wilson, Cape, c., N.T., Can. C16 96
Wilson, Mount, mtn., Ca., U.S. J7 124
Wilson, Mount, mtn., Co., U.S. G9 120
Wilson, Mount, mtn., Nv., U.S. F11 124
Wilson Lake, res., Al., U.S. H9 114
Wilson Lake, res., Ks., U.S. M9 118
Wilsons Beach, N.B., Can. H7 106
Wilsons Promontory, c., Austl. L7 70
Wilsonville, Ne., U.S. K7 118
Wilton, Me., U.S. C16 108
Wilton, N.D., U.S. D7 118
Wilton, N.H., U.S. E15 108
Wilton, Wi., U.S. G5 110
Wiltshire, co., Eng., U.K. J12 8
Wiluna, Austl. E4 68
Wimapedi, stm., Mb., Can. C15 104
Wimauma, Fl., U.S. L4 112
Wimberley, Tx., U.S. I8 116
Wimbledon, N.D., U.S. D9 118
Winagami Lake, l., Ab., Can. B18 102
Winamac, In., U.S. A10 114
Winburg, S. Afr. G8 66
Winchendon, Ma., U.S. E14 108
Winchester, Eng., U.K. J12 8
Winchester, Id., U.S. D9 122
Winchester, Il., U.S. C6 114
Winchester, In., U.S. B12 114
Winchester, Ky., U.S. B2 112
Winchester, N.H., U.S. E14 108
Winchester, On., Can. B11 108
Winchester, Tn., U.S. G10 114
Winchester, Va., U.S. H8 108
Wind, stm., Wy., U.S. G17 122
Wind, stm., Yk., Can. D27 100
Windber, Pa., U.S. G8 108
Wind Cave National Park, S.D., U.S. H4 118
Winder, Ga., U.S. F3 112
Windermere, B.C., Can. G19 102
Windfall, Ab., Can. C18 102
Windhoek, Nmb. D3 66
Windigo, stm., On., Can. E23 104
Windigo Lake, l., On., Can. F23 104
Windischgarsten, Aus. H14 10
Wind Lake, Wi., U.S. H7 110
Windom, Mn., U.S. H12 118
Windom Peak, mtn., Co., U.S. G9 120
Windorah, Austl. E5 70
Window Rock, Az., U.S. I7 120
Wind River Peak, mtn., Wy., U.S. H16 122
Wind River Range, mts., Wy., U.S. G16 122
Windsor, Austl. I9 70
Windsor, Ca., U.S. F3 124
Windsor, Co., U.S. D12 120
Windsor, Ct., U.S. F14 108
Windsor, Eng., U.K. J13 8
Windsor, Il., U.S. C8 114
Windsor, Mo., U.S. D3 114
Windsor, N.C., U.S. D10 112
Windsor, Nf., Can. D18 106
Windsor, N.S., Can. H9 106
Windsor, On., Can. H12 110
Windsor, P.Q., Can. B14 108
Windsor, Va., U.S. C10 112
Windsor, Vt., U.S. D14 108
Windsor Forest, Ga., U.S. H5 112
Windsor Locks, Ct., U.S. F14 108
Windthorst, Tx., U.S. F8 116
Windward Islands, is., N.A. H14 94
Windward Passage, strt., N.A. E7 94
Windy Lake, l., Sk., Can. D12 104
Windy Peak, mtn., Co., U.S. F10 120
Windy Peak, mtn., Wa., U.S. B6 122
Winefred, stm., Ab., Can. C4 104
Winefred Lake, l., Ab., Can. B24 102
Winejok, Sudan M4 60
Winfield, Ab., Can. E20 102
Winfield, Al., U.S. I9 114
Winfield, Ia., U.S. I4 110
Winfield, Ks., U.S. N11 118
Winfield, Mo., U.S. D6 114
Winfield, W.V., U.S. I5 108
Wing, N.D., U.S. D7 118
Wingate, N.C., U.S. E6 112
Wingene, Bel. F3 12
Wingham, Austl. H10 70
Wingham, On., Can. G14 110
Wingo, Ky., U.S. F8 114
Winifred, Mt., U.S. C16 122
Winifreda, Arg. I6 80
Winisk, On., Can. E15 96
Winisk, stm., On., Can. F15 96
Winisk Lake, l., On., Can. F15 96
Wink, Tx., U.S. H3 116
Winkana, Myan. G5 40
Winkelman, Az., U.S. L6 120
Winkler, Mb., Can. I17 104
Winlaw, B.C., Can. H17 102
Winlock, Wa., U.S. D3 122
Winneba, Ghana I9 64
Winnebago, Il., U.S. H6 110
Winnebago, Mn., U.S. G1 110
Winnebago, Ne., U.S. I11 118
Winnebago, stm., Ia., U.S. G2 110
Winnebago, Lake, l., Wi., U.S. F7 110
Winneconne, Wi., U.S. F7 110
Winnemucca, Nv., U.S. D8 124
Winner, S.D., U.S. H8 118
Winnetka, Il., U.S. H8 110
Winnett, Mt., U.S. C17 122
Winnfield, La., U.S. K4 114
Winnibigoshish, Lake, l., Mn., U.S. C1 110
Winnie, Tx., U.S. M2 114
Winnipeg, Mb., Can. I17 104
Winnipeg, stm., Can. H18 104
Winnipeg, Lake, l., Mb., Can. F17 104
Winnipeg Beach, Mb., Can. H18 104
Winnipegosis, Mb., Can. G15 104
Winnipegosis, Lake, l., Mb., Can. F14 104
Winnipesaukee, Lake, l., N.H., U.S. D15 108
Winnsboro, La., U.S. J5 114
Winnsboro, S.C., U.S. E5 112
Winnsboro, Tx., U.S. G11 116
Winnsboro Mills, S.C., U.S. E5 112
Winona, Ks., U.S. L6 118
Winona, Mi., U.S. D7 110
Winona, Mn., U.S. F4 110
Winona, Mo., U.S. E5 114
Winona, Ms., U.S. I7 114
Winona Lake, In., U.S. A11 114
Winooski, Vt., U.S. C13 108
Winooski, stm., Vt., U.S. C14 108
Winschoten, Neth. B11 12
Winside, Ne., U.S. I10 118
Winslow, Az., U.S. I6 120
Winslow, Me., U.S. C17 108
Winsted, Ct., U.S. F13 108
Winsted, Mn., U.S. F1 110
Winston, Fl., U.S. K4 112
Winston, Or., U.S. G2 122
Winston-Salem, N.C., U.S. C6 112
Wintego Lake, l., Sk., Can. C12 104
Winter, Wi., U.S. E4 110
Winter Garden, Fl., U.S. K5 112
Winter Harbor, Me., U.S. C18 108
Winter Harbour, B.C., Can. G6 102
Winterhaven, Ca., U.S. L11 124
Winter Haven, Fl., U.S. K5 112
Wintering, stm., N.D., U.S. D7 118
Wintering Lake, l., Mb., Can. C17 104
Winter Island, i., N.T., Can. C16 96
Winter Park, Fl., U.S. K5 112
Winter Park, N.C., U.S. E9 112
Winterport, Me., U.S. C18 108
Winters, Ca., U.S. F4 124
Winters, Tx., U.S. H7 116
Winterset, Ia., U.S. I1 110
Winterthur, Switz. C10 13
Winterton, Nf., Can. E20 106
Winterville, Ga., U.S. F3 112
Winterville, Ms., U.S. I5 114
Winterville, N.C., U.S. D9 112
Winthrop, Ia., U.S. H4 110
Winthrop, Me., U.S. C17 108
Winthrop, Mn., U.S. F1 110
Winthrop Harbor, Il., U.S. H8 110
Winton, Austl. D5 70
Winton, N.C., U.S. C10 112
Winton, N.Z. G2 72
Wipperfürth, Ger. D7 10
Wirāṭanagar, Nepal G12 44
Wīrgañj, Nepal G11 44
Wirral, pen., Eng., U.K. H10 8
Wirraminna, Austl. H2 70
Wiscasset, Me., U.S. C17 108
Wisconsin, state, U.S. C9 98
Wisconsin, stm., Wi., U.S. G5 110
Wisconsin, Lake, res., Wi., U.S. G6 110
Wisconsin Dells, Wi., U.S. G6 110
Wisconsin Rapids, Wi., U.S. F6 110
Wisdom, Mt., U.S. E12 122
Wise, Va., U.S. C4 112
Wishart, Sk., Can. G10 104
Wishek, N.D., U.S. E8 118
Wishram, Wa., U.S. E5 122
Wisła, stm., Pol. A18 10
Wismar, Ger. B11 10
Wismar, Guy. D13 84
Wisner, La., U.S. K5 114
Wisner, Ne., U.S. J11 118
Wissembourg, Fr. C14 14
Wister, Ok., U.S. H2 114
Wisznice, Pol. D23 10
Witbank, S. Afr. E9 66
Witbooisvlei, Nmb. E4 66
Witchekan Lake, l., Sk., Can. E7 104
Withlacoochee, stm., U.S. I3 112
Witjira National Park, Austl. E7 68
Witless Bay, Nf., Can. E21 106
Witrivier, S. Afr. E10 66
Witsand, S. Afr. J5 66
Witt, Il., U.S. C7 114
Wittenberg, Wi., U.S. F6 110
Wittenberge, Ger. B11 10
Wittenburg, Ger. B11 10
Wittenoom, Austl. D3 68
Wittingen, Ger. C10 10
Wittlich, Ger. F6 10
Wittmund, Ger. B7 10
Wittstock, Ger. B12 10
Witwatersrant, reg., S. Afr. E8 66
Witzputz, Nmb. F3 66
Wiwa Creek, stm., Sk., Can. H7 104
Wiżajny, Pol. A22 10
Włocławek, Pol. C19 10
Włoszczowa, Pol. E19 10
Woburn, Ma., U.S. E15 108
Wodonga, Austl. K7 70
Wohlen, Switz. D9 13
Wohlthat Mountains, mts., Ant. C3 73
Woi, Sudan N6 60
Woking, Ab., Can. B16 102
Woking, Eng., U.K. J13 8
Wolbach, Ne., U.S. J9 118
Wolcott, In., U.S. B9 114
Wolcott, N.Y., U.S. D10 108
Wolcottville, In., U.S. A11 114
Wolf, stm., Ks., U.S. L12 118
Wolf, stm., Ms., U.S. L7 114
Wolf, stm., U.S. G7 114
Wolf, stm., Wi., U.S. F7 110
Wolfach, Ger. G8 10
Wolf-Bay, P.Q., Can. B13 106
Wolf Creek, Mt., U.S. C13 122
Wolf Creek, Or., U.S. H2 122
Wolf Creek Lake, res., Ks., U.S. M12 118
Wolf Creek Pass, Co., U.S. G10 120
Wolfeboro, N.H., U.S. D15 108
Wolfe City, Tx., U.S. F10 116
Wolfen, Ger. D12 10
Wolfenbüttel, Ger. C10 10
Wolfenden, Mount, mtn., B.C., Can. G7 102
Wolfforth, Tx., U.S. F4 116
Wolfhagen, Ger. D9 10
Wolf Lake, Mi., U.S. G9 110
Wolf Lake, l., Ab., Can. C24 102
Wolf Lake, l., Yk., Can. F29 100
Wolf Point, Mt., U.S. B20 122
Wolfratshausen, Ger. H11 10
Wolfsberg, Aus. I14 10
Wolfsburg, Ger. C10 10
Wolfville, N.S., Can. G9 106
Wolgast, Ger. A13 10
Wolhusen, Switz. D9 13
Wollaston, Islas, is., Chile H3 78
Wollaston Lake, l., Sk., Can. E12 96
Wollaston Peninsula, pen., N.T., Can. C9 96
Wollemi National Park, Austl. I9 70
Wollogorang, Austl. A2 70
Wollongong, Austl. J9 70
Wolmaransstad, S. Afr. F8 66
Wołomin, Pol. C21 10
Wolseley, S. Afr. I4 66
Wolseley, Sk., Can. H11 104
Wolsey, S.D., U.S. G9 118
Wolsztyn, Pol. C16 10
Wolvega, Neth. C9 12
Wolverhampton, Eng., U.K. I11 8
Wolverine, Mi., U.S. E11 110
Wondai, Austl. F9 70
Wonderland, Ca., U.S. D4 124
Wonewoc, Wi., U.S. G5 110
Wŏnju, S. Kor. F15 32
Wonosobo, Indon. j14 39a
Wonotobo Vallen, wtfl, Sur. E14 84
Wŏnsan, N. Kor. D15 32
Wonthaggi, Austl. L6 70
Wood, S.D., U.S. H7 118
Wood, stm., B.C., Can. E16 102
Wood, stm., Ne., U.S. K8 118
Wood, stm., Sk., Can. I8 104
Wood, stm., Wy., U.S. G16 122
Wood, Mount, mtn., Yk., Can. F24 100
Woodall Mountain, hill, Ms., U.S. H8 114
Wood Bay, b., N.T., Can. B30 100
Woodbine, Ga., U.S. I5 112
Woodbine, Ia., U.S. J12 118
Woodbine, N.J., U.S. H12 108
Woodbridge, Va., U.S. I9 108
Woodburn, Or., U.S. E3 122
Woodbury, Ct., U.S. F13 108
Woodbury, Ga., U.S. G2 112
Woodbury, N.J., U.S. H11 108
Woodbury, Tn., U.S. G10 114
Woodenbong, Austl. G10 70
Woodfibre, B.C., Can. H11 102
Woodhull, Il., U.S. I5 110
Wood Islands, P.E., Can. G11 106
Woodlake, Ca., U.S. H6 124
Wood Lake, Ne., U.S. I7 118
Wood Lake, l., Sk., Can. C11 104
Woodland, Ca., U.S. F4 124
Woodland, Ga., U.S. G2 112
Woodland, Me., U.S. B19 108
Woodland, N.C., U.S. C9 112
Woodland Park, Co., U.S. F11 120
Woodlawn, Ky., U.S. E8 114
Wood Mountain, mtn., Sk., Can. I8 104
Wood Mountain Indian Reserve, Sk., Can. I8 104
Woodridge, Mb., Can. I18 104
Wood River, Il., U.S. D6 114
Wood River, Ne., U.S. K9 118
Woodroffe, stm., Austl. C2 70
Woodroffe, Mount, mtn., Austl. E6 68
Woodrow, N.C., U.S. D9 112
Woodruff, Az., U.S. J6 120
Woodruff, S.C., U.S. E4 112
Woodruff, Wi., U.S. E6 110
Woods, Lake, l., Austl. C6 68
Woods, Lake of the, l., N.A. B13 118
Woodsboro, Tx., U.S. K9 116
Woodsfield, Oh., U.S. H5 108
Woods Hole, Ma., U.S. F16 108
Woodside, Austl. L7 70
Woodson, Tx., U.S. F7 116
Woodstock, Il., U.S. H7 110
Woodstock, N.B., Can. F6 106
Woodstock, N.Y., U.S. E12 108
Woodstock, On., Can. G15 110
Woodstock, Va., U.S. I8 108
Woodstock, Vt., U.S. D14 108
Woodsville, N.H., U.S. C14 108
Woodville, Al., U.S. H10 114
Woodville, Fl., U.S. I2 112
Woodville, Ga., U.S. F3 112
Woodville, Ms., U.S. K5 114
Woodville, N.Z. D5 72
Woodville, Oh., U.S. F3 108
Woodville, Tx., U.S. L2 114
Woodward, Ia., U.S. I2 110
Woodward, Ok., U.S. C7 116
Woody, stm., Can. F14 104
Woody Head, c., Austl. G10 70
Woody Island, Ak., U.S. H18 100
Woolgoolga, Austl. H10 70
Woolmarket, Ms., U.S. L8 114
Woomera, Austl. H2 70
Woonsocket, R.I., U.S. E15 108
Woonsocket, S.D., U.S. G9 118
Woorabinda, Austl. E8 70
Wooramel, stm., Austl. E3 68
Wooster, Oh., U.S. G5 108
Worb, Switz. E8 13
Worcester, Eng., U.K. I11 8
Worcester, Ma., U.S. E15 108
Worcester, S. Afr. I4 66
Worden, Mt., U.S. E17 122
Wörgl, Aus. H12 10
Work Channel, strt., B.C., Can. C4 102
Workington, Eng., U.K. G10 8
Worksop, Eng., U.K. H12 8
Workum, Neth. C7 12
Worland, Wy., U.S. F18 122
Wormerveer, Neth. D6 12
Worms, Ger. F8 10
Wortham, Tx., U.S. H10 116
Worthing, Eng., U.K. K13 8
Worthington, In., U.S. C10 114
Worthington, Mn., U.S. H12 118
Worthington, Oh., U.S. G3 108
Worthington Peak, mtn., Nv., U.S. C10 124
Woudrichem, Neth. E7 12
Wounded Knee, S.D., U.S. H5 118
Wounta, Nic. D11 92
Wounta, Laguna de, b., Nic. D11 92
Wouw, Neth. E5 12
Wowan, Austl. D9 70
Woy Woy, Austl. I9 70
Wrangel Island see Vrangel'a, ostrov, i., Russia C28 28
Wrangell, Ak., U.S. H28 100
Wrangell, Cape, c., Ak., U.S. j1 101a
Wrangell, Mount, mtn., Ak., U.S. E22 100
Wrangell Island, i., Ak., U.S. H28 100
Wrangell Mountains, mts., Ak., U.S. F23 100
Wrath, Cape, c., Scot., U.K. C8 8
Wray, Co., U.S. K5 118
Wreck Reef, rf., Austl. D11 70
Wrens, Ga., U.S. F4 112
Wrentham, Ab., Can. H22 102
Wrexham, Wales, U.K. H10 8
Wright, Mount, mtn., Mt., U.S. C13 122
Wright City, Mo., U.S. D5 114
Wright City, Ok., U.S. E11 116
Wright Patman Lake, res., Tx., U.S. I2 114
Wrightson, Mount, mtn., Az., U.S. M6 120
Wrightstown, Wi., U.S. F7 110
Wrightsville, Ga., U.S. G4 112
Wrightsville Beach, N.C., U.S. E9 112
Wrightwood, Ca., U.S. J8 124
Wrigley, N.T., Can. E33 100
Wrigley, Tn., U.S. G9 114
Wrocław (Breslau), Pol. D17 10
Wrong Lake, l., Mb., Can. F18 104
Wrottesley, Cape, c., N.T., Can. B8 96
Wroxton, Sk., Can. G13 104
Września, Pol. C17 10
Wu, stm., China F8 30
Wucheng, China B2 34
Wuchin see Changzhou, China E10 30
Wuchuan, China D11 40
Wudian, China D1 34
Wudinna, Austl. I1 70
Wudu, China E7 30
Wugang, China F9 30
Wugong Shan, mts., China H2 34
Wuhai, China D8 30
Wuhan, China E3 34
Wuhu, China D7 34
Wuhua, China L4 34
Wuhuanchi, China A9 32
Wuji, China E2 32
Wujiang, China D9 34
Wukari, Nig. H14 64
Wuliang Shan, mts., China B6 40
Wum, Cam. H15 64
Wunnummin Lake, l., On., Can. F15 96
Wun Rog, Sudan M5 60
Wunstorf, Ger. C9 10
Wuping, China J5 34
Wuppertal, Ger. D7 10
Wuppertal, S. Afr. I4 66
Würenlingen, Switz. C9 13
Würzburg, Ger. F9 10
Wurzen, Ger. D12 10
Wushan, China E8 30
Wusheng, China F8 34
Wushenqi, China D8 30
Wuskwatim Lake, l., Mb., Can. C16 104
Wusong, China D10 34
Wutai, China D9 30
Wutai Shan, mtn., China D1 32
Wutangjie, China F11 34
Wutongqiao, China F7 30
Wuustwezel, Bel. F6 12
Wuvulu Island, i., Pap. N. Gui. F11 38
Wuwei, China D7 30
Wuwei, China D6 34
Wuxi (Wuhsi), China D9 34
Wuyi Shan, mts., China I5 34
Wuyuan, China C8 30
Wuzhi Shan, mtn., China E10 40
Wuzhong, China D8 30
Wuzhou (Wuchow), China C11 40
Wyaconda, Mo., U.S. B5 114
Wyaconda, stm., Mo., U.S. B5 114
Wyalusing, Pa., U.S. F10 108
Wyandotte, Mi., U.S. H12 110
Wyandra, Austl. F6 70
Wyangala, Lake, res., Austl. I8 70
Wyatt, Mo., U.S. F7 114
Wycheproof, Austl. K5 70
Wye, stm., U.K. J11 8
Wyeville, Wi., U.S. F5 110
Wykoff, Mn., U.S. G3 110
Wylie, Tx., U.S. F10 116
Wylie, Lake, res., U.S. D5 112
Wymark, Sk., Can. H7 104
Wymore, Ne., U.S. K11 118
Wyndham, Austl. C5 68
Wyndmere, N.D., U.S. E10 118
Wynndel, B.C., Can. H18 102
Wynne, Ar., U.S. G6 114
Wynnewood, Ok., U.S. E9 116
Wynniatt Bay, b., N.T., Can. B10 96
Wynona, Ok., U.S. C10 116
Wynot, Ne., U.S. I10 118
Wynyard, Austl. M6 70
Wynyard, Sk., Can. G10 104
Wyocena, Wi., U.S. G6 110
Wyodak, Wy., U.S. G2 118
Wyoming, Ia., U.S. H4 110
Wyoming, Il., U.S. I6 110
Wyoming, Mi., U.S. H10 110
Wyoming, On., Can. H13 110
Wyoming, state, U.S. C5 98
Wyong, Austl. I9 70
Wysokie Mazowieckie, Pol. C22 10
Wyszków, Pol. C21 10
Wytheville, Va., U.S. C5 112

X

Xaafuun, Raas, c., Som. F11 56
Xaclbal, stm., N.A. B3 92
Xaidulla, China B8 44
Xainza, China E4 30
Xai-Xai, Moz. E11 66
Xalapa, Mex. H11 90
Xam (Chu), stm., Asia E8 40
Xambrê, stm., Braz. G2 79
Xam Nua, Laos D8 40
Xan (San), stm., Asia G9 40
Xangongo, Ang. E3 58
Xankändi (Stepanakert), Azer. J7 26
Xánthi, Grc. H8 20
Xanxerê, Braz. D12 80
Xapecó, stm., Braz. D12 80
Xapuri, Braz. D7 82
Xapuri, stm., Braz. D7 82
Xar Moron, stm., China C10 30
Xàtiva (Játiva), Spain G11 16
Xau, Lake, pl., Bots. C7 66
Xavantina, Braz. F2 79
Xaxim, Braz. D12 80
Xcalak, Mex. H16 90
X-Can, Mex. G16 90
Xenia, Il., U.S. D8 114
Xenia, Oh., U.S. H3 108
Xertigny, Fr. D13 14
Xeruã, stm., Braz. B7 82
Xhumo, Bots. C7 66
Xi, stm., China G9 30
Xiagaixin, China C5 40
Xiagezhuang, China G8 32
Xiahe, China D7 30
Xiamen (Amoy), China K7 34
Xiamen Gang, b., Asia K7 34
Xi'an (Sian), China E8 30
Xianfeng, China J6 34
Xiang, stm., China F9 30
Xiangcheng, China B2 34
Xiangfan, China E9 30
Xianggongshi, China G2 34
Xiangheguan, China B2 34
Xiangkhoang, Laos E7 40
Xiangkhoang, Plateau de, plat., Laos E7 40
Xiangride, China D6 30
Xiangtan, China H1 34
Xianinggang, China G1 34
Xianju, China G9 34
Xianxian, China E4 32
Xianyou, China J7 34
Xiaodanyang, China D7 34
Xiaogan, China E2 34
Xiaogushan, China D11 32
Xiao Hinggan Ling, mts., China B12 30
Xiaoji, China C8 34
Xiaojiang, China J3 34
Xiaolan, China M2 34
Xiaolipu, China G4 32
Xiaoshan, China E9 34
Xiaoshi, China H5 34
Xiaoshixiang, China E5 34
Xiaoxi, China J4 34
Xiapu, China I9 34
Xiapu, China H3 34
Xiaying, China F7 32
Xibu, China D7 34
Xichang, China F7 30
Xicoténcatl, Mex. F10 90
Xié, stm., Braz. G9 84
Xielipuke, China E10 44
Xigaotun, China C10 32
Xigazê, China F13 44
Xihua, China B3 34
Xijialong, China C7 40
Xikouxu, China J6 34
Xiliao, stm., China C11 30
Ximiao, China C7 30
Xin'an, China I5 34
Xinavane, Moz. E11 66
Xinba, China I7 32
Xincheng, China J3 34
Xindian, China F2 32
Xindukou, China B6 40
Xing'an, China F9 30
Xingcheng, China C8 32
Xinghua, China C8 34
Xingkai Hu (ozero Chanka), l., Asia B13 30
Xinglong, China C5 32
Xingtai, China F2 32
Xingu, stm., Braz. D8 76
Xinguan, China B7 34
Xingyi, China B8 40
Xinhe, China F3 32
Xinhua, China F9 30
Xinhui, China M2 34
Xining, China D7 30
Xinjiaji, China G4 32
Xinjiang, China D9 30
Xinjiang Uygur Zizhiqu (Sinkiang), prov., China C3 30
Xinle (Dongchangshou), China E2 32
Xinmin, China A10 32
Xinshi, China E9 34
Xinwen (Suncun), China H5 32
Xinxian, China D3 34
Xinxiang, China H1 32
Xinxing, China M1 34
Xinyang, China C3 34
Xinzao, China L2 34
Xinzhangzi, China C5 32
Xiongjiachang, China A8 40
Xipamanu (Chipamanu), stm., S.A. D7 82
Xiping, China B3 34
Xique-Xique, Braz. F10 76
Xırdalan, Azer. I7 26
Xisha Qundao (Paracel Islands), is., China B5 38
Xishu, China G1 32
Xitole, Gui.-B. F2 64
Xiuyan, China C11 32
Xixian, China C3 34
Xiyou, China F7 32
Xizang Zizhiqu (Tibet), prov., China E3 30
Xizhou, China F10 34
Xochicalco, hist., Mex. H10 90
Xochistlahuaca, Mex. I10 90
Xuancheng, China E7 34
Xuanhua, China C3 32
Xuchang, China A2 34
Xueao, China F10 34
Xuecheng, China I5 32
Xuji, China D5 34
Xun, stm., China G9 30
Xushui, China D3 32
Xuwen, China D11 40
Xuyong, China F8 30
Xuzhou (Süchow), China A6 34

Y

Yaan, China E7 30
Yablis, Nic. C11 92
Yablonovy Range see Jablonovyj chrebet, mts., Russia G14 28
Yabluniv, Ukr. A8 20
Yacambu, Parque Nacional, Ven. C8 84
Yacaré Norte, Riacho, stm., Para. B9 80
Yaco, Bol. G8 82
Yaco (Iaco), stm., S.A. D6 82
Yacuiba, Bol. J10 82
Yacuma, stm., Bol. E8 82
Yacyretá, Isla, i., Para. D10 80
Yādgīr, India D4 46
Yadkin, stm., N.C., U.S. D6 112
Yadkinville, N.C., U.S. C6 112
Yad Mordekhay, Isr. E3 50
Yadong, China F4 30
Yafran, Libya B3 56
Yağcılar, Tur. J12 20
Yagoua, Cam. F10 54
Yagradagzê Shan, mtn., China C16 44
Yaguachi Nuevo, Ec. I3 84
Yaguajay, Cuba C5 94
Yaguala, stm., Hond. B8 92
Yaguará, Col. F5 84
Yaguaraparo, Ven. B11 84
Yaguarí, Ur. F11 80
Yaguarón (Jaguarão), stm., S.A. G12 80
Yaguas, stm., Peru I7 84
Yahara, stm., Wi., U.S. H6 110
Yahk, B.C., Can. H18 102
Yahongqiao, China D5 32
Yahualica, Mex. G8 90
Yai, Khao, mtn., Asia H5 40
Yainax Butte, mtn., Or., U.S. H4 122
Yaizu, Japan M13 36
Yakima, Wa., U.S. D5 122
Yakima, stm., Wa., U.S. D6 122
Yako, Burkina E8 64
Yakobi Island, i., Ak., U.S. G26 100
Yakoma, Zaire H5 56
Yaku-shima, i., Japan q5 37b
Yakutat, Ak., U.S. G25 100
Yakutat Bay, b., Ak., U.S. G24 100
Yakutia see Jakutija, state, Russia D18 28
Yakutsk see Jakutsk, Russia E17 28
Yala, Thai. K6 40
Yalahau, Laguna, b., Mex. G16 90
Yale, B.C., Can. H13 102
Yale, Mi., U.S. G13 110
Yale, Ok., U.S. C10 116
Yale, Mount, mtn., Co., U.S. F10 120
Yalgoo, Austl. E3 68
Yalinga, C.A.R. N2 60
Yalleroi, Austl. E6 70
Yalobusha, stm., Ms., U.S. I7 114
Yalong, stm., China E6 30
Yalova, Tur. I13 20
Yalta, Ukr. I4 26
Yalu (Amnok-kang), stm., Asia C12 32
Yamagata, Japan I15 36
Yamaguchi, Japan M6 36
Yamba, Austl. G10 70
Yambio, Sudan H6 56
Yambrasbamba, Peru A3 82
Yamdena, Pulau, i., Indon. G9 38
Yamethin, Myan. D4 40
Yamia, Niger E15 64
Yamma Yamma, Lake, l., Austl. F4 70
Yamoussoukro, C. Iv. H7 64
Yampa, Co., U.S. D10 120
Yampa, stm., Co., U.S. D8 120
Yamparaez, Bol. H9 82
Yampil', Ukr. A12 20
Yamsay Mountain, mtn., Or., U.S. H4 122
Yamuna, stm., India H9 44
Yamzho Yumco, l., China F14 44
Yanac, Austl. K4 70
Yanacachi, Bol. G8 82
Yanagawa, Japan N5 36
Yanahuara, Peru G6 82
Yanai, Japan N7 36
Yanam, India D7 46
Yan'an, China D8 30
Yanaoca, Peru F6 82
Yanbuʻ al-Baḥr, Sau. Ar. I5 48
Yanbutou, China F4 34
Yanceyville, N.C., U.S. C7 112
Yanchang, China D9 30
Yancheng, China B9 34
Yanchi, China D8 30
Yanco, Austl. J7 70
Yandev, Nig. H14 64
Yandoon, Myan. F3 40
Yanfolila, Mali F5 64
Yangcun, China L3 34
Yangguanpu, China C4 34
Yangjia, China I7 32
Yangjiang, China G9 30
Yangkoushi, China G7 34
Yangliuqing, China D5 32
Yanglousi, China F2 34
Yangon (Rangoon), Myan. B2 38
Yangp'yŏng, S. Kor. F15 32
Yangquan, China F1 32
Yangsan, S. Kor. H17 32
Yangshuling, China B6 32
Yangtze see Chang, stm., China E10 30
Yangxiaodian, China D5 34
Yangyang, S. Kor. E16 32
Yangzhou, China C8 34
Yanheying, China C7 32
Yanji, China A17 32
Yankdŏk, N. Kor. D14 32
Yankeetown, Fl., U.S. J4 112
Yankton, S.D., U.S. I10 118
Yanliumiao, China C5 34
Yanna, Austl. F7 70
Yanqi, China C4 30
Yanqing, China C3 32
Yanque, Peru F6 82
Yanṭā, Leb. A5 50
Yantabulla, Austl. G6 70
Yantai (Chefoo), China F9 32
Yantian, China H3 34
Yanzhou, China H4 32
Yao, Japan M10 36
Yaopi, China I2 34
Yaoundé, Cam. H9 54
Yaoya, stm., Nic. D10 92
Yapacaní, Bol. G9 82
Yapacani, stm., Bol. G9 82
Yapen, Pulau, i., Indon. F10 38
Yapeyú, Arg. E10 80
Yappar, stm., Austl. B4 70
Yaʻqūb, Sudan K3 60
Yaque del Norte, stm., Dom. Rep. E9 94
Yaqui, stm., Mex. C5 90
Yaracuy, state, Ven. B8 84
Yaraka, Austl. E6 70
Yarbasan, Tur. K12 20
Yardea, Austl. I1 70
Yaremcha, Ukr. A8 20
Yarí, stm., Col. H6 84
Yarīm, Yemen G4 47
Yaring, Thai. K6 40
Yaritagua, Ven. B8 84
Yarkand see Shache, China A7 44
Yarkant (Yarkand), stm., China D2 30
Yarlung see Brahmaputra, stm., Asia G15 44
Yarmouth, Me., U.S. D16 108
Yarmouth, N.S., Can. I7 106
Yarmūk, Nahr al-, stm., Asia C5 50
Yarram, Austl. L7 70
Yarraman, Austl. F9 70
Yarrawonga, Austl. K7 70
Yarumal, Col. D5 84
Yashiro-jima, i., Japan N7 36
Yasinya, Ukr. A8 20
Yasothon, Thai. G8 40
Yass, Austl. J8 70
Yasuní, stm., Ec. H5 84
Yata, Bol. E8 82
Yata, stm., Bol. D9 82
Yatakala, Niger D10 64
Yatesboro, Pa., U.S. G7 108
Yates Center, Ks., U.S. N12 118
Yates City, Il., U.S. J5 110
Yathkyed Lake, l., N.T., Can. D13 96
Yatsushiro, Japan O5 36
Yaṭṭah, W.B. F4 50
Yatuá, stm., Ven. G9 84
Yauca, Peru F4 82
Yauca, stm., Peru F4 82
Yauco, P.R. E11 94
Yauli, Peru D3 82
Yaupi, Ec. I4 84
Yauri, Peru F6 82
Yautepec, Mex. H10 90
Yauyos, Peru E4 82
Yavarí (Javari), stm., S.A. D4 76
Yavarí Mirim, stm., Peru J6 84
Yavaros, Mex. D5 90
Yavatmāl, India B5 46
Yavero, stm., Peru E5 82
Yaví, Cerro, mtn., Ven. E10 84
Yavita, Ven. F9 84
Yaviza, Pan. C4 84
Yavne, Isr. E3 50
Yawatahama, Japan N7 36
Yaxchilán, hist., Mex. I14 90
Yaxian, China E10 40
Yayuan, China B14 32
Yazd, Iran F13 48
Yazmān, Pak. F4 44
Yazoo, stm., Ms., U.S. J6 114
Yazoo City, Ms., U.S. J6 114
Ybbs an der Donau, Aus. G15 10
Ybycuí, Para. D10 80
Ye, Myan. G4 40
Yecheng, China B7 44
Yech'ŏn, S. Kor. G16 32
Yecla, Spain G10 16
Yécora, Mex. C5 90
Yeelanna, Austl. J1 70
Yegros, Para. D10 80
Yehud, Isr. D3 50
Yei, stm., Sudan N6 60
Yekaterinburg see Jekaterinburg, Russia F10 26
Yela Island, i., Pap. N. Gui. B10 68
Yelarbon, Austl. G9 70
Yele, S.L. G4 64
Yélimané, Mali D4 64
Yellow see Huang, stm., China D10 30
Yellow, stm., Ia., U.S. G4 110
Yellow, stm., In., U.S. A10 114
Yellow, stm., U.S. L10 114

Name	Map Ref.	Page